International Directory of
COMPANY
HISTORIES

INTERNATIONAL DIRECTORY OF COMPANY HISTORIES

International Directory of
COMPANY HISTORIES

VOLUME I

Editor
Thomas Derdak

Associate Editor
John Simley

Editorial Assistants
Anne Morddel (London)
Stephanie Wasserman (Chicago)

Writers and Researchers
Gretchen Antelman, Dena Bauman, Anne Bradley, Mitch Denier, Colleen Devlin, Evelyn Dorman, Veronica Drake, Michelle Duenas, Kathy Furore, David Fine, Mike Fitzgerald, Ellen Hake, David Hosansky, David Hubbard, Elise Johnson, Nina Kavin, Karen Knowles, Roberta Lamanna, Jeanne Lewis, Greg Mantell, Rob Massa, Bruce McCarthy, Chris Moran, Bruce Murphy, Karen Newton, Elizabeth Owens, Mark Pestana, Pamela Quinlan, Penny Rothfield, Charles Smith, Johanna Stoyva, Polly Trotenberg, Susan Venus, Natalie Williams, Tom Wilson, Paul Zaccarine, Jeff Zittrain

St J

ST. JAMES PRESS
CHICAGO AND LONDON

ST. JAMES PRESS
233 East Ontario Street
Chicago, IL 60611
U.S.A.

or

3 Percy Street
London W1P 9FA
England

First published in the U.S.A. and U.K. in 1988

British Library Cataloguing in Publication Data

International directory of company histories.
Vol. 1
1. Large companies, to 1987
I. Derdak, Thomas
338.7′4′09

ISBN 0-912289-10-4

Typeset by Florencetype Ltd., Kewstoke, Avon
Printed at The Bath Press, Avon

INDUSTRIES COVERED IN THE DIRECTORY ____

VOLUME I ____
Advertising
Aerospace
Airlines
Automotive
Beverages
Chemicals
Conglomerates
Construction
Containers
Drugs

VOLUME II ____
Electronics
Entertainment
—Broadcasting
—Motion Picture
—Manufacturing and
    Recreational Services
Financial Services
—Bank
—Non–Bank
Food Products
Food Services
Health and Personal Care
—Products
—Services

VOLUME III ____
Hotels
Instruments
Manufacturing
—Building Materials
—Consumer Products
—Industrial Machinery
Metals and Mining
Office Equipment and
    Personal Computers
Paper and Forestry

VOLUME IV ____
Petroleum
—Refining
—Service and Supply
Publishing
Railroads
Real Estate
Retail
—Food Products
—Non–Food Products
Service Industries
Shipbuilding

VOLUME V ____
Steel
Technology and
    Mainframe Computers
Textiles and Apparel
Tire and Rubber
Tobacco
Transportation
—Delivery
—Passenger
—Shipping
—Trucking
Utilities
—Electrical
—Natural Gas
—Telecommunications

CONTENTS

CONTENTS

EDITOR'S NOTE _____

The *International Directory of Company Histories* provides accurate and detailed information on the historical development of 1250 of the world's largest and most influential companies. The *Directory* will consist of five volumes, each containing 250 entries. The first volume covers 10 industries ranging from advertising to drugs. Volumes two through five will cover industries from electronics to utilities.

The companies chosen for inclusion in the *Directory* have met one or both of the following criteria: they have achieved a minimum of two billion U.S. dollars in annual sales or they are a leading influence in a particular industry or geographical location.

The information at the beginning of each entry includes the company's legal name, mailing address of its headquarters, telephone number, whether the company is publicly owned (when company shares of stock are traded publicly on an exchange or bourse), privately owned (when none of the company stock shares are traded publicly), or state controlled (when all stock shares and interests of the company are owned or controlled by the national government). The company's earliest incorporation date, number of employees, sales and market value (for the fiscal year 1986), and stock index (where the company is listed for the public trade of stock shares) is also included. It should be noted that throughout the *Directory* the spelling is according to the American style, and the term "billion" is used in its American sense, i.e., a thousand million.

The information that provides the basis for the histories is taken from a number of publicly accessible sources, including magazines, general and academic periodicals, books, annual reports, and material supplied by the companies themselves. St. James Press would especially like to thank the staffs of the Chicago Public Library, University of Chicago Library, Northwestern University Library (Evanston, Illinois), Illinois Institute of Technology Library (Chicago), London Library, British Library of Political and Economic Sciences at the London School of Economics, City Business Library (London), and Westminster Central Reference Library (London) for their courteous assistance and invaluable guidance.

St. James does not endorse any of the companies or products mentioned in this book. Likewise, the companies that appear in the *Directory* have neither seen nor endorsed their entries, although they have been gracious enough to allow the use of their logo for identification purposes. The *Directory* is intended solely for reference and research, for those students, job candidates, business people, librarians, historians, and investors who want to learn more about the historical development of the world's most important companies.

Thomas Derdak

ABBREVIATIONS FOR FORMS OF COMPANY INCORPORATION ————————

A.B.   Aktiebolaget (Sweden)

A.G.   Aktiengesellschaft (Germany, Switzerland)

A.S.   Aktieselskab (Denmark)

A/S   Aksjeselskap (Denmark, Norway)

A.Ş.   Anonim Şirket (Turkey)

B.V.   Besloten Vennootschap met beperkte, Aansprakelijkheid (The Netherlands)

CO.   Company (United Kingdom, United States)

CORP.   Corporation (United States)

G.I.E.   Groupement d'Intérêt Economique (France)

GmbH.   Gesellschaft mit beschränkter Haftung (Germany)

H.B.   Handelsbolaget (Sweden)

INC.   Incorporated (United States)

K.K.   Kabushiki Kaisha (Japan)

LTD.   Limited (Canada, Japan, United Kingdom, United States)

N.V.   Naamloze Vennootschap (The Netherlands)

PLC   Public Limited Company (United Kingdom)

PTY.   Proprietary (Australia, Hong Kong, South Africa)

S.A.   Société Anonyme (Belgium, France, Switzerland)

SpA   Società per Azioni (Italy)

ABBREVIATIONS FOR CURRENCY ————————

A$ Australian dollar

BFr   Belgian franc

C$ Canadian dollar

DKr   Danish krone

FFr   French franc

DM   German mark

HK$ Hong Kong dollar

L   Italian lira

¥   Japanese yen

W   Korean won

Dfl   Netherlands florin

R   South African rand

Pts   Spanish peseta

SKr   Swedish krone

SFr   Swiss franc

TL   Turkish lira

£   United Kingdom pound

$ United States dollar

B   Venezuelan bolivar

International Directory of
COMPANY HISTORIES

ADVERTISING

DENTSU INC.
FOOTE, CONE & BELDING
  COMMUNICATIONS, INC.
INTERPUBLIC GROUP INC.
JWT GROUP INC.
LEO BURNETT COMPANY, INC.
THE OGILVY GROUP, INC.
OMNICOM GROUP
SAATCHI & SAATCHI PLC
YOUNG & RUBICAM, INC.

AEROSPACE

G.I.E. AIRBUS INDUSTRIE
AVIONS MARCEL DASSAULT-BREGUET AVIATION
THE BOEING COMPANY
BRITISH AEROSPACE PLC
N.V. KONINKLIJKE NEDERLANDSE
  VLIEGTUIGENFABRIEK FOKKER
GENERAL DYNAMICS CORPORATION
GRUMMAN CORPORATION
LOCKHEED CORPORATION
MARTIN MARIETTA CORPORATION
McDONNELL DOUGLAS CORPORATION
MESSERSCHMITT-BÖLKOW-BLOHM GmbH.
NORTHROP CORPORATION
ROCKWELL INTERNATIONAL
ROLLS-ROYCE PLC
UNITED TECHNOLOGIES CORPORATION

AIRLINES

AMERICAN AIRLINES
BRITISH AIRWAYS PLC
CONTINENTAL AIRLINES
DELTA AIR LINES, INC.
EASTERN AIRLINES
JAPAN AIR LINES COMPANY, LTD.
KONINKLIJKE LUCHTVAART
  MAATSCHAPPIJ, N.V.
DEUTSCHE LUFTHANSA A.G.
NORTHWEST AIRLINES, INC.
PAN AMERICAN WORLD AIRWAYS, INC.
PEOPLE EXPRESS AIRLINES, INC.
SCANDINAVIAN AIRLINES SYSTEM
SWISS AIR TRANSPORT COMPANY, LTD.
TEXAS AIR CORPORATION
TRANS WORLD AIRLINES, INC.

UNITED AIRLINES
USAIR GROUP

AUTOMOTIVE

AMERICAN MOTORS CORPORATION
BAYERISCHE MOTOREN WERKE A.G.
BENDIX CORPORATION
CHRYSLER CORPORATION
CUMMINS ENGINE CORPORATION
DAIMLER-BENZ A.G.
DANA CORPORATION
EATON CORPORATION
ECHLIN INC.
FEDERAL-MOGUL CORPORATION
FIAT GROUP
FORD MOTOR COMPANY
FRUEHAUF CORPORATION
GENERAL MOTORS CORPORATION
HONDA MOTOR COMPANY LTD.
MACK TRUCKS, INC.
NAVISTAR INTERNATIONAL CORPORATION
NISSAN MOTOR COMPANY, LTD.
PACCAR INC.
PEUGEOT S.A.
RÉGIE NATIONALE DES USINES RENAULT
ROBERT BOSCH GmbH.
ROLLS-ROYCE MOTORS LTD.
SAAB-SCANIA A.B.
SEALED POWER CORPORATION
SHELLER-GLOBE CORPORATION
TOYOTA MOTOR CORPORATION
VOLKSWAGEN A.G.
A.B. VOLVO

BEVERAGES

ALLIED-LYONS PLC
ANHEUSER-BUSCH COMPANY, INC.
ASAHI BREWERIES, LTD.
BASS PLC
BROWN-FORMAN CORPORATION
CARLTON AND UNITED BREWERIES LTD.
CERVECERIA POLAR
THE COCA-COLA COMPANY
ADOLPH COORS COMPANY
DISTILLERS COMPANY PLC
E & J GALLO
GENERAL CINEMA CORPORATION

GRAND METROPOLITAN PLC
GUINNESS PLC
G. HEILEMAN BREWING COMPANY, INC.
HEINEKEN N.V.
HEUBLEIN, INC.
HIRAM WALKER RESOURCES, LTD.
KIRIN BREWERY COMPANY LTD.
LABATT BREWING COMPANY LTD.
MILLER BREWING COMPANY
MOËT-HENNESSY
MOLSON COMPANIES LTD.
PEPSICO, INC.
PERNOD RICARD S.A.
SAPPORO BREWERIES, LTD.
THE SEAGRAM COMPANY, LTD.
SOUTH AFRICAN BREWERIES LTD.
THE STROH BREWING COMPANY
WHITBREAD AND COMPANY PLC

CHEMICALS

AIR PRODUCTS AND CHEMICALS, INC.
AMERICAN CYANAMID
ATOCHEM S.A.
BASF A.G.
BAYER A.G.
BETZ LABORATORIES, INC.
BOC GROUP PLC
CELANESE CORPORATION
DEXTER CORPORATION
THE DOW CHEMICAL COMPANY
DSM, N.V.
E.I. DU PONT DE NEMOURS & COMPANY
ECOLAB, INC.
ETHYL CORPORATION
G.A.F.
GREAT LAKES CHEMICAL CORPORATION
HERCULES INC.
HOECHST A.G.
HÜLS A.G.
IMPERIAL CHEMICAL INDUSTRIES PLC
KOPPERS INC.
L' AIR LIQUIDE
LUBRIZOL CORPORATION
MITSUBISHI CHEMICAL INDUSTRIES, LTD.
MONSANTO COMPANY
MONTEDISON SpA
MORTON THIOKOL, INC.
NALCO CHEMICAL CORPORATION

NATIONAL DISTILLERS AND
   CHEMICAL CORPORATION
OLIN CORPORATION
PENNWALT CORPORATION
PERSTORP A.B.
RHÔNE-POULENC S.A.
RÖHM AND HAAS
SOLVAY & CIE S.A.
SUMITOMO CHEMICAL COMPANY, LTD.
UNION CARBIDE CORPORATION
VISTA CHEMICAL COMPANY
WITCO CORPORATION

CONGLOMERATES

AEG A.G.
ALCO STANDARD CORPORATION
ALLIED-SIGNAL INC.
AMFAC INC.
ARCHER-DANIELS-MIDLAND COMPANY
BARLOW RAND LTD.
BAT INDUSTRIES PLC
BTR PLC
C. ITOH & COMPANY, LTD.
COLT INDUSTRIES INC.
ELDERS IXL LTD.
FARLEY NORTHWEST INDUSTRIES, INC.
FMC CORPORATION
FUQUA INDUSTRIES, INC.
GREYHOUND CORPORATION
GULF & WESTERN INC.
HITACHI LTD.
IC INDUSTRIES, INC.
INSTITUTO NACIONAL DE INDUSTRIA
INTERNATIONAL TELEPHONE &
   TELEGRAPH CORPORATION
ISTITUTO PER LA RICOSTRUZIONE
   INDUSTRIALE
JARDINE MATHESON HOLDINGS LTD.
KATY INDUSTRIES, INC.
KIDDE, INC.
KOÇ HOLDING A.Ş.
LEAR SIEGLER, INC.
LITTON INDUSTRIES, INC.
LOEWS CORPORATION
LTV CORPORATION
MARUBENI K.K.
McKESSON CORPORATION

MINNESOTA MINING &
   MANUFACTURING COMPANY
MITSUBISHI CORPORATION
MITSUI BUSSAN K.K.
NISSHO IWAI K.K.
OGDEN CORPORATION
SAMSUNG GROUP
SUMITOMO CORPORATION
SWIRE PACIFIC LTD.
TELEDYNE, INC.
TENNECO INC.
TEXTRON INC.
THORN EMI PLC.
TOSHIBA CORPORATION
TRANSAMERICA CORPORATION
TRW INC.
VEBA A.G.
WHITTAKER CORPORATION
W.R. GRACE & COMPANY

CONSTRUCTION

A. JOHNSON & COMPANY H.B.
BARRATT DEVELOPMENTS PLC
BECHTEL GROUP, INC.
BILFINGER & BERGER BAU A.G.
BOUYGUES
DILLINGHAM CORPORATION
FAIRCLOUGH CONSTRUCTION GROUP PLC
FLUOR CORPORATION
JOHN BROWN PLC
JOHN LAING PLC
KAJIMA CORPORATION
KUMAGAI GUMI COMPANY, LTD.
LINDE A.G.
MELLON-STUART COMPANY
OHBAYASHI CORPORATION
THE PENINSULAR & ORIENTAL STEAM
   NAVIGATION COMPANY (BOVIS DIVISION)
TAYLOR WOODROW PLC
WOOD HALL TRUST PLC

CONTAINERS

BALL CORPORATION
CONTINENTAL GROUP COMPANY
CROWN, CORK & SEAL COMPANY
METAL BOX PLC
NATIONAL CAN CORPORATION

OWENS-ILLINOIS, INC.
PRIMERICA CORPORATION
TOYO SEIKAN KAISHA, LTD.

DRUGS

ABBOTT LABORATORIES
AMERICAN HOME PRODUCTS
A.B. ASTRA
BAXTER INTERNATIONAL
BECTON, DICKINSON & COMPANY
CIBA-GEIGY LTD.
FUJISAWA PHARMACEUTICAL COMPANY, LTD.
GENENTECH, INC.
GLAXO HOLDINGS PLC
F. HOFFMANN-LA ROCHE & COMPANY A.G.
ELI LILLY & COMPANY
MARION LABORATORIES, INC.
MERCK & COMPANY
MILES LABORATORIES
MYLAN LABORATORIES
NOVO INDUSTRI A/S
PFIZER INC.
PHARMACIA A.B.
RORER GROUP
ROUSSEL-UCLAF
SANDOZ LTD.
SANKYO COMPANY, LTD.
SANOFI GROUP
R.P. SCHERER
SCHERING A.G.
SCHERING-PLOUGH
G.D. SEARLE & COMPANY
SIGMA-ALDRICH
SMITHKLINE BECKMAN CORPORATION
SQUIBB CORPORATION
STERLING DRUG, INC.
SYNTEX CORPORATION
TAKEDA CHEMICAL INDUSTRIES, LTD.
THE UPJOHN COMPANY
WARNER-LAMBERT
THE WELLCOME FOUNDATION LTD.

ADVERTISING

DENTSU INC.

FOOTE, CONE & BELDING
  COMMUNICATIONS, INC.

INTERPUBLIC GROUP INC.

JWT GROUP INC.

LEO BURNETT COMPANY, INC.

THE OGILVY GROUP, INC.

OMNICOM GROUP

SAATCHI & SAATCHI PLC

YOUNG & RUBICAM, INC.

DENTSU INC.

11, Tsukiji-cho, 1-chome
Chou-ku, Tokyo 104
Japan
03-544-51111

Private Company
Incorporated: 1901
Employees: 5,662
Billings: $3.9 billion

Dentsu Advertising of Japan is the second largest advertising company in the world; only Young & Rubicam does more business. Until 1985, when it was replaced by Young & Rubicam, Dentsu was *the* top advertising firm, a notable distinction it had held proudly since 1973. Yet Dentsu is rarely mentioned in either American or Western European business journals. Even *Advertising Age,* the advertising trade magazine, covers Dentsu's affairs and enterprises only when they encroach upon American and European advertising markets. Many people are familiar with advertising firms such as Doyle Dane Bernbach and J. Walter Thompson, but hardly anyone outside Japan or the industry itself has heard of Dentsu. Few know that it does the advertising for all three of Japan's major automobile manufacturers (Nissan, Toyota, and Honda) or that it services a variety of smaller clients, including Sapporo Beer and Kikkoman Soy Sauce. In 1985 Dentsu had billings of more than $3.2 billion. How can such a large and successful company go unnoticed?

The answer is that Dentsu operates almost exclusively in the Orient where it has been the preeminent agency since before World War II. Until very recently this market had been growing fast enough to allow Dentsu a continuous and profitable rate of expansion; therefore, the company did not feel inclined to venture outside the East. In the last few years, however, it has attempted to establish a presence in the West in order to lessen the effects of an economic recession in some Oriental countries.

Regardless of the particular medium, whether print, television, or radio, Dentsu is the leading communications and advertising firm in Japan. Its influence is unparalleled and extends beyond the traditional parameters of the advertising business. It owns stock in some of Japan's largest newspapers and television networks; the company itself is partially owned (48% of available shares) by Japan's two leading news services, Kyodo and Jiji; and it also handles the largest Japanese accounts, including those of the various departments of the Japanese government. Dentsu does so much advertising that many magazines and newspapers sell Dentsu large blocks of ad space in advance; they know Dentsu will easily find the clients necessary to fill them. There are no advertising agencies in the United States or Europe which command such comprehensive control over their respective markets.

Dentsu, which derives its name from a contraction of the Japanese words for "telegraph" and "communications," was first established in 1901. At that time it was both an advertising firm and news service agency, and though the two enterprises appeared to be separate, Dentsu created an arrangement in which they were tightly connected. The company would trade its news stories to newspapers in return for advertising space and then sell the ad space to clients at a profit. The whole system was quite convenient but, as events quickly proved, not permanent. The military government which came to power in Japan during the 1930's brought all information services under its control and severely restricted the amount and types of advertising produced in Japan. Dentsu was nearly put out of business. Only after World War II, when the Japanese economy began to rebuild, was Dentsu able to reorganize and perform to its potential.

Much of the credit for Dentsu's resurgence and subsequent success belongs to the company's fourth president, Hideo Yoshida. Under his leadership Dentsu absorbed 16 smaller competing agencies, created a reputation as an aggressive business, and established its position at the top of the industry in Japan. Yoshida also made a point of hiring the sons of powerful business and political leaders, entertained clients lavishly, and was known to give expensive gifts to those whom he hoped to influence. Yoshida conducted business the old-fashioned way: he believed in "wining and dining" potential customers, establishing personal contacts, and cementing professional relationships with private promises of loyalty.

During the late 1940's and 1950's Dentsu emerged as one of the most visible companies in Japan. Those who worked at the firm were referred to as the "Demons of Dentsu," a phrase which, though meant to be unflattering, was nonetheless received with pride by the staff. The Dentsu trademark was its red and blue flag, and hundreds of flags could be seen waving from the executive limousines which crowded the Ginza at night.

Hideo Yoshida's greatest accomplishment, however, extends far beyond his ability to win clients. Dentsu, under Yoshida's direction, almost single-handedly developed the Japanese television industry and has benefited a great deal from this original investment of time, energy and money. At the end of World War II Japan had only one radio network, which was owned by the government, and no commercial television. However, Yoshida knew that commercial television would not only be possible but also highly profitable in Japan if he could arrange the initial capitalization it required. Yoshida used Dentsu's influence and resources to attract investors, promising them generous advertising exposure. Moreover, Dentsu often underwrote fledgling networks until they achieved some semblance of financial independence. Yoshida and his company remained firmly committed to keeping the Japanese print, radio, and television media solvent.

The positive effect that this relationship has had upon Dentsu's advertising business cannot be overstated. The firm is viewed by the television and radio networks as a "godfather," and as customs of loyalty dictate, Dentsu has often received preferential treatment. Dentsu commands more prime-time (7 to 10 p.m.) advertising space than all the other agencies combined.

By associating itself with the birth of Japanese television, Dentsu emerged as the pioneer agency in television advertising. Before any other company learned to do so, it successfully developed ways of using the new media in campaigns for its clients. No other company has found the means to compensate for Dentsu's head start. As television has flourished in Japan, so has Dentsu flourished with it. Ninety-nine percent of all homes have televisions, and there are 98 commercial stations carrying programs produced by five networks. It is quite possible that Dentsu's advertising is seen by every Japanese at least once each day of the year.

The Dentsu advertising company of today operates according to procedures slightly different from those of any other advertising firm in the world. Chief among these are the practices of "block-buying" and holding competing accounts. Dentsu buys "blocks" of television, radio, or print space, often before the clients needed to fill these blocks have been contracted; it purchases the space for itself and then resells it to its customers. Few other firms have the financial resources to speculate in this way. In addition, most magazines, newspapers, and television stations prefer the continuity and quality of Dentsu's clients to those of any other agency, and usually give Dentsu priority. One result of this favoritism has been to allow Dentsu to significantly undermine competing advertising companies.

The second practice, that of holding competing accounts, has long been an accepted one in Japanese advertising. No American advertising firm would handle the accounts of Ford, General Motors, and Chrysler at the same time, but Nissan, Toyota, and Honda are all Dentsu clients, and none of the three seems to care that they share the same advertising firm. Dentsu claims that its particular system of compartmentalism allows it to hold competing accounts without compromising trade secrets. Dentsu commands a large share of the Japanese advertising market (25%), and clients are willing to forego professional jealousy in order to have the widest exposure for their products. This attitude, despite encouragement from the executives of American and European advertising agencies, has yet to be adopted by clients outside of Japan.

The actual advertisements which Dentsu produces for its clients differ stylistically from those of Western advertising campaigns. The "Japanese look" in advertising tends to stress art over copy. Says international creative director Toshio Naito, "The Japanese prefer to look at entertainment types of advertising, and they don't like to be pounded with logic." The point is neither to persuade the consumer to purchase a particular product nor to purposely degrade the competition. The Japanese consider this form of advertising, which is prevalent in America, to be distasteful.

The list of the staff at Dentsu reads like a "Who's Who" of Japanese society. The sons of prominent Japanese businessmen work with sons of members of the Diet (the Japanese parliament). Women, however, are hired only in secretarial capacities. Dentsu built itself upon "old boy networks" and has remained male dominated. The firm hires the brightest young men it can find immediately after their graduation from college and then trains them in the Dentsu tradition. This includes moving the new employee from department to department in order to familiarize him with all facets of the business. One observer likened it to the way members of the military are shuttled from base to base. Dentsu executives feel this training is important in maintaining continuity and expertise at the firm. Rarely, if ever, does the agency hire staff away from other companies.

As is true in most other Japanese companies, no matter what the industry, teamwork is stressed above individual achievement. There are no creative "stars" at Dentsu, and the firm prefers it that way. Each year all Dentsu employees at the Tokyo office, including the president, make a journey to Mt. Fuji. The trip is meant to symbolize the "team ethic" at the agency and instill a sense of solidarity. Though Dentsu does not offer salaries as high as those given by U.S. firms and does not encourage individual "ladder climbing," the company does offer financial security. Once they become members of the Dentsu staff, most employees stay for life. They are paid considerably more than the average Japanese professional, have access to the nine company-operated vacation lodges at minimal cost, can obtain maid service for $2 a day, and receive generous bonuses twice a year.

Dentsu is not without its critics. The firm has drawn criticism for undermining competition in advertising, for tampering with news information, for meddling in politics, and for pressuring newspapers and magazines not to publish stories considered damaging to Dentsu or its clients. A sociologist, Kinji Ino, has written that Dentsu "threatens a free society, threatens freedom of the press, and makes it difficult for potentially good products to succeed in the market." The agency has been called Japan's *kuroko*, after the stage hand who manipulates puppets in the *banraku* theater. In spite of these and other negative reports, the everyday functioning of the company continues without interruption. Clients and the various Japanese communications media are content with their present relationship with Dentsu, and show few signs of wanting to change the status quo. Dentsu's real challenge comes not from its critics but from the conditions of the market itself.

Since the day it emerged as the largest worldwide advertising agency in 1973, Dentsu has been losing ground to the concerted efforts of American agencies to expand internationally. Unlike Young & Rubicam or McCann-Erickson, Dentsu had a slow start in the international market. In 1974 Dentsu had 14 offices outside of Japan, and only three of them were in the United States. This insularity has created problems for the company. The most important is that Dentsu has had difficulties holding on to multinational clients when they decide to advertise abroad.

Its failure to establish itself in markets outside Japan is only one of Dentsu's long-range problems. The Japanese market itself is no longer as secure and as lucrative as it used to be. Japan is thoroughly saturated with advertising. The Japanese economy, which in the 1970's expanded impressively, has been experiencing a slowdown recently. These conditions have produced a much narrower profit margin for Dentsu.

Present Dentsu president and chief executive officer Gobei Kogure has begun efforts to reduce the company's comparatively high operating costs, particularly its payroll. In 1984, for example, Dentsu paid more in bonuses to directors ($1.2 million) than it paid in dividends ($759,000) to its shareholders. Labor costs the firm 60% of its profits. Kogure, however, plans to reduce the staff by hiring fewer new people and letting attrition take its course. More importantly, Kogure must find a way to prevent Japanese multinational companies from spending their large advertising budgets abroad. In 1983, 46 major Japanese

companies purchased $1.3 billion worth of foreign advertising (mostly in the U.S.). And because Dentsu receives only 5% of its income from foreign advertising, it received a very small portion of this new business. If this trend continues, Dentsu will not be able to reclaim the title it lost to Young & Rubicam as the largest advertising firm in the world.

The irony is that the two agencies have recently come together in a joint advertising venture—DYR of Japan. With Dentsu's assistance, Young & Rubicam hopes to gain and maintain a foothold in the Orient, where it has previously failed to generate much business. With Young & Rubicam's help, the management at Dentsu thinks it will be able to establish itself more firmly in such markets as New York, London, and Frankfurt. Annual billings for DYR have already exceeded $100 million, but most of the business has come from increased spending by clients already within the respective folds of Dentsu and Young & Rubicam. The real test of this team effort is whether or not it will be able to attract new international clients.

FCB

FOOTE, CONE & BELDING COMMUNICATIONS, [INC.]

101 East Erie Street
Chicago, Illinois 60611
U.S.A.
(312) 751–7000

Public Company
Incorporated: December 1942
Employees: 6,000
Billings: $2.1 billion worldwide
Sales: $287 million
Market value: $185 million
Stock Index: New York Midwest

One of Fairfax Cone's early employers, Stirling Getchell, once sat on the floor of Cone's office and sifted through the crumpled bits of yellow paper Cone had tossed in the wastebasket. When the young copywriter asked his boss what he was doing, Getchell responded, "I'm looking to see if you've thrown away anything we can use. I'm not sure you would recognize it." Between that day in 1936 until his death in 1977 Fairfax Cone threw away many ideas, but he also learned to recognize which ones he ought to keep. The Foote, Cone & Belding campaigns for products like Clairol ("Does she or doesn't she"), Dial soap ("Aren't you glad you use Dial?"), and Hallmark Cards ("When you care enough to send the very best") are some of the classics in the industry. They established the advertising style of Foote, Cone & Belding and set the stage for the firm's early growth.

Today, the agency is responsible for such ads as the Coors Beer "serial" commercials starring television personality Mark Harmon and the atmospheric Levi Strauss "501 Blues" commercials, which are rich in both musical quality and visual imagery. This is not meant to imply, however, that the story of Foote, Cone & Belding can be traced along a creative continuum from the past to the present. On the contrary, Foote, Cone & Belding has had a varied history and, perhaps more than any other major agency, has been subject the fluctuating market conditions endemic to the ad industry.

The history of Foote, Cone & Belding begins in 1873 with the founding of the Lord & Thomas advertising agency and the career of Albert D. Lasker. It was Lasker who, along with John E. Kennedy and Claude Hopkins, revolutionized the advertising industry and brought it into the 20th century. Lasker built his agency until it became one of the largest and most successful in the world and is said to have ruled over it in an almost dictatorial manner. Furthermore, he did not take his own success lightly, nor did he wish to conceal it. In the words of the noted advertising man David Ogilvy, Albert Lasker "made more money and spent more money than anyone in the history of the business."

In the 1930's and 1940's the most important accounts at Lord & Thomas were the American Tobacco Company and the Pepsodent division of Palmolive. The former was owned and operated by the controversial George Washington Hill; its principal product, Lucky Strike cigarettes, provided nearly one-fourth of Lord & Thomas' business. Pepsodent was at the time the largest-selling toothpaste on the market, and was particularly important to Lasker who was a large shareholder in the company.

During the Depression consumer product companies and advertising agencies alike were often faced with the possibility of failure. Most corporations that survived did so because they were large enough to weather years of economic difficulty and were run by powerful, energetic men with large personal stakes in their respective companies. Albert Lasker was used to doing business with such men; he liked the challenge of bargaining with strong personalities. When the business world began to change in the early 1940's, his interest in advertising began to diminish. Fairfax Cone wrote of Lasker's relationships with his clients, that they "had been cemented at the top. When their structure began to change, when he became a supplier instead of a valued consultant, Mr. Lasker lost interest in the business. He saw that the day of the individual owner or the lasting partnership of two or three men in any large undertaking was gone. Business had become too big for that."

Lasker called together his three regional heads—Foote of New York, Cone of Chicago, and Belding of Los Angeles—to tell them that he was retiring from advertising in order to pursue other interests and that, as of December 31, 1942, Lord & Thomas would close its offices permanently. To say the least, the three men were surprised by the news. Originally, Lasker thought he could divide Lord & Thomas' business by apportioning accounts to each of the three according to geographical location. This plan meant, in effect, that the agency would be divided into three separate firms. Then Lasker changed his mind and decided it best to keep the company intact with each man directing a regional headquarters: Foote, Cone & Belding Company was born. Lasker made Foote president, Belding chairman of the board, and Cone chairman of the executive committee.

Foote, Cone and Belding did not purchase Lord & Thomas. It was willed to them by Albert Lasker. The sole financial condition was that each man raise $32,000 as security for a $100,000 loan Lasker obtained for them through a Chicago investment bank. The only other stipulation was that the name of Lord & Thomas be retired along with Mr. Lasker.

Since the change of ownership was sudden and unexpected, many people inside and outside the advertising industry were shocked. Many industry analysts did not believe that the new firm was viable. Its harshest critics expected FCB to lose most or all of its clients and fall from the ranks of the major agencies. Foote, Cone & Belding was not taken seriously, particularly by the media. A January 4, 1943 *Time* magazine article commented that, "To the advertising world it was almost as if Tiffany had announced that from now on it would be known as Jones, Smith & Johnson."

The critics, however, focused primarily on the name change and not the more salient facts. The new agency was able to retain nearly all of the old Lord & Thomas customers, the most important of which was George W. Hill's American Tobacco account. Moreover, it won a number of new lucrative accounts, including Toni home hair permanent products, Hiram Walker Whiskey, and Marshall Field and Company, not to mention ad contracts for a few Samuel Goldwyn movies.

Yet the question still remained—who are Foote, Cone and Belding? They were barely known to each other, much less to those outside the company itself.

Emerson Foote was born in Alabama and raised in California. His college career consisted of one semester at the University of California, after which he sought work in the advertising business. He tried on various occasions to obtain a job with the research department of Lord & Thomas' San Francisco office in the early 1930's, but without success. The Depression was under way and virtually no one was hiring. So in 1934 Foote opened up his own firm, Yeomans & Foote, only to find the competition within the industry too intense for the small company to survive. A short time later, Foote's work came to the attention of the J. Stirling Getchell agency which offered him a job developing an ad campaign for a new automobile manufacturer called Chrysler. Foote accepted the job, but when Getchell died in 1938 the firm was dissolved and Foote was once again seeking employment. He applied to Lord & Thomas, and this time he was hired—as an assistant account executive for Lucky Strike cigarettes. In this capacity he met George W. Hill. Foote impressed Hill and was subsequently put in charge of the entire American Tobacco Company account. Simultaneously he was promoted to the position of general manager of Lord & Thomas in New York, a position he still held at the time of Lasker's retirement.

Don Belding, the oldest of the three men and director of the Los Angeles office, was unique for an advertising man in that he avoided being transferred from city to city doing agency business. He spent all of his career in the western United States. A native of Oregon, Belding had been an artillery man in World War I, a Western Union telegraph operator, and the publisher of a small newspaper before he entered advertising. After spending a year in the hospital for a war related illness, he enrolled in a veterans' training program. Part of his training included a government paid internship at Lord & Thomas of San Francisco. Years later Lasker opened an office in Los Angeles which Belding took charge of in 1938. There he used his experience in copywriting and accounts management to provide services for clients such as Lockheed, Sunkist, Purex, and Union Oil.

Fairfax Cone, like his two partners, spent his early life in

California. He attended the University of California at Berkeley and worked for the *San Francisco Examiner* in the ad department. He had taken up drawing as a child and had become quite accomplished. He was colorblind, however, and later realized that because of this difficulty any advancement as an artist was impossible. He turned to copywriting and obtained work at a number of small San Francisco advertising agencies. When he went to work for Lord & Thomas, Cone began writing campaigns for the Southern Pacific Railroad and Dollar Lines ocean travel, and also became proficient at selling vacations as consumer products.

In 1934 Cone temporarily left Lord & Thomas to work for J. Stirling Getchell on the Plymouth and De Soto automobile accounts. During this period, Cone became afflicted with a seriously debilitating illness. What was at first thought to be a severe case of jaundice, turned out to be hypoglycemia. The correct diagnosis and proper treatment were seven years in coming, and during the interim Cone was forced to live half his life in bed.

Cone left Getchell and returned to Lord & Thomas in 1936 as manager of the agency's San Francisco office. He remained on the West Coast until 1941 when Albert Lasker asked him to move to New York to help out with a new campaign for Lucky Strikes. His stay in New York was brief. He no sooner became acquainted with George Hill than he was transferred to Chicago to work on the troubled Pepsodent account. A year and a half later, Cone found himself one-third owner of one of the largest advertising agencies in the world.

By 1946 the new firm of Foote, Cone & Belding had answered its critics and had proven itself the suitable heir of Lord & Thomas. Then publication of a book that became a best-seller threw the agency into turmoil and a three year period of readjustment. *The Hucksters*, by a former FCB copywriter named Frederic Wakeman, was supposedly a fictional account of the less reputable side of the advertising business. The two main characters of the book included an overbearing, unscrupulous owner of a large corporation and an advertising account executive who wasn't reluctant to lie in order to sell his client's merchandise. It was generally believed within the industry that the first character was patterned after George W. Hill and the second after Emerson Foote. The book caused a stir of controversy and was soon made into a major motion picture.

Because of the unflattering portrayal of the George Hill character, many people in the industry felt Hill would take the American Tobacco account away from Foote, Cone & Belding. That did not happen. Instead, he awarded the company with a new five million dollar account for Pall Mall, American Tobacco's second best-selling cigarette.

In 1948 George Hill died. Leadership of his company passed to Vincent Riggio, a man with whom Emerson Foote felt he could not do business. On Foote's recommendation the American Tobacco account, fully one-fourth of the agency's business, was terminated by the agency. Emerson Foote, suffering from manic depression and thinking that he may have given up too much in relinquishing the account, had a nervous breakdown. He subsequently sold his stock at below market value and left the firm.

The year 1948 marked something of a watershed for Foote, Cone & Belding. The agency was successful in obtaining a number of what were to become long-standing accounts. Foote, Cone & Belding began handling the advertising for, among others, Latex elastic products and Dial deodorant soap. It was also instrumental in putting the Hallmark Playhouse, precursor to the Hallmark Hall of Fame, on television.

Throughout the 1950's Foote, Cone & Belding continued to gain new clients and expand the services rendered to those already on its roster, particularly in the areas of radio and television. The firm had long employed Bob Hope as spokesman for Pepsodent and Arthur Godfrey for Toni and Frigidaire; now it had Red Skelton and George Gobel selling Johnson's Wax and Dial Soap respectively. At this time, Foote, Cone & Belding also created ad campaigns for Paper-Mate pens, Clairol hair coloring, and Kool-Aid.

The news was not all good, however. In 1951 the company lost the Pepsodent account to McCann-Erickson, leaving FCB without the two accounts (Pepsodent and American Tobacco) that had been the bedrock of Lord & Thomas' business. Pepsodent later returned to the firm, but with a much weaker market share. Then, in 1955, General Motors withdrew the Frigidaire account from Foote, Cone & Belding and took its business elsewhere.

The withdrawal of the Frigidaire account coincided with what at first promised to be the brightest chapter in the Foote, Cone & Belding story, but which turned out to be the darkest. In August of 1955, J.C. Doyle of the Ford Motor Company asked Fairfax Cone if he would be interested in doing the advertising for a new Ford automobile. Cone accepted the invitation and FCB, along with 10 other agencies, entered into the most extensive bidding competition ever seen in the ad industry. After 22 weeks and countless campaign presentations, Foote, Cone & Belding was finally awarded the account. The firm was instructed to find a suitable name for the new "E" (Experimental) car; after a month of brainstorming the agency had created the "Edsel."

The failure of the Edsel as an automobile is well-known; it cost the Ford Company close to $350 million. What is not recognized very often is that the Edsel was an advertising failure as well. The fiasco proved a cardinal rule of advertising—an advertisement, by itself, can aid or inhibit the sales of a good product, but it cannot, no matter how excellent the art and copy, save an inferior product. The Edsel was a product so out of step with prevailing market conditions that it was a losing venture from the beginning. In the words of Fairfax Cone, "The trouble with the Edsel was almost everything." Cone and company worked diligently through the years of 1956, 1957, and 1958 to make the Edsel appealing to the American consumer, but without success. In the winter of 1959 the last Edsel crossed the assembly line.

The agency's resilience was soon apparent; the Edsel did not destroy Foote, Cone & Belding, nor even hinder its growth. The company acquired new accounts for Zenith, Dole pineapple, Contac, Fritos, True cigarettes, Sunbeam, People's Gas, International Harvester, Sara Lee, Monsanto, Ralston-Purina, Merrill Lynch, and Falstaff beer.

In 1957 Don Belding retired from the firm at the age of 60, and the agency came increasingly under the direction of Fairfax Cone and company chairman Robert Carney. Carney, a shrewd lawyer and businessman, urged the agency to go public, which it did in 1962. By 1965 the company's shares were being traded on the New York Stock Exchange.

During the 1960's the agency made strides in cementing its relationships with the major clients on its roster and in enhancing their images. Its work for Kimberly-Clark, a client of Lord & Thomas since 1923, is particularly notable. Two Kimberly-Clark products, Kleenex and Kotex, have become so well known that the names themselves are now household words used to define an entire line of products. With FCB's research and marketing help, Kimberly-Clark emerged as one of the leaders in the manufacture of paper towels, napkins, paper uniforms and paper dresses. Similar work by the company was done for Armour/Dial and S.C. Johnson & Son.

Nowhere, though, was Foote, Cone & Belding advertising more visible and prolific than on television. Fairfax Cone, who had long considered advertising and television mismatched, nonetheless brought the firm to the forefront of this area of the industry. By 1969 the company was responsible for $110 million worth of advertising time on television. Products advertised by Foote, Cone & Belding were the sponsors of such shows as "Rowan and Martin's Laugh-In," "The Dean Martin Show," "The Jackie Gleason Show," "The Ed Sullivan Show," "The Smothers Brothers Comedy Hour," and "Ironside."

The 1970's marked a shift in emphasis for Foote, Cone & Belding. The agency began to focus less on advertising as an art and more on advertising as a business. Following the trend started by the other large agencies, Foote, Cone & Belding actively sought to acquire subsidiaries and build a more comprehensive international network of company offices. In January of 1972 it purchased the predominantly female-operated Hall & Levine agency (which it later sold in 1978), in 1973 it bought Whalstrom & Company, in 1975 Honig-Copper & Harrington, and in 1978 merged with Carl Byoir & Associates. In the international arena, Impact/FCB was established in Belgium and France, Jessurun/Bauduin-FCB in Amersterdam, Lindsay Smithers-FCB in Johannesburg and Capetown, and FCB/-SPASM in Sydney and Melbourne.

Expansion on this scale, however, was costly, and fiscal 1974 was marred by a $1,410,000 loss the agency suffered as a result of the failure of its FCB Cablevision venture. Any agency operating in the international market is prone to the trials and tribulations of currency fluctuations; Foote, Cone & Belding was no exception.

In June of 1977 Fairfax Cone died. With his passing, the firm and the advertising industry as a whole lost one of its most distinguished men. He had been one of advertising's staunchest defenders and most articulate critics. Foote, Cone & Belding had grown large and profitable under his tutelage. At the time of his death, it was an international agency with resources and services rivaling those of the biggest worldwide firms. Furthermore, Foote, Cone & Belding was able to achieve this eminence without resorting to what Cone called dishonest, tasteless, and gimmick-ridden advertising.

The advertising industry during the 1970's was marked by more than just business expansion. Most of the major agencies, FCB included, went through a period of creative malaise. The difficulties involved in the management of what was now a sprawling bureaucracy, and maintaining a balance between the creative and financial operations of the business, contributed to this problem.

In 1981 Foote, Cone & Belding emerged from its slump; 10 of its entries were ranked in *Advertising Age's* 100 Best Commercials, more than that of any other agency. This accomplishment revealed a renewed commitment to creativity. The approach did not always work (FCB lost Hallmark in 1981), but it revitalized Foote, Cone & Belding's image, and between 1982 and 1984 the agency won a record number of new accounts. The year 1984 was especially lucrative because Levi Strauss and a number of other major clients substantially increased their advertising budgets to meet the demand created by the Los Angeles Olympics.

Recently, however, FCB has encountered financial difficulties. The firm went on a subsidiary buying spree between 1981 and 1984, amounting to over $23 million in purchases. The fiscal strain of this expansion was felt in 1985 and made even worse by the fact that many clients, preparing for a more sluggish economy and a drop in sales following the Olympics, reduced expenditures for advertisements. The result of these developments was that despite the 1985 increase in total revenues (including subsidiaries), the agency's net income dropped 14 %, driving its share price down. Foote, Cone & Belding recently traded at less than 13 times earnings, 10% below the industry average, making it vulnerable to takeover. Among the possible suitors is the Shamrock Holding

company which, if it can gain 10 to 15% of FCB stock, may be able to obtain a seat on the firm's board.

Present chairman and chief executive officer of Foote, Cone & Belding, Norman W. Brown, is fighting to keep the firm from becoming a takeover target. With the aid of outside consultants, the company has implemented a new budgetary system that includes profit-planning models for each office. The strategy is that the decision-making process within management will be less time consuming and more efficient and that financial planning will be more far-sighted.

Management also believes that its new research techniques in non-verbal communication and consumer response will give it an advantage over the competition. Its commercials for Nestle, Sara Lee, Levi Strauss, and Coors are regarded by experts as some of the most innovative on television. The important question facing Foote, Cone & Belding is not whether there is creative talent in the team, but whether management has the acumen to provide a sound financial foundation to assure the agency's continued success in the industry.

Principal Subsidiaries: VICOM Associates, Inc.; Smith-Hemmings-Gosden, Inc.; The NCK Organization, LTD.; Wahlstrom and Co. Inc.; Lewis, Gilman & Kynett, Inc.; Albert Frank-Guenther Law, Inc.; Carl Byoir & Associates, Inc.; Golin (Harris Communications, Inc.); Deutsch, Shea & Evans, Inc.; Foote, Cone & Belding Advertising, Inc.; Foote, Cone & Belding/Honig, Inc.; FCB International, Inc.

Further Reading: Taken at the Flood: The Story of Albert D. Lasker by John Gunther, New York, Harper, 1960; *With All Its Faults: A Candid Account of 40 Years in Advertising* by Fairfax M. Cone, Boston, Little Brown, 1969.

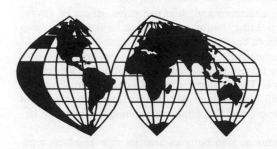

INTERPUBLIC GROUP INC.

1271 Avenue of the Americas
New York, New York 10020
U.S.A.
(212) 399–8000

Public Company
Incorporated: as McCann-Erickson in 1930; as Interpublic in 1961
Employees: 12,200
Billings: $5.5 billion worldwide
Sales: $814 million
Market value: $821 million
Stock Index: New York

Interpublic, the advertising holding company that has over $5.5 billion in worldwide billings, was the creation of Marion Harper, one of the most interesting figures in the advertising industry. Harper had long been fascinated with the way General Motors operated its corporation. GM is not one large monolithic corporation, but rather a conglomerate of separate, autonomous divisions tied to the parent company. While Pontiac, Chevrolet, Oldsmobile, and Cadillac are all General Motors cars, they cater to different tastes and different needs. Harper's desire was to create an advertising company that would mirror this structure and duplicate General Motors' success. He planned to accomplish this goal by acquiring subsidiary agencies and affiliates that, while being parts of a larger whole, were nonetheless autonomous.

In 1956 Harper, then chief executive officer and chairman of McCann-Erickson, began to implement his vision. He arranged for McCann-Erickson to buy the Marshalk Company advertising firm of New York. The move was unprecedented because Harper declared that the two agencies (McCann-Erickson and Marshalk) would be operated as competing companies. Harper's intention was to avoid the conflict of interest problem that plagued all agencies attempting to procure accounts from competing clients. He felt that if Marshalk and McCann were separately run, a camera manufacturer looking to hire McCann would not care that Marshalk did the advertising for another camera manufacturer. Most people within the industry viewed the idea with skepticism, but Harper proved them wrong. Both agencies continued to grow while often servicing rival clients.

That was only the beginning. In January of 1961 Interpublic was established as a holding company, and McCann-Erickson became its largest subsidiary. What followed was a rapid, occasionally reckless, six year period of expansion and acquisition. Harper purchased majority interest in a variety of advertising firms all over the world. The network of affiliates was global; but it was also chaotic, mismanaged, and unprofitable. In 1967 Interpublic was billing at over $700 million, yet still insolvent. Unable to repay its loans, the company nearly went into receivership. Only through a radical restructuring of management practices and sales of subsidiaries was the agency saved. One of the casualties was Marion Harper himself. He was ousted from the chairmanship of the company by the governing board.

Harper was therefore not able to personally direct his "dream-agency" to fruition. Doing so was left to others. Today Interpublic is the third largest advertising company in the world and no longer in danger of insolvency. Of the many advertising agencies selling shares to the public, it is considered by investors to be one of the best risks in the industry. Interpublic is now composed of five separate agencies: McCann-Erickson Worldwide; Marshalk; Campbell-Ewald Worldwide; SSC&B:Lintas Worldwide; and Dailey & Associates. Also included in the Interpublic family are eight diversified marketing organizations. They provide miscellaneous services such as: marketing research; public relations counseling; brochure and annual report publishing; and film and video tape production.

Although Interpublic was not officially incorporated until 1961, its history dates back 50 years. In 1911 the U.S. Supreme Court dismantled the Rockefeller Standard Oil Trust and divided it into 37 different companies. The largest of these was Standard Oil of New Jersey (now Exxon). Harrison McCann, who had been advertising manager at the Rockefeller Trust for a number of years, opened up his own ad agency and took on Jersey Standard as his first client. The age of the automobile was soon to come and with it an increase in the demand for refined petroleum products. As the advertising man for the world's largest oil company, McCann was poised for success.

In 1930 McCann merged his agency with that of Alfred Erickson to form the McCann-Erickson Company. Despite the Depression and World War II, the newly conjoined firm managed to grow in billings and importance; by 1945 McCann-Erickson was doing close to $40 million in business, making it the fifth largest advertising firm in the United States.

When Marion Harper began working at the McCann-Erickson agency in the 1930's, he was employed neither as a copywriter nor as an account executive; he was a clerk in the mailroom. After delivering the day's mail he would visit the research department and learn what he could. He proved a remarkable student; he was made manager of copy research at the age of 26 and then promoted to director of research at 30. Two years later, Harrison McCann promoted Harper again—this time to president of McCann-Erickson Advertising. In the short span of nine years Harper rose through the ranks of the agency to become president of the company.

During the period of Harper's mercurial ascendency, McCann-Erickson was experiencing the most lucrative decade of its history. In 1954 the agency surpassed $100 million in billings for the first time. Then, between 1955 and 1956, the agency added over $45 million worth of new business to its balance sheet. Among the new clients were the Westinghouse appliance division, Chesterfield tobacco, and Mennen personal hygiene products. However, these accounts were overshadowed by the fourth new customer gained by McCann at this time, namely, Coca-Cola. Though Coke was a large $15 million account in 1956, it was the soft drink company's potential for future growth that made it such an attractive customer. For McCann-Erickson, Coca-Cola was an investment in the coming era of "recreation and refreshment." Today it remains the most coveted and guarded member of McCann-Erickson's client roster.

Also at this time McCann moved to establish itself in a variety of less conventional foreign advertising markets. Long the leading agency in Latin America and Europe, the company purchased the third largest ad firm in Australia and began to actively pursue business in the Orient. By 1960 McCann-Erickson had billings of $100 million outside the U.S., with a substantial portion coming from the Asia-Pacific area.

When Marion Harper became president of McCann-Erickson the agency was considered a research-oriented firm that took a methodical approach to its advertising. It was the "organization man's" agency. Like Stanley Resor at the rival J. Walter Thompson company, Harper was a firm believer in the use of social science techniques in advertising. He was always looking for a way to accurately predict consumer response and had a bureaucrat's love for statistics. In fact, he had such reverence for facts and figures that he would occasionally sacrifice loyalty for the prospect of future earnings. In one instance he voluntarily resigned the large and long-standing Chrysler account to take on the smaller but potentially more lucrative business of General Motor's Buick division. A tireless worker, Harper would often labor at his desk for 48 hours at a stretch. He once confided in a friend, "I have been captured by what I chased." In 1960 he took his first vacation since being hired by McCann. A year later Interpublic was established, and Harper was forced to work more feverishly than ever.

Interpublic was envisioned by Harper as a family of rival sons. The various affiliates and subsidiaries would compete against each other for accounts and would operate separately. The one thing binding them together would be their mutual membership in the holding company and their ties to the parent agency's financial and informational resources. It was intended to be a "horizontal" system: the different Interpublic divisions could produce campaigns for competing products. The structure, though an ingenious way of getting around the conflict of interest problem that can make agency growth difficult, did not always work. For instance, Nestle's chocolate, a long-time McCann client, left Interpublic in 1963 after the purchase of the Erwin Wasey firm brought Carnation onto the Interpublic roster. In addition, the cost of buying so many small and medium-sized ad shops, not to mention the occasional acquisition of a large agency, was prohibitive. The overhead involved in keeping the entire business operational

was staggering. The rapid expansion of Interpublic required the one thing that Marion Harper's intellect could not provide, namely, adequate management. In 1966 Harper's sprawling conglomerate included 24 divisions, 8300 employees, a fleet of five airplanes, and billings of $711 million. Yet it rarely broke even. The following year Interpublic and Harper reached their collective nadir. The company incurred a $3 million deficit and defaulted on agreements with two New York banks. At one point in 1967 a group of investment bankers offered to buy Interpublic in its entirety for the small sum of $5 million, but the deal was never finalized.

With the danger of receivership imminent, Interpublic, needed to take drastic measures to save itself. The man responsible for instituting the changes was Robert Healy. Healy had been an executive at the firm for a number of years but went into voluntary exile in Switzerland when Marion Harper began to run the firm with what has been described as reckless authority. In the Autumn of 1967 the board brought back from Geneva to reverse the mismanaged expansion that was hurting Interpublic. After Marion Harper was ousted as the chief executive officer and chairman, Healy was put in charge. Given a short time allowance by Interpublic's creditors, Healy persuaded his employees to loan the company $3.5 million in return for convertible debentures. In addition, a number of clients agreed to pay in advance for future advertising services. These two factors permitted Interpublic to remain in business. Then, with the help of an additional $10 million in loans, the company went public in 1971.

When Marion Harper walked out of the Interpublic office he left behind the prototype of the "mega-agencies" which emerged in the late 1970's and 1980's. He also left behind a personal mystique. After being forced out of Interpublic he opened up his own small "boutique" agency, but this venture only lasted a year or two. He then kept himself out of public view for over a decade. In 1980 he was discovered living at his mother's house in Oklahoma City—penniless.

By selling public stock and reducing its comparatively high payroll costs (59% of gross income), Interpublic stabilized its finances. It began operating again at a profit. In 1973 Paul Foley succeeded Robert Healy as chief executive officer and chairman and ushered in a new era of growth at the company. Billings topped $1 billion for the first time in 1974 and plans were drawn up for renewed expansion. The Campbell-Ewald company, long-time ad agency for Chevrolet, was acquired in 1973. This move was followed five years later by the $32 million purchase of the SSC&B firm, the largest merger in advertising history at the time. These two acquisitions, along with Interpublic's strong overseas presence at a time when the American dollar was weak, led the company to record profits. At the end of 1978 Interpublic was billing in excess of $2 billion.

Throughout Interpublic's history its largest and most important clients have been Exxon and Coca-Cola. Then in the mid-1970's Lever Brothers came to Interpublic with SSC&B and Chevrolet with Campbell-Ewald. By 1979 Miller Beer would also come to rank near the top four. Miller came to McCann-Erickson as a struggling

$20 million client in 1970. Bill Backer (who had coined the phrases "Things go better with Coke" and "It's the Real Thing") and Carl Spielvogel went to work on Miller's market share. They came up with the "Miller Time" slogan and were responsible for the Miller Lite commercials which feature famous athletes. Between 1970 and 1979 Miller Beer prospered. Spielvogel thought that his success, not only with Miller but also with Coca-Cola and various other accounts, would gain him the position of Chairman at Interpublic when Foley retired. The job went to Spielvogel's rival Philip Geier. Both Backer and Spielvogel resigned and formed their own agency, taking the Miller business away from McCann-Erickson in the process. Miller was no longer a $20 million account; it was now worth over $100 million. News of the defection dropped Interpublic's stock price five points.

Coca-Cola, feeling pressure from Pepsi and upset with the departure of Backer and Spielvogel, issued an ultimatum to McCann-Erickson: "90 days to come up with a new campaign or we take our $750 million account somewhere else." Fortunately, the account was saved by the phrase "Have a Coke and a smile," and a commercial which featured Pittsburgh Steeler football player "Mean" Joe Green giving a young fan the uniform off his back.

After this initial scare Philip Geier became more comfortable as chief executive officer and chairman of Interpublic, but not too comfortable. In the 1980's Interpublic has suffered a decline of business in Europe. The offices in Great Britain and France have lost a variety of important clients (e.g., Bass Beer and Gillette), and Campbell-Ewald's European division has been operating at a loss. These difficulties are particularly troublesome to Interpublic since 65% of its billings are outside of the United States. Geier has fought back, and he has increased Interpublic's expansion in Asia where Interpublic is presently the number one American based agency.

Today Interpublic has 166 offices in 50 countries. The four company divisions create advertising for such products as: Coca-Cola, Buick, Viceroy cigarettes, Inglenook wine, Exxon, Early Time bourbon, and Kentucky Fried Chicken (McCann-Erickson); Pall Mall and Lucky Strike cigarettes, Johnson & Johnson baby shampoo, Lipton tea, Noxzema, and Bayer aspirin (SSC&B); Chevrolet and Smirnoff vodka (Campbell-Ewald); Minute Maid, Sprite, A–1 Steak Sauce, and Grey Poupon mustard (Marshalk).

Principal Subsidiaries: McCann-Erickson Worldwide; Marshalk; Campbell-Ewald Worldwide; SSC&B: Lintas Worldwide; Dailey & Associates

Further Reading: "Backer and Spielvogel Set the Standard for Growth" by Philip Dougherty, in *The New York Times*, 1 June 1980; *The Mirror Makers* by Stephen Fox, New York, Morrow, 1984.

19

JWT GROUP INC.

466 Lexington Avenue
New York, New York 10017
U.S.A.
(212) 210–7000

Public Company
Incorporated: 1980
Employees: 10,440
Billings: $4.3 billion worldwide
Market value: $354 million
Stock Index: New York

The J. Walter Thompson advertising company is the oldest among the industry's top ten agencies. Established in 1878, the company was instrumental in bringing advertising into the 20th century and making it a respectable and respected business. For six consecutive decades, from 1910 to 1970, JWT surpassed all agencies in U.S. billings. And even today, in the wake of the corporate trend, it still ranks among the leaders in advertising sales.

J. Walter Thompson was born in 1847 near Pittsfield, Massachusetts and raised in Ohio. After the Civil War Thompson travelled to New York City where he joined an advertising firm operated by a Mr. William J. Carlton. While at Carlton, Thompson became aware of the growing popularity of magazines and the sparse amount of advertising they contained. He felt magazines could be a potentially profitable medium for advertising. After he bought out Mr. Carlton in 1878 for $1300 and renamed the agency after himself, Thompson began contracting advertising space in such periodicals as *Scribner's*, *Atlantic*, *Harper's*, and the *North American Review*.

By capitalizing so quickly on magazine advertising J. Walter Thompson created a business sphere all to himself, a virtual monopoly. The agency prospered to such a degree that it developed a financial base large enough to absorb occasional loss-making accounts. The first advertising explosion of the new century was taking place, and JWT was leading it. With the agency's help companies such as Pabst Beer, Mennen toiletries, Eastman-Kodak, and Prudential Insurance became nationally known. J. Walter Thompson succeeded in making magazines commercial and magazine advertising big business.

This prosperity, however, brought complications. Administering many separate accounts was too much for a man or group of men who were also responsible for writing the ads, pursuing new clients, and keeping the books.

To handle the task of supervising campaigns of specific customers, J. Walter Thompson created the "account executive".

Nonetheless, by the end of World War I J. Walter Thompson had lost touch with his agency and the industry he had helped to build. Fortunately for the company, Thompson was smart enough to hire a young man named Stanley Resor who, with his wife Helen, was to preside over the company for over 35 years.

Stanley Resor graduated from Yale in 1901 and then joined Procter & Collier advertising of Cincinnati in 1904 as a salesman. In 1908 Resor was hired by J. Walter Thompson to supervise its new office in Cincinnati. While at the new branch, Resor offered a copywriting job to a young woman he remembered from Procter & Collier named Helen Landsdowne. Miss Landsdowne worked at the Cincinnati office for a short time and was then transferred to headquarters in New York where she was an immediate success. She offered something unique to the agency—she was female. Most JWT clients made products that were to be bought by women, but most agency copywriters were men. Helen Landsdowne avoided this problem with talent, audacity, and the encouragement of her future husband Stanley Resor. She was the first accomplished female copywriter in the history of advertising.

By 1916 Stanley Resor was in New York running the firm's headquarters. J. Walter Thompson, by this time an old man, had lost interest in the business and sold the agency to Resor for $500,000. Upon receiving title to the company, Resor did three things. First, he hired copywriter James Webb Young whose skill matched and complemented Helen Landsdowne's. Second, he reduced the client list from over 300 to 75. Third, he redirected JWT away from small local accounts toward large national ones, an orientation that continues at the agency to this day.

In 1917 Stanley Resor and Helen Landsdowne were married. Their partnership was productive both personally and professionally. As the leaders of the largest ad agency in the United States, they established between them a working division of labor. Stanley Resor was not a talented writer nor was he an artist. More than just a capable administrator, however, he was a man who possessed a very good understanding of human behavior. He used research and the help of social scientists to accurately predict public reaction to particular products. This was his gift and trade. Helen Resor, on the other hand, possessed the imagination and love for words necessary to be a successful writer. She relied more on her intuition than on research. Her ads were effective because they appeared to have been written from experience rather than from a formula.

The advertising industry experienced unprecedented growth in the 1920's, and JWT was at the forefront of this expansion. A magazine publisher, Cyrus H.K. Curtis, had taken the commerical periodical to new heights with the immensely popular *Ladies Home Journal* and *Saturday Evening Post*. These magazines were found on coffee tables all across the country, and they were Helen Resor's favorite advertising medium. J. Walter Thompson pioneered "testimonial" advertising and used it with large degree of success in Curtis' magazines. The Pond's Cold Cream ads, for instance, featured on different occasions the Queen of Rumania, Mrs. Reginald Vanderbilt, and the Duchesse de Richelieu each praising Pond's for keeping her skin young. J. Walter Thompson also became one of the first agencies to use photography in their ads. Helen Resor contracted the well known photographer Edward Steichen to work on a 1923 Jergen's lotion campaign for which he received $1000 per photograph.

By the end of the 1920's JWT had billings in excess of $37.5 million and had put more distance between itself and the N.W. Ayer Company, the number two advertising firm in the country. Accounts for such products as Libby's canned goods, Fleischmann's yeast, Kraft cheese, Yuban coffee (Resor named the brand), and Lux toilet soap kept the firm at the top.

When the Depression occurred, the advertising industry was deeply affected. Business failures became commonplace, and companies fighting for survival resorted to radical cost-cutting measures. These included, among others, a reduction in "frivolous" advertising expenditures. Total annual volume of advertising dropped from $3.4 billion in 1929 to $2.3 billion in 1931. The J. Walter Thompson agency, however, was large enough by this time to sustain itself until the economy regained its health. JWT and advertising in general weathered the Depression due in part to the advent of a new commercial medium, broadcast radio. In the 1930's J. Walter was producing radio ads for 18 clients. Performers such as Groucho Marx, Al Jolson, W.C. Fields, and Charlie McCarthy were introduced to the airwaves with JWT's help.

During this period few American advertising agencies ventured beyond the United States. Only a handful of the larger firms had offices in Europe, and they were located almost entirely in England where language posed no barrier. It was felt that what played in Peoria would not play in Paris. J. Walter Thompson, on the other hand, made a point of becoming an international company. It had opened a foreign office in Great Britain as early as 1899. In the 1920's and 1930's the company established 23 offices throughout Europe, Latin America, Asia, New Zealand, India, and Africa. This initial head start overseas afforded JWT a strong international presence. By 1960 the company had $120 million in billings abroad.

During World War II Stanley Resor and JWT gained the business of Pan American Airlines and Ford Motors, two accounts which were to help propel the company into the new age of advertising, the era of the corporate agency. In 1947 J. Walter Thompson became the first agency to surpass the $100 million mark in total billings. However, the transition to "modern" advertising was not an easy one for the Resors. They had not accurately forecast the impact of television. Following the ad style of its own copywriter, James Webb Young, the agency had traditionally produced conventional "product benefit" campaigns. Television, with its emphasis on imagery rather than words, changed the advertising terrain and forced JWT to alter its approach.

Moreover, the personnel at the agency was distinctively "old guard" and not suited to advertising's new wave of innovation. Stanley Resor had always revered the well-educated man, the social scientist, and the market researcher. As an alumnus of Yale he had a penchant for hiring fellow Ivy Leaguers; he often boasted about the number of Ph.D.'s he had on his staff. The "creative revolution" of the 1950's and 1960's was not produced by such people. Rather it was Jewish copywriters, Italian artists, and free-thinking women who led the industry through this most interesting period. The agency believed the creative fad would pass quickly and tended to ignore the fanfare attached to "artistic" and "humorous" advertising. During the 1960's the public spotlight was focused on firms such as Doyle Dane Bernbach and Ogilvy & Mather. JWT, while not exactly pushed to the background, was nonetheless overshadowed by its smaller, more innovative competitors.

In 1960 J. Walter Thompson lost the Shell Oil account (a client for 30 years) to Ogilvy & Mather. This resignation indicated a need for change. In that same year Stanley Resor, unchallenged head of the agency for nearly four decades, stepped down from his post. He was replaced as president by Norman Strouse, who instituted a reorganization of the company. The agency had in the past favored a "free-form" management structure. It was the Resor style to downplay hierarchies, divisions and departments, and definitive guidelines. Under Strouse and Dan Seymour, (who became president in 1964) J. Walter Thompson began to operate more as a corporate business; and in 1969 the agency took the final logical step in this direction by listing itself as a public company on the New York Stock Exchange.

Despite being considered the "old lady" of the advertising industry, and despite its not receiving recognition as a "creative" agency, JWT continued to expand in the 1960's. By 1970 the firm was doing $773 million in billings. However, the new decade brought additional problems to the company. 1972 was a particularly bad year. The agency lost the accounts for Ford's Pinto, Mustang, and Maverick automobiles ($17 million); Pan American Airlines ($13 million); Firestone ($8 million); and Singer sewing machines ($12 million). With these losses, the firm suffered its first billings decline since World War II.

In the early 1970's J. Walter Thompson received some publicity that temporarily damaged its public image. The Watergate break-in investigation revealed that five Nixon "operatives" were past employees of J. Walter Thompson. White House chief of staff H.R. Haldeman, press secretary Ron Ziegler, and appointment secretary Dwight Chapin were all former admen trained at Thompson. It was later discovered that the agency was indirectly connected to a public relations company that was a front for the CIA. The public relations firm named in this accusation was the Washington D.C. based Robert R. Mullen & Company. Sam Meek, who had long been the organizational head of JWT's international operations, was a principle supporter of the Mullen "agency." Even two years after the news was first reported, J. Walter Thompson remained subject to rumors linking it with the CIA. Not until the present company president, Don Johnston, issued a press release stating that the agency did not, nor will in the future, have any relationship with the CIA or any other government agency was the case finally closed.

Paralleling these scandals were a number of top management personnel changes at the firm. In October of 1974, Don Johnston became the third JWT president in a year. He succeeded Edward B. Wilson, who had very recently replaced Henry Schachte. According to *Business Week* magazine, these were the "dog-days" at JWT, and it was up to Johnston to end them. The price for a single share of company stock had fallen from $38 in 1969 to $7 in 1974. To stop the slide Johnston instituted cost-cutting measures, trimmed the payroll of its "excess talent," and set the company on a hunt for new business. In 1976 J. Walter Thompson staged a stunning recovery. It achieved a $60 million billings increase in the first nine months of the year, $30 million of which came from the newly acquired Burger King account. The company was again producing profitable advertising.

1980 was an important year for the agency. First, it incorporated as the JWT Group, thus allowing itself a way to service competing accounts by delegating them to autonomous subsidiaries. And second, it merged with the world's largest public relations firm, Hill & Knowlton, and made it part of the holding company. The acquisition of Hill & Knowlton enabled JWT to provide its customers with public relations services without having to build its own public relations department. Hill & Knowlton's clients include Texaco, Du Pont, Prudential, and Campbell Soup.

No sooner had the JWT Group showed its strength and determination in "the battle of the mega-agencies" than it was hit by another scandal. This one involved neither Watergate nor the CIA but rather fraudulent billing practices. The damage done to the company's reputation was considerable. JWT operated a television syndication service wherein spot television time on local stations would be sold to company clients. Between 1978 and 1981 the television syndication division of the company, managed by a Ms. Marie Luisi, reported tremendous profits. The figures, however, were found to be five or six times higher than their real value. Ms. Luisi had charged clients for advertising time they never received or used. The fictitious entries amounted to over $22,800,000 and affected such clients as Lever Brothers, and Burger King. The "Luisi Affair" affected company morale to such a degree that major policy changes were instituted. Salary priorities were restructured so that financial rewards could be given to staff members without their having to advance quickly through the corporate ranks. This measure was meant to curb the sort of ambitiousness that led Ms. Luisi to commit such improprieties. In addition, Johnston hired a permanent financial consultant to see that billing irregularities were, if not prevented altogether, at least discovered before becoming irrevocable.

The agency recovered from the Luisi scandal. In the first two quarters of 1983 net income at the JWT Group was the second highest in its history. This trend continued into the first quarter of 1984. Following a 17% revenue increase, net income was 254% higher than it was for the same period the year before. In 1985 J. Walter Thompson had a gross income of $450.9 million and total worldwide billings in excess of $3 billion, making it the fifth largest advertising firm in the United States.

Beginning in 1986, J. Walter Thompson encountered difficulty winning new accounts, resulting in a substantial weakening in its financial position, which in turn led to serious dissension among board members, two of whom were forced to resign after failed attempts to relieve Don Johnston of control of the company. As the financial situation continued to deteriorate, the JWT Group became identified as a target for a hostile takeover. Johnston asserted on several occasions that the JWT Group would not consider any takeover bids and would resist any hostile attempts by other companies to acquire JWT.

In late May of 1987, however, an unknown bidder began to purchase shares of the firm's stock. On June 10 a small British marketing services company called the WPP Group plc announced that it had acquired a 4.8% share of the JWT Group and intended to purchase the remaining shares for $45 each. The JWT Group rejected the offer, which was subsequently raised to $50.50 per share. Offiicials of the two companies entered into negotiations, and on June 26 reached agreement for WPP to acquire the JWT Group for $55.50 per share, or $566 million.

The takeover agreement pledged to retain Don Johnston (who later resigned) and merge the JWT Group with a unit of WPP called the Owl Group (the Owl is the unofficial symbol of JWT). The takeover raised concern that WPP, headed by former Saatchi & Saatchi financial director Martin Sorrell, would later come under the control of Saatchi and Saatchi, which at the time owned 7% of WPP. Sorrell denied any such intention.

The JWT Group, which is 18 times larger than WPP, was expected to benefit greatly from the financial expertise and good reputation of Mr. Sorrell. In the weeks following the takeover, however, JWT lost a number of very important accounts, including Goodyear and Ford.

Principal Subsidiaries: J. Walter Thompson Co.; Simmons Market Research Bureau, Inc.; Lord, Geller, Federico, Einstein, Inc.; Hill and Knowlton, Inc. The company also lists more than 35 international subsidiaries.

Further Reading: The History and Development of Advertising by Frank S. Presbrey, New York, Doubleday, 1929; *The Making of Modern Advertising* by Daniel Pope, New York, Basic Books, 1983.

LEO BURNETT COMPANY, INC.

Prudential Plaza
Chicago, Illinois 60601
U.S.A.
(312) 565-5959
Private Company
Incorporated: 5 August 1935
Employees: 4,064
Billings: $2 billion worldwide

No other advertising agency in the world has created so many memorable and marketable "product characters" as the Leo Burnett Company. The Jolly Green Giant, Morris the Cat, and Charlie Tuna are all Burnett inventions. And that is only the beginning of the list. The near-unemployed Maytag repairman, the Pillsbury doughboy, Tony the Tiger, and the legendary Marlboro Man are also examples of the Leo Burnett agency's talent for giving a product an image that endears it to the consuming public.

The operating philosophy at Leo Burnett does not, however, involve instructing agency staff to merely foster recognizeability for a client's product. Equally if not more important is the concept of "familiarity." In its advertising campaigns the Leo Burnett Company tries to establish a special rapport between producer and buyer and between agency and client. For this reason, Leo Burnett has been consistently more successful than its competitors in retaining customers for extended periods of time. Of its 29 United States accounts, half of them have been with the firm for 20 years or more.

Currently, the Chicago-based Leo Burnett Company is the eighth largest advertising agency in the world, the eighth largest in the United States, and one of two top-ten Amercian agencies not headquartered in New York City. Ironically, the firm has never made growth one of its major goals or priorities. Rather than actively pursuing numerous, varied accounts, or increasing business by extending its services through diversification, it tends to take a more conservative approach to the business of advertising. It concentrates on winning a few "blue chip" accounts and keeping them for decades. Then, as the business and advertising expenditures of its clients expand, Leo Burnett also grows.

This approach to advertising is characteristic of Leo Burnett. Born in St. Johns, Michigan on October 21, 1891, Leo Burnett attended the University of Michigan where he graduated with a degree in journalism. After college he obtained a position with Cadillac as the editor of an in-house publication and then became advertising manager in 1919. Later, he worked at Homer McKee Advertising in Indianapolis. In 1930 he was hired away from McKee by Erwin Wasey & Company of Chicago to assume the position of vice president/creative head. Five years later Leo Burnett left Wasey & Company to form his own company.

When Mr. Burnett first started his business in August of 1935 he had one account, a staff of eight, and a bowl of apples on each desk in the reception lobby. The agency's only client was the Minnesota Valley Canning Company which had formerly been with Leo Burnett's old firm. It had moved over to the fledgling Burnett agency because the management at Minnesota Valley liked Leo Burnett personally. "I want the little guy with dandruff and the rumpled suit," said the president of the company. To reward this display of confidence and loyalty, Burnett created the Jolly Green Giant.

In an industry centered in the high fashion area of Madison Avenue in New York City, the Leo Burnett Company of Chicago was something of an oddity. Rather than eastern sophistication, its ads tended to reflect a certain mid-American homeliness. The Green Giant and Kellogg campaigns typify this technique. Both have historically been aimed at the emotions of their respective audiences, protraying the products with a large degree of human warmth. Burnett used what he himself called "sod-busting corniness"—language and imagery that drive home a point by conveying a feeling of straightforward honesty. However, the "Chicago School" was more than just a creative philosophy. It was a commitment to a certain type of research and brand of workaholism.

Burnett was a firm believer in research but often felt that the questions traditionally asked in consumer surveys did not provide the advertising agency with enough information. Most surveys were conducted in order to determine which products and therefore which advertisements sold most effectively. While recognizing the importance of this type of investigation, Burnett wanted more. He wished to know whether his ads were "liked" by the consuming public. Always seeking a combination of image and language that would evoke the most positive emotional response, Burnett was one of the first to seriously use Motivational Research (MR) in advertising. This is not to say that the Burnett agency put advertising popularity above product sales. Burnett simply felt that if he could find out what people liked, he could more successfully create effective ads. Motivational research became popular among a number of advertising firms in the late 1940's and 1950's, but the technique itself came under fire in the 1960's with the rising power of consumerism. Motivational Research was thought to be what gave advertising agencies the ability to influence buying patterns and behavior through psychological conditioning. That, of course, was not what Leo Burnett meant when he spoke of motivational research. He was constantly making public speeches imploring the advertising industry to be socially responsible and never to surrender the invaluable commodity of integrity. Nevertheless, motivational research was all but abandoned in the 1960's, although during the interim Leo Burnett had learned some of what he wanted to know about the American consumer's likes and dislikes.

During this time the atmosphere around the agency ranged from the hectic to the frenzied. Stories abound of Leo calling up his copywriters at various Chicago bars on Saturday nights to ask them to come in Sunday morning to rewrite still imperfect ad campaigns. What is more, the stories go, the writers were always eager to take Leo up on his "invitation." Leo Burnett either surrounded himself with like-minded, overly industrious people or his workaholism was contagious. He himself described the grueling creative review committee meetings as "being nibbled to death by ducks." The work, however, always paid off with ad campaigns that "stuck" in the mind of the consumer. Don Tennant, former worldwide chief creative officer, says of the agency, "They put their stamp on these brands and put a stamp on the American consciousness."

During the decade of the 1950's, the years of "I like Ike" and Pax Americana, the Leo Burnett Company was able to reflect the American values of strength, tradition, comfort, and family in its advertising campaigns. This talent won for the agency a number of new and profitable clients and secured those accounts already in the Burnett agency. A good example is the work the agency did for United Airlines. United, although it had a large market share of the passenger air travel business, was feeling the pressure of new carriers coming into the industry. For years United had been associated with the cold stainless steel of its airplanes and began for the first time to worry about its image. When it received the account, Burnett focused on the people who ran the airline rather than on the plane itself. This gave rise to the "Fly the Friendly Skies" campaign. Similarly, the thematic catch phrases of "the best to you each morning" for Kellogg's and "you're in good hands" for Allstate carry with them a familial warmth and all-American appeal.

As successful as these campaign images were, none compares with the impact of the most famous Burnett creation, the Marlboro Man. In his book, *On Advertising*, David Ogilvy writes that, "Without any doubt, Leo's greatest monument is his campaign for Marlboro."

Phillip Morris, the cigarette's manufacturer, was having trouble selling the new filter-tipped Marlboros to an American public which had grown accustomed to Lucky Strikes. Filtered cigarettes were viewed as unmasculine, and Marlboro could never claim more than 1% of the market share. So Burnett went to work creating a different image for it. He came up with a character that exuded masculinity and American heritage, namely, the cowboy. Sales increased dramatically and Marlboro became the number one selling cigarette brand in the world, a title it still holds today. What was particularly striking about the ad campaign was that it translated so well from television to magazine print and billboard advertising—an absolute necessity after cigarette commercials were banned from network television in the United States in 1970.

Leo Burnett died in 1971 at the age of 79. He left behind more than a successful advertising agency. He also left a personal legacy and a philosophy that encompassed both the business and creative aspects of advertising. The motto at the Leo Burnett Company was and remains, "Reach for the stars; you may not get one, but you won't come up with a handful of mud either." Nothing could possibly capture the homespun wisdom of Leo Burnett better. He kept a file called "Corny Language" and added entries to it whenever he overheard something in a passing conversation that struck him as honest and poignant. Most fundamental to the Burnett creative philosophy, however, was what Leo called "inherent drama." He thought every product possessed this quality and that it was up to him and his copywriters to uncover it. Inherent drama, he said, "has about it a feeling of naturalness which gives the reader an emotional reward. It is what the manufacturer had in mind in the first place when he conceived the product."

Yet the discovery and display of a product's inherent drama is not supposed to make the ad more striking than the product itself. The Burnett agency tries not to create a "Burnett look" that is imposed upon its customers. Instead, the specific client is given a "look" with Burnett's help. Also, the agency tends to measure the effectiveness of its creativity by way of sales rather than awards, an attitude which occasionally draws criticism from the new breed of "idea" men presently in the industry. Recently, the agency has been criticized for being overly cute, and for creating bland, homogenous advertising. The "Chicago School," some say, is an antiquated concept that develops only provincial, child-like campaigns. "Sod-busting" honesty, it has been remarked, is passé.

This criticism has not gone unanswered. Both in the creative and business spheres, the Leo Burnett Company has become more aggressive. It pursued and won the lucrative McDonald's account (stealing it away from Needham and Harper), is actively seeking foreign markets, and is also venturing into the areas of service industries and high tech. In 1985 the firm acquired Hewlett-Packard as a client. Recognition for creativity has also come to the firm in the past couple of years. For instance, the Leo Burnett Company won more music awards at the 1985 *Advertising Age* magazine awards banquet than any other agency except J. Walter Thompson.

This shift in posture and attitude does not represent, however, a change in fundamentals. The company will no doubt retain its "blue chip" accounts and the conservative campaigns that have made those accounts profitable. The agency heads do not wish to alter Leo Burnett in any way, just allow it greater latitude in dealing with the changing industry trends. Says present chairman of the board and president John Kinsella, "We haven't been as active as we possibly should have in the past. It's a mistake we made. I'm not against growth, but growing just to be bigger is not a goal at all." The agency intends to develop the best ads it can, but will shirk innovation for the sake of innovation. As Leo Burnett would say, quoting an old boss of his, "If you want to be different, come to the office in the morning with a sock in your mouth."

It may seem odd for a company with more than $2 billion in total billings to be privately owned. In fact, private ownership is in keeping with the firm's "family" orientation. There are no anonymous share-holders at Burnett as there are at most other firms. Leo Burnett was not persuaded that public ownership would be good for his business. Indeed, the whole idea seemed counter to the operating philosophy of the agency itself. When most of the other major advertising agencies began to publicly trade shares in the 1960's, Leo Burnett was one of the few who did not.

Though Leo Burnett has been dead for over 15 years, his presence is still felt at the agency. His picture—a bald man with sloped shoulders, double chin, and a formidable lower lip wearing a crumpled suit—hangs in every office, of which there are 38 in more than 32 countries. His words, "Steep yourself in your subject, work like hell, and love, honor and obey your hunches," still direct the work of the agency's 8383 staff members. The vice presidents and executive heads in particular are dedicated to the Burnett method of advertising. Nearly all of the chief officers at the firm began their careers with the Leo Burnett Company. The agency rarely goes outside its own doors to hire its executives.

If it is indeed true that the "Chicago School" of advertising is antiquated and on the way out, no one at the Leo Burnett will concede that that is so. Nor will the agency's clients who, with Burnett's help, have become some of the largest and most successful in their respective industries. There is good reason for this confidence. "Personality" and "warmth" are the two words which most accurately characterize the long list of Burnett advertising campaigns, and clients can be sure they will not soon go out of style.

Further Reading: Giants, Pigmies, and Other Advertising People by Draper Daniel, Chicago, Crain Communications, 1974; "Leo Burnett: The Solid Sell" by David M. Elsner, in *The Wall Street Journal* (New York), 12 January 1977; "Leo" by Carl Hixon in *Advertising Age* (Chicago), 8 February 1982; *The Benevolent Dictators* by Bart Cummings, Chicago, Crain Books, 1984.

Ogilvy & Mather

THE OGILVY GROUP, INC.

2 East 48th Street
New York, New York 10017
U.S.A.
(212) 907-3400

Public Company
Incorporated: 1985
Employees: 8,817
Billings: $3.8 billion worldwide
Sales: $560 million
Market value: $495 million
Stock Index: NASDAQ London

David Ogilvy is the founder and patriarch of the expansive Ogilvy Group. After leaving Oxford without a degree he became a salesman of various products in England, occasionally writing advertising copy. Most notably, he wrote an instructional pamphlet, "The Theory and Practice of Selling the Aga Cooker," which won him a position with the London ad agency, Mather & Crowther, where his brother was an account executive.

Soon after going to work there, Ogilvy persuaded Mather & Crowther to send him to the United States for a year to study American advertising techniques. Ogilvy was so enthralled by what he saw in America that his yearlong sojourn turned into permanent residence.

He studied advertising intensely, going so far as to convince the executives at NBC to allow him to go behind the scenes to watch radio commercials being written and produced. During this time Ogilvy found himself divided between two advertising techniques or philosophies: the "image" school of MacManus and Rubicam, which stressed product "personality," and the "claim" school of Lasker and Hopkins, which relied more heavily on straightforward, product-benefit copy. "My admiration for those two opposites tore me apart," Ogilvy remembered. "It took me a long time to reconcile what I learned from both of them."

Interestingly enough, Ogilvy did not immediately enter the advertising business after his arrival in America. Instead, he went to work for George Gallup's research organization in Princeton and Hollywood. In three years, he conducted over 400 national opinion surveys, became closely acquainted with American tastes and customs, and made a lifelong friend in Mr. Gallup. The research fascinated Ogilvy with its insights into human behavior. He became aware of its value as a tool in advertising.

After his apprenticeship with Gallup, Ogilvy left the professional research business, but again did not seek a position in advertising. He bought an Amish farm and moved there with his wife and son. After a couple of years, by 1947, he had come to understand that advertising was what he wanted to do. He would have liked to work for the Young & Rubicam agency and apply his research skills to its "image" philosophy, but thought that at the age of 36 he was too old to be hired, so he never applied. Instead, he took $6,000 of his own money, borrowed major capital from Mather & Crowther and another London firm, S.H. Benson Ltd., and established his own advertising business in New York. Ogilvy then hired Anderson F. Hewitt away from J. Walter Thompson to be president, and appointed himself vice president in charge of research.

In September of 1948 the Hewitt, Ogilvy, Benson & Mather agency officially opened for business. The timing could not have been better. The Depression and World War II had driven all but the largest, well-established, advertising firms out of business and had discouraged attempts by newcomers to break into the market. However, with the war over and the American economy expanding with unprecedented vigor, and a greater public awareness of the media and its influence, advertising became a necessary element in any business practice. The potential for growth was almost limitless.

Still, the agency of Hewitt, Ogilvy, Mather & Benson did not become successful overnight. Competing with such long-standing industry leaders as J. Walter Thompson, Young & Rubicam, Leo Burnett, and BBDO was difficult. Yet Ogilvy combined good timing, a bit of luck, and some fresh ideas, and managed to make a name for his company in the early 1950's. He did it with highly innovative campaigns for three small accounts: Hathaway shirts, Schweppes quinine water, and Rolls-Royce. The Hathaway ad featured a model ("a cross between movie star Clark Gable and author William Faulkner") wearing a Hathaway shirt and an eye patch. Ogilvy called this a "story-interest" ad which imbued the product with mystique. What's more, the eye patch created immediate product identity for the consumer.

Ogilvy also created the "man from Schweppes." The British beverage company was having trouble selling its quinine water in the American market, and looked to Ogilvy for help. Ogilvy again sought product indentity through a character model. Employing the bearded, aristocratic face of Schweppes advertising manager, Commander Edward Whitehead, he was able to sell eccentric sophistication in the form of a tonic water. Not long after the campaign ads appeared in U.S. magazines, Schweppes was finally able to gain a foothold in the American beverage market.

Both the Hathway and Schweppes campaigns were clearly image oriented, which was odd in that they came from Ogilvy, a man from a predominantly research background who tended to stress copy and claim over image. Their success taught Ogilvy the power of "image" but did not bring him to abandon his belief in the "claim" school. The third ad campaign for the young agency was the one produced for Rolls-Royce. Here Ogilvy was able to bring together both approaches, claim and image, to create an effective sales technique. Below a picture of a Rolls-Royce racing along the highway was a large print caption which declared: "At 60 miles an hour the loudest noise in this new Rolls-Royce comes from the electric clock." Then, within the body of the ad, in detailed copy, Ogilvy listed 11 benefits and characteristics unique to the Rolls-Royce. Though the ad ran in only two magazines and two newspapers at a cost of $25,000, sales for the car rose 50%, and the ad became the paradigm for all subsequent automobile advertisements.

Ironically, these three highly original ads barely paid for themselves, at least in the short run. The accounts were small and therefore meant little in the way of commission. (Traditionally, agencies receive a 15% commission of the total billings revenue. For example, if a client purchases $100 worth of advertising space, the agency's share would be $15.) The fledgling firm had to rely on larger, more conservative campaigns to pay the bills. However, over the long term, the Hathaway, Schweppes, and Rolls-Royce ads demonstrated the "Ogilvy style" and attracted a number of new clients. One customer, Shell Oil, increased the agency's revenues by almost 50% when it started an account in 1960. Later, accounts were also secured from General Foods, Bristol-Myers, and Lever Brothers, to name just a few. Little of this success would have been possible, however, had it not been for the initial impression Ogilvy, Mather & Benson made in its first few years in advertising.

By 1962 the agency's billings had increased dramatically, and Ogilvy had established himself as an innovator in the business. Indeed, the 1960's and early 1970's marked a period of expansion and innovation. In 1964 Ogilvy, Benson & Mather Inc. of New York merged with Mather & Crowther Ltd. of London to become Ogilvy & Mather International. Ogilvy's firm, though, was not the only one expanding. In fact, it seemed every ad agency was undergoing some kind of expansion. The growth put new fiscal pressures on all the agencies, and one by one the companies began to sell shares of stock to mitigate expansion costs. In 1966 Ogilvy & Mather followed this trend and went public.

During this period Ogilvy & Mather also became more diverse in its range of advertising. It developed campaigns for large corporations (Sears, Weyerhauser), non-profit organizations (The United Negro College Fund, the World Wildlife Fund), whole nations (Puerto Rico, Singaore, France), and international clients whose markets were primarily outside the United States.

By 1975 Ogilvy & Mather had grown extensively. In addition to General Foods and its other base accounts the agency had established accounts with American Express, IBM, Merrill Lynch, Campbell's Soup, Morgan Guaranty, and a number of smaller manufacturers such as Mercedes-Benz. Branch offices were set up around the world to handle the large amount of international business the firm had developed and subsidiaries such as S.H. Benson Ltd. and Carson/Roberts (both acquired in 1971) were consolidated under the umbrella of the parent company.

Growth on the scale experienced by Ogilvy & Mather can also result in adverse effects. Creativity tends to become stifled as the immensity of the operation creates bureaucratic impediments. Time is spent more on administration and procedure than on innovation. With larger and larger amounts of an agency's shares under public ownership, firms have a propensity to become conservative. They feel an obligation to their shareholders to secure consistent dividends and minimize risks, and therefore shy away from the innovative in favor of going with "what has worked in the past." Ogilvy & Mather, long thought of as an "idea shop," became a victim of this kind of corporate syndrome. The agency successfully produced conservative campaigns for large companies but, creatively speaking, had stagnated. One former writer with the firm commented that Ogilvy & Mather was "working like a bank. It was a financial institution that was doing dull, predictable advertising."

Ogilvy was aware of what was happening, and on the eve of his retirement he decided to make some dramatic changes. First, in 1979 Norman Berry was brought over from England to become creative director in New York. Berry had a reputation for being dedicated to original ideas and innovative people. He was to wrest the direction of the company away from the accounts management people and put it back in the hands of the production people. He also made it clear to clients that he would stand up for his staff on issues of creativity.

Second, Kenneth Roman, a veteran account executive with a sensitivity for the wants and needs of those on the creative side of the business, was appointed president of Ogilvy & Mather U.S.A. He took on the difficult task of healing the divisions within the agency and coordinating the "art" and "business" sides more effectively.

And third, the commercial writer and producer, Hal Riney, was instructed by Norman Berry to set up an Ogilvy & Mather office anywhere he chose. He opted for San Francisco, and before long was developing innovative advertising campaigns.

Soon Norman Berry had challenged Ogilvy & Mather into actively pursuing awards and recognition for creativity and originality, something that had been avoided and frowned upon in the recent past. In 1982 Ogilvy & Mather won its first Kelly award for the inventive and sexually suggestive Paco Rabanne men's cologne campaign. In 1985 the agency for the first time started collecting its share of Clios (the Oscar of advertising), and its commercial for Hershey's chocolate covered granola bars won a silver medal at Cannes.

What did all this emphasis on creativity mean to Ogilvy & Mather? Not only was the agency able to keep those clients who had exhibited signs of dissatisfaction, but also it attracted a large amount of new business. According to a 1984 *Advertising Age* survey, Ogilvy & Mather was operating in 41 countries, was ranked third in world advertising income with $363.2 million in revenues, and had amassed over $2.4 billion in billings.

In recent years, as Ogilvy & Mather has sought to deal with the problems of expansion, their approach to the advertising business has grown and changed accordingly. Not wanting to repeat the problems that hindered its creativity in the mid-1970's, the agency has created a network of semi-autonomous subsidiaries that, while having access to the resources only a large company can provide, still work as in a "small shop" environment. According to the agency heads at Ogilvy & Mather, this method "abolishes the subsidiary stigma" and "promotes a competitive edge." An example of one such member of this network is the Scali, McCabe and Sloves Company, which in 1985 reported $390 million in billings while retaining its reputation as an "original idea" shop.

In May of 1985 Ogilvy & Mather International Inc. became The Ogilvy Group. The name change reflects the agency's increasing focus on comprehensive client services and shows a continued application of "Ogilvy Orchestration," an agency orientation conceived in 1984 to bring together Ogilvy & Mather's "many instruments and voices to form one big sound." The purpose of the program is to provide prospective clients with complete advertising assistance through coordination of the services the agency can offer.

Coupled with "Ogilvy Orchestration" is the company's persistence in diversification. This move illustrates the agency's dedication to growth and its willingness to be prepared in the event of an economic recession. In 1985 the Ogilvy Group acquired two European medical advertising firms, Zoe (France) and Pharma (Germany), formed a health care marketing group in the United States, and expanded its role in public relations. The firm has also continued to develop its direct-mail marketing, a field in which it is now the leading agency.

In the late 1970's and early 1980's Ogilvy & Mather began to experience conflict of interest problems among clients and prospective clients, making it hard for the agency to expand. In other words, it became difficult for the firm to pursue additional clients in a particular industry (brewing, for example) when it was already doing the advertising for another company manufacturing the same type of product.

Ogilvy & Mather experienced this dilemma in 1979 when it attempted to procure the Lincoln-Mercury account. Upon hearing of the firm's pursuit of Lincoln-Mercury, Mercedes-Benz USA, a long-time client of the agency, defected. Unfortunately for Ogilvy & Mather, Young & Rubicam ultimately won the Lincoln-Mercury account, leaving Ogilvy & Mather a double loser. The company is hoping that diversification through its semi-autonomous subsidiaries will "solve the perceived conflict-of-interest problem with competing accounts."

The future looks bright for the Ogilvy Group. The firm was named agency of the year for 1982 by *Advertising Age* magazine and received acclaim for its campaigns for American Express, Gallo Wines, Hershey, and International Paper. In addition, the agency is financially sound. Both 1984 and 1985 were successful years, billings having increased successively in each. It would appear that the Ogilvy Group will follow along the same course it started at the beginning of the 1980's. The company, while wanting to diversify still further, will do so selectively. Its interest now seems directed towards medical advertising, over-the-counter drug marketing, public relations and direct mail.

Principal Subsidiaries: Ogilvy and Mather Worldwide; Scali, McCabe, Sloves Group; Cole & Weber, Inc.; SAGE Worldwide; Research International

Further Reading: "The Ogilvy of the Offbeat Ideas" by Carl Spielvogel, in *The New York Times*, September 7, 1958; *Confessions of an Advertising Man* by David Ogilvy, New York, Atheneum, 1963; *Blood, Brains and Beer: The Autobiography of David Ogilvy* by David Ogilvy, New York, Atheneum, 1978.

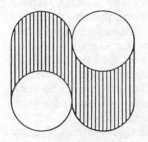

OMNICOM GROUP INC.

909 Third Avenue
New York, New York 10022
U.S.A.
(212) 935-5660

Public Company
Incorporated: 1986
Employees: 10,000
Billings: $5.5 billion worldwide
Sales: $754 million
Market value: $589 million
Stock Index: NASDAQ

In the summer of 1986 the advertising agencies of 16th-ranked Needham Harper Worldwide and 12th-ranked Doyle Dane Bernbach joined together with 6th-ranked BBDO to form Omnicom. With combined 1985 billings in excess of $5 billion and a combined income of $736 million, the new group is advertising's second largest worldwide holding company behind Saatchi & Saatchi.

The story of Omnicom has yet to write itself; at this time, it is still only the sum of its constituent parts, the three separate histories of BBDO, Doyle Dane Bernbach, and Needham Harper Worldwide.

BATTEN, BARTON, DURSTINE & OSBORN

BBDO was itself the product of a merger. In 1919 Bruce Barton, Roy Durstine, and Alex Osborn opened an advertising agency on West 45th Street in New York City. A few years later, as its business grew, Barton, Durstine & Osborn moved to the seventh floor of a building on 383 Madison Avenue. Three floors above BDO was another advertising agency, the George Batten Company. It seemed odd having competing firms sharing the same address, so a merger was proposed. On May 16, 1928 the George Batten Company joined with BDO to form Batten, Barton, Durstine & Osborn.

The most important man at the Batten agency was William Johns. Johns was more experienced and considerably older than Barton, Durstine or Osborn. He was therefore made president of BBDO while the job of chairman went to Bruce Barton. Durstine was vice-president and general manager, and Osborn ran a separate BBDO office in his hometown of Buffalo, New York.

Bruce Barton was not a typical advertising man. In fact, he admitted on numerous occasions that he and the profession were not well suited. Barton was trained in theology and philosophy, attracted to politics, and committed to his personal writing projects. He wrote two extremely popular books, *The Man Nobody Knew* (a reappraisal of the life of Jesus Christ) and *The Book Nobody Knew* (a similar reappraisal of the Bible). Then, in the mid-1930's, Barton ran for Congress. He was elected and held office for two consecutive terms. In 1940 he ran for senator but lost by 400,000 votes. Barton was involved only in the creative aspects of BBDO's enterprises.

Durstine was the opposite of Barton. He was in love with the advertising business and what it could obtain for him. Like a number of other agency heads trying to make money during the Depression, Durstine's workaholism became self-destructive. He began drinking heavily, lost his wife and Long Island estate, and was forced to retire from BBDO in 1939.

The vacancy left by Durstine's departure caused some reshuffling of BBDO's management. William Johns by now was too old to handle the day to day operations of the agency. He was "promoted" to chairman, but relieved of all administrative duties. Osborn and Barton were then required to run the agency themselves.

The readjustment proved beneficial to the agency, for BBDO was in need of a new approach to its advertising. Osborn in particular was instrumental in reorganizing the agency and directing it toward the packaged goods advertising business. From the very beginning BBDO had primarily handled accounts for "institutional" clients such as Du Pont Chemical, Consolidated Edison, and Liberty Mutual. Although they were consistent customers, these companies neither needed nor wanted extensive advertising. If BBDO was going to grow rapidly enough to compete with large and established agencies, it would have to do advertising for packaged goods. Not only are new packaged goods constantly introduced to the market, but also those already on the shelves are always being improved to keep up with competing brands. In this environment advertising flourishes—that was Osborn's important insight.

Between 1939 and 1945 BBDO gained a number of important non-institutional accounts: Lever Brothers, B.F. Goodrich, Chrysler (Dodge Division), MJB Coffee, and the 3M Company. Not even the upheaval of World War II kept BBDO from growing. Billings increased from $20 million at the height of the Depression to $50 million at the end of the war.

In 1946 management changes again took place at BBDO. Ben Duffy, a veteran account man with the agency for over 15 years, was elected president; and Charlie Brower, who was to lead BBDO in the 1950's and 1960's, became executive vice-president in charge of copywriting. Duffy was an excellent salesman who could close a deal quickly. When Foote, Cone & Belding resigned the $11 million American Tobacco Company account in 1948, Duffy went directly to see American Tobacco's George Hill and secured the account after one meeting. In Duffy's 10 years at the helm of BBDO the agency increased its billings from $50 million to over $200 million.

Unfortunately for BBDO, Duffy was prone to ill health. In 1956 he suffered a stoke in Minneapolis while visiting the chairman of General Foods. He could not continue as the head of the agency, and Charlie Brower subsequently replaced him as president. Brower was the obvious choice. He had been in charge of the creative side of BBDO's advertising for over 20 years and was responsible for much of the agency's success.

Brower had a "no-nonsense" approach to advertising. He felt that as president of BBDO he had to do four things: 1) add one million dollars to the payroll; 2) hire talent from the outside; 3) fire many of his best friends; and 4) do away with company time clocks, which he thought made the agency a factory instead of a creative enterprise.

When Duffy retired there was confusion at BBDO, and a number of important clients quit the firm. In fact, until Charlie Brower established himself as president of the company no one was actually in charge. Revlon, a $6 million customer, cancelled its account as soon as it heard of Duffy's retirement. Other clients followed Revlon's example. Brower did not allow this situation to continue for long. BBDO appeared headed toward disaster when Brower won for it the most lucrative account in its history—Pepsi Cola. Within a matter of weeks BBDO was financially healthy once again.

For BBDO the 1950's and early 1960's was a period marked by more than management readjustments and client shuffling. It was also a period in which BBDO became intimately and extensively involved in political advertising. Many agencies try to avoid producing campaigns for political movements and parties so that copywriters are not forced to sell opinions they themselves may not hold or to which they may be vehemently opposed. BBDO is one of the few firms that has accepted political advertising as a normal part of its business.

In 1948 BBDO ran its first ad campaign for a political candidate, Republican Thomas Dewey. Both candidate and agency lost this close election but, though Dewey left the political foreground, BBDO simply waited for the next election and a more marketable candidate. It found one in Dwight D. Eisenhower. In 1952 BBDO signed the Republican National Committee as a regular account, and did the advertising in Eisenhower's successful bid for the presidency. The firm was hired again four years later to handle Eisenhower's re-election campaign. Unfortunately for the Republican Party, and Richard Nixon in particular, BBDO's success ended with Eisenhower. A BBDO make-up man was responsible for the "grey shave" look of Nixon's face in his 1960 televised presidential debate with John F. Kennedy.

Outside the political realm BBDO continued to expand and sign new clients. Not only did it increase the number of its institutional customers such as CBS Broadcasting (1959) and the SCM Corporation (1961), but also it won product oriented accounts such as Tupperware (1959), Autolite (1961), McGregor Sporting Goods (1964), and Pepperidge Farm (1964). To match this domestic growth BBDO began to expand internationally for the first time in 1959, opening up offices in London, Paris, Milan, Frankfurt, and Vienna. In 1964 BBDO acquired the Atlanta-based firm of Burke Dowling Adams and with it the accounts of Delta Air Lines and the various governmental agencies of the state of Georgia. The Clyne Maxon firm of New York, with its $60 million in billings, was also merged with BBDO in 1966.

By the time of the worldwide recession during the 1970's, Charlie Brower had retired as president of BBDO. His successor was Tom Dillon, who had been the agency's treasurer since the late 1950's. Like most ad agencies BBDO suffered considerable losses in domestic billings during these years of economic stagnation. However, because of the way the company was structured, BBDO was able to endure this period without undue strain. By opening up offices in new places around the world, the agency entered advertising markets which had previously been closed to it. This international expansion served to offset losses incurred in the domestic market. In addition, BBDO began selling shares to the public in an effort to diffuse operating costs.

In 1976 Bruce Crawford was named president of BBDO. He had been head of the agency's foreign operations. During his eight year tenure billings at BBDO tripled to $2.3 billion, and his cost management measures kept the company from misusing the benefits of this growth. As one analyst said of BBDO in 1981, "I've never seen a company so conscious of cost controls."

Crawford retired on March 31, 1985 and was succeeded by another able manager, current president Allen Rosenshine. Under his tutelage BBDO has continued to expand by acquiring subsidiaries, creating for the agency a genuine worldwide network. It has traditionally been BBDO policy to allow local entrepreneurs the freedom to run their own offices, to encourage individuality and creativity. This practice is coming to an end under Rosenshine. A number of foreign and international clients have expressed concern over these "local" shops. They think there is too little direction coming from top management, and have become wary of giving business to BBDO subsidiaries. To remedy the problem Rosenshine has attempted to tighten the connections within the BBDO network and provide more centralized leadership.

So far it appears Rosenshine has instituted these changes without alienating those on the creative side of the business or retarding BBDO's ability to produce innovative advertising. In fact, in 1985 BBDO and its various sub-agencies won a total of 530 awards for creativity. Most notable of these was the Grand Prix Gold Lion at the Cannes Film Festival. The trophy is presented to the agency which produces the year's best television commercial. The ad that won this coveted award was the "Archeology" commercial made for Pepsi Cola.

BBDO is such a large and vital member of the advertising industry that there has been some question as to why it needs or wants to join in a merger, particularly when the other two potential partners are currently experiencing financial difficulty. What does BBDO have to gain?

The answer is not hard to find. BBDO was one of the last major agencies to expand internationally, waiting until 1959. This late start has proven to be a handicap and has made BBDO's overseas growth uneven. For instance, BBDO is presently the number one firm in Germany and the number two firm in Australia; but is 17th in Canada, 26th in France, and 29th in Britain (the most important European market.) The situation was complicated in 1985 by BBDO's being forced to sell its interest in a major South African subsidiary at a considerable loss. This divestiture led to a decrease in BBDO's international revenues of 94% and removed BBDO from the South African market where it had been the top agency. The merger with agency. The merger with Needham and Doyle Dane Bernbach would provide BBDO with greater international presence, particularly in France, Canada, and Great Britain. According to the policy planning heads at BBDO, this improvement of the agency's foreign business is necessary if BBDO is to maintain itself as a formidable worldwide advertising competitor.

DOYLE DANE BERNBACH

When those within the advertising industry are asked which agency most exemplifies innovation and creativity, one firm above all others is mentioned—Doyle Dane Bernbach. In the world of advertising, where imitation is the rule, the Doyle Dane Bernbach agency has made itself an exception. Most ad firms follow familiar schools of thought, but not Doyle Dane Bernbach. In the words of David Ogilvy, "They just sort of created an original school out of air."

In 1949 Ned Doyle and William Bernbach joined Maxwell Dane in the formation of a new advertising agency. Bernbach and Doyle had been trained at Grey Advertising, and Dane had owned his small ad company for a number of years. Doyle Dane Bernbach's first year billings came to just $500,000, but something about its advertising style suggested it would soon be a major force in the industry. It hired the most creative people it could find, no matter where they came from.

Among Max Dane, Ned Doyle and Bill Bernbach there existed a well-defined division of labor. Doyle was the account executive in charge of winning and retaining clients; Dane took care of administration and financial matters; and Bernbach handled the creative concerns. Rarely did they cross into each other's designated spheres.

What made the firm unique in the ad industry was Bill Bernbach and his preoccupation with the "road not taken." Born in Brooklyn and educated in English and philosophy at New York University, Bernbach was the ad man's intellectual. His ideas were fresh, striking, and more often than not, couched in subtle humor. He sympathized with the public at large, which found most advertisements boring. His quest was to make ad campaigns exciting and fun while still focusing on the product's attributes. He had little reverence for research. He felt it substituted statistics for ideas and emotions. For him advertising was an art, and as an artist he was primarily concerned with imagery, impression, and point of view.

Bernbach was also a good teacher. He was patient, precise but gentle in his criticisms, and had the ability to nurture natural ability. His "students" formed the firm's Creative Team: a small group of copy writers, artists, art directors, and photographers that produced the agency's campaigns. Bernbach led the group but not in an authori-

tarian manner. It was what he called an "horizontal hierarchy." "We are all peers here," he said.

In the 1950's Doyle Dane Bernbach displayed its style of advertising in four notable campaigns for four near-unknown companies: Polaroid Cameras, Levy Bakery Goods, Ohrbach's Department Store, and El Al Israel Air Lines. These companies, like Doyle Dane Bernbach, were attempting to establish themselves in their respective markets. Polaroid was overshadowed by Kodak, Ohrbach's by Macy's, and few people had ever heard of Levy's Bread or El Al Air. To compensate for this lack of public recognition, the agency created strikingly different ads featuring everything from a cat dressed in women's hat to an American Indian claiming that "you don't have to be Jewish to enjoy Levy's real Jewish rye." Not only did the campaigns sell large quantities of cameras, clothes, bread, and airline tickets, they sold Doyle Dane Bernbach advertising as well. In 1954 the Agency's billings were $8 million; by 1959 that figure had increased to $27.5 million.

In the early 1960's the agency won two new accounts that were to further enhance its reputation: Avis Car Rental Service and Volkswagen. In the rent-a-car business Hertz held the dominant market share. Far behind in second place, Avis wanted to increase its own market share. Most advertising is meant to portray the client in as favorable and strong a position as possible. Doyle Dane Bernbach, however, disregarded this tradition; its campaign stressed Avis' weak position vis-a-vis Hertz. "We're number two," said the ads, "We try harder. We have to." This strategy worked. In two years Avis increased its market share by over 25%.

The Volkswagen advertising campaign is a similar story. These small German cars were not what the American consumer wanted, or so it appeared. Again, Doyle Dane Bernbach converted a liability into a saleable asset. Hoping people had tired of the large and overly-embellished American-made cars of the 1950's, Doyle Dane Bernbach said simply: "Think small." The art of the ads was minimalist, usually showing a small picture of the car against a blank white backdrop. The text was equally odd. The short, simple copy was blocked in paragraphs that looked, in the words of copywriter Helmut Krone, "Gertrude Steiny." Not only did Americans purchase these "ugly" Volkswagens by the thousands, but the car became a symbol for an entire "non-conformist" generation.

Following these successes the agency won accounts from American Air Lines, Seagrams, International Silver, Heinz Ketchup, Sony, Uniroyal, Gillette, Bristol-Myers, and Mobil Oil. The 1960's were the golden age of advertising's "creative revolution," and Doyle Dane Bernbach was at the forefront of this movement.

As the 1960's gave way to the 1970's, the industry witnessed a return to conventional advertising techniques. This trend and the recession which plagued the beginning of the decade spelled trouble for the company. In 1970 Doyle Dane Bernbach lost the $20 million Alka-Seltzer account, even though the "that's a spicy meat-ball" commercial was extremely popular and a favorite of the critics. Other agency clients quickly followed Alka-Seltzer's lead. Lever Brothers, Whirlpool, Sara Lee, Quaker Oats,

Cracker Jack, Uniroyal, and Life Cereal also cancelled their accounts.

Fortunately for the agency, its growth during the 1960's provided it with enough revenue to absorb these losses, at least in the short run. Nonetheless, a company reorganization and reorientation was in order. In 1974 Neil A. Austrian joined the company as executive vice president. He had expertise in the business aspects of advertising, something that had been missing at the agency. Gradually he transformed the company into a more orderly advertising network. Subsidiaries were acquired to strengthen Doyle Dane Bernbach's worldwide presence and offer more comprehensive client services. In 1975 the agency's billings rose for the first time in the new decade, and this trend continued for seven years.

On October 2, 1982 William Bernbach died of leukemia. His absence left a void at the agency. This raised a difficult question: Could Doyle Dane Bernbach continue without Bill Bernbach?

The question haunted the firm. In 1982 earnings fell 30%. This loss was compounded in the next two years by the resignation of important accounts. American Air Lines cancelled its account in 1983. Its spot was filled by Pan Am which subsequently left the agency a few months later. Then, in 1984, Polaroid announced it would be taking its business elsewhere. The agency was particularly shocked by this resignation. Its commercials had helped make Polaroid the world's best-selling camera.

In the first half of 1986 Doyle Dane Bernbach was forced to lay off 24 staff members; it had lost almost $113 million in net earnings. The merger with BBDO and Needham Harper Worldwide represents a necessary business decision. It is doubtful that Doyle Dane Bernbach could continue if its fiscal situation were not improved. The security afforded by the Omnicom umbrella should relieve the agency of its present financial difficulties, and allow it to concentrate on what is does best, namely, innovative advertising.

NEEDHAM HARPER WORLDWIDE

In 1924 Maurice Needham opened up his own advertising agency in Illinois. It was named The Maurice H. Needham Company. This title was changed in 1929 to Needham, Louis & Brorby, Inc. The firm then merged with Doherty, Clifford, Steers & Shenfield, Inc. in 1964 to become Needham, Harper & Steers. In 1984 the company name was again changed, this time to Needham Harper Worldwide.

As a Chicago based agency, it has traditionally avoided Madison Avenue type of advertising, and is generally considered to have stronger advertising presence in the Midwest than in the East. Until becoming part of Omnicom, Needham & Harper had not ranked among the largest worldwide agencies. However, this provincialism has contributed to its success. Smaller companies, feeling neglected and disrespected by large advertising agencies, have often turned to Needham & Harper. This type of client has been the foundation of the firm's business.

In addition to that of Maurice Needham, the other name associated with the agency is that of Paul Harper. He came to the company in 1945 when it was Needham, Louis & Brorby. Harper had been educated at Yale and had spent four years in the Marine Corps fighting in the Pacific campaign. After his discharge, he walked into Needham's Chicago office looking for employment. He had no résumé, no writing experience, and no civilian clothes. Despite his scant qualifications Needham gave him a job as a copywriter, and soon Harper was making a name for himself in advertising. He worked primarily in broadcast advertising. Most notably, he produced commercials for Johnson's Wax on the "Fibber McGee and Molly" radio show.

As Harper became a man of greater importance at the agency he gradually moved from copywriter to manager. In 1964 he became president of the company and supervised the acquisition by Needham of Doherty, Clifford, Steers and Shenfield in 1965. At this time the name of the agency was changed to Needham, Harper & Steers. In 1967 he became chairman and chief executive officer of the agency, and retained this position until his retirement in 1984.

During the late 1950's and 1960's when companies were substantially increasing their expenditure on advertising, Needham, Harper & Steers, though still only a mid-size agency, grew along with the industry. It concentrated on smaller accounts but also retained a number of large Midwest clients, such as the Household Finance Corporation and the Oklahoma Oil Company. For the former it created the "Never borrow money needlessly" slogan; and for the latter it coined "Put a tiger in your tank."

In 1972 the firm followed the industry trend of publicly trading its shares. This move did not prove to be lucrative. Investors do not generally consider advertising to be a perennially stable business. More so than other industries, it is affected by the fluctuations of the economy. Smaller advertising firms are especially vulnerable and therefore pose higher risks to potential investors. Unlike the larger agencies such as Ogilvy & Mather and Interpublic, Needham, Harper & Steers was unsuccessful in drawing a strong investment interest. Four years after going public Needham & Harper "went private" again.

Though it services many small and mid-size accounts, Needham & Harper is primarily known for its "blue chip" clients. It won Xerox in 1968, McDonald's in 1970, Honda in 1977, and Sears in 1982. The agency produced the famous "Brother Dominic" commercials for Xerox, and the "you deserve a break today" slogan for McDonald's. Unfortunately for the agency, in 1984 McDonald's took its domestic business away from Needham and turned it over to Leo Burnett. The bad news continued in 1986, when Needham lost the $40 million Xerox account.

The merger with BBDO and Doyle Dane Bernbach may well alter the "personality" of Needham Harper. Even though the three agencies intend to operate as separate divisions of Omnicom, there is more to the merger than a simple name change. Already some clients have expressed displeasure with the prospect of sharing the agency with competitors. The old conflict of interest problem has become particularly pronounced. Campbell's Soup, a Needham and Harper client, will not stay with Omnicom if Heinz, a Doyle Dane Bernbach client, remains. Similar difficulties have arisen between Stroh's and Busch beer, and Honda and Volkswagen automobiles.

The most important question among Needham and Harper customers is whether they will continue to receive the same advertising attention to which they have become accustomed. "Fortunately," says one such client, "Keith Reinhard will still be around." Reinhard joined the firm in 1964, became president of NH&S/Chicago in 1980, chairman and chief executive officer of NH&S/USA in 1982, and chairman and chief executive officer of Needham Harper Worldwide in 1984. He has impressed staffers, colleagues, and customers alike with his integrity and hard work. He maintains that the merger with Omnicom will help Needham attract and retain large clients, but claims that the agency will not treat its smaller customers any differently than it has in the past. Reinhard

also hopes Omnicom will restore to Needham a presence in the New York advertising market, something it has lacked since Xerox withdrew its account in 1986.

Principal Subsidiaries: BBDO Worldwide Inc.; DDB Needham Worldwide Inc.; Diversified Agency Services

Further Reading: *The Story of Advertising* by James P. Wood, New York, Ronald Press, 1958; "Bernbach's Advertising: A Formula or Delicate Art?" by Robert Alden, in *The New York Times*, 7 May 1961; "Doyle Dane Bernbach: Ad Alley Upstart" by A. Kent MacDougall, in *The Wall Street Journal* (New York), 12 August 1965.

SAATCHI & SAATCHI COMPANY PLC.

SAATCHI & SAATCHI PLC

80 Charlotte Street
London W1A 1AQ
England

Public Company
Incorporated: 1970
Employees: 7,500
Billings: $8.2 billion worldwide
Sales: $3 billion
Market Value: $1.06 billion
Stock Index: London New York

Throughout the 1980's the advertising industry has been experiencing a fundamental change in its structure. This change has been caused primarily by a trend towards larger and larger advertising conglomerates which serve as holding companies for subsidiary agencies. The entire complexion of advertising is being altered; the industry is presently entering the era of the "mega-merger" and the "super agency." At the forefront of this trend is the Saatchi & Saatchi Company and the two brothers who operate it, Charles and Maurice Saatchi. In the short span of 16 years they have taken their operation from a small office in London's Soho district and have built it into the world's largest advertising company with offices all over the globe (the Saatchis have not even visited many of the agencies they presently own). In May of 1986 the Saatchis completed a ten-year agency buying binge with the purchase of the highly profitable Ted Bates firm. This acquisition gave Saatchi & Saatchi combined total billings of over $7.2 billion, enabling it to move past Omnicom (itself the product of a merger between BBDO, Needham Harper, and Doyle Dane Bernbach) in the race for top position in the advertising business. The price tag for purchasing Bates and attaining industry pre-eminence? $450 million.

The Saatchi-Bates agreement is interesting not only because it represents the largest acquisition in advertising history but also because it almost did not happen. Negotiations broke down numerous times and the Saatchi brothers feared they would lose Bates the same way they lost a bid to purchase Doyle Dane Bernbach before it became part of Omnicom. To secure the deal the Saatchis agreed to extraordinary payment terms: $400 million cash up-front, and another $50 million over the next two years. No one but the Saatchis would have had the financial resources to fulfill such a contract.

Most industry analysts agree that once the competing client or "conflict of interest" problem is taken care of, the Saatchi-Bates merger will be beneficial for both firms. Saatchi & Saatchi, which promises its shareholders an annual per share increase of 20%, needs wholesale growth in order to maintain its present rate of expansion; and the acquisition of Bates allows for just this kind of growth. Bates wanted to make 21 acquisitions of its own but had the resources to make only two such purchases. Says Bates chief executive officer Robert Jacoby, "Privately held, Bates would be 10th next year and 15th the year after. It was inhibiting us." With the Saatchis behind him, Jacoby is now pursuing all 21 potential acquisitions.

The Saatchi brothers have gained a reputation as men with the single-minded intention of creating the largest advertising institution in the world. When they have an opportunity to purchase an agency to further fortify this global network, they usually take it. Since 1982 they have added such important firms as Compton Communications, McCaffrey & McCall, Backer-Speilvogel, Dancer Fitzgerald Sample, and the Hay Group (a Philadelphia-based consulting agency) to their holdings. Furthermore, they have not been reticent in expressing their goals and intentions. In 1983, for example, they took out a full page ad in the *New York Times* announcing that they were moving into both Wall Street and the American advertising market.

Charles and Maurice Saatchi are first-generation Britishers of Iraqi-Jewish extraction, their father having emigrated to England to become the owner of a moderately successful textile business. Both brothers are reclusive and enigmatic. They rarely grant interviews or agree to have their photographs taken, they do not frequent advertising social circles, and seldom meet with clients. Though they actively draw attention to their agency, they try to direct it away from themselves.

Charles, who is in his early 40's, is competitive, aggressive, and often brilliant. He began his advertising career at 18 when he went to work for a small London ad firm as an office boy. In two years he became the star copywriter and then left for the United States to study the American style of magazine advertising. Upon his return to England he was hired by Benton & Bowles. From there he moved over to London's most innovative advertising firm, Collett Dickenson Pearce. He stayed at CDP long enough to make a reputation for himself and then left to start his own creative consultancy. In 1970 he joined his brother Maurice and friend Tim Bell to form Saatchi & Saatchi advertising.

Smooth and calm, Maurice is the perfect complement to his brother. While Charles and creative director Jeremy Sinclair handle the creative side of the business, Maurice takes care of the financial side. Maurice is urbane and modest. After receiving a sociology degree from the London School of Economics, he was employed briefly as a developer of new magazines. Later, when he and Charles first entered the advertising business, he used his experience with magazines to help promote the fledgling agency. In addition to his collection of other advertising firms, Charles has created one of the largest collections of contemporary art in the world and has recently established a private museum in London. Maurice, for his part, has rooms full of model trains.

The Saatchi & Saatchi Company's story is a "rags-to-riches" tale that was accomplished in only 16 years, a virtual overnight success in the advertising business. From their small office in Soho, Maurice would call prospective clients on the phone without invitation, and Charles would leak news of the agency's newly won accounts to the trade journals so as to build a reputation for the firm. In addition, the Saatchis had a skill for hiring talented people and creating innovative ads. One of their most famous campaigns was for the British government's Health Education Council which was trying to increase public awareness of birth control. The Saatchis produced an ad that featured a pregnant man with a curiously anxious expression on his face. The text asked: "Would you be more careful if it were *you* who got pregnant?'

The most important opportunity for Charles and Maurice, however, came in 1976 when they merged with the old and well established Compton agency of London. By merging with Compton the Saatchis acquired the accounts of a number of "blue chip" clients, chief among them being Procter & Gamble.

More importantly, Compton was listed on the London Stock Exchange, thus giving the Saatchis a source for generating the large revenues needed for expansion. Selling public shares in an advertising agency, however, is not an easy task. Most industry analysts and investors consider advertising companies poor risks and Compton more so than others. Its share price was a disappointing four times earnings. Maurice had to work hard to persuade the London investment community that Saatchi-Compton was a stable business capable of turning a profit regardless of economic cycles. Investors were impressed with Saatchi's steady growth and soon started buying agency stock. Eventually the price-to-earnings multiples of Saatchi stock rose above that of the overall market average.

The capital produced by selling public shares of stock enabled Saatchi & Saatchi to expand and purchase more agencies. For the Saatchis, there is more to the advertising business than just advertising. Advertising itself makes up only one of the three "pillars" of the Saatchi institution, the other two consisting of communications and consulting. To increase its financial resources for expansion, Saatchi & Saatchi offered public over-the-counter stock in the United States for the first time in 1983. And, in fact, it was the company's ability to raise capital in the stock market that made it such an attractive merger partner in the eyes of Ted Bates.

However, not all of the Saatchi mystique is the product of financial or business prowess. The agency has won numerous awards for creativity in advertising and tends to attract the most innovative people. One reason is that the Saatchis pay their creative types very well, better in fact than any other British agency. According to John Salmon of Collett Dickenson Pearce, "They've changed the salary structure of the creative market in London."

Saatchi & Saatchi is perhaps most famous for its political advertisements. The Saatchis produced a campaign for Margaret Thatcher in her successful bid to become Prime Minister of Britain in 1979 (they also helped with her 1983 re-election race.) One ad aimed at the incumbent Labour Party showed a long line of workers waiting in a "dole queue" and said simply, in a brilliant pun, "Labour isn't working." The agency was so deft at this kind of political advertising that it reportedly "changed the face of British politics." Mrs. Thatcher's campaign for prime minister proved to be a vehicle of self-promotion for Saatchi & Saatchi. By the end of 1979 it was the number one agency in Britain; two years later it was the largest agency in Europe.

The ads the agency creates usually feature provocative or arresting visual images and an economy of text. Saatchi creative director Jeremy Sinclair feels that a direct and simple message is the best kind of advertisement. This attitude helped Saatchi & Saatchi win the British Airways account over from Foote, Cone & Belding a few years ago. British Airways has now become the agency's flagship account.

Yet the main lesson the Saatchis have taught the advertising industry is that advertising is a business first and an art second. Furthermore, they have proven many times over that they will not remain complacent. They actively and aggressively seize any good opportunity for added growth, whether it involves retail growth in the way of new clients or wholesale growth in the way of new agencies. Saatchi & Saatchi feel no need to conform to the established connections and rules of the industry. For instance, the British advertising trade association forbids the stealing of clients from competitors, claiming that this kind of unsolicited "poaching" is unethical. The Saatchis believe so firmly in poaching that they have a special account team that does nothing but try to take clients away from competing firms. As for the advertising trade association, the Saatchis simply did not join.

When one listens to Maurice Saatchi explain the reasons for the agency's preoccupation with continuous expansion, the word "position" figures prominently. "We have a strong belief in building position," he says. And he thinks the Ted Bates agreement will secure its place among the three or four most profitable advertising companies for at least 20 years. Yet, for two men who are so dedicated to controlling as much of the global advertising market as they can, the Saatchis tend not to get involved with either their clients or their subsidiary firms. The rule of thumb is to purchase good agencies and then leave them alone. In fact, neither of the Saatchi brothers is on the governing board of any of their subsidiaries.

In spite of their extremely rapid and well-publicized rise to the top of the advertising industry, the Saatchis themselves see nothing unusual in their success. In their words, they are just "riding the tide of industry history." Advertising, they explain, will soon be conducted by a number of large compartmentalized holding companies which service the accounts of fewer but larger multinational clients.

If Charles and Maurice Saatchi are correct, clients will need to become accustomed to sharing a particular advertising company with competitors. (For instance, Mobil Oil and Shell Oil may in time have the same advertising agency.) And the agencies themselves will need to learn how to remain creative while the size and complexity of their operation increases. The Saatchis have further proven that greater attention must be given to financial matters if an ad firm hopes to survive. Much of what has made their agency such a successful enterprise has been its healthy approach to the stock exchanges in London, Paris and New York. Other advertising companies will have to reassess their relationship with Wall Street and the City of London if they are not to be left behind.

Critics of the Saatchis, however, are not sure their approach to advertising is good for the industry or for the Saatchis themselves. They feel Saatchi & Saatchi has perhaps stretched itself too far. Trying to do so much in such a short time often means agreeing to expensive deals. Between 1987 and 1992 Saatchi & Saatchi will have to make earnings-related payments on its recent acquisitions of up to $162 million. More frequently, though, the Saatchis are criticized less for their accomplishments and more for the way they have achieved them. The British advertising community is especially quick to point out that the Saatchis publicize only their victories while glossing

over their losses. Others say Saatchi has lost its creative edge.

Yet the Saatchis usually find ways of answering their critics. Saatchi & Saatchi is a very profitable agency with an impressive clientele. It handles 40 of the world's 200 largest multinational corporations. Furthermore, its shareholders are happy. According to Morgan Stanley, Saatchi & Saatchi's emphasis on cost controls and budgeting has allowed it to outdistance other publicly-owned agencies in profit growth.

Principal Subsidiaries: Saatchi & Saatchi Compton Worldwide; Backer & Spielvogel; KHBB (U.K.); William Esty; Ted Bates Worldwide; McCaffrey and McCall; DFS Dorland Worldwide; Saatchi & Saatchi Compton Group.

Further Reading: *Advertising in Britain: A History* by T.R. Nevett, London, Heinemann, 1982; "Consulting Arm Faces Hurdles" by Stewart Alter in *Advertising Age* (Chicago), January 5, 1987.

YOUNG & RUBICAM INC.

285 Madison Ave
New York, New York 10017
U.S.A.
(212) 210–3000

Private Company
Incorporated: as Young & Rubicam Advertising in 1923
Employees: 10,844
Billings: $4.1 billion worldwide

In 1985 Young & Rubicam Inc. became the largest advertising company in the world, unseating the Dentsu agency of Japan which had held the position since 1973. Young & Rubicam's total billings amounted to over $3.2 billion and its gross income rose to $480.1 million. The advertising holding companies of Saatchi, Saatchi & Bates, Omnicom, and Interpublic have sales figures greater than those of Young & Rubicam, but they are the combined products of numerous loosely connected agencies. Unlike these conglomerates, Young & Rubicam is one agency. In spite of its size, however, Young & Rubicam is one of the most creative ad firms in the industry. In 1979 it was named the co-agency of the year (it shared the honor with the Ayer company) by *Advertising Age* magazine, and has perennially been among the leaders in Clio awards, the advertising industry's Oscar. That Young & Rubicam is still recognized for its originality proves it has retained its commitment to Raymond Rubicam's one and only rule: "Resist the usual."

The history of 20th century advertising is populated by a handful of men. Stanley Resor, Claude Hopkins, Albert Lasker, Marion Harper, Bill Bernbach, Leo Burnett, and David Ogilvy are the names that come quickly to mind. Also included within this group would be Raymond Rubicam, the man cited by David Ogilvy as the single most important influence in his advertising career. Said Ogilvy, "He taught me that advertising can sell without being dishonest." He was only the second living person ever elected to the American Advertising Federation Hall of Fame.

Born in Philadelphia in 1882 to a family that had prospered in the import-export business, Rubicam seemed destined to lead an easy and comfortable life. However, when young Raymond's grandfather died the estate fell to his wife's side of the family instead of to Rubicam's father, who was a writer for a trade journal. The situation worsened when Raymond's father died of tuberculosis.

The young boy was then shuttled from relative to relative because his widowed mother could not care for him. Due in large part to his unconventional and lonely childhood, Rubicam was a poor and unruly student. He left school in his early teens to work as a grocery clerk in Denver and never attended school again. Later, he returned to his native Philadelphia hoping to become a short story writer, but he became an advertising man instead.

His first position was as a copywriter for the Armstrong Advertising Company in Philadelphia. The owner, F. Wallis Armstrong, was generally regarded as an autocratic tyrant who harassed his employees on a regular basis, and Rubicam more regularly than most. When offered a more lucrative position at the larger and more renowned N.W. Ayer Company, Rubicam accepted with gratitude. While at Ayer he wrote two advertisements which made him a reputation within the industry. The first was for Steinway pianos. Steinway had traditionally been averse to advertising. The owners of the company did not regard it as an estimable craft and consequently did as little of it as possible. To satisfy this particularly skeptical client Rubicam produced the famous "Instrument of the Immortals" ad. It not only caused a stir in the 1920's when it first appeared (Steinway sales rose by 70%), but has stood the test of time. It is still considered one of the most effective advertisements ever written. The other Rubicam creation of note was the "Priceless Ingredient" slogan developed for Squibb over-the-counter drugs.

Rubicam would have stayed indefinitely at the Ayer agency had the elder Ayer not died and left the business to his son-in-law. Rubicam was hoping to be made copy chief, but was passed over in favor of an older man. Because of this unpromising situation, Rubicam decided to quit Ayer in 1923. Along with another dissatisfied Ayer employee, account executive John Orr Young, he started his own advertising agency in New York. The new Young & Rubicam firm had nothing but enthusiasm to offer prospective clients, but that proved enough to persuade General Foods to give it the struggling Postom beverage account. Postum was then followed by other General Foods accounts. Young & Rubicam did the advertising for products such as Grape-Nuts, Sanka Coffee, Jell-O, and Calumet baking powder.

The office atmosphere at the Young & Rubicam agency was different from that at any other ad firm. It was markedly loose, lively, and informal; it had the imprint of its founder Raymond Rubicam. Nearly all agency directors, both in the past and in the present, have emerged from the accounting rather than from the creative department. Rubicam was different. He was the creative man *par excellence*, and he ran his agency accordingly. What the office lacked in structure and standard operating procedure (no one made it to work before 9:30 in the morning) it more than made up for in talent and vitality. An example would be what were called "gang ups" at the agency. When work on a new campaign was initiated, all copywriters, artists, photographers, and copy chiefs involved in the project would lock themselves in a room to labor over the details. These "gang ups" usually lasted well into the night and were very exhausting. Only a rare breed of person could produce effectively in that kind of environment—but Rubicam always found such people. He hired his staff on the basis of their writing and artistic skill, and their willingness to work long and odd hours. He cared little about the typical qualifications of educational background and work experience. He wanted people with innovative ideas rather than impressive résumés.

The agency grew steadily throughout the 1920's and 1930's. Even the Depression did not hinder its ability to gain new clients and increase revenues. It may have been a loosely organized advertising company, but more often than not the ad campaigns were of exceptional quality. Billings went from $6 million in 1927 to $12 million in 1935, and then jumped to $22 million in 1937. During this period Young & Rubicam gained such lucrative accounts as Travelers Insurance, Bristol-Myers, Gulf Oil, and Packard automobiles. However, it also voluntarily resigned the extremely large Pall Mall account from the American Tobacco Company. The owner of American Tobacco, George Washington Hill, was notorious for badgering those who were unfortunate enough to do his advertising. The relationship between George Hill and Young & Rubicam grew so strained that Rubicam decided it would be in the best interest of the agency to forfeit the $3 million account. Rarely has the news of a large business loss met with such a sigh of relief at an advertising firm. The $3 million loss was well worth the boost in morale.

In 1934 John Orr Young retired. He had lost interest in the business and was allowing others to slowly take over his duties. Despite the great amount of money he was making, he wanted an early retirement. His position as head of new business was filled by Sigurd Larmon, who was to become an important influence at the agency for decades. Rubicam, who had been progressively exerting more and more influence at the firm, now had majority interest in the business. In the next 10 years Rubicam led an ascending firm through the advertising industry's first "creative revolution." The agency was successful because Rubicam, while always encouraging his creative department to be original and take chances, was nonetheless careful with the gifted but fragile personalities who surrounded him. Though it is a cliché to say a business is its people, the maxim holds particularly true in advertising; an ad agency has no other form of inventory. The agency's staff was pushed but also nurtured, and resignations were rare. In the words of former copy supervisor George Gribbin, "One of the great assets of this agency is that a man here feels he can express himself as a writer."

When Raymond Rubicam retired to Arizona in 1944, Young & Rubicam was the second largest advertising company in the world. Only the J. Walter Thompson agency did more business. The void left by a man such as Raymond Rubicam could have caused confusion at the agency and left it without direction, but that scenario did not happen. Rubicam had trained his successors well, especially George Gribben. Gribben had long been one of the most influential men at the firm and, upon Rubicam's retirement, was named creative director in charge of all advertising production. He was instrumental in bringing Young & Rubicam into the second advertising "revolution" which took place in the late 1950's and 1960's. In 1951 the agency reached the $100 million mark in total billings and by 1960 that figure had more than doubled to $212 million.

In the 1960's advertising grew as an industry. Firms such as Ogilvy and Mather, Doyle Dane Bernbach, and Leo Burnett initiated a period of innovation that broke all previous advertising rules and conventions. They helped re-establish advertising as an artistic craft. Though overshadowed by these smaller, more "visible" ad agencies, the larger companies like Young & Rubicam and J. Walter Thompson also benefited from the renaissance.

More money than ever was being spent by companies on advertising. The growth in business was paralleled by staff increases and subsidiary acquisitions within particular agencies. This internal growth, however, proved to be problematic. In 1971 the worldwide economic recession brought the rapid rise in advertising expenditures by manufacturers to a quick halt. Nearly all advertising companies suffered billings losses, and many of the smaller "creative" shops were forced out of business altogether. Young & Rubicam itself was in trouble. Its payroll and other expenses were too high, and the agency was not growing. A "changing of the guard" took place among the company's management. Ed Ney became chairman and chief execu- tive officer, Alex Kroll became creative director, and Alexander Brody was placed in charge of international operations. These men were to lead the agency into a period of unprecedented growth.

Ney's first action was to reduce the staff at the New York office by one-third and relinquish some of the losing accounts that were draining the agency. One of those to go was the Bristol-Myers account; they had been a client for over 25 years. Then he set out to reorganize and increase the company's financial resources in order to renew its ability to purchase subsidiaries and broaden its range of services. Rather than sell shares to the public to raise capital, Ney instead manipulated retirement benefits and agency-held stock to generate the funds he needed. These maneuvers allowed him greater flexibility and privacy when it came time to decide when and where to use the money. For instance, in 1973 Ney supervised the acquisition of Sudler & Hennessey (a health care ad firm) and Wunderman, Ricotta & Kline (a direct marketing company). These two agencies added $62 million to the firm's balance sheet and pushed it past J. Walter Thompson to become number one in domestic billings. In a little over five years Ney had taken Young & Rubicam from third to first in the industry. Ney, however, was not yet satisfied. In addition to purchasing a number of small midwestern and southwestern ad shops, he also arranged in 1979 for Young & Rubicam to merge with the Marsteller agency, which had long been among the leaders in the public relations business. Not only did Marsteller's $306 million in billings help Young & Rubicam stay ahead of J. Walter Thompson, it also gave the agency the strong public relations department it needed.

While Ed Ney was building Young & Rubicam on the domestic front, Alexander Brody was increasing the company's presence abroad. The firm successfully broke through cultural and political barriers by linking up with Hungary's leading advertising agency (Mahir), illustrating that the Eastern Bloc countries should no longer be considered "non-markets." More importantly, Brody was instrumental in orchestrating the agency's most important joint venture to date, the 1981 merger of Young & Rubicam's Tokyo office with Dentsu's Tokyo office. Never before had the number one and number two advertising companies in the world joined together on a business venture such as this one. The new subsidiary, called DYR, gives Dentsu a firmer foothold outside Japan and strengthens Young & Rubicam's position in Tokyo. DYR's billings are presently well over $300 million. Brody, who now presides over DYR, says this figure is sure to grow. He projects that by 1990 DYR, with its strong advantage in the field of "bi-cultural advertising," will have billings in excess of $1 billion.

In 1985 Ed Ney announced that he was resigning as chairman and chief executive officer of Young & Rubicam. He named as his successor Alex Kroll, the former head of Young & Rubicam U.S.A. and the man responsible for resurrecting the agency from its creative doldrums. Under his leadership the firm reasserted itself as an "idea" shop. During a seven month period in 1977 the agency procured $77 million in new business. Accounts included Pabst beer, Oil of Olay skin cream, and Kentucky Fried Chicken. When Young & Rubicam lost the Chrysler account in 1979, Kroll's persistence helped to win the very prestigious Lincoln-Mercury account worth $65 million. Kroll is also the man who hired comedian and television personality Bill Cosby to do Jell-O Pudding commercials.

Following in the footsteps of Ney, one of the most effective administrators in the advertising industry, is no easy task. Kroll insists he will try to emulate Ney's methods and patterns of success. Remaining the number one world agency requires a commitment to growth and diversification. Kroll is prepared to take the necessary steps to secure Young & Rubicam's position at the top of the advertising industry, but not at the expense of the company's reputation for creativity.

Further Reading: "Memoirs" by Raymond Rubicam in *Advertising Age* (Chicago), 9 February 1970; *Giants, Pigmies, and Other Advertising People* by Draper Daniels, Chicago, Crain Communications, 1974; "An Interview with Ed Ney" by Bart Cummings in *Advertising Age* (Chicago), 3 January 1983; *The Mirror Makers* by Stephen Fox, New York, Morrow, 1984.

AEROSPACE

G.I.E. AIRBUS INDUSTRIE

AVIONS MARCEL DASSAULT-BREGUET
 AVIATION

THE BOEING COMPANY

BRITISH AEROSPACE PLC

N.V. KONINKLIJKE NEDERLANDSE
 VLIEGTUIGENFABRIEK FOKKER

GENERAL DYNAMICS CORPORATION

GRUMMAN CORPORATION

LOCKHEED CORPORATION

MARTIN MARIETTA CORPORATION

McDONNELL DOUGLAS
 CORPORATION

MESSERSCHMITT-BÖLKOW-
 BLOHM GmbH.

NORTHROP CORPORATION

ROCKWELL INTERNATIONAL

ROLLS-ROYCE PLC

UNITED TECHNOLOGIES
 CORPORATION

⟁ Airbus Industrie

G.I.E. AIRBUS INDUSTRIE

Avenue Lucien Servanty
BP No. 33 31700
Blagnac
France
(61) 93 33 33
Consortium
Incorporated: December 1970
Employees: 28,000 (On Reserve)

The last European jetliners to be produced in significant quantities were the French Caravelle and the BAC-111 during the 1960's. When the production runs for these airplanes came to an end, the commercial passenger jet market was soon dominated by three American companies: Boeing, McDonnell Douglas, and Lockheed. European aerospace companies were too small to carry the large investment costs of developing a new jetliner. After several unsuccessful attempts to form a trans-European aerospace group, the governments of France and West Germany concluded an agreement in May of 1969 which cleared the way for the formation of a consortium to produce commercial jets. Plans were laid for production of an airliner which later became known as the A300.

In December of 1970 the Airbus Industrie was officially formed and incorporated in France as a *groupement d'intérêt économique* (G.I.E.), a form of unlimited partnership commonly used by vinters and construction projects which involve several contractors. This style of industrial organization made success possible for Airbus because, as one official put it, "On other cooperative projects, like the Concorde, nothing could be done without unanimous agreement of all the partners. With the Airbus, they all had to be unanimous to stop us."

The Airbus consortium members were Aérospatiale of France, Deutsche Airbus (65% Messerschmitt-Bölkow-Blohm and 35% VFW-Fokker) of West Germany, Fokker-VFW of The Netherlands, and Construcciones Aeronauticas S.A. (CASA) of Spain. Originally British Aerospace was to be a full member, but it withdrew when Britain's Labour government decided that the program had no chance of success. Britain's Hawker-Siddeley, however, remained associated with Airbus through a subcontracting arrangement in which it was responsible for building aircraft wings. Nonetheless, Airbus Industrie remained primarily a French-German consortium.

The most popular medium-size American jetliners, the Boeing 727 and McDonnell-Douglas DC-9, were fitted with inefficient engines which consumed large quantities of fuel. The Airbus was designed to compete with these jetliners by incorporating the latest avionic technology and the most efficient engines available. Britain's Rolls-Royce was selected as the manufacturer for the A300's jet engines, but had to withdraw from the program when work on its RB.207 engine fell behind schedule. Airbus asked General Electric of America to supply an alternative engine, the CF6-50, which was built for use on McDonnell Douglas' DC-10. The choice of a new engine power plant forced a design change in the A300 which reduced its passenger capacity from 300 to 250. It was a fortunate turn of events for Airbus because at the time many airline companies were struggling to avoid overcapacity caused by excessively large airplanes. Rather unexpectedly the A300 had gained sudden popularity.

The A300 made its maiden flight on October 28, 1972 (ahead of schedule) and entered regular service with Air France in May of 1974. Interest in the fuel-efficient A300 increased when the 1973 world oil crisis caused fuel prices to rise dramatically. By 1975 over 40 of these airplanes had been ordered.

At this time Henri Ziegler retired as the head of Airbus. He was succeeded by Bernard Lathière, who had previously served with the French Civil Aviation Authority. Lathiére appointed an American named George Warde to be in charge of Airbus sales in America. The American aircraft manufacturers (Boeing in particular) worked very hard to prevent Airbus from entering the American aircraft market. Warde was able, however, to reach an agreement with Eastern Airlines whereby Eastern would operate four A300s on a six-month trial basis and fund the $7 million crew training and maintenance costs. It was a risky and potentially costly gamble which paid off when Eastern and Pan Am both decided to purchase the A300.

Lathière, known to airline executives around the world as "Monsieur Airbus," remained primarily concerned with aircraft sales. The engineering and production coordination was largely handled by general manager Roger Béteille from his office at Airbus' final assembly plant in Toulouse. While Lathière was president of the consortium and maintained a high public profile, it was Roger Béteille who worked behind the scenes.

In July of 1978 Airbus Industrie announced the development of a new jetliner called the A310. This smaller and more efficient version of the A300 incorporates a unique fuel-saving feature. When the A310 is in flight, fuel is pumped from an aft tank into the main wing tanks to help maintain the airliner's center of gravity. On other aircraft a device called a "trim control" automatically adjusts the tail elevators in order to maintain level flight. However, excessive reliance on the trim control causes aerodynamic drag which wastes fuel. The A310's fuel pumping scheme has since been duplicated by other aircraft manufacturers and has become a regular feature of most modern aircraft designs. In addition, the A310's wings were redesigned to make it more efficient at distances of less than 1500 miles. This became a major selling point for Airbus since three-quarters of all airline routes are distances of less than 1500

41

miles. The A310 made its inaugural flight in April of 1982 and entered service with Lufthansa a year later.

In January of 1979 Britain became an official member of the Airbus consortium when Hawker-Siddeley became a part of the state-owned British Aerospace. At this time the present capitalization ratio of Airbus was established: Aérospatiale and Deutsche Airbus each holds a 37.9% share of Airbus Industrie, British Aerospace holds 20%, and CASA of Spain holds 4.2%. In May, Belairbus of Belgium joined Fokker-VFW of the Netherlands as associated production members. Fokker, which became a subsidiary of West Germany's Vereinigte Flugtechnische Werke (VFW) in 1969, was sold back to public investors in 1980. VFW was subsequently acquired by Messerschmitt-Bölkow-Blohm, but Fokker continued to be associated with Airbus as a subcontractor.

Deutsche Airbus manufactures most of the fuselages and vertical tails for Airbus planes and transports them to Aérospatiale's assembly facilities in Toulouse where they are assembled with cockpits and center fuselages from Aérospatiale, wings from British Aerospace, and horizontal tails from CASA. The Deutsche Airbus fuselages are transported to Toulouse in the cargo hold of a "Super Guppy," a converted Boeing Stratocruiser capable of holding very large cargos.

In March of 1984 Roger Béteille resigned his post due to ill health. Lathière ended the tradition of having Frenchmen dominate the highest managerial positions at Airbus by appointing a multinational troika to take Béteille's place. Jean Pierson, a Frenchman, was named chief executive officer; Johann Schaeffler, a German, was made responsible for production; and Robert Whitfield, a Briton, was placed in charge of managing the consortium's finances.

In 1983 Airbus developed altered versions of its two jetliners, the A300-600 and A310-300, with extended flight range. Plans were also announced to manufacture a smaller Airbus called the A320 which was intended to compete with Boeing's 737-300 and McDonnell Douglas' MD-80 for short-haul passenger markets. Airbus claims the A320 is 30% less expensive to operate than its competition. Airbus received over 100 orders for the A320 before its maiden flight.

The A320 is the first commercial airliner to have a "fly-by-wire" flight system. The crew's commands are executed by a computer which electronically controls the wing flaps, rudders and elevators. Since the airplane has no direct mechanical controls, the pilot could hypothetically lose control of the airplane in the event of an electronic failure. However, Airbus insists that the fly-by-wire system has been perfected on jet fighters and on the Concorde. In fact, Airbus claims that the system provides the crew with even more control over the aircraft, thus making it all the more safer.

Boeing and McDonnell Douglas, however, are determined to make sure that the A320 has "no more than four years in the market." Both companies are meeting the Airbus challenge by developing a new generation of airliners which are as much as 40% more efficient than the Airbus. These new aircraft, the 7J7 and MD-91, use a revolutionary new engine called a "propfan" which combines the thrust of a jet engine with the efficiency of a high-speed propeller. To date, management at Airbus has no plans to develop an airliner with propfans. Airbus must convince potential customers that they cannot wait until the 1990's for propfans when its own planes are available now.

Pan Am ordered 16 A320s in 1985, and the following year NWA, the holding company for Northwest Airlines, announced that it had ordered 10 A320s with an option to purchase an additional 90. If Northwest agrees to purchase all 100 A320s, it could mean up to $3.2 billion in sales for Airbus.

The proceeds of such a large order would go a long way in defraying the consortium's record of accrued losses, which are believed to amount to between $7 billion and $10 billion. Financial statistics for Airbus are virtually impossible to find. Because of the nature of its industrial organization, Airbus Industrie is not required to publish an annual report. Different accounting methods and degrees of government involvement among the individual consortium members preclude the option of assembling data. A Boeing executive has said, "The Airbus partners aren't just hiding numbers; they don't know them."

If the consortium was a typical nationalized industry, its finances would be a matter of public record. But disclosure of Airbus' financial information has the potential to cause a great deal of opposition to the consortium in European political circles. The Airbus member governments would like to prevent the consortium's economic performance from becoming a political issue; its becoming one might lead to its dissolution. Airbus is, after all, the European Community's only technically successful non-military industrial enterprise.

The United States government has voiced its concern that the extensive subsidies Airbus receives from its member governments violate the principles of the General Agreements on Trade and Tariffs. Officials at Airbus in turn complain that the American aircraft manufacturers benefit substantially and unfairly from aeronautic research funded by the U.S. Department of Defense and the National Aeronautics and Space Administration. In particular, they have complained that the Boeing Company subsidizes the development of new commercial airliners with proceeds from its profitable 747 program and defense projects.

It is widely believed that the market for the next generation of commercial airliners is potentially worth $250 billion and that this market can only support two major aircraft manufacturers. It is believed that Boeing is in a secure position, but that McDonnell Douglas and Airbus could very likely engage in a highly competitive encounter for what remains of the market. The results could be as disastrous for one of these companies as it was for Lockheed when it challenged Boeing and McDonnell Douglas in the early 1970's. In order to avoid such a costly encounter, McDonnell Douglas and Airbus have held discussions to investigate the feasibility of jointly producing the MD-11. In the absence of a joint production agreement, the MD-11 will challenge two new Airbus jumbo jets, the twin-engine A330 and the long-range A340 with four engines.

Airbus' management was reorganized in 1985 and directorates were created for technology, planning, product support, and purchasing. In February 1986 Airbus received 500 aircraft orders. However, Airbus will require at least 400 more aircraft orders for it to remain financially healthy.

The continued existence of Airbus Industrie rests on its ability to successfully compete with companies such as Boeing and McDonnell Douglas in the aircraft market during the 1990's. Yet it won't be enough to sell only a few hundred aircraft; Airbus must substantially dominate a significant position of the airliner market. Anything less than a 25% market share may be regarded as a failure.

Further Reading: Multinational Development of Large Aircraft: The European Experience by Mark A. Lorrell, Santa Monica, California, Rand Corporation, 1980; *The Sporty Game* by John Newhouse, New York, Knopf, 1982.

AVIONS MARCEL DASSAULT-BREGUET AVIATION

BP 32
92420 Vaucresson
France
(1) 741 79 21

Public/State-owned Company
Incorporated: December 1971 upon the merger of Avions Marcel Dassault and Breguet Aviation
Employees: 15,790
Sales: FFr 14.56 billion (US$ 2.252 billion)
Market value: FFr 12.87 billion (US$ 1.992 billion)
Stock Index: Paris Brussels

Dassault-Breguet is well known for manufacturing the delta-wing Mirage jets, one of the most popular fighter planes in third world air forces. It is also the only French company of its kind to have resisted government attempts to make it a completely nationalized industry. With good reason, therefore, it may be said that Dassault-Breguet has a unique corporate character as France's most important defense manufacturer and also as one of its most capitalistic institutions.

Dassault was founded by Marcel-Ferdinand Bloch who was born in Alsace on January 22, 1892. As a schoolboy in Paris Bloch viewed his first airplane, built by the Wright Brothers, making a low pass over the city and then circling the Eiffel Tower. As a young man, still fascinated with aviation, Bloch attended the Ecole Supérieure de l'Aéronautique, France's first school for aeronautical engineering. He established a factory in a converted garage, and convinced his father-in-law to finance his small aeronautical business. During World War I Bloch developed a variable pitch propeller for the Spad fighter which gave French pilots the ability to outmaneuver their German adversaries. The Spad propeller made a great deal of money for Bloch who, after the war, went into housing construction.

Bloch began to manufacture airplanes again in the early 1930's when French military contracts were once more available. But the complexion of French politics changed abruptly in 1936 when the Socialist-Communist "Popular Front" government of Léon Blum came to power. On January 1, 1937 Bloch's aircraft factories were nationalized by the Société Nationale de Constructions Aéronautiques de Sud-Ouest (S.N.C.A.S.O.), one of six state-controlled aeronautic factories. Bloch was retained as a civil servant and invested the compensation he received for his company in a variety of North American securities. After the Popular Front fell from power, Bloch founded a new aircraft company which later produced the highly successful Bloch 152 fighter.

After the Germans invaded France at the outset of World War II Marcel Bloch, a Jew, was asked to build aircraft for the German war effort as an "honorary Aryan." Bloch refused the offer and was forced into hiding. He was later arrested in Lyon and jailed. Eight months before the war ended he was deported to the Buchenwald concentration camp where he remained until the area was liberated by American forces in May of 1945.

Bloch converted to Roman Catholicism after the war and changed his last name to Dassault, the *nom de guerre* of his brother who was a member of the French resistance. Although an "l" was added, the name literally means "on the attack." Marcel Dassault subsequently became an honored member of General De Gaulle's inner circle, but since his company had been destroyed by the war it was once again nationalized.

Dassault recruited the most brilliant engineers from the best schools in France to work for a new company, Avions Marcel Dassault. Dassault's first project was the development of a small military liaison aircraft which was later manufactured for Air France under the name Languedoc. In 1951 the company began production of its Ouragan (Hurricane) jet fighter. When production of the Ouragan ended in 1953, the company had built 441 of the planes. In 1954 Dassault introduced its next jet, the Mystère. Designed as a subsonic fighter, the Mystère was the first European jet to break the sound barrier in level flight. The Mystère was followed by the Etendard attack jet. In 1953 Dassault acquired the manufacturing license for Armstrong Siddeley's Viper turbojet engine. The Viper was the intended power plant for Dassault's delta-wing Mirage fighter jet, which made its maiden flight in 1955.

Dassault had grown quickly in 10 years. Yet the company employed only a small work force primarily comprised of engineers and designers. Most of the actual production of aircraft was subcontracted to the state-owned company Sud-Aviation. Doing so was an intentional policy of Marcel Dassault. Unlike Dassault, state-owned companies were better able to keep workers employed while demand for their products was low. As a private company, however, Dassault was free to continue developing new aircraft designs without worrying about laying off production workers. The company's engineers were less specialized than others; each was capable of designing an entire airplane. As a result, they could be moved easily from one project to the next, wherever they were needed most. In short, Dassault did not encounter the kinds of employment problems that plagued the state-operated companies.

In 1958 Marcel Dassault was elected a member of the French Parliament and represented the Beauvais region north of Paris. As a Gaullist deputy, Dassault continued to support the conservative political causes of his party. During this time France implemented a policy of independent military deterrence which culminated in the nation's

1966 decision to withdraw from the North Atlantic Treaty Organization. The defense of France was now solely the responsibility of the French military. Consequently, the demand for military equipment increased greatly, and the primary beneficiary was Avions Marcel Dassault.

Dassault owned factories in nine locations across France. The design facilities and primary factories were located at Saint-Cloud outside of Paris. The Bordeaux plant handled the final assembly of components manufactured by Sud-Aviation, while the other plants handled sub-assembly work and flight testing. The Martignas facility, however, later became primarily responsible for manufacturing missiles. Dassault also founded an electronics company in 1963 called l'Electronique Marcel Dassault. The electronics company, which was operated by Dassault's son Serge, provided his aircraft company with a variety of flight control and avionics devices.

Against the advice of several advisers, Marcel Dassault ordered the development of the Mystère into a small business jet. The civilian version of the Mystère was sold outside of France under the English name of Falcon (it was thought that this would increase its international marketability). The Mystère/Falcon later became one of the world's most popular private jets. In 1972 Dassault and Pan Am created an American subsidiary called the Falconjet Corporation for the sale and service of Falcon jets in the United States. Besides assisting Sud-Aviation in the development of the French-British Concorde SST at this time, Dassault also developed improved versions of its Mirage fighter jet. Regarded as the most successful European jet since Britain's Canberra bomber, the Mirage was sold to over a dozen foreign air forces.

In June of 1967 Avions Marcel Dassault purchased a 62% majority interest in Breguet Aviation, the French partner in the Franco-British Jaguar jet project. Breguet was founded in 1911 by the French aviation pioneer Louis Breguet. The company was nationalized in 1936, but managed to regain a significant degree of independence three years later when it repurchased three of its former factories from the government.

During June of the same year, Egypt, Syria and Jordan launched a surprise attack on Israel in what later became known as the Six Day War. Israel, however, was armed with Dassault's Mirage fighter jets which destroyed the Soviet-equipped Egyptian air force in three hours. The Mirages performed so well during the conflict that they were given much of the credit for the subsequent Israeli victory. President De Gaulle imposed an embargo on 50 additional Mirages bound for Israel. The embargo was lifted three years later by President Georges Pompidou, after it was learned that Israeli spies had acquired the plans for the Mirage and that modified versions were already being built in Israel. At approximately the same time, the French government also agreed to sell 110 Mirage fighters to Libya.

The French government, fully aware of the French aerospace industry's decreasing ability to compete internationally, campaigned for the rationalization (or merger) of several French aircraft manufacturers. The state-owned aircraft companies Sud-Aviation, Nord-Aviation, and Sereb (a missile manufacturer) were merged to form Aerospatiale in 1970. A year later, with the encouragement of the government, Breguet Aviation, a publicly traded company which was controlled by Marcel Dassault, merged with the larger, privately-owned Avions Marcel Dassault. The new company, Avions Marcel Dassault-Breguet Aviation, operated 20 factories and accounted for 35% of all French aerospace production. Marcel Dassault's reason for merging his company with Breguet was that both companies could economize their operations by eliminating duplicated facilities and bureaus. Dassault also wanted to take advantage of Breguet's public stock listings in Paris and Brussels in order to raise capital. Dassault required a $280 million line of credit in order to develop a new 134-passenger commercial jetliner called the Mercure.

The Mercure was a twin-engine airliner very similar in appearance to the Boeing 737. In fact, the Mercure competed with the B-737 for the same market. Only 10 Mercures had been sold by 1976, all of them to the French domestic airline Air Inter. The project was abandoned after the company failed to reach an agreement with McDonnell Douglas whereby the two companies would co-produce the subsequent Mercures.

Dassault-Breguet became involved in an unusual scandal during 1976 when the company's financial director, Hervé de Vathaire, disappeared with 8 million francs from the company account. As the company accountant, de Vathaire was more familiar with the company's finances than anyone. He had become disillusioned a few months earlier after the death of his wife. He reportedly began assembling incriminating evidence against Dassault-Breguet, a photocopy of which fell into the hands of Jean Kay, a French right-wing "soldier of fortune" who became known for his flamboyant terrorist activities. Kay demanded 8 million francs from de Vathaire for his copy of the dossier and threatened to turn the document over to news organizations if his demand wasn't met.

De Vathaire was introduced to Kay by his mistress Bernardette Roels, whose roommate was a friend of Kay's. Together with his mistress and Kay, de Vathaire went to Divone les Bains near the Swiss border. When French authorities began to search for de Vathaire, all three vanished. De Vathaire turned up a few weeks later in Corfu, and then returned to Paris where he surrendered to the police. In the meantime, an anonymous caller to a Paris television station announced that all 8 million francs had been turned over to Lebanese Christians for arms purchases. Marcel Dassault also confirmed that Kay had returned the document.

Details of the document's contents were published in *Le Point* in October. Among other things, Dassault was accused of diverting funds for his personal use and attempting to avoid payment of taxes. According to the allegations, Marcel Dassault used company funds to build a replica of King Louis XIV's Petit Trianon palace at Versailles. The disclosures led to tax evasion investigations of Marcel Dassault and severely damaged his political position.

In 1978 French Socialist and Communist politicians pledged to nationalize Dassault-Breguet if they were elected. Marcel Dassault, who owned 90% of the company and was believed to have been the wealthiest man in

France, stood for all that leftist politicians opposed. The leftist charged that the French government was allowing Mirage fighters to be sold to anyone who had the money to purchase them. Dassault-Breguet, they claimed, was only interested in making money by taking advantage of the ambitious military requirements of oil-rich and other third world nations. In answering these charges, Dassault maintained that these nations would purchase their arms from other manufacturers if they didn't purchase them from Dassault and that its position as an arms supplier strengthened French political influence in the third world.

The following year leftists won enough seats in the national assembly to implement their nationalization policies. The government purchased a 21% share of Dassault-Breguet for $128.5 million. This included a special 33% voting interest which under French law enabled the government to exercise veto power over company decisions. When Francois Mitterand was elected President of France in 1981, the government increased its share in Dassault-Breguet to 46%, with a special 63% voting majority. The move was regarded by many as an act of spite against the 89-year old Marcel Dassault who continued to be regarded as a political opponent.

The French arms industry broke into the newspaper headlines again in 1982 during the brief South Atlantic war between Britain and Argentina over the Falkland Islands. During the hostilities Argentina destroyed a number of British ships with Matra Exocet missiles launched from a Dassault-Breguet Super Etendard. A French embargo on additional arms for Argentina had little effect on the losses suffered by British forces, who successfully completed their invasion of the Falklands and achieved an Argentine surrender.

Nonetheless, Dassault-Breguet remained in excellent financial condition due to its continued marketing success with improved versions of the Mystère/Falcon and Mirage fighter. Generally, the company remained competitive because it avoided the costs involved in developing new aircraft from scratch. Instead, Dassault-Breguet continually improved existing aircraft the designs of which had been thoroughly proven. This was Marcel Dassault's rationale for campaigning against French participation in the four-nation *Eurofighter* program led by British Aerospace and MBB. Without a government commitment to

purchase, Dassault-Breguet developed an entirely French-built fighter jet called the Rafale, which was intended to serve as the basic instrument for the aerial defense of France.

Dassault-Breguet became involved in spacecraft engineering during 1985 when the French space agency Centre Nationale d'Etudes Spatiales assigned the company to lead the aeronautical development of the Hermes spaceplane as a subcontractor to Aérospatiale. The Hermes, similar in design to the American space shuttles, is expected to fly into space atop an Ariane 5 rocket in 1995. Despite its position in the Hermes program, Dassault-Breguet has no plans to establish a space division.

Marcel Dassault died on April 18, 1986 at the age of 94. His son Serge was placed in charge of the company. Today Dassault-Breguet remains France's most dynamic aeronautical manufacturer. In addition to the Super Etendard and Mirage and Falcon series, Dassault-Breguet is a partner with British Aerospace in the Jaguar fighter program, and with Dornier of West Germany in the Alpha jet program. In addition, the company manufactures aircraft fuselages for Fokker of the Netherlands.

It is generally believed that the nationalization program of Francois Mitterand's Socialist government has not produced its intended results. In all likelihood the state-owned Aérospatiale will be at least partially privatized, possibly by 1995. In the meantime, Dassault-Breguet will remain France's largest, and certainly its most important, aircraft manufacturer.

Principal Subsidiaries: Génerale de Mécanique Aéronautique; La Compagnie de Gestion de Rechanges Aéronautiques (COGER); Sociedad de Coordinacion Aeronautica (Spain); Dassault Aéro Service; Dassault International (USA) Inc.; Dassault International (France); Falcon Jet Corporation (USA); Corse Composites Aéronautiques (with Aérospatiale and SNECMA).

Further Reading: A Dassault Dossier: Aircraft Acquisition in France by Robert L. Perry, Santa Monica, California, Rand Memorandum No. R-1148-PR, September 1973; *A History of French Military Aviation* by Charles Christienne and Pierre Lissarrague, trans. by Frances Kianka, Washington, D.C., Smithsonian Institution Press, 1986.

BOEING

THE BOEING COMPANY

7755 East Marginal Way South
Seattle, Washington 98108
U.S.A.
(206) 655-2121
Public Company
Incorporated: July 19, 1934 as Boeing Airplane Company
Employees: 98,700
Sales: $16.34 billion
Market value: $8.259 billion
Stock Index: New York

The Boeing Company, one of America's most successful corporations, is the world's largest manufacturer of commercial aircraft. With the recent exception of the 727, every one of its 700 series jetliners is still in production (some for more than 30 years). Boeing is also an industry leader in aerospace technology.

William Boeing was raised in Michigan where his father operated a lucrative forestry business. While he was in San Diego, California in 1910 Boeing met a French stunt pilot named Louis Paulhan who was performing at the International Air Meet. When Paulhan took Boeing for an airplane ride, it marked the beginning of Boeing's fascination with aviation.

After two years of study at Yale's Sheffield School of Science, Boeing returned to Michigan to work for his father. He was sent first to Wisconsin and later to the state of Washington to acquire more timber properties for the family business. In Seattle he met a Navy engineer named Conrad Westerveldt who shared his fascination for aviation. A barnstormer named Terah Maroney gave the two men a ride over Puget Sound in his seaplane. Later Boeing went to Los Angeles to purchase his own seaplane, thinking it would be useful for fishing trips. The man who sold him the plane and taught him how to fly was Glenn Martin, who later founded Martin Marietta.

While in Seattle, Boeing and Westerveldt made a hobby of building their own seaplanes on the backwaters of Puget Sound. It became more than a hobby when a mechanic named Herb Munter and a number of other carpenters and craftsmen became involved. In May of 1916 Boeing flew the first "B&W" seaplane. The next month he incorporated his concern as the Pacific Aero Products Company. Their first customer was the government of New Zealand, which employed the plane for mail delivery and pilot training.

Boeing and his partners anticipated government interest in their company when the United States became involved in World War I. They discovered their hunch was correct when the company was asked to train flight instructors for the army. After the war, Boeing sold a number of airplanes to Edward Hubbard, whose Hubbard Air Transport is regarded as the world's first airline. The company shuttled mail between Seattle and the transpacific mailboat which called at Victoria, British Columbia. Later, when the post office invited bids for various airmail routes, Hubbard tried to convince Boeing to apply for the Chicago to San Francisco contract. Boeing mentioned the idea to his wife, who thought the opportunity looked promising. In the prospect, he and Hubbard created a new airline named the Boeing Air Transport Company. They submitted a bid and were awarded the contract.

To meet the demands of their new business Boeing and his engineers developed an extremely versatile and popular airplane called the Model 40, fitted with a Pratt & Whitney air-cooled Wasp engine. It could carry 1000 pounds of mail and a complete flight crew, and still have room enough for freight or passengers.

The Kelly Airmail Act of 1925 opened the way for private airmail delivery on a much wider scale. As a result, a number of airline companies formed with the intention of procuring the stable and lucrative airmail contracts. One of these companies was Vernon Gorst's Pacific Air Transport which won various routes along the Pacific Coast. Boeing purchased this company and then ordered a young employee named William Patterson to purchase its outstanding stock. Another airmail carrier was Varney Airlines which began operation in 1925. Operated by Walter T. Varney, the company won almost every mail contract it applied for. However, it soon became overextended and had financial difficulties. Boeing also purchased this company and added its routes to his own.

With the addition of National Air Transport, Boeing's airline holdings formed the original United Air Lines. In 1928 all these companies were organized under a holding company called the Boeing Aircraft and Transportation Company. In 1929 a larger holding company was formed, the United Aircraft and Transportation Company. Included in this group were the "United" airlines and Stout Airlines; Pratt & Whitney (engines); Boeing, Sikorsky, Northrop and Stearman (manufacturers); and Standard Steel Prop and Hamilton Aero Manufacturing (propellers). Boeing was made chairman of the company, and Fred Rentschler of Pratt & Whitney was named president.

Boeing and Rentschler became extremely wealthy in this reorganization by exchanging stock with the holding company in a method similar to J.P. Morgan's controversial capital manipulation. They multiplied their original investments by a factor of as much as 200,000 times. It was, however, entirely legal under the legislation of the day.

In 1933 the government conducted an investigation of fraud and other illegal practices in the airline industry. Boeing was called upon to testify and explain his windfall profits before a senate investigating committee. Under examination he admitted to making $12 million in stock flotations. Boeing was so infuriated with the investigation that he retired from the company (at age 52) and sold all his aviation stocks. Upon Boeing's departure the company's production manager, Phil Johnson, was named the new president.

In 1934 a government investigation of collusion in the airmail business led to a suspension of all contracts awarded. As a result, the U.S. Congress declared that airline companies and manufacturers could not be part of the same business concern. This led to the break up of the three aeronautic conglomerates: Boeing's United, the Aviation Corporation of the Americas, and North American Aviation.

All of the Boeing company's aeronautic properties east of the Mississippi became part of a new company, United Aircraft, operated by Fred Rentschler. The western properties, principally the Boeing Airplane Company, remained in Seattle exclusively manufacturing airframes. Pat Patterson was put in charge of the commercial air carriers which retained the name of United Air Lines and based its operations at Chicago's Old Orchard (later O'Hare) airport.

In 1934 William Boeing was recognized for his emphasis on innovation and experimentation in aeronautical research and development. He was awarded the Daniel Guggenheim medal, "for successful pioneering and achievement in aircraft manufacturing and air transport."

In the years leading up to World War II the Boeing company led the way in developing single-wing airplanes. They were constructed completely of metal to make them stronger and faster; more efficient aerodynamic designs were emphasized; retractable landing gear and better wings were developed, along with multiple "power plant," or engine technology; finally, directional radios were installed which enabled better navigation and night flying. Boeing had established itself as the leading manufacturer of airplanes.

When the United States launched its wartime militarization program, Boeing was called upon to produce hundreds of its B-17 "Flying Fortresses" for the Army. In the European war the B-17 became an indispensable instrument for the U.S. Air Corps. In June of 1944, when production was at its peak, Boeing's Seattle facility turned out 16 of these airplanes every 24 hours. By this time the company was also producing an improved bomber called the B-29 "Super Fortress." It was this airplane that dropped the atomic bombs on Hiroshima and Nagasaki in August of 1945.

Boeing's president, Phil Johnson, died unexpectedly during the war. He was replaced with the company's chief lawyer, William M. Allen, on the last day of the war. Under Allen's leadership Boeing produced a number of new bombers, including the B-47, B-50, and the B-52. Boeing's B-307 Stratoliner, a B-17 converted for transporting passengers, was succeeded by the B-377 Stratocruiser in 1952. The Stratocruiser was a very popular double-deck transport, most widely used by Northwest Orient. It was also Boeing's only airplane built for the commercial airline market since before the war.

In the spring of 1953 Bill Allen convinced the secretary of the U.S. Air Force, Harold Talbot, to allow Boeing the use of the government-owned B-52 construction facilities for the development of a new civilian/military jet. Boeing invested $16 million in the project, which was intended to put the company ahead of the Douglas Aircraft Company. Douglas had dominated the commercial airplane market for years with its popular propeller-driven DC series.

This new jet, the B-707, first flew on May 15, 1954. American Airlines, a loyal Douglas customer, was the first to order the new jet. Their defection so alarmed Douglas that the company accelerated development of its nearly identical DC-8 passenger jetliner. The government later took delivery of Boeing's military version of the jet, the KC-135 tanker, alternately known as the "missing 717."

Boeing, which changed its name to The Boeing Company in 1961, enjoyed a large degree of success and profitability with the 707. The company devoted its resources to the development of a number of other passenger jet models, including the 720 (a modified 707) and the 727 which was introduced in 1964. The 727 was Boeing's response to a successful French model called the Caravelle. The Caravelle's engines were located in the rear of the fuselage, uncluttering the wings and reducing cabin noise. Boeing adopted this design for its three-engine 727 which carried 143 passengers. Douglas, eager not to be left out, introduced a similar two-engine model called the DC-9 in 1965.

During this time the company also recognized a demand for a smaller 100-passenger jetliner for shorter routes. As a result, Boeing developed the 737 model. The 737 seemed to run counter to the general trend at Boeing of building larger, more technologically advanced jetliners, but it did have a place in the market and made a profit.

Boeing's next engineering accomplishment was the creation of a very large passenger transport designated the 747. This new jetliner was capable of carrying twice as many passengers as any other airplane. Its huge dimensions and powerful four-engine configuration made it the first of a new class of "jumbo jets," later joined by McDonnell-Douglas' DC-10 and Lockheed's 1011 Tri-Star.

The 747 program required such a large investment that it nearly forced the company into bankruptcy. One hundred and sixty orders were placed for the jetliner by the time it was delivered in 1969, but no more were placed until 1972. During this period, Boeing was also developing the 2707, a supersonic transport better known as the "SST." Progress on this aircraft was slow and costly. Despite the support of Senator Henry Jackson, the U.S. Congress voted not to fund further development of the SST. Shortly thereafter Boeing abandoned the project altogether.

In 1969 a new chief executive was appointed to head the organization. An engineer named Thornton Wilson took charge of Boeing in a way reminiscent of his predecessor, Bill Allen, 25 years before. Faced with an impending disaster, Wilson's response was to pare the workforce down from 105,000 to 38,000. The layoffs at Boeing had a profound effect on the local economy; unemployment in Seattle rose to 14%.

Wilson's strict austerity measures paid off quickly. Soon Boeing's jets were rolling off the tarmac and employees were called back to work. After the company's initial recovery, it received a deluge of commercial airplane orders and military contracts. Boeing started development of two new passenger jet models intended to take the company into the 21st century.

These new jetliner models, the 757 and the wide-body 767, became available in the early 1980's. Utilizing advanced technology and improved engines, these jetliners were Boeing's response to McDonnell-Douglas' MD series and the European Airbus consortium's 300 series. The current customer in the commercial jetliner market is more concerned with labor costs than fuel efficiency, owing to consistently cheaper oil. However, Boeing's newest entries are doubly efficient, requiring smaller crews as well as less fuel. Besides the 757 and 767, Boeing offered an updated 737 for the shorter-range rural "puddle-jumper" market and modified 747s capable of greater range and passenger capacity.

During this period of prosperity with commercial jetliners, Boeing made several attempts to diversify its business. Not all of them were successful. In the 1970's Boeing entered the metro-rail business, manufacturing mass transit systems for Boston, San Francisco and Morgantown, West Virginia. The systems were modern, computerized, and efficient. They were also prone to frequent breakdowns. After fulfilling its obligation to rectify the systems (at great cost), Boeing decided to discontinue its ground transport business.

Boeing now does most of its business through four principal divisions: civilian aircraft are manufactured and sold by the Boeing Commercial Airplane Company; the Boeing Vertol Company, acquired in 1960, produces helicopters for the armed services; Boeing Aerospace produces strategic and tactical missiles and space products; the Boeing Military Airplane Company builds bombers and tankers as well as high-technology surveillance aircraft.

Boeing's military business has been more stable than its commercial airlines business. That stability did not, however, ensure the company against debilitating losses in its civilian business during the 747 crisis or during the period after "deregulation" in America when demand for new jetliners declined. In fact, the percentage of Boeing's revenues from government contracts has been steadily declining. The military divisions, nonetheless, have remained viable and competitive in winning contracts, and designing and developing, and later producing, a wide variety of state-of-the-art military hardware.

Boeing's major contributions to the military include the KC-135 tanker and the versatile mainstay of the United States Air Force, the B-52 bomber. The company builds E-3 Airborne Warning and Control System aircraft (AWACs) for the Air Force, the North Atlantic Treaty Organization, and Saudi Arabia. In addition, Boeing builds the E-4 command post and the E-6 submarine communications aircraft. Under a consortium led by Northrop, it is presently developing a new bomber intended to replace the aging B-52, designated the B-1B. Boeing's other (top secret) project is a role in the development of the F-19 Stealth bomber. Boeing's Vertol facilities, located in Philadelphia, produce CH-46 and CH-47 (Chinook) helicopters.

In the aerospace division, Boeing won a $4 billion defense department contract in 1980 to manufacture the air-launched cruise missile. It builds the MX intercontinental ballistic missile and the Roland air defense missile. The company also provides modernization services for existing Minuteman ICBMs. Boeing's aerospace business includes the production of inertial upper stage boosters for satellites delivered into orbit by Titan rockets or the Space Shuttle. In addition, Boeing is developing an air-launched missile which destroys satellites.

With its wide variety of products, Boeing is America's number one exporter. It holds a 55% market share of "the most expensive product in the world not sold by the bidding process." There are more Boeings in the air than any other airplane. Boeing's advantage is its size and broad product mix.

Boeing engineers have on their drawing boards an impressive array of futuristic aircraft. Boeing's three-engine 777, originally scheduled to be introduced with the 757 and 767, attracted little interest and was shelved. Nonetheless, Boeing engineers are developing a new model, the 150-passenger 7J7, scheduled to fly in 1991. This new jet will be the first to employ fuel-efficient propfans, jet engines with rear-mounted propellers. Perhaps their strangest project is the 907 flying wing. Equipped with eight jet engines, this radically designed airplane will carry 1000 passengers, twice the capacity of a 747. Looking something like a boomerang, it is scheduled for service sometime in the next century. If this project is successful, it could allow Boeing to change the future of aviation once again.

Principal Subsidiaries: Astro, Ltd.; Logistics Support Corp.; Boeing Technology International, Inc.; Boeing of Canada, Ltd.; Boeing International Corp.; Boeing Financial Corp.; Boeing Equipment Holding Company; Boeing Leasing & Financial Corp.; Boeing International Sales Corp.; Boeing Environmental Products, Inc.; BCS Richland, Inc.; Boecon Corp.; Boeing Technical & Management Services, Inc.; Boeing Domestic Sales Corp.; Boeing Computer Services Canada, Ltd.; Boeing Engineering & Co. Southeast, Inc.; Boeing Agri-Industrial Co.; BE&C Engineers, Inc.; Boeing Electronics, Inc.; Boeing of Georgia, Inc.; Aircraft Sales & Financing Corp.; Boeing Computer Services (Europe), Ltd.; Boeing Operations International, Inc.; Hydraulic Units, Inc.; Boeing Computer Support Services, Inc.; Boeing Middle East, Ltd.; Astro II, Inc.; Boeing Sales Corp.; Boeing Investment Co., Inc.; Boeing of Mississippi, Inc.; Boeing Offset Co., Inc.; Boeing Petroleum Services, Inc,; Boeing Technical Operations, Inc.

Further Reading: *747: The Story of The Boeing Super Jet* by Douglas J. Ingells, Fallbrook, California, Aero Publishers, 1970; *The Great Gamble: The Boeing 747* by Lawrence S. Kuter, University, University of Alabama Press, 1973; *Boeing: Planemaker to the World* by Robert Redding and Bill Yenne, London, Arms and Armour Press, 1983; *Flight in America 1900–1983: From the Wrights to the Astronauts* by Roger E. Bilstein, Baltimore, The Johns Hopkins University Press, 1984.

BRITISH AEROSPACE PLC

100 Pall Mall
London SW1Y 5HR
England
(01) 930 1020

Public Limited Company
Incorporated: April, 1978
Employees: 75,823
Sales: £3.14 billion (US$ 4.601 billion)
Market value: £1.302 billion (US$ 1.903 billion)
Stock Index: London

In the years after World War II the British aircraft industry was overpopulated with manufacturers who had an increasingly difficult time competing not only with each other but with larger American manufacturers such as Boeing, Douglas and Lockheed. British companies were victimized by small orders from a government which was divesting itself of most of its empire and therefore had greatly reduced military needs. Noting that the British aircraft industry was three times larger than France's, "with no obvious justification for being so," *The Economist* asked the critical question, "Does Britain need an aircraft industry?" Throughout the 1950's the health of British aviation was a major political issue and was the subject of many Parliamentary debates. Finally, in 1960, after intense lobbying from the Minister of Aviation, Duncan Sandys, Parliament passed a bill which called for a "rationalization" of the British aircraft industry through the merger of several existing companies that were facing closure.

The purpose of the rationalization was to combine the talent and resources of about 20 companies and limit overall production, while avoiding the politically sensitive issue of creating unemployment or allowing the British aeronautics industry to fall victim to external economic pressures. It was hoped that the program would raise the intensity of technological development to a level equal of that of the Americans. It was also noted that British aeronautic companies were diversifying themselves out of aircraft production, a trend which could have left Britain without an aircraft industry of any kind.

Early in 1960 Vickers-Armstrong, Ltd., which was originally founded in 1928, merged with English Electric (founded in 1918) and Bristol Aeroplane (founded in 1910) to form the British Aircraft Corporation (BAC). The three companies continued to operate as divisions of BAC, with Vickers and English Electric each accounting for 40% of the consortium's capital, the remaining 20% coming from Bristol. In May of 1960 BAC acquired a controlling interest in another British company, Hunting Aircraft.

At the time of the British Aircraft Corporation merger, a second group of British aircraft companies were amalgamated to form the Hawker-Siddeley Aviation Company. Like BAC, Hawker-Siddeley's constituent companies, Armstrong Whitworth (founded in 1921), A.V. Roe & Company (1910), Folland Aircraft (1935), Gloster Aircraft (1915), and Hawker Aircraft (1920) were operated as subsidiaries. Each brought an area of expertise to the new company. Armstrong produced large cargo airplanes, Avro built smaller passenger liners, while Folland, Gloster and Hawker were known for their Gnat, Javelin and Hunter jetfighters. Hawker-Siddeley also acquired a controlling interest in de Havilland Holdings, Ltd. and The Blackburn Group, as well as a 50% share of Bristol-Siddeley, the airplane engine manufacturer.

The amalgamation which created British Aircraft Corporation and Hawker-Siddeley also made Westland Aircraft Britain's primary helicopter and hovercraft manufacturer. Rolls-Royce (which receives most of its publicity from its manufacture of automobiles but most of its profits from aircraft engine production) and Bristol-Siddeley, Ltd. became Britain's leading engine manufacturers. Handley Page, Short Brothers, Scottish Aviation, and British Executive and General Aviation were the only British companies which were not a part of the government's rationalizaton program.

During the 1960's BAC continued to manufacture English Electric's Lightning and Hunting's Jet Provost fighters in addition to Vickers' four-engine VC10 jetliner. The company also built a new twin-engine jetliner called the BAC-111. In 1962 BAC entered a co-production agreement with Aérospatiale of France to build the Concorde supersonic passenger transport.

Hawker-Siddeley was divided into two divisions: Aircraft, for aircraft production, and Dynamics, for missiles and rockets. The aircraft division took over production of the HS-125 executive twin-jet from de Havilland and the HS-748 turboprop airliner from Avro. In 1964 it introduced the Trident, a three-engine jetliner intended to compete against the BAC-111, Douglas DC-9 and Boeing 727. In the military field, Hawker-Siddeley assumed production of Blackburn's Buccaneer fighter and developed the HS-1182 Hawk trainer as well as a military patrol version of the de Havilland Comet called the Nimrod. The unique product of Hawker-Siddeley during the 1960's was the Harrier fighter jet.

The Harrier features thrust nozzles which the pilot can aim either straight backward or towards the ground. When the nozzles are pointed backward the Harrier can take off on a runway like a conventional jet. When the nozzles are pointed down it can take off vertically like a helicopter. The Harrier was built in two configurations, one for the Royal Air Force and one for Royal Navy aircraft carriers.

Hawker-Siddeley Dynamics produced the Seaslug, Firestreak and Red Top missiles. BAC also operated a missile division which manufactured the Vigilant, Blue

Water, Thunderbird and Bloodhound missiles. The Bloodhound was a particularly effective weapon, but created a scandal when details of BAC's high profits from the project were made public.

The success of the rationalization program was, however, limited, and by 1965 Britain's aerospace industry was again unable to compete with foreign competitors. Lord Plowden headed a special Parliamentary committee which recommended a second major restructuring of the aircraft industry. The Plowden Report proposed that Rolls-Royce and Bristol-Siddeley merge to form a single company which manufactured aircraft engines. This merger, which included the sale of Hawker-Siddeley's 50% interest in Bristol-Siddeley to Rolls-Royce, was carried out in 1966. The second proposal, a merger of BAC and Hawker-Siddeley, was abandoned.

In February of 1969 the governments of France and West Germany concluded an agreement which established a consortium called Airbus to manufacture a new passenger jetliner designated the A-300. The British government was invited to join Airbus as a full partner, but declined when it decided the project was doomed to failure. In its opinion, there was simply too little room in the commercial airliner market (already dominated by Boeing, McDonnell Douglas and Lockheed) to support another competitor. Hawker-Siddeley, however, agreed to produce wings for the A-300 as an Airbus subcontractor. Because of intense competition, BAC and Hawker-Siddeley made no plans to develop successors to the BAC-11 and Trident. Even British Overseas Airways (BOAC), Britain's state-owned international air carrier, was ordering the more advanced American-made jetliners. In addition, the American aircraft companies had extremely profitable military divisions which enabled them to devote large sums of money to the development of new commercial aircraft. BAC and Hawker-Siddeley had excellent military divisions, but the requirements of the domestic military establishment were small. At the same time, the international arms market was dominated by the American and Soviet manufacturers. American arms import restrictions prevented Hawker-Siddeley from selling its Harrier to the United States, despite interest in the jet by the Pentagon.

British Aircraft Corporation, Messerschmitt-Bölkow-Blohm (MBB) of Germany, and Aeritalia of Italy created the Panavia partnership in order to develop the Tornado Interdictor Strike fighter. Separately, BAC and Breguet of France created another consortium called SEPECAT (Société Européenne de Production de L'avion E.C.A.T.) to develop the Jaguar jet fighter. Both of these programs were a financial drain on BAC, despite substantial contributions from the British government. Finally, it became apparent that BAC was unlikely to realize a profit from its costly co-production of the Concorde with Aérospatiale. Only 16 were built (seven each for British Airways and Air France, two remain unsold), the first of which did not enter service until 1976. Once again the two largest British aerospace companies were in financial trouble and facing bankruptcy.

Engineers at Hawker-Siddeley designed a new short-haul 80-passenger jetliner called the HS-146. Convinced of the aircraft's commercial potential and the need for Hawker-Siddeley to remain in the commercial aircraft market, the British government pledged to share the development costs for the HS-146. In order to generate capital, the company's chairman, Sir Arnold Hall, authorized the sale of de Havilland of Canada to the Canadian government for $38 million. Similarly, BAC sold assembly rights for the BAC-111 to the government of Romania.

While the HS-146 was being developed, poor economic conditions and intense competition from the Americans eroded the already tenuous position of the British aerospace industry. In 1975 the Plowden merger proposal for BAC and Hawker-Siddeley had been resurrected in the form of an Aircraft and Shipping Industries Bill. The following year BAC and Hawker-Siddeley were nationalized, less in an attempt to protect their finances than to force a merger upon them. In 1977, after it had once been rejected in the House of Lords and defeated in the Commons, Prime Minister James Callaghan's Labour government successfully saw the Industries Bill through Parliament.

The Aircraft and Shipping Industries Bill merged the Aircraft and Dynamics divisions of Hawker-Siddeley with the British Aircraft Corporation and Scottish Aviation, Ltd. The new company, called British Aerospace, continued to be operated by the British government as a state-owned corporation. British Aerospace was divided into two divisions: Aircraft, based at the Hawker-Siddeley facility in Kingston, and Dynamics, headquartered at the BAC Guided Weapons plant in Stevenage.

Scottish Aviation, the third and smallest member of the British Aerospace group, was established in 1935 to create employment opportunities in aviation in Scotland. Scottish Aviation built the international airport in Prestwick, which today is the forward traffic control base for flights between London and North America. Later, Scottish Aviation manufactured a series of propeller-driven general purpose aircraft.

In 1978 British Aerospace considered partnership with foreign companies to produce a new large passenger airliner. Even in its new form British Aerospace lacked the resources to develop a commercial jetliner any larger than the HS-146 (renamed BAe-146). Airbus, for which British Aerospace was still building A-300 wings, was a candidate, as was Boeing, which was beginning work on its next generation of commercial aircraft. To join Boeing would have been politically inexpedient since Boeing was the primary source of the British aerospace industry's decline. In addition, British officials expressed concern over Boeing's size and aggressive corporate personality. Joining Airbus, on the other hand, would require a substantial entry fee for development costs already incurred by the Airbus partners.

Eventually Boeing lost interest in a partnership with British Aerospace. On January 1, 1979 British Aerospace purchased a 20% share of Airbus, pledging $500 million through 1983 for incurred costs and development of a new aircraft designated the A-310.

In 1979 Sir Keith Joseph, industry secretary for the Conservative government of Prime Minister Margaret Thatcher, announced the government's intention to privatize (or sell to the public) most of Britain's state-owned corporations, including British Aerospace. At first this announcement alarmed officials, including British Aerospace Chairman Lord Beswick, who had worked hard to reform the nation's aerospace industry. They feared that private investors would divide the company and indiscriminately sell the more profitable divisions, possibly to foreigners.

The privatization program moved slowly because of political opposition and the government's desire to offer shares only when market conditions were most favorable. In the meantime, British Aerospace appointed a new chairman to succeed Lord Beswick. The man they chose was the chairman of Esso Petroleum, Dr. Austin Pearce. Pearce was faced with the dual task of guiding British Aerospace through the privatization while ensuring that the company's orders were being filled. The increased military budget of the Conservative government contributed to the company's backlog of orders.

The unconventional method in which British Aerospace was privatized established the form of future privatizations. On December 31, 1979 British Aerospace became a private limited company with authorized capital of £7 divided into seven shares, each with a par value of £1. All seven shares were held by nominees of the Secretary of State for Industry. On January 2, 1981, pursuant to the British Aerospace Act of 1980, the seven shares were split into 14, each with a value of 50p, and an additional 79,999,986 were created, raising the company's share capital to £40 million. On the same day, British Aerospace adopted new Articles of Association and was registered as a public limited company. By February 4, 1981 British Aerospace's share capital was increased to 200 million shares, 50 million of which were made available to the public. Currently, the secretary of state holds 48.43% of the company's issued share capital. 3.14% is owned by trustees of the company's employee share ownership plan, and the balance of 48.43% is owned by private shareholders.

In its first year as a substantially public company, British Aerospace registered a pre-tax profit of £71 million. This was £6 million more than had been predicted, despite £50 million in development costs for the BAe 146 and A-310. The Panavia Tornado was past its development stages and in full production. However, the West German Panavia partner MBB prevented the consortium from realizing a substantial profit from the Tornado project by not allowing exports of the fighter to countries outside of NATO, such as Saudi Arabia.

Management at British Aerospace was reorganized on January 1, 1983. Admiral Sir Raymond Lygo was appointed to the newly created position of managing director. Under the new system all group executives were to report to Sir Raymond. This enabled the board chairman, Dr. Pearce (now Sir Austin), to more easily handle matters such as company finances. One such external matter was British Aerospace's involvement in the Airbus A-320 project.

The A-320 was designed to carry 150 passengers and featured advanced "fly-by-wire" electronic control and navigation systems. British Aerospace, which owns 20% of Airbus, persuaded the other partners to allow it a 26% share of the A-320. The British government supported the company's involvement in the new Airbus project by making a £250 million line of credit available on favorable repayment terms. Under the terms of the agreement British Aerospace would produce wings for the A-320.

As a public company, British Aerospace enjoyed greater independence in its policymaking. But like other public companies it also risked becoming a takeover target. On May 15, 1984 the chairman of Thorn EMI, Peter Laister, announced his company's intention to merge with British Aerospace. Thorn EMI was a profitable electronics and leisure conglomerate, whose assets included everything from production rights for video recorders to performance rights to Placido Domingo and the rock group Duran Duran. British Aerospace, described as a company which earns money making missiles and loses it building airliners, was also profitable but involved in an entirely different line of business. The London financial community reacted to Mr. Laister's announcement with amazement. In Parliament the Labour Party asked: "Is it sensible to allow a firm which has been successful in the fields of color television, videos and the marketing of pop groups to have the responsibility of looking after the development of Britain's largest company in civil and military aviation, in missile technology and space satellites?"

The announcement also invited criticism from the managing director of Britain's General Electric Company, Lord Weinstock: On two previous occasions when GEC expressed an interest in purchasing all or part of British Aerospace, it was privately rebuffed by the government which was concerned that GEC would become too dominant a force in the British defense industry. GEC, which was a principal owner of BAC before 1977, was fully prepared to exceed any bid submitted by Thorn EMI.

In June of 1984 British Aerospace rejected Thorn EMI's takeover proposal, and the following month did the same with GEC, citing a lack of any specific proposals. The government was satisfied with the takeover rejections because it ensured that British Aerospace would remain under British ownership and that it would continue to be a part of the Airbus group.

In 1985, confident about the company's position, the British government offered to sell its 48% of British Aerospace. The £550 million offer was tightly restricted to institutional investors. The company was also reorganized into eight functional divisions during the year, a move which was intended to economize utilization of engineering teams by having them specialize in the development of products in specific fields.

In 1986 the Lockheed Corporation reached an agreement with British Aerospace to develop new versions of the BAe-146 for military and cargo applications. Co-production agreements with American companies was nothing new to British Aerospace, whose Harrier fighter jet had been built in the United States in conjunction with McDonnell Douglas since the mid-1970's.

Today British Aerospace is one of the world's largest aerospace concerns, producing aircraft, missiles and spacecraft, in addition to parts for a variety of jointly produced commercial and military aircraft. As its name implies, British Aerospace will continue to lead the British and European aerospace industries to greater technological heights from which they can effectively compete with the American companies and their seemingly endless financial resources.

Principal Subsidiaries: British Aerospace (Insurance), Ltd.; British Aerospace (Holdings), Inc.; British Aerospace (Insurance Brokers, Ltd.; British Aerospace Australia, Ltd. (Australia); British Scandinavian Aviation AB.

Further Reading: Concorde and Dissent: Explaining High Technology Project Failures in Britain and France by Elliot J. Feldman, Cambridge, Cambridge University Press, 1985; *International Collaboration in Civil Aerospace* by Keith Hayward, New York, St. Martin's Press, 1986.

N.V. KONINKLIJKE NEDERLANDSE VLIEGTUIGENFABRIEK FOKKER
(Fokker Royal Netherlands Aircraft Factories)

P.O. Box 12222
1100 AE Amsterdam-Zuidoost
The Netherlands
020 594–9111

Public Company
Incorporated: 1919 in The Netherlands
Employees: 10,053
Sales: Dfl 444.3 million (US$ 196.7 million)
Market value: Dfl 261.7 million (US$ 115.9 million)
Stock Index: Amsterdam Brussels

The Fokker aircraft company is one of the smaller manufacturers of commercial aircraft. The company was founded in 1919 by the aviation pioneer Anthony Fokker, who is also remembered for his role as a supplier of warplanes for the Kaiser's Germany during World War I. The company has weathered the turbulent years since then by carefully observing the needs of potential customers and developing some of the most practical planes in use today.

Anthony H.G. Fokker was born on a coffee plantation on the island of Java in the Dutch-ruled Netherlands Indies, presently the Republic of Indonesia. At the age of 20 he taught himself to fly on a small home-made monoplane which he had constructed in an abandoned zeppelin hanger in Baden-Baden, Germany. With newer, improved aircraft, he won a military competition in St. Petersburg (now Leningrad). Fokker was a poor student but had an unusual talent for aviation. He intermittently attended an engineering school in Frankfurt, and in 1912 was asked by the German government to teach military aviation.

Fokker failed to gain the interest of the Italian and British governments in his aircraft. The Germans, however, were more intrigued, purchasing a number of airplanes for their air corps. When World War I broke out, Fokker was involuntarily conferred German citizenship and given orders to continue building airplanes for the Kaiser. Nonetheless, Fokker continued to regard himself as a patriotic citizen of neutral Holland.

When the French pilot Roland Garros was shot down on October 5, 1918, the Germans noticed that his airplane's propeller was fitted with steel deflectors. The deflectors allowed the pilot to operate his machine gun, oblivious to the obstruction of the propeller; bullets would ricochet off the blades rather than damage them. The propeller was taken to Berlin and shown to Fokker. Three days later Fokker returned from his factory at Schwerin with a device which synchronized the firing of a machine gun to the passing of the propeller blades. In effect, the airplane's engine operated the gun, firing bullets between the blades rather than at random.

By the end of the war Fokker had produced more than 40 types of airplanes for the Germans. He was later invited to the U.S. by the Army Air Corps. He shipped airplanes to the Air Corps and Navy until 1922, when he established a factory at Hasbrouck Heights, New Jersey, just across the river from New York. The company was called the Atlantic Aircraft Corporation and its sales were handled by Hamilton Standard, which later became a division of United Aircraft.

In 1925 Anthony Fokker brought a new tri-motor (three-engine airplane) to the U.S. from his factory in The Netherlands and won the Ford Reliability Tour. Later named the "Josephine Ford," this airplane was used by Admiral Richard Byrd and Floyd Bennett on their flight to the North Pole. Another Fokker airplane, the Southern Cross, was used by the aviator Sir Charles Kingsford-Smith for his historic trip across the Pacific and around the world.

The company changed its name to the Fokker Aircraft Corporation of America on December 3, 1927. In May of 1929 Fokker was merged with Dayton-Wright, a subsidiary of General Motors. In the summer of 1930 Fokker was reorganized by General Motors: it became a wholly-owned subsidiary of GM and was renamed the General Aviation Corporation. However, in compliance with the provisions of the Air Mail Act of 1934, General Motors was forced to dissolve General Aviation.

Fokker left General Motors because of differences in opinion over company policy. He subsequently returned to Holland where he maintained his company, the Nederlandse Vliegtuigenfabriek, which produced a variety of military and civilian aircraft. KLM (Royal Dutch Airlines) developed an air route to the Netherlands Indies for the Dutch government, using Fokker aircraft. In 1929 a U.S. Army Fokker C-2A established a duration record of 150 hours and 40 minutes. In that same year, however, Fokker lost both his second wife and his test pilot Bertus Brase. These losses depressed him so much he admitted that he no longer enjoyed flying and preferred instead to spend time either on his yacht or driving.

In March of 1931 a Fokker tri-motor crashed and killed the popular Notre Dame coach Knute Rockne. The accident was widely reported and resulted in a sudden loss in popularity of and confidence in Fokker airplanes. An investigation revealed that a rotten wooden joint in the wing assembly caused the wing to rip off during flight. Fokker favored building airplanes with wood, but his customers demanded that they be made of metal. When Douglas unveiled its all-metal DC-2, Fokker negotiated an arrangement to manufacture the airplane in Europe. He later won an agreement to build the DC-3 and Lockheed

Electra, although neither one was ever built in Holland. As an agent for Douglas, Fokker sold almost 100 DC-2s and DC-3s in Europe.

On December 23, 1939, after a three week battle with pneumococcus meningitis, Anthony Fokker died. He was survived only by his mother. The company remained in business until the following May when it was confiscated by the invading armies of Nazi Germany. Friedrich Seekatz, who had been arrested by the Dutch authorities because of his German sympathies, was reinstated by the Germans and placed in charge of the factory, which was converted to repair German military aircraft operating from Dutch air bases. For this reason the factory was heavily bombed by the Royal Air Force.

By the end of the war the factory had been looted by the German army and almost completely destroyed by Allied bombings. However, Fokker's technical staff survived the war and within a year the factory was completely rebuilt. The company's new S-series designs entered production soon after the war, some of which were produced in the United States by Fairchild and in South America by the company's Brazilian subsidiary.

Fokker developed a 44-passenger turbo-prop airplane called the F-27 Friendship in 1956. Development costs and an initially weak market for the F-27 depressed profits, but after a slow recovery hundreds were sold to airlines all over the world. The Soviet aircraft company Antonov produced an aircraft called the An-24 which was strikingly similar to the F-27. This led many to believe that Antonov merely reverse-engineered an F-27 for its own purposes. Over 1100 An-24s were built by Antonov during Fokker's production run of the F-27.

On March 21, 1960, the Republic Aviation Corporation of Long Island, New York acquired a large minority interest in Fokker. The two companies concluded a number of cooperative agreements involving the production and sale of their airplanes. At this time Fokker also began production of Lockheed F-104 Starfighters in collaboration with German and Belgian companies. In association with the Dutch electronics company Philips, Fokker manufactured parts for the Hawk missile. During the 1960's Fokker also produced parts for Northrop's Canadian-built F-5 fighter.

In 1964 Fokker's airframe division developed a 60 to 85-passenger jetliner called the F-28 Fellowship, which was designed for short to medium range airline routes. The F-28 entered service in 1969. An agreement between Fokker and Fairchild-Hiller of America to build a shorter version of the F-28 called the F-228 resulted in a production run of over 100 of these airplanes.

Fokker's aerospace division was formed in 1967. Its expertise in thermal control, maneuvering, electronics and structures gave the division important roles in the development of the ANS and IRAS scientific satellites and spacecraft with the European Space Agency (ESA) and the National Aeronautics and Space Administration (NASA). Some of its later contributions were to the ESA Giotto Halley's Comet probe and the Ariane rocket program.

In 1969 Fokker merged with the Vereinigte Flugtechnische Werke GmbH (VFW) of West Germany. The new division, which comprised the entire Dutch aircraft industry, was named VFW-Fokker B.V. Fokker continued, however, to manufacture the F-27, F-28 and VFW-614 (the first postwar German jet) in addition to various parts for other aircraft. VFW-Fokker was also chosen to manufacture a significant portion of General Dynamics' F-16 fighter jets sold to NATO.

After heavy financial losses the partnership with VFW was dissolved in 1980 and Fokker was once again brought under direct private ownership. Seventeen percent of the company's stock was acquired by the Dutch ABN-Bank, an additional 17% was acquired by VMF machining industries, 20% was acquired by the Northrop Corporation during the 1960's, and the remaining 46% was divided among a number of private investors.

During the 1970's the company developed improved designs of its F-27 and F-28. The market for small fuel-efficient turbo-props and jets was still quite lucrative, but now Fokker was facing stronger competition from other small airplane manufacturers such as de Havilland and British Aerospace in the U.K.

The Fokker 50 propjet is the successor to the F-27 turboprop. The F-50 has many of the same dimensions as the Friendship with the exception of its engine nacelles and windows. The new power plants (engines), which drive six-bladed propellers, are faster but deliver less thrust at takeoff. The F-50 incorporates improved electronic systems and features a new cabin layout and interior. It is also capable of carrying 14 more passengers than its predecessor.

In the early 1980's, after the new jets from Boeing and McDonnell Douglas were announced, Fokker recognized a gap in the airliner market for jetliners capable of serving the world's many short-haul routes. To fill that gap Fokker began development of a new jetliner designated the F-100. Fitted with more efficient Rolls-Royce Tay engines and capable of carrying 100 passengers, Fokker's new jet has the lowest break even load factor of any jet available. In other words, it has the potential to deliver a profit with only 30 % of its seats filled. Impressive statistics such as these have led a number of major airlines, including Swissair, KLM, ILFC, and USAir, to order the F-100. Because of its advanced electronic systems, the F-100 is also one of the easiest commercial jets to pilot.

Original plans to co-produce the new Fokker jet with McDonnell Douglas as the MDF-100 were cancelled when that company decided to concentrate on building an improved version of its DC-9 called the MD-80. Instead, Fokker is building its F-100 in collaboration with Britain's Short Aircraft Company and Rolls-Royce, Germany's Messerschmitt Bolköw-Blohm, and the American companies German and Collins.

The company manufactures airplane wings for Britain's Short 330 and 360 aircraft in addition to wing components for the Airbus consortium's A-300 and A-310. Fokker has begun preliminary work on a fuel-efficient prop-fan airplane they have designated the FXX. If developed, the FXX will challenge the Boeing 7J7 and McDonnell Douglas MD-91 prop-fan airplanes shortly after they become available in 1992.

The commercial airliner market is extremely competitive and overwhelmingly dominated by three companies,

Boeing, McDonnell Douglas and Airbus. In an age when smaller aircraft manufacturers are concentrating on more stable military contracts, Fokker is openly challenging the larger companies. Frans Swarttouw, chief executive officer of Fokker, is the driving force behind Fokker's aggressive character. Swarttouw was put in charge of Fokker in 1978 and was given the mission of making the company more competitive with its larger rivals. He devoted a great deal of the company's financial resources to development of the F-50 and F-100. It was regarded by many as a risky gamble, but the company's commitment to technological superiority, product versatility and reliable product support have rewarded it with a solid share of the commercial market. The company expects to receive more orders for its new airplanes in the next few years, orders that should provide Fokker with the capital it needs to develop more efficient and technologically advanced aircraft.

Principal Subsidiaries: Société Anonyme Belge de Constructions Aeronautiques S.A.B.C.A. (42.8%); Avio-Diepen B.V.; Fokker-UFW B.V.; Aircraft Financing & Trading B.V.

Further Reading: *Flying Dutchman: The Life of Anthony Fokker* by H.G. Anthony Fokker and Bruce Gould, New York, Arno Press, 1931; *Fokker: Aircraft Builders to the World* by Thijus Postma, London, MacDonald and Jane's, 1980.

GENERAL DYNAMICS

GENERAL DYNAMICS CORPORATION

Pierre Laclede Center
St. Louis, Missouri 63105
U.S.A.
(314) 889–8200

Public Company
Incorporated: 29 May 1925 as Electric Boat Company
Employees: 92,600
Sales: $8.892 billion
Market value: $3.273 billion
Stock Index: New York

General Dynamics is one of several American companies that manufacture aircraft. It is one of two submarine builders and the only manufacturer of battle tanks in the United States. The company has a long history in weapons production, a history that originates with an Irish-American inventor named John Holland.

Holland was associated with the Fenians, a secret organization founded in New York City which was sympathetic to Irish nationalists trying to end British domination of Ireland. The Fenians commissioned Holland to construct a submarine capable of destroying British naval vessels. Previous submarine designs had been attempted by other inventors, but none were effective warships. Several of Holland's first submarines sank. Before long his ill-conceived attempts at secrecy alerted American law enforcement authorities who prevented Holland from achieving his mission for the Fenians. In order to continue his work, Holland sought and later won support from various members of Congress. He arranged financial backing and on February 7, 1899 founded the Electric Boat Company.

Despite Holland's good relationship with government officials, Electric Boat was unable to interest the U.S. Navy. Then a lawyer-financier and battery and electronics magnate named Isaac Leopold Rice offered to finance the development of subsequent Holland submarines in return for an interest in Electric Boat. Holland was persuaded to relinquish his patent rights and management authority to Rice, who successfully made sales to the U.S. Navy and several other foreign naval services. Holland effectively lost control of the company and found himself earning a salary of $90 per week as chief engineer while the company he founded was selling submarines for $300,000 each.

Electric Boat gained a reputation for unscrupulous arms dealing in 1904–05 when it sold submarines to both Japan and Russia, who were at war. Holland submarines were sold to the British Royal Navy through the English armaments company Vickers (ironic, considering the company's Fenian beginnings). Submarines, which had once been denounced in Britain as "damned un-English," as too sly and cowardly for a proper gentleman's war, were now legitimized as genuine naval weapons by the world's most powerful navy.

Holland lost patience with Rice and resigned in protest at being excluded from his company's affairs. A frail man plagued by a respiratory condition since birth, Holland died shortly afterward in 1914. He was replaced as chief engineer by Lawrence Spear who, in close association with Vickers, redesigned the Holland submarine. Speed was improved, a conning tower and periscope replaced the Holland observation dome, and torpedo tubes were incorporated for the first time. The full potential of the submarine, however, was not fully recognized until World War I, when German U-boats caused serious disruptions in British shipping.

Isaac Rice died in 1915 and was replaced by his associate Henry Carse. Spear, who never liked Rice, was given greater control over the company's operations under Carse. Electric Boat had a substantial backlog of profitable orders and was financially strong enough to purchase several companies, including Electro Dynamics (involved in ship propulsion), Elco Motor Yacht (builders of pleasure boats), and New London Ship & Engine of Groton, Connecticut (manufacturers of diesel engines and civilian ships). The company's name was changed to the Submarine Boat Corporation.

When the United States became involved in World War I, Carse made the crucial decision to devote the company's resources to the construction of disposable cargo vessels rather than submarines. Then, having realized his mistake, he began to retool for submarine production, but before the process could be completed the war had ended—as a result, the company lost a great deal of money. Then, the Navy decided to devote most of its reduced post-war budget to surface ships. Faced with bankruptcy, Carse reorganized the company, emphasized production of surface ships, and brought back the Electric Boat name.

On the eve of World War II, the business practices of Electric Boat came under investigation by the U.S. government and a number of independent groups; it was accused of being a "financial beneficiary" of foreign wars. Electric Boat was also found to have inadvertently given design secrets to officials of the increasingly hostile government of Japan. In an investigation led by Senator Gerald Nye, Electric Boat was accused of profiteering, graft, and unethical business practices. Carse responded that, because the U.S. Navy had suspended all major contracts for 10 years, Electric Boat had been forced to deal with foreign governments (many of which were corrupt) in order to remain financially solvent.

The German re-militarization and hostile Japanese activities forced the Roosevelt Administration to reassess its position on military preparedness. Consequently, the government placed orders for submarines and PT (patrol/

torpedo) boats from Electric Boat facilities at Groton and the Elco plant in New Jersey. The new orders led to the revitalization of Electric Boat, now led by a man named John Jay Hopkins. Hopkins was appointed by the retiring Lawrence Spear, who himself had taken over when Henry Carse retired. While Spear continued to offer advice from his retirement, Hopkins was thoroughly in charge and fully responsible for the company's strong re-emergence.

Electric Boat and its Elco Yacht and Electro Dynamic subsidiaries mobilized for production at full capacity following the American declarations of war against the Axis powers. The sudden expansion in output caused a serious labor shortage which necessitated the hiring of women as welders and riveters.

The Electric Boat companies produced hundreds of submarines, surface ships and PT boats during the war, contributing greatly to the success of island fighting in the Pacific. When the war ended in 1945, the Navy reduced its orders for new vessels. Only 4000 of the company's 13,000 wartime employees were retained after the war, and Electric Boat stock fell in value from $30 per share to $10.

Hopkins initiated another reorganization of Electric Boat, which included a diversification into related commercial and defense industries. Electric Boat purchased Canadair from the Canadian government for $22 million. (Canadair produced flying boats and modified DC-4s during the war, but had greatly diminished in importance during peacetime.) A series of events, including the Berlin Blockade, Soviet detonation of an atomic bomb, and the war in Korea, stimulated demand for new aircraft, including the T-33 trainers, F-86 Sabres and DC-6's built under contract by Canadair. By the early 1950's, Canadair's importance overshadowed Electric Boat; their business advisers even suggested that Canadair purchase Electric Boat and operate it as a subsidiary.

With substantial profits from its Canadair subsidiary, Electric Boat purchased Convair from the Atlas Corporation. Convair manufactured a variety of civilian and military aircraft, including the 440 passenger liner, F-102 and F-106 fighters, Atlas and Centaur rockets, and the B-24, B-36, and B-58 Hustler bombers. On February 21, 1952, a new parent company called General Dynamics was established to manage the operations of Convair, Canadair, and Electric Boat.

Convair led the development of the American nuclear aircraft program, enthusiastically supported by the Pentagon. Hopkins was a strong advocate of nuclear power and its numerous applications, but the nuclear airplane, or "N-bomber," was later found to be impractical, and the project was abandoned. Electric Boat enjoyed greater success with nuclear power; in 1955 it launched the first nuclear submarine, the *Nautilus*.

The company's development of commercial jetliners came near the end of Hopkins' tenure. While Douglas and Boeing were developing their DC-8 and 707 passenger jets, Convair was unable to introduce its jetliner because the company was delayed by contractual obligations to TWA and its eccentric and intrusive majority shareholder Howard Hughes. Specifically, Convair was bound to incorporate numerous design changes suggested by Hughes. As the result of a financial crisis that postponed

TWA's purchase of jetliners, and eventually forced Hughes out of TWA, Convair was unable to recover from the delayed entry of its 680 and 880 models into the jetliner market. General Dynamics was forced to write off the entire passenger liner program with a $425 million loss.

The financial position of General Dynamics was so seriously weakened by the Convair jetliner program that the company was targeted for a takeover by Henry Crown, a Chicago construction materials magnate. Crown offered to merge his profitable Material Services Corporation with General Dynamics in exchange for a 20% share of the new company's stock. The proposal was accepted in 1959.

In the early 1960's the U.S. Defense Department invited American defense contractors to bid for the production of a new aircraft, the F-111, with which the Department intended to replace its aging fleet of B-52 bombers. General Dynamics entered the competition in partnership with the Grumman Corporation, against a design submitted by Boeing. Even though the Boeing F-111 was considered to be the better built and the more capable plane, the General Dynamics/Grumman version was consistently declared superior by Pentagon officials and industry experts. An investigation of impropriety in the selection process was interrupted when President Kennedy was assassinated in November of 1963, and was not concluded until 1972.

General Dynamics continued to develop its version of the F-111 at its Convair facility in Fort Worth, Texas. The Air Force and Navy amended their design specifications and requested the addition of so many devices that the prototype could barely fly. The F-111's utility as a replacement for the B-52 was greatly diminished. When the aircraft's role was reassessed, the project was identified by congressional critics as an example of gross mismanagement, organizational incompetency, and financial irresponsibility. The F-111 project consumed an inordinate amount of the defense budget and delayed by six years the introduction of Grumman's similar (and in many ways superior) F-14 Tomcat.

Under Roger Lewis, whom Crown had appointed chairman in 1961, General Dynamics purchased the Quincy shipbuilding works from Bethlehem Steel in 1963 for five million dollars. Quincy was an outdated facility requiring costly improvements, but held promise as a builder of surface ships.

Despite his having been appointed by Crown, Lewis removed Crown from the company in 1966 by repossessing his 18% share of non-voting company stock. Crown was paid $120 million for his shares, but lost control of both General Dynamics and Material Services Corporation. Thereafter, over a period of years, Crown continued to purchase substantial numbers of shares of voting stock, expanding his interest until he emerged in 1970 with control over the board of directors. Roger Lewis was summarily fired and replaced by David Lewis (of no relation). Crown subsequently moved the company from New York to St. Louis in February of 1971.

In 1971 the Electric Boat division of General Dynamics and its chief competitor, Newport News Shipbuilding, were awarded contracts to manufacture a new submarine, the 688, or *Los Angeles* class. Two years later General Dynamics hired a successful but ruthless businessman named Takis Veliotis to take charge of the Quincy yard. Once in charge at Quincy, Veliotis concluded an agreement to build liquified natural gas tankers in conjunction with a cold storage engineering firm called Frigitemp.

During this period the Defense Department announced a $200 million competition for the production of a new jet fighter. Careful to avoid the problems which plagued the F-111, General Dynamics initiated its development of the F-16. The F-16 program closely followed its development and budget schedules, and the first prototype exceeded specifications.

Although it was apparently chosen over the Northrop F-17 Cobra, the F-16 faced an unexpected challenge from McDonnell Douglas' independently developed F-15 Eagle. The lower-priced F-15 took a significant portion of the fighter market away from General Dynamics. However, the U.S. government compensated General Dynamics by promoting sales of the F-16 to NATO countries and other American allies. Canadair, which manufactured aircraft for Commonwealth countries, was sold back to the Canadian government in 1976 for $38 million.

The following year Admiral Rickover publicly berated Electric Boat for poor workmanship and cost overruns on 18 *Los Angeles* class submarines. Rickover was particularly upset about the U.S. Navy's contractual obligation to absorb a large portion of the overruns, which were running as much as $89 million per vessel. A dispute then arose between the Defense Department and Electric Boat, wherein Electric Boat threatened to halt production of the submarines unless its share of the losses were covered as well. General Dynamics sought the protection of Public Law 85-804, which was originally intended to protect "strategic assets" such as Lockheed and Grumman from bankruptcy due to cost overruns.

General Dynamics won a settlement from the Pentagon, but soon realized that its problems at Groton were not merely financial. Productivity was seriously compromised by absenteeism and an employee turnover rate of 35%. Management lost control over inventories, and poor workmanship resulted in costly reconstruction. In October of 1977 David Lewis transferred Takis Veliotis from Quincy to Groton, with instructions to reform the operation. Within months Veliotis had restored discipline, efficiency and financial responsibility at Electric Boat.

Veliotis left Electric Boat in 1981 to take a seat on the board of directors, and to serve as international salesman and "company ambassador." Later that year, however, Veliotis resigned in protest over a dispute with David Lewis, who Veliotis claimed had promised him the position of chief executive officer. The dispute deteriorated until Veliotis was indicted by government prosecutors for illegal business practices. He fled to Greece; he still claims to have damaging evidence of fraudulent overcharges made by General Dynamics.

In 1982 General Dynamics purchased the Chrysler battle tank division, with plants located in Warren, Michigan and Lima, Ohio. The division, renamed Land Systems, had already secured a government contract to build the Army's next main battle tank, the M-1. Developed in response to newer Soviet tanks such as the T-72, the M-1 was to be powered by a jet turbine and capable of speeds of up to 50 miles per hour. The M-1 also included a computer-guided gun aiming mechanism designed to assure a high degree of accuracy while the tank was traveling over rough terrain at high speeds.

When the first M-1 prototypes were delivered from Land Systems, a number of basic design flaws were noticed by Pentagon officials. Exhaust from the engine was so hot that infantry could not come near the tank for cover under fire. The M-1 was fast but prone to breakdown, and it required so much fuel that logistical support became questionable. Finally, the M-1's ammunition bay was too small to carry more than 40 shells. Critics recommended that the M-1 project be cancelled in favor of its predecessor, the durable, battle-tested M-60. During this same period General Dynamics won a government contract to service and maintain TAKX supply ships for the American Rapid Deployment Force.

David Lewis and other company officials were called to testify before a congressional subcommittee about their alleged overcharges for simple items, such as hammers and coffee pots, as well as about billings for personal expenses. The proceedings initiated separate investigations by the Justice Department and the Internal Revenue Service.

Soon after Admiral Rickover was involuntarily retired by Navy Secretary John Lehman, General Dynamics was awarded a government contract to manufacture a number of new boats, including the $500 million Ohio class Trident submarine. The contract eliminated many of the company's disputed charges to the Pentagon and, as a result, led to the cessation of the congressional investigation. Wisconsin Senator William Proxmire criticized these developments by remarking that "Defense contractors like General Dynamics have so much leverage against the government they can flout the laws that govern smaller companies and individuals."

David Lewis retired in 1985 and was replaced by Stanley C. Pace, formerly head of TRW. Oliver Boileau, president of General Dynamics, was passed over for the position at the insistence of the board of directors and the Crown family, all of whom wished to see an end to the policies of Lewis and his proteges. Pace made a number of changes at General Dynamics, even before Lewis had left the company. He sold the Quincy shipyard and founded a new division called Valley Systems, established to win contracts for the Reagan Administration's Strategic Defense Initiative.

The future of General Dynamics under Pace is hard to predict. The company's position as one of the world's largest defense contractors guarantees for it some degree of stability. Although the company may lose money under adverse conditions, the United States government views General Dynamics as an indispensable resource, essential to national security.

Principal Subsidiaries: Datagraphix Inc.; Material Service Corp.; General Dynamics (hereafter "GD") Manufacturing Ltd.; GD Export Sales Corp.; GD International

Corp.; GD International Services Inc.; GD Services Co.; Pantheon Inc.; Electrocom Inc.; Fore River Railroad Corp.; GD Financial Corp.; GD Credit Corp.; Braintree Equity and Maritime Corp.; Patriot Shipping Corp.; General Dynamics Land Systems, Inc.; Mines SNA, Inc.

Further Reading: *The Illusion of Choice: The F-111 and the Problem of Weapons Acquisition Reform* by Robert F. Coulam, Princeton, Princeton University Press, 1977; *Brotherhood of Arms* by Jacob Goodwin, New York, Random House, 1985; *The Defender: The Story of General Dynamics* by Roger Franklin, New York, Harper, 1986; *Running Critical: The Silent War, Rickover and General Dynamics* by Patrick Tyler, New York, Harper, 1987.

GRUMMAN CORPORATION

1111 Stewart Avenue
Bethpage, New York 11714
U.S.A.
(516) 575-3369

Public Company
Incorporated: December 6, 1929
Employees: 21,856
Sales: $3.502 billion
Market Value: $960 million
Stock Index: New York

Grumman is one of the United States' most important defence contractors, manufacturing an assortment of highly sophisticated aircraft. It has now achieved more than half a century in the national service, yet Grumman may quite literally have been founded by accident.

Leroy Grumman left the Navy in 1920 to become a test pilot and chief engineer for Grover and Albert Loening, who manufactured an airplane called the Fleetwing. In 1923 Vincent Astor's New York-Newport Air Service Company lost one of its Fleetwings over the ocean. Cary Morgan (a nephew of J.P. Morgan) was killed in the accident, which a later investigation revealed was caused when Morgan fell asleep with his foot obstructing the pilot's controls. Nevertheless, bad publicity surrounding the accident put Astor's company out of business. Grumman and a fellow worker named Leon Swirbul purchased the airline from Astor, and later transformed it into a manufacturing company, building amphibious floats for Loening aircraft.

Unlike other aircraft manufacturers who entered the business as barnstormers or hobbyists, Leroy Grumman was a graduate of the Cornell University engineering school. Leon Swirbul was a product of the disciplined military aviation program. Both men continued to work for the Loening brothers while operating their own company, which they had named Grumman Aircraft Engineering. However, when Keystone Aircraft purchased Loening Aeronautical in 1928, the entire operation was moved to Keystone's headquarters in Bristol, Pennsylvania. Grumman and Swirbul decided to remain in Long Island and operate their own company.

After building a number of experimental airplanes, Grumman Aircraft manufactured its first fighter, designated the FF-1, for the Navy in 1932. This design was improved upon in subsequent models and led to the development of the successful F4F Wildcat, Grumman's first fighter with folding wings. With folded wings, twice as many airplanes could be stored on an aircraft carrier as before. The company also manufactured a line of "flying boats" called the Goose and the Duck.

Coincidentally, a second factory for manufacturing warplanes was dedicated by Grumman on the morning of December 7, 1941, as the Japanese were bombing Pearl Harbor. At the outset of the war Grumman had an advantage over non-military manufacturers because the company didn't require retooling. Automobile manufacturers, for instance, had to be converted from the production of cars and trucks to battle tanks and airplanes, assembly lines for sewing machines had to be refitted to produce machine guns. Grumman's only task was to increase its output and develop new airplane designs.

During the war Grumman developed new aircraft such as the amphibious J4F Widgeon, the TBF Avenger naval attack bomber, and a successor to the Wildcat called the F6F Hellcat. The Hellcat was developed in response to the Mitsubishi Zero, a highly maneuverable Japanese fighter with a powerful engine. Grumman aircraft were used almost exclusively in the Pacific war against Japan, and provided the American carrier forces with the power to repel many Japanese naval and aerial attacks. U.S. Secretary of Navy Forrestal later said, "In my opinion, Grumman saved Guadalcanal."

No other aircraft manufacturer received such high praise from the military. Grumman was the first company to be awarded an "E" by the U.S. government for excellence in its work. The award further increased the high morale at Grumman. The Grumman company turned out over 500 airplanes per month. To maintain that level of productivity the company provided a number of services to its workers, including day care, personnel counseling, auto repair and errand running. In addition, employees were substantially rewarded for their efficient work. By the end of the war Grumman had produced over 17,000 aircraft. The company had always had an excellent relationship with its employees, largely as a result of policies set down by Leon Swirbul.

The sudden termination of government contracts after the war seriously affected companies such as Boeing, Lockheed, and Douglas, as well as Grumman. Many aircraft companies first looked to the commercial airliner market as an opportunity to maintain both their scale of operation and profitability. The market suddenly became highly competitive. Although Grumman manufactured commercial aircraft, it elected to remain out of the passenger transport business. Those companies which did manufacture commercial transports lost money, and some even went out of business. Grumman continued to conduct most of its business with the Navy. In addition to its F7F Tigercat and F8F Bearcat, the company developed a number of new aircraft, including the AF-2 Guardian and the F9F Panther and F10F Jaguar, Grumman's first jet airplanes.

During the 1950's Grumman developed two new amphibious airplanes called the Mallard and Albatross; new jets included the Tiger, Cougar and Intruder. It also diversified its product line by introducing aluminum truck bodies, canoes and small boats. Leon Swirbul died in 1960. During his tenure Swirbul was responsible for Grumman's production and employee relations. Grumman had been involved in design, engineering and financial matters.

Grumman created a subsidiary in 1962 called Grumman Allied. The subsidiary was established to operate and coordinate all of the company's non-aeronautical business, and allow management to concentrate on its aerospace ventures. When the National Aeronautics and Space Administration completed its Mercury and Gemini space programs, it turned its attention to fulfilling the challenge made by the late President Kennedy, namely, landing a man on the moon before 1970. The Apollo program called for several moon landings, each using two spaceships. The comman modules, manufactured by McDonnell Douglas, were intended to orbit the moon while the lunar modules, built by Grumman, landed on the moon. Grumman's contract with NASA specified construction of 15 lunar modules, 10 test modules and two mission simulators. Only 12, however, were actually built.

Design problems already faced by Grumman engineers were compounded by their limited knowledge of the lunar surface. The lunar modules had to meet unusual crisis-scenario specifications, such as hard landings, landings on steep inclines, and a variety of system failures. Nine thousand Grumman personnel were devoted to the lunar module project, representing a reorientation of the company's business—Grumman had entered the aerospace industry.

The United States made its first manned moon landing in July of 1969, with several more to follow through 1972. Grumman's spaceships performed almost flawlessly and represented a new and special relationship between the company and NASA. Grumman was later chosen by NASA to build the six-foot thick wings for the agency's space shuttles.

Through the 1950's and 1960's Grumman maintained a good relationship with the Pentagon. While that relationship continued to be good during the 1970's, it was marked by a serious disagreement over the delivery of 313 of Grumman's F-14 Tomcat fighter jets. At issue: who pays for cost overruns on a government-ordered project—the company or the taxpayer? Grumman was losing $1 million per F-14 and refused to deliver any more to the Navy until its losses were covered. The company pleaded its case in full-page advertisements in the *New York Times*, *The Wall Street Journal*, and the *Washington Post*. Grumman argued that completion of the contract under the present terms would bankrupt the company. The matter was later resolved when the Defense Department agreed to cover Grumman's losses, and the company agreed to a new contract procedure which would automatically review project costs on an annual basis and make adjustments when necessary.

Grumman's swing-wing F-14s became operational in 1973, and have since become the standard carrier-based fighter jet for the American Navy. The Tomcat's mission is to intercept attacking jets and protect carrier battle groups. It has variable geometry wings which sweep back when it is sprinting and sweep out when it is landing. It can independently track 24 targets and destroy six of them at a time. F-14s have performed successfully in intermittent raids and dogfights with Libyan pilots over the Gulf of Sidra.

In addition to the F-14, Grumman manufactures the E-2C Hawkeye, an early warning airborne command center able to track over 600 objects within three million cubic miles of airspace. The Israeli Air Force used E-2Cs to direct its air battles with Syrian pilots over Lebanon's Bekaa Valley in 1982. During those battles Syria lost 92 of its Soviet-built MiGs while Israel lost only two of its jets. In the Falkland Islands War, Britain's HMS Sheffield was sunk by an Exocet missile launched from an Argentine Super Etendard attack jet. U.S. Navy Secretary John Lehman asserted that if the British had an E-2C in the Falklands, they would have had unchallenged air superiority and would not have lost any ships to Exocet missiles. Both examples illustrate the value of the Hawkeye.

The Navy's A-6 Intruder attack bomber and EA-6B Prowler radar jammer are also manufactured by Grumman. The company has also re-manufactured 42 General Dynamics F-111 bombers for the U.S. Air Force. The new aircraft, designated EF-111, is designed to jam enemy radar surveillance "from the Baltic to the Adriatic." According to Grumman's current chairman, Jack Bierwirth, "it's one of the great exercises to fly this plane against the E-2C." This volley of electronic countermeasures shows the extent to which Grumman's only competition is itself.

The electronic sophistication of Grumman's aircraft has invited criticism from military reformers who have argued that modern weapons have become too complex and therefore unmanageable. In the 1970's these reformers, led by Gary Hart, widely publicized this view. The ultimate success of their movement could have had disastrous effects for Grumman. Following the costly disagreement over the F-14, the company's long term viability was threatened even more by these reformers under the Carter Administration.

Continued attempts to sell F-14s to foreign governments failed, as did lobbying efforts to sell more of the jets to the U.S. Navy. Consequently, Grumman made an effort to diversify its product line. The strategy was ambitious, but failed. The company's Dormavac freight refrigerators had no market (loss: $46 million), and its Ecosystems environmental management and research venture was unable to turn a profit (loss: $50 million).

In 1978 Grumman acquired the curiously named Flxible bus division from Rohr Industries. Many of the buses developed cracked undercarriage components, prompting some customers (such as the City of New York) to pull all of their Flxible buses out of service. Grumman filed a $500 million suit against Rohr, alleging that details of design flaws were not revealed prior to the sale. The suit was dismissed in court. Grumman's losses in this venture approached $200 million before the entire division was sold to General Automotive in 1983 for $41 million.

In 1981 Grumman faced a hostile takeover from LTV, a steel, electronics, and aircraft conglomerate based in Texas. Grumman's workers mobilized an enthusiastic demonstration of support for their company's resistance to LTV. Leroy Grumman, who retired from the company in

1972, raised employee morale when he voiced his support of the opposition to the LTV takeover attempt. A U.S. Court of Appeals later rejected LTV's bid to take over Grumman on the grounds that it would reduce competition in the aerospace and defense industries.

Leroy Grumman died the following year after a long illness. It was widely reported that Grumman was blinded in 1946 by a severe allergic reaction to penicillin administered during treatment of pneumonia. In fact, Grumman was not blinded. His eyesight did, however, begin to deteriorate many years later as his health began to wane.

The Grumman Corporation faced another external threat when it became involved in a scandal involving illegal bribes to government officials in Iran and Japan. After the Lockheed Corporation was accused of such improprieties, the sales practices of other defense contractors such as Grumman came under scrutiny. During the investigation of Grumman, a Japanese official named Mitsuhiro Shimada committed suicide.

After the investigations subsided, the companies in question were free to concentrate all their efforts on more constructive matters. Grumman engineers, however, had something highly unconventional on their drawing boards. Grumman's chairman, Jack Bierwirth, is credited with saying, "If you don't invest in research and development, you damned well aren't going to accomplish anything." With that in mind Grumman, in conjunction with the Defense Advanced Research Projects Agency, developed a special jet called the X-29 specifically to demonstrate the company's advanced technology. The revolutionary feature of the X-29 is that its wings sweep forward, appearing to have been mounted backwards. This feature gives the X-29 superior maneuverability. To counteract the inherent instability of such a design, the X-29 is equipped with a Honeywell computer system which readjusts the canards (wing controls) 40 times a second, maintaining stable flight.

The X-29 was tested under the auspices of NASA during 1984 and 1985. Never intended for mass production, only one X-29 was built as a "technology demonstrator." Bierwirth describes projects such as the X-29 as "marrying electronics with computer programming, then putting wings on it."

John Cocks Bierwirth is a former naval officer who became Grumman's chairman and chief executive officer in 1976. In his words, "We are essentially building the corporation of the future." Bierwirth divided Grumman's operations into nine divisions under centralized management. According to Bierwirth, Grumman's future lies with aircraft, space and electronics. However, work on such projects as a new post office truck are designed to maintain a stable and diverse product line. Bierwirth claims, "We think we are a good investment for people who are interested in the long term and are willing to grow with the company; Grumman is not a three month in-and-out investment."

Grumman, in association with Lockheed, has a contract to maintain NASA's space shuttles, despite the hiatus in the program following the tragic loss of the Challenger. Grumman also expects to win a major role in the construction of the American space station. The company is also involved in the development of controlled nuclear fusion, the energy source of tomorrow's power plants.

The largest employer on Long Island, New York, Grumman has consistently reflected the personalities of its founders. Beyond its commitment to technological innovation, Grumman has a humanistic, paternal relationship with its employees and a respect for the public in general. These two features of the "company of the future" ensure for it a powerful position in the aerospace industry for many years to come.

Principal Subsidiaries: Grumman Aerospace Corp.; Grumman Allied Industries, Inc.; Grumman Data Systems Corp.; Grumman Ohio Corp.; Grumman Credit Corp.; Grumman International, Inc.; Paurnanock Development Corp.

Further Reading: The Grumman Story by Richard Thruelsen, New York, Praeger, 1976; *Chariots for Apollo: The Making of The Lunar Module* by Charles R. Pellegrino and Joshua Stoff, New York, Atheneum, 1985.

LOCKHEED CORPORATION

2555 Hollywood Way
Burbank, California 91505
U.S.A.
(818) 847-6121

Public Company
Incorporated: 1916 as the Loughead Aircraft
   Manufacturing Company
Employees: 81,300
Sales: $10.27 billion
Market value: $3.411 billion
Stock Index: New York London Amsterdam Zurich
Basle Lausanne Geneva

"None of Lockheed's troubles ever seems to be a little one," noted *The Economist* magazine in 1981. However, after emerging from a financial crisis and a scandal that nearly ruined the company, Lockheed is more successful than ever before. Today Lockheed is one of the most important manfacturers of weapons and related systems in the United States.

The Lockheed Corporation has its origins with two brothers named Allan and Malcolm Loughead. Allan, an auto mechanic, first learned to fly in Chicago in 1912. When he returned home to San Francisco later that year he decided to build his own airplane. He and Malcolm spent their evenings in a garage, engineering and constructing a small ultralight seaplane they called the Model G. This airplane was one of the first "tractor" designs with a forward-mounted engine enclosed in the fuselage.

During this time Allan flew as a barnstormer, but later gave it up after some powerlines had ensnared his Model G. The brothers established the Alco Hydro-Aeroplane Company with financial backing from Max Mamlock's Alco Cab Company and concentrated on building airplanes. Unfortunately, they couldn't sell the airplanes, and the company was dissolved the following year.

In 1916 the brothers started another new venture, the Loughead Aircraft Manufacturing Company, based in Santa Barbara. Apparently tired of having their last name mispronounced as "lug head," Allan and Malcolm changed the spelling to match the pronunciation, "Lockheed." Likewise, the company's name was changed to Lockheed. Malcolm left the company three years later to sell hydraulic brakes. Still employed, however, was a young engineer named Jack Northrop (later the founder of the

Northrop Corporation) who helped the brothers to develop their twin-engine F-1 flying boat.

Northrop started a tradition of naming Lockheed airplanes after celestial bodies. In 1927 he helped develop the Lockheed Vega which became widely known as an explorer's airplane. When Amelia Earhart crossed the Atlantic, she flew a Vega. In June of 1928 Northrop left Lockheed to work for Avion, a subsidiary of William Boeing's United combine.

Lockheed was acquired by the Detroit Aircraft Corporation in July of 1929. An infuriated Allan Lockheed, who had little control over the turn of events, resigned his post and sold all his holdings in the company. Under new management, Lockheed's engineers produced a number of new airplanes. Most notable among them was a popular passenger transport called the Orion.

While Lockheed was still operating profitably two years into the Depression, its parent company, Detroit Aircraft, was in poor financial condition. When it went into receivership in 1932 Lockheed was put up for sale. A group of investors, Robert Gross and Lloyd Stearman among them, purchased the company for $40,000. The new owners wasted no time in developing a new airplane. In 1933 they introduced the Model 10 Electra. The Electra flew in the shadow of Douglas' DC-3, but was still popular with Northwest and Pan Am as a complement to their fleets of larger airplanes.

The following year airmail legislation and other subsequent congressional acts forced the breakup of a number of powerful aviation combines. Lockheed, however, was small enough that it remained largely unaffected.

One month after Germany annexed Austria in March of 1938, a British delegation toured the United States with the intention of purchasing airplanes for the Royal Air Force. Lockheed engineers were given only five days notice to design the reconnaissance bomber in which the British were interested. They presented the "Hudson," a modified Model 14 Super Electra fitted with more powerful engines, a bomb bay and guns. For unknown reasons, the Hudson retained the Model 14's cabin windows.

The British agreed to buy at least 200 Hudsons for $25 million. It was the largest military contract awarded before the war and marked a turning point in Lockheed's business. The Hudsons were to be built by Lockheed's Vega subsidiary, predominantly a manufacturer of military airplanes. By May of 1943 Vega had manufactured over 3000 Hudsons.

As the United States became more involved in World War II, Vega produced a number of new airplanes for the allied armies, including the Ventura, the Harpoon, and variations of Boeing's B-17 bomber. Lockheed also introduced the P-38 Lightning, an effective and versatile triple hull interceptor. The company produced about 10,000 of these airplanes and its variations.

Because the War Department required so many different types of airplanes, Lockheed converted a number of commercial designs to perform military duties. Perhaps the most impressive among these conversions was the four engine C-69 Constellation. Originally, this airplane was secretly developed by Howard Hughes and Lockheed engineers for civilian service. However, after Pearl Harbor the government prohibited further production of commercial airplanes. Nevertheless, only 15 of these planes were delivered before the war ended.

When the war finally came to a close late in the summer of 1945, Lockheed had produced 19,297 aircraft for the military—nine percent of the total U.S. production. After the war, the company concentrated on meeting the demand for commercial airplanes caused by the various airlines' expansion plans. Thus, Lockheed resumed the civilian 049 Constellation project. Variously described as "beautiful" or "romantic," several versions of this distinctive triple-rudder airplane were manufactured. It was a commercial success for Lockheed; virtually every major airline in the world ordered at least one. Lockheed also remodeled its Electra, designated L-188, and fitted it with prop-jet engines.

After the war Lockheed maintained numerous military contracts, many of them secret. One such project which the company and the armed forces had an interest in keeping quiet was the development of a jet fighter. Conventional piston-driven airplanes had propellers which simply pushed the air behind the airplane. Jets, on the other hand, sucked air into a chamber where at high pressures a spray of jet fuel was detonated. The rocket-like explosion of the fuel generated a powerful thrust. That thrust enabled an airplane to fly twice as fast as conventional airplanes. The newly created Air Force, now involved in the beginnings of the Cold War, expressed great enthusiasm for the project.

Lockheed had become interested in developing a jet during 1939, the year the Germans first tested one. Two years later the British designed and successfully built a jet. In 1943 Bell Aircraft built a jet called an Airacomet. All were test models and only Messerschmitt's Me.262 and Britain's Gloster F. 9/40 engaged in combat during World War II.

Kelly Johnson, the company's chief designer, led Lockheed's jet project at the secret Advanced Development Products (ADP) division. On January 8, 1944 the XP-80 Shooting Star was successfully flown over Muroc Dry Lake, Nevada. It later served as a prototype for more than 1700 improved variations.

The XP-80 model jet arrived too late for World War II, but was used when the Korean War broke out in 1950. Other Lockheed aircraft in action over Korea were the Neptune reconnaissance airplane, the F-94 Starfire interceptor, and the Constellation transport. "Korea," it was said, "was a Lockheed war."

The 1950's were a period of growth and innovation at Lockheed. With a steady flow of lucrative military contracts, the company expanded existing plants and built several new ones. It tested a vertical take-off and landing (VTOL) airplane, as well as a ramjet, widely regarded as the propulsion mechanism of the next century. Lockheed even made plans for a nuclear-powered aircraft. In 1953 the company established its missiles and space division which produced satellites and submarine-launched missiles.

Lockheed built a number of variously designed fighter jets for testing and use by the Air Force. Their one failure

was the F-104 Starfighter which was sold to the West German Luftwaffe in 1959. The Germans called them "widowmakers" and "flying coffins." 175 of these jets crashed, killing a total of 85 pilots. Lockheed, which initially refused to acknowledge the design problems with Starfighter, paid the pilot's widows $1.2 million in compensation during 1975.

In the commercial market Lockheed responded to Douglas' new DC-7 with an altered version of its Constellation, including new wings and a new name—the "Starliner". Two years later, in 1957, the company produced a small jet called Jetstar. These were to be Lockheed's last commercial ventures for fifteen years.

In the early 1960's Lockheed was closely associated with the Department of Defense. Robert and Courtland Gross, the company's chief executive officer and president respectively, maintained low profiles and delegated much of their responsibility to subordinates. Even after Robert died in 1961 and Daniel Haughton was named president, the direction of the company remained the same.

In military ventures the company developed transports such as the C-130 Hercules, the C-141 Starlifter and the C-5 Galaxy, the largest airplane in the world. During this period Lockheed's military products were consistently chosen over those of Boeing and Douglas for the award of Pentagon contracts.

In the decade of the 1960's Lockheed developed two very important jets, the U-2 spy plane and the SR-71. The U-2 flies at altitudes over 70,000 feet loaded with remote sensing electronic equipment. After the Cuban missile crisis of 1962, Senator Barry Goldwater credited the U-2 alone, with its reconnaissance abilities, for providing President Kennedy with precise and accurate information regarding the location of missile sites in Cuba.

The SR-71 was designed in the early 1960's and has not required any further improvement; its aerodynamics are regarded by most engineers as nearly perfect. Called the "blackbird" because it is painted black, the SR-71 has a cruising speed of over 2100 miles per hour and is able to fly at an altitude of over 85,000 feet. The SR-71's large engines create pockets of extremely low air pressure in front of the air intakes, drawing the aircraft forward. Acting like vacuums, the engines contribute to the forward motion of the airplane in this way.

In 1967 Courtland Gross stepped down as chairman, ending a 30-year era in the history of Lockheed. Daniel Haughton was promoted and Carl Kotchian was named president. These two men continued the conservative management tradition of the Grosses, but made one uncharacteristically risky venture in the commercial airline market. When Boeing announced the development of its 747, and Douglas its DC-10, Lockheed responded with a commercial wide body jetliner of its own, the 1011 TriStar. Lockheed's new jetliner first flew in November of 1970. However, the TriStar program was plagued with several major problems. Rolls-Royce, the manufacturer of the 1011's engines, went into receivership during February of 1971. Several airline companies, principally Eastern, experienced numerous equipment failures with their TriStars. Sales of the airplane began to drop, and the company faced a liquidity crisis. Even after important modifications in the design of the aircraft and increased sales, production of the L-1011 continued to lose money for Lockheed.

Lockheed's decision to compete with the new generation of commercial jetliners nearly ruined the company. By 1971 Lockheed's financial position became so grave that it required a guaranteed government loan to remain financially afloat. After producing a total of about 250 TriStars, Lockheed discontinued the program in 1981.

Lockheed, like many of its competitors, has always had a difficult time selling its jetliners in foreign markets. Their competitors have been known to use bribery to procure lucrative contracts. Lockheed made no secret that it intended to challenge its competitors on similar terms when it informed the Securities and Exchange Commission in 1975 that it would resist that agency's efforts to halt Lockheed's "sales incentives." The SEC withheld any action against Lockheed because the guaranteed loan gave the government an active interest in the company's quick financial recovery.

Lockheed was accused of bribing officials in Iran, Indonesia, Italy, the Netherlands and Japan. In 1976 a series of arrests in Japan culminated in the detention of the former prime minister, Kakuei Tanaka, whose government was brought down in the controversy. A month later, Prince Bernhard of the Netherlands was implicated in accepting Lockheed bribes. Questionable payments were made to officials in several other nations. Lockheed was successful in selling its planes, but now it was at the center of an international scandal.

The two men most closely associated with Lockheed's questionable practices were the company's president, Carl Kotchian, and chief executive officer, Daniel Haughton. Both men were compelled to resign in 1976 after details of the $30 million improprieties were publicized. Haughton, who consistently answered "no comment" to inquiries from the press, resigned peacefully. Kotchian had to be removed from his position during a four hour board meeting.

The board named an interim chief executive officer, Robert Haack, to preside over a restructuring of the company. A former president of the New York Stock Exchange, Haack deserves much of the credit for rectifying Lockheed's management and marketing problems. At the same time Lawrence Kitchen, a former vice president, was promoted to president following the departure of Kotchian. His task in this position was less to administer than to improve the damaged reputation of the company. Eighteen months later, Lockheed's chief financial officer, Roy A. Anderson, replaced Haack as Lockheed's new chief executive officer.

Today Lockheed conducts its business through 18 subsidiaries in four principal divisions: the missiles, space and electronics systems group; the aeronautical systems group; the marine systems group and the information systems group. Its major projects for the 1980's are primarily military hardware. They include building the F-19 stealth bomber and the Trident II submarine-launched missile, and maintaining the National Aeronautics and Space Administration's space shuttles. Because of its involvement in manufacturing so much military equipment, the company is regarded by the United States government as indispensable for the country's defense.

Principal Subsidiaries: Advanced Marine Systems; Lockheed Air Terminal, Inc.; Lockheed Advanced Aeronautics, Inc.; Lockheed Aircraft International A.G.; Lockheed Electronics Co., Inc.; Lockheed Missiles & Space, Inc.; Lockheed Finance Corp.; Lockheed Western Export Co.; TriStar Parts, Ltd.; Lockheed Engineering and Manufacturing Services, Inc.; Lockheed Georgia International Services, Inc.; Lockheed Shipbuilding Co.; Murdock Engineering Co., CADAM, Inc.; DIALOG Information Services, Inc.; Lockheed Data Plan, Inc.; Lockheed Space Operations Co.; Lockheed Support Systems Corp.; Lockheed Marine Company; Datacom Systems Corp.; Lockheed Jeromod Center, Inc.; Metier Management Systems (U.K.).

Further Reading: Lockheed: The Grease Machine by David Boulton, New York, Harper, 1978; *The Sporty Game* by John Newhouse, New York, Knopf, 1982; *Lockheed Horizons*, edited by Roy Blay, Burbank, California, Lockheed Corporation, 1983; *Flight in America 1900–1983: From the Wrights to the Astronauts* by Roger E. Bilstein, Baltimore, The Johns Hopkins University Press, 1984.

MARTIN MARIETTA CORPORATION

6801 Rockledge Drive
Bethesda, Maryland 20817
U.S.A.
(301) 897-6000

Public Company
Incorporated: October 10, 1961 upon the merger of the
Martin Company and American-Marietta
Employees: 69,000
Sales: $4.753 billion
Market value: $2.740 billion
Stock Index: New York

Martin Marietta is a corporation that will become increasingly better known in the next 50 years. Most recently, the company has become one of the most notable manufacturers of advanced technological equipment for the National Aeronautics and Space Administration (NASA); Martin Marietta is a leading contractor for a number of government projects, including the American space station. Yet, the company has its roots in the very foundation of American aeronautic history.

In 1905 a youthful Glenn Martin moved with his family to California. In the hills of Santa Ana, Martin built and flew his first experimental gliders. Not long afterwards Martin started a small airplane factory while working as a salesman for Ford and Maxwell cars. Martin's earnings from the auto sales went to finance his airplane business. He later performed publicly as a barnstormer in order to make money for the company and, at the same time, to attract interest in his product. During this time he hired a man named Donald Douglas to help him develop new airplanes. Soon thereafter, Douglas and Martin collaborated to produce a small flight trainer called a Model TT which was sold to the U.S. Army and the Dutch government.

On the eve of World War I, Douglas was summoned to Washington to help the Army develop its aerial capabilities. Less than a year later, he became frustrated with the slow moving bureaucracy in Washington and returned to work for Martin who had relocated to Cleveland after dissolving a short-lived partnership with the Wright company. In Cleveland, Douglas directed the development of Martin's unnamed twin-engine bomber. Neither he nor Martin was willing to compromise or shorten the period of time needed for the development of one of their airplanes.

For that reason the "Martin" bomber, for lack of a better name, arrived from the assembly line too late to see action in World War I. When Martin moved to Baltimore in 1929 Douglas left the company once again, this time to start his own aircraft company in California.

Even after the war Martin continued to impress the military with his aircraft demonstrations. In July of 1921, off the Virginia Capes, seven Martin MB-2 bombers under the command of General Billy Mitchell sank the captured German battleship *Ostfreisland*. Continued interest from the War Department led Martin's company to develop its next generation of airplanes, culminating with the B-10 bomber. The B-10 was a durable bomber, able to carry heavy payloads and cruise 100 miles per hour faster than conventional bombers of the day. For his work on the B-10 bomber Martin was awarded the Collier Trophy in 1932.

Through the 1930's, on the banks of the Chesapeake, Martin continued to manufacture bombers. He also recognized a need in the commercial airline market for a large passenger "flying boat" to traverse long distances over the water. With substantial backing from Pan Am's Juan Trippe, Martin developed the M-130 "China Clipper," the first of which was delivered in 1932. The clipper weighed 26 tons, carried up to 32 passengers and was capable of flying the entire 2500 miles between San Francisco and Honolulu. Pan Am flew Martin's planes to a variety of Asian destinations, including Manila and Hong Kong.

In the late 1930's airplane manufacturers seemed to know that a second world war was drawing near. Germany was building planes for a commercial airline that didn't exist while embarking on a massive remilitarization program. When World War II started Martin was prepared. The company produced thousands of airplanes for the Allied war effort, including the A-30 Baltimore, the B-26 and B-29 bombers, the PBM Mariner flying boat, and the 70-ton amphibious Mars air freighter. Martin invited some criticism in 1942 when he suggested that the United States could dispense with its costly two-ocean navy and defense of the Panama Canal if it had enough airplanes like the Mars.

After the war ended Martin continued to manufacture what few airplanes the Army and Navy were still ordering. In 1947 the company entered the highly competitive commercial airliner market with a model called the M-202. The development of later aircraft, the M-303 (which was never built) and the M-404, was a severe drain on company finances. Despite loans from the Reconstruction Finance Corporation, the Mellon Bank of Pittsburgh, and a number of other sources, the Martin Company was unable to generate an operating profit.

In July of 1949 Chester C. Pearson was hired as president and general manager of the company. Glenn Martin, at the age of 63, was moved up to the position of chairman. Despite the new management and an increase in orders as a result of the Korean War, the Martin Company was still losing money. There were two reasons: First, production of the 404 was interrupted which, in turn, halted delivery and therefore payment for the aircraft. Second, the company hired hundreds of new but unskilled workers, which lowered productivity.

By the end of 1951 George M. Bunker and J. Bradford

Wharton, Jr. were contacted, probably by the Mellon Bank, and asked to take over the management of the company. As part of a refinancing plan Glenn Martin was given the title of honorary chairman and his 275,000 shares in the company were placed in a voting trust. Bunker was named chairman and president and Wharton was named financial vice president. Pearson was made a vice president and later resigned. Bunker and Wharton were successful in arresting the company's losses and by the end of 1954 declared the company out of debt.

Martin substantially re-engineered a version of the English Electric Canberra bomber for the United States Air Force. Known as the M-272, the bomber was given the Air Force designation B-57. Martin built a number of scout and patrol planes, including the P5-M and P6-M flying boats, and expanded its interest in the development of rockets and missiles. One of Martin's first projects in this area was the Viking high-altitude research rocket, followed by the Vanguard missile. By the 1960's the company was a leader in the manufacture of second generation rockets like the Titan II.

Despite the company's return to profitability after the Korean War, the larger airplane manufacturers such as Boeing, Douglas and Lockheed had the advantage of size, which allowed them to compete more effectively with smaller companies like Martin, Vought and Grumman. These smaller companies, however, retained very different kinds of engineering teams which allowed them to continue developing unique aeronautic equipment and weapons systems.

Glenn Martin, who never married, died of a stroke in 1955 at the age of 69. He resigned his position in the company in May of 1953 shortly after his mother died, but remained as a company director until his death. Martin's mother, Arminta, was a enthusiastic supporter of her son. The fact that Martin often looked to his mother for inspiration and support may have had something to do with his decision to retire. George Bunker succeeded Martin as president and chairman and directed the company for the next 20 years.

The company was largely unsuccessful in achieving diversification in anything but its number of government customers. Martin aircraft was subject to the whims of the Department of Defense with its unstable pattern of purchases. By December of 1960 Martin's last airplane, a Navy P5M-2 antisubmarine patrol plane, rolled off the production line. From this point forward the company produced only missiles, including the Bullpup, Matador, Titan and Pershing among them.

The Martin Company's solution to the problem of selling one line of products to one customer was to merge with the American-Marietta corporation in 1961. Marietta was a manufacturer of chemical products, paints, inks, household products and construction materials. After convincing the government that the merger would not reduce competition in any of either company's industries, the two companies formed Martin Marietta. The diversification continued in 1968 with the purchase of Harvey Aluminum. The name of the subsidiary was changed to Martin Marietta Aluminum in 1971.

In 1969 Martin Marietta's aerospace unit was selected to lead construction of the two Viking capsules which landed on Mars in 1976. In 1973 the company was awarded a contract to build the external fuel tank for NASA's space shuttles. During the 1970's Martin Marietta had become known for its space projects, but remained a major producer of aluminum and construction materials.

Thomas G. Pownall was made Martin Marietta's president in 1977 and chief executive officer in 1982, succeeding J. Donald Rauth. The same year Martin Marietta faced the most significant challenge to its existence in its history —a hostile takeover bid from the Bendix Corporation. Bendix, which had earlier abandoned an attempt to take over RCA, was led at the time by Bill Agee. Agee's director of corporate planning, Mary Cunningham, left Bendix when questions arose regarding her relationship with Agee (who was already married). Before she resigned her position, however, she assembled a list of takeover candidates for Bendix, including among them Martin Marietta. For several years Agee had been divesting Bendix of its residual businesses, and in the process accumulated over $500 million for an acquisition "war chest." Agee later divorced his wife and married Cunningham, and together they instigated their $1.5 billion bid for Martin.

Martin Marietta responded by attempting to take over Bendix. Pownall invited his friend, Harry Gray of United Technologies, to participate in the takeover strategy. Pownall and Gray agreed to divide Bendix among them in the event that either Martin Marietta or United Technologies was successful in taking over Bendix. By a strange quirk of state incorporation laws in Maryland and Delaware (the companies' legal domiciles), Bendix and Martin Marietta could conceivably have controlled each other.

The takeover was stalemated until a three-way deal was arranged wherein the Allied Corporation agreed to purchase Martin Marietta's holdings in Bendix on the condition that Bendix abandon its bid for Martin Marietta. The deal left Allied with a 39% ownership of Martin Marietta, but it was agreed that Allied's voting share would be directed by Martin's board until such time that Allied could sell its interest in Martin. Bill Agee joined Allied's board of directors but later left the company. In the meantime, Martin Marietta went $1.34 billion into debt as a result of its takeover defense.

In 1982 one third of Martin Marietta's sales were in aerospace and two-thirds in the production of aluminum, construction materials and chemicals. Pownall's first attempt to improve his company's financial situation was to sell its cement and certain specialty chemicals operations; by 1983 the debt was reduced to $613 million. Due to the continuing deterioration of the aluminum market, Pownall sold the company's aluminum subsidiary to Comalco of Australia. The sale produced a $365 million write-off, but also generated over $400 million in cash and notes. By 1986 debt was down to $220 million, giving Martin Marietta a comfortable debt-to-total capitalization ratio of 24%.

A reorganization was already in process when Bendix launched its takeover attempt. In defending itself from Bendix the reorganization was accelerated. In retrospect, Tom Pownall recognized positive results of Bendix's takeover attempt. The company emerged from the fiasco as a more tightly managed and efficient business.

Martin Marietta would once again have been deprived of a wide base of operations were it not for astute management. Aside from its aerospace business, the company became active in the design, manufacture and management of energy, electronics, communication, and information systems, including the highly sophisticated level of computer technology known as artificial intelligence.

Even with this diversification, most of Martin Marietta's business is with the United States government from which the company derives 80% of its revenues. The company supplies the Pentagon with a number of weapons systems, including the Pershing II missile; a major part of the MX missile; the Patriot missile, designed for air defense of field armies; and the Copperhead, a "smart," or guided, cannon shell. Martin Marietta is also developing a series of night vision devices for combat aircraft.

The company continues to build external fuel tanks for NASA's space shuttle program, despite the temporary suspension of that program following the Challenger tragedy. Martin Marietta is also a major contractor for the American space station scheduled to be built in 1993. In another public project, the company is working on a new air traffic management system for the Federal Aviation Administration.

Tom Pownall is grooming a successor, a man named Norman R. Augustine. Augustine was named president and chief operating officer and is expected to assume the positions of chief executive officer and chairman when Pownall retires. Having been assured of a smooth transition of leadership Martin Marietta is looking to the future with confidence not simply as a major aerospace firm, but as one which recognizes the importance of its unique technologies and systems.

Principal Subsidiaries: Martin Marietta Energy Systems, Inc.; Hoskyns Group, Ltd. (UK); Martin Marietta Ordnance Systems, Inc.; International Light Metals, Inc. (60%); Chesapeake Park, Inc.; Orlando Central Park, Inc.

Further Reading: *Conquest of the Skies* by Carl Solberg, Boston, Little Brown, 1979; *The Sky's the Limit* by Arthur Whitehouse, London, Macmillan, 1979.

MCDONNELL DOUGLAS

McDONNELL DOUGLAS CORPORATION

P.O. Box 516
St. Louis, Missouri 63166
U.S.A.
(314) 232-0232
Public Company
Incorporated: 1967 upon the merger of McDonnell
Aircraft and the Douglas Company
Employees: 88,391
Sales: $12.66 billion
Market value: $3.220 billion
Stock Index: New York

McDonnell Douglas is not only a major United States defense contractor, but also one of the largest manufacturers of commercial aircraft. Three of every ten airliners in the free world are products of McDonnell Douglas. At present, McDonnell Douglas is a major competitor of Boeing and Airbus, and considered an important part of the Western military/industrial complex.

Donald Douglas' interest in aviation can probably be traced back to a Wright Brothers exhibition for the United States Army in 1908. He later entered the Naval Academy which, at the time, was experimenting with seaplanes. After two years at the academy he left to study mechanical engineering at the Massachussetts Institute of Technology. Douglas completed the four year curriculum in two years. Upon his graduation in 1915, he was summoned to California by the designer Glenn Martin (later of Martin Marietta). A year later, with the outbreak of war in Europe, the United States government asked him to move to Washington, D.C. in order to direct the aviation section of the Signal Corps. After a few months Douglas became frustrated with the bureaucracy of Washington and returned to Martin's company, whose headquarters had since moved to Cleveland.

Douglas left Martin in 1920 and established his own company office behind a Los Angeles barber shop. With virtually no capital at his disposal, Douglas persuaded a wealthy young man, David R. Davis, to underwrite the costs of developing a new aircraft design called the "Cloudster." With Davis' help, Douglas had enough money to hire several engineers away from Martin in order to build the Cloudster. This airplane was designed to fly coast to coast, stopping only to refuel. It also had a service

ceiling high enough to enable it to fly over mountain ranges.

In 1921 the newly renamed Douglas Company produced a torpedo plane for the Navy designated the "DT." The DT's popularity established a reputation for Douglas in the War Department which later led to an interest in Douglas' next plane, the World Cruiser or "DWC." In a 1924 demonstration the World Cruiser was flown around the world in 15 days. This accomplishment generated more interest in Douglas' small company.

Douglas, no longer with the financial support of Davis, introduced a flying boat for the commercial market in 1928 called the Douglas Dolphin. In 1934 Douglas' rival, William Boeing, secretly purchased a Dolphin which, it is rumored, he used to tender his yacht. It has been suggested that Boeing studied the Dolphin's design and later incorporated some of this design into the Boeing Company's flying boats.

Jack Frye of TWA was unable to convince Boeing to sell airplanes to his airline. Boeing chose to give top priority to the airlines owned by his own United Company. Frye responded by soliciting several alternative aircraft companies for a new all-metal tri-motor airplane capable of carrying 12 passengers at 145 miles per hour.

Douglas received one of Frye's written requests in August of 1932. His small company was an unlikely candidate to supply TWA with an airplane, but when Douglas submitted an airplane design able to carry 14 passengers, capable of speed approximating 180 miles per hour, and fitted with only two engines, Frye awarded him the contract. The airplane Frye agreed to purchase was the DC-1 (DC stood for "Douglas Commercial"). Before more than one DC-1 could be produced, the design was improved. The airplane finally delivered to TWA was a revised version of the DC-1, redesignated the DC-2. With the experience he had gained from the production of the DC-2, Douglas began work on his next design, the DC-3. New airmail legislation in 1934 increased the reliance of airlines on passenger business. As a result, the DC-3 was designed to meet new specifications, making it the "first airplane to make money just hauling passengers."

Airplane manufacturers were aware of the rising political tensions in Europe. The likelihood of war was becoming increasingly apparent. Aircraft designers knew that the large commercial airplanes could easily be converted into bombers. Many became suspicious when they learned that Hitler's Germany was ambitiously building commercial planes for routes that weren't yet charted. People wondered what Germany was doing with so many planes when the country in fact had no commercial airline. Douglas thought another war in Europe was inevitable, so the DC-3 was developed with a dual commercial/military purpose in mind.

Douglas' DC-3 was more popular than Boeing's 247. At the beginning of World War II, 80% of the airplanes in commercial service were DC-3s. During the war, the DC-3 served as a personnel carrier, and in other design variations as a B-18 bomber and a C-47 transport. Over 10,000 DC-3s of various configurations were built for service with the Army Air Corps. Douglas also produced a number of attack planes for the military, the A-20 Havoc and the

SBD Dauntless among them. A squadron of Dauntless airplanes was intrumental in the defeat of the Japanese Navy at the battle of Midway Island.

Douglas' next plane, the DC-4, was put into military service (as a C-54) before it flew commercially. The DC-4 had four engines and was nearly three times larger than its predecessor. When it finally entered commercial service in 1946, it gained an undeserved reputation for accidents. Pilot error was most often determined to be the cause of the disasters.

When the war exposed the secret development of Lockheed's revolutionary designed "Constellation," Douglas was provided with a look at what his competition would be offering after the war. Douglas began work early on a response to Lockheed's airplane, and his DC-6 entered service after the war. An improved version, the DC–6B earned substantial revenues for the airlines. A further improvement, the DC-7, was the first commercial transport to cross the United States non-stop against prevailing winds. Over 1000 airplanes in the DC-6/DC-7 series were produced. The first presidential aircraft were Douglas DCs; Roosevelt's "Sacred Cow" was a C-54, and Truman's "Independence" was a C-118, the military version of a DC-6.

Donald Douglas prepared his son, Donald Jr., for a leading position in the company, and appointed him president in 1958. The senior Douglas, however, continued to make the "important" decisions. One such important decision was to delay the development of a passenger jetliner. Unfortunately, it turned out to be a very costly decision. In Seattle, Boeing was flight testing its 707 when Douglas' DC-8 was just a model in the wind tunnel. Douglas was surprised when its most loyal customer, American Airlines, placed an order for Boeing 707's. Douglas accelerated development of its similarly configured DC-8, but Boeing's lead in designing and manufacturing a jetliner was insurmountable.

In a rather ironic turn of events United Airlines, historically associated with Boeing, placed the first order for DC-8s. When the airplane finally became available Douglas wasn't adequately prepared to meet the demand for its new jetliner, and a backlog of orders developed. The company lost some customers to Boeing and upset others by delaying delivery of the airplanes.

In 1965 the company introduced an improved jetliner designated the DC-9 in order to challenge Boeing's new 727. Once again these two airplanes were very similar. They were both designed with engines mounted on the rear of the fuselage, a feature first seen on the popular French-built Caravelle. The costly development of the DC-9 and the continuing backlog of orders resulted in a liquidity problem for Douglas. Douglas lost a great amount of money in 1966, and banks began to withhold their financial support of the company.

"Overwhelmed by prosperity," but unable to control costs, Douglas was quickly becoming a prime target for a takeover. In 1967 six companies submitted takeover bids for Douglas: General Dynamics, North American Aviation (later Rockwell International), Martin Marietta, Signal Oil & Gas, Fairchild and McDonnell Aircraft. Douglas' board of directors voted for a sale to McDonnell which had a history of effective management as well as an innovative group of middle managers. McDonnell had expressed an interest in Douglas as early as 1963, but was unable to arrange a merger until Douglas' financial position had sufficiently deteriorated. The merger encountered no problems because McDonnell had recently split its operations into three separate divisions, all independently managed. The simple addition of Douglas as a fourth division was made without difficulty and without interruption of either company's business.

James Smith McDonnell's company began as an airplane manufacturer for the military shortly before World War II. It was a major manufacturer in St. Louis by the end of the war, but it gained significant recognition only with the production of its Phantom jets in 1946. McDonnell was primarily a manufacturer of military jets, including the F2H Banshee, F3H Demon, F-101 Voodoo, and the various F-4 Phantom designs. (James McDonnell had a fascination with the occult, which may explain the origin of the names he chose for his jets.) In addition, McDonnell built the Mercury and Gemini space capsules for NASA. Since that time the company has built a number of missile systems, but its business with the National Aeronautics and Space Administration remains limited.

McDonnell had two sons, James III and John, as well as a nephew, Sanford. All three sat on the board of directors at McDonnell Douglas. Donald Douglas, Jr. was gradually excluded from the management of the company. It became harder for him to work in the shadow of the McDonnell family. Sanford McDonnell was named chief executive officer of the company upon James McDonnell's retirement in 1971, but Sanford still took directions from his uncle.

Under the continuing domination of James McDonnell, McDonnell Douglas developed a wide body "jumbo" jetliner in order to compete with Boeing's 747 in the commercial airliner market. The 450-passenger 747 was certainly larger, but McDonnell Douglas' DC-10, with only three engines, was better suited for the needs of more airline companies. Boeing had a hard time selling 747s: the airplanes were regarded as too large. Soon the company was facing a financial crisis. Then, with modifications, the 747 began to garner substantial orders. The DC-10 entered the market just as the Boeing 747 was becoming popular. As a result, McDonnell Douglas had a difficult time selling the DC-10 and recovering its development costs.

More stable business came from the Pentagon. McDonnell Douglas' military production still constitutes three-quarters of the company's business. The company is licensed to build Hawker Siddley's vertical take-off and landing Harrier "jump-jet," which played a prominent role in Britain's war in the Falkland Islands. The company also produces the popular F-4 Phantom, the F-15 Eagle, the A-4 Skyhawk and the F-18A Hornet.

McDonnell Douglas risked losing its contract to manufacture F-15s in 1970 when the U.S. Civil Rights Commission reported racially discriminatory hiring and promotion practices at the company, particularly in regard to black employees. By 1979, however, the company reported that the implementation of affirmative action programs had rectified the situation.

There have been other problems for the company. In 1979 James McDonnell III and three other company officials were indicted on charges of bribing foreign officials. According to the indictment, McDonnell Douglas was paying bribes to influence the sales of its airplanes in Korea, Pakistan, Venezuela, Zaire and the Philippines. Clark Clifford, a former secretary of defense, defended the company in court by arguing that these payments were made with the full knowledge of the U.S. government in "difficult sales environments." Nevertheless, a committee of directors recommended that non-management executives should dominate the membership of the board of directors to prevent schemes such as this from happening again.

McDonnell Douglas wasn't the only company accused of paying bribes. Lockheed, desperate to sell the L-1011 TriStar, was similarly implicated, but its activities were believed to have been far more extensive. Both Lockheed and McDonnell Douglas admitted their guilt, but while McDonnell Douglas was merely ordered to pay a fine of $55,000 and a $1.2 million civil award, the Lockheed Corporation was nearly ruined.

It was a bad year for McDonnell Douglas in another way. On May 25, 1979, at Chicago's O'Hare Airport, an American Airlines DC-10 lost an engine during take-off, crashed and killed all 273 people aboard. After a temporary grounding of DC-10s, the National Transportation Safety Board cited inherent design flaws and unapproved maintenance procedures for having caused the accident. In response, Sanford McDonnell issued a statement to remind DC-10 customers that American "damaged the plane severely by using a crude maintenance technique." Controversy persisted as the public continued to associate the DC-10 with the crash. The design problems were finally corrected and all maintenance procedures were standardized. Presently, the DC–10 has been updated, redesigned and renamed the MD-11. The MD-11 looks very much like a DC-10 with the exception of small vertical winglets located on the tips of airplane's wings.

The MD-11 is McDonnell Douglas' entry for the 1990's medium wide-bodied airliner market. The MD-11 is more fuel efficient, is capable of carrying 405 passengers, and requires only a two man crew. It also has a flying range of 8870 miles. For these reasons, airlines have shown significant interest in the airplane. It is still uncertain, however, especially in light of intense competition from Boeing and Airbus, whether McDonnell Douglas can make the MD-11 project profitable.

The official head of McDonnell Douglas is now Sanford McDonnell. After the death of his uncle, Sanford set out to change the character of the company, away from the autocratic style of his uncle and toward a more democratic corporate structure. Whether or not these policies will have beneficial results for the company remains to be seen.

During the 1980's McDonnell Douglas has attempted to compete in the commercial aircraft market without designing an entirely new jetliner. In addition to the MD-11, the company is offering an updated version of its DC-9, designated the MD-80 (the number ostensibly indicates the year of the design) to compete with Boeing's 757. This airplane seats 150 passengers and costs approximately half that of a new Boeing. In order to sell the MD-80 the company arranged to lend the jetliners to American Airlines with a later option to buy. Instead of the standard 18-year lease, the MDC–American contract has a five-year term. The move is indicative of one of the most innovative policies implemented under the direction of Sanford McDonnell. However, American could elect not to purchase the jetliners after five years. When understood in this light, the deal says something about the management's attitude toward high risk ventures.

In the conduct of its business one thing has remained consistent over the years: McDonnell Douglas has a very good credit rating. One result of 30 years success in the military field is that the company has virtually no debt. McDonnell Douglas uses its financial position to help customers purchase its jetliners; the American lease is just one example.

In regard to the future, McDonnell Douglas has started development of a new airplane, the MD-91X, fitted with new prop-fan engines. Prop-fans combine the speed of a jet engine with the economy of a propeller. The counter-rotating sickle-shaped propeller blades mounted on the rear of a jet engine are a rare sight today, but will become commonplace starting in the late 1990's. The MD-91X will enter the market in competition with Boeing's 7J7 prop-fan around 1992. In the meantime, the company will continue to manufacture its MD series and fulfill its military contracts.

Principal Subsidiaries: McDonnell Douglas Finance Corp.; McDonnell Douglas Canada Ltd.; MDC Realty Co.; Vitek Systems Inc.; Microdata Corp.; Hughes Helicopters, Inc.

Further Reading: The McDonnell Douglas Story by Douglas J. Ingells, Fallbrook, California, Aero Publishers, 1979; *Flight in America 1900–1983: From the Wrights to the Astronauts* by Roger Bilstein, Baltimore, The Johns Hopkins University Press, 1984; *The DC-3: 50 Years of Legendary Flight* by Peter M. Bowers, Blue Ridge Summit, Pennsylvania, Tab Books, Inc., 1986.

MESSERSCHMITT-BÖLKOW-BLOHM GmbH.

Postfach 80 11 09
8000 Ottobrun bei Munchen 80
Munich
Federal Republic of Germany.
(089) 6000–0

Public/State owned Company
Incorporated: 1926 as Bayerische Flugzeugwerke
Employees: 36,915
Sales: DM 6.01 billion (US$ 3.03 billion)
Market value: DM 600 million (US$ 303 million)
Stock Index: Munich Frankfurt Bonn Hamburg

Messerschmitt-Bölkow-Blohm is widely recognized as the most important aerospace company in West Germany. It is the final product of many mergers and acquisitions in German industry. Many of the companies and divisions which were absorbed by MBB were originally founded as aircraft companies, electronics firms and shipbuilders. One of MBB's component companies was Messerschmitt A.G., founded by Professor Willy Messerschmitt, whose engineering talents are often compared to such pioneers in aviation history as Anthony Fokker, Donald Douglas, and Kelly Johnson.

MBB has its origin in the Bayerische Flugzeugwerke. BFW, as the company was known, was founded in Augsburg, Germany as the successor to the Udet Flugzeugbau of Munich which ceased to exist in 1926. BFW commenced operations that year at the former works of the Bayerische Rumpler Werke in Augsburg. BFW manufactured a number of aircraft designs including two-seat light airplanes and larger transport aircraft. On the company's roll of employees was a young designer and engineer named Willy Messerschmitt.

Dr. Messerschmitt, a native of Augsburg, flew an airplane when he was 15 and designed his own airplane when he was 18. After graduating from the Munich Technical University he established his own company in 1923 and later merged its operations with BFW. In 1927 he was made BFW's chief designer, specializing in speed aviation. During the worldwide Depression, however, BFW encountered serious financial difficulties and failed. In order to stay in business Willy Messerschmitt re-established his own company, the Messerschmitt Flugzeugbau, and took over the unfinished projects of BFW. After a short period

of time, the Messerschmitt Flugzeugbau was assured solvency and reverted to the name BFW. Messerschmitt was extremely influencial in the company, of course, and by the end of the decade it was again incorporated under his name as the Messerschmitt Aktiengesellschaft.

Until the middle 1930's Willy Messerschmitt devoted most of his time to the development of civilian aircraft. Then, under the leadership of Adolf Hitler, Germany declared its intention to remilitarize and to reconstitute its air force or "Luftwaffe." As a result, Messerschmitt turned his energies toward the development of warplanes and later producted one of the most successful fighter planes in the history of warfare, namely the Me-109.

The single-seat Me-109 went into mass production at Augsburg and other factories in the latter half of 1938. Thousands were delivered to the Luftwaffe, and special versions of the airplane set new speed records. The following spring the company introduced its Me-110 two-seat escort fighter, a version of which later became the Jaguar twin-engine bomber. Later Messerschmitt aircraft included the heavily armed Me-210 fighter/bomber.

Messerschmitt airplanes were given important roles in the German war strategy of *Blitzkrieg*, or "lightning war." In 1939 Messerschmitt airplanes controlled the skies over Poland as German armies invaded that country. The following year the successful strategy was repeated in France. In the summer and fall of 1940 the Luftwaffe engaged the British Royal Air Force in one of the most bitterly fought and decisive aerial battles in history, the Battle of Britain. Despite their powerful capabilities and greater numbers, however, the Messerschmitts were unable to secure control of the skies for a German invasion of Britain.

In 1941 Messerschmitt secretly developed the Me-262, the world's first jet fighter. Messerschmitt's test pilot, Fritz Wendel, took the twin-engine jet for its first flight in July of 1942. But the German High Command, especially Hitler himself, wanted the jet to be manufactured as a bomber. The dispute caused mass production of the jet to be delayed until late in the war when Allied bombers had already destroyed most of Messerschmitt's factories.

The Me-262 was capable of attaining speeds of 550 miles per hour and reaching attitudes of 40,000 feet, far beyond the capabilities of any Allied airplane. When it was made fully operational in October of 1944, the Me-262 was shooting down as many as 45 Allied planes a day. Willy Messerschmitt later remarked that the Normandy invasion could have been repelled if Germany had had an additional 200 jets. When Soviet armies marched into Berlin in 1945 they found workers still assembling Me-262s in tunnels beneath Tempelhof airport.

By the end of the war Messerschmitt had produced about two-thirds of Germany's warplanes, including over 30,000 of the durable Me-109. Willy Messerschmitt was arrested by American forces in western Germany, detained briefly, and three years later was brought to trial in a German court, accused of being a "fellow traveller" of the Nazis. Claiming to have merely been a "reluctant beneficiary" of the German war machine, Messerschmitt was later acquitted of his involvement with the Nazi regime.

After the war the Allied occupation authorities imposed

a ten year moratorium on the production of German aircraft. The Messerschmitt factories were rebuilt to manufacture sewing machines, pre-fabricated houses, and small bubble-topped automobiles called the Kabinenroller. Unfortunately, these civilian ventures proved that Willy Messerschmitt's talents were restricted to the development and production of aircraft. By 1956 the company was nearly bankrupt and deeply in debt to the Bavarian and Federal governments. During this time Messerschmitt moved his permanent residence to Estapona near Malaga, Spain. While in Spain Messerschmitt and his team of engineers worked under contract to the Hispano Aviación company developing a line of HA-100 and HA-200 pilot trainers for the Spanish Air Force.

In 1957, after the moratorium expired, Messerschmitt returned to Germany where he developed a vertical take-off aircraft for the German Defense Ministry. The company shared a contract with the Heinkel company to assemble and later build French Fouga Magister jets in addition to building Lockheed F-104 Starfighters and the Fiat G-91. The Starfighters were an especially problematic jet for the reconstituted Luftwaffe; 175 of them crashed and killed a total of 85 pilots.

The German aircraft companies Heinkel, Focke-Wulf and Dornier, as well as Messerschmitt, never fully recovered from either the devastation of the war or the ten year production moratorium. It became a policy of the Federal government to rationalize the German aircraft industry through a process of mergers and joint ventures. Messerschmitt agreed to merge with Bölkow GmbH, a manufacturer of sport and civilian aircraft, sailplanes, electronics and small space vehicles.

The Bölkow company was founded in 1948 by a Dr. Ludwig Bölkow, as a small civil engineering firm in Stuttgart. In 1958 the company moved to Ottobrunn, near Munich, and changed its name to Bölkow-Entwicklungen K.G. On January 1, 1965, after the Boeing Company acquired a minority interest, the name was changed again to Bölkow GmbH.

The Messerschmitt/Bölkow merger was delayed for several months while the companies calculated their correct value (a component of which was future product orders). The German government, however, interpreted the delay as deliberate stalling. It announced that it would be withholding all new orders and additional funding until the companies carried out their amalgamation. On June 6, 1968 the two companies merged to form Messerschmitt-Bölkow GmbH. Willy Messerschmitt was named director of the new company and Ludwig Bölkow was made chairman of the board of directors.

The following May Messerschmitt-Bölkow merged with another aircraft company named the Hamburger Flugzeugbau GmbH. HFB, as this company was known, was founded in 1933 by the Blohm & Voss shipbuilding company and remained substantially owned by the Blohm family until the time it was sold. HFB resumed operations after the war in 1956, producing Noratlas 2501 transport aircraft under license from the French company Nord-Aviation. HFB was also involved in the production of Lockheed Starfighters, the Transall C-160 military transport, and the Fokker F-28.

To reflect the addition of HFB, the company was named Messerschmitt-Bölkow-Blohm. The major shareholder of MBB was the Blohm family, with a 27.1% interest. Other shareholders included Dr. Messerschmitt (23.3%), Dr. Bölkow (14.6%), the Boeing Company (9.7%), Aérospatiale (9.7%), and the State of Bavaria (6.5%). In July, Siemens A.G. acquired a remaining 9.1%.

The amalgamated Messerschmitt-Bölkow-Blohm maintained its commitments to joint ventures and co-production agreements with other companies. MBB developed missile systems with Nord-Aviation and Aérospatiale, and was a member of the Panavia *Eurofighter* consortium with British Aerospace and Aeritalia. MBB provided 65% of the capital for Deutsche Airbus which, in turn, constituted 37.9% of the total capitalization of the Airbus Industrie commercial jetliner consortium. MBB was also involved in the production of the Transall C-130, Fokker F-27 and F-28. MBB also modified F-4 Phantom fighters and General Dynamics' F-16s for the Luftwaffe. In addition, MBB continued to manufacture its successful BO.105-series of helicopters.

Through the 1970's MBB maintained a high profile in the commercial airliner market, mostly through its association with Airbus. MBB manufactured large portions of the A-300 and A-310 fuselage, which were then flown via "Super Guppy" (a converted Boeing Stratocruiser) to Aérospatiale facilities in Toulouse, France for final assembly. MBB also devoted its resources to the development of subsequent Airbus jetliners, including the A-320.

Dr. Bölkow retired from MBB at the end of 1977 following an unsuccessful attempt to convince the board to waive his mandatory retirement at age 65. As Bölkow was leaving, the government was once again considering a further consolidation of the German aerospace industry. MBB was financially healthy and considered an ideal candidate to take over the troubled Vereinigte Flugtechnische Werke, or VFW. A merger between the two companies, however, did not occur because the government did not consider such a merger a necessary part of the nationalization program.

On September 15, 1978 Willy Messerschmitt died following an undisclosed major surgical operation. Ironically, his death came on the day the British mark as the anniversary of the Battle of Britain. In less than a year MBB had lost both of its prominent founders.

The German aerospace industry continued to experience difficulties caused by weak markets and overwhelming foreign competition. VFW, in particular, was in deep financial trouble. VFW was formed by the merger of Focke-Wulf and Weserflug in 1963, and Heinkel in 1964. In 1969 VFW merged with Fokker of the Netherlands and was called VFW-Fokker. Despite the continuing success of Fokker's aircraft line, VFW-Fokker was unable to generate a profit. The company sold only 16 of its new VFW-614 jetliners. While Fokker facilities in Amsterdam were expanding, VFW's in Bremen were laying off workers. Because the two companies had different long-term strategies and that they were moving in different directions, a decision was made for VFW and Fokker to dissolve their partnership.

The breakup was delayed for two years while Fokker

prepared for its independence. During this time VFW regained a good measure of its financial health. The government, however, was still determined that VFW be merged with MBB. The subsequent merger was so well planned that, virtually within days of the VFW-Fokker breakup, the way was cleared for an MBB-VFW merger.

Both companies were owned by a diverse mix of industrial companies, private citizens, and state and federal governments. Settling their claims delayed MBB's absorption of VFW for several months. When it was completed, MBB owned 19 plants between the North Sea and the Alps, making it the third largest aerospace company in Western Europe. VFW's 35% stake in Deutsche Airbus was added to MBB's 65%, making it a wholly-owned subsidiary of MBB. The company also continued to participate in a number of pan-European aerospace programs, including the Panavia Tornado fighter (42.4%), Airbus Industrie (37.9%), the French-German *Eurocopter* and *Euromissle* consortiums (both 50%), and the *Eurosatellite* direct television broadcasting system (24%). Starting in 1979, MBB manufactured a new helicopter called the BK.117 in conjunction with Kawasaki Heavy Industries of Japan. The policy of involvement in joint ventures was started by Ludwig Bölkow in the 1950's and was later continued at MBB.

The company was reorganized in September 1983 after Willy Messerschmitt's nephew, Gero Madelung, who had served as MBB's chief executive, left the company. The former Military Aircraft and Helicopter divisions were merged into a new military aviation group. The Dynamics division was merged with the Special Products division, which includes marine systems and missiles. MBB's other divisions, the Space group and the Transport Aircraft group, were unaffected.

In 1984 MBB attempted to improve its slow growth by acquiring Krauss-Maffei, manufacturer of the highly successful Leopard II battle tank. Although Krauss-Maffei had significant retained earnings, its parent company, the Freidrich Flick group, was experiencing financial difficulties which induced them to sell the tank builder. MBB acquired Krauss-Maffei through its 50%-owned subsidiary RTG.

During this time MBB itself became a takeover target. The strongest candidate bidding for MBB was the Munich-based automobile manufacturer BMW. BMW, however, wanted nothing less than a 51% share of MBB. MBB's majority shareholders, the German states of Bavaria, Bremen, and Hamburg were opposed to the takeover and primarily responsible for rejecting BMW's bid. MBB has since corrected its structural deficiencies and is no longer considered a takeover target.

The German states, which together own more than 50% of MBB, have often expressed their desire to further privatize the company. Yet by holding their majority interest they can exercise control over a number of factors, including employment and additional industrial development in their regions.

In civil aeronautics MBB has taken a 31% share in production of the Airbus consortium's new A-320 jetliner (down from 35% for the A-300 and A-310). It also has a 27% share in Fokker's new short/medium range airliner

called the Fokker 100. Furthermore, MBB is a major partner in the Ariane unmanned rocket program. In military aviation, MBB is a partner in the Munich-based European Fighter Aircraft (EFA) consortium called *Eurofighter*. The EFA program was created to produce 800 high-performance fighter jets for the air forces of Britain, West Germany, Italy and Spain.

Britain and West Germany considered developing a successor to the Panavia Tornado with France. When negotiations failed the British government backed the development of an entirely British fighter jet, the P.110. The P.110 was later developed into the Agile Combat Aircraft (ACA) by the reunited Panavia partners. Fearing that the ACA would endanger a separate five-nation European fighter project, the German and Italian governments withdrew their support. The British aerospace industries, however, continued to develop the ACA and later produced a new fighter designated the EAP (for Experimental Aircraft Programme). Ironically, Britain's EAP became the prototype for the five (presently four) nation *Eurofighter*.

MBB regards its failure to support the development of the ACA into the EAP as a major mistake. It allowed the British to establish a strong lead in advanced avionic technologies. The Eurofighter partners, British Aerospace (33%), MBB (33%), Aeritalia (21%) and CASA (13%), now must decide how much of Britain's EAP is relevant to the EFA.

The Eurofighter and Airbus groups are perhaps the best examples of MBB's strong position in the European aerospace industry. The continued growth of the West German economy assists MBB by generating domestic demand as well as providing strong export markets. There is currently no need for further rationalization in the German aerospace industry, nor does it appear that there will be. The company's managing director, Hanns Arnt Vogels, has said that MBB is again very close to making a broad structural change so that it can remain a strong European competitor.

Principal Subsidiaries: MBB-Grundstucksverwaltungsgesellschaft (99.25%); Vereinigte Flugtechnische Werke GmbH; ERNO-Raumfahrttechnik GmbH; Bayern-Chemie Gesellschaft für flugchemische Antriebe GmbH; Rhein Flugzeugbau GmbH; Bölkow Anlagen GmbH; Deutsche Airbus GmbH; Flugzeug Union-Sud GmbH; MBB-Transtechnica Gesellschaft für Technologie Transfer GmbH; Junkers Flugzeug und Motorenwerke GbmH; MBB-Weitsschaftsdienst GmbH; GELMA Industrie-elektronik GmbH; MBB Helicopter Corporation (USA); MBB Helicopter Systems, Ltd. (England).

Further Reading: Messerschmitt: Aircraft Designer by Armand van Ishoven, New York, Doubleday, 1975; *The German Air Force 1933–1945* by Mathew Cooper, New York, Jane's Publications, 1981.

NORTHROP

NORTHROP CORPORATION

1840 Century Park, Northeast
Los Angeles, California 90067
U.S.A.
(213) 553-6262

Public Company
Incorporated: March 7, 1939
Employees: 41,500
Sales: $5.608
Market value: $2.323
Stock Index: New York

Jack Northrop worked as an engineer at various aviation companies in the United States for nearly 20 years before founding his own company. Donald Douglas said of Jack Northrop in the 1940's that, "Every major airplane in the skies today has some Jack Northrop in it." Douglas' observation remains true even in the last quarter of the 20th century. Northrop's many discoveries and innovations are commonly used in jetliners manufactured by Boeing, McDonnell Douglas, Lockheed and Airbus, as well as the company he founded.

John Knudsen Northrop was born in 1895. He served in World War I as an infantryman and was later transferred to the Army Signal Corps which was responsible for military aviation. In the Signal Corps he developed a skill for designing aircraft and, as a result, went to work for Donald Douglas in California after the war. As a draftsman he helped to develop the airplanes that first established Douglas' firm as a leading aircraft manufacturer.

In 1927 he went to work for Allan Lockheed. While he was there he led the development of the Vega, the airplane that made Lockheed a major company. The Vega was one of the first airplanes to have a "stressed skin" construction, meaning that the structural integrity of the outer shell of the aircraft was sufficient to eliminate the need for a weighty frame and struts. The design ushered in a new generation in aircraft design. Amelia Earhart flew a Vega on her solo flight across the Atlantic in 1932.

Northrop formed his own company in 1928, the Avion Corporation. Here he conducted research for the first all-metal aircraft and the "flying wing," a highly efficient boomerang-like aircraft with no fuselage. Two years later Avion was purchased by Bill Boeing's United Aircraft and Transport Corporation.

Jack Northrop created a second company in 1932 as a division of Douglas Aircraft. Established as a partnership with Douglas, the Northrop Corporation developed an airplane for the Army Air Corps called the Alpha. Similar to the Vega, the Alpha had a single shell, or "monocoque," construction. However, because the plane was made of metal instead of wood, it was more durable and efficient. The Alpha made a new generation of aircraft possible for Douglas, namely the DC-1, DC-2 and the DC-3. Northrop's engineering success with this type of airplane set a new standard for manufacturers; biplanes, double-skin construction and airplanes made of wood were relegated to the past.

In 1939, Jack Northrop left Douglas to establish his own company called Northrop Aircraft. When World War II erupted, Northrop devoted much of his company's resources to the development of a flying wing bomber. This revolutionary design was greeted with great skepticism. The advantage of the flying wing was that, without the "baggage" of a fuselage or tail section, the entire mass of the airplane could be employed to produce the lift needed to keep it aloft. This allowed the possibility of much greater bomb payloads. In 1940 the company flew its first experimental flying wing designated the N-1M.

Northrop later developed the B-35 flying wing bomber, and then an improved version called the B-49, which he hoped would be chosen as the primary bomber for the Air Corps. Yet the Army cancelled further development of Northrop's bomber because, as reported by the Army, the B-49 wasn't stable enough in the air and because it required powered rather than manual controls. Northrop, however, revealed shortly before he died that the Army cancelled the B-49 because he refused to merge his company with a manufacturer in Texas. Others have suggested that the Army dropped the flying wing when Northrop refused to allow other government-appointed companies to manufacture his design. Even today the real reason the B-49 was cancelled is not clear.

In spite of the B-49 fiasco, Northrop contributed to the war effort in many other ways. His company built the P-61 night fighter known as the Black Widow. He also established a prosthetics department at his company for dismembered veterans. He even employed disabled servicemen either at the plant or in their hospital beds for regular pay.

In 1952 Jack Northrop retired and relinquished his presidency to O. P. Echols. In 1958 the name of the company was changed to the Northrop Corporation and the following year the current chairman, Thomas V. Jones, took over as president. Jones led the company into a number of diversified subcontracting arrangements. Northrop built numerous airplane and missile parts, electronic control systems, and even became involved in construction.

During the 1950's and 1960's Northrop produced the F-89 jet interceptor and the curiously named Snark missile system. The company continued to produce its own jet fighters, including the popular F-5 Freedom Fighter. A total of over 2200 F-5s were flown by 30 countries, including Nationalist Taiwan, Iran and South Korea. The trainer version of the F-5, the T-38, was used by the United States Air Force and was also the jet chosen by the Thunderbirds acrobatic flying troupe.

In 1972 Jones made an illegal $50,000 contribution to the re-election campaign of President Nixon; he was fined $200,000 for this indiscretion. The scandal led to an investigation which revealed another more serious impropriety. The company admitted to paying $30 million in bribes to government officials in Indonesia, Iran, and Saudi Arabia, among other countries, in an effort to increase business.

An enraged stockholder sued the company and, as a result, won a settlement which forced Jones to resign his presidency but allowed him to remain as chairman. A further condition of the court ruling was that the board was required to seat four more independent directors, giving the non-management "outsiders" a majority. Today it is a company policy that 60% of the board seats must be held by non-management personnel.

Since the scandal the company has had considerably more trouble selling its products. David Packard, an assistant secretary of defense in the Nixon Administration, invited two finalists to compete for the job of producing America's next fighter jet; Northrop's F-17 Cobra competed against General Dynamics' F-16. Prototypes of the jets flew against each other in dogfights. In the end, the F-16 won the competition. The F-17, however, was later redesigned by Northrop in conjunction with McDonnell Douglas and renamed the F-18 Hornet.

The F-18 Hornet was to be produced in two versions in partnership with McDonnell Douglas. Douglas was the prime contractor for the F-18A carrier-based fighter, and Northrop was the prime contractor for the F-18L, a land-based version. Each company was supposed to serve as the other's subcontractor. A dispute erupted when McDonnell Douglas' F-18A outsold the F-18L, even in countries without aircraft carriers. According to Northrop, the company was being treated unfairly by McDonnell Douglas. The two companies brought legal action against each other, charging violation of their "teaming agreement," one of the first major competitor partnerships since World War II. In April of 1985 the court settled in favor of Northrop and awarded the company $50 million. McDonnell Douglas, however, was awarded the prime contractor's role for all future F-18s, with Northrop designated as the subcontractor.

Northrop had another unpleasant experience when the Carter administration called for the development of an advanced fighter jet which was expressly intended for export. Too many foreign countries were showing interest in jets which the government considered too technologically sophisticated for mass export. In response Northrop, at its own expense, developed a less sophisticated fighter called the F-20 Tigershark. It was delivered ahead of schedule and below budget. The problem was that foreign governments still wanted the more sophisticated American jets. Northrop complained that the United States government wasn't promoting the F-20 vigorously enough. The government denied a large sale of F-20s to Taiwan because it was afraid the sale would upset mainland China. In November of 1986 the U.S. Air Force selected General Dynamics' F-16 over the F-20 as its main fighter for defense of the North American continent. As a result, Northrop announced that it would halt further work on the F-20.

Today, Northrop produces a variety of defense electronics systems, including the guidance system for the MX missile, as well as various parts for Boeing's 747. It also manufactures a sizable portion of the F-18. The company is also actively involved with Lockheed in the production of the top secret F-19 Stealth bomber. This airplane has such a low radar profile that it is virtually invisible on enemy radar screens. The secrecy of this project is such a high priority that the Air Force, the Pentagon and even the manufacturers contend it doesn't exist. In addition, the Defense Department selected Northrop (with McDonnell Douglas as its subcontractor) to develop a version of an advanced tactical fighter (ATF) called the YF-23A. Northrop's ATF will compete for a government production contract against a second version called the YF-22A produced by Lockheed, Boeing and General Dynamics.

The company's business is conducted through two main divisions: the aircraft group and the tactical and electronic systems group. The nature of the company's defense-related business requires it to maintain a low public profile. In the tradition of Jack Northrop, however, company policies continue to reflect a commitment to social responsibility.

Jack Northrop died in February of 1981, but the company he left behind continues on the cutting edge of high technology defense systems. Regarding his contributions to commercial aviation, Thomas Jones said, "His many design breakthroughs helped make possible aviation as we know it today."

Principal Subsidiaries: Northrop Services, Inc.; Northrop Worldwide Services, Inc.; Wilcox Electric, Inc.

Further Reading: *Getting Off the Ground: The Pioneers of Aviation Speak for Themselves* compiled by George C. Dade and George Vecsey, New York, Dutton, 1979.

ROCKWELL INTERNATIONAL

600 Grant Street
Pittsburgh, Pennsylvania 15219
U.S.A.
(412) 565-2000
Public Company
Incorporated: December 6, 1928 as North American
Aviation
Employees: 105,759
Sales: $12.39 billion
Market value: $8.121 billion
Stock Index: New York

Rockwell International is a manufacturer of industrial machines and household appliances, as well as military hardware and aerospace equipment. It presently operates in so many unrelated businesses that it is easy to forget the company began as one of the United States' largest aviation concerns.

Charles Lindbergh's flight across the Atlantic in 1927 generated such interest in aviation that suddenly even small aviation companies were deluged with money from investors. So much capital was made available by investors (almost one billion dollars by 1929) that holding companies created hundreds of airlines and airplane manufacturers. Three companies in particular emerged in the late 1920's as the largest aeronautic concerns. They were: the Aviation Corporation of the Americas (Avco), run by Averell Harriman and the Lehman Brothers investment firm; the Boeing/Rentschler consortium known as United Aircraft and Transportation; and North American Aviation, organized by a New York financier named Clement Keys.

The engine manufacturer Pratt & Whitney had secured two airplane manufacturers and a major airline, the United Aircraft consortium, as exclusive customers. Clement Keys recognized that his company needed a similar affiliation if it was to survive. He finalized an arrangement wherein the Wright Engine Company became the exclusive supplier of engines for North American Aviation.

North American's major airline, National Air Transport, was one of 45 aviation companies operated by Keys; the list also included the Curtiss Aeroplane & Motor Company and Wright Engine. Curtiss was a successful manufacturer of such airplanes as the Condor, and Wright manufactured some of the highest quality aircraft engines

of the day. North American also owned Eastern Air Lines, the pioneer of air service along the eastern coast of the U.S., and Transcontinental Air Transport. These subsidiaries made the parent company's stock even more attractive. Money continued to flow into North American from investor groups, making the original stockholders (Keys among them) extremely wealthy.

The bright future of the aviation companies came to an abrupt end on October 24, 1929 when a financial disaster hit Wall Street. Virtually all stocks were inflated in value and backed only with borrowed funds. When investors realized that the market could no longer support the inflated values of their stock, they flooded brokerage houses with orders to sell. The large number of claims led people, banks, and companies into bankruptcy. The resulting stock market crash brought about a 10 year world depression.

In 1930 North American lost its majority control of National Air Transport to the United Aircraft company. The buyout provided temporary relief to financially troubled North American, which was purchased by General Motors four years later. General Motors was one of the few companies with capital available to refinance a business which held such promise for the future. General Motors acquired North American in an attempt to diversify, since its own product was not selling well during the Depression.

Keys retired from business in 1932 because of ill health. James Howard Kindelberger, who was with Donald Douglas during development of the DC-1 and DC-2, was made president of North American in 1935. He was trained as an engineer, but knew the automotive business so well that his managerial acumen overshadowed his engineering skills.

General Motors, which held a substantial amount of stock in Trans World Airlines, sold its holdings in that company in 1936. In the same year North American (still a subsidiary of General Motors) sold its Eastern Air Lines unit to the airline's director, Eddie Rickenbacker. The divestiture of airline companies from airplane manufacturers was forced upon the three largest aeronautic conglomerates by senator Hugo Black, who also advocated the break-up of numerous other monopolies. North American Aviation was no longer an airline company, but merely a manufacturer of airplanes and parts for airplanes.

During World War II North American manufactured thousands of P-51 Mustangs for the U.S. Army Air Corps. The P-51, one of the last mass-produced piston engine airplanes, saw action in every theatre during the war. The company also built the B-25 Mitchell bomber and T-6 Texan trainer. The company built more airplanes for the U.S. military than any other company during the war years. The rapid expansion of the company was financed mostly by the government, which was North American's largest customer.

When the war ended North American's military contracts also ended. Like Grumman, North American opted to avoid entering the competitive commercial airliner market. Instead, the company focused its resources on the development of the next generation of military aircraft, namely, jets. Working from designs and prototypes of jet aircraft which were captured from the Germans after the war, North American built its first fighter jet called the F-86 Sabre. Because the Sabre's supersonic wings were developed from German designs, the company saved millions of dollars in research and development costs.

In the years after the war North American attempted to enter the private airplane market, with a small four-passenger plane called the Navion. Poor sales of the Navion convinced company management of the futility of entering the private market. In 1947 the design and production rights to the Navion were sold to Ryan Aeronautical.

North American continued to develop new equipment for the military. The company built a number of fighters and trainers for the Navy's aircraft carriers, in addition to a new jet called the F-100 Super Sabre. North American also constructed the first experimental supersonic aircraft, the rocket-powered X-15 and X-70.

When General Motors sold its share of the company in 1948, North American diversified its product line. It became involved in the development of rockets, guidance systems and atomic energy. It created Rocketdyne, Autonetics and Atomics International as new divisions to pursue research in those individual fields. Here again, Rocketdyne was assisted by the Germans: much of its rocket and missile technology was acquired from captured German data.

Kindelberger who had been promoted to chairman, and the company's new president, J.L. Atwood, planned the company's diversification before the war ended. They both knew that in order for the company to survive the postwar environment, they would have to prove the company's worth to the government by leading the development of the newest defense systems. The government could then justifiably be asked to fund much of the costly development of any new systems.

The company's greatest success was in its Rocketdyne division, which produced the Thor, Jupiter, Redstone and Atlas rockets. The research and development of an atomic-powered missile was abandoned when the system was declared impractical and unworkable. Research from the ambitious but ill-fated project was converted for use in the development of nuclear reactors.

When the Soviet Union put Yuri Gagarin into space in 1961, the United States space program was jolted into action. North American's Redstone rocket was used to launch Alan Shepard and Virgil Grissom into space during the Mercury space program in 1961. Later, John Glenn was launched into orbit aboard a Mercury spacecraft perched on top of an Atlas rocket. North American Aviation enabled the United States to recover its technological edge in the space race with the Soviet Union.

In order to meet President Kennedy's challenge to land a man on the moon before 1970, the National Aeronautics and Space Administration contracted North American to build the three passenger Apollo space capsule. On January 27, 1967 a flash fire swept through a manned Apollo capsule during a gound test. Killed in the accident were Virgil Grissom, Edward White II, and Roger Chaffee. The astronaut's widows each received $350,000

in a legal settlement, but North American was still harshly criticized. Despite the fact that most of its business involved government contracts, the company suffered severe financial reverses which threatened it with bankruptcy. Within two months of the accident North American Aviation was a prime candidate for a takeover.

Rockwell-Standard made a $922 million bid for North American Aviation in March of 1967. Rockwell was established in Wisconsin in 1919 as a manufacturer of truck axles. At the time of the bid, Rockwell was primarily a manufacturer of industrial machinery and light and heavy vehicle parts.

Under the terms of the merger, J.L. Atwood, president and chief executive officer of North American, would assume the same duties at the new company, while Colonel Willard Rockwell, chairman of Rockwell-Standard, would serve as chairman. The merger was delayed for a few months by the Justice Department which argued that the merger would be anti-competitive. The problems were finally resolved and the smaller Rockwell, with sales of $636 million, took over North American, with sales of $2.37 billion.

Atwood said the merger was "in furtherance of North American's previously announced objective to diversify its activities into the commercial and industrial sector." What the company management really wanted was to improve its public image. Its association with the Apollo space capsule tragedy was never forgotten. The merger with the Rockwell company would recover the reputation of integrity that management thought North American deserved. It was clear that Colonel Rockwell would be firmly in charge of the new company, which was called North American Rockwell.

Rockwell's role in the U.S. space program continued, but the company maintained a low profile. It spent much of its first years after the merger manufacturing car and truck parts, printing presses, tools, industrial sewing machines, and electronic instruments for flight and navigation. The company devoted much of its resources to the development of space systems, including the enormous Saturn V rocket engines which launched later Apollo missions to the moon. Later, the company was chosen as the primary contractor for NASA's space shuttles. During this time, it also became NASA's largest contractor, and has held that position ever since. In 1973 the company changed its name to Rockwell International when it was merged with another separate company created by Willard Rockwell Jr., the Rockwell Manufacturing Company.

Willard Rockwell, Jr., who took over from his father in 1967, retired in 1979 and Robert Anderson assumed the position of chairman. Anderson had joined Rockwell in 1968 after he left the Chrysler Corporation. He was named president of Rockwell in 1970 and chief executive officer in 1974. Anderson's background in the automotive business made him a conservative and cautious manager. Generally regarded as an engineer more than as a financial manager, he had a strategy for the company's growth and expansion that was markedly different from that of his predecessor. Anderson himself later remarked, "it's fair to say that we disagreed on the direction of the company altogether."

Under the junior Rockwell the company made some

high risk acquisitions, stretching its balance sheet to an uncomfortable degree. At one point the company was losing a million dollars a day. Rockwell was trying to establish the firm's business in high profile consumer markets, like Admiral television, which Anderson sold in 1974.

Anderson, who was originally hired to smooth the transition of management and resources during the 1967 merger, had little tolerance for the waste usually associated with defense contracts. He introduced the General Motors policy, which required all company divisions to submit profit goals for various production periods. As a result of Anderson's strict management, Rockwell's debt-equity ration (the company's debt divided by its net worth) fell from 99% in 1974 to 50% in 1977 and to 9% in 1983.

Rockwell had initially planned to build the B-1 bomber, but in 1977 the Carter Administration cancelled the program, favoring instead the development of Northrop's stealth bomber. By 1983, however, the Reagan Administration had reactivated the B-1 project as part of its ambitious military program. Production of the B-1 bomber was expected to generate a profit of approximately $2 billion a year for Rockwell, but subsequent orders for more of the bombers ceased. Once again, Rockwell and its B-1 were summarily excluded from consideration for the production of the United States' next strategic bomber. The company still had other defense contracts, however: the MX "Peacekeeper" missile (designed to replace the nation's stock of aging minuteman missiles), five space shuttles, and a navigation satellite called Navstar.

Willard Rockwell, Jr. resigned as a consultant to Rockwell in 1984 due to a conflict of interest between the company and a separate concern he founded in 1979 called Astrotech. Astrotech was negotiating to purchase one or more of NASA's space shuttles in the belief that only private enterprise could make shuttle flights profitable.

That venture was indefinitely postponed by the explosion of the space shuttle Challenger in January of 1986. An investigation of the accident later revealed that one of the booster rockets malfunctioned and caused the rocket to collide with the huge external fuel tank. The resulting explosion decimated the orbiter and killed all seven of its astronauts. A few months later President Reagan announced the order for a new shuttle from Rockwell to replace the Challenger.

Shortly before the accident Rockwell was implicated in a government investigation into illegal overcharges on various government contracts. The company was banned from further contract awards until Anderson himself convinced Air Force Secretary Vernon Orr to reinstate the company in December of 1985. Anderson promised to fire senior managers involved in any illegal activities.

In 1985 Anderson engineered the first major acquisition of his career at Rockwell with the $1.7 billion purchase of the Allen-Bradley Company of Milwaukee. Rockwell was suffering from a decrease in business after the cancellation of the B-1 bomber and the completion of the space shuttles. Allen-Bradley, a successful manufacturer of industrial automation systems, provided Rockwell with a steady profit from its operations and helped to reduce the company's dependence on government contracts.

Robert Anderson is scheduled to retire in 1988. The company's president, Donald Beall, is expected to take Anderson's place. Beall, almost 20 years younger than Anderson, emphasizes creativity and innovation within the company organization. Rockwell's preliminary work on a ramjet-powered supersonic transport, capable of traversing the Pacific in approximately 45 minutes, has led Beall to comment that the jet is "a lot closer to being realized than people think."

Rockwell International is again trying to diversify its business by manufacturing more products for private companies. Colonel Rockwell once claimed that 200 companies would one day control 60 to 75% of the world's gross national product. The policy of continued diversification and expansion demonstrate Anderson's commitment to the Colonel's vision that Rockwell will be one of those 200 companies.

Principal Subsidiaries: Rockwell Graphic Systems, Inc.; Rockwell International Finance Corp.; Rockwell International of Canada (Ontario), Ltd., Rockwell International Holdings, Ltd.; Rockwell International, Ltd. (England); Rockwell International Sales Corp.; Wescom, Inc.

Further Reading: "The Truman Administration and the Enlistment of the Aviation Industry in Postwar Defense" by Donald J. Mrozek, in *Business History Review* (Boston), Spring 1974; *The Jet Makers: The Aerospace Industry from 1945–1972* by Charles D. Bright, Lawrence, Regents Press of Kansas, 1978; *Shuttle* by Nigel MacKnight, Osceola, Wisconsin, Motorbooks International, 1985.

ROLLS-ROYCE PLC

65 Buckingham Gate
London SW1E 6AT
England
01–222 9020

Public Company
Incorporated: 1971
Employees: 41,500
Sales: £1.802 billion (US$ 2.901 billion)
Market value: £1.36 billion (US$ 2.18 billion)
Stock Index: London

Rolls-Royce plc., the *aeroengine* manufacturer, has a common origin with Rolls-Royce Motors, the manufacturer of what many people regard as the finest automobiles in the world. Both companies were divisions of Rolls-Royce Ltd. until 1971, when they were separated by the British government as a means of solving the company's financial crisis. Although the distinction between the two companies can often be a source of confusion, Rolls-Royce plc concerns itself primarily with the manufacture of jet engines.

Rolls-Royce was founded in 1906 by Frederick Henry Royce, an engineer, and Charles Stewart Rolls, a London automobile dealer. Through their partnership, Rolls and Royce established a new standard in automobile production. Rolls was particularly interested in the development of powered aircraft, and in 1907 inaugurated production of aircraft engines. Subsequent models were used in some of the world's first aircraft, and Rolls-Royce gained the distinction of being one of the world's first aircraft engine manufacturers.

Charles Rolls was tragically killed in 1910 when his Wright biplane crashed from a height of only 23 feet. Royce, who did not like aircraft, nevertheless maintained his company's interest in aircraft engines. The intertwined "RR" logo, which had appeared on the company's automobile *grilles* in red, was changed to black by Frederick Royce as a symbol of mourning for his partner.

When World War I broke out in Europe in 1914, Britain was drawn into the fighting as a result of a number of secret diplomatic agreements with France and Czarist Russia. As armies began to employ more aircraft for reconnaissance and battle missions, they created more demand for Rolls-Royce engines. The company's Hawk engine was superseded by the Falcon, and later by the Eagle. By the time the war ended in 1919, Rolls-Royce accounted for more than half of Britain's total aeroengine production.

A version of the Eagle engine, the 360-horsepower Eagle VII, powered the aircraft which carried Capt. (later Sir) John Alcock across the Atlantic in 1919. A new engine, the Phantom, was introduced in 1925, and among other things served as an important prototype for subsequent models.

Royce was created Sir Henry in 1930 in recognition of his contributions to Britain's automotive and aeronautic industries. He became ill late in 1932, but continued to work on new engineering projects from his bed. His health, however, deteriorated, and he died in 1933.

During this period the aeroengine division of Rolls-Royce developed a new engine called the Kestrel. Demand for these engines remained relatively low, despite the rapid rearmament of the increasingly belligerent Nazi regime in Germany. The British government refused to acknowledge the danger that Germany posed. When the "appeasement" policies of Prime Minister Neville Chamberlain appeared to have failed, it became increasingly apparent that Britain would be drawn into a second war with Germany. When German armies invaded Poland in 1939, Britain and France declared war on Germany. France was defeated the following year, and Britain prepared for an intense aerial war against the numerically superior forces of the German Luftwaffe.

At this time Rolls-Royce introduced a new 1260-horsepower engine called the Merlin. This engine was used to power Supermarine Spitfire and Hawker Hurricane fighters. The Merlin also powered a variety of bombers manufactured by Avro, most notably the Lancaster. The Packard Company built Merlin engines in the United States for Avro and North American Aviation, which used the engine in its Mustang fighter.

Rolls-Royce suspended its automobile operations to devote all its production capability to the manufacture of aircraft engines. During the "Battle of Britain" every first line fighter in the Royal Air Force was equipped with a Merlin engine. German aircraft initially resorted to low-altitude flying in order to avoid anti-aircraft fire during raids on Britain. Rolls-Royce responded by modifying the Merlin's supercharger to give it increased power at lower altitudes. German aircraft were forced to fly at the higher altitudes at which they could more easily be shot down.

In 1941 Rolls-Royce was instructed by the Ministry of Aircraft Production to engage in the manufacture of jet engines of the kind originally developed by the inventor Sir Frank Whittle. In conjunction with Power Jets Ltd. and the Rover Company, Rolls-Royce perfected its first jet engine, the Welland, in April of 1943.

With involvement of the Soviet Union and the United States, the war began to turn against Nazi Germany. The power of British aircraft was greatly increased after Rolls-Royce introduced its 2000-horsepower Griffon engine. Despite its introduction of formidable Messerschmitt jets in the last months of World War II, Germany was forced to surrender in May of 1945. By that time, Rolls-Royce had manufactured more than 150,000 Merlin engines.

Rolls-Royce began to make deliveries of the Welland engine in 1944, but the aircraft it was intended for, the

Gloster Meteor, arrived too late for use during World War II. The Welland was superseded by the more durable Derwent engine. A parallel project produced the Nene engine, out of which developed the Tay.

Rolls-Royce resumed auto production after the war, and established a diesel engine division. Most of the company's resources, however, were employed with the production of aircraft engines. Rolls-Royce was interested only in the development of aircraft engines specifically for the military until the late 1940's, when it introduced a new turboprop engine. The turboprop provoked such strong interest from commercial aircraft manufacturers that it was introduced in commercial form in 1952 under the model name Dart.

Rolls-Royce was similarly persuaded to alter the design of its Avon jet engine for commercial purposes. The Avon was later chosen by de Havilland for its new Comet jetliner, the world's first passenger jet, and by Nord Aviation, the French manufacturer, for the Caravelle.

In 1947 Rolls-Royce signed a 10-year licensing agreement with Pratt & Whitney, which allowed that company to manufacture Tay and Nene jet engines in the United States. A subsequent agreement was signed in 1953 with Westinghouse (whose F-40 jet engine proved a failure), giving them American production rights to all Rolls-Royce jet and turboprop engines, except the Tay and Nene. Westinghouse and Rolls-Royce collaborated on a number of projects, which placed Rolls-Royce in a leading position in aircraft engine development on both sides of the Atlantic.

The Dart turboprop came widely into use in 1955 when Fokker began production of its successful F-27 Friendship. A new turboprop engine called the Tyne was chosen by Vickers to power its Vanguard when it entered service in 1960. A newer jet engine called the Conway was developed in the late 1950's and was specifically intended for use on the forthcoming Douglas DC-8 and Boeing 707 jetliners.

Rolls-Royce formed a joint venture company with Vickers and Foster Wheeler in early 1956 called Vickers Nuclear Engineering Ltd. Like similar companies in the United States, particularly Convair, the joint venture was specifically interested in investigating the feasibility of a nuclear-powered jet engine. Like Convair, however, the project was abandoned when certain logistical problems proved unresolvable.

At the beginning of the 1960's, more than 80% of Rolls-Royce's revenues were generated by the aeroengine division. The company decided to more aggressively market its aircraft engines in the United States, where companies such as Boeing, Douglas, and Lockheed were developing a variety of new jetliners, all of which were expected to have very long lives. The company chose to concentrate on the promising jumbo jet market, for which a more powerful jet engine had not yet been developed. With experience gained from the recent Spey engine program, Rolls-Royce engineers began the expensive process of designing their largest, most powerful engine to date, the RB.211.

When the design was completed in 1966, Rolls-Royce began to negotiate sales agreements with several aircraft manufacturers and airline companies. One Rolls-Royce target was the Lockheed Corporation's L-1011 Tristar. Another objective was a share of the Boeing 747 program. Strong competition with General Electric forced Rolls-Royce to greatly reduce the price of the RB.211. Company officials decided to underbid General Electric in order to gain a share of the American market and to put the RB.211 into production. Lockheed emerged as the largest customer in March of 1968; it ordered 555 engines.

Increasing development costs forced the company to divert all its profits from automobile production into the aeroengine division. The first RB.211 was assembled in the summer of 1969. After rigorous testing, however, a number of design errors were discovered, most notably with the forward compression fan. The necessary corrections consumed an even greater amount of money and placed the program far behind schedule. As a result of penalty clauses written into its contracts, Rolls-Royce was forced to compensate Lockheed and its other customers. Privately, the British financial community began to question whether Rolls-Royce could meet its obligations. The only outward sign that the program was in trouble was the company's announcement that its dividend was being reduced from four to three percent.

In November 1970 the British government suddenly announced that it was arranging a loan of £60 million to Rolls-Royce. Company officials simultaneously revealed that they were writing off £45 million for anticipated losses on the RB.211 project. The company's board of directors turned managerial control over to a four-man committee, and shareholder dividends were further reduced. Two days later the government announced in the House of Commons that it would nationalize Rolls-Royce.

The government implemented a reorganization of Rolls-Royce, which included a recommendation that the financially solvent automobile division be separated from the company and returned to the private sector. The recommendation was accepted in 1973, and Rolls-Royce Motors Ltd. was created as a public company.

With its flaws corrected, the RB.211 entered service in 1972, but not before having nearly ruined Rolls-Royce and heavily damaging Lockheed in its attempt to secure its projected L-1011 market share. The RB.211 did, however, demonstrate several advantages over other engines, including durability, efficiency, and easy maintenance.

Although the L-1011 was widely recognized as the best wide-body aircraft available, economic realities forced Lockheed to phase out the production of their plane in the early 1980's after only 250 had been delivered. With the loss of Lockheed as a customer, Rolls-Royce was forced to rely on Boeing, which had chosen the RB.211 as an alternate engine for its 747.

In the mid-1970's Boeing initiated two new commercial aircraft programs, the 757 and 767. In a move which confirmed the strong merits of the Rolls-Royce engine, Boeing chose the RB.211 for the 757. The production run of the RB.211 (currently at about 1200 engines) has been extended indefinitely.

In 1979 the chairman of Rolls-Royce, Sir Kenneth Keith, resigned in protest at the government's policies toward the company, which he characterized as a "bureaucratic contraceptive." He was replaced by Francis Scott

(Frank) McFadzean, a former managing director of Royal Dutch/Shell and chairman of British Airways.

When Conservatives regained control of Parliament in 1979, the government of Prime Minister Margaret Thatcher, an adamant opponent of nationalized industry, prepared a schedule of companies for "privatization." One of those companies was Rolls-Royce.

A delegation of workers and managers from Rolls-Royce toured their competitors' facilities in the United States in 1978 and discovered productivity rates as much as 50% greater than their own. Rolls-Royce production facilities were restructured, emphasizing automation and eliminating redundant labor. Several thousand workers were retired or released, but by the end of 1980 productivity had risen by 25%. Between 1981 and 1983 a further 20,000 workers were released.

Frank McFadzean retired in March of 1983 and was replaced by Sir William Duncan. Sir William was selected specifically to help prepare Rolls-Royce for privatization. He died unexpectedly the following November. Norman Tebbitt, the secretary for Trade and Industry, and the only man who could authorize the appointment of a successor to Sir William, was injured during an attempted assassination of Mrs. Thatcher at a hotel in Brighton. Because of these events, privatization was deferred. Despite the delay, Rolls-Royce proceeded to engage in joint ventures with General Electric and Pratt & Whitney, both of which had been established under Sir William. Then in May 1986, after years of preparation, Rolls-Royce was re-registered as a public limited company and 801.5 million shares of stock were offered for sale to the public. The government's assigned value was well below market value, causing oversubscription by speculators and triggering a "clawback" rationing provision that effectively eliminated institutional investors from the offering. The method of Rolls-Royce's privatization provoked the criticism that private investors were allowed an immediate windfall profit at the expense of the taxpayers.

Today, Rolls-Royce plc remains almost exclusively involved in the production of aircraft engines. Some models, however, have been modified for a variety of applications, including use in industrial and marine equipment.

Principal Subsidiaries: Rolls-Royce (hereafter "RR") of Australia Pty. Ltd. (Australia); RR (Canada) Ltd. (Canada); RR Capital, Inc. (USA); RR (China) Ltd. (PRC); RR Credit Corp. (USA); RR Developments, Ltd.; RR Diesels, Ltd.; RR de Espana S.A. (Spain); RR Far East Ltd.; RR Finance Ltd.; RR (France) Ltd.; RR Holdings, Inc. (USA); RR Inc. (USA); RR India Inc.; RR Industrial & Marine Ltd. (Canada); RR Industrial Turbines (Saudi Arabia) Ltd. (Saudi Arabia); RR Industries Canada Inc. (Canada); RR and Japanese Aero Engines Ltd.; RR Leasing Ltd.; RR (Middle East) E.C. (Bahrain); RR Plant Leasing Ltd.; RR Turbomeca do Brasil Ltda. (Brazil); RR Turbomeca International S.A. (France); RR Turbomeca Ltd.

Further Reading: The Engines Were Rolls-Royce: An Informal History of That Famous Company by Ronald W. Harker, New York, Macmillan, 1979.

UNITED TECHNOLOGIES CORPORATION

Hartford, Connecticut 06101
U.S.A.
(203) 728-7000

Public Company
Incorporated: July 21, 1934
Employees: 205,500
Sales: $15.66 billion
Market value: $6.897 billion
Stock Index: New York

United Technologies is one of the largest conglomerates in what President Eisenhower first termed the American "military/industrial complex." United Technologies, however, is rarely the first company to be mentioned when considering leaders in the aerospace industry. The company's low-profile reputation is primarily the result of its diversified structure. United Technologies' best known division, Pratt & Whitney, produces two-thirds of all the aircraft engines in the free world.

Pratt & Whitney was organized by Fred Rentschler in 1925 as one of the first companies to specialize in the manufacture of engines, or "power plants," for airframe builders. Pratt & Whitney's primary customers were two airplane manufacturers, Bill Boeing and Chance Vought. Rentschler was interested in securing a market for his company's engines. He convinced Boeing and Vought to form a new company with him in 1929 called the United Aircraft and Transportation Company. The three gave exclusive priority to each other's business.

United became so successful that it was soon able to purchase other important suppliers and competitors, establishing a stronger vertical and broader horizontal monopoly. The group grew to include Boeing, Pratt & Whitney and Vought, as well as Sikorsky, Stearman and Northrop (airframes); Hamilton Aero Manufacturing and Standard Steel Prop (propellers); and Stout Airlines, in addition to Boeing's airline companies.

The men who led these individual divisions of United exchanged stock in their original companies for stock in United. The strong public interest in the larger company drove the value of United's stock up in subsequent flotations. The original shareholders quickly became very wealthy. Rentschler himself turned a meager $253 cash investment into $35.5 million by 1929.

Postmaster William Folger Brown acknowledged that United was the largest airline network and the most stable equipment supplier in the country. Thus United was assured of winning the postal service's lucrative airmail contracts before it applied for them. The company's airmail business required the manufacturing division to devote all of its resources to expansion of the airline division. This meant that United wouldn't be able to sell airplanes to other airline companies for several years. In this way United controlled nearly half of the nation's airline and aircraft business. It was a classic example of an aeronautic monopoly.

In 1934 Senator Hugo Black (later a Supreme Court justice) instigated an investigation of fraud and improprieties in the aeronautics business; Bill Boeing was called to the witness stand. Black's interrogation of Boeing exposed United's monopolistic business practices, and eventually led to the break up of the huge aeronautic combine. Boeing was humiliated. He completely divorced himself from his company, sold all of his stock, and retired. In the reorganization of the corporation, all manufacturing interests west of the Mississippi went to Boeing Airplane in Seattle, everything east of the river went to Rentschler's United Aircraft in Hartford, and the transport services became a third independent company under the name of United Air Lines which was based in Chicago.

Chance Vought died in 1930, but his company, as well as Pratt & Whitney, Sikorsky, Ham Standard and Northrop, became part of the new United Aircraft Company. Sikorsky became a principal manufacturer of helicopters, Pratt & Whitney continued to build engines, and Vought later produced a line of airplanes including the Corsair and Cutlass.

When World War II erupted, business increased at United's Pratt & Whitney division. The company produced several hundred thousand engines for airplanes built by Boeing, Lockheed, McDonnell, Douglas, Grumman and Vought. Over half the engines in American planes were built by Pratt & Whitney. After the war, United Aircraft turned its attention to producing jet engines. Pratt & Whitney started late in the business because its customers were constantly demanding improvements in the company's piston-driven Wasp engine. In the meantime, Pratt & Whitney's competitors, General Electric and Westinghouse, were free to devote more of their capital to the research and development of jet engines. When airframe builders started looking for jet engine suppliers, they had no choice but to disregard Pratt & Whitney. Even United's Vought division had to go to Westinghouse to find turbojets for its Cutlass.

The division recognized the gravity of the situation quite late, but nonetheless began an ambitious program to develop a line of advanced jet engines. When the Korean War began in 1950, Pratt & Whitney was again deluged with orders. The mobilization of forces gave the company the opportunity to re-establish its strong relationship with the Navy and conduct business with its newly-created Air Force.

In the early 1950's United Aircraft experienced a conflict of interest between its airframe and engine manufacturing subsidiaries. Vought Aircraft's alternate engine suppliers, Westinghouse and General Motors' Allison division, were reluctant to do business with a company so closely associated with their competitor, Pratt & Whitney. On the other hand, Pratt & Whitney's other customers, Grumman, McDonnell, and Douglas, were concerned that their airframe technology would find its way to Vought. As a result, both of United's divisions were suffering. The members of the board decided that they had no choice but to eject Vought. In 1954 Vought was forced to resign from United Aircraft.

In 1959 Fred Rentschler, at the age of 68, died after a long illness. He was eulogized in *The New York Times*: "This nation's air superiority is due in no small measure to Mr. Rentschler's vision and talents." Indeed, it was his concern over advances in engine technology in the Soviet Union, rather than at his competitors, which drove him to re-establish Pratt & Whitney's leadership in the industry. Rentschler had served as United Aircraft's chairman since 1935. He was succeeded by the company's president, H. Mansfield (Jack) Horner. Under the leadership of Horner, United Aircraft grew significantly in size and importance.

Under Horner's stewardship United Aircraft continued to manufacture engines and a variety of other aircraft accessories into the 1960's. Much of its business came from Boeing, which had a number of Pentagon contracts and whose 700-series jets were capturing 60% of the commercial airliner market. Horner himself retired in 1968. He was succeeded by W. P. Gwinn, president of United since Rentschler's death. The changes in personnel were of little consequence to the company, which was running smoothly. United was, however, about to enter a period of crisis.

There was considerable trouble with Pratt & Whitney's engines for Boeing's 747 jumbo jet. The problem, traced to a design flaw, cost Pratt & Whitney millions of dollars in research and re-development. It also cost millions of dollars for Boeing in service calls and lost sales. Commercial airline companies suffered lost revenue from cancelled flights and reduced passenger capacity.

By 1971 the performance of the Pratt & Whitney division had begun to depress company profits. The directors of United acted quickly by hiring a new president named Harry Gray, who was drafted away from Litton Industries. As the number three man at Litton, he was once invited to tour General Electric's Evandale, Ohio facility. Litton was a trusted customer of General Electric, and consequently Gray was warmly welcomed. He was made privy to rather detailed information on GE's long range plans. A few weeks later officials at GE read that Gray had accepted the presidency at their arch-competitor United Aircraft. The officials protested Gray's actions but were casually reminded that Gray had asked not to be informed of any plans of a "proprietary" nature during his visit to the GE plant.

Harry Gray was born Harry Jack Grusin in 1919. He suffered the loss of his mother at age six and was later entrusted to the care of his sister when his father's business was ruined in the Depression. He was raised in Chicago and in 1936 entered the University of Illinois at Urbana where he later earned a degree in journalism. During World War II he fought in Europe with General Patton's

Third Army infantry and artillery. After the war he returned to Urbana to receive a Master's degree in journalism.

After moving to Chicago Harry Grusin went through a succession of jobs, working as a salesman of trucks and as a manager of a transport company. In 1951 he changed his name to Harry Gray, according to the court record, for "no reason." He moved to California in 1954 to work for the Litton Industries conglomerate. He spent the next 17 years at Litton working his way up the corporate ladder. Hindered in promotion at Litton by superiors who weren't due to retire for several years, Gray accepted the offer from United Aircraft.

One of his first acts at United was to order an investigation into and re-engineering of the Pratt & Whitney engines for Boeing's 747. Gray then sought to reduce United's dependence on the Pentagon. United Aircraft also began a purchasing program in an effort to diversify its business. In 1974 it acquired Essex International, a manufacturer of wire and cables. A year later the company purchased a majority interest in Otis Elevator for $276 million. In 1978 United added Dynell Electronics, a builder of radar systems. Next came Ambac Industries, which makes diesel power systems and fuel injection devices.

United Aircraft changed its name to United Technologies in 1975 in order to emphasize the diversification of the company's business. The acquisitions didn't stop. In 1981 United Technologies, or UTC, purchased Mostek, a maker of semiconductors, for $345 million. Two years later the company acquired the Carrier Corporation, a manufacturer of air conditioning systems. In addition, UTC purchased a number of smaller electronics, software, and computer firms.

It is reported that Harry Gray has been known to maintain a portfolio of the 50 companies he'd most like to purchase. Virtually all of his targets, including the ones he later acquired, have never wanted to become part of UTC. Some of the companies which successfully resisted Gray's takeover attempts were ESB Ray-O-Vac (the battery maker), Signal (which builds Mack Trucks), and Babcock and Wilcox (a manufacturer of power generating equipment).

During the present time, United Technologies operates four principal divisions: Power Products, including aircraft engines and spare parts; Flight Systems, which manufactures helicopters, electronics, propellers, instruments and space-related products; Building Systems, encompassing the businesses of Otis and Carrier; and Industrial Products, which produces various automotive parts, electric sensors and motors, and wire and printing products. The company, through its divisions, builds aircraft engines for General Dynamic's YF-16 and F-111 bomber, Grumman's F-14 Tomcat, and McDonnell Douglas' F-15 Eagle. In addition, it supplies Boeing with engines for its 700-series jetliners, AWACs, B-52 bombers, and other airplanes. McDonnell Douglas and Airbus also purchase Pratt & Whitney engines.

Gray, who aimed to provide a new direction for UTC away from aerospace and defense, has proven to be one of the most successful presidents the company has had. He learned the business of the company's principal product, jet engines, in a very short time. A year after he joined the company he was made chief executive officer and soon thereafter chairman. In 15 years at UTC Gray has completely refashioned the company. When Harry Gray was appointed president of United Aircraft, sales for the year amounted to $2 billion. Today the company has recorded $16 billion in sales.

UTC's directors did, however, have a difficult time convincing Gray to relinquish his power as his retirement drew near. Gray refused to name a successor. When a potential new leader appeared to be consolidating a base of power, Harry Gray would "destroy" him. About Gray it has been said, "For people who have been attuned to power, there is an awful fear of giving it up." One former UTC executive said, "Harry equates his corporate position with his own mortality."

Perhaps the only man who could have satisfied the stockholders, management, and Harry Gray as the new leader of UTC was Alexander Haig. However, Haig served on the board of UTC for less than a year after turning down a bid for the presidency of the U.S. in 1980. He left the company after being appointed Secretary of State in the Reagan administration. The members of the UTC board then created a special committee to persuade Gray to name a successor. Finally, in September of 1985, Robert Daniell (formerly head of the Sikorsky division) was appointed as chief executive officer. Yet Daniell was not the board's first choice, and more to their chagrin, Gray remained as chairman.

In light of the poor performances posted by the company's various divisions, some industry analysts were beginning to wonder if Harry Gray had lost his magical touch. His refusal to step aside threatened the stability of UTC. With the $424 million write-off of the failed Mostek unit, many analysts began talking of a general dissolution of UTC; the divisions were worth more individually than together. But the "critics" were silenced when Harry Gray announced in September of 1986 that he would retire and named Robert Daniell to take his place.

Even before the official departure of Harry Gray, however, Daniell moved quickly to dismantle the philosophy of "growth through acquisition." Hundreds of middle-management positions were eliminated and there was speculation that some of the less promising divisions would be sold. Daniell told *The Wall Street Journal,* "This is a new era for United Technologies. Harry Gray was brought here to grow the company. But now the company is built, the blocks are in place and growth will be a secondary objective." Daniell's challenge is to prove that neither Gray's overstayed welcome nor his departure will have any ill effect on the company.

Principal Subsidiaries: Pratt & Whitney Canada, Inc. (Canada); United Technologies Automotive Holdings, Inc.; Carrier Corp.; UT Credit Corp.; Inmont Corp.; Essex Group, Inc.; Otis Elevator Co.; Otis Europe S.A. (France); Norden Systems, Inc.; United Technologies Building Systems Co.

Further Reading: Excess Profits: The Rise of United Technologies by Ronald Fernandez, Reading, Massachusetts, Addison-Wesley, Publishers, 1983.

AIRLINES

AMERICAN AIRLINES

BRITISH AIRWAYS PLC

CONTINENTAL AIRLINES

DELTA AIR LINES, INC.

EASTERN AIRLINES

JAPAN AIR LINES COMPANY, LTD.

KONINKLIJKE LUCHTVAART
   MAATSCHAPPIJ, N.V.

DEUTSCHE LUFTHANSA A.G.

NORTHWEST AIRLINES, INC.

PAN AMERICAN WORLD
   AIRWAYS, INC.

PEOPLE EXPRESS AIRLINES, INC.

SCANDINAVIAN AIRLINES SYSTEM

SWISS AIR TRANSPORT
   COMPANY, LTD.

TEXAS AIR CORPORATION

TRANS WORLD AIRLINES, INC.

UNITED AIRLINES

USAIR GROUP

A'A AmericanAirlines

AMERICAN AIRLINES

P.O. Box 619616
Dallas/Fort Worth Airport, Texas 75261
U.S.A.
(817) 355-1234
Wholly-owned subsidiary of AMR Corporation
Incorporated: April 11, 1934
Employees: 37,500
Sales: $6.018 billion
Market Value: $3.304 billion
Stock Index: New York

Given the difficult conditions created for the airline industry by deregulation, the success of many airline companies is difficult to assess. American Airlines, however, has mastered the new deregulation market and has grown to become the United States' number one airline. As large as the company is, it is able to maintain a highly flexible and responsive attitude toward the changing conditions of the airline market.

American Airlines is a product of the conglomeration of a number of small airline companies. One of these founding companies was the Robertson Aircraft Company of Missouri, which employed Charles Lindbergh on the first mail run in 1926. In April of 1927 another of these small companies, Juan Trippe's Colonial Air Transport, made the first passenger run between Boston and New York. The nucleus of these and the 82 other companies that eventually merged to form American Airlines was a company called Embry-Riddle. It later organized the Aviation Corporation of the Americas, one of America's first airline conglomerates. The conglomerate was run by a Wall Street group who were not very conversant with the new airline business. This group was led by Avrell Harriman and Robert Lehman.

In 1930 Charles Coburn formally merged the various airlines into one concern named the American Airways Company. American flew a varied assortment of planes, including the Pilgrim 10A. In 1930 American was awarded the Southern airmail corridor from the East Coast to California. In 1934 the government suspended all private airmail contracts only to reinstate them a few months later. American resumed its airmail business but, due to the damage already caused by this interruption, was unable to maintain a profit.

The company was soon in financial trouble. It was rather easily acquired by a corporate raider named E. L. Cord who changed the name of the company to American Airlines. Harriman and Lehman resigned in protest when Cord installed an ineffective man named Lester Seymour as president. Both men returned to Wall Street, and Harriman later served as the wartime ambassador to the Soviet Union.

During this period of time, a Texan named Cyrus Rowlett Smith was quickly becoming a popular figure at American. Smith was originally the head of Southern Air Transport, a division later acquired by American. Cord recognized Smith's ability and later made him vice-president of American, despite the fact that they didn't like each other personally.

In the early 1930's Smith persuaded Donald Douglas to develop a new airplane to replace the popular but obsolete DC-2. Douglas' airplane company developed a larger 21-passenger airplane, designated the DC-3. Cooperation between the manufacturer and the airline throughout the project set an example for similar joint ventures in the future. American was flying the DC-3s by 1936. It became the number one airline by the close of the decade, largely as a result of the successful new plane. The DC-3, called the "flying whore" because it had "no visible means of support," proved to be a very popular airplane; its innovative and simple design made it durable and easy to service. Smith said the DC-3 was "the first airplane that could make money just by hauling passengers."

During 1937, in reaction to a public scare over airline safety, American ran a printed advertisement which directly asked, "Afraid to Fly?" Citing the statistical impossibility of dying in a crash, the copy discussed the problem in a straightforward and reassuring way. "People are afraid of things they do not know about," the advertisement read, "there is only one way to overcome the fear—and that is, to fly." The promotion succeeded in allaying passenger fears and increasing the airline's business.

When World War II started American Airlines devoted over half of its resources to the army. American DC-3s shuttled the Signal Corps and supplies to Brazil for the transatlantic ferry. Smith himself volunteered his services to the Air Transport Command. American's president, Ralph Damon, went to the Republic Aircraft Company to supervise the building of fighter airplanes.

After the war American returned to its normal operations, and Smith set out to completely retool the company with modern equipment. The modernization went smoothly and quickly. In 1949 Smith had a good laugh, so to speak, when arch-rival United was still flying DC-3s and American had already donated its last DC-3 to a museum.

American Airlines acquired a fleet of "flying boats" when it purchased Amex Airlines from American Export Steamship Lines. The steamship company was forced to sell Amex when the U.S. Congress decreed that transportation companies could not conduct business in more than one "mode." It was an attempt to prevent industrial vertical monopolies from forming. Pan Am, until then the only airline with flying boats, began to experience competition from American on its overseas routes.

In the late 1940's American suffered another financial crisis, in large part caused by the grounding of the DC-6.

The airplanes were experiencing operational problems which led to their crashing, and the federal government wanted all of them thoroughly inspected. Six weeks later they were back in service, but the interruption cost American a large amount of money. When banks restricted American's line of credit, Smith joined representatives of TWA and United on Capitol Hill to lobby for fare increases. Subsequently, as part of a compromise, American was awarded an airmail subsidy.

Still experiencing financial difficulties, company management attempted to raise cash by selling the overseas routes served by the Amex flying boats. The sale was blocked by the Civil Aeronautics Board. American needed the cash and Juan Trippe at Pan Am actually wanted to purchase the overseas routes. As a result, they jointly lobbied the Truman administration to overturn the CAB decision, but the timing was inauspicious. The time was June of 1950 and the President's mind was on the war in Korea. A few weeks later, after the Korean situation stabilized, Truman did finally rule in favor of the airlines and American was allowed the sale. In this way the company avoided a debilitating financial crisis.

American made the first scheduled non-stop transcontinental flights in 1953 with the 80-passenger DC-7. In 1955 American ordered its first jetlines, Boeing 707s. The 707s were delivered in 1959 and entered service at American with several new Lockheed Electras. With larger and faster aircraft on the drawing boards, American became interested in, and eventually purchased, jumbo B-747s in the late 1960's. The company also ordered a number of supersonic transports, but was forced to cancel these orders when congress halted funding to Boeing for their development.

C.R. Smith left the airline in 1968 for a position in the Johnson Administration, serving the President as Secretary of Commerce. Smith was succeeded at American by a lawyer named George A. Spater. After taking command, Spater changed the marketing strategy and attempted to make the airline more attractive to vacation-goers instead of to the traditional business traveler. The strategy failed. His presidency lasted only until 1973, when he admitted to making an illegal $55,000 corporate contribution to the Nixon re-election campaign. Some believe the gift was intended to procure favorable treatment from the Civil Aeronautics Board for American. As a result, the board fired Spater and drafted Smith out of retirement at the age of 74 to head the company again.

Smith retired after only seven months when the board of directors persuaded Albert V. Casey to leave the Times-Mirror Company in Los Angeles and join American. As the new chief executive officer Casey reversed the company's fortunes from a deficit of $20 million in 1975 to a record profit of $134 million in 1978. To everyone's surprise Casey decided to move the airline's headquarters from New York to Dallas/Fort Worth. Interestingly enough Casey's brother, John, was a vice chairman of Braniff International, which was also based in Dallas. Some said Casey was unhappy with his inability to gain acceptance in New York's social circles. Casey's response was that a domestic airline "belongs in Mid-America." Believing the company needed to be shaken out of its lethargy he said, "the company had to get repotted, replanted."

Soon afterwards, American introduced "Super Saver" fares during 1977 in an innovative attempt to fill passenger seats on coast-to-coast flights. TWA and United followed suit after they failed to persuade the CAB to intervene.

During that year American was also forced to rehire 300 flight attendants who were fired between 1965 and 1970 because they had become pregnant. The award also included $2.7 million in back pay. Compounding these setbacks, on May 25, 1979, American lost a DC-10 at Chicago's O'Hare airport. 273 people died in the crash, which was later blamed on inadequate maintenance procedures. As a result, American was fined a half million dollars by the Federal Aviation Administration (FAA). Although the company collected $24.3 million from insurance, it has been forced to pay wrongful death settlements averaging $475,000 per passenger.

To better protect itself from crises in the industry, Casey set up a holding company for the airline and a number of its other businesses. The new parent company was called the AMR Corporation. Many airlines created holding companies to diversify their resources in the event of serious hardship in the industry.

The Airline Deregulation Act of 1978 had the effect of making the airline industry suddenly volatile and competitive. AMR had several options with which to deal with deregulation. First, it could divest itself of the airline, selling its jetliners once they were written down, and moving into other more promising businesses. Second, it could scale down only partially, leaving a more efficient operation to compete with new airlines like New York Air and People Express. A third option was to ask employees to accept salary reductions and other concessions as Frank Borman did at Eastern. In the end, American was not forced to take any of these measures. The company secured a two-tier wage contract with its employees and this new agreement reduced labor costs by as much as $10,000 a year per new employee. In addition, workers were given a profit sharing interest in the company.

Robert Crandall, formerly with Eastman Kodak, Hallmark, TWA and Bloomingdale's, joined American in 1973 and became its president in 1980. Known for his impatient and aggressive manner, Crandall may be credited with American's successful, but not completely painless, readjustment to the post-deregulation era. Crandall fired approximately 7000 employees in an austerity drive, a decision that severely damaged his standing with the unions.

American updated its jetliner fleet to meet the new conditions in the industry during the 1980's by phasing in B-767s and MD-80s. The MD-80s have two major advantages over other aircraft: a two-person cockpit crew and high fuel efficiency. American is relying heavily on the success of the MD-80, having already received 67 of them with the option to purchase up to 100 more. Crandall says, "American is growing a new, low-cost airline inside the old one." With an interest in purchasing the MD-80s and the stretched MD-82, American is relying on McDonnell Douglas to provide much of its planned fleet of over 330 jetliners by 1990.

American's Sabre computer reservations system dominates the business, and it is widely regarded as the best in the industry. The Sabre system allows agents to assign seats, book Broadway plays or lodging, and can even arrange to send flowers to passengers. Naturally, the system is biased toward American, listing the airline ahead of all the others. The system has proved extremely successful in filling space on American efficiently and at low cost. Recently, the Sabre system has expanded by beginning operation in Europe.

American runs a major hub at Dallas/Fort Worth and at Chicago. Secondary hubs in Nashville and Raleigh/Durham are intended to more firmly establish the airline in the Southeast. In addition to a multi-hub system and the reservations database, American contracts with smaller regional carriers, called "American Eagle Partners," to feed traffic into the American system.

American owned a number of subsidiaries when it created the AMR holding company. An airline catering business called Sky Chefs was started in 1942, and serves American and a number of other air carriers. In 1977 American created AA Development Corporation and AA Energy Corporation. These subsidiaries participated in the exploration and development of oil and natural gas resources, many of which were successful. The American Airlines Training Corporation, created in 1979, services military and commerical contracts that provide for pilot and mechanic training.

In 1985 American surpassed United in passenger traffic and regained after twenty years the title of number one airline in the United States. Although the company has dealt reasonable well with disruptions in the industry, and despite its stated intention to grow internally, American announced in November of 1986 that it would acquire ACI Holdings, Incorporated, the parent company of AirCal, for $225 million. American's competitors, Delta and Northwest, recently announced cooperation agreements with western air carriers. Management at American was afraid that the company would be eliminated from the West Coast market if it did not move quickly. The addition of AirCal's western routes significantly increases American's exposure on the West Coast, and would possible lead to American services across the Pacific.

Principal Subsidiaries of AMR Corporation: American Airlines, Inc.; Flagship International, Inc.; AA Development Corp.; AA Energy Corp.; AA Training Corp.; AMR Services Corp.

Further Reading: Eagle: The Story of American Airlines by Robert Serling, New York, Dial, 1980; *The Sky Their Frontier: The Story of the World's Pioneer Airlines and Routes 1920–1940* by Robert Jackson, Shrewsbury, England, Airlife, 1983; *Takeoff! The Story of America's First Woman Pilot for a Major Airline* by Bonnie Tiburzi, New York, Crown, 1984.

BRITISH AIRWAYS PLC

P.O. Box 10
Speedbird House
Heathrow Airport
Hounslow, Middlesex TW6 2JA
England
01-759-5511

Public Limited Company
Incorporated: March 31, 1924 as Imperial Air
Transportation, Ltd.
Employees: 36,500
Sales: £3.149 billion (US$ 4.723 billion)
Market value: £482 million (US$ 723 million)
Stock Index: London

British Airways' earliest predecessor was Aircraft Transport & Travel, Ltd., founded in 1916. On August 25, 1919 this company inaugurated the world's first scheduled international air service, with a converted de Havilland 4A day bomber leaving Hounslow (later Heathrow) Airport for London and also Le Bourget in Paris. Eight days later another company, Handley Page Transport, Ltd., started a cross-channel service between London's Cricklewood Field and both Paris and Brussels.

That same year Britain's advisory committee for civil aviation proposed plans for establishing a world airline network linking Britain with Canada, India, South Africa, Australia and New Zealand. Due to the fact that airplanes capable of crossing wide stretches of water were not yet available, the committee recommended that first priority be given to a route to India operated by state-assisted private enterprise.

Progress was made quickly. Before the end of the year the British government was operating a service to Karachi and had established a network of 43 Royal Air Force (RAF) landing strips through Africa to the Cape of Good Hope. Meanwhile, strong competition from subsidized foreign airline companies had forced many of the private British air carriers out of business. By March of 1921 all British airline companies had suspended their operations. The government responded with a pledge to keep the British companies flying, using its own form of subsidization.

In January of 1923 Parliament appointed the Civil Air Transport Subsidies Committee to form a single British international air carrier from existing companies. On March 31, 1924 the Daimler Airway, British Marine Air Navigation, Instone Air Line and Handley Page merged to become Imperial Air Transport.

In 1925 Imperial Airways operated a number of European routes while it surveyed a route across the Arabian desert from Cairo to Basra in present-day Iraq. The airline was faced with a number of problems on this route. The desert was featureless, making it easy to get lost. Water stops and meteorological and radio stations were difficult to maintain. Basra was a major terminal on the route to India. However, on January 7, 1927 the Persian government forbade Britain the use of its airspace, blocking all flights to India. Negotiations reopened the airspace two years later, but not before generating a demand for longer range aircraft.

Passengers flying to India flew from London via Paris to Basel, where they boarded a train for Genoa. A flying boat then took them on to Alexandria, where they flew in stages to Karachi. The passage to India, previously three weeks by sea, had been reduced to one week by air.

Imperial Airways service to Calcutta was established in July of 1933, to Rangoon in September and to Singapore in December. In January of the following year the Australia's Queensland and Northern Territories Air Service (Qantas) inaugurated a route linking Singapore with Brisbane. The passage to Australia could be completed in twelve and a half days.

A commercial service through Africa was opened in 1931 with flying boats linking Cairo with Mwanza on Lake Victoria. In April of 1933 the route was extended to Cape Town, the trip from London taking ten and a half days. An east-west trans-African route from Khartoum in the Sudan to Kano in northern Nigeria was established in February of 1936. This route completed a world network which linked nearly all the countries of the British Empire.

The primary source of revenue on the network was not from transporting passengers but mail. However, an increase in demand for more passenger seating and cargo space generated a need for larger airplanes. Britain's primary supplier of flying boats, the Short Company, developed a new model, designated the C-class, with 24 seats and weighing 18 tons. Since it had an increased range and flew 145 miles per hour, it was able to simply bypass "politically difficult areas." The Short C-class went into service in October of 1936. A year later Imperial Airways made its first trans-Atlantic crossing with a flying boat equipped with extra fuel tanks. However, it was Pan Am, with more sophisticated and updated Boeing airplanes, which was first to schedule a regular trans-Atlantic service.

Imperial Airways was formed with the intention of being Britain's "chosen instrument" for overseas air service. On its European services, however, Imperial was competing with the British Continental airlines and an aggressive newcomer called British Airways. British Airways was created in October of 1935 by the merger of three smaller airlines companies. Three months later the company acquired a fleet of Lockheed 10 Electras which were the fastest airplanes yet available. The competition from British Airways threatened the "chosen instrument" so much that in November of 1937 a Parliamentary committee proposed the nationalization and merger of Imperial and British Airways. When the reorganization was completed on November 24, 1939, the British Overseas Airways Corporation (BOAC) was formed.

The creation of BOAC was overshadowed by the declaration of war on Germany the previous September. The Secretary of State for Air assumed control of all British air services, including BOAC. Within a year Italy had entered the war and France had fallen. Britain's air routes through Europe had been eliminated. However, British flying boats continued to ferry personnel and war cargo between London and West Africa with an intermediate stop at Lisbon in neutral Portugal. The air link to Khartoum maintained Britain's connection to the "Horseshoe Route," from Cape Town through East Africa, Arabia, India and Singapore to Australia. When Malaya and Singapore were later invaded by the Japanese, BOAC and Qantas opened a non-stop service between Ceylon and Perth in Western Australia. BOAC transported ballbearings from neutral Sweden using a route which was dangerously exposed to the German Luftwaffe. BOAC also operated a service for returning flight crews to North America after they delivered American and Canadian-built aircraft to the Royal Air Force.

When the war ended BOAC had a fleet of 160 aircraft and an aerial network which covered 54,000 miles. The South American destinations of BOAC were assigned to a new state-owned airline, British South American Airways (BSAA), in March of 1946. Similarly, the European services were turned over to British European Airways (BEA) on August 1, 1946. After the war Britain re-established its overseas services to the nations of its Empire. Some of the nations which had recently gained their independence from Britain received advice (and often finance) from BOAC.

In order to remain competitive with the American airline companies, BOAC purchased Lockheed Constellations, the most advanced commercial aircraft of the day. They were later joined by Boeing 377 Stratocruisers and Canadair Argonauts (modified DC-4s). BEA operated generally smaller airplanes and more frequent flights between the British Isles and Continental Europe. In 1948 it joined other Allied airline companies in the airlift to Berlin during the Soviet blockade.

Following a series of equipment failures at BSAA, the Civil Aviation ministry declared that the company should re-merge with BOAC. On July 30, 1949, BSAA was absorbed by BOAC.

Even though its passenger load had steadily increased, BOAC accumulated a debt of £32 million in the five years from 1946 to 1951. Much of this was due to "recapitalization," or purchasing new equipment; the British-built Handley Page Hermes and de Havilland's DH Comet 1, the world's first jetliners, were delivered to BOAC.

In January of 1954 one of BOAC's Comets exploded near Elba in the Mediterranean. Another Comet crashed near Naples only 16 days after an investigation of the first crash was concluded. As a result, the Comet's certificate of airworthiness was withdrawn and a full investigation was ordered. In the final report it was determined that the Comet's pressurized cabin was inadequately designed to withstand low air pressures at altitudes over 25,000 feet. When the airplane reached that altitude it simply exploded. The cabin was strengthened and the jet re-introduced in 1958 as the DH Comet 4.

The company was forced to purchase propeller-driven DC-7s to cover equipment shortages when delivery of its Britannia turbo-props was delayed in 1956. When the Comet re-entered service BOAC found itself with two undesirable fleets of aircraft which were later sold at a loss of £51 million ($122 million).

South American operations were suspended in 1954 when the Comet was taken out of service. Operation of the route with shorter range aircraft was too costly. At the insistence of Argentina and Brazil, which claimed Britain had "lost interest" in South America, the routes were reopened in 1960. That same year the first of 15 Boeing 707 jetliners was delivered to BOAC.

British European Airways used a wide variety of aircraft for its operations and remained a good customer for British aircraft manufacturers. In 1964 the company accepted delivery of the first de Havilland Trident 1, a three-engine airliner capable of speeds up to 600 miles per hour. A few years later, when the company expressed an interest in purchasing a mixed fleet of Boeing 727s and 737s, it was instructed by the government to "buy British" instead. BEA complied, ordering BAC-111s and improved versions of the Trident.

BOAC's cargo traffic was growing at an annual rate of 27%. However, a sudden and unexplained drop in passenger traffic during 1961 left many of the world's airline companies with "excess capacity," or too many empty seats to fly profitably. At the end of the fiscal year BOAC's accumulated deficit had grown to £64 million. The losses, however, were underwritten by the British government, which could not allow its flag carrier to go bankrupt.

BOAC and Air France agreed to commit funds for the buildings of a supersonic transport (SST) in 1962. In June the company became associated with the Cunard Steamship Company. A new company, BOAC-Cunard Ltd., was placed in charge of the trans-Atlantic air services in an attempt to capture a larger portion of the American travel markets.

The British published a "White Paper" (a statement of government policy) which recommended a drastic reorganization of BOAC. In response, the company's chairman, Sir Matthew Slattery, and the managing director, Sir Basil Smallpiece, resigned. Britain's minister for aviation appointed Sir Giles Guthrie as the new chairman and chief executive officer. Under Sir Giles BOAC suspended its unprofitable services and rescheduled its equipment purchases and debt payments. After the financial situation had improved, the company continued to purchase new equipment and expand its flight network. In April of 1967 BOAC established its second around-the-world route and opened a new cargo terminal at Heathrow.

The company's sister airline, BEA, had been paying close attention to consumer marketing for vacationers. In 1967 the company created a division called BEA Airtours Ltd., offering complete travel packages to a number of vacation spots. In May of 1969 BOAC opened a passage to Japan via the North Pole. The route was shortened even further when the Soviet Union granted BOAC landing rights in Moscow and a Siberian airlane to Tokyo.

On March 31, after six years of record profits, BOAC announced that it no longer owed any money to the government. Later, on July 17, 1972, following several recommendations on further reorganization of the state-owned airline companies, management of BEA and BOAC were coordinated under a new government agency called the British Airways Group. On April 1, 1974 the two companies were merged and renamed British Airways. A second reorganization of the internal management structure took place in 1977.

The first British Airways' Concorde was introduced in 1976. Jointly manufactured by British Aerospace and the French firm Aerospatiale, the supersonic Concorde was capable of carrying 100 passengers at the speed of 1350 miles per hour at an altitude of 55,000 feet. A seven-hour flight from New York to London was nearly reduced to half the time by the Concorde. British Airways employed additional Concordes on a number of international services, most notably London-Singapore, which was temporarily suspended through 1978 due to "political difficulties."

In 1980 Prime Minister Margaret Thatcher appointed Lord (John) King as the new chairman of British Airways. His stated assignment was to prepare the airline for privatization (sale to private stockholders). Lord King's first move was to adopt aggressive "American-style" marketing and management philosophies. As a result, he initiated a massive campaign to scale down the company and reduce costs. More unprofitable air services were terminated, and a staff reduction (begun under Lord King's predecessor, Roy Watts) was continued. A British Airways official told *Business Week* magazine that, "we had too many staff but couldn't get rid of them because of the unions." In order to utilize the excess labor, the company was forced to remain large. Lord King established a better relationship with labor, which had become more agreeable to layoffs and revisions of work rules. In three years the work force was reduced from 60,000 to 38,000 without a strike.

On July 11, 1983, no fewer than 50 senior executives were fired. The company's chief executive officer, Colin Marshall, hired in their place a team of younger executives (mostly with non-airline business backgrounds). The new executive staff initiated a series of programs to improve punctuality and service at the airline. They hired Landor Associates, a successful San Francisco-based design firm with considerable experience with airlines, to develop an entirely new image for British Airways. The result was controversial. The British Airways coat of arms and portion of the Union Jack on the airplanes' tail fin was bound to upset the more politically temperamental countries of the third world which the company serves. The familiar "Speedbird" logo which dates back to the days of Imperial Airways was removed despite employee petitions to retain it.

British Airways also recognized a need to replace older airplanes in its fleet with more modern and efficient equipment. The company's Lockheed TriStars were sold to the RAF for conversion into tankers, and the BAC-111s

were sold because they would violate new noise regulations. British Airways is currently leasing a number of airplanes until it makes a decision on new purchases. This is not likely to occur until after the privatization.

The company was plagued by its decision to retain separate European and overseas divisions. The result was a perpetuation of the previous management regimes of BEA and BOAC. To rectify this problem the operation was further divided into eight regional groups involved in three different businesses: cargo, charter and tours. Each of the eight groups has increased autonomy and responsibility for its business and profitability.

The Laker Airways Skytrain, an initially successful cut-rate trans-Atlantic airline, was forced to close down due to what its chairman, Freddie Laker, claimed was a coordinated attack by a number of airlines to drive the company into bankruptcy. Laker charged the companies, which included British Airways, with violations of anti-trust laws. He later settled out of court for $48 million, but in a subsequent civil suit British Airways was also required to issue travel coupons to passengers who claimed they were hurt by the collapse of Laker Airways.

Ironically, the company is now advocating the deregulation of European air fares in the belief that it can compete more effectively than its rivals. But Air France and Lufthansa in particular are reluctant to participate, claiming that deregulation would endanger the delicate market balance which took so many years to establish.

In 1985 British Airways was made a public limited company, but all its stock was retained by the government until such time that it could be offered to the public. The privatization of British Airways (which will be limited to a 51% sale) has been delayed by a number of problems. The company's chief domestic rival, British Caledonian, opposes British Airways' privatization claiming that the company already controls 80% of the domestic market and is too large to compete against. However, British Airways' most significant obstacle to privatization involved reducing the debt which it accumulated during the 1970s, and increasing the company's profitability. In January of 1987 the British government announced that 720.2 million shares of British Airways stock would be sold to the public for one billion pounds ($1.47 billion).

British Caledonian, or BCal, was formed in 1970 through the merger of Caledonian Airways and British United Airways. For many years, BCal was British Airways' only large domestic competitor, fighting vigorously under the direction of Sir Adam Thompson for more favorable operating rights from the British government. When Britain's Civil Aviation Authority recommended the reallocation of British Airways routes to BCal in 1984, Lord King threatened to resign. Instead, British Airways was instructed to trade its profitable Middle East routes for some of BCal's less profitable Latin American destinations. The Middle Eastern routes became much less popular during 1986 as a result of regional tensions and falling oil prices. BCal, which had been generating a fair profit, started to lose money and was faced with bankruptcy.

In July of 1987 it was announced that British Airways had reached agreement with BCal wherein it would acquire the airline for £237 million in stock. The new airline would have almost 200 aircraft, and combine British Airways' 560,000-kilometer route structure with BCal's largely unduplicated 110,000-kilometer network, forming one of the largest airline companies in the world. Several smaller independent British airline companies threatened to challenge the BA/BCal merger on the grounds that the new company would dominate both London's Heathrow and Gatwick airports, forcing them to relocate to the less accessible and underdeveloped field at Stansted.

In the event of a successful merger, British Airways would be better able to compete with other international airlines (primarily the Americans), and perhaps be more successful in its attempt to deregulate the European airline markets. As a substantially public company, British Airways has followed the example of American airline companies by increasing its size by external growth.

Principal Subsidiaries: Alta Holidays Ltd.; British Airways Tour Operations Ltd.; British Airtours Ltd.; British Airways Associated Companies Ltd.; British Airways Engine Overhaul Ltd.; Overseas Air Travel Ltd.; British Airways Helicopters Ltd.; Martin Rooks & Company Ltd.; The Airways Housing Trust Ltd.; Travel Automation Services Ltd.

Further Reading: The Rise and Fall of Freddie Laker by Howard Banks, London, Faber, 1982; *British Airways: The Path to Profitability* by Alison Cooke, New York, St. Martin's Press, 1986.

CONTINENTAL AIRLINES

America Tower
2929 Allen Parkway
Houston, Texas 77019
U.S.A.
(604) 641-2112

Wholly-owned subsidiary of the Texas Air Corporation
Incorporated: in 1934 as Varney Speed Lines
Employees: 13,500
Sales: $1.705 billion
Market value: $362 million

Robert Foreman Six, founder of Continental Airlines, was one of the few men to manage his own airline company from the birth of commercial aviation into the jet age. Over the years Six and other airline pioneers such as Juan Trippe, C.R. Smith, Pat Patterson, C.E. Woolman, and Jack Frye molded the commerical airline business within the U.S. into its current form.

Robert Six dropped out of high school after his second year and began a variety of odd jobs. He was fired as a bill collector for Pacific Gas & Electric when it was learned he was taking flying lessons on company time. In 1929, at the age of 22, he received his pilot's license, purchased a small airplane, and founded the Valley Flying Service in Stockton, California. During the week he sold scenic tours of the countryside and on weekends competed in airplane races. Six later enrolled at a flight school in San Francisco established by Boeing Air Transport in order to train airline pilots.

A short time later the Depression financially destroyed his flying service. Six sailed for Shanghai where he worked part time for the China National Aviation Company. When he returned to the United States 18 months later, he accepted a job driving a truck for the *San Francisco Chronicle* during a newspaper strike. He married Henriette Erhart Ruggles whose father, William Erhart, was chairman of the Charles Pfizer Company, one of the nation's largest drug companies.

In 1937 Six convinced his father-in-law to lend him $90,000 to purchase a 40% interest in Varney Speed Lines, the fourth airline company to be founded by Walter Varney (the first was purchased by Boeing's United Aircraft and the next two failed). Most of Six's investments was used to pay debts and little remained to purchase new aircraft. Six, however, convinced Lockheed

Corporation to sell the company three L-12s on credit. Six later persuaded the company's chairman, a man named Louis Mueller, to change the airline's name to Continental, claiming that the airline could never be successful with a name like "Varney." The following year Six was made president of the airline.

The most popular airplane in America at this time was the DC-3. While it was practical and durable, it was also too expensive of an airplane to purchase for Six. Instead, he favored a new airplane from Lockheed called the L-14 Lodestar. Continental purchased a number of Lodestars and hired its first 12 stewardesses to work aboard them.

Continental, whose network covered a circuit between Denver and El Paso, worked vigorously to add new routes. By the time Wichita and Tulsa services were opened, the Japanese had attacked Pearl Harbor and the country was mobilizing for World War II. Six placed Continental under the care of a lawyer named Terrell Drinkwater and enlisted in the U.S. Army. He was sworn in as a captain in August of 1942 and stationed in New Caledonia and later the Caribbean, where he was responsible for maintaining the military air conduit between the United States and Brazil.

After the war Continental acquired a number of DC-3s from military surplus. With the addition of San Antonio and Kansas City as destinations, Continental's route system had grown by 300%. Government contracts during the war left Continental with $900,000 in cash and a debt of only $60,000.

In light of the newer, more efficient equipment being ordered by the other major airlines after the war, Six began to plan for the eventual replacement of the DC-3s. Airplanes such as Lockheed's Constellation and Douglas' DC-4 and DC-6 (all with four engines) were too large for Continental's purposes. The company wanted to purchase twin-engine airliners, but could not decide between the Martin 202 or the Convair 240. Douglas recently cancelled plans to build its own two-engine airplane but had an employee named Ed Burton in whom Six placed a great deal of trust. When asked, Burton advised Continental to buy Convairs. Later, the Martin 202 would prove a disastrous mistake for those airlines that decided to purchase it.

Early in 1951 Continental placed orders for seven new Convair 340s and two DC-6Bs. The expenditure was $7.6 million, nearly the company's gross income for the entire year. Updating the aircraft fleet was becoming more expensive because the newer airplanes were designed to carry more passengers greater distances. Continental was still a comparatively small airline. The decision to make such an expensive investment in the company's future was typical of Six's management style.

In 1953 Continental purchased all the stock of Pioneer Airlines which included the rights to fly into Dallas/Ft. Worth and Austin, Texas. When Pioneer was absorbed by Continental, Six gained a talented young manager and confidant named Harding Lawrence, who was placed in charge of the company's finances.

The Civil Aeronautics Board granted service rights between Chicago and Denver, Denver and Los Angeles, and Chicago and Los Angeles to Continental in 1955. In order to live up to its obligation of operating the new cross-country routes, Continental would have to purchase several expensive new airplanes, including jetliners. In addition, Continental would be directly competing against American, United, and TWA, three airlines with the financial resources to drive Continental out of business.

The airline invested $60 million worth in new aircraft which included DC-7s, Viscount 810s, and Boeing's 707 jetliner. Continental's 707s were flying a full year before United Air Lines' DC-8 jetliners. Harding Lawrence established an imaginative 707 maintenance program which routinely called the jetliners out of service on a rotational basis. The program actually reduced maintenance time on the airplanes; major problems were identified and corrected before they became serious. As a result of Lawrence's "progressive maintenance" system, Continental was able to utilize its five 707s for an average of 15 hours a day, the longest in the industry.

In 1959 Six offered a position at Continental to Alexander Damm. Damm had become upset with his career at TWA and was particularly disenchanted with the company's chairman Howard Hughes. One of Damm's first proposals at Continental was that the company end its policy of leasing equipment, such as aircraft, trucks, and machinery. He noted that the two most profitable airlines, Delta and Northwest, had the lowest percentage of leased equipment. Continental canceled whatever leasing arrangements it could and began to concentrate on purchasing more equipment.

The group of bankers that forced Howard Hughes into a non-voting stock trust at the financially troubled TWA approached Six early in 1961 with a lucrative offer to become the president of TWA. Six, however, was extremely loyal to Continental and, in spite of offers to merge the two companies, he refused the group's offer.

On December 12, 1961, rather by surprise, Six and a man named Ted Baker of National Airlines (an East Coast competitor of Eastern Airlines) announced a merger of their two companies. The merger, however, was canceled as suddenly as it was announced when Six learned that Baker had already secretly negotiated the sale of National to Maytag's Frontier Airlines.

In 1962 Continental ordered four Boeing 720s (shorter but faster versions of the 707). However, the order was increased to five after May 22 when a bomb exploded aboard a Continental 707. The bombing caused a crash from which there were no survivors. It was the first crash in Continental's 24 year history.

Prior to 1963 Continental was under obligation to the Civil Aeronautics Board to operate a number of rural air services which fed passenger traffic into larger air terminals. The services were unprofitable and required government subsidization. That year, however, Continental was released from these obligations. This allowed the company to sell its smaller aircraft and reassign manpower to the profitable commercial routes. Furthermore, before the year was over Continental announced that it was moving its headquarters from Denver to Los Angeles.

Howard Hughes offered to sell his controlling interest in TWA to Continental and to make Six president of the new company (pending the approval of TWA's new board of directors). Some people regarded this as an attempt by Hughes to regain control of TWA. Six, however, knew that TWA's board was pleased with the airline's performance under Charles Tillinghast. He also knew that the new management at TWA didn't trust Hughes and was unlikely to go along with any of his proposals.

In 1964 Continental received a contract from the government's Military Airlift Command to carry out military transportation services in Southeast Asia. To perform these duties the company created a new subsidiary called Continental Air Services (CAS). CAS operated in concert with Air America, the Central Intelligence Agency's covertly run airline, but did not engage in any CIA activities.

Harding Lawrence, Six's most trusted confidant, left Continental that year to become president of Braniff Airlines. While no attempt was made to replace Lawrence, the most notable addition to Continental came a year later when the late President Kennedy's press secretary, Pierre Salinger, joined the board of directors. Salinger remained on the board for two years before he resigned during a leave of absence.

The Civil Aeronautics Board invited bids for a commercial air service linking the United States to the approximately 2500 islands in the South Pacific which comprise the American Trust Territory. Continental saw this as an opportunity to demonstrate its ability to operate the trans-Pacific services it had wanted for years. In November of 1967 Continental was awarded routes to various islands in Micronesia and Northern Mariana. A subsidiary called Air Micronesia was created in partnership with Hawaii's Aloha Airlines and a local investor group called United Micronesian. A fleet of 727s was procured, airports along the route had to be modernized, and a number of hotels were constructed for tourists.

Lyndon Johnson, in one of his last official acts as President, awarded Continental air traffic rights to Hawaii, Australia, and New Zealand. Barely a month later President Nixon canceled all three awards. The routes were later re-awarded, revoked again, and re-awarded a third time. During the cancellation period Continental had accepted delivery of four 747s. Since they could not be used, Continental was forced to put them into storage at a hanger in New Mexico at a cost of $13 million a year. Three of the 747s were later sold to Iran in 1975.

At one time Continental was one of the most financially stable airlines in the world. Its measured growth was accompanied by consistent profits. In its first 35 years it registered its only loss in 1958. However, the high cost of fuel and poor economic conditions caused business in the airline industry to decline steadily through the mid-1970's. Continental began posting losses in 1975 when it lost $9.7 million.

The Airline Deregulation Act of 1978 added to Continental's problems by exposing some of its most stable and profitable markets to competition from other airline companies. In addition, Continental was bound to honor a number of labor agreements which, because of their built-in provisions for inflation, were becoming increasingly expensive to maintain. Six stepped down from the day-today operation of the company in 1980 and was replaced by Alvin L. Feldman.

Feldman took charge of an airline which was in serious trouble. The most promising strategy available to Feldman for the survival of the airline was a merger between Continental and another financially troubled airline, Los Angeles-based Western Airlines. The merger plans collapsed in March of 1981 when Frank Lorenzo announced that his Texas Air Corporation would be increasing its ownership of Continental stock from 4.24% to 48.5% as part of an effort to take over Continental. In response, two Continental pilots named Paul Eckel and Chuck Cheeld organized a plan which would allow the company's employees to purchase the airline. Employees approved the plan by a margin of 8932 to 359, and nine banks were lined up who agreed to help finance the $185 million employee acquisition. By August, however, the banks withdrew their support. Feldman, who was still depressed over the recent death of his wife, shot and killed himself in his office at Los Angeles International Airport. A month later, Texas Air acquired a 50.84% majority of Continental stock.

At the annual meeting on March 30, 1982, Robert Six, at the age of 74, retired from Continental. He expressed confidence in Texas Air's chairman Frank Lorenzo and said he regretted that he was leaving "on a note of red ink and not black ink." It was an anti-climatic ending to his 43-year career at Continental.

Texas Air completed its acquisition of Continental on October 28, 1982. Texas International Airlines was later absorbed by Continental. On September 24, 1983 Lorenzo initiated Chapter 11 bankruptcy proceedings for the new Continental. The company's labor contracts were invalidated by the courts and new work rules and wage scales were imposed. 56 hours after winning bankruptcy protection, Continental was back in the air.

No airline had attempted to continue operating through bankruptcy. The company had to contend with striking workers and their picket lines, the possibility that travel agents would stop writing tickets for Continental, and the possibility of losing passengers from negative publicity. Management's response to this was to offer a $49 fare for any non-stop flight on Continental. The fare was planned to bring passengers to Continental in order to demonstrate that the company was committed to remaining in business. The promotion also produced a significant number of return customers.

Continental's labor opposition dissolved after only a few weeks when workers elected to return to their jobs realizing, according to Lorenzo, that "what they were getting from the unions was pure gibberish . . . The enemy isn't Frank Lorenzo, but the new competitive environment." Questionable strike tactics led Continental pilots to repudiate their union. 4000 of the original 12,000 employees were rehired at half-pay with an increased workload. By 1985 labor costs had been reduced from 36% of total operating costs to 22%.

The number of passengers flying on Continental has grown steadily since the strike. The Texas Air Corporation has acquired a number of airline companies as subsidiaries, including Eastern Airlines, People Express and Frontier. These airline companies were all acquired while they were facing bankruptcy. Together they have placed the Texas Air Corporation over $4.6 billion in debt. Continental, however, has started its debt repayment program. In September of 1986 Continental owed $925 million to its creditors. Under the current schedule Continental will be out of debt by 1997.

Continental and the other Texas Air subsidiaries have more potential to compete successfully together than separately. If it were not for Texas Air and the policies of Frank Lorenzo, Continental and the other subsidiaries would probably have failed and been dissolved. For the time being, Continental has a promising chance of regaining the financial integrity it possessed during its early years.

Principal Subsidiaries: Continental Airlines lists no subsidiaries.

Further Reading: Maverick: The Story of Robert Six and Continental Airlines by Robert J. Serling, New York, Doubleday, 1974; *The Airline That Pride Almost Bought* by Michael Murphy, New York, Watts, 1986.

DELTA AIR LINES, INC.

Hartsfield International Airport
Atlanta, Georgia 30320
U.S.A.
(404) 765–2600

Public Company
Incorporated: in 1934 as Delta Air Corporation
Employees: 39,000
Sales: $4.517 billion
Market value: $2.894 billion
Stock Index: New York

Delta Air Lines is one of the United States' most successful air carriers. With the exception of 1983, the company hasn't lost money since 1947. Originally founded as a crop dusting service in 1924, Delta was led for forty years by an agricultural scientist and pilot named Collet Everman Woolman. Until his death in 1966 Woolman dominated the operations of Delta. In this sense he was similar to his three major competitors, Eddie Rickenbacker at Eastern, Juan Trippe at Pan Am and Howard Hughes at TWA.

The company started in 1924 when Woolman and an associate joined a conversation with some Louisiana farmers concerned about the threat to their crops from boll weevils. Woolman knew that calcium arsenate would kill the insects, but the problem was how to effectively apply the chemical. Having learned to fly the boxy "flying jennys" during World War I, Woolman considered dropping the chemical from an airplane. He engineered a "hopper" for the chemical and later perfected the system, and then began selling his services to farmers throughout the region. As a result, the world's first crop dusting service, named Huff Daland Dusters, was born.

In 1925, Woolman left the agricultural extension service to take charge of the duster's entomological work. In 1928 the crop dusting operation broke away from its parent company to become Delta Air Service. Woolman continued his crop dusting business across the South and expanded into Mexico and South America. The company began to diversify by securing air mail contracts, and in 1929 inaugurated passenger service between Dallas and Jackson, Mississippi. Later, routes to Atlanta and Charleston were added.

The airline began its climb to prominence when the U.S. government awarded it an airmail contract in 1930. The company remained in business during a temporary but costly suspension in the airmail contract system in 1934.

The company, now called Delta Air Corporation, was later awarded three more airmail contracts by 1941. During World War II Delta, under contract to the War Department, devoted itself to the allied war effort by transporting troops and supplies. Delta returned to civilian service in 1945, and entered an age of growth and competition in the airline industry never seen before.

On May 1, 1953 Delta merged with Chicago and Southern Airlines and continued to prosper as a major regional trunk carrier through the 1950's and 1960's. In June of 1967 Delta merged with Delaware Airlines and officially adopted the name Delta Air Lines.

Delta's exposure to the Northeast increased with the acquisition of Northeast Airlines on August 1, 1972. In July of 1976 Delta purchased Storer Leasing, a move which added several jets to the existing fleet of about 200. Recognizing the value of high technology Delta formed two computerized marketing subsidiaries, Epsilon Trading Corporation in 1981 and Datas Incorporated in 1982. These organizations were created to coordinate and sell more passenger seats on all Delta flights.

Delta's consistent growth can be partially attributed to its successful transition of leadership. In the early days of commercial air transport airlines were run by individual men who would be better described as aviation pioneers first and as businessmen second. At American, Eastern, Pan Am, TWA, and Delta, these men established what can be described as almost dictatorial operations and retained their posts as long as they possibly could. Many of thse men were majority stockholders who categorically refused to share their power or prepare any successor to operate the company after they died. In many airline companies, when the chairman did eventually die, there was a difficult period of time readjusting to new management.

The departure of Delta's Woolman, however, was not surrounded by difficulties. He suffered a heart attack in his late 60's and was forced to relinquish some of his duties to Delta's board members. As Woolman's health deteriorated the board members gradually assumed more of his duties until he finally died at age 76. Fortunately, the airline was able to make a smooth transition to a more modern, corporate style of collective management. Although Woolman's absence was deeply felt at Delta, business continued as usual.

Delta is recognized for having one of the best planning and management teams in the airline industry. Specifically, Delta's management is agile and responsive to problems which arise. A sound financial policy allows greater flexibility in decision-making even at the highest levels. And a concensus-style of management may be said to afford Delta cohesiveness and enduring stability.

Delta has the highest productivity in the "trunk," or domestic, airline business. The company is on very good terms with its employees who are noticeably non-unionized. Their willingness to adjust to the needs of the company provides Delta with the unique ability to weather hardships in the airline industry. Actually only the pilots and the dispatchers are organized employees. The machinist's union, for example, reports that it is difficult to organize Delta employees because the company maintains pay and benefits above its unionized competition. As long as the company outperforms union contracts there is no incentive for the worker to unionize.

Delta is known for treating all of its employees as "family," and has gone a long way to avoid layoffs. During the 1973 oil crisis and the 1981 PATCO strike, for instance, the airline refused to release workers even though its profitability was compromised. In the absence of union rules and constraints, employees are able to be moved on a regular basis to other positions in order to fill temporary labor shortages. These measures are a major reason why the company remains competitive.

Although the company did not invent it, Delta was the first airline to widely employ the so-called "hub and spoke" system. Under this system a number of flights are scheduled to land at a hub airport within approximately 30 minutes. This allows passengers to make connections for final destinations conveniently and quickly. The "big push," as it is called, occurs about ten times a day at the Atlanta hub. Regarded by management as an effective marketing tool the "big push" is not, however, immune to problems caused by bad weather or maintenance delays. Delta also operates hubs at Dallas/Fort Worth, Boston, Memphis and Cincinnati in addition to Atlanta.

Delta has the most modern jetliner fleet in domestic service. They are not known for purchasing new models until they have been proven, often in a costly way at other airlines. This "wait and see" policy saved the company a large amount of money when it refrained from purchasing Lockheed's 1011. Only after competing airlines had used the L-1011 for a number of years did Delta purchase the plane. At the present time Delta is replacing its Boeing fleet of 727s with the 757, 767 and MD-88. These are technologically advanced and fuel efficient planes which Delta plans to employ for the next 20 years or longer. In fact, the decision to replace the 727 was made in the early 1970's. It is typical of Delta that a 15 year strategy for flight equipment and support facility planning is used. According to vice chairman and chief financial officer Robert Oppenlander, "success is based on the long term maintenance of a technical edge, which is cost efficiency."

Delta is known for having the most conservative balance sheet in the industry. With a debt-equity ratio that is consistently below one to one, (meaning that their debts are usually outweighed by their net worth) the company can afford to do most of its financing internally. Such a conservative character is aptly reflected in this statement by the late chairman W.T. Beebe: "We don't squander our money on things like goofy advertising."

Recently, Delta has taken on a more aggressive corporate personality. Its committment to internal growth has been threatened by a general trend in the industry toward external growth. Delta is becoming relatively smaller as companies such as TWA, Texas Air and Northwest expand through mergers. In 1986 Delta announced its intention to take over the Los Angeles-based Jet America. However, the $18.7 million deal never materialized.

Later that year Delta went ahead with the $680 million purchase of another air carrier based in Los Angeles, Western Air Lines. Delta's chief executive officer, David Garrett, explained that "for a merger to be worthwhile, two plus two has to equal seven." Enlarged by Western's hubs in Los Angeles and Salt Lake City, Delta management might be able to make that kind of math work. Yet there are problems with integrating Western's unionized workforce into Delta's system. Nevertheless, as Garrett noted, when Delta merged with Northeast Airlines in 1972 Northeast's unions dissolved.

This airline has adhered to the principles of its founder, C.E. Woolman, by placing a high value on people, both its customers and its personnel. Woolman used to ride on flights and mingle with the passengers in an effort to gauge the public opinion concerning his airline. He was once quoted as saying: "We have a responsibility over and above the price of a ticket, let's put ourselves on the other side of the counter."

Principal Subsidiaries: Chicago and Southern Airlines, Inc.; Storer Leasing, Inc.; Northeast Airlines, Inc.; Epsilon Trading, Inc.; Datas, Inc.

Further Reading: Delta: The History of an Airline by David W. Lewis and Wesley Philips Newton, Athens, University of Georgia Press, 1973; "The Delta–C & S Merger: A Case Study in Airline Consolidation and Federal Regulation" by David W. Lewis and Wesley Philips Newton, in *Business History Review* 53 (Boston), 1979.

EASTERN AIRLINES

Miami International Airport
Miami, Florida 33148
U.S.A.
(305) 873-2211

Public Company (controlled by Texas Air Corporation)
Incorporated: March 29, 1938
Employees: 37,415
Sales: $4.185 billion
Market Value: $522 million
Stock Index: New York

Eastern Airlines has been in existence since the beginning of commerical aviation in the United States. It has been led by two of the most well-known men in 20th century aviation history, Harold Pitcairn and Eddie Rickenbacker. Starting as a mail carrier Eastern has grown to become a widely recognized and successful airline serving three continents.

The story of Eastern begins with a man named Harold Pitcairn, who shocked his family when he decided to pursue aviation as a career. He was only one of many entrepreneurs drawn into the airline business by the Kelly Airmail Act of 1925 which allowed private carriers the right to bid for airmail routes. He designed an airplane called the "Pitcairn Mailwing," built six of them, and then assembled a team of barnstormers and World War I pilots to fly them. Financed by his skeptical father, Pitcairn won the New York to Atlanta route in 1928 by entering the lowest bid. Later that year, he acquired an extension to Miami, doubling the network to 1400 miles. Pitcairn increased the fleet to sixteen with improved versions of his open-cockpit single-engine airplanes. The future looked bright. However, due to two fatal plane crashes, or perhaps because his first love was airplane manufacturing, he sold Pitcairn Aviation in July of 1929. Clement Keys of North American Aviation purchased the company for $2.5 million and changed the company's name to Eastern Air Transport. Under Keys, Eastern became associated with a number of companies which later formed the Sperry Corporation. This fortunate connection gave the company's pilots an opportunity to work with state of the art flight instruments.

Airmail was the company's primary business until congress passed the McNary-Watres Act in 1928. The act changed the airmail pay scale from a poundage to a mileage basis. As a result, passenger business became profitable on a wider scale. All the airlines began transporting more passengers. Keys siezed the opportunity by inaugurating a daily-except-Sunday route between New York and Richmond, via Newark, Philadelphia, and Baltimore, using the new Ford tri-motor airplane. Over the next two years Eastern expanded its fleet and route system while maintaining an excellent safety record. By 1932 it was possible to fly a Curtiss Condor, Kingbird, or Fokker tri-motor airplane to many destinations along the Eastern Seaboard. An advertisement for their popular Florida destinations read, "From the frost to the flowers in fourteen hours."

In February of 1933 General Motors, in search of promising investments, acquired a controlling interest in Eastern's parent company named North American Aviation. The following year, however, the government decided to terminate the lucrative private airmail contracts and turn them over to the army's air service. A few months later the Air Mail Act of 1934 restored the private contracts, but not in time to save many companies from bankruptcy. At Eastern both employees and routes were substantially reduced. Despite the award of new routes and another airmail contract, the company was losing in excess of a quarter-million dollars a month. Eastern was in dire need of new and more effective management. General Motors chose the dynamic Eddie Rickenbacker to head the company.

Rickenbacker was awarded the Congressional Medal of Honor for his exploits during World War I. After the war he and a partner started Florida Airways. Yet Rickenbacker, a race car driver before the war, left the company in order to work as a sales executive at General Motors. In 1932, however, he resigned from General Motors rather than relocate. Nonetheless, he impressed company management enough to be called back to direct Eastern Air Transport. When he accepted the general manager's post in 1935 Rickenbacker vowed to have Eastern removed from its government subsidy and also vowed to make the airline profitable. In the ensuing three years Rickenbacker revised the company's management structure, reduced costs, and updated the airline fleet with Douglas DC-2s.

Seemingly, as soon as the airlines adjusted to one market condition something else happened to disturb the market again. The Black-McKeller Law, and later the Civil Aviation Act of 1938, decreed that airplane manufacturers must divest themselves of controlling interests in airline subsidiaries. When General Motors sold Eastern's manufacturing partners in the North American Aviation Consortium, management was also tempted to sell the airline. However, the Depression was still serious enough to eliminate potential buyers, and General Motors was forced to hold on to Eastern for the time.

Despite this disruption, Rickenbacker's austerity policies and careful management kept the airline in good financial condition. In fact, it was showing such promise by 1938 that a Wall Street investment group threatened to acquire it. Alfred P. Sloan, chief executive of General Motors, gave Rickenbacker the option of purchasing Eastern for himself, if he could match the $3.5 million Wall Street bid. In a frantic eleventh hour effort,

Rickenbacker succeeded in raising financial support for his own bid on Eastern. On April 22 Rickenbacker's group purchased Eastern Airlines from General Motors. Rickenbacker became president of the company and assumed almost total control of its operations.

The company's new independence was overshadowed by the Japanese attack on Pearl Harbor. Eastern joined the war effort, placing not only its equipment, but also its personnel at the disposal of the United States Army. Since Eastern had already established itself as the dominant carrier in the American Southeast, it was assigned the duty of transporting men to Brazil for the trans-Atlantic ferry in addition to shuttling priority passengers and cargo along the east coast. Under the authority of the Military Transport Division, Eastern operated over 7000 miles of supply routes across the South Atlantic. In October of 1942 Rickenbacker was temporarily lost during an airbase inspection tour when his plane was forced down in Samoa.

When he returned to the airline after the war Rickenbacker resumed strict control of the company. In his quest to achieve reliable and efficient service at the lowest possible cost, he set demanding standards for himself and expected the same dedication from all his employees. Obsessed with detail, he organized Eastern so tightly that he could determine an up-to-the-minute performance history of any one of his airplanes. The stringent management proved successful as profits rose to $14.7 million by 1956. Eastern added new routes and modernized its airline fleet, but only offered dividends when Rickenbacker thought the airline was in excellent financial condition. He surprised many of his critics by accepting the unionization of his workers, and also became the first airline president to introduce a standard 40 hour work week.

The 1950's were the golden days for Rickenbacker and for Eastern. The airline continued to generate a steady profit, maintain a modern fleet, and expand. With the merger of Colonial Airlines in 1956, Eastern added almost 3000 route miles and numerous "authorities," or destinations, to its network. The new airline served the Atlantic seaboard from Boston to Miami and the Caribbean, in addition to St. Louis and mid-Texas.

Eastern had a service monopoly on many of its destinations. As a result, they were free to operate the airline at their own convenience and at the expense of their customers. At times service became so bad that an activist group formed, called "WHEAL," for We Hate Eastern Airlines. Among other things they complained that Eastern stewardesses were curt, aloof and rude. When and where they could, customers expressed their dissatisfaction more practically by switching to Eastern's competitors.

To compound the problem, Eastern decided to purchase only a minimal number of the new passenger jetliners. Instead, they favored propeller-driven DC-7s, Super Constellations, Lockheed Electras, and Martin 404s, believing that they were better suited for the company's predominantly short-haul routes. However, Eastern's competitors invested heavily in jets. The company's major rival, Delta, actually acquired the DC-8s reserved for and later waived by Eastern. The result was disastrous for Eastern as Delta soon dominated every market involving the two companies.

At the dawn of the jet age, after 26 years leadership, Rickenbacker decided to relinquish the presidency of Eastern. While he remained as chairman, the company now had the additional burden of replacing one of the most successful airline presidents in history. Malcolm MacIntyre was chosen to succeed Rickenbacker. He was a very talented lawyer, but like many of the men who were to replace an airline's founder, MacIntyre knew very little about running an airline. Besides the poor economic climate in the industry and the divisive effect of Rickenbacker's continued meddling, the company had to contend with the Civil Aeronautics Board's opposition to regulated long-haul monopolies. The establishment of exclusive rights to certain airlines on specific routes could have meant large profits for Eastern. In addition, the public lost confidence in Eastern's main airplane, the Electra, following several crashes. After two consecutive labor strikes in three years, Eastern's record of profitability was shattered, and MacIntyre was relieved of his duties.

To his credit MacIntyre upgraded the quality of service, reduced costs, and introduced the very successful Boeing 727. Most notably, Eastern started an air shuttle service on April 30, 1961 linking Washington, D. C., New York, and Boston. The service evolved out of a need to keep jetliners from remaining idle. Since the hourly flights did not require reservations, when a plane was filled to capacity the company prepared another plane for the same route.

When MacIntyre left Eastern in December of 1963, Eddie Rickenbacker also retired and appointed Floyd Hall to head the company. Previously, Hall had improved the financial condition of TWA, and it was hoped he could do the same for Eastern. When he took over he discovered that Eastern was $70 million in debt. His "operation bootstrap" offered $100 in green stamps to employees who contributed to any of the four prescribed goals of generating more revenue, improving on-time performance, reducing passenger complaints, and increasing compliments. The operation proved so successful that WHEAL burned its charter and the airline turned a $30 million profit in 1965.

By 1967, however, the company was headed for bankruptcy again. Eastern's top-heavy management and increasingly disinterested president compounded problems of feuding between the New York and Miami offices. The plane which was to revive the airline in the 1970's, the wide body Lockheed 1011 tri-star, proved to be a financial disaster, with engines prone to breakdown, and ultimately cost millions of dollars in canceled or delayed flights.

The acquisition of Mackey Airways in 1967 and Caribair in 1973 added new routes to the Bahamas and West Indies. However, these new services to popular vacation spots could not forestall the rising tide of misfortunes which led to Hall's replacement in 1975. The new president was former astronaut Frank Borman, famous for his reading from Genesis while orbiting the moon in Apollo 8 on Christmas Eve of 1968. "The Colonel," as he was referred to by his employees, previously served as a consultant to Eastern, and was admired because of his association with the highly disciplined and efficient Apollo space program. One of his first moves was to streamline management by "reassigning" or firing half of all middle and executive level personnel. In addition, Borman secured a labor contract (later dropped in 1983) wherein employee salaries were linked to company profit and loss. These factors and the wide scale elimination of waste led Eastern to a $120 million profit through 1978.

Borman moved the main headquarters to Miami, initiated a white shirt-dark suit dress code, and emphasized "dry" business lunches. He sold Eastern's fuel-guzzling airplanes and invested heavily in new equipment. He maintained an active and high profile, often flying coach in order to talk with passengers and appearing in numerous television commericals for the company.

While Eastern was demonstrating its new viability, the Airline Deregulation Act was passed. Suddenly confronted with drastically changing industry conditions, Eastern struggled to adapt. Borman's expansion of the airline resulted in a $3 billion debt. Revenues were reduced by a shrinking market share, a result of the increased competition after deregulation. From 1979 to 1983 Eastern lost $200 million, and saved itself from bankruptcy only by wrestling concessions from creditors and employees. In return for temporary but large wage reductions, the airline gave its employees a 25% share of the company's stock and four seats on the board of directors.

In response to the advice of its creditors, Borman recognized that Eastern was in serious trouble and could only be saved by a complete reorganization or acquisition by another company. In early 1986 the company invited takeover bids, and later agreed to be acquired by Texas Air Corporation, an airline holding company. As a condition of the $676 million sale agreement, Eastern retained its management structure, employees and name. On November 25, 1986 Eastern's stockholders voted in favor of the acquisition of their company by Texas Air. Prior to that vote, Frank Borman was replaced as chairman of Eastern by Texas Air's chairman Frank Lorenzo. Borman was in turn named a vice chairman of Texas Air.

With the addition of Eastern to its other subsidiaries, including Continental Airlines, People Express, Frontier Airlines and New York Air, the Texas Air Corporation controlled a four-continent network. The Texas Air network operates major transfer hubs in Denver, New York, Miami, Atlanta, Kansas City, and Houston, and holds over 20% of the domestic airline market. However, the merger of Eastern and Texas Air ran into problems with the Department of Transport, which claimed the move would be anticompetitive in the Northeast corridor. In order to generate more competition in those markets, Eastern sold a number of its gates in the Northeast to Pan Am, which now operates a competing shuttle service.

As part of the new group, Eastern can increase the entire network's ability to compete on a low-fare basis with its computerized reservations system called SODA. Eastern brings a strong north-south route network to Texas Air, and is compatible with Continental's predominantly east-west route structure.

Eastern Airlines has survived the most difficult conditions of the post-deregulation era. Since having engineered the successful Texas Air acquisition, the company has been more fortunate than other airlines dismembered by the new market conditions. As a subsidiary it is insulated from periodic hardship in the industry by its well-diversified parent company.

Principal Subsidiaries: Eastern Airlines, S A (Mexico); Eastern Airlines of Puerto Rico, Inc.; Dorado Beach Estates, Inc.; Dorado Beach Development, Inc.

Further Reading: From the Captain to the Colonel by Robert Serling, New York, Dial, 1980; *The U.S. Airline Industry: End of an Era* by Paul Biederman, New York, Praeger, 1982.

JAPAN AIR LINES COMPANY, LTD.

Tokyo Building
7–3, Marunouchi, 2-chome
Chiyoda-ku, Tokyo 100
Japan
284-2081

Public/State-owned Company
Employees: 20,367
Sales: ¥781.5 billion (US$ 4.909 billion)
Market value: ¥2311 billion (US$ 14.51 billion)
Stock Index: Tokyo

In 1952 the governments of Japan and the United States signed a bilateral agreement which established normal air services between the two countries. During the postwar American occupation Northwest and Pan Am were the two principal air carriers serving Japan. The formation of a Japanese airline was not permitted until the occupation ended in 1951. At that time Japan Air Lines was established and placed in charge of domestic flight services between a number of major Japanese cities. In 1952, however, it was in need of capital. The Japanese government purchased an entire JAL stock issue which doubled the company's capital, but also gave the government a 50% interest in the airline.

The airline suffered from a shortage of experienced pilots. Nearly all Japanese aviators were drafted into the air service during the war and very few survived. As a result, American, British, and other Commonwealth aviators were required to operate the company's fleet of aircraft (which consisted of Martin 202s leased from Northwest and, later, a number of DC-4s) until Japanese pilots could be trained and assimilated into the flight crews.

Japan Air Lines grew quickly under the leadership of Seijiro Yanagida. In early February of 1954, JAL inaugurated its first international route, a semi-weekly service which connected Tokyo, Honolulu, and San Francisco. Plans were made to extend JAL services to Hongkong and Sao Paulo, Brazil, the center of a large Japanese community in South America. Also that year, JAL opened offices in Los Angeles, San Francisco, and Chicago. A route connecting Tokyo and London was established when the airline purchased several de Havilland Mark II Comet jetliners.

In its first year of operation JAL secured a significant share of the trans-Pacific market. However, the company lost money, despite a $3 million government subsidy. In its rush to acquire the latest aircraft, JAL purchased production orders for DC-6Bs from other airlines. This plan for securing early delivery of the airplanes obliged JAL to pay a compensatory premium. Another costly factor was the training program which placed an unusually high number of employees on the payroll. In addition, JAL's maintenance and repair work was being performed by United Airlines until Japanese personnel could be trained.

Japan Air Lines offered its first issue of public stock in May of 1956. ¥500 million (US$1.38 million) was raised to finance the purchase of several new DC-8 passenger jets from the Douglas Aircraft Company. The company made a number of subsequent public offerings and had increased its share capital to ¥5.3 billion (US$14.7 million) in 1960. That figure was increased to ¥11.7 billion (US$32.5 million) in 1962 and ¥18.2 billion (US$50.5 million) in 1965. The increased capital at JAL's disposal enabled it to implement a rapid expansion program.

In 1958 JAL extended its Bankok service to Singapore, marking a significant return to Southeast Asia for Japanese interests. The Japanese occupation of Malaya and the East Indies during World War II has remained a politically sensitive issue for Southeast Asian governments. The return of the Japanese flag to Singapore on commercial terms began a normalization process between Japan and Southeast Asia.

Japan Air Lines created a subsidiary in 1957 called the Airport Ground Service Company, which provides a variety of maintenance services to JAL and other airlines serving Japan. The company's personnel training programs were completed that same year, and for the first time JAL was operating regular flights with all-Japanese crews. Two years later a JAL crew training center was opened at Tokyo's Haneda Airport.

The company began a Tokyo to Paris service in conjunction with Air France in 1960. This route was unique because it was one of the first regular services to fly over the North Pole. Air France provided the Boeing 707 jetliners which were required for the long stretch over the Arctic.

Later that year JAL received its first DC-8 commercial jetliners. Less than a month later it was put into service on the Tokyo to San Francisco route. By the end of the year JAL DC-8s were flying to Los Angeles, Seattle, and Hongkong. The company ended its arrangement with Air France and inaugurated its own DC-8 service from Tokyo to London and Paris via Anchorage on June 6, 1961.

The next jetliner to enter service with JAL was the Convair 880 which was used primarily on domestic and Southeast Asian routes. After appropriate arrangements were concluded with various governments, JAL established a "Silk Road" service between Europe and Japan via Hongkong, Bangkok, Calcutta, Karachi, Kuwait, Cairo, Rome, and Frankfurt. The route was inaugurated in October of 1963 with the new Convair jets.

The Boeing Company sold its first airliner, a 727, to JAL in 1965. This purchase marked the beginning of a close relationship between the airline and Boeing. Over the years JAL would become Boeing's best foreign customer. In addition, that same year JAL adopted the *tsuru* (which means crane) as its official symbol. The crane is a symbol of good luck in Japan and is regarded as an appropriate motif for the Japanese airline.

Shortly after setting up a new computerized reservations system called JALCOM early in 1967, Japan Air Lines completed a route network which stretched around the world. The trans-Pacific service to San Francisco was linked to New York and London, where it connected with the "Silk Road" back to Japan. It is a honor for an airline to boast around-the-world service. Few have been able to maintain them for more than just a few months. JAL's worldwide service, however, lasted for six years.

A dispute over the Soviet occupation of several Japanese islands has prevented a full normalization of relations between those two countries ever since World War II. Once again, Japan Air Lines has helped to promote a normalization of relations between Japan and a foreign country. In 1967 JAL inaugurated a service in conjunction with the Soviet airline Aeroflot which linked Moscow and Tokyo. The Soviets provided the aircraft (a Tupelov 114) and flight crew, but the cabin attendants were a combination of JAL and Aeroflot personnel.

JAL created a subsidiary called Southwest Airlines on June 22, 1967. The new airline operated domestic services between Japanese cities and vacation spots in the Ryukyu Islands in southern Japan. JAL's tourist business continued to grow as the country became more affluent. In 1969 the company founded another subsidiary called JAL Creative Tours, whose purpose was to market travel packages and excursions.

On July 22, 1970 Boeing delivered the first of several 747s to JAL. Three months later the aircraft was introduced on the Tokyo-Los Angeles route. In addition to jumbo jets, JAL had three Concorde and five Boeing supersonic transports (SSTs) on order. These jetliners were later canceled when the price of a Concorde increased and the Boeing project was abandoned.

Shizuma Matsuo, who succeeded Seijiro Yanagida as president of the airline in 1961, was promoted to the position of chairman in 1971. Another company officer, Shizuo Asada, took Matsuo's place. During this period of time questions were raised about JAL's management. A series of major accidents throughout 1972 culminated with the crash of a JAL DC-8 after takeoff from Moscow's Sheremetyevo Airport. These accidents were blamed on the pilots' lack of experience. Commercial pilots in western nations usually come from the military where they gain thousands of hours of flight experience. Japan, however, has only a small "self-defense force" whose pilots are forbidden from taking higher-paying jobs in civilian aviation. As a result, less experienced JAL pilots (it was reported) tended to lack certain instinctual skills during crisis situations. The airline investigated this problem, but in the meantime the loss of its DC-8 created an equipment shortage which forced JAL to cancel the London-U.S. portion of its around-the-world service. Consequently, the company took a number of steps to ensure that accidents of this kind would not occur in the future.

On April 21 of 1974, as part of a wider government campaign to normalize relations with the People's Republic of China, Japan Air Lines suspended its service to Taipei. Taipei is the capital of Taiwan, an island which has been ruled by a rival Chinese government since the Communists came to power on Mainland China in 1949. Six months later JAL opened air service between Osaka and Shanghai in the People's Republic of China. The following year JAL created a separate subsidiary called Japan Asia Airways which resumed the air service to Taiwan.

Japan Air Lines continued to add Boeing 747s to its growing airliner fleet. However, in 1977 a number of Japanese politicians were implicated in a scandal which involved illegal payments from the sale of Boeing airplanes. An investigation by the Japanese government led to the resignations of several Japanese officals before any formal charges of wrongdoing could be initiated. Boeing's chief competitor, McDonnell Douglas, hadn't sold a new airplane to JAL in over 10 years. That company's latest entry in the commercial jetliner market was the wide body DC-10. The DC-10 was smaller than Boeing's 747, but it was also more suitable for a number of JAL's routes. Soon thereafter, the airline purchased a number of DC-10s and introduced them on routes previously served by DC-8s, which were converted for freight service.

Boeing, however, was still JAL's number one aircraft supplier. JAL had a special need for aircraft capable of carrying very large numbers of passengers and only Boeing manufactured an airliner as large as the 747. In 1980 JAL accepted delivery of its first 747SR, a special 747 capable of carrying 550 passengers. It was used mainly for domestic flights between Tokyo and Okinawa.

Japan Air Lines was recognized for its numerous successes when it was chosen "1980 Airline of the Year" by the editors of *Air Transport World.* And while JAL had made its mark in the air, it was also very active on the ground. Tokyo's Narita Airport was built to accommodate Tokyo's growing air traffic and relieve the pressure of air traffic at the older Haneda Airport. The problem with Narita, however, is that it is located 66 kilometers from downtown Tokyo. JAL officials had long expressed an interest in developing a high-speed train which would cover the distance in 20 minutes. After many years of experimentation, JAL introduced the HSST (high speed surface transport), built in conjuction with Sumitomo Electric Industries and Tokyo Car Manufacturing Company. The HSST (also known as a "mag-lev" vehicle because of the way it works) does not touch the rails it rides over. The train is magnetically suspended approximately one centimeter above the rails. Since it never touches the rails, there isn't any friction and, as a result, the train can travel at greater speeds. On February 14, 1978 the HSST achieved its intended operating speed of 300 kilometers per hour. It was demonstrated on a special 400 meter track at the Tsukuba Exposition in 1985 with the hope that it may attract buyers searching for a high-speed public transportation system.

Shisuo Asada announced his retirement as president of JAL in 1981. He was succeeded by Yasumoto Tagaki. Under Tagaki, Japan Air Lines entered a new phase in the world airline market. Deregulation in the United States inspired increased airline competition in foreign markets. By 1983 a committee recommended that JAL should be operated more like a commercial operation, and perhaps even privatized.

In 1985 the Japanese government authorized JAL's domestic rival, All Nippon Airways, to fly international routes and operate cargo services in competition with JAL. In return, JAL was given the authority to fly more domestic routes in competition with All Nippon, which had a monopoly on many Japanese routes. It was also suggested that Toa Domestic Airways and a number of other foreign airlines be given greater freedom to operate in Japan.

During this period JAL suffered from a number of brief but highly publicized strikes. Perhaps the biggest blow to the company's credibility came in February of 1982, when the pilot of a JAL jet (who was later diagnosed as a schizophrenic) crashed his airplane into Tokyo Bay, killing 24 passengers. Many air travelers subsequently avoided JAL, severely depressing the company's earnings.

On August 12, 1985, JAL flight 123 from Tokyo to Osaka took off with 524 passengers. Shortly after takeoff, while the cabin was pressurizing, the rear bulkhead ruptured and severely damaged the 747's tail fin. The airplane had no manueverability but stayed aloft for 30 minutes before crashing into a mountainside killing all but four passengers. This was the most serious single-airplane accident in aviation history, and it kept thousands of customers away from JAL. Yasumoto Tagaki assumed full responsibility for the tragedy and offered his resignation to Prime Minister Yasuhiro Nakasone, who publicly berated Tagaki for lax discipline. Japan Air Lines held memorial services and offered to pay all educational costs of any children who lost parents in the crash. Later, Tagaki personally went to visit the surviving members of the crash victims, offering one last apology before his resignation took effect.

Susumu Yamaji was appointed JAL's president in December of 1985 and Junji Itoh was named the airline's chairman in June of 1986. Mr. Itoh became the first chairman of JAL with a background in marketing. Under Itoh's leadership JAL was restructured and organized under three main operating divisions: international passenger service, domestic passenger service, and cargo (including mail) service. Itoh also made progress with the company's strained state of labor relations.

The most obvious feature of chairman Itoh's leadership is the company's emphasis on marketing. Under the previous management the loyalty of Japanese customers was largely taken for granted. In a more deregulated market, however, JAL is forced to fight for its share of the market. The American airline companies are expected to compete intensely in Japan. JAL has prepared for their arrival by securing agreements with Delta Air Lines and Western Airlines which link JAL to an extensive American flight network.

The Japanese government's ownership of Japan Air Lines has been reduced to 34.5%. It is expected that the government will sell its share of JAL to the public in 1987. When this privatization is complete, JAL will still be the tenth largest airline in the world, serving six continents with the world's largest fleet of 747s numbering 47.

Japan Air Lines has diversified its operations into a number of wholly- and partially-owned businesses, including its chain of Nikko International Hotels, and Japan Creative Tours Company, Ltd. (JALPAK), a packager of international tours. In addition, JAL operates Southwest Airlines (in Japan) and Japan Asia Airways, and the Airport Ground Service Company, an aircraft maintenance division.

Principal Subsidiaries: Japan Creative Tours Co., Ltd. (50.2%); Airport Ground Service Co., Ltd. (85%); Japan Air Lines Development Co., Ltd. (67.1%); Nikko Trading Co., Ltd. (72.9%); Southwest Airlines Co., Ltd. (51%); Japan Asia Airways Co., Ltd.

Further Reading: Empires of the Sky: The Politics, Contests, and Cartels of World Airlines by Anthony Sampson, New York, Random House, 1984.

Royal Dutch Airlines

KONINKLIJKE LUCHTVAART MAATSCHAPPIJ, N.V. (KLM Royal Dutch Airlines)

55 Amsterdamseweg
Amstelveen
The Netherlands
(020) 499123

Public/State-owned Company
Incorporated: October 7, 1919
Employees: 19,193
Sales: Dfl 5.65 billion (US$ 2.50 billion)
Market value: Dfl 1.78 billion (US$ 791 million)
Stock Index: New York, Amsterdam

Royal Dutch Shell, Philips, Fokker, and DeBeers are just a few Dutch companies with international reputations. The Dutch airline KLM is no less important a member of that group. As the national flag carrier KLM is the country's most obvious commercial ambassador and serves 119 destinations in 75 countries on six continents.

KLM was organized by a young aviator lieutenant named Albert Plesman. In August and September of 1919 Plesman, with the financial support of an Amsterdam shipping company, sponsored the "Elta" aviation exhibition in Amsterdam to satisfy the public's fascination with the airplane. Over half a million people attended the air show. When it closed a number of Dutch commercial interests decided to establish a Dutch air transport company and Plesman was nominated to head the company.

The Royal Dutch government lent its support to Plesman's project by offering to allow him use of the title *Koninklijke*, meaning "Royal," in the company's name. On October 7, 1919 the Koninklijke Luchtvaart Maatschappij, or "KLM," was founded in The Hague. It was one of the world's first commercial airline companies. In its early years KLM transported passengers, freight and mail to a growing number of European destinations linking Dutch cities with London, Paris, Oslo and Athens. At that time the Netherlands had a world-wide empire with colonies in Asia and the Caribbean. Soon KLM was charting routes to link these colonies with Holland. Services to Curacao and Trinidad were opened, and in 1927 KLM established a route from Amsterdam to Batavia (later Djakarta) on the island of Java in Dutch Indonesia. The 8700 mile trip took eleven days.

At the start of World War II German armies invaded the low countries and closed KLM operations. Plesman was understandably upset by the occupation and frustrated with his inability to convince the Germans to relax their grip on the Netherlands. One summer night Plesman's determination to take action led him to awaken one of his house guests, a Swedish KLM pilot named Count von Rosen. Plesman asked the Count, "What can I do to stop this?" Von Rosen replied, "You could talk to my Uncle Hermann." Suddenly Plesman realized he was speaking to the nephew of the German Reichmarschall Hermann Goering. A few days later Plesman was in Berlin discussing the possibility of a peace treaty between England and Germany with Goering.

Plesman formulated a document which was later forwarded to Churchill's office in London. The peace terms would leave the British Empire intact, but give Germany control of the European continent and the United States control of the Americas. The matter was "studied with much interest" and receipt of the document was acknowledged by Lord Halifax. Goering, however, became displeased with Plesman's initiative and later had him jailed. He was released in April of 1942 and told to remain at his house in Twenthe in the woods of eastern Holland until the end of the war. During this time he kept himself occupied by formulating strategies for the postwar operation of KLM.

When the war ended in the spring of 1945 Plesman was largely forgiven by the public for his attempts to make peace with the Germans earlier in the war. Soon afterwards he traveled to the United States to negotiate the purchase of surplus warplanes for KLM. The company wasted no time rebuilding its network, but since the Dutch East Indies were in a state of revolt Plesman's first priority was to re-establish KLM's route to Batavia. By the end of the year KLM was again flying to Indonesia. By 1948 services were opened to Africa, North and South America, and the Caribbean. Also during the immediate postwar period, the Dutch government expressed interest many times in gaining a controlling interest in KLM. Plesman, however, was a fiercely independent man and kept the company under private control while conceding only a portion of KLM's ownership to the government.

Indonesia (formerly the Dutch East Indies) gained its independence from The Netherlands in 1949. The following year the Indonesian government established its own national airline called Garuda. KLM assisted Garuda from the time of its inception and continued to aid the company with technical and financial assistance until 1982. KLM later helped to establish a number of other airlines in developing nations, including Philippine Airlines, Nigeria Airways, Viasa (Venezuela), Egyptair, and Aerolineas Argentinas.

In 1950 KLM entered into an agreement with Swissair and Belgium's Sabena airlines which led to the establishment of a spare parts pool. The BeNeSwiss agreement laid the ground for a future maintenance pool called the KSSU group which included KLM, Scandinavian Airlines, Swissair, and the privately operated French airline UTA. KLM also continued to modernize and expand during the 1950's. It was the first European airline to fly new versions of the Lockheed Constellation and Electra. In addition, a number of destinations in western North America were added to KLM's route structure. In 1954 the company created KLM Aerocarto N.V., an aerial survey and photography service.

Albert Plesman died on December 31, 1954 at the age of 64. Praised and decorated as a hero of the Netherlands, Plesman also received decorations from Denmark, Belgium, Sweden, Czechoslovakia, Greece, Tunisia, Lebanon and Syria. The company he left behind was entering a difficult period in commercial aviation history. A sudden and unexplained decline in ridership caused financial reverses at KLM and most of the world's other airlines. The company also faced the burden of financing a costly conversion to jet airplanes. And by this time the government had increased its ownership of the company to two-thirds by purchasing new KLM stock issues. The board of directors, however, remained under the control of the private shareholders.

In 1961 KLM reported its first year of losses. The company's president, I.A. Aler, resigned and was replaced by Ernst Hans van der Beugel. Yet the change in leadership was not enough to reverse the company's financial difficulties. Aler enlisted McKinsey & Company, an airline consulting firm, to make recommendations for returning the company to profitability. Their study concluded that KLM should reduce its staff and number of airplanes. Aler, however, had already reduced the staff by one-seventh and refused to release any more personnel. In January of 1963 Aler resigned from KLM and later checked into a hospital suffering from exhaustion.

KLM's board of directors then elected Horatius Albarda to the company's presidency. Albarda initiated a reorganization of the company which involved further cutbacks in staff and air services. But Albarda's tenure of presidency ended when he was killed in a private plane crash during 1965. Albarda was succeeded by KLM's Deputy President Gerrit van der Wal. Van der Wal adopted Albert Plesman's attitude toward government involvement in KLM. Before his appointment to KLM Van der Wal reached an agreement with the government that, despite its major financial holding in the company, KLM would be run as a private enterprise without interference from the government. By 1966 the Dutch government interest in KLM had been reduced to 49.5%.

In 1965 the airline created a subsidiary called KLM Helicopters to transport oil workers to and from oil drilling rigs in the North Sea. The division has since expanded its range of operations to include specialized and chartered airlift services. KLM created another subsidiary in 1966 to operate domestic passenger air services in the Netherlands. NLM Dutch Airlines connected a number of smaller Dutch cities with the nation's international airports in Rotterdam and Amsterdam. NLM later included flights to other European cities and in 1976 the division's name was changed to NLM CityHopper.

In an attempt to better utilize its facilities at Amsterdam's Schiphol Airport, KLM initiated a promotion called Distrinet in conjunction with a number of Dutch shipping and transport companies. Distrinet was intended to co-ordinate these various Dutch companies in order to establish Amsterdam as the primary continental port of entry and distribution for European cargo.

KLM was a regular customer of the McDonnell Douglas Corporation. When the airline introduced jet service in 1960 it decided to employ the Douglas DC-8 rather than the Boeing Company's 707. In 1969 the company purchased DC-9s rather than Boeing's similarly configured three-engine 727. In 1971, however, KLM purchased the first of a number of Boeing 747 jumbo jets. McDonnell Douglas campaigned very hard to prevent KLM from purchasing more Boeing products. Nevertheless, KLM remained neutral. KLM preferred to recognize the unique qualities of each company's product and avoid becoming the exclusive customer of any one company.

McDonnell Douglas' response to Boeing's production of the 747 was to manufacture the DC-10 which became available shortly after the 747. The DC-10 is smaller than the 747 and somewhat more efficient at lower passenger load factors (when a number of seats remain empty). In 1972 KLM purchased the first of several DC-10s to provide the airline with a more flexible fleet. Boeing and McDonnell Douglas, however, soon had more than just each other for competition. A number of airline companies, most of them European and including KLM, placed orders for a new airplane being developed by Airbus, the European aerospace consortium. KLM ordered ten Airbus A-310 passenger jetliners scheduled for delivery beginning in 1983.

Difficult economic conditions caused by the oil crises in 1973–74 forced KLM to seek government assistance in arranging debt refinancing. In return for the government's money KLM issued additional shares of stock to the government. By the late 1970's the government held a 78% majority of KLM stock. Company management, however, remained under the control of private shareholders.

Sergio Orlandini (his father was Italian and his mother Dutch) became KLM's president in 1973. Upon taking office he was confronted with a problem common to all international carriers at that time, namely, overcapacity. KLM was flying planes with too many empty seats. The solution at other airline companies was to offer discounted fares in the belief that some income from a given seat was better than none at all. Orlandini chose another approach. His idea was to reconfigure KLM's 747s (with its huge capacity for passengers) so that it could carry a combination of passengers and freight. A partition separated the passenger cabin from the cargo hold in the rear of the airplane. Later 747s delivered to KLM (called "combis") were specifically designed for combinations of passengers and freight.

Presently one-sixth of KLM's earnings are from non-airline operations which include management consulting, technical services, staff training, hotels, duty-free shops, catering, and ground handling. Under the terms of the KSSU agreement, KLM performs maintenance on 747s and overhaul of CF6 engines. The company's diversity has enabled it to survive difficult periods in the airline passenger market.

The Dutch government's share of KLM was reduced to 54.8% in 1986 and is expected to be reduced even further to 36.6% in 1987–88. KLM has also cooperated with British Airways and a number of American airline companies who are lobbying to relax airline regulations in Europe. This cooperation may one day lead to a European form of airline deregulation.

Principal Subsidiaries: KLM Aerocarto; NLM City-Hopper; KLM Helicopters; Golden Tulip International; Service Q. General Service Co.; KLM International Finance Co.; Weblock; Highmark International.

Further Reading: Pictorial History of KLM, Royal Dutch Airlines by Roy Allen, London, Ian Allen, 1978.

DEUTSCHE LUFTHANSA A.G.
(Lufthansa German Airlines Incorporated)

Von-Gablenz-Strasse 2–6
D–5000 Koln 21
Federal Republic of Germany.
(0221) 8261

Public/State-owned Company
Incorporated: 1926 as Deutsche Luft Hansa
Aktiengesellschaft
Employees: 31,575
Sales: DM 9.287 billion (US$ 4.782 billion)
Market value: DM 3.169 billion (US$ 1.632 billion)
Stock Index: Frankfurt

The West German national flag carrier Lufthansa is regarded as one of the five major airlines in the Western world. Its history parallels the development of aviation in Germany, dating back to a time when the first aviators were just beginning to fly. However, it wasn't established as a commercial airline in Germany until the 1920's.

After World War I the German government favored the development of a national airline sytem made up of a number of associated regional airlines. One of the largest airline companies, Deutscher Aero Lloyd, was incorporated in 1923 and centered its operations around Berlin's Temple Field. The following year Junkers Luftverkehr was founded. Junkers built airplanes in addition to operating an airline. Together the two companies dominated German aviation.

The two companies merged with all the other German aeronautic concerns in 1926 to form Deutsche Luft Hansa Aktiengesellschaft (the name "Hansa" was taken from the north-German Hanseatic trading league which had contributed most of the airline's private capital). Luft Hansa was a government-private monopoly; the chosen instrument for all German air services. The company's logo was taken from Aero Lloyd and its blue and yellow colors were taken from Junkers. By May of 1926 Luft Hansa served 57 domestic and 15 international airports.

In 1934, under the new name "Lufthansa," the company opened an airmail service between Stuttgart and Buenos Aires. As an instrument of state commerce and diplomacy Lufthansa flew to numerous destinations around the world including Beijing, New York, Cairo, Bangkok and Tokyo. Regarded as an instrument of the state Lufthansa increasingly came under the control of the ruling Nazi party. Lufthansa began service to destinations in the Soviet Union during 1940. These routes provided the German Luftwaffe (air force) with valuable strategic information used in Hitler's surprise invasion of the Soviet Union two years later. In 1941 the Luftwaffe assumed control of Lufthansa's airplanes and converted many of them for military use. As the war continued many Lufthansa employees were drafted into military service in support of the Luftwaffe; by the end of the war in 1945 many had lost their lives.

After the war Germany was occupied by the Soviet Union, the United States, France and Britain. The Soviet occupied zone later became the German Democratic Republic (East Germany), and the American, French and British zones became the Federal Republic of Germany (West Germany). A general state of belligerency between the Soviet Union and the Western allies further divided East and West Germany. Under the conditions of the occupation both East and West Germany were forbidden to establish their own airline companies. British, French and American airlines had a monopoly on air service in West Germany, while the Soviet airline Aeroflot assumed all air services in East Germany.

By 1951 the re-establishment of a national airline for West Germany was proposed. The following year the West German government in Bonn set up a preparatory airline corporation, and then in 1953 Luftag was created. Hans Bongers, who joined Lufthansa in 1926, was reinstated as director of the national airline. Luftag began service with four Convair 340s, later joined by three DC-3s, and four Lockheed Constellations.

Luftag's airplanes were piloted by foreign airline personnel while former Lufthansa pilots were retrained in the United States. The Germans later flew as co-pilots until 1956 when all-German crews were assigned. In 1954 Luftag instituted its old name, Lufthansa, and in the following years re-established its services to North and South America and the Middle East.

Lufthansa began flying Boeing 707 passenger jets on its international routes in 1961. The introduction of jets marked the beginning of an equipment rotation at Lufthansa. The older propeller-driven airplanes were slowly phased out and replaced by passenger jets. With this new equipment Lufthansa had firmly re-established itself as one of the world's premier air carriers.

The expansion of Lufthansa continued with the reintroduction of services to Africa. The airline established service to Nigeria in 1962 and later that year began service to Johannesburg, South Africa. Despite the heavy investment required for the airline's expansion, Lufthansa was able to declare its first profitable year in 1964. Previously the airline had charged its losses to the Federal government.

Lufthansa joined a maintenance pool called ATLAS in 1969. As a member of ATLAS, Lufthansa cooperates with Air France, Alitalia, Sabena, and Iberia in the repair and maintenance of aircraft and other equipment. Lufthansa's Hamburg facility has been designated to perform repairs for the pool's B-747s, DC-10s and A-300s.

The updating of equipment at Lufthansa continued over

the next few years as the airline introduced Boeing's 737 for short distance shuttle routes, and a 747 jumbo jet for heavily traveled long distance services. In addition to the 747, Lufthansa purchased several McDonnell Douglas DC-10s. The new aircraft replaced the older propeller-driven airplanes, the last of which was removed from the fleet in 1971. During this period Lufthansa developed its air freight services with a fleet of 747s specially designated to haul cargo. The airline constructed automated freight handling facilities in a number of destinations across the world. Lufthansa recognized the importance of cargo services before most of its competition. The company established one of the most modern freight handling systems in the world. Cargo services have been a major source of revenue for Lufthansa.

Being a European airline Lufthansa was dangerously exposed to terrorist activities during the 1970's. Security was inadequate at many airports served by the company, which made it easy for terrorists to board and later commandeer an airplane. However, not one Lufthansa passenger has lost his life despite numerous hijackings on the airline. The chairman of the company during the 1970's was Rolf Bebber and he must be credited for Lufthansa's success in ending the hijacking peacefully. He established a crisis management procedure which enlisted the diplomatic influence of the West German government. Through this procedure the company could respond quickly to terrorist demands in order to resolve a crisis. In addition, security at all Lufthansa airports was significantly upgraded.

The airline experienced considerable problems with German air traffic controllers who staged a "go-slow" from May to November 1973. Lufthansa estimates that it lost $71 million due to flight cancellations during that period. The controllers, who are civil servants, have been demonstrating their displeasure with working conditions in this manner since 1962. Lufthansa has tried to persuade the Federal government to change the status of the controllers in an effort to avoid future slowdowns but has thus far been unsuccessful.

Lufthansa received its first A-300 jetliner in 1976 from Airbus, the French-German-British-Spanish aircraft consortium. The A-300 was the first commerical aircraft to be built primarily by Germans in over 30 years. The German member of the Airbus group, Messerschmidt-Bölkow-Blohm (MBB), continued to contribute to the development of more advanced Airbus jetliners and Lufthansa continued to add them to its fleet. In 1983 the airline commissioned its first A-310 and has since expressed interest in the consortium's A-320 and A-340 jumbo jet projects.

MBB has been particularly willing to involve Lufthansa in the Airbus projects. Since both companies are German they are encouraged by the Federal government to co-ordinate and serve each other's economic interests. As a result, Airbus is especially sensitive to Lufthansa's design requirements. And because Lufthansa is a highly respected modern air carrier, the jetliners built to its specifications are, in turn, more marketable to other airline companies.

In 1982, 80% of Lufthansa's stock was owned by the West German government. The board of directors, however, was appointed by Lufthansa's private investors. On June 22 of that year the board of directors narrowly elected a new chairman to succeed Herbert Culmann. Culmann was a popular chairman, but he retired two years early to save his company embarrassment over allegations of kickbacks to travel agents.

The new chairman was Heinz Ruhnau, a career bureaucrat with strong affiliations with the West German Social Democratic Party. His appointment generated an unusual amount of concern because many feared the ruling Social Democrats were attempting to politicize the airline. Ruhnau was an Under Secretary in the Transport Ministry and a former chief assistant to the head of West Germany's largest trade union, IG Metall. He did not, however, have experience in private enterprise, and Lufthansa was being prepared for a further privatization of its stock. In 1985 the Federal government held 74.31% of Lufthansa, 7.85% was held by government agencies, and the remaining 17.84% was held by private interests.

Ruhnau assumed his post on July 1, 1982 in a smooth transition of leadership. Ruhnau's immediate tasks were to improve Lufthansa's thin profit margin and win the support of the company's 30,000 skeptical employees. The company's performance in 1982 was impressive and resulted in its election as airline of the year by the editors of *Air Transport World*.

Much of Lufthansa's future growth depends on its ability to remain competitive in an increasingly difficult world airline market. To this end, it has entered a number of markets which are not immediately recognized as potential commercial successes. For instance, Lufthansa's service to Lagos, Nigeria is extremely popular. Lufthansa is also one of the first major airline companies to establish regular service to Beijing, where it is investing in a new 400-room hotel and business center. Given the growing economic importance of the Far East, China may also become one of Lufthansa's more popular destinations.

Principal Subsidiaries: Condor Flugdienst GmbH; German Cargo Service GmbH; Lufthansa Commercial Holding GmbH; Delvag Luftuersicherungs AG.

Further Reading: The Lufthansa Story by Joachim Wachtel, Cologne, Lufthansa German Airlines, 1980.

NORTHWEST AIRLINES, INC.

Minneapolis/St. Paul International Airport
St. Paul, Minnesota 55111
U.S.A.
(612) 726-2111

Wholly-owned subsidiary of NWA, Inc.
Incorporated: April 16, 1934
Employees: 30,000
Sales: $4.517 billion
Market value: $1.807 billion
Stock Index: New York

Northwest claims to be the second oldest commercial air carrier in the United States. Like the other original airline companies established during the 1920's, its first business was hauling mail under contract to the U.S. postal service. Over the years Northwest established itself as the United States' northern regional air carrier, serving New York, Seattle and Anchorage. Northwest's expanded services to Asia inspired a new but unofficial name, Northwest Orient, which appears on its jetliners today.

After passage of the Kelly Airmail bill in 1926 the Ford Transport Company, a subsidiary of the auto manufacturer, was later awarded the Chicago to St. Paul airmail route. They commenced business on June 7 of that year, but a series of airplane crashes over the summer forced Ford to sell the company to Northwest Airways by October. Northwest ran Ford's open-cockpit single-engine biplanes until the winter weather compelled them to cease operations. In the spring of 1927 Northwest resumed business. By July the company was hauling passengers on their short trunk routes. Once again, however, the harsh northern winter obliged them to close for the season.

During the flying seasons of 1928 to 1933 Northwest secured an expansion of routes through the Dakotas and Montana, and eventually to Seattle, Washington. The man largely responsible for the company's westward growth was Croil Hunter. While only occupying a position in middle management, it was Hunter's initiative to enter new markets and win new airmail routes that gave Northwest its early pre-eminence. By 1933 Hunter was vice-president and general manager of the airline.

In the years before World War II Northwest directed its expansion eastward to New York. The company survived the government's temporary suspension of airmail contracts in 1934 with virtually no loss in business, and began operating mail services and passenger routes along the northern corridor. Moreover, new and modified airplanes enabled Northwest to continue operations through the winter. In 1937 Croil Hunter, who had been credited with the airline's success, was named president of the company.

In the attempt to establish northern routes to Asia, Northwest pilots made expeditions to Alaska and across the Aleutian Islands. The northern route had been passed up by Pan Am, which was unable to win landing rights in the Soviet maritime provinces and Japan. Instead, Pan Am decided to open a route to the Philippines and China, via Hawaii and Guam. Pan Am crossed the ocean first, but Northwest held the promise of a faster route.

When the Americans became involved in World War II in 1941, Northwest was chosen to operate the military support routes to the strategically important Aleutian Islands. The airline's experience with cold weather aviation and its predominance in the region made it a logical choice. The Army Air Corps flew its C-46s, C-47s, B-25 and B-26 bombers directly from the production line to Northwest facilities in Minneapolis, Minnesota and Vandalia, Ohio in order for them to be modified for cold weather and long distance routes. Northwest's expertise in this area contributed significantly to the effectiveness of the Allied war effort.

During the war passenger flights were strictly limited to people with priority status. Regardless of the suspension of commercial business, however, Northwest benefited from the war. With a healthy military allowance from the War Department, Northwest improved its facilities and upgraded its technology.

When the war ended Northwest lobbied the Civil Aeronautics Board to award the airline rights to fly to the Orient from Alaska. This so-called "great circle" route was actually about two thousand miles shorter than Pan Am's transpacific route. When congress rejected airline magnate Juan Trippe's proposal to make Pan Am America's international flag carrier, the Civil Aeronautics Board was free to certify Northwest for "great circle" routes to the Orient.

With the government's reaffirmation of competition within the industry, all the companies hurried to modernize their airline fleets. It was both a matter of cost efficiency and prestige. Northwest looked to the Martin Company, with its new 202 airliner, to replace the aging DC-3 model, and complement the company's fleet of Boeing 377 Stratocruisers. The Stratocruiser, with its lower level bar and intimate "honeymoon suites" was extremely popular with newlyweds and business travelers. The Martin 202, however, did not remain in service for very long; its reputation for malfunctioning became widespread. Fortunately, the 202 was quickly replaced with the new DC-4.

When the Korean War started in 1950, Northwest employed many of its DC-4s to assist the United Nations forces. They ferried men and transported equipment, including bomber engines and surgical supplies, to various points in Japan and Korea. The military utilization of the airline, which lasted for several years, was carried out without any interruption of its regular commercial services.

In 1952 Hunter relinquished the presidency to Harold R. Harris, but retained his position as chairman of the board. After two uneventful years Harris was replaced by Donald Nyrop. After he received his law degree, Nyrop served in the military transport group during World War II. Later, he headed the Civil Aeronautics Board. For many years after joining Northwest he set an austere tone for the organization. For example, the Minneapolis headquarters was located in a large windowless building that he planned would become a maintenance hangar at some point in the future. Nyrop also had a chart showing the inverse relationship between the number of vice presidents and profits. Needless to say, Northwest had a minimal number of vice presidents.

On the other hand, Nyrop brought Northwest into the jet age quickly, purchasing the Lockheed L-188 prop-jet Electra, the DC-8, and Boeing 707 and 727. Through the early 1960's Northwest consolidated its service across the northern United States and along the "great circle" to its Asian destinations. Profits were consistent and growth remained slow and cautious.

Perhaps the one outstanding event of the period occurred on Thanksgiving Eve of 1971. A man who identified himself as Dan Cooper boarded a Northwest 727 in Portland, Oregon bound for Seattle, Washington. He claimed to have a bomb and demanded $200,000 and two parachutes. His demands were met and the airplane departed. Somewhere over southwestern Washington, at about 25,000 feet, Cooper ordered the airplane's rear bottom door opened. He walked down the stairs and jumped into the densely clouded, cold and black night. Cooper and most of the money were never found. He was, however, rumored to have died in a New York hospital in 1982.

In 1978, after 24 years in charge, Donald Nyrop retired. He was replaced by Joseph M. Lapensky, an accountant who was promoted from within the company. Many industry analysts expected Lapensky to continue Nyrop's management policy. In fact, Lapensky must be regarded an interim figure; one who represented a definite but subtle change in direction for the company.

Lapensky inherited the leadership on the eve of deregulation. For many of the large airlines the new era of competition resulted in the loss of large amounts of revenue. Northwest, however, was quite firmly established in its various markets, and remained for the most part unchallenged. Lapensky's most important problem, however, was the ruptured state of labor relations which resulted from his predecessor's attempts to weaken the unions. In one instance, when Northwest employees threatened to strike, Nyrop decided to confront the unions. He enlisted the help of a 15 airline mutual aid fund established to enable the companies to withstand the effects of a longterm strike. When Nyrop realized the effort was stalemated, he gave in to union demands. Nyrop's union problem became Lapensky's union problem, and before long Lapensky retired.

In October of 1983 Steven G. Rothmeier became Northwest's new president. Rothmeier gained Lapensky's favor after writing a paper on a deregulated airline market as a student at the University of Chicago. Rothmeier's case study of Northwest so impressed people at the airline that they offered him a job in 1983. Like Lapensky, he rose through the company, albeit quickly, to the top executive position. Under new management the airline formed a holding company, Northwest Airlines, Inc., which assumed responsibility for the airline and its subsidiaries. On Janaury 1, 1985 Rothmeier was named chief executive officer confirming his position as the leader of Northwest.

In 1985 United Airlines proposed to buy the Asian and Pacific routes of Northwest's competitor Pan Am. Rothmeier led the opposition to the sale, arguing that it would leave only two airlines competing in Asia. Northwest invested many years of negotiation and costly waiting to achieve and maintain its Pacific markets. According to Rothmeier, it was hardly fair that United could simply purchase a competitive share. Regardless of the opposition, the sale of Pan Am's Asian routes to United was approved in 1986.

Until recently Northwest suffered from not having a computerized reservations system. As a result, Northwest purchased a large share of TWA's Pars system, which the two companies jointly operate. The company has also made arrangements with four smaller independent airlines to generate more "feeder" traffic to Northwest.

In 1986 Northwest purchased its regional competitor Republic airlines. The $884 million sale barely won federal approval since the two airlines operated many of the same routes. At first the Civil Aeronautics Board was concerned that Northwest would operate monopolies in too many markets. Republic had established hubs in Detroit and Memphis, in addition to Minneapolis. However, Republic's north-south route structure provides the ideal "feeder" for Northwest's longer-haul east-west structure, despite a certain amount of overlap. In the end, the merger was approved. As a result of this merger, John F. Horn was named president of Northwest and NWA, Inc. Rothmeier, still chief executive officer, assumed the position of chairman, vacant since Lapensky's retirement in May of 1985.

Northwest and Republic operate approximately 290 airplanes, including Boeing 727s, 747s and 757s, A320s, DC-9s, DC-10s and MD-80s. The two companies employ about 30,000 people each, but this number, like the number of jetliners, is expected to decline as the merger is fully implemented. Prior to the merger, Republic flew to over 100 cities in 34 states, Canada and the Caribbean. Northwest's network covered 74 cities in 27 states and 16 countries in Western Europe, the Far East and the Caribbean. The new Northwest is the third largest American airline in terms of route miles.

Until the purchase of Republic Airlines, Northwest had always been "underleveraged," or virtually free of debt. Northwest's management used to be proud of this fact, but today recognizes that, for tax and other purposes, it is good to carry "some debt." In this respect Northwest and Delta are very similar. They are both underleveraged and very sensitive to new developments in the airline market. Unlike Delta, however, Northwest's employees are thoroughly unionized and generally paid less than at other airlines.

To deal with the more rigid costs and unstable market conditions created by deregulation, Northwest's parent company operates a number of diversified subsidiaries. NWA owns Sun Country Airlines, a charter operator, Mainline Travel, a nationwide vacation packager, and NWA Aircraft, a retailer of used airplanes.

Aside from the diversification and the decision to finance operations through debt, another legacy of Rothmeier's tenure has been a more "corporate" style of leadership, emphasizing the role of the board and the primacy of effective marketing. His success with the airline can be attributed to his strategy to bring Northwest into the 1990's as a modern and competitive concern.

Principal Subsidiaries of NWA, Inc.: Northwest Airlines, Inc.; Montana Enterprises, Inc.; Affiliated Enterprises, Inc.; Compass 315, Ltd.

Further Reading: Airlines of the U.S. Since 1914 by R.E.G. Davies, London, Putnam, 1972; *The Sky Their Frontier: The Story of the World's Pioneer Airplanes and Routes 1920–1940* by Robert Jackson, Shrewsbury, England, Airlife, Ltd., 1983.

PAN AMERICAN WORLD AIRWAYS, INC.

Pan Am Building
New York, New York 10017
U.S.A.
(212) 880-1234

Wholly-owned subsidiary of Pan Am Corporation
Incorporated: March 14, 1927
Employees: 27,700
Sales: $3.038 billion
Market value: $592 million
Stock Index: New York

Pan Am is one of America's largest airline companies and has had an important role in aviation history. Until the 1950's it was America's most widely recognized airline; it was the closest thing the United States had to a national flag carrier. Pioneering regular flights to Europe, Asia and South America, the company took on an ambassadorial character. Recently, however, "the world's most experienced airline" has been forced to reduce the scale of its operations. At the present time the company transports passengers, freight and mail to 32 destinations in the U.S. and its territories, in addition to 51 cities in Europe, the Carribean and South America.

The architect of Pan Am's prominence, and ironically of its later decline, was a man named Juan Terry Trippe. Upon graduation from Yale in 1920 Trippe worked for a year in his father's bank. However, soon thereafter he left the bank in order to pursue a career in the airline business. Without any warning his father suddenly died and with his inheritance he purchased nine Navy "Jennys" for his Long Island Airways. Unable to generate enough business the company failed.

Trippe and two wealthy friends from Yale then organized a second airline after the passage of the Kelly Air Mail Act. Their company, Colonial Air Transport, won the first airmail contract establishing a route between New York and Boston. They purchased two three-engine Fokker airplanes the following year which enabled them to transport passengers as well as mail. A dispute among stockholders that year resulted in the sale of the company to what later became known as American Airlines. Trippe and his partners were excluded from both the decision and their airline.

Shortly afterwards Trippe's group purchased Aviation Corporation of the Americas with the intention of bidding on the Key West-Havana mail route. In 1928 the company merged with Pan American Airways and Atlantic, Gulf and Caribbean Airways. The new company retained the Pan American name and flew the Havana route which was the first scheduled international commercial destination.

Pan Am had difficulty reserving the eight seats on each flight because people were afraid of flying over the 90 miles of water. Pilots were known to enter Cuban bars and dare American tourists to fly back to Florida. In Miami the company tried a different advertising campaign: "Fly with us to Havana, and you can bathe in Bacardi rum four hours from now." Pan Am lost one of its three Fokker airplanes in the ocean in 1928. In spite of this, however, air travel grew in popularity. The introduction of direction-finding radio, amphibious aircraft and other safety measures convinced the public to accept the advantages of air travel.

Trippe was now planning Pan Am's expansion in the Caribbean. Due to a lack of airports in the region he supported the development of the water-landing Sikorsky S-38 "flying boat." Pan Am purchased 25 of the five-ton airplanes, which could travel 100 miles an hour and had a range of 300 miles. In anticipation of the U.S. Postal Service opening several new routes Trippe had his flying boats make survey flights beyond Cuba over routes that, at his insistence, were to be selected for airmail contracts. He also dispatched advance men to secure landing rights, mail contracts and other concessions so that when the post office finally invited airmail bids Pan Am would be the preferred choice. In this way the company secured routes to Puerto Rico, Panama, and other points throughout the Caribbean.

In 1930 Postmaster General Walter Brown forced Pan Am's biggest airmail contract competitor, the New York, Rio and Buenos Aires airlines, to merge with Pan Am. Trippe's airline doubled its fleet and was awarded the extremely lucrative South American East Coast airmail contract. These routes served as a springboard for future business. Pan Am emerged as the world's largest airline and the "chosen instrument" for flying the U.S. flag abroad.

By employing the flying boats Pan Am consolidated its coverage of the Caribbean and turned its attention to traversing the oceans. The airline used the newly developed China Clipper (a Martin M-130), with a range of 2500 miles, to transport passengers and mail from California to the Orient. Overcoming huge obstacles of diplomacy, financing and engineering, Pan Am established service to Europe in June of 1939 using the larger and faster "Dixie Clipper" aircraft.

Pan Am's aeronautical pioneering was quite costly. Trippe was said to have been obsessed with the idea of "having a plane in every airport in the world." This left little money for dividends and, as a result, the stockholders voted to replace him with his old friend and associate "Sonny" Whitney in March of 1939. Whitney, however, was an ineffective manager and unable to maintain control of the company. Less than a year later Trippe was asked to return.

During the early 1940's Pan Am, the only established American international airline at the time, played a major role in the war effort when it placed itself at the disposal of the U.S. government. In November of 1940 Pan Am signed a contract with the War Department providing for the construction of airbases and remote supply, radio and weather stations. In October of 1942 the airline established a war transport service from the United States across the South Atlantic to West Africa and from there to points in the Middle East. Pan Am was rewarded handsomely for having devoted up to three-quarters of its resources to the armed forces during the war years. When the war ended the company's hegemony over international air routes was at its peak.

Trippe thought the interests of the United States would be served best by the creation of one official airline to compete with foreign carriers. On Capitol Hill he proposed that Pan Am be made a regulated monopoly, not unlike utility companies. Congress rejected his proposal and opened the door for the competition Pan Am had never previously experienced. With an eroding market share Pan Am looked to the future, hoping that the development of Boeing's first jetliner, the 707, would help regain what it had recently lost. The delivery of the first 15 of these airplanes precipitated the jet age and forced Pan Am's competitors to follow suit.

In the early 1950's Pan Am acquired American Overseas Airlines. Trippe also diversified Pan Am's operations and selected related businesses such as hotels, corporate jet aircraft, and National Aeronautics and Space Administration (NASA) support services, all of which were profitable (particularly a New York real estate deal involving the building and leasing of the Pan Am building which was dedicated in 1963).

In the late 1960's Juan Trippe announced his plans to retire. The airline had suffered some recent setbacks, and Trippe's failure to plan for his successor aggravated, if not precipitated, a series of new problems. When Najeeb Halaby, former head of the Federal Aviation Administration and Trippe's hand-picked successor, assumed the founder's post in 1969 he found himself presiding over an airline on the verge of bankruptcy. Halaby inherited an 81,430 mile route system which was the result of Trippe's quest to have a plane in every airport in the world. The system could not be maintained without the award of a government subsidy or a compensatory monopoly, neither of which were likely to be granted. The company became so overextended that Halaby referred to it as "an airline without a country." All of these problems added up to losses of $364 million from 1969 through 1976 with debt estimated in excess of one billion dollars.

In 1977 Pan Am, helped by tax-loss credits, made a profit for the first time since 1968. The man responsible for this was William Seawell, who was brought in to replace Halaby in 1972. Unable to obtain subsidy relief from either the Civil Aeronautics Board or the White House in 1974 and 1975, or possible funding from the Shah of Iran, Seawell instituted austerity measures in 1976 and renegotiated the company's debt. Abandoning Trippe's grand strategy, he reduced the system 25% by severing money losing services. He reduced personnel by approximately 30% and approved an offer by employees to accept a wage cut. By these measures complete financial ruin was averted.

Late in 1979 Pan Am received approval for the acquisition of National Airlines. Now in possession of a strong domestic network, Pan Am's plans to build a profitable division were mitigated by the Airline Deregulation Act. Pan Am was confronted with strong competition from new domestic and foreign carriers. The company was once again on the brink of financial ruin. Only by selling a large portion of its assets, including the Pan Am building headquarters, was it able to avoid bankruptcy.

Edward Acker became chairman in September of 1981. A cautious but optimistic manager, he continued the divestiture of Pan Am's resources. In 1985 the company sold its Asian routes to United Airlines for $715.5 million. The fast growing Pacific market was one of the few profitable areas Pan Am could rely on. However, the company had a liquidity problem and needed an infusion of cash immediately. In the aftermath of the deal there was speculation that United and Pan Am were coordinating their operations, with Pan Am serving the Atlantic routes and United serving the Pacific routes.

On September 14, 1984 Pan American Airways created a holding company called Pan Am Corporation. The parent company assumed ownership and control of the airline and the services division.

Pan Am's present fleet of about one hundred jetliners consists of B-727s, 737s and 747s, as well as L-1011s, Airbus A-300s, and one DC-10. Its route system in the American East is perhaps Pan Am's last area of competitive viability. Eastern Airlines, which operates a lucrative shuttle service between Boston, New York and Washington, D.C., sold several of its gates in those cities to Pan Am. The FAA ordered the sale to prevent Texas Air (Eastern's parent company) from establishing a monopoly on the northeast corridor shuttle service. In October of 1986 Pan Am began its own shuttle service in competition with Eastern.

The new shuttle services will provide Pan Am with a reliable cash flow. However, it is only with good management and cooperation of the kind demonstrated in the agreement with United that Pan Am will have a chance to fully recover and re-establish its historic pre-eminence in the airline industry.

Principal Subsidiaries: Pan American World Airways, Inc.; Pan Am World Services, Inc.

Further Reading: Empire of the Air: Juan Trippe and the Struggle for World Airways by Mathew Josephson, New York, Harcourt Brace, 1944; *Flying the Oceans: A Pilot's Story of Pan Am* by Horace Brock, New York, Jason Aronson, 1978; *Crosswinds: An Airman's Memoir* by Najeeb E. Halaby, New York, Doubleday, 1978; *The Perilous Sky: U.S. Aviation Diplomacy and Latin America 1919–1931* by Wesley Philips Newton, Coral Gables, Florida, University of Miami Press, 1978; *The Chosen Instrument* by Marglin Bender and Selig Altschul, New York, Simon and Schuster, 1982.

PEOPLExpress

PEOPLE EXPRESS AIRLINES, INC.

Former Address: Terminal C
Newark International Airport
Newark, New Jersey 07714
U.S.A.
(201) 961-2935

Absorbed by Continental Airlines
Incorporated: 1980
Employees: 7,500
Sales: $586 million
Market value: $192.5 million (Prior to acquisition
   by Texas Air)

People Express Airlines was a result of the 1978 Airline Deregulation Act. With innovative management and rapid but careful growth, People Express successfully competed with established airlines in regional markets. Until recently it usually won that competition. The airline had a no-frills reputation which made it very attractive to a certain type of customer. People Express was primarily a passenger air carrier serving about forty airports, mostly in the Northeast, and offering cut-rate transatlantic service to London.

The principal founder, Don Burr, has had a life-long fascination with aviation. As a boy he used to coax his parents into taking him to Bradley Field outside of Hartford, Connecticut in order to watch the airplanes. Burr quickly became involved in the airline industry after receiving his MBA from Harvard. His first job was working as a securities analyst with National Aviation, a Wall Street firm specializing in the aerospace industry. In six years he ascended to the presidency of the firm. In 1973, at the age of 30, he moved to Texas International Airlines, a struggling regional carrier. It was Burr's idea to introduce the "peanut" fares at his new company in an attempt to increase passenger volume. The scheme was very successful in raising the company's net income from $2.5 million in 1976 (when he was named chief operating officer) to $41.4 million in 1979.

Burr may have continued at Texas International, but chose instead to take advantage of the opportunities created by deregulation. Conditions were ideal for the entry of new low-cost airline companies capable of quickly acquiring a significant share of the market. In 1980 Burr and twelve others resigned their positions at Texas International in order to start such an airline in Newark, New

Jersey, the site of the proposed "hub," or traffic center. In July of that year People Express became the first airline to apply for certification after passage of the Airline Deregulation Act. People Express began operation on April 30, 1981 with three Boeing 737s.

Deregulation significantly changed the character of the airline industry. Either in an attempt to prepare for it or as a result of it, many established airlines avoided possible competition by reducing their operations. Scaling down their operations meant selling a number of airplanes, which created a buyer's market for inexpensive aircraft. People Express seized every opportunity to expand and purchased 17 more 737s, in addition to 727s and 747s.

People Express originally flew to Buffalo, New York, Columbus, Ohio and Norfolk, Virginia from Newark, but the PATCO air traffic controllers strike in 1981 temporarily halted expansion plans and crippled the existing network. To prevent their jets from remaining idle, People Express introduced flights to Florida from its northern markets. These new routes brought a profit of $500,000 on revenues of $8 million, helping the airline to financial success only seven months after its inception despite the PATCO strike.

In January of 1982 the company reported its one millionth customer; this was evidence of a very large volume after only nine months of operation. In May of 1983 People Express inaugurated a service to London, confident of filling the opening left by the failure of Freddie Laker's Skytrain. However, today's temperamental airline industry is highly "leveraged," or debt-ridden. This means that even minor swings into profit or loss columns can have a major impact on a company's viability. This is no less true of what happened to People Express.

Late in 1984 the company's meteoric rise came to an abrupt end. Plagued by a persistent overcapacity (too many empty seats) despite consistent growth in passenger traffic, and also faced with the unionization of its flight managers, the airline suffered a $14.2 million operating loss for the final quarter of 1984. This disappointing performance came after seven straight profitable quarters. Employee benefits were sharply reduced and the company's stock value fell by 50%.

Burr responded to the crisis by freezing salaries, curtailing expansion, and limiting expenses. Rather unexpectedly Burr fired his managing officer, Lori Dubose, who was largely responsible for the company's initially successful "humanistic" worker-involved labor/management policy. This heavy-handed response seems to have worked as People Express returned to profitability in the second quarter of 1985. However, Burr's authoritarian management style estranged a number of the company's co-founders. Some of them defected to competing airlines. Most conspicuously, Harold J. Paretti, the president of People Express, and about a dozen other managers left the company to form their own company called Presidential Airlines in January of 1985.

Over the years, Burr acquired a healthy disrespect for bureaucratic and typical corporate management. Instead of a highly structured hierarchical organization, People Express established only three management levels. There were no vice presidents or secretaries. Employees were expected to share the responsibility of helping the company to run smoothly and efficiently. This required them to perform many different tasks. For example, pilots double as schedule drafters, cargo specialists and inventory managers. To maintain uniformity managing officers rotated positions. Other jobs such as aircraft maintenance, baggage handling and telephone reservations were subcontracted.

People Express was founded on the principle that employees should have a financial stake in the company; the logic behind this is that if all workers were owners, this commitment would make them more productive. In fact, when they were hired, employees were required to purchase 100 shares of the company's stock (made available to them at a 70% discount). This unique relationship between the employees and the company resulted in lower labor costs and higher productivity. These conditions allowed the airline to begin operations and maintain a competitive edge until it became firmly established.

Passengers were also required to bear the burden of reduced costs. Many services once taken for granted were made optional. For example, the airline charged three dollars to check a piece of luggage, offered sandwiches for one dollar, and coffee for 50 cents. Other features, such as hot meals, baggage transfer to other airlines, and ticket desks in terminals were entirely eliminated. Due to these options and lower prices, People Express was successful in winning passengers over from other airlines, railroads and bus lines (and even out of their own automobiles).

Much of the airline's success resulted from being prepared, indeed, even designed for deregulation. It maintained the lowest costs in the industry largely because of the way its airline fleet was employed. People Express flew its aircraft an average of ten or eleven hours a day, about three hours more than the industry average. By doing this the airline more than doubled aircraft productivity without increasing capital costs or compromising safety standards. For years People Express saved money by using a dilapidated low-rent wing of Newark airport's north terminal as a headquarters. It was financially secure enough at one point to renovate and improve the facility to make it larger, more efficient and attractive. These measures were essential to facilitate the airline's growth.

Deregulation has allowed regional carriers like People Express to enter new markets without prior government approval. As a result, many airlines are no longer exclusively regional. The Civil Aeronautics Board has reclassified these companies as "large/trunk" carriers, serving a geographically diverse number of destinations. As these companies struggle to grow in the shadow of the larger airline companies, they must establish secondary hubs.

People Express acquired Britt Airways and Provincetown-Boston Airlines, two small "feeder" lines, in late 1985. In October the company purchased Frontier Airlines for $300 million. As part of the acquisition the company gained 56 more airplanes and numerous destinations, including a second hub in Denver.

The impetus for large/trunk airlines to expand comes from a threat by the larger airlines to "cross subsidize" flights in certain competing markets. This practice involves devoting capital from more profitable routes to subsidizing a price war with a competitor until the weaker airline surrenders its share of the market. The larger established airlines usually win. American Airlines successfully employed this technique with their "ultra super savers" in early 1985, but was forced to discontinue the practice when competitors alerted the CAB.

1986 was the beginning of a new era for People Express. The company announced its intention to convert into a full service airline in order to attract the business traveler. Faced with the enormous task of first changing their image from a no-frills to a full service airline, analysts gave People Express an expiration date rather than a chance for survival. The airline's infrastructure was not prepared for the new marketing strategy. Flight delays, maintenance problems, overbooking and lost luggage resulted in successive quarters of financial loss for People Express.

Burr responded to the crisis by selling the company's excess airplanes and by placing Frontier Airlines up for sale. United Airlines offered to buy Frontier for $146 million, and the deal would have been finalized if the United Airlines pilot's union hadn't rejected the proposal for absorbing the Frontier Airline pilots.

In the end, the board of directors at People Express was reported to have taken away a large degree of Don Burr's power. By August of 1986 Frontier closed down and filed for bankruptcy. Soon afterwards People Express was secretly put up for sale. At that time Texas Air publicly offered to purchase the company and all its subsidiaries for $301 million in stock reciprocation and cash.

People Express, "hardly a Procter & Gamble" when it comes to effective management, was expected to survive under the "savvy" and well-disciplined direction of Texas Air. With the acquisition of People Express and Frontier, Texas Air became the largest airline system in the United States and second in the world only to the Soviet airline Aeroflot. Texas Air is merely a holding company, but with its other subsidiaries, including New York Air, Continental and Eastern Airlines, it held over 20% of the domestic airline market, and dominated hubs in New York, Miami, Denver and Houston.

The reorganization in the industry which was expected to take place soon after deregulation has finally materialized. At present there are only a fraction of the independent airline managements that existed in 1980. People Express, the nation's first company to search for success in the deregulated airline market, has unfortunately become a victim of that deregulation. In January 1987 it was announced that People Express would be absorbed by its fellow Texas Air subsidiary, Continental Airlines. Since there was no consumer loyalty left to exploit, People Express was completely dissolved the following February.

Further Reading: Airline Deregulation: The Early Experience edited by John R. Meyer and Clinton V. Oster, Jr., Boston, Auburn House, 1981; *The Corporate Warriors: Six Classic Cases in American Business* by Douglas K. Ramsey, Boston, Houghton Mifflin, 1987.

SCANDINAVIAN AIRLINES SYSTEM

Ulvsundavagen 193
S-161 87 Stockholm-Bromma
Sweden.
46–8–780 10 00

Public/State-owned Company
Incorporated: August 1, 1946
Employees: 19,000
Sales: SKr 19.84 billion (US$ 2.917 billion)
Market value: SKr 2.55 billion (US$ 364 billion)
Stock Index: Copenhagen, Oslo, Stockholm

SAS, the Scandinavian Airlines System, is a unique example of international cooperation between three culturally similar but independent nations. Late in the 1930's three independent Scandinavian airline companies, Det Danske Luftartselskab (DDL) of Denmark, Det Norske Luftfartselskap (DNL) of Norway and Aktiebolaget Aerotransport (ABA) of Sweden, made plans for a collaborative trans-Atlantic passenger service. But their plans for the Bergen-New York service had to be postponed when Denmark and Norway were invaded by Nazi Germany. During the war the three companies secretly continued to arrange their consortium. Since Sweden remained neutral its investors were relatively free to conduct their own business. The private owner of Sweden's share of SAS, Swedish Intercontinental Airlines (SILA), negotiated to purchase American airplanes when the war ended. They hoped this would give SAS an auspicious start and enable it to begin operations immediately after the war. In 1943, SILA, the purchasing agent for SAS, placed the first order for seven Douglas DC-4s. At great risk the Danes smuggled their share of the downpayment to Sweden.

When the war ended SILA purchased a number of American B-17 bombers. These airplanes were acquired by SILA for only one dollar each. The "Flying Fortresses" were converted for passenger service by the Svenska Aeroplan Aktiebolaget (SAAB). On June 27, 1945, barely two months after the fall of Germany, ABA inaugurated their trans-Atlantic service to New York from Stockholm employing the refitted B-17s. A year later the DC-4s went into service. SAS's three-nation flag and logo were created that year, and south Atlantic DC-4 service to Brazil and Uruguay was also inaugurated. The Atlantic services of DDL, DNL and ABA were combined under SAS, but their European and domestic services continued to operate independently until 1948. That same year SILA acquired all of ABA's privately held stock. In 1951 the European, Atlantic, and domestic services of the three companies were combined, and SAS became the international flag carrier of Norway, Denmark and Sweden.

DDL, DNL and ABA are each 50% owned by the governments of Denmark, Norway and Sweden, respectively. Together the three companies form the SAS Consortium. DDL and DNL each own two-sevenths of the SAS Consortium while ABA owns three-sevenths. The SAS Group includes a number of businesses, the largest of which is their airline consortium. From its inception SAS was operated as an unsubsidized instrument of the Scandinavian trade and commerce.

In 1949 SAS expanded its intercontinental service to Bangkok via Europe and central Asia. Two years later service was extended from Bangkok to Tokyo. In 1954 SAS pioneered a polar route to Los Angeles and three years later to Tokyo. It was the first airline to fly the Caravelle, a revolutionary French-built jet with its engines mounted on the rear of the fuselage. The airline also ordered special cold-weather versions of the DC-8 and DC-9 from Douglas.

About this time SAS was confronted with a basic problem in airline economics. Most of its destinations were European, which meant that most of its flights were of short duration. This, in turn, translated into frequent takeoffs and landings and increased wear on the airplane. Moreover, the cost of preparing an aircraft for another flight was incurred more frequently. There was, therefore, an economic incentive to operate "long haul" flights to more distant points. During this period SAS also suffered from "overcapacity," or simply having too many airplanes. A solution to these problems arose when SAS was approached by officials from Thailand who wished to establish their own international airline services. SAS was chosen over other airline companies because Thailand regarded the Scandinavian countries as politically neutral. In 1959 an agreement was reached and a new company called Thai Airways International, Ltd. was formed. Under the agreement SAS contributed 30% of that company's total capital of $100,000. Thai Airways would be sole concessionaire on all routes to foreign destinations for 15 years. SAS would provide the management, support, and flight personnel in addition to leasing the necessary aircraft. Thai Airways began operations in 1960 and recorded its first profit five years later. Today, Thai companies are sole owners of TAI, Ltd. but technical, operational, and commercial cooperation with SAS continues.

SAS began a limited related diversification in 1960 when it purchased the Royal Hotel in Copenhagen. Later SAS established a catering subsidiary and a charter airline called Scanair. In 1965, SAS created the first Europe-wide computerized reservation service (or "CRS"), providing the company with a significant advantage over its larger European competitors.

In February of 1970, SAS formed an inter-airline association with KLM (Royal Dutch Airlines), Swissair and UTA (Union de Transports Aeriens of France), known as the KSSU group. Together they established a maintenance pool which offered cooperative operational and technical services. As one unit they were better able to compete with major airlines such as BOAC, Air France and Lufthansa. SAS spent much of the 1970's expanding its service area and updating its fleet. The combined "internal" and "external" expansion programs made SAS a major international air carrier by the end of the decade.

After 17 profitable years SAS suffered its first loss in 1980. It was threatened by increased competition from the recently deregulated American airline companies and low-cost operators like Freddie Laker's trans-Atlantic "Sky-train." Compounding this problem was SAS's overly conservative management style. Not only was there less concern for passengers or service on SAS, but entrenched management was broadening its scope of authority and centralizing the bureaucracy. Indeed, a number of employee responsibilities were taken away. Many changes were needed if SAS was to remain competitive, and the first step was to install more enlightened leadership.

The man chosen by the board of directors was Jan Carlzon, formerly the head of Linjeflyg, a domestic Swedish air carrier and subsidiary of SAS. Applying an innovative management style, Carlzon first recommended treating expenses as resources in an effort to find ways of raising efficiency. He declared, "All three Scandinavian countries can only survive by doing business in foreign markets; business travel is the backbone of SAS traffic; the first purpose of a Scandinavian airline must be to serve business." Since SAS failed to consistently attract the business traveler, Carlzon initiated a strong compaign to standardize and improve the company's business class passenger service. As a result, one year later SAS recorded a $24.6 million profit for the airline operation, and more than doubled that the following year. Moreover, SAS invested millions of dollars in programs for staff training and motivation, urging employees to "work smarter, not harder." And finally, in the effort to bring about changes in management most of the airline's principal managers were replaced as a new organizational structure was introduced.

Carlzon also launched a campaign aimed at making SAS the most punctual airline in the world. He even had a computer terminal installed in his office so that he was constantly apprised of every flight. When a delay threatened the departure of an airplane he would telephone the crew and investigate the problem personally. On time efficiency was raised to 90%, making SAS the most punctual airline in Europe. Carlzon then took steps to improve flight operations by selling or leasing older jets and purchasing the most recent state-of-the-art equipment. The airports of Copenhagen and Bangkok were designated as the airline's European and Asian hubs. All flights were designed to connect at these hubs to facilitate passenger transfers. Much of Copenhagen Airport's traffic includes passengers flying on to other destinations. The other airports, Oslo's Fornebu and Stockholm's Arlanda, are secondary hubs connecting SAS with smaller domestic services.

In 1984, SAS began operating hovercraft between Copenhagen Airport and the southern Swedish port of Malmö. Malmö is a busy port for passenger traffic from southern Sweden. The 17 mile trip across the Oresund strait directly to the airplane tarmac in Copenhagen can be made in 30 minutes. The hovercraft (British Hovercroft Corporation AP-188s) are impervious to water, land and ice. Although they are owned by DSO (a subsidiary of Danish State Railways), SAS operates the hovercraft under its name with its own personnel.

Believing that little more could be done to improve the "air travel" of SAS, Carlzon concentrated on what happens to the customer on the ground. A new service concept called SAS Business Hotels and Destination Service was introduced which enabled passengers to confirm reservations and arrange rental cars and hotel rooms with one phone call. In addition, SAS created Business Travel Systems which expanded the capabilities of its computerized reservations system.

SAS is currently investigating the feasibility of a second teaming arrangement with Sabena of Belgium and Finnair of Finland. An agreement would involve coordination of flight schedules to more efficiently utilize their share of certain highly competitive markets. Due to its size and pragmatic character SAS has been compared with Delta Air Lines in the United States. SAS flies to 90 cities in 40 countries, operating 96 aircraft, including DC-8s, DC-9s, DC-10s, B-747s, and F-27s. The airline will accept delivery of 16 new aircraft to cover expansion plans for the 1988–1990 period. Its air cargo business, with a hub in Cologne, West Germany, is one of the most sophisticated in the world. The facility's computerized cargo system was developed by SAS. Presently the company is offering to sell the model for this system to airlines which don't compete with SAS in the same markets.

The SAS Group operates a number of subsidiaries aside from the airline. These include Vingresor, the largest tour operator in Scandinavia, and Service Partner, a profitable catering service. In addition the Group operates SAS International Hotels which includes a network of 11 first class hotels in Scandinavia, Vienna and Singapore. The SAS Group also operates the Olson & Wright air cargo company, the Scanair charter airline service, and an insurance company.

Principal Subsidiaries: SAS Service Partner; Vingresor AB (Sweden); Nyman & Schultz Affarsresebyraer AB (Sweden); AB Olson & Wright (Sweden); Danair A/S (Denmark); SAS Royal Hotel A/S (Hotel Scandinavia) (Norway); SAS-Invest A/S (SAS Royal Hotel) (Denmark); A/S Dansk Rejsebureau (Denmark); SAS Cargo Center A/S (Denmark); Hotel Scandinavia K/S (Denmark).

Further Reading: The Politics of International Air Transport by Betsy Gidnitz, Lexington, Massachusetts, Lexington, 1980.

SWISS AIR TRANSPORT COMPANY, LTD.
(Swissair)

P.O. Box CH 8058
Zurich-Airport
Switzerland.
(01) 812 12 12

Public/State-owned Company
Incorporated: March 26, 1931
Employees: 16,652
Sales: Sfr 3.646 billion (US$ 2.240 billion)
Market value: Sfr 1.866 billion (US$ 1.147 billion)
Stock Index: Zurich, Frankfurt

The Swiss Air Transport Company (Swissair) was formed on March 26, 1926, upon the merger of Balz Zimmerman's Basle Air Transport (Balair) and Ad Astra Aero, which was operated by Walter Mittelholzer. Both companies were originally founded in the early 1920's and operated a number of air routes between Switzerland and Germany. Swissair's fleet consisted of several aircraft built by Fokker, Dornier-Merkur, Messerschmitt and Comte. Later the company added Lockheed Orions, Curtiss-Condors, DC-2s and DC-3s to its fleet. At this time Swissair also became the first European airline to employ stewardesses.

Walter Mittelholzer was killed in a climbing accident in 1937. Balz Zimmerman died unexpectedly only a few months later. Swissair, however, survived the deaths of its founders and continued to operate successfully throughout Europe. Yet Swissair was forced to cancel all operations indefinitely at the end of August, 1939. Nazi Germany had started a war in Europe which neccessitated the closure of all air services. Switzerland, which was determined to maintain strict neutrality, waited nearly six years for the war to end.

The war brought important technological advances in aeronautics. And after the war many well designed and highly sophisticated airplanes became available. At the same time, railroads and highways were severely damaged and took years to repair. These conditions led to rapid growth in commercial aviation. Swissair, which was designated the national airline in February of 1947, later inaugurated a trans-Atlantic route from Geneva to New York using four-engine Douglas DC-4s.

European air fares were based on the British pound which was devalued in 1949. The devaluation affected business at Swissair so adversely that the government, which acquired a 30% stake in the company in 1947, was asked to render it assistance. The government purchased two DC-6Bs and leased them to Swissair; Swissair later purchased these DC-6Bs from the government in 1965.

In 1950 Swissair was reorganized into four divisions: Finance and Economics, Traffic and Sales, Engineering and Maintenance, and Operations. In addition, Dr. Walter Berchtold, director of the Swiss Federal Railways, was named the new president of the airline. In the next several years Swissair opened new routes to Lisbon and Dakar and from there across the Atlantic to Rio, Sao Paulo, Buenos Aires, Montevideo and Santiago. A route to the Far East included Bangkok, Hongkong, Manila and Tokyo.

Newer aircraft were becoming available which were capable of carrying more passengers at greater speeds. Swissair continued to update its fleet with these new aircraft which included propeller-driven DC-7s and Convair 440s, as well as DC-8 and Convair 880 passenger jets. Swissair also shared a number of Convair 990 and French Caravelle jetliners with SAS as part of a cooperation agreement signed in 1958. Later Swissair became one of the first airlines to order DC-9s, and Boeing 747 and DC-10 jumbo jets. By the winter of 1968–69 Swissair had a fleet comprised entirely of jet aircraft.

On September 6, 1979 a Swissair DC-8 en route from Zurich to New York was hijacked by terrorists from the Front for the Liberation of Palestine. The jet was forced to land at Dawson Field near Zerga in northwestern Jordan. The hijackers demanded the release of three terrorists being held in a Swiss prison. A settlement was reached and the terrorists were exchanged for the hostages. During this time, however, a civil war erupted in Jordan. The Swissair jet was allowed to leave, but in the fighting a TWA 707, a BOAC VC-10, and a Pan Am 747 were exploded at Zerga and completely destroyed.

Swissair concluded an agreement with SAS in 1958 and with KLM in 1968 which provided for the establishment of a joint maintenance pool. The privately-owned French airline UTA joined the group in 1970. Each company performed a specialized task in the maintenance of certain airplanes. Later the "KSSU Group" jointly negotiated with McDonnell Douglas for the purchase of 36 DC-10s.

Swissair's president, Dr. Berchtold, retired at the end of 1971 upon reaching the mandatory retirement age. He was succeeded by Armin Baltensweiler, an administrator with a strong background in aeronautical engineering. Swissair under Baltensweiler continued to expand and modernize its fleet. One of the airplanes it was particularly interested in purchasing was the A-310, produced by the European Airbus consortium. Swissair later ordered 10 of these airplanes.

The Swiss Federal Railways, one of the most efficient railroad systems in the world, opened a terminal at Zurich airport in 1980 providing passengers with access to local and intercity rail service directly from the airport. Swissair also concluded an agreement with the Swiss national domestic airline Crossair defining each company's respective area of activity and establishing areas of cooperation.

Swissair opened routes to Beijing and Shanghai in 1975. The commercial value of these destinations was minimal, but it reflected the Swiss government's interest in normalizing relations with all countries. In a similar move ten years later Swissair opened a route to Tirana, Albania, one of the poorest and most politically repressed nations in Europe.

Armin Baltensweiler, who served as president of the International Airline Transport Association from 1981 to 1982, was promoted to board chairman when the previous chairman, Fritz Gugelmann, reached the mandatory retirement age in 1982. As a result, the company's deputy president, Robert Staubli, was named president.

The airline encountered financial difficulties in 1982 due to declining passenger traffic and rising expenses. The previous year Swissair posted a record operating loss of $27.6 million. In an effort to lower costs Swissair reduced a number of customer services. Ekkehard Endrich, a Swissair executive, told *The Wall Street Journal* that "The results were OK on the financial side, but the echo from passengers was horrible." Even economy-class passengers began to complain about such things as plastic wine glasses and sandwiches (instead of hot meals). Consequently, Swissair looked to other areas to implement their austerity measures.

Swissair's employees are among the highest paid in the world, and even though they did offer to defer pay increases the airline decided instead to concentrate on keeping as many seats as possible filled with full-fare passengers. To this end, Swissair introduced a business-class service to appease passengers who complained that regular economy-class was too spartan and first-class was too expensive. It is interesting to note that Swissair does not offer cut-rate tourist fares.

Determined to avoid the popular notion that flight attendants are merely "waitresses in the sky," Swissair has developed strict selection and training programs for all flight personnel. Flight attendants are also required to be fluent in at least three languages. The meals served on Swissair are among the best available. Those which are not prepared in Swissair kitchens come from caterers whose work is supervised by Swissair chefs. In addition, Swissair has trained security people on most of its flights. They are provided by the Swiss government and are trained to deal with such terrorist acts as hijackings and bomb threats.

Swissair lost revenue on its passenger services from 1979 to 1983, but offset these losses with non-operating income from activities such as selling airplanes. Despite operating losses and the high cost of fuel, Swissair has remained profitable since 1954. Some of that success can be attributed to the airline's high aircraft utilization rate; all operational aircraft are transporting passengers.

Swissair has been described as the "bank that flies." In fact, dividends are so stable that the company's stock performs more like a bond. Swissair's finances are very conservatively managed. As a result, the airline has considerable liquid financial resources. If it is unable to secure a loan with favorable terms, it can easily make purchases with cash. In fact, over the last 15 years 80% of the company's investments have been funded from its cash flow.

Swissair's corporate strategy is long-term, usually five to ten years. However, "In U.S. terms," Staubli told *Forbes* magazine, "strategic planning is 'What am I doing next week?' " An example of Swissair's strategy is its decision to be the launch customer (first to order) for the new Fokker 100 passenger jet from Fokker Aircraft. Swissair was searching for a new jetliner to replace its aging and noisy DC-9s. Swissair is not as concerned with the resale value of its older jets as with the efficiency of the newer models becoming available. In some passenger markets the Fokker 100 can generate a profit with only 30% of its seats occupied. Government regulations in Switzerland require that a tax be paid on airplanes that produce a large amount of noise. And because the next generation of fuel-efficient airplanes (the McDonnell Douglas MD-91 and Boeing 7J7) are noisy "propfans," the Fokker 100 will continue to serve as Swissair's main medium capacity passenger jet.

In Swiss cities such as Zurich noise pollution is a serious ecological concern. Since the area around Klosten airport is residential, Swissair has spent a large amount of money to make engine maintenance procedure as quiet as possible. The 20-minute ground tests are conducted either in sound-proof hangars or in front of large "detuner" muzzles on the tarmac. Moreover, the use of thrust reversers (exhaust shields which redirect engine thrust forward after landing) is discouraged in favor of wheel brakes.

Another problem faced by Swissair is the perpetual fog which hovers over Zurich's Klosten and Geneva's Cointrin airports. During World War II the Swiss air force burned petroleum along the runways to lift the fog. Research in other fog lifting systems is currently in progress, but in the meantime Swissair is using sophisticated electronic devices to assist aircraft in finding the runway during low visibility.

The company's efforts to make its passenger business more profitable have been successful. In 1985 Swissair generated an operating surplus of over $11 million. In addition, the company's two vacation charter subsidiaries, Balair and CTA, turned in equally good performances. A third Swissair subsidiary, Swissair Associated Companies, Ltd., did well enough in 1985 to offer a dividend for the first time. The Associated Companies division controls (to various degrees) 29 subsidiaries of its own, including hotels, catering services, tour packagers, business consultants and insurance and real estate companies.

Principal Subsidiaries: Balair, Ltd., Basle (57%); Compagnie de Transport Aerien (CTA), Meyrin (57%); Swissair Associated Companies, Ltd., Basle. *Principal Subsidiaries* of Swissair Associated Companies, Ltd.: Swissair Nestle Hotels, Ltd. (51%); ICS Catering Services, Ltd.; Swissair Photo and Surveys Ltd.; Kuoni Travel, Ltd. (50.2%); Swissair Auditing, Ltd.; Uto AG (75%); Avireal AG; Meier und Wirz AG; Interconvention, Ltd.

Further Reading: Empires of the Sky: The Politics, Contests, and Cartels of World Airlines by Anthony Sampson, New York, Random House, 1984.

TEXAS AIR CORPORATION

4040 Capital Bank Plaza
Houston, Texas 77002
U.S.A.
(713) 658-9588

Public Company
Incorporated: June 11, 1980
Employees: 20
Sales: $4.407 billion
Market value: $1.272 billion
Stock Index: American

The Texas Air Corporation is not an airline, it is an airline holding company. In the decade after deregulation Texas Air has challenged many rules in the airline industry. A relatively young company, the story of Texas Air parallels the story of its founder Frank Lorenzo.

Frank Lorenzo was born and raised in New York City. He graduated from Columbia and received his MBA from Harvard. Due to his life-long fascination with aviation, he spent the next three years working in the financial departments of TWA and Eastern Airlines. In 1966 he and a colleague from Harvard, Robert J. Carney, established an airline consulting firm. In 1971 their company was appointed by the Chase Manhattan Bank to arrange a complex $35 million refinancing for the troubled Texas International Airlines. Lorenzo and Carney established a second company in 1969 called the Jet Capital Corporation, an aircraft clearing house and leasing organization. By 1971 Jet Capital had amassed $1.5 billion in equity, an amount sufficient to afford Lorenzo the opportunity to acquire Texas International, or "TXI."

In 1972 Jet Capital, which was largely owned by Lorenzo and Carney, absorbed Texas International. Lorenzo was named president and chief executive officer while Carney became chief financial officer. In 1977 a TXI vice president named Donald C. Burr introduced a new low-cost "peanut fare" to attract more passengers. The cut-rate scheme temporarily revived the airline and increased the cash flow, but it also invited challenges from competing airlines.

The following year Congress passed the Airline Deregulation Act which effectively eliminated government control over airline markets and fares. Donald Burr, who had recently been named president of TXI, resigned from the company along with several associates and established an airline called People Express. Based in Newark, New Jersey, People Express became synonomous with cut-rate air fares and no-frills service.

Meanwhile, Texas International initiated a cost-cutting campaign. Through Jet Capital the company replaced its older Convair jets with durable and efficient DC-9s. In addition, TXI eliminated cross subsidization (the practice of financing money-losing routes with profitable ones). Under deregulation Texas International was free to discontinue any unprofitable route it deemed necessary.

In June of the following year Lorenzo created a holding company for TXI called the Texas Air Corporation. The following September Texas Air created a new airline using excess TXI equipment. The new carrier, New York Airways, was created to lure business away from Eastern Airlines' profitable northeastern routes. It maintained lower labor costs because its employees were non-union. Burdened with a significant debt, but also possessing a large amount of cash generated from TXI and New York Air, Lorenzo launched his bid for another troubled airline, namely, Continental.

Lorenzo has described his success at takeover attempts as including an element of good timing. The strategy is to wait until a company with sufficiently high debt is found, which makes it easy to acquire. Then take note of its labor contracts. If these are due to expire, then purchase the company and rewrite the labor agreements in order to bring costs into line. If necessary, challenge the unions and hold out until they compromise their demands. This philosophy has provided Lorenzo with a reputation as a union breaker. It has also given him a reputation for saving failing airlines and, ultimately, many thousands of jobs.

With that in mind, Texas Air increased its holdings in Continental to 48.5% in March of 1981. By September the company had a majority interest in Continental and completed the takeover the following year. Shortly afterwards, TXI was merged with Continental and ceased to exist as a separate airline.

The new Continental Airlines had serious labor problems which threatened to close the airline. On September 24 Continental filed for reorganization under Chapter 11 of the Bankruptcy Code. At the same time it imposed new work rules and wages scales, and filed suit in court to have the old contracts voided. Operations resumed on September 27 despite thousands of workers on strike. According to Lorenzo, the strikers later "returned to Continental with a changed attitude" because they realized that "what they were getting from the unions was pure gibberish." In the end Frank Lorenzo had defeated Continental's unions.

In 1985 Lorenzo initiated a takeover of debt-ridden TWA. He was challenged, however, by well known corporate raider Carl Icahn. In the ensuing takeover attempt both parties drove up the value of TWA's stock. However, just when it appeared that Icahn was ready to cancel his bid and sell his TWA stock (at a large profit), he strengthened his position by enlisting the support of the airline's unions. Instead it was Lorenzo who canceled the bid. Texas Air earned $26 million from the "raid" it never intended to make, and Icahn found himself in charge of an airline he probably didn't intend to own.

Texas Air was at a disadvantage since it had no computerized reservation system (CRS) which travel agencies use to arrange itineraries. Continental was a member of the Neutral Industry Booking System, but that network couldn't compete with American Airline's Sabre (which dominates the market) or United Airline's popular Apollo system. To some extent it was for the CRS that Frank Lorenzo attempted a takeover of TWA. TWA operated a well-established CRS called Pars. If Texas Air could acquire TWA, then it could acquire Pars. With Pars the Texas Air system would be better able to compete with American and United.

The following year Texas Air turned its attention to Eastern Airlines. Eastern was in unstable financial condition. It had become a takeover target because of its enormous debt. Eastern's employees, who owned 25% of the company's stock, were "shell-shocked" by successive crises at the airline. They wanted a labor settlement and were willing to compromise, but only if offered a fair deal. Eastern also had an established CRS, called System One, or "SODA."

Texas Air's $676 million takeover bid for Eastern was approved by the Federal Aviation Administration (FAA) in 1986, despite that agency's protests that the new complexion of Texas Air would give it a near monopoly in certain markets. Conditional upon the FAA's approval was Eastern's pledge to sell a number of boarding gates in the northeast to Pan Am. With these gates Pan Am could more effectively compete with Eastern and New York Air on profitable shuttle flights between Washington, New York and Boston.

Barely a month later Donald Burr's People Express re-entered the scene. It attempted to sell its bankrupt Frontier Airlines unit to United Airlines, but the deal was rejected by the United Airlines pilot's union, which couldn't agree on a formula for absorbing the pilots from Frontier. People Express then offered itself for sale, with Frontier included. It was at this time that Frank Lorenzo made his offer of $125 million for People Express and $176 million for Frontier. (Texas Air subsequently purchased the two airlines at a lower price.) The settlement was initiated in September of 1986 and was later approved by

People Express stockholders and the FAA. Once again Donald Burr found himself working for Frank Lorenzo.

In January 1987 it was announced that People Express and New York Air would be absorbed by Continental Airlines. They would cease to exist as separate organizations, and their airplanes would be either repainted in the red and gold Continental pattern or sold. The consolidation left Texas Air with two separate airline companies which are roughly equal in size: Eastern Airlines which is characterized by excessive labor and operating costs (31% higher than Continental); and Continental Airlines which is characterized by low labor costs and profitability.

The new Texas Air Corporation controls over 20% of the domestic airline market. However, Lorenzo seems to have foreseen this. He told *Fortune* magazine that, "In the post deregulation era, first there was the new airline phase. Then came the consolidation and cost-cutting phase. Now we're heading into the megaline phase, which will leave the U.S. with five to eight major carriers, instead of a dozen or so today."

Becoming the largest of those "megalines" has put Texas Air $4.6 billion into debt. The ratio of debt to equity (net worth) is almost eight to one. This is not a problem for Lorenzo, who maintains that a substantial debt is "okay as long as you maintain significant liquidity and profitability." Nevertheless, for the time being Texas Air is not likely to acquire any more airline companies. Lorenzo was quoted in *The Wall Street Journal* as saying, "Three years from now you'll see the same Texas Air that you see today. Whatever growth we're going to have from this time on, we can satisfy internally."

Principal Subsidiaries: CCS Automation Systems, Inc.; Continental Airlines Corp.; Eastern Airlines, Inc.

Further Reading: Deregulation and the New Airline Entrepreneurs by J.R. Meyer and Clinton V. Oster, Jr., with Marni Clippinger, Cambridge, MIT Press, 1984; *Deregulating the Airlines* by E.E. Bailey, D.R. Graham, and D.P. Kaplin, Cambridge, MIT Press, 1985.

TRANS WORLD AIRLINES, INC.

605 Third Avenue
New York, New York 10158
U.S.A.
(212) 692-3000

Public Company
Incorporated: 1928 as Transcontinental Air Transport
Employees: 20,871
Sales: $3.145 billion
Market value: $608 million
Stock Index: New York

Trans World Airlines, or TWA, has a long and eventful history which dates back to the mid-1920's. From rather humble beginnings the airline has grown to serve airports on four continents and operate a complete round-the-world route system. Such well-known people as Charles Lindbergh, Amelia Earhart, Jack Frye and Howard Hughes were closely associated with the company. The company established a reputation for leadership and innovation and was widely regarded as one of the United States' leading airlines. In recent years, however, TWA has been forced to reduce its size in order to remain competitive.

TWA was established through the merger of several small airline companies in the 1920's. One of those small companies was Maddux Air Lines, which began a luxury passenger service between Los Angeles and San Diego on July 21, 1927. Maddux and a number of other carriers were organized by a group of investors who sought to establish a transcontinental passenger line using a combination of airplane flights and railroads. The group, Transcontinental Air Transport, hired Charles Lindbergh to survey the route. On July 7, 1929, TAT inaugurated the "Lindbergh Line." It began by boarding the Pennsylvania Railroad in New York in the evening. The next morning passengers flew from Columbus, Ohio to Waynoka, Oklahoma. From there the Sante Fe Railroad took them overnight to Clovis, New Mexico. From Clovis the passengers flew on to either Los Angeles or San Francisco. TAT offered coast-to-coast transportation in about 48 hours.

In the early days of commercial aviation, airlines made most of their money hauling mail for postal services. The United States Postmaster, Walter Folger Brown, was responsible for assigning three transcontinental airmail routes. American Airlines won the southern route,

Northwest Airlines won the northern route, and TAT was awarded the central route, but only on the condition that the company merge with Western Air Express. By the end of August of 1930, the two companies joined to form Transcontinental and Western Air Lines. In October the new company, "TWA," mastered the coast-to-coast route completely with airplanes, in light of the failure of the previous scheme. The trip was reduced to 36 hours and then later to 24.

Bill Boeing manufactured what were generally regarded as the best airplanes of the day; however, he refused to sell them to any company except his own. Excluded from the Boeing market, TWA's general manager Jack Frye solicited designs from a number of manufacturers. A small California operation run by Donald Douglas proposed an impressive design which outperformed Frye's basic specifications. TWA accepted Douglas' offer, and the first DC-1 was built. The DC-1, however, became obsolete before it could be mass produced. It was lengthened and otherwise improved. The new plane, the DC-2, was every bit as practical as the DC-1, but more difficult to fly.

Since there were breaches in pilot discipline and frequent equipment failures, a number of TWA airplanes crashed. At one point, the airline was losing 5% of its personnel annually to such accidents. The company was further troubled when the Roosevelt administration decided to cancel all government airmail contracts with private carriers in 1934. Many airlines depended on mail contracts for their profitability, and like them, TWA was adversely affected.

During this crisis TWA was sold to another group led by the Lehman Brothers and John Hertz of the Yellow Cab Company. The government decided to restore the airmail contracts a few months later and reopened the bidding. Curiously, companies that had held contracts before were barred from bidding. In order to get around this stipulation, the company responded by merely adding "Incorporated" to its name. It was re-awarded 60% of its original airmail system and, over a period of a few years, recovered the rest.

Under the new owners Jack Frye, a vice president and former Hollywood stunt pilot, was promoted to president. Under this new management TWA made major improvements in its training, flight efficiency and also upgraded its airport facilities. TWA employed directional "homing" radar and installed runway lights to facilitate night flying. The DC-3 became the company's new workhorse while business improved significantly.

In the 1930's airline companies became especially vulnerable to buyouts. General Motors acquired Eastern Airlines in 1933 and American Airlines was taken over by the auto magnate E.L. Cord. When General Motors purchased stock in TWA, the airline worried that it would be forceably merged with some other GM interest. In 1938, when TWA had fully recovered from the airmail fiasco, the Lehman/Hertz group sold the airline to another group of investors. During this time Frye personally convinced millionaire Howard Hughes to invest in TWA. It is very likely that Frye wanted Hughes' interest in the company so that he could help to defend it from any hostile takeover bids, ostensibly from GM.

Frye and Hughes respected each other as aviators and businessmen. Frye was a daredevil flier, a man totally enthralled with aviation and its possibilities. Hughes was an equally eccentric young man who was devoted to breaking aviation records. From his father he inherited ownership of the extremely lucrative Hughes Tool Company, the primary supplier of oil well drilling bits. Using his large fortune Hughes purchased 25% of TWA's stock. In 1941 he gained a controlling interest in the airline and later increased his share to 78%.

One of Hughes' first activities at TWA was to begin development of a new airplane in association with Lockheed. The airplane was the L-049 Constellation. While the Constellation was still being developed Hughes approved Frye's proposal to buy another new airplane, Boeing's 307 Stratoliner, for the interim. The Stratoliner had a pressurized cabin and was able to reach an altitude of 20,000 feet. As a result, it could fly over bad weather rather than be forced to navigate through it.

TWA was one of the first American airline companies to serve during the Battle of Britain in 1940. Even before the U.S. government had committed itself to the war effort, TWA was helping the Army Air Corps assist the British. When the U.S. became fully involved in 1941, TWA was assigned two military supply routes: the North Atlantic to Prestwick, Scotland; and the South Atlantic from Brazil to Liberia and points east.

The airline had the distinction of flying President Roosevelt and a number of other government personnel to and from various meeting places during the war, most notably, Casablanca. The war gave TWA the opportunity to upgrade and expand its facilities worldwide in anticipation of the allied victory. The U.S. War Department actively supported the airline's activities during the war. It would be fair to say that TWA served the country well and that it also profited handsomely. When TWA's military service was over it had flown 40 million miles for the Army, and was exposed to hundreds of new destinations.

The major overseas carriers after the war were Pan Am, American and TWA. All these airlines requested licensing for commerical use of much of their wartime network. TWA was granted two transatlantic routes to Europe, one via the "great circle" near the Artic, and the other via the Azores to the Mediterranean. From there TWA flew on to India, Southeast Asia and Japan.

Hughes and Frye had grandiose plans for the airline whose name they had changed to Trans World Airlines. The Constellation they helped to develop first flew in 1944, served briefly during the war, and was now in wide commercial use. However, it was at this time that the two men began to disagree. Hughes, who was injured in the crash of a test plane during the war, had changed. He had developed a very difficult personality and was known to hold up major business decisions for weeks while he agonized over minute details. He even disappeared for several days with a Constellation, only to turn up in Bermuda making endless test landings.

TWA didn't have enough business on its 21,000 miles of postwar international routes to generate a profit. Frye's efforts to rectify the problem collided with the plans of Hughes' financial manager Noah Dietrich. Dietrich charged that Frye had mismanaged the airline into a financial crisis and dangerous overexpansion. Hughes offered to provide money for TWA from the Hughes Tool Company, but only on the condition that Frye resign. In January of 1947 Frye left TWA.

TWA suspended many of its plans for further expansion. The headquarters was moved from Kansas City to New York. The man brought in to replace Jack Frye was Ralph Damon, who had previously been with American Airlines. Damon was an old-school engineer and airplane manufacturer. He was known for his careful attention to detail. Damon's numerous successes at the airline, however, were hindered by Hughes' continued interference and manipulation. Hughes insisted that the company reduce its advertising and promotion at a time when it was probably most needed. Regardless, TWA went off its postwar government subsidy in 1952, and a year later was healthy enough to declare a 10% stock distribution. Two years later Damon died at work, a victim of pneumonia and exhaustion. Doctors suggested that his poor health was exacerbated by the unrelenting pressure of running an airline for Howard Hughes.

Damon's successor was Carter Burgess, a former Assistant Secretary of Defense. Burgess lasted only 11 months, during which time he had never even met Hughes. TWA's next president was Charles Thomas. Thomas kept a low profile and followed all of Hughes' orders. He worked hard to keep the company in good financial condition.

When Thomas took over in the mid-1950's, all of the airlines were competing to be the first to have jetliners in their fleets. While the other leading companies were laying their plans and placing orders, TWA's order was delayed by Hughes' indecision over which airplane to buy, the Boeing 707 or the DC-8. Weeks later he finally decided to order 76 airplanes from Boeing and Convair. The jetliners would cost $500 million, much more than TWA could afford. Hughes' plan was to have his successful tool company purchase the planes and lease them to the airline. He wanted to keep TWA's profits low, channel money out of the Tool Company, and thereby avoid paying large penalty taxes.

However, a world oil glut hurt the Hughes Tool Company so badly that it was unable to pay for the new airplanes. As a result, TWA was forced to turn to a group of Wall Street investment bankers for financial support. The bankers were aware of Hughes' reputation as a successful tycoon, but also recognized that his interests were probably not the same as those of the airline. As a condition for their financial assistance, they required that Hughes' majority voting interest in TWA be placed in a trust under their control. Negotiations lasted until the bankers' deadline when Hughes finally conceded.

One of the first actions of the bankers was to install Charles Tillinghast as president of TWA. Tillinghast, a lawyer, promptly filed an antitrust suit against Hughes, alleging violations of the Sherman Act and the Clayton Anti-Monopoly Act, and accusing him of monopolizing aircraft purchases for his own benefit and to the detriment of TWA. Hughes responded to the bankers with a countersuit, charging that they swindled him out of his airline. The litigation continued for many years and cost TWA over $10 million. In the end, there was no clear decision by the courts.

Tillinghast reorganized the airline quickly and completely; management was restructured and pared down. TWA placed orders for newer B-727s and French-built Caravelles. In addition, Tillinghast attempted to change the company's public image. In light of its association with Hughes, TWA was regarded as being overly concerned with speed, glamour and style, and not enough with dependability, efficiency and safety.

TWA emerged from its troubles with stable and consistent profits through 1966, largely due to the direction of Charles Tillinghast. Ironically, the chief beneficiary of TWA's improvement was Howard Hughes. In 1966 he sold his stock in the airline for $546.5 million; he received $86 per share. Three years earlier TWA stock sold for only $7.50.

Aside from the large profits and the Hughes fiasco, the 1960's were important in another way. It was at this time that Tillinghast made perhaps his most important contribution. Hoping to provide the company with protection against the unpredictable and unstable airline business, he initiated a diversification program aimed at strengthening the airline's capital structure and cash flow.

TWA's diversification began in 1964 with a contract to provide base support services to the National Aeronautics and Space Administration at Cape Kennedy. In 1967 TWA purchased Hilton International, the operator of all Hilton Hotels outside the United States. Later, TWA acquired the Canteen Corporation, Spartan Food Services and Century 21, a real estate firm. The company was the first to diversify into non-airline businesses, and its timing was auspicious. The airline was suffering from the recession of 1970-71. In addition, TWA's B-747s and L-1011's were flying with nearly empty passenger cabins. The original decision to purchase the jetliners was made in response to Pan Am's huge orders, and not based on TWA's needs. As a result, the airline was plagued with overcapacity; it owned too many of the wrong kind of airplanes.

To make matters worse, TWA suffered a crippling six-week flight attendant's strike in 1973. By 1975 several payrolls could only be met by the immediate sale of six 747s to the Iranian Air Force. It was an unfortunate financial transaction for TWA (which sold the jetliners for about one-sixth their actual value), but the airline was desperate for cash. TWA was also losing money on its transpacific route which had been awarded during Johnson's presidency. For the first time in its history TWA's network stretched around the world, but even this would soon come to an end.

Amid these numerous crises Tillinghast retired. He was succeeded in January of 1976 by Carl Meyer. Meyer navigated the airline through a series of changes in the airline passenger market. Costs were reduced as international traffic expanded. The Airline Deregulation Act of 1978 allowed TWA to establish a more efficient dual hub system: St Louis for domestic traffic and New York for international traffic. Moreover, under Carl Meyer TWA reduced its fleet and its staff. The company purchased more fuel-efficient airplanes while selling the "gas-guzzlers" as soon as their value had completely depreciated.

On January 1, 1979, TWA created a holding company called the Trans World Corporation. "TWC" assumed parent ownership of the airline and the various subsidiaries. Four years later, a curious thing happened. Other airline holding companies have been known to sell their non-airline subsidiaries in periods of financial difficulties. When hard times came to Trans World Corporation, however, it sold the airline.

TWA was acquired by the corporate "raider" Carl Icahn early in 1986. Icahn's style of "raiding" usually involves buying up enough of a company's stock to threaten the other stockholders with a controlling interest, or takeover. This drives the price of the stock up to a point where the raider decides to sell, usually at a large profit. With TWA, however, Icahn was battling Texas Air Corporation. He enlisted the support of the airline's labor unions by pledging to honor their numerous demands. With the unions behind him, Icahn held out with a bid of $18.17 per share and found himself the new owner of the airline. Unfortunately, the company Icahn purchased was not fully prepared for the trauma of a corporate raid. As owner, however, Icahn was free to reorganize management as he thought necessary. He fired the popular president, Richard Pearson, and replaced him with Joseph Corr.

TWA's labor relations and economic condition deteriorated after Icahn took control. 4,000 striking flight attendants were more or less fired, which reduced the number of flights at a time when TWA should have experienced a period of growth. In response, Icahn purchased TWA's smaller competitor, Ozark Airlines. TWA had long considered acquiring Ozark, but it took Carl Icahn to finally commit the airline to the purchase. In accordance with the terms of the acquisition, TWA would receive four dozen older, but popular, jetliners which could be sold for cash. TWA also sold 50% of its successful IBM Pars computerized reservations system to Northwest Airlines. Joint use of the Pars system will introduce a significant degree of cooperation between TWA and Northwest. In addition, Northwest's payment for Pars in installments will guarantee TWA scheduled infusions of cash for some time to come.

At the present time TWA no longer operates its transpacific routes. Despite a brief rash of terrorism in 1985, TWA continues to fly in the Mediterranean, but has reduced its routes there. Instead, the airline has shifted its excess capacity to European and domestic routes, following the popular demand for alternative vacation spots.

Presently, TWA is in the middle of a series of changes: changes in identity, purpose, size and character. Icahn has surprised many of his critics by devoting the time and money necessary to return the airline to profitability. The conditions created by deregulation hinder any airline from carving out a niche which guarantees security or certainty. TWA is by no means an exception to these prevailing conditions.

Principal Subsidiaries: Trans World Airlines, Inc., lists no subsidiaries.

Further Reading: The U.S. Airline Industry: End of an Era by Paul Biederman, New York, Praeger, 1982; *Howard Hughes' Airline: An Informal History of TWA* by Robert J. Serling, New York, St. Martin's Press, 1983.

UNITED AIRLINES

P.O. Box 66100
Chicago, Illinois 60666
U.S.A.
(312) 952-4000

Wholly-owned subsidiary of Allegis, Inc.
  (formerly UAL, Inc.)
Incorporated: December 28, 1934
Employees: 43,800
Sales: $9.918 billion
Market Value: $2.966 billion
Stock Index: New York

United Airlines is one of the world's largest airline companies. United is a product of several mergers of airline companies which were originally founded in the 1920's. Through the years United experienced steady growth as a major domestic airline, pioneering the use of modern aircraft and equipment. After 34 years under the leadership of William "Pat" Patterson, United has recently suffered from inept management, inconsistent profits, and strong competition. Despite this, United has overcome many of its problems and achieved its long-time goal of expansion across the Pacific.

United Airlines was created in the early 1930's by Bill Boeing's aeronautic conglomerate in order to exploit demand for air transport and to serve as an immediate market for Boeing aircraft. At first United was similar to a consortium, involving the participation of several independent airline companies. One of those companies was Varney Air Lines, credited with being America's first commercial air transport company. Varnay's 460-mile network between Pasco, Washington and Elko, Nevada was linked with Boeing Air Transport, which operated an airmail service between Chicago and San Francisco. This route crossed Vernon Gorst's Pacific Air Transport network, which ran mail between Seattle and Los Angeles. The National Air Transport Company, operated by New York financier Clement Keys, connected with Boeing in Chicago, flying mail south to Dallas. Stout Air Services, which had the financial backing of Henry and Edsel Ford, operated an air service between Chicago, Detroit and Cleveland with Ford tri-motor airplanes.

These airline companies cooperated with Boeing, who manufactured aircraft in Seattle, and Pratt & Whitney, an aircraft engine manufacturer in Connecticut operated by Frederick Rentschler. Together these companies formed a "vertical" aeronautic monopoly, restricting the delivery of new aircraft to its constituent partners and devoting its resources to eliminating competition on its air services. The airline group became known as United Air Lines in 1931.

Among other things, the group was responsible for the introduction of air-to-ground radio and stewardesses. The radio improved communication and safety. The stewardesses, all eight of whom were registered nurses, were actually hired to allay passengers' fear of flying. A United executive at the time commented, "How is a man going to say he's afraid to fly when a woman is working on the plane?"

In 1934 National, Varney, Pacific and Boeing officially merged under the name United Air Lines Transportation Company. Pat Patterson, a banker and Boeing official, was placed in charge of the airline at the age of 34. That year, however, congressional legislation outlawed the type of monopoly United had formed with Boeing and Pratt & Whitney. The airline was forced to divorce itself from the conglomerate and subsequently became an independent company based at Chicago's Old Orchard (now O'Hare) airport.

In 1936, after several airplane accidents, a series of syndicated newspaper stories appeared which sensationalized the horror of airplane crashes. These stories incited a virtual state of panic which drove passengers back to railroads by the thousands. The airline industry was so deeply affected that many smaller companies were faced with bankruptcy. United responded by retaining a popular military test pilot named Major R.W. Schroeder, who was hired to oversee the company's implementation of new safety codes. With this action United helped to rebuild the public's confidence in air travel.

As one of the nation's larger airline companies United maintained a position of leadership in the industry, constantly demanding newer, more advanced aircraft. United funded many of the developmental costs of Douglas' DC-4, the first four-engine passenger plane. However, when the United States became involved in World War II, all DC-4s were devoted to the war effort before ever having carried a commercial passenger. The company's name was shortened to United Air Lines in 1943 and new plans were made for the airline in anticipation of the war's end. When the war ended two years later United redeployed its aircraft and resumed commercial flying.

In 1954 United became the first airline to employ flight simulators as part of its training and pilot testing programs. The following year United placed an order with Douglas aircraft for DC-8s, the airline's first passenger jetliners. Although Boeing's 707 jetliner actually became available a few months before the DC-8, United preferred the DC-8 because of its seating arrangement and other cost advantages.

In spite of United's favorable position in the industry, its competitors were growing rapidly and in many cases outperforming United. In short, the company was in a brief period of decline. However, when United acquired Capital Airlines in 1961 its network in the eastern U.S. was strengthened, helping the company to regain its position as the nation's number one airline.

United's president Pat Patterson retired in 1966. The man elected to replace Patterson was George Keck, an engineer who rose to the top position from the company's maintenance department. Keck was generally regarded as arrogant and secretive. It has been reported that his abrupt manner and authoritarian personality offended many people within the airline, as well as in the Civil Aeronautics Board and the company's unions. As a result, this severely limited his effectiveness and ability to manage the airline in many ways. In 1971 Keck was forcibly removed in what was described as a "corporate coup" instigated by two members of the company's board, Gardner Cowles and Thomas Gleed.

In 1967, during Keck's first year, United became the first airline to surpass $1 billion in annual revenue. On December 30, 1968 United created a subsidiary called UAL to operate its non-airline businesses. On August 1 of the following year United Air Lines became a subsidiary of UAL. Western International Hotels was acquired by the UAL holding company in 1970. Western's name was later changed to the Westin Hotel Company and linked to another UAL subsidiary which arranged travel packages. Westin's operations later grew to represent about one-twelfth of UAL's total business.

Eddie Carlson, who had a record of success while in charge of the Westin Hotel subsidiary, was named to succeed Keck as UAL's new chief executive officer. Carlson had a warm and personable demeanor which motivated everyone working for UAL, in every division and at every level. He flew 186,000 miles one year, inspecting the facilities and terminating the employment of what he regarded as redundant company bureaucrats. Despite his lack of experience in the airline industry, Carlson was successful in reversing the company's discouraging trends.

Carlson began to prepare a successor for his position in anticipation of his retirement. The man he chose to run the company was Richard Ferris, whom he had promoted from the Westin hotel subsidiary. When Carlson was named chairman of UAL and United, Ferris was made president of the airline. In 1978 Ferris was promoted to chairman of United and president of UAL. Carlson remained as chairman of UAL until his retirement in 1983.

Notwithstanding efforts to improve the relationship the company has with its unions (which deteriorated during the leadership of George Keck), United remains on cautious terms with its employee representatives. In 1976 the airline agreed to a million dollar pay-back settlement with women and minority employees in an anti-discrimination suit. In 1979 United lost $72 million, largely as the result of a month-long labor strike that year.

Under the leadership of Richard Ferris the airline reached a compromise with its pilots' union. The agreement guaranteed that layoffs would not be authorized in return for more flexible work rules. The lower operating costs which resulted from the agreement were passed on to the consumer with the formation of a discount air service called "Friendship Express." The service was also intended to allow the company to more effectively compete with cut-rate airlines such as People Express and New York Air.

In 1978 and 1979 UAL continued to diversify its operations when it acquired Mauna Kea Properties and the Olohana Corporation in Hawaii for $78 million. As resort developments, these acquisitions allowed UAL to take more advantage of the tourist business in the airline's most popular destination.

In 1978 Congress passed the Airline Deregulation Act. Under the new legislation airline companies were free to enter new passenger markets without prior government approval. United was the first major airline to support deregulation. When the Act was passed, however, United was forced to scale down its operations in order to compete profitably. Richard Ferris later commented, "If we did make a mistake, it was in not recognizing the intensity of pricing competition that deregulation would bring, and getting structured to cope with it." Executives with smaller airline companies expressed their fear that the larger airlines would concentrate their resources on contested markets with the goal of forcing the smaller companies out of business. One executive poignantly remarked, "What Ferris wants is to have us for lunch, and I don't mean at McDonald's."

In 1985 United acquired Pan Am's Asian traffic rights for $715.5 million. The agreement also included 18 jets, 2700 Pan Am employees, and all of Pan Am's facilities in Asia. The addition of 65,000 route miles and 30 destinations to United's network made other acquisitions pale in comparison. Ferris said, "We could spend two or three lifetimes and never get all the traffic [rights] we're buying from Pan Am."

The sale of these routes helped Pam Am out of a short-term financial crisis. United is better suited than Pan Am to operate the Pacific routes because of its well-established network in the western U.S. It may, however, be years before the acquisition pays for itself. The most unique feature about the transfer of these routes is that they were sold as an independent business entity, as if the routes were a subsidiary. The Pan Am routes agreement also provides insight into Richard Ferris' long-term plans for United.

Ferris joined the board of directors at Procter & Gamble in 1979 with the intention of studying its successful marketing formulas and applying them at UAL. He restructured UAL in order to reduce costs and improve marketing. Since 1982 costs have been controlled, productivity has risen, and profits have stabilized. Part of the new marketing strategy involves the establishment of additional passenger transfer points, or "hubs." In addition to its main facility at Chicago's O'Hare airport, United operates secondary hubs in Denver, San Francisco, and Dulles airport near Washington, D.C.

In 1986 United's purchase of the bankrupt Frontier Airlines unit from People Express was canceled when the United pilot's union failed to reach an agreement with management over the manner in which Frontier pilots were to be absorbed by United. The $146 million acquisition promised to ease competition at Denver's Stapleton airport, where United, Frontier and Continental were engaged in a costly battle for passengers. People Express closed Frontier in August of 1986 and declared it bankrupt. Less than a month later People Express was acquired by Frank Lorenzo's Texas Air Corporation, and Frontier was liquidated. The following February People Express was absorbed into Continental Airlines. Still competing with United in Denver, Texas Air now controls airlines with 20% of the domestic airline market, compared to United's 16% share.

United has started to replaced its fleet of B-727s with newer wide-body B-767s on more heavily traveled routes. After 25 years United is the last major airline company which still operates DC-8s. Federal regulations on noise pollution, however, have forced United to replace the engines on its DC-8s with quieter models. In addition to these aircraft, United flies large numbers of B-737s, B-747s, and DC-10s.

United lost its number one rank in passenger volume to American Airlines in 1985. In spite of this apparent setback, United's immediate prospects are very good. Early in 1987 it was decided to change the name of UAL in order to distance it from the initials of its airline subsidiary. UAL was renamed "Allegis," a curious computer-generated choice which combined portions of the words "allegiance" and "aegis." With an airline, a hotel chain, the Hertz Rent-a-car company, and the Apollo computerized reservations system to coordinate them all, Allegis has become an integrated full-service travel company.

Shortly afterwards, Allegis encountered a number of problems with Ferris' strategy to create a travel conglomerate. Several investor groups noted that Allegis' subsidiaries would be worth more as separate companies than as divisions of Allegis. On May 26, Coniston Partners announced that it had acquired a 13% share of Allegis stock, and that it would be purchasing more in an attempt to gain control of the board and remove Richard Ferris. The Allegis board initiated an anti-takeover defense in which the Boeing Company was given a 16% stake ($700 million) in the company in return for a $2.1 billion aircraft order. The defense failed in June, forcing Ferris and several other board members to resign. The new board appointed Frank A. Olson chairman of Allegis, and later as president and chief executive office of United. The board also announced its intention to sell Westin, Hilton International, and Hertz, in addition to a portion of its Apollo reservations system. The board also expressed a desire to change Allegis' name back to UAL.

Principal Subsidiaries of Allegis: United Airlines, Inc.; Westin Hotel Company; Mauna Kea Properties, Inc.; The Hertz Corp.

Further Reading: The U.S. Airline Industry: End of an Era by Paul Biederman, New York, Praeger, 1982.

USAIR GROUP

1911 Jefferson Davis Hwy.
Arlington, Virginia 22202
U.S.A.
(703) 892–7000

Public Company
Incorporated: March 5, 1937 as All American
Aviation, Inc.
Employees: 13,789
Sales: $4.407 billion
Market value: $1.222 billion
Stock Index: New York

In 1978 Allegheny Airlines conducted a passenger survey in which customers were asked to rate the different airline companies. Included in the list of choices was a non-existent airline called "USAir." The customers rated USAir highly, in fact, it was even ranked ahead of Allegheny. After deregulation, when Allegheny was searching for a new name that didn't give the impression of being a small and regional airline, it chose USAir.

The company was originally incorporated in Delaware in 1937 as All American Aviation by a glider pilot named Richard C. du Pont, of the Delaware du Ponts. On May 12, 1939 the airline began to deliver mail around the mountains of Pennsylvania and West Virginia. Since many communities did not have airstrips, the company devised a system employing hooks and ropes that enabled the mailplane to drop off one mailbag and pick up another without landing. Du Pont's method brought regular mail service to a number of once-isolated communities and was widely imitated. Later, All American began transporting passengers on its limited network. Despite the addition of more destinations the airline remained a small operation, serving many remote communities throughout the Alleghenies.

When the United States became involved in World War II, du Pont went to work on the Army's glider program in California. In 1943 du Pont was killed in a glider crash. The mailbag snare he developed, however, was adapted by the Army's Air Corps and used to rescue downed pilots behind enemy lines. In addition, he helped to develop a glider which could be picked up by an already airborne airplane. This system was used in the evacuation of Allied troops from the Remagen beachhead in Germany.

After the war the company changed its name to All American Airways. On January 2, 1953 the name was changed again to Allegheny Airlines. That same year the government chose Allegheny to operate shuttle services between smaller eastern cities and major cities or destinations served by larger airline companies. Allegheny was provided a subsidy to operate these services to communities which otherwise would have had no air service.

The company experienced a period of healthy growth for several years in the 1950's and 1960's. The old DC-3s it was flying were replaced with new Convair 440s, Convair 540s and Martin 202s. The operations and maintenance base was also relocated from Washington, D.C. to a modern complex in Pittsburgh. Allegheny began buying jets in 1966. On July 1, 1968 the company acquired Lake Central Airlines and on April 12, 1972 purchased Mohawk Airlines. By the mid-1970's Allegheny had become a major regional airline.

Concurrent with this steady growth, Allegheny was obliged to operate the government-assigned "feeder" services. Starting in 1967, however, Allegheny began subcontracting these routes to smaller independent carriers. This arrangement satisfied Allegheny's obligations to the Civil Aeronautics Board. The independents were able to make a profit on the routes because they had lower costs, they were not unionized, and their equipment was better suited for the rural "puddle jumper" routes. The CAB was more than pleased to release Allegheny from its obligations (and discontinue the subsidies) and therefore supported the company's subcontracting arrangements. Since the independents fed passengers mostly to Allegheny, the company itself had become a large regional airline.

Even as a larger airline, however, passengers had a particularly low opinion of Allegheny. It became widely known for its nickname "Agony Air." In many cities the airline had a monopoly on air service, so there was no incentive to improve, or even maintain, a certain level of customer service. The company's on-time record was poor, its customer service was described as unpleasant, and flight cancellations were common.

Fortunately for Allegheny its chairman and president, Edwin Colodny, had previously served with the CAB. This provided him with the experience and knowledge of how to acquire and protect the company's right to fly to certain destinations, and how to successfully raise fares. Before any of his policies could be put into effect, however, the Airline Deregulation Act of 1978 was passed. Vigorously opposed to the passing of this Act, Colodny argued that permitting all airlines to freely enter into any market deregulation would allow the larger airlines, with their vast resources, to raid markets served by smaller companies with the intention of driving them out of business. This did not happen. Instead, the larger airlines used their new freedom under deregulation to contend with their more immediate competition, namely, each other. Regional operators like Allegheny were virtually unaffected. But deregulation did have an effect on the regional air carriers. For the first time Allegheny was allowed to operate long haul routes to Texas and the West Coast. With such an opportunity, the company clearly required an improvement upon its "Agony Air" reputation. Colodny decided to begin with a new name. He chose

"USAir" over several other names, including "Republic Airlines" (which was later used by the old Minneapolis-based North Central Airlines). Allegheny officially became USAir on October 28, 1979.

Under the name of USAir the company launched an advertising campaign which claimed that they "carry more passengers than Pan Am, fly to more cities than American, and have more flights than TWA." This coincided with the inauguration of new routes to the southwest. These new services were originally intended to prevent company jets from remaining idle during the traditional winter slump in the northeastern markets. In addition, USAir planned to implement a Pittsburg–London route, but withdrew the application due to fears of "overambition." According to Colodny, "overexpansion is the most tempting of all possible sins of airline managements under deregulation. And, if overdone, it can result in a serious bellyache. In designing a route system, a carrier must limit its ego." As a result, the airline has concentrated on consolidating its current markets and strengthening its central Pittsburg hub.

Colodny claims that two-thirds of American air travel is in markets under 1000 miles. USAir has made it a point to avoid "overambition" and has instead concentrated on developing these local markets. However, the short duration of these flights means that the airplanes must make more take-offs and landings. The frequency of these take-off and landings, in turn, increase maintenance costs. This explains why there is so little difference in the price of a ticket for a 100-mile flight and a 400-mile flight.

Presently classified as a "major/trunk" carrier, the company flies DC-9s, B-727s, 737s, and even a few British Aerospace BAC-111s. The 111s are expensive to fly but inexpensive to maintain. Recently, USAir has ordered new unpainted jets except for the logo and markings, to lower aircraft weight and save money on fuel and maintenance.

The airline's on-time record has significantly improved as a result of strict attention to scheduling and the "first flight of the day" standard, which prevents late starts from pushing back the whole day's schedule. The airline has also perfected a system of efficient bad-weather maintenance. These measures have contributed to what campany officials claim is the second lowest number of complaints to the CAB (Delta is first) based on passenger volume.

In order to remain competitive with other airline companies which are merging into even larger companies, the USAir Group announced in December 1986 that it would be acquiring Pacific Southwest Airlines (PSA) for $400 million. The announcement surprised many industry analysts because USAir's predominantly East Coast airline network has few integration points with PSA which is concentrated along the West Coast. PSA is operated as a subsidiary of the USAir Group and will later be absorbed by USAir. The merger increased the amount of traffic on USAir by 40% and gave USAir landing rights in a number of cities on the West Coast.

USAir is presently in a strong financial position, having obtained and protected a significant share of passenger traffic in its various markets. Barring unforeseen difficulties with its normal but "industry-volatile" debt-equity ratio, a labor dispute, or a competitor's attempt to penetrate one of its markets, the airline should continue to experience steady growth and consistent profits.

Principal Subsidiaries of USAir Group: USAir; Pacific Southwest Airlines, Inc.

Further Reading: Airlines of North America by Robert Shives and William Thompson, Sarasota, Florida, Crestline, 1984.

AUTOMOTIVE

AMERICAN MOTORS CORPORATION

BAYERISCHE MOTOREN WERKE A.G.

BENDIX CORPORATION

CHRYSLER CORPORATION

CUMMINS ENGINE CORPORATION

DAIMLER-BENZ A.G.

DANA CORPORATION

EATON CORPORATION

ECHLIN INC.

FEDERAL-MOGUL CORPORATION

FIAT GROUP

FORD MOTOR COMPANY

FRUEHAUF CORPORATION

GENERAL MOTORS CORPORATION

HONDA MOTOR COMPANY LTD.

MACK TRUCKS, INC.

NAVISTAR INTERNATIONAL CORPORATION

NISSAN MOTOR COMPANY, LTD.

PACCAR INC.

PEUGEOT S.A.

RÉGIE NATIONALE DES USINES RENAULT

ROBERT BOSCH GmbH.

ROLLS-ROYCE MOTORS LTD.

SAAB-SCANIA A.B.

SEALED POWER CORPORATION

SHELLER-GLOBE CORPORATION

TOYOTA MOTOR CORPORATION

VOLKSWAGEN A.G.

A.B. VOLVO

American Motors Corporation

AMERICAN MOTORS CORPORATION

American Center
27777 Franklin Road
Southfield, Michigan 48034
U.S.A.
(313) 827-1000

Public Company
Incorporated: July 29, 1916 as Nash Motors Company
Employees: 22,500
Sales: $3.4 billion
Market Value: $525 million
Stock Index: New York

In 1953 two leading manufacturers of automobiles, Hudson Motor Car Company and Nash-Kelvinator Corporation, suffered sudden, serious setbacks in their positions in the United States car market. Both firms were confronted with sharp reversals in their financial performances, and in the following year their separate corporate existences were brought to an end. On May 1, 1954 Hudson Motor Car Company merged with Nash-Kelvinator Corporation to form the American Motors Corporation.

The merger, which was widely viewed as an essential move in a struggle for survival by the relatively small independent manufacturers of automobiles, did not provide immediate solutions to the problems of the companies; indeed, it seemed that the new firm might not be able to survive.

From 1954 through 1957 the company did not report a profit. For each of its first four annual reports, American Motors recorded losses before tax adjustments varying from a low of approximately $12 million to a high of almost $29 million per year, the firm's largest loss having occurred in 1956. The situation became so serious that officials of the company publicly acknowledged that American Motors could not survive very long if such heavy losses continued.

Although they came close to failure in their automotive operations, American Motors survived the ordeal. In fact, the company staged one of the most impressive comebacks in the history of American business, earning more than $25 million before taxes in 1958, $105 million in 1959, and equally large profits in the following years.

American Motors Corporation began business May 1, 1954 under the leadership of George Mason. However, less than six months later Mr. Mason died suddenly at the age of 63. On October 12, 1954 George Romney, who was second in command at the firm, was elected chairman of the board of directors, president, and general manager of American Motors Corporation. Romney took control at a crucial and difficult time. Competition within the industry was at an all-time high and American Motors had had little time to forge an effective management team from the personnel of the two previously separate and ailing companies.

For several months after the merger American Motors continued to produce the 1954 Hudson and Nash models that had been previously introduced. Late in 1954, however, the firm brought out new Nash and Hudson models based on the former Nash body shell. The previous Hudson bodies were dropped entirely, and the 1955 Hudson models were really Nashes with slight exterior differences. With the introduction of its 1956 models in December of 1955, American Motors began to place greater emphasis on its Rambler series. The 1956 Rambler models were described as "completely new" in that they were small-sized, and were considered the new "basic volume" car of the firm. Separate facilities were provided at Kenosha, Wisconsin for the assembly of the Rambler model. During the same time, the Milwaukee plant was used for the assembly of Nash and Hudson models using the full-sized body shell. However, even though Rambler had begun to show greater sales promise, the executives at American Motors were undecided as to whether the company should return to the role of a specialist producer.

Such an image of the company was acknowledged by George Romney himself. While promoting his firm's small-sized Rambler models, Romney predicted, "There will be a smaller percentage of mechanized dinosaurs in the American driveways of the future. However, if you still want them, we've got them, too, built a better way – our dinosaurs are smoother, safer, and roomier."

In September of 1957 American Motors reported a further consolidation of its operations. The full-sized Nash and Hudson models, whose sales had been disappointing since the merger, were discontinued. They were replaced by the Rambler Ambassador, which used many of the basic body parts of the regular 108-inch wheelbase Rambler line on a 117-inch wheelbase car. The 108-inch wheelbase was first introduced on Ramblers in 1954. In addition, the earlier 100-inch wheelbase model was again put into production in late 1957 and reintroduced in January 1958 as the Rambler American. This was probably the only time that a discontinued car was ever reintroduced. It used the basic body of the earlier 100-inch wheelbase Rambler which had been discontinued after 1955, but it had altered hood, rear deck, and fenderlines. Thus, by the end of 1957, American Motors was still producing cars using different basic bodies, but they were all known as Ramblers, including the Rambler, Rambler Ambassador, and Rambler American. In late 1957, three years after the merger, American Motors reported that its manufacturing consolidation program was complete. The firm's automotive lines had been simplified, and company officials believed that significant savings had been made possible through the elimination of duplicate facilities.

From 1954 through 1957, then, extensive changes were

imposed upon the combined Nash and Hudson organizations. As a result, American Motors finally became a profitable operation. In 1958 the company was able to show its first annual profit. Moreover, it was the only domestic automobile manufacturer to improve its position in 1958. Factory sales of its cars rose almost 60% and dollar sales of the firm rose more than $108 million above the amount of 1957. An operating profit of $25 million was obtained. American Motors became the pacesetter for the industry, leading the way with its compact car and enjoying exceptional profitability ratios. The company's Kenosha plant became the most used assembly plant in the industry. And, although the other domestic firms followed its product leadership into the compact car class, American Motors' sales remained at high levels.

In abandoning the broader line, which it initially had sought through the merger, American Motors based its strategy for survival and prosperity "on cars that are distinctive and unique – cars that do not compete head on with automobiles of the Big Three" (Ford, Chrysler and General Motors). The improvement in company sales was a direct result of the rising popularity of its Rambler model.

Credit for the turnaround in the firm's fortunes must also be given to the executives at American Motors. Although many managers had favorable offers of higher pay from other companies, they remained loyal. The five highest paid executives even accepted a voluntary reduction in salary averaging 25.9% in 1957. Much of this perseverance must be attributed to the corporation's charismatic leader, George Romney.

In 1956, Romney was appointed chairman of a citizen's committee on education. The exposure he received made him popular with the many Americans who sought a strong leader able to address pressing national issues and command bipartisan support. When he resigned as President of American Motors in 1962, Romney successfully ran for the governorship of Michigan. Later, he was to become a widely respected candidate for president, losing to Richard Nixon in the 1968 Republican primaries.

The Rambler models, perhaps more than any other single factor, made American Motors a profitable company. They won acclaim from many sources including, among others, selection as a "best buy" by *Consumer Reports*, and as "car of the year" by *Motor Trend* magazine. Even more important was the acclaim the car received from consumers.

The decade of the 1970's found American Motors once again in the position of fighting for its existence. Not only were its car sales running 30% behind those of the previous decade, but it was burdened with an aging product line, a shortage of cash to finance model changes, and growing competition in the small car market. Whereas its Gremlin and Pacer had once dominated the small car market, strong competition from other car makers, especially Chrysler, now jeopardized the company's market share. Successive chairmen, such as Roy Abernathy, Roy Chapin, William Lundberg, and Gerald Meyers, seemed unable to stem the tide against them, and between 1974 and 1978 the company watched its share of total U.S. sales shrink from 3.8% to 1.2%. It was only

through profits from the company's Jeep and AM General (bus and government vehicles) divisions that AMC offset losses in auto operations.

By the late 1970's it was clear to most industry analysts that American Motors needed a partner who could fund a badly needed line-by-line overhaul. In 1978 it was announced that the company would link up with Renault in a reciprocal agreement to sell and eventually build cars designed by the French company. The new strategy initially had a positive impact. By 1982, when the merger actually took place (Renault acquired a 46% stake), American Motors' automotive operations reported net profits of $38.8 million, compared with losses totaling $89 million in the three previous years. But this did not last long. By 1985, sales of its sub-compact cars, especially the Alliance and Encore, had started to decrease and Renault had lost approximately $1 billion of its own money. Most of American Motors' profit continued to come from its popular four-wheel drive Jeep specialty vehicles, not from its hard won 2% share of the U.S. passenger car market.

The burden of such figures would fall on Jose Dedeurwaerder, a Belgian who controlled American Motors' operations as president from 1982 to 1986. An engineer and 23-year veteran of Renault, Dedeurwaerder is credited with streamlining many of the company's arcane management techniques. He also instituted important improvements in plant layout and cost and quality control.

Yet by 1986 the struggle to avert bankruptcy remained formidable. Leadership of the company passed to Joseph E. Cappy whose conservative management promised a return to profitability. By striking a favorable agreement with the United Auto Workers, by reducing costs by 25%, and by improving the product development, company executives predicted 1987 would bring a turnaround in American Motors' performance. But the prediction was not fulfilled. The company's share of the U.S. car market has continued to decline, operations continue to post losses, and production has stabilized at about 49% of capacity.

Early in 1987, the Chrysler Corporation offered to buy the 46% stake in American Motors held by Renault. The final bid, enhanced from $4 per share to $4.50 per share, gained the approval of American Motors Corporation's board of directors. The total purchasing price will ultimately depend on the amount of royalties paid to Renault for the sale of its AMC Jeep and Premier models. The royalties, which will be paid through 1991, could increase the bidding price to $350 million. Although the merger offer is a friendly one, the position of Joseph Cappy, company president and chief executive officer, remains uncertain.

Principal Subsidiaries: American Motors Sales Corp.; American Motors Realty Corp.; American Motors Leasing Corp.; Evart Production Co.; Coleman Products Co.; American Motors Pan American Corp.; Jeep Corp.; McDonald Molding, Inc.; Mercury Plastics Co.; Rantoul Products, Inc.; American Motors (Canada) Inc. Additional subsidiaries and affiliates include American Motors

Corporation de Venezuela, CA; American Motors Financial Corp.; Arab American Vehicles Co.; Beijing Jeep Corp.; Jeep Australia Pty., Ltd.; Jeep de Venezuela, SA; Mahindra & Mahindra, Ltd.; Vehiculos Automotores Mexicanos, SA.

Further Reading: The Automobile Industry since 1945 by Lawrence J. White, Cambridge, Harvard University Press, 1971; *The Decline and Fall of the American Automobile Industry* by Brock Yates, New York, Empire Book, 1983.

BAYERISCHE MOTOREN WERKE A.G.

BMW Haus, Petuelring 130
Postfach 40 02 40
Federal Republic of Germany
(89) 38951

Public Company
Incorporated: 1917
Employees: 54,000
Sales: DM 15.6 billion (US$8.065 billion)
Market Value: DM 8.719 billion (US$4.490 billion)
Stock Index: Vienna Berlin Stuttgart Bremen
Düsseldorf Frankfurt Hamburg Hanover Munich

Bayerische Motoren has not always been known as a car maker. It was originally an aircraft engine manufacturer and is also a major producer of motorcycles. In terms of annual car production, the 71-year old firm is rated sixteenth worldwide. But overall, BMW is the seventh largest automobile company, and its growth rate in the late 1980's is more vigorous than most of its competitors.

Although not officially established until 1917, BMW can trace its heritage back to 1913 when Karl Rapp started to build aircraft engines for Austria in anticipation of World War I. Rapp-Motorenwerke's top customer was Franz Josef Popp, general inspector of Emperor Franz Josef's army. Popp hired Max Friz, an aircraft engine designer from Austro-Daimler; together in Munich they established Bayerische Werke based on the engineering ideas of Rapp.

Popp, an engineer, took charge of administration while Friz served as senior designer. A third associate, Camillo Castiglioni from Vienna, looked after the accounts. The trio began their enterprise at the old Rapp factory, then moved to the Moosacher Strasse factory, also in Munich, in 1918. There Friz designed and built the company's first aircraft engine.

At the end of the war, Bayerische Motoren turned to the production of train brakes, and when in 1922 the Moosacher Strasse factory was sold to Knorr-Bremse, BMW employees moved to another Munich location, the former Ottowerke plant on the Lerchenauer Strasse. (Ottowerke had been founded by Gustav Otto, son of Nikolaus August Otto, inventor of the four-stroke internal combustion engine.)

Despite the 1923 Treaty of Versailles' ban on aircraft production in Germany, Bayerische Motoren continued to operate and thrive. Their 12-cylinder engines were used on international flights by ace pilots such as Lpuschow, Gronau, and Mittelholzer, and more than a thousand BMW VI engines were sold to the Soviet Union. Production continued to rise steadily through the 1930's.

The company's interests in motorcycle manufacture developed rapidly in the early 1920's. The first model, the R32, consisted of a flat twin engine and drive shaft housed in a double-tube frame, with valves in an inverted arrangement to keep the oil clean. Ernst Henne, riding an R32, broke the world motorcycle speed record at 279.5 kph (173.35 mph) in 1929; his record held until 1937.

In 1928 Bayerische Motoren acquired the ailing Fahrzeugwerke Eisenach, and a year later the Dixi, BMW's first luxury car, was produced at the Eisenach site. The Dixi won the 1929 International Alpine Rally, covering the mountain route in five days. But despite its success, the Dixi created major financial problems for BMW, and a merger with Daimler-Benz was discussed in detail. Meanwhile, a partnership contract was agreed; Dr. Wilhelm Kissel, Daimler-Benz's chairman, and Popp, at Bayerische Motoren, joined each other's supervisory boards. However, a smaller 6-cylinder model of the Dixi proved to be a most effective competitor in the Daimler-Benz market, and Popp dropped the merger plans.

Another Dixi, the DA2, based on the 6-cylinder model, was introduced in Berlin in July 1929. It featured improved handling, better brakes, and a more attractive interior. Despite the stock market crash in October 1929 and the subsequent depression (17,000 German firms were forced into bankruptcy, including one of Bayerische Motoren's shareholders, the Danat-Bank) the company avoided financial disaster. 5,390 DA2's, the "mini car at a mini price," were sold in 1929; this was increased the following year to 6,792 cars.

When Hitler assumed power in 1933, Bayerische Motoren, along with other German automotive companies, was required to manufacture airplane engines for the new air force (Luftwaffe). In the same year, BMW acquired licenses to produce the 525 bhp Hornet engine and to develop small radial engines for sports planes. The company also launched its 300 automobile series with the 303, the first car to feature the long-familiar "kidney" shape. Lighter than comparable models, the 303 was 50% more powerful. Its success encouraged BMW to introduce two popular compact sports models, the 315 and the 319. Early in 1936, the 326 model was launched in both sedan and convertible versions. The all-steel bodied 327 was also introduced that year, and in September Popp unveiled the standard-production 328, which proved to be the fastest sports car of its time; it won the Italian Mille Miglia race in 1938.

The company's rising production of aircraft engines and armored motorcycles resulted in an expansion of facilities at the Milbertshofen plant on the Lerchenauer Strasse which had previously been devoted to motorcycle manufacturing. A 1939 edict of the German Ministry of Aviation required Brandenburgische Motorenwerke to merge with Bayerische Motoren, and a new factory, Allach, was constructed with government money. The Allach buildings, tucked away in woods near Munich, were constructed at a distance from one another to minimize damage in the event of an air raid.

BMW played an important role in the German war effort and at the height of Nazi domination the company operated plants as far afield as Vienna and Paris. In two crucial areas of military technology, BMW was in the vanguard: with the guidance of Dr. Hermann Oestrich of the German aviation test center, the company developed the 003, the first jet engine to enter standard production; and under conditions of intense secrecy, it opened a rocket testing and production plant at Zuhlsdorf.

Intent on maintaining a plentiful supply of military aircraft, the Nazi government instructed Bayerische Motoren in 1941 to halt all motor car production. Popp, who had been at the company helm for 25 years, refused. He was forced to resign and narrowly avoided internment in a concentration camp. It was left to his successor, Fritz Hille, to institute Bayerische Motoren's automatic system of monitoring production—a mechanical forerunner of the computer.

After the defeat of the Nazis, Allied Command ordered the dismantling of many BMW facilities; at the same time, reconstruction of the now-divided Germany got underway. In the immediate post-war years, few West Germans were in a position to buy cars, but by 1948, the year of German currency reform, there was a substantial need for motorcycles. BMW produced a new model out of spare parts provided by dealers. Known as the R24, this motorcycle was put into production and in 1949 almost 10,000 machines came off the assembly line. 1950's production increased to 17,000, 18 percent of which were exported.

Bayerische Motoren's return to car manufacturing in 1951 proved to be a disappointment. The 501 model, a 6-cylinder conservatively styled car with few technical innovations, was not well-received; neither was its successor, the 502, which featured a V8 engine. The company pinned its hopes on the 503 and 507 models, highlights of the 1955 Frankfurt Motor Show. Both cars were designed by Albrecht Graf Goertz and were powered by Alex von Falkenhausen engines. However, they proved to be too expensive for the majority of West German motorists. To add to BMW's woes, their motorcycle sales dropped drastically and the Allach factory had to be sold.

The company's fortunes revived a little in the late 1950's during the era of the "bubble car." Their Isetta mini-car, a mere 2.29 meters (7.51 feet) in length and fitted with motorcycle engines, reached a speed of 53 mph. Customer interest in the machine was short-lived, but it enabled BMW to recoup some of its recent losses.

To capitalize on the increasing market for cars—albeit inexpensive ones—Bayerische Motoren introduced the rear-engined 700 LS model in August 1959. Available as a coupé or convertible, and powered by motorcycle engines, the 700 LS was initially unprofitable. By 1965, however, when annual sales reached 18,000 units, the car had become the company's first long-term success of the post-war years.

BMW's fortunes further improved with the launching of their 1500 model. Indeed, this first "sports sedan" secured the company's prominence in the automotive market for the foreseeable future. The balance sheet showed a profit of DM 3.82 million in 1963 and a 6 percent dividend was paid. By the end of the decade, the company's long-suffering shareholders were much happier. Nine more models had been introduced, sales for 1969 set a new record of 144,788 cars, and turnover was up to DM 1.4 billion.

The 1970's, a period of dramatic growth in Western Europe, proved to be a time of significant reorganization and development at BMW. All motorcycle production was moved to West Berlin, a new plant was opened, the popular 520 sports sedan was launched (1972), the Dingolfing plant in Lower Bavaria was further expanded (providing jobs for 15,000 farmworkers), and following the establishment of the European Economic Community, BMW subsidiaries were set up in member countries. Halfway through the decade, a United States importing, marketing, distribution, and support subsidiary was formed in Montvale, New Jersey, and later in the 1970's the company built a car plant at Steyr in Austria.

It had appeared early in the 1970's that Bayerische Motoren's interests in motor racing, operated by BMW Motorsport GmbH, might be curtailed; in fact, the company was able to expand its racing activities. For some years, BMW had been the leading producer of racing car engines in the classification known as Formula 2; the company now decided to compete in the Formula 1 market as well. Success was swift. In 1975 Nelson Piquet won the Formula 1 World Championship in a BMW-powered Brabham. This was the first turbo-charged engine to win in the 34-year history of Formula 1 racing.

The Steyr plant in Austria commenced operation in the early 1980's as a producer of turbo-charged diesel engines. Now, the factory is a major petrol engine manufacturer and at full capacity can turn out 150,000 engines a year. Another factory, at Spandau in West Berlin, opened in the spring of 1984 to make BMW's new four-cylinder, water-cooled K series of motorcycles. This machine won the January 1985 Paris-Dakar Rally, the world's toughest and longest off-road race. The company's motorcycles won this rally four times in its first six years.

BMW's car sales in the last couple of decades have increased along with the demand for higher-priced models, and healthy domestic sales have been enhanced by the successes of foreign subsidiaries. In 1984, for example, BMW of North America sold 71,000 cars. On the other hand, motorcycle sales have suffered. High unemployment, high interest rates, and loan restrictions have decreased the purchasing power of a crucial motorcycle market—young Europeans; and competition from Japan has been fierce.

BMW Group's present chairman, Eberhard von Kuenheim, has ably survived the industry's ups and downs and is frequently cited as one of West Germany's most astute businessmen. Director Paul Hahnemann, hired as part of the new management team in 1961, is now in charge of both production and sales. He has been instrumental in the development of the company's "New Class" line. BMW is hopeful that these middle price-range cars, emphasizing speed, styling, and luxury, will be widely popular among young executives.

Principal Subsidiaries: BMW Motorrad GmbH; BMW Holding Corp. (USA); BMW of North America Inc. (USA); BMW Leasing; BMW Marine GmbH; BMW Machinenfabrik Spandau GmbH; BMW Motorsport GmbH; Bavaria Wirtschaftsagentur GmbH; Bavaria-Lloyd Reiseburo GmbH (51%); Schorsch Meier GmbH. The company also has subsidiaries in the following countries: Australia, Belgium, Canada, Curacao, England, Italy, Japan, The Netherlands, New Zealand, South Africa, Spain, and Switzerland.

BENDIX CORPORATION

Incorporated: April 13, 1929 as the Bendix Aviation
Corporation
Absorbed by the Allied-Signal Corporation
Allied-Signal, Inc.
Columbia Road and Park Avenue
Morristown, New Jersey 07960
U.S.A.
(201) 455-2000

The Bendix Corporation ceased to exist in 1983 after its failure to succeed with an acquisition attempt. Bendix was purchased by the Allied Corporation (later Allied-Signal) and subsequently dissolved. While certain former Bendix divisions continue to use the Bendix brand name and "blue banana" logo, the company has been completely assimilated into Allied-Signal.

The corporation bears the name of its founder, Vincent Bendix, an automotive engineer who perfected a method of mass-production for triple thread screws essential for the application of electric starters to automobiles. In 1913 Bendix licensed his method to the Eclipse Machine Company, a bicycle parts manufacturer. The following year, Eclipse began selling integrated starter drives to major automobile manufacturers.

By 1919 substantial production royalties enabled Bendix to purchase the Winkler-Grimm Wagon Company, a manufacturer of large utility vehicles, located in South Bend, Indiana. It was later rumored that the Studebaker Company (also in South Bend) persuaded the city council in 1920 to purchase its fire engines from a source other than Bendix, fearing that the company had the potential to become a rival.

While visiting Europe early in 1923, Vincent Bendix met the French engineer Henri Perrot, who needed a more efficient braking system for his line of taxicabs. Bendix developed a four-wheel braking system, and the two men formalized their business relationship in November 1923 by establishing the Perrot Brake Company in South Bend. The following year the company's name was changed to the Bendix Corporation, and shares of stock were sold to the public.

In 1928 Bendix acquired a majority interest in the Eclipse Machine Company. General Motors, Eclipse's largest customer for starter drives, offered to help finance the transaction by accepting $6.8 million in notes. That year Bendix held approximately 25% of the available market for brakes.

Although he did not like to fly, Vincent Bendix maintained a strong interest in aviation. His company developed and manufactured a number of products for the aviation industry and later sponsored transcontinental air races. Even though only eight percent of company sales were derived from aviation products, the company's name was changed to the Bendix Aviation Corporation in 1929.

One of several companies acquired by Bendix in 1929 was the Stromberg Carburetor Company, which was subsequently moved from Chicago to South Bend. Bendix Aviation experienced very strong growth in the five years after its incorporation. Its stock, purchased for $26 in 1924, sold for $420 in 1929. The company had successfully diversified into a variety of automotive and aeronautic systems and thereby controlled a substantial share of the market. In October 1929, however, confidence in the American stock market collapsed, precipitating a severe economic depression.

Bendix, like many American industrial companies, did not suddenly "crash", rather, it deteriorated slowly over a period of years. In 1932 Bendix was forced to discontinue share dividends, and the following year stock that had been purchased for $104 at the end of 1929 was worth only $4.37. But throughout the slump, the company continued to develop new automotive systems, including power brakes and power steering, and made significant improvements in its existing product lines. By 1935 business had recovered enough to permit the reinstatement of dividends.

During the mid-1930's the Hydraulic Brake Company, a Bendix subsidiary, permitted two young engineers to use a Bendix machine shop to refine a new washing machine they had developed. Officials at Hydraulic Brake later persuaded Vincent Bendix to lend his name to the product in return for a 25% share of the washing machine company, incorporated in 1936 as Bendix Home Appliances. Aside from producing a few parts, however, Bendix had almost nothing to do with the popular washer. The company disposed of its share of Bendix Home Appliances in 1940.

Unsatisfactory business conditions during 1937 led General Motors, which by this time held a 25% share of Bendix, to install two board members and initiate a reorganization of the company; operations were streamlined, management centralized, and costs reduced. Bendix subsidiaries were made into divisions, transforming Bendix from a type of holding company into an operating company.

While Bendix Aviation experienced its most profitable year in 1939, Vincent Bendix was forced to declare bankruptcy, having speculated badly in real estate over a number of years. In the spring of 1942, Vincent Bendix resigned as president and chairman of Bendix Aviation, and two years later he formed a new company, Bendix Helicopters, Inc., as part of an attempt to develop a four-seater helicopter for families. He died on March 27, 1945.

Ernest R. Breech, a board member installed by General Motors, was elected president upon Vincent Bendix's resignation. The following year, Bendix headquarters were relocated to Detroit, the home of General Motors. The company's early years in Detroit were lucrative ones.

During World War II Bendix received a substantial number of military contracts. By 1944 the company controlled over $100 million worth of government facilities and employed 70,000 workers.

A few months before the end of the war government contracts worth one billion dollars were cancelled and the company faced a financial crisis. Ernest Breech left Bendix to become an executive vice president of the Ford Motor Company, and Malcolm P. Ferguson was elected to return Bendix to profitable peacetime operation. A $12 million operating loss in 1946 was followed by a return to profitability the following year, largely on the strength of Bendix's automotive products.

In the second half of the 1940's Bendix developed a number of new systems for the defense industry, including the TALOS surface-to-air missile. Bendix outgrew its facilities at South Bend and in 1951 established a second, larger plant in the nearby city of Mishawaka. That same year it re-entered military production schemes at the outbreak of the Korean War. But this time, Bendix managed its war supply operations as strictly temporary enterprises.

While Bendix continued to manufacture products for the aviation industry, it remained heavily involved with manufacturing products and equipment for use in a wide variety of industries. For this reason, it was decided in 1960 to drop the word "Aviation" from the company's name; once again it became known as the Bendix Corporation.

The level of unemployment in South Bend rose dramatically in 1967 when Studebaker merged with the Worthington Corporation and halted its local manufacturing operations; thousands of employees lost their jobs; many also lost their pensions. Bendix reaffirmed its commitment to the community and helped to preserve the local economy.

During the early 1960's Bendix conducted nearly 80% of its business with the government, primarily in the area of defense systems. The company also continued its policy of growth through the acquisition of profitable subsidiaries, including the Fram Corporation, a manufacturer of air and oil parts for automobiles. But at the same time, Bendix followed a policy of diversification and successfully reduced its dependence on the progressively less stable automotive and defense-related businesses.

Bendix headquarters were again relocated in 1971, this time to nearby Southfield, Michigan. On November 30, 1973 Bendix acquired the Autolite spark plug operation from the Ford Motor Company for $27 million. Ford had been ordered to sell Autolite as part of a Supreme Court ruling, which also required Ford to purchase most of its spark plugs from Bendix until 1983.

In 1976 William (Bill) A. Agee became chairman of Bendix, replacing W. Michael Blumenthal who was appointed treasury secretary in the Carter Administration. Agee, a 38-year-old director who left Boise Cascade for Bendix in 1972, had a reputation as a headstrong businessman overly concerned with short-term financial performance. He was, however, an excellent portfolio manager and invested company funds in businesses which were later sold at a great profit.

When Blumenthal was dismissed by President Carter in 1979, Agee prevented him from returning to Bendix and blocked his readmittance to the board. Blumenthal joined the Burroughs Corporation, where he was reportedly being prepared to succeed Paul Mirabito as chief executive officer. Agee raised eyebrows by trying to persuade the Burroughs board to elect himself and offering to serve concurrently as head of both companies. His proposal was rejected.

During 1978 and 1979 Agee engineered the acquisition of two metals processing companies, ASARCO and Bass & Company. In 1981 he initiated a large-scale divestiture of Bendix assets, including the $425 million sale of Bendix Forest Products Corporation, the $336 million sale of ASARCO, and the sales of Bass and the United Geophysical Corporation for $28.8 million and $80 million, respectively. Proceeds from the sales were invested in government securities, suggesting to industry analysts that Agee was preparing to acquire a large company.

Bill Agee came under strong criticism during 1980 for his relationship with Mary Cunningham, a graduate of the Harvard Business School, whom he had hired as his executive assistant in 1979. Cunningham quickly became involved in decisions of the highest importance, causing alienation between Agee and many of his executives. Jerome Jacobson, executive vice president for strategic planning, resigned, and Agee promptly hired Mary Cunningham to replace him. When Bendix president William Panny confronted Agee about Cunningham, Panny was asked to resign. Although he refused to do so, Agee announced Panny's resignation anyway. Amid rumors that Agee was romantically involved with Cunningham, Agee was suddenly divorced in August of 1980. Executives in the company attributed Cunningham's rapid promotions to her relationship with their chairman. Agee called a meeting the following month to address Cunningham's position within the company and did such a poor job presenting his case that Mary Cunningham was forced to resign.

Early in 1981 Bill Agee announced to the board that Bendix had an opportunity to purchase a major high-technology firm. This acquisition, he said, would require the resignation of several board members who were based in Detroit and who, because they were also board members of Burroughs, faced a possible conflict of interest. Agee upset several more board members by refusing to name the company he intended to purchase. By August it became apparent to board member Robert Purcell that Agee was bluffing in order to purge board members thought to be too closely associated with Michael Blumenthal and Burroughs. Purcell resigned in protest.

Before Mary Cunningham left Bendix she prepared a list of takeover targets that Bendix could acquire by utilizing its $500 million cash reserve. In March 1982 Bendix announced that it had acquired a 7.2% share of the RCA Corporation for $100 million. RCA management immediately took measures which prevented Bendix from gaining a larger share, commenting that Agee had "not demonstrated the ability to manage his own affairs, let alone someone else's."

Bendix announced in August of the same year that it would attempt to acquire the Martin Marietta Corporation for $1.5 billion. At the same time, Martin Marietta's price per share of stock was undervalued because of weak performances by its aluminum and cement divisions. Martin Marietta, intent on remaining independent, responded on August 30 by announcing that it intended to acquire Bendix for $1.8 billion.

With the two companies heading for a deadlock, Martin Marietta chairman Thomas Pownall enlisted the help of United Technologies chairman Harry Gray, a personal friend of his, whom the *New York Times* described as "an acquisition hunter operating at several orders of magnitude beyond Mr. Agee" On September 7, 1982 United Technologies pledged to match Marietta's bid for Bendix and to divide Bendix between itself and Marietta in the event that either company eventually acquired Bendix.

Matters were further complicated on September 20 when Bendix announced that it had acquired a 70% share of Martin Marietta. Martin Marietta later revealed that it had acquired a 45% share of Bendix and was completing the purchase of an additional 6%. At that point it would have been possible for Martin Marietta and Bendix to control each other, an arrangement certain to invite judicial intervention. Bill Agee may have assumed that because his tender offer would precede Marietta's by five days, Bendix would have no trouble gaining control of that company. Martin Marieta, however, was incorporated in Maryland where state law requires ten days before a shareholder's meeting can be called to dissolve the board. But Bendix, incorporated in Delaware, could be taken over by a majority shareholder immediately. In effect, Martin Marietta could take control of Bendix five days before Bendix could take control of Martin Marietta.

On September 22 the Bendix board hastily agreed to consider an alternative takeover by the Allied Corporation for $85 per share, or $1.9 billion. Two days later, an Allied-Bendix agreement was concluded in which Bendix would be absorbed by Allied and Martin Marietta would remain independent. Martin Marietta would surrender its Bendix shares to Allied, and Allied would retain a 39% share of Martin Marietta until Marietta could repurchase its own stock.

Without much effort the Allied Corporation, whose chairman Edward L. Hennessy used to work for Harry Gray, acquired Bendix at comparatively little cost. But the arrangement left Martin Marietta heavily in debt, and United Technologies lost an opportunity to acquire the Bendix automotive and industrial divisions.

The 60-year-old Bendix Corporation ceased to exist after an ill-conceived 31-day takeover attempt planned and executed almost entirely by Bill Agee. Mary Cunningham, whom Agee married in June 1981, served as an executive consultant to Agee during this period and reportedly undermined Agee's effectiveness in meetings with Pownall and others. While Hennessy later appointed Agee president of Allied, former Bendix president Alonzo McDonald and 4000 Bendix employees lost their jobs. On February 8, 1983 it was announced that Bill Agee would resign from Allied after having been eliminated from consideration for the post of chief operating officer.

Bendix was operated as a subsidiary of Allied (later Allied-Signal) until September 1985 when its operations were assimilated into the divisional structure of Allied-Signal. Many of the former Bendix enterprises became part of the Allied-Signal Industrial Group, which was sold in 1986. The former Bendix automotive, aerospace, and electronics operations, however, have remained with Allied-Signal. The company continues to use the Bendix name for purposes of brand identification in its Automotive Group.

Further Reading: *Till Death Do Us Part* by Hope Lampert, New York, Harcourt Brace Jovanovich, 1983; *Merger* by Peter F. Aartz, New York, Morrow, 1985.

CHRYSLER CORPORATION

12000 Chrysler Drive
Highland Park, Michigan 48203
U.S.A.
(313) 956-5252

Public Company
Incorporated: June 6, 1925
Employees: 107,850
Sales: $22.5 billion
Market Value: $7.7 billion
Stock Index: New York London

With famous lines of passenger cars, numerous major manufacturing subsidiaries, and a variety of important interests in foreign countries, the Chrysler Corporation would appear to be a strong, viable company. But in the late 1970's Chrysler, the 14th largest industrial firm in the United States, was fighting for its life. It took a massive injection of government and private capital, extremely careful management, and some brilliant marketing to restore the ailing giant. The company's comeback is now legendary, but it would be premature to assume that Chrysler's problems are all in the past.

The company was incorporated in 1925 by Walter Percy Chrysler, a former vice president of General Motors. Resigning from GM over policy differences, Chrysler went on to restore the Maxwell Motor Corporation to solvency; in the process he designed Maxwell's Chrysler automobile. First exhibited in 1924, the car was an immediate success and before year's end the company sold 32,000 cars at a profit of more than $4 million.

The enthusiasm with which the vehicle was met encouraged Walter Chrysler to design four additional models for the coming year: the 50, 60, 70, and Imperial 80. These model numbers referred to the maximum velocity that the cars could reach on a level stretch of road. Until that time, Ford's Model T had enjoyed the reputation of the fastest car, achieving a modest 35 mph. Alarmed by Chrysler's technological breakthrough, the Ford Motor Company closed its doors for nine months and emerged with a replacement for the Model T. However, by 1927 the Chrysler Corporation (as it had been called since 1925) had firmly established itself with a sale of 192,000 cars, becoming the fifth largest company in the industry.

Walter Chrysler realised that in order to exploit his firm's manufacturing capacities to their fullest, he would have to build his own plants. Since he could not afford the estimated $75 million to achieve this, he approached the New York banking firm of Dillon Read and Company. Dillon Read had bought the Dodge Corporation of Detroit from the widows of the Dodge brothers and was happy to reach an agreement with the now highly regarded Walter Chrysler. In July 1928 Dodge became a division of the Chrysler Corporation; overnight, the size of the company increased fivefold.

But Walter Chrysler, carefully avoiding the dangers associated with rapid growth, discontinued his policy of manufacturing as many parts as possible for his cars. While he paid more for components than other car makers, he was able to maintain greater flexibility in models and designs. This proved to be extremely important in an age of rapid technological advance. Indeed, Walter Chrysler's farsightedness helped the company to survive the 1930's Depression far better than most in the industry, and his strategy of spending money on research, "no matter how gloomy the outlook," may have been responsible for his firm's sound financial standing until well into the 1940's.

Along with the rest of Detroit's motor industry, Chrysler converted to war production during World War II. The manufacture of its Chrysler, Dodge, and Plymouth cars was put on hold while the corporation specialized in defense hardware such as small arms ammunition and submarine nets. But chief among its war products were B-29 bomber engines and anti-aircraft guns and tanks. Chrysler's wartime service earned it a special Army-Navy award for reliability and prompt delivery.

The corporation's problems started in the immediate postwar period. The ambition and spirit which drove the company to constant innovation and experimentation in the early days had been lost. The auto market had exhausted fundamental engineering breakthroughs and American tastes had changed. It seemed that the public was more excited by the sleeker, less traditional, and sometimes less reliable models being produced by Chrysler's rivals. In short, the car industry was becoming a "marketer's game," and Chrysler's management wasn't playing.

In 1950 L.L. Colbert, a lawyer hired by Walter Chrysler in 1929, became the corporation's president. By this time, some major overhauling was necessary and Colbert hired the management consulting firm of McKinsey and Company. Three reforms were instituted: Chrysler developed international markets for its cars, its management was centralized, and the role of the engineering department was redefined.

Colbert's reforms did little to revive the company's flagging fortunes and two years later there was another change of management. Lynn Townsend, the new corporate head, proved to be more effective. He consolidated the Chrysler and Plymouth car divisions, closed some unproductive plants, and generally tightened operations; he also reduced the work force and installed an IBM computer system to replace 700 members of the clerical staff. Most importantly, he enhanced sales by improving the quality of the Chrysler automobile, introducing the best warranty the industry had yet seen and instituting a more aggressive marketing policy. In less than five years, Townsend had revitalized the corporation.

Success led to expansion: a space division was formed

and Chrysler became the prime contractor for the Saturn booster rocket. By the end of the 1960's Townsend's international strategy yielded plants in 18 foreign countries. But before the decade was over, the domestic market was undergoing major changes. Inflation was taking its toll on U.S. auto manufacturers, imports of foreign vehicles had substantially increased, and the price of crude oil had risen drastically. Chrysler's troubles were compounded by internal factors: it was more concerned with competing against Ford and General Motors than in adapting itself to the rapidly changing market; it did not produce enough of its popular compact cars to meet consumer demand; and it had an overstock of larger vehicles.

The corporation reported a $4 million loss in 1969 and was operating at only 68% of its capacity; the previous year it had earned profits of $122 million. Car prices were substantially reduced, but this did little to solve the underlying problems. John J. Riccardo, an accountant, succeeded to the presidency and immediately set about reducing expenses. Salaries, work force, and budget were all cut and the company experimented with the marketing of foreign-made cars.

Unfortunately, Chrysler seemed incapable of reading the public mood: it narrowed and shortened Dodge and Chrysler models to bring prices down, but sales also tumbled; it continued to make Imperials long after Cadillacs and Lincolns had demonstrated their superiority in the luxury market; and it greeted the 1973–74 Arab oil embargo with a large inventory of gas-guzzlers. 1974 losses totalled a massive $52 million, but the next year's deficit was five times that amount.

The company experienced a brief respite in 1976 and 1977. Its trucks were in demand and foreign subsidiaries turned in good results, but domestic car sales remained a problem. Riccardo further consolidated North American operations and increased manufacturing capacity for compact cars. However, by the time Chrysler became a significant contender in that market, American car buyers were showing a distinct preference for the reliable and relatively inexpensive Japanese compacts. The days of United States manufacturing hegemony appeared to be over.

A loss of $205 million in 1978 led many industry-watchers to wonder if Chrysler's roller-coaster finances could rebound from this latest big dip. The syndicate of banks (with Manufacturers Hanover Trust in the vanguard) which for years had been pouring money into Chrysler, panicked. Incredibly, many of the smaller banks had agreed to virtually unlimited lines of credit on the assumption that the company would never need to use them.

But complex and highly charged negotiations eventually saved Chrysler from bankruptcy. The federal government agreed to guarantee loans up to $1.5 billion provided Chrysler raised $2 billion on its own. However, politicians could not justify such a massive bail-out without changes in Chrysler's management. Riccardo, who had diligently fought against heavy odds, had to go.

It was left to the charismatic Lee Iacocca to preside over Chrysler's comeback. An ex-Ford man with a flair for marketing and public relations, Iacocca took Chrysler's problems to the people, explaining that the company's failure would mean the loss of hundreds of thousands of jobs and could seriously damage the economy of the State of Michigan. But despite popular mythology and the near-adulation of Iacocca in some quarters, Riccardo was largely responsible for forging the agreement that gave Chrysler a new lease of life.

Nevertheless, Iacocca's skills as a communicator and as a super television salesman have been of crucial importance. Remarkably, Chrysler's recovery has been solid enough to enable it to buy from Renault its 46% stake in the Detroit-based American Motors Corporation. Iacocca claims that this acquisition will enhance Chrysler's competitiveness in the 1990's and he believes that his company can substantially increase sales of the AMC Jeep. Even so, high expectations are tempered by doubts about the economy. In November 1987 Chrysler announced the temporary lay-off of workers at two plants to allow time for inventories to be reduced.

Principal Subsidiaries: Automotive Financial Serices, Inc.; Chrysler Overseas Capital Corp.; Chrysler Realty Corp.; Gulfstream Aerospace Corp.; Chrysler Financial Corp. The company also has subsidiaries in the following countries: Canada, Mexico, and the Netherlands Antilles.

Further Reading: *International Labor Relations Management in the Automotive Industry: A Comparative Study of Chrysler, Ford, and General Motors* by Duane Kujawa, New York, Praeger, 1971; *Going for Broke: The Chrysler Story* by Michael Moritz and Barrett Seaman, New York, Doubleday, 1981; *Iacocca* by David Abodaher, New York, Macmillan, 1982; *Iacocca: An Autobiography* by Lee Iacocca with William Novak, New York, Bantam, 1984; *The Iacocca Management Technique* by Maynard M. Gorden, New York, Dodd Mead, 1985; *The Complete History of Chrysler Corporation, 1924–1985* by Richard M. Langworth and Jan P. Norbye, New York, Beekman House, 1985; *New Deals: The Chrysler Revival and the American System* by Robert B. Reich and John D. Donahue, New York, Time, 1985.

CUMMINS ENGINE CORPORATION

500 Jackson Street
P.O. Box 3005
Columbus, Indiana 47202
U.S.A.
(812) 377-5451

Public Company
Incorporated: February 3, 1919
Employees: 19,624
Sales: $2.304 billion
Market Value: $855 million
Stock Index: New York

Cummins Engine Corporation, founded in 1919 by a chauffeur who worked on motors in his employer's garage, is a leading supplier of diesel engines for trucks and heavy industry. Its worldwide subsidiaries design, manufacture and sell diesel engines, components, and replacement parts. While Cummins does not produce its own trucks, its engines are offered as options by every major U.S. truck manufacturer—even those that manufacture their own diesel engines and compete with Cummins. In addition to trucks, Cummins' diesel engines are used for drilling rigs, boats, industrial locomotives, compressors, pumps, logging equipment, agricultural equipment, and municipal and school buses. The company that didn't turn a profit for its first 18 years has presently surpassed $2 billion in total sales.

The company's founder and the man who made Rudolf Diesel's engine design practical was Clessie L. Cummins, the chauffeur of a 1909 Packard touring car owned by Will G. Irwin, a rich industrialist and philanthropist in Columbus, Indiana. Cummins was regarded by Irwin as indispensable since he was the only man who could keep the Packard in running condition. When shortly before World War I, he demanded a pay hike to $85 a month, Irwin threatened to fire him. However, the two men reached a compromise. Cummins would accept a salary reduction if the family garage was equipped with tools so that he could do engine repair work. In 1917 Cummins began making wagon hub caps for the Army, while reading news about Germany's diesel-powered U-boats. Most diesel engines at that time were large and smoky, and entirely impractical for any kind of transportation.

Cummins started working fulltime on diesels in 1919 when he heard that Sears, Roebuck & Co., would buy 3-horsepower farm diesels made on a European patent. He persuaded Irwin to negotiate a contract with Sears and established the Cummins Engine Corporation. The beginning was inauspicious; Sears said the engines were defective, and Irwin had to financially rescue his chauffeur. Neither Irwin nor Cummins was quitting, however. Irwin gave Cummins $10,000 to correct the initial defect, and eventually poured more that $2.5 million into the company.

The problem with diesel engines at that time was that engineers kept adding devices to them to give them more power. Cummins accepted only one common premise, that of "combustion ignition," or fuel oil in the cylinder bursting into flames to provide power, and systematically disposed of other parts. He initially reduced engine horsepower, but ultimately got his diesel to run faster than other models. For ten years his experimental engines ripped the bottoms out of fishing boats or tore themselves to remnants, but Cummins still would not quit. His breakthrough was what he called "the Sneezer," a device that discharged every last particle of fuel oil into the cylinder to ensure that no oil was released as smoke. He also created a fuel injector experts described as "simpler than a fountain pen."

With his diesel at last perfected, he installed it in a Packard and drove the 792 miles from Columbus to New York City on $1.88 of heating oil without refueling. He then exhibited the car in the 1930 New York Automobile Show. When skeptics suggested he had used more fuel than he admitted, Cummins proved them wrong by driving across the country on $9.36 of fuel. He also raced the Packard in the Indianapolis Speedway and finished 13th while establishing a record speed for a diesel-driven car of 80.389 mph.

Cummins' fuel pump and injector were now regarded as the best in the industry, but truck manufacturers refused to use them and continued to manufacture gas engines, while trying to design their own diesel engine. Irwin came to Cummins' rescue by having the engines of delivery trucks used by his chain of Purity Stores in California replaced by Cummins' diesel engines. The truckers liked these new engines, which were powerful, fuel-efficient, and reliable. As these truckers recommended the engine to their colleagues, the business began to flourish.

Cummins, however, was no salesman. So Irwin's grandnephew, J. Irwin Miller, a young man with a pronounced taste for Greek and Latin, but without any business training, was appointed as head of the company. Miller was an unlikely manager. He had stuttered as a child, was something of an outcast at school, and knew nothing about engines. But he had expected to inherit some facet of the family business, and he applied himself rigorously to the business at hand.

Miller replaced the chauffeur's hand tools with production equipment and constructed a fullscale plant. He then neutralized a threatened CIO strike by helping the company form its own union, the Diesel Workers Union, and solicited business during the depression by pointing out to cash-starved truckers that they would save money if they bought only those trucks that offered Cummins engines as options. Miller referred to this strategy, namely, going to the users and not the suppliers, as a "back-door approach." Fortunately for the young company, the trucking business prospered in the 1930's due to improved roads and demand for point-to-point deliveries. Diesel engines for large trucks that needed maximum fuel efficiency were more and more in demand. In 1937 the young company turned its first profit. Selling engines to competitors was an uncertain way of doing business, but it worked and it continues to be, however unorthodox, the Cummins approach. Miller, who became an admired scholar and philanthropist, and the first layman president of the National Council of Churches, later acknowledged, "We're in the business of selling engines to engine makers, which is surely not the smartest way to make a living."

The company was not just unorthodox in its marketing approach. It contributed five per cent of its profits each year to charity or to Columbus architecture projects, and was a local leader in labor relations and desegregation. Years later, Cummins became one of the first companies in its industry to hire blacks for other than janitorial jobs. Miller's sense of justice and his scholarly background helped him at times decide against prevailing social attitudes. When asked why Cummins was resisting pressure to diversify, Miller told *Forbes*, "This may be counter to trends, but we believe that by diversifying you are liable to lose confidence in the value of a good product."

The company doubled its sales in five years and continued to double sales every five years into the 1960's. Sales in 1946 hit $20 million; a decade later they reached more than $100 million. Cummins' best-selling engine was a 2,590-pound diesel for trucks of 13 tons or more. In order to maintain the high demand for Cummins engines, the company had to stay ahead of the competition, which soon included Mack Trucks, Caterpillar, and GM's Detroit Diesel. In 1952 the company unveiled a turbo-diesel which used exhaust gases to turn a gas turbine supercharger. The device, without raising fuel consumption, increased the horsepower of each Cummins engine by 50%. That year Cummins demonstrated the engine in the Indianapolis Speedway where it malfunctioned. Miller was non-plussed. "We have progressed from failure to failure," he said, confidently predicting that the turbo-diesel would soon be perfected and marketed, which it was.

Cummins stayed way ahead of its competition in the 1950's by securing up to 60% of the heavy truck market. Its in-line 6-cylinder engines were renowned for their power and longevity. Cummins distributors, who handled nothing but Cummins engines, were regarded as highly reputable because of their expertise with the single product line. Although it faced competition from Caterpillar and Euclid, Cummins also began selling engines for off-the-road construction. "We'll build the roads and then we'll run on them," said Miller.

However, the heavy truck market appeared to be saturated by 1960. To expand into alternative markets Cummins crafted a new line of V-6 and V-8 engines, based on an "oversquare" gasoline engine design. Since the diameter of the cylinder in oversquare engines is greater than the piston stroke, the engines produce more power at high speeds. Diesel engines had been long-stroke, but

Cummins' engineers found the right combination of fuel and air to inject into the combustion chamber and make their engines workable.

The new engines, the Vim, a V-6 model with 200 horsepower, the Vine, a V-8 with 265 horsepower, and the Val, a V-6 with 120 horsepower, represented the first time Cummins attempted to penetrate the lighter truck market. At that time, 44% of trucks 13 tons and over had diesel engines, but fewer than 1% of the trucks from eight to 13 tons were diesel-powered. With heavier trucks representing just 6% of the market, and the lighter trucks 22%, management concluded that manufacturing smaller engines would raise revenues. But the lighter truck market proved difficult to enter. Gas was cheap and diesel engines, which at that time cost $1,000–$4,000 more than gasoline engines, were seen as economical only if the vehicles were driven approximately 4,000 hours per year.

In the early 1960's the Cummins Engine Corporation began a slow decline. Sales and profits fluctuated. A new line of engines with more than 300 horsepower, introduced by the company in 1962, failed to gain a dominant market share for more than two years. Management was criticized for being behind in both product development and market share.

Part of the problem was Cummins' policy of diversification. Beginning in the late 1950's Cummins started acquiring an interest in companies that produced diesel-related products. By the late 1960's it had become genuinely diversified, purchasing a ski manufacturer, a bank, and even an Irish cattle feeding outfit. Management had decided to make these acquisitions due to the slow growth of the diesel market. While Cummins' sales averaged 15% annual growth, the diesel market was projected to expand at half that rate. A number of new diesel competitors, such as GMC Division and Perkins, compounded the problem.

By 1967 Cummins' share of the crucial heavy-truck market had slipped to less than 45%. Earnings were off 78%. A strong truck market helped sales rebound in 1968, reaching a record of $365 million. Vigorous sales continued over the next few years, but earnings were erratic. Miller's hand-picked young successor, Henry Schacht, who joined the company after graduating from Harvard Business School and assumed the presidency just two years later, blamed surprisingly strong demand for the thin margins. Instead of preparing for an increased truck demand, Cummins had diverted resources to its non-diesel holdings. To catch up to the competition, Cummins operated its factories 24 hours a day, seven days a week, and paid a large amount in overtime wages. A two-month long strike only exacerbated the company's difficulties.

"We clearly left the door open to competitors," Schacht told *Forbes*. Demand exceeded supply, and customers went elsewhere. There was criticism that Cummins met the demands of only its biggest customers and that smaller consumers were forced to buy from the competition. Cummins' share of the large truck market reached a low point of less than 40% in the early 1970's. The company elected to sell its other holdings and concentrate on meeting the unexpectedly high diesel demand.

The main challenge was to devise a marketing strategy

for engines that remained about five per cent more expensive than the competition's. The company refused to downgrade its product line. Management believed that the most significant problem for truckers who drove their vehicles 240,000 miles and more a year was downtime. So the company's response to its slipping market share was to make its engines more powerful, which in turn made them more reliable. In this way Cummins held on to its largest customers.

Furthermore, the company expanded its overseas operations. It had a worldwide network of 3,000 service outlets, and a computerized analysis of 50,000 miles of major highways, allowing it to match the best engine to the customer's requirements. Its reputation helped it gain access to new markets. By the mid-1970's, 25% of the company's revenues came from overseas, and additional profits were being made in the agriculture, construction, and marine enterprises for which Cummins was designing extra-large motors of 1,200 horsepower.

Then Cummins made an apparent mistake and introduced a line of 450-horsepower engines. This was 50% more power than a truck needed to haul a loaded rig at 65 mph on a level highway. Cummins was marketing power in its engines, but the problem was the new 55 mph speed limit. The company confronted this issue with an advertising campaign that stressed "reserve power." According to the ads, the new engines could easily maintain 55 mph even on uphill grades, so truckers would not have to lose more speed than they had to by law. Furthermore, constant speed and less shifting would actually increase fuel efficiency.

The new engines didn't sell very well at first, as the truck market in 1975 slumped 40%. The following year, however, the market rebounded, and Cummins took the lion's share. Sales reached $1 billion and earnings were $59 million. Cummins benefited from the erratic enforcement of the 55 mph speed limit. Furthermore, the company outperformed its competitors by introducing a turbo-charged, slower-running version of its large-block engine, offering five per cent better economy.

Nonetheless, management was increasingly concerned about the volatile truck market. While automating company plants in order to stay competitive within the truck engine industry, Cummins increased its profit from non-highway engines until they accounted for nearly 25% of revenues. This stabilized the company. The demand for agricultural and construction equipment ran in cycles that were unrelated to the demand for truck engines. Cummins also established plants in Scotland, England, and France to penetrate the European market while avoiding European tariffs. It faced new rivals, such as Renault in France and Iveco in Italy, which placed only their own engines in trucks they were manufacturing. But Cummins, which had faced a similar obstacle in the 1930's, was undeterred. New laws allowing trucks of up to 38,000 pounds on European highways, in addition to the escalating costs of fuel, persuaded the Cummins management that Europe was the new market for Cummins' diesel engines. For Cummins, the European market grew slowly but steadily.

While planning to enter markets outside North America and Europe the Schacht management team also launched an austerity program. About 2,000 employees at the Columbus, Indiana, plant were laid off. Interest payments were cut sharply, and the debt–equity ratio reduced to 0.5 to 1.

Looking to the future, Cummins agreed to a $350 million joint venture with the J. I. Case Co. in the early 1980's to produce a new line of fuel efficient 3, 4, and 6-cylinder engines with a range of 55 to 250 horsepower. The engines, it was hoped, would reach the crucial middle-size truck market. At the same time, Cummins initiated a $750 million program to protect its share of the heavy-duty truck market. By 1984 Cummins surpassed a 60% share of that market once again. The next year, however, sales decreased.

In 1986 the company, confronting a soft truck market and declining profits, began to consolidate its worldwide operations and reduce its work force by 17%. It planned to close four plants, reducing its worldwide engine manufacturing and distribution floor space by 19%. While sales remained strong, new models such as the L-10 were not successfully entering the market. That and the cost of consolidation were leading the company into financial difficulty.

Principal Subsidiaries: Cummins Americas, Inc.; Cummins Corp.; Atlas Crankshaft Corp.; Fleetguard, Inc.; McCord Heat Transfer Corp.; HSE Consultants, Inc.; VI Holdings, Inc.; Diesel Recon, Inc.; Cummins Engine Holding, Co.; Advance Drivetrain Corp.; and Diesel Controls Technology, Inc. The company also has subsidiaries in the following countries: Australia, Barbados, Brazil, Britain, Canada, Colombia, France, Italy, Japan, Mexico, N. Antilles, and Singapore.

DAIMLER-BENZ A.G.

Mercedesstrasse 136
Postfach 202
D-7000 Stuttgart 60
Federal Republic of Germany
(0711) 17–0

Public Company
Incorporated: 1926
Employees: 232,000
Sales: DM 58.5 billion (US$30.1 billion)
Market Value: DM 52.1 billion (US$26.8 billion)
Stock Index: Berlin Düsseldorf Frankfurt Hamburg
Munich Stuttgart

Daimler-Benz has an image befitting the manufacturer of the Mercedes-Benz. Conservative and stable, the automaker has a history that goes back to the very beginnings of the gasoline-powered engine. Yet, in addition to being a manufacturer of luxury cars, Daimler-Benz is Europe's largest commercial truck producer and makes more heavy (over six-ton) trucks that any other company in the world. And when the company unexpectedly bought three large conglomerates (between February 1985 and February 1986), the list of Daimler-Benz products grew to include everything from spacecraft systems to vacuum cleaners. The acquisitions also made Daimler-Benz the second largest industrial company in West Germany and its second largest defense contractor.

The roots of this company go back to the mid-1880's and two engineers, Carl Benz and Gottlieb Daimler. Most authorities cite them both as the most important contributors to the development of the internal combustion engine. Yet, although concerned with the same idea at virtually the same time, and living within 60 miles of each other, the two apparently never even met. They certainly never envisioned the 1926 merger of their two companies.

Although Benz drove his first car in 1885 and Daimler ran his in 1886, neither was actually the first to create gasoline-powered vehicles. However, they were the first to persist long enough to make them viable as transportation. At this time the obstacles to motorized vehicles were enormous: gasoline was considered dangerously explosive; roads were poor; and few people could have afforded an automobile in any case. Nevertheless, Benz dedicated himself to revolutionizing the world's transportation with the internal combustion engine.

Early in 1885 Benz sat in a car and circled a track next to

his small factory, while his workers and his wife stood nearby. The car had three wheels and a top speed of 10 m.p.h. This engineering triumph was only slightly marred by Benz's first public demonstration which took place shortly afterwards. He forgot to steer the car and smashed into the brick wall around his own house. Despite this inauspicious debut, Benz's cars quickly became known for their quality construction and materials. By 1888 he had 50 workmen building his three-wheeled car. Two years later, he began making a four-wheeled vehicle.

Daimler's convictions about the internal combustion engine were as intense as Benz's. Originally a gunsmith, Daimler later trained as an engineer, studying in Germany, England, Belgium and France. After working for a number of German and British firms, he became technical director for the Gasmotorenfabrik Deutz. Disillusioned by the company's limited vision, however, he and researcher Wilhelm Maybach resigned in 1882 to set up their own experimental workshop. They tested their first engine on a wooden bicycle. Later, they put engines into a four-wheeled vehicle and a boat. Daimler sold the French rights to his engines to Panhard-Levassor (which later fought him for the use of his name). In 1896 he granted a patent license to the British Daimler company, which eventually became independent of the German Daimler-Motoren-Gesellschaft.

The story of how Daimler found a new brand name for its cars has become legendary. In 1900, Austro-Hungarian Consul-General and businessman Emil Jellinek approached the company with a suggestion. He offered to underwrite the production of a new high performance car. In return, he asked that the vehicle be named after his daughter—Mercedes.

Daimler's Mercedes continued to make automotive history. In 1906 the young engineer Ferdinand Porsche took the place of Daimler's oldest son, Paul, as chief engineer at the company's Austrian factory. (Paul Daimler returned to the main plant in Stuttgart.) In the five years that Porsche was with Daimler, he produced 65 designs, which makes him one of the most influential and prolific automotive designers ever. Approximately the same time, in 1909, the Mercedes star emblem was registered; it has embellished the radiators of all the company's cars since 1921.

In 1924 the Daimler and Benz companies began coordinating designs and production, but maintained their own brand names. They merged completely in 1926 to produce cars under the name Mercedes-Benz. The merger undoubtedly saved the two companies from bankruptcy in the poverty and inflation of post-World War I Germany.

The company continued to grow throughout the 1930's. The most consistently successful participant in automobile racing history, Mercedes-Benz scored international victories that added to its reputation. The company's racing success was also used as propaganda by the Third Reich in the years before World War II. The Mercedes-Benz became Adolph Hitler's parade transportation. Whenever he was photographed in a vehicle, it was a Mercedes.

In 1939 the state took over the German auto industry, and during the war Daimler-Benz developed and produced trucks, tanks, and aircraft engines for the Luft-waffe. The company's importance to the German war machine made Daimler-Benz a primary target for Allied bombing raids. Two weeks of air strikes in September of 1944 destroyed 70% or more of the company's plants.

Although little was left of the company, workers returned to resume their old jobs after the war. To the surprise of many people the factories recovered, and the company again became one of the most successful auto manufacturers in the world.

Much of Daimler-Benz's growth in the 1950's occurred under the direction of stockholder Friedrich Flick. A convicted war criminal, Flick lost 80% of his steel fortune at the end of the World War II. Yet he still had enough money to purchase a 37½% interest in Daimler-Benz between 1954 and 1957. By 1959 his $20 million investment was worth $200 million, and he had become Germany's second ranking industrialist.

Flick's holdings allowed him to push the company to buy 80% of competitor Auto Union, in order to gain a smaller car for the Daimler product line. The acquisition made Daimler-Benz the fifth largest automobile manufacturer in the world and the largest outside of the United States.

The acquisition probably lessened the impact of new U.S. compact cars in the 1950's as well. However, Daimler-Benz was less worried than other European automakers for another reason. Mercedes' appeal was to the wealthy, status-conscious customer, and that appeal grew steadily. By 1960 Daimler-Benz already had 83,000 employees in seven West German plants. Additional plants were located in Argentina, Brazil and India, and the company had established assembly lines in Mexico, South Africa, Belgium and Ireland.

Daimler-Benz's conservative outlook is evident in its strategy of gradual growth, concentration on areas of expertise, foresight, and willingness to sacrifice short-term sales and earnings for long-term benefits. This conservatism helped to soften the effect of the recession and gasoline shortages that had severely affected other automakers by mid-1970. While many manufacturers were closing facilities and cutting workers' hours, Daimler-Benz registered record sales gains.

Chairman Joachim Zahn, a lawyer, said the company had foreseen "the difficult phase" the auto industry was about to confront. Between 1973 and 1975 Zahn had set aside some $250 million as "preparation" for bad times. And while other automakers had spent time and money on model changes, Daimler-Benz had invested in engines powered by inexpensive diesel fuel. These vehicles comprised 45% of its output by the mid-1970's.

The company was not without some problems during these years. High labor costs and the increasing value of the deutsche mark were making Mercedes-Benz automobiles more expensive than ever. Rather than reducing costs or cutting corners, however, the company began to speak of its cars as "investments."

Although primarily known for its passenger cars, Daimler-Benz has a commercial truck line that was its largest source of profits for many years. The company profited from the oil-price increase of the late 1970's, when demand for its commercial vehicles rose dramatically in the Middle East. Most of the company's trucks are made outside of Germany, unlike its cars. Later, the commercial line did lead the company into one risk that was stalled by unfortunate timing. In 1981 Daimler-Benz purchased Freightliner, a manufacturer of heavy trucks, just as sales ground to a halt in the face of America's recession.

Some risk-taking was inevitable, of course. And usually it paid off. Daimler-Benz increased its car production from 350,000 to 540,000 units a year between 1975 and 1983. Most of the increase was due to the introduction in 1983 of its 190 model, a small version of its saloon car. There was a chance that sales of the 190 would detract from sales of its larger cars, rather than add to them. Yet, the 190 not only attracted new customers, but the updated image of the new model lowered the average age of a Mercedes owner from 45 to 40.

As a manufacturer of luxury automobiles, Daimler-Benz was less vulnerable than most automakers to shifts in demand during the early 1980's. Most Mercedes-Benz customers were rich enough to rise above concerns about finance rates, inflation, recession, gasoline prices or tax breaks. In early 1985, for example, German lawmakers vacillated over tax breaks for buyers of cars with lower exhaust emissions. And many Germans delayed purchasing a car until they could see which way the balance would swing. While other auto manufacturers suffered through the resultant falling sales, Daimler-Benz was unaffected. Not only were its diesel-powered cars producing fewer fumes, but most Mercedes drivers were unconcerned about tax perks.

Another traditional safeguard for Daimler-Benz is its long-standing policy of making only as many cars as it can expect to sell, especially during a recession. The result has usually been a backlog of demand when the recession ends. In addition, since the company's sales are good even when the market is bad, Daimler-Benz does not have to cater to demands from dealers. Although the U.S. is Daimler-Benz's largest market (after West Germany), its 500 American dealers unsuccessfully requested more cars in 1985.

Why wouldn't Daimler-Benz increase shipments? One reason is that sharp upswings in supply tend to lower the value of used Mercedes. That means owners are less likely to sell and buy a new one. And resales are vital to the company's success; 90% of West German owners buy another Mercedes when they change cars. In foreign markets, the rate of repurchasers is as high as 80%.

Due to the limitations that the company places on production and exports, a "gray market" in Mercedes-Benz cars operates in America. Dealers import recent models from other countries without Daimler-Benz's authority, often illegally. Then they modify them to meet U.S. safety and emission standards and sell them for less than regular dealer franchises. Daimler-Benz tries to protect its carefully controlled market against these "gray market" dealers, but with little success.

During the mid-1980's Daimler-Benz was confronted with a dramatic increase in competition for the luxury car market, the fastest growing segment of the automobile business. Along with this market competition is the increasing speed and sophistication of competitors' automotive research. For example, pioneering Daimler-Benz engineers spent 18 years developing anti-skid brakes that enable drivers to keep control of their vehicles during sudden stops. A few months after the company introduced the breakthrough in the United States, Lincoln brought out a similar system as standard equipment.

Competition and the high price of research and development were two of the factors that precipitated the sudden moves Daimler-Benz made between February 1985 and February 1986. Industry analysts were surprised when the company acquired, in quick succession, three large conglomerates. This was a departure from Daimler-Benz's tradition of gradual growth. In February of 1985 Daimler-Benz acquired Motoren-und-Turbinen-Union, which makes aircraft engines and diesel motors for tanks and ships. Daimler already had a 50% interest in the company, and when MAN (a Daimler-Benz partner and manufacturer of heavy trucks and buses) wanted to acquire some cash, the company bought MAN's share for $160 million. Motoren-und-Turbinen-Union sales were $768 million in 1984.

The second acquisition followed in May of 1985. Daimler-Benz spent $130 million for 65.6% of Dornier, a privately-held manufacturer of spacecraft systems, commuter planes and medical equipment. The company was up for sale because of disputes within the Dornier family. Dornier sales were about $530 million in 1984.

In early 1986 Daimler-Benz made its third acquisition. The company paid $820 million for control of AEG, a high technology manufacturer of electronic equipment such as turbines, robotics and data processing, as well as household appliances. Although annual sales in 1984 were an impressive $3.7 billion, the company had just emerged from bankruptcy after losing $904 million in nine years building nuclear power plants.

Many industry-watchers were dubious about the diversification of a company that was already doing so well. Profits had increased every year but one between 1970 and 1985; in 1985 they increased more than 50%. Some analysts questioned the speed of Daimler-Benz's purchases, as well as management's ability to hold such a large and diverse enterprise together.

Yet Werner Breitschwerdt, chairman of Daimler-Benz's management board, claimed full confidence in the moves. Breitschwerdt, an electrical engineer, joined the passenger car division of the company in 1953 and served as head of styling and product development. He became a member of

the managing board in 1977 and chairman in 1983 after the death of his predecessor Dr. Gerhard Prinz. Breitschwerdt is the first engineer to head the company in decades, and the only research and development expert to hold that position.

By bringing the technical and research expertise of the new subsidiaries to Daimler-Benz, Breitschwerdt hoped significantly to expand the company's research base. The prospects were highly promising for the automotive division, whose engineers were already interested in developing "intelligent" cars. In this area, the radar technology of AEG and the materials expertise of Dornier would be extremely useful.

However, the Deutsche Bank which owns 28% of Daimler-Benz, became increasingly troubled by Breitschwerdt's apparent lack of a clear program for integrating the company's recent acquisitions. In July 1987 Breitschwerdt announced his resignation. Despite the major reservations of several board members, but with Deutsche Bank's full approval, Edvard Reuter, the company's chief strategic planner, was appointed to succeed Breitschwerdt.

These recent upheavals seem to have had little impact on Daimler-Benz's performance; it has emerged as the largest industrial concern in West Germany. And notwithstanding its recent diversification, the company remains closely identified with its line of expensive automobiles.

Principal Subsidiaries: Holzindustrie Bruchsal GmbH; Machinenfabrik Esslingen AG (97.3%); Hanomag-Henschel GmbH; Industriehandel Handels-und Industrie-ausruestungs-gesellschaft mbH; Mercedes-Leasing-GmbH; Daimler-Benz Wohnungsbau Gesellschaft mbH; Daimbler-Benz of North America Holding Co.,Inc.; Mercedes-Benz of North America, Inc.; Freightliner Corp. The company also has subsidiaries in the following countries: Argentina, Australia, Austria, Belgium, Brazil, Canada, England, France, Greece, India, Indonesia, Iran, Italy, Japan, Mexico, The Netherlands, Nigeria, Saudi Arabia, South Africa, Spain, Switzerland, and Turkey.

Further Reading: The Star and the Laurel: The Centennial History of Daimler, Mercedes, and Benz, 1886–1986 by Beverly Rae Kimes, Montvale, N.J., Mercedes Benz of North America, 1986.

DANA CORPORATION

4500 Dorr Street
P.O. Box 1000
Toledo, Ohio 43697
U.S.A.
(419) 535-4500

Public Company
Incorporated: October 12, 1916 as Spicer Manufacturing
Company
Employees: 38,200
Sales: $3.695 billion
Market Value: $1.829 billion
Stock Index: New York London

Executives at the Dana Corporation are proud of the fact
that the company grew up with the motor vehicle industry.
The company has good reason to emphasize this since
Dana Corporation has managed to remain both a flexible
growth company throughout the changes in the automotive industry, as well as a leader in its field.

The Dana Corporation began with an idea that would
improve automotive equipment. In 1902 Clarence Spicer
invented the Spicer universal joint to replace the chain and
sprocket devices that were being used for automobiles at
that time. With this invention, Clarence Spicer founded
the Spicer Manufacturing Company of Plainfield, New
Jersey.

Clarence Spicer was president of the company from
1910–1914, and Charles A. Dana was appointed to the
position in 1916. Dana, a well-known philanthropist, New
York lawyer, and legislator remained at the head of the
Corporation for more than half a century. In 1946 the
Spicer Manufacturing Company was renamed Dana Corporation in his honor.

Dana graduated from Columbia University with both a
bachelor of arts and law degree. After college, he practiced law for the State of New York, becoming assistant
prosecutor in 1907. Dana went on to serve as a state
legislator for six years before becoming president and then
chairman of the Corporation. Dana also served as director
or officer of over 20 additional companies.

In 1930 the company moved to Toledo, Ohio where its
headquarters have remained. Dana had to resort to numerous layoffs over the years, and in 1945 the company fired
4,000 workers because of a steel shortage. Two months
before this layoff, Dana had managed to end a 55-day
strike at the Pottstown, Pennsylvania plant when 1,820

employees stopped work because personnel with low
seniority were rehired after the dismissal of some of their
colleagues with "super-seniority" rights.

By 1952 Dana considered closing down the Pottstown
plant because it was no longer competitive. But through
careful, and lengthy, negotiations with the United Auto
Workers union, the management agreed to a four year $5
million modernization process that would enable the plant
to regain its competitive edge. This meant several concessions on the part of the UAW, including 21 revisions in its
union contract, but by 1959 the plant was productive once
again.

During the 1960's the Dana Corporation grew from
strength to strength and by 1967 was one of the largest
independent suppliers of automotive components and
replacement parts throughout the world with $500 million
in sales. Dana saw itself as a "growth company" and not a
conglomerate. Management was watching for new developments within the transportation industry.

Dana became a leader in the after-market industry early
in the 1960's with the acquisition of Perfect Circle Corporation, a manufacturer of piston rings and related products,
and in 1963 with Victor Manufacturing and Gasket
Company. By 1968 the company's impressive customer list
included General Motors, Ford, International Harvester,
Chrysler, and American Motors.

In the late 1960's, Rene C. McPherson was appointed
president of the company. Described by *Fortune* magazine
as a "maverick," McPherson is important in the history of
Dana Corporation because of his progressive policies on
management and employee relations. He is credited with
turning a large, somewhat unwieldy, auto parts manufacturer into a "model of productivity." One of the first
decisions McPherson made was to cut 350 people from a
500 person staff at company headquarters in Toledo and
replace a 17-inch stack of company operating manuals with
a brief policy statement.

McPherson decentralized the corporate bureaucracy by
requiring managers to make decisions and encourage
personnel to participate in a Dana stock plan. At his
insistence, managers met with employees instead of sending memos, and in a unique move, time clocks were abol-
ished and managers helped personnel to establish their
own production goals.

Another innovation was the establishment of "Dana
University," an in-house training program for employees
who wanted to move up the ranks of the company. The
progressive policies of the company led one security
analyst to note that McPherson brought "Japanese-style
management to Dana before most people even knew what
it was."

McPherson's strategy was to make careful, small acquisitions while maintaining low costs and high productivity.
As a result, Dana was considered one of the nation's best-
run companies and maintained a sound financial record in
the 1970's. During this decade, McPherson moved Dana
away from its reliance on the original-equipment market
and toward the light trucks market, which ultimately
represented 35% of its 1970's sales.

Dana has been praised for its ability dramatically to
improve its acquisitions. For example, in 1974 Dana

acquired Summit Engineering Corporation, a manufacturer of numerical controls for machinery. At the time the company's sales were at $900,000. Under Dana's direction, sales increased to $18 million by 1979.

Between 1963 and 1980 Dana Corporation purchased 24 companies that were outside its original-equipment vehicle business and it saw profits rise from $62 million in 1975 to $164 million by 1979. There were now three distinct areas to the corporation's business: original-equipment auto and truck parts, replacement parts, and industrial machine components.

The changes implemented by McPherson were carried on by Gerald B. Mitchell in 1980 after McPherson retired. Dana's continuing commitment to its workers' concerns was made difficult for Mitchell because of problems brought on by the recession of the early 1980's. But Mitchell well understood the validity of his company's approach, having started as a Dana machine operator at the age of 16.

The emphasis on light truck parts in the 1970's caused a dependency that resulted in a 40% earnings drop in the 1980's when the light trucks no longer appealed to the consumer. 1982 earnings were 46% below those of 1980; Dana had to close five plants and lay off one-third of its employees in its American operations.

One United Auto Worker officer stated that Dana's management principles "are very nice while everything is going good. But when things turn bad, Dana is just like every other company." However, Dana's concern for its employees was demonstrated to some degree. The company offered its unemployed workers preferential hiring at other plants and assisted with relocation expenses. Lists of laid-off employees were sent to other manufacturers in the area and a two week job counseling program was provided when Dana plants were shut down.

Suddenly in 1983 Dana's original equipment parts business had an excellent year; earnings rose 119% to $112 million. However, Mitchell believed that Dana's best prospects for the future were probably in the replacement market for its auto and truck parts. In 1984, Mitchell was anticipating that the replacement parts business would make up 40% of the company's net earnings by 1989, while the original-equipment business would make up only about 30%.

Dana began manufacturing gears in 1984 that were identical to those designed for a line of Clark Equipment Company truck transmissions. Through this tactic, it is possible for Dana to "skim the cream off the top of Clark's

replacement sales." A competitor commented in *Business Week* that "Gerry Mitchell has drive and nerve, but our attitude is: We are going to watch him slip on that banana." But Mitchell did manage to direct Dana through a difficult period to a position of moderate security.

During the early 1980's Dana also diversified into the financial service industry. The company had earlier developed an internal financial service as protection against anticipated insurance costs. However, its acquisition of Cherokee Insurance Company, a small property and casualty insurance company, was not successful. In 1984 Cherokee failed and Dana wrote off $6 million of its investment. While Dana declared it had no further liability for Cherokee Insurance, other companies felt differently, particularly because Cherokee had been unable to fulfill reinsurance obligations. Dana was subsequently sued for $1.7 million by St. Regis Corporation in 1985 and other insurance companies involved with Cherokee were reviewing the matter.

During 1985 Dana spent $120 million on "Project 90," a program for investment in new technology, better use of existing facilities, and a new system of incentive payments which could be tied to higher productivity. The company hopes to reduce its costs to 90% of those of its major competitors. Dana is experiencing another transition because of the trend of car manufacturers' to make parts in-house or to use foreign-made parts. Although it has now limited its manufacture of passenger car components, Dana has expanded its production of engine parts for trucks.

Dana's future is inextricably bound to the automotive industry. However, over the years the company has learned to survive the industry's ups and downs. The changes that are occurring within Dana at the present time are a result of management's realistic, and optimistic, attitudes.

Principal Subsidiaries: Dana Equipamentos Limitada (Brazil) (99.9%); Racing-Hidraulica Ltd., (Brazil); Dana World Trade Corp.; Hayes-Dana Inc. (Canada) (52%); Diamond Printing and Mailing; Boston Industrial Products; Dana Domestic International Sales Corp.; Wix Corp.; Maumee Holdings BV (Netherlands); Albarus SA (Brazil) (56%); Warner Electric Brake & Clutch Co.; Dana Distributing Inc. The company also has subsidiaries in France and West Germany.

EAT•NEAT•N

EATON CORPORATION

1111 Superior Ave. N.E.
Cleveland, Ohio 44114
U.S.A.
(216) 523-5000

Public Company
Incorporated: 1911 as the Torbensen Gear & Axle
Company
Employees: 43,000
Sales: $3.675 billion
Market Value: $2.347 billion
Stock Index: New York

The Eaton Corporation is one of the world's largest automotive components manufacturers. In recent years, however, Eaton has attempted to reduce its exposure to the cyclical passenger automobile industry by entering new markets in high-technology products. Although the company has existed for over 60 years, its greatest growth occurred during the 1960's. Eaton is counting on a similar expansion again during the 1990's, when a number of new products from its electronics division become available.

Joseph Oriel Eaton established a small machine shop in Bloomfield, New Jersey in 1920. With a small staff, he started to manufacture heavy-duty truck axles for the expanding automotive transportation industry. But it soon became apparent that truck buyers preferred to purchase fully integrated vehicles; so Joseph Eaton targeted a new customer—truck manufacturers. In May 1923 the Eaton Axle Company was acquired by the Torbensen Gear & Axle Company and moved to Cleveland, in order to be closer to the auto manufacturers there and in Detroit. Over the next few years the new company, Eaton Axle & Spring, acquired a number of smaller auto parts manufacturers, and in the process diversified the company's product line. It was during this period that Eaton began to manufacture parts for aircraft engines.

The Company weathered the economic depression of the 1930's and managed to finance the purchase of several companies which were nearing bankruptcy. By the late 1930's industrial growth was stimulated by President Roosevelt's New Deal program, and demand for products of the Eaton Manufacturing Company (a name change was registered in May 1932) increased slowly but steadily. When the United States became involved in World War II Eaton, as a primary manufacturer of vehicle parts, produced a variety of items for the war effort.

After the war, in 1946 Eaton purchased the Dynamatic Corporation, and a year later established a joint sales and engineering company with two British firms, Rubry Owen and E.N.V. Engineering. These companies soon became suppliers of axles and gears to Ford and General Motors in England. In 1953 Livia, a small Italian manufacturer of engine valves acquired technological assistance and a production license from Eaton. Within a few years Livia had grown to become the exclusive supplier of engine valves for Simca of France as well as for all trucks built by Fiat. Livia was purchased by Eaton in 1961.

John C. Virden was named president of Eaton in 1958 and followed the company's policy of diversifying its lines of business. He was a strong believer in "divisional autonomy," insuring that Eaton's subsidiaries and divisions maintained a large degree of managerial independence. Under the direction of John Virden, Eaton made no less than 23 major acquisitions from 1958 to 1973. Eaton entered the automotive transmission business when it acquired Fuller Manufacturing in 1958. But the company's most important acquisition came in 1963, when it purchased the Yale & Towne Manufacturing Company.

Yale & Towne was founded in the 1870's by the inventor Linus Yale, Jr. He developed a revolutionary pin-tumbler cylinder lock which has remained basically unchanged since it was invented. When Yale died at the age of 47, Henry Towne took over the company and remained in charge for the next 50 years. Yale & Towne was acquired by Eaton on October 31, 1963 and a full merger occurred on January 1, 1966 when the company became known as Eaton Yale & Towne.

The Eaton auto parts division had suffered a temporary setback in 1965. General Motors, one of Eaton's primary customers, reduced its orders from Eaton when model changes and higher wages forced it to scale down production. Yale & Towne, however, remained profitable and its divisions supported the company until demand for Eaton's products recovered. The following year, Eaton Yale & Towne experienced record growth in sales and profits, largely as a result of an expansion in industrial growth.

Eaton and Yale & Towne executed a careful integration of managerial personnel. Officials at Yale & Towne were given important permanent positions in the new company. Gordon Patterson, formerly president of Yale & Towne, was named vice chairman. John Virden was promoted to chairman in 1963. He was replaced as president by Elliot Ludvigsen, a former president of Fuller Manufacturing. When Virden retired in 1969, E. Mandell de Windt, who joined the company as a production clerk, was elected chairman. The company's name was changed once again on April 21, 1971 to Eaton Corporation.

The lowered demand for American cars in the 1970's severely affected the three largest manufacturers of automobile components, Bendix, Rockwell, and Eaton. All three companies attempted further diversification of their operations. Bendix acquired new product lines, but never held on to them long enough significantly to broaden its markets. Rockwell attempted to increase sales of its consumer lines by adding electronics products but its fortunes remained bound to the defense department and NASA. Eaton, in contrast, began to emphasize the less volatile truck components market and expand in foreign markets. It also initiated a $470 million diversification program to develop a new line of factory automation products.

In 1978, with the automotive market still sluggish, Eaton made three acquisitions—Samuel Moore & Company, a manufacturer of hydraulic motors and transmissions, Kenway, a company specializing in robotic warehouse storage systems, and, most importantly, the electronics company Cutler-Hammer. The AIL electronics division of Cutler-Hammer had developed the ALQ-161 advanced radar counter-measures system for Rockwell's B-1 bomber and had also been chosen by NASA to build the landing system for the Space Shuttles. Eaton's intention was to combine the resources of these three companies in order to develop a new line of factory automation products. But during the development stage, dollar investment was high and product profits low. Eaton's position was worsened by its continued exposure to the weak automotive business and the Yale & Towne division's marginally profitable ventures with forest equipment and lift-trucks. 1980 was a particularly bad year for the corporation.

During 1981 Eaton sold or closed down 18 subsidiaries whose profits were marginal or non-existent. The forestry equipment and lift-truck businesses were written off and sold in 1982 for $200 million. That year Eaton registered its first loss in 50 years, $189.6 million on sales of $2.4 billion. Determined to reduce the company's exposure to the vagaries of the automotive components business, E. Mandell de Windt declared that Eaton had now dedicated itself to becoming a "high technology company servicing the growth markets of the 1980's."

Ironically, the automotive division generated most of the company's profit the following year. Eaton's major automotive customers, International Harvester, Ford, General Motors, and Paccar, had fully recovered from the recession of the mid-1970's and were once again selling a wide range of trucks. Even so, automotive components, which had accounted for 79% of Eaton's sales in 1977, were down to 46% in 1983. Twelve of the company's automotive components plants were closed and employment was reduced from 63,000 in 1979 to 41,000 in 1984. But sales from the electronic components division had risen dramatically from 21% of turnover in 1977 to 54% in 1983.

Jim Stover, president and chief operating officer of Eaton since 1979, was named chairman and chief executive officer when E. Mandell de Windt retired on April 23, 1986. Stover maintained de Windt's commitment to the company's substantial foreign markets, remarking that Eaton had learned from the recession that "you compete on a global basis or you don't compete at all." (The company's strong foreign presence currently accounts for 13.4% of sales.) Stover took over after Eaton had reported a 1985 profit of $231 million on sales of $3.7 billion. At the beginning of 1986 Eaton had one billion dollars available for financing acquisitions. By July it had purchased three more companies, Pacific-Sierra Research (defense and computer systems), Singer Controls (switches and valves), and Consolidated Controls (precision instruments). Despite continued emphasis on developing its high-technology and electronics business, the automotive division continues to provide the largest share of Eaton's profit. Stover's goal is to achieve equality in profits between the two divisions, but this is not expected to occur until the early 1990's.

Principal Subsidiaries: Analytical Assessments Corp.; Pacific-Sierra Research Corp.; Eaton International Corp.; AIL International, Inc.; Cutler-Hammer Export Sales Corp.; Eaton DISC Company; Yale Materials Handling Corp. (59%); Eaton Consulting Services Corp.; Eaton-Kenway, Inc.; Yale & Towne Company; Kenway Handling Systems, Inc.; Eaton I.C.S.A. (Argentina); Eaton Pty., Ltd. (Australia); Cutler-Hammer Australia Pty., Ltd.; Samuel Moore Europe S.A. (Belgium); Eaton Yale, Ltd. (Canada); Milmer Road Enterprises, Ltd. (Canada); Eaton Controles Industriales S.A. (Costa Rica) (97.78%); Eaton S.A. (France); Eaton Technologies, Ltd. (Hong Kong); Eaton S.p.A. (Italy); Eaton EST S.p.A. (Italy) (99%); Eaton Controls S.p.A. (Italy); Eaton Automotive S.p.A. (Italy); Eaton Nova S.p.A. (Italy); Eaton Japan Company, Ltd.; Eaton International, Inc. (Liberia); Cutler-Hammer Anstalt (Liechtenstein); Condura, S.A. de C.V. (Mexico); Cutler-Hammer Mexicana, S.A. (Mexico) (66.7%); Eaton s.a.m. (Monaco); Eaton B.V. (Netherlands); Eaton Finance N.V. (Netherlands Antilles) (71.05%); Cutler-Hammer New Zealand, Ltd.; Cutler-Hammer Nigeria, Ltd.; Cutler-Hammer (South Africa), Ltd.; Eaton Truck Components (Proprietary), Ltd. (South Africa); Cutler-Hammer Babelegi (Proprietary), Ltd. (South Africa); Cutler-Hammer Igranic Properties (Proprietary), Ltd. (South Africa); Eaton, S.A. (Spain) (50.14%); Productos Eaton Livia S.A. (Spain) (52%); Cutler-Hammer Espanola, S.A. (Spain); Cutler-Hammer Svenska A.B. (Sweden); Eaton, Ltd. (U.K.); Cutler-Hammer Europa, Ltd. (U.K.); Eaton Foreign Sales Corp. (U.S. Virgin Islands); Eaton, GmbH. (West Germany); Cutler-Hammer, Ltd. (Zambia); C.H.I. Properties (Private), Ltd. (Zimbabwe) (80%).

ECHLIN

ECHLIN INC.

100 Double Beach Rd.
Branford
Connecticut 06405
U.S.A.
(203) 481-5751

Public Company
Incorporated: January 13, 1959
Employees: 9,500
Sales: $933 million
Market value: $1.193 billion
Stock Index: New York

Echlin Inc., founded by the Echlin brothers in 1924, is a leading manufacturer of automotive replacement parts, including brake parts, engine parts and transmissions. The company has made at least 22 acquisitions since 1964, establishing subsidiaries across the United States and in eight foreign countries. Despite the corporate trend to diversify, most of Echlin's expansions have been within the low-profile and often volatile automotive parts business. Its non-automotive items, such as security access control products, industrial wire and cable products, and fork lift truck replacement parts, accounted for less than 10 percent of total sales in 1985.

Jack and Earl Echlin founded Echlin and Echlin in San Francisco in 1924. They made pistons, piston pins and similar parts at first, but then turned to manufacturing replacement parts such as ignitor gears and oil pump gears. Eventually, they bought the ignition business of another company and went on to become one of the United States' leading ignition manufacturers.

While Earl established a small machine shop, Jack appointed himself salesman of the firm and attended a night class to learn the rudiments of his job. Soon thereafter he devised a one-evening sales clinic for salesmen of auto parts stores whose training had been largely neglected. Salesmen from out of town began asking for the class, and soon Jack was traveling to cities across the country conducting his one-evening workshop. Jack Echlin expanded his class into a technical as well as a sales clinic, in which students were taught the value of replacement parts. His workshop and through it, his company, achieved a national reputation, and his classes became the cornerstone of Echlin's marketing program.

In 1928 the company signed a contract to supply oil pump and ignition gears to the National Automotive Parts Association (NAPA) which, in turn, distributed those parts to garages across the country. The contract proved lucrative, and soon Echlin began supplying ignition parts as well. The company and the association, which still work together, have grown faster than the industry as a whole, and NAPA is presently recognized as one of the most efficient distributors in the automotive parts market.

Continuing to demonstrate their understanding of the industry's needs, the Echlin brothers commenced publication of an ignition catalogue in 1929. It was the first time an entire list of ignition parts was listed within a single *Car Guide* and proved to be a boon to mechanics. The standard is still used today in parts catalogues. The brothers followed this innovation with another—the Echlin Visumatic Business System, a specially designed cabinet in which a mechanic could organize a small inventory of popular replacement parts. This device (in effect, an inventory management system) moved automotive parts into the repair facility, where the mechanic had immediate access to them. The cabinet has been used by Echlin ever since, and is the model for parts cabinets made by other manufacturers.

Echlin struggled through the Depression, an era when many people decided that buying replacement parts for their car was less expensive than acquiring a new one. But the high costs of operating in San Francisco forced the company to move to New Haven, Connecticut in 1939.

During World War II the company profited by manufacturing parts for aircraft automatic pilots. Jack Echlin served on the advisory boards of the War Production Board and the Office of Price Stabilization. When the war ended, sales rose dramatically after the years of parts shortages.

Jack Echlin remained as head of the company until 1969. He established a consistent annual sales growth rate of 15%, while adhering to a policy that kept the firm from expanding into unrelated areas. But within the field of automotive parts, Echlin made a number of acquisitions and developed new product lines. The most important of these were hydraulic brake parts, which became the second largest product line of the company, with sales in 1985 of $308.6 million. Management next added fuel systems parts, thus providing a more efficient service for its customers.

Echlin acquired Ace Electric Company in 1970, a manufacturer of components for alternators, generators, and starters. Soon the company was producing electronic voltage regulators, the first electronic product to appear in automobiles. Despite warnings to stay out of the voltage regulator business because the new units would supposedly have a very long life, Echlin continued to produce replacement units. It was a wise decision since the original voltage regulators did not prove to be as durable as some had anticipated. Echlin then introduced replacement parts for electronic ignition systems, which were standardized by all car manufacturers in 1975.

Echlin's acquisition in 1971 of the Berg Manufacturing Sales Company, a small producer of air brakes for trucks, also paid off handsomely. Initially, it allowed Echlin to broaden its base in the truck and trailer service industry. Then, in the mid-1970's, the federal government imposed safety regulations mandating stopping distance and straight line braking requirements on heavy-duty trucks and truck trailer rigs. Those stopping requirements could only be met through the use of advanced, electronically controlled anti-skid systems. A joint venture between Berg and Italy's Fiat led to the development of an anti-skid system which became standard equipment on a number of truck trailers.

Another successful acquisition was that of Lift Parts Manufacturing, a producer and distributor of parts for industrial lift trucks. This acquisition provided the company with a foothold in the off-road equipment and construction markets.

Echlin remedied its neglect of high-performance ignition systems with a program started in the 1970's. Racing quality ignition parts were marketed under the brand name ACCEL which, despite fierce competition, soon became the leading name in its field. Echlin backed up its ignition parts business with high performance clutches and a turbocharger for both car and truck engines. The popular turbocharger, first marketed for just $700, provided extra horsepower and improved efficiency.

Echlin recognized the importance of foreign markets and, beginning in 1969, established subsidiaries in West Germany, England, Australia, Canada, South Africa, Brazil, Venezuela, and the Virgin Islands. In 1986 Echlin agreed to a joint venture with Lucas Girling of Birmingham, England to manufacture and distribute brake parts for heavy-duty applications in Europe. Management had remained mindful of what Joe Scott, a president of Echlin, had said in 1976, "The growth in both passenger car and truck registrations outside the United States is about three times the rate of growth in North America. We view our international operations as money in the bank, ready to bring us increasing returns as our markets expand well beyond those of 1975."

The success of Echlin's policies were amply demonstrated by its revenues. Income climbed from $204.5 million in 1976 to $771.4 million in 1985. Profits over the same period rose from $13.2 million to $45.6 million.

The company still relies on sales of its products to warehouse distributors; its other major customers are mass merchandisers, oil companies, truck and trailer manufacturers, and other auto parts replacement manufacturers. Its broad product line currently divides into four categories: engine systems, brake parts, hard parts, and non-automotive parts. Engine systems include condensers, distributors and distributor caps, ignition coils, rotors, carburetor and emission control parts, fuel pumps, catalytic converters, and other items. The brake parts category comprises hydraulic brake master cylinders, items for both drum and disc brake systems, hoses and controllers for electrical brakes, and a variety of parts for the heavy-duty brake market. Hard parts consist of clutches, transmission parts, and water pumps. In the non-automotive category, Echlin produces small engine parts, fork lift truck replacement parts, security access control products, and industrial wire and cable products.

Due to the expected market growth in fuel systems products, heavy-duty brake products, rebuilt parts, and the export business, Echlin will probably continue to record a 15% annual increase in revenue. But while Echlin's foreign subsidiaries position it favorably for the growing international market, the company faces stiff foreign competition, and it will have to remain abreast of trends within the industry.

Principal Subsidiaries: Ace Electric Company, Inc.; Automotive Controls Corp.; Blackstone Manufacturing Co., Inc.; Brake Systems, Inc.; BWD Automotive Corp.; Echlin International , V.I., Inc.; Echlin-Ponce, Inc.; EPE, Inc.; Exhaust Controls Corp.; The Echlin Sales Company; Lift Parts Mfg. Co., Inc.; Lipe Corp.; Pacer Industries, Inc.; Midland Brake, Inc.; Ristance Corp.; Roto-Master, Inc.; Sierra Supply Company; Tekonsha Engineering Company; Continental Hydraulic Hose Corp.; and Vialle USA, Inc.. The company also has subsidiaries in the following countries: Australia, Brazil, Britain, Canada, Puerto Rico, Venezuela, and West Germany.

FEDERAL-MOGUL CORPORATION

P.O. Box 1966
Detroit, Michigan 48235
U.S.A.

Public Company
Incorporated: May, 1 1924
Employees: 12,500
Sales: $942 million
Market Value: $568 million
Stock Index: New York Pacific

Federal-Mogul Corporation had its origins in the Muzzy-Lyon Company, which was founded in Detroit, Michigan, in 1899 to sell mill and factory supplies. This firm, which became a national producer of bearings and bearing alloys, combined in 1924 with Federal Bearing and Bushing to form a new company called the Federal-Mogul Corporation. The growth of the organization through a series of expansions and acquisitions made it an important defense supplier during World War II. That growth continued with the acquisition of Bearing Company of America in 1953, the merger of Bower Roller Bearing Company into Federal-Mogul in 1955, and the acquisition of National Seal in 1956. In more recent years, the company has acquired a number of other units in both the United States and abroad. With headquarters in Southfield, Michigan, Federal-Mogul presently operates some 40 plants, more than 50 distribution centers, and four major research facilities throughout the world. Its product line ranges from a variety of precision parts for the transportation, farm equipment, construction and manufacturing industries, to aerospace components.

The history of Federal-Mogul goes back to the turn of the century when two young Detroit mill supply vendors began searching for ways to produce better babbitt metal. Babbitt metal, an alloy of tin, antimony, and copper, had been patented in 1839 by Issac Babbitt as an antifriction agent surrounding moving metallic locomotive parts. It remained the principal means to prevent rotating metallic shafts from overheating and wearing out. However, the 19th century methods were unsuitable for 20th century combustible engines. J. Howard Muzzy and Edward F. Lyon's success in developing new formulas for and applications of babbitt metal would help to make more efficient automobile engines possible.

Muzzy and Lyon left secure jobs to begin their new

business. As employees of J.T. Wing and Company, a vendor of mill and factory supplies, their friendship and business acumen had gradually matured. Determined to be their own bosses in the market they knew best, the two partners wasted no time opening the doors to their first building in 1900. The mill and factory supply business was highly competitive at the turn of the century. Many producers offered shoddy merchandise at inexpensive prices. The business also required a large running inventory of slow moving items, which would stretch the new firm's limited capital. Nonetheless, the partners established a reputation for quality items and made it through the early years, putting most of their profits back into the business. They also used aggressive and imaginative advertising, providing money-back guarantees and coupons good for prizes ranging anywhere from pocket rulers to firearms.

Whatever time Muzzy could spare from his primary responsibility of managing the financial and manufacturing end of the business he devoted to endless experimentation with babbitt metals. Lyon, when not on the road selling company products, joined his partner in blending new formulas of tin, antimony and lead. Their hard work paid off with major orders from Clark Motor Company and the Sheffield Motor Company. As a result of the increased business, the partners formed a subsidiary company called the Mogul Metal Company.

An inquiry from Sheffield's parent organization, the Fairbanks Morse Company, started Muzzy-Lyon on its next important breakthrough. The traditional method of making motor bearings was to pour molten babbitt metal directly onto the motor block and to shape the metal to fit by hand. Mechanics replaced worn bearings by laboriously gouging out the old metal and then pouring in the new. Why not die cast metals into standard size bearings? The partners purchased a typecasting machine and began modifying it. They were able to make some of the new parts themselves and commissioned various machine shops to produce the rest. In this way, the design and construction of their new machine remained a secret. Neither partner had any mechanical or engineering experience, but the machine worked.

The potential of the die casting machine so impressed the partners that they decided to drop the mill supply business completely. The company would devote its entire resources to manufacturing and mechandizing automotive bearings and babbitt metals. Soon orders for Mogul's die cast bearings began to arrive. The year 1910 brought an important order for 10,000 connecting rod bearings for the massive Buick 10. That same year the partners nearly lost a large order from the Hudson Motor Company when they refused to compromise their secret processes by allowing Hudson engineers to inspect the plant.

Despite a difficult business climate, the Muzzy-Lyon management retained enough confidence in the future to expand in 1923. The most significant events began when Muzzy learned that Douglas-Dahlin, a large Kansas City-based parts distributor, stood in danger of bankruptcy while owing the company a large sum of money. S.C. Reynolds, vice president of Federal Bearing and Bushing, called Muzzy to discuss the situation. His company was also faced with losing a large sum of money; consequently, the two men traveled together to Kansas City to protect their interests. On the trip they became friends and, when they compared their companies and assessed their relative strengths and weaknesses, they realized the advantages of a merger. The Federal Bearing employees were expert bronze foundrymen but lacked the capacity to produce babbitt. Muzzy-Lyon, on the other hand, operated a complete babbitt foundry but purchased bronze on the market. It seemed like a perfect partnership. The names of Muzzy-Lyon Company and Federal Bearing were replaced by Federal Mogul Corporation.

To protect its investments, Federal-Mogul took over the near-bankrupt Douglas-Dahlin Company. Suddenly Federal-Mogul was in the service business. Other acquisitions followed shortly. In 1927 Federal-Mogul purchased U.S. Bearings Company, an Indiana distributor that resold replacement bearings. The following year, Federal-Mogul's involvement in the service business increased substantially with the acquisition of the Watkins Manufacturing Company of Wichita, Kansas. Following this major expansion, Federal-Mogul also purchased the Pacific Metal Bearing Company in San Francisco, primarily to supply its West Coast branches. The corporation acquired the Indianapolis-based Superior Bearings Company in 1936. In 1937 the service division went international with the acquisition of the former Watkins Rebabbitting Limited that had locations in Toronto, Montreal, and Winnipeg, Canada. By 1939 Federal-Mogul operated 53 service branches across the North American continent.

World War II led to further expansion. By 1941 Federal-Mogul plants exhibited signs such as, "Defense Plant, part of the Arsenal of Democracy," and over 50 of their facilities were devoted to military production. Federal-Mogul plants turned out millions of bearings, bushings and seals for military applications. Their marine division won highly competitive U.S. Navy tests for PT boat propellers and secured orders for over 24,000 Super Equi-poise wheels for every PT boat propeller used by all the Allied navies, including the Soviet Union. From 50 employees in 1942, the marine division grew to a workforce of nearly 1,000 by the end of the war. From September of 1939 to July of 1945, the total area of Federal-Mogul plants had increased nearly threefold. The workforce had grown correspondingly and annual sales were more than double the best prewar amounts.

Employee layoffs after the war failed to impede the additional acquisition of compatible companies. In 1953 Federal-Mogul merged with Bearings Company of America to mark the single largest acquisition in its history. The merger of the Bearings Company brought 610 new employees and approximately 121,000 square feet of manufacturing space into the organization. Even more significant growth occurred in 1955 when the Bower Roller Bearing Company merged with Federal-Mogul. The relationship that had begun with a 1950 sales agreement had culminated into a union of the two businesses. The ink had scarcely dried on the Bower agreement when the corporation announced its third major merger in as many years. The National Motor Bearing Company would join the new Federal-Mogul-Bower Bearing Corporation in

1956. The acquisition earned the company its first listing in the *Fortune* magazine ranking of the 500 largest American companies. It ranked 350 in 1956 with sales that exceeded $100 million that year.

As the 1950's drew to a close, the corporation could look back on a decade of substantial growth. The service division alone had gone from 58 to 96 branches, and the number of customers had doubled to over 10,000. The mergers and increased efficiency of the 1950's had increased annual sales to four times their 1949 level.

Further successes marked the 1960's. The corporation's timely response to the changing face of world automobile production ultimately resulted in large dividends. The early 1960's saw a steady increase in the market share commanded by foreign automobile manufacturers. The worldwide spread of mass production technology, the development of the European Common Market, and increasing nationalism threatened American export sales. Federal-Mogul management noted this trend and in March of 1960 started to invest in foreign manufacturing operations and purchased interests in various major European bearing firms. Domestic expansion also continued and the firm turned more and more to specializing in the highly sophisticated missile market. In 1964 the company opened a new facility that was publicized as the most highly mechanized oil seal plant in the world. In 1965 the company purchased Steering Aluminum, a piston factory, and the Vellumoid Company, a manufacturer of gaskets and gasket materials.

The early 1970's marked a domestic expansion into the southern states. A highly automated new plant in Princeton, Kentucky opened in late 1970. The 50,000 square foot facility was devoted to production of super alloy metal powders. In 1971 a new plant in Virginia started to manufacture aluminum sleeve bearings while another plant emphasized the manufacture of bimetal bushings and bearings. An additional powdered metal parts plant in Ripley, Tennessee opened in 1972. The following year a new 360,000 square foot plant in Hamilton, Alabama began producing tapered rolling bearings ranging up to eight inches in diameter.

The 1975 recession caused management at Federal-Mogul to reassess its long-term strategy. Earnings were too closely tied to the original-equipment automotive industry which traditionally led the national economy into and out of recessions. However, 1976 brought the beginning of economic recovery. The integration of the international manufacturing operations with domestic product lines paid off and as the decade of the 1970's drew to a close it was apparent that Federal-Mogul had made a rapid recovery from the 1975 recession. Despite a depressed automotive market, 1979 marked Federal-Mogul's fourth consecutive year of record sales and earnings.

Tom Russell, the current president of Federal-Mogul, is said to be placing an emphasis on the strategy of diversification. In 1985 the corporation acquired the Mather Company, a manufacturer of high performance sealing products for the automotive and industrial markets and a leader in Teflon technology. The purchase of the Carter Automotive Company, a manufacturer of fuel systems with significant sales, further strengthened Federal-Mogul's position.

The days when an expanding automobile industry made for a good future in the bearing business have given way to a time when large numbers of stockholders expect constant growth and high dividends. For Federal-Mogul, this will result in a continued strategy of diversification and reorganization in the years to come.

Principal Subsidiaries: Huck Manufacturing Co.; Federal-Mogul World Trade Corp.; Federal-Mogul World Trade, Inc.; Mather Co. The company also has subsidiaries in the following countries: Brazil, Canada, England, France, Italy, Mexico, and West Germany.

FIAT GROUP

10 Corso Marconi
Turin
Italy
(011) 65651
Public Company
Incorporated: March 8, 1906 as Societa Anonima Fabbrica
   Italiana di Automobili
Employees: 226,222
Sales: L26.6 trillion (US$19.679 billion)
Market value: L26.9 trillion (US$19.905 billion)

The name Fiat is commonly associated with automobiles, but the company also manufactures commercial vehicles, construction machinery, thermomechanics and telecommunications equipment, metallurgical products, engine components, rail road stock, tractors, and airplanes. One of Europe's largest companies, Fiat also has interests in bio-engineering, transportation, and financial services companies; additionally, it owns one of Italy's leading newspapers, *La Stampa*.

Fiat was founded in 1899 by Giovanni Agnelli, an ex-cavalry officer, and a few other Turin businessmen. The city of Turin, often known as "Italy's Little Detroit," was developed with Fiat money and half of its population, either directly or indirectly, still depends on Fiat for a livelihood.

The company began manufacturing automobiles and engine parts for the automotive industry very early in the 20th century. With the advent of World War I, however, Fiat significantly expanded its production line, and as the years passed, the company became a conglomeration of various manufacturing enterprises. By the early post-war years, Fiat was manufacturing so many products that Agenlli felt it was time to improve central administration.

To help him in his reorganization efforts, Agnelli hired Vittorio Valletta, a university professor and former consulting engineer, in 1921. Their aim was to control all of the manufacturing processes as completely as possible, thus reducing their dependence on foreign suppliers. Soon, Fiat was pouring its own steel and producing its own plastics and paints. Thus, the company became even more diverse, and in a further reorganization, Agnelli formed a holding company, the IFI (Industrial Fiduciary Institute), in 1927. To this day, IFI is one of the wealthiest and most influential holding companies in Europe; and it remains a closed company, owned and operated by Agnelli's heirs.

In its first two decades, Fiat produced only two types of automobile; the basic, limited options model, and the de luxe model. The company had little incentive to offer other models since it was protected by the Italian government's high tariff policy (known as "kept capitalism"); as a result, imported cars were far beyond the reach of the average Italian. Indeed, more than 80% of all the cars sold in Italy were Fiats, and much of the remaining 20% of the country's car sales consisted of expensive Italian-made Lancias and Alfa Romeos.

Finally sensitive to Italian complaints that Fiat's "cheap" car was too expensive, the company developed the Topolino, or "Little Mouse," a four-cylinder, 16 horsepower two-seater which averaged 47 miles per gallon. It was an immediate success and accounted for 60% of the Fiats sold in Italy up until the mid-1950's.

Fiat flourished in World War II as it had done in World War I, and profits increased significantly under Mussolini's much heralded modernization program. But the company's production of planes, cars, trucks, and armored vehicles for the European and African campaigns of the Axis forces made its plants prime targets for Allied bombing raids.

Fiat faced the post war era with war-torn plants and antiquated production facilities, and at the height of its disarray, in 1945, Giovanni Agnelli died. Valletta was named president and managing director and immediately set about reviving the company's fortunes, aided by Agnelli's grandson, Giovanni Agnelli II, who became a senior vice president.

Once the Allied effort to rebuild post-war Europe was under way, Valletta applied to the U.S. Government for a loan to renovate and modernize company facilities. He reasoned that Fiat was crucial to Italy's recovery and should therefore be entitled to special help. Well aware of the political benefits of a strong Italy, the Americans granted Fiat a $10 million, six-month revolving loan. Other loans soon followed and the company was back in business, gearing up for full production ahead of most of its West European competitors. By 1948 Fiat's holdings represented six percent of Italy's industrial capital.

But fewer people were able to buy cars than before the war, and Fiat, like other car manufacturers, felt the effects of a smaller market. However, the company faced its problems squarely: to reduce its production costs substantially, Fiat built a plant for its 600 and 1300 models in Yugoslavia which was able to produce about 40,000 automobiles yearly. Other foreign expansion followed rapidly. Additionally, the company managed to secure a lucrative manufacturing contract from NATO.

Fiat's foreign forays were a mixed blessing; its Italian workers began to fear for their jobs and worker agitation became a severe problem. On a few occasions Valletta was held prisoner in communist-led worker uprisings in Turin. The political situation did not ease until the mid-1950's when the U.S. government tied an anti-communist clause to its $50 million offshore procurement contracts with Fiat. This resulted in the firing, relocation, and political re-education of many Fiat employees, as well as improvements in the company's already elaborate (by U.S. standards) social welfare program. The Italian workers formed three unions, the largest of which cooperated closely with company management.

Valletta spent $800 million in expansion and modernization in the 15 years following World War II and built the most impressive steelworks in Italy. By 1959 Fiat sales reached $644 million, representing one third of its country's mechanial production and one tenth of its total industrial output. The price of Fiat's stock quintupled between 1958 and 1960; even so, Fiat did not reduce the relative price of its cars.

Still running the company in 1960 at the age of 76, Valletta was a keen supporter of Italy's membership of the European Economic Community. He was sure that Italian companies were strong enough to survive direct competition from the other five members. Fiat itself had the advantage of a highly trained staff, the swiftest production lines in Europe, and listed assets of $1.25 billion. But Italy's organization of manufacturers, Confindustria, opposed EEC membership, believing that France and Germany would quickly dominate the market. Nevertheless, by the end of the first year of membership, Italian companies made 283 deals with companies in other EEC countries; but the only deal involving the giant Fiat was a sales arrangement with the French automaker Simca.

Valletta's confidence in his company's competitiveness within the EEC was seriously questioned when, in 1961, intra-community tariffs were lowered and import quotas were dropped. At the same time, American automakers such as General Motors, Ford, and Chrysler were significantly expanding their European operations. It quickly became apparent that Fiat had underestimated the potential sales of foreign-made cars in Italy. Unwilling to wait months for delivery of a Fiat, or simply tired of its models, Italians were more than ready to consider the increasing array of foreign vehicles. Moreover, Fiat misjudged its domestic market and failed to introduce a model that might appeal to the many Italians moving from the lower to the middle income bracket. In three years, from 1960 to 1963, Fiat's domestic sales dropped a massive 20%, from 83% to 63%.

The company filled the gap in its product line with its 850 sedan, and by 1965, Italian car imports had dropped to 11%. But part of the revival in Fiat's domestic sales was effected by less positive means: the company launched a vigorous campaign against car imports enlisting the aid of its newspaper, *La Stampa*. This campaign was aided and abetted by the Italian government which angered car exporting countries by imposing a supposedly non-discriminatory anti-inflation tax on automobiles.

Meanwhile Fiat's exports improved and sales to underdeveloped nations flourished. In addition to its assembly plants in Germany and Austria, the company built plants in numerous other countries, including India, Morocco, Egypt, South Africa, Spain, and Argentina. Fiat also signed an agreement with the Soviet Union in 1965 for a facility capable of producing 600,000 units a year by 1970.

After running Fiat for 21 years, Vittorio Valletta was succeeded in 1966 by Giovanni Agnelli II, the founder's grandson. Under Agnelli's leadership, the company's annual sales came close to $2 billion by 1968, and for a short time Fiat edged out Volkswagen as the world's fourth largest automaker. At that time Fiat's cooperative arrangement with the French car maker Citroen made it the world's sixth largest non-American firm; the company operated 30 plants and employed 150,000 workers. Agnelli candidly credited Fiat's success to the company's near monopoly of its domestic market for half a century, but he warned that more sophisticated production methods were required if Fiat was to survive in the international market. He imposed a schedule for new models of two years from drawing board to assembly line and standardized many car parts to allow more interchange between models.

Agnelli also sought further to diversify Fiat's products to lessen its dependence on autos and trucks which accounted for 86% of its revenue. At the same time he set about improving the company's flagging sales performance in underdeveloped countries, and in 1969 he made two notable acquisitions. Fiat took full control of the Italian car manufacturer Lancia and announced a merger with Ferrari, the famous Italian racing car company. When Ferrari's problems had surfaced in 1962, owner Enzo Ferrari had turned down the Ford Motor Company but accepted financial backing from Fiat. Further losses forced Ferrari to sell, and his company was reconstructed as Fiat's racing car division.

While the Ferrari and Lancia acquisitions were good for Fiat's image both at home and abroad, its domestic situation worsened. The company had to contend with Italy's 7.3% inflation rate and a series of strikes; 1972 production fell short by 200,000 vehicles. For the first time in its history, Fiat failed to show a profit or pay an interim dividend. Fortunately, news from abroad was good. Agnelli's younger brother, Umberto, who had doubled sales at Fiat France in 1965–70 and constructed successful plants in Argentina and Poland, had gone on to direct American sales. The number of Fiats sold there doubled between 1970 and 1972 and Fiat cars became the fourth largest selling import in the U.S. Umberto returned to Italy as second-in-command to help his brother with the pressing problems at home.

But events appeared to be beyond the brothers' control and Fiat's domestic fortunes deteriorated to the point where the company seemed a likely candidate for partial state ownership. In 1973 Fiat slipped $30 million into the red, and after a three-month strike in 1974, Italy's Socialist Labor Minister granted the union a monthly pay increase significantly higher than Fiat's final offer. Amidst Fiat's loud protests, the government also imposed ceilings on the prices the company could charge for its automobiles—and this at a time when sales were down 45% because of worldwide apprehension over the energy crisis. Finally, it seemed, the days of government protection for Fiat were over; the politicians were having to listen to their constituents, many of whom, at that time, viewed the industrial bosses as enemies of the people. Fiat's case was not helped by the Agnelli brothers' refusal to reveal the value of IFI, the family-owned holding company whose funds— in Swiss banks—were beyond Italian government scrutiny.

However, Fiat's foreign holdings continued to offset its severe troubles on the home front, and the company thrived in the less saturated markets of Eastern Europe, Turkey, and South America. Its largest overseas investment was an $86 million plant in Brazil which became operational in 1976. Other foreign ventures included a project with the American Allis Chalmers company, an important manufacturer of earth-moving equipment with units in the United States, Italy, and Brazil, and under an arrangement with Colonel Khadafi in 1976, Libya acquired a 10% interest in Fiat. This purchase cost Moammar Khadafi $415 million and Fiat shares immediately rocketed on the Milan Exchange. Since Libya paid almost three times the market price, serious questions were raised about Khadafi's long-term motives. But Fiat had no such qualms; Khadafi's purchase eased its cash flow at a time when the company earned less than $200,000 on sales of about $4 million and had dipped into reserves in order to pay shareholders.

Meanwhile, the company's domestic woes continued. In 1974, with a heavy backlog of unsold cars to keep it going, Fiat fired all of its Italian workers with violent records. A year later, the company laid off a massive 15% of its Italian work force and was able to weather the ensuing strike.

Fiat's management was convinced that it could beat its powerful competitors by producing cars at the lowest possible price. Through its subsidiary Comau, a leader in the automation field, Fiat retooled and partially robotized its factories and standardized yet more Fiat car parts. The assembly robots provided the company with much greater flexibility on production lines, since the machines could easily be programmed to perform a variety of tasks on a variety of models. Further worker layoffs were justified by Fiat by the rise in production rates. Annual output per worker in 1979 was 14.8 units; in 1983 the output was up to 25 units per worker.

Fiat's bold and successful moves to modernize were matched by major changes abroad. The company entirely removed itself from the U.S. market, choosing not to compete against General Motors, Ford, Chrysler, and Japanese imports. In South America the company closed operations in Uruguay, Chile, Colombia, and Argentina, retaining only its facility in Brazil. Fiat's international operations were also brought under the aegis of a new holding company, the Fiat Group.

Since its recovery Fiat has been building a light truck engine designed by Peugeot, has developed a car underbody and components with Alfa Romeo, and with Ford of Britain has formed a venture to manufacture heavy trucks. As Fiat moves toward the next decade it has highly automated production lines, a diverse range of products, and a firmer grasp of its international finances. Management is hopeful that its recent achievements will enable the company to be a major factor in the automobile industry of the 1990's.

Principal Subsidiaries: IHF S.A.; Iveco B.V.; Fiat-Allis B.V.; Bioengineering International B.V.; Fiat France S.A.; Deutsch Fiat GmbH.; Fiat do Brasil S.A.; Fiat Concord S.A.; Fiat USA; Fiat Financing Holding B.V.; Fiat Auto S.p.A.; Fiat Trattori S.p.A.; Teksid S.p.A.; Fiat Componenti S.p.A.; Comau Finanziaria S.p.A.; Fiat-impresit S.p.A.; Fiat Ferroviaria Savigliano S.p.A.; Fiat Aviazione S.p.A.; Fiat TTG S.p.A.; Telettra S.p.A.; Ventana S.p.A.; Itedi S.p.A.; Fidis S.p.A.

Further Reading: *Il signor Fiat: Una biografia* by Enzo Biagi, Milan, Rizzoli, 1976; *Giovanni Agnelli: La Fiat dal 1899 al 1945* by Valerio Castronovo, Turin, Einaudi, 1977.

FORD MOTOR COMPANY

The American Road
Dearborn, Michigan 48121
U.S.A.
(313) 322–3000

Public Company
Incorporated: July 9, 1919
Employees: 383,300
Sales: $62.17 billion
Market value: $21.2 billion
Stock Index: New York Boston Pacific Midwest
Toronto Montreal London

Until recently, the Ford Motor Company has been one of the most dynastic of major American enterprises, a factor which has both benefited the company and brought it to the brink of disaster. Today, Ford is the second largest manufacturer of automobiles and trucks in the world, and its operations are well diversified, both operationally and geographically. The company operates the world's second largest finance company in the world, and is a major producer of tractors, glass, and steel. It is most prominent in the United States, but also has plants in Canada, Britain, and West Germany, and facilities in almost 100 other countries.

Henry Ford, the founder of the Ford Motor Company, was born on a farm near Dearborn, Michigan in 1863. He had a talent for engineering, which he pursued as a hobby from boyhood, but it was not until 1890 that he commenced his engineering career as an employee of the Detroit Edison Company. In his spare time Ford constructed experimental gasoline engines, and in 1892 completed his first "gasoline buggy." Dissatisfied with the buggy's weight, he sold it in 1896 to help fund the construction of a new car. Ford's superiors at the electric company felt his hobby distracted him from his regular occupation, and despite his promotion to chief engineer, he was forced to quit in 1899.

Shortly afterwards, with financial backing from private investors, Ford established the Detroit Automobile Company. He later withdrew from the venture after a disagreement with business associates over the numbers and prices of cars to be produced. Ford advocated a business strategy which combined a lower profit margin on each car with greater production volumes. In this way, he hoped to gain a larger market share and maintain profitability.

Working independently in a small shed in Detroit,

Henry Ford developed two four-cylinder, 80-horsepower race cars, called the "999" and the "Arrow." These cars won several races and helped to create a new market for Ford automobiles. With $28,000 of capital raised from friends and neighbors, Henry Ford established a new shop on June 16, 1903. In this facility, a converted wagon factory on Mack Avenue in Detroit, the Ford Motor Company began production of a two-cylinder, eight-horse-power design called the Model A. The company produced 1,708 of these models in the first year of operation.

The Ford Motor Company was sued by the Licensed Association of Automobile Manufacturers, an industrial syndicate which held patent rights for "road locomotives" with internal combustion engines. Ford responded by taking the matter to the courts, arguing that the patent, granted to George B. Selden in 1895, was invalid. During the long process of adjudication, Ford continued to manu-facture cars and relocated to a larger plant on Piquette and Beaubien Streets. A Canadian plant was established in Walkerville, Ontario on August 17, 1904.

Henry Ford and his engineers designed several automo-biles, each one designated by a letter of the alphabet; these included the small, four-cylinder Model N (which sold for $500), and the more luxurious six-cylinder Model K (which sold poorly for $2500). The failure of the Model K, coupled with Henry Ford's persistence in developing inexpensive cars for mass-production, caused a dispute between Ford and his associate Alexander Malcolmson. The latter, who helped to establish the company in 1903, resigned and his share of the company was acquired by Henry Ford. Ford's holdings then amounted to 58½%. In a further consolidation of his control, Ford replaced John S. Gray, a Detroit banker, as president of the company in 1906.

In October 1908, despite the continuing litigation with the Selden syndicate, Ford introduced the durable and practical Model T. Demand for this car was so great that Ford was forced to enlarge its production facilities. Over 10,000 Model Ts were produced in 1909. Able to vote down business associates who favored more conventional methods of production, Henry Ford applied his "assembly line" concept of manufacturing to the Model T.

In developing the assembly line, Ford noted that the average worker performed several tasks in the production of each component, and used a variety of tools in the process. He improved efficiency by having each worker specialize in one task with one tool. The component on which the employee worked was conveyed to him on a moving belt, and after allowing a set time for the task to be performed, the component was moved on to the next operation. Slower workers thus needed to increase their work rate in order to maintain production at the rate determined by the speed of the belts.

Ford's battle with the Selden group led to a decision by the Supreme Court in 1911, eight years after the initial suit. The Court ruled that the Selden patent was invalid. The decision freed many automobile manufacturers from costly licensing obligations; it also enabled others to enter the business.

When the United States became involved in World War I (April 1917), the Ford Motor Company placed its resources at the disposal of the government. For the duration of the war, Ford Motor produced large quantities of automobiles, trucks, and ambulances, as well as Liberty airplane motors, Whippet tanks, Eagle "submarine chasers," and munitions.

In 1918 Henry Ford officially retired from the company, naming his son Edsel president, and ceding to him a controlling interest. But in fact, Henry continued to direct company strategy, and spent much of his time developing a farm tractor called the Fordson. He also published a conservative weekly journal, *The Dearborn Independent*. Edsel, who was more reserved and pragmatic than his father, concerned himself with routine operations.

At the end of the war Henry and Edsel Ford disagreed with fellow stockholders over the planned expenditure of several million dollars for a large new manufacturing complex at River Rouge, near Detroit. The Fords eventually resolved the conflict by buying out all the other shareholders. Their company was re-registered as a Delaware corporation in July 1919. The River Rouge facility, built shortly afterward, was a large integrated manufacturing and assembly complex which included a steel mill of substantial capacity.

Between January 1 and April 19, 1921 the Ford Motor Company had $58 million in financial obligations due, and only $20 million available to meet them. Convinced that Ford Motor would be forced into bankruptcy, representatives of several large financial houses offered to extend loans to the company, on the condition that the Fords yield financial control. When the offer was refused, the bankers retreated, certain that they would soon be called upon to repossess the company.

With little time available, Henry Ford transferred as many automobiles as possible to his dealerships, who were instructed to pay in cash. Almost immediately, this generated $25 million. Next, Ford purchased the Detroit, Toledo & Ironton railroad, the primary medium of transportation for his company's supplies. By rearranging the railroad's schedules, Ford was able to reduce by one-third the time that automotive components spent in transit. This allowed him to reduce inventories by one-third, thereby releasing an additional $28 million. With additional income from other sources, and reduction in production costs, Ford had $87 million in cash by April 1, $27 million more than he needed to pay off the company debts.

The Ford Motor Company's only relationship with banks after this crisis was as a depositor. And despite poor financial management, Ford maintained such strong profitability that it offered to lend money on the New York markets, in competition with banks. With large quantities of cash still available, Ford acquired the financially troubled Lincoln Motor Company in 1922.

Edsel Ford was more enthusiastic about the development of the aircraft industry than his father, and in 1925 persuaded his fellow shareholders (all family members) to purchase the Stout Metal Airplane Company. His close friend William Stout, who was retained as vice president and general manager of the company, developed a popular three-engine passenger aircraft known as the Ford Trimotor. 196 of these aircraft were built during its production run.

After 18 years producing the Model T, the Ford Motor Company faced its first serious threat from a competitor. In 1926 the General Motors Corporation introduced its Chevrolet automobile, a more stylish and powerful car. Sales of the Model T dropped sharply. After months of experimenting with a six-cylinder model, Ford decided to discontinue the Model T in favor of the new Model A. On May 31 1926, Ford plants across the country were closed for six months while assembly lines were retooled.

That year Ford voluntarily reduced its work week to five days declaring that workers should also benefit from the success of the company. Ford was also one of the first companies to limit the work day to eight hours, and to establish a minimum wage of $5 per day. At Henry Ford's own admission, these policies were instituted more to improve productivity than to appease dissatisfied (and unrepresented) workers.

The British Ford Company was formed in 1928 and shortly thereafter the German Ford Company was founded. Henry Ford recognized the Soviet Union as a market with great potential, and like a number of other American industrialists, he fostered a relationship with officials in the Soviet government. Later, Ford participated in the contruction of an automobile factory at Nishni-Novgogrod.

The economic crisis of October 1929, which led to the Great Depression, forced many companies to close. Ford Motor managed to remain in business, despite losses of as much as $68 million per year. By 1932 economic conditions became so difficult that the Ford minimum wage was reduced to $4 per day. But for its Model A, which sold 4.5 million units between 1927 and 1931, Ford's situation would have been much worse.

The economy of Detroit was heavily dependent on large, locally based industrial manufacturers and when companies less successful than Ford were forced to suspend operations, a banking crisis developed. The Ford Motor Company, and Edsel Ford personally, extended about $12 million in loans to these banks in an effort to maintain their solvency. But these efforts failed and the banks were forced to close in February 1933. Ford lost over $32 million in deposits and several millions more in bank securities. The principal Ford bank, Guardian National, was subsequently reorganized by Ford interests as the Manufacturers National Bank of Detroit. Ford's largest business rival, General Motors, having suffered a similar crisis, emerged with control over the National Bank of Detroit.

The implementation of President F.D. Roosevelt's "New Deal," made conditions more favorable to the organization of labor unions. But Henry Ford, who had supported President Hoover in the election, advised his workers to resist union organization, and in 1935 raised the company's minimum wage to $6 per day.

In 1937 the United Automobile Workers union began a campaign to organize Ford workers by sponsoring the employee occupation of a Ford plant in Kansas City. The conflict was resolved when Ford officials agreed to meet with union representatives. That same year there was trouble at the River Rouge complex. Several men distributing UAW pamphlets at the gates were severely beaten by unidentified assailants, believed to have been agents of the Ford security office. Following an investigation by the National Labor Relations Board, Ford was cited for numerous unfair labor practices. The finding was contested, but eventually upheld when the Supreme Court refused to hear the case.

In 1940 Henry Ford, who opposed American involvement in World War II, cancelled a contract (arranged by Edsel) to build 6000 Rolls-Royce Merlin aircraft engines for the British Royal Air Force, and 3000 more for the United States Army. In time, however, public opinion led Ford to change his mind. Plans were made for the construction of a large new government-sponsored facility to manufacture aircraft at Willow Run, west of Dearborn.

Unionization activities climaxed in April 1941 when Ford employees went on strike. The NLRB called an employee election, under the terms of the Wagner Act, to establish a union representation for Ford workers. When the ballots were tabulated in June, the UAW drew 70% of the votes. Henry Ford, an avowed opponent of labor unions, suddenly altered his stand. He agreed to a contract with union representatives which met all worker demands.

The company devoted its resources to the construction of the Willow Run Aircraft plant. Eight months later, in December 1941, the Japanese bombing of Pearl Harbor resulted in a declaration of war by the United States against Japan, Germany, and Italy. Willow Run was completed the following May. It was the largest manufacturing facility in the world, occupying 2.5 million square feet of floor space, with an assembly line three miles long. Adjacent to the plant were hangars, covering 1.2 million square feet, and a large airfield. The airplanes produced at this facility were four-engine B-24E Liberator bombers, the Consolidated Aircraft version of the Boeing B-24. Production of aircraft got off to a slow start, but after adjustments the rate of production was raised to one plane per hour, 24 hours a day. During the war, other Ford Motor plants produced a variety of engines, as well as trucks, jeeps, M-4 tanks, M-10 tank destroyers, and transport gliders. The company also manufactured large quantities of tires, despite the removal of its tire plant to the Soviet Union.

Edsel Ford died unexpectedly in May 1943 at the age of 49. At the time of his death, Edsel was recognized as a far better manager than his father. Indeed, Henry Ford was often criticized for repeatedly undermining his son's efforts to improve the company, and the managerial crisis which occurred after Edsel's death is directly attributable to Henry Ford's persistent failure to prepare capable managers for future leadership of the company.

Edsel had been responsible for much of the company's wartime mobilization and his absence was deeply felt by his aging father, who was forced to resume the company presidency. In need of assistance, Henry Ford sought a special discharge from the Navy for Edsel's son Henry II. The navy complied, citing the special needs of Ford management during wartime. Henry Ford vigorously prepared his grandson to succeed him.

By the end of the war, when the Willow Run plant was turned over to the government, Ford had produced 8600 B-24E bombers and over 57,000 aircraft engines.

In September 1945, Henry Ford II, aged 28, was named president of the Ford Motor Company. The inexperienced man could not have started at a worse time. No longer supported by government contracts, the company began to lose money at a rate of $10 million per month. The source of the problem was Henry Ford I's financial management policy, specifically designed to perplex the Internal Revenue Service and discourage audits. The severe economic conditions after the war made Ford's finances an albatross.

Unable to bring the company's finances under control, Henry II hired Ernest R. Breech, a General Motors executive and past chairman of Bendix, in 1946. Breech was placed in charge of two groups—a managerial group and a financial one. The first one was comprised of several managers hired away from General Motors, and the second group was made up of ten talented financial experts who had served with the Air Force Office of Statistical Control. The Air Force group included Robert S. McNamara, J. Edward Lundy, Arjay Miller, and Charles "Tex" Thornton; they spent several years reconstructing the company's system of financial management.

Henry Ford I, who had retained the title of chairman since 1945, died in April 1947 at the age of 83. Henry II and Ernest Breech were then able to implement their own strategies for recovery, and these included the adoption of the proven General Motors management structure, and the decision to establish the Ford Motor Company in foreign markets. In its first year under Breech, the company registered a profit and it continued to gain strength in the late 1940's and early 1950's. Breech's top priority was strict adherence to a financial plan with strong profit margins; unfortunately, this proved to be at the expense of developing automobiles for an increasingly complex market.

Over the previous two decades, the Ford Motor Company had been a notable pioneer and achiever in the industry, and it was the first company to cast a V-8 engine block (1932). Ford had produced its 25 millionth automobile in 1937 and the following year, its Lincoln Division introduced the Mercury line which proved highly successful in the growing market for medium-priced automobiles. Ford's good image had been further enhanced by its contributions to the Allied effort in World War II; even Josef Stalin had kind words for the enterprising American company.

Before he died, Henry Ford I had created two classes of Ford stock. The B Class was reserved for family members and constituted the controlling 40% voting interest. The ordinary common shares were to be retained by the company until January 1956, when they were to be offered to the public for the first time.

Two years after Henry I's death, in 1949, the company unveiled a number of new automatic styles. But while the cars were practical, and to a degree fashionable, the company no longer appeared to be a pioneer; indeed it gained a reputation, not wholly justified, as being an imitator of General Motors.

Regaining its initiative, the Ford Motor Company decided to introduce a new model to fill a gap in the market between the Ford and Lincoln-Mercury lines. In 1958 the much heralded, 410 horsepower Edsel made its debut. It was a terrible flop. Ford's market researchers had been very wrong; there was no gap in the market for the Edsel to fill. After just two years, production of the ill-fated car ceased. 110,847 units had been produced, at a loss of some $250 million.

The 1960's saw many changes at Ford: dissatisfied with his secondary role in the company decision-making, Henry Ford stripped Breech of his power, replacing him with Robert McNamara. But McNamara left the Ford Motor Company in 1961 to serve as Secretary of Defense in the Kennedy administration. Many of McNamara's duties were taken over by Arjay Miller, who succeeded the interim president, John Dykstra, in 1963.

The Ford Motor Company purchased the Philco Corporation in 1961 and established a tractor division in 1962. The following year Ford introduced its highly successful Mustang; more than 500,000 of these cars were sold in 18 months. The man most responsible for developing the Mustang was a protégé of Robert McNamara named Lee Iacocca.

In another move intended to assert his authority over management, Henry Ford dismissed Arjay Miller in 1968 and named Semon E. Knudsen as president. Knudsen, a former executive vice president at General Motors, known for his strong personality, found himself in constant conflict with Henry Ford, and after 19 months he was replaced by Lee Iacocca. Iacocca was a popular figure, highly talented in marketing and sales, but like Knudsen, he frequently disagreed with Henry Ford.

Ford Motor Company subsidiaries in Europe entered a period of strong growth and high profitability in the early 1970's, and these subsidiaries produced components for the Pinto, a sub-compact introduced in the U.S. in 1971. Pinto models from 1971 to 1976 and similarly configured Bobcats from 1975 to 1976 drew a great deal of attention after numerous incidents in which the car's gas tank exploded in rear-end collisions. The unfavorable publicity from news reports damaged Ford's public image, as did the wrongful death litigation.

In April 1977 Henry Ford reduced Iacocca's power by creating a new executive triumvirate. Iacocca was a member of this, along with Ford himself and Philip Caldwell. But a year later, Henry Ford added his brother William Clay Ford to the group and relegated Iacocca to a subordinate position; then within a few months, Ford suddenly fired Iacocca and installed Caldwell as president. Henry Ford was battling stockholder allegations of financial misconduct and bribery at the time and his dismissal of Iacocca made him more unpopular than ever.

Henry Ford made a critical decision and a very misguided one. He cancelled development of a small car which had been proposed by Iacocca and which was intended to succeed the aging Pinto. Thus, as the Japanese compacts became increasingly popular in the U.S., Ford found itself quite unable to compete. Adding to its woes, Ford Motor, along with other U.S. car manufacturers, was obligated by Congressional legislation (particularly the Clean Air Act) to develop automobiles which would emit less pollutants.

Henry Ford relinquished his position as chief executive officer to Philip Caldwell in October 1979. The following March, Ford retired and gave the chairmanship to Caldwell, but he retained his seat on the board of directors.

The Ford Motor Company encountered severe economic losses as a result of a reduction in market share, and high costs incurred by labor contracts and the development of automobiles that met the new federal standards. In 1980 the company lost $1.54 billion, despite strong profits from the truck division and European operations. Ford lost a further $1.06 billion in 1981 and $658 million in 1982 while trying to effect a recovery; its market share fell from 23.6% in 1978 to 16.6% in 1981.

Company officials studied Japanese methods of industrial management, and worked more closely with Toyo Kogyo, the Japanese manufacturer of Mazda automobiles (Ford gained a 25% share of Toyo Kogyo in November 1979, when a Ford subsidiary merged with the company). Ford imported Mazda cars and trucks, and in many ways treated Toyo Kogyo as a small car division until the Escort, its successor to the Pinto, reached the showrooms. This new compact was modelled after the Ford (Europe) Erika; another version of it, the Lynx, was produced by Ford's Lincoln-Mercury division.

Caldwell transferred the talented manager Harold Poling from the European division to the United States in an attempt to apply successful European formulas to the American operation. In the restructuring which followed several plants were closed and more than 100,000 workers were dismissed. Ford's weakness in the market was a major concern of the unions; consequently, the company inaugurated a policy of employee involvement in plant operations and was able to secure more favorable labor contracts. Productivity improved dramatically.

In 1984, with costs reduced, Ford started to repurchase 30 million shares (about 10% of the company's stock). Its production of cars in Mexico was increased, and through its interest in Kia Motors, output was stepped up in South Korea. The following year Ford introduced the Taurus (another version, the Salde, was produced by its Mercury division), a modern full-size automobile which had taken five years to develop at a cost of $3 billion. The Taurus proved highly successful and won several design awards.

Sales and profits reached record levels in 1984, and in 1986 Ford surpassed General Motors in income for the first time since 1924. In addition, Ford's market share increased to just under 20%. Ford Motor purchased several companies in the mid 1980's, including the First Nationwide Financial Corporation and the New Holland tractor division of Sperry, which was later merged with Ford Tractor. Ford also purchased a 30% share of Otosan, the automotive subsidiary of the Turkish Koc Group. The attempted acquisition of the Italian car maker Alfa Romeo in 1986 failed, due to a rival bid from Fiat.

Philip Caldwell retired as chairman and chief executive officer in February 1985 and was succeeded by Donald Petersen. While Ford family interests continue to control the Ford Motor Company, it is unlikely that a Ford family member will play an active role in the management of the company for some time to come.

Principal Subsidiaries: Rouge Steel Co.; Ford Aerospace & Communications Corp.; Ford Electronics and Refrigeration Corp.; Ford Export Corp.; Ford International Capital Corp.; Ford International Finance Corp.; Ford Motor Credit Co.; Parker Chemical Co.; The American Road Insurance Co.; Ford Leasing Development Co.; Ford Motor Land Development Corp.; First Nationwide Financial Corp.; First Nationwide Savings; Ford Motor Company Ltd. (England); Ford Motor Credit Company Ltd. (England); Henry Ford & Son (Finance) Ltd. (England); Ford-Werke A.G. (West Germany); Ford Credit Bank A.G. (West Germany); Ford Motor Company of Canada Ltd.; Ensite Ltd. (Canada); Ford Glass Ltd. (Canada); Ford Motor Company of Australia Ltd.; Ford Motor Company of New Zealand Ltd.; Ford Brasil S.A. (Brazil); Ford Motor de Venezuela; Ford France S.A.; Ford Motor Company (Belgium) N.V.; Ford Credit N.V. (Belgium); Ford Italiana S.p.A. (Italy); Ford Credit S.p.A. (Italy); Ford Leasing S.p.A. (Italy); Ford Motor Argentina S.A.; Ford Motor Company A/S (Denmark); Ford Motor Company S.A. (Mexico); Ford Nederland B.V. (Netherlands); Ford Espana S.A. (Spain); Ford Credit S.A. (Spain); Ford Leasing S.A. (Spain); Ford Credit A.B. (Sweden); Ford Credit S.A. (Switzerland); Transcon Insurance Ltd. (Bermuda); Mazda Motor Corporation (Japan); Ford Motor Company (Japan) Ltd.; Ford Lio Ho Motor Company Ltd. (Taiwan). Ford also has 262 American and 81 foreign vehicle dealerships and 162 other American and foreign subsidiaries.

Further Reading: *The Public Image of Henry Ford: An American Folk Hero and His Company* by David L. Lewis, Detroit, Wayne State University Press, 1976; *Henry Ford, "Ignorant Idealist"* by David E. Nye, Port Washington, New York, Kennikat Press, 1979; *Henry Ford, the Wayward Capitalist* by Barbara Gelderman, New York, Dial Press, 1981; *The Five Dollar Day: Labor Management and Social Control in the Ford Motor Company 1908–1921* by Stephen Meyer, Albany, State University of New York Press, 1981; *Working for Ford* by Huw Beynon, London, Penguin, 1984.

FRUEHAUF

FRUEHAUF CORPORATION

10900 Harper Ave.
Detroit, Michigan 48232
U.S.A.
(313) 267–1000

Public Company
Incorporated: Feb. 27, 1918 as Fruehauf Trailer Company
Employees: 26,500
Sales: $2.56 billion
Market value: $2.1 billion
Stock Index: New York Pacific Midwest

A leader in the volatile truck trailer manufacturing industry, Fruehauf has had more than its share of ups and downs. So far, it has managed to recover from its bouts of financial instability and it has successfully fought off an unfriendly takeover bid. But the company is still trying to live down a period of poor management and a damaging tax fraud conviction against two of its chief executives.

August Fruehauf, born on a small Michigan farm, became apprenticed to a blacksmith in 1882. By 1903 he had begun to raise a family in Detroit and was gaining a reputation as an expert carriage builder. In 1914 a Detroit lumber merchant, Frederic M. Sibley, Sr., asked Fruehauf to make him a type of dray that could hook onto his Model-T Ford. The lumber merchant owned a boat and wanted to transport it to his summer house.

Fruehauf's semi-trailer, a two-wheeler with a pole acting as tongue and brake, worked so well that Sibley commissioned Fruehauf to build another one to haul the merchant's lumber. The result was a stronger semi-trailer with a platform, and it proved both practical and economical. Fruehauf began to canvass manufacturers and advertise. His maxim was "A horse can pull more than it can carry . . . so can a truck." Orders poured in and Fruehauf had to operate both a day and night shift; even so, his supply could not keep up with demand. Recognizing that he needed to raise capital to expand his meagre facilities, he incorporated as the Fruehauf Trailer Company in 1918.

Constant improvements and new designs characterised the Fruehauf Trailer Company for many years. The manual coupler in which the semi-trailer's jacks were replaced by wheels was introduced in 1919, and in the same year Fruehauf developed a reversible four-wheeler trailer. Soon thereafter, the Fruehauf van-type trailer became popular with haulers such as small-item manufacturers who had once operated with horse and dray. In the early

1920's Fruehauf introduced the first refrigeration trailer, which had a trap door on the roof into which ice and salt were poured.

By 1926 Fruehauf had made an automatic version of his semi-trailer; coupling and uncoupling were now accomplished mechanically by the engine's power. Another very useful innovation was the drop-frame semi-trailer onto which a tank was mounted. This enabled haulers to transport gasoline and oil more efficiently and economically. In 1929 the company's sales climbed to $3,759,000.

The following year August Fruehauf retired from active management. He remained chairman of the board, but died in 1931. His son, Harvey, became president and continued August's tradition of innovation, introducing the tandem axle in the early 1930's. Trailer lengths and heights were increased, and the larger payloads brought greater profits. Even the Depression did not harm the company; since trailers were so practical and economical, the demand for them remained healthy. The company next introduced a "frameless" van which was much lighter but very durable; this satisfied the trailer weight restrictions of states where Fruehauf's heavier trailers could not go.

As the company expanded, relations with its work force worsened. Harvey Fruehauf opposed the Wagner Act which permitted collective bargaining, but in 1937 the Supreme Court upheld the Act and Fruehauf was forced to comply.

Throughout World War II the business expanded rapidly because of the increased demand for truck trailers to mobilize troops and supplies. Then, in 1953 Roy Fruehauf, another son of the founder, wrested control of the corporation from his brother Harvey. Roy had an excellent reputation as a salesman, but his lack of expertise in other business areas was to prove costly.

In 1954 the company introduced a longer trailer, the 35-foot Volume Van, and by 1956 68% of all vans purchased were of this length. (Previously, most vans had measured 32 feet; today most new vans are 40 to 45 feet long). Another important step for Fruehauf was the acquisition of Hobbes Manufacturing and Hobbes Trailer and Equipment of Texas. With these facilities, the company was able to expand its production of flat-bed trailers, tank trailers, and vans. Fruehauf also acquired the Steel Products Engineering Company in order to increase its range of supplies to the aircraft industry. Then came the acquisition of the Independent Metal Products Company, a manufacturer of quality tank vessels for trailers.

Despite these important developments, no one in the organization controlled manufacturing costs and there was heavy borrowing to finance excessive inventories. Roy Fruehauf's solution was to reduce costs, and one of his methods, initiated in 1955, later involved the company in damaging litigation. But long before the details of Roy Fruehauf's cost-reductions became public knowledge, he was indicted on federal charges involving a 1954 loan to the Teamster union's president, Dave Beck.

At the heart of Fruehauf's cost-cutting measures was a scheme to reduce the company's excise tax burden. Fruehauf officially lowered the price of truck trailers to customers, thereby reducing the excise. Then he billed the customers for a variety of "services," including advertising and record keeping which were not subject to excise tax, to make up the revenue difference. The company's counsel considered the scheme legal, but only on the condition that all "services" billed were actually performed. But when the IRS issued a regulation forbidding the exclusion of advertising costs from a manufacturer's excise tax base, Fruehauf simply changed the word "advertising" to "printed matter, catalogues, etc." without any study of the company's true cost for such materials.

Roy Fruehauf's questionable bookkeeping methods did not get the company out of debt, and creditors asked William Grace, who had been a major stockholder at Hobbes Trailer before Fruehauf acquired it, to try to resolve the financial problems. Grace succeeded brilliantly by reducing inventories, cutting expenses, and setting prices above cost. A loss of $5.5 million in 1958 swung to pre-tax profits of $27 million in 1959. In that year, the board removed Roy Fruehauf and installed Grace as president and chief executive officer (Fruehauf remained as chairman until 1961).

Under Grace's leadership, the Fruehauf Trailer Company continued to expand and diversify. In order to reflect its broader interests, the company changed its name in 1963 to the Fruehauf Corporation. Then, in 1964 Fruehauf announced its "total transportation" philosophy, seeking to participate in businesses covering all phases of the transportation industry. To that end, it acquired the Magor Railcar Company of New Jersey in 1964, expanded into manufacturing cargo containers, as well as cranes and other unloading equipment for ships. In 1968 Fruehauf acquired the Maryland Shipbuilding and Drydock Company of Baltimore and the following year took over the Jacksonville Shipyards in Florida.

After IRS reviews in 1969, the Department of Justice brought charges of tax evasion against Fruehauf and accused its two highest officers, William Grace and Robert Rowan, of criminal tax fraud. But the case against the company and its chief officers did not go to trial until 1974, by which time Rowan was serving as president and chief executive officer. Grace maintained that since Fruehauf's excise tax plan had ben declared legal by company accountants and lawyers, he had no reason not to continue the plan. However, in 1974 both Grace and Rowan were convicted of tax fraud, each charged $10,000 and given 6-month jail terms. The jail terms were later reduced to probation and community service. Grace and Rowan appealed all the way to the Supreme Court, but in 1979 the Court upheld their convictions. The two men resigned, but were reinstated by the stockholders because of their success in returning the company to profitability.

During the decade clouded by the tax fraud case, the company continued its policy of expansion. Most significant was its 1973 acquisition of the Kelsey-Hayes Company, a leading supplier of wheels, brakes, and automotive components. Fruehauf went on to acquire subsidiaries of Kelsey-Hayes, thus providing it with holdings in Australia, Japan, Europe, South America, and South Africa.

Over the years, Fruehauf had developed a nationwide network of more than a hundred service centers for its customers. It also developed the popular Model F Plus line, including closed dry freight trailers, open top units, trailers for railroad piggybacking, and warehouseman models. In 1980 the company introduced the Spacelite Refrigerated Van line for perishable cargo, which significantly improved thermal efficiency for the industry.

Fruehauf's performance in the 1980's has been inconsistent, at times depressed by down-swings in the market, at other times bolstered by favorable changes in legislation. 1982 was a particularly bad year with overall losses of $30.4 million. However, the Transportation Act of 1982 allowed manufacturers to build larger trailers, resulting in a substantial increase in orders for Fruehauf. Improved sales both at home and abroad, and cost cutting measures, gave the company an $8.4 million profit in 1983. Revenues were further enhanced by the deregulation of the industry. Many carriers consolidated, and this resulted in new customers for the company. During the 1984 record-breaking year in the U.S. transportation supply industry, Fruehauf received more orders than any of its competitors.

But after 1984 the industry experienced another downturn. Sales were off 8% to $2.6 billion, earnings dropped 26% to $118 million, and the company developed cash flow problems. Fruehauf's woes prompted a takeover attempt in May 1986 by Asher Edelman, whose Plaza Securities investment group already owned almost 10% of Fruehauf stock. Stock prices rose in anticipation of the bidding contest, but fell sharply as Edelman's attempt failed. In August 1986 Rowan was again in court, this time on charges of infringing upon the rights of stockholders by agreeing to a management buy-out at a price below that offered by Edelman.

Since other takeover attempts may follow, Fruehauf is considering various cost-reduction plans, including the possibility of sizable cuts in the number of its white collar workers. The company currently has 55 manufacturing plants and 115 sales, service, and rental branches. It is the only U.S. company of its kind to operate local service centers, part of its "total transportation" philosophy.

Principal Subsidiaries: Ackermann-Fruehauf oHG (West Germany); Crane Fruehauf (England); Decatur Aluminum; Fruehauf International Ltd.; Fruehauf Canada, Inc. (91%); Fruekel, Inc.; Fruehauf International Sales Corp.; Jacksonville Shipyards, Inc.; Kelsey-Hayes Co.; Paceco, Inc.; Rentco International Corp.; Trailer Rentals, Inc.

Further Reading: *Over the Road to Progress! Fruehauf Truck Trailers* by Roy Fruehauf, New York, Newcomen Society, 1957.

GENERAL MOTORS CORPORATION

3044 West Grand Blvd.
Detroit, Michigan 48202
U.S.A.
(313) 556-5000

Public Company
Incorporated: October 13, 1916
Employees: 748,000
Sales: $102.814 billion
Market Value: $24.952 billion
Stock Index: New York

The beginning of General Motors can be traced back to 1892 when R.E. Olds collected all his savings in order to convert his father's naval and industrial engine factory into the Olds Motor Vehicle Company, where the new horseless carriages known as automobiles were to be built. For a number of years, however, the Oldsmobile (as the product came to be known) did not get beyond the experimental stage. In 1895 the first model, a four-seater with a petrol engine that could develop 5 hp and reach 18.6 mph, went for its trial run.

Olds proved himself not only an innovative engineer but also a good businessman and was very successful with his first model, of which a relatively few were built. As a result of his success, he founded the first American factory in Detroit devoted exclusively to the production of automobiles. The first car was a luxury model costing $1,200, but the second model was introduced at a list price of $650 and was very successful. Two years later, at the turn of the century, Olds had sold over 1,400 cars.

That same year, an engineer named David Buick founded a factory under his own name in Detroit; and a third factory was also built in Detroit, the Cadillac Automobile Company. This company was founded by Henry Leland, who was already building car engines with experience gained in the Oldsmobile factory, where he worked until 1901. By the end of 1902 the first Cadillac had been produced—a car distinguished by its luxurious finish. In the following year, tiller steering was replaced by the steering wheel, the reduction gearbox was introduced, and some cars were fitted with celluloid windscreens. Oldsmobile also reached their projected target of manufacturing 4,000 cars in one year.

By 1903, a time of market instability, so many different manufacturers were operating that the financially weak-

est disappeared and some of the remaining companies were forced to form a consortium. William Durant, a director of the Buick Motor Company, was the man behind the merger. The son of a Michigan governor, and a self-made millionaire, Durant believed that the only way for the automobile companies to operate at a profit was to avoid the duplication that occurred as many concerns manufactured the same product. General Motors was thus formed, bringing together Oldsmobile and Buick, and joined in 1909 by Cadillac and Oakland (renamed Pontiac). Positive financial results were immediately seen from the union, although the establishment of the company drew little attention.

Other early members of the General Motors family were Ewing, Marquette, Welch, Scripps-Booth, Sheridan, and Elmore, together with Rapid and Reliance trucks. General Motors' other U.S. automotive division, Chevrolet, became part of the Corporation in 1918. Only Buick, Oldsmobile, Cadillac, and Oakland continued making cars for more than a short time after their acquisition by GM. By 1920 more than 30 companies had been acquired through the purchase of all or part of their stock. Two were forerunners of major GM subsidiaries, the McLaughlin Motor Company of Canada (which later became General Motors of Canada Limited) and the Fisher Body Company, in which GM initially acquired a 60% interest.

By 1911 the company set up a central staff of specialists to coordinate work in the various units and factories. An experimental or "testing" laboratory was also established to serve as an additional protection against costly factory mistakes. General Motors' system of administration, research, and development is one of the largest and most complex in private industry.

About the same time that General Motors was establishing itself in Detroit, an engineering breakthrough was takin place in Dayton, Ohio—the electric self-starter, designed by Charles F. Kettering. General Motors introduced Kettering's invention in its 1912 Cadillacs, and with the phasing out of the dangerous and unpredictable hand crank, motoring became much more popular. Kettering's Dayton Engineering Laboratories were merged into General Motors during 1920 and the Laboratories were relocated in Detroit in 1925. Kettering later became the scientific director of General Motors, in charge of its research and engineering programs.

During World War I General Motors turned its facilities to the production of war materials. With no previous experience in manufacturing military hardware, the American automobile industry completed a retooling from civilian to war production within 18 months. Between 1917 and 1919, 90% of General Motors' truck production was for the war effort. Cadillac supplied Army staff cars along with V-8 engines for artillery tractors and trench mortar shells, and Buick built Liberty airplane motors, tanks, trucks, ambulances and automotive parts.

It was at this time that Alfred P. Sloan, Jr., who went on to guide General Motors as president and chairman until 1956, first became associated with the company. In 24 years, Sloan had built a $50,000 investment in the Hyatt Roller Bearing Company to assets of about $3.5 million.

When Hyatt became part of General Motors, Sloan joined the corporate management.

General Motors suffered greatly under the effects of the Depression, but it emerged with a new, aggressive management. Coordinated policy control replaced the undirected efforts of the prior years. As its principal architect Sloan was credited with creating not only an organization which saved General Motors, but a new management policy that was adopted by countless other businesses. Fundamentally, the policy involved coordination of the enterprise under top management, direction of policy through top-level committees, and delegation of operation responsibility throughout the organization. Within this framework management staffs conducted analysis of market trends, advised policy committees, and coordinated administration. For a company comprised of many varied divisions, such a system of organization was crucial to its success.

By 1941 General Motors accounted for 44% of the total U.S. automotive sales, compared with 12% in 1921. In preparation for America's entry into the Second World War, General Motors retooled its factories. After Japan struck at Pearl Harbor in 1941, the industrial skills that General Motors had developed were applied with great effectiveness. From 1940 to 1945 General Motors produced defense material valued at a total of $12.3 billion. Decentralized and highly flexible local managerial responsibility made possible the almost overnight conversion from civilian production to wartime production. General Motors' contribution included the manufacture of every conceivable product from the smallest ball bearing to large tanks, naval ships, fighting planes, bombers, guns, cannons and projectiles. The company manufactured 1,300 airplanes and one-fourth of all U.S. aircraft engines.

Car manufacturing resumed after the war, and postwar expansion resulted in increased production. The decade of the 1950's was characterized by automotive sales records and innovations in styling and engineering. The public interest in automatic gears convinced General Motors to concentrate their research in this field; by 1950, all the models built in the United States were available with an automatic gearbox. Car body developments proceeded at the same time and resulted in better sight lines and improved aerodynamics.

During the Korean war, part of the company's production capacity was diverted into providing supplies for the United Nations forces (although to a smaller extent than during the Second World War). The reallocation reached 19% and then leveled off at about 5% from 1956 onwards. Between 1951 and 1955 the five divisions which today form General Motors—Buick, Chevrolet, Pontiac, Oldsmobile, and Cadillac—all began to feature a new V-8 engine with a higher compression ratio. Furthermore, the electrical supply was changed from 6 to the more reliable 12 volts. Power assisted steering and brakes appeared on all car models and the window dimensions were increased to further enhance visibility. Interior comfort was improved by the installation of the first air-conditioning systems. Also during this period General Motors completely redesigned its classic sedans and introduced front seat safety belts.

The period between 1950 and 1956 was particularly prosperous in the United States, with a rise in demand for a second car in the family. However, Americans were beginning to show real interest in smaller European cars. By 1956, a year of decreasing sales, Ford, Chrysler and General Motors had lost some 15% in sales while imports were virtually doubling their market penetration. The longer Detroit's automobiles grew, the more popular imports became. In 1957 the United States imported more cars than it exported, and despite a recession, imports accounted for more than 8% of U.S. car sales. Although General Motors promised that help was on its way in the form of smaller compact cars, the new models failed to generate much excitement; the company's market share slipped to just 42% of 1959's new car sales.

The 1960's were difficult years in Detroit. Riots in the ghettos surrounding General Motors' facilities forced management to recognize the urban poverty that had for so long been in their midst and began to employ more workers from minority groups. Much of the new hiring was made possible by the expansionist policies of the Kennedy and Johnson administrations. General Motors prospered and diversified; its interests now included home appliances, insurance, locomotives, electronics, ball bearings, banking, and financing. By the late 1960's after-tax profits for the industry in general reached a 13% return on investment, and General Motors' return increased from 16.5% to 25.8%.

Like the rest of the industry, General Motors had largely ignored the importance of air pollution control, but new, costly federal regulations were mandated. However, by the early 1970's, the high cost of developing devices to control pollution was overshadowed by the impact of the oil embargo. General Motors' luxury, gas guzzling car sales were down by 35% in 1974, but the company's compacts and subcompacts rose steadily to attain a 40% market share. Ford, Chrysler and General Motors had been caught unaware by a vast shift in consumer demand, and General Motors suffered the greatest losses. The company spent $2.25 billion in 1974 and 1975 in order to meet local, state, and federal regulations on pollution control. By the end of 1977 that figure had doubled.

Under the leadership of its current president, F. James McDonald, and current chairman, Roger Smith, General Motors has reported earnings losses since 1985. Management's strategy is to pursue strategic initiatives that reflect the kind of foresight that was missing in previous years. McDonald and Smith have attempted to place these losses in perspective by arguing that they are necessary if General Motors is to develop a strong and secure position on the worldwide market. Since the start of the 1980's, General Motors has been in the process of redesigning most of its cars and modernizing the plants that produce them. Between 1980 and 1986 this program cost over $60 billion. In addition, the company recently acquired two major corporations, Hughes Aircraft and Electronic Data Systems. The purpose of these expensive takeovers is to provide General Motors with the best technology in advanced computer services, micro electronics, and systems engineering. Despite these important moves, however, many industry analysts believe that the future of

General Motors will depend even more on decisions that the U.S. government makes and has made with regard to the tax code, and trade and budget deficits.

Principal Subsidiaries: General Motors Electronic Data Systems Corp.; General Motors Commercial Corp.; General Motors Development Corp.; General Motors Export Corp.; General Motors Interamerica Corp.; General Motors Overseas Corp.; General Motors OI Leasing Corp.; General Motors Hughes Electronics Corp.; Delco Electronics Corp.; Hughes Aircraft Corp.; General Motors Trading Corp.; Saturn Corp. The company also has subsidiaries in the following countries: Australia, Austria, Belgium, Brazil, Canada, Chile, Colombia, England, Finland, France, Greece, Ireland, Italy, Japan, Luxembourg, Mexico, The Netherlands, New Zealand, Norway, Portugal, South Africa, Sweden, Switzerland, Uruguay, Venezuela, West Germany, and Zaire.

Further Reading: *My Years with General Motors* by Alfred P. Sloan, Jr., New York, Doubleday, 1964; *Paradise Lost: The Decline of the Auto-Industrial Age* by Emma Rothschild, New York, Random House, 1973; *R.E. Olds, Auto Industry Pioneer* by George S. May, Grand Rapids, Michigan, Eerdmans, 1977; *The Dream Maker: William C. Durant, Founder of General Motors* by Bernard A. Weisberger, Boston, Little Brown, 1979; *Chrome Colossus: General Motors and Its Time* by Ed Cray, New York, McGraw Hill, 1980; *On a Clear Day You Can See General Motors* by John Z. De Lorean, London, Sidgwick and Jackson, 1980; *The Corporate Warriors: Six Classic Cases in American Business* by Douglas K. Ramsey, Boston, Houghton Mifflin, 1987.

HONDA

HONDA MOTOR COMPANY LIMITED
(Honda Giken Kogyo Kabushiki Kaisha)

1-1, Minami-Ayama, 2-chome
Minato-Ku, Tokyo 107
Japan
(03) 423-1111

Public Company
Incorporated: September 24, 1948
Employees: 53,730
Sales: ¥2341 billion (US$14.7 billion)
Market Value: ¥1269 billion (US$7.973 billion)
Stock Index: Tokyo Osaka Niigata Nagoya Kyoto Fukuoka Supporo Hiroshima New York

Prior to 1960 the image of the motocyclist in America was that of an unsavory teenager who belonged to a group of unruly characters known by such names as "Hell's Angels" and "Satan's Slaves." In general, motorcyclists were regarded by the American public as troublemakers who wore leather jackets. By the mid-1960's, however, Honda and its American subsidiary had successfully transformed that image, and at the same time established the company as the leading motorcycle manufacturer in the world. The story of how this happened has firm roots in the company's early history.

In 1959 Honda established an American subsidiary, named the American Honda Motor Company, which was in sharp contrast to other foreign manufacturers who relied on distributors. Honda's strategy was to create a market of customers who had never given a thought to owning a motorcycle. The company started its enterprise in America by producing the smallest, lightweight motorcycles available. With a three speed transmission, an automatic clutch, five horsepower (an American cycle had only two and a half), an electric starter and step-through frame for female riders, Honda sold its unit for $250 retail compared to $1,000-$1,500 for the American machines. Even at that early date Honda was probably superior to other companies in its productivity. By 1959, with sales of $55 million, Honda was already the largest motorcycle manufacturer in the world.

Honda followed a policy of developing the American market region by region. The company started on the west coast and moved eastward over a period of five years.

During 1960 2,500 machines were sold in the U.S. In 1961 it established 125 distributors and spent $150,000 on regional advertising. Honda's advertising campaign, which was directed to young families, included the slogan, "You meet the nicest people on a Honda." This was a deliberate attempt to disassociate their motorcycles from the undesirable elements in American society. Honda's success in creating a demand for lightweight motorcycles was impressive. Its U.S. sales skyrocketed from $500,000 in 1960 to $77 million in 1965. By 1966 the market share revealed the ascendancy of the Japanese manufacturer and its success in selling lightweight motorcycles.

Any description of the company's success must take into account the unusual character of its founders Soichiro Honda, and his partner, Takeo Fujisawa. Soichiro Honda's achievements as a mechanical engineer are said to match those of Henry Ford's. Working in his machine shop in 1938, Honda concentrated his efforts on casting a perfect piston ring, and finally succeeded in casting a ring that met his standards. Two years after rejecting Honda's first batch of piston rings, the Toyota Corporation placed a large order, but because the country was preparing for war, Honda was unable to obtain cement to construct a factory. Undaunted, he built the plant by learning how to make his own cement.

Honda's factories survived bombing attacks during World War II but were then destroyed by an earthquake. Undaunted, Honda sold his piston ring operation to Toyota and went on to manufacture motorbikes. He had designed his first bike in the early post war years when gasoline was very scarce.

To form a company, Honda joined efforts with Takeo Fujisawa. Honda and Fujisawa had known one another throughout the 1940's. In 1949 Fujisawa provided the capital, as well as the financial and marketing strategy, to begin a new company with his friend. Honda's motivation for establishing the company was not purely commercial but to provide a secure financial base so that he might pursue other ambitions. In 1950, after his first motocycle had been introduced in Japan, Honda stunned the engineering world by doubling the horsepower of the conventional four-stroke engine. With this technological innovation, the company was poised for success. By 1951 demand was brisk, yet production was slow. It was primarily due to design advantages that Honda became one of the four or five industry leaders by 1954 with 15% of the market share.

The two owners of the company had different priorities. For Fujisawa the engine innovation meant increased sales and easier access to financing. For Honda the higher horsepower engine opened the possibility of pursuing one of his central ambitions in life—motorcycle racing. Indeed, winning provided the ultimate confirmation of his design abilities. Success came quickly, and by 1959 Honda had won all of the most prestigious racing prizes in the world.

Fujisawa, throughout the 1950's, attempted to turn Honda's attention away from racing to the more mundane tasks of running a successful business venture. By 1956, as the technological innovations gained from racing began to pay off in vastly more efficient engines, Fujisawa prompted Honda to adapt this technology for a commercial motorcycle. Fujisawa had a particular segment of Japanese society in mind. Most motorcyclists in Japan were male and the machines they used were primarily an alternative form of transportation to trains and buses. There were, however, a large number of small commercial establishments in Japan that still delivered goods and ran errands on bicycles. The finances of these small enterprises were usually controlled by Japanese housewives who resisted buying conventional motorcycles because they were expensive, dangerous, and difficult to handle. Fujisawa suggested to Honda that, with his knowledge of racing, he might be able to design a safe and inexpensive motorcycle that could be driven with one hand (to facilitate carrying packages).

In 1958 the Honda 50cc Supercub was introduced. It featured an automatic clutch, three-speed transmission, automatic starter, and the safe, friendly look of a bicycle. Its inexpensive price was due almost entirely to its high horsepower but lightweight 50cc engine. Overwhelmed by demand, the company arranged for an infusion of capital in order to build a new plant with a 30,000 unit per month capacity. By the end of 1959 Honda had climbed into first place among Japanese motorcycle manufacturers. The company's total sales that year of 285,000 units included 168,000 Supercubs.

Honda had experimented with local Southeast Asian markets in 1957-58 with little success. The European market, while larger, was heavily dominated by its own name brand manufacturers, and the popular mopeds dominated the low price, low horsepower products. Fujisawa decided to focus attention on the United States.

In the spring of 1963 an undergraduate advertising major at UCLA submitted, in fulfillment of a course assignment, an advertising campaign for Honda. Its theme was: You meet the nicest people on a Honda. Encouraged by his instructor, the student submitted his work to a friend at Grey Advertising. Consequently, the "Nicest People" campaign became the impetus behind Honda's sales. By 1964 nearly one out of every two motorcycles sold in the U.S. was a Honda.

As a result of the growing number of medium income consumers, banks and other consumer credit companies began to finance the purchase of motorcycles. This involved a shift away from dealer credit, which had been the traditional purchasing mechanism. Seizing the opportunity created by a soaring demand for its products, the company set in motion a risky plan. Late in 1964 Honda announced that soon thereafter it would cease to ship motorcycles on a consignment basis and would require cash on delivery. Management prepared itself for a dealership revolt. Yet, while nearly every dealer either questioned or complained about the decision, not one relinquished his franchise. By this one decision, Honda transferred the financial authority (and, the power that goes with it) from the dealer to the manufacturer. Within three years this became the basic pattern of the industry and the Honda motorcycle had the largest market share of any company in the world. By 1981 Honda Motor's total motorcycle production reached some 3.5 million units and one-third of those were produced or sold outside of Japan.

As early as 1967, when Honda was on its way to becoming the world's leading motorcycle manufacturer, it also began to produce cars and trucks. In addition, the company started to manufacture portable generators, power tillers, lawn mowers, pumps, and outboard motors. In 1967 and 1968 the company introduced two lightweight passenger cars which performed poorly in both the Japanese and American markets. It was not until 1973 and the introduction of the Honda Civic that the company became a real presence on the international automobile market. The world was in the grip of the oil crisis, and the energy-efficient Japanese compacts suddenly found a worldwide market.

In the last 15 years, Honda has maintained a significant presence in the automobile industry; but not surprisingly its ascendancy over the two-wheeled vehicle market has not been repeated in the passenger car market.

Honda Motor Company has already become a world enterprise since its products are being manufactured by 43 plants in 28 countries. BL Limited (formerly British Leyland), Britain's largest car manufacturer, which is owned by the government, decided to manufacture one passenger car model under license from Honda. In this particular case, Honda sold a technical license to BL Limited, marking the first time Japanese cars were to be built in an industrialized nation of the West under license. The company also has joint agreements with South Africa, Yugoslavia, France and China.

The current director of Honda is Kiyoshi Kawashima, a man who believes strongly in what is called the system of "collective leadership." It has been said that he has done more than any other modern corporate leader to improve working conditions for his employees. At the same time, he has more than doubled the gross production output of Honda during his tenure. His innovations to improve working conditions include shorter hours and the fostering of "communion" among members of the corporation through the common understanding of their similar interests. Such improvements promise to have a large influence upon the American car industry. So much so that *Forbes* magazine ran a 1986 cover story comparing factories run by Honda and an American corporation. *Forbes* concluded that the different approaches constituted "two separate worlds," and implied that Kawashima's management system was superior to that employed in American-owned automobile factories. As word continues to spread, the unusual style of this Honda president is likely to have a noticeable influence on the future of industrial capitalism.

Market saturation has forced the automotive industry to undergo radical changes. To a large extent, the focus is now on compact cars where a growing demand can be expected, despite the finite size of the international market. Under these circumstances, special attention is being paid to what has been called the "global" or the "world" car. The major automotive companies' strategy is concerned with how to achieve an efficient and high quality production standard of vehicles through the international division of labor. The success or failure of the "world" car will, to a large extent, determine the future of these corporations. For this reason, most of the major international auto companies are now investing capital in foreign automakers or cooperating with them in the fields of research and development, production, and sales.

In Japan the domestic automobile market reached a point of saturation in the late 1970's, and Japanese automakers have since been growing primarily by increasing their exports. In Honda's case, growth has occurred through the introduction of entirely new fuel efficient models such as the popular Accord and CRX. However, as the increasing export of Japanese automobiles has created economic and political problems in the West, Japanese auto manufacturers have begun to reduce their exports to the United States, Canada, and the European Economic Community. Japan now believes that its automotive industry can prosper in the future only through the promotion of multinationalization and by cooperating in the global reorganization of the industry. In order to survive the difficulties of the present international market, an auto manufacturer must have researched and developed some technological advantages in production processes, especially in the field of compact cars; without such an edge, even the ability to raise capital will be limited.

Principal Subsidiaries: Honda Research and Development Co., Ltd.; Honda Engineering Co. Ltd.; Honda International Sales Corp.; Honda SF Corp.; Honda Minami Tokyo Co. Ltd.; Honda Motor Service Co. Ltd.; ACT Trading Corp.; Press Giken Co. Ltd. (98.2%); Seiki Giken Co. Ltd. (98%); Honda and Co. Ltd. (86.6%); Honda Research of America Inc.; Honda Sogo Tatemono Ltd. (70%); American Honda Motor Co. Ltd.; Honda of America Mfg. Inc. The company also has subsidiaries in the following countries: Australia, Belgium, Canada, France, The Netherlands, Thailand, United Kingdom, and West Germany.

Further Reading: *Honda Motor: The Men, The Management, The Machine* by Tetuus Sakiya, Tokyo, Kadonsha International, 1982; *The Corporate Warriors: Six Classic Cases in American Business* by Douglas K. Ramsey, Boston, Houghton Mifflin, 1987.

MACK TRUCKS, INC.

2100 Mack Blvd.
Allentown, Pennsylvania 18105
U.S.A.
(215) 439-3011

Public Company
Incorporated: 1967
Employees: 13,300
Sales: $1.712 billion
Market Value: $577 million
Stock Index: New York

It was by hauling heavy artillery pieces through the mud of World War I battlefields that Mack trucks first earned their famous nickname. Legend has it that a British officer, trying to free an artillery piece that was mired in mud, coined the name "bulldog" when he called out to a Mack driver, "Bring that bulldog over here." Management liked the term. In 1932 Mack began putting the bulldog emblem on the front of all trucks and in the 1960's, to raise company morale, Mack produced bulldog pins, carpets, flags, T-shirts, and other items. The square-shouldered grimly determined bulldog is an appropriate symbol. Mack, a quality-conscious, pioneering truck manufacturer has a history of cash flow problems and near collapses.

The youngest of five brothers, 14 year old Jack Mack ran away from his Pennsylvania home in 1878 to join the Teamsters and work as a stationary mechanic. In 1893 Jack, with his brother Augustus, purchased a small carriage and wagon building firm in Brooklyn, N.Y. The firm was ruined by the financial panics of the 1890's, and the two brothers were forced to enter the business of maintaining and repairing engines, rather than manufacturing them.

During this time they began to experiment with new types of self-propelled vehicles. The Macks had exacting standards, and both an electric car and a steam-powered wagon were dumped into the East River for having too many mechanical flaws. But in 1900, after eight years of testing, the brothers finally produced a vehicle that satisfied them. "Old Number One," the first successful bus built in America, was a chain-driven vehicle that featured a Mack-built four-cylinder engine, a cone-type clutch and a three-speed transmission. It conveyed 20 sightseers at a time through Brooklyn's Prospect Park. The vehicle, which was converted into a truck in 1908 and finally retired in 1917, was the first Mack "million-miler."

Orders for more buses came rapidly, and Jack and Augustus, joined by their other brothers, incorporated Mack Brothers Company in New York with a capitalization of $35,000. In addition to manufacturing buses, the young company pioneered the design of custom-built, heavy-duty trucks. This ran against the prevailing wisdom on such matters. Automakers at that time considered trucks a poor relation to the automobile, and manufactured them from surplus or obsolete auto parts. They made trucks in order to keep their shops busy during periods of slow business. Jack Mack, however, anticipating that the days of the horse and wagon were numbered, decided to make trucks with a capacity of 1 to 7½ tons. He introduced the "seat-over-engine" truck, made a 7-ton, 5-cubic-yard dump truck for the construction of the New York city subway, and began manufacturing rail cars and engine-driven fire trucks. By 1911 the Mack Brothers Company, manufacturers of "The Leading Gasoline Truck in America," had 825 employees producing about 600 units a year.

Due to depressed market conditions the demand for trucks slowly diminished and the company, which had relocated to Allentown, Pennsylvania, merged first with the Saurer Motor Company and then the Hewitt Motor Company. The new management did not meet the approval of Jack and three of his brothers, and they left the company. Though regrettable, their departure didn't end Mack innovation. The new chief engineer, Edward R. Hewitt, designed a medium-duty Mack truck that was the mainstay of the market from 1914 until 1936. The AB Mack featured a four-cylinder engine with a three-speed transmission, a worm drive rear axle, and two large inspection ports that allowed a quick inspection of the crankshaft and rod bearings. Hewitt's successor, Alfred F. Masury, designed the Mack AC, a heavy-duty, chain-driven truck that featured clutch brakes to prevent its gears from clashing. This was the truck that hauled artillery pieces in Europe during World War I. Its performance there gave rise to the phrase, "Built like a Mack truck."

With improved roads and an increased demand for point-to-point delivery, the truck industry prospered in the 1920's. For Mack, which was producing more than 7,000 units by 1927, sales rose from $22 million in 1919 to $55 million in 1927. The company added improved cooling systems, four-speed transmissions, dual-reduction drive and the Mack Rubber Shock Insulator (the first major breakthrough in vibration dampening since automobiles were first introduced) to the AB and AC models.

At the end of the decade Mack launched a line of high-speed, six-cylinder trucks. These models, designated the BJ, BM, BX, and BQ, marked the beginning of the transition from slow, four-cylinder trucks to high-speed transports. Mack also manufactured the country's first practical off-highway dumper designated the AP. It was used in the construction of the Hoover Dam.

The Depression had a devastating effect on Mack. In addition to the drop in demand, light-duty trucks introduced by other manufacturers created competition for Mack's large models. Mack sales dropped 75% between 1929 and 1932. But the company fought back. Instead of reducing production Mack offered a new line of small trucks, and introduced the CH and CJ cab-over-engine models. The cab-over-engine design, the best way of getting a 1/3–2/3 distribution by weight on the front and rear axles, was necessitated by laws restricting axle loading, gross vehicle weights and overall lengths. Despite the depression, Mack's new line was successful. Those manufacturers in financial distress, needing more efficient ways of transporting goods, turned to the transportation that offered the lowest cost per ton per mile, namely, the truck. Furthermore, the urban demand for public transit ensured a strong bus market.

Mack's leadership of the industry continued in 1938 with the introduction of the Mack Diesel, the first diesel engine made by a truck manufacturer. In 1940 Mack sales hit $44 million on domestic deliveries of 7,754 units, with a net profit of $1.8 million. By making heavy-duty trucks, small delivery trucks, dump units, buses and fire trucks, Mack offered the most comprehensive product line of any truck manufacturer.

As early as 1940 Mack began producing the NR military six-wheeler, a tank transporter that would be used for British General Montgomery's North African campaign. After Pearl Harbor, Mack produced virtually nothing but military equipment, including power trains for tanks, military trucks, torpedo bombers, and the "MO" which pulled 150 mm field guns. Since it suspended civilian truck production for the duration of the war, Mack set up an extensive maintenance network which enabled those trucks to remain in running condition. Its contribution to the war effort won the company numerous government awards.

But that contribution meant little in the post-World War II environment. Strikes and new taxes resulted in a loss of profits for the company in 1946, while contract renegotiations and a soft market made the late 1940's a financially difficult period in general for Mack. In 1952 the manufacturer again reversed its fortunes by introducing the best-selling "B" series. These trucks featured a widened chassis frame in front for easier maintenance, a wider front axle for improved maneuverability, and rounded fenders with a sleek hood and cab. This appearance was a significant change from earlier long-nosed and box-shaped trucks. By the time the "B" series was discontinued in 1966 approximately 127,000 models had been sold.

Another major innovation was the END 673 "Thermodyne" diesel engine which was introduced in 1953 and featured direct fuel injection, allowing for greater power (170 horsepower) and reliability. Close to 80 percent of the heavy-duty "B" trucks were sold with Thermodyne engines.

These innovations notwithstanding, Mack's financial condition declined drastically in the 1950's and early 1960's. Finance oriented executives, with no experience in truck manufacturing, deferred maintenance and allowed facilities to deteriorate in order to maintain a strong cash flow. Corporate offices were moved to Montvale, New Jersey, effectively isolating management from union employees. This management style, in conjunction with repeated work stoppages and strikes, left the company with reduced sales. From 1959 to 1964 earnings fell from $15.8 million to $3.4 million. A proposed merger with

Chrysler Corporation, which might have saved the company, was not approved by the Justice Department.

In 1965 a dispirited management offered the presidency to career trucking executive Zenon C.R. Hansen. He eagerly accepted the challenge. "Many well-informed individuals advised me that I was taking over a sinking ship . . . that Mack was too far gone to save . . . that Mack would either go under or be absorbed by one of our competitors," Hansen said later. "But I thought they were wrong. Mack still had a great name, a great product, and above all it had the people."

Hansen assured employees that there would be internal promotions and a cessation to the firings, and he distributed bulldog flags, jewelry, rugs and other items to boost morale. He set up an accelerated program to improve all the previously deferred maintenance. Corporate offices were moved back to Allentown, and a new assembly plant was built on the West Coast. He also approved manufacture of the "Maxidyne" diesel engine, which produced constant horsepower over a wide operating range. It featured a simple five-speed transmission, compared with earlier transmissions which had 10, 13, or 15 speeds.

These reforms helped Mack improve its financial situation by 1967. But the company remained plagued by a lack of capital. It was forced to stockpile millions of dollars of parts to ensure production of enough trucks during high demand periods, while at the same time advancing millions of dollars in loans to customers. In order to ease this crisis, Mack agreed to become an affiliate of Signal Oil & Gas Company in 1967 on the condition it was guaranteed complete autonomy.

However, Mack did not stay abreast with the industry innovations during the 1970's. Because profits went back to the parent company, Mack could not modernize its plants. It did introduce an air-to-air intercooled diesel engine in 1973, the ENDT 676 "Maxidyne," which featured 285 horsepower, 1,080 pound/feet of torque. But industry deregulation and foreign competition drained Mack's profits, and those of other American truck manufacturers as well.

To cope with these problems the new president, John Curcio, persuaded the French auto manufacturer Renault to purchase 41% of Mack from Signal for $228 million in the early 1980's. Renault not only contributed new capital, but also helped to distribute the Mack light trucks. In 1983 the company went public, although it was unable to pay dividends. Cost-cutting measures by Curcio, which reduced expenses $160 million in four years, returned the truck manufacturer to a sound financial condition in 1984 for the first time since 1980. Sales increased by 73% to $2.1 billion. But a write-off on the antiquated Allentown plant led to $58 million in losses during 1985.

Early in 1986 Mack announced it was moving its main production plant from Allentown to an $80 million computerized facility in Winsboro, South Carolina. The Allentown plant, built in 1926, was so old that trucks were still spray-painted by hand. Parts had to be moved by forklifts since there was no robotic technology. Furthermore, in Pennsylvania unionized labor cost close to $23 an hour including benefits, compared to labor costs of about $12 an hour in the south.

In 1986 Curcio told *Forbes* magazine that truck transportation had become more efficient, causing the demand for trucks to drop to 125,000 a year. The country's seven largest manufacturers had a combined production capacity of 230,000 trucks a year. "In the next five years, we expect a major skirmish, if not a major war," he said.

But Mack may be safe for some time. Curcio's policies have reduced the break even point for the company from 37,000 units to 19,000 units and Renault-built buses and medium-size trucks are keeping the Mack network of 230 dealers and 503 service stations prosperous. Furthermore, Japanese manufacturers aren't expected to introduce Class 8 trucks (those weighing 33,000 pounds and over) until the 1990's. Mack increased its market share of these large trucks from 15% to 18.5% between 1983 and 1985. Recent

policy should ensure that Mack enters the 1990's in a fairly strong position.

Principal Subsidiaries: Mack Americus, Inc.; Mack Canada, Inc.; Mack Properties, Inc.; Mack Truck Worldwide Ltd.; Mack Truck Australia Pty., Ltd.

Further Reading: The Legend of the Bulldog by Zenon C.R. Hansen, New York, Newcomen Society, 1974; *A History of Motor Truck Development* by Ernest R. Sternberg, Warrendale, Pennsylvania, Society of Automotive Engineers, 1981.

NAVISTAR

NAVISTAR INTERNATIONAL CORPORATION

401 N. Michigan Ave.
Chicago, Illinois 60611
U.S.A.
(312) 836-2000

Public Company
Incorporated: March 1966 as International Harvester
Employees: 15,000
Sales: $3.374 billion
Market Value: $1.718 billion
Stock Index: New York

Navistar International Corporation, which can trace its history back to the 1830's and Cyrus McCormick's invention of the first practical mechanical reaper, manufactures and markets medium and heavy-duty diesel trucks. Although Navistar is a giant among truck manufacturers, it is less than half the size of the company that, under the name International Harvester, was a leading manufacturer for the agriculture, construction and truck industries and boasted, in 1980, 47 manufacturing plants comprising 38 million square feet. Years of staggering losses compelled Harvester to sell its agriculture and construction business, its name and its symbol, lay off thousands of workers, and reduce sales by more than 50%. Management hopes the new name and the new "diamond road" symbol portend a brighter future. Though the company in 1986 had only eight plants with 7.5 million square feet, most of its debts had been paid and profitability seemed close at hand.

The company's beginning was hardly indicative of a multi-billion dollar business. Cyrus McCormick, a guiding light to both Harvester and the agricultural machinery industry, had quite a struggle to promote his 1831 invention. It took him 10 years to sell his first reaper, and then his patent expired. To stay ahead of the competition he was compelled to invent such sales techniques as the warranty and extended credit. Early reapers were bulky and noisy, and at the Great Exhibition in London in 1851, The *Times* of London disparagingly referred to McCormick's entry as a "cross between . . . a chariot, a wheelbarrow, and a flying machine." But The McCormick Harvesting Company did eventually market its reapers and other farm machinery. The new farm machinery was so successful that whereas in 1831, the year the reaper was invented, it took nine Americans on the land to feed themselves and a tenth person in the city, 100 years later one American farmer could feed himself and five city dwellers.

After McCormick died, his company merged with four other struggling agriculture machinery manufacturers to form International Harvester. The new firm boasted $120 million shares of stock. The 1902 merger provoked cries of "foul" from anti-trust loyalists, and for more than 20 years the company battled a number of anti-monopoly suits. These suits whittled away certain parts of the company and sparked some competition in the agriculture field, but left it essentially intact. Cyrus H. McCormick, descendant of the inventor and the company's first president, defended the merger by arguing that it gave the new company opportunities and resources that were beyond the reach of smaller companies. "Presently," he wrote, "there was afforded to the business world the unique spectacle of five competitors in one line coming together for the preservation of their concerns and of the industry, and for the fulfillment of their hopes of a future that was to count for much in the swelling total of American enterprise . . ."

The courts agreed that Harvester, which at one point held an 85% share of the agriculture market, did not raise prices or stifle competition. There was, in fact, a general consensus that Harvester was helping farmers by producing a whole range of new equipment. The company would eventually make everything conceivable to speed the production of useable food, including manure spreaders, disk harrows, harvester combines, feed grinders, and more. The diverse product line and continuous patents began to reap rewards at home and abroad. By 1908 Harvester had 75,000 employees and owned iron mines, coal mines and acres of forest. Sales climbed from $53 million in 1903 to $125 million in 1912, capitalization more than doubled, and foreign sales rose 388% to $51 million. More than 36,000 dealers in 38 countries were selling Harvester products.

In 1907 Harvester quietly introduced a new piece of farm equipment called the auto wagon. This high-wheeled, rough vehicle was designed to carry a farmer, his family and his produce over rutted mud roads to the marketplace. It was well-designed for farmers, and it sold well. Harvester unveiled a low-wheeled truck that featured water and air-cooled engines. Wooden wheels were replaced with solid tires.

Although Harvester suffered a huge loss during the 1917 Russian Revolution when its Russian interests were taken over by the new government, the company had a number of strong years. In the 1920's the economy was expanding, new roads were built for trucks, and the international demand for agricultural equipment seemed endless. Harvester continued to manufacture everything farmers could possibly need (in the late 1930's, for example, it would launch a line of walk-in freezers) while diversifying into other fields. Although it dominated the agricultural industry, the company tried to promote competition by not invoking tariffs, and by not protecting its patents for more than five years (by 1949 the company had some 1,300 patents). The company also experienced vigorous competition in both the construction and the truck industries, while building up a vast dealer and supplier network.

Harvester did not implement any corporate restructuring while expanding. As a result, the company grew in a rather haphazard fashion; new divisions were added and line managers were not given autonomy. Even minor decisions required a clearance through the central office. Harvester soon earned a reputation for conservatism, for antiquated management techniques, and strictly in-house promotions, which saw it through the depression and into World War II, but did not prepare it for the post-war environment.

The war itself helped to increase Harvester sales. In 1940 Harvester accepted $80 million in defense contracts from the government. Even before Pearl Harbor, 20% of the company's total output was defense-related. Harvester employed its dealer network to haul in millions of tons of ferrous scrap from the fields of farmers, and also sent its mechanics into the army in order to service and maintain military vehicles. Its contributions to the war effort won it a *Business Week* cover story and numerous awards; its wartime goods sold for $1 billion. Subsidiaries in Britain during the war were able to raise agricultural production there by a third.

However, the war left Harvester financially weakened and without a strategy for the future. High taxes and a concentrated research effort cut profits; in 1945 the company reported $24.4 million profit on $622 million in sales. That compared poorly with the 1941 earnings of $30.6 million on $346.6 sales. A Harvester official complained to *Forbes* that, "The company's leadership in many articles of farm equipment is almost too well-established to bear expansion without charges of monopoly."

Nonetheless, the company continued to expand when and where it could. It entered the consumer market with air conditioners and refrigerators; it introduced a mini tractor, the Farmall Cub, for small farmers; for the construction market it manufactured an 18-ton crawler tractor. A mechanical cotton-picker, introduced in 1942, sold well, as did a self-propelled combine and pickup baler. Sales rose in four years from $741 million to $1.28 billion. Furthermore, the company's overall market changed. By 1948 farm equipment accounted for less than half of the company's total sales. Trucks were the company's single largest item; construction equipment and refrigeration equipment comprised the remainder of its product line.

These new units and a capital improvement program improved profits, which rose to $66.7 million in 1950. It was a performance Harvester could not match for nine years due to an overextended budget, conservative management and intransigent unions. When Harvester tried to reduce labor costs, it was opposed by some of its 80,000 workers and 28 unions. An innovative pension fund program and in-house promotions placated workers, but even more difficulties arose when Harvester tried to reduce wages during the McCarthy era. The company accused the leaders of the Farm Equipment Workers union of being communists or communist sympathizers; the workers accused the company of using "red smoke screens" to cover up wage cuts. Meanwhile, Harvester won an "Industrial Statesmanship Award" from the National Urban League for establishing racially integrated plants in Memphis and Louisville. "Fair employment," said a Harvester manager, "is good business."

The combination of high labor costs, bad management, a poor organizational structure and the failure to introduce genuinely innovative products (competitors said Harvester merely redesigned existing machines instead of making new ones) kept the company's profit margin dangerously narrow. Harvester's much-touted policy of in-house promotions was actually stifling research and technological advances. New management was needed, but most Harvester officers stayed with the company for as long as 30 years. In 1955 Harvester sold its line of refrigeration equipment, but kept its other losing ventures and failed to modernize antiquated plants. The company, intent on conserving its resources and maintaining its market position, did not consider company growth important and began a slow and steady decline. "For too many years, as long as there was cash to cover the dividends, few executives really cared about how much the company made," a Harvester director said later. Tradition was valued to a fault. For example, a poor-selling truck was kept on a main assembly line for years simply because it had always been there. And although Harvester retained its market share, competitors alleged that it did so only by making government and fleet deals at cost.

Beginning in the late 1950's a series of company presidents attempted to reverse the economic fortunes of the company. Frank W. Jenks, president from 1957–1962, standardized production, reduced district offices by half, reduced the number of dealers from 5,000 to 3,600 and increased expenditure for research and development. In 1961 Harvester re-entered the consumer market with a jeep called the Scout and a small lawn and garden tractor named the Cub Cadet. It also expanded its promotional campaign for a station wagon, the Travelall, that looked like a scaled-down truck. All three products could be produced inexpensively, the company did not have to retool its plants to manufacture them, and sold them through its already existing distributor network. The new products increased sales, but profits only rose temporarily. By then Harvester found itself ranked the number two company in the farm machinery industry, John Deere & Company having surpassed it. Management tried to improve upon Harvester's 10–15% share of the construction industry, but could not gain any ground on Caterpillar and other companies. The only viable product was trucks, which comprised close to half the company's total sales by 1964. Harvester had the largest market share of the heavy-truck market—31%.

Throughout the 1960's profits declined as the company used more and more capital and went deeper and deeper into debt. Its labor costs were higher than General Motors; its management had poor communication channels; and low-selling products, such as the in-city truck, named the Merco, continued to be produced at high volume. The decentralization policy was not implemented in the correct way. Plants in different countries did not share research and did not make interchangeable parts. Although these plants began to work more closely during the 1970's, Harvester's construction products were still sold under several brand names and competed against each other. In 1974 they were finally combined as PayLine to present "a united front to the industry."

It was too late, however, since Harvester was already overextended. Even though it was larger than most of its competitors, it was ranked the number two company, or worse, in each of its three industries. Cyrus H. McCormick's grandnephew, Brooks McCormick, took charge in 1968, and closed a number of inefficient plants, including the famed McCormick Works in Chicago. Younger people were hired for management, dealerships were reduced and a Chrysler executive by the name of Keith Mazurek was appointed head of advertising. Mazurek promptly doubled the advertising budget, put the best-selling models on the main assembly lines, reorganized the district dealer network into regions and changed the name of his division from the old-fashioned "motor-truck" to simply "truck." But profits continued to decline. Sales in 1971 passed $3 billion, but profits reached a mere $45 million. *Forbes* described the company as virtually all sales and no profits and warned that Harvester's profits were far behind all its main competitors.

In 1977 Harvester brought in the number two man at Xerox Corporation, Archie R. McCardell, who quickly reduced costs and engineered a profit increase from $203.7 million to $370 million in his first year. But his cutbacks led to a crippling strike in 1979–1980. The company suffered more than $1 billion in losses and fell $4.2 billion into debt. When McCardell resigned in 1982, industry experts predicted that the company would soon file for bankruptcy. New managers tried to restructure the company, but as one observer said, "The new management is doing some very good things, but it is like putting a band-aid over a massive stomach wound."

Harvester's share in the construction and farm markets continued to decline, and it fell to a number two ranking in heavy trucks behind Ford. Troubled by soft markets and persistent creditors, Harvester sold its construction line and then its agricultural holdings. The sale of its agricultural line to Tenneco for $488 million in 1985 helped the company reduce its long-term debt to less than $1 billion.

Harvester sold its name as well as its equipment. This enabled the directors to declare it a reborn company in 1986 and name it Navistar, a word that implies high technology and a futuristic outlook, exactly what the old Harvester company had lacked for so many years. The company also left the gasoline-powered truck market, relying instead on a line of diesel-powered medium and heavy-duty trucks. It manufactured diesel engines for the medium trucks, and used engines from other companies for the heavier trucks. The emphasis on fuel-efficiency, along with the solid construction and reliability of the trucks, encouraged Navistar to advertise them as "LCO," or lowest cost ownership. The low operating costs of the trucks should make it attractive to consumers. This fact, in combination with Navistar's agreement to import Japanese medium-duty trucks, will improve the company's financial condition. Industry analysts have praised the company's restructuring, cost-efficiency and strong foreign sales and not only give it a good chance of surviving, but of returning to profitability in the future.

Principal Subsidiaries: International Harvester Co. of Belgium, S.A./N.V.; International Harvester Co. Ltd.; International Harvester France; International Harvester Mexico, S.A. de C.V.; ASPECT AG (Switzerland); Seddan Diesel Vehicles Ltd. (UK); International Harvester Export Co.; International Harvester Domestic International Sales Co.; Iowa Industrial Hydraulics; Victor Fluid Power, Inc.; International Harvester Credit Corp.; International Harvester Acceptance Corp., Ltd. (Bermuda); International Harvester Overseas Finance Co., NV (Netherlands Antilles); International Harvester Finanz AG (Switzerland); and International Harvester Credit Corp. of Great Britain, Ltd.

Further Reading: "International Harvester in Russia: The Washington–St. Petersburg Connection?" by Fred V. Carstensen and Richard Hume Werking, in *Business History Review 57* (Boston), Autumn 1983.

NISSAN MOTOR COMPANY, LTD.

17-1, Ginza, 6-chome
Chuo-Ku, Tokyo
Japan
543-5523

Public Company
Incorporated: 1933
Employees: 59,700
Sales: ¥3439 billion (US$21.6 billion)
Market Value: ¥1446 billion (US$9.086 billion)
Stock Index: Tokyo Osaka Niigata Nagoya Kyoto Fukuoka Supporo Frankfurt

Established in 1933, Nissan Motor Company was a pioneer in the manufacturing of automobiles. 54 years later, Nissan has become one of the world's leading automobile manufacturers, with more than 57,000 employees and an annual sales of approximately ¥3,750 billion. In addition to its most popular automobile, called Datsun, Nissan also produces textile machinery, forklifts, marine engines, watercraft, and even the solid-propellant launch vehicles used in Japan's space program.

In 1911 Masujiro Hashimoto, an American-trained engineer, founded the Kwaishinsha Motor Car Works in Tokyo. Hashimoto dreamed of building the first Japanese automobile, but lacked the capital. In order for his dream to come true, he contacted three men, Kenjiro Den, Rokuro Auyama and Keitaro Takeuchi, for financial support. To acknowledge their contribution to his project Hashimoto named his car DAT, after their last initials. In Japanese, "dat" means "escaping rabbit" or "running very fast."

The first DAT was marketed and sold as a 10-horsepower runabout. Another version referred to as "datson" or "son of dat," was a two-seater sports car produced in 1918. One year later, Jitsuyo Jidosha Seizo Company, another Nissan predecessor, was founded in Osaka. Kwaishinsha and Jitsuyo Jidosha Seizo combined in 1926 to establish the Dat Jidosha Seizo Company. Five years later, the Tobata Imaon Company, an automotive parts manufacturer, purchased controlling interest in the company. Tobata Imaon's objective was to mass produce products that would be competitive in quality and price with foreign automobiles.

In 1932, "Datson" became "Datsun," thus associating it with the ancient Japanese sun symbol. The manufacturing and sale of Datsun cars was controlled by the Jidosha

Seizo Company established in Yokohama through a joint venture between Nihon Sangyo Company and Tobata Imaon. In 1934 the company changed its name to Nissan, and one year later, the operation of Nissan's first integrated automobile factory began in Yokohama under the technical guidance of American industrial engineers.

However, Datsun cars were not selling as well as expected in Japan. Major automobile companies of the United States, such as General Motors and the Ford Motor Company, had established assembly plants in Japan during this time. These companies dominated the automobile market in Japan for 10 years. And as a result of the Depression in 1929, foreign companies were discouraged to export to the U.S.

In 1941 World War II began. At this time, Nissan's efforts were directed toward military production. During this wartime interlude the Japanese government ordered the motor industry to halt production of passenger cars and produce much-needed trucks.

After World War II, and the complete recreation of the Japanese auto industry, technical assistance contracts were established with foreign firms such as Renault, Hillman, and Willy's-Overland. In 1952 Nissan contracted a license with the United Kingdom's Austin Motor Company Ltd. With the help of American technical assistance and improved steel and parts from Japan, Nissan was capable of producing small, efficient cars, which later provided the company with a marketing advantage in the U.S.

The U.S. market was growing, but very gradually. Nonetheless, Nissan felt the U.S. needed low-priced economy cars, perhaps as a second family car. Surveys of the American auto industry encouraged Nissan to display its cars at the Imported Motor Car Show in Los Angeles. The exhibition was noticed by *Business Week* magazine, but as a staff member wrote in 1957, "With over 50 foreign car makers already on sale here, the Japanese auto industry isn't likely to carve out a big slice of the U.S. market for itself."

Nissan sifted through this criticism while struggling to improve domestic sales. Small-scale production resulted in high unit costs and high prices. In fact, a large percentage of Datsun cars were sold to Japanese taxi companies. Yet Kawamata, the company's new and ambitious president, was determined to increase exports to the U.S. Kawamata noted two principal reasons for encouraging exports to the U.S.: "Increased sales to the U.S.A. would give Nissan more prestige and credit in the domestic markets as well as other areas and a further price cut is possible through mass producing export cars."

By 1958 Nissan had contracted two U.S. distributors, Woolverton Motors of North Hollywood, California and Chester G. Luby of Forest Hills, New York. Sales did not improve, however, as quickly as Nissan had hoped. As a result, Nissan sent two representatives to the U.S. in order to help increase sales. They were Soichi Kawazoe, an engineer and former employee of GM and Ford, and Yutaka Katayama, an advertising and sales promotion executive. Each identified a need for the development of a new company. They recommended that a U.S. company be established to sell and service Datsuns in America. By 1960 Nissan U.S.A. had 18 employees, 60 dealers and a sales total of 1,640 cars and trucks. Yet it was the success of the Datsun pickup truck in the U.S. market which actually encouraged new dealerships.

Datsun assembly plants were also built in Mexico and Peru during the 1960's. In 1966 Nissan merged with the Prince Motor Company Ltd., and two years later Datsun passenger cars began production in Australia. During the year of 1969 cumulative vehicle exports reached one million units. This was a result of Katayama and Kawazoe's efforts to teach Japanese manufacturers to build automobiles comparable to American cars. It meant including mechanical similarities and engine capacities that could keep up with American traffic.

With the introduction of the Datsun 240Z, foreign sports cars made their debut in the American market. Datsun began to receive good reviews from automotive publications in the U.S. and sales began to improve. It was also at this time that the first robotics were installed in Nissan factories to increase production.

After the establishment of specialized aerospace techniques, Japan launched its first satellite on a Nissan rocket in 1970. Only five years later, Nissan export sales reached $5 million. But allegations were made to the effect that Nissan Motor Company in the U.S. was "pressuring and restricting its dealers in various ways: requiring them to sell at list prices, limiting their ability to discount, enforcing territorial limitations," according to author John B. Rae. In 1973 Nissan Motor Company U.S.A. agreed to abide by a decree issued from the U.S. Department of Justice that prevented Nissan from engaging in such activities.

The 1970's marked a slump in the Japanese auto industry as a result of the oil crisis. Gasoline prices started to increase and then a number of difficulties arose. President Nixon devalued the dollar and announced an import surcharge; transportation prices went up and export control was lacking. To overcome these problems Nissan U.S.A. brought in Chuck King, a 19 year veteran of the auto industry, to improve management, correct billing errors and minimize transportation damages. As a result, sales continued to increase with the help of Nissan's latest model, the Datsun 210 "Honeybee," that featured the capability of 41 miles to the gallon of gas.

In 1976 the company began the production of motorboats. During this time, the modification of the Datsun model to American styling also began. These additions included sophisticated detailing, roof racks and air conditioning. New styling of the Datsun automobiles was highlighted with the introduction of the 1980 model 200SX.

The 1980's marked the establishment of production in Italy, Spain, West Germany and the United Kingdom. An aerospace cooperative agreement with Martin Marietta Corporation was also concluded. The Nissan CUE-X and MID4 prototypes were also introduced.

The new generation of Nissan automobiles offers high-performance luxury sedans. They feature electronic control, variable split four-wheel drive, four-wheel steering, an "intelligent" engine, a satellite navigation system, as well as other technological innovations. Clearly, the management of Nissan has made a commitment to increase expenditures for research and development. In 1986 Nissan reported that the company's budget for research and development reached ¥170 billion, or 4.5% of net sales.

Presently, Nissan is in the process of evaluating future consumer trends. From their analysis of consumer trends conducted so far, Nissan expects consumers to prefer a car with high performance, high speed, innovative styling, and versatile options. All of these factors will be taken into account to get "a clear image of the car in the environment in which it will be used," says Yukio Miyamori, a director of Nissan. Cultural differences are also considered in this evaluation.

The use of robotics and computer-aided design and manufacturing will also reduce the time required for computations on aerodynamics, combustion, noise and vibration characteristics, enabling Nissan to have an advantage in both the domestic and foreign market. The strategy of Nissan's new management is to improve the company's productivity and increase future competitiveness. Currently ranked fourth worldwide in the automotive industry, Nissan will continue to provide intense competition for its rivals Toyota and Honda.

Principal Subsidiaries: Nissan Aichi Machine Industry Co., Ltd.; Atsugi Motor Parts Co., Ltd.; Ikeda Bussan Co., Ltd.; Japan Automatic Transmissions Co., Ltd.; Japan Electronic Control Systems Co., Ltd.; Kanto Seiki Co., Ltd.; Kiriu Machine Mfg. Co., Ltd.; NDC Co., Ltd.; Nihon Radiator Co., Ltd.; Nissan Credit Corp.; Nissan Diesel Motor Co., Ltd.; Nissan Koki Co., Ltd.; Nissan Motor Car Carrier Co., Ltd.; Nissan Motorist Service Co., Ltd.; Nissan Motor Sales Co., Ltd.; Nissan Real Estate Co., Ltd.; Nissan Rikuso Co., Ltd.; Nissan Shatai Co., Ltd.; Nissan Trading Co., Ltd.; Rhythm Motor Parts Mfg. Co., Ltd., Tokyo Sokuhan Co., Ltd.; Tsuchiya Mfg. Co., Ltd.; Yokohama Transportation Co., Ltd. The company also has subsidiaries in the following countries: Australia, Canada, Italy, Mexico, The Netherlands, New Zealand, Peru, Spain, Switzerland, United Kingdom, and the United States.

Further Reading: *The Japanese Auto Industry and the U.S. Market* by C.S. Chang, New York, Praeger, 1981; *Car Wars: The Untold Story* by Robert Sobel, New York, Dutton, 1984.

PACCAR INC.

P.O. Box 1518
Bellevue, Washington 98009
U.S.A.
(206) 455–7400

Public Company
Incorporated: 1924 as Pacific Car & Foundry Company
Employees: 9800
Sales: $1.796 billion
Market Value: $1.018 billion
Stock Index: NASDAQ

The history of Paccar began with a steel foundry established in Bellevue, Washington (near Seattle) in 1904. At that time, the major industries in Seattle were forestry and shipping, neither of which had any use for primary steel products. Unable to find a market for the steel, the company's founder, William Pigott, decided to establish a second facility to manufacture finished steel products. In 1905 the company began production of "bunks," the steel clasps used to secure logs to railroad flat cars. Shortly afterwards, the company began to produce railroad cars, and took the name Pacific Car & Foundry Company.

Over the ensuing 20 years Pacific Car & Foundry developed a variety of special transportation equipment but remained primarily involved in railroad car production. Pacific Car was incorporated in April 1924, and was acquired four years later by the American Car & Foundry Company. In May 1931 Pacific Car acquired the Arrow Pump Company and plants belonging to the Bacon & Matheson Drop Forge Company.

Severe economic conditions during the Depression forced American Car & Foundry to close its Pacific Car plant at Renton, south of Seattle. William Pigott's son, Paul, repurchased the facility in 1934, and initiated production of refrigerated box cars. The box cars, or "reefers," were bought by railroads and agricultural combines to transport perishable goods to distant markets. Production of the company's refrigerator cars was highly profitable despite continuing poor economic conditions, and generated enough surplus capital to permit the acquisition in 1936 of Heisers Incorporated, a manufacturer of motor buses.

During World War II Pacific Car produced railcars for the transportation of war materiel from production plants to major ports. The company also manufactured special vehicles and mechanical components. Following a re-

organization in 1943, the company retired its common stock, and compensated stockholders with new preferred shares. The reorganization brought Pacific Car under close family control.

In January 1945, as the war neared its end, Pacific Car & Foundry purchased the Kenworth Motor Truck Corporation, located in Seattle. Kenworth specialized in the production of powerful diesel trucks, and achieved a reputation for quality.

Transportation needs in the western United States grew during the late 1940's and 1950's. Despite the growth of smaller communities in the west, it was uneconomic for railroad companies to construct new lines. This created a demand for large trucks capable of climbing steep mountain grades and crossing long stretches of flatland. Kenworth trucks were perfectly suited for this kind of work, and, while expensive, they were also highly dependable and popular.

In 1953 Pacific Car & Foundry bought the Seattle facilities of the Commercial Ship Repair Company. Five years later the company purchased the assets of the Dart Truck Company, a Kansas City-based manufacturer of large "off-highway" construction equipment such as earth movers and giant dump trucks; then in the following year, 1954, Pacific Car acquired the Peterbilt Motors Company, a truck manufacturer like Kenworth, located in Newark, near San Francisco.

When Paul Pigott died in 1961, Robert O'Brien was named to succeed him as president of the company. O'Brien placed greater emphasis on truck sales and structural steel production. As a result of these efforts, Pacific Car experienced an average 23% annual increase in earnings between 1961 and 1966. In 1965 Robert O'Brien was promoted to chairman of the board, and replaced as president by Charles Pigott, grandson of the founder.

Pacific Car purchased a Canadian producer of automotive transmissions and industrial winches called Gearmatic, and in early 1967 completed its acquisition of Sicard Incorporated, a manufacturer of snow removal equipment and airport vehicles.

Workers at all three Pacific Car plants in Seattle staged a crippling labor strike from April 5 to July 22, 1968. This precipitated a 12–week strike at the Gearmatic Division in British Columbia, and a three–week strike at the Dart facility in Kansas City. The strikes cost Pacific Car over $1 million in lost production, but caused no lasting damage to the vehicle divisions.

Pacific Car & Foundry continued to produce railroad cars at its Renton Division. Although railroad car production contributed only a fraction to company earnings, it remained stable and profitable. Structural Steel, the weakest Pacific Car division, was one of the first American steel manufacturers to suffer from the effects of outdated technology and a market restricted by imported steel. While efforts were made to cut costs and increase productivity, Structural Steel continued to perform marginally.

In November 1971 Pacific Car & Foundry created a holding company, incorporated in Delaware, called Paccar Incorporated. On February 1, 1972 Paccar absorbed Pacific Car & Foundry. Company divisions such as Kenworth and Peterbilt retained their names, but other subsidiaries (particularly in finance) adopted the Paccar name.

Unlike competing truck manufacturers, Paccar was insulated from severe shifts in market demand by maintaining virtually no manufacturing facilities. Kenworth and Peterbilt trucks were merely assembled from parts produced by Eaton, Rockwell International, Cummins Engine, and Caterpillar Tractor, among others. This permitted Paccar to avoid costly investments in manufacturing facilities, and easily reduce production when demand fell. In addition, Paccar had the freedom to purchase components from a variety of competing manufacturers, allowing it to custom build trucks to a customer's specifications and take full advantage of the newest products.

Inflation and high oil prices in 1974 led trucking companies to utilize their equipment more efficiently which, in turn, caused a decline in new truck orders. Demand for higher quality Kenworth and Peterbilt trucks, however, was not seriously affected and production losses during 1974 were due more to the reoccurrence of strikes than to poor market conditions. Many labor disputes between 1974 and 1978 were caused by wage disputes as labor contracts expired.

In November 1979 Paccar failed in an attempt to gain control of the Harnischfeger Corporation, which produced cranes and earth-moving equipment. But eleven months later Paccar successfully completed a takeover of Fodens Ltd., a British manufacturer of heavy-duty trucks. Fodens, which had been bankrupt since July, sold trucks in Britain, Europe, and Africa. The company's operations were taken over by a newly created Paccar subsidiary, Sandbach Engineering.

A second oil crisis in 1979, and the subsequent implementation of deregulation in the trucking industry, once again compelled operators to utilize their equipment more efficiently. This caused sales of Class 8 trucks (those over 33,000 pounds in gross vehicle weight, and the only type produced by Kenworth and Peterbilt) to fall 58% between 1979 and 1982. However, despite an overall 35% drop in sales, Paccar remained profitable.

The Freightliner subsidiary of Daimler-Benz and the merged operations of Volvo White and General Motors became particularly aggressive in the mid-1980's, forcing Paccar's share of the Class 8 truck market to drop from 23% in 1983 to 18% in 1986. Plagued by overcapacity, Paccar was forced to close a Kenworth plant in Kansas City in April 1986, and a Peterbilt plant in Newark, California the following October.

In an effort to reduce its dependence on the depressed Class 8 truck market, Paccar announced its intention to purchase Trico Industries, a manufacturer of oil exploration equipment based in Gardena, California. After initial resistance, Trico agreed to be acquired for $65 million.

During this time Paccar also announced that it was negotiating with the Rover Group, the state-owned British automotive company, for the purchase of its British Leyland truck division. However, Rover management, with substantial support in Parliament, elected to sell the truck division to DAF, a Dutch automotive concern.

Paccar continued to experiment in new markets, and in early 1987 concluded an agreement with Volkswagen do Brasil to import Class 7 trucks (26,001 to 33,000-pound gross vehicle weight) for sale in the United States. The Class 7 market, however, is overwhelmingly dominated by Navistar, General Motors, and Ford. Paccar also remains interested in acquiring the Bell Helicopter division of Textron, a unit it first attempted to purchase in 1985.

A recovery in demand for Class 8 trucks in early 1987 reinforced Paccar's position that Kenworth and Peterbilt should not be merged. While truck production continues to provide Paccar with about 90% of its operating income, the company has yet to find a viable alternative to the cyclical demand and production of Class 8 trucks.

Principal Subsidiaries: Paccar of Canada, Ltd.; Paccar International, Inc.; Paccar Financial Corp.; Truck Acceptance Corp.; Paccar Financial Services, Ltd.; Paccar Insurance Co., Ltd.; Paccar Leasing Corp.; Paccar Australia Pty., Ltd.; Paccar Acceptance Pty., Ltd.; Paccar U.K., Ltd.; Railease, Inc. (90%); Paccar Machinery Corp.; Paccar Rail Leasing, Inc.; Vilpac, S.A. (49%).

Further Reading: *Paccar: The Pursuit of Quality* by Alex Grones, Bellevue, Washington, Documentary Book Publishers, 1981.

PEUGEOT

PEUGEOT S.A.

75, avenue de la Grande Armée
F–75761 Paris 16
France
(1) 502 11 33

Public Company
Incorporated: 1896
Employees: 187,500
Sales: FFr 97.4 billion (US$15.1 billion)
Market Value: FFr 18.9 billion (US$2.94 billion)
Stock Index: Paris

One of the prominent French families of the past century, the Peugeots have built their success on a painstaking approach to the assembly and quality of their automotive products. The company inspects every individual component that comes into the plant, test running every engine and gear box for about 10 minutes (about one in ten is either rejected or sent back for rebuilding), and track testing every finished car for approximately one hour. On average, seven faults are corrected per vehicle. Some 10% of the total work force of about 60,000 at Peugeot is occupied with quality control.

The manufacture of automobiles at Peugeot began in 1891 when a factory previously devoted to the construction of quadricycles dedicated nearly all of its resources to the construction of the automobile as we know it today. The founder of the company was Armand Peugeot, a Frenchman with a highly individualistic nature. Peugeot's success in the manufacture of machine tools resulted in his gaining recognition and influence, and many of his colleagues feared the risks entailed in devoting his complete resources to the manufacture of an automobile. However, this did not deter Peugeot. In 1891 he traveled to Germany in search of the perfect twin-cylinder engine, resolved that he would not come back empty-handed. Two months later he returned with the 525-cc version which was being manufactured by Daimler for its own hand-built cars. This purchase, Peugeot told his colleagues, was the beginning of something "grand."

Within fifteen years Peugeot had established manufacturing facilities throughout France. The first Peugeot factories were established in Valentigney and Audincourt, and then in Lille and Sochaux. For a few years after the Sochaux plant was opened, production primarily involved the manufacture of trucks. The first of these to bear resemblance to modern trucks was the type 109 which, with a maximum load of 3 tons, could still reach 20 km/hr. Industrial vehicle production increased dramatically during World War I, but as the war ended it began to recede.

In the period leading up to the war Peugeot cars won many races, including the 1913 Indianapolis 500. During this time the company was producing a complete range of vehicles for all uses with one salient feature which still distinguishes its product line today—its cars were sturdy and dependable vehicles with an excellent finish. Peugeot specialized mainly in the production of utilitarian models like the Bebe. The Quadralette engineered along the same lines as the Bebe and introduced at the Brussels Motor Show in 1920, subsequently led to the development of the model 5 CV which hit a record production figure of 83,000 chassis.

The history of the modern Peugeot automobile, however, did not begin until the 1929 Paris Motor Show with the debut of the 201 model. This completely new car, which was originally fitted with an 1122-cc engine, earned Peugeot its reputation as a manufacturer of reliable vehicles. What distinguished Peugeot from other car companies of its time was the number of technological developments that the company incorporated into its product designs year after year. Indeed, a steady stream of innovations form the core of the company's history during its first century.

By 1932, for example, the company had produced the more refined 301 model, also available in a family version. The lines of the 201 and 301 had become more elegant and attractive, creating a distinctive style very much in keeping with the current trends of the time. In 1934 the first aerodynamic tests were conducted on the 301 model and Peugeot introduced the 401 model and the six-cylinder 601, but no other model could match the 201. Before the 201 finally went out of production in September 1937, 142,000 units had been produced. The aerodynamic series began in 1935 with the 402 prototype model, which had its headlights set behind the grill. It was with this model that the numbering system which Peugeot still uses today to identify its cars began. Peugeot launched the 302 model at the 1936 Paris Motor Show; this was a new and scaled down version of the 402. Its most significant innovation was the use of the synchromesh gearbox, and it was also the first touring car fitted with a diesel engine.

Production slowed during World War II and almost ground to a halt as a result of the damage incurred by Allied bombing. It picked up again immediately after the war with the 202 model which had originally been introduced in 1938. This was replaced towards the end of 1947 by the 203 model, of which over 685,000 vehicles were built. With a unitary body and a 1300-cc 45 hp engine, this remained in production for almost 12 years without any major modifications.

It was only after World War II that the overwhelming difference in scale between Peugeot and the massive American companies like General Motors became clear. Armand Peugeot's successor, Roland Peugeot, found himself asking the question: should the small French family business "go public" in order to enlarge its operations? Many members of the board of directors believed that the additional capital which would be derived from such a share offering was necessary if the company was to compete in the same markets with Detroit. Furthermore, such a move was bound to create many new jobs.

Ultimately, what was at stake was the image of the company itself. On the one side, there were men like Roland Peugeot who believed that the careful and elaborate approach to the production of a small number of cars was the key to the company's survival. On the other side, there were the board of directors who were largely convinced that the company would be more successful producing several million cars per year. The debate was finally settled by Roland Peugeot when he convinced the board of directors in 1954 that manufacturing a small number of sturdy and reliable cars was more profitable than developing larger numbers of more glamorous vehicles which the Europeans perceived Detroit to be making already. "Quality" and "reliability" had been the focal points of a successful marketing strategy for a long time, and the company made a firm decision to concentrate on selling to that part of the public which viewed the car as a basic utility rather than as a status symbol. In this type of market a premium would be placed on a high quality car which could be depended upon to have a long and reliable performance.

In April of 1955 Peugeot began its association with the bus company Pininfarina. Since then, their cars have been produced with the marque of the Lion Rampant, first used on the modern 403. This car was given an 1800-cc 48 hp diesel engine in 1959. A more modern version of the 403 was launched in May 1960 and designated the 404. This car model was available with a 1485 or 1618 cc carburetor petrol engine (the fuel injection model was brought out later) or a diesel engine of almost 2 liters. An important feature of the 404 model was its versatility; it was available as a family car, a coupe, or an all purpose van. A total of 2,450,000 of these models were built.

Meanwhile, in the commercial sector, the front wheel drive J7 van which featured a large carrying capacity, was introduced. It was one of the few vans in its category in which a man could stand upright and it was available with the same petrol or diesel engines as the 403 model. In April of 1965 front wheel drive was introduced in the small, new 204 model car, which had a 1130-cc 58 hp petrol engine. The "04" series expanded over the years to include the 304 car (a more powerful 204 model with a different body) and the 504 car which was the flagship of the company until the arrival of the 604 model.

By the mid-1960's Peugeot was already making headway in popularizing its brand of cars abroad. Production levels of its handmade vehicles were increasing at a steady pace and, by the time of the oil crisis in 1973, the company had gained a significant share of the automotive market in America. As the European economic recession grew worse in 1973, many of the international automobile companies began experiencing depressed markets, but Peugeot was largely unaffected. Its 1973 output was 14.1% higher than the previous year, a better performance than the average 10% gain of the previous five year period.

Turnover for the year was 18.4% higher than 1972. Profits, however, were less substantial, partly as a result of the energy crisis. And sales to leading export markets, such as West Germany and Switzerland, decreased during the closing months of 1973.

While Peugeot was by no means immune to the conditions that influenced the international motor car industry, the economic situation did not convince management to abandon all thought of growth during 1974. Francis Rouge, the new president of Peugeot, was encouraged by the company's strong market position in the developing countries of Africa and Latin America. Company management was to learn that the automotive markets in Third World countries were useful in offsetting the declining demand in industrial countries.

In recent years the company has experienced severe financial losses. Many industry analysts believe that company management made a mistake by first acquiring Citroen, and then a division of Chrysler. The current president of the company, Jacques Calvet, is said to favor stringent modernization programs to return to profitability. When Calvet was appointed in 1984, many analysts speculated that he would be an "Iacocca type" of manager. By this they meant that he would be willing to be the architect of controversial cuts in employment. Fortunately, such a move has been obviated by recent successes, most notably the modernization program which has led to the production of the 205 car.

The future of Peugeot, at least during the next decade, will depend in part upon the continued success of cars like the 205, with carburetor and fuel-injected petrol engines, as well as Turbo-charged diesels. Under the direction of Calvet's modernization strategy, it is likely that the company's continuous attempts to improve the automobile will result in some advantageous developments for the automobile industry.

Principal Subsidiaries: Automobiles Peugeot; Automobiles Citroen; Aciers et Outillage Peugeot; Cycles Peugeot; Engrenages et Reducteurs; Société de Constructions Mécaniques Panhard et Levassor; Gefco; Société de Crédit à l'Industrie Automobile-Socia; Société Financière de Banque-Sofib; Compagnie Générale de Crédit aux Particuliers-Credipar; PSA Wholesale Ltd.; Anglo French Finance Co., Ltd.; Peugeot Finance International NV; PSA Finance Holding. The company also has subsidiaries in Belgium, Italy, The Netherlands, Spain, Switzerland, and West Germany.

Further Reading: *In First Gear: The French Automobile Industry to 1914* by James M. Laux, Liverpool, Liverpool University Press, 1976; *The Automobile Revolution: The Impact of an Industry* by Jean-Pierre Bardou, Chapel Hill, University of North Carolina Press, 1982; *The New France* by Pierre Lefebre, London, Penguin, 1984.

RÉGIE NATIONALE DES USINES RENAULT

34 Quai du Point du Jour BP 103
Boulogne-Billancourt 92 109
France
609-1530

State-owned
Incorporated: 1945
Employees: 215,844
Sales: FFr 121.7 billion (US$18.9 billion)

The closest parallel in the French automobile industry to Henry Ford was Louis Renault. His youthful interest in mechanical contrivances, especially steam engines and electrical devices, was accepted by his well-to-do family and he was allowed to have his own workshop on the family's property.

Soon after he finished his military service and his father had passed away, Louis convinced his older brothers Fernand and Marcel to each invest FFr30,000 to build an automobile firm which would be called Renault Freres. In 1899 Renault Freres received its first down payments for motor cars at FFr1,000 per vehicle. Primarily an assembly operation in the early years, Renault Freres expanded operations as fast as it could acquire components and erect buildings. Engines, tires, radiators, gears, steel, and electrical equipment all came from other companies. Already by 1899, the industry had generated a considerable range of specialist component firms. Marcel Renault soon joined the active management of the company in order to lessen some of Louis' work load, since he preferred to work in the shop rather than attend to commercial details. By 1901 the company had become the eighth largest firm in the automobile industry, based on the manufacture of a small, inexpensive, and reliable car. Its success should not be measured only by its sales and profits, however, but by its imitators; Louis Renault's transmission system was eagerly copied by other small car manufacturers.

Perhaps the most important ingredient in the firm's early success was the publicity Renault's cars received as a consequence of their racing prowess. Both Marcel and Louis Renault were expert racing drivers and they were victorious in numerous international events. But in 1903, while competing in the Paris–Madrid race, Marcel Renault was killed. Louis immediately withdrew his cars from the racing circuit and his company did not compete again for several years.

After 1905 Renault's taxicab became his largest selling product. Work began on this line late in that year when the company won an order for 250 chassis. The large orders for cabs soon made Renault the most important French automobile producer.

The firm did considerable export business during this period. In 1912, for example, nearly 100 Renault cabs were in service in Mexico City, and Renaults outnumbered all the other types of taxicabs in Melbourne. By 1914 the company had 31 dealers in foreign countries, from Yalta to Shanghai. Louis Renault himself did not take as much interest in these marketing matters as he did in the technical aspects of his business. He considered himself more of an inventor than anything else, and took out in his own name about 700 patents for devices that he had made personally or that had been developed in his factory.

Like several other automobile firms, Renault participated in the development of aviation in France. In 1907 the company began to experiment with aircraft engines, attempting to extract the most power possible from light-weight, air-cooled motors. While somewhat successful technically, this activity brought no profits at the time. Nevertheless, the discoveries and the experience which resulted found their justification in the war that soon followed. During World War I the company became an important manufacturer of all sorts of military equipment, including aviation engines and the light tanks that proved so effective in 1918.

After the war, the Renault factory expanded. But while the firm remained among the top producers in France during the inter-war period, Louis Renault was slow to adopt new technical and organizational ideas. This reluctance significantly hindered the company's growth. Then, when Paris was liberated, near the end of World War II, Louis Renault was jailed on a charge of Nazi collaboration. He died in prison before his case could be examined and the de Gaulle provisional government nationalized his company. The government installed some inspired technocrats to operate the company along commercial lines, and they made it into a showpiece of French industry. The firm built up its own production of machine tools and its factory was the first in Europe to use automation. In 1948, the company began to manufacture a miniature car called the Quatre Chevaux (4 CV or hp) which had been planned secretly during the war by Renault technicians.

The Quatre Chevaux proved to be a symbol of the social philosophy which has guided Renault ever since, first under Pierre Lefaucheux and then under his successor Pierre Dreyfus. An idealistic kind of technocrat, Dreyfus regarded the car as a social instrument which every family had a right to possess. Therefore, the firm concentrated on a large production of relatively small and inexpensive cars, the models gradually growing in size as French incomes and living standards rose. The other feature of this social philosophy was the idea that a firm owes its workers not only a wage, but also as full and happy a life as possible. With state support Renault led the field in welfare and labor relations.

It is possible to view the introduction of the Quatre Chevaux either as an example of effective business management or as the use of a state firm to provide a lower cost product. During the 1950's and 1960's the company maintained its record for effective product innovation. The Dauphine was manufactured in order to fit into the market opening between the inexpensive economy models and the higher priced models. The new model soon became quite popular and outsold all others for the next five years. A second distinctive aspect of Renault's success has been its emphasis on exports. It was one of the first companies in the automobile industry to make a serious effort to develop a sales organization in the United States.

Due to the interest in Renault cars within the United States, the company was initially aiming to penetrate the market by supplying 1000 cars per month. However, the United States ordered no fewer than 3000 cars in only one month. Consequently, Renault increased their daily production rate from 300 to approximately 500 units; company production facilities were near capacity for months in advance. Continued expansion into the world automobile markets remained one of the company's main concerns for years, and plans were therefore made for the construction of plants abroad. Sales agreements using existing local networks were made in Brazil, Argentina, Algeria, and India.

By the end of 1959 Renault was estimated to be the sixth largest automobile manufacturer in the world. At the beginning of 1960, when the American automobile market began to shrink, sales of the Dauphine dropped by 33% in comparison with the previous year. It was a period of stagnation on the U.S. domestic market and, as a result, Renault was faced with the problem of adjusting to the specific requirements of the American motorist.

In France, meanwhile, preparations were underway for new car models which would be known as the R-4 and the R-8. These were vehicles which had a third side window on a four door body. Subsequently, an error was made on a project which was to have been a large six-cylinder vehicle. Once the accounts had been completed it was discovered that the price of the car ought to have been 25% higher than originally planned. The swift and decisive intervention of Renault's chairman, Pierre Dreyfus, established the parameters of the new car, which was to have four cylinders, a functional styling, and a competitive price. The result was the R-16, which remained in production until the mid 1970's and had features that are still retained on more recent models. As a parallel development to car production, Renault had also begun to manufacture the Estafette, a commercial vehicle for door-to-door deliveries, which was replaced by another model in the beginning of the 1980's.

During the 1970's Renault went through a period of significant expansion. The success of the R-5, a particularly well-designed and highly reliable vehicle, allowed Renault to stay at the top of the European league of manufacturers. At the same time, a widely based program initiated in 1977 enabled the firm to purchase 46.4% of the shares in American Motors in 1980. The U.S. company then began production of the Alliance and the Encore, corresponding to European versions of the Renault.

The relationship began in 1979 when the two corporations signed an agreement. American Motors became the exclusive North American importer and distributor of Renault cars, while the French corporation would market American Motors products in France and several other countries. This was followed by the direct purchase of approximately $500 million in American Motors securities. American Motors chairman Gerald Meyers resigned in 1982 and was replaced by Paul Tippett, Jr., who then named Renault's Jose Dedeurwaerder president and chief operating officer. Other Renault personnel took their places in the corporation and on the board of directors as the first modern trans-Atlantic company was established.

By the mid-1980's, however, Renault's small deficit had turned into a one billion dollar loss. Georges Besse arrived in 1985 with a mandate to prevent any further losses. Besse, a pragmatic engineer who rescued the state-owned Pechiney Metals Group, was unable to go much beyond symbolic measures in helping the company. The Socialist government in France had backed away from tough industrial decisions that it feared would hurt the party in national elections. In addition, Besse's timing was unfortunate since powerful French communists had been arguing that Renault should worry more about upgrading French operations and protecting French jobs than spending money abroad on American Motors. The communists claimed that there was an imbalance between investments needed at home and expansion abroad. AMC's losses in 1986 made those arguments more compelling in the view of many Frenchmen.

In November of 1986 Besse was assassinated by the French terrorist organization, "Direct Action." This unfortunate event, however, was not the only one that had an adverse effect on Renault. The company was also suffering from a series of poor marketing judgments which had reduced its share of the domestic auto market. Once the largest car manufacturer in Europe, Renault has slipped to sixth place.

In March 1987 Renault announced it would withdraw from the U.S. market by selling its share in American Motors to the Chrysler Corporation. Under this agreement, which American Motors voted to accept, Renault will be paid upwards of $200 million dollars for its AMC shares and bonds over a period of five years.

Renault will also receive royalties from Chrysler's marketing of AMC's newly launched Premier. In exchange, Renault will export between two and three billion dollars worth of automatic components to Chrysler.

Renault's deal with Chrysler has been criticized by some industry observers; while increasing Renault's political standing, they say, the deal could ultimately do more harm than good. Renault's U.S. business had provided 6,000 jobs in France. Yet Christian Martin, Renault's export director for Europe, stands by the company decision, claiming management reached a compromise in order to avoid an imminent financial crisis.

Principal Subsidiaries: Renault Vehicles Industriels; Renault Industries Equipements Et Techniques (99.9%); Renault Agriculture; Europcar; Société Nouvelle De Roulements (86%); Chausson (35%); Diffusion Industrielle Et Automobile Par Le Crédit-Diac; Société De Financement Pour L'Extension de L'Industrie-Sofexi.

Further Reading: *In First Gear: The French Automobile Industry to 1914* by James M. Laux, Liverpool, Liverpool University Press, 1976; *Renault: The Cars and the Charisma* by J. Dewar McLintock, Cambridge, Stevens, 1983.

BOSCH

ROBERT BOSCH GmbH.

Robert-Bosch-Platz 1
Gerlingen-Schillerhöhe, Stuttgart
Postfach 50
7000 Stuttgart 1
Federal Republic of Germany
(07 11) 811 1

Private Company
Incorporated: 1886
Employees: 61,400
Sales: DM 18.37 billion (US$ 7.459 billion)

Bosch is West Germany's leading manufacturer of ignition, fuel injection, and lighting equipment, and a major contributor to German automotive engineering. The company has been described as a mixture of paradoxes—alternately conservative and daring, reflective and enterprising. Bosch's unique blend of management acumen and foresight has kept it at the forefront of the automotive components field.

The company was founded in Stuttgart in 1886 by a highly motivated, self-educated electrical engineer named Robert Bosch. More talented as an administrator than as an engineer, Robert Bosch gained a reputation for innovation in industrial relations. He instituted an eight-hour work day (which was uncommon at the time) and paid employees at a higher standard rate in the belief that superior working conditions would encourage better employee performance. Bosch readily acknowledged ability and creativity in his employees, assigning the most talented among them to positions in the most promising areas. He also recognized the need for a diverse, high-quality product line as the most direct means to growth.

Bosch entered the automotive industry in the early 1890's, when the company introduced a hand-crank motor starter. Near the turn of the century, on the strength of the growing American automobile market, Bosch became the world leader in ignition systems. By 1914, 70% of the company's sales were in the United States. The outbreak that year of World War I resulted in an American trade embargo against Germany. Bosch was prevented from doing any more business in the United States and forced to rely solely on European sales under a wartime economy.

When the war ended in 1918, the German economy was in a state of complete disarray. The nation fell into a serious economic depression during the 1920's, which caused many businesses to fail. Bosch, however, managed to remain in business, partly as a result of its diversification and good management. As the economic situation stabilized, public discontent in Germany began to rise. Bosch, which expanded modestly during this period, purchased the radio manufacturer Blaupunkt-Werke in 1933. That same year, the Nazis under Adolf Hitler seized power and initiated a new economic order characterized by industrial growth and rearmament.

The company enjoyed several periods of strong growth during the 1930's, primarily due to a strong demand from German industry and the military for electronic and mechanical products. The company's growth necessitated a new form of organization, and in 1937 it was incorporated as a private limited company. German military adventurism and territorial expansion precipitated a second World War which again eliminated foreign markets for companies such as Bosch. Robert Bosch died in 1942, during the height of Germany's success in the war, and was succeeded by a man named Hans Walz.

For Germany, the remainder of the war was characterized by severe shortages of all kinds and extensive war damage. At the end of the war Germany was partitioned into occupied Soviet and Western Powers zones (later East and West Germany). The more heavily industrialized western zone, where Bosch was located, was in ruins. Bosch reorganized and its factories were rebuilt. The American market, however, remained closed to Bosch after the war, again forcing the company to strengthen its connections with smaller European manufacturers. New efforts were made to develop more advanced products, and by 1949 Bosch perfected a mechanical fuel injection system.

West Germany was "readmitted" to the world market system in the early 1950's, during which time Bosch became a major supplier of automotive products to foreign manufacturers. During the 1950's the consumer automobile market experienced a strong growth, due this time to an expanding world economy and new levels of prosperity.

Hans Walz retired in 1962 after 20 years as the company's chief executive. He was replaced by Hans Merkle, a self-taught and apprenticed engineer and businessman, known for his ability to predict changing market conditions. Merkle recognized pollution control and fuel economy as key factors in future automobile sales. Under Merkle's leadership, Bosch began to devote more of its resources to the development of electronic products, and later produced a new fuel injection system which promoted a smoother running engine and reduced fuel consumption.

Potential competitors of Bosch, including Siemens and Bendix, largely ignored the potential of fuel injection systems while Bosch continually perfected new and better versions. When strict new antipollution regulations were enacted in the United States, automobiles equipped with Bosch fuel injectors, such as the Volkswagen Beetle, became extremely popular. Soon afterwards, other European manufacturers, including Daimler-Benz and Volvo, decided to integrate the Bosch system into their product line. When the 1973 OPEC oil crisis caused dramatic increases in the price of petroleum, the highly efficient Bosch fuel injection systems became virtually indispensable.

By the mid 1970's, Bosch had made strong progress in regaining its prewar market share in the United States. Bosch purchased a plant in Charleston, Virginia in 1974 to produce fuel injection systems in the U.S. The company also acquired a 25% share of American Microsystems, a manufacturer of integrated circuitry, and a 9.3% share of Borg-Warner, which was well-established in the area of microcircuitry. Bosch planned to apply technologies developed by these two companies to produce even more advanced automotive systems.

The Charleston plant was subsequently expanded three times, and today remains the company's base of operations in the United States. Through the late 1970's fuel injection systems, Bosch's primary product, became the most important electronic component to automobile manufacturers. By 1984, nearly half of the cars sold in the U.S. were equipped with fuel injection systems. That number is expected to grow to more than 80% in the 1990's.

Several other manufacturers have recently initiated efforts to reduce Bosch's share of the worldwide automotive components market. Marcus Bierich, who was named chief executive officer of Bosch in 1984, reacted quickly to these threats by expanding the company's product line and diversifying its operations.

One of the most important products to emerge from this new initiative was the ABS, or anti-skid braking system. This device prevents brakes from locking by means of an electronic gauge which is wired to the brake pedal. In addition to being an important safety feature, it makes a number of other wires and cables redundant, allowing room for "cruise control" and other features. The Bosch ABS system is standard on many European automobiles, and was introduced on American luxury cars in 1985. Despite competition in this area from Alfred Teves (a subsidiary of ITT) and Honda, Bosch is planning to open an ABS plant in the United States in 1990, when it estimates sales to American automobile manufacturers will reach 100,000 units.

As car features grow more sophisticated, Bosch continues to develop systems to aid the driver. A new device called the digital trip meter calculates the course and direction of a car by measuring heat levels of the terrain and posting a computerized map on the driver's dashboard. In addition to making the driver aware of the most efficient available routes, the meter can also detect traffic jams. This product is expected to be introduced on 1990 model cars.

Strong competition in high-technology electronics has drawn Bosch into the growing mobile cellular telephone industry. Bosch's Blaupunkt subsidiary (highly respected for its state-of-the-art car stereo systems) is preparing to enter the cellular telephone industry, particularly in Europe, where its network of service centers can more easily facilitate installation and repair.

In order to assist its technical development, Bosch recently purchased Telefonbau und Normalzeit, a German telecommunications company, and Telenorma, the exclusive supplier of communications systems to Bundespost, the national postal and telecommunications group. Bosch has also entered into a partnership with AEG-Daimler, Germany's second largest electronics manufacturer.

Bosch has several other affiliations under consideration, including joint ventures with Nixdorf (computers), SEL (telecommunications), and CGE (the French manufacturer of telephone switching devices). The company would like to establish a link between Telenorma and CGE to create a French-German cellular telephone network using cellular telephones manufactured by Blaupunkt and fiber optic cables made by Bosch.

Fierce competition and a 1984 metalworkers strike seriously affected the company's production for several months, and weakened its lead over competitors. For virtually the first time, clients were forced to evaluate alternative suppliers. These developments have raised the most important question in Bosch's future—whether or not the company should remain privately owned. In over 100 years of operation, Bosch has been controlled by only four leaders. Its earnings are directed into a trust fund which provides funding for research and development, and corporate acquisitions. With plans for substantial investments in the United States, and expansion in the telecommunication and information management industries, Bosch's ability to remain private is uncertain. The company will, however, remain a strong competitor in the automotive components industry.

Principal Subsidiaries: BTS Broadcast Television Systems GmbH.; Blaupunkt-Werke GmbH.; Robert Bosch Electronik GmbH.; Teldix GmbH.; Telefonbau und Normalzeit Lehner & Co. The company also has subsidiaries in the following countries: Argentina, Australia, Austria, Belgium, Brazil, Canada, Denmark, England, France, Italy, Japan, Malaysia, Mexico, The Netherlands, Norway, Portugal, South Africa, Spain, Sweden, Switzerland, Turkey, and the United States.

ROLLS-ROYCE MOTORS LTD.

Pym's Lane
Crewe, Cheshire CW1 3PL
England
0270 255155

Subsidiary of Vickers, plc
Employees: 5,029
Sales: £216.8 million (US$311.7 million)

The Rolls-Royce name is not as old as that of Panhard, Daimler, or Napier, all three of whom established automotive companies in the 19th century, but as C.S. Rolls & Company advertised in November of 1905, "No greater mistake can be made than to suppose that the older the manufactury the better the car." Certainly, the Rolls-Royce name implies not only the finest craftsmanship, but comfort, money, power, and elitism. The distinctive radiator *grille* has transcended its function to become a powerful symbol of luxury and quality. An American art historian recently authored a paper entitled *The Ideological Antecedents of the Rolls-Royce Radiator*.

The history of Rolls-Royce begins with its founders, an engineer named Frederick Henry Royce, and Charles Stewart Rolls, an automobile dealer and an engineer himself. Royce manufactured electric cranes and dynamos at his company, called Royce, Ltd., which was established in Manchester, England in 1884. Early in 1904, he purchased his first two-cylinder car, a French Decauville. Far from being an inferior model, Royce was nonetheless dissatisfied with its performance. He decided to build a car of his own by "taking an existing part and making it better." On April 1, he emerged from his workshop on Cook Street with three two-cylinder, 10-horsepower cars.

Royce automobiles, known for their silent and vibration-free ride, featured an engine which could be kept idling and then speeded up to 1000 rotations per minute without the problematic adjustments required with other engines. The successful Royce automobiles soon came to the attention of Henry Edmunds, a friend of Charles Stewart Rolls, who at the time operated a London dealership for French Panhard automobiles. Strongly interested in the Royce automobile, however, Rolls later arranged to meet Royce at the Midland Hotel in Manchester in May of 1904. He was immediately impressed by Royce's determination and creativity. The two men later agreed to establish an automobile partnership, and pledged that Rolls-Royce vehicles would never again be built with merely two cylinders.

Rolls and Royce believed that by combining their own expertise and dedication with the latest technologies, they could produce the finest automobile possible. By the end of the year, newly-engineered four-cylinder, 20-horsepower Royce cars had won several important races, and had become one of the most popular luxury cars available.

Charles Rolls and Henry Royce formalized their partnership on March 15, 1906 when they founded Rolls-Royce Ltd. The company's first product, the "40/50" (horsepower), made its debut at the Paris Motor Show in 1906, featuring a distinctive arched top radiator. The car was fitted with a powerful new six-cylinder engine which enabled it to reach a top speed of 65.2 miles per hour. Claude Johnson, an associate of Charles Rolls, later named it the "Silver Ghost," because of its metallic appearance and because its engine was "quiet as a ghost."

In order to expand, the company moved in 1907 from Manchester to Derby, 50 miles south, in the English Midlands. Soon afterwards Rolls-Royce established a technical inspection service which made house-calls. This service later formed the basis of the Rolls-Royce driving school.

Under the supervision of Charles Rolls, the company began to manufacture small aircraft engines in 1907. Three years later, however, Rolls was tragically killed when his Wright biplane crashed from a height of only 23 feet. As a symbol of mourning, the intertwined "RR" logo on the radiator plate was changed from red to black.

Royce introduced a statuette called the "Spirit of Ecstasy" (or alternatively, the "Flying Lady") mounted on the radiator of the 1911 Silver Ghost. The winged figure was modeled by Charles Sykes at the behest of Lord Montagu, a well-known motoring enthusiast, and served to further enhance the appearance of the radiator. Electric starter motors became increasingly popular after their introduction in 1914. Royce, however, was cautious about making drastic design changes in his automobile line until the starter device had been properly developed. The electric starter was finally built into Silver Ghosts in 1919. Rolls-Royce continued to develop its hand-crafted automobiles for an increasingly exclusive (and wealthy) clientele. New models were resistant to change, maintaining a practical and traditional appearance.

Despite the death of his partner, Henry Royce remained committed to the development of new engines for the aeronautics industry. During World War I Rolls-Royce accounted for half of Britain's total aircraft engine output. The company's automobiles, however, were also well employed during the war. T.E.Lawrence (Lawrence of Arabia) waged several battles with a fleet of nine armored Rolls-Royces, which in the desert, he claimed, were "prized above rubies."

When the Silver Ghost went out of production in 1925, more than 6000 models had been built. It was replaced by a newer, uncharacteristically light model called the Phantom. Subsequent improved versions of the Phantom came out in later years, including one with a 12-cylinder engine. In 1931 Rolls-Royce purchased Bentley Motor Ltd., a consistently undercapitalized English manufacturer of high-performance automobiles. Henry Royce, who was conferred a baronetcy in 1930, died on April 22, 1933 after a long illness.

The aircraft engine division of Rolls-Royce spent much of the interwar period developing a series of engines, including the Kestrel. On the eve of World War II, a successor to the Kestrel, the more powerful Merlin, was developed. The Merlin engine was used to power Supermarine Spitfire and Hawker Hurricane fighters, the primary instruments of the Royal Air Force.

Rolls-Royce halted its production of automobiles during World War II and instead concentrated its resources on the production of aircraft engines. When the war ended in the spring of 1945, over 150,000 Merlin engines had been built in Great Britain and under license in the United States.

Auto production resumed after the war at a new Rolls-Royce plant in Crewe, near Derby. The company ceased building each car to a customer's specifications, and instead standardized the product line. A separate diesel engine division was also established which produced large engines, primarily for construction machinery.

Rolls-Royce developed a number of jet engine designs for military aircraft, and was the first company to introduce a turboprop engine, which gave the company an interest in the commercial airplane market for the first time. With the development of commerical jets during the 1950's, Rolls-Royce altered the design of its Avon jet engine for use in the de Havilland Comet and the French Nord Aviation Caravelle. A new engine, called the Conway, was specifically designed for the American Douglas DC-8 and Boeing 707. During the 1960's, a new line called the Spey went into production.

Throughout most of the company's history, the aircraft engine division accounted for over 80% of Rolls-Royce's total revenues. A decision was made in the early 1960's to raise this figure by entering the competitive American aircraft engine market. This necessitated the development of a larger, more powerful engine for the emerging jumbo jet market.

In 1966 Rolls-Royce completed a design for the new engine, which was designated the RB.211. A concerted sales effort resulted in the sale of 555 RB.211s to the Lockheed Corporation for installation in their new line of L-1011 Tristar jetliners. The sale, however, was extremely costly to Rolls-Royce, which was forced to lower its price in order to beat a counter offer from General Electric. In order to meet the increasing cost of the project, any available capital from the automobile division was systematically diverted to the aero-engine division.

The construction of the first RB.211 commenced in the summer of 1969. When the engine was tested, however, it became apparent that several design flaws would seriously delay the project. As a result of penalty clauses written into its supply contracts, Rolls-Royce was obligated to remit substantial payments to its customers. This forced the company to announce in October that its interim dividend would be reduced from 4 to 3%. Moreover, company officials refused to address specific problems with the RB.211. The situation continued to deteriorate for over a year, when the gravity of Rolls-Royce's condition was finally revealed.

On November 11, 1970 the British government announced that it was extending a loan to Rolls-Royce totaling £60 million. Three-quarters of this sum was for anticipated losses on the RB.211 project, and the remaining £15 million was earmarked for operating expenses. In addition, it was revealed that executive control of Rolls-Royce would be turned over to a four man committee. Two days later it was announced in the House of Commons that the government would nationalize Rolls-Royce.

As problems with the RB.211 were gradually resolved, the British government continued to meet the company's financial obligations and oversee its restructuring. To many it seemed ironic that the world's premier automaker, a symbol of British prosperity, had become a symbol of Britain's decline. The British government, which was uncomfortable with this situation, decided to prepare the automotive and diesel divisions for privatization. Consequently, Rolls-Royce Motors Ltd., comprising the automobile and diesel engine operations, was created as a separate company in 1973 and returned to private stockholders. The aircraft engine division, which was not profitable, remained under government ownership.

David Plastow, who was placed in charge of the automobile operation after the nationalization, initiated a modernization program for Rolls-Royce Motors, which included a £20 million investment in new plant and equipment. The company's annual output increased from 2000 to 3500 cars, and its diesel division won a contract to produce 1600 engines for Chieftain battle tanks intended for sale to the Shah of Iran. The government, however, canceled the tank sale after the Shah fell from power in 1978. Rolls-Royce produced 270 engines, none of which were delivered, but was protected from losses by its contract with the government.

In 1979 higher interest rates and a stronger pound reduced demand for automobiles. Further difficulties with the economy weakened the diesel operation despite its having won a contract to produce a line of MBT-80 battle tanks for the British government. The company's financial situation required urgent action in order to prevent it from falling into bankruptcy. In September of 1980, 90% of Rolls-Royce's stock was acquired by Vickers plc, a well-known British engineering firm which had a long history as a defense contractor, and with whom Rolls-Royce had frequently collaborated. Rolls-Royce Motors Ltd, subsequently became a subsidiary of Vickers, and Plastow was named the parent company's new chief executive officer.

Even the Rolls-Royce automobile division encountered difficult times as Britain entered a serious economic recession. The company's output of vehicles dropped from 3018 in 1980 to only 1567 in 1983, and was forced to lay off 1000 workers. A five-week labor strike in 1983 forced the company to change its marketing strategy and lower the price of its automobiles.

Rolls-Royce has recently found itself vulnerable to many of the same pressures that have plagued large automakers. The present chief executive of Rolls-Royce is Richard W. Perry, who it is said plans to place greater emphasis on the company's Bentley line, with the introduction of two new models, intended primarily for European customers. Once the cornerstone of Rolls-Royce, Bentley sales have fallen off in recent years, and at one point the company considered its discontinuation. Yet

Perry, who believes in effective marketing, believes he can increase sales of Rolls-Royce cars with more enlightened strategies. The advertising budget will be increased by 40%, and a new audience is currently being targeted, namely, younger people with assets of $500,000 or more. Despite the optimism that flows from such a strategy, company executives concede that the days are over when the carmaker could routinely depend on strong profits from a captive clientele.

Further Reading: *Rolls-Royce in America* by John Webb De Campi, London, Dalton Watson, 1975; *Rolls-Royce from the Wings: Military Aviation 1925–71*, Oxford, Oxford Illustrated Press, 1976, and *The Engines Were Rolls-Royce: An Informal History of That Famous Company*, New York, Macmillan, 1979, both by Ronald W. Harker; *The British Motor Industry 1896–1939* by Kenneth Richardson, Hamden, Connecticut, Archon, 1977; *Rolls-Royce: The Growth of a Firm, The Years of Endeavour* by Ian Lloyd, London, Macmillan, 2 vols., 1978; *The Future of the United Kingdom Motor Industry* by Krish Bhaskar, London, Kegan Paul, 1979; *The Decline of the British Motor Industry: The Effects of Government Policy 1945–1979* by Peter J.S. Dunnett, London, Croom Helm, 1980; *Rolls-Royce: The Formative Years 1906–1939* by Alex Harvey-Bailey, Derby, Rolls-Royce Heritage Trust, 1983; *Rolls-Royce: The History of the Car* by Martin Bennett, Yeovil, Oxford Illustrated Press, 1983; *In the Beginning: The Manchester Origins of Rolls-Royce* by Mike Evans, Derby, Rolls-Royce Heritage Trust, 1984; *Rolls-Royce: The Cars and Their Competitors 1906–1965* by A.B. Price, London, Batsford, 1986.

SAAB-SCANIA

SAAB-SCANIA A.B.

S-581 88 Linköping
Sweden
13 18 00 00

Public Company
Incorporated: April 1937 as Svenska Aeroplan
Aktiebolaget
Employees: 47,000
Sales: Skr 33.6 billion (US$4.944 billion)
Market Value: SKr 13.8 billion (US$2.038 billion)
Stock Index: Stockholm

During the 1980's many larger automotive corporations in the United States and Western Europe purchased aerospace companies, partly in order to gain access to advanced technology in the aviation and space industries. Saab-Scania, however, has had such access for four decades. One of the world's oldest automotive manufacturers, Saab-Scania has a history which begins at the end of the 19th century.

In the early 1890's the English bicycle manufacturer Humber built a factory in Malmö, Sweden called the Svenska AB Humber & Company. Near the turn of the century, the plant was sold to Swedish interests and the name was changed to Masinfabriks AB Scania. Initially the plant manufactured vacuum cleaners and paper machines as well as bicycles. New bicycle models introduced in the early 1900's cost the average consumer the equivalent of six months wages, so ownership was limited to the wealthy. At the time, the company was also manufacturing a primitive type of motor vehicle, consisting of a French gasoline-powered engine with an English carburetor fastened to the bicycle frame. The construction of this vehicle was important in that it gave the company practical experience in combustion engines.

In 1901 a new managing director, Hilding Hessler, and a new plant manager, 23-year old Anton Svensson, assumed control of company operations. The two men began focusing on the manufacture of automobiles. During 1901 and 1902 the company's best engineers, Fridolf Thorssin and Tomas Krause, built at least three experimental models. All were constucted with the engine and gearbox under the driver's seat. Svensson, however, believed that the engine should be placed in the front of the car. This disagreement led to Thorssin's departure from the company, at which time Svensson decided to establish a regular production model based on his own ideas.

At the beginning of 1903 Scania offered three models: the four-seat Model A, the two-seat Model B, and the Model C, a larger luxury car, with one, two and four cylinder engines, respectively, ranging from 4.5 to 24 horsepower. The engines were purchased from the Kemper Motorenfabrik in Berlin, thus enabling Scania to concentrate on the development of a chassis. The new vehicles were remarkably advanced for their time, featuring a track-rod steering system and central chassis lubrication. The Scania Model A featured a rear seat which could be converted into a small loading platform.

In 1911 Scania merged with the Vagnfabriks Aktie Bolaget in Södertälje (Vabis), a railroad car manufacturer which had also been producing automobiles since 1897. The new company, Scania-Vabis, developed the world's first "purpose-built" bus. In 1924 Scania-Vabis decided to concentrate its efforts on the manufacture of larger trucks and buses, and in 1929 discontinued automobile manufacture altogether. The company introduced its first diesel engine in 1936.

With the threat of another war in Europe, it became imperative for Sweden to improve its defenses. Not least important was the need for a domestic aircraft industry large enough to supply the Swedish forces with military aircraft. This led to the formation in April 1937 of the Svenska Aeroplan Aktiebolaget, abbreviated SAAB. Two years later, SAAB, with headquarters in Trollhättan, took over the aircraft division of the Aktiebolaget Svenska Järnvägsverkstäderna, or Swedish Railroad Works, located in Linköping. SAAB subsequently transferred its corporate headquarters and construction and design departments to Linköping.

Construction was accelerated at both the Linköping and Trollhättan plants, which were building aircraft designed by Bristol, Junkers, and Northrop. During this period work proceeded on the first SAAB aircraft, the Svenska B-17 dive bomber, which made its first flight in 1940. When war came to Europe, however, Sweden declared itself neutral. As a result the country was spared from occupation by Nazi troops which had already taken control of its Scandinavian neighbors Norway and Denmark.

Plans for car production at the SAAB plant at Trollhättan started evolving as World War II was nearing an end, and management sought to widen the production program to meet an expected decline in military aircraft requirements. The success of small European cars in the Swedish market just prior to the war provided management with the confidence that cars of the same type should also prove popular in the future, and that demand would be steady enough to ensure the success of a SAAB automobile.

A talented aircraft engineer named Gunnar Ljungström was placed in charge of the development of the SAAB auto, the first prototype of which, the 92001, was ready by the summer of 1946. The body design, however, was neither practical nor aesthetically pleasing. The car was reintroduced in 1947 with an improved external design, and designated the 92002. The design of this model was to characterize SAAB automobiles for the next 30 years. Streamlining helped to reduce fuel consumption and engine wear, and enabled the car to reach speeds of 60 miles per hour. Despite a number of minor shortcomings, the car's road performance was excellent, and its appearance was stylish and popular.

Improved versions of Ljungström's original design appeared throughout the 1950's, and by 1955 SAAB automobiles had become the most popular in Sweden; one car was leaving the assembly line every 27 minutes. In order to meet anticipated demand, more plant space was required, and a new factory was established at Göteborg to manufacture engines and gearboxes.

During the previous 20 years, Scania-Vabis developed and produced heavy vehicles, particularly trucks and buses. While somewhat less dynamic in character than SAAB, the company managed to make several innovations in Swedish industry, including the introduction of a turbocharged diesel engine in 1951.

SAAB continued to develop a variety of aircraft, particularly military fighter jets. The first of these was introduced in 1949, and production in various forms was maintained throughout the 1950's. The SAAB aircraft division also held licenses to manufacture foreign-designed aircraft and produce aircraft components for foreign manufacturers.

As early as 1953 SAAB management started exploring the possibilities of selling cars in the United States, but hesitated from entering that market until 1956, when a more promising atmosphere had developed. Using New York City as a base of operations, an American subsidiary was created to import SAAB automobiles, and a depot was established near Boston to receive cars and store spare parts. It was a modest beginning for a small foreign company in the world's largest automobile market, and growth was difficult and slow.

During the 1960's the scope of SAAB's operations expanded from automobiles and aircraft into satellites, missiles, and energy systems. On May 19, 1965, as its business continued to grow, the company changed its name to Saab Aktiebolag (the acronym had become so popular as to warrant the elimination of the old name). Over the next four years, officials of Saab and Scania-Vabis began to investigate the viability of operating as a single corporation.

Saab and Scania-Vabis merged their operations during 1969, and absorbed two other military contractors, Malmö Flygindustri and Nordarmatur. All automotive operations of Saab-Scania AB were centered at the facility in Södertälje, and the aircraft division headquarters, which produced the JAS-35 Draken and JAS-37 Viggen fighter jets, remained at Linköping. Also in 1969, Saab-Scania, in cooperation with the Finnish company Oy Valmet AB, established an automobile factory at Uusikaupunki, Finland.

Saab-Scania decided to focus its efforts on competing for a significantly larger share of the American automobile market, the main goal being to define its cars as a better choice than those offered by BMW, Mercedes-Benz, and Volvo. These cars had been highly successful with more affluent American consumers. The expanded marketing campaign produced few results over the first half of the decade, but by 1978 began to pay off handsomely. The company's sales increased by 19% in America and by 17% in Scandinavia.

In 1980 the company introduced a new line of Scania trucks based on a unique method of modular construction. These trucks are primarily class 7 vehicles (26,001 to 33,000 pounds in gross vehicle weight), which have recently become extremely popular in the United States. Meanwhile, the automotive division was preparing to introduce a restyled line of cars in its 9000 series; they were introduced in 1984 and proved to be popular. However, problems related to retooling production plants thwarted a planned expansion of production capacity by 10% during 1985.

Saab-Scania entered into a joint venture with Fairchild Industries of the United States in 1980 to develop a new 30–36 passenger commercial airliner called the SF340. However, a corporate restructuring of Fairchild forced the company's withdrawal from the project in 1985. Saab-Scania took complete control of the SF340 in November of that year and completed the project in 1986. The SF340 is currently in service with a number of airline companies, providing connection services between small airports in outlying areas and major airports. The aircraft division has also started development of the JAS-39 Gripen fighter jet, expected to enter service in 1992.

In the late 1980's, Georg Karnsund, the current president of Saab-Scania, is expected to place greater emphasis on marketing programs in Europe, particularly in France and Italy, and in Australia and Japan. Karnsund believes that Saab's ability to develop advanced technology will give its cars a distinct advantage in increasingly competitive international markets.

Principal Subsidiaries: VAG Sweden Group (67%); Bill & Buss Group; Saab-Ana Group (Sweden); Saab-Scania of America, Inc.; Saab (Great Britain) Ltd.; Saab-Scania Combitech Group; Saab-Scania Enertech Group (Sweden); Oy Saab-Valmet AB (50%); Oy Scan-Auto AB (Finland) (50%); Scancars AG (Switzerland) (25%); Scania Nederland BV (Netherlands). The company also has subsidiaries in the following countries: Argentina, Australia, Austria, Belgium, Brazil, Denmark, France, Great Britain, Norway, and West Germany.

SEALED P⚡WER

SEALED POWER CORPORATION

100 Terrace Plaza
Muskegon, Michigan 49443
U.S.A.
(616) 724–5011

Public Company
Incorporated: 1912 as Piston Ring Company
Employees: 6,000
Sales: $666 million
Market value: $416 million
Stock Index: New York

This Fortune 500 company celebrated its 75th anniversary in 1986 with a record year, but as the president of Sealed Power, Robert D. Tuttle, has remarked, "It would be less than candid to say that Sealed Power is a household name, although we are very well known and respected within the industries we serve." Sealed Power is the world's largest supplier of automotive engine replacement parts, and has numerous other major businesses. The company is divided into four areas: replacement products, powered products, service products, and industrial products. Even though most U.S. consumers do not recognize the company name, they do a large amount of indirect business with Sealed Power.

While the automobile was gaining popularity in the United States around the turn of the century, an enterprising man named Charles E. Johnson was busy gaining experience in a wide range of occupations, including farming, woodworking, cabinetmaking, and toolmaking. He also designed camshafts and held a number of patents. But most importantly, Johnson had arrived at a new method for manufacturing piston rings. At that time, it was normal procedure to cut or slice off piston rings from a long cylinder of cast iron. Johnson suggested that piston rings should be cast individually, "with proper tension pre-cast." A small section of each ring would then be removed so that when a ring was placed and compressed against a perfectly round cylinder wall, it would make a perfect fit.

Johnson approached his friend, Paul R. Beardsley, a bookkeeper for a Muskegon, Michigan department store, and the two men formed a partnership and took their idea to Detroit. There they learned that most engine manufacturers made their own rings. Undaunted, Johnson and Beardsley combined their life savings of $3000 and borrowed additional capital to establish the Piston Ring Company. Working nights in their factory, while maintaining regular day employment in order to support their families, the two men made 200 sample piston rings. Beardsley strung some of the samples on his arm and walked across the street to show them to the purchasing agent at the Continental Motors Corporation. The agent had never heard of the Piston Ring Company, but Continental Motors tried the rings, like the quality and the price, and placed an order.

The growth of the Piston Ring Company was dramatic. Almost immediately the company needed larger quarters, and in its first year of operation—1912—it produced 348,000 rings. In 1913 a foundry was added to the main factory so that castings did not have to be purchased from an outside source. The company sold one million rings the following year, and by 1916 the foundry was doubled in size and a four-story machine shop was constructed. The company retooled its factory during World War I to manufacture piston rings for military trucks, airplanes, tanks, and naval vessels. Later, in 1921, the Piston Ring Company decided to enter the replacement parts market, one of the few expanding areas during the 1920–21 recession.

In 1925 the company created an Export Department and within a year 38 foreign countries were purchasing its products. The name Sealed Power Corporation was adopted in 1932 and an aggressive advertising campaign was launched. Salesmen began to call on auto parts suppliers, the company built a facility in Canada and a number of acquisitions were made. Sealed Power was now able to add pistons and heavy-duty cylinder sleeves to its products.

Facilities were expanded during World War II and new ones were created to handle the increase in military demand. Paul Beardsley died shortly after the war in 1947, and after Charles Johnson died in 1952, Johnson's son, Paul, assumed leadership of the company. Other significant events of the 1950's included the company's first public offering of common stock shares and the acquisition of the American Hammered Automotive Replacement Division of Koppers, one of the most respected names in the replacement parts business. But despite Sealed Power's expansion and diversification, engine rings continued to be the company's main product. The introduction of the SS-50, the first stainless steel oil ring in the industry, proved to be most successful and it has remained at the core of Sealed Power's replacement parts business.

The 1960's and 1970's were marked by diversification and internationalization. Sealed Power acquired facilities in the United States and Mexico which enabled the company to further expand its product lines with items such as automatic transmission filters, powered metal parts and components, hydraulic valve tappets, and zinc and aluminum die castings. Net sales rose from $82.2 million in 1971 to $141.9 million in 1975. During the same five year period, Sealed Power's net income rose from $4.9 million to $7 million.

Despite the early 1980's slump in the auto market, Sealed Power did not suffer badly. Once again, consumers tended to have their cars repaired rather than purchase new ones. While original equipment sales were down, the sales of replacement parts, especially for the popular compacts, kept the company profitable. Sealed Power's large distribution network of over 30 facilities throughout the United States and its team of more than 100 trained field salespeople also helped to give the company an advantage over its smaller rivals.

Anxious to ensure steady growth in the foreseeable future, and well aware of the uncertainties of its markets, the company management decided to expand beyond original equipment and replacement parts. In the past, the company logo identified Sealed Power as a piston ring company; a new logo was adopted to reflect not only Sealed Power's increased line of engine parts but also its new products. In 1982 the company acquired the Kent-Moore Corporation, a leader in special service tools. This was followed in 1985 by the acquisition of another large tool firm, Owatonna Tool Company, active in the automotive electronics field and a manufacturer of high pressure hydraulics and window and door hardware.

Today Sealed Power is organized into four major divisions. Replacement parts, the first division, still remains the largest segment, generating 38% of sales. These parts include engine components, transmission oil filters, chassis parts, and service tools. Powered products, the second division, accounts for 30% of sales, and includes Sealed Power's piston rings, transmission rings, valve tappets, cylinder sleeves, transmission filters, and a variety of die cast or powered metal parts. In the third division, service products, Sealed Power is a world leader in designing,

engineering, manufacturing, and marketing special service tools and electronic diagnostic instruments. These products are primarily for the auto and heavy duty industrial markets, but also for agricultural, construction, and the refrigeration/air conditioning industries. Presently, the service division produces 18% of the company's income. The fourth segment, the industrial division, which contributes 14% of income, manufactures a wide range of products, including hardware, hydraulic pumps and rams, special purpose equipment for dispensing fluids, and threaded fasteners.

Sealed Power is growing steadily. Sales increased 7 percent between 1985 and 1986, up to $665 million from $625 million. Net income has risen from $9.9 million in 1976 to $29.9 million in 1986. However, it appears that the company has no intention of resting on its laurels. Current president Robert Tuttle recently said: "Our major effort . . . is to provide quality by preventing mistakes. We are directing our efforts toward better training, toward re-engineering the product where feasible, and toward redesigning the workplace."

Principal Subsidiaries: Sealed Power Corp. of Canada, Ltd. (40%); Sealed Power de Mexico, S.A. (40%); Cia Americana-Mexicana, S.A. (40%); Kent Moore Corp.; Owatonna Tool Co.; Truth, Inc.; Tri-Mark Corp.; Twin Tool, Inc.

SHELLER-GLOBE CORPORATION

1505 Jefferson Avenue
P.O. Box 962
Toledo, Ohio 43697
U.S.A.
(419) 259-6000

Wholly-owned subsidiary of NEAC, Inc.
Incorporated: February 23, 1929 as City Auto Stamping
Company
Employees: 12,000
Sales: $917 million

Sheller-Globe's recently developed policy of looking outside the U.S.A. for joint ventures which will help it to utilize advanced foreign technologies is characteristic of the company. Throughout its history, and through its various mergers and acquisitions, Sheller-Globe has demonstrated an ability to survive and prosper by careful planning for the future.

Sheller-Globe was not established until 1966, but its history can be traced to the 1882 establishment of the Cincinnati-based Globe Files Company. The Corporation now supplies North American and European automotive manufacturers with parts, components and assemblies for cars, trucks and other vehicles. It also furnishes component parts and materials to other industries, including office products and accessories, microprocessor based instruments and related equipment, nuclear radiation monitoring systems and special purpose electronic components. Employing more than 12,000 people, the company has manufacturing, research and development, and warehouse facilities in 75 locations, as well as affiliates in eight countries outside the United States.

The original purpose of the Globe Files Company was to manufacture file cabinets and other office equipment. Two years after the company was formed its first catalogue was released. As business expanded into diverse areas the company's name was changed to the Globe Company.

In 1890 a New York office was opened and the company acquired a factory to manufacture office furniture and other products. By the turn of the century, the Cincinnati operation had outgrown its original facility. A new block-long building in down-town Cincinnati was constructed. At the same time the Michigan-based Wernicke Company was acquired. Wernicke, also a office supply company,

was well-known for its "elastic" bookcase model, the predecessor of today's sectional office equipment.

The merger was an immediate success. Together, Globe-Wernicke developed the first vertical filing cabinet. This model can now be seen on display at the Smithsonian Institution in Washington, D.C. By the turn of the century, four different models of these cabinets were available.

In the early decades of the 20th century Globe-Wernicke expanded greatly. During the depression years, under the leadership of J.S. Sprott, the company persevered through ingenuity and resourcefulness. By 1939, the year Sprott died, Globe-Wernicke was already immersed in wartime production. Over 90% of its production capacity was directed toward the war effort, while peacetime items also experienced an increased demand.

In the 1950's Globe-Wernicke was acquired by the Toledo-based City Auto Stamping Company. This die maker of automotive body parts and other large stampings was founded in 1916 by Amos Lint. As an automotive engineer, Lint worked for a variety of automobile companies before he determined the need for another firm that would be completely devoted to the manufacturing of parts which automobile manufacturers could not make themselves in a cost-effective way. Products included grilles, light fixtures, console and arm rests.

In 1957 a decision was made to rename the company Globe-Wernicke Industries, Inc., with the metal office furniture and office supplies operations of the Globe-Wernicke company assuming a subsidiary position but remaining prominent. The dye making and stamping operations became the Stamping and Metal Fabrication Division which remained active until the division was sold in 1985. Further acquisitions included the Aluminum Seating Corporation of Akron, Ohio.

When a "safety explosion" began in the design of passenger cars and trucks in the mid-1960's, Globe-Wernicke took a close look at the Detroit-based Sheller Manufacturing Corporation. Sheller, which had begun in 1916 as a wood rim steering wheel manufacturer in Portland, Indiana, had produced the first recessed safety steering wheel and padded dash safety package offered by Ford in 1958. A merger of the two companies which took place on December 30, 1966 resulted in the Sheller-Globe Corporation, a combination with extensive complementary capabilities in metal stamping, die casting, plating, injection molded plastics, molded and extruded rubber items, and cork/rubber products.

Sheller-Globe's survival, which depended upon its ability constantly to adapt to a changing environment, demanded innovation. In the case of the original merger, it was new federal safety regulations that brought about the union of two companies which independently could never have capitalized on changes in the market. The history of this newly created corporation is, in turn, the story of company mergers and takeovers.

The company was to grow substantially in 1974 through the merger of the Cleveland-based VLN corporation with Sheller-Globe. The merger substantially expanded Sheller-Globe's product presence in its existing markets. VLN's Leece-Neville divisions were long established suppliers of heavy-duty alternators and related equipment to the automotive industry, and fractional horse power motors for automotive and industrial customers. Its Paramount Fabricating division in Detroit also expanded Sheller-Globe's automotive product lines with stampings and assemblies, while the Accurate Parts line of starter motor components significantly strengthened Sheller-Globe's position in the automotive aftermarket. Another part of VLN, Victoreen Instrument Company of Cleveland, had been a leader in developing and producing electronic components and equipment.

In 1981 Sheller-Globe acquired Radiation-Medical Products Corporation, a manufacturer of radiation medical instruments and x-ray measuring instrumentation. The acquisition of this particular company had little to do with the automobile industry, and the decision to become involved in an unrelated area reflected a new disposition to capitalize on any market that looked extremely productive. Radiation Medical's operations were therefore merged into Victoreen.

In 1982 Sheller-Globe acquired the automotive business of Detroit-based Olsonite Corporation, a manufacturer of steering wheels and injection-molded plastic parts and components for supply to the domestic vehicle manufacturers. In 1984 Sheller-Globe acquired Northern Fibre Products Company, a manufacturer of insulation and sound deadening materials and components for cars and trucks. Northern Fibre's advanced technology would provide Sheller-Globe with an additional resource in the development of new materials and products for vehicle interiors.

The company's plastics manufacturing capabilities were also expanded in 1984 with the addition of the Engineered Polymers Company, a wholly-owned subsidiary that was acquired from Amoco Chemical. The subsidiary is a custom molder of structural foam cabinets for computers, word processors, work station components, communications devices, networking systems and other business machines, a proprietary line of reusable pallets for the food and pharmaceutical industries, and injection molded parts for appliances and consumer products. The acquisition would permit the use of Sheller-Globe technology in electro-magnetic and radio frequency shielding of electronic components in a promising market.

As a consequence of many of Sheller-Globe's acquisitions, the automotive related divisions of the company supply an extremely wide range of original equipment parts, components and assemblies to the vehicle manufacturers. Products include thermoplastic, urethane and leather wrapped steering wheels for cars and trucks; instrument panel pads, padded consoles, arm rests and other padded components; tail lamp assemblies and a larger number of other products for vehicles.

In developing a strategy for growth during the next decade, Sheller-Globe has placed its emphasis on what it calls the "team concept." In dealing with its automotive customers, the company provides a full complement of engineers and technical personnel who work closely with the automakers several years in advance of a manufacturing program.

Chester Devenow, the current chairman of Sheller-Globe, is now in his 70's, but he plans to lead the company into its next decade of expansion. The man is viewed within the industry as an executive with a talent for organizational change, as he has brought about a number of significant modifications in the structure and management of Sheller-Globe. In 1986 Devenow attempted to maximize technical and manufacturing efficiency by consolidating the operations of various units which had been duplicating functions. In addition, Devenow began to sell those businesses which were even slightly unproductive.

However, perhaps most important to the company's future was Devenow's decision to enter into joint ventures with foreign manufacturers that possess technologies which do not exist in the United States. The basic strategy for future development at Sheller-Globe is to diversify within the automobile industry by merging with companies whose superior technology has no base in America. In 1985, for example, Sheller-Globe acquired a 60% interest in Etablissement Mesnel, a leading French manufacturer of auto body parts and window sealing systems whose processes had been adopted by the Ford and Mercury model cars. Even more significant to the future of the company was a joint venture with Ryobi Limited of Japan. The new entity, Sheller-Ryobi Corporation, will utilize Japanese technology in the United States to manufacture precision aluminum die castings for supply to the North American auto industry. According to industry analysts, Sheller-Globe's involvement with the Japanese manufacturer will place it in an excellent position to continue its tradition of technological innovation and adaptation in a changing automobile market.

In June 1986 an investment group headed by Shearson Lehman Brothers purchased all the outstanding common and preferred shares of Sheller-Globe for $482 million. A holding company called NEAC was created by Shearson Lehman Brothers, Knoll International Holdings (the holding company for General Felt Industries), and members of Sheller-Globe management. Through NEAC, Knoll International emerged with the largest share of control. Chester Devenow retained his position as chairman and chief executive, and Alfred Grava was named president the following March.

The transfer of Sheller-Globe to private ownership invited a great deal of interest from federal authorities who suspected that arbitrageurs, particularly Ivan Boesky, had engaged in illegal speculation. Boesky allegedly profiteered through a 9.2% interest in the company when Sheller-Globe stock appreciated from $28.50 per share to $43. Nevertheless, Boesky was convicted on other charges, and the allegations of illegal activity involving Sheller-Globe were never raised in court.

Since Devenow still runs Sheller-Globe, his plans for the company's future are expected to continue.

TOYOTA

TOYOTA MOTOR CORPORATION

1 Toyota-cho
Toyota City, Aichi, 471
Japan
0565-28-2121

Public Company
Incorporated: July 1, 1982
Employees: 62,000
Sales: ¥6324 billion (US$39.7 billion)
Market Value: ¥4599 billion (US$28.8 billion)
Stock Index: Tokyo NASDAQ

In 1933 a Japanese man named Kiichiro Toyoda traveled to America where he visited a number of automobile production plants. Upon his return to Japan, the young man established an automobile division within his father's loom manufactory and in May 1935 produced his first prototype vehicle. General Motors and Ford were already operating assembly plants in Japan but U.S. pre-eminence in the worldwide automotive industry did not deter Toyoda.

Since Japan has very few natural resources of its own, the company had every incentive to develop engines and vehicles that were highly fuel efficient. In 1939, the company established a research center to begin work on battery powered vehicles. This was followed in 1940 by the establishment of the Toyoda Science Research Center (the nucleus of today's Toyota Central Research and Development Laboratories, Inc.) and the Toyoda Works (presently Aichi Steel Works, Ltd.). The next year Toyoda Machine Works, Ltd. was founded for the production of both machine tools and auto parts.

As Japan became embroiled in World War II, the procurement of basic materials for automobile manufacturing became more and more difficult. At one point Toyoda was manufacturing trucks without radiator grills, brakes only on the rear wheels, wooden seats, and a single headlight. Pushing toward the limits of resource conservation as the course of the war began to cripple Japan's economy, the company started piecing together usable parts from wrecked or worn-out trucks in order to build "recycled" vehicles.

When the war ended in August of 1945 most of Japan's industrial facilities had been wrecked, and Toyoda's (or Toyota as it was known after the war) production plants had suffered extensively. It had 3,000 employees, but no working facilities; and the economic situaton in Japan was chaotic. But the Japanese tradition of dedication and per-

severance proved to be Toyota's most powerful tool in the difficult task of reconstruction.

Just as the Japanese motor industry as a whole was beginning to recover, there was mounting concern that American and European auto manufacturers would overwhelm the Japanese market with their economic and technical superiority. Japan's automakers knew that they could no longer count on government protection in the form of high import duties or other barriers as they had before the war.

Since American manufacturers were concentrating their efforts on medium size and larger cars, Toyota's executives thought that by focusing on small cars the company could avoid a head-on market confrontation. Kiichiro Toyoda likened the postwar situation in Japan to that in England. "The British motorcar industry," he said, "also faces many difficulties, but its fate will be largely determined by how strongly American automakers feel they should concentrate on small cars." It was January 1947 when Toyota engineers completed their first prototype for a small car: its chassis was of the backbone type—never used before in Japan; its front suspension relied primarily on coil springs; and its maximum speed was 54 mph. After two years of difficulties the company seemed headed for success.

However, this was not to be accomplished as easily as expected. Two years later, in 1949, Toyota suffered its first and only serious conflict between labor and management. Nearly four years had passed since the end of the war, but Japan's economy was still in poor condition: goods and materials of all kinds were in short supply; inflation was rampant; and, worst of all, people in the cities were forced to trade their clothing and home furnishings for rice or potatoes in order to keep themselves alive. That year the Japanese government took measures to control runaway inflation in ways that severely reduced consumer purchasing power and worsened the already severely depressed domestic automotive market. Japanese auto manufacturers found themselves unable to raise the funds needed to support their recovery efforts, for the new governmental policy had discontinued all financing from city banks and the Reconstruction Finance Corporation.

Under these conditions the company's financial situation deteriorated rapidly. In some months, for example, the company produced vehicles worth a total of ¥350 million while income from sales reached only ¥250 million. In the absence of credit sources to bridge the imbalance, Toyota was soon facing a severe liquidity crisis. It should be noted here that, largely because of wartime regulations and controls, Toyota had come to place strong emphasis on the production end of the business, so that in the early postwar years not enough attention had been paid to the proper balance between production and sales. The Japanese economy at that time was suffering from a severe depression, and because the Toyota dealers were unable to sell cars in sufficient quantities, these dealers had no choice but to pay Toyota in long term promissory notes as inventories kept accumulating.

Finally, Toyota was unable to meet its regular payroll. Delayed payments were followed by actual salary reductions and then by plans for large-scale layoffs—until April of 1949 when the Toyota Labor Union went on strike. Negotiations between labor and management dragged on with the union leaders bitterly opposed to any layoffs. As a result, Toyota was compelled to reduce both production and overhead. Workers staged demonstrations to press their demands, and all the while Toyota kept falling further into debt, until the company finally found itself on the verge of bankruptcy.

Production dropped to 992 vehicles in March of 1949, to 619 in April, and to 304 in May. Crucial restructuring efforts included a proposal to incorporate Toyota's sales division as a separate company, leading eventually to the formation of Toyota Motor Sales Company Ltd., in April 1950. Toyota Motor Sales Company handled all domestic and worldwide marketing of Toyota's automotive products until July of 1982 when it merged with Toyota Motor Company.

In the meantime, discussions between labor and management finally focused on whether to admit failure, declare bankruptcy and dissolve the company, or to agree on the dismissal of some employees and on a rebuilding program. In the end management and labor agreed to reduce the total work force from 8,000 to 6,000 employees, primarily by asking for voluntary resignations. At the management level, President Kiichiro Toyoda and all of his executive staff resigned. Kiichiro, Toyota's founder and a pioneer of the Japanese automotive industry, died less than two years later.

Not long after the strike was settled in 1950, two of the company's new executives, Eiji Toyoda (now chairman of Toyota Motor Corporation) and Shoichi Saito (later chairman of Toyota Motor Company) visited the United States. Seeking new ideas for Toyota's anticipated growth, they toured Ford Motor Company's factories and observed the latest automobile production technology. One especially useful idea they brought home from their visit to Ford resulted in Toyota's suggestion system in which every employee is encouraged to make suggestions for improvements of any kind. However, on their return to Japan the two men inaugurated an even more vital policy that remains in force at Toyota today, namely, the continuing commitment to invest in only the most modern production facilities as the key to advances in productivity and quality. Toyota moved quickly and aggressively in the 1950's, making capital investments in new equipment for all the company's production facilities. Not surprisingly, the company began to benefit from the increased efficiency almost immediately.

Along with improvements in its production facilities, Toyota also worked to develop a more comprehensive line of vehicles in order to contribute toward the growing motorization of Japanese society. During 1951, for example, Toyota introduced the first 4WD Land Cruiser. Moreover, as the domestic demand for taxis rapidly increased, production of passenger cars also rose quickly, from 50 units per month to 250 units per month by 1953.

In production control, Toyota introduced the "Kanban System" (Synchronized Delivery System) during 1954. The idea was derived from the supermarket system where "consumers" (those in the later production stages) took "products" (parts) from the stock shelves, and the "storekeepers" (those in the earlier production stages) replenished the stock to the degree that it was depleted. This "Kanban System" became the basis for Toyota's entire present-day production system.

By the early 1950's, just as Toyota had anticipated, the Japanese market was crowded with vehicles from the United States and Europe. It soon became apparent that to be competitive at home and abroad, Toyota would not only have to make additional investments in manufacturing facilities and equipment, but also undertake a major new research and development effort as well. This was the reasoning behind Toyota's decision in 1958 to build a full-scale research center for the development of new automobiles (which was also to become Japan's first factory devoted entirely to passenger car production). Toyota also began to offer a more complete line of products. Beginning with the Crown model, introduced in 1955, Toyota quickly expanded its passenger-car line to include the 1000cc Corona, then added the Toyo-Ace (Japan's first cab-over-truck) and a large size diesel truck.

Throughout these years Toyota was also working hard on another important, if less conventional, approach to adapting itself to the rapid motorization of Japan, brought about by a remarkable increase in national income. When, for example, Toyota Motor Sales was capitalized at ¥1 billion, 40% of that amount (¥400 million) was immediately invested to establish an automobile driving school in an effort to help citizens acquire driver's licenses. Through this and similar efforts, Toyota made a major contribution to Japan's growing motorization in the years following 1965, a trend that was to lead to a mass domestic market for the automobile.

In 1955, ten years after its defeat in World War II, Japan became a member of GATT (the General Agreement on Tariffs and Trade); but the Japanese auto industry, remained one of Japan's least competitive industries in the field of international trade. Toyota, foreseeing the coming age of large-scale international trade and capital liberalization in Japan, decided to focus on lowering its production costs and developing even more sophisticated cars, while at the same time attempting to achieve the highest level possible of quality production. This was a joint effort cxonducted with Toyota's many independent parts suppliers and one which proved so successful that ten years later, in 1965, Toyota was awarded the coveted Deming Prize for its quality control achievements. That was also the year that the Japanese government liberalized imports of foreign passenger cars. Now Toyota was ready to compete with its overseas competitors—both in price and quality.

In subsequent years Japan's GNP expanded rapidly, contributing to the impressive growth in auto sales to the Japanese public. The Toyota Corolla, which went on sale in 1966, quickly became Japan's most popular family car and led the market for autos of its compact size. Toyota continued to make major investments in new plants and equipment in order to prepare for what it believed would be a higher market demand. In 1971 the government removed controls on capital investment. In the wake of this move, several Japanese automakers formed joint ventures or affiliations with different companies of the United States' largest automakers.

Two years later, the 1973 Middle East War erupted and the world's economy was shaken by the first international oil crisis. Japan, wholly dependent upon imports for its oil supply, was especially affected. The rate of inflation increased and demand for automobiles fell drastically. Yet, in the face of the overall pessimism that gripped the industry and the nation, Toyota's chairman Eiji Toyoda proposed a highly aggressive corporate strategy. His conviction was that the automobile, far from being a "luxury," had become and would remain a necessity for people at all levels of society. As a result, Toyota decided to move forward by expanding the company's operations.

The 1973 oil crisis and its aftermath were valuable lessons for Toyota; the crisis demonstrated the necessity for a flexible production system which could easily be adaptable to changes in consumer preferences. For example, Toyota did away with facilities designed exclusively for the production of specific models, and shifted instead to general-purpose facilities which could be operated according to changes in market demand for the company's various models.

In December of 1970 the United States Congress passed the Muskie Act which set limits on automobile engine emissions. In the U.S. the enforcement of this law was eventually postponed, but in Japan even stricter laws were promulgated during the same time with no postponement of enforcement deadlines. When the Muskie Act was first proposed, automakers all over the world were opposed to it. They argued that it would actually prohibit the use of all internal combustion engines currently used, and they requested that the enforcement of the law be postponed until new technology, able to meet the law's requirements, could be developed.

Notwithstanding these developments, Toyota moved forward on its own to develop a new generation of cleaner and more fuel efficient engines. After studying all the feasible alternatives, including catalytic systems, rarefied combustion, rotary engines, gas turbine and batter-powered cars, Toyota settled on the catalytic converter as the most flexible and most promising, and succeeded in producing automobiles which conform to what are the world's toughest emissions control standards. (Meanwhile, imported cars were given a three year grace period to conform to Japan's strict emissions control standards.)

In 1980 Japan's aggregate automobile production was actually better than that of the U.S. In the same year,

Toyota ranked second only to General Motors in total number of cars produced. Although Toyota made continuous efforts over the years to improve the international cooperation between automakers in such ways as procuring parts and materials from overseas manufacturers, Japan's successes in the world auto market have nonetheless resulted in the Japanese automobile industry becoming a target of criticism.

The current president of Toyota, Yukiyasu Togo, possesses a solid understanding of the nature of American culture. Togo is said to believe that Toyota's future success depends in part on the way that it handles public relations with the United States, a nation that he preceives to be extremely bitter about losing trade battles with Japanese industry. By means of intense advertising and controlled public relations under Togo's direction, Toyota has tried to elevate the principle of free competition in the minds of the American people. At the same time, Togo is carefully committing his company to greater international cooperation in both technological and managerial areas. In the fall of 1985, for example, Toyota announced that it would build an $800,000 production facility near Lexington, Kentucky. The plant, which is expected to begin assembling 200,000 cars per year by 1988, will create approximately 3,000 jobs. Moreover, the General Motors and Toyota joint venture, called New United Motor Manufacturing, Inc., will also begin building up to 50,000 vehicles a year to be sold by Toyota dealers. This strategy, it is hoped, will help to ease the tensions between the U.S. and Japan over their inequitable trade relations.

Principal Subsidiaries: Kanto Auto Works, Ltd. (49.06%); Towa Real Estate Co., Inc. (49%); Toyota Machine Works, Ltd.; Toyota Central Research & Development Laboratories, Inc. (54%); Calty Design Research, Inc. (60%); New United Motor Manufacturing Inc. (50%); Toyota Motor Sales, USA, Inc.; Toyota Motor Manufacturing USA, Inc.; Toyota Technical Center, USA, Inc. (80%).

Further Reading: *My Life with Toyota* by Shotaro Kamiya with Thomas Elliott, Toyota City, Toyota Motor Sales Co., 1978.

VOLKSWAGEN A.G.

Postfach 3180
Wolfsburg
Federal Republic of Germany
(0 53 61) 90

Public Company
Incorporated: 1938
Employees: 259,047
Sales: DM 47.2 billion (US$24.3 billion)
Market Value: DM 12.5 billion (US$6.446 billion)
Stock Index: Berlin Düsseldorf Frankfurt Hamburg
Munich Stuttgart Zurich Basle Geneva Vienna
Brussels Antwerp Luxembourg Amsterdam

Volkswagen AG, a company born in the shadow of Nazism, has risen to become one of the world's premier automobile companies. Volkswagen has long been the industry leader in West Germany where it holds 28 percent of the automotive market, but the company's interests are truly international: it maintains plants in the United States, Brazil, Mexico, South Africa, Nigeria, Yugoslavia, Argentina, and Belgium. In addition to its automotive subsidiaries, Volkswagen owns computer and office equipment concerns. Yet, however large and diverse the company becomes, it will perhaps always be most strongly associated with the idea from which it derives its name, "the people's car."

Volkswagen was founded in 1937 as the "Company for the Development of the German Volkswagen." It embodied the dreams of two men: Ferdinand Porsche and Adolf Hitler. Porsche, an engineer, had designed powerful luxury automobiles for Austro-Daimler, but had been dreaming of a small low-priced car for the ordinary consumer since the early 1920's. Porsche had tried in vain to find financiers for his venture. Always interested in technical innovation, Porsche had designed a rear-engined, air-cooled vehicle with independent suspension. The radical design had to be perfected, however, and Porsche's first sponsor had little patience for torsion bars that exploded under pressure and engines that malfunctioned after a few miles.

Porsche's meeting with Hitler in 1934 changed everything. By 1938 his roundish, odd-looking car had become the center of a plan to build an ideal worker's city, and a factory was started at Wolfsburg. During the war, however, the Volkswagen plant produced vehicles for the German military, largely with the slave labor of prisoners.

By the end of the war the factory had been virtually destroyed by bombing. Hitler's "people's car" never materialized.

The Volkswagen factory was operated by the British occupation forces from 1945 to 1949. The company became the focus of the effort to rebuild the German auto industry, and within a decade Volkswagen was producing half of Germany's automobiles. Ironically, it was the British administrators of Volkswagen who started the production of passenger rather than military vehicles, and thus made the dream of the people's car a reality.

The company came under the control of the German federal government and the state of Lower Saxony in 1949. The man the British selected to head the company, Heinz Nordhoff, was largely responsible for Volkswagen's impressive recovery, and the conversion of a reminder of Nazi aspirations into the most popular car ever built. His success is the more surprising, given that he was no fan of Volkswagen prior to his arrival there. Nordhoff, an engineer, had been employed by the Adam Opel Company, owned by General Motors, before and during the war. Opel management resented Hitler's Volkswagen because they were hoping to develop a similar automobile of their own.

Unlike Porsche, it was not Nordhoff's skill as an engineer (though he was responsible for innovations), but his managerial ability, that made such a contribution to the success of Volkswagen. (Porsche could not take part in the realization of his dream; his health was ruined by nearly two years spent in a French prison on charges of war crimes for which he was later acquitted. Porsche died in 1951.) Nordhoff was able to assemble around him a talented team of executives, and inspired his sometimes despairing and hungry workers. He actually slept in the factory for six months, and instituted the quite novel practice of addressing the workforce on a regular basis. Nordhoff, however, also gained a reputation for being autocratic and even arrogant, perhaps due to his unrelenting managerial approach.

Success came slowly, particularly in the United States. Nordhoff sorely needed U.S. dollars, but his first trip to the United States in 1949 was a failure, and only 330 Volkswagens were sold there in 1950. The car's Nazi associations continued to haunt it, and though American interest in foreign cars grew during the mid-1950's, it was really not until 1959, when the firm of Doyle Dane Bernbach took over the advertising for the car, that it began to appeal to large numbers of Americans. It was Doyle Dane that coined the name "Beetle" for the Volkswagen. In a series of award-winning advertisements, the ad agency took what had been the car's drawbacks and turned them into selling points with such slogans as "Think Small" and "Ugly is Only Skin-deep." Even the car's apparently invariable design from year to year was exploited, with an advertisement that had no photography at all and claimed there was nothing new to display about the more recent models. Changes were made internally, however, and the Volkswagen became renowned for its durability. The Beetle eventually had a record production run of over 40 years, during which over 20 million cars were produced. During the 1960's, the Volkswagen became what might be called a "cult classic" in the U.S.

In 1960 Volkswagen was, in essence, denationalized, with the sale of 60% of its stock to the public. The remaining 40% of the stock was divided evenly between the federal government and the government of Lower Saxony. A foundation was also established to promote research in science and technology, and received all dividends paid to the two governments. These measures settled the disagreement between the federal government and Lower Saxony over the ownership of the company. Nordhoff was glad to have an end to the question, but did not benefit directly since he and other Volkswagen executives in high income brackets were not eligible to purchase stock by the terms of the sale.

Annual production of the Beetle peaked in 1968 at 400,000 units, but by the early 1970's the Beetle was finally regarded as outdated. In 1974 Volkswagen was brought to the brink of bankruptcy. Diminishing sales, rising labor costs, increasing competition from the Japanese automakers, and the end of fixed exchange rates had all contributed to the dramatic decline. New models were introduced, but they suffered from a poor reputation.

A development program was instituted to create a successor to the Rabbit, the company's major automobile after the Beetle. Meanwhile in 1981 Volkswagen's U.S. workforce was cut from 10,000 to 6,000, and a plant in Michigan was sold to Chrysler. In 1983 the company lost $144 million in the United States alone.

When the new Golf was finally unveiled, it looked very much like the Rabbit, but it had a larger engine, more interior space, and better overall performance. The changes paid off; sales rose 25% in 1985, profits doubled and Volkswagen became the leading European auto manufacturer. The Golf GTI was named "Car of the Year" by *Motor Trend* in 1985. In the luxury car market sales of the Audi were up 50%, a second straight record year (Volkswagen had acquired the Audi automobile manufacturer in 1965). Even more remarkable was that sales of the Jetta, a model costing about $1,000 more than the Golf, jumped 120%.

From the company's point of view, it is significant that the gap between Volkswagen and the competition has been narrowed. It used to be that the German cars cost 20% more than their Japanese rivals, but the base price of the Golf is now lower than those of competing vehicles from Honda and Toyota. These gains may be due to Volkswagen's policy of automating its factories. The company spent $194 million on its Halle 54 at the Wolfsburg factory (the largest single automobile factory in the world) where 25% of final assembly is performed by robots. The automation provides a time savings of 20%.

Not everything has been promising for Volkswagen, however. The company recalled 77,000 Golf and GTI models because the innovative high-density polycarbonate fuel tank which fits under the rear seat and over the axle failed to meet crash test requirements. The cost of the recall could run as high as $18 million. Additionally, 18,000 Vanagons and Campers have been recalled for a potential problem with the latches on their sliding doors. Finally, the New York attorney general and two consumer groups have asked the Transportation Department to recall 200,000 Audi 5000's, claiming that the cars can suddenly accelerate when shifted out of the park position; Volkswagen has said that the accidents reported are the result of driver error, but it has replaced some damaged cars or paid repair costs.

Volkswagen sales fell in the first quarter of 1986, partially, at least, because of a drop in the value of the U.S. dollar. And while the Westmoreland, Pennsylvania plant is operating at half capacity, there is an order backlog for Golfs in Europe. A plan has been considered to produce 21,000 to 30,000 Jettas at the Westmoreland plant which would allow the European operation to increase its capacity, but it would take a year to retool the factory. Without such an adjustment the Westmoreland factory, where 18,000 workers are already on layoff, could face further cuts. There has been talk of building Surbarus at Westmoreland with Fuji Heavy Industries, but discussions are presently suspended. Plans have also been made to close a West Virginia parts plant and substitute parts from Mexico and Brazil. (UAW autoworkers in the U.S. make $20 per hour, whereas their Brazilian counterparts collect an hourly wage of $2.)

In 1986 the company sold Royal Business Machines, one of its office equipment subsidiaries, and it has purchased a majority interest in Spain's Sociedad Española de Automobiles del Turismo S.A. (SEAT), which had been a money-losing venture. The Spanish government agreed to absorb the company's $1 billion debt and to provide a cash infusion of $114 million. With SEAT, Volkswagen could acquire 25% of the Spanish car market.

Agreements have been made with East Germany and China for the production of 300,000 and 100,000 automobile engines, respectively, with options for Volkswagen to buy back some of the engines, which would help alleviate its capacity problems. The company has also negotiated with the Soviet Union for the building of an engine plant, and it has entered into a licensing agreement with Nissan for the production of kits to build Nissan Santanas. A possible production merger has been discussed by Ford Argentina and Volkswagen of Brazil, in order to increase capacity by 30% and meet consumer demand. And, with Renault, Volkswagen is planning development of a four-wheel-drive/automatic transmission system. Almost every Volkswagen model brought out between now and the end of the decade is slated to be available with a four-wheel-drive option. The company also has ambitious plans to compete with the Yugoslavian Yugo and South Korea's Hyundai Excel by introducing a Brazilian-built, low-priced car, currently referred to simply as Project 99. Volkswagen hopes sales of this will reach 100,000 cars per year. Meanwhile, the company will continue its current Golf design, but its Scirroco sports model, introduced several years ago, will shortly be replaced with a car along the lines of the Porsche 944.

Volkswagen chairman Carl C. Hahn, who worked under Heinz Nordhoff, is stressing German engineering and advanced technology as the key to the company's competitiveness. He has set his sights on rebuilding the public's confidence in Volkswagen in the United States, and hopes to boost the company's return on sales from 1% to 3% to match the U.S. automakers. Hahn also aims to cut costs and raise profit margins by making use of newly acquired

SEAT and other Volkswagen operations in developing countries. Capital spending will be boosted 25% in the next five years, with $13 billion aimed at operations outside Germany. It is uncertain what labor's reaction will be to the increasing use of foreign resources; the German auto industry was plagued by strikes in 1984.

Hahn has gained valuable experience in the American market; he headed the Volkswagen operation in the U.S. during the Beetle's heyday. Later Hahn became chief of continental Gummi Werke, where he turned a money-losing business into an industry leader. Like his predecessor, Hahn seems capable of taking forceful steps where necessary to control the direction of the company, and he appears more than willing to circumvent inflexible bureaucratic corporate culture that frequently afflicts large German firms. If he proves to be as forthright and determined as Nordhoff, then Volkswagen should remain a major force in the worldwide automotive industry.

Principal Subsidiaries: AUDI AG (99%); V.A.G. Kredit Bank GmbH; V.A.G. Leasing GmbH; VOTEX GmbH; VW KRAFTWERK GmbH; VW Siedlungsgersellschaft mbH; InterRent Autovermietung GmbH; V.A.G. Marketing Management Institut GmbH. Volkswagen also has subsidiaries in the following countries: Belgium, Brazil, Argentina, Canada, France, Italy, Japan, Mexico, The Netherlands, Netherlands Antilles, South Africa, Sweden, Switzerland and the United States.

Further Reading: *Small Wonder: The Amazing Story of the Volkswagen* by Walter H. Nelson, Boston, Little Brown, 1967; *The Volkswagen Story* by K.B. Hopfinger, Cambridge, Massachusetts, R. Bentley, 1971.

VOLVO

A.B. VOLVO

S–405 08
Göteborg
Sweden
(031) 59 00 00

Public Company
Incorporated: in 1926 as a subsidiary of AB Svenska
Kullagerfabriken
Employees: 67,857
Sales: SKr 80.3 billion (US$11.8 billion)
Market Value: SKr 26.3 billion (US$3.86 billion)
Stock Index: Stockholm London Düsseldorf Frankfurt
 Hamburg Oslo Paris

Volvo is a diversified international group of companies operating primarily in the areas of transportation equipment, energy, and food. The parent company, AB Volvo, is Scandinavia's largest industrial enterprise; it generates more than $11 billion in annual sales and employs more than 70,000 people worldwide. Although Volvo manufactures a wide variety of products, it is best known for its automobiles.

Established as a subsidiary of AB Svenska Kullagerfabriken in 1915, Volvo began to assemble cars and trucks in 1926. It was established as an independent company in 1935 under the leadership of Assar Gabrielsson and Gustaf Larson. Gabrielsson was working in France as the sales manager for a Swedish ballbearing company which was a major supplier to the French automotive industry. In the early 1920's he saw a great deal of potential in the establishment of Swedish auto manufacturing and thus entered into discussions with Larson, who had worked for several years in the British auto industry and had intended to start such a company. Larson's technical ability and Gabrielsson's economic and marketing skills complemented one another quite well.

At an early stage in the development of the company, Gabrielsson decided to concentrate on volume rather than immediate profit. He safeguarded engine deliveries by acquiring a majority interest in AB Pentaverken in 1930 and integrated it completely into Volvo five years later. Gabrielsson, not averse to taking risks, ordered 10,000 revolutionary crankshafts in 1933 for overhead-valve engines. The new shaft was forged in one piece, in direct contrast to the multiple-forging shafts used until that time by automakers around the world. In 1925 Volvo was entered on the Stockholm Stock Exchange. "We've now

become the property of all the Swedish people," declared Gabrielsson.

In 1941, a majority interest was acquired in a Swedish precision engineering company, Svenska Flygmotor AB, and the following year Sweden's leading gearbox manufacturer was also purchased. Gabrielsson's bold ambitions could not be dampened even by World War II. While Europe was in turmoil, he authorized the development of the innovative Volvo PV144 auto and instigated the development of two versions of diesel engines, one featuring pre-ignition chamber fuel injection for a more solvent operation and the other featuring direct fuel injection for greater fuel economy. In 1942, the company produced its first bogie axle, thus increasing the load capacity of its trucks; a year later, Volvo manufactured its first tractor.

Gabrielsson and Larson jointly controlled all aspects of the company's two main operational areas. By 1947, twenty years after its founding, Volvo was one of the largest companies in Sweden. Between 1945 and 1946 sales of Volvo trucks doubled while sales of buses increased sixfold. By 1949 Volvo had produced more than 100,000 vehicles, one-fifth of them for export. During this same period Volvo's 10,000th tractor rolled off the production line.

Volvo began the 1950's with the acquisition of Bolinder-Munktell, a Swedish manufacturer of farm machinery with its own line of diesel engines. This increased Volvo's capacity to produce components for the expanding automotive market, while also making it possible to concentrate Volvo's tractor assembly operation in Bolinder-Munktell's plants. Now known as Volvo BM, the company took over production of tractors in 1951 and soon afterwards one out of every five tractors sold in Sweden was being made by Volvo. Passenger car volume also surpassed that of trucks and buses, partly due to heavy demand for the PV444 model. In 1951 about 25,000 PV444's were produced; five years later the figure was 100,000. The creativity of Volvo designers was underscored in 1954 when the company introduced the first test model of the Volvo Sport. The sports car, a convertible, featured a unique plastic body and puncture-proof tires.

Assar Gabrielsson retired in 1956. He was succeeded, in the midst of the Suez Crisis, by Gunnar Engellau, who had been directing Volvo Flygmotor. The closing of the Suez canal at that time disrupted the flow of oil to many countries. In Sweden alone sales of Volvo cars were reduced by one-third, and Gunnar Engellau was obliged to implement a four day work week and other cost-cutting measures. "Those months were some of the most dramatic I experienced at Volvo," Engellau noted later. "But my gamble on the date when the Suez crisis would be settled was successful. During the spring of 1957 Volvo was able to meet a sudden surge in demand with full-capacity resources."

In the mid-1950's exports set one record after another, increasing an impressive 82% between 1955 and 1956. In 1954 Volvo was the first manufacturer to introduce turbo-charged diesel engines in trucks and buses. The power of Volvo's largest truck, the Titan, was increased 25% while the weight of the engine increased a mere 3%. Truck production rose steadily, reaching 1,400 units in 1956. The following year, the first Volvo Amazon appeared on the road, and the company exported some 5,050 PV444s and Duets. Engellau himself directed international marketing strategy.

1958 was another eventful year for Volvo: the PV544 was introduced; the 100,000th Volvo automobile was exported; and the first Volvo truck was sold in the United States. A new foundry opened in Skovde during 1951 and two years later a large assembly plant was constructed in Göteborg. Up to 15,000 buses and trucks could be produced annually on the two assembly lines, and by 1959 more than 89,000 commercial vehicles had been produced at the Göteborg plant. Almost 50% of production was exported. Volvo announced preliminary plans to build a new automobile plant in Torslanda, a suburb of Göteborg. In January 1959 the company earned accolades for its introduction of the revolutionary Aquamatic drive for boats—the world's first commercially successful solution to the problem of an inboard engine with an outboard drive.

Volvo continued its successes in the 1960's, and there were numerous major developments, including the establishment of Forsakrings AB Volvia, an insurance company; the 50,000th automobile in the PV444 and PV544 series was shipped to the U.S.; the P-1800 sports car model was introduced; a new tractor plant was built in central Sweden; Volvo developed its most powerful truck, the Volvo L495 Titan; the engine factory at Skovde was rebuilt to handle larger capacity production; and a plant was opened in Malaysia.

The Volvo Trucks division also introduced a revolutionary new model, the L4571 Raske-Tiptop, a forward control truck with a tilt cab. In Nova Scotia, Canada, Volvo built its first assembly plant for automobiles outside Sweden. Volvo became the first automotive manufacturer to introduce argon-shielded short arc welding. By the mid-1960's Volvo had nearly 25,000 employees and its products were assembled in eight foreign countries.

Sweden decided against membership of the European Economic Community in the 1960's, but Volvo nevertheless established operations in Ghent, Belgium, where a passenger car plant with a capacity of 14,000 units per year was inaugurated in 1965. The plant was Volvo's largest foreign investment and enabled the company to avoid EEC tariffs on cars imported from outside the Common Market. Volvo's exports increased more than eightfold between 1954 and 1964.

In 1966 Volvo introduced its 144 model which won acclaim as the "Car of the Year." In the same year, the company commenced truck production in Peru, and construction began on a new auto assembly plant in Halifax, Canada. In the United States Volvo sales increased rapidly, and facilities in Ghent were expanded to handle the growing demand.

Volvo turned 1969 into its best year despite some labor problems in Sweden. Sales rose 14% and paved the way for an investment program projected for the 1970's. The planned capital expenditure program included such projects as: assembly plants for passenger cars and trucks in Belgium; civilian projects in Volvo Flygmotor; and investment in sales companies in Germany and France. In-

creased sums were also allocated for product development.

During the 1960's Volvo had concentrated largely on investments to increase production. The growth of the automotive market and the development of production technology had made it profitable to manufacture large quantities of each auto series. Since Volvo's line of automobiles was limited, however, it was obvious that the company could achieve only a relatively small share of the markets. Yet Volvo's share of the Swedish market, and of the Scandinavian market in general, was so large that there was little room for expansion; continued growth could only be achieved by an even more vigorous export program in the 1970's.

But at the same time the company felt that in the long-term it must reduce its dependence on cars. The Volvo Truck Corporation had been plagued by serious problems relating to quality control and profitability, and during the latter half of the 1960's the company had been considering terminating the operation. Instead, management decided to take the opposite course and expand the truck business.

There was no assurance, in the mid-1970's, that Volvo would be able to survive as an independent auto manufacturer. The crucial problem was how to solve the high costs of product development. Volvo's profits, which decreased in 1976 and 1977, were clearly inadequate to finance a comprehensive product updating program. The recent past pointed towards well established firms having to merge or undergo a restructuring program in order to survive. In Volvo's case, the natural course was to explore the potential effects of a merger with Saab-Scania, Sweden's other major car manufacturer. In May 1977 the two Swedish car makers announced that they planned to merge. After some weeks, however, opposition to the merger began to develop and by August of that year the plans had been abandoned. The same month, the company initiated discussions with Norway's prime minister, Oddvar Nordli. Volvo management wanted to link its future industrial development with the oil industry and it was particularly interested in Norway's offshore oil supplies. Ultimately, however, it was not possible to obtain the support of shareholders for the far-reaching proposals.

While Volvo was engaged in these negotiations, a substantially larger transaction, the acquisition of the Beijerinvest Group, was taking shape. Volvo was particularly attracted by Beijerinvest's oil trading firm, the Scandinavian Trading Company (STC). The Beijerinvest Group also operated a profitable food processing business, several engineering concerns, and many smaller companies. The acquisition took place and profits for Volvo in 1978 were twice as large as in 1977.

Meanwhile, Volvo sold Renault a 9.9% interest in its car division, which, in combination with the proceeds of a new share issue, assured the company of funds it needed for continued growth. At this time, the sale of Volvo cars became increasingly profitable and the price of Volvo shares began to rise. The new issue of shares in 1979 was followed by second and third issues in 1981 and 1982. The latter was the largest in the history of Swedish industry.

The present chief executive officer of the company is Pehr G. Gyllenhammar. He has seen Volvo become

Sweden's largest industrial company and expects his company's 1987 sales to exceed $10 billion—12% of Sweden's gross domestic product.

Under Gyllenhammar's leadership the company has diversified in order to reduce its sensitivity to fluctuations in the world economy. During 1986 Volvo acquired shares representing slightly more than 25% of each of two pharmaceutical companies, Pharmacia and Sonesson, and its acquisitions within the food industry continued to increase. At the same time, acquisitions are becoming more difficult for Gyllenhammar. The political context within which his company operates is complex. Sweden's socialist government prohibits acquisitions abroad and many industry analysts believe the government will not look favorably on the company's anticipated growth within Sweden itself.

Principal Subsidiaries: Volvo Car Corp.; Volvo Truck Corp.; Volvo Components Corp.; Centro-Morgardshammar AB; Volvo Bus Corp.; AB Volvo Pentaverken; Volvo Flygmotor AB; Kockums Jernverksaktiebolag AB; Volvobil Svenska Bil AB; STC Scandinavian Trading Company AB; Provender Food AB; Volvo Energy Corp.; Volvo Transport AB; Volvo Data AB; Forsakrings AB Volvia; Fastighets AB Volvo-City; Volvo International Development AB; Volvo Aktiesparfondforvaltning AB; Wilh Sonesson AB (30%); AB Custos (16%); AB Gambrinus (25%); Pharmacia AB (27%); AB Catena (48%). The company also has subsidiaries in the following countries: Argentina, Australia, Belgium, Brazil, Denmark, Finland, France, Hong Kong, Iran, Mexico, The Netherlands, Norway, Peru, Singapore, Switzerland, United Kingdom; United States, and West Germany.

Further Reading: "How Volvo Adapts Work to People" by Pehr G. Gyllenhammar in *Harvard Business Review 55* (Cambridge, Massachusetts), Summer 1977; *Job Redesign and Management Control: Studies in British Leyland and Volvo* by F.H.M. Blackler, Farnborough, Hampshire, Saxon House, 1978; *Volvo: The Cars—from the 20s to the 80s* by Björn-Eric Lindh, London, Osprey, 1984.

BEVERAGES

ALLIED-LYONS PLC

ANHEUSER-BUSCH COMPANY, INC.

ASAHI BREWERIES, LTD.

BASS PLC

BROWN-FORMAN CORPORATION

CARLTON AND UNITED
    BREWERIES LTD.

CERVECERIA POLAR

THE COCA-COLA COMPANY

ADOLPH COORS COMPANY

DISTILLERS COMPANY PLC

E & J GALLO

GENERAL CINEMA CORPORATION

GRAND METROPOLITAN PLC

GUINNESS PLC

G. HEILEMAN BREWING
    COMPANY, INC.

HEINEKEN N.V.

HEUBLEIN, INC.

HIRAM WALKER RESOURCES, LTD.

KIRIN BREWERY COMPANY LTD.

LABATT BREWING COMPANY LTD.

MILLER BREWING COMPANY

MOËT-HENNESSY

MOLSON COMPANIES LTD.

PEPSICO, INC.

PERNOD RICARD S.A.

SAPPORO BREWERIES, LTD.

THE SEAGRAM COMPANY, LTD.

SOUTH AFRICAN BREWERIES LTD.

THE STROH BREWING COMPANY

WHITBREAD AND COMPANY PLC

ALLIED-LYONS PLC

Allied House
156 St. John Street
London EC1P 1AR
England
(01) 253-9911

Public Company
Incorporated: April 13, 1961 as Ind Coope Tetley Ansell Ltd.
Employees: 70,301
Sales: £3.643 billion (US$5.356 billion)
Market Value: £3.01 billion (US$4.425 billion)
Stock Index: London Brussels Amsterdam

Allied-Lyons is the largest beverage company outside the United States and fourth largest in the world. Although its operations are centered around the production of beer and wine, Allied-Lyons also operate retail shops, ice cream parlours, and hotels. The company was formed in 1961 when three breweries, all of them in existence for more than 100 years, merged to form Allied Breweries.

Allied Breweries' earliest predecessor was an outdoor brewhouse built by Edward Ind as an extension of the Star Inn in Romford, Essex, which he had purchased in 1799. Appreciated by both travelers and the local population, the Ind ales grew steadily in popularity. In 1845 the Ind Brewery merged with the Coope Brewery, operated by the brothers George and Octavius Coope. Together the two companies established the Ind Coope Brewery in 1856 at Burton-upon-Trent, the beer capital of England. Over the next one hundred years, Ind Coope ales remained dominant brands throughout southern England.

The second brewery group was founded in 1822 when Joshua Tetley purchased the brewing operations of William Sykes. Located in Leeds, the Tetley brewery went on to produce a variety of beers that gained great popularity in northern England. The third brewery was that of Joseph Ansell, a "maltster" and hops merchant who established the Ansell Brewery in 1881; it soon gained a reputation for its mild ale in Birmingham and throughout the Midlands.

During the 19th century, and into this century as well, beer drinkers in England tended to identify strongly with beers that were locally produced. Ind Coope, Tetley, and Ansell each grew within its own region of influence, competing with each other in only a limited number of areas. Despite strong brand loyalty on the part of the public, that situation has now greatly changed. The grad-ual demise, since World War II, of the "tied house" system (in which pubs agreed to serve only the products of one brewery) brought greater competition to the English brewing industry, intensified in the 1940's and 1950's with the introduction by the breweries of more efficient distribution networks. These factors helped to change the economics of beer production; only larger companies could experience greater growth.

In order to achieve a larger and more profitable scale of operation, Joshua Tetley and Son merged with Walker Cain in 1960 to form a new company called Tetley Walker. The following year the directors of Ind Coope, Tetley Walker, and Ansell agreed to merge their operations, and on 13 April 1961 they formed Ind Coope Tetley Ansell Ltd. Each company could now take advantage of the others' regional establishments; as well, each company was now dedicated to the common goal of increasing total sales for the group. The company's name was changed on 1 March 1963 to Allied Breweries Ltd.

The amalgamation was successful in strengthening the collective profitability of the original companies and in making their brands available in new markets throughout Great Britain. Indeed, Allied Breweries' success was so great that management was able to make a strategic acquisition in 1968, that of the wine and spirits conglomerate SVPW.

Like Allied Breweries, SVPW was itself an amalgamation, formed in 1961 when three alcoholic beverage companies—Whiteways, Vine Products, and Showerings—were merged. Whiteways of Whipple was founded in 1903 by Henry Whiteway; the company produced a popular alcoholic apple cider called Cydrax. Vine Products, a vintner established in Fulham by Alexander Mitzotakis in 1905, produced a popular variety of sherries and sparkling wines. Showerings was founded in 1953 by Francis Showering; it was known for a sparkling perry (a fermented beverage made from pears) called Babycham.

As a result of its acquisition SVPW (later called Allied Vintners), Allied Breweries gained a dominant position in the British beverage market. The companies that together made up Allied Breweries continued to operate separately as associated companies, and Allied spent much of the 1970's consolidating and refining its new organizational structure as well as evaluating its marketing strategies. Those strategies were successful, and as a result management could consider diversifying the company's operations.

In 1978 Allied Breweries made an offer for J. Lyons and Company, which owned Tetley Tea and the Baskin-Robbins ice cream shops. Some financial observers considered the take-over to be ill-advised; Allied Breweries, they noted, had not yet achieved a strong enough position in the marketplace to consider taking over so large a company as Lyons (1978 sales: £788 million). Allied felt differently. Because of consistently poor performance, Lyons was significantly undervalued. With proper management, Lyons could be transformed into a much more profitable company—and Allied believed it could provide the necessary expertise. In August of 1978 Allied Breweries sold its share of the Trust Houses Forte hotel and restaurant group for £48 million; a week later Allied bought Lyons for £60 million.

As were Allied Breweries' other subsidiaries, J. Lyons and Company was at first administrated as a separate company (it was not until October 1981 that the combined company adopted the name Allied-Lyons). Yet, as older members of the Lyons board retired, they were replaced by talented managers from Allied who applied new business methods and strategies. And in 1982 Sir Derrick Holden-Brown, an accountant by training and head of the Allied beer division, was elected chairman of Allied-Lyons.

Sir Derrick became chairman at a time when Allied-Lyons was initiating a plan to expand overseas. A new division, Allied Overseas Trading Ltd., was established to promote exports to franchises on five continents. Over the next two years changes were also made in the organization of several companies in the spirits division. In 1984 R. N. Coate, and its sister company William Gaymer and Son (which makes Gaymer's Olde English Cyder) merged with Showerings. In June of 1986 Vine Products merged with Whiteways to form Vine Products and Whiteways Ltd. That same year the Victoria Wine Company, a retail chain with 960 outlets, was transferred from the wine and spirits group to the beer division. Allied-Lyons was now both a more aggressive and a more efficient company.

In late 1985 the Australian brewery and finance conglomerate Elders IXL announced its intention to take over Allied-Lyons for £1.68 billion. A few months later, in a separate takeover battle, Gulf Canada (controlled by the Reichmann family of Canada) attempted to take control of the Canadian beverage firm of Hiram Walker. Hiram Walker agreed to sell its liquor division, Gooderham and Worts, to Allied-Lyons for C$2.64 billion, thus providing Walker with sufficient cash to thwart the Reichmanns. Other takeover problems in Australia forced Elders to turn its attention away from Allied-Lyons and eventually to rescind its bid. Meanwhile, the Reichmanns succeeded in acquiring Hiram Walker, but they then refused to honor that company's agreement to sell its liquor division to Allied-Lyons. This agreement was highly important to Allied-Lyons: it provided the company with the means to establish itself as an important presence in North America, something it had long desired. Sir Derrick produced a copy of the contract; he claimed it bound the Reichmanns to comply. Before the matter had gone to litigation, Allied-Lyons reached a second agreement with the Reichmanns: the sale was permitted on the condition that 49% was sold back to Gulf Canada. Thus Allied-Lyons ended up with 51% of Hiram Walker-Gooderham and Worts, which it purchased for C$831 million. The remaining interest in Hiram Walker was acquired by Allied-Lyons late in 1987 in a deal worth C$1.3 billion, and which transferred a 10% share in Allied-Lyons to a company controlled by the Reichmanns.

Allied-Lyons has now emerged as one of the most important beverage companies in the world. It has been organized into three divisions: brewing; wine, spirits, and soft drinks; and food. The brewing group produces a variety of beers, including Skol, Tetley Bitter and Mild, Long Life, Löwenbräu, Oranjeboom, Ansell's Bitter and Mild, and John Bull Bitter. The wine, spirits, and soft drinks group is responsible for producing Harvey's Bristol Cream, Teacher's Scotch, Babycham, and Cockburn, a popular port. The foods group, created in 1978, sells Tetley Tea (no relation to Tetley beer), Lyons coffee, Hales cakes, Maryland biscuits, and Lyons Maid ice cream. Allied-Lyons' Embassy hotels unit is also managed by the foods group. The company's most successful foreign operations are the Hiram Walker-Gooderham and Worts business in Canada and the Baskin-Robbins ice cream shops, located mainly in the United States.

Principal Subsidiaries: Allied Breweries Ltd.; Allied Vintners Ltd.; J. Lyons & Company Ltd.; Allied-Lyons Investments Ltd.; Allied-Lyons Overseas Ltd.; Financiering Maatschappij d'Oranjeboom BV (Netherlands).

Further Reading: *Wine for Sale: Victoria Wine and the Liquor Trade 1860–1984* by Asa Briggs, Chicago, University of Chicago Press, 1985.

ANHEUSER-BUSCH COMPANY, INC.

One Busch Plaza
St. Louis, Missouri 63118
(314) 577-2000

Public Company
Incorporated: February 21, 1979
Employees: 39,769
Sales: $7.677 billion
Market Value: $9.683 billion
Stock Index: New York

Anheuser-Busch is the nation's leading brewer of light, premium, and super-premium beers. Expensive European hops and beechwood-chip aging in eleven breweries across the country distinguish Anheuser-Busch beers such as Budweiser, Michelob, and Busch from much of their competition. Although principally a brewer, Anheuser-Busch has diversified, via various subsidiaries, into food products, refrigerator cars, metal containers, corn syrup, starch, and baker's and brewer's yeast. The company has also established two entertainment parks. These non-beer enterprises account for only 10% of Anheuser-Busch profits, but they are indicative of the company's success.

In 1852 Eberhard Anheuser, a prosperous soap manufacturer in St. Louis, bought a failing brewery from a Bavarian immigrant named Sneider. Although the brewery's cool underground caverns near the Mississippi River were conducive to good brewing, and although he had the will to succeed, Anheuser lacked one crucial ingredient for success—experience. He therefore hired his son-in-law, Adolphus Busch, another recent German immigrant schooled in the art of brewing, to be his general manager. That which the two men separately brought to the enterprise—an aggressiveness in business and a knowledge of quality brewing—has informed Anheuser-Busch's history ever since.

Although the true story of the founding of Anheuser-Busch is interesting enough, the company's executives have sometimes preferred a different one, that in the 1870's Adolphus Busch stopped at a German monastery and was given the recipe for the beer the monks were brewing there. They also gave him some of their brewer's yeast, the secret of their excellent beer. That recipe became the basis of Anheuser-Busch beers, and the original strain of yeast is still used in the beer brewed today (indeed, the original yeast was preserved for years in

Adolphus' ice-cream freezer!). The story is fictitious, but it does serve to illustrate the dominant philosophies of Anheuser-Busch—that only the finest "European" ingredients are to be used, that the recipe of the beers does not change with time, that the founders of the company established precedents that continue to be followed.

During 1853 Anheuser and Busch increased the rejuvenated brewery's capacity from 3,000 to 8,000 barrels per year and began to expand their sales effort into Texas and Louisiana as well as their home state of Missouri. Cowboys, we are told, deserted their beloved red-eye whiskey for the light taste of Budweiser, Adolphus Busch's 1876 imitation of a light Bohemian beer (the rights to the name were not purchased from the Bohemian brewer of "Budweis" until 1891). Because of constant innovations in the brewing industry, Budweiser's formula was soon improved. Beer was now pasteurized and preserved for longer periods. The newly invented refrigerated railroad cars permitted the transport of beer across state borders, and the bottling of beer allowed for easier distribution throughout the country. Regional brewers lost their advantage to large breweries such as Anheuser-Busch, which had found the means to supply beer to every state in the union. Despite the growth of its market, however, Anheuser-Busch still referred to itself as a "regional brewery"—an institution that understood the distinct needs and tastes of local people.

Anheuser gave over the day-to-day operations to Busch in the 1870's. The company continued to prosper. As Anheuser-Busch grew, so did the number of its employees. Adolphus Busch initiated the idea (much imitated since) that his employees were somehow members of a family, cared for and nurtured by the company, loyal to the company for a lifetime. The relation between employer and employee is thus intimate and co-operative, and it is that co-operation that results in an outstanding product. In the 1890's Pabst, a competitor, was the best selling beer in the United States. Busch and his "family" thwarted the competition with the introduction of Michelob in 1896. Forceful and frequent advertising cunningly suggested that Budweiser and Michelob were uniquitous—and therefore popular. By saying it often enough, the company achieved what it had proposed: by 1901 Anheuser-Busch was the leading brewery in the country.

Busch died in 1913, and his son (also called Adolphus) took over; he was soon to prove that one of the company's virtues was its flexibility. The first diesel engine was patented by Busch and installed in the brewery to increase production. With the coming of World War I, Busch founded a subsidiary to produce the engines for Navy submarines. As well, the Anheuser-Busch family purchased sufficient war bonds to finance two bombers—appropriately named "Miss Budweiser."

Then one war ended as another began: in November 1918 President Wilson signed the bill that instituted Prohibition. Anheuser-Busch had already stopped producing beer in October of 1918, but it did not wait for imminent collapse. Instead, Busch used this hiatus to the company's advantage, by diversifying into related fields. Malt syrup was canned and sold to people who required malt for their homemade brews. A refrigeration car company was established to transport perishables. Bevo, a soft drink made from ingredients similar to those in beer, was a great success for three years; it later failed when Prohibition laws concerning the use of yeast forced the company to change ingredients. Thus, Anheuser-Busch early began a trend toward diversification that would thereafter characterize the history of the company.

When Prohibition ended, Anheuser-Busch experienced an unforeseen problem: people had become used to the sweet taste of the soft drinks and homemade brews that were available during Prohibition, and were not willing to return to the bitter taste of beer. In response, many brewers changed their formulas to achieve a sweeter taste. However, since one of the philosophies of the Anheuser-Busch company is that it must maintain successful traditions, Busch refused to alter the formula for best-selling Budweiser. Dr. Robert Gall, the company's post-Prohibition brewmaster, agreed with this decision. The company initiated a major advertising campaign: Busch challenged consumers to a "five day test." He predicted that after five days of drinking Budweiser the consumer would not drink a sweet beer again. The advertising campaign was successful and established a trend for future consumer appeals.

During World War II the company, now led by Adolphus Busch III, again made substantial contributions to the war effort: Anheuser-Busch supplied ammunition hoists, in production at a new Anheuser-Busch subsidiary, to the military. The distribution of Budweiser beer was withdrawn from the Pacific Coast in order to supply the government with additional freight cars for war essentials. Spent grain was sold to financially troubled war-time farmers for poultry and livestock food. These patriotic actions elevated sales and advanced Anheuser-Busch's image as a patriotic company.

Between 1935 and 1950 the demand for Anheuser-Busch beer always exceeded the supply. In 1941 three million barrels of beer were produced; in 1950 six million barrels were produced. Production was at its highest, and the industry was no longer hampered by wartime restrictions. The death of Adolphus Busch III in 1946 momentarily caused the company to relinquish its lead in the industry. But with the succession of his brother, August Busch, Jr. (Gussie), the company became the nation's top brewer once again.

The advertising policy of August Busch, Jr. did not significantly differ from the high-pressure ads used by his brother and father. Adolphus had advertised his beer through the distribution of pocket knives and gold pieces. Patriotic art such as "Custer's Last Stand" was employed in advertisements. In 1933 the famous Clydesdale horses were introduced and still remain an advertising legend. After the war, August Busch required an even more expansive approach to entice the public to drink Anheuser-Busch's beer. Thus, Anheuser-Busch became the first brewery to sponsor a radio network. Positive consumer response prompted William Bien, the vice-president of marketing, to design a legendary advertising campaign: "pick-a-pair-of-six-packs." The campaign cost $2.5 million for two months, but was the most successful promotion in the history of the beer industry.

Despite its successful promotions, Anheuser-Busch entered a close competition at the beginning of the 1950's with Carling beer. At first, August Busch did not acknowledge the severity of the competition. A holiday had just been declared in Newark, New Jersey in honor of the opening of a new Anheuser-Busch factory in that city. This established an industry precedent: no other beer company had ever been so honored. But the new facility and new equipment necessitated a price increase. Carling profited when its lower-priced beer attracted disaffected Anheuser-Busch customers. Busch countered with a low-priced lager beer in 1954. Busch Bavarian soon replaced the lager and was better received. Again Busch had vied against the competition and won. This victory spurred more aggressive advertising promotions in keeping with the brewery's tough marketing strategy. In 1953 Anheuser-Busch bought the St. Louis Cardinals baseball team and created a new arena in which to advertise its product. In addition, a new category of consumers, sports fans, could be targeted for advertising campaigns.

It was not long before another brewery attempted to displace Anheuser-Busch from its number one market ranking. By decreasing the price of its beer in the 1960's, Schlitz hoped to force Anheuser-Busch into a price war just as Carling had attempted to do in the 1950's. However, August Busch, Jr. believed that the consumer recognized the quality of Anheuser-Busch beer and could not be swayed by a lower-priced competitor. By committing several marketing and advertising mistakes, however, Schlitz made it unnecessary for the public to decide between the two beers. Competent marketing and product confidence were once again the tools of Anheuser-Busch's success.

At the end of the 1960's August Busch III began to prepare to take on the position of chief executive officer held by his father, August Busch, Jr. He attended college for two years in Arizona and then transferred to a Chicago school where he learned the art of brewing. He started at the bottom of the Anheuser-Busch company ranks and advanced according to merit. He even joined the union, but formally withdrew when he became the chief executive officer in 1979. August Busch III vowed to uphold Adolphus Busch's philosophy that natural ingredients must be used to distinguish the company's fine brewing from the lower quality brewing of other beers. During the 1970's and 1980's Miller Brewing Company challenged this philosophy. August Busch III, however, had already devised a unique method of dealing with the competition, including: 1) the introduction of new brands; 2) an increase in the advertising budget; and 3) the expansion of the breweries. Although Busch's aggressive plan was effective for a short period, Miller introduced a light, low calorie beer to the market in 1974. Consumers were impressed and Miller Lite became the best selling beer for a few months. Shortly after the popularity of the new beer peaked, Anheuser-Busch edged back into the top ranking but since then has always been closely followed by the Miller brewery.

Anheuser-Busch introduced two light beers in 1977, Natural and Michelob Light, with Budweiser Light soon to follow. Moreover, August Busch instigated more focused marketing. He hired a team of 100 college graduates to promote the sale of Anheuser-Busch beers on college campuses. He also targeted new advertisements to specific consumer groups such as youth and the working class. The marketing budget was quadrupled, and sales were increased by focusing on the tastes of categories of people rather than on the general public.

August Busch III manages the brewery with a style different from that of his father, grandfather, or great-grandfather. The use of a "management control system" has increased the efficiency of the company, making it more a modern corporation than a small family business. According to August Busch III, the following three principles are the core of his management control: 1) planning; 2) teamwork; and 3) communications. Without these controls, Anheuser-Busch's image as a regional brewery, which produces different beers to satisfy the tastes of the local residents, would, ironically, be impossible.

Anheuser-Busch has continued to rank number one in the brewing industry into the 1980's. In 1980 sales had reached 50 million barrels and in 1982 sales increased to 54.5 million barrels and have since gone higher. Competition with Miller is still intense. In 1980 Miller was 5% behind Anheuser-Busch in beer sales. Despite this slim margin, Anheuser-Busch's aggressive sales techniques and diversification into associated markets ensures its future success.

Anheuser-Busch purchases subsidiaries with regard to their efficacy in providing products which will further popularize the name of Anheuser-Busch. The malt plants in Wisconsin and Minnesota, the beer can factories in Florida and Ohio, and the yeast plants in Missouri, New Jersey, California, and Florida are directly related to the production of beer. The St. Louis Refrigerator Car Company inspects and maintains the 880 refrigerated railroad cars which are used to transport the company's beer across the country. Manufacturers Railway ships Anheuser-Busch beer after it has been manufactured at the brewery with help from the malt and yeast subsidiaries.

Other Anheuser-Busch subsidiaries, however, are not beer-oriented, but they are more relevant to the company's strategy than they at first appear to be. Campbell-Taggart, Inc., the second largest bakery in the United States, acquired in 1982, associates Anheuser-Busch's name with the food industry. In fact, 6.7% of Anheuser-Busch's operating income is spent on food products. The production of baker's yeast in the already existent brewer's yeast factory further develops Anheuser-Busch's interest in the food industry. Eagle Snacks, Inc. nationally distributes food products to bars, taverns, and convenience stores. This subsidiary's most threatening competitors are Frito-Lay and Planters Peanuts. Despite intense competition, Eagle Snacks has brought Anheuser-Busch's reputation into an arena where consumers are most likely to buy Anheuser-Busch beer along with the food products.

Within the entertainment industry, Anheuser-Busch has developed theme parks, called Busch Gardens, in Virginia and Florida. The Tampa, Florida park, "The Dark Continent," boasts one of the world's largest collections of wildlife under private ownership. "The Old Country," in Williamsburg, Virginia is modeled after villages in 17th-century Europe. Although operation of these theme parks

is not profitable, exposing Anheuser-Busch's name to a new target group, the younger generation and their parents, justifies the investment in the subsidiary. Furthermore, the educational theme parks confirm the Anheuser-Busch World War I policy of contributing to the public welfare while improving the Anheuser-Busch reputation.

That Anheuser-Busch owns the St. Louis Cardinals also helps to popularize Anheuser-Busch products with Cardinal and other sports fans. In fact, name association is the key factor in any Anheuser-Busch decision to purchase prospective subsidiaries. A subsidiary may not be linked to beer but if the name and reputation of the company can improve Anheuser-Busch's image, then Anheuser-Busch concludes that it can improve the sale of beer.

The immediate future of Anheuser-Busch will be devoted to the foreign market. It has already exported beers to ten foreign countries, but only experienced successful results in Canada and Japan. In Japan, Budweiser is second only to Heineken in the imported beer market because of the company's success in promoting Budweiser as a beer for the young adult. In Canada, Budweiser is successfully marketed as a beer for all ages. However, in England Budweiser's specific qualities rather than its unique consumer appeal are promoted. English beer is heavy, so Budweiser is merchandised as a "lighter" beer. Anheuser-Busch entered the German beer market with a partner, the Oetker Group of Germany, and a different advertising style. Advertisements spotlight the Old West by using dubbed voices of familiar wild west screen actors. These complementary advertising techniques have resulted in exported beer sales equal to 15% of the total Anheuser-Busch sales and 10% of the total profits.

Despite the emphasis on the foreign market, Anheuser-Busch will also be compelled to focus on the declining beer consumption of Americans. The company introduced LA, the first low alcohol beer on the market, in 1984. Perhaps other such alternatives will be introduced. Perhaps subsidiaries to produce non-alcoholic beverages will be considered. Whatever methods August Busch III uses to approach the problems of the next decade, Anheuser-Busch is certain to remain one of the dominating influences in the brewing industry.

Principal Subsidiaries: Anheuser Busch, Inc.; Busch Entertainment Corporation; Manufacturers Railway Company; St. Louis Refrigerator Car Company; St. Louis National Baseball Club, Inc.; Busch Properties, Inc.; Metal Container Corporation; Container Recovery Corporation; Metal Label Corporation; Anheuser Busch International, Inc.; Busch Creative Services Corporation; Busch Agricultural Resources, Inc.; Busch Industrial Products Company; Civic Center Corporation; Eagle Snacks, Inc.; Campbell Taggart, Inc.; and Anheuser Busch Beverage Group, Inc.

Further Reading: Making Friends Is Our Business: 100 Years of Anheuser-Busch by Roland Krebs, St. Louis, Cuneo Press, 1953; *Brewed in America: A History of Beer and Ale in the U.S.* by Stanley Wade Baron, New York, Arno Press, 1972.

ASAHI BREWERIES, LTD.

7–1, Kyobashi, 3-chome
Chuo-ku, Tokyo
Japan

Public Company
Incorporated: September 1, 1949
Employees: 2,672
Sales: ¥236 billion (US$1.482 billion)
Market Value: ¥245.7 billion (US$1.543 billion)
Stock Index: Tokyo Osaka Nagoya

The history of the Asahi Breweries is linked with that of virtually every other brewery in Japan. The first brewery built by the Japanese was a government enterprise; it was established in the early days of the Meiji restoration on Hokkaido, the northernmost of the islands of Japan. In the 1880's the government sold its Hokkaido brewery to private interests—and thus the Osaka Beer Brewing Company, Japan Beer Brewery Company, Sapporo Brewery, and Nippon Brewing Company all came into being. In 1888 a man named Hiizu Ikuta was sent to Germany by Osaka Beer Brewing Company to study brewing at the famous School of Weihenstephen in Bavaria. He returned the following year and was appointed manager and technical chief of the Suita Brewery, one of the individual breweries controlled by Osaka. One year later, in 1890, his creation, Asahi beer, was released for sale.

Soon after the turn of the century the Osaka Beer Brewing Company, Sapporo Brewery, and Nippon Brewing Company were amalgamated into the Dai Nippon Brewery Company. Asahi, now a separate division of the new company, began a long history of producing non-alcoholic beverages as well as beer. Asahi pioneered the soft drink industry in Japan with both Mitsuya Cider and Wilkinson Tansan, a mineral water. Mitsuya Cider was released for sale in 1907, 17 years after Asahi beer had first been introduced to the market.

In 1949 Dai Nippon Brewery was divided into two parts—Asahi Breweries and Nippon Breweries. Since that time, the growth of Asahi has been impressive. In 1951, Asahi mineral water was introduced to the Japanese market. That year also saw the introduction of Japan's first fruit-flavored soft drink, Bireley's Orange. Asahi's first plant exclusively devoted to the production of soft drinks was opened in Kashiwa in 1966. Six years later another Asahi soft drink plant began production in Fukushima. Soft drink sales now account for 27% of the company's

total sales (a lower percentage than during the mid-1970's when soft drinks accounted for 35% of sales). Asahi now plans vigorously to expand its sale of soft drinks in the Japanese market. In 1971, in a joint venture with Nikka Whiskey Distilling Company, Asahi established Japan International Liquor to important foreign liquors, primarily Scotch whiskeys (Dewars and King George IV).

1978 was a banner year for Asahi: the company's net profit passed the billion yen mark for the first time. From 1973 to 1985 the company's sales increased by almost 100%.

In February of 1986 Asahi made a move that was virtually unprecedented in the brewing industry—it changed the yeast that it had traditionally used to brew beer. This bold move was prompted by the slow but still steady decline that the company had been experiencing in its share of the Japanese beer market. The move was not made without extensive marketing research: in 1985 Asahi conducted an extensive series of studies that indicated that Japanese drinkers actually preferred beer quite different in taste from that traditionally brewed by Asahi (Asahi's beer had a strong taste of hops). The company decided to change the yeast fungus it had been using in order to achieve a taste that it believed would be more palatable to the Japanese beer drinker.

This change was the first for Asahi of such magnitude in almost 30 years: the existing yeast had been used since 1957. The change in Asahi's yeast was accompanied by a change in its label. Such changes would not have been contemplated by the company if it were Japan's leading brewery; so dramatic a switch in taste and presentation would have been considered too risky. Asahi's initiative was rewarded: within a very short period the company has managed to recover a good portion of its lost market share.

Asahi has also enjoyed other kinds of success. Its Central Research Laboratory, charged primarily with quality control, has also developed new products, including "Ebios," a day brewer's yeast renowned in Japan for its medicinal properties; the company introduced Ebios in the 1930's and has been manufacturing it ever since. Laboratory staff also invented the world's first outdoor fermentation and lagering tank (the "Asahi Tank"); the West German beer plant construction firm of Ziemann soon negotiated with the company for a license to build the tank.

Asahi's soft drink division received new impetus in the mid-1980's when the company concluded an agreement with Schweppes: several Schweppes brands are now manufactured in Japan by Asahi—Tonic Water, Golden French (an apple and ginger drink), Passion Orange, and Grapefruit Dry. Asahi has entered into other partnerships, notably to import foreign beers and wines into Japan. In 1983 the company concluded an agreement with the Löwenbräu Company of West Germany to produce Löwenbräu beer under license in Japan. The following year Asahi formed a partnership with the Australian wine company Lindemann's: Asahi now sells eight kinds of Australian wine under the "My Cellar" brand. Asahi also imports the German Drathen Company's "Tafelwein."

Exports are also coming to play an increasingly important role in company strategy; in fact, Asahi was the first Japanese brewery to have its beer produced overseas under license. In 1971 Asahi concluded a technical assistance agreement with United Breweries of New Guinea, and a brewery was subsequently constructed at Port Moresby. In January 1986 a technology transfer agreement was reached with the San Miguel Corporation of Indonesia for the local production of Asahi beer. Another technical transfer agreement had previously been reached in 1979 with this same company for the use of Asahi's automatic beer gauge system for beer fermentation at other plants under San Miguel control. This system had been jointly developed by Asahi and the Toshiba Corporation.

Asahi beer is now exported to more than 30 countries around the world. The United States is Asahi's major customer, and the company now maintains offices in New York and Los Angeles to oversee its export activity. Sales to the United States account for more than 60% of Asahi's exports, but the company's beer is also exported to Australia, the Peoples Republic of China, the U.S.S.R., Iraq, Vietnam, and Iran (obviously, political differences with some of these countries have not interfered with the export program).

Asahi has recently entered the restaurant business. Subsidiary companies—Asahi Kyoei and New Asahi—manage more than 100 restaurants in western and eastern Japan respectively. The company has also entered into a joint venture with the American company Pizza Hut to establish Pizza Hut restaurants in Japan.

Asahi also owns subsidiary companies involved in transportation and manufacturing. The company's four transportation subsidiaries all began as companies expressly involved in transporting and distributing only Asahi products; however, Asahi has recently initiated a program to broaden the scope of their activities. Similarly, the Shin-Nihon Glass Company, another subsidiary, began life as the exclusive producer of bottles for Asahi but now has clients outside the Asahi group. In fact, Shin-Nihon Glass Company has developed so many "outside" clients that most of its business is now with companies unrelated to Asahi. Other subsidiaries include the Mitsuya Foods Company, which continues to be involved in maintaining and promoting Asahi's sales networks and in maintaining Asahi's vending machine operations. Asahi is currently expanding its operations into such fields as printing, real estate, life and accident insurance, building management and construction.

Asahi Chemical Industry (despite their similar names, the companies were not previously related) acquired 22 million shares of Asahi Brewery in October 1981. An agreement was concluded between the two companies concerning relations involving personnel, technology, and sales. Asahi Chemical is now the major shareholder of the brewery—with a 10% holding. Only slightly more than half of Asahi's 400 million authorized shares have actually been issued (of that number, only .08% are owned by foreigners).

Despite their relatively small share of the Japanese beer market, Asahi would seem to have a bright future. Now part of the Sumitomo Group, Asahi remains the third largest brewer in Japan, and it has recently instituted a program to revitalize its management. Most recently, company chairman Tsutomu Murai and president Hirotaro Higuchi have devised a "New Century" plan, which they hope will both guide the company and reinforce its corporate identity well into the 21st century.

BASS PLC

30 Portland Place
London W1N 3DF
England
01-637-5499

Public Company
Incorporated: August 17, 1967 as Bass Charrington Ltd.
Employees: 71,207
Sales: £2.41 billion (US$3.45 billion)
Market Value: £3.25 billion (US$4.77 billion)
Stock Index: London Brussels Amsterdam

Employees of Bass once proclaimed that they worked for the best firm within the British brewing industry. While many of these employees would still say that this adequately describes the company's beer, they would probably also admit that in the recent past the company has suffered from some myopic management policies. Yet, when the industry trend toward consolidation fostered the growth of large national companies, Bass emerged as an industry leader. Today, in addition to brewing, the company manages diverse holdings in growing international markets.

The founding of Bass & Company dates back to 1777 in the ancient town of Burton-on-Trent in Staffordshire. Although monks had been brewing beer in this town since the twelfth century, it was William Bass who laid the foundation for securing Burton's status as the focal point of Britain's brewing activities. William Bass inhabited the house next to the gateway of his brewery; it was here that his son and grandson, both future company leaders, were born. By 1791 Michael Bass, William's son, was actively engaged in his father's business.

By the turn of the century the increased volume of brewing, now 2000 barrels per year, compelled the family to expand the High Street brewery to twice its original size. In 1821 the company became one of the first brewers to export ale to India after discovering that it was a suitable product for warm climates. Thus was born the "East India Pale Ale" which many other brewers soon imitated.

Michael Thomas Bass, William's grandson, assumed control of the brewery in 1827 when brewing capacity had reached nearly 10,000 barrels per year. By 1837 the company was known by the name of Bass, Ratcliffe & Gretton, after two fellow businessmen, John Gretton and Richard Ratcliffe, formed a partnership with Bass. The expansion of the railways greatly benefited the growing business; Burton ales, transported across the nation, became widely recognized as premier brands. With Bass' output surpassing 140,000 barrels a year by 1853, a second brewery was needed. By 1860 volume had increased threefold; a third brewery was constructed.

Michael Thomas Bass, became not only an important figure in the industry but also a widely recognized civic leader. He financed the construction of several churches, recreation facilities, and a public library. Moreover, he served in Parliament for 33 years as a member for Derby.

By 1876 Bass was recognized; it was now Britain's largest brewing company. Its bottled ale was so popular that the company was forced to become the first firm in England to make use of the Trade Marks Registration Act of 1875 to protect its red pyramid trademark. A few years prior to Michael Bass' death in 1884, the business was organized as a private limited company. The old brewery on the High Street was renovated, but now the Bass empire covered 145 acres of land, the largest ale and bitter beer brewery in the world.

In 1888, under the leadership of Michael Bass' eldest son, Michael A. Bass, later Lord Burton, the company was incorporated as Bass, Ratcliffe & Gretton Ltd. with a share capital of £2.7 million. Output neared one million barrels a year; more than 2,500 men and boys were employed at the breweries.

In the same year that Lord Burton incorporated the company, Gretton's son, John Gretton Jr., joined the firm. After assuming control of the malting department in 1893, Gretton went on to join the board of directors. Gretton also served as a Conservative MP between 1895 and 1943. Among his many political causes, Gretton opposed the Licensing Bill of 1908 and trade restrictions on the brewing industry during World War I. Upon Lord Burton's death in 1908, Gretton assumed the title of Bass' chairman.

During the next decades Bass' management, unlike that of many competitors, adhered to the free trade system whereby the company relied on small traders to bottle and stock its products. Increasingly, the more common practice for British brewers was to run their own "public houses" as outlets to retail their beer. Bass did own a few public houses, but preferred to depend on the continuing national popularity of its brands to achieve expansion. As long as Bass remained in such high demand, the retailing could be left to the free trade customers. While competitors chose to invest money in the improvement of their public houses, Gretton ignored the trend and neglected his properties.

During World War I overall consumption of beer decreased. The brewing industry (through taxation) was used by the government as a source of income. This led to an increase in the price of beer. The advent of radio, cinema, and other modern leisure activities drew patrons away from the public houses. These changes in social attitudes gave further impetus to the brewers to improve their properties. Public houses were increasingly converted to comfortable places where customers could enjoy an evening of food, drink, and conversation.

Yet Gretton chose to continue rejecting the general trend toward improved public houses. Instead, his company spent the decade of the 1920's acquiring several other breweries. In 1926 Bass purchased control of Worthington & Company Ltd., a long-established competitor also located in Burton-on-Trent. The Worthington label, like that of Bass, enjoyed a national reputation. This acquisition, however, did not lead to the kind of merger common in today's market; Worthington remained virtually an autonomous operation.

While Bass continued making acquisitions that included the purchase of a wine and spirit operation, further changes in the industry occurred which were at odds with Bass' traditional approach. The small but growing firm of Mitchells & Butler not only set an industry example by improving its public house properties, but also led a trend in initiating a policy of direct brewery management. Formerly most brewery-owned houses were run by tenants who were given a free hand to operate the business. Mitchells & Butler imposed new regulations on the tenant managers; it compelled them to sell more of the firm's own beer rather than national brands such as Bass and Worthington. This policy ensured higher earnings and therefore a greater return on their investment. Such actions undercut Bass' market position.

Bass' continuing reliance on the free trade system became increasingly anachronistic. However, it was not only changing social attitudes and industry trends that contributed to Bass' declining sales in the postwar years; the economic conditions of the early 1930's created further obstacles. As a result of worldwide depression, factories shut down and unemployment increased, and Bass was forced to cut back production.

Gretton had become preoccupied with his non-business activities. He was deeply involved in political life, a vocal advocate of conservative causes. Bass management was not entirely asleep, however. When awareness of hygiene and quality drew consumers to pasteurized and bottled products, Bass capitalized on the trend: it introduced its "Blue Triangle" brand in 1934. Sales of this bottled version of the older "Red Triangle" grew steadily.

After Gretton died in 1947, Arthur Manners, a longtime Bass executive, assumed the title of chairman. Like Gretton's, his management style was conservative. Yet between the late 1940's and the late 1950's Bass' net profits increased by 123%. Expansion took the form of share acquisitions in the equity of fellow brewers. Bass acquired holdings in William Hancock & Company and Wenlock Brewery Company.

Over the next few years, however, Bass' failure to adopt a more modern business approach helped to create competition that previously did not exist. Because of the "tied house" system, Bass beer was lost in popularity to more aggressively marketed national brands and regionally brewed pale ales. The company refused to update its pricing system or adjust to changing public tastes toward milder beers. Even Bass' holdings in other companies were mismanaged; integration was nonexistent and redundant operations put a strain on profits. Although Bass operated an extensive trading network, controlled 17 subsidiaries across the United Kingdom, and still manufactured a venerated beer, a major change was in order.

When Arthur Manners retired as chairman in 1952, his position was filled by C.A. Ball, a 65-year-old executive who had started his career as Manners' typist. While Ball recognized the need to modernize by hiring professional managers, Bass' decline had progressed too far. Ball died in 1959 and was succeeded by the nearly 70-year-old Sir James Grigg, a former cabinet minister under Churchill. Grigg's first action as chairman was to find a suitable merger to help the company solve growing financial difficulties.

H. Alan Walker, the dynamic chief executive director of Mitchells & Butler, approached Grigg, and an agreement was soon finalized. Walker had built Mitchells & Butler into one of the most efficient and financially successful breweries in the industry. By closing down unprofitable operations, by modernizing marketing and production, and by acquiring other breweries, he had significantly improved the company's performance. Yet Walker's company was not large enough to protect itself against any potential takeover bid; he was looking for a merger of his own choosing. Bass, Ratcliffe and Gretton merged with Mitchells & Butler in 1961.

At virtually the same time, another industry merger occurred that would play an important role in Bass' future. In 1962 Charrington & Company Ltd., a London brewery whose history dates back to 1766, merged with United Breweries, the brewers of the national brands of Carling Lager and Jubilee Stout. While Charrington functioned in many ways as a family concern, United was a new consortium of medium-sized brewers from various parts of the United Kingdom.

The formation of Charrington United Breweries created a well-balanced national company with strong ties to London and an established distribution network across the United Kingdom. Almost the exact same thing could be said of the Bass, Mitchells & Butler merger. With Walker assuming the title of chief executive and Grigg maintaining his position as chairman, the management began a program of rationalization to integrate and modernize the companies' operations.

However, by the late 1960's the management of both newly formed companies recognized the unfulfilled potential in their firms' performance. While Charrington United Breweries controlled a variety of regional brands, the company lacked a premium draught beer such as Bass or Worthington. Bass, Mitchells & Butler, lacked a spirit and soft drinks business as successful as that of Charrington United Breweries' Canada Dry subsidiary. Although the mergers improved the two companies' national distribution networks, areas of weakness existed for both firms. In 1967 a new merger was arranged between Charrington United Breweries and Bass, Mitchell's & Butler.

The Bass Charrington company was an immediate success. The easy integration process was followed by years of effort to improve market position. This improvement slowed for a short time between 1973 and 1974 as a result of rising inflation and economic recession. By 1975, however, company performance once again improved, and Bass Charrington began to garner the benefits from its investments and expansion.

By the early 1980's the newly renamed Bass plc had registered an 18% increase in its earnings. Under the leadership of chairman Derek Palmar, Bass now managed more pubs in the United Kingdom than any other industry competitor. Furthermore, the company successfully capitalized on the growing market for lager. Yet in many ways Bass maintained its conservative management policies. A "Bass package" of regional ales continued to be distributed by the free trade system. Similarly, Bass' property improvements, while generous, were more concerned with promoting family establishments than catering to younger clients. A program of diversification led Bass to create a leisure division. While mostly profitable, their subsidiaries, which included a hotel business and betting shops, contributed less than 20% to profits. Bass remained one of the least diversified of the major brewers.

Recently, however, Bass' leisure activities have assumed a greater role in the company. The hotel division, through its Coral and Crest subsidiaries, has enjoyed healthy financial gains. Crest is now one of the fastest growing British companies in Europe.

In May 1987 Bass announced an agreement with the U.S.-based Holiday Corporation to purchase eight European Holiday Inn hotels for £152 million. With its other leisure holdings, Bass hopes its non-brewing interests will now account for 25% of total profits. The company's current formula for combining well-chosen acquisitions with the traditional business of brewing premium beer has proven a success.

Principal Subsidiaries: Bass Investments Public Limited Co.; Bass Holdings Limited; Bass European Holdings NV; Bass Continental Finance NV; Bass UK Limited; Bass Mitchells & Butler Limited; Bass North Limited; Bass Wales & West Limited; Charrington and Company Limited; Tennent Caledonian Breweries Limited; Bass Ireland Limited; Bass Brewing Limited; Bass Maltings Ltd.; Bass Off Licences Ltd.; Bass & Tennent Sales Ltd.; Bass Horizon Hotels Ltd.; Bass Leisure Ltd.; Coral Racing Ltd.; Bass Hotels & Holidays Ltd.; Coral Social Clubs Ltd.; Britannia Soft Drinks Limited; Hedges & Butler Limited; Alexis Lichine et Cie SA; Bass Export Limited; Bass Computer Services Ltd.; Chandos Insurance Co. Ltd.; White Shield Insurance Co. Ltd.

Further Reading: Bass: The Story of the World's Most Famous Ale, Burton-on-Trent, Bass, 1927.

BROWN-FORMAN CORPORATION

850 Dixie Highway
Louisville, Kentucky 40210
U.S.A.
(502) 585-1100

Public Company
Incorporated: 1933
Employees: 6,550
Sales: $1.06 billion
Market Value: $1.60 billion
Stock Index: American

Brown-Forman is a diversified company with most of its sales in the liquor market. A full-line distiller, Brown-Forman markets Bols Liqueurs, Bolla and Cella wines, Korbel champagne and brandy, Ushers scotch, Jack Daniels whiskey, Southern Comfort liqueur, and Early Times and Old Forester bourbon. Brown-Forman's success is due to its timely diversification into different areas of the liquor industry as well as into other unrelated fields.

George Garvin Brown and John Forman founded the Brown-Forman Distillery in Louisville, Kentucky in 1870. From the beginning Brown-Forman marketed Old Forester bourbon. Before Brown and Forman marketed its own brand, bourbon had been sold to taverns in barrels. The bartenders were responsible for decanting the barreled alcohol into special bottles with the name of the tavern on the label. Brown poured the bourbon into bottles at the distillery, he corked and sealed the bottles, labelled them, and warned taverns not to buy the bourbon if the seals were broken. As an additional innovation, all of the labels were handwritten and included a guarantee on the quality of the bourbon. Old Forester sold well as a result of these innovations—but John Forman was dubious: in 1902 he sold his interest in the Brown-Forman Distillery because he believed that Brown-Forman's success would diminish as soon as the novelty of packaging began to fade. The Brown family purchased all of John Forman's interest in the company. From that time, the company has always produced top-grade alcohol, and has always had a Brown in charge.

In 1905 Brown-Forman Distillers Corporation continued their packaging innovations by bottling Old Forester in pear-shaped bottles. Old Forester's tavern sales increased significantly as a result. These increased sales led to a certain amount of bitterness among other distillers in Kentucky. Some competitors went so far as to slip iron nails into barrels of Brown-Forman whiskey to make it turn black.

Brown-Forman's bourbon was aged in barrels in large warehouses. At that time, warehouses were not heated, and labels on bourbon bore the expression "summers old," a reference to the fact that bourbon can age only in a warm climate. As a result, during the early decades of this century it took many years for the bourbon to be prepared for the market. Consequently, the word "old" became a common prefix in any brand name.

Old Forester, produced, marketed and distributed by Brown-Forman Distillers, continued to be very successful under the private ownership of the Brown family, which had no plans to diversify. All the company's advertising concentrated on marketing Old Forester, which it promoted as a product that would restore health: "Many, many times a day, eminent physicians say, Old Forester will life prolong and make old age hale and strong." Although this advertising was effective, Prohibition threatened to close Brown-Forman Distillers. To prevent this from happening, Brown-Forman went public just prior to Prohibition, but the Browns maintained control of the company.

The pre-Prohibition advertising had been valuable: the Brown-Forman company was one of four distillers permitted by the government to sell alcohol for medicinal purposes during Prohibition. The marketing of Old Forester had saved the company from the kind of downfall that other distillers suffered.

Brown-Forman spent the decade between the end of Prohibition and World War II readjusting to the fact that it could now legally sell Old Forester as bourbon. The bourbon now needed to be advertised as an alcoholic beverage rather than as a health tonic, in order to change the image it had acquired during Prohibition. However, the extensive advertising of the late 1930's and early 1940's was largely futile; the production of alcoholic beverages was once again severely curtailed during World War II. This time Old Forester could not be advertised as a health tonic since even this type of alcohol was now illegal. In spite of this development, the Brown family was not pessimistic about the future of their distillery. They investigated ways in which their alcohol could be used to help the war effort, and during the war Brown-Forman produced alcohol that was used in making both gun powder and rubber. The Browns also planned for the end of World War II and the future of the Brown-Forman company. They wanted their bourbon to have a headstart in the postwar market.

During World War II Brown-Forman's executive committee considered the fact that it took at least four years to age a marketable bourbon. They attempted to predict when the war would end and correctly decided on 1945. By starting the aging in 1941, they could have Old Forester ready for sale immediately following the war. As the competition's bourbon would not be marketable until 1949, Brown-Forman could monopolize the bourbon market for the first four post war years.

Because the executive committee's predictions were correct and resulted in impressive sales, the Brown-Forman executives decided to create a committee system of management. Finance, marketing, and production committees were created, in addition to the executive committee, to discuss and implement policies that could lead to the future success of the company.

In 1945 the management at Brown-Forman implemented an annual training course for 10 to 20 selected individuals from outside the firm. These individuals worked in all areas of the company, from the lowest to the highest positions. Approximately one half of them were then hired by other companies, and half continued with Brown-Forman in management positions. In this way, Brown-Forman created for itself an adequate supply of employees for management positions from outside the company itself. However, the remaining other employees were hired according to a policy of planned "nepotism."

Since George G. Brown founded Brown-Forman in 1870, the Browns have supported this type of company "nepotism." In 1945 the executives at Brown-Forman publicly stated that nepotism was good for their business and would be encouraged. They believed that if a father enjoyed working at Brown-Forman, his son would feel just as comfortable working there. Brown-Forman executives, as a policy, encourage the children and grandchildren of good employees to work for the company.

One of the effects of the limited production of alcohol during World War II was that postwar consumers favored whiskey blends which did not have a strong alcohol taste. The executives at Brown-Forman, however, did not pay attention to this new trend. They continued to sell bourbon with high alcohol content. By 1956 Brown-Forman had diversified into the rye whiskey business by purchasing the Jack Daniels distillery in Lynchburg, Tennessee. The acquisition cost $20 million, but this deal confirmed Brown-Forman's movement away from being a company that produced only bourbon. Later the company went on to purchase companies in other areas of the wine and spirit industry.

At the beginning of the 1960's, Brown-Forman continued its diversification program by purchasing the Joseph Garneau Company. This company imports scotch whiskies and European wines. Although Brown-Forman had not followed consumer trends after World War II when blends were popular, they succumbed to the high demand for scotch in the 1960's. By 1962 scotch held 9% of the liquor market, while the popularity of wine was increasing steadily.

Despite the diversifications, Brown-Forman portrayed itself as a medium-sized company. This stance worked in favor of the company during the 1960's. Before 1963, 80% of all hard liquor in the U.S. was sold by the four largest distilling companies, and the remaining 20% was sold by Brown-Forman, Heublein, James B. Beam Distilling Company, and the American Distilling Company. However, in 1963 these smaller companies increased their sales by 70% while the larger companies did not increase their sales at all. Consumer tastes during the 1960's favored the small, independent distilling companies. One reason for this change was that consumers in increasing numbers were switching from blended whiskey, popular after World War II, to straight whiskey.

In order to continue its expansion in the broader

market, during 1964 Brown-Forman purchased all outstanding stock of the Oertel Brewing Company, a small Louisville brewery. This company produced beer which was distributed in Kentucky, Tennessee, Indiana, Ohio, and Alabama. The brewery later became unprofitable, and Brown-Forman sold its interest in the company during the late 1960's. Yet the purchase of Oertel was proof of Brown-Forman's willingness to diversify into new areas of the alcohol market.

In 1966 Daniel L. Street was appointed president of Brown-Forman, the first time that a man outside of the Brown family had been president of the company. Street joined Brown-Forman as a lawyer in 1938 and advanced to the position of executive vice president in 1953. He continued Brown-Forman's program of diversification while president. In 1967 he authorized a merger with Quality Importers, Inc., which provided Brown-Forman with a "top scotch and good gin," according to Street. Quality Importers produces Ambassador Scotch, Ambassador Gin, and Old Bushmills Irish Whiskey. By 1968 sales had risen to $180 million as Brown-Forman continued to expand under the direction of Street.

Although Daniel Street effectively diversified Brown-Forman, William F. Lucas replaced him as president in 1969. Lucas, as well, was not part of the Brown family. He had joined Brown-Forman as an engineer in 1935 and advanced through the ranks. Lucas concentrated on marketing Brown-Forman's premium-priced products— President's Choice, Jack Daniels, Old Forester, and Early Times. Lucas did not spend large sums advertising Brown-Forman's low profit brands, because he felt that, as higher quality whiskey could be made for pennies more per fifth, and could be sold at a much higher price, only the expensive brands merited increased advertising expenditures.

In 1969 Lucas purchased the Bols line of liqueurs and Korbel champagne and brandy. These purchases expanded Brown-Forman's premium product line. In the early 1970's, as the demand for wine soared, Lucas initiated the purchase of Bolla and Cella Italian wines. This purchase was followed by the company's development of another product called Gold Pennant Canadian Whiskey. This whiskey was designed especially for women. Each bottle sold was accompanied by a horoscope pamphlet with "love potion" recipes for each astrological sign.

Lucas then bought six year old barrel-stored whiskey from Publicker Industries. In the 1960's Publicker had decided to make light whiskey but had later, when it was unsuccessful, reversed this decision. Lucas used Publicker's misfortune to Brown-Forman's advantage by purchasing their light whiskey, triple filtering it, and marketing the clear 80 proof product. Light whiskey is a clear beverage because it is aged in used barrels that have already given color to the whiskey previously stored in them. The clear whiskey is then distilled at a higher proof so it is lighter in taste. The term "light whiskey" actually refers to the type or body of the whiskey and not to its color.

In December of 1970 Schenley Industries, National Distillers and Chemical Corporation, and American Distilling Company filed an injunction against Brown-Forman to bar introduction of Brown-Forman's light whiskey called Frost 8/80. There was insufficient evidence for a ruling, and the injunction hearing was denied.

Under government restrictions light whiskey was not permitted to be marketed until July of 1972. Although Brown-Forman's light whiskey was distributed before it was allowed to be, Brown-Forman's competition dropped its suit because Frost 8/80 was already on the market. As a result, Brown-Forman was free to advertise its new product as a "dry, white whiskey" with which "the possibilities are endless." By advertising the whiskey as easily combining with any mixers, Brown-Forman tried to capture a share of the vodka and lighter Canadian whiskey market. The difficulty was that consumers did not buy Frost 8/80; they were used to drinking whiskey with color and, moreover, they could not associate Frost 8/80 with identically colored vodka: the flavors were different.

By 1973, $6 million had been invested in Frost 8/80 without a profitable return. Brown-Forman had extensively researched the popularity of a white whiskey and had received positive consumer response in various areas of the United States. However, consumers were confused by the company's advertising promotions and did not purchase the product. The extensive market research which Lucas had consulted before distributing Frost 8/80 had been incorrect.

Although light whiskey was not successful, Lucas still believed that American tastes were turning to lighter alcoholic drinks. For this reason, in 1971, Lucas contacted Lester Abdson and Oscar Getz who owned Barton Brands of Canada. Barton Brands bottled Canadian Mist, a blended whiskey. Brown-Forman could not purchase the entire company because of strict antitrust laws, so Lucas negotiated an agreement with Getz and Abdson to buy Canadian Mist and its distillery without buying the entire company. (This was the first time that a major brand of liquor was sold separately from the remainder of the company.) Lucas' determination to satisfy the American taste for lighter drinks was not diminished by the strict antitrust laws or the failure of Frost 8/80. By 1973 sales of such products had significantly increased.

Brown-Forman's success dwindled in the late 1970's as the bourbon market declined. Lucas moved aggressively to concentrate on faster growing segments of the alcoholic beverage market. In 1979 Brown-Forman spent $35 million in advertising its full line of alcoholic products. Lucas significantly increased Brown-Forman's wine and liqueur revenue to 22% of total sales. Most importantly, in 1979 Lucas purchased privately held Southern Comfort for $90 million. This purchase provided Brown-Forman with greater access to foreign markets since one-fifth of Southern Comfort sales were overseas.

The acquisitions of Southern Comfort and Jack Daniels were similar because both companies were small and privately held. Also, each company had developed a distinctive character for their single product. Unlike Jack Daniels, Southern Comfort is a liqueur and does not need to be aged. It can be produced and sold at a much faster rate. Before the Brown-Forman acquisition, Southern Comfort was already the number one selling liqueur. Brown-Forman simply enhanced its success. The company

was equally successful with Jack Daniels: From 1970 to 1979 Brown-Forman tripled Jack Daniels' sales to 1.7 million cases by creating the image of a quaint distillery nestled in a Tennessee hollow.

In 1979, W.L. Lyons Brown, Jr. was appointed president of Brown-Forman. He is the great grandson of George Garvin Brown who founded Brown-Forman in 1870. After two presidents who were not related to the Brown family, W.L. Lyons Brown, Jr. re-established the tradition of a Brown at the head of the business. The restoration of the family was a good omen: Brown-Forman advanced to sixth in the alcohol industry and became the fastest growing full-line distiller.

Despite overall growth, the company experienced a setback with Southern Comfort in 1982; as competition increased, the share held by Southern Comfort in the market decreased. Brown-Forman responded to this weakening market share with another innovative idea, one and three-quarter liter plastic bottles to replace the one-half gallon glass bottles. After petitioning the Bureau of Alcohol, Tobacco, and Firearms, the company was granted permission to begin using the plastic bottle in 1983. However, later tests indicated that a loose molecule of plastic could contaminate the alcohol, and the container was soon prohibited.

In 1983, Brown-Forman acquired Lenox Inc., even though Lenox fervently fought the acquisition. Lenox makes crystal, china, giftware, and luggage, products that presented special problems for Brown-Forman. Drastically different methods of distribution were needed to market the Lenox products. Yet management at Brown-Forman understood the need for a transition. This was apparent in their name change from Brown-Forman Distillers Corporation to Brown-Forman Corporation in 1984. Nevertheless, the company's diversification did not exclude the acquisition of other alcoholic products; Brown-Forman bought California Cooler Inc. in 1985 for $63 million.

In the foreseeable future Brown-Forman will continue to diversify into fields which are not associated with the liquor industry. Such diversification is evidence of Brown-Forman's management flexibility. And, as the list of Brown-Forman's subsidiaries increases, the sales of this company should also continue rise.

Principal Subsidiaries: Jack Daniel Distillery, Lem Motlow, Prop. Inc.; Canadian Mist Distillers, Ltd.; Blue Grass Cooperage Co.; Jos. Garneau Co.; Southern Comfort Corp.; Mt. Eagle Corp.; B-F Spirits, Ltd.; Brown-Forman International Ltd.; Thoroughbed Plastics Corp.; Clintock Ltd.; Longworth Ltd.; Lenox Inc.; Early Times Distillers Co.; Art Carved Class Rings; Art Carved/Keepsake; Lenox Awards; Lenox Candles; Lenox China; Lenox Collections; Lenox Crystal; Lenox Gallery of Gifts.

Further Reading: *Nothing Better in the Market: Brown-Forman's Century of Quality 1870–1970* edited by John Pearce, Louisville, Newcomen Society, 1970.

CARLTON AND UNITED BREWERIES LTD.

16 Bouverie Street
Carlton, Victoria 3053
Australia
(03) 342–5511

Wholly-owned subsidiary of Elders IXL Limited
Incorporated: 1907
Employees: 6,000
Sales: A$1.585 billion (US$1.055 billion)

As manufacturers of the extremely popular Foster's Lager, Carlton and United Breweries have achieved impressive sales both in and outside Australia. Although Foster's export history dates back to 1901, the company's major international market thrust initiated in the 1970's is realizing its full potential only at the present time. Moreover, since becoming a subsidiary in 1986 of Elders IXL Limited, an Australian conglomerate, the brewery has seen its worldwide marketing position significantly enhanced. Today, sales of Foster's ranks it in the top ten of the world's most successful beers.

Carlton's growth is synonymous with the growth of Australia. During the gold rush era of the 1850's inhabitants of Victoria were forced to confine their drinking to what was available: only English style ale, first imported and then brewed locally, was available to the growing population of fortune seekers and frontier people. Served at room temperature, the traditional ale was ill-suited to the warm climate. Immigrant tastes, however, could not be mollified for long; soon the market expanded to include locally brewed and more appropriate lagers.

Among the early entrepreneurs were two immigrant brothers, W.M. and R.R. Foster. Together in 1888 they built a modern lager brewery in the Melbourne suburb of Collingwood. To capitalize on the thirst-quenching quality of their product, the Foster brothers made sure the lager was served in its proper chilled form. They achieved this through the marketing ploy of supplying free ice with each sale.

Soon afterwards, they brought over a refrigeration engineer from New York to install an ice-making machine alongside the brewery. Before long a cold serving of Foster's lager could be purchased in many of Victoria's numerous hotels. Eventually, consumers of lager outnumbered patrons of traditional ale; the Foster brothers are given much of the credit for winning over local tastes.

In 1907 the Foster company joined an amalgamation of six Melbourne breweries to form the Carlton and United Breweries Proprietary Limited, the forerunner of Australia's largest brewery. The founding partners included in the merger were the Victoria, Carlton, Castlemaine, McCracken's, Shamrock and Foster's companies. Today several of these labels continue to exist in Carlton's product line, yet Foster's remains the most popular of these brands.

In 1901 Australian soldiers serving in the Boer War in South Africa could enjoy the hometown taste of Foster's. This marked the first time the lager was exported outside Australia. During World War I and II Australian troops overseas spread the name of Foster's throughout the world. It is said that Australian servicemen and women revealed their nationality through their loyalty to Foster's.

Despite the lager's growing international fame, it was not until the 1970's that the company embarked on concerted marketing policy to enhance Foster's worldwide popularity. Among the many cities where the beer could be found were London, Hong Kong, and Manama, Bahrain. Foster's marketing network was further enhanced by an agreement with Watney Mann and Truman Brewers, the large British brewery, to sell Foster's in all of its 12,000 United Kingdom outlets. Today Carlton's lager can be found in 80 countries. The U.S. and British sales of Foster's recently benefited from a popular advertisement campaign. Actor and comedian Paul Hogan endorses the product using Australian colloquialisms and examples of local custom.

Carlton Breweries has long been recognized for its commitment to quality. In the earliest years, the Foster brothers hired a German-American brew-master to supervise operations at the new facility. The yeast strain that is said to give Carlton's products their unique flavor was brought over from Europe in the 1920's. During World War II all the original cultures were destroyed except one batch in Melbourne. Today the surviving Melbourne strain is kept active in the company's control laboratory.

Carlton's reputation as quality brewers increased with the development of their own hop variety. Unsatisfied with imported strains, Carlton scientists created the "Pride of Ringwood" variety. Today this variety is recognized around the world for its flavor. Carlton's advanced technology achieved even wider fame with their development of an innovative method for extracting hops.

Further innovative achievements include their advancement of malt technology and their application of uses for genetic engineering. Of all Carlton's research and development activities, yeast genetics appears to be the one with the most potential. Whereas in the past the company was compelled to import technical knowledge, breweries around the world now turn to Carlton for its expertise.

Carlton's brewing stages begin with a germination process to convert barley into malt. Next the malt is stored in grist bins, mixed with hot water, and transferred into a mash "tun" (tank) where it is allowed to stand. Here the temperature changes the starch to fermentable sugar. The mixture is then passed to a lauter tun where the liquid is separated from the residue. This liquid, called brewing "wort," is placed in a kettle where sugars are added. The whole mixture is allowed to boil, coagulating the proteins into "trub." The trub is then removed from the wort.

Fermentation begins with the chilling of the wort in order to allow the yeast to grow. This process continues until all fermentable sugars are consumed. The fermenter is then chilled to 4°C causing the yeast to drop to the bottom of the vessel. This is removed and the beer is placed in a storage vessel. After it is cooled to 1°C, the hop concentrate is added. The beer is then stored for a specified period of time. After storage the beer is passed through a filter and packaged into bottles and cans.

Carlton's products are recognized for their consistency in taste and long shelf-life. To guarantee quality, 45 brewers, 40 engineering specialists, and 80 scientists and technicians oversee the brewing process.

Today Carlton's achievements are a source of pride to Australians. The product line celebrates the diversity of local tastes by including a wide range of regional beers. The company is recognized for its commitment to environmental protection and the Australian economy. A recycling effort to recover bottles and cans finds the company working alongside many community organizations. Carlton is also a sponsor of many sports activities and social welfare programs.

In 1983 the largest takeover in Australian history occurred when Carlton and United Breweries was absorbed by the Australian conglomerate Elders IXL Limited. Elders' operations are divided into five major groups, including brewing, agribusiness, international, finance and Elders resources. In addition to managing Carlton's activities, the brewing group operates a hotel business, a wine and spirits division, and a beer marketing organization. In 1986 the group's brewing business was augmented by its purchase of the Courage Brewing Group in the United Kingdom and the Canadian company Carling O'Keefe Limited.

Carlton's market position has been enhanced by its subsidiary status. With Elders' financial backing the brewing company has now launched a highly effective international marketing campaign. As Carlton's products grow in popularity in worldwide markets, Foster's lager remains the company's most important brand.

Principal Subsidiaries: Carlton Brewery Pty. Ltd.; Carlton & United Breweries (Queensland) Ltd.; Carlton & United Breweries (Rockhampton) Pty. Ltd.; Corner Pty. Ltd.; Court House Hotel Pty. Ltd.; C.U.B. Fibre Containers Pty. Ltd.; Derrimut Hotel Pty. Ltd.; Duke of Wellington Hotel Pty. Ltd.; Durham Hotel Pty. Ltd.; Edinburgh Hotel Pty. Ltd.; Edwardes Lake Hotel Pty. Ltd.; Joseph Pease (Pty.) Ltd.; Joseph Pease (Cairns) Pty. Ltd.; London House Pty. Ltd.; Marrara Hotel Pty. Ltd.; Max Cohn & Co. Pty. Ltd.; Melbourne Brewery Co. Pty. Ltd.; Middlesex Hotel Pty. Ltd.; Moorabbin Hotel Pty. Ltd.; Norfolk Hotel Pty. Ltd.; N.T. Brewery Pty. Ltd.; Pease Investments Pty. Ltd.; Penang Pty. Ltd.; Petroleum Distributors Pty. Ltd.; Production Investments Pty. Ltd.; Queensland Brewery Pty. Ltd.; Royarc Pty. Ltd.; Samuel Allen & Sons Ltd. (91.4%); The Castlemaine Brewery Co. Melbourne Pty. Ltd.; The Foster Brewing Co. Pty. Ltd.; The Manufacturers' Bottle Co. of Victoria Pty. Ltd.; The Oakleigh Pty. Ltd.; The Shamrock Brewing Co. Pty. Ltd.; Victoria Brewery Pty. Ltd.

CERVECERIA POLAR

Apartado 2331
Carmelitas Zona 101
Caracas
Venezuela 1070
239-68-11

Private Company
Incorporated: 1940
Employees: 3,600
Sales: B 13.25 billion (US$ 1.767 billion)

Little-known Cerveceria Polar, a Venezuelan brewing company, supplies 85% of that nation's beer. In just under 50 years, Polar has grown from a small family operation to become Venezuela's largest private company. It now ranks 13th among the world's breweries.

Dr. Lorenzo Mendoza Fleury, a Venezuelan lawyer, inherited a soap factory from his family during the late 1930's. Although this factory proved to be a financial failure, Fleury established a business style worthy of future success; he soon sold the soap factory in pursuit of a more profitable industry. The search ended in 1941 when he established a brewery in Antimano, a suburb of Caracas. The rapid expansion that followed is the legacy of Mendoza Fleury's far-sighted decision.

The Antimano facility enjoyed sufficient success that by 1950 a second brewery, Cerveceria de Oriente, could be established in the Venezuelan city of Barcelona. A year later production demand required the construction of a new brewery with large scale capacity. Also located in Caracas, this establishment eventually became the headquarters for all Polar's activities. The company trademark, a polar bear looking across a body of blue water, emerged from this facility.

By 1960, at a time when large Venezuelan corporations lacked confidence in the country's beleaguered economy and thus turned their attention to overseas markets, Cerveceria Polar decided instead to expand at home. This decision marked a significant turning point in establishing Polar as the pre-eminent Venezuelan brewery. Soon Cerveceria Modelo, the company's newest brewery, was in operation in Maracaibo in Western Venezuela.

During the following decade Cerveceria Polar captured 50% of the domestic market. The continual pursuit of product stability and production quality required adaptation to climatic conditions and the eventual automation of all Polar's activities.

Beer sales tripled during the 1970's. To maximize existing capacity, the company introduced a number of improvements in the production process. They included the implementation of high-gravity brewing, first fermenting wort of 14% extract and then correcting this to 11.3% extract. Three week cycles of fermentation and storage followed this process. Tight production schedules were maintained.

By the end of the decade yet another brewery, Cerveceria Polar del Centro, began operations in the city of San Joaquin. A major innovation, signifying a technological breakthrough in the brewing process, was initiated at this site: the San Joaquin facility became the first brewery in the world to use a one-tank system with cylinder-conical tanks from the start of production. The efficiency of the process marked the end for the company of the kind of beer supply shortages which had occurred in the past. The small Antimano brewery now outlived its usefulness and was duly closed.

Cerveceria Polar's brewing process begins with water, supplied by municipal sources, that is passed through sand and activated carbon filters and then decarbonated by weak-acid ion exchangers. Since Venezuela's climate precludes the cultivation of malt or hops, these supplies are imported from countries as diverse as Canada, Finland, Czechoslovakia, and Australia. Pre-cooked rice flakes are used as an adjunct, and wort is extracted by the infusion mashing method and lautering. Flavor stability is guaranteed through the separation of the hot trub.

The fermentation process follows over the next 21 days. Except at the Caracas brewery, where conventional fermentation continues, all other Polar facilities use cylinder-conical tanks. Fermentation occurs at 11° to 14°C. Then after reducing total diacetyl to under .1 mg/l, the beer is cooled until it reaches 1°C.

Automation at the Cerveceria Polar breweries takes the form of milling, mashing, lautering and wort boiling. Later, automation is used for filtration and cleaning. The company's future plans to automate the one-tank fermentation process promises to increase production capacity. The bottling process, using both European and American equipment, involves two different size glass bottles and standard aluminum cans. Once in the containers the beer is pasteurized in tunnel pasteurizers.

Cerveceria Polar conducts its operations with careful attention to water conservation and environmental protection—the recycling of condensates, the use of air coolants for diesel engines, and the condensation of exhaust steam. Waste water is treated with activated sludge to eliminate 95% of the organic load. In an attempt to extend their environmental activities, the company has recently begun to demineralized treated waste so that it can be reused for indirect processes. Polar works in close cooperation with Venezuelan universities in conducting research on uses for sludge produced in waste water treatment. Possible uses for the sludge range from improving sandy soils to forming an ingredient in cattle feed.

Research and development at Polar concentrates on process innovation. Numerous laboratory tests involve investigations into methods of improving beer flavor stability. Venezuela's climate subjects the country to year-round sunshine; high temperatures cause product variability. At Polar laboratories a method was devised to deal with this problem peculiar to tropical climates. A simple means of measuring oxygen content in the bottles eliminated flavor instability. The method has subsequently been adopted by other breweries around the world.

Distribution of Polar products takes place under the direction of eight wholly-owned regional distributors, and Polar beer can be found in even the most remote regions of Venezuela. Although transportation conditions are at times precarious, Polar has succeeded in the consistent delivery of its products.

Polar also operates its own in-house advertising agency, Cadesa, which directs a highly effective campaign using patriotic messages. A popular example is the short film entitled, "Traveling with Polar." Here viewers share in the celebration of images of national scenery and cultural heritage.

By 1984 Cerveceria Polar controlled an 85% share of its domestic marketplace. New areas of expansion include the production of alcohol-free malt beverages and the penetration of overseas markets. The establishment of a food division has signalled Polar's attempt to become a more diversified business. Prior to their use of rice flakes, the company had used imported cornflakes as an adjunct to the brewing process. Corn, however, is an indigenous crop to Venezuela. Instead of continuing to import, Polar purchased a small local corn mill to produce cornflakes. This operation was the precursor of Polar's food divisions which now produces corn oil, animal feed, and the traditional Venezuelan "arepa." Today, over 500,000 tons of corn are processed annually. The company has subsequently expanded into other agricultural activities, including poultry farms, pork production and slaughterhouses.

Over the course of its history Polar has acquired several subsidiaries to augment company growth—Superenvases Envalic, a manufacturer of two-piece aluminum cans; Plasticos Metalgrafica, a manufacturer of plastic beer cases; and Industria Metalgrafica, producers of crown corks. All three of these subsidiaries supply products not only to Polar but also to industry competitors.

Whether Polar will always remain a private company remains to be seen. The need for capital to support Polar's growing activities might encourage the public listing of shares. In the meantime, the company continues to capture a majority of Venezuela's market for beer. All accounts indicate that Cerveceria Polar will maintain this strong market share in the future.

Principal Subsidiaries: H.A.T., C.A.; Cadesa; Transpolar, C.A.; C.A. Inversora Exitos 2000; Plasticos Metalgrafica S.A.; Industria Metalgrafica; Superenvases Envalic, C.A.; Fabrimonca, San Joaquin; C.A. Suplidora Venezolana.

THE COCA-COLA COMPANY

310 North Avenue, NW
Atlanta, Georgia 30313
U.S.A.
(404) 676-2121

Public Company
Incorporated: September 5, 1919
Employees: 38,520
Sales: $8.669 billion
Market Value: $17,929 billion
Stock Index: New York Frankfurt Zurich Basle

The ubiquity of Coca-Cola in the world today makes it difficult to comprehend that the beverage and the company that produces it have a definite history. Now, a century after its creation, Coca-Cola is sold in approximately 140 countries and is advertised in over 80 different languages. Its red and white trademark is probably the best-known trademark on earth. And the Coca-Cola Company, the largest soft drink company in the world, which for a long time was a one-product concern, has in recent decades diversified into such industries as food products, entertainment, and clothing.

The inventor of Coca-Cola, Dr. John Styth Pemberton, came to Atlanta from Columbus, Georgia in 1869. Since 1885, when he set up a chemical laboratory and went into the patent medicine business, Atlanta has been the headquarters of the Coca-Cola Company. Pemberton invented such products as Indian Queen hair dye, Gingerine, and Triplex liver pills. In 1886 he concocted a mixture of sugar, water, and extracts of the coca leaf and the kola nut. He added caffeine to the resulting syrup so that it could be marketed as a headache remedy. Through his research Pemberton arrived at the conclusion that this medication was capable of relieving indigestion and exhaustion in addition to being refreshing and exhilarating.

The doctor and his business partners could not decide whether to market the mixture as a medicine or to extol its flavor for its own sake. In *Coca-Cola: An Illustrated History*, Pat Watters cites a Coca-Cola label from 1887 which states that the drink, "makes not only a delicious . . . and invigorating beverage . . . but a valuable Brain Tonic and a cure for all nervous affections." The label also claims that "the peculiar flavor of Coca-Cola delights every palate; it is dispensed from the soda fountain in the same manner as any fruit syrup."

The first newspaper advertisement for Coca-Cola appeared exactly three weeks after the first batch of syrup was produced, and the famous trademark, white Spenserian script on a red background, made its debut at about this time.

Coca-Cola was not, however, immediately successful. During its first year in existence Pemberton and his partners spent $73.96 advertising this unique beverage, and made a mere $50.00 from sales. The combined pressures of poor business and ill health led Pemberton to sell two-thirds of his business in early 1888. By 1891 a successful druggist named Asa G. Candler owned the entire enterprise; it had cost him $2,300 to purchase the business. Dr. Pemberton, who died three years earlier, was never to know the enormous success his invention would have in the coming century.

Asa Candler, a religious man with excellent business sense, infused the enterprise with his personality. Candler became a notable philanthropist, incidentally associating the name of Coca-Cola with social awareness. He was also an integral part of Atlanta both as a citizen and as a leader. Candler endowed Emory University and its Wesley Memorial Hospital with more than $8 million. Indeed, the University could not have come into existence without his aid. In 1907 he prevented a real estate panic in Atlanta by purchasing $1 million worth of homes and reselling them to people of moderate income at affordable prices. During World War I Candler helped to avert a cotton crisis by using his growing wealth to stabilize the market. After he stepped down as the president of Coca-Cola he became the mayor of Atlanta, and introduced such reforms as motorizing the fire department and augmenting the water system with his private funds.

Under Candler's leadership, which spanned a 26 year period, the Coca-Cola Company grew quickly. Between 1888 and 1907 the factory and offices of the business were moved to eight different buildings in order to keep up with the company's growth and expansion. As head of the company, Candler was most concerned with the quality and promotion of his product. He was particularly concerned with production of the syrup, which was boiled in kettles over a furnace and stirred by hand with large wooden paddles; in fact, he improved Pemberton's formula with the help of a chemist, a pharmacist and a prescriptionist. In 1901, responding to complaints about the presence of minute amounts of cocaine in the Coca-Cola syrup, Candler devised the means to remove all traces of the substance. By 1905 the syrup was completely free of cocaine.

In 1892 the newly incorporated Coca-Cola Company allocated $11,401 for advertising its drink. Advertising materials included signs, free-sample tickets, and premiums such as ornate soda fountain urns, clocks, and stained-glass lampshades, all with the words "Coca-Cola" engraved upon them. These early advertising strategies initiated the most extensive promotional campaign for one product in history. Salesmen traveled the entire country selling the company's syrup, and by 1895 Coca-Cola was being sold and consumed in every state in America. Soon it was available in some Canadian cities and in Honolulu, and plans were underway for its introduction into Mexico. By the time Asa Candler left the company, Coke had also been sold in Cuba, Jamaica, Germany, Bermuda, Puerto Rico, the Philippines, France, and England.

An event which had an enormous impact on the future and very nature of the company was the agreement made between Candler and two young lawyers that allowed them to bottle and sell Coca-Cola throughout the United States: the first bottling franchise had been established. Three years later, in 1904, the one millionth gallon of Coca-Cola syrup had been sold. In 1916 the now universally recognized, uniquely-shaped Coke bottle was invented. The management of all company advertising was assigned to the D'Arcy Advertising Agency, and the advertising budget had grown to $1 million by 1911. During this time all claims for the medicinal properties of Coca-Cola were quietly dropped from its advertisements.

World War I and the ensuing sugar rationing measures slowed down the growth of the company, but the pressure of coal rations led Candler's son, Charles Howard, to invent a process whereby the sugar and water could be mixed without using heat. This process saved the cost of fuel, relieved the company of the need for a boiler, and saved a great amount of time: there was now no need for the syrup to go through a cooling period. This method of mixing is still in use today.

Although Candler was fond of his company, he became disillusioned with it in 1916 and retired. One of the reasons for this decision was the new tax laws which, in Candler's words, did not allow for "the accumulation of surplus in excess of the amount necessary for profitable and safe conduct of our particular business." (It has also been suggested that Candler refused to implement the modernization of company facilities.)

Robert Winship Woodruff became president of the company in 1923 at the age of 33. His father had purchased it from the Candler family in 1919 for $25 million, and the company went public in the same year at $40 a share. After leaving college before graduation, Woodruff held various jobs, eventually becoming the Atlanta branch manager and then the vice-president of an Atlanta motor company, before becoming the president of Coca-Cola.

Having entered the company at a time when its affairs were quite tumultuous, Woodruff worked rapidly to improve Coca Cola's financial condition. In addition to low sales figures in 1922, he had to face the problem of animosity toward the company on the part of the bottlers as a result of an imprudent sugar purchase that management had made. This raised the price of the syrup and angered the bottlers. Woodruff was aided in particular by two men, Harrison Jones and Harold Hirsch, who were adept at maintaining good relations between the company and its bottling franchises.

Woodruff set to work improving the sales department; he emphasized quality control, and began advertising and promotional campaigns that were far more sophisticated than those of the past. He established a research department that became a pioneering market research agency. He also worked hard to provide his customers with the latest in technological developments that would facilitate their selling Coca-Cola to the public, and he labored to increase efficiency at every step of the production process so as to raise the percentage of profit from every sale of Coca-Cola syrup.

Through the 1920's and 1930's such developments as the six-pack carton of Coke, which encouraged shoppers to purchase the drink for home consumption, coin-operated vending machines in the workplace, and the cooler designed by John Stanton expanded the domestic market considerably. And, by the end of 1930, as a result of the company's quality control efforts, Coca-Cola tasted exactly the same everywhere.

Considered slightly eccentric, Woodruff was a fair employer and an admired philanthropist. In 1937 he donated $50,000 to Emory University for a cancer diagnosis and treatment center, and over the years gave more than $100 million to the clinic. He donated $8 million for the construction of the Atlanta Memorial Arts Center. Under his leadership the Coca-Cola Company pioneered such company benefits as group life insurance and group accident and health policies, and in 1948 introduced a retirement program.

Woodruff was to see the Coca-Cola Company through an era marked by important and varied events. Even after the stock market crashed and during the depression the company did not suffer—the result of Woodruff's cost-cutting measures. When Prohibition was repealed, Coca-Cola continued to experience rising sales. However, it was World War II that catapulted Coca-Cola into the world market and made it one of America's first multinational companies.

Woodruff and Archie Lee of the D'Arcy Advertising Agency worked to equate Coca-Cola with the American way of life. Advertisements had, in Candler's era, been targeted at the wealthy population. In Woodruff's time the advertising was aimed at all Americans. By early 1950 blacks were featured in advertisements, and by the mid-1950's there was an increase in advertising targeted at other minority groups. Advertising never reflected the problems of the world, only the good and happy life. Radio advertising began in 1927, and through the years Coca-Cola sponsored many musical programs. During World War II Woodruff announced that every man in uniform would be able to get a bottle of Coke for five cents no matter what the cost to the company. This was, intentionally or not, an extremely successful marketing maneuver, and provided Coke with good publicity. In 1943, at the request of General Eisenhower, Coca-Cola plants were set up near the fighting fronts in North Africa and eventually throughout Europe in order to help increase the morale of American soldiers. Thus, Coca-Cola was introduced into the world market.

Coke was available in Germany prior to the war, but its survival there during the war years was due to a man named Max Keith who kept the company going even when there was little Coca-Cola syrup available. Keith developed his own soft drink, using ingredients available to him, and called his beverage Fanta. By selling this beverage he kept the enterprise intact until after the war. When the war was over the company continued to market Fanta. By 1944 the Coca-Cola company had sold one billion gallons of syrup, by 1953 two billion gallons had been sold, and by 1969 the company had sold six billion gallons.

The years from after World War II to 1980 were years of

extensive and rapid change. Although Woodruff stepped down officially in 1955, he still exerted a great amount of influence on the company over the coming years. There was a series of chairmen and presidents to follow before the next major figure, J. Paul Austin, took the helm in 1970; he was followed by Roberto Goizueta in 1981. In 1956, after 50 years with the D'Arcy Advertising Agency, the Coca-Cola Company turned its accounts over to McKann-Ericson and began enormous promotional campaigns. The decade of the 1950's was a time of the greatest European expansion for the company. During this decade Coca-Cola opened approximately fifteen to twenty plants a year throughout the world.

The company also began to diversify extensively, beginning in 1960 when the Minute Maid Corporation merged with Coca-Cola. Four years later the Duncan Foods Corporation also merged with the company. In 1969 Coca-Cola acquired the Belmont Springs Water Company, Inc. which produces natural spring water and processed water for commercial and home use. The following year Aqua-Chem, Inc., producers of desalting machines and other such equipment, was acquired, and in 1977 Coca-Cola acquired the Taylor Wines Company and other wineries. These last two companies were sold later under Goizueta's leadership.

In addition to its diversification program, the Coca-Cola Company also expanded its product line. Fanta became available in the U.S. during 1960 and was followed by the introduction of Sprite, Tab and Fresca, along with diet versions of these drinks. One reason that Coca-Cola began to introduce new beverages during the 1960's was competition from Pepsi Cola. Pepsi's success also motivated the Coca-Cola Company to promote its beverage with the slogan "It's the Real Thing," a subtle, comparative form of advertising that the company had never before employed.

Things have not always run smoothly for Coca-Cola. When Coke was first introduced to France, the communist party, as well as conservative vineyard owners, did what they could to get the product removed from the country. They were unsuccessful. Swiss breweries also felt threatened, and spread rumors about the caffeine content of the drink. More consequential was the Arab boycott in 1967 which significantly hindered the company's relations with Israel. In 1970 the company was involved in a scandal in the United States when an NBC documentary reported on the bad housing and working conditions of Minute Maid farm laborers in Florida. In response, the company established a program that improved the workers' situation. In 1977 it was discovered that Coca-Cola, for various reasons, had made $1.3 million in illegal payments over a period of six years, mostly to executives and government officials in foreign countries.

During the 1970's, under the direction of chairman J. Paul Austin and president J. Lucian Smith, Coca-Cola was introduced in Russia as well as in China. To enter the China market, the company sponsored five scholarships for Chinese students at the Harvard Business School, and supported China's soccer and table-tennis teams. The beverage also became available in Egypt in 1979, after an absence there of 12 years. Austin strongly believed in free trade and opposed boycotts. He felt that business, in terms

of international relations, should be used to improve national economies, and could be a strong deterrent to war. Under Austin, Coca-Cola also started technological and educational programs in Third World countries in which it conducted business. For example, it introduced clean water technology, and sponsored sports programs in countries too poor to provide these benefits for themselves.

Austin's emphasis was on foreign expansion. Furthermore, under Austin management of the company became more specialized. Where Woodruff was aware of all facets of the company, Austin would delegate authority to various departments. He would, for example, give general approval to an advertising scheme, but would not review it personally. Smith was responsible for the everyday operations of the company, and Austin would, among other things, set policies, negotiate with foreign countries, and direct the company's relations with the U.S. government.

Roberto Goizueta became chairman in 1981 replacing Austin. Less than a year later he made two controversial decisions. First, he acquired Columbia Pictures for about $750 million in 1982. Goizueta thought that the entertainment field had good growth prospects, and that it would benefit from Coca-Cola's expertise in market research. Secondly, without much consumer research, Goizueta also introduced Diet Coke to the public, risking the well-guarded trademark that until then had stood only for the original formula. Something had to be done about the sluggish domestic sales of Coca-Cola and the intense competition presented by Pepsi. In 1950 Coke had outsold Pepsi by more than 5 to 1. By 1984 Pepsi had a 22.8% share of the market and Coke had a 21.6% share. Goizueta's decisions were correct. Diet Coke is presently American's number one diet soft drink, and Columbia Pictures has performed well.

In 1985 Goizueta took another chance. Based on information gathered from blind taste tests, Goizueta decided to reformulate the 99-year old drink in the hope of combating Pepsi's growing popularity. The move was not enthusiastically greeted by the American public. It appears that Goizueta did not take into account the public's emotional attachment to the name "Coca-Cola" and all that it stands for: stability, memories, and the idea of a "golden America." Within less than a year the company brought back the "old" Coke calling it Coca-Cola Classic. Coca-Cola continues to produce both brands (Classic Coke considerably outsells "new" Coke), and the company has gained back some of its lost share.

In September of 1987 Coca-Cola agreed to sell its entertainment business to Tri-Star Pictures, which was approximately 30% owned by Coca-Cola. In return, Coca-Cola's interest in Tri-Star was increased to 80%. Coca-Cola's holding in Tri-Star will be distributed as a special dividend to Coca-Cola shareholders until the company's interest is reduced to 49%. It is expected that Tri-Star will then change its name to Columbia Pictures Entertainment, and seek its own listing on the New York Stock Exchange.

The sale of Columbia to Tri-Star was regarded by financial analysts as an attempt to increase the profitability of Coca-Cola's entertainment company so that it could itself fund other acquisitions.

In an article in the *New York Times* during 1984 Goizueta stated that he saw Coke's challenge as "continuing the growth in profits of highly successful main businesses, and (those) it may choose to enter, at a rate substantially in excess of inflation, in order to give shareholders an above average total return on their investment." Goizueta projected that by 1990 his new strategy would nearly double the company's net income to $1 billion.

Principal Subsidiaries: Caribbean Refrescos, Inc.; Coca-Cola Bottling Company of Baltimore; Coca-Cola Bottling Enterprises, Inc.; Coca-Cola Bottling Company of California; Atlanta Coca-Cola Bottling Company; Coca-Cola Bottling Company of New England; Coca-Cola Bottling Company of Michigan; Ore-Cal Coca-Cola Bottling Co.; Coca-Cola Interamerican Corp.; L Communications; P Communications; Tandem Acquisition Corp.; Coca-Cola Export Corp.; Refreshment Sales Inc. The company also lists subsidiaries in the following countries: Argentina, Brazil, Canada, Cayman Islands, Colombia, West Germany, Italy, Japan, Spain, and the United Kingdom.

Further Reading: *Asa Griggs Candler* by Charles Howard Candler, Atlanta, Emory University, 1950; *The Big Drink: The Story of Coca-Cola* by Ely Jacques Kahn, New York, Random House, 1960; *Coca-Cola* by Pat Watters, New York, Doubleday, 1978; *The Cola Wars* by J.C. Louis and Harvey Z. Yazijian, New York, Everett House, 1980; *The Corporate Warriors: Six Classic Cases in American Business* by Douglas K. Ramsey, Boston, Houghton Mifflin, 1987.

Coors

ADOLPH COORS COMPANY

12th and Ford Streets
Golden, Colorado 80401
U.S.A.
(303) 279-6565

Public Company
Incorporated: June 12, 1913
Employees: 10,000
Sales: $1.315 billion
Market Value: $1.027 billion
Stock Index: NASDAQ

The Coors family has owned and operated this American brewery for more than 100 years, and Coors has the distinction of being the only family brewery to survive the amalgamation process of the 1960's intact. Coors is also one of very few brewing companies in the enviable position of having never accumulated any long-term debt.

Adolph Herman Joseph Coors founded the business in 1873 after having come to America from Germany in 1868 and settling in Colorado. Coors formed a partnership with Jacob Schueler: Coors contributed $2,000 to the endeavor, while Schueler provided $18,000. In May of 1880 Coors bought out Schueler and, since that time, the Coors brewery of Golden, Colorado has remained within the family.

The Coors family seems always to have had the ability to brew beer that people enjoy. The fledgling brewery's sales increased steadily. In 1887 the brewery sold 7,049 barrels of beer (31 gallons per barrel). Three years later that figure more than doubled, reaching 17,600 barrels. Over the years Adolph Coors slowly expanded his market. By the time he officially incorporated his brewery as the "Adolph Coors Brewing and Manufacturing Company," Coors' beer was being distributed throughout Colorado.

Even at this early point in the company's history, the distinctive Coors philosophy was emerging. The main tenets of this philosophy have been followed by three successive generations of Coors beermakers, each generation further refining the knowledge inherited from the preceding generation. Adolph Herman Joseph Coors believed in sparing no effort or expense in producing the best beer possible. To this end, he believed that only Colorado spring water was good enough for his beer. He also commissioned farmers to grow the barley and hops that he needed for his brewing process. The second tenet of the philosophy was that his family always came first, without exception. The Coors family brewery has remain-ed a tight-knit, protective and almost secretive enterprise. The last tenet is that "a good beer sells itself." Until 1980 Coors spent substantially less on advertising than any other brewer.

Prohibition came early to Colorado. In 1916 the Colorado legislature passed a law banning the production and consumption of alcoholic beverages within the state. Obviously, Prohibition was detrimental to Adolph Coors' brewery; however, some business historians would say the company was strengthened by it. During Prohibition the company's name was changed to its present one, the "Adolph Coors Company." This change in name reflected a change in Coors' product line. From 1916 through 1933 the company produced "near beer," with an alcohol content of less than 3%, and malted milk. In addition, it was during this time that Adolph Coors and his son, Adolph Jr., diversified the company, creating what was eventually to become a small-scale vertical monopoly: Coors owned all that it needed to produce its beer, from the oil wells that created the energy necessary to run the brewery to the farms that grew the ingredients, and from the bottling plant that made the containers to the trucks used for distribution. This expansion was financed entirely with family money.

The repeal of Prohibition did not result in a dramatic sales increase for Coors as it did for many other producers of alcoholic beverages. Instead, the Adolph Coors Company, now under the direction of Adolph Jr., expanded its market slowly. While breweries in the East and Midwest were aggressively competing with each other with advertising and sponsorship of sports events, trying anything to increase their market shares, Coors hardly advertised at all. In 1970 Coors spent 60¢ to 70¢ per barrel on advertising, while its competition spent as much as $3.50 per barrel. Only in the 1980's has Coors changed its advertising policy.

If Coors growth and development in the decades following the repeal of Prohibition is unexciting compared to that of companies such as Anheuser-Busch and Miller, it remains impressive just the same. In 1933 Coors sold 123,000 barrels of beer. Just 30 years later that number had increased more than 20 times to 3.5 million barrels. Until 1959 Coors had never been among the top 15 brewers in the country. Sales of 1.649 million barrels in 1959 put Coors in 14th place. A year later, Coors reached 11th place. By 1969, Coors had moved up to seventh place. In 1973, Coors position had peaked at number four. What makes such growth impressive is that Coors managed its climb to the top when "regional" breweries were being squeezed out of the market. In 1947 there were 450 independent breweries. By 1967 that number had dwindled to 120.

So how did Coors grow 1500% between 1947 and 1967, with only one product, made in a single brewery, and sold in only ten states? The quality of their product is certainly one reason for Coors' success. Through the 1970's Coors was the leading beer in nine of the 11 western states in which it was sold. In California, the second largest beer market in the country (New York is first), Coors at one time held an astonishing 43% of the market. Another reason is a unique marketing ploy that Coors perfected during the 1960's. When Coors entered a new market, it would lead with draught beer only. The company would sell kegs to taverns and bars at a price under that of its lowest competition. Then Coors would encourage the barkeepers to sell the beer at a premium price. Once Coors' premium image was established, the company would then introduce the beer in retail stores. Since Coors spent so little on advertising, the company was able to offer a better profit margin to its wholesalers. These profit incentives to both wholesalers and retailers worked well.

However, neither marketing nor product quality can account for what is now considered one of the strangest phenomena in American business history. Beginning in the late 1960's and culminating in the mid-1970's Coors developed, without any effort by the company, a mystique which made it "cult" beer. Limited availability created intense demand on the east coast. Westerners, keen to flaunt their perceived superiority to easterners, got caught up in a "we have what you want" syndrome and unwittingly became the company's unpaid advertisers. As a result, Coors virtually eliminated its competition in nine western states. Those nine states provided Coors with all the market it needed to become the fourth largest brewery in America.

Even at the height of the company's success in 1974, there were already signs of impending trouble. Since 1960, when Adolph III was kidnapped and murdered, the Coors have believed that they were the targets of radical terrorists. Over the years the family grew more insulated, cautious and secretive. They were highly careful in their hiring practices, utilizing polygraphs and sworn statements of loyalty. Outsiders saw these practices as both unfair and as a means of enforcing racial discrimination: the limited numbers of blacks and Hispanics employed by the company seemed to support this view. Lawsuits were filed alleging discrimination and, more importantly, a boycott was organized by a coalition of minority and interest groups filed lawsuits alleging discrimination and, more importantly, they organized a successful boycott. The boycott and lawsuits provoked more public scrutiny of the Coors dynasty. A series of articles appeared in the *Washington Post* in May of 1975 documenting Joe Coors' political philosophy and activism. Not only did these revelations exacerbate the boycott, they also influenced the average consumer and generally undermined Coors' market position.

At first, the Coors family response was retrenchment and litigation. However, when sales dropped 10% in California in 1975 (at the time that state accounted for 49% of total sales), the family changed their tactics. They settled the lawsuits, agreeing to a minority hiring plan. They began advertising campaigns aimed at showing the company's "good side." Television advertisements revealed a rainbow of minorities working happily in the brewery. Bill Coors took the initiative on environmental issues and proclaimed that Coors was well ahead of the industry and the government in keeping the environment clean. The replacement of pull-tabs with "pop-down" tabs and the first aluminum recycling program were cited as proof of Coors' commitment.

After a decrease in sales through the late 1970's, the company appeared to revive in 1980. Barrel sales dropped by one million between 1976 and 1978, bottoming out at 12.5 million before rebounding in 1980 to 13.7 million, 200,000 barrels ahead of 1976. Bill and Joe Coors, the third generation of the family and now in charge, concluded that their sales problem resulted from their image problem and that they had successfully solved both.

Two separate situations, one in 1975 and the other in 1976, should have signaled that the company's problems went beyond that of image. In 1975 the Coors family, for the first time, was forced to offer shares to the public to raise $50 million to pay inheritance tax for a family member. The original offering was successful, raising over $130 million. The stock sold was of a non-voting variety, so the family did not relinquish any control over the company. It was remarked by analysts at the time that the reluctance with which the company undertook the offering disclosed a disdain for modern methods of capitalization. The second situation involved a Federal Trade Commission (FTC) ruling, later upheld by the Supreme Court, striking down Coors' strongarm tactics over distribution. Coors refused to sell its product to distributors that the company regarded as unable to handle the beer properly. Once again, many industry analysts remarked that the company exhibited a disdain for mass marketing techniques.

With Anheuser-Busch and Miller growing rapidly, Coors believed that it should continue to do that which made the company successful in the first place, produce a beer superior in quality and present it to the consumer with a low-key approach. The two larger companies were spending billions of dollars on promotion in a market which they continually expanded with new products. In 1982 Coors sales dropped under 12 million barrels for the first time in 10 years.

Bill and Joe Coors had run the family business for 20 years, sharing the credit for the company's success and the blame for its reverses. Joe was better known for his politics than his business accomplishments, even though he directed Coors' most successful subsidiary. As president of Coors Porcelain Company he created a profitable high technology operation which, among other endeavors, supplied material for the National Aeronautics and Space Administration (NASA) space shuttle project.

In 1986 Jeffrey and Peter Coors, Joe's sons, took over the top positions in the company. Having worked their way up through various aspects of the business, they are responsible for Coors' success since 1983. More open to modern business strategies, they have experimented successfully in expanding Coors' product line. "Coors Light," introduced in 1978, was the second best selling beer in its category in 1986 (behind "Miller Lite"). Other new products include "Herman Joseph's 1868," "George Killians' Irish Red," and "Coors Extra Gold." Coors' distribution, which expanded slowly through the 1970's, was officially "nationwide" for the first time in 1986. Also in 1986 Coors opened a huge distribution center in Elkton, Virginia which now receives refrigerated shipments by train directly from Golden, Colorado. Future plans call for a second brewery at this site. Perhaps the place where the recent change in leadership has been felt the most is in market research and advertising. The Coors brothers have, for the first time, hired top level professionals to manage Coors' marketing strategy.

Principal Subsidiaries: Advantage Health Systems; Coors Biotech Products Co.; Coors Ceramics; Coors Distributing Co.; Coors Energy Co.; Coors Food Products Co.; Coors Packaging Co.; Coors Transportation Co.; Golden Recycle Co.; Rocky Mountain Water Co.

DISTILLERS COMPANY PLC

Distillers House
33 Ellersly Road
Edinburgh EH12 6JW
Scotland

Absorbed by Guinness plc
Incorporated: April 24, 1877

The Distillers Company Limited was once one of the most important and powerful companies in the United Kingdom. Distillers dominated the Scotch Whisky industry, controlling over 80% of the domestic market and almost 75% of the worldwide market. Distillers' brands included Dewar's, the number one Scotch in the U.S., Johnnie Walker, Red and Black labels, the most popular Scotches in the world, Gordons vodka and gin, and over 60 other labels. The company successfully diversified into industrial and medical chemicals, yeast production, glass production, and plastics. Profits were impressive, and this conservative 19th century company reinvested wisely.

Yet, the company's markets began to shrink as its competition became more aggressive, and lawsuits and their settlements crippled both its profits and public image. In 1986 Distillers, founded in 1877, was purchased by Guinness plc, the brewery company, for £2.5 billion. The new owners quickly moved to absorb the company, rather than operate it as a subsidiary. Distillers Company Limited, once synonymous with Scotch Whisky, disappeared forever.

Distillers was founded at a time when technology was transforming what had been essentially a cottage enterprise into a modern industry. For centuries pot stills had been the only way to make whisky. A pot still is a large iron pot suspended over an open fire. Pot distillers used only barley, which they boiled, mashed, and fermented to form a "wort." This wort was the key to a single malt Scotch whisky. In the second half of the 19th century a new kind of still was invented. The "patent still" is a sealed pressure unit which makes use of various cereals including, but not limited to, barley. The product of patent stills is generally called "grain, or neutral spirits." The main difference between the two processes is that the patent still produces a larger volume less expensively. It is generally conceded that pot stills produce a better quality product. Certainly, pot or malt distillation produces a distinct product, full bodied, with a peat smoke flavor. (The barley is dried in peat kilns in the pot still process.) The "neutral

spirits" distilled by the patent process were blended with the "malt spirits" made in pot stills, creating "blended Scotch whisky." The quality of these blends varied greatly, according to the amount of malt in the blend.

The industry which Distillers eventually was to control reacted adversely to the technological innovations. Pot distillers, patent distillers, blenders, farmers, and whisky brokers all fended for themselves. Since the consumption of whisky was on the rise, it appeared that there was enough room for everyone. An attempt to form a trade association merely revealed that differences in the industry were great. All that came out of this attempt to organize was a limited association of malt distillers called the Northern Scotland Malt Distillers Association. The association was composed of 61 independent malt distillers who gathered regularly to express their opinions. No one distiller produced sufficient whisky to have any control or even influence over the others, consequently little was accomplished. The one issue upon which they were all agreed was that they needed a government approved definition of "Scotch Whisky" which recognized malt spirits as the distinguishing factor.

The patent distillers had a more modern attitude toward business. Though consumption was rising sharply, the unrestricted competition between individuals was seriously damaging profit margins. In 1877 six patent still operators joined forces and formed a company which they called Distillers Company Limited. Although it was not involved in either malt distillation or blending, Distillers quickly acquired a large share of the grain spirits market. The largest blenders—Buchanan, John Walker & Sons, and the Dewars brothers—immediately recognized the power Distillers had in controlling 70% of the grain spirit market vital to their blending. For more than 30 years the three blenders competed intensely with Distillers, going so far as opening their own distillery, a project they quickly abandoned because of prohibitive costs. Though these three largest companies refrained from distilling, many others took their place. The 1890's were the best years for whisky makers; they could not produce enough to meet demand. Distilleries could be found all over Scotland. Even Distillers, which had already firmly established its reputation as a conservative firm, purchased two distilleries and built a third (all were malt distilleries, a first for the company).

This prosperity did not last for long. In the 10 years prior to 1900, the peak of the demand for whisky, the number of distilleries in Scotland nearly doubled. When the Scotch market went dry due to a combination of general economic turmoil, high taxes, and temperance movements, many of these new distilleries were left with large quantities of well-aged, unsellable Scotch whisky. Distillers, meanwhile, had been conserving its resources and expanding at a comparatively slow rate. After the market suffered the downturn, Distillers instituted its policy of consolidation. Using profits from its newly diversified subsidiaries in industrial alcohol and yeast, the company purchased competing patent stills at reduced prices and subsequently closed them; the company also bought the excess stocks of whisky; other stills purchased were transformed into additional industrial alcohol and yeast plants. By 1922 Distillers owned all but one patent still in Scotland, all but one in Ireland, and all but two in England. If the three largest blenders were worried when Distillers controlled 70% of the patent market, they were in a state of near panic in 1923. As a result, in 1925 Buchanan, John Walker & Sons, and Dewars amalgamated with Distillers; they had little other choice. The men in charge of each of these blending companies received a seat on Distillers' board of directors.

Distillers also survived World War I intact, while many other companies failed. War restrictions affected the industry severely. High taxes, import restrictions on foreign grain, and a general feeling that whisky hurt the war drive all served to place constraints on the industry.

Throughout the war Distillers continued its policy of consolidation. After the war and after the absorption of the three largest blenders, management at Distillers decided to continue its acquisition program. Its next target was the northern malt distillers. Prior to 1925 Distillers owned only three of more than 70 pot stills in the country (the amalgamation with the blending companies brought them several more). Depression conditions after 1929 left many independent stills ready for takeover. By 1934 Distillers dominated all three phases of the Scotch whisky trade: it had purchased many pot stills and now owned or had a large share in 54 malt distilleries. These random and haphazard new holdings were organized as the company's Scottish Malt Distillers subsidiary. Distillers now controlled the largest grain and malt distilleries and the largest blending facilities.

Interestingly enough, this large company, controlling over 90% of the world's Scotch whisky market, remained almost anonymous. Distillers never printed its name on a bottle of Scotch, and its operations often seemed to be those of a kind of ultimate secret conglomerate. Only one man, up to this time, made a name for himself and garnered a degree of publicity. William Henry Ross gained distinction with Distillers for his role as the company's arbitrator to the rest of the industry and the government. He became managing director of Distillers in 1900 and its chairman in 1925. He was said to be responsible for the consolidation policy which proved to be so successful during the early part of the century.

Sometime during the mid-1920's a Canadian bootlegger named Sam Bronfman approached the Distillers board seeking aged whisky stock that would be in demand after the end of Prohibition in the United States. Bronfman already had a previous agreement with Distillers to distribute their liquor in North America. Sam Bronfman now offered Distillers cash and a share of his company, which he expected to grow rapidly, in order to procure the aged whisky. He had already made a deal in Canada, giving him control of a large distillery and the "Seagram" name which went with it. Distillers did not have any marketing structure in North America, and they reached an agreement with Bronfman. The Bronfman company's name became Distillers Corporation–Seagrams Limited.

Bronfman's firm was small, and he had to make a successful entrance into the American market if he was going to accomplish his dream of a liquor empire. Prohibition ended in 1933, and Bronfman thereafter did quite well. So well, in fact, that he thought he was entitled to a better price on the whisky he imported from Distillers. The board of directors at Distillers disagreed, Bronfman traveled to Scotland to argue his case: the conservative management at Distillers and Bronfman abruptly ended their business relationship when Bronfman was thrown out of the board room. Bronfman vowed to take revenge on Distillers, and he accomplished his goal. His Canadian blends dominated the important U.S. market for some 40 years. His Cutty Sark Scotch even ranked number one in sales in America for a short period of time. Bronfman kept the word "Distillers" in the company name and did nothing to counteract public confusion (the company name was eventually changed to Seagram Corporation by his sons in 1979).

World War II brought back many of the same problems that Distillers had faced during World War I. This time, however, Distillers was so large and diversified that the war proved to be a benefit. Even though the whisky market was depressed, the company more than compensated for any loss of profits with earnings from its chemical and biochemical subsidiaries: industrial alcohol and solvents, yeast and grain were all crucial to the war effort.

The late 1940's and 1950's were a successful time for Distillers. The company did not release any market statistics during this time, but experts say that the company retained its impressive share of the Scotch whisky market. That success was extended into new markets in South America, Africa and Asia, with Japan emerging as a particularly important new market. Distillers also added other liquors to its product line, including Gordon's gin and vodka. Distillers' subsidiaries were doing as well, or better, than the parent company. Distillers Company Biochemical had become an important manufacturer of drugs in the United Kingdom. It was from this company's activities, however, that the beginning of the end came for Distillers.

In the late 1950's the German pharmaceutical company Grunenthal created, tested and won government approval for a new sedative which it believed to be the safest sleeping pill to date. In addition to its other attributes, Thalidomide was suicide-proof. The company said that it was almost impossible for an overdose to cause death.

Distillers Company Biochemical purchased the rights to manufacture and market Thalidomide in the United Kingdom and Commonwealth. It was a doctor in Perth, Australia who connected Thalidomide to an occurrence of birth defects in late 1962. Others soon verified his initial findings, and Thalidomide was taken off the market. However, before the tragedy ended some 100 British babies (almost 10,000 worldwide) were stricken with defects ranging from missing limbs to severe mental retardation. Distraught parents immediately brought lawsuits against Distillers Company Biochemical and its parent company Distillers.

For ten years Distillers engaged in litigation, slowly settling with several individual families. A large number of families, 62 altogether, banded together in the hope of a larger settlement. This group was led by the father of a "Thalidomide child" named David Mason. Mason became something of a national hero in his battle against the large company. Distillers had argued all along that while the company had conducted tests on its own, the drug had been approved by both the West German and British governments and that the sole responsibility for the effects of the drug should not rest solely with the company. For a time there was public sympathy for the company's position. However, as litigation began to seem interminable, the public came to believe that Distillers was attempting to avoid compensation for the children and their families. By 1973, after 10 years of litigation, Distillers' reputation was badly damaged. Members of Parliament, along with various interest groups, were beginning to speak against the company. The company eventually settled the joint suit by establishing a £25 million fund for the support of the Thalidomide children throughout their lives.

In 1969 Distillers sold its entire chemical holdings to British Petroleum for £90 million of British Petroleum stock and cash. Distillers' chemical interests had provided a steadily growing source of revenue since 1900. The loss of this income was to hurt the company in the 16 years leading to its demise. Distillers had always relied on its subsidiaries during the frequent downturns in the volatile whisky market.

The early 1970's were, despite the lingering litigation over Thalidomide, a profitable and busy time for Distillers. The company entered joint operations in both glass and plastics. It expanded its brands to include a line of Australian wines and brandies, and it acquired control of the popular Tanqueray gin. In 1973 the company took over the popular Pimms flavored gin line. Profits reached £100 million for the first time in 1980. During this time the company also built a large new distillery capable of producing one million gallons of spirits a year.

The steady rise in profits fell sharply in the early 1980's. In 1978 the company became involved in a feud with the European Economic Community (EEC). The EEC ordered Distillers to refrain from charging British wholesalers more for Scotch which was to be exported than for Scotch which was to be sold domestically. Chairman J.R. Cater did not appreciate what he considered meddling in the company's internal affairs. The very same day that the EEC notified him of its decision, Cater removed all Johnnie Walker Red Scotch from the British market. At the time, Johnnie Walker Red was the most popular Scotch in the world with approximately 15% of the total world market. Estimates place the popular Scotch at 75% of the European market. While the feud and boycott lasted six months, Johnnie Walker Red lost market shares that it has been unable to replace since.

The fall in profits is also blamed on poor marketing in the United States. Distillers had always allowed American companies to distribute its liquor. While the company lost a considerable amount of profit to these distributors, it believed that was an effective means of marketing the company's products in the United States. That may have been so; by the early 1980's it had ceased to be true. The indigenous competition was more aggressive, and Distillers' U.S. market share eroded rapidly. Another weakness, traditional with Distillers, was in advertising. Distillers' competitors had better, more up-to-date advertising strategies.

Profits for the company peaked in 1983 at £139.2 million. 1984 profits dropped by more than £11 million. Industry analysts warned that the company's management was not active enough. In 1985 Distillers started to sell some of its British Petroleum stock for ready cash. The ploy did not provide enough cash to halt the slide in profits, and soon Distillers was ripe for a takeover. Argyll, a British supermarket chain, took advantage of the opportunity in December of 1985 in a hostile takeover attempt. When it became obvious that Distillers could not successfully defend itself, Guinness offered its services and soon became the company's choice in the takeover battle. Before another year passed Distillers had been absorbed by Guinness.

Further Reading: Suffer the Children: The Story of Thalidomide by the Insight Team of the Sunday Times of London, New York, Viking Press, 1979.

E & J GALLO

P.O. Box 1130
Modesto, California 95353
U.S.A.
(209) 579-3111

Private Company
Employees: 3,000
Sales: $1 billion (estimated)

The Gallo winery is a highly secretive private business which does not offer public tours or display its name on its company headquarters. It produces 55 types of wine ranging from premium corked varieties to popular low priced "jug" wines. Ernest Gallo's marketing skills and business acumen complement his brother Julio's concern for both quality control and improvement of the wines. This combined attention to consumer needs and wine quality has ensured Gallo a leading position in the wine industry.

Joseph Gallo, Ernest and Julio's father, purchased a 230 acre vineyard in California after he emigrated from Italy during Prohibition. Although most alcohol was banned during this period, wine could be sold for religious and medicinal purposes. Joseph, however, could not profitably sell his grapes; he was competing with too many other struggling vineyards established prior to Prohibition. The prospect of a grim future induced Joseph to kill his wife, attempt to kill Ernest and Julio, and finally to kill himself. This family tragedy was actually the catalyst for Ernest and Julio's founding of Gallo wines immediately after Prohibition. They pooled their inheritance of $5,900 to establish a winery in Modesto, California. With a recipe borrowed from a pamphlet in the Modesto Public Library, Ernest and Julio began what was to become a wine empire.

Initial labor costs for producing the wine were minimal. Ernest convinced his wife to help prepare wine in the shed which served as their winery. The exhausting and sacrificial labor yielded positive returns: the Gallo brothers sold their one gallon jug wine for one half the price of their larger competitors' wine. Ernest used aggressive marketing skills to increase the sales of the jug wine. He flew to Chicago and sold a contract for 6000 gallons of Gallo wine at fifty cents per gallon to a major distributor. Within the first year Ernest and Julio had earned $34,000 in profits.

Since the founding of Gallo wines, Ernest's aggressive business tactics have underlined his quest for perfection—in wine as well as in life. If Ernest believes, for example, that a business agreement has not been executed in the proper manner, the person at fault is instantly reprimanded, sometimes fired. Ernest has also gained a reputation for reading his market: he has continously and successfully predicted consumer tastes. His brother Julio oversees the quality of the wine. Julio personally tastes every batch at eleven o'clock each day. He also flies over the Gallo vineyards to inspect the growth and quality of the grapes. Thus, Julio's striving for the finest quality wine mirrors his brother's quest for managerial perfection.

In 1938 Ernest and Julio established their own bottling company in Modesto; in 1940 they purchased bottling companies in Los Angeles and New Orleans. Through these acquisitions Ernest believed that the winery could become self-sufficient and thereby accumulate additional profits.

At the outbreak of World War II distributors bought wine at low prices because the wine market was diminishing and there was a surplus. Then these distributors forced their retailers to purchase the wine at high prices as a condition of buying the hard liquor that was in great demand. After the war, the distributors caused the price of wine to rise again because they controlled most of the available stocks—the result of their purchases during the war. Gallo took the opportunity to sell its wine to the distributors at the high price of $1.50 per gallon in 1946. In 1947 Gallo bought back the same wine for $.50 per gallon when the wine market declined.

As a result of having this revenue at its disposal, Gallo was the first to automate its winery. At Julio's insistence, Gallo was the first to hire research chemists. This industry innovation transformed wine making into an exact science; the taste of Gallo wines was now more stable than the taste of that of its competitors. The revolutionary use of stainless steel storage bins instead of wooden storage bins also led to a beneficial change; the wines no longer retained the taste of bacteria infested wood. The Gallo winery was also the first to computerize its records.

In 1957 Gallo introduced "Thunderbird," a red wine with 20% alcohol flavored with lemon juice, which sold for one dollar per bottle. Ernest introduced this wine because people in the south had been flavoring strong wines with juice for years. An unprecedented 2.5 million cases were sold in less than one year. Ernest Gallo had recognized a consumer trend before the competition and had profited handsomely. The success with Thunderbird also had a negative effect on the company: it established Gallo in the public consciousness as a purveyor of cheap wine—a reputation the company would later find it difficult to overcome.

Gallo's power was enhanced during the 1960's as increasing numbers of small vintners, unable to keep up with the wine industry's ever-rising expenditures for advertising and marketing. In 1930 there had been 800 vintners in California; in 1963 there were 241. Gallo improved and increased its advertising to ensure that it maintained its position in the industry against the larger wineries which were expanding through acquisitions of smaller vintners. In 1963 Gallo spent $5 million on advertising; the entire wine industry spent only $12 million. As well, Gallo maintained a tight rein on its distributors, insisting that they accept modest profit margins, to keep prices low for the consumer, to provoke more Americans to drink wine.

The per capita consumption of wine in America had been steadily rising: in 1959 consumers spent $650 million on wine while in 1962 they spent $745 million. Gallo capitalized on this increase by encouraging the sale of table wines more vigorously than the sale of sweet dessert wines. In 1963 the sweeter wines still outsold the table wines by a 2 to 1 ratio (86 million gallons to 40 million gallons). But the wine advisory board of California supported Gallo's crusade for table wines by levying a tax of two cents per gallon on dessert wines and one cent per gallon on table wines. The advisory board also established wine-tasting sessions and wine study courses. Their efforts went a long way in helping to destroy the myth prevalent in the U.S. that wine should be consumed only on special occasions. Still, Americans were reluctant to drink wine with meals although Europeans had been doing it for centuries. During the mid-1960's the typical Frenchman drank 35 gallons of wine in one year, the typical Italian drank 31 gallons, and the typical American drank 1 gallon.

Gallo's competitors were not just the other California wineries: European winemakers began to invade the domestic market. Gallo emphasized the superiority of American wine to consumers by explaining that its stability and predictable flavor were due to the constant California climate. Domestic winemakers cross-bred grapes to improve the flavor of wines while Europeans relied on the same grapes every year. A 1965 federal directive supported the Gallo contention of American wine "superiority": only American wines may be served at U.S. embassies and U.S. related functions abroad.

While Gallo attempted to improve the image of American wines, it also battled for rights to the best grapes in the country. In 1967 Gallo offered grape growers a fifteen year contract at a minimum price of $75 per ton of grapes or the going market price that year, whichever was higher. Gallo proposed this contract because of a shortage of certain grapes: the company wished to overwhelm its competition by capturing a large portion of the grape market. By offering a fifteen year contract for grapes, Gallo also hoped that growers would specifically plant grapes for Gallo consumption only. This action would exclude the competing wine companies and force them to use other, perhaps more expensive, grapes.

Gallo introduced the first "pop wines" in 1969. Under the Boone's Farm Apple Wine label, Gallo marketed the first wine flavored with juice and carbonated. This later version of Thunderbird captured the market; by 1972 it had 88% of the pop wine sales in the United States. By 1969 Gallo was number one in the wine industry, producing 66 million gallons of wine per year (wine sales for the industry as a whole were 172 million gallons).

Despite record wine sales, Gallo continued to struggle with the pressures of being a private business without the financial resources of a public company. The shortage of available capital limits Gallo's potential growth. It is difficult for Gallo to make acquisitions because the company cannot issue shares on the open market; it must rely on retained earnings or go into debt to purchase any new business.

However, there are advantages in being a private business that sometimes outweigh the disadvantages. A private business can be more daring and introduce new products which might easily fail—without answering to irate shareholders. The company's directors have more freedom. Finally, more latitude is allowed the company in how it spends its profits. It can either reinvest in the operation of the company or initiate a new line of products. Both Ernest and Julio recognize these advantages and have resisted all outside suggestions to transform Gallo into a public company. The personalities of the founders, especially Ernest, do not allow for restrictions in making decisions about new product lines or consumer trends.

It was Ernest Gallo's decision to promote the image of wine as an everyday drink and not a sophisticated European drink, and that decision was a correct one; he boosted sales of table wines. As Gallo sold more of its "hearty burgundy" and less of the pop wines, its profits increased. Consumers switched from sweet dessert wines to lighter table wines. Champagne and sparkling wines also became drinks for any occasion. The surge in American travel to Europe also helped build a new market for table wines. It also greatly helped the sales of European wines in America: imported wines enjoyed 10.5% of the market in 1956, 21% in 1970.

California's share of the national wine market declined from 90% to 73%. However, Gallo was not adversely affected: it continued to increase sales by increasing its share of the domestic wine market. By 1971, along with United Vintners, it shipped 60% of all California wines.

The 1970's were also a period of difficulty for the company. In 1973 the United Farm Workers (UFW) boycotted Gallo wines. Cesar Chevaz's union had represented the Gallo workers, but in 1973 Gallo workers decided to change to the rival Teamsters Union. Chevaz charged Gallo with illegal tactics, and the dispute lasted for two years. In 1975 Gallo allowed its employees to vote for a new union of their choice. They did not vote to reinstate the UFW. Again, Chevaz charged unfair labor practices; he received support from senators Walter Mondale and Alan Cranston; 200 California stores removed Gallo wines from their shelves; protests were organized by other unions. Gallo continued to claim that the company paid workers well above the industry average and had not changed unions without the consent of the employees.

Despite these difficulties Gallo continued to dominate the wine market. It also began to upgrade the types of wine for which it was known. In 1974 Gallo introduced its first premium wines made with varietal grapes. To enhance the premium image that the company wished to establish, Gallo sealed its varietals with corks (in the past Gallo had sealed its wines with screw caps). Despite these efforts to upgrade the Gallo image, wine writers were still embarrassed to recommend Gallo wines; its reputation as a maker of cheap wines continued to haunt the company. Gallo attempted to erase this negative image by spending more money in promoting its new premium wines.

Its problem with the unions also continued to plague the company. In 1976 Gallo again felt the repercussions of its decision to switch unions. Gallo wine ads were banned from some college newspapers while others gave free ad space to the UFW in papers where Gallo already advertised. To add to its difficulties, Gallo was forced to consent to an FTC order barring anticompetitive dealings with its wholesalers for ten years. The FTC charged that Gallo set up "exclusionary marketing policies which it enforced by coercing distributors." Gallo acceded to this consent agreement, but would not admit that it had committed any inproprieties.

Gallo was limited as a result of this consent agreement, and its competition took advantage of this restraint. The Coca-Cola Company's wines, such as Taylor, challenged Gallo's market share with extensive ad campaigns and lower prices. In response, Gallo offered discounts and initiated a new advertising campaign to counteract Coke's growing influence on consumers. Soon, Coke's war with Pepsi monopolized its ad budget, and thus thwarted Coke's fight with Gallo. Coke sold its product line of wines to Seagram in 1983.

Although Gallo sales were high, Ernest Gallo became increasingly annoyed with the limits on the winery's dealings. In 1982 the company petitioned the FTC to lift the consent agreement barring Gallo from exclusive dealership. Since its market share had declined, Gallo argued that it was not the same threat as it had been before. The FTC agreed and revoked the consent agreement. Several grape growers were not so pleased with Gallo. Steven Sommer, a Sonoma grower, filed a grievance with the California Department of Agriculture after Gallo had downgraded his harvest from $475 per ton to $275 per ton; Bernard Rutman sued Gallo because Gallo had rejected his grapes for no apparent reason after 40 years of service. Growers became victims of Gallo's quest for perfection; the grapes that had been used for years suddenly did not meet Gallo standards.

While Julio upgraded wine quality, Ernest continued to predict successfully new consumer trends. The success of Gallo's wine cooler, Bartles and Jaymes, is a result of Ernest Gallo's careful consideration of the needs and tastes of the public in different age and career groups. Bartles and Jaymes appeals to an older audience because of its sleek bottle and smooth taste. California Cooler, the competition, appeals to a young audience primarily because it is available in different flavors. However, the clever advertising, product positioning, and dynamic marketing of Bartles and Jaymes have helped it to sustain its number one position among wine coolers throughout the 1980's. Ogilvy and Mather handles the $20 million ad budget for the cooler—a substantial portion of the total $35 million Gallo advertising budget.

Gallo premium wines, aged in a newly built cellar in rows of twelve foot casks made from Yugoslav Oak, are Ernest Gallo's pride. Gallo recently increased its advertising budget to $40 million, and the premium wines as well as the wine cooler will be the focus of future Gallo advertising and marketing efforts.

Ernest Gallo's strong character is the prime force behind the success of Gallo wines. He allows himself no leisure: in his spare time he invites politicians, businessmen, and winemakers to his house to discuss business. Ernest does not waste time socializing with people who do not understand the wine business. As Julio says, "We don't socialize much. There's not much to talk about." The goal of perfection may be obsessive, but the Gallo bothers do sell wine. Ernest is rigorous in following certain practices to increase the sale of Gallo wines. He teaches retailers how to sell Gallo wine by forcing them to read a 300 page manual entitled *How to Maximize Your Wine Profits.* He trains them in the shelf positioning of Gallo wines. He employs more Ph.D.'s than all the other wineries combined to work in the Gallo research laboratories. Finally, he imposes on Gallo's top executives the most ambitious marketing strategy in the industry. Three-quarters of the top people in the wine industry have at one time or another worked for the Gallo winery.

The future of Gallo not only lies in the success of its premium wines but also and more importantly in the direction of the winery after Ernest and Julio Gallo die. Ernest and Julio's brother, Joseph, claims that he owns one-third of the business; the inheritance with which Ernest and Julio began their first winery should have been shared with him. However, his claim will probably not be upheld in court. Julio's son, Robert, and his son-in-law, James Coleman, are the most likely successors; they already oversee most of the day-to-day operations of the winery. Ernest's sons, David and Joseph, also work in the business. Yet many observers feel that what the brothers have in mind for the future is most likely to be a professional manager answering to a family board of directors.

The Gallo winery has consistently dominated the market since its founding by accepting small profit margins and occasional losses. In 1986 Gallo led the industry in champagne (Andre), brandy (E & J), and wine coolers (Bartles and Jaymes). A long time aide to Ernest and Julio has remarked that "the wine-maker is a warrior." If that is so, then it must be added that the Gallo brothers have combined the combative spirit with persistence and a quest for perfection—and it is that combination that is the secret of their success.

Principal Subsidiaries: Fairbanks Trucking Company; Midcal Aluminum Company.

GENERAL CINEMA CORPORATION

27 Boylston Street
Chestnut Hill, Massachusetts 02167
U.S.A.
(617) 232–8200

Public Company
Incorporated: 1950 as Mid-West Drive-In Theatres, Inc.
Employees: 13,000
Sales: $1.069 billion
Market value: $1.604 billion
Stock Index: New York

General Cinema is regarded by many Wall Street analysts as an investment firm; it has interests in radio and television stations, clothing stores, and real estate. Yet the company's diverse holdings and overall financial success are founded upon, and closely tied to, the public's consumption of carbonated beverages and attendance at movie theatres. General Cinema is presently America's largest independent bottler of soft drinks and its biggest operator of multi-screen theatres.

Originally part of a corporation established in 1939, Mid-West Drive-In Theatres was entirely independent by 1950. Small in size at first, under the management of Philip Smith the company created 53 drive-in theatres throughout the United States, all of which were modestly profitable. Evolving demographic and sociological conditions in America, however, changed the direction of his company forever.

Smith was well aware of the fact that box office receipts in large urban movie houses were dwindling rapidly because of the rise of television and a reluctance on the part of suburban dwellers to travel into the city for entertainment. Throughout the 1950's population growth in the cities of America had been predominantly in their suburbs. More people lived farther from the central city, and its movie houses, than ever before. In the late 1940's, 90 million Americans viewed a film every week; the money they spent amounted to $1.7 billion in 1948. By 1958, the average weekly movie attendance was down to 39.6 million, and box office receipts had slipped below $1.2 billion.

Smith decided it was the perfect time to open a theatre in a newly constructed suburban shopping center—the suburban equivalent of "downtown". The mall increasingly became the equivalent of a town square, the center for both shopping and entertainment, and business boomed

for Mid-West. Indeed, the mutually beneficial relationship between retail stores and movie theatres was too promising for Mid-West's competitors to resist; of the approximately 180 indoor theatres built in 1961 and 1962, one-third were in shopping malls.

Renamed General Cinema in 1964 to reflect the shifting focus of its operations, the firm continued to expand rapidly. It acquired the Mann Theatres Chain of Minneapolis for $6.6 million in cash and notes during 1970. Two years later, the company purchased an interest in 47 indoor theatres located in Louisiana and Florida from Loews Corporation for nearly $16 million.

Although General Cinema is well known for its extensive network of movie theatres, the soft drink industry is the one in which the company achieved its most impressive financial returns. In 1968 General Cinema began the gradual acquisition of beverages companies which eventually made it America's largest independent bottler. General Cinema's beverage division has exclusive franchise agreements with Pepsi-Cola Inc., Dr. Pepper Company, and the Seven-Up Company; the company has the right to produce and sell Pepsi-Cola, Diet Pepsi, Pepsi Light, regular and diet Pepsi Free, and Mountain Dew, in the District of Columbia and specific areas in California, Florida, Georgia, Indiana, and West Virginia.

More recently General Cinema's market position in both the soft drink and entertainment industries has become less secure. There have been predictions by Wall Street analysts that income from the theatre business will decline because of the rise of cable television and video cassettes. Additionally, U.S. census statistics indicate a coming decline in the percentage of the population from 10 to 20 years of age, the age group that comprises 80% of all moviegoers. As well in April 1986 the company revealed that it was under investigation by the Federal Government for antitrust violations in its beverage business and ticket price-fixing in its theatre operations.

Despite these difficulties, General Cinema has an efficient and dependable management team upon which to rely. Richard A. Smith, who became chief executive officer of the company after the death of his father in 1961, has a reputation for hiring businessmen with proven talent for solving financial, legal, and managerial problems. Two of his most notable "finds" are Robert J. Tarr and J. Atwood Ives. Tarr, president and chief operating officer since 1985, arrived at the company in 1976 after a career as an investment banker at Paine Webber. Ives, chairman and chief financial officer since 1985, also joined the company after a stint at Paine Webber.

Lately, amid rumors of a change in leadership, Smith has denied that the appointments of Tarr and Ives signal the beginning of a competition for his job. What the appointments do signify, however, is Smith's plan to change General Cinema's reputation from that of being a one-man company to that of a company in which decisions are made collectively among the top executives. Yet Smith is finding it hard to downplay his own business acumen. According to one investor, "You're not really betting on soft drinks or movies. You're betting that Dick Smith is going to make another smart deal."

In fact, Smith has done remarkably well. Fiscal 1985

marked the 12th consecutive year, and the 24th out of its 25 years as a public company, in which General Cinema posted record operating results. In the past few years, it has been the beverage division, rather than the theatre operation, that is the strongest cash generator; it has accounted for more than 70% of the company's annual operating earnings. Walter Mack, present of Pepsico for many years, has made a number of insightful remarks on generating cash in the soft drink business: "Take a bottler whose plant and machinery cost him in the neighborhood of a million dollars. With any luck at all he's probably making five million a year, so he's getting his money back fives times over from now until doomsday. It's a sweetheart business . . . ." Keeping in mind that Mack's figures are based on a company's owning its bottling plants, one must conclude that profit must be potentially even greater for General Cinema, which leases rather than buys or builds it plants.

General Cinema's forays into the larger marketplace have also proved rewarding. With its characteristic low profile, the company began purchasing stock in Heublein Inc. Attempting to thwart a perceived takeover by General Cinema, Heublein was finally forced to seek a higher-priced bid from another company. The result—Smith sold his holdings in Heublein for a significant profit. Clearly, the management of General Cinema knows when to be aggressive.

It also knows when to send mixed signals to the market —as in its pursuit of Carter Hawley Hale stores. Carter Hawley Hale is America's tenth largest clothing retailer, with Bergdorf Goodman and Neiman Marcus under its control. In 1984 the Los Angeles-based firm found its market share eroding in the competitive environment of California, and was soon confronted with a unwanted takeover bid from a clothing store chain. Here was an opportunity for Smith to put into action his plan to "consider a major investment in another company, provided it is one with involvement." By "investment with involvement" Smith meant that "after making a significant minority investment in a company, we would participate actively in strategic decisions but leave day-to-day responsibilities to operating management." Carter Hawley Hale subsequently issued one million shares of preferred stock which General Cinema purchased for $300 million, providing it with a 37% interest in the company—the largest interest of any single shareholder.

General Cinema's interest in Carter Hawley Hale caused Carter's share value to increase dramatically, despite the fact that the company's profits were well below what had been expected on Wall Street. Perhaps investors were expecting General Cinema to institute major operational changes at Carter Hawley Hale. They were mistaken. General Cinema signed an agreement with the company which will expire in 1991: General Cinema's interest in Carter Hawley Hale is frozen, and restrictions have been placed on the sale of its stock.

In regard to both the Heublein and Carter Hawley Hale transactions, Smith insisted at first that he wanted to purchase the company, but he later admitted he was playing with stock instead. Smith recently revealed that, "At the moment, the investment activity is ahead of the operating activity," and has made known to Wall Street investment bankers his intention to purchase another operating division in either consumer package goods or services. However, Smith is very selective. He has rejected opportunities to acquire Entenmann's (a food products concern), Wm. Underwood (a theatre chain), and Wometco Enterprises (a Coca Cola bottler). In Smith's estimation, each of these companies is overvalued.

The faith of investors in management's ability to spot a potential moneymaker has given rise to the description of General Cinema as an "investment firm." Yet, more than anything else, the company's future depends on its success as a soft drink bottler and movie exhibitor. According to Smith, the beverage division is growing at a rapid pace, and the long-term effects of home videos on movie attendance will be negligible. If he is correct, General Cinema's goal of increasing its earnings at a rate of five to ten percent above inflation is quite feasible.

Principle Subsidiaries: Airway Drive-In Theatre Co., Inc.; Beta One Leasing, Inc.; Cinema AD-Ventures, Inc.; Coral Television Corp.; Dazzle, Inc.; Dedham Cinema, Inc.; GCC Beverages, Inc.; GCC Beverages of Mass., Inc.; GCC-Communications, Inc.; GCC Films, Inc.; GCC Theatres, Inc.; Holiday General Corp.; Jersey Division Realty Corp.; Joliet Cinema, Inc.; Kokomo Cinema, Inc.; Laconia Theatre Corp.; Newport Plaza Cinema, Inc.; Pepsi-Cola Bottlers of Akron, Inc.; Route 42 Cinema, Inc.; Southdown Cinema Corp.; Super Video, Inc.; Timonium Concessions, Inc.; Timonium Drive-In Theatre Corp.; Bedford Mall Cinema, Inc.; College Square Cinema, Inc.; Des Moines Drive-In Theatre Co.; Hanover Mall Cinema, Inc.; Jarundale Cinema, Inc.; Lincoln Realty Corp.; Meyerland Cinema, Inc.; Nashua Mall Cinema, Inc.; Natick Auto Theatre Corp.; Polk Realty Corp.; Shoregate Cinema, Inc.; Westgate Brockton Cinema, Inc.; Southwest Bottlers of Florida, Inc.

Further Reading: *No Time Lost* by Walter Mack with Peter Buckley, New York, Atheneum, 1982.

GRAND METROPOLITAN

GRAND METROPOLITAN PLC

11–12 Hanover Square
London W1A 1DP
England
01–629–7488

Public Company
Incorporated: 1934
Employees: 137,195
Sales: £5.287 billion (US$7.772 billion)
Market value: £5.064 billion (US$7.445 billion)
Stock Index: London

Grand Metropolitan is a highly diversified British-based company. It began as a property company, but its subsidiaries now cover a broad base of consumer products and services, including hotels, casinos, breweries, dairies, distilleries, and health care services. Maxwell Joseph, the founder of Grand Metropolitan, encouraged the rapid growth of his company by supporting acquisitions in profitable fields; its diversification has been indicative of the company's quest for maximum profits and maximum control of selected markets.

Born in 1910, Maxwell Joseph left school at the age of 16 to begin a career with local real estate agents in north London. He was paid the equivalent of six dollars per week for selling houses and other property. Shortly after mastering the intricate sales techniques and valuation skills of a successful realtor, Joseph established his own property firm in 1926, and that firm has grown to be Grand Metropolitan, now one of Britain's largest and most diversified companies.

Throughout the late 1920's and the 1930's, Joseph attempted to purchase good properties which would bring a high return when resold by his firm. However, because the English economy was in the midst of a depression, there were few prospective buyers and even fewer who could offer the kind of money that would meet his profit criteria. The advent of World War II deflated Joseph's hopes for a prosperous business.

Joseph's firm finally began to move toward success, after the war, with the purchase of the blitz-damaged Mandeville Hotel in the Marylebone district of London in 1946. Throughout the 1950's and 1960's Grand Metropolitan expanded through the development and purchase of new hotels. Joseph later admitted that he bought these hotels for "chicken feed." "Between 1950 and 1965," he said, "there wasn't a real estate man in the country who knew the value of hotels." Joseph did; moreover, he understood what they would be worth in the future.

Grand Metropolitan's base of operations widened as Joseph continued to purchase both more profitable and more prestigious hotels. The first such acquisition was London's Mount Royal Hotel, acquired in 1957 for $2.8 million. Grand Metropolitan quickly followed that takeover with purchases of a number of other luxury hotels throughout Europe. In Paris, Joseph purchased the Lotti Hotel; in Cannes, the Carlton Hotel; in Copenhagen, the Hotel d'Angleterre. By the end of the 1960's, Grand Metropolitan had established a significant presence in the European hotel industry.

Because of the financial success of the Grand Metropolitan hotels, Maxwell Joseph felt confident enough to embark on a new strategy of diversification. He initiated the purchase of Express Dairies in 1969. The two-part purchase was completed in 1970 with approval from the shareholders of Grand Metropolitan and the former owners of Express Dairies. Because this purchase had received firm shareholder support, Grand Metropolitan went on to purchase Berni Inns, Ron Nagle, and Truman Hanburg. Of these varied acquisitions, the Truman Hanburg deal was the most significant because it was Grand Metropolitan's first brewery. This particular acquisition also involved the largest takeover deal in Britain up to that time—the purchase price amounted to £400 million.

Seeking a financially equivalent takeover in 1972, Joseph purchased the Watney-Mann brewery. His purchase of Watney was fully justified in terms of company strategy. Grand Metropolitan already had a 49% stake in Carlsberg, a Danish brewer. Stanley Grinstead, the deputy chairman of Grand Metropolitan, and Maxwell Joseph were concerned that although they owned almost half of Carlsberg, they had no control over what brands were brewed. At the time, Carlsberg brewed only the Carlsberg and Tuborg brands of beer. Grand Metropolitan felt that, if it wished to expand in the beer market, it must acquire and control a less parochial beer company such as Watney-Mann.

Despite the future positive effects which all of these extensive purchases could have produced, Grand Metropolitan had incurred a large debt, particularly as a result of the purchases of Truman Hanburg, Express Dairies, and Watney-Mann. There were management failures at Watney-Mann which exposed Grand Metropolitan to severe financial losses. Furthermore, the company's expansion into Italy and France could not be effectively controlled from London. The company learned that it had to send special advisers into the foreign country in order to establish partnerships and gain a share of the market—but that, too, was a costly lesson.

In 1974 the company's debt peaked at £528 million, and Grand Metropolitan was forced to sell some of its smaller businesses to decrease that debt. For example, Joseph decided to sell the Royal Manhattan Hotel of New York and close the Vandenheuvel Brewery, which was one of Watney-Mann's three breweries in Belgium; neither enterprise had been particularly profitable. To further decrease debt, Grand Metropolitan also sold its shares in Carlsberg beer for £5.39 million. By these and other similar moves,

Grand Metropolitan began to reduce debt substantially and to reposition itself for a more careful acquisition strategy.

Grand Metropolitan's 1977 purchase of 20% share in Pleasurama, a casino operator, was one of its most important of the decade. Pleasurama and Grand Metropolitan already operated a joint venture, the A.M Casino, an enterprise located in Grand Metropolitan's Ritz Hotel in London. With the Pleasurama purchase, Joseph increased shareholder's equity above the level of debt for the first time since 1969.

Jospeh had passed the usual retirement age of 65 in 1975, but he had refused to relinquish his chairmanship. He continued to distrust younger and less experienced associates with business decisions, and he insisted on personally approving all major transactions. Under Joseph's guidance, Grand Metropolitan embarked in the late 1970's on a second series of acquisitions in which "leveraged buyouts," takeovers that incur huge debt, were carefully avoided. Occasionally, too, Joseph disposed of companies that were, in fact, profitable. Grand Metropolitan had purchased the Savoy Hotel Group from Trafalgar House in 1978. The Savoy Group was profitable, but it yielded only a 2% return. Joseph sold the Savoy Group to the Rothschild Investment Trust for £8.4 million, and Grand Metropolitan subsequently invested in other higher-yielding businesses.

For many years the Liggett Group, an American tobacco and liquor company, distributed Grand Metropolitan's J&B brand Scotch whisky in the United States. In 1980, on reported sales equivalent to $6.2 billion, Grand Metropolitan made a $415 million tender offer for Liggett—a move that also signalled a change in Joseph's attitude toward the American market, which he had in the past avoided. In purchasing Liggett, Grand Metropolitan would also gain control of Austin Nichols, a Liggett subsidiary well-established in the American liquor market. Shortly after Grand Metropolitan had made its bid, however, Liggett sold Austin Nichols to Pernod Ricard for $97.5 million. The Paddington Corporation, the Liggett subsidiary responsible for marketing J&B Scotch, therefore became Grand Metropolitan's main concern in the tender offer.

Liggett's management was strongly opposed to a takeover by Grand Metropolitan, fearing above all that Joseph would replace them with managers from Grand Metropolitan. As Liggett mounted a legal battle to thwart Grand Metropolitan, Standard Brands entered a competing bid of $513 million. Determined to succeed, Grand Metropolitan raised its tender offer to $590 million—a price that Standard Brands could not top and Liggett shareholders could not refuse.

In a separate, less successful bid, Grand Metropolitan failed to gain control over the Coral Leisure Group during 1980. The company's bid, valued at £85 million, was opposed by many shareholders who lacked confidence in Coral's ability to generate profit or future growth. Yet the decision to abandon Coral was, in effect made by the English Monopolies Commission, which ruled against the takeover.

The continued involvement of the Monopolies Commission in Grand Metropolitan's affairs brought to light an increasingly urgent shortcoming in the company's position: Grand Metropolitan had overemphasized its growth within Britain. With nearly 90% of its profits generated domestically, Grand Metropolitan would face other charges of monopoly control over certain markets if it continued to invest in British enterprises. The company's overexposure within the British economy became problematic in 1980, when the country entered a period of recession. In response, Grand Metropolitan inaugurated three- and four-year management plans, intended to improve short-term planning until the company could diversify geographically.

Grand Metropolitan achieved greater financial stability in 1981, largely due to Liggett's success in selling Bailey's Original Irish Cream and J&B Scotch in the United States. Increased sales of these products justified larger advertising budgets for them, which, in turn, helped to maintain their increased market shares. In order to derive greater profits from liquor sales in Britain, Grand Metropolitan attempted to enter the retail liquor business. But because the British government did not permit producers and distributors of liquor to own retail outlets, Grand Metropolitan was forced to adopt a different strategy: the company sub-leased its bars and restaurants to "outside" management, and thus circumvented the restrictions, while drawing at least a portion of the profits earned from retail liquor and food sales.

By 1982 Grand Metropolitan owned 66 hotels in Europe and the Middle East. That year, the company agreed to purchase the Intercontinental Hotel chain, consisting of 110 hotels, from Pan American World Airways in exchange for $500 million, Grand Metropolitan's Forum Hotel chain, and several other smaller hotel properties. The Monopolies Commission, however, became so involved in this transaction that Grand Metropolitan at last decided to end its concentration on European markets. Thereafter, the company redirected investment capital to the largely unrestricted markets of the United States, where it established an American subsidiary called GrandMet USA Inc. This company was given direct responsibility for the operations of Liggett and three new companies: Western Dairy Products, in California; Express Foods Inc., in Vermont; and Dry Milks Inc., in Kentucky.

In Britain, Grand Metropolitan divested itself of both marginally performing subsidiaries and companies the operations of which were considered peripheral to Grand Metropolitan's "core" industries. CC Soft Drinks Ltd., a subsidiary which bottled and distributed Coca-Cola in southern England, was sold to the Coca-Cola Export Corporation in 1984. The following year, Grand Metropolitan sold its Express Dairy subsidiary to Northern Foods for £51 million. Northern Foods subsequently purchased four other Grand Metropolitan dairies and a distributor, reducing Grand Metropolitan's share of the dairy market by one-third. Proceeds from these divestments were used to strengthen Grand Metropolitan's hotel and entertainment division, which in 1985 purchased the profitable Mecca Leisure group for £95 million.

During 1985, however, Grand Metropolitan again altered its corporate strategy. Because they correctly anticipated the phenomenal growth of health care services in the

United States, the company's board decided to make investments in that industry a company priority. Grand Metropolitan acquired Quality Care Inc., a large home health care and medical equipment company, and soon afterwards purchased an interest in Pearl Health Services. After it was taken over by Grand Metropolitan, Pearl established a large chain of dental and eye care centers intended to exploit opportunities in the American market for medical services in shopping malls and retail thoroughfares.

Despite the promising new health care ventures, Grand Metropolitan remained committed to its profitable hotel and entertainment division. After some deliberation, the company even refused a $900 million offer from Trafalgar of California to purchase the Intercontinental Hotel chain.

Grand Metropolitan appointed a new chief executive officer, Allen Sheppard, in 1987. Although the company had only recently entered the health care field, Sheppard believed that opportunities in this industry had already been exploited; he advocated the sale of Quality Care before the industry became unprofitably competitive. Grand Metropolitan thus halted its expansion in health care and resumed its purchases of "core" enterprises. In March 1987 Grand Metropolitan acquired Heublein Inc. from RJR Nabisco for $1.3 billion. Heublein had lost many of its non-beverage operations while a subsidiary of RJR Nabisco, but its beverages included such brands as Smirnoff vodka, Arrow liqueurs, Harvey's Bristol Cream sherry, and Guinness Stout beer—brands now controlled by Grand Metropolitan.

Grand Metropolitan may be expected to remain primarily a hotel, entertainment, and beverage company. Its expertise and ability to maintain stable operations in these fields suggest that Grand Metropolitan's future is relatively secure, particularly if it can continue to avoid the kind of debt that threatened to undermine its activities during the early 1970's.

Principal Subsidiaries: Samuel Webster and Wilsons Ltd.; Ushers Brewery Ltd.; Watney-Mann and Truman Maltings Ltd.; Watney Combe Reid & Co., Ltd.; Truman Ltd.; Phoenix Brewery Company Ltd.; Drybrough and Company Ltd.; Watney-Mann and Truman Brewers Export Ltd.; Watney-Mann National Sales Ltd.; Watney International Ltd.; Brouwerij Maes NV; Stern Braueri Carl Funke A.G. (78.3%); The Berni and Host Group Ltd.; Mecca Bookmakers Ltd.; London Clubs Ltd.; Compass Contact Services (UK) Ltd.; Grandmet International Services Ltd.; GM Health Care Ltd.; GrandMet USA Inc.; Alpo Petfoods Inc.; Atlantic Soft Drink Co.; Pepsi-Cola San Joaquin Bottling Co.; Liggett Group Inc.; Manns Northampton Brewery Co., Ltd.; Norwich Brewery Co., Ltd.; Diversified Products Corp.; Children's World Inc.; Eden Vale Ltd.; Heublein Inc.; Pearl Health Services Inc.; Intercontinental Hotels Corp.; International Distillers and Vintners Ltd.; Paddington Corp.; Carillon Importers Ltd.; Gilbey Canada Inc.; International Distillers and Vintners France S.A.; Selviac Nederland BV; Gilbey Vintners Ltd.; Morgan Furze & Co., Ltd.; Peter Dominic Ltd.; W&A Gilbey (South Africa) (Pty) Ltd. (51%); Justerini & Brooks Ltd.; Gilbey's of Ireland Ltd.; Croft Jerez S.A.; Croft & Ca Ltda.; International Distillers (Developments) Ltd.; Grand Metropolitan Information Services Ltd.; Grand Metropolitan Biotechnology Ltd.

GUINNESS

GUINNESS PLC

Bodiam House
Twyford Abbey Road
London NW10 7ES
England
01–965–7700

Public Company
Incorporated: 1886
Employees: 18,616
Sales: £1.187 billion (US$1.744 billion)
Market value: £4.71 billion (US$6.924 billion)
Stock Index: London

The dark creamy stout brewed by Guinness for more than two centuries is a product that is regarded as synonomous with the drinking habits of the Irish. Yet Guinness stout is now purchased in many foreign countries; through ingenious marketing strategies and adept management, Guinness has achieved the status of a multi-national corporation. This success, however, has recently been threatened by a scandal surrouding the firm's first non-family leader: it has severely disrupted brewing operations and thrown doubt on the company's future independence.

In 1759 Arthur Guinness, an experienced brewer, leased an old brewery at James Gate in Dublin. Besides renting the brewery Guinness signed an unusual 9,000 year lease for a mill, a storehouse, a stable, a house, and two malthouses. As it turned out, he didn't require so long a lease—in just four years significant quantities of ale and table beer were emerging from the new workplace.

Soon after the brewery was in full operation, Arthur Guinness began to establish a reputation in both business and civic affairs. The company secured an active trade with pubs in towns surrounding Dublin and also became one of the largest employers in the city. As a vocal participant in public life, Guinness supported such diverse issues as penal reform, parliamentary reform, and the discouragement of dueling. Furthermore, although a Protestant, he strongly supported the claims of the Irish Catholic majority for equality.

The business nearly came to an abrupt end in 1775 when a dispute over water rights erupted into a heated exchange between Guinness and the mayor's emissaries. The argument centered around the City Corporation's decision to fill in the channel that provided the brewery with water. When the sheriff's men appeared at James Gate, Guinness grabbed a pickaxe from a workman and with a good deal

of "improper language" ordered them to leave. For fear of escalating violence, the parties to the dispute finally settled by means of a tenant agreement.

In 1761 Arthur Guinness married Olivia Whitmore; of the 21 children born to them only 10 survived. Their eldest son, Hosea, became a clergyman. Consequently, after the founder's death in 1803, the thriving company was passed on to the second son, Arthur, who, like his father, soon became active in both civic and political affairs. He served in the Farming Society of Ireland, the Dublin Society, the Meath Hospital, and the Dublin Chamber of Commerce. Most importantly, as an elected director in the Bank of Ireland, he played a significant role in settling currency issues. In politics, Arthur adhered to his father's beliefs by advocating the claims of the religious majority.

From the very beginning of his career, it appears that Arthur's main concern was not so much in managing the company as in pursuing his banking interests. Nonetheless, brewery records indicate that from the end of the Napoleonic Wars to the end of the Great Famine in 1850, the company's production output increased by 50%. For this reason, Arthur is often credited with making the Guinness fortune.

A great deal of that success, of course, can be attributed to Arthur Guinness's decision to shift most of the firm's trade from Ireland to England. Yet the growth of Guinness was a result not only of management's business acumen and the firm's financial strength but also of the myths surrounding the beverage: from its earliest days Guinness stout was considered a nutritional beverage and promoter of virility. Although the company was once accused of mashing Protestant Bibles and Methodist hymn books into the brew in order to force ingestion of anti-Papal doctrine, Britain's leading medical journal during the mid-19th century claimed the drink was ". . . one of the best cordials not included in the pharmacopoia." This notion formed the basis of the company's advertisement campaign of 1929, which suggested that drinking Guinness could lead to the development of "strong muscles," "enriched blood," and the alleviation of "exhausted nerves." Somewhat surprisingly, this tradition still continues in Britain: the national health insurance system underwrites the purchase of Guinness for nursing mothers.

When Arthur died in 1855, his son, Benjamin Lee, assumed control of the company. Fifty-seven years old at the time, he had already worked for nearly 30 years at the brewery. During his tenure as head of the firm, the James Gate facility became the pre-eminenet porter brewery in the world. Following the tradition of his family, he was also intimately involved in civic affairs. He was awarded a baronetcy in 1867 for his contributions to the restoration of St. Patrick's Cathedral and other services; he died a year later.

Although Benjamin Lee Guinness, in his will, divided the responsibility for running the firm equally between his two sons, Edward Cecil and Arthur Edward, Edward soon emerged as the more astute of the two. The younger of the brothers, he was said to be an energetic yet excitable man. His decisions were controversial and, apparently, overwhelming: after eight years Arthur decided to leave the brewing business, and the partnership was dissolved.

In the tradition of his family, Edward became a leading figure in both civic affairs and in English social life. After his marriage to his cousin Adelaide, he seems to have "arrived," and the young couple circulated freely in elite circles. Among the many dignitaries entertained at their opulent 23,000 acre estate in Suffolk was King Edward VII.

Edward Guinness's wealth, prestige, influence, and mainly his philanthropies eventually earned him the title of Lord Iveagh. He drew heavily from the family fortune to contribute to worthy causes. He established the Iveagh Trust to provide basic necessities for 950 indigent families. He donated money for the continuing restoration of St. Patricks' Cathedral. He was, as well, recognized as an enlightened employer, ahead of his time in providing pension plans, health services, and housing for his employees.

In 1886 Guinness became a public company, its shares traded on the London exchange (Dublin, at that time lacked its own exchange). The company raised six million pounds on its shares, and embarked on an ambitious period of expansion in Ireland, England, and abroad. Guinness's unique brewing process ensured that the quality of the produce would not be impaired by long voyages to foreign markets. By the 1920's Guinness had reached the shores of East and West Africa and the Caribbean.

In 1927 leadership of the company passed to the next generation. The second Lord Iveagh is recognized primarily for his role in creating a modern brewery at Park Royal in London, built to service the company's growing business in southeast England. The facility became operational in 1936, and it is there that Guinness Extra and Draught Guinness were first brewed for the British market. By 1974 production at this plant exceeded that at James Gate by 100%.

Construction of the Park Royal facility was completed under the supervision of a civil engineer named Hugh E. C. Beaver. He formed a close association with managing director C. J. Newbold yet turned down Newbold's invitation to join the Guinness board of directors. After World War II Lord Iveagh personally asked Beaver to join the company as assistant managing director—and this time Beaver accepted. When Newbold died in the late 1940's, Beaver assumed the position of managing director. He is credited with modernizing the company's operations, introducing new management and research policies, increasing exports, and diversifying the company's product base. On his initiative the company was officially divided into Guinness Ireland and Guinness U.K. (control of both concerns remains with a central board of directors).

Beaver was also a strong advocate of generating new ideas through "brainstorming sessions." One now-famous product to emerge from these meetings was Harp lager. When Britons began taking their holidays abroad during the 1950's, they returned home with a new taste for chilled lager. Beaver sensed this changing preference, and during one of the "brainstorming sessions" company executives decided that Guinness should become the first local firm to market its own lager. Named for the harp on the label of Guinness's traditional product, Harp lager soon became the most successful product in the growing British lager market.

Beaver is also recognized as the founder of the extraordinarily successful publication, *Guinness Book of World Records*. Initially created as something of a company lark, the book has been such a success, throughout the world, that it is now a company tradition. The *Guinness Book of World Records* now sells some five million copies in 13 different languages.

Beaver, now Sir Hugh, retired in 1960, but throughout the next decade Guinness continued to expand—notably abroad, in countries with warm climates. Consistent with this strategy, the company constructed new breweries in Nigeria and Malaysia—then a second and third brewery in Nigeria as well as breweries in Cameroon, Ghana, and Jamaica. Guinness also developed a new product during this period, Irish Ale, which was exported to France and Britain. To offset the declining market for stout, the company began to diversify into pharmaceuticals, confectionary, and plastics, as well as other beverages.

Although both sales and earnings per share had doubled between 1965 and 1971, Guinness entered the 1970's confronting a number of problems. Compared to those of its competitors, the company's shares sold at modest prices, largely because Guinness operated outside the tied-house system (the five largest brewers owned and operated most of the country's 100,000 pubs), and investors felt the other breweries had the advantage for growth. The London financial community reasoned that Guinness was at a disadvantage because the company had to absorb the added costs of retailing.

There were also problems at the James Gate brewery. The Park Royal facility continued to outproduce the older Dublin site, and the company and its employees' union reached an agreement whereby the James Gate work force would be reduced by nearly one half. This solution temporarily solved the problem of decreasing profits at the James Gate facility and allowed operations to continue at the highly esteemed landmark facility. By 1976, however, the cost-cutting plan was seen to have achieved less than had been expected.

The company's diversification efforts were also, during this period, less than stellar; in the event, the company had gone on a purchasing spree in which 270 companies, producing a wide variety of products from baby bibs to car polish, had been acquired, and many of these companies were operating in deficit.

Even in the base brewing business, Guinness had its share of troubles. Its witty advertisements certainly appealed to the middle class but ignored the working class that provided the bulk of Guinness's custom. A new product, designed to combine the tastes of stout and ale, was a three-million-pound mistake.

The Guinness share price continued to decline.

To remedy the situation, Guinness executives called in the first non-family professional manager to take over leadership of the company. The sixth Lord Iveagh, as well as numerous Guinness relations, remained on the board, but Ernest Saunders, a former executive at J. Walter Thompson and Nestlé, stepped in as chief executive officer.

Saunders saw his first task as reducing the company's disparate holdings. He sold 160 companies. The companies that remained were all retail businesses. He then reduced the work force and brought in a new management team to develop and market the company's products. He made a large investment in increased and more eclectic advertising. He made cunning acquisitions in specialty foods, publishing, and retailing (including the 7-Eleven convenience stores). Brewing, according to Saunders, would in the future comprise only half of Guinness's total volume.

Financial analysts, and the City of London in general, were pleased with Saunders's efforts. The Guinness share price began noticeably to climb.

By mid-1985 Saunders seemed to have conquered. During his tenure the company's profits had tripled, its share price increased fourfold. He had accomplished a dazzling takeover of Distillers Company (Dewar's White Label, Johnnie Walker, Gordon's). That Guinness could—and would—pay £2.5 billion for a company twice its size surprised many industry analysts, yet Saunders's wish to create a multi-national company on the scale of Nestlé seemed to justify the expense. There were rumors that Saunders might be honored with a knighthood.

Within a matter of months, however, there were other kinds of rumors in the City—rumors concerning Saunders's methods in making the Distillers acquisition. In order to make possible the Distillers takeover, Saunders, with two of his fellow directors, allegedly had orchestrated an international scheme to provoke the sale of Guinness shares, thus raise their value and make possible the acquisition. Outside investors were indemnified in various ways against any losses incurred in purchasing huge numbers of Guinness shares. Bank Leu in Switzerland purchased Guinness shares with the understanding that the company would eventually buy them back. In return, Guinness deposited $75 million (in a non-interest-earning account) with the bank. The bank's chairman happened to be Saunders's ex-boss at Nestlé and a Guinness board member. Ivan F. Boesky, the American arbitrageur who has now admitted to "insider trading" in numerous deals, has been cited as the primary source of information about the Distillers takeover. Boesky is himself believed to have played a large role in the takeover; Guinness made a $100 million investment in a limited partnership run by Boesky only one month after Boesky had made significant purchases of Guinness shares. Boesky is now believed to have been only the tip of the iceberg, only one of various international investors who bought Guinness shares in an effort to increase their value. The company's auditors have discovered some $38 million worth of invoices for "services" rendered by various international investors during the takeover.

The charges, if true, are extremely serious—and obviously a violation of British company laws. Since late 1986, events have moved quickly. In December of that year the British Trade and Industry Department instigated an investigation of Guinness. In January of 1987 the Guinness board of directors asked for Saunders's resignation, and subsequently, in March, brought legal action against Saunders and one of his fellow directors, John Ward. In May the British government brought charges of fraud against Saunders: the claim is that Saunders knowingly destroyed evidence during the Trade and Industry Department investigation. The case remains unresolved. Throughout these events, Saunders has continued to deny all charges brought against him.

The Guinness share price has tumbled as a result of the continuing scandal. To prevent any further decline, Anthony Tennant, Guinness's new chief executive officer, has announced a plan to sell the company's subsidiary businesses and hereafter to concentrate solely on brewing. Clares Equipment, a manufacturer of shopping equipment, was sold for £28.5 million. Plans to sell the remaining holdings are presently being implemented. Tennant seems determined to rescue Guinness, even to bring it back to its days of glory. Whether his strategy will enable Guinness to survive, and to maintain its independence, obviously remains uncertain.

Principal Subsidiaries: Arthur Guinness Son & Co. (Great Britain) Ltd.; Arthur Guinness Son & Co. (Belfast) Ltd.; Irish Bonding Co. Ltd. (N. Ireland); Croft Inns Ltd. (N. Ireland); Martin the Newsagent plc; Guinness Enterprises Ltd.; Clares Equipment Ltd.; R. Gordon Drummond Ltd. (Scotland); Lavells Ltd.; The Harp Lager Co. Ltd.; Guinness Ireland Ltd.; Arthur Guinness Son & Co. (Dublin); Guinness Group Sales; Harp Ireland Ltd.; Irish Ale Breweries Ltd.; Murtagh Properties Ltd.; Meadow Meats Ltd.; Guinness Overseas Ltd.; Guinness Exports Ltd.; Guinness Malaysia Berhad (Malaysia); Guinness Cameroun SA (Cameroon); Guinness-Harp Corp. (U.S.A.); Arthur Bell & Sons plc; The Distillers Co. plc; The Champneys Group Ltd.; Neighborhood Stores plc; Richter Brothers Inc.

G. HEILEMAN BREWING COMPANY, INC.

100 Harborview Plaza
La Crosse, Wisconsin 54601
U.S.A.
(608) 785–1000

Wholly-owned subsidiary of Bond Corporation Holdings Ltd.
Incorporated: April 3, 1918
Employees: 7,000
Sales: $1.169 billion

G. Heileman Brewing Company is America's fastest growing brewer of premium beer, "near beer," malt liquor, and low-calorie beer. Krausening, or "double brewing," in 12 breweries across the nation under 34 different brand names distinguishes Heileman's beer from that of its competitors. Heileman manages the largest number of wholesalers in the brewery business, which ensures each brand's distribution across the United States. In fact, high quality and wide distribution are primary elements of Heileman's success.

In 1853 Gottlieb Heileman, a recent German immigrant to the United States, and his partner John Gund, the proprietor of a La Crosse, Wisconsin brewery, founded the City Brewery on Third and Mississippi Streets in La Crosse. The City Brewery competed locally only with Schaefer and Leinenkugel until 1858. However, growth of the large Milwaukee breweries engendered competition for local breweries. Gund wanted to invest in a larger brewery in order to compete effectively against Milwaukee, so he and Heileman dissolved their partnership in 1872 and Gund founded the Empire Brewery, later known as the John Gund Brewing Company. It soon became the largest brewery in La Crosse, but it went bankrupt during the Prohibition in the 1920's.

The City Brewery became the Heileman Brewing Company when Gund left. It was managed by Gottlieb Heileman until his death in 1878. His widow, Johanna, ran the brewery until she died in 1917.

In the 1850's the growing number of German immigrants in Wisconsin and the rest of the country generated a sudden increase in the number of breweries. The Wisconsin state legislature instructed the state Commission of Immigration in 1852 to distribute pamphlets describing Wisconsin's advantages to prospective immigrants from Europe, especially Germans. Great numbers of Europ-

eans responded, and consequently a large number of breweries were founded in Wisconsin to satisfy the tastes of the growing German population. However, outside Milwaukee there were few sources of the supplies needed for brewing.

Later in the decade the spreading network of railroads brought the needed resources within reach for brewers outside Milwaukee. The state's wheat growers could now transport their wheat in bulk to La Crosse, for instance. Local brewers already had access to barley, another important beer ingredient.

Two historical events helped boost Heileman's sales in the 1860's and 1870's. With the outbreak of the Civil War in 1861 the federal government instituted war taxes. Hard liquor was taxed at a rate of $1 per gallon, while beer was taxed at $1 per barrel. Beer thus became less expensive than other alcohol, so Americans began to consume it in greater quantities. Secondly the Chicago fire of 1871 ruined many breweries in that city. Wisconsin brewers seized the opportunity to extend their market into a major metropolitan area.

In 1900 Wisconsin was fourth nationally in the output of malt liquors, after New York, Pennsylvania, and Illinois, but Heileman had remained a comparatively small brewery by expanding its facilities slowly and increasing production marginally. Slow expansion and attention to beer quality distinguished Heileman from other local brewers of the period. While its competitors hastened production for maximum profits, Heileman maintained that "We don't aim to make the most beer, only the best." The brewery's location in a cool climate (with plentiful natural ice, an important commodity in the time before electric refrigeration) aided production of good beer. Moreover, labor and cooperage were inexpensive in La Crosse. Free from the high production costs of larger breweries, Heileman was able to invest additional money in making better quality beer.

Johanna Heileman copyrighted Heileman's most popular beer, Old Style, in 1902. Old Style is still produced using Heileman's unique krausening method, in which the beer supplies its own malt because natural carbonation absorbs carbon dioxide and locks it into the beer. The beer is then stored for several months before being put on sale.

Before World War I Old Style had become a regionally popular beer due to railroad distribution to various midwestern states. During the war Heileman and other brewers benefited from lenient war taxes on beer. Heileman's sales grew after the war as a new wave of German immigrants entered America.

Though a state-wide referendum in 1851 determined that the majority of Wisconsin residents wanted a prohibition law, by the time the national prohibition amendment was passed in 1918 the "wets" outnumbered the "drys." Even so, President Wilson signed a bill instituting it. The impact on breweries was devastating.

Under the Volstead Act of Prohibition, only beverages below 0.5% alcohol were legal. This led Heileman to produce "near beer," which contained a lower than legal amount of alcohol. The production of "near beer" also gave rise to another area of Prohibition-era revenue: the retail sale of malt to those who wished to brew beer privately. R. A. Albrecht, manager of the brewery after Johanna Heileman's death, supervised the "near beer" and malt sales which rescued Heileman from the economic ruin that shut down many of the nation's breweries.

Thousands of unemployed brewery workers exerted pressure on the government to legalize beer; finally, on "New Beer's Eve," April 6, 1933, the Volstead Act was repealed.

Harry Dahl became president of Heileman as the company reorganized and made post-Prohibition plans. His first act was to raise the price of malt syrup used in home brews in order to discourage consumers from brewing their own beer. This measure alone was not enough to restore Heileman's former prosperity, however, because competition among the nation's 700 brewers mounted after the repeal of Prohibition. Dahl understood that there were many different tastes to cater to, and under his direction Heileman began to assume the role of a local brewery producing beer for varying tastes in specific regions.

With the advent of World War II in 1941 the company instituted some major changes—none of which the public liked. Under President Albert D. Bates, Heileman introduced new beer can labels, changed its advertising approach, and revised its beer recipe. Promotions had previously stressed the beer's unique qualities, but now emphasized price and general consumer appeal. Most damaging however, was Bates's decision to alter the recipe to produce a richer flavor; by the end of World War II sales were lower than they had been in twenty years.

Ralph T. Johansen accepted the Heileman presidency in 1951 and spent five years trying to revive the company's sales, but to no avail. The turnaround began when company treasurer Roy E. Kumm took over the presidency in 1956.

Kumm revived the brewery's image as one that, first and foremost, cared about quality. In Kumm's first year as president Heileman ranked 39th in the industry; by 1960 it had moved up to the 31st position. But the company still remained a local rather than a national brewery. Kumm decided to change this state of affairs by instituting an aggressive acquisition policy.

From 1959 to 1980 Heileman bought 13 breweries, thereby increasing sales and profits considerably and adding regional name brands to those Heileman already produced. And since the purchase of small, regional breweries proved much less expensive than building new breweries, Heileman was able to extend its sales area in the most economical way. Between 1956 and 1966 sales rocketed from $15 million to $31.9 million, and shares climbed from $1.36 to $3.54. Through careful acquisitions Heileman had become a major producer of regional brands of beer.

Jet, Heileman's "near beer" brand originated during Prohibition, had remained popular in its relatively small market until 1965. At that time, concerned citizens protested distributions of "near beer" because of the common belief that it primed youths for alcoholic beer. Kumm's response was that Jet was meant for adults with medical problems, for dieters and for people living where alcoholic beer was unavailable; he also remarked that Jet was better

for a person's teeth than sugary soda. Nevertheless, Jet sales suffered because Oklahoma, Alabama, and Michigan banned the sale of any beverage with less than 0.5% alcohol which resembled an alcoholic drink.

Heileman's growth continued through the second half of the 1960's. In 1966 the company produced 972,000 barrels of beer and outperformed the larger breweries on the rate of return on stockholders' equity (15.6% as compared to 10.9% at the four largest brewers).

By the end of 1967 Heileman had risen to 22nd in the industry. Its higher-priced premium lines such as Special Export, Old Style, Heidelbran Pilsner, Fox Head De Luxe, Weber Special Premium, and Wisconsin Premium had become the most profitable; nevertheless Kumm was dissatisfied, noting that the United States' top five brewers still controlled a third of the total beer market. The company thus became even more aggressive. With the purchase of Wiedemann Brewing Company in Kentucky in 1967, Heileman's total production capacity rose to two million barrels of beer. By 1968 Heileman had further improved its rank in the industry to 18th.

Kumm, concerned that Heileman still retained its regional image, purchased the nationally known Blatz Breweries in 1969. Blatz's sales had been declining since 1964 and Kumm seized the opportunity to acquire it at well below market value.

Kumm's son-in-law, Russell Cleary, who had joined the company in 1960, took over as president in 1971 and continued the policy of making inexpensive acquisitions of ailing breweries. Between 1971 and 1980, five more breweries, including Rainier and Carling, were purchased and Heileman's midwest and east coast presence was considerably enhanced.

As part of Cleary's plan to broaden the product line, he introduced a line of light beers in the 1970's. Miller, the first brewery to use the term "light" beer, wanted exclusive rights to the description and sued Heileman. However, the court denied Miller's claim. Anheuser-Busch filed a similar suit against Heileman for using the term "LA" on low-alcohol beer. In this case, too, the court found in favor of Heileman. As competition increased among the top brewers, law suits such as this became more prevalent and characterized the rivalry among breweries during the decade.

In 1973 one of Heileman's many brewery purchases resulted in an antitrust action. The Justice Department ruled that Heileman could retain the three breweries it had bought from Associated Brewing Company if it divested itself of several brands. A later antitrust agreement prohibited Heileman from buying breweries in eight midwestern states for ten years.

Beer sales began to rise in the second half of the 1970's as the standard of living increased and social drinking became more popular; at the same time there was an unprecedented expansion of the number of people in the 21-to-34 age group (from 13.4 million to 46.5 million in a decade). Heileman, like most American brewers, augmented its marketing program to attract the new consumers. Additionally, local competition decreased as the larger brewers, Heileman included, dominated the new market. In 1933 there had been 700 brewing companies in the United States; in 1975 there were 54.

Other factors helped increase Heileman's sales during the 1970's. First, Schlitz's sales dropped in Minnesota and Heileman's Grain Belt beer became number one in that region. In 1976 Anheuser-Busch suffered severe economic losses after a long strike and Heileman stepped into the breach, further expanding its markets. And the company greatly increased the size of its bakery division in 1976 by purchasing the Trausch Baking Company of Iowa.

While other brewers suffered a series of financial misfortunes in the late 1970's, Heileman saw significant growth. Schlitz, Pabst and Coors all experienced a decrease in sales in 1978, but Heileman shipped 7.1 million barrels that year, up 14% from 1977 and second only to Miller. But despite Heileman's many acquisitions 90% of its sales in the late 1970's were in a 15-state region from western Pennsylvania to the Dakotas and south to Missouri. However in terms of consumption, these states, which have large Scandinavian and German populations, accounted for 50% of the nation's beer. In several areas Heileman's brands were ranked first in 1977, including Old Style in Chicago. By this time the company had become the seventh largest brewer in the country.

In 1980 Heileman was merchandising 34 brands of beer, many of which held the top rank in specific regions; and between 1976 and 1981, equity rose 30.2%. Despite record results, Cleary was still concerned that Heileman did not have a truly national identity. He therefore proposed a merger with Pabst which ultimately led to the purchase of Pabst in 1983. Stroh and Schmidt brewers filed an antitrust suit against Heileman claiming that sales in the upper midwest would be monopolized by the combined company; but a year later the court ruled in favor of Heileman.

At this time the company acquired the Lone Star Brewing Company, thus expanding sales in Texas and other southern states.

In the summer of 1987 Heileman itself became an acquisition target. Bond Corporation Holdings Ltd., a large brewing conglomerate based in Perth, Australia, offered $38 per share ($1.01 billion) for the company, but the Heileman board dismissed the amount as inadequate. The Wisconsin state legislature enacted special laws to prevent the takeover until certain economic guarantees could be secured. A subsequent offer from Bond valuing shares at $40.75 ($1.22 billion) was accepted in September, with guarantees that Bond would not move the company out of Wisconsin or attempt to change any current business or labor agreements. Heileman was expected to benefit greatly from the managerial expertise of the Bond Corporation.

The company is now competing for a larger share of the southeastern United States market; it has lowered its prices there and increased its promotion in the region. However, industry analysts believe that Heileman will have to glamorize its image across the country if it is finally to achieve a national identity and challenge the likes of Miller and Anheuser-Busch.

Principal Subsidiaries: Machine Products Company; Heileman Baking Company, Inc.; Nesco Signs Corporation.

Further Reading: *Brewed in America: A History of Beer and Ale in the U.S.* by Stanley Wade Baron, New York, Arno Press, 1972.

HEINEKEN N.V.

2E Weteringplantsoen 21
1000 AA Amsterdam
The Netherlands
(020) 709 111

Public Company
Incorporated: January 27, 1873
Employees: 28,749
Sales: Dfl5.45 billion (US$2.296 billion)
Market value: Dfl4.557 billion (US$2.074 billion)
Stock Index: Amsterdam Antwerp Brussels
Luxembourg

Founded more than 100 years ago, the Heineken brewing company is today one of the world's largest and most respected breweries. The family-run business built a solid reputation early in its history for maintaining high standards for its beer, standards Heineken still adheres to in the 1980's. Currenty ranked fifth in revenue among the world's beer makers, Heineken has operations in many countries outside its base in the Netherlands, though it has no brewing facilities in the United States, by far the company's largest export market.

In 1864 Gerard Adriaan Heineken convinced his mother that there would be fewer problems with alcoholism in Holland if the Dutch could be induced to drink beer instead of gin, and, moreover, that beer brewed in Holland was of such poor quantity that he felt a personal obligation to produce a high-quality beer. Heineken's mother bought him an Amsterdam brewery known as De Hooiberg (The Haystack) which had been established almost 300 years before. Heineken was only 22 when he assumed control of De Hooiberg, one of Amsterdam's largest breweries. He was so successful that after four years he built a new, larger brewery and closed the original facility. His business continued to grow rapidly, and after six more years, in 1874, he purchased a Rotterdam brewery to add to his operation.

Carl von Linde developed a new cooling technique for the wort which in 1873 gave Heineken the ability to brew year-round at a consistent quality level. Heineken was one of the first breweries in the world to eliminate the brewer's traditional dependence on seasonal natural ice.

In 1879 Heineken hired a Dr. Elion, a former student of Louis Pasteur, to research yeast. Over the next 13 years Elion systematically bred and selected a specific yeast cell which came to be known as the "Heineken A-yeast" (yeast

is the source of alcohol and carbon dioxide in beer). The Heineken A-yeast has been used for more than a century now, and is shipped from Holland to all breweries owned or operated by the company. Because the A-yeast has been studied comprehensively and its action in the brewing process fully cataloged, regular use of it lends uniformity to Heineken products. Heineken now operates plants in very different climates around the world, so consistency control is crucial.

The Dutch have always been interested in business opportunities outside their small country. Heineken actually began to export just 12 years after the De Hooiberg purchase. Exporting to the U.S. began soon after the founder's son, Dr. H. P. Heineken, assumed control of the company in 1914. Traveling on the Dutch liner *Nieuw Amsterdam* to New York, he met Leo van Munching, the liner's bartender. Impressed by van Munching's knowledge of beer, Heineken offered him a position as the company's importer in New York. The bartender quickly accepted.

Van Munching distributed Heineken beer to the finer restaurants, taverns, and hotels in the New York area until Prohibition forced him to stop the importing operation in 1920. After repeal of Prohibition in 1933, Heineken was the first beer imported into the United States. World War II once again brought importing to a temporary halt while van Munching served in the U.S. Navy. In 1945 he formed Van Munching and Company, Inc. and established a nationwide distribution system to build the beer's market beyond the New York area.

Since the 1940's the U.S. has been extremely important to Heineken; it has grown to become the beer's largest market outside the Netherlands. Heineken used Van Munching's distribution system over the years to become the dominant beer import in most of the United States. Most other imported beers (there are over 200) are still available only in major metropolitan areas or in narrow geographical regions. Heineken, on the other hand, is available in 70% of the nation's retail outlets handling alcoholic beverages. The company commands 40% of the imported beer market in the U.S. Heineken beer is also the leading import in Japan, Canada, and Australia. Today the majority of Heineken beer destined for America is brewed at the company's Hertogenbosch brewery, where special production lines accommodate the varied labelling requirements of the different states.

Currency fluctuations have little effect on the company itself, largely because Heineken sells its beer to Van Munching, which pays the brewer in guilders and thereby assumes all currency risks.

In 1930 the company entered the first of many joint brewing ventures in countries to which it had previously exported. That year Malayan Breweries was formed in Singapore in association with a local partner. This was followed closely by participation in a brewery in Indonesia. In 1949 the company built the first of four breweries in Nigeria; the fourth opened in 1982. Between 1958 and 1972 the company also built four breweries and two soft drink plants in Zaire. Heineken has breweries in Rwanda, Chad, Angola, the People's Republic of Congo, Ghana, Madagascar, and Sierra Leone as well.

During the late 1940's H.P. Heineken sent his son Alfred to New York to learn about Van Munching's marketing operation. The young Heineken took advertising and business courses in the evening and spent his days canvassing New York on foot with Van Munching's sales staff. His return to Holland in 1948 marked the beginning of a new era in the company's marketing strategy. Alfred Heineken had been impressed with the changes in the American lifestyle brought about by electrical refrigerators and modern supermarkets, and he foresaw the eventual impact of modern conveniences on the Dutch way of life. He prompted the company to implement marketing techniques that capitalized on these habits. Recognizing the importance of the take-home market, for instance, the company began selling beer in grocery stores (with store displays designed by Alfred Heineken). In addition, Heineken began advertising its beer on the radio. Previously, advertising had been considered unnecessary because tavern owners were tied to specific breweries.

In the 1960's the company institutionalized its meticulous quality control efforts under its technical services group, Heineken Technisch Beheer, or H.T.B. High quality has always been the company's hallmark. The brewing process of medium-quality beers usually takes three days and aging lasts a week at most. Heineken, however, brews its beer for eight days and ages it for six weeks. The H.T.B. unit operates out of the company's laboratory at Zoeterwoude in the Netherlands and provides laboratory services, research on raw materials, project engineering, and other services for all breweries associated with the company. There is also a tasting center at the Zoeterwoude laboratory. Samples of all beers brewed under Heineken supervision are shipped there each month to be tested by panels of taste experts. The tests at Zoeterwoude augment the taste testing that is carried out at each individual brewery.

Product diversification began relatively late in Heineken's history, because the company's emphasis had been on expanding its markets. However, in 1968 the company purchased the Amstel Brewery, Holland's second largest, founded by Jonkheer C. A. de Pesters and J. H. van Marwijk Kooy in 1870 and the first in Holland to brew lager beers. Amstel's export market was firmly established by the time Heineken purchased the operation. Heineken entered the low-calorie beer market with Amstel Light soon after the purchase. Amstel beers now sell in more than 60 countries.

Shortly after the Amstel purchase, the company changed its name from Heineken's Beer Brewery Company to Heineken. The company's remarkable success outside the Netherlands has in recent years led management to emphasize Heineken's international presence rather than casting it as a Dutch company with a significant international operation. In fact, the company now looks upon all of Europe as its domestic market. Heineken Holland has headquarters at the Zoeterwoude brewery. Its various breweries contract with Heineken World to supply worldwide beer shipments. Heineken World headquarters remain in Amsterdam and are housed in an addition to the Heineken family home.

In 1970 Heineken entered the stout market by buying the failing James J. Murphy brewery in Cork, Ireland. In addition to Murphy's Irish Stout, the brewery now produces Heineken light lager brew under license.

Wines, spirits, and soft drinks are becoming increasingly important Heineken products. Soft drinks are made at Bunnik by Vrumona B.V., and the company bottles Pepsi-Cola and 7-Up under license. Heineken and its affiliates also sell Royal Club, Sisi, Sourcy, and B3 soft drinks; Royal Club and Green Sands shandies; and non-alcoholic beers such as Amstel Brew. Spirits and wines include Bologna, Hoppe, Coebergh, Glenmark, Grand Monarque, and Jagermeister brands. In 1971 Heineken purchased the Bokma distillery. Bokma *genever* is now Holland's most popular gin. The distillery at Zoetermeer is the headquarters of Heineken's Netherlands Wine and Spirits Group B.V.

The French market has proven to be the most difficult part of Heineken's European operations, and since entering France in 1972, Heineken has had only one profitable year there. The situation was considered so bleak that in 1986 the company and its French partner cut 500 jobs and closed down three breweries and a bottling plant in France. (The company offered displaced employees retraining and outplacement.) From 1983 to 1986 Heineken invested more than Dfl 550 million in Sogebra S.A. (Société Générale de Brasserie), trying to sustain the company's French activities. Heineken holds 51% of the shares of Sogebra, the second largest brewery in France.

In the 1980's the company has been victim of a series of criminal incidents. In 1982 two unsuccessful blackmail attempts were made against the brewery, followed the next year by an extortion attempt. The most serious incident was the November 1983 kidnapping of the company chief, Alfred Heineken, and his chauffeur. The two were held for 21 days and released after the company paid out an estimated 30 million guilders for their return (though the actual amount was never made public).

Heineken spends tens of millions of guilders each year to bolster its image as a prestigious import. The company's refusal to brew in the United States, even though its beer is brewed under license in many other countries, is in part attributable to a need to maintain the image. Löwenbräu's experience was not lost on Heineken; when Miller began brewing Löwenbräu under license in the United States the German brand lost a major portion of its market share. It appears that Americans enjoy the "snob appeal" of an import. The premium price they pay for Heineken beer lends credence to the image.

Management policies at Heineken have changed little over the years. The family retains control over virtually all aspects of the company, which is managed by a small team selected by the head of the family. The group is kept small—presently three men—in order to prevent factions from developing. However, as in the past, the family head of the company is involved in Heineken's day-to-day functions. Alfred Heineken, grandson of the founder and owner of 50% of the shares in the company, directly supervises research and development, finance, and public relations.

Heineken is unquestionably a powerful force in the brewing industry in the 1980's. In revenues it ranks fifth in the world behind Anheuser-Busch, Miller, Britain's Allied and Japan's Kirin. Its share of the world beer market increased from 2.61% to 2.82% between 1977 and 1981. Total sales of beer brewed under Heineken's supervision was 42.1 million hectolitres in 1986 (the figure includes the beer output of affiliates, as well as that brewed under license by third parties). In the future Heineken is certain to remain a family business; the current major stockholder and director, Alfred Heineken, has publicly stated that he will pass his shares along to his daughter Charlene.

Principal Subsidiaries: Heineken Nederlands Beheer BV; Heineken Brouwerijen BV; Heineken Nederland BV; Heineken Technisch Beheer BV; Heineken Internationaal Beheer BV; Heineken Reken Centrum BV; Heineken Assurantie Bemiddeling BV; Heineken Exploitatie Maatschappij BV; Inverba Holland BV; Amstel Brouwerij BV; Amstel Internationaal BV; Panden Exploitatie Maatschappij BV; Vrumona BV; Bokma BV; Coebergh BV; Gedistilleerd en Wijngroep Nederland BV; Mouterij Albert NV (Belgium); Ibecor S.A. (Belgium); Atheniean Brewery S.A. (Greece), 98.3%; Birra Dreher S.p.A.; Duncan Gilbey & Matheson (U.K.); Murphy Brewery Ireland Ltd. (Ireland); Heineken Finance N.V. (Netherlands Antilles); Windward & Leeward Brewery Ltd., 82.7%; Heineken do Brasil Comercial Leda (Brazil); Amstel Brewery Canada Ltd. The company also lists subsidiaries in Angola, Burundi, France, Indonesia, New Caledonia, People's Republic of Congo, Rwanda, Sierra Leone, Singapore, Spain, Trinidad, and Zaire.

HEUBLEIN, INC.

P.O. Box 388
Farmington, Connecticut 06034–0388
U.S.A.
(203) 240–5000

Wholly-owned subsidiary of Grand Metropolitan plc
Incorporated: December 2, 1915
Employees: 28,500

When Heublein was acquired by R. J. Reynolds in 1982, it was a diversified alcoholic beverage and food products company. Shortly afterwards, Reynolds merged with Nabisco, and many of Heublein's non-beverage operations were sold to other divisions or companies. Heublein itself was sold to Grand Metropolitan in March of 1987; it was then essentially a distiller of vodka (Smirnoff, Relska, Koskarva, Arrow, and Popov brands), and importer of other beverages, such as Harvey's Bristol Cream sherry, Bell's scotch, Guinness Stout, Bass Ale, and Rose's lime juice.

In 1875 Gilbert and Louis Heublein were working in their father's restaurant in Hartford, Connecticut. The Connecticut Foot Guards hired the Heublein restaurant to prepare one gallon of martinis and a lesser amount of manhattans for their annual picnic. The picnic, however, was cancelled by rain and the cocktails were stored. After several days, Gilbert and Louis's father instructed an employee to throw away the mixtures, but the curious clerk tasted the cocktails and declared that they were still good. Gilbert and Louis later decided to sell pre-made cocktails in the restaurant, and when demand for them increased, the two brothers established a distillery to mass-produce the product.

Gilbert and Louis Heublein increased sales by bottling their cocktails for the carriage trade. Their success in this field was facilitated by promotions and creative advertisements which emphasized the "charms, conviviality, and good taste" of the martinis and manhattans.

In 1892 the Heubleins bottled the first pre-mixed cocktails sold to hotels and restaurants, and later offered the cocktails for sale directly to consumers. As the Heubleins' product gained wider popularity, the distillery introduced a line of whiskies: Heublein Private Stock, Old Waverly, Powderhorn, and Forest Park. Gilbert and Louis invested the profits from their growing operation in smaller companies such as the A-1 Steak Sauce Company, which they purchased in 1906.

With the advent of Prohibition, Heublein's profits from alcohol were completely eliminated. The steak sauce operation, which was heavily undervalued when it was acquired, helped to maintain the company's profitability as its only marketable product.

In 1933, after Prohibition had ended, Heublein's distillery operations were revived by John G. Martin, who was named president of the company upon the retirement (and subsequent death) of his grandfather, Gilbert Heublein. Martin's first act as president was to diversify the company's line of alcoholic beverages. In 1939 Martin purchased the trademark and distilling process of Smirnoff vodka from a Russian emigré named Rudolf Kunett. Kunett originally purchased an American franchise for Smirnoff vodka from Vladimir Smirnoff, whose vodka recipe had remained with his family since 1818, but whose vodka was neither popular nor profitable in Russia. Due to competitive pressure and the American public's lack of enthusiasm for vodka, Kunett's franchise soon became unprofitable. As a result, the Smirnoff rights were greatly undervalued when they were purchased by Heublein for only $14,000.

Shortages during World War II led to heavy restrictions on alcohol production. Heublein was not permitted to sell Smirnoff until the war ended. The company was, however, allowed to continue manufacturing its pre-mixed cocktails, because they contained less alcohol and were therefore not as strictly regulated. When the war ended, however, Americans had become unaccustomed to the strong alcoholic taste of regulated spirits such as vodka. Heublein inaugurated an advertising compaign intended to restore the American taste for liquor—in favor of Smirnoff vodka. The campaigns promoted Smirnoff as the vodka that "leaves you breathless," and emphasized its versatility, as it could be combined with a variety of mixers. Vodka's supposed lack of odor attracted noontime drinkers. Sales of Smirnoff increased.

Heublein became the American sales agent for Grey Poupon mustard in 1946. Despite this broadening of the product line, other distillers felt that Heublein relied too heavily on vodka sales. But instead of diversifying into other alcoholic beverage lines, Heublein popularized more diverse uses for Smirnoff; bloody marys, screwdrivers, and Moscow mules were the trendy and popular drinks of the 1950's.

By 1960 vodka consumption had risen to 19.4 million gallons from 1.3 million in 1951, largely as a result of aggressive promotion. In 1961 Martin introduced nine new pre-made cocktails intended for consumers who were inexperienced as home bartenders. Despite the growth and success of the cocktails and Smirnoff, Martin continued to feel pressure to diversify from industry analysts who believed that Heublein would be devastated if either its cocktails or vodka lost popularity. In response, Martin purchased Timely Brands, which made cake decorating products, and Escoffier Ltd., which produced London brand specialty foods. These purchases were particularly timely, as increasing competition in the vodka market depressed profits.

Still, Martin aggressively promoted Heublein's less expensive vodka labels, Relska and Popov. When asked what the difference was between Relska and Smirnoff, Martin admitted that the two liquors were of approximately the same quality, but differed in "pricing policy." The cheaper brands grew in popularity during the 1960's. Heublein's earnings grew to $115 million in 1963—four times the figure in 1959. At this time 73% of Heublein's sales volume was derived from vodka.

In an effort to continue Heublein's diversification, Martin decided to purchase the Arrow liqueur line in 1964. Martin also negotiated the rights to distribute such products as Harvey's Bristol Cream sherry (imported from England), Lancer's rosé (from Portugal), Bisquit cognac (from France), Bertani table wines (from Italy), and Jose Cuervo tequila (from Mexico).

Ralph A. Hart was elected president upon Martin's retirement in 1965. Formerly an executive with Colgate-Palmolive, Hart brought to Heublein a marketing philosophy which permitted the addition of new product lines only on the conditions that they had great sales potential and were compatible with existing distribution channels and marketing techniques.

True to that philosophy, Hart purchased the Theo Hamm Brewing Company of St. Paul, Minnesota, the nation's eighth largest brewer. The company's beer was sold in 31 states, although principally in the American midwest and far west. This acquisition caused a sharp controversy among Heublein executives because it was the first time Heublein had purchased an established firm. Hart, convinced of Hamm's potential, encouraged the brewery's introduction of the first draft beer in a can. The success of this raised prospects for Hamm's and proved Hart's ability to identify superior takeover targets.

In the 1960's many consumers shifted from drinking in saloons to drinking at home, and showed a growing preference for a wider variety of liquors. Through advertising, Hart asked consumers to try more drinks mixed with vodka, noting that, unlike other liquors, one did not have to "acquire a taste" for vodka.

Hart was promoted to chief executive officer in 1966. He was replaced as president by Stuart D. Watson, a marketing expert. Watson was aware of the company's continued over-reliance on sales of vodka. Hamm's had failed to consolidate its market share; the beer lost popularity because store managers were not instructed to rotate their inventories of Hamm's beer. As a result, much of the beer was sold stale—a problem which disenchanted even loyal Hamm's drinkers. Watson acquired the Beaulieu Winery and United Vintners, the second largest winemakers in the U.S., for $33 million. He also decided that Heublein should expand its food production operations, a sector which at the time accounted for only 5% of total sales. The firm purchased the Coastal Valley Canning Company, which produced tomato juice and Ortega brand salsa sauce. The tomato juice addition was particularly beneficial since it could be promoted as a complement to vodka in advertisements featuring bloody marys. These acquisitions, and a much larger advertising budget, led to sales of $384 million in 1968—a 337% increase from 1963.

Sales of A-1 steak sauce in 1968 had increased 113% over 1961; Lancer's rosé was the fastest growing seller of its type in the United States, Arrow liqueurs generated $17

million in sales; and Smirnoff was being produced in 32 countries. Watson's corporate diversification strategy had reduced Heublein's reliance on vodka production, and led to positive growth in all its markets.

Heublein acquired Kentucky Fried Chicken in 1971 as part of Watson's desire for the company to move into more "contemporary" consumer product lines. By 1973, however, Kentucky Fried Chicken's sales growth had slowed dramatically, causing the division to lose some of its market share to competitors.

Heublein's financial position was further compromised by United Vintners, which, as a result of price controls, was prevented from passing on radically increased grape costs to the consumer. These developments weakened Watson's position as leader of Heublein, and prompted him to form an "office of the chairman," consisting of four group vice presidents and himself. The goal of this committee was to set corrective marketing policies and to form future strategies. Another group, the corporate management committee, was comprised of other executives who concentrated solely on administrative matters and shifted the burden of more routine operating decisions to lower management levels. Both groups later recommended the sale of Hamm's to Olympia Brewing, as Heublein was unable to revive the operation.

Watson was replaced as president by Hicks B. Waldron, Jr. in 1975. Unlike Watson, he believed that the entire staff should contribute to corporate decisions rather than just the top executives. He made the executives, middle managers, and line foremen aware of their contributions to Heublein's earnings.

A year earlier, Waldron authorized the expansion of Kentucky Fried Chicken's menu to include fried codfish. This, however, prompted a law suit from Colonel Harland Sanders, the founder of Kentucky Fried Chicken, who claimed that Heublein could not use his name to promote any product but chicken. The codfish proved unsuccessful in any case, and was withdrawn from most franchises.

Kentucky Fried Chicken, however, suffered from several more crucial problems; cleanliness and quality control were low, individual stores were managed poorly, and even Colonel Sanders proclaimed its chicken the worst he had ever tasted. Waldron assigned two Heublein executives, Mike Miles and Dick Mayer, to restore the operation. They recommended more centralized management control, the renovation of many outlets and a reduction in their number, greater promotion of lunchtime business and more disciplined quality control. Heublein undertook all of these measures at great cost, and despite intense competition from Church's Fried Chicken and grocery store frozen brands, Kentucky Fried Chicken's sales began to increase.

In the beverage markets, United Vintners lost a substantial market share to Gallo, and growth in vodka sales slowed to 3% annually, largely as a result of competition. With the exception of isolated successes in some foreign markets, sales of Heublein products had declined.

In 1977 Waldron became ill and relinquished the company presidency to his predecessor Stuart Watson. Watson, however, was unable to reverse Heublein's decline until 1979. That year, United Vintners' sales recovered, largely due to the increased popularity of its Inglenook label—despite a brief (and belated) accusation by the Federal Trade Commission that Heublein's acquisition of United Vintners, ten years before, was anti-competitive. (In 1980, however, the Commission dropped its charges.)

In cooperation with the Reverend Jesse Jackson's Operation PUSH program, Heublein spent $180 million between 1982 and 1986 to create 9000 jobs in the black business community—mostly at black-owned Kentucky Fried Chicken franchises.

With an improved public image and profits restored, Heublein petitioned the Bureau of Alcohol, Tobacco, and Firearms to alter its definition of distilled spirits. The Bureau classified liquor of less than 40% alcohol as "diluted," a term which was unattractive to many consumers. The request, however, has yet to be reviewed.

At this time, R. J. Reynolds Industries, a food, tobacco, energy, and shipping company, purchased Heublein for $1.2 billion. Soon after the acquisition, Reynolds sold some of Heublein's select wineries and brands to Allied Grape Growers, and though this did not have a significant impact on the company's earnings, it did mark the beginning of a planned restructuring for Heublein. Heublein continued to sell a variety of products, and it had the added financial and marketing support of Reynolds when experimenting with new products.

Heublein's international sales increased substantially in the 1980's. A new vodka distillery was built in Brazil, a growing market, where the population was expected to rise from 112 million to 200 million by the year 2000. In 1985 Heublein formed a joint venture with the Mitsubishi Corporation, called Heublein Japan. The company was also forced to abandon its business in Iran, which had become unworkable since the Ayatollah Khomeini came to power in 1979. In the United States, Heublein became the American agent for Wild Turkey Bourbon and other Austin Nichols brands.

During a corporate restructuring in which R. J. Reynolds merged with Nabisco (to form RJR Nabsico), Kentucky Fried Chicken was made a wholly owned subsidiary and was later sold for $800 million. Another subsidiary, the Heublein Grocery Products Group, was subsequently merged with RJR Nabisco's Del Monte group. RJR Nabisco reduced the Heublein product line to a core of beverages, and in March of 1987 sold Heublein to Grand Metropolitan for $1.3 billion.

John Furek, president and chief executive officer of Heublein, and John A. Powers, chairman of the board, have remained in charge of Heublein since shortly after the company was acquired by R. J. Reynolds. Under their direction, Heublein has concentrated much of its marketing strategy on emerging tastes in the American market for lower-alcohol beverages. In fact, attention to satisfying the demands of the American public is the unique factor which had led the Heublein company to its past success. Now, as a subsidiary of Grand Metropolitan, Heublein will largely depend on this consideration for its future success.

Further Reading: *Heublein at 100*, Farmington, Connecticut, The Company, 1975.

HIRAM WALKER RESOURCES, LTD.

1 First Canadian Place
Toronto, Ontario M5X IC5
Canada
(416) 864–3300

Wholly-owned subsidiary of Gulf Canada Ltd.
Incorporated: 1858
Employees: 10,300
Sales: C$3.765 billion (US$2.726 billion)

Hiram Walker began as a small grocery business in 1856. Today it is one of the three largest distilleries in the world, exporting products to over 150 countries. Through growth and expansion, the company now consists of three Canadian distilleries and four American marketing subsidiaries, as well as a bottling facility, a glass company, and a distillery. It owns 11 Scottish distilling plants and has holdings in France, Mexico, Argentina, and Spain. The diversified Hiram Walker Resources has two businesses besides the distilling unit: an oil company and a gas distribution facility.

The founder of the distilling company, Hiram Walker, was born in Massachusetts in 1816. It is ironic that an American did more than anyone else to give Canadian whiskey a distinct identity. Young Walker learned about grain on his family's farm and at the age of 22 moved west to the Detroit area. In Michigan he started a grocery business; one of the commodities he sold was whiskey, in bulk and unbranded. Through his business Walker became a successful grain merchant selling to Canadian millers and distillers.

In the 1850's United States temperance laws were uncertain. Concerned about prohibitionist activities and legal licensing, and attracted to the potential of Canada's markets and natural resources, Walker decided to move his business across the river to Canada. With some of the $40,000 he had earned in Michigan, Walker purchased 468 acres of Canadian land. By 1858 he was operating a combined mill and distillery in Ontario, using his perfected grain for whiskey and turning the rest into flour. Walker believed that the purity of the yeast in a whiskey's fermentation is responsible for the whiskey's flavor.

After Walker opened his business in 1858 he began to build a town around it for his workers. Walkerville included schools, a church, a music hall, modest homes for company employees, and mansions for company execu-

tives. Walker personally hired the members of the town's police force and fire department. In 1890 he commissioned construction of a new set of executive offices in the Florentine style.

In its time, Walkerville created quite a stir. An 1890 *Detroit Journal* article entitled "Neither Town Nor City: The Queerest Place in All Christendom" attacked the town's lack of government, officials, and taxpayers, and contended that Walker was as much a dictator as was the Russian czar. It appears, however, that Walker's employees—the inhabitants of Walkerville—were treated fairly and were content. Walker was known as a charitable man who would pay an employee's medical bills, and he also provided most of the funds for the Children's Free Hospital in Detroit. Walkerville became a part of Windsor, Ontario in 1935.

A year after Walker began his business, John McBride joined it as a salesman. In 1863 McBride and Walker formed a partnership, and the business became known as Hiram Walker and Company. McBride left the company four years later, and in the 1870's, after Walker's sons Edward Chandler and Franklin Harrington joined the enterprise, its name was changed to Hiram Walker and Sons.

The company then introduced its Walker Club Whiskey in the United States, cleverly giving a name to a product that previously had been sold generically. The whiskey's popularity caused American distillers to complain that consumers were unable to differentiate between American and Canadian products. Toward the end of the 1880's, Congress passed legislation requiring the country of origin to be shown on all labels. Walker abided by the law naming his product "Canadian Club." This trademark became such a success that some retailers began falsely to label their whiskies "Canadian." In the courts and in advertisements, Walker accused them of fraud. Soon afterward, Walker faced another obstacle when the Pure Food and Drug Act of 1906 defined blended whiskey as imitation whiskey. Three years later the law was reinterpreted so that blended whiskey would be considered true whiskey as long as its type was specified.

By the beginning of the 20th century Canadian Club was an established favorite in Canada and the United States, and the company had opened offices in Paris and London to introduce its whiskey to the rest of the world.

Hiram Walker retired in 1895 after suffering a stroke that left him paralyzed; he died in 1899. The business remained in the Walker family until 1926, run by Walker's sons and grandsons, including Edward Chandler, Franklin Hiram, James Harrington, and Harrington Walker. During this time the Walker family held all 50,000 of the company's shares. The successful enterprise was earning a yearly average of $1.5 million.

The Walkers faced a problem, however, when Prohibition went into effect in the United States in 1919. While they were Canadian distillers, they were still American citizens and, it seemed, ought to comply with the American law. They found their position uncomfortable, and decided to sell control of the company. Not burdened by the guilt over border trade that so bothered the Walkers, Harry C. Hatch, a Canadian businessman from Toronto, purchased the distillery in 1926. He paid $14 million for the company, $9 million of which was for the "goodwill" associated with the Canadian Club trademark.

Hatch, born in 1883, was the son of a Canadian hotel-keeper. By the time he was 20 years old Hatch was the proprietor of whiskey stores in Whitbey, Toronto, and Montreal, and the general manager of the Corby distillery of Consolidated Distillers Ltd., Montreal. He was a lively and jovial man with a natural flair for sales. He sold liquor by delivery service to customers he could not reach over the counter; he survived Canada's fluctuating prohibition laws by selling by mail order when he could not sell liquor directly; and he sold Corby's overseas when he lacked home markets. By 1923 he was a millionaire. With two friends Hatch purchased Canada's oldest distillery, Gooderham and Worts, which had been established in Toronto in 1832. With his purchase of Hiram Walker and Sons and the consequent merger of the two companies, Hatch came to own the largest distillery in Canada. Together the Walkerville and Toronto plants had a capacity of eight million gallons a year, exceeding that of Distillers Corporation-Seagrams Limited. The combination formed the kernel of the enterprise that exists today, Hiram Walker-Gooderham & Worts, Ltd. Hatch, with a penchant for growth, continued to expand the company until his death in 1946.

For three years after Hatch's takeover the company was highly successful. In 1929, however, the Canadian government decided to help the U.S. enforce the Volstead Act, which governed prohibition. The price wars among Canadian distillers, who now had to continue their cross-border traffic via the French islands of St. Pierre and Miquelon, caused Hiram Walker's profits to fall from their 1929 high of $4 million to $255,000 the next year.

The company's fortunes changed when U.S. prohibition of liquor sales ended in 1933. Hatch had 14 million gallons of whiskey accumulating and ripening in warehouses, and $5 million in Canadian government bonds available to purchase property for an American plant. By opening a plant in the United States, Hiram Walker would avoid the tariffs imposed on sales across the Canadian-American border. William Hull, formerly a member of Congress, persuaded Hatch to locate the new plant in his home town, Peoria, Illinois. Peoria seemed a perfect site for the Walker facility: it had excellent limestone water just below the ground; it was situated in the center of the midwestern cornbelt and a large coal region; and it was on 15 rail lines and the Illinois River, which links the Great Lakes and Mississippi River shipping routes. The Peoria distillery opened in 1934 with William Hull serving as sales manager in the U.S.

In 1936 the company purchased Ballantine & Son Ltd., a Scotch whisky maker. Two years later the firm completed Europe's largest distillery, in Dumbarton, Scotland. In 1943 Walker bought a distilling company in Buenos Aires which produced Old Smuggler and a distinctive Argentinian whiskey, and in the mid-1940's Walker built a bottling company in California.

After Hatch's death in 1946, Howard Walton assumed the presidency. He remained in the post for the next 15 years, during which the company acquired Courvoisier and Salignac Cognacs and established associations with Drambuie and Peter Heering. Walton's successor, Burdette E. Ford, retired in 1964. An important expansion during Ford's years was the purchase of a small plant in Mexico City which today produces Kahlua, the best-known name in coffee liqueurs. H. Clifford Hatch, son of Harry C. Hatch, then took over the presidency of the parent company.

In the 1960's the company formed Hiram Walker International, which introduced the distiller's products in markets outside the U.S. and Canada. Based in London, the international company accounts for 24% of Hiram Walker's sales. By 1969 Hiram Walker's total sales had increased 8.8%, and the company's earnings surpassed $47 million. Canadian Club remained Walker's best-selling brand, but Imperial Blended Whiskey also became very popular.

In 1971 the company built its Okanagan Distillery in British Columbia. The plant handles the company's full domestic line, as well as Canadian Club for Canada and the west coast markets of the U.S. In the same year Hiram Walker (Europe) S.A. completed a distillery in Spain. The operation manufactures a variety of products for the Spanish market, Doble-V being the best known. In 1972 expansion doubled the production capacity of the Walkerville Distillery; seven years later the Peoria plant closed and a new ultra-modern distillery opened in Fort Smith, Arkansas. The plant was better equipped to produce the cream liqueurs that were becoming a large part of Hiram Walker sales.

In 1975 *Time* magazine reported that Hiram Walker and other distilleries had reduced the proof of their whiskeys from 86 to 80 (the lowest legal proof of a whiskey) without lowering prices or publicizing the change. Whiskey sales had been slow for three years, and production costs had soared. Distillers were suffering financially, but were hesitant to raise the price of their products for fear their customers would turn to less expensive beer and wine.

Of growing importance during the 1980's was the company's emphasis on advertising and marketing. Sales had dropped significantly between 1980 and 1984, largely because of widespread public concern over issues of health and drunk driving, and the company recognized the need to update the image of its products. With advertising of Canadian Club directed toward the young, upwardly mobile consumer, the new marketing strategy focused on the changing roles of men and women and the obsession with calories and fitness. One advertisement depicted a woman with a glass of the drink in her hand asking her husband/boyfriend what he was making for dinner. Noted for its light taste, Hiram Walker now began to emphasize this aspect of its product for the first time to attract the young and health-conscious public.

Hiram Walker continued its tradition of growth and expansion in the 1980's. Research began for Canadian Club Classic, a 12-year-old barrel-blended whiskey that was introduced in 1984 and advertised in prestigious magazines. Every aspect of the production of Canadian Club Classic was influenced by market research results. Thirty-two formulas were tried before the final one was chosen. In the same period, the company bought a bourbon distillery in Kentucky, producer of Maker's Mark, and control of Tia Maria Limited. The company entered the cream liqueur category when it introduced the Haagen Dazs line. Hiram Walker also acquired Callaway Wines in California. The growing duty-free business led to the organization of Hiram Walker Consolidated International Brands Limited, which covers duty-free shops, military bases, and airlines. In 1983 Courvoisier received a prestigious French award, *Diplome du Prestige de la France*, honoring its sales performance, progressive personnel policies, and consistently high production standards.

To further consumer recognition throughout the world, Hiram Walker began sponsoring many well-known sporting events. Canadian Club sponsors the annual Golf Challenge Award, Kahlua promotes cross-country skiing events, and Ballantine Scotch supports Scottish highland games in Canada. Hiram Walker also associates its name with rodeos, lobster fishing, and sailing.

In 1980, under pressure from HCI Holdings Ltd., which had begun making large purchases of Hiram Walker's stock in 1979, president Hatch merged his company with Home Oil Company Ltd. and Consumer's Gas Company Ltd. The former is a major presence in the Canadian oil and gas industry and has investments in the United States, the North Sea, Indonesia, and Australia. The latter is a large and efficient gas distribution utility. Hiram Walker Resources is also the largest shareholder in Interprovincial Pipeline Ltd., a major oil pipeline operator. 29 percent of the company's assets are accounted for by its distilled spirits division, with 40% and 31% of its assets in Home Oil and Consumer Gas, respectively.

Falling oil prices in 1981 forced Hiram Walker Resources to make several valuation write-downs on petroleum assets (one $737 million portfolio proved to be worth only about half that amount). Management therefore decided to strengthen the company's financial position by reducing debt, curtailing acquisitions, and reinvesting a greater share of profits. This process depressed short-term earnings and caused share prices to fall. As a result, Hiram Walker was undervalued and began to attract the interest of corporate raiders.

In March 1986 the Reichmann family of Toronto began bidding for shares of Hiram Walker through Gulf Canada, a petroleum resources company they controlled. On April 1, Hiram Walker agreed to sell its liquor operations (Gooderham & Worts) to Allied-Lyons plc for C$2.64 billion. The sale raised cash which Hiram Walker used to resist the Reichmann bid, and at the same time helped Allied-Lyons mount its own defense against a hostile takeover by the Australian conglomerate Elders IXL.

A week later, TransCanada Pipelines made a C$4 billion counter-offer for Hiram Walker. The offer still permitted the sale of liquor operations to Allied-Lyons. By May, however, Gulf Canada had prevailed in its acquisition of Hiram Walker, yet refused to respect the terms of the sale of liquor operations to Allied-Lyons. The matter was taken to court, but was later settled when Allied-Lyons agreed to sell 49% of the liquor division to Gulf Canada for C$800 million. Late in 1987 Allied-Lyons announced it would buy back full control of Hiram Walker. Under the terms of the deal, a 10% stake in Allied-Lyons would go to GW Utilities, Ltd., which took over the assets of Gulf Canada in 1986.

Further Reading: *Hiram Walker and Walkerville from 1858*, New York, Newcomen Society, 1958.

KIRIN BREWERY COMPANY LTD.

26-1, Jingumac 6-chome
Shibuya-ku, Tokyo 150
Japan
03-499-6111

Public Company
Incorporated: 1907
Employees: 7,519
Sales: ¥1.225 trillion (US$7.699 billion)
Market value: ¥2.020 trillion (US$12.694 billion)
Stock Index: Tokyo Osaka Nagoya Kyoto Hiroshima Fukuoka Niigata NASDAQ

Ranking as both the largest brewery in Japan and the third largest in the world, the Kirin Brewery Company Ltd. is internationally renowned. With over 100 years of experience in the brewing business, Kirin now applies its fermentation technology to areas such as plant genetics, pharmaceuticals, and bioengineering. While the brewing operation still remains the core of Kirin's activities, the company anticipates a large future market for these research-intensive projects.

William Copeland, a naturalized U.S. citizen of Norwegian descent, arrived in Yokohama in 1864. Japan had recently reopened its ports to Western commerce, and Copeland hoped to make his fortune there. He first established a drayage business and later a dairy firm; both of these ventures were modestly successful. However, in 1869, responding to the large foreign contingents' demand for domestically brewed beer (Japan had no brewing industry to speak of at this time), Copeland opened the Spring Valley Brewery. In 1872 Copeland left Yokohama temporarily to search for a bride in Norway; later, he returned with his wife, but she died in 1879. Shortly thereafter Copeland, who seemed dogged by misfortune, found that he lacked the necessary capital to improve and expand the business. By 1884 he closed the brewery and sailed for the United States.

A year later W. H. Talbot and E. Abbott, both foreign entrepreneurs, entered into partnership with two Japanese businessmen, Yonosuke Iwasaki and Eiichi Shibusawa, to reopen Copeland's brewery. With sound financial backing, the newly formed Japan Brewery soon became a profitable enterprise. And by 1888, all its beer carried the "Kirin" label. According to ancient Chinese legend, the

Kirin, which is half horse and half dragon, heralds good fortune to those able to catch a glimpse of it.

Although Copeland's association with the company that would one day control a major share of the Japanese beer market was relatively short and difficult, he is credited with founding the only Yokohama brewery that has survived until the present with some degree of continuity. Copeland returned to Yokohama during the late 1880's to open the Spring Valley Beer Garden next door to his old brewery. He operated his establishment with a new wife, but it was not a success and he again left Yokohama. He returned once more in 1901 and died a year later. But to this day, employees pay tribute to the founder by leaving cans of Kirin beer at his grave.

Initially, many foreigners were involved with the company: Americans and Englishmen filled the executive ranks while German technicians supervised the brewing process. Over the years, however, their presence gradually diminished. By 1907, when the firm was incorporated under its current name, management had been taken over entirely by the Japanese.

It was not long before Kirin began rapidly to expand; in 1918 the company constructed a brewery in Amagasaki and later built another facility to house the operations of the Toyo Tozo company which Kirin had taken over. On the eve of World War II, Kirin even ran its own bottling factory. Clearly, the novel attraction of beer had developed into a large market demand; the company achieved record sales figures during the mid-1930's.

With the start of World War II, the government imposed strict controls over the entire brewing industry. Sales of Kirin beer dropped drastically. Despite a reduction in operations, however, Kirin established the foundation for its future research and development efforts. In January 1943 the company created the science laboratory at the Yokohama brewery and the research department at the Amagasaki brewery.

Over the years, Kirin's research and development activities outgrew the original facilities. Consequently, in order to co-ordinate long-term projects and centralize its scientific investigations, the firm built a new laboratory in Takasaki. The General Research Laboratory, completed in 1967, placed Kirin in the forefront of brewing technology. At Kirin's Takasaki laboratory scientists offered the first explanation for the mechanics of diacetyl formation in the brewing process. Based on this discovery, Kirin devised a way to control metabolism during the period of fermentation. Another noteworthy research effort included the development of the "Amagi-Nijo" strain of malting barley which today commands over a 50% share of the worldwide market. More recently, company bacteriologists have learned how to control a virus known to destroy the bitter flavor of hops.

Sales improved dramatically after the war; during the 1950's the average increase was 17% a year. By the end of the decade, beer had replaced sake as Japan's most popular beverage and Kirin had established itself as the nation's leading brewery. A little more than 10 years later, Kirin's sales figures were exceeded by only one other brewery in the world—the St. Louis-based Anheuser-Busch company. Much of Kirin's success is attributed to its controlling over 60% of Japan's beer market which was itself growing by an annual rate of eight percent.

During the early 1970's Kirin's management decided to diversify into new areas. A partnership was announced with Joseph E. Seagram & Sons Inc., the U.S. subsidiary of the Montreal-based liquor company; Kirin-Seagram operated a distillery to produce scotch whisky. The company also launched a variety of new soft drinks, and Kirin's Lemon Fizz and Orangeade were generating large sales. Later, dairy items and fruit juices were added to its product line. Additionally, using its expertise and knowledge acquired from years of developing fermentation technology, Kirin introduced new drugs to the health care field.

Kirin's beer sales reached a record high in 1977. But threatened with an antitrust suit, the company president, Yasusaburo Sato, initiated a temporary program of self-imposed regulation. The plan was to control production, ration distribution, and tone down the advertising campaign. By the following year, Kirin achieved a stabilization in beer sales and still increased revenues because of its successful diversified businesses.

Kirin suffered a setback in the fiscal year of 1979–80. Following the yen's depreciation, import costs for barley and fuel reduced the company's operating profits by 22.2%. Moreover, the increased price of domestic barley and wheat, which Japanese brewers are forced to use by government decree, contributed to Kirin's unimpressive performance. The company had to raise the price of its beer; two years later Kirin reported an increase in operating profits.

Kirin had been deterred from selling its beer in foreign markets because of high transportation costs. But in the early 1980's a licensing contract was arranged with Heineken N.V., the Netherlands-based brewing company, whereby Kirin produced Heineken for the Japanese market and Heineken produced Kirin for the Dutch market.

As Japanese cuisine became popular with Americans, the demand for Kirin beer increased. The firm established the Cherry Company Ltd., a wholly owned subsidiary in Hawaii to supervise Kirin's U.S. market distribution. Kirin USA was then established in New York to promote sales.

By 1986 Kirin's international operations encompassed Europe, North America, South America, Asia, and Australia. In West Germany, Kirin contracted Krones A.G. to market empty bottle inspection machinery. (This equipment marked the introduction of intelligent robots to the brewing industry.) In Brazil, Kirin holds a majority interest in a food and beverage company; in China, the company is constructing a soft drink production factory; in Australia, the Kirin Australia Pty. Ltd. subsidiary manu-

factures and supplies Kirin products to the Australian market.

In the 1980's, management initiated major changes in Kirin's research and development program. The company's laboratory was divided and reorganized along three major fields of investigation—brewing science, pharmaceuticals, and plant bioengineering. New departments were also added at the administrative level to coordinate fund-raising activities for research projects.

Lately, a number of joint ventures established with American companies have increased Kirin's participation in the field of biotechnology. In 1984 Kirin completed a 50–50 venture with Amgen, a California-based company, to develop and market a synthetic human hormone to treat anemia. This pharmaceutical, called Erythropoietin, was created to help patients undergoing kidney dialysis. In the past, many patients commonly became anemic and required blood transfusions during treatment. Another potential application is as a drug for cancer patients suffering blood-cell reduction from chemotherapy. Kirin also combined its resources with an agricultural biotechnology company, Plant Genetics Inc. Together, the partners plan to develop synthetic seeds for a variety of agricultural products.

Kirin's most recent expansion activity includes a successful chain of beer pubs called Kirin City. Started in the Roppongi district in 1983, the company now controls 11 pubs across Japan. Similarly, the Kirin Food Service Company Ltd., another recently established subsidiary, operates a restaurant franchise. Kirin has also constructed a number of health clubs and sports complexes across the nation. The latest addition to Kirin's list of subsidiaries is the Flower Gate company which produces African violets developed by an innovative tissue culture process.

According to industry analysts, Kirin's profits will continue to rise with the purchase of inexpensive raw materials from overseas and the growth of the company's diversification program. While the company actively pursues a wide variety of applications for its biotechnological investigations, the business of brewing beer will remain the most important of its operations.

Principal Subsidiaries: Kirin-Seagram Ltd. (50%); Kirin Lemon Services Co., Ltd.; Hokkaido Kirin Lemon Service Co., Ltd.; Tsurumi Warehouse Co., Ltd.; Nagano Tomato Co., Ltd.; Koisai Products Co., Ltd.; Kirin Echo Co., Ltd.; KCB Food Service Co., Ltd.; Serealia Co., Ltd.; Kinki Coca-Cola Bottling Co., Ltd.; Kirin City; Kirin Food Service Co., Ltd.; Flower Gate Inc.; Kirin Sports Club; Kirin's Seaside Tennis Club; The Cherry Co., Ltd. (Hawaii); Kirin USA; KW Inc.; Industria Agricola Tozan SA (Brazil); Kirin Australia Pty., Ltd. (Australia); KBB Malting Company Pty., Ltd.

LABATT BREWING COMPANY LTD.

150 Simcoe Company
London, Ontario N6A 4M3
Canada
(519) 673–5050

Wholly-owned subsidiary of John Labatt Ltd.
Incorporated: 1911 as John Labatt Ltd; 1979 as Labatt
Brewing Company Ltd.
Employees: 14,200
Sales: C$1.274 billion (US$922 million)

In 140 years the Labatt Brewing Company Ltd has grown from a local enterprise into Canada's largest brewing company, with Labatt beverages distributed around the world. As the business expanded, production diversified into new areas, eventually warranting creation of a separate brewing group controlled by the John Labatt Ltd holding company.

Company founder John Kinder Labatt was born in Ireland in 1803. His family heritage can be traced back to the Huguenots in France. Fleeing prosecution, Labatt's ancestors resettled outside Dublin. As a young man Labatt moved to London, England, where he met and married Eliza Kell. Together the couple set sail in 1833 for Canada and arrived in London, Ontario. Labatt became a farmer and sold prize-winning malting barley to the local innkeeper who had built a small brewery in 1828. Contact with the innkeeper gave Labatt the idea of becoming a brewer himself, an idea in which he became so interested that in 1847 he formed a partnership with Samuel Eccles, an experienced brewer. The two bought the London Brewery from the innkeeper.

Early annual production capacity was 400 barrels, In 1853 Labatt bought his partner's share of the business and increased annual brewing capacity to 4,000 barrels. The newly renamed John Labatt's Brewery had six employees. Despite its remarkable production increase, the young enterprise remained a local operation. The situation changed, however, with the growing presence of the railroads. When the tracks of the Great Western Railway connected London to other cities, Labatt began shipping beer and ale to Montreal, Toronto, and the Maritimes.

John Labatt's third son, John Labatt II, apprenticed as a brewer in Wheeling, West Virginia. John's two older brothers, Robert and Ephraim, had meanwhile gone into their own brewery business. Their departure left the John Labatt Brewery without a brewmaster, as it had been assumed that one of the older brothers would eventually fill the position. As a result, at age 26 John Labatt II accepted his father's offer of the post.

In his new capacity, John II was instrumental in establishing a product with international appeal, India Pale Ale, based on a recipe he had learned in Wheeling. By 1878 the ale had earned high marks and honors at the Canada Exposition in Ottawa, the International Centennial in Philadelphia, the Exposition in Australia, and the International Exposition in France.

In 1866, just two years after John II returned to the brewery, the founder died, leaving the company to his wife. Eliza Labatt formed a partnership with her son and renamed the business Labatt & Company. Mother and son operated the brewery together until 1872, when John II bought his mother's interest and became the sole owner.

Before the new company leader had much opportunity to establish himself, fire destroyed the London Brewery. Fortunately, however, insurance coverage enabled Labatt to build a modern facility at the cost of $20,000. Annual production now reached 30,000 barrels.

In addition to introducing an award-winning ale and expanding production, John II is credited with modernizing the company through the use of refrigeration and distribution networks. Labatt products also reached distant Canadian provinces; by 1900 customers in Manitoba and the Northwest Territories could purchase the brewer's products.

At the turn of the century John II's two sons, Hugh and John III, joined the family business. John III had earned a brewmaster's certificate from the brewing academy in New York after graduating from McGill University.

In 1911 John II incorporated his company under the name John Labatt Limited. All but four of the 2,500 shares issued were retained by him. The remainder went to his two sons, a nephew, and his lawyer. Total capitalization amounted to $250,000.

John Labatt II died in 1915 at age 75, and the company presidency went to John III. At that time the various provinces were debating possible Prohibition laws. Unlike the United States, where the liquor industry was regulated by a blanket federal law, in Canada each province created its own standard. While almost all of Canada was legally rendered dry by 1916, several provinces allowed the manufacture of alcoholic beverages for export. By the end of Prohibition only 15 of Ontario's 65 breweries still survived. Labatt was not only one of the surviviors, but was also the only such firm to have maintained management continuity through the era.

During the 1920's and 1930's the brewery implemented a number of innovative employee policies. In the 1920's Labatt workers became some of the first Canadian employees to receive annual vacation pay. In 1932 Labatt set an industry standard by establishing a group insurance plan for its employees, and six years later an annuity plan was created to build pension benefits.

While the nation struggled through the years of the Depression, the Labatt family underwent its own period of misfortune. On August 15, 1934, John Labatt III, already a widely recognized business and community leader, was kidnapped on the way from his summer home in Sarnia to a company board meeting. Later his empty car was discovered with a note instructing John's brother, Hugh, to pay a ransom of $150,000 for the safe return of the victim. For the next several days the story of the mysterious disappearance appeared in the headlines of major newspapers around the world. The incident was the first kidnap assault in Canadian history. Detectives concentrated their search around the Detroit, Michigan areas as suspicion mounted about the possibility of gangster involvement. During Prohibition, American gangsters had transported alcoholic beverages from Canada into the United States in rowboats down the Detroit River. Authorities believed Labatt had been abducted in a similar fashion. After a few days Labatt was released unharmed. The search for his assailants continued over the next several months until the severely shaken Labatt identified a Canadian bootmaker. Labatt retired from public life for the remaining years of his presidency.

After World War II the company prepared to undertake a major expansion. To raise capital John Labatt Ltd became a public company and issued 900,000 shares. Many employees were among the over 2,000 original shareholders. In 1946 the company completed its first acquisition, the Copland Brewing Company in Toronto, which doubled Labatt's brewing capacity.

The 1950's saw a number of new beverages added to Labatt's product line. Fiftieth Anniversay Ale, nicknamed "Annie" or "Fifty," commemorated John and Hugh Labatt's years of activity in the company. It later became Canada's most popular ale. Pilsner Lager Beer was Labatt's successful venture in the international market.

In 1951 the company presidency passed from John III to his brother Hugh, the former vice president. A year later John died at age 72. The company continued to expand during the decade, most notably with the purchase of Shea's Winnipeg Brewery Ltd., a company dating to 1873. The new subsidiary introduced Labatt into the hotel industry. Labatt also acquired the Lucky Lager Brewing Company of San Francisco. Construction of a $6.5 million brewery in Ville La Salle, Quebec in 1956 marked Labatt's expansion into other provinces.

When Hugh Labatt died in 1956, W.H.R. Jarvis became the first non-family president of Labatt. The following year he oversaw formation of a Feed Products Department, the company's first entrance into an industry outside brewing. The division manufactured animal feed additives using brewing by-products.

Jarvis died of a heart attack during a board meeting in the early 1960's. John H. Moore assumed the post and supervised the further expansion of Labatt's operations. Acquisition of breweries in Newfoundland and Saskatoon, and later in Halifax and Waterloo, strengthened Labatt's position in the national market.

Major structural changes occurred at Labatt in the next few years. The first came in the mid-1960's when the Milwaukee-based Joseph Schlitz Brewing Company attempted to gain a 40% interest in the Canadian brewery. The family trust agreed to sell half its shares and many public shareholders were also willing to sell, but the acquisition was eventually halted by U.S. antitrust laws. An investigation led by then-U.S. Attorney-General Robert F. Kennedy alleged that Schlitz wanted to control the California market through a Labatt subsidiary. In 1967 Schlitz was forced to sell its approximately one million shares to a consortium of three Canadian investment groups. From then on Labatt would take pride in maintaining its strictly Canadian identity.

Another major structural change occurred in 1964 when John Labatt Ltd. became a holding company to manage all the various company activities. Brewing fell under Labatt Breweries of Canada Ltd. The parent company proceeded to make acquisitions in other areas. Labatt's first purchase in the wine industry was of Parkdale Wines, in 1965. In 1973 Labatt consolidated its many wine holdings under the Chateu-Gai brand name. The Ogilvie Flour Mills Company purchase led Labatt into the dairy and processed food industry. Other food product purchases followed over the next several years. By 1974 company operations fell into three main divisions, brewing, consumer products, and agricultural products. Brewing operations were later divided into the Canadian and International groups.

A major expansion campaign at the London facility in 1965 increased annual capacity to 1.3 million barrels, making it one of the largest breweries in the world. At the same time, Labatt announced plans to form a joint venture with Guinness Overseas Ltd. to produce the famous Irish stout in Canada.

At the end of the decade Moore announced he would leave Labatt to take charge of a company that represented Labatt's largest shareholder. N.E. Hardy, formerly president of Labatt Breweries of Canada Ltd., succeeded Moore.

Labatt participated in the construction of a brewery in Trinidad and purchased an interest in Zambia Breweries and a Brazilian brewing company during the 1970's. It also established Labatt Importers Inc. in New York to develop aggressively Labatt's presence in the U.S. market. The company also acquired a 45% interest in the Toronto Blue Jays, an American League baseball franchise.

The company continues to grow in the 1980's. The Labatt Brewing Company Ltd., as the brewing operations are now named, engages in such innovative activities as biotechnology. (The company offers a consulting service through its research on the genetic manipulation of yeast.) Today Labatt is Canada's largest brewing company, and is involved in many other enterprises. In all its ventures, the company continues to take pride in remaining loyal to its original product and its Canadian heritage.

Principal Subsidiaries of John Labatt Ltd: Sports Network; McGavin Foods Ltd.; Catelli-Primo Ltd.; Allelix Inc,; Casco Co,; Canada Malting Co. Ltd.

MILLER BREWING COMPANY

3939 West Highland Boulevard
Milwaukee, Wisconsin 53201
U.S.A.

Wholly-owned subsidary of Philip Morris, Inc.
Incorporated: 1888
Employees: 11,000
Sales: $2.92 billion

Between the establishment of the Miller Brewing Company in 1855 and the death of its founder in 1888, the firm's annual productive capacity increased from 300 barrels to 80,000 barrels of beer. This impressive growth has continued to the present day: Miller now operates six breweries, five can manufacturing plants, four distributorships, a glass bottle production facility, a label and fiberboard factory, and numerous gas wells. Beginning with a staff of 25, Miller now employs some 11,000 people. The company currently produces more than 40 million barrels of beer per year and is the second largest brewery in the U.S.

The founder of the Miller Brewing Company, Frederick Miller, was born in Germany in 1824. As a young man he worked in the Royal Brewing Company at Sigmaringen, Hohenzollern. In 1850, however, at the age of 26, he emigrated to the United States. Miller wanted to start his own brewery and regarded Milwaukee as the most promising site, probably because of the large number of beer-drinking Germans living there.

In 1855 Miller bought the Plank Road Brewery from Charles Lorenz Best and his father. These two men had been slow to modernize their operation, but Miller's innovative techniques made him successful, indeed famous, in the brewing industry.

The Bests had started a "cave-system" which provided storage for beer in a cool undisturbed place for several months after brewing. Yet these caves were small and in poor condition. Miller improved upon the Best's system: his caves were built of brick, totaled 600 feet of tunnel, and had a capacity of 12,000 barrels. Miller used these until 1906 when, due to the company's expansion and the availability of more modern technology, refrigerator facilities were built.

After his death, Miller's sons Ernest, Emil, and Frederick A., along with their brother-in-law Carl, assumed control of the operation which was incorporated as the Frederick Miller Brewing Company. By 1919 production had increased to 500,000 barrels, but it was halted shortly thereafter by the enactment of Prohibition. The company managed to survive by producing cereal beverages, soft drinks, and malt-related products.

Ernest Miller died in 1922 and was succeeded as president by his brother Frederick A. Miller. Frederick A. remained president and chief executive until 1947 when his nephew, Frederick C., became head of the firm. Frederick C. instituted a program of expansion, and was instrumental in bringing major league baseball (the Braves) to Milwaukee, thus strengthening the relationship between the beer industry and the sporting world. The cultivation of this relationship led to increased sales for Miller. But tragedy struck when Frederick C. was killed in a plane crash in Milwaukee during 1954. At the time of his death, the Miller Brewing Company was ranked ninth among American brewers.

The expansion program initiated in 1947 was continued by Norman Klug who became president following Miller's death. Under Klug's management, Miller purchased the A. Gettelman Company in 1961, and four years later bought the General Brewing Corporation of Azusa, California. That same year, the firm purchased a Carling O'Keefe brewery in Fort Worth, Texas. By this time Miller had formed a can manufacturing company in Milwaukee with the Carnation Corporation. The plant produced approximately 150 million beer cans a year.

Just before Klug's death, arrangements had been made for a diversified shipping firm, W.R. Grace, to acquire 53% of the brewing company. The Miller stock was owned at that time by Mrs. Lorraine Mulberger and her family, descendents of Frederick A. Miller. The Mulbergers were paid $36 million but Grace soon discovered that its purchase was significantly undervalued.

Because of its cash reserves and growing importance within the industry, Miller was a prime acquisition target; in 1969 management at Grace decided to sell its interest in Miller to PepsiCo for $120 million. Yet suddenly, and without warning, Grace cancelled the agreement and almost immediately sold its shares to Philip Morris for $130 million. PepsiCo filed suit in federal court to prevent this, but the suit failed.

Philip Morris purchased the remaining shares of Miller's stock from the De Rance Foundation of Milwaukee in the following year (1970). In 1971 Miller extended its production activities in Fort Worth, obtained a tract of land in Delaware as a possible site for a new brewery, and also acquired Formosa Springs, a Canadian brewery. By 1972 Miller Brewing ranked seventh in the beer industry.

Under the Philip Morris management, Miller's marketing strategies and advertising campaigns became more important than ever before. Aiming to replace Anheuser-Busch as the nation's largest brewer, the company expanded its range of brands and penetrated all segments of the market. As a result, production rose from seven million barrels in 1973 to 31 million barrels in 1978.

Led by John Murphy, a Philip Morris executive trained as a lawyer and with notable marketing ability, the company began a thorough study of American beer drinking trends. Miller had been known previously as "The Champagne of

Beers," and its advertising campaigns were directed to appeal to a specific group of white-collar consumers. Murphy revised this strategy and reoriented it toward the large blue-collar market with an emphasis on the work-reward relationship. Miller's new slogan was: "If you've got the time, we've got the beer." This slogan, and the marketing plan behind it, led to increased sales.

By 1985 reduced calorie beers accounted for 20.5% of all beer sales. Miller has the distinction of initiating this market with its Miller Lite, which still remains the number one product in this category. Rather than marketing Miller Lite as a diet beer, the company emphasized its lower calorie content and its unique flavor. Once again it was clever advertising that accounted for Miller's success. Television advertisements showed brawny men enjoying Miller Lite; the slogan proclaimed: "Everything you always wanted in a beer. And less." The Miller Lite allstars, included such personalities as Rodney Dangerfield and John Madden, have continued this approach in the beer's award-winning commercials. In 1986 the tagline emphasized the beer's uniqueness: "There's only one Lite beer. Miller Lite."

Miller's rivals soon responded with low calorie beers of their own, and the company tried to prevent brewers such as Schlitz and Heileman from using the world "Light." Fortunately for Miller's rivals—and for the English language—the U.S. Supreme Court ruled that Miller did not have exclusive rights to the word.

Shortly after the introduction of Miller Lite, the company began to market a domestically brewed version of Löwenbräu—a German beer with a 600-year old history—to which Miller owned the U.S. distribution rights. In an $11 million advertising campaign, Miller captured 10% of Anheuser-Busch's Michelob market. Anheuser-Busch promptly filed suit with the Federal Trade Commission accusing Miller of using deceptive packaging and advertis-

ing in order to convince consumers they were buying an imported beer. Later, when Anheuser-Busch introduced its "Natural Light" beer, Miller retaliated by pointing out that there was nothing natural about Anheuser-Busch's product. The publicity garnered from these "beer wars" helped Miller to improve its standing within the brewing industry; by the early 1980's, Miller was in second place behind Anheuser-Busch.

After Miller brew beer, it is filtered, aged, and finally packaged. Most packaged beers are pasteurized, but two Miller products are unique because they require no pasteurization; in effect, they are real draft beers in a bottle. Plank Road Original Draft and Miller Genuine Draft are made with special cold filtering process (purchased from Sapporo Breweries in 1985) that removes the yeast residue and allows the beer to be packaged without pasteurization (which, because it involves heating the beer, affects its flavor). Although the shelf life for these two items is the same as other packaged beer (approximately 120 days), consumers have noticed the difference in taste. Sales have skyrocketed since their introduction.

Miller's presidents since Murphy—John Cullman, George Weisman, and the current president William Howell—have resolutely continued their company's efforts to dislodge Anheuser-Busch as America's largest brewery. Yet the company still has a long way to go. At present, Miller sells 40 million barrels of beer a year and has a 20% market share, as compared with Anheuser-Busch's 67.8 million barrels and 36.6% market share. The competition between the two largest breweries in the U.S. continues.

Further Reading: Heritage Born and Pledged Anew, Milwaukee, Miller Brewing Company, 1955; *Brewed in America: A History of Beer and Ale in the U.S.* by Stanley Wade Baron, New York, Arno Press, 1972.

MOËT-HENNESSY

30 avenue Hoche
75008 Paris
France
(1) 563–0101

Public Company
Incorporated: 1971
Employees: 7063
Sales: FFr7.477 billion (US$1.162 billion)
Market Value: FFR14.183 billion (US$2.205 billion)
Stock Index: Paris Brussels

Moët-Hennessy, whose product lines includes Christian Dior perfurme, Dom Pérignon champagne, and Hennessy X.O. cognac, is a well-established and extremely successful French enterprise. What began as the business of a talented French vinter almost 250 years ago is now a world leader in the production of wines, spirits, cosmetics, and perfumes.

Claude Moët considered the Champagne region east of Paris, in the Marne River valley, to be an ideal location for wine production. He established a vineyard near Epernay, but became frustrated dealing with the *courtiers en vin*, or distributors, who took his wine to market. Instead of depending on them to sell his wine, Moët decided to buy one of the offices of *courtiers en vin* and sell the wine himself.

In 1743 Moët et Cie (Moët and Company) was formed. Joined by his son Claude-Louis, Moët quickly established customer accounts which included a number of landed gentry and nobles. In 1750 father and son established an account with Madame du Pompadour, who regularly ordered Moët champagne for the royal court at Compiègne. That same year Moët began selling champagne in Germany, Spain, Eastern Europe, and America.

Claude Moët died in 1792, leaving the company to his grandson Jean-Rémy, who laid the groundwork for the later success of Moët et Cie. He expanded the base of operations at Epernay by purchasing the vineyards of the Abbey of Hautvillers, where a century earlier the Benedictine monk Dom Pérignon perfected the double fermentation of wine to create champagne. However, it was Jean-Rémy's friendship with Napoleon that helped the company attract a loyal international following.

Jean-Rémy became mayor of Epernay in 1802 and first met Napoleon two years later. Napoleon and his entourage were lavishly wined and dined by Jean-Rémy in newly built guest houses at the firm's address, 20 avenue de Champagne. Champagne historian Patrick Forbes wrote of the period: ". . . everybody who was anybody in Europe was passing through the Champagne district en route from Paris to the Congress of Vienna and they all wanted to visit the celebrated champagne maker. . . . His 10 years in the Napoleonic limelight had made him the most famous wine-maker in the world and orders for his champagne began pouring in with such profusion that he hardly knew how to fill them." Later, before abdicating, Napoleon rewarded Jean-Rémy for his generosity by giving him his own Officer's cross of the Legion of Honor. Moët later dedicated its Brut Imperial in Napoleon's honor.

Jean-Rémy's customer list in the early 19th century had grown to include such famous people as Czar Alexander of Russia, Emperor Francis II of Austria (Napoleon's father-in-law), the Duke of Wellington, Madame de Staël, Queen Victoria, and the Prince Royal of Russia (later to become emperor of Germany).

In 1832 Jean-Rémy retired and relinquished direction of the company to his son Victor and son-in-law Pierre-Gabriel Chandon de Briailles. To reflect the new partnership, the company's name was changed to Moët et Chandon.

Victor and Pierre expanded the firm's operations, and by 1879 Moët et Chandon dominated the Marne Valley with its introduction of more flavorful grapes from Cramant, Le Mesnil, Bouzy, Ay, and Verzenay. At this time Moët et Chandon employed close to 2000 people working as cellarmen, cork cutters, clerks, vineyard farmers, tinsmiths, needlewomen, basketmarkers, firemen, packers, wheelwrights, and stableboys. The company had even established a social security system for employees, which included free medical attention, housing assistance, pensions, maternity benefits, sick pay, and free legal aid.

Moët's average annual sales were believed to have been about 20,000 bottles during the 1820's. By 1872 that figure had risen to two million, and by 1880 it had reached 2.5 million. At the turn of the 20th century, Moët et Chandon's clientele remained primarily within the upper echelons of society.

During World War I, bombs demolished the offices and guesthouses where Napoleon had dined. (Today the only remaining structures from the original property are two salons, used as reception rooms for visitors.) Despite the destruction, Moët et Chandon reaffirmed its place in the market in the late 1920's by creating the Dom Pérignon brand of vintage champagne. Described by connoisseurs as the most perfect champagne available, Dom Pérignon also became the most expensive. The introduction of Dom Pérignon initiated a trend other champagne houses later followed: that of creating a premium brand, which placed other regular vintages second in status. Dom Pérignon, however, emerged as the most successful premium champagne.

Despite interruptions in its business during World War II, Moët et Chandon recovered quickly after the war, as a result of its prompt modernization of facilities. From the installation of new wine presses to a comprehensive system of work incentives, the goals of fairness and efficiency were emphasized in all aspects of production.

Count Robert-Jean de Vogüé, one of France's most important wine buyers in the mid-1950's, led the company to even greater success. Under de Vogüé, Moët et Chandon experienced its most rapid period of growth to date, marked by its transformation from a family-owned venture into a Société Anonyme, or corporation. A series of acquisitions, mergers, and diversifications expanded the company's product line.

Moët et Chandon gained control of Ruinart Père et Fils (France's oldest champagne house and Moët's chief competitor) in 1962. The company acquired Mercier, another rival champagne house, in 1970, and soon thereafter purchased an interest in Parfums Christian Dior, marking the company's first undertaking outside the champagne business. Moët et Chandon later completed its takeover of Dior, whose perfume products include Miss Dior, Dioressence, and Eau Savage.

Moët et Chandon merged with Jas. Hennessy & Company, France's second largest cognac producer, in 1971. The new company, called Moët-Hennessy, enjoyed a broader financial base and was better able to stimulate the growth of its interests abroad. The merger of Moët and Hennessy was brought about mainly as a result of a 1927 statute which limited the Champagne growing region to 34,000 hectares. (The statute was intended to protect the quality of French champagne by discouraging price competition). While less than 25,000 hectares were under cultivation in 1970, Robert-Jean de Vogüé believed that growing demand for champagne would exhaust the supply of land by the year 2000. Until other regions suitable for champagne production could be found, de Vogüé decided that diversification through a merger with Hennessy would insure a stable future for Moët.

Moët-Hennessy established a firmer presence in the United States in 1973 when it opened the Domaine Chandon winery in Napa Valley, California, a location which proved ideal for the production of sparkling wines. The production of sparkling wines at Domaine Chandon grew dramatically and enabled Moët-Hennessy to expand in one of its most important foreign markets. The winery also reduced, somewhat, demand in North America for French champagne, whose production was still restricted by law.

Alain Chevalier, a protegé of de Vogüé, was chiefly responsible for the success of Domaine Chandon. He was named chief executive officer in the mid-1970's, and has since transformed Moët-Hennessy into a less conservation company with more aggressive marketing strategies. After de Vogüé's, death in 1976, Chevalier continued the diversification program started by his predecessor.

In 1977 Moët-Hennessy purchased the Rozes companies in Portugal and France in an effort to raise demand for champagne. The following year, the company purchased Roc, a French cosmetics firm specializing in hypoallergenic make-up. The company also acquired Delbard, a French rose company, which was unable to continue financing the development of special new rose hybrids. The company also purchased Armstrong Nurseries of Ontario, California, the largest farmer of rosebushes in America. Moët-Hennessy is trying to apply rosebush cloning techniques to grape vines in order to produce better hybrids. As a result of these acquisitions, Moët-

Hennessy became the world's leading producer of roses. Chevalier, who became president of Moët-Hennessy in 1982, told *Business Week*, "Roses are a commodity. We can make them a brand name like champagne." Losses incurred by both Roc and Armstrong, however, depressed Moët-Hennessy's earnings. The introduction of a popular new perfume from Dior called Poison, however, largely covered those losses.

Continuing its expansion in the United States, Moët-Hennessy acquired its American sales agent, Schieffelin & Company, one of the oldest wine and spirit distributors in North America. Moët-Hennessy is one of the first French companies to use European Currency Units (or "ECU's"), which are more stable in value against the dollar, and are therefore preferable for funding investments in the United States. Moët-Hennessy has yet to realize fully an $11.7 million investment in research and development made during 1983 and 1984. The company has, however, succeeded in creating advanced technology for the *in vitro* method of cultivating roses and vines. Moët scientists are also developing a method which uses encapsulated yeast pellets to speed fermentation without changing the taste of the product. This technique will reduce labor costs and create as much as 15% more space for aging. The company plans to license the technology to competitors if the experiments are successful on a larger scale.

In June 1987 Moët-Hennessy announced plans to merge with Louis Vuitton, a champagne and luggage concern. A new holding company called LVMH was formed to operate three separate businesses: Moët-Hennessy, Louis Vuitton, and Dior. Alain Chevalier was named chairman of LVMH, and Henry Recamier, the septuagenarian chairman of Louis Vuitton, was named executive vice-president. The merger strengthened Moët-Hennessy's family control, and settled the question of management succession at Louis Vuitton. In addition to announcing the merger, Moët-Hennessy also completed a separate agreement with Guinness, the Irish brewing company, to cooperate in the distribution and marketing of each other's products.

Moët-Hennessy is presently France's leading champagne producer and exporter, its second largest cognac exporter, and the world's largest exporter of perfumes and cosmetics. In keeping with its prestigious reputation for quality and innovation, Moët-Hennessy may be expected to develop new products while protecting and maintaining those which have made it famous.

Principal Subsidiaries: Jas. Hennessy & Co. (99%): Champagne Moët & Chandon (99.9%); Parfums Christian Dior Paris (98.8%); Setric Genie Industriel (99.9%); Pellisson (99.8%); Taransaud (99.9%); Distillerie de la Groie (99.9%); Champagne Ruinart (99.9%); Rozes France; Fines Specialties S.A. (99.9%); France Champagne (99.9%); Provital (99.7%); Champagne Mercier (99.9%); Roc (97.1%); Richemont (UK); Armstrong Nursuries Inc. (USA) (93.3%); Schieffelin & CO. (USA); Simi Winery (USA); Domaine Chandon (USA). The company also lists subsidiaries in Belgium, Brazil, Canada, Italy, Japan, Mexico, The Netherlands, Panama, Portugal, Switzerland, the United Kingdom, and West Germany.

MOLSON COMPANIES LTD.

1555 Notre Dame Street East
Montreal, Quebec H2L 2R5
Canada
(514) 521–1786

Public Company
Incorporated: December 4, 1930
Employees: 1100
Sales: C$1.639 billion (US$1.186 billion)
Market Value: C$652 million (US$472 million)
Stock Index: Toronto Vancouver Montreal

Established in 1876, Molson is the oldest brewery in North America. The modern brewery's operations are extensive, and Molson beers are now sold throughout Canada and in most of the United States. The company is also licensed to brew the German Löwenbräu beer for distribution in North America and, under contract with Adolph Coors Company of Colorado, distributes Coors and Coors Light beers in Canada.

Founder John Molson did not limit his attention to brewing; in the early 19th century he invested in farming, lumber, banking, and various civic enterprises. He is also known for lending his support to development of the first Canadian steamboat line and railroads. Later the company shed all its interests in non-brewing fields and concentrated on its original business for a century. In the 1960's Molson began to diversify and today has divisions in various industries, particularly sanitation products, retail home improvement outlets, venture capital, and television production.

The history of Molson brewing began soon after the 18-year-old Molson emigrated from Lincolnshire, England during the late 18th century. He arrived in Montreal in 1782. A year later Molson became a partner in a small brewing company outside the city walls on the St. Lawrence River. In 1785 he became the sole proprietor of the brewery, closed it temporarily, and sailed to England to settle his estate and buy brewing equipment. Upon his return in 1786, with a book entitled *Theoretical Hints on an Improved Practice of Brewing* in hand, the novice started brewing according to his own formula. By the close of the year, Molson had produced 80 hogsheads (4300 gallons) of beer.

In 1787 Molson remarked, "My beer has been almost universally well liked beyond my most sanguine expectations." His statement in part reflects the quality of the brew, but it also indicates that Molson had excellent timing; he faced very little competition in the pioneer community.

Molson believed that an elemental part of brewing high-quality beer and keeping operating costs low was local production of barley and hops; to that end, he brought seeds back with him to distribute to local farmers. Today the brewery is particularly proud of the yeast it uses, praising the superiority of live cultures imported from England when shipping time was shortened in the 19th century. The corporation's literature professes that the "purity of yeast cultures is protected in high security yeast rooms. The descendants of that first transatlantic yeast shipment are hard at work today in some Molson breweries." Admittedly, the recipes and tastes for beer have changed over the past 200 years, but John Molson's insistence that the brewery produce only high-quality beer persists.

Before electrical refrigeration became available in 1900, Molson was confined to a 20-week operating season because it had to rely on ice from the St. Lawrence River. Nevertheless, production grew throughout the 1800's as the Montreal brewery steadily added more land and equipment. Population growth and increasingly sophisticated bottling and packaging techniques also contributed to Molson's profitability in the early days.

It was not long before Molson became an established entrepreneur in Montreal, providing services in the fledgling community that contributed to its growth into a major Canadian city. Molson first diversified in 1797 with a lumberyard on the brewery property. A decade later he launched the *Accommodation*, Canada's first steamboat, and soon thereafter he formed the St. Lawrence Steamboat Company, also known as the Molson Line. The steam line led to Molson's operation of small-scale financial services between Montreal and Quebec City; in turn, the services became Molson's Bank, chartered in 1855.

In 1816 John Molson signed a partnership agreement with his three sons, John Jr., William and Thomas, ensuring that the brewery would remain under family control. He was elected the same year to represent Montreal East in the Canadian Parliament, and opened the Mansion House, a large hotel in Montreal that housed the public library and post office and Montreal's first theatre.

The Molson's established the first industrial-scale distillery in Montreal in 1820. Three years later, the youngest brother, Thomas, left the organization after a severe disagreement with his family. In 1824 he moved to Kingston, Ontario, where he established an independent brewing and distilling operation.

The elder John Molson left the company in 1828, leaving John, Jr. and William as active partners. He served as president of the Bank of Montreal from 1826 to 1830, and in 1832 was nominated to the Legislative Council of Lower Canada. Possibly his most foresighted venture was his contribution of one quarter of the cost of building Canada's first railway. He died in January 1836 at age 72.

Thomas Molson returned to Montreal in 1834 and was readmitted to the family enterprise. Over the next 80 years new partnerships formed among various members of the Molson family, prompting several more reorganizations.

The first in the third generation to enter the family business was John H.R. Molson, who joined the partnership in 1848. He became an increasingly important figure in the company as William and John Jr. devoted more of their time to the operation of Molson's Bank.

In 1844 the Molson brewery, now called Thos. & Wm. Molson & Company, introduced beer in bottles which were corked and labelled by hand. Beer production grew faster than bottle production, though, necessitating the company's purchase of a separate barrel factory at Port Hope, Ontario in 1851. In 1859 Molson started to advertise in Montreal newspapers, while also setting up a retail sales network and introducing pint bottles.

The company became John H.R. Molson & Bros. in 1861 following the establishment of a new partnership with William Markland Molson and John Thomas Molson. In 1866 the Molsons closed their distillery, citing poor business, and in 1868 they sold their property in Port Hope.

By 1866, the brewery's hundredth year exclusively in Molson hands, its production volume had multiplied 175 times but profit cleared on each gallon remained the same—26 cents. In the early years of the 20th century, the company incorporated pasteurization and electric refrigeration into its methods. Additionally, electricity replaced steam power, and mechanized packaging devices sped the bottling process. In 1911 the company became Molson's Brewery Ltd. following its reorganization as a joint share company. The family's direct interest in banking ended in 1925 when Molson's Bank merged with the Bank of Montreal.

The first half of the 20th century was a period of rapid growth for Molson. Production at the Montreal brewery rose from 3 million gallons in 1920, to 15 million in 1930, to 25 million in 1949. Molson adopted modern marketing and advertising methods to enhance market penetration, and in 1930 began producing its first promotional items—despite founder John Molson's contention that "An honest brew makes its own friends."

In the mid–1950's Molson management recognized a need to expand operations significantly. By concentrating their resources, other Canadian breweries had finally begun to compete successfully against perennial leader Molson. Molson decided that the appropriate strategy was to have a brewery operating in each Canadian province, as distribution from its base in the pronvice of Ontario to other provinces was subject to strict government regulations. With operations in the other provinces, Molson could further build its market throughout Canada.

Thus, a large-scale expansion began when Molson announced a second brewery would be built on a ten-acre site in Toronto. Modernizations at the Montreal facility had, it was felt, fully maximized output there. The new Toronto installation opened in 1955. It became the home of Molson's first lager, Crown and Anchor. In the next few years Molson acquired three breweries: Sick's Brewery, bought in 1958; Fort Garry Brewery in Winnipeg, 1959; and Newfoundland Brewery, 1962. By the late 1980's Molson had nine breweries in Canada.

The expansion effort resulted in good returns for Molson investors; between 1950 and 1965 earnings more than doubled. Even so, Molson leaders recognized that expansion potential within the mature brewing industry was limited, and further, that growth rates in the industry would always be slow. It was clear that even the most successful brewing operation would soon reach the limits of its profitability. Thus Molson began an accelerated diversification program in the mid-1960's which heralded in Canada the era of the corporate takeover.

In 1968 Molson made its first major non-brewing acquisition in more than a century. Ontario-based Anthes Imperial Ltd. was a public company specializing in steel materials, office furniture and supplies, construction equipment rentals, and public warehousing. The Anthes executive staff was known to be highly talented in acquisitions and strategic management, two areas in which Molson needed expert help to pursue its goal of diversification. However, because the various Anthes companies required different management and marketing strategies, the acquisition did not benefit Molson as much as its directors had hoped. Soon Molson sold off most of the Anthes component companies. The company had learned that future acquisitions should be of firms that were more compatible with Molson's long-standing strengths in marketing consumer products and service.

By the early 1970's Molson was again searching for an acquisition to establish for the company a foothold outside the brewing industry. Management felt the ideal candidate must be a Canadian-based firm; it must be involved in above-average growth.

The "do it yourself" material supplies market seemed to be the ideal candidate for everything the brewery wanted to accomplish in its diversification program. There seemed to be a new trend—consumers doing their own home improvements—and Molson recognized the potential for rapid growth of this market in urban areas, which at that time had few or no lumberyards or similar outlets. Molson began acquiring small hardware, lumber, and home furnishings companies. In 1972 it spent $50 million buying more than 90% of the shares of Beaver Lumber, a large Canadian company. During the remainder of the decade Beaver acquired several smaller hardware and lumber operations. Molson's service-center division grew to encompass 162 retail stores, most of them franchises, selling anything from paint to home-building supplies. In the mid-1980's Beaver began importing competitively priced merchandise from Asian countries.

In July 1973 the company's name was changed to Molson Companies Ltd., a reflection of its diversification. The brewing operations were now called Molson Breweries of Canada Ltd.

Although Beaver's sales climbed steadily throughout the 1970's, profits lagged behind what Molson had anticipated, and initially the company considered the Beaver purchase only a modest success. Struggling at first to integrate the brewing and home improvement divisions, Molson eventually learned that the two industries, and marketing therein, are very different. The beer industry operates in a controlled market; governments regulate sale and manufacture of alcoholic products. The hardware industry, on the other hand, operates in a relatively free market. Furthermore, in brewing, manufacturing efficiency is the key to a profitable enterprise, but the success of a home improvement retail operation hinges on the ability to provide a broad variety of products at competitive prices.

The challenge of integrating two companies operating in such different markets led Molson to a careful reassessment of its diversification criteria; in the future, the company would concentrate on marketing specific product brands. W.J. Gluck, vice president of corporate development wrote: "We only wanted to go into a business related to our experience—a business in which marketing, not manufacturing, is the important thing." The search for another acquisition began.

In 1978 Molson offered $28 per share of stock in Diversey Corporation, a chemical products manufacturer based in Northbrook, Illinois. Diversey stockholders contested the offer, hoping for a more lucrative takeover bid, but later Molson was able to buy Diversey for the $55 million it had originally offered to pay. Diversey was Molson's first large acquisition in the United States, though most of Diversey's clients and manufacturing plants were in fact located outside the U.S. in Europe, Latin America, and the Pacific basin.

Two years later Molson paid $25 million for another American company, BASF Wyandotte Corporation, a manufacturer of chemical specialties products related to food services and commercial laundries. The subsequent merger of BASF and Diversey made the chemical products division Molson's second largest earnings contributor. Prior to the merger, Diversey was a weak competitor in the U.S. sanitation supplies market. BASF Wyandotte, however, was a leader in the U.S. kitchen services market. Thus the marriage was a sound move for Diversey, which had found a relatively inexpensive way to increase its share of its market in the United States.

The chemical specialties division now has the greatest worldwide presence of any company in the chemical industry; it is represented in 36 countries with 52 manufacturing plants. In order to sustain the advantage, Diversey emphasizes the development of products and technologies with worldwide applications. In recent years Diversey has considered entering the metal products industry and expanding into markets in Mexico and the People's Republic of China.

In the mid-1980's Molson is fully established as a branched conglomerate and appears to concentrate less on major new acquisitions than on refining its management techniques and on organizing its three main divisions. The company's excursions into new markets and services have been on a smaller scale in the past decade. For example, Grayrock Capital, a venture capital firm with approximately $23 million worth of interests in U.S. oil and gas exploration, specilty retailing, health care, communications, and biotechnology, had profits of just $3 million in 1986. It is not, as a result, counted among Molson's major divisions. The television production company, Ohlmeyer Communications, is also a smaller-scale member of Molson Companies Limited, as are Molson's various interests in amateur and professional sports.

In 1986 the brewing group accounted for more than half of the Molson's sales and a third of its profits. The chemical specialties group contributed almost twice as much to sales and profit as the retail merchandising group did in 1986, but both the non-brewing groups cleared a healthy profit relative to sales.

Principal Subsidiaries: Molson Breweries of Canada Ltd.; Molson Newfoundland Brewery Lrd.; Molson's Brewery Quebec; Molson's Brewery (Ontario) Ltd.; Molson's Western Breweries Ltd.; Aikenhead Hardware Ltd.; Beaver Lumber Co., Ltd.; Molson Mont Laurier Ltée.; Wilson Office Specialty Ltd.; C-N-W Leasings Ltd.; C.W. Henderson Cartage Ltd.; Cotnoir & Pleau Ltée.; Curlew Investments Ltd.; Molson Breweries International; Club de Hockey Canadien, Inc.; Le Club de Soccer Manic de Montreal Inc.; Diversey Corp.; Seaway/Midwest Ltd.; Kipling Properties Ltd.; L'Arena des Canadiens Inc.; Molson Abitibi Ltée.; Molson Baie Comeau Ltée.; Molson Gaspesie Ltée.; Molson Levis Ltée.; Molson (Quebec) Ltée.; Molson Sept-Iles Ltée.; Molson (Sherrybrooke) Ltée.; Molson St-Hyacinthe Ltée.; Molson Valleyfield Ltée.; Michel Fuller Ltée.; Saveway Lumber & Building Supplies Ltd.; Sick's Bohemian Brewery Ltd.; Warden Lumber Distributors Ltd.; Yves Bourre Ltée.; A Ben Mathieu Inc.

Further Reading: The Barley and the Stream: The Molson Story by Merrill Denison, McClelland and Stewart, 1955.

PEPSICO, INC.

Purchase, New York 10577
U.S.A.
(914) 253–2000

Public Company
Incorporated: September 18, 1919 as Loft, Inc.
Employees: 150,000
Sales: $9.29 billion
Market Value: $9.11 billion
Stock Index: New York

When Caleb D. Bradham concocted a new cola drink in the 1890's, his friends' enthusiastic response convinced him that he had created a commercially viable product. For twenty years, "Doc" Bradham prospered from his Pepsi-Cola sales. Eventually, he was faced with a dilemma; the crucial decision he made turned out to be the wrong one and he was forced to sell. But his successors fared no better and it was not until the end of the 1930's that Pepsi-Cola again became profitable.

Fifty years later, PepsiCo, Inc. is a mammoth multi-national supplier of soft drinks, snack food, and fast food. The company has finally dislodged Coca-Cola as the number one soft drink company in America. But there is little enough to distinguish between the quality, variety, and taste of the products offered by either company. PepsoCo's slight edge is almost entirely the result of its management style and the phenomenal success of its television advertising.

Doc Bradham, like countless other entrepreneurs across America, was trying to create a cola drink similar in taste to Coca-Cola, which by 1895 was selling well in every state of the union. At his pharmacy in New Bern, North Carolina on August 28, 1898, Bradham gave the name Pepsi-Cola to his most popular flavored soda. Formerly known as Brad's Drink, the new cola beverage was a syrup of sugar, vanilla, oils, cola nuts, and other flavorings diluted in carbonated water. The enterprising pharmacist followed Coca-Cola's method of selling the concentrate to soda fountains; he mixed the syrup in his drugstore then shipped it in barrels to the contracted fountain operators who added the soda water. He also bottled and sold the drink himself.

In 1902 Doc Bradham closed his drugstore to devote his attention to the thriving new business. The next year, he patented the Pepsi-Cola trademark, ran his first advertisement in a local paper, and moved the bottling and syrup-making operations to a purpose-built factory. Almost 20,000 gallons of Pepso-Cola syrup was produced in 1904.

Again following the successful methods of the Coca-Cola company, Bradham began to establish a network of bottling franchises. Entrepreneurs anxious to enter the increasingly popular soft drink business, set themselves up as bottlers and contracted with Bradham to buy his syrup and sell nothing but Pepsi. With little cash outlay, Pepsi-Cola reached a much wider market.

Bradham's first two bottling franchises, both in North Carolina, commenced operation in 1905. By 1907, Pepsi-Cola had signed agreements with 40 bottlers; over the next three years, the number grew to 250 and annual production of the syrup exceeded one million gallons.

Pepsi-Cola's growth continued until World War I, when sugar, then the main ingredient of all flavored sodas, was rationed. Soft drink producers were forced to cut back until sugar rationing ended. The wartime set price of sugar—5.5 cents per pound—rocketed after controls were lifted to as much as 26.5 cents per pound in 1920. Bradham, like his rivals, had to decide whether to halt production and sit tight in the hope that prices would soon drop, or stockpile the precious commodity as a precaution against even higher prices; he chose the latter course. But unfortunately for him the market was saturated by the end of 1920 and sugar prices plunged to a low of 2 cents per pound.

Bradham never recovered. After several abortive attempts to reorganize, only two of the bottling plants remained open. In a last ditch effort, he enlisted the help of Roy C. Megargel, a Wall Street investment banker. However, very few people were willing to invest in the business and it went bankrupt in 1923. The assets were sold and Megargel purchased the company trademark, giving him the rights to the Pepsi-Cola formula. Doc Bradham went back to his drug dispensary and he died 11 years later.

Megargel apparently lacked marketing ability and after continuous losses, reorganized the firm as the National Pepsi-Cola Company in 1928. But after three years he had to declare bankruptcy. That same year (1931), Megargel met Charles G. Guth, a somewhat autocratic businessman who had recently taken over as president of Loft Inc., a New York-based candy and fountain store concern. Guth had fallen out with Coca-Cola for refusing the company a wholesaler discount and he was on the lookout for a new soft drink. He signed an agreement with Megargel to resurrect the Pepsi-Cola company, and acquired 80% of the new shares, ostensibly for himself. Then, having modified the syrup formula, he cancelled Loft's contract with Coca-Cola and introduced Pepsi.

Loft's customers were wary of the brand switch and in the first year of Pepsi sales the company's soft drink turnover was down by a third. By the end of 1933, Guth had bought out Megargel and owned 91% of the insolvent company. But resistance to Pepsi in the Loft stores tailed off in 1934, and Guth decided further to improve sales by offering 12 ounce bottles of Pepsi for a nickel—the same price as six ounces of Coke. The Depression-weary people of Baltimore—where the 12 ounce bottles were first introduced—were ready for a bargain and Pepsi-Cola sales increased dramatically.

Guth established Pepsi-Cola Company of Canada in 1934 and the following year formed Compania Pepsi-Cola de Cuba. He also moved the entire American operation to Long Island City, New York and set up national territorial boundaries for the bottling franchises. In 1936, Pepsi-Cola Ltd. of London commenced business.

Guth's ownership of the Pepsi-Cola Company was challenged that same year by Loft Inc. In a complex arrangement, Guth had organized Pepsi-Cola as an independent corporation, but he had run it with Loft's employees and money. After three years of litigation, the court upheld Loft's contention and Guth had to step down, although he was retained as an adviser. James W. Carkner was elected president of the company, now a subsidiary of Loft Inc., but Carkner was soon replaced by Walter S. Mack, Jr., an executive from the Phoenix Securities Corporation.

Mack established a board of directors with real voting powers to ensure that no one person would be able to wield control as Guth had done. From the start, Mack's aim was to promote Pepsi to the hilt so that it might replace Coca-Cola as the world's best-selling soft drink. The advertising agency Mack hired worked wonders. In 1939, a Pepsi jingle—the first one to be aired nationally—caught the public's attention: "Pepsi-Cola hits the spot. Twelve full ounces, that's a lot. Twice as much for a nickel, too. Pepsi-Cola is the drink for you." The jingle, sung to the tune of the old British hunting song "D'Ye Ken John Peel," became an advertising hallmark; no-one was more impressed, or concerned, than the executives at Coca-Cola.

In 1940, with foreign expansion continuing strongly, Loft Inc. made plans to merge with its Pepsi subsidiary. The new firm, formed in 1941, used the name Pepsi-Cola Company since it was so well-known. Pepsi's stock was listed on the New York Stock Exchange for the first time.

Sugar rationing was even more severe during World War II, but this time the company fared better; indeed, the sugar plantation Pepsi-Cola acquired in Cuba became a most successful investment. But as inflation spiralled in the postwar U.S. economy, sales of soft drinks fell. The public needed time to get used to paying six or seven cents for a bottle of Pepsi which, as they remembered from the jingle, had always been a nickel. Profits in 1948 were down $3.6 million from the year before.

In other respects, 1948 was a notable year. Pepsi moved its corporate headquarters across the East River to midtown Manhattan, and for the first time the drink was sold in cans. The decision to start canning, while absolutely right for Pepsi-Cola and other soft drink companies, upset the franchised bottlers, who had invested heavily in equipment. However, another decision at Pepsi-Cola—to ignore the burgeoning vending machine market because of the necessarily large capital outlay—proved to be a costly mistake. The company had to learn the hard way that as canned drinks gained a larger share of the market, vending machine sales would become increasingly important.

Walter Mack was appointed company chairman in 1950, and a former Coca-Cola vice president of sales, Alfred N. Steele, took over as president and chief executive officer; he brought 15 other Coke executives with him. Steele continued the policy of management decentralization by giving broader powers to regional vice presidents, and he placed Herbert Barnet in charge of Pepsi's financial operations. However, Steele's outstanding contribution was in marketing. He launched an extensive advertising campaign with the slogan "Be sociable, have a Pepsi." The new television medium provided a perfect forum; Pepsi advertisements presented young Americans drinking "the Light refreshment" and having fun.

By the time Alfred Steele married the movie star Joan Crawford in 1954, transformation of the company was well underway. Crawford's adopted daughter Christina noted in her bestseller *Mommie Dearest*: "[Steele had] driven Pepsi into national prominence and distribution, second only to his former employer, Coca-Cola. Pepsi was giving Coke a run for its money in every nook and hamlet of America. Al Steele welded a national network of bottlers together, standardized the syrup formula . . . brought the distinctive logo into mass consciousness, and was on the brink of going international . . . ." In fact, Pepsi-Cola International Ltd. was formed shortly after Steele's marriage.

Joan Crawford became the personification of Pepsi's new and glamorous image. She invariably kept a bottle of Pepsi at hand during press conferences and mentioned the product at interviews and on talk shows; on occasion she even arranged for Pepsi trucks and vending machines to feature in background shots of her movies. The actress also worked hard to spread the Pepsi word overseas and accompanied her husband, now chairman of the board, on his 1957 tour of Europe and Africa, where bottling plants were being established.

Steele died suddenly of a heart attack in the spring of 1959. Herbert Barnet succeeded him as chairman and Joan Crawford was elected a board member. According to the film version of *Mommie Dearest*, the Hollywood star took an active interest in company policy and did not mince her words at board meetings.

Pepsi-Cola profits had fallen to a postwar low of $1.3 million in 1950 when Steele joined the company, but with the proliferation of supermarkets during the decade and the developments in overseas business, profits reached $14.2 million in 1960. By that time, young adults had become a major target of soft drink manufacturers and Pepsi's advertisements were aimed at "Those Who Think Young."

Al Steele and Joan Crawford had been superb cheerleaders, but a stunt pulled in 1959 by Donald M. Kendall, head of Pepsi-Cola International, is still regarded as one of the great coups in the annals of advertising. Kendall attended the Moscow Trade Fair that year and persuaded U.S. Vice President Richard Nixon to stop by the Pepsi booth with Nikita Khrushchev, the Soviet premier. As the cameras flashed, Khrushchev quenched his thirst with several Pepsis and the grinning U.S. Vice President stood in attendance. Next day, newspapers around the world featured photographs of the happy couple, complete with Pepsi bottle.

By 1963 Kendall was presiding over the Pepsi empire. He had been an amateur boxing champion in his youth and joined the company as a production line worker in 1947 after a stint in the U.S. Navy. He was later promoted to syrup sales where it quickly became apparent that he was destined for higher office. Ever pugnacious, Kendall has been described as abrasive and ruthlessly ambitious; beleaguered Pepsi executives secretly referred to him as White Fang. Under his long reign, the company's fortunes skyrocketed.

Pepsi-Cola's remarkable successes in the 1960's and 1970's were the result of five distinct policies, all of which Kendall and his crew pursued diligently: they advertised on a massive, unprecedented scale; they introduced new brands of soft drinks; they led the industry in packaging innovations; they expanded overseas; and, through acquisitions, they diversified their product line.

The postwar baby-boomers were in their mid-to-late teens by the time Kendall came to power. "Pepsi was there," states a recent company flyer, "to claim these kids for our own." These "kids" became the "Pepsi Generation." In the late 1960's Pepsi was the "Taste that beats the others cold." Viewers were advised "You've got a lot to live. Pepsi's got a lot to give." By the early 1970's, the appeal was to "Join the Pepsi people, feelin' free." In mid-decade an American catch-phrase was given a company twist—"Have a Pepsi Day," and the 1970's ended on the note "Catch the Pepsi Spirit!"

The Pepsi Generation wanted variety and Pepsi was happy to oblige. Company brands introduced in the 1960's included Patio soft drinks, Teem, Tropic Surf, Diet Pepsi—the first nationally distributed diet soda—and Mountain Dew, acquired from the Tip Corporation. Pepsi Light, a diet cola with a hint of lemon, made its debut in 1975, and a few years later Pepsi tested the market with Aspen apple soda and On-Tap root beer. The company also introduced greater variety into the packaging of its products. Soon after Kendall's accession, the 12-ounce bottle was phased out in favour of the 16-ounce size, and in the 1970's Pepsi-Cola became the first American company to introduce one-and-a-half and two-liter bottles; it also began to package its sodas in sturdy, lightweight plastic bottles. By the end of the decade, Pepsi had added 12-pack cans to its growing array of packaging options.

The company's expansion beyond the soft drink market began in 1965 when Kendall met Herman Lay, the owner of Frito-Lay, at a grocer's convention. Kendall arranged a merger with this Dallas-based snack food manufacturer and formed PepsiCo, Inc. Herman Lay retired soon thereafter but retained his substantial PepsiCo shareholding. The value of this stock increased dramatically as Frito-Lay products were introduced to Pepsi's nationwide market.

In the late 1960's and early 1970's Kendall acquired two well-known fast-food restaurant chains, Taco Bell and Pizza Hut; naturally, these new subsidiaries became major outlets for Pepsi products. But Kendall also diversified outside the food and drink industry, bringing North American Van Lines, Lee Way Motor Freight, and Wilson Sporting Goods into the PepsiCo empire.

Overseas developments continued apace throughout Kendall's tenure. Building on his famous Soviet achievement, he negotiated a trade agreement with the USSR in 1972; the first Pepsi plant opened there two years later. Gains were also made in the Middle East and Latin America, but Coca-Cola, the major rival, retained its dominant position in Europe and throughout much of Asia.

By the time PepsiCo greeted the 1980's with the slogan "Pepsi's got your taste for life!," Kendall was busy arranging for China to get that taste too; production began there in 1983. Kendall put his seal of approval on several other major developments in the early 1980's, including the introduction of Pepsi Free, a non-caffeine cola, and Slice, the first widely distributed soft drink to contain real fruit juice (lemon and lime); the latter was aimed at the growing 7-Up and Sprite market. Additionally, Diet-Pepsi was reformulated using a blend of saccharin and aspartame (NutraSweet). "Pepsi Now!" was the cry of company commercials, and this was interspersed with "Taste, Improved by Diet Pepsi."

In 1983 the company claimed a significant share of the fastfood soft drink market when Burger King began selling Pepsi products. A year later, mindful of the industry axiom that there is virtually no limit to the amount a consumer will buy once the decision to buy has been made, PepsiCo introduced the 3-liter container.

By the mid-1980's the Pepsi Generation was over the hill. Kendall's ad agency, no expense spared, heralded Pepsi as "the Choice of a New Generation," using the talents of superstar Michael Jackson, as well as those of singer Lionel Richie and the Puerto Rican teenage group Menudo. Michael Jackson's ads were smash hits and enjoyed the highest exposure of any American television commercial to date. The company's high profile and powerful presence in all of the soft drink markets—direct results of Kendall's strategies—helped it to weather the somewhat uncertain economic situation of the time.

On only one front had Kendall's efforts failed to produce satisfactory results. Experience showed that for all its expertise, PepsiCo simply did not have the managerial experience required to run its subsidiaries outside the food and drink industries. A van line, a motor freight concern, and a sporting goods firm were indeed odd companies for a soft drink enterprise; and Kendall auctioned off these strange and ailing bedfellows, vowing never again to go courting in unfamiliar territories.

With his house in excellent order, the PepsiCo mogul began to prepare for his retirement. He had bullied and cajoled a generation of pepsi executives and guided them ever upward on the steep slopes of Pepsi profits. But he had one last task—to lead Pepsico to victory in the Cola Wars.

Hostilities commenced soon after the Coca-Cola Company changed its syrup recipe in the summer of 1985 and with much fanfare introduced New Coke. Pepsi, caught napping, claimed that Coca-Cola's reformulated drink failed to meet with consumer approval and pointed to their own flourishing sales. But serious fans of the original Coke were not about to switch to Pepsi and demanded that their favorite refreshment be restored. However, when blindfolded, it became manifestly apparent that these diehards could rarely tell the difference between Old Coke, New Coke and Pepsi; indeed, more often than not, they got it wrong. In any event, the Coca-Cola Company acceded to the public clamor for the original Coke and remarketed it as Coca-Cola Classic alongside its new cola.

Some advertising analysts believed that the entire "conflict" was a clever publicity ploy on the part of Coca-Cola to demonstrate the preeminence of its original concoction ("It's the Real Thing!"), while introducing a new cola—allegedly a Pepsi taste-alike—to win the hearts of waverers. More interesting perhaps than the possible differences between the colas were the very real differences in people's reactions. Four discrete fields could be identified: the totally wowed (possibly caffeine-induced); the rather amused; the slightly irritated; and the distinctly bored.

The latter group must have nodded off in front of their television sets when Pepsi took the Cola Wars beyond the firmament. "One Giant Sip for Mankind," proclaimed the ads as a Pepsi "space can" was opened up aboard Challenger, the U.S. space shuttle. Presumably, had a regular can been used, Pepsi-Cola would have sloshed aimlessly around the gravity-free cabin. This scientific breakthrough, together with the almost obligatory hype and hoopla, and more mundane factors such as the continued expansion in PepsiCo's outlets, boosted sales to new heights; and Pepsi's ad agency glittered with accolades. The debate still continues, at least within Coke and Pepsi corporate offices, as to who won the Cola Wars. The answer would appear to be that there were no losers, only winners; but skirmishes will inevitably continue.

D. Wayne Calloway replaced Donald M. Kendall as chairman and chief executive officer in 1986. Calloway had been instrumental in the success of Frito-Lay, helping it to become PepsiCo's most profitable division. By the time he took command, 195 independent owners operated 380 Pepsi-Cola franchise territories in the U.S., and a further 38 territories were owned directly by the company. Additionally, there were 600 PepsiCo plants worldwide, located in 148 countries and foreign territories.

In the last couple of years, PepsiCo's Slice has become a real winner and there have been several additions to this soft drink line, including Diet Slice, Mandarin Orange, Cherry Cola, and Apple. Marketing analysts see continuing strength in the company's advertising program, citing in particular a second agreement with Michael Jackson and PepsiCo's sponsorship of concerts and sporting events. It is expected that PepsiCo will end the 1980's as it started them: rich, aggressive, and second to none.

Principal Subsidiaries: Ainwick Corporation; Darlyn Realty Corp.; Frito-Lay Corp.; Recot, Inc.; Arizona Specialty Breads, Inc.; California Exceptional Breads, Inc.; National Beverages, Inc.; Franklin Bottling Co.; Pizza Hut, Inc.; Taco Bell Corp.; Taco Bell Royalty Co. PepsiCo also lists subsidiaries in the following countries: Argentina, Australia, Bermuda, Canada, Chile, France, Ireland, England, West Germany, Mexico, the Netherlands Antilles, Spain, and Turkey.

Further Reading: Twelve Full Ounces by Milward Martin, New York, Holt Rinehart, 1962; *Soda Pop* by Lawrence Dietz, New York, Simon and Schuster, 1973; *The Cola Wars* by J.C. Lousi, New York, Everest House, 1980; *No Time Lost* by Walter Mack and P. Buckley, New York, Atheneum, 1982; *The Other Guy Blinked: How Pepsi Won the Cola Wars* by Roger Enrico and Jesse Kornbluth, New York, Bantam, 1986.

PERNOD RICARD S.A.

142 Boulevard Haussmann
75008 Paris
France
4359–28–28

Public Company
Incorporated: 1974
Employees: 10,618
Sales: FFr10.4 billion (US$1.617 billion)
Market Value: FFr8.54 billion (US$1.327 billion)
Stock Index: Paris Frankfurt

If it were not for the French tradition of gathering for a pre-dinner apéritif, Pernod Ricard might not be the largest alcoholic beverage company in Continental Europe. As it is, the customary French toast "to health" (à santé) has helped to keep Pernod Ricard in excellent condition. Indeed, the company is now also the largest soft drink beverage producer on the Continent.

Pernod Ricard was formed in 1974 through the merger of the Pernod and Ricard companies, two of France's largest suppliers and distributors of aniseed beverages. The group, whose anise-based drinks account for 70% of the French market, also produces and distributes a variety of wine-based apéritifs, liquers, spirits, and wines, as well as fruit juices and mixers, cider, syrups, and soft drinks. Pernod Ricard also distributes Coca-Cola, and controls 75% of the French cola market.

Anise, a distinctively flavored aromatic seed, gained popularity during the 18th century as a substitute for absinthe. Absinthe, discovered some years earlier by a Swiss doctor, was mixed with wormwood and other herbs and used as a medical elixir. The drink became popular, and in 1797, an aspiring businessman named Pernod purchased the recipe. But absinthe was later determined to cause nerve damage and was banned from France, Swtizerland, and the United States. Pernod altered the recipe by substituting anise or pastis for absinthe, and thereby created two new beverages which were found to stimulate the palate.

Pernod founded a company in 1805, and though it was the first to produce anise-flavored apéritifs, it remained small. Pernod introduced a variety of brands, including Pernod, Pastis 51, Byrrh, and Cinzano, as inexpensive alternatives to wine apéritifs. After over 100 years as a modest family-run company, Pernod acquired the Suze company, a firm which made bitters from the distilled roots of the gentian plant.

The expansion of Pernod encouraged imitators to establish competing firms in the early 1930's. Once such imitator, Paul Ricard, introduced his own aniseed aperitif in 1932. Ricard's extensive and often innovative marketing methods maintained the popularity of anise, despite growing demand for whiskey and wine apéritifs. Ricard established foundations to sponsor art and cultural activities (an unheard of practice for French business at that time) and a world yacht race, and to build on auto race track. Additionally, Ricard donated several Mediterranean islands to the French government to promote tourism. In recognition of Ricard's support for auto racing, an annual contest, the Circuit Paul Ricard, was named in his honor. Ricard's publicity stunts paid off handsomely, and by the time of his retirement in 1968, his 15% stake in the company was worth $104 million.

The merger of Pernod and Ricard, termed "the equivalent of a merger between General Motors and Ford," enabled the new company to solidify its base as a major French beverage company in order to launch an export business. Since the merger, the Pernod Ricard group has embarked on a massive reorganization and diversification campaign. Paul Ricard's son Patrick became a major force within the company after being named general manager in 1967. Patrick was an astute businessman, was well-trained by his father, and had gained considerable experience outside the company.

In 1976 Pernod Ricard purchased Cusenier of Argentina, which makes liquers from the extracted essences of plants, fruits, and grains. Cusenier is also the Argentine distributor of Cutty Sark, Gilbey's gin, and Ambassadeur apéritifs, in addition to champagnes, fruit juices, and syrups. At this time, Pernod Ricard purchased Campbell, a whisky distiller whose brands included White heather and Aberlour scotch, in addition to Dubonnet and Clan Campbell liquers.

By 1979 it was clear that Pernod Ricard had to continue to look outside of France to maintain its sales growth. Even though the group recorded a 3.2% increase (by volume) in sales of anise apéritifs, liquor sales domestically had only increased 1.3%. While other Pernod Ricard brands fared slightly better, the company recognized that its French earning growth would be limited.

During 1980 Pernod Ricard spent $48 million on a marketing campaign in England, Spain, and Germany. Much of this money was spent in sales promotion, including posters, taste tests, and product giveaways at discos (intended to introduce young adults to the taste of anise and pastis liquers). "It's the third glass that makes a convert," Patrick Ricard said at the time, "so we have to put glasses of Pernod in people's hands." In England, where Pernod had a small following, the campaign succeeded brilliantly and sales increased by 34%. So that it might solve a distribution problem caused by the increased demand, Pernod Ricard purchased its English distributor, the J.R. Parkington Company.

Continuing its expansion program, Pernod Ricard bought its American sales agent, Austin Nichols, a well-known wine and spirits firm, whose best-selling brand is

Wild Turkey bourbon. This acquisition increased Pernod Ricard's turnover in 1980 to about FFr280 million.

In a 1980 interview with *Management Today*, Patrick Ricard said, "Ours is a young export country, and for too long we were held back by an official attitude that it was unpatriotic to invest abroad, though that is now changing. That's why we're following a policy of buying companies in prime markets, such as Austin Nichols. It would take too long to start from scratch, building up our own distribution and sales organization."

Another reason behind the Austin Nichols purchase was the fact that Americans simply weren't excited about anise beverages—what Patrick himself once termed "a strange drink with a funny taste." In addition, an overall trend toward declining alcohol consumption compelled Pernod Ricard to seek opportunities in the soft drinks business.

The company's most important acquisition occurred in 1983, with Française des Produits d'Orangina, makers of Orangina soda, which contains 12% real fruit juice—more than the 10% of Slice, and the 3% in Minute Maid orange soda. Orangina was first introduced in the United States in 1984 as the "French quench," and the "soft drink with juice you can taste." Patrick Ricard intends to make Orangina a worldwide brand name by the year 2000. Other companies, such as PepsiCo and Canada Dry followed suit by test marketing their own brands of natural soft drinks. Pernod Ricard officials told *BusinessWeek* in 1984 that the company had planned for Orangina to take a one percent market share (all orange drinks together consitute only six percent of the soda market).

Besides Orangina, Pernod Ricard also markets fruit juices (Fruidam, Banga, Pampryl, and Pam Pam) through its JAF-Pampryl subsidiary. Pernod Ricard ventured into the fruit preparation business in 1982, with the purchase of a 66% interest in SIAS-MPA, the world's leading producer of fruit preparations for dairy products. Despite poor economic conditions during the early 1980's, Pernod Ricard's sales grew an average of 20% per year. Altogether, the company has spent some $250 million on its acquisition strategy in an attempt to establish its products in every French soft drink category.

In order to increase liquor sales, the company arranged an agreement in 1985 with Heublein, an American alcoholic beverage company, which would give Pernod Ricard access to Japanese and Brazilian markets, and better exposure in the United States. Through a 15% interest in Heublein's Japanese subsidiary, Pernod Ricard sells Wild Turkey and Bisquit brandy in Japan. In Brazil, Pernod Ricard purchased a 30% interest in Heublein Industria e Commercia, Brazil's leading spirits distributor. Pernod Ricard officials said they joined Heublein in international markets to increase the company's foreign sales by five to ten percent, despite the fact that the market was growing smaller. Foreign liquor sales accounted for 19% of group turnover, compared to 13% when Pernod and Ricard merged in 1974.

Pernod Ricard's export subsidiary SEGM (Société pour l'Exportation de Grandes Marques) acquired Ramazotti, an Italian apéritif producer, and established a joint venture with Deinhard of West Germany to sell Dubonnet, Pernod, Bisquit, and Ricard brands. SEGM also orchestrated the acquisition of Perisem in Swtizerland and Prac in Spain. Pernod Ricard also purchased an additional 45% interest in the Société des Vins de France (SVF), France leading table wine group, which is Pernod Ricard's largest subsidiary in terms of sales. As recently as February 1987, however, Pernod Ricard was negotiating the purchase of yet another European group, called Cooymans, a Dutch firm founded in 1829. Cooymans operates three plants and controls half of the Dutch liquor market, and had sales of $37 million in 1986.

Company officials expect a strong increase in earnings during the late 1980's, primarily from its expanding line of non-alcoholic drinks, which in 1986 represented 36% of group activities. Foreign sales of soft drinks accounted for 25% of the company's sales. In France, the group recently introduced Pacific, the first non-alcoholic aniseed drink; it was an immediate success. Pernod Light, another new low-alcohol beverage, is presently being prepared for exportation. Brut de Pomme (an apple soft drink) is the company's newest low-calorie soda. In addition, Orangina is being marketed in Southeast Asia and Malaysia, but company executives regard China as its most promising market.

For the moment, however, Pernod Ricard has focused its future development on the domestic production of the fennel and licorice plants necessary for the production of anise-based drinks. Previously, these plants were imported from China and Vietnam, but high import costs have forced the company to seek other alternatives. Pernod Ricard scientists are also experimenting with the cultivation of aromatic plants for more unique ciders and wines.

Although the company derives 32% of its sales from anise-based drinks, Pernod Ricard is clearly dedicated to the diversification of its product line and of its market. The company expects to match, and even surpass, its recent successes. The time when Pernod was a modest family operation, content to rest on its laurels, is over.

Principal Subsidiaries: Ricard; Pernod; Société pour l'Exportation des Grandes Marques; JAF-Pampryl; Société Parisienne de Boissons Gazeuses (99.77%); Besserat de Bellefon (98.04%); Sopagly; Santa Lina; SIAS-MPA; Société des Vins de France; Société Raison (66.1%); Compagnie Française des Produits d'Orangina; SIFA; GJFF; EVC (98.88%); Fruidam. The company also lists subsidiaries in Argentina, the United Kingdom, and the United States.

SAPPORO BREWERIES, LTD.

10–1, Ginza 7-chome
Chuo-ku, Tokyo 104
Japan
(03) 572–6111

Public Company
Incorporated: September 1949 as Nippon Breweries, Ltd.
Employees: 3,819
Sales: ¥379.9 billion (US$2.386 billion)
Market Value: ¥365.7 billion (US$2.297 billion)
Stock Index: Tokyo Osaka Nagoya Sapporo

The American largely responsible for renewing trade relations with Japan, Commodore Matthew Perry, brought several cases of beer to Japan as a gift for the Tokugawa Shogunate. The beverage was so well liked that the Japanese government soon decided to establish a brewing industry. After an extensive search for a suitable area, wild hops were found growing on the island of Hokkaido, the northernmost island in the Japanese archipelago. As a result, in 1876 the Commissioner-General for the development of Hokkaido founded Japan's first brewery in the town of Sapporo.

The original government facility was designed by the brewmaster Seibei Nakagawa who had returned to Japan after studying beer-making techniques in Germany. The first product brewed in the factory was called Sapporo cold beer or German beer, and even some of the early labels were printed in German as well as in Japanese.

In 1886 the brewery was sold by the government to Okura-Gumi, a private limited partnership. Two years later, Okura-Gumi itself was purchased by a group of Japanese businessmen, who then reorganized the brewing operations under the name Sapporo Brewery Ltd. A number of other breweries, which would soon figure prominently in Sapporo's development, were also started during this time, including Nippon Brewing Company Ltd., Osaka Brewery, Kirin Brewery Company Ltd., and the Nippon Beer Kosen Brewery.

In the first decade of the 20th century, the Sapporo Brewery, the Nippon Brewing Company, and the Osaka Brewery was amalgamated into the Dai Nippon Brewery Company Ltd. This process of amalgamation and consolidation continued for 20 years until, in 1933, the Nippon Beer Kosen Brewery was also absorbed by Dai Nippon.

During the 1920's and 1930's Japanese militarists, implementing their plan to make Japan the dominant economic power in Asia, began to centralize the brewing industry. By 1943, the merger of all Japanese breweries was virtually complete: Dai Nippon and Kirin were the only two brewing companies left in Japan. In fact, the militarists were powerful enough to force the Sapporo division of Dai Nippon to establish joint ventures in the occupied territories of Korea and Manchuria.

At this stage, local markets were dominated by particular brands. Dai Nippon sold Sapporo beer in the region north of the Kanto district, primarily in Hokkaido. The company also manufactured Yebisu and Asahi brand beers; the former was popular in the Tokyo area and the latter in the Kansai area. Not surprisingly, because of the increased demand for beer (it was rapidly superseding the traditional drink sake), its production continued throughout the war.

The current structure of Japan's brewing industry originated after World War II during the U.S. occupation. In 1949 the Dai Nippon Brewery, which had cornered nearly 70% of the beer market in Japan, was divided into Nippon Breweries Ltd. and Asahi Breweries Ltd. Initially, Nippon Breweries marketed beer exclusively under its own brand name; it was not until 1957 that beer displaying the Sapporo label was reintroduced.

Nippon's growth during the postwar was impressive, primarily because of an expanding product line; from 1951 to 1981 production at the company's facilities increased by a factor of 15. During that same period, the brewery's sales increased from ¥20 billion to ¥330 billion, and its capitalization from ¥100 million to over ¥14.1 billion.

It was not until 1964 that the Nippon Breweries changed its name to Sapporo Breweries, Ltd. Shortly thereafter, arrangements were made to merge the Sapporo and Asahi breweries. By this time they had become the second and third largest breweries, respectively, in Japan. (Kirin had captured the largest share of the domestic beer market.) However, the merger never materialized.

The formation of a joint venture with Guinness plc, called Sapporo-Guinness, also took place in 1964. This agreement led to the sale of Irish stout in Japan. By 1976 the consumption of stout beer had risen dramatically and a sales war ensued with the Kirin brewery (which had its own version of the beverage). Even though the cost of Guinness's product is twice that of Kirin's, Sapporo has managed to maintain about 45% of the domestic stout market by relying heavily on Guinness's quality image.

Sapporo entered the wine market in 1971 when it formed a joint venture with Mitsui and Company Ltd. to import both wine and liquor. Sapporo Liquor Company Ltd. first began to import Nicolas, Hoch, and Melini wines. The company then started to produce its own wines at the Katsunuma Winery west of Tokyo in 1976; its Polaire brand of wine now includes the top five best sellers in Japan. After the Okayama Winery was established in 1984, a wine cooler, a sparkling wine, and Hyosai, a white brandy, were also added to the growing domestically produced beverage line. In addition, the Sapporo Liquor Company imports Baileys Irish Cream, Bombay Gin, Green Island Rum, and several scotches, including J and B Rare, Dunhill, Knockando, and Spay Royal.

Sapporo brand name beer is brewed exclusively in

Japan, but much of the barley and hops used in its manufacture is imported from Canada, Australia, West Germany, and Czechoslovakia. However, the company's supply of yeast comes from a strain originally developed at the Sapporo laboratory.

In the mid-1970's the Sapporo laboratory developed a technique for the ceramic filtration of beer. Since the introduction of pasteurization in the early part of the 20th century, beer had been sterilized by means of a heating process. This was necessary because the yeast residue in beer rendered it unsuitable for extended storage or long-distance transportation. Yet the problem with heating beer is that the high temperature affects its flavor. Sapporo's unique ceramic filtration method removes the yeast residue from beer without having to heat it. The beer is filtered at a constant temperature of zero to one degree centigrade through a long ceramic cylinder; a thin coating of diatomaceous earth in the tube traps the yeast residue. The first draft beer made with this new process went on the market in 1977, and in 1985 the filtration technology was exported to South Korea and to the Miller Brewing Company in the United States. Even so, Sapporo still pasteurizes many of its products.

The Sapporo laboratory presently conducts research in fields such as soft drinks, and the application of beer yeast to the development of food seasonings and health food products. Sapporo scientists are also investigating the utilization of recent discoveries in biotechnology to develop new plant breeds, agricultural chemicals, and pharmaceuticals.

Sapporo's diverse holdings also include real estate firms, the largest of which is the Seiwa Fudosan Company Ltd. Primarily a leasing agency, Seiwa Fudosan is also in charge of the current development of Sapporo's Ebisu properties in Tokyo. In addition, an enormous sports and leisure center in Tokyo is operated by Sapporo's affiliate, the Seijo Green Plaza Company Ltd.

Throughout its history, rising prices for raw materials have reduced company profits. During the 1970's the Japanese government made matters worse by requiring brewers to purchase domestically grown barley; this accounted for 20 to 25% of the barley used in the entire industry. Originally intended to protect farmers who had switched from the cultivation of rice (which was in surplus) to barley, the domestic strain cost the brewers 3.7 times as much as imported ones.

In spite of such problems, Sapporo has grown consistently over the last 35 years. In fact, from 1985 to 1987 the company has enjoyed record sales and earnings. Sapporo attributed this success to reduced materials costs, a decreasing interest payment burden, and effective management of surplus funds. Furthermore, the appreciation of the yen and the consequent lower price of foreign malt have also helped.

Sapporo seems set for continued growth: recent overtures have been made concerning the construction of a brewery in China, and domestically, Sapporo is now the second largest brewer in Japan with nearly 20% of the market share. Although beer presently accounts for almost 90% of the company's total sales, forays into fields such as real estate and biotechnology promise to be highly profitable in the near future.

Principal Subsidiaries and Affiliates: Sapporo Lion Ltd.; Tokyo Ribbon Service; Sapporo Wines Ltd.; Sapporo Liquor Co., Ltd.; Seiwa Real Estate Ltd.; Seijo Green Plaza Co., Ltd.; Nihon Glass Manufacturing Co., Ltd.; Sapporo Beer Transporting Co., Ltd.; Sapporo Nosan-Kako Malting Co., Ltd.; Nihon Suishitsu Kenkyujo Co., Ltd.

THE SEAGRAM COMPANY, LTD.

1430 Peel Street
Montreal, Quebec H3A 1S9
Canada
(514) 849–5271

Public Company
Incorporated: March 2, 1928 as Distillers Corporation
Employees: 14,000
Sales: C$3.309 billion (US$2.398 billion)
Market Value: C$8.219 billion (US$5.956 billion)
Stock Index: New York Paris Toronto Montreal
London Vancouver

In 1889 the Bronfman family fled Czarist anti-Semitic pogroms in Bessarabia to make their home in Canada. A wealthy family, they were accompanied by their rabbi and two servants. In the century since, the Bronfmans (whose name, ironically, means "liquor man" in Yiddish) experienced a brief period of poverty but then went on to build the world's largest distilling business. The Seagram Company Ltd. and its subsidiaries sell more than $2 billion worth of liquor a year and market 600 brands in more than 175 countries. Almost a million and a half bottles of Seagram liquor are sold every day. On an international level, the Bronfmans operate one of the largest family-controlled capital pools in the non-Arab world.

Soon after the family's arrival in Canada, patriarch Yechiel Bronfman learned that tobacco farming, which had made him a wealthy man in his homeland, was incompatible with the cold Canadian climate. The Bronfmans found themselves without a livelihood, and Yechiel was forced to leave his family to work as a laborer clearing the right-of-way for a line of the Canadian Northern Railway. He bought a shed for $12 for his family and after a short time moved to a better job in a sawmill. Yechiel Bronfman and his sons then started selling firewood, making a fairly good living, and began a trade in frozen whitefish to earn a winter income. Eventually they turned to trading horses, a venture through which they became involved in the hotel and bar business. On reaching adulthood, two of Yechiel Bronfman's sons, Harry and Sam, took charge of the family's business interests. Harry Bronfman owned his first hotel in 1903 when he was 17 years old.

When Prohibition came to Canada in 1916, the Bronfmans decided to leave the hotel business and enter the whiskey trade. Canada had implemented Prohibition only to appease foes of drinking; in reality, alcohol consumption remained high in Canada. The Bronfmans took advantage of the imprecise Canadian Prohibition laws to maximize their bottlegging profits. Sam Bronfman bought the Bonaventure Liquor Store Company, conveniently located near the downtown railway in Montreal, in 1916. People traveling to the "dry" west could stock up on liqour before boarding the train. Business was brisk until March 1918, when a law was passed that prohibited the manufacture or importation of alcohol containing more than 2.5% spirits.

The prohibition excluded alcohol intended for medicinal purposes, so Harry Bronfman promptly went into the drug business. He bought a Dewar's whiskey sales contract from the Hudson Bay Company and began selling straight liquor through drugstores and to processors who made "medicinal" mixtures. One such concoction was known as a Dandy Bracer—Liver and Kidney Cure; it contained sugar, molasses, bluestone, 36% alcohol, and tobacco

When the Volstead Act instituted Prohibition in the U.S. in 1919, the Bronfmans imported 300,000 gallons of alcohol from the United States, enough to make 800,000 gallons of whiskey. They reduced 65-overproof white alcohol to the required bottling strength by mixing it with water, some real whiskey and a bit of burnt sugar to provide color. A shot of sulphuric acid brought on a quick simulated aging process. The Bronfmans' mixing equipment could fill and label 1,000 bottles an hour. All the whiskey came out of the same vats, but it was bottled under several different labels to raise the liquor's value. Materials cost of the whiskey mixture was no more than $5.25 per gallon. Bottled, the whiskey sold for the equivalent of $25 a gallon.

In 1924 the Bronfmans opened their first distillery in La Salle, across the St. Lawrence River from Montreal. In the same year they incorporated under the name Distillers Corporation Limited.

Two years later the family sold a 50% interest to Distillers Company, an amalgamation of British distillers that controlled more than half the world's scotch market and from which the Bronfmans had been importing scotch in bulk. In exchange for a half share in Distillers Corp., the British Enterprise gave the Bronfmans Canadian distribution rights for its brands, which included Haig, Black & White, Dewar's, and Vat 69.

At about the same time the Seagram family's distilling business became a public company. The enterprise had begun in 1883 when Joseph Emm Seagram became sole proprietor of a distillery in Waterloo, Ontario where he had worked since the 1860's. Seagram later turned to politics (he was a Conservative member of Parliament from 1896 to 1908), and also devoted much of his time to horse racing. His company was a leading Canadian rye producer with two popular brands, Seagram's '83 and V.O., which was introduced in 1909. (Joseph Seagram's racing colors, black and gold, still appear on the labels of V.O. bottles.)

In 1928, two years after Seagram went public, the Bronfmans' Distillers Corp. acquired all stock in the distillery and itself became a public company. The merged company took the name Distillers Corp-Seagram Limited.

W.H.Ross was president and Sam Bronfman was vice president. In its first year the company netted $2.2 million in profits, most of it from the Bronfman's busy bootlegging work. In 1929 Sam Bronfman prepared a $4.2 share offering to finance expansion in the highly successful export business. By 1930, however, company profits were declining, and the share offering had to be postponed.

By that time the border between Canada and the United States was extremely dangerous for illegal alcohol transport, so most trading was done by sea. The Bronfmans had established warehouses on the coast and subsidiaries called Atlantic Import and Atlas Shipping. Schooners shipped the contraband goods into the U.S. in the dead of night. Prohibition ended in the U.S. in 1933. The next year a conservative lawyer, Richard Bedford Bennett, was chosen to head the Canadian Conservative Party and immediately launched an investigation into the liquor smuggling industry. The Bronfmans were arrested, and a year later they were tried. The judge threw the case out of court.

In 1928 Sam Bronfman had anticipated the end of Prohibition and begun to stockpile and age whiskey. Now the company owned the largest private stock of properly mellowed whiskey. This lucrative position enabled it in 1933 to acquire 20% of Schenley, whose product line included the well-known Golden Wedding brand of rye whiskey. When Sam Bronfman informed the Distillers Company board in Scotland of the move and requested an increase in whiskey prices, he was told at an acrimonious board meeting that Distillers would not agree to either proposal. In response, the Bronfman brothers raised $4 million and bought out the Distillers Company's holding in Distillers Corporation-Seagrams Limited. W.H. Ross resigned after the split, and Sam Bronfman became president.

The company then purchased the Rossville Union Distillery in Lawrenceburg, Indiana, and set up Joseph E. Seagram and Sons Inc. to operate the U.S. venture. Schenley's board of directors suggested an equal partnership in the American operation, but when Sam Bronfman found out that Golden Wedding was not aged before it was sold, he immediately rejected the plan. Soon afterward, Seagram and Schenley parted company. Schenley held the top position in the whiskey market until 1937, lost it to Seagram until 1944, regained it until 1947, then lost it to Seagram for good.

Blending and aging became Seagram's hallmark. Sam Bronfman wanted to quash the somewhat dubious image of drinking whiskey that had developed in the bootlegging era and replace it with a more respectable and refined one. In promoting his products he would use one of three descriptions of the blending process: a formal outline of the details of the process; a short definition ("Distilling is a science; blending is an art"); and an informal explanation ("Look, when a man goes into a store for a bottle of Coca-Cola, he expects it to be the same today as it will be tomorrow. . . . The great products don't change. Well, our product's not going to change either"). Seagram still has "blending libraries" at its offices in New York, Montreal, and Paisley, near Glasgow, where samples of the company's different types of straight whiskies are continually catalogued and tested.

The company purchased Maryland Distillers, Inc and its Calvert affiliate in Relay, Maryland in 1934 and imported its own aged Canadian stock to blend with its new American distillates. The resulting product came out under the Five Crown and Seven Crown labels. A few years later the company built a new distillery in Louisville, Kentucky. By 1938 Distillers-Seagram had approximately 60 million gallons of whiskey aging in its three American plants.

The Bronfman brothers revolutionized liquor marketing by selling their products to distributors already bottled. Other distillers sold liquor to local rectifiers in barrel consignments, thereby losing control over the final product. The Bronfmans' method allowed Seagram to maintain the kind of quality control that builds brand loyalty. The practice is now industry standard. By the end of 1936 Seagram sales were up to $60 million in the United States, with another $10 million in Canada. By 1948 total sales exceeded $438 million, and the company posted an after-tax profit of $53.7 million.

Sam Bronfman had always been impressed with British aristocracy. When George VI and Queen Elizabeth visited Canada in 1939, Bronfman blended 600 samples of whiskey before creating the prestigious Crown Royal brand in their honor. He also purchased the Chivas distillery in Aberdeen, Scotland because its operators owned a grocery store that served the royal family when they were in Scotland. Chivas Regal is now the best-selling deluxe scotch whiskey in the world.

In the 1940's Seagram expanded from the whiskey business into the larger liquor industry. Its entry into the wine markets began with a 1942 partnership with German vintners Fromm & Sichel to purchase the Paul Masson vineyards in California. (Seagram sold its 96% interest in Paul Masson in the mid-1980's). Eight years later the company bought a majority interest in Fromm & Sichel. During World War II Seagram imported rum from Puerto Rico and Jamaica and acquired several West Indies distilleries which would later introduce the Captain Morgan, Myers's, Woods, and Trelawny labels. Seagram also purchased Mumm's Champagne, Perrior-Jouet Champagne, Barton & Guestier, and Augier Frères.

Sam Bronfman took the company in a dramatically new direction in 1950 when he invested in the Alberta oil company Royalite. He later sold his interest in Gulf and purchased the Frankfort Oil Company. In 1963 Seagram acquired the Texas Pacific Coal and Oil Company for $276 million.

In 1957 Edgar Bronfman, Sam Bronfman's son, became the company's president. He resurrected Calvert Reserve by remarketing it as Calvert Extra and promoting it with a personal tour. He also expanded Seagram's brands of rum, scotch, and bottled cocktails (manhattans, daiquiris, whiskey sours, and martinis), and began to import wine on a large scale. By the end of 1965 the company was operating in 119 countries and had surpassed $1 billion in sales.

Between 1961 and 1971, sales of blended whiskey by all makers dropped from 60% to 20% of the total hard liquor market, but Seven Crown, V.O., Chivas, and Crown Royal continued to capture an increasing share of their shrinking markets and Seagram revenues and profits maintained their growth. In 1975, however—a year after the company name was changed to The Seagram Company, Ltd.—Seagram's earnings slipped 9% to $74 million. Seven Crown sales dropped by 600,000 cases, and V.O. was down 300,000 cases. Edgar Bronfman decided to reorganize the company's board of directors and management. A new executive committee was formed with another Bronfman brother, Charles, at its head. In 1977 Seagram recorded a net income of $84 million on sales of $2.2 billion.

In the late 1960's Edgar Bronfman decided to get involved in the film industry. He bought $40 million of MGM stock, and in 1969 replaced Robert O'Brien as the studio's chairman. MGM lost $25 million in the next year, and Bronfman resigned from the studio. Seagram lost about $10 million in the short-lived venture. He found some success in the entertainment industry later when his Sagittarius Productions Inc. staged several Broadway successes.

The fabulously wealthy Bronfman family received extensive media attention in the 1970's. Details of Edgar's private life, exposed in divorce proceedings, were eagerly reported in the tabloids; and in 1975, the family had to contend with the alleged kidnapping of Edgar's 23-year-old son, Samuel II. The incident and subsequent trial became headline news in many countries. Mel Patrick Lynch, the defendant (a fireman from Brooklyn, New York) was acquitted of kidnapping charges but convicted of extortion. Throughout the trial, Lynch maintained that Sam II was his lover and that the kidnapping was a hoax cooked up by Bronfman in order to lay his hands on some of the family cash. Sam II was reunited with his father; both of them hotly denied Lynch's version of events.

In 1980 Seagram sold Texas Pacific to the Sun Company for $3 billion, but when Edgar wanted to reinvest the money in St. Joe Minerals, he was turned down even though he offered $45 a share for stock that had been selling at $28 a share. Conoco also rejected Seagram's advances. Du Pont, Seagram's third choice, accepted a bid on 19% of the company's stock. Seagram remains the single largest shareholder in Du Pont.

Seagram has continued to diversify in the 1980's. In 1981 the company formed Westmount Enterprises to finance its beverage ventures and market its new gourmet frozen dinners. Seagram also manufactures and markets premium mixers jointly with the Coca-Cola Bottling Company of New York. In addition, the company has purchased 11.6% of Biotechnica International and has ventured increasingly into the wine industry through its Seagram's Vinters division.

In 1985 Seagram underwent a thorough reorganization of its companies, brands, and personnel. It also launched a new advertising campaign aimed at upgrading the image of liquor consumption, and Edgar Bronfman asked the television networks to suspend their ban on advertising for distilled spirits. The three major broadcasters all refused to air a commercial comparing the alcohol content of whiskey, wine, and beer.

At any one time, four million barrels of spirits and 42 million gallons of wine are aging in Seagram warehouses. The Bronfmans, wealthier than the Rockefellers, own real estate, shopping malls, office complexes, and the Club Mediterranée, among their many other assets. Most labels owned by the family make no reference to their Seagram connection, and many apparently independent producers are nothing more than Seagram subsidiaries.

Principal Subsidiaries: Centenary Distillers, Ltd.; Seagram International BV; Seagold Vineyards Holding Corp.; Gold Seal Vineyards, Inc.; Joseph E. Seagram & Sons, Inc.; Distillers Products Sales Corp.; General Beverage Co.; Gonzales & Co., Inc.; The Taylor Wine Company, Inc.; Jerome Distributors, Inc.; JES Developments, Inc.; Vintners Associates, Inc.; Brandy Associates of California, Inc.; Vie-Del Co. (87%); Seagram Investments, Inc. The company also lists subsidiaries in the following countries: Argentina, Australia, Austria, Bahamas, Belgium, Bermuda, Costa Rica, France, Israel, Italy, Japan, Mexico, Portugal, Spain, Thailand, the United Kingdom, Venezuela and West Germany.

Further Reading: King of the Castle: The Making of a Dynasty: Seagrams and the Bronfman Empire by Peter C. Newman, New York, Atheneum, 1979.

SOUTH AFRICAN BREWERIES LTD.

P.O. Box 1099
Johannesburg 2000
South Africa
(011) 339–4711

Public Company
Incorporated: 15 May, 1895 in London
Employees: 73,500
Sales: (Group) R5.747 billion (US$2.587)
Market Value: (Group) R4.118 billion (US$1.853 billion)
Stock Index: Johannesburg London

In many ways the history of South African Breweries is the history of the South African brewing industry; the largest breweries in South Africa were forced to merge in 1956 by government order. South African Breweries owes much of its success to a consistently strong demand for beer, or what the company refers to as "thirst."

The discovery of gold on the Witwatersrand (a region encompassing Johannesburg) in 1875 brought large numbers of prospectors to South Africa. Small outposts for white settlers were transformed into busy cities with new industries. Several brewmasters, most with little experience, began to produce a variety of beers which immediately gained popularity with the settlers.

In 1889 a British sailor named Frederick Mead left his ship in Durban and took a job working in the canteen of a local army garrison at Fort Napier. While there, Mead, who was only 20, became acquainted with a businessman in Pietermaritzburg named George Raw. Neither of them knew anything about brewing, but they persuaded the local residents to help establish the Natal Brewery Syndicate. After purchasing a factory site, Frederick Mead returned to England to procure machinery and raise capital. In need of brewing expertise, Mead approached W.H. Hackblock, head of Morgan's Brewery in Norwich. The two men became friends and Hackblock agreed to serve as chairman of Mead's company, which was registered in 1890 as the Natal Brewery Syndicate (South East Africa) Limited. The company brewed its first beer in July 1891.

Mead remained interested in establishing a brewery in the rapidly growing Witwatersrand. In 1892 he purchased the Castle Brewery in Johannesburg from its proprietor Charles Glass. The expansion of this facility, however, was beyond the means of the Natal Brewery Syndicate, and

Mead returned to England to attract new investors. In the final arrangement, Mead formed another larger company based in London called the South African United Breweries. This company took over the operations of both the Natal Brewery Syndicate and the Castle Brewery.

After construction of the new Castle Brewery, South African United Breweries made additional share offerings which were purchased by South Africa's largest investment houses. Subsequent growth precipitated a restructuring of the company and reincorporation in London on May 15, 1895 as the South African Breweries Limited.

In 1896 South African Breweries purchased its first boarding houses. That same year, Frederick Mead moved to England for reasons of poor health, but continued to occupy a seat on the board of directors and frequently returned to South Africa. From London, Mead directed the purchase of machinery for brewing lager beer from the Pfaudler Vacuum Company in the United States. Patent restrictions and mechanical difficulties delayed production of Castle lager until 1898. The beer gained such widespread popularity that competing breweries rushed to introduce their own lagers.

South African Breweries, or SAB, was listed on the London Stock Exchange in 1895, and two years later became the first industrial company to be listed on the Johannesburg Stock Exchange. Through these listings SAB had greater access to additional investor capital.

On October 11, 1899 a war broke out between British colonial forces and Dutch and Huguenot settlers known as Boers. The war drove residents of Johannesburg out of the city and forced the Castle Brewery to close for almost a year. When British troops recovered the area, the brewery had sustained little or no damage. British authorities regarded the plant as an essential industry, and encouraged the company to resume production in August 1900. Disrupted supply lines caused shortages of yeast and other raw materials, but within a year production had returned to full capacity.

The Boer War ended in 1902, but was followed by a severe economic depression. The brewing industry was not as adversely affected as others, however, and SAB was able to continue its expansion across southern Africa. The company acquired the Durban Breweries and Distillers company, and established a new plant at Bloemfontein. SAB purchased Morgan's Brewery in Port Elizabeth in 1906, and five years later acquired another brewery in Salisbury, Rhodesia (now Harare, Zimbabwe). At its northernmost point, SAB established a brewery at Ndola, Northern Rhodesia (now Zambia).

W.H. Hackblock died in 1907 and was succeeded as chairman by Sydney Chambers. In 1912 Chambers led the company into an innovative arrangement with its competitor, Ohlsson's Brewery, to cultivate hops jointly at a site near the city of George, midway between Port Elizabeth and Cape Town. A joint subsidiary called Union Hop Growers spent many years developing new hybrids, which delayed the first commercial use of South African-grown hops until 1920.

After Frederick Mead died in August 1915, John Stroyan, who succeeded Sydney Chambers a few months earlier, became the most important figure in SAB management. Stroyan faced a serious challenge the following year when hostilities during World War I interrupted the supply of bottles to South Africa. SAB decided to establish its own bottle-making plants in 1917. Actual production, however, did not begin until 1919, the year the war ended.

Another economic depression beset South Africa after the war, but steady growth in the demand for beer reduced many of the detrimental effects of the depression. SAB was financially strong enough in 1921 to purchase the Grand Hotel in Cape Town, an important addition to the company's lodging business. SAB gained an interest in the mineral water business in 1925, when it purchased a substantial interest in the Schweppes Company.

The Great Depression of the early 1930's had little effect on the South African brewing industry; SAB continued to expand its operations and improve its facilities. The company's biggest problems were shortages of labor and capital.

The Spanish Civil War and rising political tensions in Europe during the mid and late 1930's caused a distruption in the supply of cork to South Africa. Faced with a severe shortage of cork seals for its beer, SAB developed a method of recycling old cork until a new supplier of cork could be found.

Castle Beer accompanied South African soldiers to the East African and Mediterranean theatres of World War II, but apart from its involvement in Europe, South Africa was relatively unaffected by World War II. When hostilities ended in 1945, SAB turned its attention to further modernization and expansion. Arthur Griffith-Boscawen, who had succeeded John Stroyan as chairman in 1940, died in 1946, and was replaced by John Stroyan's son, Captain John R.A. Stroyan. Under the leadership of the younger Stroyan, SAB concentrated on the establishment of a South African barley industry as an extension of the joint agricultural project it operated with Ohlsson's.

South African Breweries entered a new stage of its development in 1950. That year, in the midst of a large corporate modernization program, SAB decided to move its head office from London to Johannesburg. In 1951 the company acquired the Hotel Victoria in Johannesburg, and a second brewery in Salisbury. Captain Stroyan retired the following year and returned to England. His successor, a talented barrister named J.K. Cockburn Millar, died after only four months in office, and was replaced by a solicitor, S.J. Constance.

After producing nothing but beer for more than 60 years, SAB began to introduce a range of liquor products. The incentive to diversify was provided by increased taxes on beer. Consumption of beer in South Africa fell for the first time on record and showed every indication of further decline.

Officials of the three largest brewing companies in South Africa, SAB, Ohlsson's Cape Breweries, and United Breweries, met on several occasions in London and Johannesburg to discuss the viability of competition under deteriorating market conditions. In 1956 these officials decided that the three companies should merge their operations into one large brewing concern. SAB acquired all the shares of Ohlsson's and United Breweries, thus retaining the South African Breweries name, and B.C. Smither of Ohlsson's and M.W.J. Bull of United Breweries joined the SAB board of directors.

Although the new company controlled 90% of the market for beer in South Africa, antiquated production facilities narrowed profit margins. In response, company activities were centralized in the Transvaal and the Western Province, areas where the three companies had previously competed. In addition, the old Castle Brewery in Johannesburg was closed in 1958. After succeeding Constance as chairman in 1959, M.W.J. Bull initiated a further diversification into wines and spirits. In 1960 SAB acquired the Stellenbosch Farmers Winery and later added Monis Wineries. Bull retired at the end of 1964 and was replaced by Dr. Frans J.C. Cronje, an economist and lawyer with substantial experience in government.

The company encountered a severe financial crisis in 1966 when Whitbread and Heineken entered the South African beer market. The most damaging market developments, however, came from government quarters; successive increases in excise duties made beer the most heavily taxed beverage per serving. Consumers began to abandon beer for wine and sorghum beer. SAB was able to reduce the effect of this crisis by increased sales of products from the Stellenbosch winery.

South African Breweries chief executive Ted Sceales was instrumental in the creation of a new subsidiary called Barsab, jointly held by SAB and Thomas Barlow & Sons Ltd. (later Barlow Rand), the rapidly expanding mining services group. Barsab permitted SAB and Barlow to invest in each other and pool their managerial and administrative resources. It also provided SAB with the resources needed to adapt to rapidly changing market conditions. Sceales died following an auto accident in 1967, but the success of Barsab continued under the new chief executive, Dick Goss.

South African Breweries first attempted to move its legal domicile from Britain to South Africa in 1950, but was prevented from doing so by complex tax obligations to the British government. Consequently, SAB, which still derived about one-third of its income from investments in Rhodesia and Zambia, was bound to observe the British trade embargo against Rhodesia in 1967.

Parliamentary motions to permit the reincorporation of SAB in South Africa were initiated in 1968. These motions, however, did not gain approval until March 17, 1970. On May 26, 1970, after 75 years as an English company, SAB became a *de jure* South African company.

During the late 1960's SAB began brewing a number of new beers, including Guinness, Amstel, and Rogue. The company also acquired the Old Dutch and Stag brands, as well as Whitbread in South Africa. While sales of wine and spirits continued to rise, SAB sold a number of its liquor-oriented hotels, and reorganized those that remained under a new subsidiary called the Southern Sun Hotel Corporation. Southern Sun, which operated 50 hotels in South Africa, was formed by the merger in 1969 of the existing SAB hotel interests with those of the Sol Kerzner family.

The South African government barred SAB from further investment in the liquor industry and limited its ability to invest overseas. The company then made several attempts to diversify its operations. In 1972 SAB and Barlow rand decided to alter their collaboration and dissolve Barsab. As a result, two former Barsab holdings, the Shoe Corporation, and Afcol, South Africa's largest furniture manufacturer, came under SAB control. The following year, SAB acquired OK Bazaars, a large discount department store chain. Certain other investments were disposed of, however, including ventures in banking and food products.

Several brewing interests attempted to challenge SAB's dominant position in the South African market. Various German interests set up breweries in Botswana and Swaziland in a failed attempt to gain a foothold in South Africa. Louis Luyt, a South African entrepreneur, also failed, and sold his breweries to the Rembrandt group in 1973. The Luyt breweries, which formed the core of Rembrandt's alcoholic beverage group, were later incorporated as the Intecontinental Breweries. Determined to succeed, Rembrandt's chairman, Dr. Anton Rupert, committed his company to a scheme of competition based on control of liquor retail outlets. In 1978 Rembrandt acquired a 49% share of Gilbey's, the third largest liquor group in South Africa. The addition of Gilbey's 100 retail outlets gave Rembrandt access to a total of 450 stores. South African Breweries responded by acquiring Union Wine, an independent liquor retailer with 24 hotels and over 50 retail outlets.

Once again, market conditions were not conducive to competition. Therefore, the government proposed a rationalization program in which SAB would take over Rembrandt's brewing interests and turn over its wine and spirits operations to an independent subsidiary called Cape Wine and Distillers. The program, executed in November of 1979, also called for Rembrandt to turn over its Oude Meester wine and spirits operations to Cape Wines, in which SAB, Rembrandt, and the KWV wine growers cooperative each owned a 30% interest. The remaining 10% interest was sold to private investors.

By the early 1980's the South African government's system of racial separation (*apartheid*) and deteriorating social conditions for Blacks had become international issues, and highly sensitive ones for the predominately apolitical English-speaking business establishment. Many business leaders openly called for change, but the government still prevented companies such as SAB from transferring capital out of South Africa through foreign investments. Often these companies had little choice but to reinvest their surplus capital in South African ventures, which in turn has given them a more crucial interest in the resolution of social and human rights problems within South Africa.

Many foreign-owned companies, which face fewer restrictions on divestment, have sold their South African subsidiaries and closed their offices in South Africa. This trend has made acquisitions by South African companies easier. SAB took over control of the ABI soft drink concern from Coca-Cola, and later added several clothing retailers, including Scotts Stores and the Edgars chain. A government order in 1979 for SAB to sell its Solly Kramer retail liquor stores was completed in 1986, five years before its deadline.

South African Breweries remains a public company, but is actually controlled by its majority shareholder, the Anglo American Corporation, a large South African mining and finance group. SAB continues to derive most of its operating income from the production of beer at its ten breweries. Under the company's new chairman, Murray B. Hofmeyer (who succeeded Dr. Cronje in 1987), SAB will remain strongly interested in the resolution of social tensions caused by *apartheid* in order to maintain a stable and profitable business environment.

Principal Subsidiaries: Alrode Brewing Company (Pty.), Ltd.; Amalgamated Beverage Industries (Pty.), Ltd. (55%); Appletiser Pure Fruit Juices (Pty.), Ltd.; Bier en Mout Beleggings (Edms.), Bpk.; Ohlsson's Brewery Transkei (Pty.), Ltd. (70%); Ohlsson's Cape Breweries, Ltd.; Southern Associated Maltsters (Pty.), Ltd. (55%); United Breweries (Pty.), Ltd. (70%); Amalgamated Retail, Ltd. ("Amrel") (69%); Edgars Stores, Ltd. (61%, indirect); OK Bazaars (1929), Ltd. (70%); Associated Furniture Companies, Ltd. ("Afcol") (65%); SA Footwear, Ltd.; Southern Sun Hotel Holdings, Ltd. (68%); Sabfin (Pty.), Ltd.; Sabre Finance, Ltd.; Shoecorp Properties, Ltd.

THE STROH BREWING COMPANY

100 River Place
Detroit, Michigan 48207
U.S.A.
(313) 446–2000

Public Company
Incorporated: 1850
Employees: 6,800
Sales: $1.65 billion

The Stroh family began brewing beer in a family-owned inn during the 18th century in Germany. In 1848, during the German Revolution, Bernhard Stroh, who had learned the brewing trade from his father, emigrated to the United States. In 1850 he founded a brewery which has been owned and operated by the family for more than 130 years. While the company has expanded considerably in recent decades, it is still directed by a Stroh, and all of its stock shares are in the hands of 27 Stroh family members.

Bernhard Stroh established his brewery in Detroit when he was 28 and immediately started producing Bohemian-style beer, which had been developed at the municipal brewery of Pilsen, Bohemia, in 1840, In 1865 he purchased additional land and expanded his business. He adopted the Lion's Crest from the Kyrburg Castle in Germany and named his operation the Lion's Head Brewery. The company still uses the crest in its advertising.

Bernhard Stroh, Jr. took charge of the brewery on the death of his father, the founder. He changed the brewery's name to the B. Stroh Brewing Company. With the introduction of pasteurization and refigerated rail cars, Stroh was able to ship some of his beer to Florida and Massachusetts. In 1893 Stroh Bohemian Beer won a blue ribbon at the Columbian Exposition. In 1908 Bernhard Stroh's brother Julius took over the brewery and renamed it the Stroh Brewing Company. After a tour of famous European breweries, he introduced the European fire-brewing method in the Stroh brewery. Today Stroh's is the only fire-brewed beer on the American market. Common in Europe before World War I, the fire-brewing process uses a direct flame rather than steam to heat beer-filled copper kettles. The company claims that the resulting higher temperatures bring out more of the beer's flavor.

During Prohibition Julius Stroh operated the business under the name The Stroh Products Company, producing near beer (beer with its alcohol extracted), soft drinks, malt products, and ice-cream. Though production of most of these items ceased when Prohibition ended in 1933, a special unit of the brewery still makes Stroh Ice Cream. The product is sold in retail groceries and independent ice-cream parlors in Michigan.

Upon Julius Stroh's death in 1939, his son Gari assumed the presidency. Gari's brother John succeeded him in 1950 and became Stroh's chairman in 1967. Gari's son Peter, who had joined the company following his graduation from Princeton in 1951, became president in 1968. He is now chairman of the board. At present, Stroh's president is Roger Friedholm.

In 1964 the company made its first move toward expansion from its traditional position as a small but successful producer of one brand of beer and ice cream when it bought the Goebel Brewing Company across the street. At the same time, Peter Stroh directed the company into a period of large-scale changes motivated principally by two causes: the 1958 Michigan beer strike, and the mergence of the Anheuser-Busch and Miller brewing companies as corporate leaders in the beer industry.

In 1956 Stroh sold 2.7 million barrels of beer. A long statewide beer strike two years later enabled out-of-state beers to capture larger shares of the Michigan market, and while Stroh remained the largest brewer in the state in 1968, it still had not fully recovered the ground lost in the strike. Sales were low in Michigan that year and far behind the sales of 12 years earlier. Recognizing that half the company's production was sold outside Michigan, Peter Stroh ended a 40-year relationship with Stroh's advertising agency to search for a large national agency that would help develop the company's growing business on a national scale.

By 1971 the Stroh Brewery Company had moved from 15th to 13th place in the national beer market. In 1972 it entered the top ten for the first time and had a market area of nine states. A year later it was the eighth-largest brewery in the United States, selling four million barrels of beer per year in 17 states.

At the same time Miller and Anheuser-Busch entered into intense competition; Anheuser wanted to maintain its position as America's dominant brewer, while Miller attempted to rise from its seventh-place rank to overtake Anheuser's position. The large advertising budgets, wide distribution areas, and efficient production methods used by the two breweries through the 1970's proved impossible for many regional breweries to match. Peter Stroh's willingness to depart from years of tradition enabled Stroh to survive, though his family's pride in the brewery's heritage made many of his revolutionary changes difficult to implement. It is not surprising that Peter's decisions would have seemed radical to many in a company that had produced only one brand for nearly 130 years. Stroh himself had prevously seen his role as "more a braumeister than a promoter," but the soft-spoken man now remarked that "as the industry changed I've had to become more marketing oriented. Deep in my heart I know it's either grow or go."

Peter Stroh broke the company's old-world management tradition by recruiting outside experts from such companies as Pepsico and Procter & Gamble to manage the brewery's affairs. He also expanded the product line by introducing Stroh's second brand, Stroh's Light, in 1978. Adamant in the conviction that his brewery should not sacrifice its product's taste, however, Stroh insisted that the light version be held to 115 calories rather than being cut to the 96 calories of most other light beers. At 115, Stroh's Light was 25% lower in calories than Stroh's regular beer.

The 1973 increase of market area to 17 states had caused the brewery nearly to outgrow its production capacity by 1978, when it produced 6.4 million barrels of beer. The Detroit family was 66 years old and had a capacity of seven million barrels annually. As it became difficult to make efficient shipments to new markets in the east, the company recognized that it must build a new brewery.

A solution presented itself in the form of New York's F&M Schaefer Brewing Corporation, one of the regional breweries that had been a victim of Miller's growing market share. Stroh, planning to purchase all of Schaefer's stock to gain control of the brewery, paid an initial $800,000 for 8.5% of the total shares. After the takeover was complete in 1981, the combined breweries ranked seventh in beer sales. Under the terms of the deal, Stroh gained access to Schaefer's Allentown, Pennsylvania brewery. With its capacity of a million gallons it is one of the industry's most efficient United States operations. In addition, Stroh was able to take advantage of Schaefer's distributors in the northeastern part of the country. The acquisition also brought Stroh three new brands: Schaefer and Piels beers, and Schaefer's Cream Ale. The company now had a volume of over 40 million barrels and 400 distributors in 28 states, Washington, D.C., Puerto Rico, and other Caribbean islands. The Stroh brewery Company began to take the form of a smaller version of the industry leaders.

Early in 1982 Peter Stroh made a bid on 67% of the Schlitz Brewing Company, the first step in acquiring the third-largest brewery in the United States. By April of that year, Stroh had purchased the entire company for $17 a share. Schlitz became a wholly owned subsidiary of the Stroh Brewing Comany, making Stroh the third-largest brewery in the United States. The acquisition was by no means simple. Schlitz resisted the takeover by taking Stroh to court. Schlitz finally accepted the takeover when Stroh raised its offer from an initial $16 per share to $17, and the U.S. Justice Department approved the acquisition once Stroh agreed to sell either Schlitz's Memphis or Winston-Salem breweries.

Along with the expansion of Stroh's brewery came a departure from the company's traditional marketing approach. Stroh had always been marketed as a popularly priced "blue-collar" beer, with a six-pack selling at 25¢ less than national premium brands. Commercials noted the fire-brewed flavor of the beer. A large part of Stroh's national market, however, began to find it difficult to reconcile the brew's low price with its advertised quality. The new premium beers recently introduced by Miller and Anheuser became more popular with the working class that had previously purchased Stroh beer. In order to revive blue-collar sales, Stroh reduced the price of Schlitz to below the premium level.

Stroh divested itself of the Schlitz-run Geyser Peak Winery in order to concentrate on beer products. Despite the success of its light beer, Stroh initially moved with typical caution in introducing new products. Because of its two major acquisitions the company now marketed regular and light versions of Schlitz, Stroh, and Old Milwaukee, as well as Goebel, Piels, and Schlitz Malt Liquor. Even so, it was not until four years after the introduction of Stroh's Light that the company introduced another new product of its own. Stroh Signature marked the brewer's entry into the premium market.

The move from a regional market into the national arena was especially challenging for Stroh's advertising and promotional efforts. As mentioned above, the company did away with the emphasis on its fire-brewing process when consumers seemed unable to reconcile Stroh's reputed high quality with its relatively low price. Ad campaigns became more upbeat, first using an "Alex the Dog" commercial where Alex would fetch, buy, or pour beer for his master. The company then turned to the "From One Beer Lover to Another" campaign that had science-fiction and phantasmagorical themes. The brewery won two awards for its "Beer Lover" ads. In 1985 Stroh moved to the good times-good friends-good beer theme popular in the beer industry. Its slogan was "Stroh's is Spoken Here." The company felt the theme was more relevant to the all-American beer drinker and showed more confidence in the beer, rather than being merely entertaining.

In the 1980's the company also turned to corporate sponsorship to gain needed national publicity. In 1982 Stroh was a sponsor of the World's Fair in Knoxville, Tennessee, an event that strengthened Stroh's new national standing considerably. For many years Stroh had received little television exposure because of an agreement between the major networks and Anheuser and Miller which allowed the two top brewers exclusive advertising rights. Stroh fought the agreement and in 1983 was allotted advertising time on ABC's Monday Night Baseball, on two NBC boxing events, and on other popular U.S. television sports shows. Confronted with nearly prohibitive network costs, the company began "The Stroh Circle of Sports" on cable television and independent stations. The program featured live events with reporting and analysis. Stroh also looked to such sports as hockey, which had been overlooked by Anheuser and Miller, for increased publicity opportunities. Stroh sponsored broadcasts of National Hockey League games on the USA cable network. The company sponsored the Formula One stock car race with Valvoline Motor Oil. The event was considered an important boost for Stroh's international name recognition. "High Rollers," a contest for amateur bowlers, was also developed and sponsored by the company. Stroh's most popular non-sports promotion is the "Schlitz Rocks America" concert series.

Americans' increased health and moderation awareness caused beer sales to drop considerably in the first half of the 1980's. Stroh's challenge, therefore, was to maintain strong profit margins in the declining beer industry. In attempting to do so, Stroh has begun to consider itself a general beverage company rather than strictly a brewery.

In 1985 it introduced White Mountain Cooler, a citrus-, orange-, or berry-flavored drink that contains 5% alcohol. The cooler is not wine-based like its competitors; instead Stroh uses its beer technology to make a malt-based beverage that has been successful. Stroh differentiated the cooler from its beer brands by forming the Colorado Cooler Company division to market the new product.

Other new subsidiaries are Stroh Foods, Inc. (formerly the Pacific Health Beverage Company), the Great Northern Import Company, and Stroh International, Inc. Creation of Pacific Health in 1985 marked Stroh's entry into the competitive soft drink market. The division produces and markets Sundance 100% Natural Juice Sparklers, which contain 70% pure fruit juice and 30% sparkling water. Great Northern has expanded Stroh's product line by importing alternative beverages, including Koenig, Germany's top-selling beer, and Barbican, a non-alcoholic malt beverage from England. Finally, Stroh International introduces Stroh products into world markets.

Stroh now owns six breweries, in Pennsylvania, North Carolina, Tennessee, Texas, Minnesota, and California. The company operates two container manufacturing plants and a growing network for recycling aluminum beverage containers. Stroh products are available in many European countries, as well as in Asia, the Middle East, and the Caribbean.

The flurry of new and successful activity started in 1985 appears to promise a healthy future for Stroh. Company management clearly is able to anticipate consumer trends and market Stroh products to the best advantage.

Principal Subsidiaries: F&M Schaefer Corp.; Joseph Schlitz Brewing Co.; Stroh Brewery Co.

Further Reading: Brewed in America: A History of Beer and Ale in the U.S. by Stanley Wade Baron, New York, Arno Press, 1972.

WHITBREAD

WHITBREAD AND COMPANY PLC

Brewery, Chiswell Street
London EC1Y 4SD
England
01–606 4455

Public Company
Incorporated: July 24, 1889
Employees: 21,866
Sales: £1.533 billion (US$2.253 billion)
Market Value: £1.164 billion (US$1.711 billion)
Stock Index: London

Whitbread is one of the most prestigious of London's older breweries; it will celebrate its 250th anniversary in 1992. Its history closely parallels that of the Whitbread family, which has retained continuous control of the company since 1742. Since that date, Whitbread has also maintained its headquarters on Chiswell Street in central London.

Samuel Whitbread, at the age of 14, was sent to London by his mother in 1734 to become an apprentice to a brewer. Whitbread, raised as a Puritan, proved to be an extremely hard worker. Six years after coming to London, he established his own brewery with a £2000 inheritance and additional underwriting from John Howard, the renowned prison reformer. As the brewery became successful, Howard's investment became more lucrative—it even led to a reciprocation of financial support by Whitbread for Howard's reform movement.

By 1750 Whitbread had acquired an additional brewery located on Chiswell Street. At this time there were over 50 breweries in London, but, despite intense competition, the Whitbread brewery expanded rapidly. By 1760 its annual output had reached 64,000 barrels, second only to Calvert and Company.

Whitbread was enthusiastic about new brewing methods. He employed several well-known engineers who helped to improve the quality and increase the production volume of the company's stout and porter (a sweeter, weaker stout).

The Whitbread family had a long history of involvement in English politics. Samuel Whitbread's forefathers fought with Oliver Cromwell's Roundheads during the English Civil War and later developed a connection with the Bedfordshire preacher and author John Bunyan. Samuel Whitbread himself was elected to Parliament in 1768 as a representative of Bedford. His son, Samuel II, succeeded him in Parliament in 1790, and Whitbread descendants served in Parliament almost continuously until 1910.

Samuel Whitbread died in 1796. Samuel II assumed control of the brewery, but was so preoccupied with Parliament that by 1799 he was compelled to take on a partner. The partnership, however, was short-lived. The brewery entered into seven more partnerships over the next 70 years, only two of which were successful. Most notably, Whitbread's 1812 partnership with the Martineau and Bland brewery resulted in a full merger of the two companies' brewing operations. The Martineau and Bland facility at Lambeth, however, was later closed down and its equipment was moved to Chiswell Street.

During the early 19th century the bulk of Whitbread's business was conducted with "free houses," public houses—or pubs—neither owned by, nor bound to sell only the products of one brewer. These pubs numbered several hundred, and their business remained fairly stable. But when the Drury Lane Theatre burned down in 1809, Samuel II saw an opportunity to profit from its renovation. He led a committee to restore the theatre, invested heavily in the project, and persuaded several friends to join him. The venture yielded only a small dividend when the theatre was reopened, and cost Whitbread the friendship of many of his fellow investors. In Parliament, Whitbread opposed the resumption of war with Napoleon, a position which made him even more unpopular. In July of 1815, shortly after Waterloo, Samuel Whitbread II committed suicide.

Whitbread's sons, William Henry and Samuel Charles, inherited their father's interest in the brewery. Whitbread family control, however, had been greatly diminished by the company's nine partners. It was not until 1819 that the Whitbread brothers were able to re-establish direct family control over the operation. The number of partners was reduced, and the brewery remained under Whitbread control for many years.

In 1834 Whitbread introduced ale to its product line. The ale gained immediate popularity and resulted in a substantial increase in turnover for the brewery. Whitbread expanded even more dramatically after 1869, when the family established its last partnership.

During the 1880's, a sudden and significant decline in demand for beer caused many "free houses" to sell their leases to breweries (and thereby become "tied houses"). Breweries such as Whitbread, which had established numerous tied houses, were forced to extend loans to public house operators so that they could remain in business. The capital required to purchase free house leases and to extend loans could only be satisfied by the public through share flotations. Therefore, when Whitbread's partnership agreement expired in 1889, the partners decided to transform the brewery into a public company.

An attempt by brewers to raise the profitability of tied houses by reducing beer prices backfired; their tenants competed on price and went even further into debt. A recession in 1900 forced Whitbread to write down the value of its tied house properties—a move which may have saved the company. Demand for beer recovered steadily and permitted Whitbread to increase its production every year from 1899 to 1912. Accordingly, the value of tied houses recovered as they became profitable. Just prior to World War I, however, the government raised its license duty on tied houses, rendering many of them financial liabilities. Whitbread stopped buying tied houses, and instead concentrated on expanding its bottled beer trade.

While Whitbread weathered this difficult period virtually intact, many competitors were forced to close. Whitbread's ability to survive was attributed to three factors: the maintenance of a harmonious relationship between the brewer and the publican (public house operator), sustaining a good public image of the brand, and keeping influence in government.

Francis Pelham Whitbread, the director of the brewery at the time, devoted his energies to maintaining a stable atmosphere for profitable brewing; as chairman of the Brewers Society, he promoted better brewer-vendor relations. Later, as chairman and treasurer of the politically active National Trade Defence Association, he lobbied against the temperance movement in Parliament. After World War I he played a major role in the formation of policies within the brewing industry, and was particularly opposed to the proliferation of tied houses.

During the interwar period Whitbread took over the Jude Hanbury brewery. As its situation with vendors remained unsettled, Whitbread concentrated further on the expansion of bottled beer sales. Whitbread beer had become available throughout the world. Francis Whitbread, however, became increasingly divorced from the everyday operation of the brewery; his position as a spokesman for the industry and his dedication to philanthropic activities occupied most of his time.

On December 29, 1940, German incendiary bombs landed in five separate areas of the brewery. Each of the fires was put out by the company fire brigade, with the exception of a malt fire which, like burning coal dust, is very difficult to extinguish. It was finally doused a week later. Damage to the brewery and the surrounding area was great. Nevertheless, Whitbread resumed brewing almost immediately.

Francis Pelham Whitbread died in 1941. His leadership of the brewery was highly conservative—especially when compared to the policies of his successors. Francis was in many ways a popular figurehead for the company. Much of the actual burden of management fell on the shoulders of Samuel Howard Whitbread, who served with the company from 1915 until his death in 1944. William Henry Whitbread assumed leadership of the company that year, but was forced to postpone his plans for the rehabilitation of the brewery until after the war.

Though the war ended less than a year later, the British economy continued to suffer from after-effects for many years. Conditions were so grave that Whitbread was unable to begin its modernization until 1950. At that time Whitbread undertook a sweeping rationalization program which included the concentration of human resources and retooling of machinery.

Other smaller breweries were in less stable condition, and many were threatened with bankruptcy. Whitbread, however, offered an amalgamation scheme to these breweries. Under this formula, called the "Whitbread Umbrella," failing breweries agreed to coordinate their operations and distribution networks with Whitbread. Many of these arrangements resulted in Whitbread's eventual acquisition of the smaller brewers. In the period from 1951 to 1970 Whitbread took over 26 breweries and expanded its number of tied houses from less than 100 to 10,000.

Some of the breweries acquired by Whitbread were large well-established companies. Beginning with the Dutton brewery in 1964, Whitbread took over Rhymney in 1966, Threlfall and Fremlin in 1967, Strong in 1968, and Brickwood in 1971. These additions to Whitbread also gave the company greater geographical coverage—Threlfall's was located in the northwest port of Liverpool, and Brickwood's was in Portsmouth, on the south coast.

The 1970's were characterized as a period of streamlining for Whitbread. The company disposed of many of its marginally profitable or outdated operations—even the Chiswell Street brewery was closed in 1976. Still, Whitbread suffered from the after-effects of a serious economic recession during the mid-1970's, and the company came very close to bankruptcy. A gradual economic recovery led to improvements in the market which greatly strengthened Whitbread's financial position.

However, as popular demand shifted from ale to lager, total beer consumption began to fall. Whitbread started to de-emphasize certain brewing assets and instead invested heavily in restaurants (including a large Pizza Hut franchise), discos, and other more diverse interests. Today Whitbread derives only slightly more than 50% of its profits from brewing.

William Henry Whitbread, who turned 87 in 1987, gave up day-to-day control of the company during the 1970's. The current managing director is Samuel Whitbread (a fifth generation descendant of the company's founder). Under his leadership, Whitbread has continued to add new product lines, mainly in the areas of soft drinks, wines, spirits, and food. Whitbread has even negotiated British brewing rights for severl imported beers. But as long as demand for beer remains in a downward trend, Whitbread may be able to compensate for earnings losses in brewing with profits derived from its other operations.

Principal Subsidiaries: Long John International Ltd.; Stowells of Chelsea Ltd.; Whitbread North America Inc. (USA); Langenbach GmbH (West Germany); Kaltenberg Bauerei GmbH (West Germany); Highland Distillers Corp. of California; Whitbread International Trading Ltd.; Calvet S.A. (France).

CHEMICALS

AIR PRODUCTS AND CHEMICALS, INC.
AMERICAN CYANAMID
ATOCHEM S.A.
BASF A.G.
BAYER A.G.
BETZ LABORATORIES, INC.
BOC GROUP PLC
CELANESE CORPORATION
DEXTER CORPORATION
THE DOW CHEMICAL COMPANY
DSM, N.V.
E.I. DU PONT DE NEMOURS
  & COMPANY
ECOLAB, INC.
ETHYL CORPORATION
G.A.F.
GREAT LAKES CHEMICAL
  CORPORATION
HERCULES INC.
HOECHST A.G.
HÜLS A.G.
IMPERIAL CHEMICAL INDUSTRIES PLC

KOPPERS INC.
L' AIR LIQUIDE
LUBRIZOL CORPORATION
MITSUBISHI CHEMICAL
  INDUSTRIES, LTD.
MONSANTO COMPANY
MONTEDISON SpA
MORTON THIOKOL, INC.
NALCO CHEMICAL CORPORATION
NATIONAL DISTILLERS AND
  CHEMICAL CORPORATION
OLIN CORPORATION
PENNWALT CORPORATION
PERSTORP A.B.
RHÔNE-POULENC S.A.
RÖHM AND HAAS
SOLVAY & CIE S.A.
SUMITOMO CHEMICAL
  COMPANY, LTD.
UNION CARBIDE CORPORATION
VISTA CHEMICAL COMPANY
WITCO CORPORATION

AIR PRODUCTS

AIR PRODUCTS AND CHEMICALS, INC.

P.O. Box 538
Allentown, Pennsylvania 18105
U.S.A.
(215) 481-4911

Public Company
Incorporated: October 1, 1940 as Industrial Gas
Equipment Co.
Employees: 18,700
Sales: $2.040 billion
Market value: $2.632 billion
Stock Index: New York

As a teenager George Pool, founder of Air Products, sold oxygen to industrial users. By the age of 30 Pool was district manager for Compressed Industrial Gases. In 1938, when Pool began his work, the oxygen market was dominated by large companies like Linde and the Air Reduction Company which avoided price wars and did not intrude in each other's sales territory. Oxygen is inexpensive to distill and the raw material from which it is distilled, namely air, is free. When Pool founded his company, now the second largest of its kind, the chief cost of oxygen to the customer was the cost of shipping it in heavy containers. Pool's idea was to distill oxygen in the customer's plant. The cost of this plan would have been prohibitive unless a cheap oxygen generator could be designed.

Pool, the son of a boiler-maker, had only a high school education, but he set out to design the generator he needed. He hired a young engineer by the name of Frank Pavlis to work with him. The design they came up with was revolutionary because it used a compressor lubricated with liquid oxygen and graphite. The competitor's compressors were lubricated with water due to the fear that the compressed oxygen, in contact with a lubricating oil, would ignite when exposed to the smallest spark. However, when oxygen was compressed using water, several steps were required to then remove the water from the oxygen. Pool's generator could skip these steps and, as a result, it was less expensive to build, install and maintain.

By 1940 Pool and Pavlis had a functioning generator. Pool quit his job, sold his insurance policy and borrowed all the money that his wife (a school teacher) had saved. With this money he founded Air Products Inc., and opened shop in a building that had been a mortuary. A mortuary was an appropriate place to start a new business given the gloomy business climate that prevailed during the last years of the Depression. In the beginning, Pool had a great deal of difficulty selling his generators.

The situation improved for Air Products during World War II because it manufactured mobile oxygen generators for the armed services and heavy industry. When the war ended Air Products found itself without customers and was forced to aggressively pursue new accounts. Although Air Products could provide oxygen at a cost 25% lower than its competitors, it had to convince its customers of the benefits of the new system, where the customer leased the generator on a 5–10 year basis. Air Products maintained the generator and taught the customer's employees how to operate it. Many potential customers liked the idea, but were locked into long term contracts with a company that shipped oxygen to their plants.

In desperation, Pool went to Pittsburgh and used a sales technique called "door-stepping" to win a major contract with Weirton Steel. This sales technique involved staying at the customer's plant until the contract was signed. Pool said years later, "God, we just *lived* at Weirton Steel when we learned they were interested in our proposition." Indeed, Weirton was practically Air Product's only customer.

Air Products knew it was in a precarious position and said as much in the prospectus they sent out to potential investors when the company needed funds for a new plant. "The Company . . . has no background in prewar civil business . . . proposes to compete by a new method of distribution in a well-established field against experienced competitors who have much greater resources . . . expects to operate at a loss following the completion of its government contracts." The company's boldness and candor impressed investors and the necessary 300,000 dollars was raised. Soon Air Products installed generators at a number of chemical companies and built a huge generator for Weirton Steel (a generator 100 times larger than any that had been built before).

Air Products was a combative little company and part of its success was due to the "tiger pack" as Pool called the group of aggressive young salesmen-engineers that he surrounded himself with. Pool occasionally assumed the role of manager, dealing out a tongue-lashing to any of those young men who had misled a customer or lost a sale. Otherwise, he was reputed to have a good sense of humor and to take care of his employees.

In the mid-1950's Air Products gained an opportunity from the launching of the first Sputnik, which American scientists surmised was powered by liquid hydrogen. The U.S. also wanted liquid hydrogen, and Air Products was asked to supply it. As a security precaution the new Air Products Company plants were provided with code names like "Baby-Bear" and "Project Rover." One large plant was disguised as the "Apix Fertilizer Company."

Air Products was now making liquid hydrogen and also branching out into new areas of chemistry like fluorine chemistry and cryogenics (the science of ultra-low temperatures). The oxygen business continued to grow. The company no longer leased generators, but built multimillion dollar operations near major customers like Ford and U.S. Steel, and sold any excess capacity to smaller customers.

Throughout the 1960's the company was very successful. In the course of the decade sales rose 400% and earnings rose 500%. The expansion into merchant gas (gas sold in tanks) was profitable for the company, although Air Products was a latecomer to the field. Air Products used its Johnny-come-lately status to its advantage by conceding the saturated markets to its well-established rivals, Linde and Air Reduction Co., and sought out smaller, more receptive markets instead. During the time that Air Products saw its fortunes rising, competitors like Linde saw its profits decreasing.

In the 1960's oxygen-fired furnaces became more popular for steel-making than older, hearth-style furnaces, and this increased oxygen consumption. Nitrogen, another Air Products specialty, was in demand as a refrigerant. Air Products not only sold gas, but also the implements to handle it: welding tools, anesthesia equipment and cryogenic systems were numbered among its wares. Gases and gas-related equipment accounted for approximately ¾ of Air Product's profits during the 1960's. The remainder came from chemicals and engineering services.

The diversification of Air Products into chemicals began in 1962 with the company's purchase of Houdry Chemicals and later Air Company, a specialty chemical company. Air Products had better luck with Air Company than the previous owners. When the plant was purchased it was losing money, but the management at Air Products took Air Company's acetylic chemicals and made them into specialty chemicals which fetched a higher price. The plant became profitable right away. In 1969 Air Products purchased Escambia Chemicals (for cash) at a price well below its market value. Escambia's attraction lay in a product called DABCO, supposedly the best catalyst for making urethane foam.

Due to the energy crisis and a recession, the 1970's was a difficult period of time for many chemical companies. Air Products could not sustain the phenomenal growth it experienced in the 1960's, but each year its sales and profits increased at least 9% in bad years and over 20% in good ones. The company held a strong position in industrial gases both in the U.S. and abroad, and its gases were used by virtually every major industry. Its chemical division performed erratically, and during the recession its engineering services division (which designs pipelines and plants) yielded disappointing results, but industrial gases kept the company afloat.

The energy crisis had a strong influence on the company in both positive and negative ways. The industrial gases division, which consumed a large amount of electricity, was sensitive to rising utility rates. However, as the price of organic fuels rose oxygen became a more attractive fuel to burn. The increased production costs of petro-chemicals and plastics were offset by higher demand for cryogenic equipment and gases to liquify natural gas. Air Products, like many other successful chemical companies, found a bright side to high energy prices.

The oil embargo convinced the management at Air Products to invest in synthetic fuels. In 1980 Air Products, Wheelbraton Fry Inc., the State of Kentucky and the U.S.

Department of Energy formed a joint venture to produce a high energy, low pollution fuel from coal. Air Products invested $45 million in the project; however, the bulk of the money, $748 million, came from the Federal Government. None of the various synfuel projects were successful, so Air Products' only consolation was the high levels of oxygen consumed in the unsuccessful venture. Yet Air Products remains interested in energy development. In 1985 it bought a methane recovery plant and accelerated development of a plant that converts garbage to steam and electricity.

Despite the disappointment of the synfuel project, Air Products sales grew an average of 20% per year throughout the 1970's. A 12-year $281 million contract to supply liquid hydrogen for the space shuttle helped, and so did the discovery of expanded uses for industrial gases. For instance, the food industry increased its use of hydrogen for hydrogenating vegetable oils and flash-freezing, a process which requires nitrogen, became an increasingly more popular technique.

In the 1970's and the early 1980's as well, Air Products shared certain qualities with other highly successful chemical companies of the same size. One was finding a way to turn the energy crisis to its advantage, even if escalating petroleum costs posed some minor problems. The second was having a product that was used by a myriad number of industries so that the company was not in a situation where the fortunes of its staple products were linked to the fortunes of a cyclical industry. For example, the American steel industry is a major customer for Air Products oxygen, but there are so many other customers for its industrial gas that the depressed market for steel is not fatal to the company. In its annual reports Air Products rarely mentions the obvious advantages it has over other chemical companies with a less diverse product mix. Instead, it attributes its success to its employees, in particular, to those with technical training.

Although statements about the importance of "people-power" are obligatory in its annual reports, nevertheless, Air Products emphasis on employees at times is more than a mere recitation of platitudes. One indication of this is the company's recruitment policy. Rather than leaving recruitment to professionals the company President, Edward Donley, the vice-presidents, and the 57 line managers all spend some time interviewing graduating engineers, chemists and M.B.A.'s. Donley has said that he likes to visit college campuses in order to find the best possible job candidates. The high level company executives, he says, are better judges of an applicant's potential than a professional recruiter. The applicants who are eventually hired by Air Products may spend up to three years working in different departments of their choice in order to decide where their skills will be best employed. Air Products believes the exposure of engineers and chemists to management positions will be helpful later on in their careers.

The company's attitude towards the health of lower echelon workers compares favorably with most other chemical companies. In the 1970's, when three employees died from PVC induced cancer, Air Products periodically tested 492 other workers at two plants for possible exposure. Steps were taken to minimize health risks. At the same time, the company initiated a legal challenge to OSHA regulations, which it claimed were unfeasible to implement.

For the next decade or two Air Products will most likely continue its slow but steady growth. Industrial gases will remain a staple product, and should be relatively safe from most economic problems. The company plans to invest in its core industries: gases, chemicals, engineering equipment and engineering services. Amines and urethane will continue to be important chemicals. The chemical division, while profitable, has never realized Donley's goal of providing 50% of total profits. Its contribution to company profits tends to hover around 30%, but Donley has no intention of giving up. In fact, the chemical division will likely be strengthened by the acquisition of small companies. The company has no plans for diversification into unfamiliar areas. If any division causes a problem it will be the engineering services division which provides 5–10% of revenues and is not recession-proof.

Principal Subsidiaries: Air Products, Inc.; Air Products Capital Corp.; Air Products Manufacturing Corp.; American REF-FUEL Co. of Texas; Arcain Co.; Catad, Inc.; Catalytic, Inc.; GSF, Inc.; GSF Energy Inc.; Middletown Oxygen Co., Inc.; Prodain Corp.; Stearns-Catalytic Corp.; Stearns-Roger, Inc.; Stearns-Roger Manufacturers, Inc. Air Products also has subsidiaries in the following countries: Belgium, Brazil, Canada, France, The Netherlands, United Kingdom, Virgin Islands and West Germany.

AMERICAN CYANAMID

One Cyanamid Plaza
Wayne, New Jersey 07470
U.S.A.
(201) 831-2000

Public Company
Incorporated: July 22, 1907
Employees: 36,432
Sales: $3.816 billion
Market value: $4.478 billion
Stock Index: New York London Basle Amsterdam
 Frankfurt Geneva Lausanne Zurich

When William Bell became president of American Cyanamid in 1922, he is reported to have said "even a fool could see what we need is diversification." Thus began a prolonged program of diversification. Once only a manufacturer of fertilizer, American Cyanamid now makes products as different as Pine Sol cleaner and L'Air du Temps perfume.

American Cyanamid was founded in 1907 by Frank Washburn, a Cornell-educated civil engineer. Cyanamid is a compound of lime, carbide and nitrogen that is suitable for use in fertilizer. Washburn had been a consultant to a nitrate operation in Chile, and had also built three dams in the southern United States. Intent on discovering new industrial uses for hydro-electric power, he saw the perfect opportunity in a revolutionary new way of extracting nitrogen from the air through use of an electric arc. He bought the North American rights to this process, as well as the rights to a new method of binding nitrogen, carbide and lime.

For Washburn, the beauty of these new methods of producing cyanamid lay in the fact that they required large amounts of electricity. He had originally planned to build his first plant and the dam it would require in Alabama, but his hydro-electric project became "a political football," so to speak. For this reason, the first Cyanamid facility was built in Ontario, Canada, its power supplied by Niagra Falls.

The first carload of cyanamid rolled out of the plant on December 4, 1909. After seven years of producing only this carbide, nitrogen and lime mixture, Washburn traded holdings in American Cyanamid for stock in Ammo-Phos, a company owned by James Duke (of Duke University). This arrangement provided American Cyanamid with an inexpensive supply of phosphoric acid. Phosphoric acid, combined with the nitrogen in cyanamid, produces ammonium phosphate, a good plant food.

The demand for American Cyanamid's products came almost exclusively from those people engaged in producing agricultural products. In the deflation that followed World War I farmers were especially affected, and with them, American Cyanamid. The once busy Ontario plant began to operate at 14% of its former capacity. Washburn became seriously ill in 1921 and died the following year. His successor, a Quaker and lawyer named William Bell, did not have an easy job ahead of him.

When Bell became head of American Cyanamid in 1922, the company had two principal raw materials: calcium cyanamid and phosphate rock, which were combined to form products for use in agriculture. The challenge for Bell was to find uses for these materials in less cyclical industries. Fortunately for American Cyanamid, while the economic aftermath of World War I had reduced the demand for fertilizers, it had increased the demand for cyanide, which had formerly been supplied by Germany. At the time, cyanide was principally used in the extraction of gold and silver from their ores. American Cyanamid began to manufacture cyanide from cyanamid, thereby broadening its market by supplying mining companies with a necessary chemical. The company also started to produce hydrocyanic acid, an important ingredient in the vulcanization of rubber.

By the mid 1920's American Cyanamid's expansion of its line of products, along with a revival in the fertilizer industry, put the company in a position to grow even larger. In the first three or four years of Bell's leadership the company had pursued a conservative policy of vertical diversification, that is, it concentrated on finding new markets for the same basic material, cyanamid. However, during the years of the 1920's, with a general improvement in the economy, and an increase in the value of American Cyanamid's securities in particular, the company embarked on a slightly more aggressive plan of diversification. American Cyanamid, a public company, began to exchange its common stock for holdings in other companies. Some of the first companies acquired in this way were Kalbfleish (heavy chemicals,) Selden (sulfuric acid) and Calco (dyes.) In retrospect, Lederle Labs, acquired in 1930, was the company's most important acquisition.

The period between the post war deflation and the crash of the U.S. stock market in 1929 was a time of expansion for many companies. American Cyanamid, with a total of 30 subsidiaries, was one of the most diversified companies in the chemical industry. Chemical companies as a whole weathered the Depression well in comparison with other businesses. In the mid-1930's, direct sales to consumers (drugs, plastics) helped to offset the sharp decline in the industrial demand for American Cyanamid's products.

With the onset of World War II American Cyanamid's fortunes improved considerably. The war cut off trade between American companies and their European suppliers so American Cyanamid enjoyed an expanded domestic market. The bulk of their business, however, was from the government. American Cyanamid's most important contributions to the war effort came from their pharmaceutical division which supplied typhus vaccine, gangrene anti-toxin and dried blood plasma to the armed forces. A subsidiary, Davis and Geck, was a major supplier of surgical sutures.

American Cyanamid received its share of commendations for its part in the war effort; however, questions were raised about the size of the company's financial rewards. In 1942 the parent company was charged with a violation of anti-trust laws and fined $453,461.00, a large fine considering that American Cyanamid's net profit for the previous year was $5,666,901.00. Mr. Bell, writing in the company's annual report, was understandably reticent about the affair, but he did hint that Calco (a subsidiary which produced dyes) was involved, and that a member of the board of directors had been indicted.

The company had a good year in 1950 when its sales increased from $237 million to $322 million. This increase in sales was largely due to a series of breakthroughs made by Lederle Labs. In 1947 Lederle researchers had succeeded in synthesizing vitamin B. In 1948 they discovered Aureomayacin, an antibiotic that was used to treat pneumonia. By 1953 they were producing tetracycline, one of the first broad-spectrum antibiotics. An oral polio vaccine went on the market in 1954. The demand for Lederle's vaccines and antibiotics was such that new plants were built to keep up with the demand, both at home and abroad. In 1957, for instance, plants to manufacture Lederle's antibiotics were built in England, Brazil and Argentina. Growth was slow during the 1950's for many of Cyanamid's products, and overseas pharmaceutical sales were important to the company's financial stability. At times Lederle accounted for almost half of the company's profits.

During the 1950's the leadership of American Cyanamid changed four times. William Bell died in 1950 and his replacement, a Mr. Gaugler, died within the year. Kenneth Towe succeeded Gaugler, but in 1957 switched places with Mr. Allegaert, who had been chairman of the board. While the top executives were busy swtiching places, the workers were frequently on strike. There were four work stoppages in 1954 alone.

In the early 1960's American Cyanamid received increased attention from the press for its new corporate headquarters in Wayne, New Jersey. The company was, and is, decentralized. Its major divisions are scattered around New York, New Jersey and Connecticut, and it has subsidiaries in 27 countries at last count. Industry analysts have remarked, however, on the remarkable coordination that exists within the company.

The company is run by the management-finance team, which consists of the president and the four executive vice-presidents. These five managers control the capital expenditures of each department. Siverd, president during the 1960's summed up company fiscal policy at that time when he said "we can't have managers running wild with capital."

The 1960's was not a particularly good decade for American Cyanamid. The chemical industry as a whole was not performing well. In 1967 American Cyanamid suffered a major setback with its conviction for restraint of trade. Along with Pfizer and Bristol-Myers, American Cyanamid was accused of conspiring to monopolize the marketing and manufacturing of tetracycline from 1953 to 1961. The 81 treble damage suits the company had to contend with in 1967 "hung over American Cyanamid like a sword of Damocles" according to Siverd, who became president in 1969. The company finally settled for $48.5 million, which represented more than 50% of the net profit for that year.

Despite its legal difficulties and conservative fiscal policies, the decade had some bright spots. One of the company's strengths has always been the Research Coordinating Committee, which makes sure that research is shared among different divisions. In the 1960's, part of the formula for Breck hair conditioner was discovered in the textile labs, while the chemical basis for an anti-tuberculosis drug was discovered by chemists working on products for the rubber industry.

For American Cyanamid, the 1970's began with a slump in profits. Industrial sales were down, in part due to a series of prolonged strikes in the rubber and automobile industries. As petroleum companies diversified into chemicals, an overcrowded market developed which depressed chemical prices at a time when inflation was increasing operating expenses.

During the 1970's Lederle continued to carry the company. Its six cent return on the dollar was not impressive however, when other pharmaceutical companies enjoyed a return of over 15 cents. The consumer products division, which had a number of lucrative brands, began to lose a portion of its market share. The best-selling Breck Shampoo was overtaken by Johnson's Baby Shampoo and Prell; Davis and Geck had once led the market in sutures, but now it was second to Johnson and Johnson.

The company was also affected by unfavorable publicity from labor disputes and environmental abuses. In 1973 the Georgia State Water Quality Control Board forced Cyanamid to stop killing fish by dumping sulfuric acid in the Wilmington and Savannah rivers. When workers at the Bound Brook, New Jersey plant charged in 1978 that employee health was being compromised by exposure to carcinogens, they found management unsympathetic. 1,300 workers decided to strike in order to protest health hazards at the plant only to be told by plant manager Eldon Knape that, "we don't run a health spa." When the company decided that exposure to lead compounds at the Willow Island, Virginia pigments plant might cause birth defects, women of child-bearing age in the plant were ordered to quit, accept demotion or be sterilized. A large amount of adverse publicity resulted from this last incident, after five women admitted to having themselves sterilized in order to keep their jobs.

Whereas the strategy of American Cyanamid had once been to diversify, the strategy of the 1980's has been to eliminate unprofitable product lines. Current president George Sella has sold the Formica and titanium divisions because their markets were too cyclical. The fertilizer division may be sold because it is also subject to periodic downturns. Another problem with the fertilizer division is that American Cyanamid cannot extricate itself from an expensive phosphate contract, and is purchasing that commodity at a price well above what other fertilizer companies must pay.

Sella is pinning the firm's hopes on a higher research budget. The increase in research and development began in 1979 and is beginning to show results. For example, Lederle Labs has a promising new anti-cancer drug, Novantrone, on the market in Europe and its approval for the United States is imminent. Lederle Labs still accounts for a major portion, nearly 44%, of Cyanamid's earnings.

The company's future is bright enough to make it an attractive candidate for a takeover bid. To guard against this, the company is building up large cash reserves and has rewritten the company by laws to make a takeover more difficult. Should a serious attempt threaten the company, industry analysts say that the consumer products division might be sold to buy back shares in a new Cyanamid.

In the coming years American Cyanamid will be facing more foreign competition in its domestic and international chemical markets, and will have to weather yet another downturn in the fertilizer industry. Cyanamid will probably follow the industry wide trend to concentrate on consumer products, pesticides and specialty chemicals. If the company continues to invest in research and avoids the illegal activities that have proven costly in the past, this corporation will maintain its good standing in the worldwide chemical industry.

Principal Subsidiaries: Acufex Microsurgical, Inc.; Cyanamid Inter-American Corp.; Cyanamid International Corp.; Cyanamid Metals Corp.; Cyanamid International Sales Corp.; Cyanamid Overseas Corp.; Davis & Geck, Inc.; Glendale Protective Technologies, Inc.; Jacqueline Cochran, Inc.; Lederle Parenterals, Inc.; Lederle Piperacillin, Inc.; La Prairie, Inc.; Shulton, Inc.; Toiletries, Inc. The company also lists subsidiaries in the following countries: Australia, Bermuda, Brazil, Canada, Costa Rica, France, India, Italy, Japan, Korea, Mexico, The Netherlands, Netherlands Antilles, Pakistan, Peru, Philippines, Portugal, Switzerland, United Kingdom, Venezuela, and West Germany.

ATOCHEM S.A.

La Defense
10 Cedex 42
92091 Paris
France
(1)49 49 00 80 80

Wholly-owned subsidiary of Société Nationale Elf Aquitaine
Incorporated: 1983
Employees: 11,800
Sales: FFr 19.98 billion (US$ 2.646 billion)

Atochem was created in 1983 as part of a government-sponsored program to "rationalize" the French chemical industry, which during the previous decade had lost its ability to compete effectively with foreign companies in both domestic and international markets. The rationalization program created three large chemical product producers, CdF Chimie, Rhône-Poulenc and Atochem. Each company's product line was restructured to reduce competition in the domestic market so that they could better compete with foreign companies in the international market.

The merger, from which Atochem was created, combined three chemical companies, Ato Chimie, Chloé Chimie and Produits Chimiques Ugine Kuhlmann (PCUK). The largest of these companies was Ato, which was formed in 1971 as a joint subsidiary of Aquitaine and Total. Chloé was created in 1980 as a second joint subsidiary which specialized in the production of chlorine and ethylene. PCUK was an independent company specializing in chlorine and fluorine.

Aquitaine, which merged with Elf-Erap in 1976, and Total continued to operate Ato and Chloé until 1982, when the government's rationalization program was announced in May. At that time Total announced its intention to sell the 50% interest it held in both companies for $406 million. Later that year Elf Aquitaine agreed to take over ownership and responsibility for a new company formed from Ato, Chloé and PCUK.

As part of a restructuring program in 1983 Atochem sold its ethylene oxide operations at Choques to Imperial Chemical Industries of Britain in exchange for ICI's polyethylene plant at Rozenburg. Other changes were made which further narrowed the scope of Atochem's operations to three product lines. In basic chemicals, Atochem's "steam crackers" at Feyzin and Gonfreville produced raw materials for chemicals and plastics, including ethylene, propylene, benzene and styrene. In the area of plastics, Atochem manufactured a variety of technical and fluorinated polymers (finished plastics made from basic chemicals). Atochem was also a world leader in specialty chemicals such as hydrazine (a fuel), thio-chemicals (sulfer derivatives), and chlorofluorinated products.

Elf Aquitaine's chemicals director René Sautier was placed in charge of Atochem. He expressed confidence that Atochem could be made profitable by 1986, but only if the government would ease price controls. At the time chemical product prices were about 20% lower than in other European Community countries. By October several of Atochem's secondary plants were either sold, exhanged, or closed.

At the end of 1983 Atochem reported a $188 million loss. During the next year, however, the company's sales of speciality chemicals increased sharply. Stronger demand for Atochem's ethylene products kept its factories operating at nearly full capacity. By the end of 1984 sales increased by 14% to $2 billion. The company's profit, however, was only about $5 million.

In November the executive commission of the European Economic Community charged five European chemical companies with conspiracy to fix prices and supplies of chemical products between 1961 and 1980. The commission fined Atochem, Solvay, L'Air Liquide, Degussa and Laporte a total of $6.7 million.

Atochem reported a $3 million profit in 1985 on sales of $3 billion. During the year, however, the company increased its investment in itself by 20% to about $148 million. With the restructuring almost completed, Atochem's production of ethylene and vinyl chloride was reduced by 30%. In addition, Atochem's plants at Feyzin, Lavéra and Jarrie were closed. When the ICI plant at Choques closed, production was transferred to Atochem's facilities at Mont and Balan. Atochem also continued to be adversely affected by the high cost of electricity being supplied by Electricité de France, an issue which Atochem protested strongly.

BP Chimie, the French chemical subsidiary of British Petroleum, combined its polypropylene (PP) production with Atochem's. In the summer of 1986 the two companies merged their PP operations. According to Atochem's president Jacques Puéchal, "In petrochemicals, the zone of action is Western Europe." Individually the two companies lacked sufficient capacity to compete effectively in the Western European PP market. A second Atochem-BP joint venture called Appryl was established to produce resins at a lower cost.

The determination to break into foreign markets is very strong at Atochem. Jacques Puéchal told *Chemical Week,* "In 1983 there was a piercing realization that [French] companies lacked international penetration." The company has since established additional joint ventures to produce hydrogen peroxide with L'Air Liquide in Quebec and Dainippon Ink and Chemicals in Japan.

Early in 1985 Elf Aquitaine redistributed its chemical operations around two "poles." Non-organic chemical materials were assigned to Atochem, while organic materials, or biotechnology, was turned over to Elf Aquitaine's other chemical subsidiary, Sanofi.

In March of 1986 a conservative government was elected to serve the last two years of socialist President Mitterand's 7-year presidential term. The government announced that it would be drastically reducing its share of ownership in state-controlled companies, including Rhône-Poulenc and Atochem's parent company Elf Aquitaine. During this period, however, the declining value of the American dollar made French products less

competitive in international markets. For the time being, at least, Atochem's value will be depressed as long as the franc remains strong against the dollar.

Principal Subsidiaries: Atochem, Inc. (USA)

Further reading: The Origins and Early Development of the Heavy Chemical Industry in France by John Graham Smith, Oxford, Clarendon Press, 1979.

GmbH, Kassel; Kali-Transport Gesellschaft mbH, Hamburg; Kali-Union Verwaltungsgesellschaft mbH, Kassel; Kohlen-Handelsgesellschaft Auguste Victoria oHG, Marl; Montangesellschaft mbH, Cologne; SAWIKO Salzvertriebsgesellschaft mbH, Kassel; Taberg Grundstucks-Gesellschaft mbH, Hamburg; Tensid-Chemie Vertriebsgesellschaft mbH, Dueren; Twyford Pharmaceuticals GmbH, Ludwigshafen; Untertage-Speicher-Gesellschaft mbH, Nordenham; Vitamultina Pharmazeutische Praparate GmbH, Hamburg; Wintershall Beteiligungs-GmbH, Kassel; Wohnbau Salzdetfurth

GmbH, Bad Salzdetfurth; Dr. Wolman GmbH, Sinzheim; BASF-Altershilfe GmbH, Ludwigshafen; Dr. Heinrich von Brunck Gedachtnis-Stiftung fur Werksangehorige der BASF GmbH, Ludwigshafen (95%); Gewerkschaft Victor Chemische Werke; Unterstutzungskasse GmbH i.L. Castrop-Rauxel

Further Reading: Industry and Ideology: IG Farben in the Nazi Era by Peter Hayes, London, Cambridge University Press, 1987.

BASF

BASF A.G.

Carl-Bosch-Strasse 38
D-6700 Ludwigshafen-Rhine
Federal Republic of Germany
(0621) 601

Public Company
Incorporated: 1952 as Badische Anilin & Soda Fabrik
A.G.
Employees: 130,173
Sales: DM 36.193 billion (US$ 18.637 billion)
Market value: DM 14.722 (US$ 7.581 billion)
Stock Index: Munich Frankfurt Bonn Hamburg
Zurich Basle Geneva Paris Vienna Brussels
Antwerp London Amsterdam

Since its founding in 1865 Badische Analin und Soda Fabrik AG (now known as BASF) has been a major influence in the world chemical industry. As one of the three largest German chemical companies, BASF's influence from 1924 to 1947 extended far beyond dyes and nylons. When joined with Bayer and Hoechst to form the world's largest chemical cartel, one of the most powerful cartels in history, BASF was instrumental in helping to secretly re-arm Germany.

For its role during these years the chemical cartel, known as the IG Farben, was broken up by the Allies, and BASF again existed as an independent company. Despite the fact that almost half of its plant in Ludwigshafen, West Germany was reduced to rubble during World War II, BASF has been able to re-establish its presence in the chemical industry. It is now the world's fourth largest chemical company (after Du Pont, Hoechst and Bayer). Its main production facilities in Ludwigshafen extend for three and a half miles. BASF holds a significant share of the international market in mineral oil, natural gas, plastics, intermediaries for synthetic fibers, nitrogen compounds, and its original product, dyes.

BASF was founded in 1861 by Frederick Englehorn, a jeweler, along the banks of the Rhine River at Mannheim. Using the discoveries of the English scientist William Perkins, BASF became one of the first companies to manufacture dyes from coal tar. Its specialty was the bright bluish purple known as indigo. The attraction of BASF's process lay in the fact that it took coal tar, a messy byproduct of gas distillation, and transformed it into something that replaced a more expensive and unreliable organic substance.

BASF's synthetic dyes were less expensive, brighter, and easier to use than organic dyes. Profits from these dyes were used to finance BASF's diversification into inorganic chemicals later in the century as well as new production facilities across the river in Ludwigshafen.

By the early twentieth century journalists were calling BASF "The World's Greatest Chemical Works." In 1910 the company employed over 8,000 people and by 1926 this number had grown to 42,000. Its production facilities in Ludwigshafen alone covered 2,787 acres. American journalists were impressed by BASF's charity and reported that, "The company has given a great deal of attention to welfare work; especially to housing, hygiene and the care of the sick."

BASF's sanatoriums and dispenseries, along with its main production facilities, were financed in part by business arrangements that would be illegal today in either Germany or the U.S. Beginning around 1900 leaders of the German chemical industry began to dream of what was, in effect, the merger of most German chemical companies. Should this cartel be formed, said Carl Duisberg, the man who eventually set up the IG Farben, ". . . the now existing domination of the German chemical industry, especially the dye industry, over the rest of the world would then, in my opinion, be assured."

By 1904 two major cartels had been formed. The first of these cartels included Bayer and BASF, the second cartel was anchored by Hoechst. Not only did these firms avoid competition and fix prices, but they also set up a quota system and even shared their profits. For instance, a marketing agreement was reached for the sale of indigo which was one of the most profitable dyes.

Both cartels played an important role during World War I. Not only was dye necessary for garments, but the basic chemical formulas for dyes could be altered slightly to make mustard gas and munitions. Companies like BASF provided gas and explosives for German troops and, previous to America's entry into the war, they initiated economic activities that stunted the growth of the chemical companies important to the American war effort. For instance, BASF had sold aniline at below market prices to U.S. firms in order to discourage aniline production by U.S. companies. As part of the dye cartel it had also engaged in a practice called "full-line forcing." If a dealer wanted to purchase item A for example, available only from BASF, the dealer was forced to purchase the whole product line, effectively eliminating U.S. producers.

After the war the German government recognized the importance of the chemical industry, especially the dye industry. Not only did the chemical industry bring in needed foreign currency, but it was critical to defense. Since the build-up of the chemical industry was so important to Germany, the cartels were granted government loans as well as a ten year tax deferment. The cartels also received a special allotment of coal, which was very scarce at the time.

In 1925 the top men in the chemical industry decided that the duplication of product lines and the maintenance of separate sales forces was wasteful. As a result, hundreds of German chemical companies formally merged with BASF. This new corporation, headquartered at Ludwigshafen, was renamed the Interessen Gemeinschaft Farben-werke, or IG Farben. Later, the executives of IG Farben feared that leftists might triumph in Germany's unstable political climate and that IG Farben itself would be nationalized. This led to the IG Farben's support for Adolph Hitler. As early as 1931 its directors made secret contributions to the Nazi Party.

During World War II the IG Farben grew very large. At its peak it had controlling interest in 379 German firms and 400 foreign companies. It has been noted that one of the historic restraints on Germany was its lack of colonies to supply necessary products, like rubber for instance. During this time the IG Farben, synthesizing many of the country's chemical needs with a native product, provided Germany with the self-sufficiency it lacked during World War I.

Near the end of the war the BASF production facilities at Ludwigshafen were bombed extensively. While factories built during the war were often camouflaged, the old BASF factories were more visible to American bombers which often flew over Ludwigshafen on the way back from other bombing raids and dropped any left-over bombs on the ammonia and nitrogen works. During the war BASF factories sustained the heaviest damage in the IG Farben with 45% of BASF buildings destroyed.

With the surrender of Germany, IG Farben's problems had only just begun. From the very beginning the Allies disagreed over the fate of the IG Farben. The British and French favored a break-up of the company into large separate companies, while many American officials advocated that the company be divided into smaller and therefore less influential firms. Negotiations over the cartel's fate lasted for several years. The French and British plan eventually prevailed.

In 1952 the IG Farben was divided into three large firms, including Bayer, Hoechst and BASF, and nine smaller firms. After this reorganization BASF was once again a small corporation located on its original Ludwigshafen site. Its share of the 30,000 IG Farben patents had been taken away; some of its trade secrets had been sold for as little as $1.00. It was isolated from its previous suppliers in Eastern Europe and, in fact, most of its basic supplies, such as coal, were insufficient. The 55% of its buildings that hadn't been destroyed were filled with outdated equipment.

West Germany, lacking money to import chemicals from abroad, was in dire need for chemicals produced at home. By 1957, BASF's sales of nitrogen and ammonia products were approaching their wartime levels. BASF initially lagged behind both Bayer and Hoechst in profits, in part because its product line included such items as fertilizers, plastics and synthetics which were easily challenged on the market by competitors. Between 1957 and 1962 sales grew 59%, less then either Bayer or Hoechst. As prices for plastics and fertilizers stabilized in 1963, however, sales for the company increased 19% in one year.

BASF's growth during the post-war period was impressive. In the 10 years after the dissolution of the IG Farben, the company increased its capital from DM 81 million to DM 200 million. Employing only 800 workers in the late 1940's, it employed 45,000 by 1963. Although BASF had lost all of its patents in 1952, within 10 years it had recovered a large number of them.

BASF began its second decade of independence from the IG Farben with a switch to oil as a base for most of its old, coal-based formulas. With the purchase of Rheinisch Oelfinwerke, BASF added petroleum to the long list of raw materials it was able to provide for itself. The company soon became the world's largest producer of plastic, and provided an astonishing 10% of the international requirement for synthetic fibers.

Despite these gains, BASF was still faced with problems. It was the possessor of the old IG soda and nitrogen works, but these products were often in oversupply. BASF competed with other European producers who were not burdened with this product and who were situated in more petroleum-rich countries. Nevertheless, the company reached the DM 1 billion in sales during 1965. Chairman Bernard Timm attributed the company's performance in 1965 to a judicious mix of plastics, farm chemicals, raw materials for coatings, dyes, and raw materials for fibers.

1968 was another significant year for BASF. BASF purchased Wintersall, which had half of the German potash market and produced a quarter of the country's natural gas. This acquisition was the largest in German history, and with it BASF jumped over Bayer to become the nation's second largest chemical company. A large new plastics plant at Antwerp made PVC, polyethylene, and caprolatum (a nylon intermediary) at an accelerated rate.

After the impressive growth of BASF during the 1960's, the 1970's started slowly. After much encouragement by the state of South Carolina in the U.S. to build a $200 million dye and plastics plant in an impoverished area near Hilton Head, the company's plans were thwarted by an unlikely coalition of outside agitators, local residents, and Southern gentry who feared damage to the beautiful Carolina coastline. In 1971 large investments in fibers and plastics were lost due to overcapacity. Synthetic fibers, whose prices were low in relation to the petroleum used in their manufacture, continued to plague BASF throughout the decade.

Despite the problems with fibers, however, the company continued to grow. The growth plan favored by Bernard Timm, a research chemist who had directed BASF since 1954, featured vertical integration, expansion abroad, and emphasis on consumer products. Of the three successors to the IG Farben, BASF was the one left with the least attractive product line. In order to remedy this situation, BASF marketed its line of magnetic cassette tapes (a product it claims to have invented) and then ventured into video tapes. As for vertical integration, the company had ample access to raw materials and chose to modify existing raw materials rather than diversify into unfamiliar fields.

The expansion into foreign markets is, and has been, a cornerstone of BASF's strategy for growth. There is little room to grow in Germany. In order to avoid U.S. tariffs BASF has formed numerous partnerships with American companies and has acquired others. Wyandotte was a major acquisition in 1969. The 1980's began with the purchase of Fritzsche, Dodge and Ollcott, the third largest U.S. producer of flavors and fragrances, not to mention Cook Industrial Coatings and Allegheny Ludlums. This last acquisition puts BASF among the top 15 pigment manufacturers in the U.S. Although BASF's foreign ventures are by no means limited to the U.S. (it does business in 33 countries), its emphasis on American expansion is understandable. The U.S. consumes 1/3 of the world's chemical production. The company's holdings in the U.S. also cushion BASF against fluctuations in the value of the deutschemark and the dollar. In general, a strong dollar works to BASF's advantage, as U.S. chemical companies are eliminated from the international market.

Until recently, news coverage of BASF centered on its ventures into the U.S. market, but in 1986 labor problems received a large amount of publicity. The Oil, Chemical and Atomic Worker's union decided to strike at a wholly-owned subsidiary called BASF Corporation located in Geismar, Louisiana. Union allegations of unsafe working conditions have prompted the U.S. Congress to investigate conditions at the plant, but no conclusive evidence has yet surfaced. The union has announced a campaign of negative publicity directed against the company. The strike surprised the management at BASF which, with the exception of World War II, has generally treated workers well. Asked about the labor difficulties, a highly ranked BASF executive said, "We haven't had a strike since 1924, except a work stoppage in 1947 to protest our president being tried for war crimes."

Under the guidance of Matthias Seefelder, BASF seems well-positioned for the future. In the 1970's the company had the foresight to move away from commodity chemicals and towards specialty chemicals. Its long range goals, including a broad international market and the establishment of a base in the U.S., are achieving success. The company has also invested 4 to 5% of sales (twice the U.S. average) on research and development in order to overcome a potential weakness, namely, the original heavy investment in the unprofitable chemicals that were its legacy from the IG Farben during World War II. Since its founding in 1861, BASF has been one of the world's most important and successful chemical companies. This is unlikely to change in the foreseeable future.

Principal Subsidiaries: BASF Farben & Fasern AG, Hamburg; BASF Kraftwerk Mark GmbH, Marl; Dr. Beck & Co. AG, Hamburg; Burbach-Kaliwerke AG, Kassel (98.9%); Chemag AG, Frankfurt/Main; Chemische Fabrik Kalk GmbH, Cologne; Chemische Fabrik WIBARCO GmbH, Ibbenbueren; Chemische Werke Minden GmbH, Minden; CompaktaWerke Baustoff-GmbH, Traunreut; COMPO GmbH Produktions-ub Vertriebsgesellschaft, Muenster-Handorf; Deltaplast Kunststoff-Technik GmbH, Lemfoerde; Elastogran GmbH, Lemfoerde; Elastogran Kunststoff-Technik GmbH, Lemfoerde; Elastogran Maschinenbau GmbH, Lemfoerde; Elastogran Polyurethan-Systeme GmbH, Lemfoerde; Erdol-Raffinerie Mannheim GmbH, Mannheim; Gewerkschaft Auguste Victoria, Marl; Gewerk-

schaft Victor Chemische Werke, Castrop-Rauxel; Guano-Werke AG, Hamburg (98.5%); Kali und Salz AG, Kassel (71.7%); Knoll AG, Ludwigshafen; LUWOGE Wohnungsunternehmen GmbH, Ludwigshafen; M.R. Kunststofftechnik GmbH, Diepholz; Nordmark-Arzneimittel GmbH, Vetersen; Schiwa GmbH, Glandorf; Transpharm GmbH, Ludwigshafen; Vaerst (AG & Co.), Hamburg (87.5%); Wintershall AG, Celle/Kassel; Wintershall Mineralol GmbH, Duesseldorf; Wintershall Roholversorgungs-GmbH, Kassel; Ammonia Unie B.V., Utrecht (50%); BASF America Corporation, Parisppany, New Jersey; BASF Antwerpen N.V., Antwerp; BASF Argentina S.A., Buenos Aires; BASF Australia Ltd., Melbourne; BASF Brasileira S.A., Industrias Quimicas, Sao Paulo; BASF Canada Inc., Montreal; BASF de Mexico, S.A de C.V., Mexico, D.F.; BASF Espanola S.A., Barcelona; BASF Farben & Fasern Ges. m. b. H., Vienna; BASF Finance Europe N.V. Arnhem; BASF India Ltd., Bombay (50%); BASF Japan Ltd., Tokyo; BASF Nederland B.V., Arnhem; BASF Osterreich Ges. m. b. H., Vienna; BASF Quimica Colombiana S.A., Medellin; BASF Rohstoffhandelsgesellschaft mbH, Ludwigshafen; Elastogran Polyurethan-Elastomere GmbH, Lemfoerde; Haidkopf GmbH, Celle/Kassel; BASF Belgium S.A., Brussels; BASF Corporation, Parsippany, New Jersey; BASF Danmark Als. Copenhagen; BASF Inmont Canada Inc., Brampton, Ontario; Fishburn Printing Ink Co. Ltd., Watford; Inmont Italiana S.p.a., Milan; Inmont Ltd., Wednesfield; Inmont S.A., Clermont-de-l'Oise (99.7%); Mitsubishi Yuka Badische Co. Ltd., Yokkaichi (50%); Pigmenti Italia S.p.a., Cesano Maderno; Wintershall Nederland B.V., The Hague; BASF (Schweiz) AG, Waedenswil, Au; BASF Svenska AB. Goeteborg; BASF United Kingdom Ltd., Cheadle, Cheshire; BASF Venezolana S.A., Caracas; Compagnie Francaise BASF S.A., Levallois; Delfzee Dubai Petroleum N.V., The Hague; Glasurit-Beck Ltd., Slinfold; Glasurit do Brasil Ltda., Sao Bernardo do Campo; Glasurit S.A., Madrid (99.6%); Interknoll AG, Liestal; Knoll AG, Liestal; Knoll S.A., Rio de Janeiro; Laboratoires BIOSEDRA S.A., Malakoff; Nupharma AG, Liestal; Peintures & Encres BASF S.A., Le Bourget (95.1%); Produits et Engrais Chimiques du Rhin S.A., Ottmarsheim (50%); Rheinische Oelfinwerke GmbH, Wesseling (50%); Suma S.A., Gilen (Loiret); Yuka Badische Company Ltd., Yokkaichi (50%).

Unconsolidated Subsidiaries: Auguste Victoria-Grundstucke oHG, Marl; BADICHEM Chemiegesellschaft GmbH, Ludwigshafen; BASF Beteiligungs-GmbH, Ludwigshafen; BASF Handels-und Export-Gesellschaft mbH, Ludwigshafen; BASF Terratec GmbH, Ludwigshafen; Chemische Dungerfabrik Rendsburg GmbH, Rendsburg; Deutscher Strassen-Dienst GmbH, Kassel; Erdol-Raffinerie Franken GmbH, Eggolsheim; Fritzsche Dodge & Olcott GmbH, Hamburg; Gewerkschaft Beienrode, Koenigslutter/Kassel (89.9%); Gewerkschaft des konsolidierten Steinkohlenbergwerks; Breitenback, Ludwigshafen; Gewerkschaft Rochling, Marl; Gewerkschaft Uchte, Uchte; Gewerkschaft Ummendorf, Kassel; Glasurit GmbH, Hamburg; Herbol GmbH, Cologne; Kali und Salz Consulting GmbH, Kassel; Kali-Bank

GmbH, Kassel; Kali-Transport Gesellschaft mbH, Hamburg; Kali-Union Verwaltungsgesellschaft mbH, Kassel; Kohlen-Handelsgesellschaft Auguste Victoria oHG, Marl; Montangesellschaft mbH, Cologne; SAWIKO Salzvertriebsgesellschaft mbH, Kassel; Taberg Grundstucks-Gesellschaft mbH, Hamburg; Tensid-Chemie Vertriebsgesellschaft mbH, Dueren; Twyford Pharmaceuticals GmbH, Ludwigshafen; Untertage-Speicher-Gesellschaft mbH, Nordenham; Vitamultina Pharmazeutische Praparate GmbH, Hamburg; Wintershall Beteiligungs-GmbH, Kassel; Wohnbau Salzdetfurth

GmbH, Bad Salzdetfurth; Dr. Wolman GmbH, Sinzheim; BASF-Altershilfe GmbH, Ludwigshafen; Dr. Heinrich von Brunck Gedachtnis-Stiftung fur Werksangehorige der BASF GmbH, Ludwigshafen (95%); Gewerkschaft Victor Chemische Werke; Unterstutzungskasse GmbH i.L. Castrop-Rauxel

Further Reading: Industry and Ideology: IG Farben in the Nazi Era by Peter Hayes, London, Cambridge University Press, 1987.

BAYER A.G.

5090 Leverkusen
Bayerwerk
Federal Republic of Germany
0214-301

Public Company
Incorporated: in 1952 as Farbenfabriken Bayer A.G.
Employees: 63,954
Sales: DM 36.441 billion (US$ 18.765 billion)
Market value: DM 18.715 billion (US$ 9.637 billion)
Stock Index: Munich Bonn Hamburg Frankfurt Paris Luxembourg Vienna Zurich Basle Geneva London Brussels Antwerp

Bayer, along with BASF and Hoechst, is heir to the German chemical cartel known as the IG Farben, which the Allies disbanded in 1952. Rising above its past, Bayer has again assumed a commanding position in the world chemical industry. The company now makes polyurethane, organic and inorganic chemicals, synthetic rubber and agrichemicals, as well as its original products which include dyes and pharmaceuticals.

Bayer A.G. was founded in Elberfield, West Germany by Friedrich Bayer. Bayer's first product of note was a synthetic magenta dye. The works at Elberfield, built in 1865, were followed by additional production facilities at Leverkausen (1891) Uerdingen (1907) and Dormagen (1913). The man who presided over the expansion of Bayer, Carl Duisberg, also organized the IG Farben.

Although Bayer was a world leader in dyestuffs, its place in the history of early 20th century chemistry was secured by its contributions to pharmacology. A Bayer chemist, Felix Hoffman, discovered aspirin at the turn of the century. In 1908 the basic compound for sulfa drugs was synthesized in Bayer laboratories. The immediate application of the compound was a reddish orange dye, but it was soon discovered to be effective against pneumonia, a major health hazard in the early years of this century. Despite the lives that could have been saved if the sulfa drug had been released immediately, Bayer held on to the formula. Frustrated French chemists were forced to duplicate the drug in their own laboratories in order to introduce it to the market.

Bayer chemists regularly tested dye compounds for their effectiveness against bacteria. In 1921 they discovered a cure for African sleeping sickness, an infectious disease that had made parts of Africa uninhabitable. Aware of the

political, as well as the pharmacological implications of its compound, Bayer offered the British the formula to the drug, known as Germanin, in exchange for African colonies. Britain declined the offer. This led to the policy during World War I where Bayer deprived the Allies of drugs and anesthetics whenever possible.

In 1925 the president of Bayer, Carl Duisberg, organized a merger of the major German chemical companies into a single entity known as the Interessen Gemeinschaft Farbenwerke, or I.G. Farben. Almost from its inception the German chemical companies had been organized into a series of progressively more powerful trusts, but with the IG Farben the last vestiges of competition in the chemical industry were extinguished. Other industries, such as steel, were undergoing a similar process in Germany.

The IG Farben set quotas and pooled profits. But this large trust was more than an economic institution—it was a political organization. The chief political concern of the I.G. Farben was the possibility of a leftist uprising that would establish worker control over industry. In order to prevent such an uprising from occurring, the IG Farben financed right wing politicians and attempted to influence domestic policy in secret meetings with German leaders. Bayer also played a major role in the political influence exercised by the German chemical cartel abroad. In the years preceding America's entrance into the war Bayer's various foreign agencies gave an estimated 10 million marks to Nazi Party associations in other countries. The money was also designated for propaganda. In 1938 Bayer forced an American affiliate, Sterling Drug, to write its advertising contracts in such a way that the contracts would be immediately canceled if the publication presented Germany in an unflattering light.

Bayer, and the IG Farben in which it was an important member, profited handsomely from their support of Adolph Hitler and his foreign policy. By 1942 the IG Farben was making a yearly profit of 800 million marks more than its entire combined capitalization in 1925, the year the cartel was formalized. Not only was the IG Farben given possession of chemical companies in foreign lands (the IG Farben had control of Czechoslovakian dye works a week after the Nazi invasion), but the captured lands provided its factories in Germany with slave labor. In order to take full advantage of slave labor, IG Farben plants were built next to Maidanek and Auschwitz.

Many of the IG Farben plants contracted during the war were built in remote areas, often with camouflage. These factories did not sustain much physical damage in comparison to the many German cities which were completely destroyed. By IG Farben's account, only 15% of productive capacity was destroyed by the Allies. The worst damage was sustained by the extensive BASF works and also the factories in eastern Germany, which were destroyed by IG Farben employees so that the buildings would not fall under Russian control.

Immediately after the war many members of the Vorstand, or board of directors of the IG Farben, were arrested and indicted for war crimes. There was a large amount of written evidence incriminating the Vorstand, most of it written by the directors themselves. IG Farben executives were in the habit of keeping copious records, not only of meetings and phone calls, but also of their private thoughts on the IG Farben's dealings with the government. However, despite the quantity of written evidence and testimony from concentration camp survivors, the Vorstand was dealt with leniently by the judges at Nuremberg. Journalists covering the 1947 proceedings attributed the light sentences, none of which was longer than four years, to the fact that all the sentences in the trials were becoming less severe towards the end, and to the judges' unwillingness to lower the standards for active participation in war crimes to include businessmen.

The Potsdam Agreement referred to the necessity of dismantling the IG Farben in the interests of "peace and democracy." From 1947 until 1952, when the cartel was disbanded, IG Farben plants operated under Allied supervision. The cartel was finally broken up according to the wishes of the English and the French, who insisted that it be split into sizable chunks instead of the scores of small firms the U.S. envisioned. The division of IG Farben generally adhered to the boundries of the original companies; for instance, the works at Leverkausen and Elberfield reverted to Bayer. Bayer also received the AGFA photographic works.

In the first five years of its independence from IG Farben, Bayer concentrated on replacing outdated equipment and on supplying Germany's need for chemicals. By 1957 Bayer had developed new insecticides and fibers, as well as new raw and plastic finished materials. Bayer's resiliency in recovering from the war impressed U.S. investors who held 12% of the company's stock.

A plan of overseas expansion was implemented in the late 1950's; and by 1962 Bayer was manufacturing chemicals in eight different countries including India and Pakistan. Most of the work done was "final stage processing," that is, small amounts of active ingredients were sent from Germany and mixed with locally obtained inert ingredients that would be expensive to transport overseas. Final stage processing arrangements allowed Bayer to manufacture products, mostly farm chemicals and drugs, in Third World countries that would not have been profitable otherwise.

In addition, high tariffs in the U.S. and high labor costs in Germany provided incentives for Bayer to acquire production facilities in America. In 1954 Bayer and Monsanto formed a chemical company known as Mobay in order to manufacture engineering plastics and dyestuffs. At that time Bayer did not have sufficient funds to build a plant in the U.S., so it provided the technical expertise while Monsanto provided the financial resources. Even though Bayer had part and eventually full interest in Mobay, Mobay was never allowed to mention Bayer's name in any promotional material. The American rights to the Bayer trademark were given to Sterling Drug after World War I in retaliation for Bayer's suppression of American dye companies during the early years of this century.

Realizing that West Germany offered only limited opportunity for growth, even Bayer's domestic facilities worked on developing products with the United States chemical market in mind. The emphasis was on exporting value-added products for which Bayer held the patents, including pesticides, polyurethane, dye stuffs and engineering plastics. The 1960 discovery of the urethane compound that forms the familiar "crust" on urethane used in auto dashboards is an example of the technical innovation that allowed Bayer to penetrate the U.S. market. Before Bayer's discovery, the porous quality of urethane limited its usefulness. During this period Bayer consolidated and slowly expanded its international operations, especially in the U.S. Overall, the decade of the 1960's was a good one for Bayer as domestic production increased 350% while foreign production increased sevenfold.

In the early 1970's, Bayer began to increase its already substantial investment in the U.S. Between 1973 and 1977 its investment rose from $300 to $500 million, which went to expand production capacity and add to its product line. Bayer still manufactured dyes, drugs, plastics and synthetic rubber, and rather than adding new product lines Bayer diversified within them. Although all patents held by Bayer before 1952 had been taken away as war retribution, by the mid-1970's Bayer had expanded its product line to include 6,000 items, many of them patented by the company.

Bayer increased its capacity by both expanding existing plants and purchasing new ones. In 1974 Bayer purchased Cutter Laboratories, a manufacturer of nutritional products and ethical drugs which had financial difficulties until 1977. Later, Allied Chemical sold its organic pigments division to Bayer. In 1977 a U.S. anti-trust suit forced Bayer to buy Monsanto's share of Mobay which, with $540 milllion in sales, was an expensive transaction. The following year Bayer purchased Miles Laboratories, manufacturers of Alka-Seltzer and Flintstones vitamins.

Bayer had strong incentives to expand its U.S. operations. Due to the prevalence of strikes in Europe, U.S. retailers were wary of European suppliers who did not have large stockpiles in America should the flow of a certain product from Europe be interrupted by a strike. Lower energy and labor costs made America even that much more attractive to Bayer. U.S. holdings also cushioned the impact of the high Deutsche Mark. Since, by the mid-1970's, 65% of Bayer's sales came from outside of Germany, it was important that Bayer protect itself against currency fluctuations.

At the beginning of the 1980's Bayer's world-wide holdings expanded to the point where its corporate structure needed to be reorganized. German law mandates a two-tier structure for corporations. One tier consists of a management board similar in function to the board of directors of an American corporation. Above the management board there is a supervisory board consisting of major stockholders, labor representatives, and outside interests. This board serves a supervisory capacity as well as approves major decisions and appoints board members. In 1982 Bayer created a third tier below the management board. This board consists of upper management and corporate staff who took over the responsibilities for specific product lines which had previously been the responsibility of board members. Board members are now assigned a specific region. Bayer's matrix structure, where executives are responsible to more than one supervisor, was left intact at the lower levels of the company.

Bayer began the 1980's by increasing its already large debt. The company's response to the oil crisis, when things looked particularly bleak at home, was to increase its expenditures in the U.S. Between 1976 and 1983 Bayer doubled its indebtedness. At home and abroad Bayer found it necessary to extricate itself from the fibers business and commit itself more deeply to chemicals.

1982 was a difficult year for Bayer because AGFA, Bayer's photographic materials division, was hurt by the high price of silver and the Mobay plastic intermediaries plant was closed. However, in 1983 Bayer wisely used its improved cash flow to make large purchases of raw materials whose prices went up shortly thereafter. In addition, the performance of the U.S. dollar worked to Bayer's advantage in 1984 and helped to increase pre-tax profits 73%. "We couldn't be happier with the high dollar," Bayer's finance director remarked, "the dollar is knocking out U.S. competition in foreign markets."

Bayer's transition from one of the members of the IG Farben to one of the four largest chemical companies in the world is impressive, but not unexpected. Bayer was a member of that group of German dye companies from which modern industrial chemistry evolved. Furthermore, whatever one may think of the company's well-documented relation to the Nazi regime, Bayer remains unequaled in technical ability and financial management. Since its rebirth in 1952, the company has attempted to expand abroad, especially in the United States. Unlike the American chemical companies which are trying to adapt to changing market conditions by moving into specialty chemicals, Bayer is forging ahead with pharmaceuticals which require less capitalization. Agricultural chemicals, in which Bayer is a world leader, will also be important to the company's future.

Principal Subsidiaries: Bayer Chemiefaser Verkaufsgesellschaft mbH; Bayer Verwaltungsgesellschaft für Analgevermogen mbH; Bayer Diagnostic Electronic GmbH; Bayer Diagnostik GmnH; Bayer-Anhydrit-Verkaufsgeswellschaft mbH; Bayer-Kaufhaus GmbH; Bayropharm GmbH; Bunawerke Huls GmbH; Correcta GmbH; Drugofa GmbH; Dunning & Krausse GmbH; EC Erdolchemie GmbH; Esarom GmbH; Farbenfabriken Bayer GmbH; Faserwerke Lingen GmbH; Filofarm Arzneimettel GmbH; Fluß-und Schwerspatwerke Pforzheim GmbH; Formflex GmbH; Frucade Essenzen GmbH; GbR Deutsche BP AG, Hamburg, und Bayer AG; GbR Suddeutsche Zucker AG, Mannheim, und Bayer AG; Gerhard Peter KG; Gesellschaft für Farben-und Chemikalien-Handel mbH; GVC Gesellschaft für Venture Capital Beteiligungen mbH; GVW Garnverediungswerke GmbH; Haarman & Reimer GmbH; Hansa Beteiligungsgesilschaft mbH; KVP Pharma-und Veterinar-Produkte GmbH; LINDAUER ZAHNE DENTAL GmbH; Makroform GmbH Chemiewerkestoffe; Maschinenfabrik Hennecke GmbH; Metzeler Kautschuk GmbH; Metzeler – Lord Gimetall GmbH; Metzeler Schaum GmbH; Palatinit Su Bungsmittel GmbH; Pallas Versicherung Aktiengesellschaft; Pro Chemie Handelsgesellschaft mbH; Rhein-Chemie Rheinau GmgH; Rheinhold & Mahia GmbH; Sauerstoff-und Stickstoffrohrleitungegesellschaft mbH; Schimmel & Co. GmbH; SEKUSA-Spezialgipsfabrik GmbH; Suberit Kork GmbH; Troponwerke GmbH & Co. KG; Troponwerke GmbH; Wolff Walsrode Aktiengesellschaft; Ylopan Folien GmbH. The company also lists subsidiaries in the following countries: Angola, Argentina, Australia, Austria, Bangladesh, Barbados, Belgium, Bermuda, Bolivia, Canada, Chile, Colombia, Costa Rica, Denmark, Dominican Republic, Ecuador, El Salvador, Ethiopia, Finland, France, Greece, Guatemala, India, Indonesia, Iran, Italy, Ivory Coast, Japan, Kenya, Luxembourg, Malaysia, Mexico, Morocco, Namibia, The Netherlands, New Zealand, Nigeria, Norway, Pakistan, Peru, Philippines, Singapore, South Africa, Spain, Sweden, Switzerland, Thailand, Turkey, United Kingdom, United States, Venezuela, Zaire, and Zimbabwe.

Further reading: Industry and Ideology: IG Farben in the Nazi Era by Peter Hayes, London, Cambridge University Press, 1987.

BETZ LABORATORIES, INC.

4636 Somerton Road
Trevose, Pennsylvania 19047
U.S.A.
(215) 355-3300

Public Company
Incorporated: February 21, 1957
Employees: 2,540
Sales: $344 million
Market Value: $772 million
Stock Index: NASDAQ

The inauspicious beginnings of a father and son partnership in 1925 gave little indication of Betz Laboratories' major participation in the future development of the water treatment industry. William H. Betz and L. Drew Betz founded their modest business in Philadelphia to produce a water purification compound. Fifty years later Betz Laboratories, its international sales alone exceeding $6 million, reaped the benefits of a growing movement in favor of pollution control. With the enactment of the 1971 Clean Water Act and increased government incentives to place the burden of regulation on the industries themselves, the company's customer base grew to include the accounts of major oil refineries and steel mills. However, recent developments in these industries, reflecting problems of overcapacity in petrochemicals and a drastic reduction in domestic steel production, placed Betz' future expansion at a turning point. Although much of its traditional customer base is now significantly diminished, Betz management proved to be considerably adept at conforming to a changing market.

Betz' first product, K-Gel, a colloidal substance used in the purification of boiler water, remained on the manufacturer's list for fifty years. After just one year of sales, this product made the company approximately $30,000. Despite the difficulties of the Depression, Betz fared well in the 1930's. With sales surpassing $100,000 the company announced the addition of Collogel to its product line. This chemical compound dispersed sodium alginate in domestic water systems. Two years later a third product line, named Adjunct for its use in connection with K-Gel, entered the market. Although the company experienced two years of decreased sales, by 1936 a consulting service had been started that would eventually grow large enough to warrant a separate division.

As the company expanded into new areas, its older operations benefited from a more integrated production. A new processing plant on the coast of Maine exploited natural resources available in the ocean floor. Using algin and alginic acid extracted from ocean kelp, this plant successfully processed ingredients later used in the production of K-Gel. Although initially successful, the plant was subsequently sold when a 1945 hurricane destroyed the kelp beds. Interestingly, at this point in Betz' history, the company's services, now widely recognized as a reputable leader, were solicited in order to fulfill an unusual request. To ensure the comfort of their unprecedented visit to the White House in 1939, George VI and Elizabeth, the reigning monarchs of the United Kingdom, were given tea brewed with synthetic London water. Betz was given the honor of synthesizing and bottling this water.

In 1940, John Drew Betz, the son and grandson of the company founders, officially joined the partnership. The young executive's tenure at Betz began while still in high-school; John Drew worked as a sample-bottle washer in the summer of 1932. Eight years later the company embraced its third generation of family management, enabling this newest partner to participate in the manufacturing of Betz' first patented product. Remosil, a chemical compound of magnesium oxide used in the treatment of water containing silica, received U.S. patent approval in January of 1943.

By the end of the decade Betz entered its first foreign market through a Canadian partnership. During this period of time research was also underway to combat pitting and tuberculation in industrial cooling water systems. This research ultimately produced a line of patented products under the name Dianodic, and due to their innovative uses established Betz' position as an industry leader. One such product, a zinc-Dianodic, so effectively protected systems against corrosion that it remained a preferred product for years. In addition to these achievements sales surpassed, for the first time, the $2 million mark.

Water treatment chemicals were not the sole representatives of Betz' product line. In entering the paper processing industry the company developed biocides and other products useful to the manufacture of paper. In 1957 the original partnership established over 30 years earlier was transformed into a corporation and renamed Betz Laboratories, Inc. Two years later, while serving as chairman of the board, William H. Betz died. L. Drew Betz then stepped up to the position of chairman and John Drew assumed the title of president. The company issued its first common stock in 1965 signaling the transition from private to public ownership.

After observing the inauguration of Betz de Mexico, L. Drew Betz retired as chairman of the board of directors on the same day he turned 71. However, his list of achievements continued to grow until his death in 1971. The company's board of directors conferred upon him the position of chairman emeritus and several years later the Drexel Institute of Technology awarded him an honorary doctorate in engineering. Following L. Drew's retirement John Drew assumed the title of chairman and a young executive by the name of John J. Maguire, who was not a family member, was promoted to executive vice president. Only two years later Maguire assumed the position of company president, signifying the end of the founding family's traditional tenure in this position.

Under the new president's leadership, industry observers watched the company consolidate its newly initiated European operations (including a joint venture with the British B.T.I. Chemicals Limited and a marketing office established in Belgium) into Betz International. This wholly-owned subsidiary held the responsibility of guiding Betz' entrance into the international market. By 1972 Betz International successfully established operations in Central and South America, the Caribbean, Africa, the Middle East and parts of Asia. In addition, an office was established in Austria for the purpose of penetrating communist bloc countries in Eastern Europe, and an office was established in Taiwan to arrange for Betz products to enter the market of the Republic of China.

The company's consulting business, operating under an independent division, similarly experienced a period of expansion during the later 1960's and early 1970's. First acquiring Albright & Friel, a consulting firm with over 75 years of experience, and then purchasing Fridy-Gauker & Fridy, a planning and architectural company, Betz' consulting services grew to achieve industry prominence. So important did this aspect of Betz' operations become that it was consolidated in 1971 into Betz Environmental Engineers, and later cited as a catalyst in the company's ability to secure customers. While Betz' product line consisted in commonplace bulk chemicals, its marketing of the uses and benefits of these products tallied the figures of the company's success.

By 1975 consolidated sales surpassed $100 million as compounded annual earnings growth reached 20%. The company's success was due not only to increased foreign operations and expanding services but also to a highly favorable economic and political climate. The enactment of the 1971 Clean Air Act, as well as the summit accord reached between President Nixon and Premier Brezhnev to cooperate on environmental protection issues, created an constructive environment for the pollution control industry. With estimates high for domestic expenditures needed to protect national resources, the government searched for ways to defray costs. These attempts included tax relief incentives for industry to regulate itself, tax-exempt pollution control bonds, and federal legislation. In addition, the high price of oil served to bolster Betz' profit margins. Scale deposits on boilers increased fuel bills; Betz' products removed scale deposits and therefore decrease the cost for maintenance.

While Betz continued to control an impressive 18% market share during 1984, fluctuations in the economy reflected a changing market configuration. The company, on the whole, operates independently from the drastic effects of economic cycles; no matter how much industry suffers through a recession, few companies would forgo the cost of basic maintenance. Yet fundamental changes in the economy demanded a realignment of Betz' customer base. 75% of the U.S. market for water treatment chemicals can be attributed to under 12 companies. The reason for this market dominance was due to the fact that these customers represented four heavy industries, including oil refineries, petrochemical plants, and steel and paper mills. Yet production overcapacity in both the petrochemical and paper industries as well as the virtual disappearance of many domestic steel companies and oil refineries found Betz searching for new customers.

Much of John F. McCaughan's tenure as Betz' current chief executive officer focused on this issue of securing new markets. Despite the difficulties surrounding Betz' four major industry customers, McCaughan pointed to the company's success in consolidating business in the "middle" market, such as the auto and textile industries. Similarly, Betz executives emphasized the fact of dropping levels of water tables as an incentive for future growth. Since water represents a finite resource, some industries find themselves searching for alternative coolants, including the use of treated sewage water. Furthermore, an innovative new product called Dianodic II, an organic water treatment compound, entered the marketplace in a company effort to conform with the Environmental Protection Agency's policy on discontinuing the use of allegedly toxic chemicals contained in some water treatment compounds.

So successful was McCaughan's careful management of this period of market transition that he was honored by *The Wall Street Transcript* in 1986 with the bronze award for best Chief Executive in Specialty Chemicals. Citing his "conservative, carefully calculated course," the award commended McCaughan for the company's market strategy in a time of heavy industry consolidation, avoiding long-term debt, and capitalizing on growing demands for customized water treatment systems.

While the award recognized Betz' successful market transition, industry observers suggest the company's customer base will continue to change. The future market, according to one analyst, will be in the municipal as opposed to the business sector. While this represents a market susceptible to political vagaries, it nonetheless provides the potential for future growth.

Principal Subsidiaries: Betz International, Inc; Betz Entec, Inc.; Betz Process Chemicals, Inc.; Betz Europe, Inc.; Betz PaperChem, Inc.; Betz, Inc.; Betz Energy Chemicals, Inc.

BOC GROUP PLC

Chertsey Road
Windlesham, Surrey GU20 6HJ
England
(0276) 77222

Public Company
Incorporated: 1886 as Brin's Oxygen Co., Ltd.
Employees: 39,936
Sales: £1.942 billion (US$ 2.856 billion)
Market Value: £1.374 billion (US$ 2.020 billion)
Stock Index: London

Although oxygen had been used in an extremely limited capacity since the late 18th century as a respiratory agent, the development of chemically produced oxygen was hampered by costly methods, yielding only small amounts of relatively impure gases. Commercially produced oxygen was largely confined to "limelight," used to illuminate the stages of theatres and music halls, and that popular means of entertainment and enlightenment, the lantern lecture.

In 1885 two French brothers and chemists, Arthur and Leon Quentin Brin, traveled to the Inventions Exhibition in South Kensington, London, and erected a demonstration of their recently patented method of making oxygen by heating barium oxide, with a view to attracting financial support. They found it in Henry Sharp, an English stoneware manufacturer. In January of 1886 the brothers established Brin's Oxygen Company Limited.

In the spring of 1886 the fledgling company hired its first foreman, a young Scotsman by the name of Kenneth Sutherland Murray. A man of remarkable mechanical ingenuity, Murray redesigned the plant in his first year on the job. In 1888 the new plant went into operation and production increased from nearly 145.000 to 690,000 cubic feet of oxygen. One year later the plant installed an automatic gear, invented by Murray, and improved Brin's production to nearly a million cubic feet of oxygen a year.

From the beginning, however, limelight was a limited market and so the company board members searched for new ideas to develop oxygen sales. They promoted the use of oxygen in preserving milk, bleaching sugar, manufacturing saccharine, vinegar and linoleum, maturing whisky, and in the production of iron and steel. They hired a horse and carriage for the express purpose of "pushing business."

As a result, sales of oxygenated water in any form, flavored or not, increased dramatically. Moreover, the beverage found favor among temperance groups. The company published signed physicians' testimonials extolling the virtues of this new "health" drink, prescribing it as a sort of universal remedy.

The company then turned its attention to the means of gas containment and distribution. The early method of storing and distributing gas, the gas bag, was an inefficient method which resulted in a significant loss of both gas and profit, and was soon replaced by the sturdier iron cylinder. However, even with this vast improvement over the gas bag, the new method of containment was cumbersome and costly. The cylinder itself weighed and cost more than the gas it held, making the product economically impractical to distribute over a large geographical area.

Consequently, in 1887, under the guiding hand of Henry Sharp, Brin's began granting licenses to a handful of independent companies throughout Great Britain to produce oxygen under the patented Brin process. In 1890 Brin's introduced another improvement in containment, a steel cylinder, which soon became the standard of gas containment worldwide, and expanded its production to related products, such as valves and fittings.

At the same time, in a move that marked the beginning of the company's international growth, Brin's began exporting oxygen in cylinders to Australia for medical use, and developed plants in France, Germany and the United States, granting them sole rights to operate under the Brin process.

In the decade that followed, Brin's did little more than consolidate its operations and improve its market share. The company took over two of the British companies which had been granted licenses earlier to produce its product. The company also elected its second chairman, Edward Badouin Ellice-Clark. After several years into his chairmanship, Ellice-Clark expressed some regret that the industry had produced no advances in the application of industrial oxygen.

By 1900, however, a new method of producing oxygen by converting air to liquid had been devised independently in Britain, the United States and Germany. The German scientist reached a patent office first, and the patent went to Dr. Carl von Linde. Brin's almost immediately negotiated an agreement to use the Linde patents and within several years abandoned both its now dated barium oxide method of oxygen production and the company name. In 1906 Brin's Oxygen Company Limited became the British Oxygen Company Limited, or BOC.

There followed steady expansion spurred by development of new technologies using oxygen in metal cutting and welding. In 1914 Britain declared war on Germany, and business increased significantly. No previous war had equaled the output of munitions, and the essential element of oxygen was apparent in almost every aspect of munitions production. Every means of transport, including ships, tanks and trucks, involved either metal cutting or welding, usually both.

BOC continued to grow in the immediate post-World War I years through acquisitions and through development in the commercial use of products such as acetylene and the rare gases. These various gases, with their exotic sounding names of argon, krypton, helium, neon and xenon, were developed and marketed for use in such products as the neon light, fog lamps, miner's lamps, respiratory gas in obstetric analgesia, and as protection for divers against the "bends."

In 1920 BOC acquired a London company called Sparklets Ltd. A major producer of small arms munitions during World War I, Sparklets had originally formed for the purpose of manufacturing small bulbs of carbon dioxide for carbonated drinks. Ten years later, BOC merged with Allen-Liversidge Ltd., a South African company with whom BOC had collaborated throughout the 1920's in further developing the acetylene welding process. In 1925 Kenneth Sutherland Murray, the company's first foreman, was appointed chairman.

As an adjunct to its admittedly limited production of medical oxygen, and in response to a request by the National Birthday Trust Fund, BOC designed a machine for use by midwives in 1935 called the "Queen Charlotte's Gas-Air Analgesia Apparatus." Soon afterwards, BOC introduced an improved anaesthetic gas, called "Entonox," used extensively to ease pain in childbirth and which was available in ambulances for use during emergencies.

That same year, in a pioneering accomplishment, the company set up a separate medical division equipped to install oxygen which would be available "on tap" by means of an extensive circuit of copper pipes connecting hospital wards and operating theatres to a battery of cylinders usually located in the basement of a hospital. Four years later, the company developed a machine which was the forerunner of surgical anaesthetic equipment in use today. In an effort to further increase its welding interests, during 1936 BOC acquired The Quasi-Arc Company, a British company which had a refined welding electrode instrument that improved the process of arc welding.

With the onset of World War II, BOC produced gases for munitions and for medical needs. The Air Ministry enlisted the assistance of the company to produce oxygen and equipment designed to withstand high pressures for the Royal and allied Air Forces. Sparklets again began producing a variety of its unique bulbs, including bulbs used to inflate lifejackets; bulbs filled with insecticide, used to protect soldiers against malaria; bulbs used to lower landing gear in emergencies; and larger bulbs, filled with ether, enabling engines to quick-start in the below freezing Russian temperatures.

By 1950 BOC had formed subsidiary companies in over 20 countries. It was a decade that brought with it a revolution in the manufacture of steel when an increased demand for automobiles also led to increased productivity in both the steel and the gases industries. The common method of tanking liquid oxygen to various industries to be evaporated, pressurized and then fed to furnaces proved inadequate to the new demands of steel-making. The search for a new method gave rise to the production of "tonnage" oxygen.

A variation of medical oxygen on tap, tonnage oxygen is, as the name suggests, the production of oxygen by the ton. Rather than tank in the oxygen, and then have it converted, tonnage plants were built on or near the customer site to pump in the already converted oxygen by pipeline. Toward the end of the 1950's BOC was supplying tonnage oxygen to Wimpey for use in rocket motor testing and liquid oxygen for the launching sites of the Thor and Blue Streak missiles. For use in manufacturing semiconductor devices, BOC began supplying argon to Texas Instruments.

In 1957 the British Monopolies and Restrictive Practices Commission published a report stating that the company's prices for oxygen and dissolved acetylene were "unjustifiably high" and operated "against the public interest." According to the report, BOC had deliberately set out to build a monopoly. Successfully so, it would seem, as by this time the company had managed to secure 98% of the British market. The commission disclosed BOC's practice of providing plant equipment under highly restrictive conditions, and stated that BOC had concealed ownership of several of its subsidiaries while at the same time pretending to be in competition with them in a deliberate effort to drive up prices.

The report was the most scathing ever produced by the commission, according to one reporter. However, at the same time, the commission admitted there was nothing to suggest that BOC was operating under substandard levels of efficiency in any area, as might otherwise be expected in a company of similar standing and resources. The commission also noted that not one of the company's customers had actually complained about the high prices.

BOC drew criticism again in 1962 when The Board of Trade released the company from some of its obligations to the Monopolies and Restrictive Practices Commission. In response to the board's action, and immediately following a recent 6% price raise, the British division of Air Products of America noted that BOC still controlled 95% of the British market and argued that the action would restore the company to a monopoly.

New applications for liquid nitrogen prompted the company to develop new markets in refrigeration, food preservation and packaging, preserving medical tissues, and storing and transporting bull semen for artificial insemination. Along these lines, BOC set up BOC-Linde Refrigeration Ltd, with Linde AG of Germany in 1968, acquired Ace Refrigeration Ltd., and J. Muirhead Ltd., quick frozen food suppliers, in 1969, and held Batchelors Ltd., Ireland, a food processor, from 1969 to 1973.

The 1960's and 1970's were marked by an accelerated program of diversification at BOC. Under Chairman Leslie Smith, the company began planning for the 1980's, particularly with an eye to expansion in the Far East, by setting up British Oxygen (Far East) Ltd., in Tokyo. Diversification took BOC even farther afield into such areas as fatty acids, resins and additives produced for paints, inks, and adhesives. In 1970 the company began producing cutting and welding machines which incorporated sophisticated techniques using lasers and electron beams.

The company also began developmental work on underwater welding techniques, producing DriWeld, a system that made structural welds possible at depths of 600 feet. Factories, joint ventures and new holdings were established in Jamaica, Holland, South Africa, Sweden and Spain for a variety of products, including transformers, magnetizing equipment, frozen foods, stable isotopes and radioactively-labeled compounds and cryogenic systems. Furthermore, in 1971 the company installed the largest mainframe computer in Britain, linking a network of computers throughout the country. In a move characteristic of BOC, the company sold computer time to outside customers and, as a result, BOC found itself suddenly in the computer business.

In the wake of the 1973–74 oil crisis, BOC reassessed its portfolio and decided to divest itself of its more peripheral interests in order to concentrate on its primary business, especially the gases and health-care markets. This was done with the intention of expanding production in these areas, particularly in Europe, the Americas and the Far East.

Perhaps the most important and far-reaching move in the history of BOC involved the acquisition of one of America's major industrial corporations called Airco, a company whose history, in terms of products and growth, nearly mirrored that of BOC. It was an acquisition that came after 11 years of litigation in which the U.S. Federal Trade Commission instigated antitrust proceedings against BOC in order to force the company to divest itself of all Airco stock. The decision was appealed and then delayed, but in 1978 Airco became a 100% owned subsidiary of BOC. This doubled the size of the company, and consequently the British Oxygen Company changed its name to the BOC Group.

Today the BOC Group is one of the world's five largest producers of industrial gases essential to almost every manufacturing process, supplying a variety of gases to the petroleum, electronic, steel manufacturing, metal producing and fabricating, construction, ceramic, food and beverage industries. Its principal related companies reside everywhere on the globe, including Australia, India, Hong Kong, Japan, Malaysia, Singapore and Taiwan.

Although its health care division is secondary to its gas production, BOC continues to be a world leader in researching and manufacturing completely integrated anaesthesia systems, including the Modulus II Anaesthesia System, one of the most technologically sophisticated anaesthesia devices ever produced. Indeed, it is here that the bulk of the group's health care effort is concentrated, in its anaesthetic pharmaceuticals and equipment, and with critical care and patient monitoring.

The group's health care market is largely concentrated in the United States. Encouraged by the U.S. government's determination to contain hospital costs, the company is aggressively promoting home health care services. It is ironic that while the U.S. government is promoting the same policy, it is at the same time reducing reimbursement for home health care services.

In 1982 BOC acquired a U.S. company called Glasrock Home Health Care, which provides oxygen therapy and medical equipment to chronically ill and, for the most part, elderly patients at home. In 1986 Glasrock became the exclusive national distributor of the first portable defibrillator designed for home use and of the Alexis computer-controlled, omnidirectional wheelchair. An immediate and urgent need the company expects to meet in the near future is providing AIDS patients with the long-range, in-home care that hospitals are not equipped to handle.

BOC's current chairman and chief executive officer, Richard Giordano, who came to the Group along with the acquisition of Airco, noted in 1987 that the likely future markets for further development in health care services will be in wealthier countries such as the United States and Germany, followed by Sweden and Switzerland. In the United Kingdom, he stated, home health care is "in the hands of the politicians," and he complained that, "The health service is absolutely neanderthal." Japan is an additional possibility for the expansion in health care services, according to Giordano, since it is a country burdened with an aging population.

The group's third important area of business, the graphite division, which principally makes graphite electrodes for arc furnaces, has been described as a "slow leak in BOC's earnings performance." This was a business which, like Giordano, came to BOC along with the Airco acquisition. During 1980, in an act that has been described as a fit of misguided loyalty, Giordano invested in two new U.S. graphite plants; in 1985 the group experienced a loss of six million British pounds.

Under the leadership of Giordano, the BOC Group continues to streamline its portfolio through divestments and liquidations, concentrating on its two strongest businesses of gases and health care. Thirty of the companies acquired during the 1960's and 1970's diversification program have been sold, and the work force trimmed by about 20,000. Says Giordano, "We have to walk a narrow line between watching short-term profitability and making sure we don't cheat the business."

Principal subsidiaries: Anaquest Ltd; BOC Cryoplants Ltd.; BOC Health Care; BOC Investments Ltd.; BOC Ltd.; BOC-Overseas Finance Ltd.; BOC Technologies Ltd.; BOC Transhield Ltd.; GL Baker (Transport) Ltd.; Thermit Welding (GB) Ltd. (50%); The BOC Group Inc.; BOC Inc.; Edwards High Vacuum Inc.; Fraser Harlake Inc.; Glasrock Home Health Care Inc.; US Viggo, Inc. The company also list subsidiaries and affiliates in the following countries: Aruba, Australia, Bangladesh, Belgium Brazil, Brunei, Canada, Colombia, Denmark, Fiji, Finland, France, India, Indonesia, Italy, Japan, Kenya, Malawi, Malaysia, Mauritius, Namibia, The Netherlands, New Zealand, Nigeria, Norway, Pakistan, Papua New Guinea, Philippines, Puerto Rico, Singapore, Solomon Islands, South Africa, Spain, Sweden, Switzerland, Taiwan, Tanzania, Thailand, Uganda, United States, Venezeula, Western Samoa, Zambia, and Zimbabwe.

CELANESE CORPORATION

1211 Avenue of the Americas
New York, New York 10036
U.S.A.
(212) 719-8000

Wholly-owned subsidiary of Hoechst A.G.
Incorporated: January 5, 1918 as the American Cellulose and Chemical Mfg. Co., Ltd.
Employees: 33,000
Sales: $3.046 billion

The Celanese Corporation began as a small company with a simple concept and eventually became a diversified corporate giant. The fortunes and the character of Celanese changed as the business world changed. As Celanese expanded, its leadership lost its single-minded purposefulness as it struggled to direct the complex and vulnerable organization it created.

The American Cellulose and Chemical Manufacturing Company was founded in 1918 by the Swiss chemist Dr. Camille E. Dreyfus and his brother Dr. Henri Dreyfus. In 1927 the name was changed to the Celanese Corporation. Camille Dreyfus was president of the organization from 1918 to 1945, when he became chairman of the board.

The origins of this international corporation can be traced to a small shed in Basle, Switzerland. As early as 1904 the Dreyfus brothers conducted chemical experiments inside a shed in their father's garden. By 1910 they had developed cellulose acetate lacquers and plastic film. This film was used to develop a nonflammable motion picture film base that eventually replaced the volatile cellulose nitrate base. They built a plant in Basle to manufacture these products for markets in France and Germany. This plant, Cellonit-Gesellschaft Dreyfus & Cie., was the parent company of what would become the international Celanese Corporation. The brothers Dreyfus continued their experimentation and by 1913 they had produced high quality acetate fiber yarn in the laboratory. World War I temporarily postponed further acetate yarn research. During the war the brothers produced a flame-resistant acetate lacquer coat for fabric used to cover airplane wings and fuselages. In November 1914 the British Government invited Dr. Camille Dreyfus to come to England to manufacture "dope," as the acetate lacquer coat was commonly called. This was the beginning of British Cellulose and Chemical Manufacturing Company, Ltd., forerunner of British Celanese Ltd. Two years later a French and Italian

company were formed to manufacture the acetate coat in those countries. In less than six years, a small Swiss company was now a force in the international manufacturing community. In 1918, after a year of negotiations and delays, Cellulose & Chemical Manufacturing Company, Ltd. was opened in Cumberland, Maryland to produce acetate dope for the U.S. military.

After the war the brothers resumed production of acetate yarn in the England and Maryland plants. In 1921 the British plant produced the first commercial cellulose acetate yarn, dubbed "artificial silk." The initial product was imperfect but its price of $9.00 per pound fared well against silk's $20.00 per pound price, and the company was soon running at a rate close to its initial capacity. The early yarn was sold for use primarily for crocheting, trimming, and effect threads, and for popularly priced linings. The following year the British Company offered a prize of five pounds for a trademark, and the name Celanese was created and eventually adopted by all the related companies. In 1923, with about $13,000,000 of orders on its books, a textile depression rapidly blighted the rosy prospects of the new British company. All of its orders were cancelled and the yarn could not be sold.

While the plant in England was having financial problems, the textile plant in Cumberland was having trouble getting off the ground. Twice the construction work was halted by flooding from the Potomac river. The first flood, in May 1924, caused severe damage and delayed the start of production until December. On Christmas day, 1924 the Amcelle plant produced its first spool of acetate yarn. The first U.S. yarn met with resistance from consumers reluctant to try a new product and from silk manufacturers who maintained the product's inferiority to silk. At the time acetate was introduced in the U.S. practically all better dresses were made of silk; by the 1950's less than two percent were silk.

Although the "artificial silk" initially met resistance, by 1939 the business began reporting huge profits. A practical method of dying the yarn, developed by the brothers Dreyfus, Dr. René Clavel, a Swiss dye chemist, and George Holland Ellis, an English chemist, greatly improved the product's salability. By that time the company had expanded beyond its acetate yarn into the production of industrial chemicals and plastics.

Celanese's burgeoning success met with the apparent fortuity of high textile demand between World War II and the Korean War. Yet the high demand was more artificial than real. Government contracts were responsible for the high demand during World War II. Following the war, the demand for soft goods, repressed during the war, was tremendous. Then scare buying associated with the Korean War presented another artificial stimulus.

By the early 1950's Celanese, along with Avisco and Du Pont, dominated the cellulose fiber market. Yet at the same time new synthetic fibers, such as nylon, polyester, and acrylic made a dramatic entrance into the market. These fibers, which were only in the laboratory or early production stage at the end of World War II, held their shape better than acetate, were more wrinkle-resistant, and dried more quickly. To compound things, the advent of the new fibers was accompanied by a sudden style shift toward natural fibers such as cotton. As demand for acetate plunged, prices dropped and Celanese was in serious trouble.

Camille Dreyfus was contemptuous of the new fibers and was known to collect newspaper clippings of Du Pont's early troubles with nylon. Dreyfus's dogged reliance on acetate as the company's main product could have spelled disaster for Celanese. Yet under the leadership of Harold Blancke, president of Celanese from 1945 to 1969, Celanese diversified by expanding into the production of polyester, nylon, triacetate, chemicals, plastics, paint, petroleum, and forest products. Blancke realized before the new fibers damaged acetate demand that Celanese depended too heavily on acetate fiber. Blancke believed that Celanese should develop new product lines related to its existing raw materials, products, and markets. He also believed that the new products should serve human needs and thereby have a built-in growth potential. Finally, Blancke wanted products that could be marketed overseas, away from the crowded American economy.

Ironically, Blancke's decision to diversify signalled the beginning of a cycle of diversification and concentration that has plagued Celanese's attempts to remain a dominant force in the chemical industry. The chemical division of Celanese Corporation had its origin in the necessity for developing, at a low cost, a volume source of acetic acid to supplement the then existing supplies. Acetic acid was used in the making of many of the company's products, including acetate yarn. A pilot plant was put into operation at Cumberland in 1941 and a larger plant was opened in Bishop, Texas in 1945. Under Blancke's diversification program Celanese's sales rose from $264 million to over $1 billion. But by the late 1960's many of the foreign ventures went sour and Celanese began selling off many operations it had acquired during the diversification program. Adding to Celanese's troubles was a fashion change in which double-knits replaced single-knits, wiping out around 20% of the acetate market.

John W. Brooks, who ran the acquisitions program under Blancke, succeeded him in 1968, just as the selling-off process was beginning. Brooks assumed the helm in the face of sagging prices and severe criticism of Celanese's technological abilities. Critics charged that Celanese had been a laggard in synthetic fiber technology. Instead of developing a full-market line of various synthetic fibers, Celanese had throughout the 1960's remained too heavily oriented towards acetates and polyesters. This orientation left Celanese at the mercy of the vagaries of the ever-changing fashion industry. Critics argued that Celanese, instead of developing new technologies, had relied on marketing products developed by others. This, according to the critics, resulted in Celanese's lingering dependence on acetates.

To revive the faltering company's fortunes, Brooks planned diversification into building materials, health care, and hospital supplies, among other things. He also instigated a massive corporate restructuring program. In 1973 Brooks's actions seemed to meet with success. Foreign demand for Celanese's synthetic fibers, plastics, and chemicals sent prices rising. But soon thereafter the Arab oil embargo began, causing severe price increases and shortages in raw materials.

In response to the apparent vulnerability to cyclical swings in synthetic fibers, John MacComber, who succeeded Brooks as president, planned another diversification campaign in the early 1970's. Yet MacComber's diversification plan, like Blancke's, in the end failed to produce positive results. In 1976 Celanese registered the lowest return on stockholders' equity among the 13 diversified companies in Forbes's yardstick.

In another attempt to revitalize the company, MacComber employed a new management technique. He created a six-man managing group similar to the European approach, which MacComber believed would lead to "open and frank participatory management." Secondly, diversification having failed, MacComber decided to concentrate on the company's chemical business. Unfortunately, Celanese's dependence on industrial chemicals and fibers left it prone to the cyclical nature of world markets. MacComber was criticized for not diversifying to relieve Celanese's dependence on commodity chemicals and fibers and to create a cushion for losses. Commentators speculated that Celanese's unwillingness to pay high acquisition costs explained its failure to diversify.

One casualty of the failed diversification campaign was Celanese's proposed stock-swap merger with the Olin corporation. MacComber thought that the acquisition of the $1.5 billion producer of brass, water treatment chemicals, and other products would provide Celanese with needed economic balance. The deal, however, fell through.

Some analysts believed that Celanese's need for developing a "recession-proof" business should have overcome its hesitation over making expensive acquisition. Yet MacComber avoided diversification and concentrated on boosting the efficiency and productivity of existing operation. This policy led some observers in 1979 to wonder whether Celanese was priming itself as a takeover candidate.

The takeover, however, never occurred. Celanese had its three most profitable years in history between 1979 and 1981, earning a record $144 million on sales of nearly $3.8 billion in 1981. MacComber's strategies seemed to have been vindicated.

However, earnings dipped in 1982. Several factors contributed to Celanese's downturn that year. First, the Chinese government severely restricted polyester imports which eliminated a 200,000 ton per year market for Celanese. Secondly the oil glut hurt Celanese's sales of guar gum, a drilling mud thickener. Finally, just as the company's Mexican affiliate began production, the Mexican economy weakened and the peso was devalued. The company recovered, however, and by 1983 stock was trading at near-record highs.

The company also developed new lines in the 1980's, such as methanol, polybenzimadole, and high conductivity graphite fibers. The company initiated a major research program into methanol-fueled cars in the early 1980's. Proclaiming methanol "the fuel of the future," the vice-president of marketing, John Luaer, said that the chemical's potential as an auto fuel was enormous. While less efficient than unleaded gas, methanol offered significant benefits as well. Its proponents argued that methanol would improve air quality because it burned cleanly, produced low amounts of particulates and sulfur, and reduced levels of nitrous oxide and ozone formation. Moreover, because methanol can be produced from nearly any hydrocarbon, it was seen as a significant ingredient in the country's progress toward energy self-sufficiency.

In 1983 Celanese build a $20 million plant to produce polybenzimadole (PBI). PBI was invented by a former E.I. Du Pont de Nemours and Co. chemist with research backing from the Air Force. Unlike most thermal-protective fabrics, PBI did not melt, produce a stiff char, or dissipate into smoke even when directly exposed to flame.

The Air Force promoted the production of PBI because of its potential to improve the safety of fighter pilot suits. When the Air Force decided to produce the chemical outside the laboratory in the 1960's Celanese was awarded the contract over Du Pont. The company then designed the manufacturing process for PBI. After the fire that killed three Apollo astronauts in 1967, NASA incorporated PBI into the outer shell of its space suits. Celanese began full-scale production of PBI in the 1980's under the leadership of manager Bob Stultz.

While the company struggled to find its economic identity in the 1980's it was not without legal troubles as well. In 1980 the manager of a Celanese plant in South Carolina was sent to jail for four years after pleading guilty to federal charges of transporting stolen goods across state lines and racketeering. The government charged that the plant manager illegally supplied Mitsubishi with Celanese technology for specialized film used in, among other things, satellites, rockets, computers, and x-ray films. The estimated value of the technology was $6 million.

In 1985 former employees of Celanese's defunct Hilliard, Ohio plant filed a $1.1 billion lawsuit, charging the corporation, its subsidiaries, a former plant manager, and other chemical manufacturers with an intentional tort, negligence, and loss of consortium after the workers allegedly were exposed to polyvinyl chloride and vinyl chloride monomers. The plaintiffs suffered various illnesses, including lung and throat cancers, throat polyps, skin rashes, and several nerve disorders.

Despite these and other setbacks, the corportion's stock price tripled between 1984 and 1986, due to the efforts of

then Chairman John D. MacComber. He accomplished this feat through restructuring and buybacks. Unfortunately, such gains were temporary and still did not address Celanese's major problem of non-diversification. Celanese's greatest obstacle to growth and financial security has always been its dependency on a single market. That problem was resolved, at least for Celanese's executives when the company was acquired by Hoechst, a West German chemical company. Hoechst acquired the company on November 3, 1986 in a friendly takeover for $2.8 billion dollars, roughly $245.00 a share.

The takeover was a major investment for Hoechst, and was perceived by industry analysts as an effort by Hoechst to take on Bayer and BASF (two larger West German chemical companies) for their share of the U.S. chemical market. Hoechst's move was taken with skepticism by some investors. News of the acquisition caused Hoechst's stocks to decline by $4.48 per share.

Hoechst admits that the acquisition will initially depress earnings. However, the company plans to use Celanese's marketing clout and network to distribute new products and use Celanese's strong cash flow for further research and development of new products. In the short term, Hoechst's takeover of Celanese may be just what Celanese's doctor ordered. However, only time will tell if the acquisition of Celanese was the cure for what ailed Hoechst.

Principal Subsidiaries: Celanese Fibers Operations; Celanese Ltd.; Celanese Speciality Operations; Pama Manufacturing Inc.; Celanese SA; Celanese do Brasil Fibras Quimicas Ltd.; Celanese Canada Inc.; Celanese Chemical Co., Inc.; Indal Industries do Alfarroba Ltda.; Meyhall Chemical AG; Celanese Research Co.; Virginia Chemicals Inc.; Celanese International Co.; Virchem SA/NU; Virchem Canada Inc.; Celanese France SARL; Celanese Japan Ltd.; Amcel Industra e Participacoes Ltda.

Further Reading: Celanese Corporation of America: The Founders and the Early Years by Harold Blancke, New York, Necomen Society in North America, 1952.

THE DEXTER CORPORATION

One Elm Street
Windsor Locks, Connecticut 06096
U.S.A.
(203) 627-9051

Public Company
Incorporated: July 1914 as Dexter Corporation
Employees: 5,500
Sales: $650 million
Market Value: $648 million
Index: New York

The Dexter Corporation, at 220 years old, is the oldest company listed on the New York Stock Exchange. Founded in 1767, the company, owned and operated by members of the same family since its founding, originally comprised a saw and grist mill. However, the company's interests are now as diverse as specialty plastics and adhesives, high strength fiber materials, products for cell and molecular biology, and generic pharmaceuticals. Having expanded dramatically in both the domestic and international markets since the late 1950's, the company is expected to remain a driving force in the chemicals field in the years to come.

When Thomas Dexter, an educated scholar and a farmer, arrived in America in 1630, he came determined to make his fortune. By the time he died in 1677, he had amassed a significant farming estate. In the early 1700's, Seth Dexter, Thomas's great-great-grandson, settled in the area today known as Windsor Locks, Connecticut, and started a clothing business. In 1767, Seth's son, Seth II, a wealthy clothier, bought 160 acres of timberland and a saw mill, and founded the company today known as the Dexter Corporation. In 1784, with the help of his brother-in-law and business partner, Jabez Haskell, Seth II built a grist mill and annexed it to the company.

By the time Seth II's son, Charles Haskell Dexter, joined his father's business, the company included the handling of Turk Island salt, in addition to both mills. In the late 1830's in the basement of the old grist mill, C.H. Dexter began papermaking experiments, where he successfully made wrapping paper from Manila rope by employing the waste power from the mill. The discovery yielded little or no remuneration at the time, but laid a foundation for future products.

In 1847, with his brother-in-law, Edwin Douglas, a noted engineer, C.H. Dexter reorganized the business under the name C.H. Dexter & Company. When Douglas left, Dexter continued to operate the company alone. C.H. made the company self-sustaining, while simultaneously helping to increase Windsor Lock's water power and industrial versatility.

In 1867, after his son, Edwin, and his sons-in-law, B.R. Allen and Herbert R. Coffin, joined the business, C.H. again reorganized the firm. This time the name was changed to C.H. Dexter and Sons. Allen, however, quit soon after to go into the insurance business in Hartford, Connecticut. Herbert R. Coffin assumed the supervision of the paper mill, which, under his guidance, became a principal part of the company. In 1873 a fire severely devastated a large portion of the paper mill. However, by 1875 a new mill, equipped with up-to-date machinery and a solid brick structure, was built and in operation. When Edwin Dexter died in 1886, Herbert R. Coffin assumed full control of the property and the business. He improved the company's products and distribution which led to increased sales.

After Herbert Coffin's death, his two sons, Arthur and Herbert II, operated the business as a partnership. After incorporation in July of 1914, Arthur D. Coffin became President and Herbert II became Vice-President.

In 1922, Arthur Coffin hired a young M.I.T. graduate, Fay Osborn. Osborn played a principal part in the development of the porous long fiber tea bag paper which Dexter introduced in the 1930's. This same technology led to the development of the fibrous meat casing, as well as the stencil base tissue, and a general line of absorbent and filter paper still being produced and developed today.

Innovation and experimentation led Dexter to the forefront of new paper products. Dexter marketed the first packaged sheet of toilet paper, which was packaged with a wire loop so that it could be hung on a convenient hook or nail. It came in two grades of paper, but was discontinued in the early 1930's. The company also introduced the first catalogue cover paper, as well as the "electrolytic absorbent capacitor" paper, and patented a metal tarnish preventative tissue which sold extensively to the silverware manufacturers.

In 1936, when Arthur's son, Dexter, became president of the company, its only products were short fiber paper products, such as carbonizing tissue, light weight air mail writing papers, and condenser tissues for the electrical industry. The company produced long fiber paper only on a limited basis. However, under Dexter Coffin's administration the company devoted 100 per cent of its production to long fiber paper and webs for industrial uses.

By the time David L. Coffin became Dexter's president in 1958, the company had gained a reputation as being a stodgy, old New England relic which was approaching stagnation. The company produced only paper products, opposed hiring from outside the Windsor Locks area, and prohibited borrowing from lending institutions. The company lacked an organized sales force, and almost one-third of its personnel was 65 or older.

To modernize the company's approach to business, David Coffin hired young professional managers and restructured the family-controlled executive board to include outsiders. He instituted strong cost controls, and trained and organized a sales force. (Coffin had himself started out as a salesman for the company in 1948). He also established a plan for acquiring and divesting companies to achieve growth. Coffin's target was the field of specialty chemicals. In 1958 the Dexter Corporation acquired the assets of Standard Insulation Company, manufacturer of laminates, pre-impregnated products, and closure materials. Dexter sold Standard, however, when the company decided to narrow its focus to the area of specialty formulators of industrial finishes. Dexter bought Chemical Coatings Company in 1961, Lacquer Products Company in 1962, and Midland Industrial Finishes Company in 1963.

In 1967, on its 200th birthday, the Dexter Corporation offered its shares to the public. In November of that same year, the company merged with Hysol Corporation (currently a division of the company). In 1973 the company bought Puritan Chemical Company, maker of chemical specialties for the sanitation industry, for $6.9 million. Dexter purchased Howe and Brainbridge Inc. for $11.1 million in 1976, and acquired the Mogul Corporation for $50 million in 1977.

In 1981 Dexter purchased Fre Kote Inc., a plastics release agent firm, and merged it with the Hysol Division. In 1983 the company acquired Bethesda Research Labs and merged it with the GIBCO Corporation (formerly a wholly-owned subsidiary) to form Life Technologies, Inc. (now 64% owned by Dexter). LTI's major product is a DNA-based test to determine the presense of cancer in the cervix.

In 1985 the company launched a two-year restructuring program—New Directions—which was intended to stimulate productivity and ensure healthy return on investments. The company became more centralized, divested its low-margin holdings, and sought new areas of investment in materials technology and development which displayed a growth potential.

Dexter targeted seven main business areas it planned to enter: specialty thermoplastics, high performance formulated chemicals, advanced composites, specialty materials for packaging, specialty industrial services, environmental services, and bio-technology supplies and products. To build on its existing business, Dexter acquired several businesses in the areas of advance composites, with applications in both the aerospace and housing industries (the tough plastics are used as frames and moldings for windows because they do not conduct heat), as well as specialty thermoplastics targeted for the automotive industry (the light-weight durable plastics replace metal parts in cars).

In 1985 Dexter's Hysol Division, producer of epoxies, Courtaulds PLC of Britain, a pioneer in the development of carbon fibers, and several other investors joined to form Hysol Grafil Composite Components Company (HGCC), a small custom molder of high-tech aerospace and defense parts. HGCC's biggest markets are the large aerospace engine manufacturers, such as General Electric. Dexter and Courtaulds share a 50-50 investment in research, development, and marketing in the company. HGCC, one of only eight companies licensed to produce the aerospace resin patented and licensed by the National Aeronautics and Space Administration, was the first to sell this resin in liquid form.

The federal government selected Dexter to supply carbon fiber and resin to major defense contractors competing for contracts to manufacture the government's new LHX helicopter. The company currently supplies the industry with other products, such as adhesives used in McDonnell Douglas AH-64 Apache helicopters.

The purchases of Research Polymers International (RPI), a leading manufacturer of thermoplastic polyolefin compounds, in September of 1986, and Rutland Plastics, a specialty plastics firm, in December of the same year, signaled Dexter's entrance into the high-performance thermoplastics market. The company has divided its thermoplastics businesses into two divisions in order to focus on different market segments. RPI/Dexter will direct its attention to automotive plastics, while Dexter Plastics will concentrate on the medical, appliance, and electrical markets. Plastics now comprise 20% of Dexter's $650 million sales.

Rutland, a leading manufacturer of plastics screen inks primarily for use with textiles, is also one of only a few companies (the others are small ventures) to serve the automotive market with specialty plastics. Rutland, however, faces the uncertain and financially damaging cyclical nature of the industry, even with an annual growth rate of 15–20% for plastics in the automotive industry.

In October of 1986, Life Technologies Incorporated offered its stock to the public. In the following spring, Dexter entered an overseas venture with Toyota Gosei of Japan. Hysol Aerospace & Industrial Products Division, makers of thermoplastic adhesives, formulated resin systems, and mold parts and release agents, struck a deal with Toyota Gosei (an affiliate of Toyota Motor), a manufacturer of parts based on rubber and other polymers for most Japanese car makers, to license its engineering adhesives.

The dramatic expansion of the Dexter Corporation since the late 1950's has signaled the end of an old era and the start of a new one. Shedding its views of a limited, family-based company, Dexter has grown to be an important force in the chemicals industry.

Principal Subsidiaries: Alpha Chemicals & Plastics Corp.; Bob-Ex Corp.; C.H. Dexter Europe, S.A. (Belgium); C.H. Dexter Holdings, Ltd.; C.H. Dexter, U.K. Ltd. (U.K.); Contour Chemical Intl. Inc.; Contour, Inc.; Dexter DISC, Inc.; Dexter Far East Holdings Ltd. (H.K.); Dexter (Far East) Inc.; Dexter Fibers, Inc.; Dexter Hysol Ltd. (U.K.); Dexter International Corp.; Dexter Leasing Ltd. (U.K.); Dexter Materials Ltd. (Can.); Dexter Midland Company Ltd. (70%) (Japan); Dexter Midland Coatings Ltd. (U.K.); Dexter Miki, Inc. (70%) (Japan); Dexter Netherlands, B.V.; Dexter Overseas, Ltd. (U.K.); Dexter Singapore Private Ltd.; Dexter Specialty Chemicals Ltd. (Can.); Dexter Specialty Chemicals Ltd. (U.K.); Dexter Specialty Materials Ltd. (U.K.); EXORN Corp.; Frekote, Inc.; GIBCO/Europe, Ltd. (Scotland); H & R Realty Corp.; Howe & Bainbridge (Aust.) Pty. Ltd. (Australia); Howe & Bainbridge, B.V. (Neth.); Howe & Bainbridge, Inc.; Hunter Chemicals, Inc.; Hysol Canada,

Inc.; Hysol Hong Kong Ltd.; Hysol Japan, Ltd.; Life Technologies, Inc. (64%); Mercer Plastics Co., Inc.; Mercer Properties, Inc.; Mogul, B.V. (Neth.); Puritan/Churchill Chemical Co.; Société de Méchanique General S.A. (France); Société des Vernis Bouvet S.A. (97%) (France); Société Française des Non Tissés (95%) (France); Dexter GmbH (W. Germany); Mogul Corp.; Mogul Corp. (U.K.) Ltd.

THE DOW CHEMICAL COMPANY

2030 Willard H. Dow Center
Midland, Michigan 48674
U.S.A.
(517) 636-1000

Public Company
Incorporated: June 11, 1947
Employees: 53,200
Sales: $11.113 billion
Market value: $15.779 billion
Stock Index: New York Amsterdam Antwerp Basle
Lausanne Brussels Duesseldorf Frankfurt Geneva
Hamburg Hanover London Paris Toronto Tokyo
Zurich

To say that Dow is a very large chemical company is an understatement. Its annual sales are roughly equal to the Gross National Products of Kenya and Uganda combined. At last count the company offered two thousand different products. More than half of Dow's income comes from basic chemicals, but plastics, specialty chemicals, consumer products and pharmaceuticals are also important to the company.

Herbert Dow began his career around 1890, when he convinced 3 Cleveland businessmen to back his latest project which involved the extraction of bromide from brine. Dow's idea was to extract the huge underground reservoirs of brine, souvenirs of prehistoric times when Lake Michigan had been a sea. This brine was being used for salt, but Dow was determined to distill bromides and other chemicals from it. His first venture, called Canton Chemical, failed and was superceded by Dow Chemical.

Dow's use of an electric current to separate bromides from the brine was revolutionary. He was experimenting with electrolysis at a time when the electric lightbulb was still viewed with suspicion. (At the time, President Harrison refused to touch the newly installed light switches in the White House for fear of electrocution.) However, Dow constructed primitive cells from wood and tar paper, and began producing bromides, as well as bleaching agents, for another fledgling company by the name of Kodak.

In the first years of this century Dow began to sell his bromides abroad, but the Deutsche Bromkonvention, a powerful group of German bromide producers, declared an all-out price war against Dow Chemical. German and British bleachmakers (bromide is used in bleach) reduced the price of their product from $1.65 to 88 cents a pound in the United States, which was less than cost. Dow's plants depended on a price of $1.65 in order to make a profit. While other American bleachmakers closed for the duration of the price war, Dow went deeper into debt and fought for his share of the domestic and foreign markets. One of his successful tactics was to purchase the imported bromide that the Germans were selling in New York at a price below cost, and then resell it in Europe where the price of bromide was still $1.65 per pound.

After the bromide war came World War I which, among other things, ended German domination of the world chemical industry. The German naval blockade forced American industry to turn to American chemical makers for essential supplies. Dow was pressed into the manufacture of phenol, used in explosives, and magnesium. At the time these two substances had limited use outside of munitions, but they were later to play an important role in the development of Dow Chemical and chemical technology in general. Phenol would later be required for the manufacture of plastics, and magnesium, a metal that would make aviation history.

After the war Congress protected the fledgling American chemical industry by imposing tariffs, so that the country would not become dependent on foreign chemical manufacturers again. By 1920 Dow Chemical was selling four million dollars worth of bulk chemicals like chlorine, calcium chloride, salt and aspirin every year. By 1930 sales had climbed to $15 million and the company stock had split four times. Before the stock market crashed in 1929 the price per share had climbed to $500.

Dow's success drew the attention of Du Pont which wished to acquire the midwestern bromide manufacturer until Herbert Dow threatened to leave the company and take his engineers with him. Without Herbert Dow's leadership and ingenuity the company was not regarded as worth the price of purchase and Du Pont subsequently withdrew its offer.

Herbert Dow died just as the Great Depression began and was replaced by his son Willard. Willard Dow, like his father, considered research, as opposed to production or sales, the key to the company's future. Despite the state of the economy, Willard Dow approved expenditures for research into petrochemicals and plastics. The company's product line expanded to include iodine, ethylene and materials to flush out oil from the ground. A new plant was constructed that would extract bromine from sea water. There was also a rumor on Wall Street that Dow's new method could also extract gold from the seawater, which turned out to be true. However, for every $300 worth of gold, $6,000 worth of bromine could be recovered.

During World War II Dow Chemical's new research resulted in handsome rewards. Even before America's entrance into the war, Dow had started to expand in preparation for future hostilities. One of its first wartime contracts was for the British who desperately needed magnesium, some of which was produced by the company's new plant in Freeport, Texas, which derived magnesium from seawater. Dow later supplied the metal to the United States and even shared its patented process with other companies.

Before World War II the potential value of magnesium in the manufacture of airplanes had gone unnoticed, and during this time Dow Chemical was the only U.S. magnesium producer. Yet even with a monopoly on the metal, the company lost money on its production. This was typical of Dow Chemical, namely to invent a product and then patiently wait for a market. During the war Dow produced over 80% of the magnesium used by the United States, which later led to federal investigations into whether or not Dow had conspired to monopolize magnesium production in the country. The U.S. press, however, sided with Dow and eventually the charges, which had included accusations of a conspiracy with German magnesium manufacturers, were dropped.

Besides manufacturing magnesium the company also made styrene and butadiene for synthetic rubber. After the bombing of Pearl Harbor the Japanese had conquered the rubber plantations of the Far East and soon the commodity was in short supply. Due to the fact that Dow had persisted in plastics research during the Depression, it was at the forefront of manufacturing synthetic products. Besides making styrene and butadiene, it molded Saran plastic, now known as a food wrap, into pipes or had it woven into insect screens to protect soldiers fighting in the tropics.

After the war the company had to adapt to the post-war economy. One of management's concerns was that Dow Chemical had placed such a strong emphasis on research and development in the past that it sometimes ignored the fact that it was supposed to be making profits. The marketing and sales departments were reluctantly increased. Said one man employed at the time, "You got the feeling that Willard looked on sales as a necessary evil."

Despite the fact that Dow had to share trade secrets with its competitors during the war, it was the sixth largest chemical company in the country and well-positioned to take advantage of the increasing peacetime demand for chemicals. Its product line was extensive and included chemicals used in almost every conceivable industry. Bulk chemicals accounted for 50% of sales, plastics accounted for 20% of sales, while magnesium, pharmaceuticals and agricultural chemicals each accounted for 10% of sales.

Dow expanded significantly during the postwar period, going heavily into debt in order to finance its growth. The man who presided over this expansion was Willard Dow's brother-in-law, Lee Doan (Willard Dow having been killed in a plane crash). One of Doan's first tasks was to reorganize the company and make it more customer-oriented. Willard and Herbert Dow's tenures had been previously described by insiders as "capricious." The emphasis now was on long-range planning.

In the year of Willard's death, 1949, sales were $200 million, but ten years later they had nearly quadrupled. Products such as Saran Wrap began to make Dow a high profile company. Dow's growth surpassed that of its competitors, and the company was ranked fourth in the industry. The company's plants had previously been located in Texas and Michigan, but during the 1950's important production centers were built elsewhere. Foreign partnerships like Ashai Dow in Japan were formed, and the company expanded its presence in the European market.

Dow began the 1960's with a change of leadership. Ted Doan succeeded his father and, with Ben Branch and Carl Gerstacker, reorganized the company. Communication had become a problem because of Dow's vast size, so the company was broken into more manageable units which could be run like small businesses. Marketing, however, became more centralized. The management liked to think of their company as democratic, with overlapping lines of responsibility. The structure of the company was deliberately arranged so that employees would use their own initiative to invent new products and to manufacture existing products at a lower cost. The strategy worked.

Throughout the 1960's Dow's earnings increased approximately 10% each year. Among the company's hundreds of products, however, one began to receive an inordinate amount of publicity—napalm. Beginning in 1966 the company became the target of anti-Vietnam War protests. Company recruiters were overrun on college campuses by large numbers of placard-waving students. Dow defended its manufacture of the searing chemical by saying that it was not responsible for U.S. policy in Indochina and that it should not deprive American fighting men of a weapon that the Pentagon thought was necessary. Critics charged that the gruesomeness of the weapon made it imperative for the company not to cooperate with the government. Right or wrong, the public outcry against Dow demoralized a company that wanted to be associated with Handy Wrap rather than with civilian Vietnamese casualties.

At the beginning of the 1970's *Forbes* magazine predicted that Dow would have trouble growing because of its indebtedness. In 1974, however, the same *Forbes* reporter was subjected to criticism by chief executive officer Carl Gerstacker because Dow had a record year. The oil embargo was beneficial for Dow since it had its own petroleum feedstocks with which to manufacture its various specialty chemicals, while its competitors could not find the necessary petroleum. Noted Gerstacker: "Price wasn't the problem in '74; it was availability." Dow increased the price of many of its chemicals and its earnings increased, despite a strike in its hometown of Midland, Michigan. After the six month strike, Dow gave the strikers a 10% bonus and gave each pensioner two thousand dollars worth of bonds. The stockholders did not mind management's sudden display of generosity; that year they received a 30% return on equity.

The year 1975 was followed by an oversupply of petrochemicals and a business slowdown, and the company's earnings began to slide. Since the company was doing almost half of its business overseas, an unfavorable rate of exchange added to the above problems with the result that earnings also decreased.

By 1978 a change of leadership was necessary; Gerstacker's retirement from the board of directors was the end of an era. Gerstacker's management strategy was that, "you should have as much debt as you can carry." During recessions and slowdowns, borrowed money was used for research and development as well as for plant expansion. He was an administrator in the tradition of Herbert Dow, but the moves that had catapulted Dow to a position of leadership in the chemical industry seemed unwise in the business climate of the late 1970's. P.F. Oreffice, who Gerstacker had referred to as "a little old lady in tennis shoes" because of his conservative fiscal policy, became president and chief executive officer.

Soon after his promotion, Oreffice reorganized Dow as most of his predecessors had done after their appointment. These frequent reorganizations were less a testimony to the inadequacy of the previous organization than an admission that the company was outgrowing previously successful arrangements. This time management was reorganized on a geographical basis, since Dow had plants all over the world. In 1980, the year of the reorganization, sales exceeded $10 billion for the first time.

In the early 1980's a pattern of write-offs which depressed earnings began to emerge. In 1983 the write-off of two ethylene plants and a caustic soda plant caused earnings to drop 16%. Ethylene, a lead additive which prevents knocking in automobile engines, had been an important product for Dow at one time. In 1985 earnings fell 90% from the previous year as additional ethylene plants were closed.

Another factor that depressed 1985 products was the decrease in price and demand for basic chemicals. Dow still derives 50% of its income from commodity chemicals that are sold by the ton. Foreign competitors, Arab chemical companies in particular, are invading the American market in the same way that Dow once invaded the European bromide market. To make matters worse, the market for commodity chemicals is sensitive to world economic conditions. Dow's position as an American company complicates matters further. When the dollar is strong, as it was in 1984 and part of 1985, the company's exports are harder to sell and its foreign earnings, when converted to dollars, are smaller.

Recently the company has shifted to specialty chemicals and consumer products (the latter being recession-proof). In 1981 Dow purchased Merrell Drug, thus expanding its pharmaceutical division. In 1984 Dow purchased Texize, which has a strong line of detergent products, from Morton Thiokol. Research spending remains at almost 90% of cash flow (a very high figure). Extra-strong ceramics and plastics for the electronics industry are among the numerous specialty chemicals that Dow hopes will account for two-thirds of its sales in the 1990's. The company still places a premium on innovation and anticipates placing 15 to 25 new products on the market each year, adding to the 2,000 products it already makes. In addition, the expansion into pharmaceuticals, specialty chemicals and household products will require a new

approach to management. According to an analyst with Kidder and Peabody, "If you're running a monolithic chemical business, management is the same across all products. Now they're going to have hundreds of small businesses to manage."

Dow's dependence on commodity chemicals makes the chemical company potentially vulnerable to market fluctuations, but it is presently taking the necessary steps to protect itself. The company also has a new chairman of the board, Robert Lundeen, and a new ad campaign in which working for Dow is equated with "doing something for the world." Dow is eager to rid itself of the adverse publicity surrounding topics such as Vietnam and environmental abuse. As a result, it actually supported an increase in the Environmental Protection Agency's budget and a strengthening of rules regarding hazardous waste. This is quite a turnaround for a company that had argued against a ban on dioxin in the 1970's. Whatever its difficulties, however, one thing is certain—Dow will remain a highly visible presence in the world chemical industry.

Principal Subsidiaries: Admiral Equipment Co.; Boride Products, Inc.; Cayuse Pipeline, Inc.; Dofinco, Inc.; Domoclean International Inc.; Dorinco Reinsurance Co.; Dow Chemical Delaware Corp.; Dow Chemical Inter-American Ltd.; Dow Chemical International Energy Co.; Dow Chemical International Inc.; Dow Chemical International Ltd.; Dow Consumer Products, Inc.; Dow Corning Corp. (50%); Dowell Schlumberger Inc.; Dow Engineering Co.; Dow Financial Services Corp.; Dow Interstate Gas Co.; Dow Pipeline Co.; Great Western Pipeline Co., Inc.; Louisiana Gasification Technology Inc.; Merrell Dow Pharmaceuticals, Inc.; Metal Mark Inc. (50%); Midland Pipeline Corp.; The Cynasa Co. (90%). The company also lists subsidiaries in the following countries: Argentina, Australia, Belgium, Brazil, Canada, Chile, China, Colombia, Ecuador, Finland, Greece, Indonesia, Italy, Japan, Kenya, Malaysia, The Netherlands, Netherlands Antilles, New Zealand, Norway, Panama, Philippines, Saudi Arabia, Singapore, South Africa, Spain, Sweden, Switzerland, Thailand, United Kingdom, and Venezeula.

Further Reading: A History of the Dow Chemical Company by Alan Blair Poland, Ann Arbor, University Microfilms, 1980; *Dow vs California: A Turning Point in the Envirobusiness Struggle* by Christopher J. Duerksen, Washington, D.C., Conservation Foundation, 1982.

DSM, N.V.

Hef Overloon 1
6400 AB Heerlen
The Netherlands
(045) 788111

Public Company
Incorporated: 1902
Employees: 28,610
Sales: Dfl 15.885 (US$ 7.229 billion)
Market Value: Dfl 14.693 billion (US$ 6.686 billion)
Stock Index: Amsterdam

Near the turn of the century many Dutch companies had tried and failed to establish operations, or even purchase an interest in Holland's energy supply. All coal production, including that within the country and that imported, was held entirely by foreigners. Not only did this leave Holland vulnerable to political and economic changes in other countries, but there was the fear in Holland itself that the continuing exploitation of the coal mining concessions by foreigners would lead to destruction of the local agrarian communities. More experienced in trade than in production and mining, Dutch businesses repeatedly failed to form their own energy companies. For this reason, the government decided to take measures to rectify the situation.

In 1902 the government established Dutch State Mines, a government owned but competitively operated company. The company was run by a politically independent managing board of directors and given full authority to create company objectives based on economic and competitive principles rather than on any state ideology. The company staff was not comprised of civil servants, but was given separate status and pay competitive with that in private industry, enabling the company to attract talented businessmen. The Ministry of Finance was responsible for the overall expenditures of the company, but profits could be retained by the company to finance its own operations. Since 1939 the company has paid taxes on those profits, as well as dividends to the state, the sole shareholder. DSM increased its holdings to include four large mines and two coking plants operated in Dutch Limburg. Soon afterwards, the company's production of anthracite and bituminous coal grew to 12 million tons per year, about two-thirds of all Dutch output.

The company later formed its own coke and gas production business. However, when coke oven gas was no longer used exclusively for the public gas supply, DSM moved into other areas. In 1929 the company's nitrogen works, utilizing the coke oven gas, were established to produce fertilizers. Gradually, DSM began to produce other chemicals. Yet it was the post-war energy shortage that stimulated significant growth for the company through the coal and coke production facilities. After 1945 a large corporate research laboratory was established and the chemical works expanded to include the production of plastics. Up to 1960 DSM remained small internationally, occasionally adding to its production line items such as yarn and fiber feedstocks.

In the 1960's Holland's national government, like many other European governments, was forced to accept the fact that coal was an outmoded energy source, and that it was time to close the country's collieries and coking plants. The coal and coke operations had given DSM nearly two-thirds of its total sales and profits. However, with this source of its profits gone, this company had to expand its chemical works simply to survive. Therefore, from 1965 to 1979 a major investment program was carried out with two objectives—continuity of the company and profitability. In 1967 DSM became a Naamloze Vennootschap (an unquoted public limited company). The company was no longer dependent upon the Ministry of Finance, but would have to continue operations on investments from the capital markets. DSM also hoped to enter into joint ventures with other companies, which would not have been easily done if it remained under the Ministry of Finance. The state's control was reduced to the appointments of the Board of Supervisory Directors, and to the final approval of company policy.

By 1970 all coal mining operations in The Netherlands had been phased out. During this time, the gas distribution operations were transferred from DSM to N.V. Nederlandse Gasunie. The company's use of coke oven gas was replaced by natural gas and petroleum products for chemical production. In the northern part of Holland there was a supply of naphta gas, and pipelines were constructed to transport this gas inland from Antwerp and Rotterdam on the coast. More pipelines were built to exchange ethylene, an important chemical intermediate, with other companies. In co-operation with a number of Dutch companies, DSM moved into the production of industrial chemicals, plastics, and resins, while spinning off its European fertilizer businesses into a wholly owned subsidiary called Unie van Kunstmestfabrieken (UKF).

With European chemical production becoming extremely competitive during the 1960's and 1970's, particularly in West Germany, DSM concentrated not only on expanding its market share, but on what it could produce from the basic materials obtained from its own cracking installations. DSM also improved its marketing organization by acquiring controlling interests in companies that already had captive markets and by creating a worldwide sales organization. To market its own discoveries from company research laboratories, DSM established another subsidiary called Stamicarbon. Much of DSM's early expansion occurred in the United Kingdom, the United States, Mexico, Brazil, Belgium and West Germany. By 1976 DSM ranked 61st in the *Fortune* 500 list of non-U.S. firms, employed 32,000 people, and had achieved sales of nearly 10 billion guilders.

DSM presently handles the state's 40% interest in the distribution operations of the Dutch natural gas reserves through its subsidiary DSM-Aardgas B.V. Nevertheless, the national government still has direct control over the sale and pricing policy of the gas and retains final power of approval on all export contracts.

In the 1980's management at DSM considers that its major investment and expansion programs are completed, and that work must now begin on streamlining company operations. While continuing to emphasize the production of bulk chemicals, DSM has recognized that sales for these products will grow more slowly in the future, and that the company must increase the number of special and fine chemicals in its product line. With the fall in oil prices and the low dollar, profits for the past two years have been unimpressive but steady. In 1986 sales dropped by 34% in fertilizers, by 25% in chemical products, and by 32% in plastics. However, resins sales did rise by 8%. DSM's operating profits for the year were Dfl 727 million. With this decline in sales, DSM has again increased funds for its research and development division. Quite a number of

new polymer blends have been developed, as well as new production techniques. DSM hopes to build its future on these innovations.

Principal Subsidiaries: Columbia Nitrogen Corp.; Unie van Kunstmestfabrieken BV; UKF Deutschland GmbH; Chemische Industrie Rijnmond BV; Chemische Fabrik Chem-Y GmbH; Methanol Chemi Nederland VoF (50%); Nederlandsche Benzol Maatschappij (60%); Nederlandsche Verkoopkantoor voor Chemische Production BV (55%); Nipro Inc.; DSM Transportmaatschappij BV; DSM Resins BV; DSM Kunstharze GmbH; DSM Resins Ltd.; Custom Chemicals Corp.; Daniel Products Co.; VP-Vereingte Pulverlack GmbH; DSM Aardgas BV; DSM Energie BV; Ck Addison and Co., Ltd.; Curver BV; Firma Robert Travernier NV; Fardem Group BV; Belton Son BV; Calmont BV; Coban BV; Royal MOSA BV; Ontwikkelung Bouw-en Exploitatie Maatschappij BV; Teewen BV; BV Computer Centrum Nederland; DSM Assurantiekantoor BV; DSM Limburg BV; DSM North American Inc.; Macintosh NV Stein (57%); Stamicarbon BV.

E. I. DU PONT DE NEMOURS & COMPANY

1007 Market Street
Wilmington, Delaware 19898
U.S.A.
(302) 774-1000

Public Company
Incorporated: September 4, 1915
Employees: 146,017
Sales: $27.148 billion
Market value: $27.533 billion
Stock Index: New York

Du Pont is the oldest family name in American pre-industrial wealth. Its reputation is synonymous with organic chemistry. Founded in 1802, the company began as a partnership in gunpowder and explosives. Du Pont grew from a family business to the multinational conglomerate it is today through the acquisition of companies it was in competition with, and through the diversification of product lines.

Founder Éleuthère Irenée duPont de Nemours was born to French nobility. He studied with the chemist in charge of manufacturing the French government's gunpowder, Antionne LaVoisier. The years of turmoil preceding the French Revolution caused him to emigrate to the United States in 1797. To build his production facilities he chose a site on the Delaware's Brandywine River, which was central to all the states at the time and provided sufficient water power to run the mills. Du Pont rapidly established a reputation for superior gunpowder. Irenée died in 1834, leaving his sons Alfred and Henry to buy out French financiers and continue the business. His sons expanded Du Pont's product line into the manufacture of smokeless powder, dynamite and nitroglycerine.

One century after its founding, the gunpowder and explosives combine faced dissolution when senior partner Eugene duPont died at the age of 62, after having served 42 years. With no new leadership the surviving partners decided to sell the company to the highest bidder. Alfred I. duPont, a distant relative of the founder, purchased the firm with the aid of his cousins. Alfred was serious about saving the family business. Although he had grown up working in gunpowder yards, he lacked the organizational skills needed to run the firm. His cousins Pierre S. duPont and Thomas Coleman possessed the financial acumen and led the family company to unprecedented success. The purchase price was set at $12 million but secret investiga-

tions by the cousins unveiled company assets conservatively valued at $24 million. The old partnership also held a great deal of undervalued shares in other companies, among them their direct competitors in the gunpowder business, Hazard and Laflin & Rand. Not having the initial capital for the purchase, the young cousins negotiated a leveraged buy-out giving them a 25% interest in the new corporation and 4% paid on $12 million over the next 30 years. Coleman was president, Pierre treasurer and Alfred vice-president of E.Il du Pont de Nemours & Company. The only cash involved in the takeover was $8500 in incorporation fees.

Sound management, luck, and hidden wealth resulted in the acquisition of 54 companies within 3 years. Pierre set out to dominate the industry through pay-offs and by purchasing minority shareholders and vulnerable competitors. When the cousins first incorporated in 1902, the company controlled 36% of the U.S. powder market. By 1905 Du Pont held a 75% share of the market. Du Pont alone supplied 56% of the national production of explosives, with $60 million in estimated assets; it was now one of the nations largest corporations.

A new method of operation was required to keep track of the rapidly growing organization. The cousins solicited the aid of Amory Haskell and Hamilton Barksdale, managers who had reorganized their dynamite business into an efficient organization. They remodeled the unwieldy company using elaborate family tree charts composed of levels of managers. The new structure revolutionized American business and gave birth to the modern corporation. The system of organization worked so well that Pierre bailed out the then struggling General Motors Corporation, buying 23% of the shares and applying the skills Du Pont had perfected. (The Department of Justice later ordered Du Pont to divest its General Motors holdings in 1951.)

Du Pont grew to command the entire explosives market. So dominant were they by 1907 that the U.S. government initiated antitrust proceedings against them. Du Pont was deemed a gunpowder monopoly in 1912 and ordered to divest itself of a substantial portion of its business. In addition, early years of incorporation were fraught with tension between Alfred and his more practical cousins. Arguments ensued over the modernization of the Brandywine yards. Coleman and Pierre saw modernization as the only way to fully utilize the plant. The quarrel, along with other incidents, prompted Coleman and Pierre to take away Alfred's responsibilities in 1911. In effect, this left Alfred a vice president in name only.

Modernization, diversification, good management and a command of the market characterize Du Pont's industrial era phase. The experiments of Du Pont chemists with a product known as guncotton, an early form of nitroglycerine, led to the company's involvement in the textile business. The end of World War I proved the peacetime use of artificial fibers to be more profitable than explosives. In the 1920's Du Pont acquired French rights for producing cellophane. Du Pont made it moistureproof, transforming cellophane from a decorative wrap to a packaging material for food and other products. Du Pont also produced the clothing fiber Rayon in the 1920's, and used a stronger version of the fiber for auto tire cord.

Du Pont gradually moved away from explosives and into synthetics. Their most important discovery, Nylon, was created in 1930 by a polymer research group headed by Wallace H. Carothers. The synthesis of nylon came from the hypothesis that polymeric substances were practically endless chains held together by ordinary chemical bonds. Long chain molecules could be built one step at a time by carrying out well understood reactions between standard types of organic chemicals. Carothers chose one of natures simplest reactions—alcohols reacting with acids to form esters. By reacting compounds with alcohol groups on each end with analogous acids, polyesters were produced. Super polymers were later formed when a molecular still was used to extract the water that was formed in the reaction. The excess water had created a chemical equilibrium that stopped reaction and limited chain growth. Experimentation with diamine-dibasic pairs produced a molten polyamide which could be drawn into filaments, cooled and stretched to form very strong fibers. Du Pont later marketed a 6-6 polymer which was made from the inexpensive starting compound Benzene. The new fiber proved remarkably successful. It was employed as a material for undergarments, stockings, tire cord, auto parts and brushes.

A large number of plastics and fibers followed. Products such as Neoprene (synthetic rubber), Lucite (a clear, tough plastic resin), and Teflon (a resin used in non-stick cookware) became commonplace. Fibers like Orlon (a bulky acrylic fiber), Dacron polyester and Mylar became household names. Du Pont quickly became known as the world's most proficient synthesizer. The range of textiles which they supplied reoriented the whole synthetic field.

Not every Du Pont invention was a success however. Corfam, a synthetic leather product proved to be a disaster. Lammont duPont Copeland, the last duPont to head the company, invested millions of dollars into promoting Corfam in the 1960's. The product was not successful due to the fact that, although the material lasted practically forever, it lacked the flexibility and breathability usually found in leather products. Lammont relinquished the chief executive post in 1967 and was succeeded by Charles B. McCoy, son of a Du Pont executive. Irving Shapiro took the post in 1974. Shapiro had served Du Pont well, acting as the principal lawyer negotiating the anti-trust suit brought against Du Pont and General Motors Corporation.

Shapiro lead Du Pont for six years during a period when the fibers industry stagnated from overcapacity. Du Pont's stream of synthetic fiber discoveries had led it into a trap, for it left them content to exploit the fiber market without looking elsewhere for new products. The demand for fibers collapsed in the mid-1970's, causing a halt in the company's main business. Climbing raw material costs and declining demand combined to depress the market in 1979. The innovator of a new technology had been the last to recognize that the market it created was losing momentum. The collapse compelled Du Pont to concentrate exclusively on repairing its old business, delaying actions to create a new base. Du Pont's rebuilding efforts were also hindered by reducing its commitment to research and development. Continued reliance on fibers caused Du Pont to be one of the worst hit chemical companies in the 1980 recession.

Du Pont's continued attention to the fibers business, however, resulted in an important discovery in 1980. Kevlar was added to the company's assemblage of synthetic textiles. Du Pont scientist Stephanie Kwolek discovered the solvent which unclumped the hard chains of molecules comprising an intractable polymer. The resultant revolutionary material proved to be light yet strong, possessing a tensile strength five times that of steel. Fabrics made of Kevlar are heat and puncture resistant. When laminated, Kevlar outstrips fiberglass. Du Pont made the largest financial gamble in its history, investing $250 million in a Kevlar plant expansion. Applications for Kevlar range from heat resistant gloves, fire resistant clothing, and bullet resistant vests to cables and reinforcement belting in tires. Kevlar has already proven successful in the fabrics industry; one half of the police in the United States now wear Kevlar vests. Kevlar's true success, however, will depend on the price of its raw material—oil. At present Kevlar shows no threat of becoming a steel replacement, since the price of its production is considerably higher.

Du Pont reacted to the depressed market in textiles by arranging mergers and aquisitions of other companies in other industries. Du Pont's takeover of the Conoco Oil company (American's number two petroleum firm) was the largest merger in history. Issues of anti-trust were prevalant in negotiation for the merger, but in the end Du Pont bought Conoco for $7.8 billion. Du Pont merged with Conoco to protect itself from the rise in crude oil prices. As oil supplies dwindle, a supply of Conoco oil and coal as raw material for Du Pont's chemicals will provide a competitive advantage. Conoco's sites in Alberta, Canada and off the north slope of Alaska are presently providing large amounts of these resources. Du Pont's only disadvantage in the Conoco takeover was the introduction of Edgar Bronfman, chairman of Seagram's, the world's largest liquor distiller, into a minority position in Du Pont-Conoco. Conoco had been a major aquisition target of Seagrams. The merger left Seagrams with 20% of Du Pont. Bronfman sees himself as a long term investor in Du Pont and would like an important voice in the company's direction. However, Seagram's and Du Pont have arrived at an agreement whereby Seagram's cannot purchase more than 25% of Du Pont stock until 1991.

Growth and greater financial security came to Du Pont in 1980 when they bought Remington Arms, a manufacturer of sporting firearms and ammunition. The Remington Arms unit of Du Pont has made a number of multi-million dollar contracts with the army to operate government owned plants. Du Pont also expanded its scope in the early 1980's with other major purchases. New England Nuclear Corporation, a leading manufacturer of radioactive chemicals for medical research and diagnosis, was acquired in April of 1981, and Solid State Dielectrics, a supplier of dielectric materials used in the manufacture of multilayer capacitors, was acquired in April of 1982.

Du Pont management is determined to reduce the company's dependence on petrochemicals. It has decided to take some risks in becoming a leader in the life sciences by delving into development and production of biomedical products and agricultural chemicals. In April of 1982 Du Pont purchased the agrichemicals division of SEPIC. In November they acquired the production equipment and technology for the manufacture of spiral wound reverse osmosis desalting products. In March of 1986 Du Pont acquired Elit Circuits Inc., a producer of molded circuit interconnects.

In addition to mergers and acquisitions, Du Pont is heavily involved in joint ventures. Du Pont has agreements with P.D. Magnetics to develop, manufacture and sell magnetic tape. It is also involved with PPG Industries to manufacture ethylene glycol. Aided by Olin Corporation, it will construct a chlor/alkali production facility. Du Pont also has extensive connections with Japanese industry. The 1980's have thus far united them with Sankyo Company (to develop, manufacture and market pharmaceuticals), Idemitso Petrochemicals (to produce and market butanediol), Mitsubishi Gas Chemical Company and Mitsubishi Rayon Company.

Furthermore, Du Pont has established connections in Europe. They are partners with N.V. Phillips (to produce optical discs), EKA AB (to produce and market the Compozil chemical system for papermaking processes), and British Telecom (to develop and manufacture opto-electronic components).

In addition to stock chemicals and petrochemically based synthetic fibers, Du Pont presently looks to the life sciences and other specialty businesses to produce earnings. Edward G. Jefferson, a chemist by training, succeeded Shapiro and directed the company into the biosciences and other specialty lines. Du Pont is supporting these businesses with large amounts of capital investment and research and development expenditures. The fields of interest are genetic engineering, drugs and agricultural chemicals, electronics, and fibers and plastics.

Du Pont has the kind of multi-national marketing capability and the resourses to become a major influence in the life sciences. Du Pont is presently seeking ways to restructure living cells to mass produce specific micro-organisms in an attempt to produce commercial quantities of interferon, a human protein that is potentially useful in fighting viruses and cancer. Du Pont claims to be the first company to have purified fibloblast interferon, one of the three types of human interferon in the mid-1970's. Du Pont is developing a blood profile system, artificial blood, and a test for acquired immune deficiency syndrome. They have created drugs which control irregular heartbeats, aid rhematoid arthitis pain, and are anti-narcotic agents. In addition to new drugs, Du Pont is working to develop new pesticides and herbicides. Du Pont has already built a $450 million business as a major supplier to the electronics industry, provided sophisticated connectors and the dry film used in making printed circuits. Du Pont is also developing new high performance plastics. Their scientists have developed a process called group transfer polymerization for solvent based polymer acrylics. This is the first major polymerization process developed since the early 1950's.

Du Pont has approximately 90 major businesses selling a wide range of products to different industries, including petroleum, textile, transportation, chemical construction, utility, health care and agricultural industries. Business operations exist in more than 50 nations worldwide. Du Pont has eight principle business segments: biomedical products; industrial and consumer products; fibers; polymer products; agricultural and industrial chemicals; petroleum exploration and production; petroleum refining, marketing and transportation; and coal. Total expenditure for research and development amounted to over one billion dollars in 1985. Over 6000 scientist and engineers are engaged in research activities. This alone attests to the fact that Du Pont is well prepared for the future.

Principal Subsidiaries: Conoco Coal Development Co.; Conoco Inc.; Conoco Shale Oil Inc.; Consolidated Coal Co.; Continental Pipe Line Co.; Continental Overseas Oil Co.; Douglas Oil Co.; Du Pont International Sales Corp.; Fairmont Supply Co.; Kayo Oil Co.; Louisiana Gas System, Inc.; Remington Arms Co.; Inc. The company also lists subsidiaries in the following countries: Argentina, Australia, Belgium, Brazil, Canada, Colombia, Dubai, Finland, France, Guatemala, Indonesia, Italy, Japan, Liberia, Libya, Luxembourg, Mexico, The Netherlands, New Zealand, Norway, Peru, Philippines, Puerto Rico, Singapore, Spain, Sweden, Switzerland, Taiwan, Thailand, United Kingdom, and Venezuela.

Further Reading: *Pierre S. duPont and the Making of the Modern Corporation* by Alfred D. Chandler, Jr. and Stephen Salsbury, New York, Harper and Row, 1971; *Blood Relations: The Rise and Fall of the duPonts of Delaware* by Leonard Mosley, New York, Atheneum, 1980; *duPont Dynasty* by Gerard Colby, Secaucus, New Jersey, Lyle Stuart, 1984; *Du Pont and the International Chemical Industry* by Graham D. Taylor and Patricia E. Sudnik, Boston, Twayne, 1984.

ECOLAB, INC.

370 Wabasha Street
Ecolab Centre
Saint Paul, Minnesota 55102
U.S.A.
(612) 293-2233

Public Company
Incorporated: February 18, 1924
Employees: 6,800
Sales: $845 million
Market value: $813 million
Stock Index: New York

For the first 60 years of its existence Ecolab was managed by members of the Osborn family. Merrit J. Osborn, founder of the originally named Economics Laboratory, abandoned his occupation as a Michigan salesman and organized a specialty chemical manufacturer in 1924. The company's first product was a rug cleaner for hotels. While the Osborns no longer hold management positions at Ecolab, many of the company's products remain directed toward institutional markets.

In the 1950's the company's product line grew to include consumer detergents and institutional cleaning specialties for restaurants, food processors and dairies. This area of business came to represent the cornerstone of the company's success; between the years 1970 and 1980 the chemical specialties business quadrupled, generating $640 million by the end of the ten-year period. Yet early in its history the company actively pursued customers outside of the consumer and institutional markets.

By purchasing the Magnus company in the early 1950's, Economics Laboratory gained access to the industrial specialty market. Magnus' primary business, the selling of cleaning and specialty formulas to numerous industries, including pulp and paper, metalworking, transportation, and petrochemical processing, contributed to $12.1 million in sales during 1973.

The company grew large enough by 1957 to become a public corporation. Earnings per share rose higher than an average 15% annually for the next 20 years. The mid-1960's marked a high point in the company's history as earnings grew 16% every year. This was only exceeded by a three year performance between 1974 and 1977 where profits eventually reached a 19% growth rate. By 1973 Economics Laboratory was divided into five divisions. The institutional division manufactured dishwasher products

and sanitation formulas. In the consumer division, home dishwasher detergent as well as coffee filters, floor cleaners, and laundry aids were produced. The Klenzade division provided specialty detergents to the food processing industry. Overseas sales were controlled by the International division. This division was started by future chairman and chief executive officer Fred T. Lanners who, it is said, paid his first employees out of his own expense account. And finally, as mentioned earlier, the Magnus division produced items for the industrial market.

Of all the company's individual products, detergents for household dishwashers became its most important in sales. Second only to Proctor & Gamble's automatic dishwasher detergent in domestic sales, Economics Laboratory's detergents were pre-eminent in overseas markets. In the early 1970's, despite the fine company performance, Economics Laboratory attempted to expand its business by offering several new service and equipment packages. One such package offered on-premise laundry services for hospitals and hotels. This business was strengthened by the purchase of three subsidiaries all engaged in the laundry industry. Another package offered sanitation and cleaning service to the food industry. The company's dishwashing operation service, for example, addressed every aspect of the procedure from selecting the detergent to training the employees.

This trend toward offering services to supplement specialty chemical products represented Economics Laboratory's new market strategy. According to Fred Lanners, Jr., Economics Laboratory's president, service activity was indispensible to building markets and the single most important asset to offer customers. Prospective company employees were hired according to whether they had the ability to give an impression of total commitment to the needs of clients. Aside from laundry and sanitation, future plans included offering a comprehensive cleaning service to food establishments and a chemical surveillance service to food maufacturers and handlers. The ideas for the structure and implementation of these service packages emerged from Economics Laboratory's research and development department. The increasing importance of this department resulted in hiring a staff of 200 by 1973.

In 1978 the company underwent a number of changes. Unlike in previous years, the profit margin only increased 10%. Sales of dishwashing detergent had slowed down and the expansion of international operations resulted in a temporary adverse effect on profits. Both causes for the reduced profit gains appeared easily correctable and no major reorganization was in order. Yet the disappointing figures happened to occur at the same time new executives filled positions in Economics Laboratory's management.

E.B. Osborn, son of the founder Merrit J. Osborn, ended his long tenure as chief executive officer so that Fred Lanners, the first non-family member to achieve such high executive status, could assume the new title. Lanners began at Economics Laboratory in the research and development department, becoming first the chief scientist and then the assistant to the research and development director. At the time of the management shift E.B. Osborn's experience at the company covered a timespan of 50 years. The third generation descendant, S. Bartlett Osborn, stepped up to the positions of executive vice president and chief operating officer.

By 1979 business had resumed at an accelerated pace. Sales reached a 16% increase and earnings per share rose 16.6% over the previous year. International sales now increased at a faster pace than domestic sales. Profits, however, did not substantially increase; the unimpressive 6.6% was traceable to the effects of a large hiring campaign. The 130 new employees in marketing represented the largest sales personnel increase ever in the course of one year.

The hiring of new staff marked only one tactic in management's strategy for growth. In addition to a larger sales force and continued expansion into foreign markets, Economics Laboratory announced plans to use some of its supply of cash to acquire Apollo Technologies for $71.2 million. This manufacturer of chemicals and pollution-control equipment was purchased to improve the company's industrial market share. As the company's traditional lines of business in consumer and institutional products neared the limits of market penetration, Economics Laboratory looked for ways to supplement the operations of the Magnus division. Company management hoped that the acquisition of Apollo could offer that supplement.

At first the subsidiary served this function well and both companies found the relationship mutually beneficial. Apollo gained the financial backing necessary to enter new markets, particularly overseas, and Economics Laboratory broadened its business in the industrial sector. The Apollo subsidiary now held the responsibility for selling all Economics Laboratory's industrial chemical specialties. In addition to marketing coal additives, catalysts, and dust-control products to the electrical utility and mining industries, Apollo's sales staff was given the added task of selling lubricants, pulp-processing compounds, and temperature reducers to the metal processing and paper industries.

The major advantage Apollo's business activities held for its parent company was the ability to raise the industrial service operations to the same level of success as the Economics Laboratory's institutional services. Prior to the acquisition, Economics Laboratory's industrial business suffered from an inability to offer comprehensive services to its customers. With the purchase, Economics Laboratory acquired not only a company, but also technical service engineers to supervise product implementation.

In 1981 Philip T. Perkins assumed the title of president and chief operating officer. The new top executive joined Economics Laboratory in 1968 as vice president of the company's consumer division. As a graduate of Michigan State University, Lanners used his self-created bachelor's degree in food distribution to assume a number of positions in consumer operations both at Economics Laboratory and other companies. His experience in Economics Laboratory's consumer division attracted the attention of his colleagues; after three years of employment he was chosen as the company's most valuable employee. Prior to becoming president and chief executive officer Perkins held the position of executive vice-

president and chief operating officer of the international division.

Announcing his executive affinity with President Reagan, Perkins placed a bowl of jelly beans, the president's favorite candy, on his desk. As a new top executive, Perkins was considered particularly useful in overseeing the international operations. Before assuming his new title he had developed a plan to consolidate the program into a highly efficient network. His plan is credited with helping to maintain the division's impressive growth rate. Aside from continuing to expand international operations, Perkins planned to increase research and development by spending 25%.

The last remaining promotion entitled to Perkins was the advancement to chairman and chief executive officer. Although it was generally assumed that Perkins was being prepared for this final promotion, tradition at the company protected the incumbency of its older chairmen. For this reason, no one expected the 62 year old Fred Lanner, current chairman and chief executive officer, to be relinquishing his duties in the near future.

Perkins' promotion, however, never materialized. In a surprise move Economics Laboratory recruited and hired its new top executive from outside the ranks of its employees. This abrupt shift in 1982 is said to have been managements' response to a sharp decline in sales of pollution-control chemicals. In attempting to remedy the situation, operating units were restructured and a new leader was sought with a strong background in chemistry and experience in the industrial sector. The recruitment process singled out Richard C. Ashley, former president of Allied Chemical and a group vice-president of the parent company, as Economics Laboratory's new leader. Ashley's degree in chemistry and his successful experience in the chemical field fulfilled the company's qualifications.

Ashley's talents were expected to be particularly useful in addressing the ailing Apollo subsidiary. Sales, dropping precipitously to $5 million, had been adversely affected by the depressed industrial sector and by revisions in the Clean Air Act. The move to realign operating units represented the first in a series of steps devised to increase Apollo's business.

Yet before industry analysts could evaluate how successful Ashley's program would be, the new leader was killed in a fatal car accident soon after his promotion. Once again Economics Laboratory recruited outside the company for a new chairman and chief executive officer. Early in 1983 Pierson M. "Sandy" Grieve, a 55-year-old executive from the consumer goods company Questor, filled the vacated position. Grieve's experience in acquisitions and corporate planning, as well as his aggressive and articulate style, were his most valuable assets.

Just a week after assuming his new title, Grieve displayed his talent for decisive strategic planning; the Apollo subsidiary was to be shut down. The closing of the operation caused a $43 million write-off but eliminated the possibility of continuing adverse effects on profits. Grieve's next strategic move involved reorganizing the Magnus division, issuing ultimatums on sales performance for certain foreign markets not up to standards, and hiring 100 new salesmen to market expanded product lines.

Although sales had reached $670 million, ranking the company fourth among six of the top manufacturers of domestic cleaning products, debts over the past years had accumulated and the institutional market, representing Economics Laboratory's largest customer base, had shrunk.

Grieve's decision to close Apollo was just one major company decision of the many required early in his tenure. Only months later, a significant attempt by an industry competitor to replace the nation's top dishwashing detergents caused Economics Laboratory's product to slip from second to third place. Lever Brothers, a large consumer product company, released its Sunlight brand detergent and captured a sizeable portion of the market. To prevent any further erosion of the company's market share Grieve issued a plan to develop new products internally. Moreover, for the first time in ten years, he increased allocations for product promotion by adding $5 million to the soap products' advertising budget.

A final cause for concern emerged with the aggressive maneuvers of the Molsen Company, a Canadian brewing concern. In an attempt to capture a share of Economics Laboratory's U.S. institutional and industrial markets, Molsen purchased the Diversey Corporation, a specialty chemical company. Diversey successfully increased Molsen's presence in the U.S. and in five years the company tripled its sales.

Despite these concerns, Grieve's strategy to regain certain markets appeared effective. By 1986 $55 million in assets had been sold, including the pulp and paper division, the domestic portion of Magnus, the coffee filter business, and several plants. Other consolidation measures involved the laying off of employees and the implementation of new packaging processes. Long-term debt was reduced by an equivalent of $10 million and the company once again controlled a comfortable amount of cash. The acquisition of Lystads, an exterminating service, and ICE, a pest control operation, indicates Economics Laboratory's attempt to broaden its customer base in its institutional division. Similarly, with the purchase of Foussard Associates, a laundry product and service operation, the company sought to augment growth in its institutional division. And finally, the release of several new detergent products and the opening of a unit in South Korea indicates that the revitalization of Ecolab (the company's newly adopted name) is almost complete.

Principal Subsidiaries: Detergent Service, Inc.; E.L. Manufacturing Corp.; E.L. Caribbean, Inc.; ELSO, Inc.; Economics Laboratory International Ltd.; Raburn Europe S.a.r.l. (France); E.L. Southeast Asia Ltd.; Economics Laboratory Finance N.V. (Curacao); Environmental Systems Management AG (Switzerland); Lystrads Inc. (U.S.A.). Ecolab's Soilax subsidiaries are also in the following countries: Denmark, Finland, France, Germany, Ireland, Italy, Jamaica, Lebanon, Mexico, The Netherlands, New Zealand, Norway, Spain, Sweden, Switzerland and the United Kingdom.

ETHYL CORPORATION

330 S. Fourth Street
Richmond, Virginia 23217
U.S.A.
(804) 788-5000

Public Company
Incorporated: February 1887 as Albermarle
Paper Mfg. Co.
Employees: 10,500
Sales: $1.579 billion
Market value: $3.755 billion
Stock Index: New York Toronto

In 1962 when the Albermarle Paper Company purchased the Ethyl Corporation, a chemical company five times Albermarle's size, the headline in the *Wall Street Journal* read "Jonah Swallows the Whale." There is a consensus among the business press that Albermarle's acquisition of Ethyl, the largest producer of anti-knock compounds for fuel, was the business coup of the decade. At the present time, Albermarle, which adopted the name of its most famous acquisition, may have another triumph with its acquisition of First Colony, a life insurance company.

The Albermarle Paper Company was founded in 1887 by a group of businessmen in Richmond, Virginia who were convinced that paper was a growth area for the 19th century. Situated by the James River, the company's mill produced both kraft and blotter paper. The company's early history was uneventful until 1918 when Floyd Gottwald grew impatient with his job as an assistant paymaster for the Richmond, Fredricksburg and Potomac Railways and went to work for Albermarle. By the 1940's Gottwald was presiding over the company's plantation-style Richmond headquarters.

Floyd Gottwald Sr. was described by *Forbes* magazine as a "curmudgeon" with "a passion for anonymity." But what Gottwald lacked in congeniality he made up for in business acumen. The market for blotter and kraft paper was frequently depressed, but Gottwald knew exactly what to do in order to improve their situation. In the 1950's, for instance, polyethylene completely replaced paper as the material of choice for launderers dry-cleaning garment bags. This would have been quite a setback to a kraft paper manufacturer like Albermarle, except for Gottwald's positive attitude. It is not surprising that Albermarle went into plastics and began to manufacture polyethylene.

In 1962 Albermarle invested even more heavily in plastic manufacturing with its surprise purchase of Ethyl. The Ethyl Corporation was founded after the 1917 discovery that a lead additive would prevent car engines from knocking. General Motors, in partnership with Standard Oil, began to manufacture the patented additive called tetra ethyl. The additive held on to a substantial share of the market for years, even in the 1950's when the patent expired.

Contradictory stories circulated about Albermarle's motivation for purchasing the Ethyl Corporation. In one version, Albermarle was interpreted as wanting to buy chemicals for bleaching paper from Ethyl, and the larger company was said to reject any agreement. "That made us mad, so we waited two years and bought Ethyl for ourselves," Gottwald was quoted as saying. In another version, Albermarle was interpreted as wanting to buy Ethyl for its ethylene, a necessary ingredient in polyethylene garment bags.

Whatever led to the purchase, it is clear that Albermarle benefited from the then prevelant anti-trust laws. The obvious potential buyers for the Ethyl Corporation were large chemical companies like Dow Chemical or Du Pont, but they were prevented from buying Ethyl for legal reasons. Standard Oil, although happy to sell its share of Ethyl, had never put its shares up for sale for just this very reason. When Standard Oil was approached by Albermarle an agreement was quickly decided upon for 200 million dollars.

Wall Street·was surprised that Albermarle, a paper company with 1961 earnings of 1.8 million dollars, could raise the necessary funds. It did so with the help of four insurance companies (including Prudential), several investment houses, and Chase Manhatten Bank, each of which put up cash in exchange for notes. Albermarle immediately used Ethyl's depreciation to reduce its 100% debt to 80%. Nonetheless, the new Ethyl Corporation had a high debt to equity ratio.

The new company was reorganized so that Albermarle Paper became a subsidiary of the company it had recently purchased. The new company derived 60% of its sales from tetra ethyl and the rest from paper and plastics. In 1963 Gottwald bought Union Carbide's VisQueen, a major producer of polyethylene film used for food packaging. In 1966 it developed the capacity to produce plastic bottles and became a leader in the manufacture of PVC. These new acquisitions meant that Ethyl carried a burden of debt that would have been almost unthinkable in the 1970's or 1980's. But as one industry analyst pointed out, "In an economy where interest payments are tax-deductible, it makes sense to keep money in business rather than retire debt."

Ethyl Corporation soon entered the European market selling its lead additives in bulk. In the first four years after Albermarle had purchased Ethyl its profits went up 80%, setting the pace for Ethyl's subsequent growth. With the exception of an occasional year off, Ethyl has historically grown between 10 and 20% a year.

Ethyl's acquisitions did not stop at plastics. In 1966 it bought the William Bonnel Company which made shaped aluminium and in 1967 the Oxford Paper Company became part of Ethyl. The old Albermarle Paper Company had always wanted to manufacture bleached paper; rechristened as Ethyl it owned one of the larger makers of fine printing paper and paper for books. Oxford brought with it 195,000 acres of timberland. The old Albermarle division was sold, along with Interstate Bag and Halifax Timber.

For many stock market analysts the radical, albeit successful, diversification policies of Ethyl during this period typified the business climate of the 1960's. In the period of a few years a paper company of moderate size became a major force in markets as diverse as fuel additives, food wrap and PVC, and had substantial aluminum holdings. In the late 1960's, however, Ethyl confronted another trend, namely, a growing concern for the environment. This lead to the eventual extinction of Ethyl's main product — lead additives for gasoline.

In the mid-1960's a Dr. Clair Patterson was tracing lead isotopes in the Artic and the Pacific in order to discover clues about the formation of the Earth. However, his research led him to some frightening conclusions about the present; he became convinced that air-borne lead was poisoning people. Patterson showed that urban dwellers had 50% more lead in their blood than their counterparts in rural areas. Scientist after scientist blamed leaded gasoline. Ethyl, which derived the bulk of its earnings from the leaded additives which many scientists claimed were polluting the atmosphere, was in a precarious position.

The Ethyl Corporation's official stance was that the studies of Patterson and other like-minded scientists were incorrect. Unleaded gasoline, the company said, would require expensive changes in automobiles and refineries, resulting in severe economic repercussions. In addition, one Ethyl advertisement claimed that, "Taking the lead out of gasoline can increase more than the price. It can increase the smog." This claim referred to the theory that inefficient, knocking engines would release more hydrocarbons than smoothly running engines which consumed leaded gas. Congress was not convinced and, in the Clean Air Act, mandated stricter emissions controls for cars. General Motors, Ethyl's old owner, signed the death warrant for tetra ethylene by opting for a catalytic converter on new cars rather than the lead converter that Ethyl proposed. Catalytic converters, of course, run on lead-free gas.

Some chemical companies have invested in so called "mature" industries, that is, those with little growth potential. Ethyl was in what many analysts regarded as a declining industry. The price of Ethyl stock shares, by its own admission, dropped precipitously. Earnings, however, did not. This was due to the fact that lead-free gas was phased in gradually, so Ethyl had time to withdraw from its dependence on tetra ethylene. A sizable European market for its lead additives also did not hurt. Most of all, management at Ethyl had the intelligence to diversify. In 1970, for instance, the year after the decline in its stock, Ethyl bought a company that manufactured instruments to measure auto emissions. In 1971, despite a decline in lead sales, the company had a record year as paper and chemicals surged ahead. In 1975 Oxford Paper was sold because the company was expanding more towards chemicals and away from paper. The push into chemicals intensified in 1975 when Ethyl began to make detergent intermediaries, more plastic products, and dispensers for personal care products. The advent of disposable diapers was a boon — Ethyl makes the plastic lining for Pampers. The demand for anti-knock additives steadily diminished, but even so the company managed to grow, although its growth slowed to 1% during some years.

In 1981 Ethyl bought First Colony Life Insurance. At the time it made this purchase Ethyl was deriving its income primarily from specialty chemicals and fuel additives. Ostensibly, the decision to purchase a life insurance company seemed a bit odd, but in retrospect it was a wise one. First Colony was making a large amount of money by breaking all the traditional rules for selling insurance. For instance, it sold special policies to individuals in high risk groups, including diabetics and people with heart problems. Another innovation on the part of First Colony was to convince salespeople from other companies to sell First Colony life insurance when their own companies didn't have a comparable policy. This means that First Colony didn't have to train career agents, which was an expensive project.

Floyd Gottwald Jr., who had taken over the company from his father, defended the purchase by pointing out that it is good for a specialty chemical company to have some products that do not require expensive research and development. First Colony flourished under its new ownership; its earnings quadrupled between 1982 and 1984 from $10.8 to $39.4 million. With the addition of the newly acquired insurance company, Ethyl had a record year in 1984 as its earnings rose 25%. The company's chemical product mix was well balanced between bromides, semiconductor chemicals, herbicides, anti-oxidents, paper chemicals and fuel additives.

Not to be defeated in its old market, Ethyl persists in selling a manganese substitute for lead as a fuel additive and has small investments in coal and oil. These last investments are referred to in the industry as "Ethyl's revenge."

By 1985 Ethyl's product line had gone through a complete metamorphosis. Lead additives counted for only 10% of profits and were easily eclipsed by the company's plastic and aluminum divisions. This former manufacturer of anti-knock compounds is now a major supplier of reusable bottle caps. It is also one of the U.S. manufacturers of ibuprofen, a pain killer now approved for over-the-counter sales. Recently, Ethyl shares have out-performed almost all other chemical company shares. In the last four years the value of Ethyl stock shares have risen 364%.

In 1985 Ethyl made $117 million against a profit of $132 million the year before. This was a good showing considering that the company had an extraordinary loss of $20 million for the closing of a major fuel additive plant. Insurance was, after specialty chemicals, the company's most lucrative division followed by plastics, aluminium and energy. In fact, the company has been so pleased with First Colony that it purchased another life insurance company named the Barclay Group, a leader in life insurance policies paid for through payroll deductions.

Ethyl has seen its major products of anti-knock additives and paper falter, yet it has managed to remain a vibrant and profitable company. It has protected itself by diversification into unfamiliar markets such as insurance, although the same radical diversification strategies pursued by Ethyl have proven disasterous for other companies. Ethyl's success is a tribute to the way the company is run, namely, as a family business. The Gottwald family owns 17% of the stock shares, and the directors and employees own another 15%. Says one insider, "They treat the company like it is their very own, and it is." In a 1986 feature story on executive salaries *Business Week* singled out president Floyd Gottwald Jr. as the most economical chairman of the board of an American company. With a $1.7 million salary his personal financial future is bound up with that of his company; he is not a corporate so to speak, who will begin a diversification strategy and not see it through to completion. This sort of personal commitment to a company has paid off handsomely for

shareholders. With the chemical industry as a whole facing a quickly changing, ever-more competitive marketplace, Ethyl's creativity and ability to adhere to long-term plans bode well for the company's future.

Principal Subsidiaries: Capitol Products Corp.; Interamerica Terminal Corp.; William L. Bonnel Co., Inc.; Hardwicke Chemical Co.; Massie Tool and Mold, Inc.; Libby G. Corp.; Joy Corp.; Justine Shipping Corp.; First Colony Life Insurance Co.; Morgan Semiconductor, Inc.; Fiberlux Products, Inc.; Transcontinental, Coal Processing, Inc.

Further Reading: Ethyl: A History of the Corporation and the People Who Made It by Joseph C. Robert, Charlottesville, University Press of Virginia, 1983.

G.A.F.

1361 Alps Road
Wayne, New Jersey 07470
U.S.A.
(201) 628-3000

Public Company
Incorporated: April 26, 1929 as American I.G. Chemical
Corporation
Employees: 4,300
Sales: $754 million
Market Value: $1.469 billion
Stock Index: New York

GAF Corporation is a chemicals and building materials producer that is currently achieving successes previously unequaled in its 60-year history. During that period, control of the company has been transferred from the hands of the founding German corporation, to the U.S. government, to the American public. After decades of unclear direction of its management and its industry concentration, the company has shed the characteristics that had contributed to its historical reputation of an underachiever; in the 1980's GAF finally stands on solid ground as a leader in specialty chemicals and roofing products.

GAF had auspicious beginnings, founded in April, 1929, as an American arm of the enormous German chemicals trust, I.G. Farben-industrie. Known throughout the world as I.G. Dyes, the German corporation was involved in most areas of the worldwide chemicals industry, pressing forward with massive investments in research, and in 1929 it was classed as the largest industrial corporation in Europe. Six executives from I.G. Dyes joined with a handful of prominent American businessmen—among them Edsel Ford, president of the Ford Motor Company; Walter Teagle, president of the Standard Oil Company of New Jersey; Charles Mitchell, chairman of the National City Bank; and Paul Warburg, chairman of the Industrial Acceptance Bank—to form the board of directors of the American I.G. Chemical Corporation.

For its plant facilities, the new corporation acquired substantial interests in Agfa-Ansco Corporation of upstate New York and General Aniline Works, Inc., which operated in New York and New Jersey. Agfa-Ansco, whose roots dated to a photographic supply shop set up in New York City in 1842, ranked second to Kodak in the U.S. in the production of photographic materials and film, and General Aniline Works, formerly the Grasselli Dyestuffs

Corporation, had established itself as a major manufacturer of synthetic organic chemicals and dyestuffs since its founding in Rensselaer, New York, in 1882.

The plans for American I.G. were to provide competition to other American chemicals firms and to exploit the patents of I.G. Dyes in the new American market, which it did over the next decade. Initially, the company's trump card was its process for the hydrogenation of coal, which produced gasoline as a by-product; this largely accounted for the initial interest that the presidents of Ford and Standard Oil had in the new corporation. Other products that were developed and distributed by American I.G. include dyestuffs, pharmaceuticals, solvents, lacquers, photographic products and films, synthetic silk and other fabrics, a range of nitrogen products including chemical fertilizers, and an array of other organic and inorganic chemicals.

In 1939 the company changed its name to the General Aniline and Film Corporation, after having acquired all of General Aniline Works and merged with Agfa-Ansco, of whose stock it owned 81%. By that time it had earned approximately 3900 patents for its vast stock of chemical formulations.

From the beginning, General Aniline was designed to be largely controlled by and dependent upon German direction and research. Almost all its research took place in Germany, then chemical intermediates were manufactured there and sent to the U.S. plants for final preparation. The company's consistent successes were earned through a steady performance in the fields of dyes, chemicals, and photographical products. In fact, it was the leading U.S. manufacturer of dyestuffs until du Pont caught up in the late 1930's. An acquisition which had impact on the company's future was that of the Ozalid Corporation, a producer of copying equipment, in 1940.

General Aniline and Film survived some early criticisms of its very existence by Americans who questioned the prudence of such a large German concern operating in the United States. The company's record was legitimate, but the direct participation in its management by German citizens had raised some cautious eyebrows on Wall Street and in Washington; soon after it became apparent that the United States would be an active participant in World War II, General Aniline was seized by the U.S. government in February, 1942, under the Trading with the Enemy Act. It was the largest asset taken over by the U.S. in World War II.

This move developed into a long-standing legal dispute between the U.S. government and I.G. Chemie, a Swiss holding company that was the majority stockholder of General Aniline. Prior to 1940, I.G. Chemie had been a branch of I.G. Dyes, but it contended that it broke all relations with Germany during that year, becoming an independent corporation called Interhandel; the U.S. view was that I.G. Chemie remained a front for I.G. Dyes, despite its claims to the contrary. An out-of-court settlement between the Justice Department and Interhandel was finally reached over twenty years later—General Aniline would be sold to the public, with proceeds from the sale being split 60%–40%, the U.S. receiving the majority.

Between 1942 and 1965, General Aniline was managed by government-appointed directors, and it was a turbulent, minimally profitable time for the company. All told, during this period the company had seven different chief executives and over 80 directors. In several regards, the government's hands were tied, preventing it from acting as freely and spontaneously as most managers could and did at the time. The rapid turnover of directors in itself created a barrier to long-term planning. The directors were excessively cautious, in most cases focusing on immediate rather than long-term results, never knowing when the company would be sold to the public. The pending lawsuit with Interhandel created an atmosphere laden with modest risk-taking, as each potential move by General Aniline was accompanied by threats of further legal action by Interhandel. For instance, one injunction obtained by Interhandel in 1957 (to prevent dilution of its equity) prohibited General Aniline from issuing its shares for acquisitions or from entering the equity and capital markets for money on which to expand. As the Board President Jack Frye stated in 1953, "One of the problems of this company is that, due to its ownership situation, the management, the boards of directors, and all concerned are extremely cautious about making expenditures. In trying to avoid mistakes, they actually move more slowly than do their competitors."

Consequently, General Aniline was growing in terms that were stagnant compared to its competitors in each of its fields of interest. In film and photographic equipment, it competed chiefly with Kodak, in chemicals, with du Pont, and in copying equipment with Xerox. All these firms, indeed each of the industries in question, experienced unprecedented growth and diversification that lasted through the postwar period and into the 1970's.

Regardless of its cautious management and modest overall growth, General Aniline did achieve some significant successes in the 20 years after the government takeover. One bright spot was the work of the brilliant chemical engineer Dr. Jesse Werner, who led the surge in replicating the formulas of all the important compounds that were formerly produced at the parent company in Germany. A central research laboratory for the dyes and chemicals divisions was set up in Easton, Pennsylvania, in 1942, employing 400 chemists; the management was more venturesome in this area than in others, and spent a good deal of money on product and market research and development on chemicals. These divisions produced an array of substances; among the successful were a chlorine-caustic plant set up in New Jersey in 1956, and the company's pioneering efforts in the field of synthetic detergents. The most important technical triumph was the company's success with acetylene derivatives, a fledgling branch of chemistry at which the company far surpassed any competitor's progress.

In the 1920's an I.G. Dyes chemist named Julius Walter Reppe found a way of handling acetylene under pressure without explosion, something that was previously thought by classical chemists to be impossible. Reppe's patented processes were found in General Aniline's American vaults in 1940, and were used as a basis for research by the chemists in Easton. Some of the earliest marketable uses of acetylene-based chemicals were the PVP (polyvinyl-pyrrolidone) family of products, which use a white powder that is the product of the pressurized combination of acetylene and formaldehyde; some of its uses are as a blood volume expander, suspending agent, tablet binder, and a fungicide, and also include a component in cosmetics, photographic chemicals and ink, paints, adhesives, detergents, and glass.

As of 1962, General Aniline remained the sole producer of acetylene derivatives in the United States, even though they were immensely profitable. The commercial successes of acetylene products can be largely attributed to Dr. Jesse Werner, who had risen through the technical ranks of the company in the 1940's and who was named director of commercial development in 1952, charged with the responsibility of exploitation of the chemists' discoveries. He implemented large-scale plans for the growing industrial uses of acetylene compounds, and eventually became company president in 1962; he was the first chief executive of General Aniline to have worked his way up from the laboratory.

Equal to the money poured into chemicals and dyestuffs research was the glaring lack of funds directed to the photography and copying equipment divisions. Two discoveries by researchers in the Agfa-Ansco labs would have had heavy impact on the industry, had they only received attention and funds for marketing. In the mid-1940's, a chemist named Vsevolod Tulagin invented a new dye system for color photography. His scientific peers believed it was better than what was on the market, but the business managers had little confidence that they could have a product that was of higher quality than Kodak's offerings. Then in 1951–52, Ansco developed a color movie film that was far more realistic than the super-real colors being viewed on movie screens at the time. In addition, the Ansco film could be developed within ten hours, on location, which was unheard of in the industry. Again, the circumspect General Aniline board refused to allocate the funds for an Anscofilm plant which would make production feasible.

The Ozalid division of copying equipment received a similar lack of support. Its development of small office copiers and all-purpose copiers was sluggish in a booming industry, and its marketing organization was underequipped with money and personnel. In addition, Ozalid's management was even more erratic than that of parent General Aniline; between 1957 and 1963 Ozalid had eight chief executives.

Despite all the shortcomings in Ansco and Ozalid, each maintained steady profit levels through the 1960's; the industries were expanding rapidly, so even the decreased percentage-market shares of Ozalid and Ansco amounted to steady profits. Ansco's concentration during this period shifted from the amateur photographic market to the commercial market, and it handled substantial government contracts as well. As a point of interest, the camera used by the astronaut John Glenn was a modified Ansco Autoset. Ozalid's chief market share was in the engineering field; its process involving the use of diazo-sensitized paper to produce an image upon exposure to ammonia was one of the best and cheapest at the time, and achieved great success in the reproduction of engineering drawings.

A benchmark in the company's history came on March 9, 1965, when the 23-year control by the U.S. government was ended in the biggest sale of stock at competitive bidding in Wall Street history. Dr. Werner, who had been appointed president and chief executive officer of General Aniline in 1962, and was voted chairman of the board on October 5, 1964, stood at the reins of the company as it entered its "second debut." He consolidated the company into two divisions: dyestuffs and chemicals, and photography and reproduction. In the 23 years since the U.S. seizure of General Aniline, its research program had earned almost 2000 patents of its own, and optimism for the company's future ran high.

Unfortunately, General Aniline was actually entering a new 20-year era of questionable management, during which Werner ran through a diverse roster of managers, products, and industries that never quite panned out as his plans predicted. As of 1981, the firm's shares were selling for less than one-third their 1965 offering price, and the company placed 1004th out of 1023 in the profitability rankings in *Forbes* magazine that year. Werner stated his original plans to be growth in the company's four existing fields, because, as he said in 1966, "We have too many product lines, too much diversity for our size." The only significant acquisition during his tenure was the merging in 1967 of Ruberoid Corporation, which added roofing, flooring, and related products to the company's lines.

The general trend between 1962 and 1982 was that research, development, and marketing outlays consistently fell short of what would have been necessary to forge market leaders out of GAF's divisions (the acronym GAF was adopted as the official company name in April 1968). The photographic and copying business serves as a case study. It offered a product line which was much narrower than its competitors', including no color film for its offset printers; its annual research and development expenditures averaged 1% of revenue from the division; a GAF customer observed in 1979 that "GAF's salesmen are very good, but there are just not enough of them."

Obviously, GAF must have experienced some positive feedback for its efforts or it wouldn't exist today; likewise, Werner's record showed enough merit to withstand the pressures of a proxy fight in 1971, which was led by a family of stockholders who claimed he had "grossly mismanaged" the company during his career. Much of the profitable experience occurred in the chemicals division, where there was consistent progress in production and sales of acetylene drivatives, surfactants (detergents), engineering thermoplastics, and mineral granules used for roofing shingles. Surfactants and acetylene products are sold worldwide to the pharmaceuticals, cosmetics, plastics, automotive, agricultural, textiles, oil and gas, paints, and paper production industries. GAF is one of only two worldwide producers of butanediol, itself an acetylene derivative, which is in turn used in the formulation of thermoplastic polyester compounds which have an enormous range of uses in the automotive, electrical/electronics, appliances, and other industries. The company also produces iron powders for the aerospace and electronics industries, products which were developed during the Werner years.

The roofing and flooring businesses achieved growth as well, more in the residential than in the commercial market. Indeed, during the 1970's GAF became the market leader in roofing products, partially led by its pioneering work in the production of fiberglass-based shingles.

In 1978 Dr. Werner sold the consumer photo and processing operations and the dyes and pigments interests because of continued poor showings. This was the beginning of a massive five-year divestment program which by the end of 1982 left GAF with only its two strongest lines, the chemicals and building materials, and the New York City classical radio station WNCN, which it had purchased in June 1976; all in all, over half of GAF's assets were shed during this period. Werner had seemingly played all his cards, and just when the trimmed-down company's future again began to shine, another proxy fight hit GAF, this one much more bitter and hard-fought than the one in 1971. After a two-year battle, Werner lost out to an aggressive stockholder named Samuel Heyman, a real estate brokerage owner who had no previous corporate management experience.

Heyman entered his GAF directorship on December 14, 1983, with promises to trim all but the most profitable operations, including plans to liquidate all of the chemicals division. However, after thoroughly examining all the company's records, he saw great potential for growth in building supplies *and* chemicals. He first eliminated some management positions, slashed operating expenses by 23% in his first nine months, and moved the company's headquarters from Manhattan to quiet Wayne, New Jersey. And to instill a better sense of teamwork at the company, he decentralized management; Werner had called virtually all the shots himself, but Heyman wanted to spread decision-making responsibilities among regional and divisional managers.

The first 20 months of Heyman's leadership brought remarkable success to GAF, based on cost-cutting and effective management more than on expansion of lines of business. Still, under Heyman capital expenditures were far greater, as were research and development outlays, than they had been in the Werner years.

In September, 1985, Heyman stated " We have no plans to take over other companies, but we are looking at the possible acquisition of businesses that would complement our existing chemical lines." Yet over the following 18 months, GAF attempted hostile takeovers of engineering plastics and specialty chemicals concerns, Union-Carbide Corporation and Borg-Warner; both takeovers were ultimately thwarted, but each netted huge amounts of cash for GAF through the company's sale of its stock shares in the other firms. GAF's shares in Union-Carbide brought close to $250 million to its coffers, and the stock in Borg-Warner, purchased by eventual Borg-Warner-buyer Merrill Lynch, earned over $190 million for GAF. For the future, Heyman doesn't rule out the possibility of another takeover attempt, especially if he finds an appropriate opportunity for expansion.

Typical of Heyman, he has steered much of these cash surpluses back into research for the building supplies and chemicals divisions. GAF sold its engineering plastics business in 1986, but is still one of only two producers of butanediol, which has achieved steady increases in demand throughout the last decade.

The building materials division has retained its status of market leader in residential roofing since the 1970's, and has made big steps in the commercial roofing market over the last several years. Even during the new home-building lag in the early 1980's, GAF was earning steady profits; since then, business has boomed in new home roofing, and even more so in premium re-roofing products designed to upgrade the appearance and value of homes. GAF has led the trend toward fiberglass as well as simulated woodshake roofing products.

The chemicals division has continued its progress in research, selling its products to industrial users across the United States and through 18 subsidiaries and branches throughout the world. Two of the most important recent chemical breakthroughs for GAF are its fixative polymers, used as a primary ingredient in hair mousses and sprays, and its Gantrez resin, used as an active ingredient in tartar-control toothpastes. GAF's acetylene chemicals business has held the company steadfast as one of the two world leaders in the industry.

Principal Subsidiaries: GAF Broadcasting Co., Inc.; GAF Export Corp.; GAF International Corp.; GAF Realty Corp.; General Aniline & Film Corp.; GAF Chemicals Corp.; Jay & Co., Inc.; Mayfair Investments, Inc. The company also lists subsidiaries in the following countries: Australia, Austria, Belgium, Bermuda, Brazil, Canada, France, Italy, Japan, Korea, Singapore, Sweden, Switzerland, South Africa, United Kingdom, and West Germany.

GREAT LAKES CHEMICAL CORPORATION

P.O. Box 2200
West Lafayette, Indiana 47906
U.S.A.
(317) 463-2511

Public Company
Incorporated: April 11, 1933 as McClanahan Oil Company
Employees: 3,700
Sales: $300 million
Market Value: $735 million
Stock Index: New York

Great Lakes Chemical is one of the world's largest manufacturers of bromine and brominated chemical products. Bromine, an acrid red liquid which irritates the skin, mixes easily with hundreds of organic compounds, producing thousands of toxic and non-toxic chemicals. While bromine compounds are not its only products, Great Lakes Chemical relies heavily on bromine for much of its revenue.

Great Lakes Chemical was originally founded as an oil and gas exploration company called the McClanahan Oil Company. Its founder, W.L. McClanahan, established the company to take advantage of a growing oil industry centered near Mount Pleasant in Central Michigan. The company remained small for many years, restricted both by competition from larger companies and limited oil reserves in Michigan.

In 1946 a geologist and Wall Street financier named Charles Hale became the largest shareholder of the McClanahan Oil Company, and later assumed its presidency. As part of his goal of creating a natural resources conglomerate, Hale engineered the company's acquisition of the Great Lakes Chemical Corporation in March of 1958. Great Lakes Chemical held titles to oil and gas reserves, as well as some bromine wells near Filer City, Michigan. In May of 1950 the two companies merged to form the Great Lakes Oil & Chemical Company.

During the 1950's Great Lakes expanded its petroleum interests by purchasing the Olds Oil Corporation in December of 1951, and the Cleveland Oil Company in October of 1952. These companies were later merged with Great Lakes Oil & Chemical as part of a program to rationalize production. The company's ability to compete in its traditional petroleum markets began to erode during the late 1950's. Faced with impending bankruptcy, Great Lakes was forced to alter substantially its business strategies.

Earl T. McBee, a professor of industrial chemistry at Purdue University, and a consultant to Great Lakes since 1953, advocated the company's gradual withdrawal from the petroleum industry, favoring instead the expansion of its bromine operation. Charles Hale agreed with McBee and in 1957 authorized the sale of the company's oil properties in California. Through the sale of additional California real estate during 1960, Great Lakes raised enough capital to purchase a 50% share of Arkansas Chemicals Inc., which owned several bromine-rich brine wells in Arkansas. As a result, Great Lakes became a major bromine products company by gaining a stake in the best deposits before the industry leader Dow Chemical.

The company changed its name to Great Lakes Chemical Corporation on May 9, 1960, and continued its reorganization process by attempting to diversify into financial services. The venture was unsuccessful, however, and was discontinued in 1963.

At the time, the largest application for bromine was ethylene dibromide, an additive to leaded gasoline. Ethylene dibromide, however, was a simple commodity chemical with a low profit margin. In an effort to create a line of more profitable specialty chemicals, Great Lakes Chemical devoted 5% of its sales to develop new bromine compounds in a joint venture with PPG Industries. Applications were found for bromine in a wide variety of products, including biodegradable soil fumigants and herbicides, dyes, cleansing powders, synthetic rubber, refrigerants, photographic papers, and flame-retardant additives for plastics.

In 1969 Great Lakes Chemical purchased the Cavedon Chemical Company and the Microseal Corporation, in addition to Lunevale Products Ltd. of Lancaster, England. The following year Great Lakes Chemical formed a joint venture with Pechiney Ugine Kuhlmann of France called Sobrom. Sobrom was established to develop brominated soil fumigants for the European market. The company increased its presence in France in 1972 when it formed another company called Microfral with Compagnic Français des Lubricants. Through these companies, Great Lakes Chemical enlarged its marketing network on an international scale.

Earl McBee died of a heart attack in 1973. He was replaced by Emerson Kampen, an employee of many years who gained a reputation for strong central management. Kampen continued many of McBee's policies, including that of cooperation with French companies. In February of 1976 Great Lakes Chemical agreed to form an American joint venture with Pechiney Ugine Kuhlmann called the Forex Chemical Corporation, which was established to develop fire extinguishing compounds.

In the later half of the 1970's other chemical manufacturers accidentally released bromine fire retardants into rivers, causing cattle to be poisoned in Michigan and raising questions about the safety of these retardants in children's pajamas. Great Lakes Chemical maintained that its bromine products were safe, but was forced to observe costly new regulatory measures imposed on the industry.

Great Lakes Chemical had become highly profitable, taking advantage of higher demand and new applications for bromine. The company nearly doubled its brine reserves near El Dorado, Arkansas when it purchased the bromine operations of Northwest Industries' Velsicol subsidiary in 1981. In doing so, Great Lakes Chemical prevented competitors like Dow and Ethyl from increasing their bromine assets. The Federal Trade Commission, however, filed suit to prevent the takeover on antitrust grounds. After several years of litigation the matter was finally settled in March of 1984, when the FTC agreed to permit the takeover on the condition that Great Lakes would license its technologies to PPG Industries, in order to make it a "viable competitor."

In 1984 the federal government banned ethylene dibromide for non-fuel uses. As a result of the ban, Great Lakes Chemical only lost 2% of profits; the increased use of unleaded gasoline during the late 1970's forced the company to de-emphasize production of ethylene dibromide.

One of the areas Great Lakes Chemical chose to expand was biotechnology, and in 1982 took control over the Enzyme Technologies Corporation. Another promising area was oil field chemicals. Clear fluids containing bromine salts are effective agents in flushing oil out of the ground. In July of 1982 Great lakes purchased a fluids company called Mobley Chemical, and in October acquired a 63% share of the Oilfield Service Corporation of America.

In September of 1983 Great Lakes Chemical purchased the Inland Specialty Chemical Corporation for $10 million. The acquisition marked the entry of Great Lakes into the area of electronic chemicals, where it sought to apply its halogen-based X-ray resist technology to semiconductors.

The leadership of Emerson Kampen was repeatedly called into question and described as "abusive" by senior managers. As a result of Kampen's refusal to delegate greater authority, five vice presidents resigned from Great Lakes Chemical between 1975 and 1984. One of those vice presidents was Kenneth Karmel, who left in 1982 to head Ethyl's new Bromine Chemicals Division. Fearing that its industrial secrets would be compromised, Great Lakes Chemical challenged Karmel's contract with Ethyl in court.

Largely through the benefit of licensing agreements with other companies, Great Lakes Chemical claims to be the largest producer of bromine products in America. While Emerson Kampen denies that he dominates Great Lakes Chemical, he is equally insistent that his is not a one-product company. Bromine chemistry accounts for over 80% of Great Lakes' products, but the company has several hundred different products. In the meantime, the company's attempts at diversification continue. In April of 1985 Great Lakes purchased Purex Pool Products for $20 million.

Principal Subsidiaries: Great Lakes Chemical (Europe) Ltd.; Great Lakes Chemical International, Inc.; GLK International Corp.; Arkansas Chemicals, Inc. (50%); E/M Corp.; WIL Research Laboratories, Inc.; Enzyme Technology Corp.; Oilfield Service Corporation of America; Hydrotech Chemical Corporation; Inland Specialty Chemical Corp.

HERCULES INC.

Hercules Plaza
Wilmington, Delaware 19894
U.S.A.
(302) 594-5000

Public Company
Incorporated: October 18, 1912 as Hercules Powder
Company
Employees: 25,448
Sales: $2.615 billion
Market value: $3.312 billion
Stock Index: New York London Basle Zurich Geneva

The Hercules Powder Company was one of the several small explosives companies acquired by the Du Pont Company in the 1880's. By the beginning of the 20th century Du Pont had absorbed so many of its competitors that it was producing two-thirds of the dynamite and gunpowder sold in the United States. In 1912 a federal court, citing the Sherman Anti-Trust Act, ordered Du Pont broken up. It was through this court ordered action that the Hercules Powder Company was reborn, a manufacturer of explosives ostensibly separate from Du Pont.

The division of the Du Pont Company into Du Pont, Atlas Powder Company, and Hercules Powder Company, was intended to foster competition in the explosives industry, but in reality the anti-trust agreement allowed the connection between Hercules and the parent company to remain intact. The new company was staffed by executives who had been transplanted from the Du Pont headquarters across the street into the main offices of Hercules in Wilmington, Delaware. As *Fortune* magazine remarked in 1935, "The Hercules headquarters is in Wilmington and breathes heavily Dupontizied air." Not only did the Du Pont family retain a substantial financial interest in Hercules, but as late as 1970 the president of Hercules was related to the Du Pont family.

The Hercules Powder Company was set up as a fully developed business entity, complete with several explosives factories, a healthy segment of the explosives market and a five million dollar "loan" in its treasury. It operated successfully and made a profit from its very first year. Given its early advantage it is not surprising that Hercules developed into one of the larger chemical companies in the United States.

Hercules began as an explosives company serving the mining industry, gun owners and the military. In the first month of operation its facility in Hazardville, N.J. exploded. Hercules had plants up and down the East Coast, however, and the loss of the Hazardville plant was not financially disastrous. Like other manufacturers of explosives, Hercules preferred many small plants to a few large ones. Due to the risks involved in transporting their product, these plants were located in proximity to customers, rather than near the source of raw materials.

The company's first big break came in 1916 when Hercules signed a lucrative contract to supply Britain with acetone, a contract that stipulated, however, that no known sources of acetone be used. Hercules sent ships out to the Pacific to harvest giant kelp, which was used to produce the solvent Britain needed. That same year Hercules paid large dividends on its stock shares. The company also benefited from its sale of gunpowder to the army.

In 1920 Hercules began to manufacture cotton cellulose from the lint left over from cotton seeds once the high quality cotton has been extracted. Cotton cellulose is a fiber that has hundreds of industrial uses. When treated with nitroglycerine it becomes nitrocellulose, important in the production of laquers and plastics. Hercules quickly became the world's leading maker of cotton cellulose. This early effort at diversification in no way threatened Du Pont, which also manufactured nitrocellulose, but only for its own uses.

Throughout its history Hercules has been successful at transforming a previously worthless substance into something useful. But for every time Hercules has succeeded in this kind of endeavor, it has also failed. The company's foray into naval stores is an example of this. Naval stores is a term that refers to products derived from tree sap, and recalls the early use of pitch to caulk boats. Gums, turpentine, and various adhesives are all referred to as naval stores. In 1920 a Senate Committee predicted that the virgin pine forests from which high quality naval stores were derived would soon be exhausted and that there would be no naval stores industry lcft in the U.S. The management at Hercules saw, or thought it saw, a chance to corner the naval stores market.

Hercules joined forces with Yaryan, one of the few companies that distilled rosin from tree stumps rather than pitch. After buying rights to pull stumps and building a new rosin distilling plant, Hercules quickly became the world's largest producer of naval stores. But a problem soon arose: the expected shortage of naval stores never materialized. Hercules, the Senate Committee, and the naval stores industry overlooked the fact that pine trees grow back rather quickly, and that with proper management there would be plenty of pitch. Hercules was stuck with fields full of stumps, facilities to process the stumps, and a large amount of inferior turpentine. Turpentine derived from stumps is dark in color and hence unsuitable for some uses in finishing and painting furniture.

Endowed with sufficient capital (a legacy from Du Pont) Hercules was able to salvage its naval stores division by developing a paler turpentine and convincing its customers that wood (as opposed to pitch) naval stores were a bargain. By 1935 naval stores, the second largest of the company's investments, provided the smallest percentage of company sales. Naval stores and products derived from them eventually became a mainstay of the company, albeit one with slow growth. Not until the mid-1970's did the naval stores division emerge as a profitable endeavor. It was the explosives division which ensured the company's financial stability throughout the Depression.

By 1935 Hercules had five divisions: explosives, naval stores, nitrocellulose, chemical cotton and paper products. Chemical cotton is made from the short fibers of cotton unsuitable for weaving, which are pressed into sheets and sold to industries as a source of cellulose. The paper products division began in 1931 with the purchase of Paper Makers Chemical Corporation which provided 70% of U.S. demand for the rosin "sizing" used to stiffen paper.

At the time of America's entrance into World War II Hercules was the country's largest producer of naval stores and the third largest producer of explosives. Business was good during the war and company coffers were stuffed with legitimate and illegitimate gains. Hercules, Atlas, and Du Pont were convicted of a joint price-fixing scheme, and Du Pont was assessed a $40,000 dollar fine. Hercules' Annual Reports during this period concentrate on plans for reducing the company's size once the war ended because the demands of the war had swelled the company's workforce to twice its previous size.

Three years after the war ended Hercules emerged from what a later industry analyst called "a big sleep." The demand for nitrocellulose, paper chemicals and naval stores, products Hercules was depending on in peacetime, was growing at a snail's pace. Sales were averaging an unremarkable $200 million a year. However, in the 1950's the company diversified into two markets it was later to dominate: DMT and polypropylene.

Consistent with its "waste not, want not" approach to new chemicals, Hercules began to use waste gases from refineries to manufacture polypropylene, an increasingly important type of plastic. Polypropylene was used for food packaging, among other things. DMT is the chemical base for polyester fiber and was sold as a commodity to both chemical and polyester makers like Du Pont. Besides these new products Hercules continued to look for new uses for naval stores from which it already derived chemicals used in insecticides, textiles, paints and rubber.

Between 1955 and 1963 Hercules saw its sales double, but this was due in large part to government contracts. In 1959 Hercules diversified into rocket fuels and propulsion systems for the Polaris, Minuteman and Honest John missiles. Sales of aerospace equipment and fuels accounted for almost 10% of sales in 1961, 15% in 1962 and 25% in 1963. Throughout the Vietnam War Hercules continued to derive approximately 25% of its profits from rocket fuels, anti-personnel weapons and specialty chemicals such as Agent Orange and napalm.

The man who presided over Hercules in the 1960's was George Thouron, a relative of the Du Ponts. He described Hercules' policy towards expansion as "sticking close to profit-producing fields." A profile in *Fortune* magazine describes Thouron as a quiet man. As the article noted, "his main interest is in his prize Guernsey cattle."

Thouron knew that the war in Indochina would not last forever, and undertook an ambitious reorientation of the company toward the production of plastics, polyester and other petrochemicals. A contemporary observer remarked that "few companies have expanded further or faster than Hercules Inc." Herculon, the company's synthetic fabric, had garnered almost 11% of the market for upholstry material. A water soluble gum called CMC also made money for the company. CMC was as versatile as Herculon was stain-resistant: it made its way into products as diverse as ice cream, embalming fluid, diet products and vaginal jelly. "From womb to tomb," one company pundit quipped.

The 1960's and early 1970's was an auspicious time for Hercules. Although the foray into plastics had required large capital and research expenditures that depressed earnings, Hercules was a profitable and steadily growing company. High inflation actually helped the synthetics industry since the prices of natural fibers outpaced the cost of synthetics. In 1973, however, Hercules learned that oil can be as volatile as nitroglycerine. The Arab Oil Embargo was a disaster for the petrochemical industry. And if the embargo were not enough, two years later the demand for naval stores crashed just months after a rosin shortage had been predicted. Hercules, anticipating a shortage, had ordered millions of pounds of rosin at twice the usual price. Around the time that the first rosin-laden ships arrived it became clear that Hercules' customers, also fearful of a shortage, were overstocked with the material. The rosin problem, combined with a drop in the fibers market, caused sales to drop 90%. Hercules stock went down 17%. 1975 was not a good year for most chemical companies, but the difficulties that Hercules experienced were more than its share.

Werner Brown was the company's president during these years. In 1977 he was promoted, and chose Alexander Giacco to be the next president. Hercules had become an inordinately large company, its overheads and the size of its workforce were both excessive. In his first year as president Giacco fired or forced into retirement 700 middle managers and 3 executive vice presidents. Giacco has a managerial style that differs from that of the mild-mannered Brown, and Giacco's restructuring of the company reflects that. Giacco streamlined Hercules to make it more of a monarchy. "He runs the company like an extension of himself," said one analyst. In order to stay in touch with the various divisions, Giacco invested in advanced communications equipment and computers. He also reduced the managerial levels between himself and the foremen from twelve to six. His position in the company is suggested by his description of a new product. "I heard Gene Shalit say that candy wrapping paper made too much crinkling noise in movie houses. So we developed a candy wrapper that has no crinkle."

In many ways Giacco's plan for Hercules resembles the strategy his mentor, Werner Brown, mapped out in the early 1970's: shift from commodity to value-added (specialty) chemicals, get rid of unprofitable divisions, and derive more profits from existing product lines. After the fiasco in 1975 when two unrelated markets crashed at the same time, Hercules has experimented with the proper combination of products, taking to heart the teachings of economist Charles Reeder: "There's a simple two word answer to why chemical company earnings vary all over the lot. The words are 'product mix.' "

This product mix has eluded Hercules. One thing is certain, however; Hercules' mix will not include petrochemicals. In 1975, 43% of its fixable assets were in petrochemicals, but within a decade these assets had been liquidated. Naval stores may soon be out of the picture; in 1985 they were responsible for a decline in operating profits. Demand for CMC, the binding agent, declined because the oil industry was not using it for drilling. Propylene fibers and film, food flavors and fragrances (relatively new ventures), paper chemicals, aerospace, and graphite fibers are included in the future recipe for success. The company's plants for manufacturing DMT and explosives have been sold.

Hercules has a wide variety of product lines, and this makes it particularly hard to predict what the next decade will bring. One thing is certain, however, specialty chemicals, a company bulwark, will face increased competition at home and abroad. The other large chemical companies are also shifting from commodity to specialty chemicals.

Nonetheless, in the area of international sales Giacco thinks that the Pacific Basin will be a growth area, along with the more stable countries in South America.

Hercules possesses some strong divisions and the success of these, in combination with the elimination of dangerously cyclical product lines, would eventually result in a well balanced and financially sound company.

Principal Subsidiaries: Caribbean Lumber Co.; Esgraph Inc.; Champlain Cable Corp.; Hercules Chemical Corp.; Hercules Credit, Inc.; Lextan Inc.; Mica Corp.; Simmonds Precision Products, Inc. Hercules also has subsidiaries in the following countries: Austria, Burmuda, Brazil, Canada, Finland, France, England, West Germany, Japan, Mexico, Netherlands, Netherlands Antilles, Denmark, Belgium, Italy, Spain, Sweden, and Taiwan.

Further reading: Hercules Incorporated: A Study in Creative Chemistry by Werner C. Brown and Alexander F. Goacco, New York, Newcomen Society in North America, 1977.

Hoechst

HOECHST A.G.

Frankfurt-(M)-80
Federal Republic of Germany
(0611) 305-1

Public Company
Incorporated: 1952 as Farbwerke Hoechst A.G.
Employees: 180,561
Sales: DM 33.994 billion (US$ 17.505 billion)
Stock Index: Munich Hanover Bonn Frankfurt
Hamburg Basle Zurich Brussels London Paris
Antwerp Amsterdam Vienna

Hoechst is the largest of the three chemical companies formed in 1952 after the Allies disbanded the German chemical cartel known as the IG Farben. A well-diversified company, Hoechst is particularly focused on pharmaceuticals, and would like to see its subsidiary, American Hoechst, attain a prominent position in the U.S. drug market. This is not an unreasonable aspiration for a firm that was, until Du Pont's takeover of Conoco, the largest chemical company in the world.

Hoechst started out in 1863 on the Main River, near Frankfurt. At the time its entire capital consisted of a three horsepower steam engine and a small boiler in which anilin oil and arsenic acid, boiling together, produced a synthetic fuschia dye. By 1874 this primitive machine gave way to a new chemical plant. In a period of 20 years the Hoechst workforce grew from 5 to 1900 employees. By the end of the century, Hoechst had several thousand workers and a good reputation as an employer. The company reduced the traditional 12 hour day to 8 hours, and provided its employees with athletic facilities, mid-wives and prenatal care.

Throughout the late 19th and early 20th centuries, dye-stuffs accounted for 90% of Hoechst's sales. Although an 1883 brochure alloted the company's work in pharmaceuticals only one sentence, this work was, in retrospect, significant for both Hoechst and the history of pharmacology. At first glance, a dye company like Hoechst seems an unusual setting for pioneering work in drugs, but it must be remembered that the German dye industry, with its ties to major universities, had a degree of technical expertise unrivaled in the world. Furthermore, many dyes and drugs shared a similar chemical composition.

In 1883 a Hoechst chemist working with quinine discovered Antipyrin, one of the first analgesics. The company cooperated with leading researchers Koch and Erlich to produce the Novocaine familiar to dental patients, and also Salvarsan, the first effective treatment for syphilis. Salvarsan was one of the first disease-specific medicines. Most 19th century drug discoveries were, like aspirin, general remedies.

The list of Hoechst's achievements in pharmacology includes the 1906 synthesis of adrenalin and the 1923 isolation of insulin. Despite its contributions to medicine, Hoechst was not popular with American chemical manufacturers. Along with other German companies, including Bayer and BASF, Hoechst waged an intense price war against its U.S. rivals in the dye industry. One tactic of the German dye trust was "dumping"—selling chemicals below cost in order to eliminate indigenous competitors in the American dye market.

Although the American chemical companies fought back, the German chemical trusts, of which Hoechst was a leading member, did impede the growth of the U.S. chemical industry. The political implications of the German trade wars became apparent during World War I when the Americans found themselves at a technical and productive disadvantage for waging war. Before the advent of nuclear weapons, chemical companies played a leading role in arming a country. Not only did they produce gun powder and mustard gas, but they made hundreds of synthetic substitutes for what were blockaded organic materials necessary to the war effort.

After the outbreak of World War I the German chemical industry rushed to fill military requests for inorganic chemicals, pharmaceuticals, explosives and photographic chemicals. While domestic business increased Hoechst, along with the others, lost its share of the American market and all its U.S. assets. After the war laws were passed to protect the American dye and drug industry from the aggressive policies of the German chemical companies.

England, France, the United States, and Germany had all developed elaborate orgnizations to coordinate chemical production during the war. When peace came, however, all of the countries except Germany quickly dismantled these organizations. The survival of these organizations in Germany, coupled with American protectionism, encouraged the formation of the IG Farben in 1925.

Early in the century two large chemical cartels had been formed within Germany, one of which was centered around Hoechst. In 1925 it was decided by the leaders of the chemical industry that the two cartels should merge into a single company called the Interessen Gemeinschaft Farbenwerke, or IG Farben. From an early date the IG Farben was active in politics, especially in urging that Germany re-arm itself.

That such a large cartel should wield political power comes as no surprise, but the extent of the IG's influence and the nature of its activities gives it a special distinction. After developing its own spy network and placing its directors in the German senate or Reichstag the IG Farben, as the representative of Germany's most important industry, was very influential in the 1933 elections. The man the IG Farben supported was Hitler.

The IG Farben profited greatly from Nazi Germany's

political policies. Hitler's plans for world domination coincided neatly with the IG Farben's plans to monopolize the international chemical industry. After the fall of France the Nazis requested that the IG Farben formulate plans for managing the chemical industries in conquered lands, and the cartel complied.

After the war the directors of the IG Farben were charged with war crimes. Their indictment at the Nuremberg trials stated that due to the activities of the IG Farben "the life and happiness of all peoples in the world were adversely affected." This was a serious charge, to which charges of fomenting war and killing slave laborers were added. Despite the gravity of the accusations and the large amount of evidence taken from the IG Farben's own records, no director received more than a four year prison sentence. A few even returned to sit on the board of directors at Bayer and Hoechst.

Since the German cartel was closely connected to the Nazi regime, the Allies wanted the IG Farben broken up into smaller and less influential companies. The plan for dismantling the IG Farben into three large and nine small companies was less radical than the original plan proposed by the U.S., but by the year of the plan's implementation, 1952, the focus of U.S. foreign policy had shifted away from Germany and toward Russia. Enmeshed in the Cold War, a distracted U.S. finally agreed with France and England not to break the IG Farben into smaller pieces.

The companies absorbed into the IG Farben had lost their corporate identity and this posed a problem for the Allied bureaucrats charged with the task of dividing up the cartel. In general, the largest three companies were given back their pre-1925 holdings. This meant that Hoechst inherited its original Frankfurt works. Over the objections of some Allies, Hoechst also managed to obtain Bobingen AG, a fiber manufacturer.

The newly organized Hoechst grew quickly. The German economy, rebounding from the war, needed chemicals, and Hoechst's factories had survived the Allied bombing attempts. In its first year of independence from the IG Farben, Hoechst had sales of DM 211 million. The next year, 1953, Hoechst obtained world rights (exclusive of the U.S.) to manufacture polyester. In 1954 the company began work with polyethylene and polyolefins; in 1956 it began to manufacture petrochemicals. By 1960 the company was clearly on its way to regaining its stature as one of the world's leading chemical companies. By the end of the decade, Hoechst achieved a compounded growth rate of 15.4% a year. To put this figure in perspective, one of the fastest growing American chemical companies during the 1960's, Union Carbide, had a compounded growth rate of 6.8%.

Hoechst's growth was much quicker than that of Bayer and BASF, because unlike the other two companies Hoechst did not invest in expensive petroleum projects, instead it purchased oil and gas through large term contracts. Hoechst also had a well-diversified product line that protected it from the volatility of the marketplace. Its largest division, paints and plastics, represented only 22% of sales. Plastics, fibers, agricultural chemicals, and pharmaceuticals completed the product line.

In 1963 Hoechst acquired a Dutch company that made plastic moldings. In 1965 the company built a Trevira polyester plant in neighboring Austria. In France that same year a venture in oxo-alcohols was started. In addition, Hoechst began manufacturing polystyrene in Spain.

Hoechst began the 1970's with sales of well over two million marks. In the early 1960's the company was only a third as large. On paper, the company's profit margin had decreased 9%, which is quite a decrease for an American firm. German businesses, however, have different bookkeeping procedures. They tend to minimize profits where American companies tend to inflate them.

The decrease in profits did not stop Hoechst's program of international expansion. Berger, Jenson and Nicholson, Britain's largest paint maker, was on the Hoechst shopping list, along with plans for expansion in India. Moreover, the United States, with its lower labor costs, was also an attraction. Germany was in the midst of a labor shortage, and the presence of Arabic and Mediterranean guestworkers was becoming a sensitive issue. American workers accepted lower salaries, were entitled to fewer fringe benefits, and were more amenable to layoffs than German workers.

In the midst of Hoechst's foreign expansion, pharmaceuticals emerged as a significant market. Hoechst had almost gained control of the entire diuretic market, and was a leader in oral medication for diabetics. During this time problems emerged with the maturation of some established drugs and also with drug pirating in Italy. However, pharmaceutical sales still managed to grow at a rate of 13% a year despite these setbacks. The growth was fueled by a production of antibiotics, serum and steroids, as well as a new hookworm medicine popular in Asia and Latin America.

By 1978 Hoechst was fortunate to possess a large line of pharmacological products because the company suffered losses in the fibers market. *Forbes* magazine estimated that in a period of three years Hoechst lost one billion marks. The earlier purchase of the Hercules Corporation's share of the South Carolina based Hystron Fibers Incorporated was of little comfort. Feedstocks were rising, prices were down, and patents had expired. There was little Hoechst could do but be thankful that its product line was well diversified.

During this time, the company continued its program of overseas expansion. In 1980 Hoechst built a $100 million plant in Freeport, Texas, the largest single investment it had made. With the addition of this plant Hoechst became larger than Du Pont. American Hoechst president John Brookhuis was proud of Hoechst's growth. "When our parent company celebrated its centennial there was especial joy that Hoechst world-wide had just passed Celanese Corporation in sales. Today Hoechst's sales are five times Celanese's."

Encouraged by its 20 years of growth, the management of Hoechst became determined to secure a larger share of the U.S. drug market. This would not be an easy task, even for Hoechst. Up to this point, a diuretic named Lasix accounted for 80% of U.S. sales. The first plan of action was to double the U.S. sales force, and also to target hospitals, the major customers for ethical drugs. The drive into America was part of Hoechst's long range plan to raise its share of international sales from three and a half to five percent of the world-wide market. Furthermore, as part of its strategy to make U.S. Hoechst one of the largest pharmaceutical houses, Hoechst has also been investigating the possibility of genetic engineering. A joint project with Massachusetts General Hospital has been arranged in order to use this new technology to create insulin in the laboratory.

One reason for Hoechst's expansion into the drug market, which began in the early 1980's and continues to the present day, is that the returns for drugs are higher than they are for basic chemicals. However enthusiastic the company had been in regard to international expansion, Hoechst will not expand in Venezuela or Italy. In Venezuela the company has not been allowed to raise its prices for 21 years and Italy's price controls and drug pirates make it "a drug market to forget," in the words of one German executive.

The expansion of the world's second largest chemical company is not, of course, limited to pharmaceuticals. In an ambitious move, Hoechst purchased the industrial ceramics division of Germany's largest fine china maker named Rosenthal. The Japanese presently control 90% of the market for semi-conductor ceramics, but Hoechst is determined to take away some of Japan's share. Hoechst will have to invest a substantial sum of money in the business to be competitive, but with profits increasing 80% in 1984, company management is not anticipating a cash flow problem.

Hoechst's future appears to be quite promising. Since 1970 it has been larger than the IG Farben from which it sprang. The company has a few worries including protectionism and a high debt to equity ratio, but its worldwide market, foreign production facilities and diversified product line will insulate it from many undue economic and political trends. With its de-emphasis on basic chemicals and synthetic fibers, the threat from oil-rich chemical industries faced by many American producers is minimal for Hoechst.

Hoechst plans to increase its product line in pharmaceuticals and industrial ceramics, whose success depends on technical superiority. To that end, Hoechst has continued to spend approximately four percent of total sales on research and development, which is more than Du Pont. The company's large research budget is evidence of the fact that Hoechst management thinks in terms of long term rather than short term benefits. According to one Hoechst executive, "American corporations have to show they can make more and more profits from quarter to quarter. We are not using that yardstick." If, as this quote implies, Hoechst measures its success by how well it is positioning itself for the future, then it is a successful company indeed.

Principal Subsidiaries: Ruhrchemie AG; Behringwerke AG; Asid Bonz und Sohn GmbH; Hoechst Veterinaer GmbH; Uhde GmbH; Uhde Services und Consulting GmbH; Herberts GmbH; Helmstedter Lack-umd Chemische Fabrik GmbH; Permatex GmbH; Spies, Hecker GmbH; Standox GmbH; Hoffmann & Engelmann AG; Marbert GmbH; Balenciaga GmbH; Wohnungsbau Hoechst GmbH; Decker & Eisenhardt, Essigessenz-Verk. GmbH; Boehringer & Reuss GmbH; Farbw.Schroeder & Stadelmann GmbH; Goldbach GmbH; Hoechst Versicherungs-AG; Peralta Handel GmbH; Ernst Michalke GmbH & Co.; Spinnstofffabrik Zehlendorf AG (96.7%); Hoechst Ceram Tec AG; Messer Griesheim GmbH (66⅔%); Oxytechnik GmbH; Oxysaar Huettensauerstoff GmbH (75%); Cassella AG (over 75.59%); Jade Cosmetic GmbH; Cassella-Riedel Pharma GmbH; Riedel-de Haen AG (over 76%); Cassella-med GmbH (51%); Albert Roussel Pharma GmbH (74.9%); Ticona Polymerwerke GmbH (59%); Wacker-Chemie GmbH (50%); SIGRI GmbH (50%); Benckiser-Knapsack GmbH (50%); Abieta Chemie GmbH (50%).

Further Reading: Around the World with Chemistry by Kurt Lanz, New York, McGraw Hill, 1980; *Industry and Ideology: IG Farben in the Nazi Era* by Peter Hayes, London, Cambridge University Press, 1987.

HÜLS A.G.

Paül Baumean-Strasse 1
Postfach 1320
D-4370 Marl 1
Federal Republic of Germany
(02365) 49-1

Subsidiary of Veba A.G.
Incorporated: 1953
Employees: 14,711
Sales: DM 6.544 billion (US$ 3.369 billion)

Hüls was founded in 1938, but it really should celebrate the year 1888. That was when tires were invented, and without tires and the consequent demand for rubber, there would have been no synthetic rubber. Without synthetic rubber, there would have been no Hüls. The first patent for synthesising rubber was filed in 1909, but the process was too expensive for commercial exploitation. After the automobile increased the need for tires, experiments began in earnest again. Based on the work of the Nobel prize-winners Carl Bosch, Fritz Haber, and Friedrich Bergius, Buna was created. First made in 1926, Buna was an economical synthetic rubber, based on coal and using sodium as a catalyst.

In the fall of 1935, the first experimental plant for the production of Buna was built by I.G. Farbenindustrie. A year later, the German Government issued its second Four Year Plan, in which the importance of Buna production to the country's strength was stressed. On 9 May 1938 Chemische Werke Hüls GmbH was founded specifically for the production of Buna, with a capital stock of 30 million marks. I.G. Farbenindustrie owned 74% and Bergwerksgesellschaft Hibernia A.G. owned 26% of the new company. The first managing directors were Otto Ambros and Friedrich Brüning, and on the board were Dr. Fritz ter Meer and Wilhelm Tengenmann. All four men were representatives of the shareholding companies.

Construction of new factories was difficult during wartime, yet labor was obtained because the Nazis urgently needed Buna. The factory was built very quickly and, in August 1940 production began. The annual capacity for production was 18,000 tons of Buna. The capital stock was immediately increased to 80 million marks. The company also produced chlorine, antifreeze, and other chemicals. In 1941 the production of Buna was increased to 40,000 tons annually. From this time, the chemists at Hüls began to work on the production of solvents, softening agents,

and resins. Production was increased to 50,000 tons in 1942 and capital was raised to 120 million.

It was not until 1943 that the war began to affect Hüls negatively. The company had great difficulty in obtaining raw materials and surviving bomb attacks. The worst was a heavy daylight air raid on 11 June 1943, when 1,560 bombs were dropped on Hüls factories. The works were devastated, 186 people were killed, and 752 were wounded. Production stopped for three months. In spite of more heavy bombing of the hydrogenation plants to stop the supply of raw materials, by 1944 the Hüls works reached maximum production capacity again, though they were still a main target of the bomb attacks. On 29 March 1945 a special unit of the German Army appeared with orders to blow up all of Hüls. It was Hitler's command that "the enemy should find nothing." The unit was persuaded to disobey these orders by Dr. Paul Baumann. Two days later, American troops marched into the factories.

Paul Baumann was one of the chemists who had worked on the development of Buna. He fought in World War I, then studied in Heidelberg with the Nobel prize-winner Philipp Lenard. Baumann received his doctorate in 1923, and first worked for I.G. Farbenindustrie, spending time at their offices in Baton Rouge, Louisiana. At Hüls he was quickly promoted to production manager. In 1945, when the British troops replaced those of the Americans, Baumann was made manager of works, then chairman of the board.

In 1945 the British, who were paying high prices for natural rubber at home, allowed the resumption of the production of Buna. At their orders, the company's name changed to Chemische Werke Hüls. The Potsdam agreement then forbad the production of Buna in Germany, and in order to survive the company had to change its products immediately. As the country was short of everything after the war, Hüls had no problem coming up with new products, but there were other problems, chiefly with the customers. Hüls sold a preparation that was meant to be used against scabies. When it was discovered that this was being used to make illegal liquor, the product had to be withdrawn. A lice-killer also had to be withdrawn when it was learned that people were using it as a substitute for petrol. The list of other products Hüls was permitted to make in 1945 included softening agents, artificial resins, detergents, gasses, colorings, antifreeze, and pharmaceuticals. Its mains product, after the erratically produced Buna, was acetic acid.

In November 1945 the entire company was taken over by the Allied authorities and put under a financial control office. The "de-Nazification" included the dismissal of Hans Gunther and Ulrich Hoffman. Other dismissals were planned but, as they would have meant the administrative collapse of the company, were not effected. The I.G. Farbenindustrie sales offices, Hüls's main outlets, were closed by the Allies. Hüls then co-operated with other companies on sales, but as this was regarded as joint operations, it too was stopped. All production of Buna was formally stopped by the British in 1948, partly as English, French, and Dutch colonies were experiencing a natural rubber boom, but also because the production of synthetic rubber was seen as potentially useful in the rebuilding of a German military effort. Hüls was faced with large numbers of employees and not enough work for them. The company began to produce vinyl chloride, propylene oxide, emulsifiers, and the polyvinyl chloride called Vestolit, but even so in 1949, many employees were made redundant, and plant works capable of producing 900 tons had to be dismantled.

In 1948 Hüls rather cleverly created "produkt 1973," a synthetic rubber made by the same process as that for Buna but with a few steps reversed. (It was also called "umgekehrte Buna," literally "Backward Buna.") This was to be used in linoleum. Both the forward and the backward Buna required butadien for production. In 1949 the Allied governments banned all butadien. Hüls protested, but, as it was one of the few companies to escape the total disbanding of its works by the allies, it restrained its protests. Generally, Hüls was better treated than other companies after the war, in part because of its ability to change its production to acceptable areas, and of the ability of Paul Baumann to get on so peaceably with the Allies. Additionally, Hüls was a major producer of fertilisers, which were considered vital to the agricultural economy.

In 1950, when the rest of the world dreaded that the Korean War might become World War III, Hüls was pleased to record a turnover increased by 50.4%. Colonial unrest cut off the supply of natural rubber to the Allies, and in 1951 the production of some 6,000 tons of Buna was permitted. This was on the condition that all coal export agreements were honoured first. The mines of Germany could not produce enough coal, so Hüls was forced to import coal from the United States. Not enjoying this arrangement, Hüls built its own small, temporary mine until the German mines could increase production.

The I.G. Farbenindustrie was disbanded by the Allies in Frankfurt in 1952. On 19 December 1953 Hüls was released from Allied control and converted to a joint stock company with a capital stock of DM 120 million. The following year, the company invested DM 85 million to expand plant production capacity. New products included Vestolen, a high-density polyethylene, and Vestopal, a polyester resin.

For some time, the production of Buna had ceased to be profitable, and the company had been working on ways to improve and modernise the antiquated production procedures. A new plant was proposed and a new company, Bunawerke Hüls GmbH, was formed in 1955. The shareholders were Hüls, with 50%, and its old partners from I.G. Farbenindustrie, in the guise of that company's three successors. Dr. Baumann was the managing director. In a very short time, Bunawerke was the largest producer of synthetic rubber in Europe.

Hüls grew apace. It built Power Station II, the first coal power station to operate on supercritical steam. In 1956 Quimica Industrial Huels do Brasil Ltda. was formed in Brazil. Plants were either converted or constructed to produce latices and reinforcing agents, phthalic anhydride, and more acetylene. In 1961 the capital stock was increased to DM 120 million and Faserwerke Hüls GmbH was founded, with a capital of DM 33.6 million, to produce synthetic fibers.

In 1959, quarter of a century after Hüls had begun manufacturing heavy detergents, it was discovered that they were major polluters of the environment. A law was passed in 1961 requiring that all detergents be reduceable by 80% by the existing sewage plants. Three years later Hüls produced Marlon, a biodegradable surfactant. The whole episode was a minor setback in the phenomenal growth of Hüls, which continued to form new companies, introduce new chemicals, and establish new partnerships until, in 1971, its capital reached DM 310 million.

VEBA and Bayer had long been owners of equal amounts of Hüls stock. This led to squabbles. In 1978, VEBA bought out Bayer, increasing its shareholding of Hüls to 87.6%, and thus acquiring control. A reorganisation was arranged, transferring all of VEBA-Chemie A.G. (now VEBA Oel A.G.) to Hüls. Throughout the early 1980s, Hüls built plants all over Germany for a variety of functions, from sludge burning to the production of n-butl-ene and powdered rubber. In 1985, The Chemische Werke Hüls changed its name to Hüls Aktiengesellschaft. In 1986, total sales were DM 6,544.5 million for the group; Hüls A.G. employed 14,711 people, down from the 1980 high of over 18,000, for whom it provided nearly 10,000 housing units. As the chemical arm of VEBA, the company has gained security and support and expects to continue to expand.

Principal Subsidiaries: Bunawerke Huls GmbH (50%); Phenolchemie GmbH; GAF-Huls Chemie GmbH (50%); Verwallungsgesellschaft Huls mbH; Buna France S.A.R.C. (50%); RUHR-STICKSTOFF AG; Katalysatorenwerke Huls GmbH; Kunststoffwerk Hohn GmbH (99%); Faserwerk Bottrop GmbH (99%); Deutsche Hefewerke GmbH (98.3%); Gipswerk Embsen GmbH & Co. Baustoffproduktion KG (50%); Rohm GmbH Chemische Fabrik (43.3%); Salzgewinnungsgesellschaft Westfalen GmbH (25%); Westgas GmbH (50%); Gemeinnutziges, Wohnungsunternehmen CWH GmbH (98%); Vestischer Vermittlungsdienst fur Versicherungen GmbH; Chemische Fariek SERVO B.V. The company also lists subsidiaries in the following countries: Belgium, Brazil, Denmark, France, Italy, Japan, The Netherlands, Spain, Sweden, Switzerland, United Kingdom and the United States.

IMPERIAL CHEMICAL INDUSTRIES PLC

Imperial Chemical House
Millbank, London SW1P 3JF
England

Public Company
Registered: December 7, 1926
Employees: 118,600
Sales: £10.114 billion (US$ 14.868 billion)
Market Value: £7,038 billion (US$ 10.346 billion)
Stock Index: New York London

Imperial Chemical Industries was formed by the 1926 merger of Great Britain's four major chemical companies: Nobel Industries Limited, the United Alkali Company, the British Dyestuffs Corporation and Brunner, Mond and Company Limited. The birth of the ICI coincided with the rise of the two other great chemical cartels, namely, Du Pont and the IG Farben. Unlike its foreign competitors, however, the ICI was never dismantled by the government.

Perhaps the most famous of the four companies that merged into the ICI was the dynamite business founded by Alfred Nobel. Before Nobel's invention of dynamite, blasting for engineering purposes had been done with gunpowder. Previous experiments with nitroglycerine, a more powerful substance, had ended disastrously. Nobel's contribution to explosives was twofold. He first mixed nitroglycerine with porous clay so that the nitroglycerine became relatively safe to handle. He then invented a detonating device that controlled the blast. Nobel's dynamite, more powerful and predictable than gunpowder, made ambitious civil engineering projects like the Suez canal possible. Dynamite was also important in clearing land for railroad tracks.

By 1883, 12 years after its founding, Nobel had built his British Dynamite Company into a company with £1 million in annual sales. Due to the dangers associated with making dynamite, Nobel's first large plant was located in a rural area of Scotland. Transportation was a problem for the company because Parliament had passed stringent laws concerning the transport of nitroglycerine. Many shipments of the explosive liquid had to be smuggled to factories—sometimes even in hat-boxes.

Like the Swede Alfred Nobel, the founder of Brunner, Mond and Company was also a foreigner. Ludwig Mond was a university-educated German Jew who emigrated to England, first of all, because the alkali industry was there and, secondly, because anti-semitism was on the rise in Germany. Despite an inauspicious beginning, in 1871 Mond and his partner John Brunner were able to build a strong alkali business on the grounds of a former girl's school. Mond and Brunner's contribution was to produce alkalis using the Solvay, rather than the Leblanc process.

The third alkali manufacturer that would become a part of the ICI was the United Alkali Company. The United Alkali Company began as an association of Lancashire producers who engaged in price-fixing and also set production quotas. Like its rival, the Brunner, Mond Company, the UAC conducted a large business in China and Japan in the mid-nineteenth century.

The fourth segment of the ICI, the British Dyestuffs Company, was formed much later than its three fellow companies. The BDC was formed as a response to the embargo of German dyes during World War I, which had seriously depressed some segments of British industry. In comparison with their American and German peers, British dye-makers were not technologically advanced. This was in part due to the large English textile industry which used its political and economic resources to keep dye prices low and thereby discourage research into more sophisticated production methods.

At the beginning of World War I the dynamite company founded by Nobel was a major supplier of ammunition. As the war progressed, however, there was less open warfare than predicted. Instead, the war developed into an extended seige and, as a result, high explosives rather than bullets were needed. These high explosives were very different in composition from Nobel's gunpowder. The TNT and lyddite that were required for English troops to blast their way through German defenses were coal tar derivatives, and these, of course, came from the dye industry. So the British Dye Company, to its surprise, found itself a manufacturer of armaments. Since TNT could be used more economically when mixed with ammonium nitrate, the Brunner, Mond Company, which by then was a major supplier of ammonia, was also pressed into service, along with the United Alkali Company.

In 1926 Nobel Industries Limited and the Brunner, Mond Company were the two largest companies in the otherwise enervated British chemical industry. Both companies had been shaken by the 1925 merger of many German chemical firms into the IG Farben—the largest cartel the world had ever seen. Since the IG Farben was in direct competition with British companies for exports, it was feared more than the Du Pont cartel which operated primarily in the United States.

Both Nobel and Brunner, Mond Company initially considered joining the IG Farben, but were unable to reach a satisfactory agreement with the Germans. After months of negotiations it was decided that a British cartel would be formed. The architects of this British cartel were Sir Harry McGowen of Nobel Industries and Sir Alfred Mond. British Dyestuffs and the United Alkali Company, weakened by a world-wide depression, were in no position to withstand pressure from their more powerful competitors and also agreed to the merger. The newly formed British cartel was soon in contact with Du Pont, Allied

Chemical and the IG Farben. According to Sir Harry McGowen, the formation of the Imperial Chemical Industries was "the first step in a comprehensive scheme . . . to rationalize the chemical manufacture of the world."

The newly formed Imperial Chemical Industries was divided into nine groups: alkalis, cellulose products, dyestuffs, explosives, fertilizers, general chemicals, "leathercloth" (rubberized fabric), lime and metals. Early in the ICI's history, fertilizers were chosen as the company's main growth area, and 10% of its capital was concentrated in a fertilizer plant in Billingham, England. By 1929 the onset of the Depression in the U.S. caused the demand for fertilizer to fall and the native demand was not large enough to support the huge Billingham works. In order to partially protect its investment the ICI signed an agreement with the IG Farben which established production quotas for nitrogen, the main ingredient in fertilizer. In 1935 it was agreed that the IG Farben would sell nitrogen in all of Europe, except for Spain and Portugal, and also South and Central America, while the ICI would control the markets in the United Kingdom, Spain, Portugal, Indonesia and the Canary Islands. It was agreed by both groups that the Asian market would be shared.

Despite the agreement with the IG Farben, nitrogen sales for the ICI decreased and the Billingham works were eventually closed. The ICI's return on equity dropped to 4% in the early 1930's. The company then tried to produce oil from coal, but despite government subsidies the oil produced by the ICI could not compete with regular oil. In the mid-1930's, with two failed plans behind it, the ICI finally began to give more attention to its neglected dyestuffs division.

Unlike American and German dyemakers, British dyemakers had never used their knowledge of chemistry to diversify into plastics, specialty chemicals or pharmaceuticals. The dyestuffs division, with only a small research budget, was able to begin production of agricultural and rubber chemicals around 1929. It was the alkali division and not the dyestuffs division which discovered polyethylene, one of the ICI's few contributions to the industry.

Polyethylene is a versatile plastic produced when ethylene is subjected to extreme pressure. Previous polyethylene experiments had exploded; therefore, in 1933 the ICI forbade its scientists to pressurize ethylene. However, in 1935 ICI researchers Perrin and Manning defied the ban and produced 8 grams of the polymer. Despite infighting over whether polyethylene would be developed by the alkali or plastics division, it was patented and sold as an insulating material.

ICI's work with polyethylene was interrupted by World War II. When Britain's rearmament began in 1935 ICI became a major producer for the British government. This pre-war production raised a problem for ICI in that the new plants built for the war effort would stand idle after hostilities ended and, consequently, could lead to bankruptcy for the company. ICI was reluctant to imitate Du Pont's policy and charge higher prices for their products in order to pay for the new construction. Fortunately an agreement was reached between the ICI and the British government whereby the government paid for the construction of new plants and the ICI managed them for a reasonable fee.

Almost every industry in Britain required ICI chemicals. In addition, munitions, light metals and guns were manufactured in ICI managed plants. During this time the ICI attempted to make an atomic bomb, but did not succeed. A disagreement between the director of the Manhatten project and the ICI resulted in company researchers not being allowed to work with American scientists on atomic research.

The end of the war brought two major changes for ICI. The first was a result of the anti-trust suit brought by the U.S. against the 800 various agreements the ICI had signed with Du Pont to regulate competition. Although the legal decision against the ICI-Du Pont partnership was not rendered until 1952, the exchange of technical information and cooperation on prices and markets ended in 1948. The second important post-war event was the 1952 opening of a huge chemical complex in Wilton, England. The Wilton works included a 4,000 ton nylon polymer unit as well as ammonia and hydrogen plants, and production facilities for phenol and organic chemicals. Despite this new complex, however, most of the ICI's productive capacity was obsolete.

ICI, unlike the largest German and American chemical companies, did not prosper during the 1950's. There were two reasons why this happened. The first reason was that the company had lost its monopoly over the chemical markets of Britain and her colonies. The second reason was its outmoded productive capacity and old-fashioned managerial style. ICI was not in a position to either defend its old territory or take advantage of the opportunities that "decartelization" offered.

Until the mid-1960's, the ICI continued on their same course. It was a small company in relation to its product line and rather than specializing in a few products that it could have efficiently manufactured in large plants, ICI manufactured hundreds of products inefficiently. *Forbes* magazine, in describing this stage in ICI's history, said that, "Nothing short of a full-scale industrial revolution could have saved ICI."

Increased exports and larger and more efficient plants saved the company from bankruptcy. Beginning in 1965, the ICI initiated an ambitious building plan that included an ethylene cracker in Britain, fiber spinning operations in Germany, and a huge PVC plant in Bayonne, New Jersey. The course pursued by the ICI had some inherent risks, and most important of these was over-capacity. Nonetheless, the expansion permitted ICI to produce chemicals at a more competitive price. After the building plan was underway in 1967, sales in Europe increased an average of 33% a year until the end of the decade.

While ICI expanded externally in the late 1960's, internal changes were also taking place, the most important of which was a change in labor relations. Shop employees began to be paid weekly rather than hourly wages, and most enjoyed substantial raises. In return for the increase in their wages these workers began to assume duties and responsibilities that had previously been the concern of supervisors. By the early 1970's productivity had climbed 11%, although ICI remained behind its competitors in this respect.

The 1970's did not begin well for ICI. Between 1970 and 1972 ICI's profits declined 13% while profits for the largest U.S. chemical manufacturers increased between 18% and 26%. Throughout the decade profits were erratic. For example, the year 1974, when profits climbed to £568.6 million, was followed by a 33% drop in 1975. Despite inexpensive natural gas from the North Sea, plastics and fibers depressed profits in 1975 and subsequent years.

Although Britain had joined the Common Market in 1972, ICI focused its attention not on Europe but on the U.S. In 1971 ICI purchased Atlas Chemical Industries and was almost immediately issued a restraint of trade judgement. As a result, Atlas's explosives division had to be sold. Perhaps it was due to this experience that convinced management at ICI to concentrate more on American investments rather than on any further acquisitions. ICI's U.S. investment in 1977 included a paraquat plant in Bayport, Texas and a new laboratory for ICI Stuart Pharmaceuticals division.

In Britain the company's fertilizer division proved to be a consolation. After the discovery of natural gas in the North Sea during the previous decade, ICI had signed a long-term contract for inexpensive gas. ICI's feedstock for its ammonium nitrate fertilizer was so inexpensive that it would sell fertilizer for £60 a ton when the market price was £80. By 1975 ICI controlled over one half of the British market for ammonium nitrate. Prices fell so low that other fertilizer producers requested the British government to raise ICI's prices. The government, mindful of ICI's price-cutting escapades during the 1920's, threatened to introduce a pool-price system unless ICI increased its prices and refrained from keeping competitors out of the market.

All in all, the chemical company did not perform substantially better in the 1970's than it had in the previous two decades. It was still a large but often inefficient company committed to many products which were not profitable. The future began to look more promising in 1982, however, when Sir John Harvey-Jones took over the reins of ICI.

One of Harvey-Jones' major accomplishments was to end ICI's dependence on bulk chemicals which had accounted for 40% of profits in 1979. After three years of his stewardship, this figure was reduced to 16%. Harvey-Jones also deemphasized polyethylene and concentrated on higher margin products like drugs and specialty chemicals instead. The results were impressive. By 1983 profits had climbed to $939 million, which was more than double the year before.

As part of ICI's revitalization program, Harvey-Jones began to look for additions to the company's product line. One of the more interesting products was polyester produced by genetically engineered bacteria fed on starch and water. This bacteria produced polyester has yet to make its

way into clothes manufacturing, but has had success as a surgical stitching.

In 1984 ICI launched a major acquisition campaign that has yet to end. ICI's first step was to buy Beatrice's chemical division for $750 million. This purchase was followed by many smaller purchases and then the 1986 purchase of Glidden Paint. Since the acquisition of Glidden ICI's paint shipments have been increasing at a healthy rate of 7%, twice the industry average.

An ICI executive was quoted in 1986 as saying that ICI has enough cash to acquire two more companies the size of Glidden. Indeed, the company seems poised for such acquisitions since it has asked to extend its borrowing limit from $7.5 to $10 billion. However, the company still confronts many problems. During 1985 profits slipped 12%. ICI blamed the decline on the strength of the pound, but *The Economist* magazine cited a continuing problem with bulk chemicals and also a decrease in fertilizer sales. Additionally, the plastics market was plagued by overcapacity, as usual. ICI has reduced its dependence on low-margin products like fertilizers and bulk chemicals, but it also must become less dependent on its former staples.

In 1964 Forbes reported that ICI's problems were inveterate in that ICI had been designed to dominate the British Empire, leaving the U.S. to Du Pont and Europe to the IG Farben. However, as the British Empire dissolved the ICI found itself laden with slow moving products and, as a result, unable to compete with the other international companies. This theory has been corroborated by the ICI's post-war performance. Under Harvey-Jones ICI has finally started to re-orient itself towards more profitable goods, but this program will take time.

Harvey-Jones retired in 1987, and the future of ICI may depend on the shrewdness of his successor, Denys Henderson. Most western chemical companies have reached the same conclusion as ICI, namely, that drugs and specialty chemicals are the wave of the future and that bulk chemicals are no longer profitable. As ICI continues to diversify into more value-added products it is going to confront increasingly intense competition. Only time will tell if ICI's upward trend can sustain itself.

Principal Subsidiaries: ICI Petroleum Ltd.; ICI Finance Ltd.; Nobel's Explosives Co., Ltd.; Scottish Agricultural Industries plc (62%). The company also lists subsidiaries in the following countries: Argentina, Australia, Canada, China, France, India, Japan, Malaysia, The Netherlands, New Zealand, Pakistan, South Africa, West Germany, and the United States.

Further reading: Imperial Chemical Industries: A History by W.J. Reader, London, Oxford University Press, 1970; *Chemical Foundations: The Alkali Industry in Britain to 1926* by Kenneth Warren, London, Oxford University Press, 1980; *The Spatial Organization of Multinational Corporations* by Ian M. Clarke, London, Croom Helm, 1985.

KOPPERS

KOPPERS INC.

1400 Koppers Building
Pittsburgh, Pennsylvania 15219
U.S.A.
(412) 227-2000

Public Company
Incorporated: September 30, 1944
Employees: 11,128
Sales: $1.396 billion
Market Value: $1.099 billion
Stock Index: New York

Although Koppers began as a manufacturer of by-product recovery coke ovens in 1912, its circuitous route through a number of acquisitions and diversified products classifies it as an early predecessor to a modern day conglomerate. From its long association with the Mellon family interests in Pittsburgh's heavy industry, to its forays into chemicals, plastics, wood products, and even buttons, the company has struggled to secure its own identity in the face of cyclical markets and dependence on capital goods spending. While the impressive returns earned during the 1970's expansion into chemicals were interrupted by a depressed market in the 1980's, Koppers' recent growth is a result of its operations as an integrated paving contractor.

In the 1920's an entrepreneur from Virginia purchased a small coke oven company in an attempt to build a consortium of companies to integrate all aspects of coal production. Henry B. Rust then solicited support from Andrew Mellon, one of the nation's leading financiers and industrialists, and was soon operating a vast network of holding companies engaged in mining, railroad transportation, shipping, utilities, and steel mills. Rust's conglomerate, named Kopper United, successfully exploited all the potential uses of coal and subsequently became the favorite of Mellon's industry operations. However, their empire was short lived. The Depression came and with it Roosevelt's Public Utility Holding Company Act which forced the company to sell the Eastern Gas & Fuel Associates. By losing this division that directed the coal, utility and railroad operations, the company relinquished control of its integrated coal orientation. Of the remaining former empire, the manufacturing and engineering divisions evolved into what is today known as Koppers Incorporated.

The traditional business of manufacturing by-product coke ovens and products related to coal such as tar

became, once again, Koppers' major source of income. Yet sensing the company had lost its direction, the Koppers board of directors (with the Mellon family representing a major presence) appointed Brehon Burke Somervell, a World War II four-star general, to assume control of the operations. As chief executive officer, Somervell proposed that the company follow a delineated course of action by imposing a strict military hierarchy. Minutiae of detail demarcating job responsibilities, limits of authority, and centralized powers were codified in books. While many found this method of leadership incompatible with the industry, Somervell's plan was to create an environment conducive to generating new technologies. The General's tenure at Koppers was shortened by illness; upon his death in 1955 he had only directed the company for five years.

Although the rigid organizational structure was abandoned after Somervell's death, the World War II veteran had successfully launched a campaign into the new areas of chemicals and plastics. Fred Foy, a company executive who had served under the General during the war, assumed Somervell's position and continued his predecessor's program of diversification. Before joining Koppers, Foy worked as vice president at J. Walter Thompson and also worked at Ford. By 1956 sales gained from the company's plastic operations heralded a long awaited revitalization of the almost 50-year old company. Unfortunately, intense competition from large companies in petroleum caused a volatile price war. After this price war had ended, Koppers reported low profit figures.

The results from the plastic campaign did not represent Koppers' only disappointment; the old product line also suffered from poor performance figures. Shares earning $5.01 in 1956 now earned almost half that at $3.01. To prevent any further profit decrease Foy, along with his energetic young president Fletcher L. Byron, held a policy planning meeting. Together the two executives decided on strict measures to reduce costs and consolidate businesses. 19 plants producing low profits were closed and the Engineering and Construction division, which builds plants for the steel and iron industries, acquired a general contracting firm. This subsidiary, purchased for $20 million, released the division from sole dependence on the cyclical steel industry by encouraging business in other fields. By 1960 the first nine-month earnings figures posted a healthy 50% increase. While much of these encouraging numbers resulted from sales in the Engineering and Construction division, closer inspection revealed a backlog of orders carried over from the previous year had artificially increased the new year figures.

The entry into the chemicals field, initiated 12 years earlier under Somervell, remained a disappointment. While some 60% of the $300 million sales could be traced to chemicals, Koppers' profits remained far behind competing chemical companies. This discrepancy resulted from the company's dependence on old-line products at the expense of new technologies. While competitors manufactured innovative plastics such as styrene, polystyrene, and polyethylene, Koppers produced age-old products such as roofing pitch and road-paving items. A major integration of plastics operations did not occur until the mid-1950's, well behind the industry-wide movement. To remedy this situation, Foy announced plans to market an innovative plastic building panel and double capacity projections for polystyrene production. By bolstering the chemical operations through the sale of new plastics, as well as attempting to provide an entry for old products into new markets, Foy hoped to mitigate the effects of chronic fluctuations in the market for engineering and construction products.

Working alongside Foy in this major revision of company operations was the indefatigable Byron. The company president joined Koppers as an assistant to a division manager soon after World War II and in the following thirteen years he assumed eight different positions of increasing responsibility. The son of a coal buyer at the American Steel & Wire Company, Bryon decided at an early age that his career was in the steel industry. After college he joined the same company that employed his father and began working as a sales trainee. During World War II Bryon took a leave from the company to work as a coordinator for a research project at the Naval Ordnance Laboratory in Washington. After participating in the conceptualization of surface-to-air missiles, Byron decided at the end of the war to return to the steel company. When American Steel responded with only lukewarm enthusiasm, Byron applied for a job at Koppers.

In three years he was promoted to plant superintendent after helping negotiate a compromise to a strike at a West Virginia plant. In a daring act of independence, Bryon spent $500,000 to replace aging equipment without the authority of his supervisor. When the replacement equipment upgraded plant productivity so that in just over a year profits jumped from negative figures to $2 million, Bryon's grateful superiors forgave him his impetuosity. The company then sent the young executive to a management training program at the Harvard Business School where he was exposed for the first time to an intellectual environment full of different ideas and philosophies. This exposure eventually led to the implementation of a highly decentralized, yet intellectually demanding, approach to business which would characterize Byron's 15 year tenure as chief executive officer at Koppers.

In 1960 Foy, retaining titles of both chairman and chief executive, promoted Byron to president. This promotion came after initially rejecting the candidate as too young. Four years later the Byron-Foy team had successfully molded a company whose revenues surpassed the $1 billion mark. By identifying expandable markets, Koppers began producing piston rings for high-speed diesel engines which accounted for over 50% of net income in one year. Similarly, Koppers ranked fifth among domestic producers of polyester resins and ranked high among those producing phthalic anhydride. One particularly successful branch of Koppers polyester resin business was the manufacture of buttons. By 1976 this business alone generated a $6 million revenue.

The foray into plastic building panels proved less successful because marketing of the unusual product demanded time-consuming and expensive planning. Similarly, an attempted partnership to produce polyethylene

from Koppers plastic division using ethylene manufactured by the Sinclair Oil Company also failed to generate hoped for profits. Despite an impressive beginning the joint venture fell victim to intensive competition from other oil companies. This failed venture ended Koppers' participation in the thermoplastic and petrochemical markets.

Notwithstanding these disappointments, Koppers' overall performance in the 1970's caused common stock shares to triple in value as management announced a two-for-one split. By 1979 earnings reached a high of $3.21 a share. To encourage growth, Byron guided Koppers into several high technology projects. Purchasing 30% of Genex Corporation, a recombinant-DNA research company, Byron's strategy suggested many benefits for Koppers' organic chemical production. It was hoped that the research would discover the process to genetically engineer resorcinol, a product previously manufactured by a traditional method. Additional plans were underway to explore synfuel processes such as coal gasification.

By 1980, however, company equity dropped from 20.3% to 17.1%. A depressed market started by a recession in the economy once again had adverse effects on company performance. Apart from the cyclical nature of the market, industry observers began blaming internal structural problems for Koppers' ailing profit margins. While Byron's decentralized policy of encouraging middle managers to assume greater responsibility in decision making actually allowed for a certain number of mistakes, the costs of these mistakes started to reflect on productivity. Miscalculations and faulty equipment forced write-offs and reduced profit margins.

While Byron promised better returns once an assured turn in the economy revived capital spending, he continued to pursue his unorthodox policy of management. This policy promoted the delegation of authority to such a degree that much of Byron's time was actually spent outside the area of daily decision making. By giving priority to the intellectual and civic responsibilities believed to be incumbent upon himself as a business leader, Byron functioned more as a spiritual guide then an actual company director. Not only did he traverse the country on a lecture circuit where he spoke in front of audiences from prominent universities and businesses, he also conducted tri-monthly seminars for his own young executives to examine the philosophies of such thinkers as John Kenneth Galbraith, John Maddox and Michael Harrington.

By 1981 profits dropped $2.4 million to a total of $51.8 million. Instead of patiently waiting for the recession to end, management announced an effort to reduce capital outlays and sell unprofitable businesses. Selling up to 18% of poorly performing operations in all four of the major divisions, as well as allotting just $110 million for capital spending, Koppers' management hoped to find immediate relief for the company's disappointed shareholders. High-technology research remained a protected project as maturing operations in the wood and forest division were terminated. The ascension of Charles R. Pullin to the positions of chairman and chief executive officer gave further impetus to this consolidation effort.

A former president of Koppers' Road Material group Pullin, unlike his predecessor, throughly immersed himself in day-to-day operations. The new company leader grew up in West Virginia as the son of a steel worker. A high school summer job with the state highway department directed his ambitions toward the roadbuilding industry. From the time he joined Koppers in 1946 as a technical service engineer to his final promotion to top management, Pullin was employed in the roadbuilding industry. Although some of that time was spent at another construction company, he returned to Koppers when the new road materials division needed an experienced leader.

While Pullin continued to invest money in high technology research, Koppers' most impressive results emerged from the division closest to Pullin's experience, namely, Road Building. Two new ventures in innovative production increased research spending to $88 million in 1984. These projects included the exploration of engine technology and the development of plant disease diagnostic equipment. Koppers' recovery, however, did not result from revenues generated from these new technologies; rather it was traditional blacktop roadway production that symbolized the beginning of the company's revitalization. During the first six months of 1984 the Road Building division generated $274.5 million of the $811 million in total revenues. By developing an integrated operation, independent of subcontractors, Koppers emerged as the first nation-wide paving comany. Furthermore, the five-cent-a-gallon fuel tax included in the Surface Transportation Act allocated funds for the rehabilitation of the nation's highways. Koppers moved to capitalize on this growing market.

As road building emerged as the mainstay of company profits, Pullin reduced Koppers investment in technological research. The 30% stake in Genex failed to produce the sought after financial rewards. As a result, it was sold along with several other mature businesses. Some $360 million in assets were generated from the sale of the coke ovens, button, and several wood product operations. This housecleaning included the sale of Koppers' original steel industry construction business; a hard decision for many of Koppers' executives. In addition, Pullin reduced capital spending by reducing Koppers' work force.

Thus as nationwide spending for bridge and road construction increased 17% between 1983 and 1986, Koppers successfully exploited the market trend. The price of common stock, decreasing in 1985, increased to a high of $27 per share in 1986. While federal spending on road repairs remains subject to the volatility of political decisions, Pullin nevertheless announced plans to generate a 18% return on equity in the near future. This goal appears over-ambitious to many industry observers. Wall Street analysts, however, predicted a healthy 10% return by the end of 1987. The company's greatest potential appears to be in the traditional business of road paving—quite a detour from its diversified operations of 75 years.

Principal Subsidiaries: Broderick & Gibbons, Inc.; Cherokee Crushed Stone, Inc.; Eastern Rock Products, Inc.; Echols Brothers, Inc.; Fairfield Bridge Co, Inc.; General Crushed Stone Co.; Sim J. Harris Co.; Ivy Steel & Wire Co., Inc.; Kaiser Sand & Gravel Co.; Kentucky Stone Co.; Koppers Engineered Products Ltd.; Lycoming Silica Sand Co.; The McMichael Co.; Nello L. Teer Co.; Sloan Construction Co.; Sterling Paving Co.; Sterling Sand & Gravel Co.; Sully-Miller Contracting Co.; Thiem Corporation; Western Paving Construction Co.

L'AIR LIQUIDE

75 Quai d'Orsay
75007 Paris
France
5554430

Public Company
Incorporated: 1902
Employees: 25,000
Sales: FFr 19.162 billion (US$ 2.979 billion)
Market Value: FFr 28.380 billion (US$ 4.412 billion)
Stock Index: Paris

L'Air Liquide, one of the world's largest producers of industrial gases, currently commands approximately 25% of the world market. Industrial gases find multiple applications in a diversity of products. The areas of chemistry, industry, agriculture, pharmacy, electricity, biology, papermaking, glassmaking, and medicine all use industrial gases. The company conducts operations in four sectors: industrial gases, welding and cutting, engineering and construction, and chemicals and sundries. Founded in 1902, the company prospered under the acclaimed chemist Georges Claude. L'Air Liquide presently operates more than 430 plants in 55 countries. Five research centers, the newest located in Chicago, contribute to the continued achievements of the company.

Georges Claude received his diploma in chemistry from the School of Physics and Chemistry in 1889. From 1896 to 1902 he worked as a chemist at Compagnie Française Houston-Thompson. While employed there he attempted to develop a process for handling acetylene. The chemical, discovered only a few years earlier, posed several difficulties for industrial use; in particular the expense of production and storage made it economically unfeasible for wide-scale use. At the age of 26, Claude solved these problems and discovered a method for liquefying acetylene. Professor Land, a German chemist, had succeeded earlier in separating oxygen and nitrogen. However, the gases converted by Land's "counter-current procedure" contained 40% impurities. The triumph of Claude's process, acclaimed by the Academy of Science and Chemistry, returned gases with less than 1% impurities.

Claude's research led him to believe that air gases, produced and stored economically, could serve as viable and inexpensive sources of energy. He envisioned oxygen and nitrogen as sources of power for combustion engines. Claude's process for separating air gases resulted in the emission of large quantities of heat. However, many of his early experiments failed. They were expensive to undertake and the young chemist had no financial resources of his own to rely upon. Good ideas, Claude realized, needed financing if they were to become anything more than ideas.

Paul Delorme, a former schoolmate and co-worker at Houston-Thompson, encouraged his friend Frédéric Gallier to match his own financial contribution to Claude's research. In November of 1902 Delorme and Gallier each contributed FFr 50,000 to the fledgling enterprise; the company was formally constituted, and Paul Delorme was named president, a position which he held until 1945. The bulk of the company's original 26 shares were entrusted to Claude.

During the early years the company suffered from financial hardships, but the business skills of Paul Delorme carried L'Air Liquide through these difficult times. In 1903 Delorme issued 725 new shares and offered 100 of these shares for sale. By the third quarter of 1906, L'Air Liquide had overcome its financial problems, and during that year the company earned its first dividends. Since that time L'Air Liquide has continued to prosper and has, without interruption (even during the war years), earned dividends.

Under the direction of Delorme, L'Air Liquide established plants in Belgium and Brazil in 1906, and continued to expand into overseas markets; plants were set up Spain (1910), Japan (1911), and Canada and Sweden (1913). One of the earlier inventions of Claude, neon lighting, appeared on the streets of Paris in 1910. (He had applied for the first patent on neon tubes in 1907.) In 1908 L'Air Liquide began producing oxygen and is now one of largest producers in Europe. Immediately prior to and during World War I, Claude designed machinery to improve the production of ammonia. His work with liquid oxygen at this time led to technological innovations in explosives.

The inter-war years were ones of continued overseas expansion for L'Air Liquide . Plants were established in Greece, Singapore, Hong Kong, Malaysia, Portugal, and Senegal. In this period Claude concentrated his efforts on the separation and utilization of rare atmospheric gases. His engineering skills overcame the practical difficulties and Claude was able to improve on his process for separating hydrogen. Through several stages of cooling, using liquid carbon monoxide as the coolant, hydrogen was compressed. His success with hydrogen produced a lubricant which could be used for driving motors. Employing nitrogen, the gas was injected into the motor and provided an efficient lubricant down to −211 degrees fahrenheit. No other lubricant product had proved to be so efficient at this temperature.

Claude regarded the oceans as the most abundant yet untapped source of energy on the globe, and during the 1930's he began experimenting with thermodynamic principles to take advantage of this energy source. His efforts in this area did not have any immediate practical results, but following World War II the Academy of Sciences used his principles of thermodynamics and started to build a thermodynamic plant off the coast of Cuba. An accident caused the project to be cancelled, but L'Air Liquide continues to develop oceanic products; the company currently manufacture special equipment for deep-sea diving.

Following World War II the French High Court accused Claude of collaborating with the Nazis. Unconfirmed charges claimed that the development of the "flying bomb" resulted from Claude's work. In his defense, Claude stated that he believed in German victory under the auspices of Pétain in Vichy France. The Court, however, sentenced him to life imprisonment and stripped him of all honors. He was released from prison in 1950.

During the 1960's gas sales declined, and most of the major industrial gases manufacturers began to diversify their companies. But Jean Delorme, Paul Delorme's son, believed the potential market for gases remained strong, and under his leadership L'Air Liquide did not follow the movement to diversification. This decision improved the company's leading position in the industrial gases market. At the same time, L'Air Liquide pursued a policy of expansion through cautious acquisition, Delorme seeking to acquire only companies with an established customer base.

Unlike most industries, gases producers usually perform well during a recession; the real cost of gases actually declined during the 1970's. With other fuel costs rising, the incentive to use combustion engines, which use oxygen, increased. Improved technologies resulted in the intensified use of more efficient combustion engines. Recession, though, adversely affects the customer base which consumes industrial gases. Heavy industry, like steel manufacturing, was adversely affected by the recession of the 1970's, resulting in the reduction of demand for L'Air Liquide products. This trend continued into the 1980's as European and American steel makers reduced their capacities. In order to compensate for its losses, L'Air Liquide sold its unprofitable sectors.

Technological innovations pose another major threat to L'Air Liquide's markets. For example, new technologies have allowed steel manufacturers to do away with blast furnaces and the oxygen used to power them. However, L'Air Liquide recognized that these innovations have resulted in more efficient blast furnaces which, in turn, have maintained a demand for oxygen.

Welding accounts for 11% of L'Air Liquide's sales. This sector traditionally used oxy-acetylene in all its welding equipment. Oxy-acetylene, the hottest and most concentrated fuel gas, provided light before the invention of the electric light bulb. Yet the welding market for L'Air Liquide has recently declined. Laser technology now provides cleaner, safer machinery, replacing the traditional gas-fueled torch.

The smallest customers of industrial gases producers tend to be hospitals which purchase gases in cylinders. United States industrial gases manufacturers leave this market to the smaller producers. In Europe the larger manufacturers sell and cylinder gases, and then lease the cylinder. To some degree this practice insulates them against cyclical changes in the marketplace. However, the demand for cylinder gases, mainly oxygen and acetylene, is usually met by local producers since these gases can not be liquified and are dangerous to transport. Reductions in social security drug reimbursements and lower health care expenditures have led some gases manufacturers in Europe to believe that the market may decline in this sector. These governmental policies, along with exchange rate fluctuations, have recently contributed to declining profits and sales for L'Air Liquide.

As early as 1916 L'Air Liquide entered into a joint venture with Rockefeller and Hollingsworth to form L'Air Reduction Company in the United States. After World War II, however, the French government forced L'Air Liquide to sell its U.S. holdings in order to assist France in diminishing its war debts. Not until 1969 did L'Air Liquide return to the United States. The highly international character of L'Air Liquide makes the company susceptible to parity changes between the French franc and the U.S. dollar. Recent efforts to increase L'Air Liquide's share of the United States market has contributed to this volatility. As L'Air Liquide's presence in the U.S. market grows, this vulnerability increases in importance. The limiting effects of the European Monetary System make this a lesser concern in the European markets; these markets account for 53% of the net sales of L'Air Liquide.

L'Air Liquide, however, acquired Big Three Industries of Texas in 1986 for $1.6 billion. This acquisition makes L'Air Liquide the second largest industrial gases manufacturer in the United States. The deal, financed by cash and U.S. borrowing, increased the company's United States market from approximately 14 to 20%. However, the Federal Trade Commission required L'Air Liquide to divest part of its holdings by selling certain sections of the company to ensure free competition and guard against monopolization of the industry within the U.S. by L'Air Liquide.

Air Products and Chemical, Inc., a leading U.S. competitor hoping to acquire a portion of L'Air Liquide's customer base, has begun building small plants, approximately one-eighth the size of the larger L'Air Liquide sites. Air Products believes that the structure of the larger firm slows down its ability to respond quickly to changing market conditions. Air Products hopes this will give it a competitive edge against L'Air Liquide.

Nevertheless, L'Air Liquide can expect to maintain a substantial share of its customer base in the U.S. First, the size of the company allows for large expenditures on research and development. Second, the nature of the industrial gases market entices companies to build plants next to established customers. Traditionally, the customer and the supplier enter into long-term contracts for 15 to 25 years. The supplier installs pipelines to the customer site and pumps the gases directly to the plant, alleviating expensive shipping costs.

AGA of Sweden and L'Air Liquide recently dissolved a 15-year co-operative agreement. The decision not to renew the agreement resulted in the increased presence of L'Air Liquide in Belgium and Luxembourg, while AGA increased its holdings in Germany, Holland, and The Netherlands. L'Air Liquide's management believes the termination of the agreement renders fewer constraints upon pursuing market opportunities throughout Europe, though the monopoly of the British market by BOC leaves Britain virtually inaccessible.

Business attitudes in France began to shift during 1986 in reaction to policies previously implemented by the former Socialist government. The trend toward an open economy with an emphasis on denationalization is also developing. L'Air Liquide, now a public company, can be expected to take greater advantage of these domestic trends.

The success of L'Air Liquide, represented by a doubling of its markets over the past five years, is impressive. De Royere, its current vice chairman, asserts that the company will continue to double its earnings every five years. During this time sales in the United States, Canada, Australia, Asia, and Africa increased from 20 to 36%, while the gas sector alone accounted for approximately 66% of net sales.

Although technological innovations potentially threaten the continued use of gases, L'Air Liquide exhibits its capability to adapt to changing market conditions. In 1985 the company entered into a joint venture with Whemo Denko of Japan to supply NASDA, the Japanese Space Agency, with liquid hydrogen. In addition, the rapidly growing electronics industry in Japan requires vector gases, nitrogen and hydrogen. The purification techniques developed by L'Air Liquide provide quality products for this market, with less than one part per billion of impurities. L'Air Liquide is second only to Nippon Sanso in this Japanese market.

New techniques in food processing require the use of carbon dioxide and nitrogen. The company has therefore started to package food products in inert atmospheres, another example of L'Air Liquide's response to changing market demands. The sale of agricultural fertilizers, utilizing air gases, declined in 1986, as part of an overall decline in the agricultural sector as a result of poor weather conditions and a weaker U.S. dollar. This sector of the business accounts for only 10% of the domestic market in France.

Although L'Air Liquide maintains a virtual monopoly in its home market, it continues to apply innovative measures to sustain its strong position. Products developed over the past 10 years account for more than 40% of current sales. The outlook for L'Air Liquide's continued growth appears positive. The company has always recognized the importance of responding to changing market conditions; this flexibility and foresight makes L'Air Liquide one of the most successful industrial gases manufacturers in the world today and will assist the company in maintaining its present market share.

Principal Subsidiaries: L'Air Liquide SA; Air Liquide International; Société Chimique de la Grande Paroisse (64.79%); Compagnie Française de Produits Oxygenes (99.85%); Société Anonyme de Fabrication de Genilis (99.99%); Société Industrielle des Gaz de l'Air (99.96%); SOGIF (98.84%); Compagnie Industrielle Commerciale et Financiere des Gaz; CRYOLOR (79.99%); ALM (60%); SEPAL (50.95%). The company also has subsidiaries in the following countries: Argentina, Australia, Austria, Belgium, Cameroon, Canada, Denmark, Gabon, Ghana, Greece, Italy, Luxembourg, The Netherlands, Nigeria, Paraguay, Portugal, Senegal, Sweden, Tunisia, United Kingdom, United States, and West Germany.

Further Reading: The Origins and Early Development of the Heavy Chemical Industry in France by John Graham Smith, Oxford, Clarendon Press, 1979.

LUBRIZOL CORPORATION

29400 Lakeland Blvd.
Wickliffe, Ohio 44092
U.S.A.
(216) 943-4200

Public Company
Incorporated: July 31, 1928
Employees: 5,200
Sales: $985 million
Market value: $1.533 billion
Stock Index: New York

When scrutinizing Lubrizol, the world's largest manufacturer of petroleum additives, industry analysts have to pinch themselves to make sure they aren't dreaming. Until recently the company had no long term debt. For decades at a time the stockholders consistently received a return of over 18% on their equity. And due to the nature of its product the company thrives on changes in the economy. When the price of oil is high, there is a greater demand for additives that extend the longevity of oils and lubricants. When the price of oil is low, people drive more and therefore use more motor oil, which expands the market for another kind of Lubrizol additive. Technical know-how and an ability to turn almost any economic situation to its advantage explain why even hardened analysts refer to Lubrizol as "gold-plated" and "a jewel."

The company was founded in 1928 by the Smith brothers–Kelvin, Kent and Vincent, the Nason brothers–Frank and Alex, and their friend Thomas W. James. The three Smith brothers had all worked at Dow Chemical, a company their father, a professor of chemistry, had helped to establish.

From its beginning the growth of Lubrizol, originally known as The Graphite Oil Products Company, was tied to the expansion of the petroleum and automobile industries. By working closely with manufacturers, or, in the case of short-sighted automobile makers, by staying one step ahead, Lubrizol was able to carve out an unassailable niche for itself. The company's first product, a suspension of graphite in oil, was formulated to prevent car springs from creaking.

After this initial success, the young men addressed a more serious problem. Early automobile engines were lubricated with mineral oil, which meant that the engines overheated frequently, and that their pistons would stick because of the heat or accumulated sludge. When this

happened the driver had to pull over and wait for the engine to cool. The chemists at Graphite Oil discovered that by adding chlorine to lubricants the problem of overheating was alleviated. This new product, and later the whole company, was named Lubrizol, although no one knew what the "zol" stood for. Soon auto repair shops and car dealers were ordering the strangely named oil, along with specialty lubricants tailor-made for specific models of engines.

In 1935 Alex Nason traveled to Detroit to promote his small company, but General Motors scoffed at the idea of adding chemcials to oil in order to increase engine performance. At the time, G.M.'s diesel engines became so clogged with impurities that they had to be stripped and cleaned every 500 hours. Eventually the auto manufacturer was convinced of the value of gasoline and lubricant additives, and added Lubrizol products to its list of recommended products for car care.

During World War II Lubrizol supplied its products to the military. In order to keep its equipment in optimum running condition the government established scientific tests and rigorous performance standards for all lubricants. After the war standards for lubricants used in passenger cars were also set. Since Lubrizol had patented important processes and ingredients in the manufacture of high quality lubricants, it profited from the new regulations. In 1942 the company decided to abandon the manufacture of oils and lubricants, and to concentrate solely on petroleum additives like oxidation inhibiters, detergents, and chemicals to reduce oil breakdown at high temperatures. These additives were then sold to the major oil refineries.

By the 1950's Lubrizol was selling more petroleum additives than any other company in the world, yet it was still a privately held corporation with less than 5,000 employees. There were many factors in its success. One factor was the nature of the additive industry. Lubrizol sold its additives primarily to oil companies and, interestingly enough, its only competitors were oil companies. When a company like Exxon needed an additive it did not manufacture itself, it preferred to buy the additive from Lubrizol rather than a rival oil company. Additionally, Lubrizol's status as an independent company often appealed to nationalized oil industries for political reasons. In the 1960's Lubrizol was the sole supplier of additives to the nationalized oil industry in Peru which was, for ideological reasons, reluctant to deal with the major companies in the petroleum industry.

But Lubrizol's position as a supplier to a handful of huge companies was not without a certain amount of risk. This became apparent in the mid-1950's when Texaco decided to make its own fuel additives. This single corporation had purchased nearly a quarter of Lubrizol's total output, so its defection was painful. Today defections such as Texaco's are less likely because inflation has increased the already formidable start-up costs for an additives operation.

Despite its problem with Texaco the company flourished. It did not, however, expand. The company philosophy has always been "to grow, but not get big" in the words of one executive. The president at the time, Mr. Clapp, said "Our goal is to increase earnings to shareholders in a business we understand." Consequently, Lubrizol was reluctant to diversify. Until the acquisition of Agrigenetics Corporation in 1985, company policy was to buy companies only as strong as Lubrizol, and there were not many chemical firms that fit this description. In the 1950's the company made its first acquisition, the R.O. Hull Company, which made rust-proofing chemicals. This company, which rarely accounted for more than 2% of Lubrizol's sales, has since been sold.

In the 1960's Lubrizol continued to watch its revenues steadily increase. In 1960 it became a public company, and by taking advantage of the stock options that the company offered many employees became rich. The company has had a good relationship with its employees, in part because salaries are generous and employees are eligible for profit-sharing, including those on the shop floor.

Lubrizol's approach to management is distinctive. Job descriptions are flexible, and employees have a high degree of autonomy in deciding what tasks they should do and in what manner. The company's success has always depended on staying at the forefront of research on additives, and technicians have historically comprised a high percentage of Lubrizol's workforce. Upper management is also saturated with chemists, although in the 1970's a prominent lawyer joined their ranks. The ordinarily mild-mannered Lubrizol is extremely combative in guarding its patent rights.

Unlike many chemical companies, Lubrizol applauded the country's growing concern with pollution. Lead-free gas and catalytic converters opened up a new demand for lubricants to replace the lubricating action of leaded fuel. Any change in engine design is beneficial for Lubrizol because a new design requires new additives, and the company is well-equipped to meet the latest demands before its competitors are able to. It is possible that larger profits have something to do with Lubrizol's enthusiasm for environmental protection; however, to its credit the company has never been indicted for polluting the environment.

By the early 1970's Lubrizol was recognized as an excellent investment. Although ranked by size in the lower four hundred of the *Fortune* 500, it was one of the top 40 companies in terms of stock performance. The company seemed impermeable to the various economic problems that arose during the 1970's. For instance, although some of its additives are derived from petroleum products, and many of its products are used in passenger cars, the company prospered as a result of the oil crisis. This is because high gasoline prices encouraged auto makers to design new, energy efficient cars, and these design modifications required new fuel additives, transmission fluids, and gear lubricants.

Even the recession had a beneficial effect on Lubrizol, which also makes additives used in the production of oils for heavy industrial machinery. During the recession it became imperative for large industrial companies to lower repair costs, and quality lubricants and additives were a good place to start. Lubricants are one of the least likely places for a company to economize. As then president Mastin said, "In relation to these factors (high maintenance costs) the price of superior lubricants is minor, but the benefits are significant."

In the late 1970's Lubrizol started a cautious program of diversification. Its first new purchase (1979) was the Althus Corporation, a firm that makes lithium batteries. In the early 1980's Lubrizol purchased a biotechnology company which uses recombinant DNA for medical uses. Both of these firms are small (200 employees) and financially sound.

In the last few years Lubrizol has narrowed its interest in diversification to companies that are perfecting genetic engineering with plants. Using genetic engineering, Lubrizol hopes to develop improved seed oils which could be employed in the manufacture of the additives and specialty chemicals that are likely to remain Lubrizol's main product line. In 1985 Lubrizol purchased the Agrigenetics Corporation, one of the leaders in the small field of plant genetics. This company became the first to modify a plant using recombinant DNA when it spliced a bean gene to that of a sunflower.

The purchase of Agrigenetics may appear to be an uncharacteristic move for Lubrizol, especially since Agrigenetics was operating at a loss of nearly 40 million dollars. Agrigenetics was by far the largest acquisition in Lubrizol's history, and one that required the company to go into debt. Industry analysts have pointed out, however, that there are only 20 firms capable of developing recombinant DNA techniques for plants, and that corporations who want to diversify into this particular field may soon find it impossible to acquire a plant genetics subsidiary.

As mentioned previously, although it had a long-standing policy to only buy companies that were financially sound, Lubrizol itself once seemed like a risky venture. In the seven years between its founding and its endorsement by G.M., Lubrizol did not always turn a profit. It is as if the management of Lubrizol saw in Agrigenetics a reflection of the Graphite Oil Products Co.

Nevertheless, there is more than nostalgia behind the acquisition of Agrigenetics. Although the company denies it, for the last thirty years there have been predictions that the additives industry will eventually mature. Additives have become so highly specialized and effective that there may be no pressing need for new ones. Nothing short of a return to draft animals could overcrowd the market, yet the day may come when there will be little room for growth. Plant genetics, while risky, provides unlimited possibilities for new technologies, and Lubrizol wants the patents.

Agrigenetics was purchased at a time when Lubrizol proved itself to be vulnerable to economic trends. Lubrizol has always been able to turn adverse economic conditions to its advantage, but in 1985 the world wide recession began to cut into demand. Despite the rising concern over maintenance, enough machines and vehicles were out of operation to slightly depress the additives market.

Lubrizol responded to this situation by restructuring the company. There has been a shift towards fewer employees in manufacturing and more in the development of specialty chemicals. The workforce has been pared down, but this was accomplished through voluntary early retirement plans rather than layoffs.

1985 was by no means an unprofitable year for Lubrizol.

The additives industry as a whole is more insulated than other industries to an economic recession. And as the U.S. economy improves so will the world economy. Coupled with a weaker dollar, this should expand the demand for Lubrizol's products abroad, which accounts for over two thirds of its sales. The future remains bright for Lubrizol, and the purchase of Agrigenetics provides it with long term growth potential.

Principal Subsidiaries: LBD Enterprises, Inc.; Genetechs, Corp.; Agrigenetics Corp.; Lyneville Seed Co.;Sungene Corp.; and SVO Enterprise Corp. The company also had subsidiaries in the following countries: Switzerland, Canada, Chile, Spain, Philippines, France, Austria, West Germany, Britain, Australia, Italy, Mexico, South Africa and Japan.

MITSUBISHI CHEMICAL INDUSTRIES, LTD.

5-2, Marunouchi 2-chome
Chiyoda-ku, Tokyo 100
Japan
03-283-6111

Public Company
Incorporated: June 1950
Employees: 8,135
Sales: ¥ 810.8 billion (US$ 5.092 billion)
Market value: ¥ 865.9 billion (US$ 5.438 billion)
Stock Index: Frankfurt Tokyo Osaka Nagoya Kyoto
Hiroshima Fukuoka Sappora Niigata

The Mitsubishi industrial empire was founded by Yataro Iwasaki late in the 19th century, and expanded rapidly into general trading and a variety of industrial occupations. So great was its influence that it became known as a *zaibatsu*, or "money clique." As Mitsubishi grew, it purchased factories from bankrupt or failing companies and established new divisions to operate them.

Nippon Tar was founded by Mitsubishi in 1934 to take over the operations of the Makiyama coking factory in northern Kyushu. Makiyama, which had been in existence since 1897, was modernized and reorganized. Renamed the Kurosaki plant, it later became Nippon Tar's primary facility for coke and coke products, fertilizer, and ammonia products. In 1936 the company's name was changed to Nippon Chemical Industries.

The following year Japan became involved in military hostilities in China. By the end of 1941 Japan was at war with the United States and Great Britain. Chemical production was essential to the industries which manufactured ships, aircraft, and weapons. Nippon Chemical, by its association with Mitsubishi (famous for its deadly Zero fighter plant), was intimately involved in the Japanese war effort.

Japan surrendered to Allied powers in the late summer of 1945 and was placed under the administrative authority of an Allied military commander. The occupation authority enacted a series of industrial reorganization laws which included stringent anti-monopoly laws. The financial empires of the *zaibatsu*, principally Mitsui, Sumitomo, and Mitsubishi, were divided into thousands of independent companies.

When Nippon Chemical was separated from Mitsubishi in 1950, its glass making and rayon divisions were re-established as separate companies called Asahi Glass and Shinko Rayon (presently Mitsubishi Rayon). The "new" Nippon Chemical Industries, a public limited company, was established in June of 1950.

In 1950 Japan was still recovering from the destruction and ruin caused during the war. Ironically, Japanese industries encountered a period of extreme growth later that year as the result of another war. The same month that Nippon Chemical resumed its operations, Communist forces from North Korea invaded South Korea. Japan was used as a staging base for United Nations forces which were sent to Korea to repel the attack. As a result of their proximity to the battle, Japanese companies, including Nippon Chemical, were contracted to furnish a variety of provisions and supplies.

In 1952 the company's polyvinyl chloride (PVC) division was turned over to a company called Monsanto Chemical Industries (presently Mitsubishi Monsanto), a joint venture created by Nippon Chemical and Monsanto of the United States. Later that year Nippon Chemical changed its name to Mitsubishi Chemical Industries Ltd. (or MCI), reflecting the company's growing ties with companies formerly associated with the Mitsubishi *zaibatsu*.

When an armistice was signed in Korea in 1952, many supply contracts with Japanese companies were canceled. Japan experienced a serious recession which forced hundreds of companies to merge in order to survive. In 1953 Mitsubishi Chemical absorbed the Toho Chemical company, later called the Yokkaichi plant, which produced ethyl hexanol, and synthetic rubber and textile products. With additional resources and improving market conditions, Mitsubishi Chemical began to expand at a faster rate. The company established a carbide division and laid the groundwork for a petrochemical division.

By the end of the decade Mitsubishi Chemical derived 38% of its revenues from coke, gas and tar production. The rest of the company's operations consisted of agricultural chemical products (29% of revenues), organic chemical products (12%), sundries (12%), and inorganic chemical products (9%).

Mitsubishi Chemical constructed an aluminum rolling mill in 1963 under a joint venture with the Reynolds company of the United States. The mill was designated the company's Naoetsu plant, and later became Japan's largest aluminum facility. During the 1960's Mitsubishi Chemical constructed another coke plant at Sakaide, which was opened in 1969. Production of aluminum at the Sakaide plant commenced two years later.

In 1970 Mitsubishi Chemical resumed pharmaceutical manufacturing (suspended in the early 1950's), as part of its expansion into "bio-industry." The following year the company established the Mitsubishi-Kasei Institute of Life Sciences at Yokohama, which has since acquired an excellent reputation for research.

The world oil crisis of 1973 compelled Mitsubishi Chemical Industries to reduce its work force in order to remain profitable. In addition, the company was forced to sell its aluminum division (later called Mitsubishi Light Metal Industries, Ltd.). As raw material costs continued to rise, particularly in petrochemicals, Mitsubishi Chemical placed greater emphasis on pharmaceutical and fine chemical production, and initiated a program to reduce energy consumption. The company's financial position strengthened, and as oil prices began to fall, the petrochemical operations became less of a burden. The transfer of the light metals division to Mitsubishi Light Metal Industries was completed in 1976.

In 1983 the *Mainichi Shimbun* and *Nihon Keizai Shimbun*, two Japanese newspapers, reported that the United States Defense Department forced the American division of Mitsubishi Chemical to sell its Optical Information Systems unit to the McDonnell Douglas Corporation. Although the stories were denied, the reports said that Pentagon officials considered the company to be in possession of sensitive laser technologies, which they felt could not remain secret unless controlled by an American company. The unit, which Mitsubishi Chemical purchased from Exxon in 1981, was reported sold for about $7 million.

In a continuing effort to expand its pharmaceutical division, Mitsubishi Chemical purchased the Mitsubishi Yuka Pharmaceutical company from the Mitsubishi Petrochemical Company in 1985. The transaction included the transfer of over 200 researchers to the company's research institute.

Mitsubishi Chemical lost ¥ 8.5 billion in 1983 and was forced to suspend dividends. This lowered demand for the company's stock and prevented it from recapitalizing. This left the company with a weak financial structure, despite modest profits. In 1986, however, stronger profitability returned and the five yen dividend was reinstated.

Although it is an independent company, Mitsubishi Chemical remains closely associated with other Mitsubishi companies. Managers of Mitsubishi Chemical regularly attend the *Kinyo-kai*, or "Second Friday Conference," a monthly meeting of Mitsubishi Corporation affiliated companies, where joint business strategies are formulated.

Mitsubishi Chemical has declared that in the future it will emphasize its "functional products," namely pharmaceuticals and biotechnology products. Carbon products (coke) have been reduced to a 28% share of the company's revenues. The largest share of income is derived from petrochemicals (40%), followed by chemicals (17%) and agricultural chemicals (9%).

Principal Subsidiaries: Diafoil Co., Ltd.; Kasei Naoetsu Industries, Ltd.; Matsuyama Kasei, Ltd.; Mitsubishi-Kasei Food corp.; Mitsubishi Kasei Technoengineers, Ltd.; Mitsubishi Kasei Vinyl Co.; Mitsubishi Monsanto Chemical Co.; Mitsubishi Plastics Industries, Ltd.; Ryoka Industry Co., Ltd.; Ryoka Light Metal Industries, Ltd.; Ryo-Nichi Co., Ltd.; Ryosei Sangyo Co., Ltd.; The Kansei Coke and Chemicals Co., Ltd.

Monsanto

MONSANTO COMPANY

800 N. Lindbergh Blvd.
St. Louis, Missouri 63167
U.S.A.
(314) 694-1000

Public Company
Incorporated: April 19, 1933 as Monsanto Chemical
 Company
Employees: 56,100
Sales: $6.879 billion
Market value: $6.077 billion
Stock Index: New York Zurich Geneva Brussels
 Amsterdam Frankfurt London Paris

Weight-conscious Americans at the turn of the century may have not known it, but after 1901 America was finally producing saccharin, the low-calorie sweetener. John Francisco Queeny, a purchaser for a wholesale drug house, was unable to persuade his firm to produce saccharin rather than import it from Germany. As a result, with $5000 Queeny began his own company in St. Louis, Missouri and called it the Monsanto Chemical Works after his wife's family name. Eighty-four years later, the company returned to its roots with the purchase of G.D. Searle, a pharmaceutical company known for its extremely successful low-calorie sweetener Nutra-Sweet. Along the way, Monsanto grew from a one-product company to one of the United States' largest corporations and one of its most important agrichemical concerns.

By 1905 John Queeny's company, now producing caffeine and vanillin as well as saccharin, was beginning to turn a profit. In 1908 Queeny felt confident enough about his firm's future to leave his part-time job with another drug house, and become Monsanto's full-time president. The company continued to grow, with sales surpassing the million dollar mark for the first time in 1915.

Until the start of World War I, America relied heavily on foreign supplies of chemicals. However, with the U.S. entry into the war becoming more of a possibility with each passing year, it was clear that the country would soon need its own domestic producer of chemicals. Looking back on the significance of the war for Monsanto, Queeny's son Edgar remarked, "There was no choice other than to improvise, to invent and to find new ways of doing all the old things. The old dependence on Europe was, almost overnight, a thing of the past." In fact, Monsanto was forced to rely on its own knowledge and

nascent technical ability. Monsanto researchers discovered that pages of technical descriptions of German chemical processes had actually been ripped out of library books. Yet Monsanto produced a number of strategic products, including phenol, used as an antiseptic, and acetylsalicyclic acid, or aspirin. Even today, Monsanto is the world's largest producer of bulk aspirin, with plants in St. Louis, Thailand and the United Kingdom.

With the purchase of an Illinois acid company in 1918, Monsanto began to widen the scope of its factory operations. A postwar depression during the early 1920's depressed profits, but by the time John Queeny turned over the company to Edgar the financial situation was much brighter. Monsanto had gone public, a move that paved the way for future expansion. At this time, the company had 55 shareholders, 1000 employees and owned a small company in Britain. It was under Edgar's direction, however, that Monsanto began to substantially expand and enter into an era of prolonged growth.

At preparatory school, and later in the chemical department at Cornell University, Edgar had been an indifferent student. Because of this, according to Monsanto company historian Dan Forrestal, Edgar's father was quite concerned about his ability to lead the firm. However, from 1928, when John Queeny stepped down after learning he had an incurable form of cancer, to 1962, Edgar directed Monsanto with a large degree of success.

Monsanto, now the Monsanto Chemical Company, began to expand rapidly during the 1930's under Edgar's supervision. Acquisitions expanded Monsanto's product line to include the then new field of plastics, and to include the manufacture of phosphorus. Queeny also made significant changes in the shareholder's reports, making them more understandable and informative. Although Queeny strongly opposed Roosevelt's New Deal policies, he nonetheless felt it necessary to point out, in one of these reports, that the 40 hour employee work week had been a Monsanto policy since 1932.

By the time the United States entered the war in 1941, the domestic chemical industry had attained far greater independence from Europe. Monsanto, strengthened by a number of acquisitions, was also prepared and able to produce such strategic materials as phosphates and inorganic chemicals. Most importantly, however, was the company's acquisition of a research and development laboratory called Thomas and Hochwalt. The well-known Dayton, Ohio firm strengthened Monsanto at the time, but also provided the basis for some of its future achievements in chemical technology. One of its most important discoveries was styrene monomer, a key ingredient in synthetic rubber and a crucial product for the armed forces during World War II. Another important development occurred in 1949, when Monsanto entered the synthetic fiber era. Problem after problem plagued the joint venture with American Viscose, but a later agreement with Du Pont made it into a successful operation.

Generally considered a low profile company in the public eye, Monsanto's early attempts to directly market consumer goods were beset with difficulties. However, attempts to refine a low-quality detergent led to important developments in grass fertilizer. The postwar housing increase had created a strong market of homeowners eager to have perfect lawns.

Monsanto undertook two substantial ventures in the mid-1950's, and a major reorganization in 1954. One of these ventures involved urethane foam which was flexible and easy to use; it later became crucial in making automobile interiors. With the acquisition of Lion Oil in 1955, the second of the company's ventures, Monsanto assets increased more than 50%. Stockholders during this time numbered 43,000.

Having finally outgrown its downtown headquarters, Monsanto moved to the suburban community of Creve Coeur in 1957. And, in 1960, Edgar Queeny turned over the chairmanship of Monsanto to Charles Thomas, one of the founders of the research and development laboratory so important to Monsanto. Charlie Sommer, who joined the company in 1929, became president. Under their combined leadership Monsanto saw a number of important developments, including the establishment of the Agricultural Chemicals division, created in order to consolidate Monsanto's diverse agrichemical product lines. European expansion occurred as well, with Brussels becoming the permanent overseas headquarters in 1962.

In 1964 Monsanto changed its name to Monsanto Company, a long overdue acknowledgement of the current diversity of the company's product line. Monsanto now consisted of eight divisions, ranging from petroleum and fibers to building materials and packaging.

According to Monsanto historian Dan Forrestal, "Leadership during the 1960's and early 1970's came principally from . . . executives whose Monsanto roots ran deep." In 1964 Edward O'Neal became chairman. O'Neal came to Monsanto in 1935 with the Swann Corporation acquisition. He was the first chairman in company history who had not first held the post of president. Another company leader was Edward J. Bock, who had started working at Monsanto in 1941 as an engineer. He rose through the ranks to become a member of the board of directors in 1965, and president in 1968. Bock was the first president to rule "Queenyless" when Edgar Queeny, who left no heirs, died in 1968.

Although Bock had a reputation for being a committed company executive, a number of factors contributed to his volatile term as president. High overhead costs and a sluggish national economy led to a dramatic 29% decrease in earnings in 1969. Sales were up the following year, but Bock's implementation of the 1971 reorganization caused a significant amount of friction among members of the board and senior management. In spite of the fact that this move was widely praised by security analysts, in which Monsanto separated the management of raw materials from the company's subsidiaries, Bock resigned from the presidency in February of 1972.

The acceptance of Bock's resignation led to another major problem for Monsanto. Since there was no immediate replacement for Bock, indications of a lack of management developed in Monsanto. This feeling ended in 1972 when, after a nine month search, John W. Hanley, a former executive with Procter and Gamble, was chosen as president. Hanley also took over as chairman in 1975.

Under Hanley, Monsanto more than doubled its sales and earnings between 1972 and 1983. Toward the end of his tenure, Hanley put into effect a promise he had made to himself and to Monsanto when he accepted the position of president, namely, that his successor would be chosen from Monsanto's ranks. Hanley and his staff chose approximately 20 young executives as potential company leaders and began preparing them for the head position at Monsanto. Among them was Richard J. Mahoney. When Hanley joined Monsanto, Mahoney was a young sales director in agricultural products. In 1983 Hanley turned the leadership of the company over to Mahoney. Wall Street immediately approved this decision with an increase in Monsanto's share prices. Mahoney is currently listed as Monsanto's chief executive officer.

Public concern over the environment began to escalate during the 1960's. Ralph Nader's activities and Rachel Carson's book *Silent Spring* were two important influences in increasing the U.S. public's awareness of activities within the chemical industry. Monsanto responded in a number of ways to the pressure. In 1964 the company introduced biodegradeable detergents and later, in 1976, Monsanto announced plans to phase out production of polychlorinated biphenyl (PCB).

Although Monsanto did make an effort to respond to public concerns about pollution, the past came back to haunt the company in 1979 when a suit was filed against Monsanto and other manufacturers of Agent Orange, a defoliant used during the Vietnam War. Agent Orange contained a highly toxic chemical known as dioxin, and the suit claimed that hundreds of veterans had suffered permanent damage because of the chemical. In 1984 Monsanto and seven other manufacturers agreed to a $180 million settlement, immediately prior to the beginning of the trial. With the announcement of a settlement Monsanto's share price, depressed because of the uncertainty over the outcome of the trial, rose substantially.

Also in 1984, Monsanto lost a $10 million antitrust suit to Spray-Rite, a former distributor of Monsanto agricultural herbicides. The U.S. Supreme Court upheld the suit and award, finding that Monsanto had acted to fix retail prices with other herbicide manufacturers.

In August of 1985, Monsanto purchased G.D. Searle, the "Nutra-Sweet" firm. Nutra-Sweet had generated $700 million in sales that year. Monsanto needed what Searle had to offer, namely, a marketing and a sales staff, and a real profit potential. Since the late 1970's the company had sold nearly 60 low margin businesses and, with two important agriculture product patents expiring in 1988, a major new cash source was more than welcome. What Monsanto didn't count on, however, was Searle's Intrauterine Device called the Copper 7.

Soon after the acquisition, disclosures about hundreds of law suits over Searle's IUD surfaced and turned Monsanto's takeover into a public relations disaster. The disclosures, which inevitably led to comparisons with those about A.H. Robins, the Dalkan Shield manufacturer that eventually declared Chapter 11 bankruptcy, raised questions as to how carefully Monsanto management had considered the acquisition. In early 1986 Searle discontinued IUD sales in the United States, but the matter remains far from resolved.

In the next decade Monsanto will face continued challenges from a variety of sources, including government and public concern over harzardous wastes, fuel and feedstock costs, and import competition. At the end of the 99th Congress, President Reagan signed a $8.5 billion, five-year cleanup Superfund reauthorization act. Built into the financing is a surcharge on the chemical industry created through the new tax reform bill. Biotechnology regulations are only just now being formulated and Monsanto, which already has types of genetically engineered bacteria ready for testing, can be expected to be an active participant in that field.

In keeping with its strategy to become a leader in the health field, Monsanto and the Washington University Medical School entered intc a five year research contract in 1984. Monsanto provided the school with $23.5 million for research focusing on proteins and peptides. Two-thirds of the research is to be directed into areas with obviously commercial applications; one-third of the research is to be devoted to theoretical work. One particularly promising discovery involves the application of the bovine growth factor, a way to greatly increase milk production.

In the burgeoning low-calorie sweetener market, challengers to Nutra-Sweet are putting pressure on Monsanto. Pfizer Inc., a pharmaceutical company, is hoping to soon market its product, called alitame, which it claims is far sweeter than Nutra-Sweet and suitable for baking.

In an interview with *Business Week*, senior vice-president for research and development Howard Schneiderman said, "To maintain our markets—and not become another steel industry—we must spend on research and development." Monsanto, which has committed 8% of its operating budget to research and development, far above the industry average, may emerge in the 1990's as one of the leaders in the fields of biotechnology and pharmaceuticals that are only now emerging from their nascent stage.

Principal Subsidiaries: Bolgen NV Collagen Corp.; Fisher Controls International, Inc, Monsanto PLC; Monsanto Canada Inc.; Monsanto Electronic Materials Co.; Monsanto Enviro-Chem Systems Inc.; Monsanto Europe S.A.; Monsanto International Sales Co., Inc.; Monsanto Oil Co.; Monsanto (Suisse) S.A.; Nutra Sweet Co.; Polyamide Intermediaries Ltd. (50%); RDI Inc.; G.D. Searle & Co.

Further Reading: *Faith, Hope, and $5,000: The Story of Monsanto: The Trials and Triumphs of the First 75 Years* by Dan J. Forrestal, New York, Simon and Schuster, 1977.

� MONTEDISON

MONTEDISON SpA

Foro Bonaparte 31
Milan 20121
Italy
(02) 63331
Public Company
Incorporated: July 1, 1966 as Montecatini Edison S.p.A.
Employees: 70,104
Sales: L11.638 trillion (US$ 8.608 billion)
Market Value: L6.534 trillion (US$ 4.833 billion)
Stock Index: Rome Florence Milan Amsterdam Brussel
   Geneva

Montedison was formed on 7 July 1966 on the merger of Montecatini and Edison. Edison had been an electric power utility company that had moved into chemicals, while Montecatini had been a chemical company buying and building power plants. The two had had intertwined histories for years, at times with the same man on both boards co-ordinating their growth, at other times with nothing in common but rivalry.

Edison had been formed as a power utility in 1884 in Milan. Like nearly all the early electrical companies, it grew quickly and steadily. The long strikes by workers in 1913 and the two World Wars barely effected its fortunes. In the 1930's, while the rest of the world was in a depression, Edison began to diversify widely and, in the 1950's, began its acquisition of petrochemical companies. By 1960, Edison was Italy's second largest chemical concern.

Montecatini was formed in 1888 as a pyrite mining business in Tuscany. It was run by the Donegani family, in particular by Guido Donegani, who was made director in 1910. Born in Livorno in 1877, he had studied industrial engineering, and was utterly a man of his time. He served in Parliament in 1921, was vice president of the Banca Commerciale Italiana at the peak of his business career, and soon became the president of his profession's fascist organisation.

Within ten years of taking over as Montecatini's director, Donegani had begun to build the small mining company into a much larger enterprise. While he had some domestic backing from the Banca Commerciale and the Credito Italiano, it was mainly through the heavy funding from four Parisian financial and industrial backers that he was able to involve Montecatini in the production of phosphates, fertilizers, and sulphuric acid. The development of all of Italy's chemical industry at the time depended not only on French financing and sales agreements, but on the colonial ventures in phosphate mining in French Tunisia. Montecatini had one of the main mining contracts there, and built much of its later strength on this early co-operation with the French. At the same time, the Banca Commerciale was investing heavily in public utilities, especially the electric ones like Edison. One of the bank's managers, Guiseppe Toeplitz, worked closely with the Donegani brothers to arrange Montecatini's monopolization of the fertilizer and sulphates production in Italy. With the Banca Commerciale and Donegani directing the growth of both companies, there was no real competition between them, but the ground was obviously prepared for it to begin whenever the leadership of the companies would be different.

After World War I a second phase of growth began for Montecatini. It branched out into aluminum, purchasing its own sulpher phosphate factories, and gradually took over the country's explosives industry. It built the first synthetic ammonia plant in Italy, and then added marble works. Even so, it was a small company by international standards, its 1928 capital being a little over the equivalent of £1 million.

World War II was more drastic, and reduced the company's installations by a third. Reconstruction led to some managerial changes: in 1945, Guido Donegani had been arrested as a collaborator but, like so many, was freed almost immediately, for "negative evidence." His release caused Montecatini's workers to strike in protest. Though he remained free, he disappeared and, in April 1947, died of heart disease.

By 1948, Montecatini had managed to regain its former size, with 57,000 workers, 110,000 shareholders, and a working capital of 18 million lire. It was mining or producing sulpher, bauxite, marble and granite, lead, zinc, and aluminum. The chemical production had expanded from fertilizers to insecticides, pharmaceuticals, and man-made fibres. The company's own electrical production was 1 billion 300 million kilowatts, from its eight hydro-electrical and one thermoelectrical plants. New ventures included rope making, packaging, and investment in research. It built Europe's first petrochemical plant, at Ferrara. In one of its research facilities, Professor Giulio Natta created the process for manufacturing isotactic polypropylene, of major importance in the production of thermoplastics. (For this work, he was awarded the Nobel Prize in chemistry in 1963.)

By this time, the company had overextended itself. Royal Dutch Shell became a large investor in Montecatini's petrochemical business, while preparation also had to be made for what seemed to be the inevitable nationalisation. The 1966 merger with Edison was partly a result of the difficulties brought to Montecatini by overextending and to Edison by nationalisation. Before the merger, Edison had lost its electrical generating interest to nationalisation, and was having trouble getting paid for it. Edison's president, Giorgio Valerio, began negotiating the merger of the two companies, which would compensate for Edison's great losses, in such complete secrecy that even Montecatini's president, Carlo Faina, knew nothing about it. When he was ultimately presented with the finalised merger terms, it was something of a fait accompli, though he did try to turn the tables and suggest that Montecatini take over Edison instead. The battle was loud but ineffectual, and the result, Montedison, was a huge conglomerate centred on chemicals and electricity.

Two years later, the Ente Nazionale Idrocarburi (ENI) acquired an interest in Montedison which, combined with that of Istituto per la Riconstruzione Industriale (IRI) gave the state 18.4% of the company. Small shareholders were outraged, claiming the move was "surreptitious nationalisation." In the riotous annual meeting of 1969, they stood up, shouted, and threw coins and copies of the annual report at the chair. Despite the noise, the state retained its shares.

The 1970's brought a disastrous period when the company, under Eugenio Cefis, fell to undeclared bankruptcy. While chairman of Montedison, Cefis was called the most powerful man in Italy, but he had studied at the Modena military academy and seemed to have a greater understanding of politics than of industry. As chairman, he operated from within a personal and highly political clique. At the same time, the government thought that the company could come in handy for a massive job creation scheme in the south of the country, and set up businesses through it which had no hope of making a profit. While the government supported the company's debts, Cefis over-extended into numerous other industries, and continued to play political games. In 1974 there was a scandal over his receipt of daily reports from military counter-intelligence on politicians and industrialists, among them the Prime Minister. By then, Montedison's losses were averaging 100,000 million lire per year, but Cefis did not resign for another three years. He was followed by another man not up to the job, a former minister of agriculture, Giuseppi Medici, who resigned in 1980.

The hero of Montedison's survival is Mario Schimberni, who became chairman in April 1980. Originally a lecturer in industrial technology, he moved into industry and worked his way up the managerial ranks of Montefibre and Montedison. As soon as he took over the latter, he fired seven senior managers and nearly 100 middle managers, in some cases replacing them with younger people having a more internationalist view of business. When ENI sold its shares in 1981, they were bought by Gemina, putting more of Italy's traditionally powerful businessmen among the shareholders, and giving Schimberni a group of people with whom he could work to manipulate the shareholders' decisions about the company. In a major rationalisation program, activities in subsidiaries, particularly Montefibre, were cut back. Montedison's 200 or more companies were then divided into groups based on what they produced, and the workforce was cut from 149,000 to 69,000. Even though Montedison was short on cash, Schimberni used his considerable skill to acquire controlling interest in other corporations whose assets helped to lower the company's debts significantly and to raise the cash flow to over 1,200 billion lire.

The result of Schimberni's brilliant nursing of the company back to health has been that it was heartily pursued by another. Italy's huge agri-industrial group, Ferruzzi, bought 40% of Montedison's chemical concerns by early 1987. It cost Ferruzzi over $1.7 billion to become the single controlling shareholder of a company whose dividends still yield less than Italy's treasury bonds, but the purpose seems to be to build Ferruzzi into the world's third largest agri-industrial group, after Unilever and Nestlé. Mr. Gardini of Ferruzzi and Schimberni seem to have big plans of working together on exciting new projects, many of them in developing countries, but until Ferruzzi gains a full 51% of Montedison, these plans are dependent upon goodwill and co-operation. Certainly, this public boost of Montedison's desirability could increase its strength in the future.

Principal Subsidiaries: ACNA Chimica Organica SpA; Cledia Srl (99.9%); CUAI SpA (74%); Esercizio Raccardi Ferraviari di Porto Marghera SpA (60.4%); Ferroleghe SpA; Fertimont SpA; Fidenza Vetraria SpA (58.5%); Farmoplant SpA; Iniziativa ME.T.A. SpA; Istituto G. Donegani SpA (93.2%); Immobiliare Lido Di Spina Sas; Mira Lanza SpA (38.2%); Mondedipe SpA (99.9%); Mondedison International Holding Co. (Switzerland); Mondefibre SpA (70%); R.O.L. SpA (51%); Ausimont SpA (85.5%); Sade Finanziaria SpA (65%); SE FI MONT SpA; SEGEM SpA (80%); S.I.F.I. SpA; S.I.M.E. SpA; Simmont SpA (99.9%); Società Editrice Il Messaggero SpA; Sviluppo Linate SpA; Vinavil SpA (55%); Vitrofil SpA (99%); Montepolimeri Belgio S.A. Feluy; Nedermont B.V.; Distribuzione Fibre SpA (70%); Industria Tessile De Vercelli SpA (70%); Pettinatura De Ivrea SpA (70%); Sicrem-Società Industriale Cremonese SpA Pizzighettone (CR) (35%); S.I.P.A.-Società Italiana Prodotti Acrilici SpA (70%); Società Italiana Poliestere SpA (NA) (70%); ARCA SpA (51%); A.TE.CA. SrL; Ausind SpA; LARAC SpA (95.2%); Dutral SpA (85.5%); Montefluos SpA (85.5%); Farmitalia Carlo Erba SpA (55%); Lark SpA (72%); OTE Biomedica SpA (55%); Vetem SpA (55%); Vega Oil SpA (95.5%); Alba Imballaggi Sud SpA; Commerciale Mira Lanza SpA (56%); Società Approvvigionamenti Industriali SpA; Vedril SpA; Venuti SpA (56%); C.A.F.-Compagnia Amministratricc Fiduciaria Srl (53.3%); CAGISA-Compagnia di Amministrazioni e Gestioni Immobiliare SpA (53.3%); DATAMONT SpA (53.3%); EUROMERCATO SpA (37%); Fiduciaria Valore SpA (53.3%); Finanziaria Milanese SpA (53.3%); Finanziaria Valori SpA (53.3%); MA.Part SpA (53.3%); MA.PA. Le Srl (53.3%); Montedil SpA (53.3%); Montedison Servizi Agricoltura SpA (53.3%); S.I.S.IM. SpA (53.3%); Teonimont SpA (53.3%). The company also lists subsidiaries in the following countries: Australia, Belgium, Brazil, Canada, France, Greece, Hong Kong, Indonesia, Japan, Mexico, Netherlands, Netherlands Antilles, Panama, Peru, South Africa, Spain, Sweden, Switzerland, United Kingdom, United States, Venezuela, and West Germany.

Further Reading: *The Chemical Industry, 1900–1930: International Growth and Technical Change* by Ludwig F. Haber, Oxford, Clarendon Press, 1971; *Industrial Imperialism in Italy 1908–1915* by Richard A. Webster, Berkeley, University of California Press, 1975.

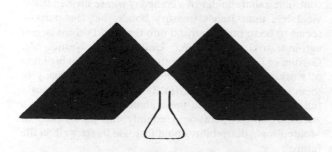

MORTON THIOKOL, INC.

110 N. Wacker Drive
Chicago, Illinois 60606–1560
U.S.A.

Public Company
Incorporated: September 2, 1969
Employees: 17,900
Sales: $1.919 billion
Market value: $2.261 billion
Stock Index: New York

Morton Thiokol was established in 1982 when Morton Industries, recently separated from Norwich Pharmaceuticals, saw Thiokol as a company that would be able to save it from any possible takeover attempt. Morton, because of its steady income from salt, was attractive to Thiokol, whose lucrative aerospace and specialty chemicals business required a large research budget that the income from salt could be used to finance.

Thiokol was founded during the Depression. Its main product was discovered by two chemists, J.C. Patrick and Nathan Mnookin, who were trying to invent an inexpensive antifreeze. In the course of an experiment involving ethylene dichloride and sodium polysulfide they created a gum whose outstanding characteristic was a terrible smell. To make things worse, it clogged a sink in the laboratory and none of the solvents used to remove it were successful. Then the frustrated chemists realized that the resistence of the material to any kind of solvent was a useful property. They had invented synthetic rubber, which they christened "Thiokol," from the Greek words for rubber and sulfur.

Mnookin and Patrick negotiated with Standard Oil to develop the product. However, the two men could not reach an agreement with the company. Finally, a salt merchant named Bevis Longstreth provided the financial support for the construction of a plant in Kansas City, Missouri. Yet the plant smelled so bad that its neighbors asked the mayor to remove the company from the area. As a result, Thiokol Inc. was forced to move to New Jersey.

When World War II began the company hoped that the rubber shortage would increase demand for Thiokol, but organic rubber was recycled instead. Thiokol Inc. was thus relegated to making hoses for specialized uses during the wartime period. Dow Chemical purchased 30% of Thiokol in 1948, but sold its share of the company during 1953 on the open market. According to Wall Street analysts, Thiokol was not a promising takeover candidate. In 1944,

when Bevis Longstreth died, no one on the board of directors was willing to replace him so Joseph Crosby, a department head, ended up in Longstreth's position.

When it was brought to Crosby's attention that the jet propulsion laboratories at the California Institute of Technology were buying 5–10 gallons of the company's solvent resistant polymer, he decided to talk to some of the Institute's scientists. It turned out that this solvent resistant polymer was the best rocket fuel the scientists had ever used.

In the 1950's, the first rockets were powered by liquid fuel. These markets required heavy tanks to hold not only the fuel and the oxidizer, but also the binding agent that held them together. Rocket fuel was so dangerous that one part fuel was mixed with four parts oxidizer to reduce flammability. The attraction of Thiokol's polymer was that it was fuel and binding agent in one.

Management at Thiokol decided to go straight to the armed forces with its product, and the Army agreed to finance a laboratory. Research began even before the building was finished. The company's research director recalled mixing propellant late at night in a room illuminated by his car's headlights before any electric lights had been installed.

The Korean War benefited Thiokol a great deal. Solid rocket fuel began to displace liquid, and the company's solvent resistant sealants were selling very well. During this period of time Thiokol began to design and manufacture rocket engines, and with a 70% share of the solid rocket fuel market the company achieved a significant measure of success.

During the 1960's the company worked on the propulsion systems for the Minuteman 3 rocket, the Poseidon submarine, and Sam-D missiles. It also provided flares and other pyrotechnic devices for the war in Vietnam. Almost two-thirds of the company's business came from the government; in fact, Crosby spent as much time in Washington as he did at the company's headquarters in Trenton, New Jersey. Although Thiokol conducted most of its business with the government at this time, during the 1960's it also had an educational division which operated training programs for the hardcore unemployed and for American Indians. Housing programs for low income residents of Gulfport, Mississippi and Raleigh, North Carolina were also administered by Thiokol. Thiokol's extensive contact with the military gave it an edge in the competition for these educational and housing programs which were government funded.

Government contracts are lucrative, but undependable, since programs are funded according to the policies of the political party in power. As a result, Thiokol used its income from aerospace contracts to diversify into specialty chemicals, fibers, off-road vehicles, and household products like Spray-n-Wash. These products were also somewhat cyclical, but demand was not linked in any direct way to the political climate in Indochina or the outcome of a presidential election, factors that influenced the size and number of the government programs that Thiokol depended on. The need to partially disassociate itself from the U.S. government became clear in 1970 when fewer government contracts caused sales to drop from $245 million to $205 million. After the market for synthetic fibers turned for the worse in 1975, Thiokol again reappraised its situation and decided to concentrate on specialty chemicals as the division that would provide the company with financial stability in case aerospace contracts were discontinued. The fiber and off-road operations were sold.

In the 1970's Thiokol enjoyed a growth of 20% during certain years. The specialty chemicals and the Texize household products divisions were performing well, while the military contracts remained lucrative. At this same time Thiokol's future partner, Morton Industries, was experiencing mixed results in its diversification program.

Morton Salt began as a small agency that distributed salt in the midwest part of the United States. At the time, salt was shipped from the eastern seaboard on the Erie Canal. After the Civil War, in Chicago the demand for salt kept pace with the expansion of the meat-packing industry. In 1879 a 24 year old clerk by the name of Joy Morton joined the agency and by the age of 30 he owned it.

Morton soon came to dominate at least a third of the salt market, and was (as it is presently) the only nation-wide distributor. Salt was extracted by brine pumping, solar evaporation and dry mining. The mining of salt is incomparably safer than coal or diamond mining due to the fact that black lung disease, cave-ins, and fires do not occur. And since salt is used in so many basic industries, demand for salt is steady. The only factor that tends to depress demand is a mild winter, which means that less salt will be sprinkled on sidewalks and roads.

In certain respects, Morton Industries was quite successful. Not only did it have a large share of a stable and profitable market, but the traditionally low price of salt did not attract many competitors. The drawback to salt was that the industry was fully matured. So in 1965 Morton Industries, hitherto private, went public and decided to diversify. Its first major acquisition was Simonize, a maker of auto wax and household cleaners. Four years later, in 1969, Morton merged with Norwich Pharmaceuticals, which manufactured prescription drugs as well as over-the-counter products like Unguentine, Chloraseptic and Pepto-Bismol.

The problem with the Morton-Norwich merger was that Morton did not possess the financial resources to improve Norwich as it required. Despite its established product line, Norwich was slowed in its growth by an inadequate research and development budget. Although it can cost $50 million to market a new drug, in 1981 Morton-Norwich's entire research budget was still only $27.5 million. As a result, from 1969 to 1971 Morton-Norwich's dividends remained negligible. Its stock shares sold for only eight times dividends, which was low for pharmaceutical companies. To remedy the situation Morton-Norwich went into partnership with Rhone-Poulenc, a French drug manufacturer. In exchange for 20% of its stock, Morton-Norwich received right of first refusal on any of Rhone-Poulenc's new products. Moreover, Rhone-Poulenc had ample research facilities.

Unfortunately, the partnership with Rhone-Poulenc was beset with difficulties. "We couldn't run our business with those people," said Charles Locke, then president of Morton. To make matters worse, Rhone-Poulenc was eventually nationalized by Mitterand, and decided to sell its stock in Morton-Norwich. The French company did not abide by an earlier agreement to refrain from selling its share of Morton-Norwich to a single buyer, so Morton-Norwich found itself a potential takeover candidate.

In 1982 Morton sold Norwich and used part of the proceeds to buy back its stock from Rhone-Poulenc. However, Morton was still a potential candidate for a takeover due to the steady income from its salt operation. Its stock was selling for $30 a share, but with only $20 a share cash reserves the management at Morton decided to take action. As a result, management began to look for an eligible specialty chemicals company to purchase or merge with. Earlier, in the 1950's, Morton had diversified into specialty chemicals, including bromides, adhesives, dye stuffs and polymers.

Thiokol, with its 20% annual growth rate, was Morton's prime candidate for a merger. It had 40% of the solid rocket fuels market, not to mention the Texize division, which manufactured cleaners such as Glass Plus. Indeed, the household products divisions of both companies would blend quite well together. In 1982 the two companies completed the finalization of their merger. Yet one year later there was a severe disagreement between the upper management of each company. As a result, the top management at Thiokol walked out. Among the defectors was Robert Davies, president of Thiokol, considered one of the brightest executives in either the aerospace or chemical industries. Four other high level executives with experience in aerospace either retired or quit when Davies decided to leave. That left Charles Locke, from Morton, in complete control of both companies.

Despite these defections, few industry analysts have questioned the wisdom of the Thiokol-Morton merger. In the first year after the merger the company posted record earnings. Two years later there was a 26% increase in earnings per share. Morton's and Thiokol's specialty chemicals divisions had blended well, and the new company offered chemical purification products, metal recovery chemicals, coatings, polymers, and chemicals for the electronics industry. The household products division saw many of its items, including Glass Plus, Yes Detergent and Spray & Wash, achieve a 10–20% market growth in a crowded and highly competitive field. To further strengthen its position in the household products market, Morton Thiokol began to manufacture its own packaging materials, the first company to do so. However, in 1985 the household products division was sold to Dow Chemical Company in order to prevent an attempted takeover by that chemical firm.

The explosion of the space shuttle *Challenger* in January of 1986 can be attributed to the malfunction of Morton Thiokol's O-rings, which reportedly froze before the launch. Despite warnings from their engineers, Thiokol executives approved the launch of the space shuttle at that time. The company received even more adverse publicity when it demoted two of the engineers who had testified before the U.S. Congress that they had advised against the space shuttle launch. The men were later reinstated, but only after pressure was applied on the company from the

U.S. Congress itself.

The consequences of the space shuttle accident have not yet been fully revealed. At first the accident lowered share prices. Soon afterwards, Locke told the *Wall Street Journal* that, "we think this shuttle thing will cost us 10 cents a share." The share prices revived, but Locke's statement was cited by many people inside and outside the industry as an example of the company's insensitivity. The family of astronaut Robert McNair has filed a multi-million dollar suit against Morton Thiokol and is advocating for a jury trial. This suit may be a harbinger of legal problems to come. The shuttle disaster resulted in a great deal of acrimony and accusation between Thiokol executives and NASA officials, and a coveted contract was awarded to an industry competitor. Nevertheless, the company hopes to win a contract to redesign the booster rockets for the 1988 space shuttle launch.

Morton Thiokol has strong market positions for almost all of its products. And the company has purchased Bee Chemicals in order to compensate for its loss of Texize. If a real problem emerges for the company, it will be in the field of aerospace. *Standard and Poor's* expects U.S. defense programs to shrink due to deficit reduction plans. This decrease is not expected until 1988, however, as old contracts expire and new contracts become more difficult to procure.

Principal Subsidiaries: Bee Chemical Co.; Southwest Salt Co. The company also lists subsidiaries in the following countries: Bahamas, Belgium, Canada, England, France, Italy, Japan, Liberia, Mexico, The Netherlands, Singapore, and West Germany.

NALCO CHEMICAL CORPORATION

One Nalco Center
Naperville, Illinois 60566-1024
U.S.A.
(312) 961-9500

Public Company
Incorporated: April 21, 1928 as National Aluminate
Corporation
Employees: 5,065
Sales: $736 million
Market value: $1.36 billion
Stock Index: New York

Nalco Chemical Company began in 1928 as National Aluminate Corporation—the result of a merger between Chicago Chemical Company and Aluminate Sales Corporation. Founded by Herbert A. Kern and P. Wilson Evans as a water treatment chemical supplier, Nalco is now engaged in the production and sale of chemicals and technology used in water treatment, pollution control, oil production and refining, steel making, energy conservation, paper-making, and mining. Within the past 59 years, the company has grown to be one of the largest specialty chemical companies in the United States.

Both the Chicago Chemical Company and the Aluminate Sales Corporation manufactured and sold sodium aluminate. Chicago Chemical Company, organized in 1920 by Herbert A. Kern, sold the chemical to industrial plants for boiler feed-water treatment, while Aluminate Sales Corporation, founded in 1922 by P. Wilson Evans, sold sodium aluminate to railroads for the treatment of water used in steam locomotives.

At its inception, Kern's Chicago Chemical Company marketed a water treatment product called Colline to industrial plants in the Chicago area. Unfortunately for the company, the chemical, while very effective on Chicago water, was not quite so effective on other water supplies. Kern found that water is not the same everywhere, and that treatments would vary. He did, however, discover that the chemical compound, called sodium aluminate, was more effective and more universally marketable than Colline. By 1922 Chicago Chemical Company began marketing Kern's Water Softener, KWS Sodium Aluminate.

Both companies held patents on liquid sodium aluminate. Kern contracted Evans' Aluminate Sales Corpora-

tion to supply the chemical for Chicago Chemical's water treatment business. Soon afterwards, however, the Chicago Chemical Company constructed a new plant in the Clearing Industrial District for the manufacture of sodium aluminate for both companies.

Aluminum Company of America (Alcoa) held several patents, during this time, on the manufacture of dry sodium aluminate. In 1928 Alcoa merged its interests with Chicago Chemical Company and Aluminate Sales Corporation to form National Aluminate Corporation. In 1929 National Aluminate Corporation founded Visco Products Company, manufacturer of chemicals used in drilling oil wells. This company established National Aluminate within the oil industry. National's sales for the year 1929 totaled more than one million dollars.

In 1933 Emmett J. Culligan, then a chemist at National, persuaded Herbert Kern to allow National Aluminate to produce a water softening, gel-type chemical zeolite. Culligan was appointed manager of the new zeolite department at the Clearing Facility. The plant was ultimately forced to expand because of the large amount of space needed to manufacture the zeolite. Drying the material required several blocks of streets, leased from the Village of La Grange Park, Illinois. In 1935, after Emmett Culligan left National on friendly terms to start his own water softening company (now known as Culligan International), the company replaced the zeolites with more efficient synthetic icon exchange resins.

In 1937 the company constructed one of the first windowless, air-conditioned plants in the country, across the street from the old factory. National's sales for the year 1939, near the end of the Depression, had grown to more than $3.8 million.

From the years 1940 through 1944 the company's sales grew rapidly. During World War II National Aluminate, which provided water treatment for steam locomotives, was classified as part of an essential war industry thus keeping production at peak levels. Immediately after the war, when steam locomotives were replaced by diesel, National was forced to change its products and its market. The company developed combustion catalysts, coding system treatments, and fuel oil additives for diesel engines. In 1949 National Aluminate introduced a new diesel cooling system treatment in pellet form.

In the 1950's the company experienced a rapid expansion in both the domestic and international markets. In 1951 National incorporated its first foreign subsidiary Nalco Italiana S.p.A. in Italy. By 1959 National had acquired several other foreign subsidiaries: Deutsche-Nalco-Chemie G.m.b.H. in Germany (1954); Nalco Espanola S.A. in Spain (1955); and Nalco Venezuela C.A. (1959).

Also in the 1950's, National added two new plants for catalyst production and oil field chemicals. To mark expansion into several new markets, National changed its railroad division's name to the transportation division. The company also penetrated the nuclear power field as a consultant on the land-based prototypes of the first atomic submarines, the first nuclear aircraft carrier, and the nation's first nuclear power plant at Shippingport, Pennsylvania.

In April of 1959, National Aluminate Corporation changed its name to Nalco Chemical Company. The name change signaled the company's expansion into new areas. By this time, Nalco manufactured a wide range of specialized chemicals in addition to sodium aluminate, the company's first product. By the end of the 1950's, its sales were approaching $50 million.

During the 1960's the company again expanded in size and scope. With its new polymer technology, Nalco maintained a solid position in the water treatment industry, and set standards in the areas of waste management and pollution control. In 1964 Nalco opened a new factory at Freeport, Texas, for the production of lead antiknock compounds for gasoline. The company employed a new electrolytic process recognized as a major achievement in chemical engineering technology. In October of that same year, Nalco's shares changed hands on the New York Stock Exchange.

Imperial Chemical Industries of the United Kingdom, or ICI, an important part of Nalco's development since the 1930's, was particularly instrumental in the company's growth in the second half of the 1960's. ICI and Nalco shared joint ventures in Katalco in the United States (1966), Nalfloc in Britain (1967), and Anikem in South Africa (1968). Katalco (which has subsequently been sold) produced catalysts for the manufacture of synthetic natural gas, ammonia, and hydrogen. Anikem was the product of a merger between the operations of the Alexander Martin Company of Johannesburg, South Africa (acquired by Nalco in 1967) and part of the operations of another South African company. Nalco's sales for 1966 rose to $100 million, and increased to almost $160 million in 1969.

Because of increased business and growth opportunities, Nalco expanded and consolidated several of its domestic operations during the 1970's. The company established a separate Water Treatment Chemicals Group and a Pulp and Paper Chemicals Group within its Industrial division. The Transportation Chemicals Group's name was changed to Specialty Chemicals and became part of the Industrial division.

Nalco also sold, or closed, several of its operations during this period. The company sold its vegetation control business in 1974, and its Environmental Sciences Group in 1978. Industrial Bio-Test Laboratories, which was purchased in 1965 to conduct the toxicological studies for both governmental and industrial clients, discontinued operations in 1978 because of its inability to recover from a poor image following litigation and questions raised by two federal agencies regarding operation procedures.

Nalco's philosophy of consolidation and expansion continued into the 1980's. W.H. Clark, elected president in 1982, emphasized acquisitions and new product development. To capture more of the world's markets, Nalco reorganized its International Division into three regions, including Nalco Europe, Nalco Pacific, and Nalco Latin America. Nalco also formed wholly-owned subsidiaries in Argentina, Ecuador, Japan, and Hong Kong and established a new affiliate, P.I. Nalco Perkasa, in Indonesia. The company also expanded its operations in Singapore and South Africa.

In 1984 the federal Environmental Protection Agency's restrictions on the use of lead antiknock compounds in gasoline (first announced in the late 1970's), in addition to the shrinking market for leaded gasoline, forced Nalco to discontinue its antiknock compound business. Production at the antiknock manufacturing plant in Texas was discontinued in 1985, and demolition and decontamination of the plant was to be completed by 1988.

Nalco made several important acquisitions during the first half of the 1980's which allowed Nalco to penetrate several new fields. In 1982 the company purchased Crescent Chemical, and in 1983 Nalco formed an Automotives Chemicals Group, both of which established the company in the automotive industry market. In June of 1985 Nalco also purchased the remaining 80% interest in Adco Products, a specialty chemicals manufacturer for the automotives, industrial, and construction industries, for $18 million in cash. In early 1986 Nalco purchased Penray, a group of three companies which markets a line of automotive chemicals to service professionals, and automobile owners, for $15.6 million in cash.

In 1984 *Fortune* magazine named Nalco one of the thirteen "Corporate Stars of the Decade" based on the 21.5% return on shareholder's equity over the period of a decade. In 1985 *Forbes* magazine also commended Nalco's stock performance on a five year return on shareholder's equity of 22.8%.

In the aftermath of the accident at the Union Carbide plant in Bhopal, India, where a toxic gas leak killed 2,000 people and injured 15,000 in December of 1984, Nalco paid special attention to safety procedures. In August of 1985, for the first time in its history, Nalco opened its Clearing plant, the company's oldest and largest factory, for public inspection. In 1986 Nalco moved its executive offices to Naperville, Illinois.

Nalco has grown from a manufacturer of water treatment chemicals into one of the largest specialty chemicals companies in the United States. While the company has had its share of disappointment in several markets, namely oil-products and gasoline, the outlook for the future is optimistic. By consolidating its divisions and expanding its domestic as well as international holdings, Nalco Chemical Company will continue to be a leader in its field.

Principal Subsidiaries: Day-Glo Color Corporation; The Penray Companies; Chicago Chemical Company (Illinois); Circuit Services Corporation (Minnesota); Industrial Bio-Test Laboratories, Inc. (Delaware); Visco Products, Inc. (Texas); Nalco International Sales Company (Delaware); Nalco Resources Investment Company (Texas); Adco Products, Inc. (Michigan); W.R. Hatch, Corporation; Deutsche Nalco-Chemie, G.m.b.H. (Germany); Nalco Capital Corporation, A.G. (Switzerland); Nalco Chemical A.B. (Sweden); Nalco Chemical B.V. (Holland); Nalco Chemical Company (Philippines) Inc. (Philippines); Nalco Chemical Gesellschaft m.b.H. (Austria); Nalco Chemical (H.K.) Limited (Hong Kong); Nalco de Venezuela, C.A. (Venezuela); Nalco Espanola, S.A. (Spain); Nalco Europe S.A.R.L. (France); Nalco France S.A.R.L. (France); Nalco Italiana, S.p.A. (Italy);

Nalco Limited (England); Nalco Productos Quimicos de Chile Limitada (Chile) (80%); Nalco Productos Quimicos de Chile Limitada (Brazil); Nalquimica del Ecuador S.A. (Ecuador); Nalquimica, S.A. (Argentina); Quimica Nalco de Columbia S.A. (Columbia); Suomen Nalco Oy (Finland); Nalco Saudi Company Limited (Saudi Arabia) (60%).

NATIONAL DISTILLERS AND CHEMICAL CORPORATION

99 Park Ave.
New York, New York 10016
U.S.A.
(212) 949-5000

Public Company
Incorporated: April 18, 1924 as National Distillers
Products Corporation
Employees: 10,600
Sales: $1.730 billion
Market value: $1.992 billion
Stock Index: New York

National Distillers's product line includes Gilbey's gin, polyethylene, titanium, and blankets. Although National Distillers operates as unlikely a mixture of businesses as found in the United States, the company is quite successful. At present, the company's energy products make up a large portion of its total sales.

National Distillers began operating in 1887 as the Distillers and Cattle Feeders Trust, popularly known as the Whiskey Trust. The link between cattle feed and whiskey came from the fact that the sour-mash grain residue left over from distillation was fed to cows. At first, the trust consisted of 65 southern and midwestern distilleries which were supposed to abide by production quotas and price guidelines. The trust agreement was legally unenforceable, however, and recalcitrant members (and competitors) were controlled by intimidation.

Due to its habit of purchasing independent distillers only to close them, National Distillers and Cattle Feeders was exposed to anti-trust suits. After 1895 the Trust was broken into autonomous units, but it remerged once again in 1899. After the turn of the century, however, independent distillers were able to successfully compete with the Whiskey Trust, now officially known as Distiller's Securities.

Until Prohibition most of the alcohol consumed within the United States was in the form of whiskey, so the market was very large. Almost all the whiskey sold was blended with neutral spirits, which are even less expensive to make than whiskey, but the trust left the profitable business of blending, bottling, and distribution to other companies. Consequently National Distillers's profits began to decline. Dividends, which were reported at five dollars in 1902, were negligible in 1913.

World War I temporarily revived Distiller's Securities when the company turned to the manufacture of industrial alcohol. However, prohibition, originally a temporary measure designed to conserve grain and glass, proved politically popular. As a result, prohibition was made law in 1919. Soon afterwards, Distiller's Securities changed its name to the U.S. Food Products Company and began dealing in yeast, vinegar and cereal products. In 1921 the market for these products was overcrowded, and the company was put into receivership. The banks that provided the financial resources for U.S. Food Products called in the engineering firm of Sanderson & Porter to decide whether the company should be recapitalized or dismantled. The firm voted to continue operation of the company and installed junior partner Seton Porter as president.

Porter changed the name of U.S. Food Products to National Distillers and directed it toward making medicinal alcohol, yeast and maraschino cherries. National was close to bankruptcy again when it had the good fortune to be sued for 20 counts of patent infringement by Fleischmann, the yeast maker. Porter convinced Fleischmann that the lawsuit would generate unfavorable publicity for Fleischmann, and charmed the Fleischmann representative so much that the company not only suspended the lawsuit, but also offered to buy the yeast business for $250,000. After the representative's generous offer, Porter reported that he felt "like hugging him." Nevertheless, Porter refused the offer, even after it was raised to $1.5 million. When, after a few more months of watching National exploit Fleischmann's patents, Fleischmann's offer rose to $4 million, Porter finally acquiesed. The money from the sale of the yeast subsidiaries was used to reduce National Distillers' debt and to buy 9 million gallons of pre-prohibition whiskey.

Porter sensed that the repeal of prohibition was coming soon. In order to prepare his company for the repeal, and return to its original business, Porter first secured the help of Redmond & Company, a New York stockbroker. Having examined Porter's books and having assured itself of Porter's sound business practices, Redmond & Company began to promote National Distillers' shares. With the money raised by the sale of this stock share, Porter began to amass almost half of all the pre-prohibition whiskey in the country. Porter knew there would be a three to four year period of time between the time the whiskey could legally be distilled and the time it would be ready for sale.

Prohibition ended in December of 1933 and National reported $15 million worth of sales in that month alone. Not only had National acquired a large market share of the available whiskey, but it also owned 200 brand names and three of the seven legal distilleries in the country. Moreover, as the nation's largest owner of aged whiskey, National was confronted with an important choice. It could either blend its aged whiskey with younger whiskey and sell it inexpensively, or it could cultivate a reputation for quality by selling its aged whiskey straight. Porter chose the latter course, and created a market for the company in the "bonded" whiskey market that it still occupies to this day.

After the repeal of prohibition four major distillers

emerged, two of them Canadian. By 1937 National Distillers had the smallest gross sales of the four, but the largest profits—seven million dollars. National used its profits to purchase other quality distillers such as W. & A. Gilbey, Limited, a gin maker, and John de Kuyper and Son, Inc., a maker of liqueurs.

Company sales and profits continued to climb during World War II, despite what appeared to be adverse circumstances. Some of the company's facilities were needed for the production of industrial alcohol for the war effort, a less lucrative product than liquor. Furthermore, rations on necessary materials reduced the production of most of National Distillers' brands. The nationwide shortage of liquor, however, only served to drive prices up, consequently profits continued to grow. These favorable market conditions lasted until 1949.

In 1949 Seton Porter selected James Bierwirth, then president of New York Trust, to succeed him as president. Bierwirth, a teetotaler, at first declined Porter's offer, but later accepted when Porter agreed that the company could diversify into chemicals. The justification for National Distillers' move into the chemical market came from the nature of the liquor industry itself.

The liquor industry never has been what could be called a growth industry. The size of the market is a product both of demographics and major social trends. Liquor manufacturers are reluctant to try and expand their market by encouraging non-drinkers to drink and drinkers to consume more. Thus, a larger market share can only be achieved at the expense of other distillers. This is not easy given the brand loyalty and regional variations that exist. Not only is it hard to expand the market share, but price-wars and cost-cutting are also ineffective. Furthermore, actual cost of the liquid contents of a bottle represents only a tenth of what one pays for it, so less expensive grain is not the answer.

Given the unusual conditions that exist in this industry, it is understandable that National Distillers would want to use its steady income from liquor to finance growth in a less stable field with higher rewards. The chemical industry was the perfect choice. Du Pont had designed an $11 million metallic sodium plant whose sodium it needed, but fear of an anti-trust suit caused it to delay construction. As a result, Du Pont sold the plans and the necessary patents to National Distillers for a mere $500,000, and signed a contract to buy one-third of the plant's production. To finance the plant Bierwirth sold certain assets like the White Rock Corporation and Swiss Colony Wines.

The metallic sodium plant was soon bringing in $8.5 million in sales, and had the highest profit margin of any division within the company. In 1952 National Distillers merged with U.S. Industrial Chemicals, a manufacturer of industrial alcohol, insecticides, anti-freeze and resins. Soon afterwards, the U.S. Industrial Chemicals division of National Distillers formed a joint venture with Panhandle Eastern Pipe Company in Tuscola, Illinois. This venture was soon expanded beyond industrial alcohol and ethyl chloride to include ammonia and polyethylene products.

The diversification of National Distillers into chemicals was well-timed due to the fact that the company's liquor sales were depressed. The decline in sales was due in large part to consumer preference for blended whiskey over National Distillers' 100 proof bourbon.

During the 1960's the company's diversification strategy yielded mixed, and often surprising, results. Polyethylene, for instance, did not sell well on the market and its failure came as a surprise because National Distillers was one of the first companies to manufacture this particular kind of plastic. In addition, management at the company thought its plan to manufacture fertilizer from hydrogen, a by-product of its ethyl production, would garner large sales. Unfortunately, several oil companies had the same idea and the market for ammonia fertilizer was soon over-crowded.

During the 1960's there were also some pleasant surprises for National Distillers. One of these was Bridgeport Brass, purchased in 1961 to help increase titanium sales. Although titanium sales never did increase during this time the brass works, once separated from an unprofitable aluminum division, did quite well. In 1968 brass accounted for a third of the company's earnings. Another profitable acquisition was Beacon Manufacturing, the world's largest producer for non-woven blankets. This company was purchased as an outlet for polypropylene fibers to be produced by a joint venture with Phillips Petroleum. The polypropylene venture was not approved by the Justice Department, but Beacon did very well for a number of years.

Despite the success of its U.S. Industrial Chemicals division and its acquisitions in other fields, 60% of the company's earnings still came from liquor during the 1960's. By 1967 bourbon was popular once again and this helped to increase liquor sales. National Distillers added to its product line of wines and spirits by purchasing Alberta Distillers, Holland House, a producer of cocktail mixes, and Almaden Vineyards. When wine sales dramatically increased during the 1970's the Almaden purchase paid off handsomely.

One major change in the mid-1970's was that the diversification into chemicals, once a drain on bourbon profits, began to show signs of recovery. Profits of $44 million in the first half of 1974 were almost twice as high as profits for both halves of 1973 combined. The strong showing by the chemical division came just in time however, because bourbon sales were decreasing. Fortunately, the company had already acquired Gilbey's, a gin producer, to capitalize on the trend towards less strongly flavored spirits.

During this time, rising oil prices convinced the management at National Distillers to slowly move away from chemicals derived from petroleum feedstocks. As a result, the company became increasingly interested in alcohols and chemicals made from renewable resources. One important purchase by the company at this time was that of Emery, a manufacturer of fat and tallow-based specialty chemicals. National Distillers also perfected a new process of making ethanol from grain that reduced the cost of ethanol by almost a third. Despite its interest in chemicals made from renewable resources, polyethylenes and acetates (made from petroleum) remained an important part of the company's total sales figure.

Perhaps the most notable suprise of the 1970's was the

performance of National Distillers' titanium subsidiary. Purchased in 1955, the company went for years without making a satisfactory profit. However, President Bierwirth, and later President Drummond Bell, continued to believe in the titanium project. They were rewarded when titanium profits increased from $6 million in 1977 to $30 million in 1980 as the government required more of the metal for its military jets.

National Distillers celebrated its titanium success with Almaden wine, which was making a profit of $20 million on sales of $144 million. An insurance company agency purchased by National Distillers in 1979, the Indiana Group, was another cause for celebration.

During the 1980's the company was fortunate it had previously invested in oleochemicals because petrochemicals were affected by low demand and low prices. 1982, a recession year, was particularly bad in the petrochemical market, sales dropped from $506 million to $456 million. Sales rebounded strongly in 1984 and rose to $775 million, but decreased again in 1985. Sales for oleochemicals, on the other hand, increased steadily from $250 million in 1981 to $307 million in 1985.

Energy related products have become increasingly important to National Distillers. Revenues from this division increased from $71 million to $571 million in 1985. This increase was largely due to the acquisition of Surburban Propane and Pargas, both propane distributors. While energy sales increased, profits from the Indiana Group decreased as the company endured major underwriting losses. It was subsequently sold. Holland House, the manufacturer of cocktail mixes, was also sold because the distribution of its products through grocery stores made it incompatible with the parent company's distribution of wines and spirits through liquor stores.

In the early and mid-1980's, the entire liquor industry was adversely affected, in part because of public concern with drunk driving and alcohol abuse. Like most other distillers, National Distillers experienced a decline in profits from wines and spirits. Under these difficult market conditions National Distillers introduced Peachtree Schnapps, which soon became one of the most successful new entrants in industry history. Peachtree Schnapps helped to increase profits in the liquor division from $648 million to $680 million during 1985, a year when the industry as a whole watched profits drop.

Standard & Poor's expects liquor consumption to decline by 1%–2% a year until 1990. Whiskey consumption is expected to decline at a slightly faster rate. This is not good news for the company, but since 80% of its profits are unrelated management is not worried. Sales of plastic are expected to increase, and this will be helped by a low dollar. At the same time, propane sales should remain consistently high.

Principal Subsidiaries: Actagen, Inc; Almaden Vineyards, Inc.; Caves Lanrent Perrier, Inc.; Cooling-Grumme-Mumford Co., Inc.; DR Insurance Co.; John de Kuyper & Son, Inc. (N.Y.); Emery Chemicals; Emery Export, Inc.; NDCC Export Corp.; National Distillers Products Co.; National Helium Corp.; National Hydrocarbons, Inc.; National Petro Chemicals Corp.; Pargas Inc.; RMI Co.; Suburban Propane Gas Corp.; Buzzini Drilling Co., Inc.; Plateau, Inc.; SPG Energy Exploration Corp.; Vangas, Inc.; Syngas Co. (Tex.); U.S. Industrial Chemicals Co. The company also lists subsidiaries in Brazil, Canada, and Mexico.

OLIN CORPORATION

120 Long Ridge Road
Stamford, Connecticut 06904
U.S.A.
(203) 356–2000

Public Company
Incorporated: August 13, 1892 as Mathieson Alkali Works
Employees: 14,900
Sales: $2.29 billion
Market value: $1.097 billion
Stock Index: New York

According to the frontispiece of its 1985 annual report, the Olin Corporation manufactures chemical products and metal products with emphasis on electronic materials for the defense and aerospace industries. Only three years before the company's emphasis, after its chemical and metal production, was on cigarette papers, cellophane, skiing equipment, ammunition and homebuilding materials. Throughout its 26 year history Olin has been a protean corporation.

The Olin Corporation is the offspring of a merger between the Mathieson Chemical Company (which manufactured ammonia and caustic soda) and the munitions and brass business started by Franklin Olin. After World War II these previously conservative companies used their newly acquired fortunes to go on a corporate spending spree, and purchased numerous small businesses in new fields. In 1954 Tom Nicholls, the youthful president of Mathieson, and John Olin, Franklin's sixty year old son, decided to merge their two companies. This merger formed the fifth largest chemical company in the U.S. Within a few years it became apparent that this union exacerbated the tendency of both companies to overextend themselves.

At the time of the merger Olin Industries was a promising corporation which manufactured gun powder. It had been founded in 1892 by a conservative ex-baseball player named Franklin Olin. In 1909 Olin was nearly replaced by the Du Pont family and their Gunpowder Trust, which acquired 49% of Franklin's company, then known as the Western Powder Company. Franklin scrambled for the remaining 51% and retained control. This incident, however, subsequently shaped Franklin's approach to conducting business.

Franklin deliberately kept his company small. Western's first acquisition, Winchester Arms, was a defensive move against Du Pont, which might have purchased the company in order to deprive Western of a customer for its gunpowder. During World War I, Franklin refused to expand his production capacity to keep up with wartime demands, although in World War II, as one of the country's larger armaments producers, he had no choice but to expand. The Winchester plants, famous for "the guns that won the West," acquitted themselves admirably during the war. For instance, they put an important new gun, the M1 Carbine, into production in just 13 days. Besides the gunpowder and munitions factories, Western Powder also operated a brass works at that time. This remains one of the operations that keeps the present Olin Corporation solvent.

After the war Franklin found himself with a large company, something he did not want. Consequently, he retired and kept most of the Western Powder Company stock for himself and divided the rest between his two sons, Spencer and John. They consolidated all Western's properties and renamed the new enterprise Olin Industries. Soon Olin Industries began to diversify into paper, rocket fuel, petrochemicals, cellophane and lumber.

After Franklin's departure Olin was managed by John and Spencer Olin and Bill Hanes. All three were in their 60's and the lack of a suitable candidate to succeed John, who was president, was the major concern of a company that was otherwise in excellent shape. While Olin Industries had high growth potential, the best and brightest of the nation's corporate elite were not eager to become Olin's president-in-training. For one thing, it was not likely that the strong-minded president would retire early. And when he did retire, he would not be the kind to easily relinquish his power.

The lack of a logical successor was an important factor in John's proposal to Tom Nicholls, the 44 year old president of Mathieson and a rising star in the chemical industry. Starting in 1947 Nicholls, with the help of his friend John Leppart, had transformed Mathieson, a small regional chemical company which concentrated on a few commodity chemicals, into a company with $366 million in sales. This represented a 600% increase over Mathieson's performance before Nicholls took over. This dramatic turnaround was accomplished by a diversification towards less cyclical products and companies with strong marketing organizations. One of the factors which had slowed the growth of Mathieson was the narrowness of its market i.e., it sold only to manufacturers. Through the acquisition of feed companies, however, it was able to bring its ammonia and phosphate products directly to farmers.

John Olin and Tom Nicholls were friends, in fact, they often went hunting together. The idea of a merger was first broached in 1951, but discarded because a satisfactory division of power did not seem possible. Nicholls headed a company almost equal to Olin in size, and neither he nor John Olin wanted to be subordinate to the other. Nevertheless, a merger remained tempting because it would further Olin's new expansion into chemicals and bring Mathieson closer to consumers. The companies had previously cooperated on a rocket fuels venture which proved they could work together.

During the initial discussions of a merger between the

two corporations, Mathieson purchased Squibb, a company only slightly smaller than itself. Nicholls seemed possessed by a drive for mergers that would eventually prove ill-advised, though the purchase of Squibb, a well-known manufacturer of pharmaceuticals, did not seem like a bad idea at the time.

In 1953, while on a hunting trip, Olin finally convinced Nicholls that a merger was possible. Within a matter of days Bill Hanes had arrived at a satisfactory division of power. The new Olin-Mathieson would be run by a triumverate of John Olin, Nicholls and Hanes. Olin would be chairman, Nicholls president and Hanes would be in charge of finance.

Although it was later to condemn the merger, the press offered its congratulations in 1953 when the agreement took place. Many analysts remarked on the compatability of the Olin and Mathieson operations: Mathieson made many products of the commodity chemicals Olin Industries used. Furthermore, the direction in which the two companies were moving appeared to dovetail: Mathieson was moving from basic chemicals to consumer goods while Olin, a manufacturer of consumer goods, was moving into basic chemicals. The only indication of trouble came from inside the company. Said an Olin-Mathieson executive soon after the merger, "We'll have to keep Tommy (Nicholls) from expanding for the present; this is a time to digest."

However, the desire to diversify continued to triumph over prudence. Within 18 months of its incorporation the Olin Mathieson Chemical Company had purchased three new businesses: Marquardt Aircraft, Blockson Chemical and the Brown Paper Mill Company. This last purchase alone cost 90 million dollars. By 1958 Olin Mathieson was producing one of the widest assortments of products of any company in the United States, yet their strategy was unsuccessful. Sales for that year were a disappointing $20 million, although Bill Hanes had said in 1956 that sales would soon be hitting $1 billion. The causes of Olin Mathieson's poor performance were manifold.

The August 1958 issue of *Fortune* magazine accused the company of allowing itself to be constantly side-tracked. Indeed, Olin Mathieson seemed to lack direction. Part of the problem lay in its strategy of diversification and part in the structure of the new company itself. Olin and Nicholls had thought that their companies could be joined like two halves of an apple although, in fact, it was an apple and an orange that were combined. This led to insufficient communication between the two. Again, *Fortune* magazine called the management of Olin Mathieson "a loose confederation of tribal chieftains." This charge was born out by a 1958 meeting where the 36 research chiefs met for the first time and two of them discovered that they had been doing identical research on a fuel additive.

The lack of communication and poor diversification strategy led to the 1957 purchase of an aluminum plant. The aluminum industry was an expensive one to enter and the purchase of the aluminum works put Olin Mathieson into debt. In addition, the timing of the purchase could not have been worse because of the imminent soft market. The business community was surprised at the poor planning of the aluminum operation because Olin Mathieson had not secured a source of bauxite, a principal ingredient in aluminum manufacture and one that was frequently in short supply. For the next two decades Olin Mathieson would find its fortunes rising and falling with the profitability of aluminum.

After this had occurred Nicholls was soon "promoted" to the board, John Olin became chairman of the executive committee, and Stan Osborne became president. Osborne was a fiesty but accessible administrator. He was also a Spanish history buff; in fact, he was engaged in writing a book on that very subject when he was promoted. Determined to avoid the corporate equivalent of the sinking of the Spanish Armada, he began to dispose of unprofitable and incompatible product lines. Moreover, a bauxite supply was assured. Cost control measures were also undertaken, including a $20,000 cut in his own salary. The business press praised his damage control.

After the two bad years of 1957 and 1958 when sales declined, the balance sheet began to improve. In 1959 profits increased 17% over the previous year, but that rate of growth did not continue. Although Osborne's cost-cutting measures kept the company from disaster, he was obviously frustrated with the company's slow progress. He resigned in 1963 for a career in banking.

Throughout the 1960's Olin Mathieson continued to be plagued by the same problems that had come to light in 1958. In 1967 the new president, a man named Grand (the fourth president in the company's 14 year history), initiated a program that sounded similar to Osborne's recovery plan. Unprofitable divisions were ordered to show an 8% yearly increase in profits. This was not an unattainable figure for most of the divisions. Even Squibb, which was responsible for a quarter of the company's sales, was producing a mediocre 5% return on assets. In 1967 Grand planned a program of expansion into recreation, housing, lumber and chemicals that was to have either unexciting or negative results for the company. In 1969, the company adopted its present name of Olin Corporation.

In what was developing into a disheartening pattern, Olin celebrated the new decade with a decline in profits. The prolonged strike by American autoworkers decreased the market for aluminum. Furthermore, the new pollution regulations were expensive. Two plants, one manufacturing DDT and the other soda ash, had to be shut down because they could not meet environmental protection standards. These closings resulted in a $26 million loss. The timing of Olin's new housing venture recalls the aluminum disaster since the market went into a depression soon after Olin entered it.

Sporting goods, sold through the Winchester division, became one of the company's priorities. Olin ski equipment was marketed and sold quite successfully, though another product, Wingo, did not fare as well. Wingo was a game in which a player shot at hollow balls of ice released by a computer operated by the opposing player. Played in a building the size of a forty lane bowling alley, it was symbolic of management strategy that characterized Olin at the time.

In 1974 the new Olin president, James Towey (Grand had died suddenly in 1971), was able to boast an 80%

jump in earnings. This increase was brought about largely through the sale of the aluminum operations and the polyester film factories which had been depressing earnings. The aluminum works had earned $19 million over a 10 year period and had lost $32 million. It's disappearance from the balance sheet was salutary. The chemicals division, always a company mainstay, performed well, and the agricultural products division prospered. Brass and paper, steady sources of income, held their ground. In 1975 the company continued to sell unprofitable product lines such as the parka business it had bought a few years before.

In the late 1970's housing and Winchester Arms took on the role of the ill-fated aluminum works in suppressing profits. Winchester's operating profits plunged 37% in one year, despite the quality of its guns and their name recognition. Olin has a history of watching quality products yield mediocre financial gains. In 1968, for example, the head of Squibb convinced Olin to sell that division so that it could realize its full earnings potential.

Forbes magazine once referred to Olin as the world's longest running garage sale. Indeed, the company had, and still has, a habit of buying unprofitable businesses and then selling them within a few years, often at a loss. In 1985 the profitable but slow growing paper division was sold, along with the last of the home-building concerns. The company's most recent round of divestment caused shareholders equity to drop 25%, although its shares went up three points.

At present Olin is looking to metal and chemical products, especially chemicals that are used by the electronics industry, to reinvigorate the company. This began with the expansion in electronics and aerospace during 1980. In 1985 Olin acquired Rockcor Inc., which produces rockets, gas generators and data systems for battlefield intelligence, as well as devices to measure the strength of underground nuclear tests. It has also offered to produce nerve gas for the government, if the liability issue can be resolved. Another anticipated growth area is water purification, a logical extension of their chlorine products for swimming pools. Ultra-purified water is used in the electronics and defense industries.

Olin's future may look like its past. The company has again shifted its focus to an industry (electronics) that almost immediately went into a slump. Chemicals, Olin's largest business, will have to contend with a weak world economy and tough foreign competition. In addition, the company's product mix is not particularly strong. The company's major commodity chemicals are ammonium and sodium phosphate, two products that have had problems with low prices, over-capacity and high production costs. In 1985 Olin lost twice as much money as it made the previous year. Industry analysts maintain that if the present president and chief executive officer, J.M. Henske, is to revive the company, he must find a stable product line and stick with it.

Principal Subsidiaries: Olin Hunt Speciality Products, Inc.; Rockcor, Inc.; Larse Corp.; Pacific Electro-Dynamics, Inc.; Physics International Co.

PENNWALT CORPORATION

Three Parkway
Philadelphia, Pennsylvania 19102
U.S.A.
(215) 587-7000

Public Company
Incorporated: September 25, 1850 as Pennsylvania Salt
Manufacturing Co.
Employees: 9,901
Sales: $1.108 billion
Market value: $660 million
Stock Index: New York

Five young Quakers started the Pennsylvania Salt Manufacturing Company in 1850 with a small budget and a great deal of hope. They combined their conservative outlook with some calculated risks and that early philosophy has been the trademark of this diversified chemical corporation ever since.

The two primary founders of Pennsylvania Salt, George T. Lewis, a commission merchant, and Charles Lannig, a manufacturer, combined their resources with three other Philadelphia Quakers to begin the process of producing alkalies from salt. At the start of this venture the partners had in their favor $100,000 in capital, a plant located on a salt deposit near Pittsburgh, and a patent for the process. The future looked promising, but after five years of attempting to manufacture salt and its derivatives, the group despaired of making the company a success. Although operating expenses were draining the company's resources, the partners decided to give the company one final try. That gamble paid off, and the company soon made a name for itself.

The first success of the company was not in salt production however. Around 1856 the company started selling lye soap for household use, and the idea was an instant success. In 1856 the company reported its first profitable year. Due to the success of the soap manufacturing business, Pennsylvania Salt Manufacturing was able to finance the restructuring of its salt processing system.

Pennsylvania Salt Manufacturing Company is notable for many innovations within the industry. In 1865 the company had begun to use some of its other raw materials. Specifically, cryolite, which is a natural fluoride of sodium and aluminum that was used at the time as a whitener in the production of glass and ceramic ware, became an important addition to the company product line. In 1864 the company signed a contract with the Danish government to obtain cryolite from the only known site in Greenland. The company was also the first to ship liquid chlorine (1907) and anhydrous hydrofluorine acid for the use in high-octane aviation fuel (1931) by tank car.

During World War II the company signed a contract with the U.S. government to manufacture synthetic cryolite. This government contract was primarily responsible for increasing the company's earnings from $9.5 million in 1939 to $26 million in 1944. In addition, unlike many companies of this time, Pennsylvania Salt did not have to reconvert its products for war time usage.

After the war the company implemented a progressive policy of research and development which led to an increased use of raw materials that diversified the essentially one-product business. By 1945 the company was manufacturing a wide range of chemicals for use within the aluminum, glass and ceramic industries, and the chemical manufacturing and farm operations industries, including such items as chlorine and chlorine compounds, acids, disinfectants, germicides and insecticides, soap and bleaching compounds, and weed killers.

The company policy of adding new products, developing new processes and expanding its facilities was established to solidify its earning potential in the years after the war. By 1950 Pennsylvania Salt was experiencing a faster rate of growth than before the war. In addition, Pennsylvania Salt could boast that it had plants located throughout the United States, including the east, midwest, south and northwest.

In 1950 Pennsylvania Salt celebrated its 100th anniversary; it was one of the oldest companies in the chemical business. It had established a reputation for being one of the "soundest firms" in the industry, with a "conservative" and "well-heeled" image. This solid reputation is exemplified by the company's report to its shareholders in 1878 that its credit rating was one of the best in the industry, and that it was a company that paid cash for everything it purchased. In 1947 Pennsylvania Salt called on its shareholders to support a share issue plan for a $7.5 million facility expansion program. This was the first time that the company had ever issued preferred stock shares, and this move symbolized a new direction for the firm.

Leonard T. Beale was president during this time and is credited for establishing new priorities for the company, not only through financing schemes, but also in terms of diversification. Beale was elected president in 1928 and continued in that post until 1949 when he was appointed chairman. Beale's management strategy included diversifying the company by acquiring dairy sanitation specialty lines, a laundry and dry cleaning compound manufacturing firm, and a chlorate plant in Portland, Oregon.

Beale's diversification policy was continued by William P. Drake who was appointed chief executive officer in 1955. Drake was interested in moving the company away from the commodity cycles that harmed its earnings and into specialty chemicals. Under Drake's direction the company diversified even further into equipment manufacturing lines, and he also emphasized new product research. Within a ten year period sales doubled to $144.4 million in 1964.

The company name was changed in 1957 to Pennsalt Chemical Corporation, although the company had been referred to as Pennsalt for many years preceding the change. At this time, Pennsalt was lagging behind the larger chemical companies such as Du Pont that had made nylon, Teflon, and Dacron household words. While Pennsalt was not able to compete with the larger corporations, it was busy putting significant amounts of money and personnel behind more than 600 products that had limited markets. These limited markets were of no interest to the "giants" of the industry and so Pennsalt was able to use them to its earning advantage.

Drake's philosophy was one of combining thriftiness with a sense of daring, a philosophy that was shared by the founders of the company. If he saw a profit in a product then Pennsalt would sell it. This philosophy led to the company's diverse line of products in the late 1950's and throughout the 1960's. The company's plan at this time was a strong emphasis on improvement, expansion, and product additions.

Drake diversified even further by moving into the processing equipment industry in 1962 with the acquisition of Sharples Company, a manufacturer of centrifuges, and in 1963 with the absorption of I.J. Stokes Corporation, a $23 million producer of tabulating machines, plastic molding machines and high-vacuum equipment. These acquisitions were the first step toward diversifying the company in order to maintain a competitive edge against the larger chemical firms.

In addition, Pennsalt was establishing an international presence, through both its expansions and acquisitions. In 1960 Pennsalt had only a single chlorine and caustic plant in Mexico, but with the acquisition of Sharples, Pennsalt inherited plants in England, France and Germany. At the same time, the company was acquiring a Dutch chemical and plastic concern. By 1965 Pennsalt had four chemical plants, and 11 equipment or combined plants in Western Europe, Mexico and South America.

Drake's interest in quality rather than quantity made 1964 a notable year in terms of research and development. Eighty new chemical products were released. Some of the most significant products were fluorine-based refrigerants, aerosol propellents, and foaming agents called Isotron. In the plastics field, another important product was Kynar 500, a paint additive that provided durability to outside wall finishes. Kynar 500, in particular, was a product that would provide significant financial reward to Pennsalt in the years to come.

Although Pennsalt had shown itself to be a promising company under the direction of Drake, the late 1960's spelled near-disaster for the company, even though sales increased from $79.8 million in 1957 to $268 million in 1968. The steadily rising earnings suddenly dropped off in the late 1960's. The cause of this crisis was blamed on the two large acquisitions and a depression in the basic chemicals market.

One of the acquisitions made in the late 1960's was S.S. White Dental Manufacturing Company, which gave Pennsalt an important position in the dental products field, but drained Pennsalt's resources because the acquired company needed significant modernization of its facilities. The dental health products business would later turn out to be poor investment. At the time, however, Drake was interested in moving the company away from a dependency on the chemical industry, and its highly volatile cycles, which hurt the company's earnings.

Another important acquisition of this period was Wallace and Tiernan, a chemical, equipment, and health care concern that added related, but noncompetitive product lines to Pennsalt. Upon the merger the company changed its name to its present title of Pennwalt Corporation. Drake viewed Wallace & Tiernan as a company that would add to the existing product mix without creating a reliance on any one product to increase the company's earnings. At the time of the merger, each company was dependent on the chemicals industry as its primary source of earnings, but the merger also added to the equipment and health care groups as well.

Along with the downswing of the chemicals market and the acquisition of S.S. White, which needed significant modernization, there were also management problems that appeared as a result of the merger with Wallace & Tiernan. Drake stated that the company had experienced a "bellyful of acquisition indigestion" because of the problems presented by management changes. Some executives died, others retired or quit; by the end of the merger only three of the original management team of Wallace and Tiernan were left. However, with the average age of the top management at 51, Drake was confident that some of the original executives would be around to witness the implementation of the 10-year plan: "We'll have our youth and vigor and still have some gray-haired expertise."

The problems experienced in the late 1960's came to an end by 1973 when Pennwalt went through a turnaround phase. The chemical operations began to pay off, even though Drake had earlier reduced the dependency on the chemical group to 55% of the company's earnings. Yet even though the chemicals group, the original product of the company, had reversed Pennwalt's streak of bad luck by 1978, Drake was looking at pharmaceuticals to provide the company's significant earnings by 1980.

Upon Drake's retirement in 1978, Edwin E. Tuttle took over as president. Tuttle was no stranger to the company; he had first arrived at Pennwalt in 1951, six years before Drake was named president. Tuttle was fresh out of Harvard's MBA program when he joined the financial division of Pennwalt. Tuttle moved up through the company, both in the financial division and as assistant to the president in 1957, and again in 1961. With the acquisition of Sharples Company, Tuttle became secretary-treasurer of the company for a year and a half before returning to Pennwalt. Tuttle's management style was patterned after the direction set by Drake—smart acquisitions that would maintain the company's growth, with particular emphasis on the acquisitions of pharmaceutical companies, considered by both men to be the direction of Pennwalt's future.

In 1981 Tuttle began a restructuring program that focused on diversifying the company in "leadership areas." What this meant was that the company began divesting itself of some of its less profitable subsidiaries. In particular, the dental business had shown itself to be a disappointment and by 1985 S.S. White Dental Corporation was sold because it was not "consistent" with the company's "long-term strategic plans."

The pharmaceutical industry was the main interest during this restructuring program. Tuttle predicted that Pennwalt's $82 million pharmaceutical operation of 1982 would increase to $250 million by 1986. Part of Tuttle's enthusiasm for the pharmaceutical industry was based on the development of the time-release decongestant capsule known as PennKinectic CD2. This product was used in such over-the-counter drugs as Allarest products. Tuttle saw this new product development as an opportunity to sell the technology to other companies in order to raise the cash to support the research and development efforts of Pennwalt's pharmaceutical efforts. Tuttle was not concerned with having to compete, once more, with the larger companies in the pharmaceutical industry, but his $250 million prediction fell short. In 1984 the pharmaceutical division earned only $109 million. At the time, Tuttle blamed the slow growth on the difficulty of getting FDA approval for Pennwalt's controlled-release drugs.

While the pharmaceutical industry appeared to be a new direction for the future growth of Pennwalt, the chemical operation was still proving its value. By 1983 Pennwalt saw a halt to three straight years of failing profits. In 1982 the chemical operations were 60% of the company's $1.06 billion sales. In addition, the company was pursuing an ambitious expansion plan with a $60 million Kynar-brand plant in New Jersey.

By 1985 Pennwalt had closed its Michigan chlorine soda/caustic unit because of a poor midwestern market. Besides implementing cost-cutting measures in the subsidiaries, Pennwalt implemented another restructuring program that included employee layoffs. In his 1985 annual message, President Tuttle explained that this restructuring was being done in order to "provide solid growth in future earnings." Emphasis was on more efficient use of resources and a future focus on high-return businesses.

Pennwalt's future depends on management's ability to successfully restructure the company and make sound acquisition investments that will complement Pennwalt's existing subsidiaries. Pennwalt's long and productive history, with its philosophy of conservative risk taking, will undoubtedly play an important role in any future decisions made by management.

Principal Subsidiaries: Automatic Power, Inc.; Cook's Industrial Lubricants, Inc.; Delaware Chemicals Corp.; Mayo Products Co.; Pennwalt, Inc.; Pennwalt Foreign Sales Corp.; Pennwalt International Corp.; Western Hemisphere; Pennwalt International Sales Corp.; Turco Products, Inc.; Turco Purex Industrial Corp.; Wyandotte Southern Railroad Co. The company also has subsidiaries in the following countries: Belgium, Canada, France, Italy, Mexico, The Netherlands, Netherlands Antilles, Spain, Switzerland, United Kingdom, and West Germany.

PERSTORP A.B.

S-28480
Perstorp
Sweden
46435-38000

Public Company
Employees: 5,347
Sales: SKr 3.941 billion (US$ 579.3 million)
Market value: SKr 3.295 billion (US$ 484.3 million)
Stock Index: Stockholm London

At a small mill on the edge of a beechwood forest in the southern tip of Sweden, Wilhelm Wendt founded Perstorp A.B. in 1881. Stensmölla Kemiska Tekniska Industri, as it was originally called, was initially dedicated to product development and refinement of its only source of raw materials, the beechwood forest. Today the company is no longer dependent upon wood products; however, it still produces many of its original product line begun almost a century ago. Perstorp presently concentrates its efforts on integrating its refining process and focusing its resources on the international market.

Originally, charcoal was the only commercial product at the Stensmölla Kemiska Tekniska Industri. However, after he had established his own company Wendt, an engineer, built a purification plant to separate useful products from waste in the fene gases captured during the carbonizing process to produce acetic acid and wood alcohol. The production of acetic acid began in 1884.

Wilhelm convinced skeptical Swedish housewives that this new acetic acid vinegar made from beechwood was better than the alcohol-base vinegar that they had used and trusted for years. The new stock lasted longer, tasted better, was less expensive, and stayed fresh longer than its competitor. The acetic acid won many prizes at exhibitions in Chicago, Lubeck, Copenhagen and Göteberg. When combined with a winning advertising campaign, this helped Wendt to achieve the first commercial success at his new company.

By 1888, the company grew to employ 16 people in the production of charcoal and acetic acid. During this time Wendt also shortened the company's name to Skånska Ättiksfabriken. Due to the fact that he did not always have access to the raw materials he needed, Wendt decided that he would have to maximize the refining process to make the company profitable. In 1898, therefore, he built a refinery to separate wood alcohol into pure methanol,

chemical acetin, an acetin substitute and woodnaphta denaturating methanol.

From 1900 to 1904 the company was confronted with financial problems. In order to overcome these problems Wendt constantly reinvested all of the liquid assets back into the company. In 1904 Wendt built a new plant to produce cresote, carbinoleum and pitch from pine tar and other carbonization processes. During the Russo-Japanese War cresote was issued to Japanese soldiers to prevent dysentery. Wendt sold all of the cresote his company could manufacture to Japan. In 1905 Wendt built a new factory designed to convert methanol to formalin. Formalin, or formaldehyde, was first sold as a disinfectant.

Between the years 1907 and 1914 the company barely met operating costs. Despite the company's dismal financial outlook and Sweden's continuing economic crisis, Wendt continued to heavily fund his product development experiments. At the start of World War I in 1914, however, acetic acid sales were so optimistic that Wendt built a glass factory to produce the bottles for the acid. Sales in the new glassworks were supplemented by the production of commercial lighting glass for export to England.

As World War I continued, Wendt realized that he could capitalize on Germany's inability to export products. He began producing acetyl acid which had previously been imported from Germany. The company's pharmaceutical factory, begun in 1905, expanded its product line to include urotropine, or hexamethylenetetramine, which during those days was considered effective against polio and other diseases.

During this time the sawmill became an integral part of the company's raw materials production. The timber from the mill was now distributed so that the best pieces would go to the newly established furniture factory; pieces would go to the packaging plant for acetic acid bottles; some would go for producing butter churns, which had been a product at the mill since Wilhelm Wendt's father started the mill; and the worst pieces would be used to fire the burners in the mill.

During the war years Wendt employed a well-educated Indian chemist named Das Gupta in the company's pharmaceutical laboratory. Das Gupta's job was to develop a new pharmaceutical product that would compete with the German manufacturers after the war was over. He discovered, after many experiments, a substitute shellac with excellent insulating properties named "indolac." Das Gupta then took the indolac, mixed it with pitch and tar, and created a plastic, or Isolit, as it was called at Skånska Ättiksfabriken. The new raw material was the Swedish version of the German bakelite, which had been on the market for years and was protected by a large number of patents. Fortunately for the company, the Germans decided not to take the matter to court.

In 1917 Skånska began manufacturing its first plastic product, a handle for electrical knife switches. The first products were riddled with problems and were discarded in the stream that ran through the area. When factory officials decided this was not safe, Skånska dumped the defects in a designated area behind the plant. Isolit's production constituted the birth of Scandinavia's first plastic products.

The radio industry soon became the primary customer of Isolit products. In 1923 Skånska Ättiksfabriken began producing laminates, or the strong, brown board in a radio which electrical parts are mounted on. The industrial grade laminate began as (and still remains) the single, largest-selling product for the company. Also, the company's furniture factory became Sweden's largest manufacturer of radio cabinets.

In the early 1920's Skånska's chemists, after adding a shiny surface to the industrial laminate, discovered decorative laminates. This new product resisted wear and tear, heat and chemicals. In the mid-1930's Skånska Ättiksfabriken introduced beech parquet. However, because the beech parquet, used as floorboards, had been dried too much, expanded, and subsequently caused a number of household accidents, the company became involved in many lawsuits and was forced to pay substantial damage costs.

During World War II Skånska refined many tons of charcoal used to manufacture a substitute gas for Sweden's passenger cars. Again, Skånska's production suffered from lack of raw materials. To fuel the modern charcoal plant Wendt's son, Otto, was forced to cut up millions of parquet boards, which actually turned out to be more economical for the company at this time than selling them on the open market.

When World War II ended in 1945, and as the European countries began piecing their industries and economies back together again, Skånska's production was no match for its competitors. Skånska, although no longer the only plastics company in Scandinavia, was the largest with a product line of more than 10,000 items.

After the war, when Swedish gasoline was placed back on the market, Skånska was faced with disposing of many tons of charcoal. The solution to this problem involved selling the excess charcoal to the carbon bisulphide industry. Thus, in the early 1950's the company began breaking the dependency link between coal and chemicals. The company did not completely stop operations at the charcoal burning plant until 1970 when environmental controls also became a factor. However, with the purchase of a small barbecue charcoal and industrial coal plant, Skånska never really eliminated coal from its activities.

The company's carefully established chain of raw materials network was finally broken in 1952 when Skånska began using methanol purchased from outside sources to manufacture its formalin. And, in 1967, the saw mill, another important part of the raw materials chain, closed its operation.

After an illness during the early 1950's, Otto Wendt was forced to relinquish some management of the day to day operations of the plant. For the first time at Skånska Ättiksfabriken new methods of planning, budgets, market analysis were implemented. The company placed new emphasis on quality and on long-term low risk projects, rather than the short-term speculation that had characterized its operations before 1945. Skånska also began making efforts to establish business contacts in export markets. It was during this time that the company established a plant in Brazil for the production of laminates.

The next twenty years became the era of the decorative laminate. It was so successful that Skånska could not produce enough to meet the demand of the Swedish market. Since this lack of production was due largely to a constant labor shortage because of the lack of housing for employees, the company helped solve the problem by collaborating with the town of Perstorp to develop new housing facilities.

In 1955 Skånska began producing the polyalcohol trimethylolopropane, intended primarily for the paint industry. The company's interest in polyalcohols began in the 1940's when Otto Wendt used profits from the charcoal operations to fund a study at the University of Lund. As a war concession at the end of World War II, the German chemical industry was forced to open up the contents of its patents and process descriptions. Like other chemical companies at the time, Skånska incorporated many of the German ideas into its production methods. Some of these ideas were incorporated into Skånska development of a polyalcohol based on formalin called pentaerythritol.

In 1955 Otto Wendt relinquished the daily management of the company to his brother-in-law, Olle Nauclér. Prior to this appointment, Nauclér served as chairman of the board of directors for ten years. Otto Wendt, however, continued to serve as chairman of Skånska Ättiksfabriken.

By 1956 the company turned its attention to the export market. Despite intense competition, the company was quite successful. Skånska's success was due to three critical factors: first, the company carefully chose its agents abroad; second, it invested funds to maintain a large inventory; and third, the company also instituted a successful marketing strategy aimed directly at the consumer.

Formalin, the primary raw material in Skånska's polyalcohols, was also an important ingredient in several other products. In 1958, in a mutual exchange of information with Reichhold Chemicals, Skånska received valuable information about several products, one being formalin. In 1959 Skånska began using Reichhold's inexpensive method of producing formalin called Formox.

Like Otto Wendt, Olle Nauclér advocated increased research, especially in the field of thermoplastics. During this period, Nauclér established the Perstorp Research Foundation for research projects. During his 15 years as president, he prepared the company for a larger market. To ensure the company's access to private venture capital and to reduce the chance of a takeover, Nauclér extended ownership of the company and placed its shares on the open market. He also added new members to the board of directors that were outside the circle of family relations. In addition, Skånska Ättiksfabriken A.B. officially changed its name to Perstorp A.B.

In 1970 Perstorp's shares went on the open market. More than 700 employees took advantage of Perstorp's special offer and became some of Perstorp's initial shareholders. Olle Nauclér retired in 1970 and Gunnar Wessman took over as president of Perstorp. This marked the first time in the company's 90 year history that a member of the Wendt family was not among the executive management staff. The Wendt's were (and still are), however, represented on the board of directors. The company then began its program of international expansion first initiated in the 1950's.

In 1970 Perstorp acquired one of the largest laminate producers in Great Britain. Perstorp also purchased a polyalcohol plant in the United States. Gunnar Wessman, during this time, began a modernization of Perstorp's organizational structure. Under the motto "Security is based on change," Wessman introduced divisionalism whereby Perstorp decentralized its decision-making processes.

Karl-Erik Sahlberg became president of Perstorp in 1975. Under his direction, all product development was concentrated in the separate divisions. Perstorp created Pernvo A.B., Perstorp's New Business Development, in order to ensure that long-term projects were not neglected for the short-termed return on investments employed by the divisions. In 1984 Perstorp again changed its organizational structure to represent the nine market-oriented business areas. These include: Perstorp additives; Perstorp Chemitec; Perstorp compounds; Perstorp electronics; Perstorp specialty chemicals; Perstorp components; Perstorp plastics systems; Perstorp surface materials; and Pernvo.

In 1982 Perstorp bought the amino plastics operation of Italy's Resem SpA. With this purchase, Perstorp became the world's leader in the production of amino plastics. In 1983 Perstorp acquired Pispalan Werhoomo Oy and Tunhems Industri A.B. In the fall of 1984 Perstorp entered the biotechnology field. Perstorp Analytical, a division of Perstorp Biotec, acquired Lumac BV of Holland, a manufacturer of analytical systems for industrial microbiology, from 3M Corporation of the United States. In addition, Perstorp A.B. acquired the Swedish company, ServoChem A.B., which develops analytical instruments for the brewery industry.

In November of 1985 Perstorp Chemitec acquired LaBakelite S.A. of France. LaBakelite is one of the largest manufacturers of resins and phenolic molding compounds in Europe. In the same year Perstorp acquired the seamless flooring and wall covering portion of the Swedish Gunfred Group, which has been incorporated into Perstorp Chemitec. Pernvo Inc. of the United States acquired minority shareholdings in Health Products Inc. (Michigan) and R Cubed Composites Inc. (Utah), while selling all of its shares in Composite Craft Inc.

Perstorp has managed to integrate new items into its product line, some of which the company has produced for almost one hundred years. By dividing the activities of the company to cater to different markets, Perstorp will continue its success. The future for the chemical industry on the whole depends on product development as well as market share. Perstorp's commitment to developing both new products and a larger market share will give the company a definite advantage in the years to come.

Principal Subsidiaries: Drycolor A.B.; Pernvo-Perstorp New Business Development A.B.; Perstorp Administration A.B.; Perstorp Biotec A.B.; Perstorp Chemitec A.B.; Perstorp Compounds A.B.; Perstorp Contilam A.B.; Perstorp Elektronik A.B.; Perstorp Far East A.B.; Perstorp Finanskon A.B.; Perstorp Form A.B.; Perstorp Kemi A.B.; Perstorp Komponent A.B.; Perstorp Konsument A.B.; Perstorp Plastsystem A.B.; Perstorp Pressmassor A.B.; Perstorp Produkter A.B.; Perstorp Regeno A.B.; Perstorp Specialkemi A.B.; Perstorp Ytmaterial A.B.; Perform A.B.; System Dishman A.B.; Perstorp do Brasil Industria e Comercio Ltds (Brazil); Perplast B.V. (Amsterdam); Skogens Kol A.B. (Kilfors); Perstorp Ltd (Toronto); Perstorp Oy (Helsinki); Perstorp S.A. (Paris); Perstorp SpA (Milan); Sythecolor S.A. (Paris); LTIS S.A. (Matra); Lumac B.V. (Holland); Pharma SpA (W. Germany).

RHÔNE-POULENC S.A.

25 Quay Paul-Doumer
92408 Courbevoie
France
(1) 768 1234

State controlled
Incorporated: 1895 as Société Chimiques des Usines du Rhône
Employees: 12,600
Sales: FFr 48.938 billion (US$ 7.608 billion)

Rhône-Poulenc began, as did many other large industrial firms, in the smallest of establishments. Its early history has been called "a history of mergers," and a complex series of mergers actually did characterize its early days, along with an active interest in diversity. The most critical period of its history, however, has been the last two decades, when increasing losses and nationalization have influenced the direction of this important French chemical firm.

Rhône-Poulenc is the product of not one, but two historical lines reaching back into the 19th century. The first of these paths began in Paris in 1858, when a pharmacist named Etienne Poulenc purchased a small drug store. It was not long before Poulenc's interests extended to more than apothecary supplies. He began to produce his own specialty products, featuring a line of photographic supplies and products. This early interest in diversification, even in such a small establishment, was characteristic of the firm as it grew.

In 1900 Etienne Poulenc's two brothers joined him in his business, and the company became known as the Etablissement Poulenc-Frères. Over the next two decades, they became associated with other firms in France and abroad. The brothers first joined forces with the Comptoir des Textiles Artificielles (CTA), founded by the Gillet and Carnot families. Collaboration between Poulenc chemists and doctors from the CTA led to the production of many drugs used to treat soldiers during World War I. The 1922 acquisition of the British firm May and Baker strengthened the Poulenc-Frères position in the pharmaceutical industry.

As the Poulenc brothers were building their chemical company, another series of important events was beginning in Lyon. In 1895 the Société Chimiques des Usines du Rhône was formed for the manufacture of dyestuffs and of raw materials for perfumes. However, there were obstacles along the way for the company. At the turn of the century, for example, German domination of the chemical industry caused difficulties for this and many other French firms. The Usines du Rhône was forced to stop production of its dyestuffs line, and the company was taken over by the banks. The banks, in turn, put the company's management into the hands of Nicolas Grillet, one of their chemical engineers. New products then began emerging from the company, among them Rhodine, which became aspirin, and a perfume called Rodo. The latter, exported to Rio de Janeiro for Carnival, brought in as much as three-quarters of the company's profits during this period. Another major development of the firm prior to World War I was the manufacture of cellophane. A 1922 merger between the Gillet family's CTA and the Usines du Rhône produced the firm known as Rhodiaceta.

By the 1920's a union was developing between Poulenc-Frères and the Usines du Rhône, due largely to their shared association with CTA. It seemed that even greater benefits were to be found in combining their resources. Thus, in 1928, the two firms merged to form the Société des Usines Chimiques Rhône-Poulenc (SUCRP). Two new subsidiaries, Prolabo and Spécia, were created at approximately the same time.

The early growth of the new firm was hampered by the worldwide depression beginning in 1929, which forced SUCRP to consolidate its laboratories into two sites and reduced the company's holdings to three factories. Notwithstanding these events, the company's English subsidiary May and Baker continued with its research and production; a notable discovery of this period was a sulfamide drug made in their laboratories, which was used to cure Winston Churchill of pneumonia. While the firm was able to continue production through the depression, the onset of World War II nearly 10 years later limited options even further by creating a shortage of supplies. Even with these limitations, however, SUCRP was involved in two important chemical developments: nylon, which was in only limited production during the war, and the first French production of penicillin. These two innovations gave SUCRP the capital it needed after the war in order to finance the restart of many of its factories.

After the war, Rhône-Poulenc's policies exhibited a growing commitment to research and development. Research became a high priority, as the company relegated four and a half to five percent of its new sales for research. Over time, the firm was divided into five groups, including chemistry, health, textile, agricultural chemicals, and films. This last group, a relatively new endeavor, hearkened back to the days of Etienne Poulenc.

Elsewhere in the industry, there were changes which would again reshape the corporate structure of SUCRP. The Gillet family, whose firm CTA had been so important for Rhône-Poulenc's early development, formed a holding company known as CELTEX in 1952 to consolidate their various interests. Meanwhile, SUCRP continued its moves into pharmaceuticals with the 1956 acquisition of Théraplix, another manufacturer of health products. These two groups were brought together in a critical merger during 1961, with the formation of a holding company to combine SUCRP and its various subsidiaries. Also forming part of this company was CELTEX. Additions in the areas of textiles and films were immediately apparent; the new group's sales were about 60% in the textile area.

Rhône-Poulenc continued to build its resources. Between 1963 and 1968 it acquired majority interests in two research facilities, the Laboratoire Roger Bellon and the Institut Merieux. Two smaller chemical firms, Progil and Péchiney Saint Gobain, were acquired in 1969. These moves strengthened the group's position in the basic products area, as well as in heavy and agricultural chemicals; the former in particular provided the company with a long overdue branch in petrochemicals. These acquisitions prompted further internal restructuring, with the formation of Rhône-Progil from the two most recent additions, and that of Rhône-Poulenc Textile, from CTA and Rhodiaceta. They also changed the distribution of sales once again, moving chemicals to the forefront. As early as 1969 Rhône-Poulenc had become the largest company in France. This series of mergers, acquisitions, and restructurings helped to develop its corporate identity into the shape it held throughout the mid-1970's.

Despite its size and position, however, the seeds of trouble were already sown at Rhône-Poulenc. It maintained a strict policy of anonymity, as well as a rather provincial attitude towards expansion. As long as French tariffs remained high, this strategy was effective; its business was conducted internally, and it retained the largest share of the French market for many of its products. Yet tariffs began to fall with the advent of the Common Market, international competition in the French market increased, and Rhône-Poulenc's market position within the industry began to decline. The company management had also made some grave policy mistakes during this period, whose damages now began to be felt. An example was the company's licensing of the major tranquilizer Thorazine, widely used in the treatment of the mentally ill. Instead of manufacturing Thorazine in the United States, where its sales were very high, the company accepted royalties on the product from American pharmaceutical manufacturers Smith Kline and French, for whom it was enormously profitable.

Some of the problems in Rhône-Poulenc's market position were solved by the acquisitions of the late 1960's, which shifted the company's emphasis away from a textile market which was slipping in profitability. The move towards international expansion initiated at this time was much too late; had it been carried out some time before, it might have assured long-lasting financial health for the company. The delay in making such a move left the company with a very small international market share. In addition, Rhône-Poulenc had the misfortune to expand internationally at the time of an industry-wide slowdown. Attempts to turn around the company's downward slide were severely hampered by a combination of management procrastination and bad timing. The French government's attempts to lower inflation added a further strain on the firm, which was one of many important French manufacturers to show a large deficit by the mid-1970's. The strain necessitated the layoff of 20,000 workers in 1974.

The downward trend continued throughout the 1970's, despite impressive profits from a number of licensing deals. A new managing director, Jean Gandois, failed to effect a notable change after his appointment in 1976. As a result of these combined events, Rhône-Poulenc found itself in a difficult position. A change in the French government was the catalyst which altered Rhône-Poulenc's status as a public company. The new socialist government determined to reverse the fortunes of what it perceived as a failing French industry. The device it used to intervene was the most straightforward available, namely, nationalization. In February of 1982 Rhône-Poulenc's management was assumed by the government.

Among the major changes made by the government in its nationalization of Rhône-Poulenc was the appointment of a new chairman, Loïk Le Floch-Prigent. His predecessor, Gandois, resigned after the nationalization because of irreconcilable differences with the Socialist program. Le Floch, a former civil servant, had no such ideological difficulties. There were, however, other surprising elements in the government's choice. One was Le Floch's young age, 39, at the time. Another was his lack of experience as an industrialist; his prior experience within the government was confined to research direction in the Industry Ministry. This background had a clear influence on his policy, giving research a high priority in his plans for the future of the company. At the time he assumed control, he acknowledged that the firm would need large infusions of government cash if it were to return to prosperity. He also made extensive changes in top management, replacing older executives with younger men. Another key to Le Floch's strategy was to work more effectively with the unions, whose leaders had earlier criticized Rhône-Poulenc for the massive layoffs.

Yet Le Floch's was not the sole voice dictating company policy. One of the government's primary concerns in its nationalization program was the reorganization of the chemical industry by means of redistributing product lines among different companies. In the process, Rhône-Poulenc lost its status as the largest chemical company in the nation, giving up its fertilizer and petrochemicals divisions. However, it gained a large number of specialty chemical and pharmaceutical product lines. This action served to give unity to a company which had suffered from a fragmented product mix in recent years, as well as suiting the government's desire to concentrate the industry's various activities in particular companies.

A combination of business changes and good fortune strengthened Rhône-Poulenc's prospects for renewal in the following year. The good fortune was the European market, which began showing a greater demand for chemicals. The additional influences of new management and restructuring, along with extensive financial input from the government, gave rise to a noticeable improvement in the company's financial condition. By the end of 1983 Rhône-Poulenc was making a profit for the first time since 1979. Le Floch began making plans to realize what he saw as the company's full potential. He began closing plants in profitless areas and reducing the workforce, in part through an emphasis on early retirement plans. New areas of production included high-growth products such as the recently strengthened pharmaceuticals division. The company also devoted a large amount of funds for research in these areas, as well as for investment in foreign countries. With this new vitality, Rhône-Poulenc planned on making a significant profit by the government's deadline of 1985.

Le Floch's policies were in many ways an extension of Gandois'. Enough differences existed, however, that the new management and the favorable economic conditions paid off in a revival of Rhône-Poulenc's fortunes. A key factor in this economic revival was its expansion into foreign markets, particularly in the U.S. and Japan. In the mid-1980's, Rhône-Poulenc began a number of diverse ventures in Japan, in such areas as agricultural chemicals, pharmaceuticals, and rare earth materials. Many of these Japanese moves were made as joint ventures; Rhône-Poulenc and Mitsui Petrochemical cooperated to produce computer print boards, while Sumitomo Metal Industries was the firm's partner in its rare earths venture.

In the summer of 1986 Loïk Le Floch-Prigent left Rhône-Poulenc. Its chairmanship passed to Jean-René Fourtou, another government appointee. Fourtou continued the trend of investment outside France. The company's most significant expansion at this time occurred in its farm chemicals area, with the acquisition of all related interests of the Union Carbide Corporation. A large investment for the still-embattled company, the purchase was made feasible at least in part by the fall of the dollar, and through the first U.S. dollar-denominated perpetual floating rate note for a corporate borrower. This transaction provided Rhône-Poulenc with the needed size and influence in the competitive U.S. market, the largest farm chemical market in the world. The move was made particularly favorable by the two firm's complementary product lines. Rhône-Poulenc's line was left much more complete than it had been, giving it an additional edge in the U.S. market. Notably, the acquisition did not include Union Carbide's assets in India, where a gas leak at Bhopal had killed some 1750 people two years earlier.

By late 1986 Rhône-Poulenc appeared to be financially healthy once again. While earnings were down slightly from the previous year, they were expected to rise again in 1987. One of the best indicators of the company's revival was Fourtou's advocating early privatization by the government. Government aid was no longer required, and returning to the private sector would allow the company to increase its equity. However, privatization may not take place until as late as 1988. The company is still considered to be in the middle of major changes. Management's attempt to move into the U.S. market indicates significant amount of restructuring which is still in its early stages. Yet while this makes the company's near future hard to predict, its renewed profits and quest for privatisation make Rhône-Poulenc's longterm future, after many years of uncertainty, appear quite stable.

Principal Subsidiaries: Rhône-Poulenc Chimie de Base; CIM; SIAC; Butachimie; Maprochim; Petrosynthese; Sodes; Methanolaco; Acquitainechimie; Gazechim; Rhône-Poulenc Spécialités Chimiques; Dietetique et Santé; Distugil; Givaudan-Lavirotte; Lacto-Labo; Prolabo; Vuinax; Rhône-Poulenc Santé Specia; Theraplix; Institut Merieux; Laboratoire Roger Bellon; A.E.C.; S.F.O.S.; IBP Rhône-Poulenc; Pharmuka; Rhône-Merieux; Rhône-Poulenc Agrochimie; Pepro-Rhodic; L.T. Piver; Buhler-Fontaine; Rhodiagri; S.O.P.E.M.; Rhône-Poulenc Fibres; Rhovyl; Cellatex. The company also lists subsidiaries in the following countries: Australia, Austria, Belgium, Cameroon, Canada, Greece, Guatemala, Indonesia, Italy, Ivory Coast, Japan, Madagascar, Mexico, Morocco, The Netherlands, Portugal, Senegal, Spain, Switzerland, and West Germany.

Further Reading: The Origins and Early Development of the Heavy Chemical Industry in France by John Graham Smith, Oxford, Clarendon Press, 1979.

RÖHM AND HAAS

Independence Mall West
Philadelphia, Pennsylvania 19105
U.S.A.
(215) 592–3000

Public Company
Incorporated: April 23, 1917
Employees: 11,840
Sales: $2.067 billion
Market value: $3.009 billion
Stock Index: New York

Röhm and Haas is a specialty chemical company that is best known for the invention of Plexiglas. Polymers and acrylics are its staple products, but the company looks to the areas of electronic chemicals, biotechnology, water treatment, engineering plastics and adhesives for long-term growth. In the 1970's Röhm and Haas engaged in the same ill-considered diversification that many chemical companies are still attempting to recover from. What sets Röhm and Haas apart from many other chemical companies is that it managed to control its own diversification and is now growing in an orderly way.

Röhm and Haas began in 1904 when a German man named Otto Röhm noticed that the stench from the local tannery was similar to the smell of the gas water produced by the Stuttgart Gas Works, where he was dissatisfied with his job as an analytical chemist. The bad odor of the gas water came from the combination of carbon dioxide and ammonia, and Röhm wondered if these chemicals could be used to soften (bate) leather. At the time, tanners bated leather as they had for centuries: with fermented canine feces which varied in composition and hence yielded inconsistent results. The unpredictability of the bating process, coupled with the inherently disgusting nature of the bating agent, made tanners eager to break with tradition. However, not even the German chemical industry, the most advanced in the world at the time, understood the chemical nature of bating, and no satisfactory replacement for the bating agent had been discovered.

Hoping to make a name for himself in chemistry, Otto Röhm attempted to solve the problem. By 1906 he had developed a solution of gas water and salts that appeared to sufficiently soften leather. He then wrote to his friend Otto Haas, a young German who had emigrated to America a few years before. Haas agreed to join Röhm in his venture, with the understanding that Haas would bring the process back to America. The new bating agent was christened Oroh, derived from the two owners initials.

By the time Haas returned to Germany, there was bad news waiting for him. Oroh was not performing as well as expected. The two men went back to the laboratory and studied the chemical process of bating, a process that had been debated a good deal in the leather industry. Röhm eventually concluded that the two prevailing schools of thought, the first, that the bating action was caused by bacteria and the second, that the action was caused by lime reacting with bate, were both partially correct. Reaction with a bate removed the lime used to dehair the hide, and then something in the organic bate softened the hide. But what?

In 1907 Eduoard Buchner discovered enzymes, the chemical compounds from living cells that caused fermentation. Röhm saw the applicability of Buchner's Nobel prizewinning work for his own research on leather chemistry. He realized that enzymes in organic bate softened leather by decomposing it, while his product merely delimed it.

Röhm set out to isolate enzymes cheaply, and by 1907 had applied for a patent for a bate made with enzymes derived from animal pancreas. Combining his own initials with the Greek word for juice, Röhm called the solution Oropon. He then developed a technique to measure the strength of Oropon so that the solution could be sold in standard strengths.

That year Röhm and Haas legally formed the company that bears their names and established their first plant in Esselingen, a city outside of Stuttgart. The first order of business was to manufacture large quantities of Oropon, which they made by squeezing animal pancreas in a manual press and collecting the juice. When the basement of the building became filled with rotting, ground-up pancreas, Haas is said to have thrown packages of it into the Neckar River on his nightly walks.

As more tanneries began to use Oropon, Haas and Röhm were able to hire men to squeeze the pancreas for them, and turned their attention to marketing the product in Germany, England and France. This early marketing effort established a style of salesmanship that still characterizes Röhm and Haas: technically proficient salesmen working closely with manufacturers. The company did so well that in 1909 Haas was able to return to open a branch in America. Due to the large number of tanneries in the area Haas decided to settle in Philadelphia.

By 1914 Haas was able to expand and open a plant in Chicago in order to serve midwestern tanners. His product line had increased to leather finishes, fat-liquors and a mordant for dyeing. The timing of this expansion was fortunate since, with the advent of World War I, there was a dramatic need for leather chemicals to replace the ones which had come from Germany which was still the world's leading producer.

Röhm and Haas' chemicals were needed for army boots, yet the firm's German origins meant that it was under surveillance by the U.S. government. This was due to the fact that a few companies run by German-Americans were discovered to be in collaboration with the Kaiser's

Germany. Although there was no evidence that Haas was a collaborator, the government nevertheless ordered that 50% of the company's stock shares (held jointly by the two owners) be sold to outsiders. A tanner's group, which was afraid of a disruption in their production of necessary leather chemicals, arranged to buy the shares and become a friendly partner with the firm.

While these legal maneuverings were taking place Röhm and Haas diversified into textile chemicals and then, in 1920, acquired one of its suppliers going out of business. That same year Haas purchased the North American rights to a German synthetic tanning agent and also supervised his company's expansion into synthetic insecticides. When the Depression began the management's growth policies helped the company through this difficult period. The company expanded its product line, but still concentrated on serving the leather and textile industries, which continued to produce goods albeit at a reduced rate. This, coupled with Haas' policy of high liquidity and low dividend payments, meant that the company not only survived the Depression without layoffs but also managed to grow.

In 1927 Haas established a company called Resinous Products with a German scientist, Kurt Albert, who had developed a synthetic resin that was useful in making varnishes. Like Oropon this new product replaced a variable and unpredictable organic product. The new company was run separately from Röhm and Haas, and from its research into resins came a whole range of chemicals used in the coating and plywood industries.

Haas was satisfied with the success of his two business ventures but unhappy with the ownership agreement, so he arranged to purchase the shares held by the tanner's association and set up a trust for Röhm who had been deprived of his interest in the American branch of the company.

Haas reaped many benefits from his continued association with Röhm. One of them was the introduction of Plexiglas, which was discovered by accident in Röhm's laboratory located in Darmstadt, Germany. Röhm had started his work with acrylics in 1927. He had originally intended them for use as drying oils in varnishes, but soon realized that they could also be used as a coating for safety glass. In 1935 one of his research associates was experimenting with an acrylic polymer to see if it would bind two sheets of glass. Instead of acting as an adhesive, however, the polymer dried into a light weight, clear plastic sheet that was immediately considered a promising glass substitute.

It was another three years until Plexiglas could be manufactured inexpensively and applications for it found. Röhm himself experimented with various uses: he replaced the glass in his car and even the glass in his spectacles with Plexiglas. Among the many uses Röhm's researchers explored were musical instruments; one such instrument, the acrylic violin, while striking in appearance produced a terrible sound. The Plexiglas flute was more successful. The most important applications of Plexiglas was not to see-through flutes, however, but to airplanes.

It was through such frivolities as the acrylic violin that company researchers learned how to stretch and shape

Plexiglas sheets into cockpit enclosures. By 1934, when these techniques were almost perfected, the Nazi government had placed restrictions on the transmission of technical reports abroad. Haas got around these restrictions by sending one of his own chemists from the U.S. over to the company's German laboratory and having this man memorize the technology.

The U.S. Army Air Force was immediately interested in Plexiglas because it was light weight and durable, and the design of war planes was altered to take advantage of this new, shatter-proof material. The U.S. branch of Röhm and Haas, anticipating the entrance of America into the war, enlarged its capacity to manufacture Plexiglas so that the discovery made in Nazi Germany could benefit the Allies.

During the war Plexiglas accounted for two thirds of Röhm and Haas' sales. In the last year before the war sales had reached $5.5 million and by the end of the war this figure had swelled to $43 million. However, Plexiglas was not the company's only contribution to the war effort. In 1934 an employee hired by Hass named Herman Bruson discovered a synthetic oil additive. It was not until the war that the significance of his discovery was revealed. Designers of military aircraft had difficulty finding a hydraulic fluid that would function at a sufficiently wide temperature range. That is, until a review of potentially useful patents turned up Bruson's formula. Bruson often took credit for the Russian victory at Stalingrad since his hydraulic fluid kept Russian equipment from freezing, unlike the German hydraulic fluid which was rendered useless by the cold.

When the war ended Röhm and Haas experienced a dramatic decrease in the demand for Plexiglas and, as a result, the company struggled to expand the civilian uses of acrylic polymers. Illuminated signs and car lights were one use, along with additives for coatings and fuel. The company's major undertaking in the decade following the war was building a huge plant in Houston, Texas that was used to make the ingredients for acrylics. Along with acrylics the company also attempted to increase its holdings in markets for insecticides and fungicides. Exports, especially fungicides, were used to expand the company's European markets which Haas had previously left underdeveloped in order not to compete with his friend Röhm.

In 1959, the 50th year of Röhm and Haas' American operation, Otto Haas retired, leaving the company in excellent shape. He was described as a hard-driving administrator who was by turns kind and unfair to his employees. One incident that typified Haas' attitude towards his employees took place during World War II when a new guard refused to allow Haas into a company munitions plant without a pass. Haas immediately fired the man and then rehired him the next day with a raise in pay. John Haas, Otto's son, was a less colorful president. John's style of administration stressed teamwork among the top executives, while his father's administration had stressed obedience.

One of the first projects John Haas undertook was the ill-fated diversification into fibers and health products. At the time Röhm and Haas was the main producer of Plexiglas in the country, and had a sensible product mix of paper, leather, textile and agricultural chemicals. The expansion into fibers was motivated by the fear that one of the large chemical companies would challenge Röhm and Haas in the Plexiglas and acrylic emulsion markets that Röhm and Haas dominated. Yet the challenge from the major chemical companies never materialized, and it was the measures taken to prevent the company from being hurt that caused the damage. The new divisions, health and fibers, were profitable in only one of their 14 years of existence.

The fibers division was especially costly. The company intended to enter the crowded field through technological breakthroughs and specialized markets; this was how it had succeeded with leather chemicals and acrylics. The company had high hopes for a new synthetic fiber named Anim/8, which was supposed to give fabrics added stretch without altering their appearance. Anim/8 failed in part because Röhm and Haas misunderstood the nature of the fibers market. While an aerospace manufacturer might pay the higher dollar amount for a superior hydraulic fluid, consumers did not care that Anim/8 had slight advantages over its competitors, Spandex and Lycra, when it was 20–30% more costly. Secondly, Röhm and Haas entered the field just as women were abandoning girdles and other undergarments which were a major market for stretch fabrics. The *coup de grace* was the crash of the entire synthetic fabric industry in 1975 when current president Vincent Gregory said, "You couldn't give the stuff away."

Earnings were depressed in the late 1960's and early 1970's as the losses incurred by the two divisions cancelled out the gains made by the specialty chemicals. The company's troubles were not only of a financial nature however. In 1975, just as the fabric industry was reaching its nadir, Röhm and Haas was deluged with bad publicity surrounding the deaths of workers who were exposed to a carcinogenic chemical called BCME. In 1962 a suspicious pattern of lung cancer deaths emerged at the company's Bridesburg, Pennsylvania plant where resins for water purification purposes were produced. The company took measures to minimize employee exposure to chemicals at the plant, but its efforts were not strong enough. In 1974 the Health Research Group, founded by Ralph Nader, accused Röhm and Haas of concealing the dangers at the plant where 54 people had died, probably from BCME induced cancer.

Vincent Gregory, who had become president in 1970, was confronted with a difficult situation. Not only did he have a public relations fiasco on his hands, but he also had to accept some of the blame for the company's financial situation since he should have divested Röhm and Haas of the fiber and health divisions immediately upon his promotion. By 1975 the company began to lose money and there was speculation that Gregory would be relieved of his duties. However, the chairman of the board, John Haas, assumed his share of the blame for having started the ill-fated diversification into areas the company was not altogether familiar with. The board decided that Gregory had had "an expensive education," so to speak, and retained him to help revitalize the company.

The solution to the company's difficulties turned out to be a combination of cost-cutting (including extensive layoffs), the sale of unprofitable plants and a few judicious acquisitions. One acquisition was the Borg-Warner PVC modifier plant, a business that was inexpensive to purchase and that had not been profitable for a while. Röhm and Haas, with its experience in plastics, returned the plant to profitability by 1982, a year after it was purchased for $35 million. Röhm and Haas currently has 55% of the PVC modifier market. These modifiers make PVC more malleable.

The company decided to keep their slow-growing but profitable staples such as Plexiglas and paint and floor finishes. For faster growth it turned to herbicides, which the company started working with in the 1930's. A herbicide called Blazer, used on soybeans, has the largest sales in its specialized market. By building on its experience with resins Röhm and Haas has made coatings for electronic components a part of their product line. This is evidence of the fact that by 1984 Röhm and Haas had returned to the company's early strategy: relying on businesses and product lines it was well acquainted with, concentrating on value-added chemicals, and increasing its market share rather than its size. This old-fashioned approach resulted in record profits. In 1985 sales were down slightly, but given the difficult economic conditions that existed that year for chemical companies, the performance of Röhm and Haas was regarded by many industry analysts as satisfactory.

Röhm and Haas gives every indication of having learned its lessons about diversification and expansion. Management is now clearly focused on one goal: to be the largest and most successful specialty chemical company. The specialty chemical industry is cyclical and because of this the company will be confronted with obstacles in the years ahead. However, Röhm and Haas is especially well-equipped to deal with the industry's inherent problems. One reason is that Röhm and Haas has a substantial share of the speciality chemical market. It also has a healthy mixture of stable and fast-growing products. Most important, perhaps, is that Röhm and Haas has the capacity to rectify, and learn from, its mistakes.

Principal Subsidiaries: Comex, Inc.; Hydraulics; Plaskon Electronic Materials, Inc.; Electro-Materials Corp. of America; Furane Products Co.; Romicon, Inc.; Southern Resin and Chemical Company. Röhm and Haas also have subsidiaries in the following countries: Australia, Bermuda, Brazil, Canada, Colombia, England, France, W. Germany, Italy, India, Japan, Mexico, New Zealand, Philippines, South Africa, Spain and Sweden.

Further Reading: Building G: The Tragedy of Bridesburg by William S. Randall and Stephen D. Solomon, Boston, Little Brown, 1977.

SOLVAY

ṠOLVAY & CIE S.A.

Rue du Prince Albert 33
B-1050 Brussels
Belgium
(02) 516 61 11

Public Company
Incorporated: July 1, 1967
Employees: 44,461
Sales: BFr 195.9 billion (US$ 4.842 billion)
Market value: BFr 65.075 billion (US$ 1.608 billion)
Stock Index: Brussels Antwerp Amsterdam Basle
Berlin Dusseldorf Frankfurt/Main Geneva Paris
Zurich

Although Solvay & Cie was not incorporated as a public company until 1967, its roots go back to the 1860's and the discovery by its founder, Ernest Solvay, of a new industrial process for producing soda ash, an essential element in glassmaking. Under his guidance and, until recently, the management of his family, the firm became one of the largest in Belgium, combining chemical innovation with social projects and intellectual programs.

The foundations of Solvay & Cie were laid when Ernest Solvay devised his process for the manufacture of artificial soda ash. At the time, the method in use was that discovered by Nicolas Leblanc in the late 1700's. Leblanc's method, while valuable as an industrial process, had serious drawbacks, most prominently its production of large amounts of alkali wastes. Although this fact called for alternative methods, none were available. In 1861 Solvay filed a patent for a method which involved the reaction of ammonium bicarbonate and salt, the product being heated to yield sodium carbonate, or soda ash. Despite his enthusiasm, his "discovery" met with indifferent or negative response on virtually all sides.

On the advice of an attorney, Solvay consulted patent records, only to find that the process was not original after all. It had in fact been proposed half a century earlier, in 1811, by Augustin Fresnel. Large-scale implementation of the process, however, was made difficult by the volatility of ammonia. Over the course of those 50 years, many chemists had attempted to devise a way to make the procedure industrially viable. All had met with failure. The propositions of the young Solvay, therefore, were seen as little but the repetition of old mistakes. While a few encouraged him, most chemists looked with disfavor on his efforts.

The ammonia-soda process may never have achieved its influence had Solvay been inclined to admit defeat. His character, however, had been marked since youth by intense curiosity about scientific questions and by dedicated application to whatever such problem was at hand. Although illness had cut short his formal studies, he had maintained this deepset curiosity and educated himself. The small encouragement he received, added to this dedication, was enough for him to continue his research. Not only would his process eliminate the problem of waste, but he believed that it could drastically lower the price of soda ash, reducing it by three-quarters or more.

In order to continue the work, he and his brother Alfred formed Solvay & Cie in 1863, and embarked on the difficult route to finding a workable procedure. The perfection of the process on a large scale was far more difficult than its invention had been; the setbacks faced by the young firm were enough to drive it to the brink of bankruptcy by late 1865. With their family's help and support, the brothers decided to try one last time. This time, they were successful, producing large amounts of soda ash. The key to their system and Solvay's greatest single achievement was the Solvay carbonating tower, which permitted the important but problematic reaction of carbon dioxide and ammoniacal brine to take place effectively and safely. By 1869, with the implementation of this invention, the Solvays were confident that they would become a strong presence in the market for artifical soda ash.

Having worked out the procedure, Solvay & Cie faced another difficult problem, that is, persuading others that the method was viable. The very novelty of the technique rendered it unfavorable in many eyes, and for a long while Solvay faced intense competition from adherents to the Leblanc process. Even this competition, however, had its benefits; one of its side effects was a reduction in the price of sulfuric acid, employed to treat phosphates for use in agriculture. The end result of this was increased productivity from crops treated with these products, in turn lowering the price of such staples as bread.

Agricultural benefits aside, Ernest Solvay had many difficult years attempting to establish his method in the industry. Eventually, however, as it became clear that the Solvay method produced soda ash at a lower cost than the Leblanc process, it became more and more widely accepted. By the turn of the century, Solvay-method production had risen from 300 tons per year in the 1860's to 900,000 tons per year, at a price around three times lower than it had been before Solvay entered the field.

The Solvay method permitted the clean production of inexpensive soda ash, with Ernest Solvay holding patents on all key phases of the process. The market share which this was to give to the company, however, was not enough for him. Ernest knew that no firm could survive by resting on one past achievement, therefore he encouraged diversification into other related areas. Most notable among these, in this phase of the company's history, was the production of chlorine and caustic soda by electrolysis. As early as 1886, Solvay wanted to proceed in the direction of chlorine manufacture. It was not until 1895, however, that the company was able to work electrolysis into its industrial scheme. The production of chlorine eventually led to the one of the company's largest modern branches, chlorinated products, including plastics. Caustic soda also combined with soda ash to provide a profitable new product area.

With the success of their first factory, located in Couillet, Belgium, the Solvay brothers began to expand their firm. The initial consideration of international growth, proposed for England, came in 1872. In the following year several British plants were constructed, in addition to one in Dombasle, France. The last two decades of the century saw rapid growth of the firm. In 1881 both the United States and Russia became sites for Solvay works: in the U.S. the cities of Syracuse and Detroit eventually housed Solvay factories, while three Russian locales were selected. The company continued its international growth in the following years by building in Austria, Hungary, Germany and, in the early years of the 20th century, Spain and Italy. In all, by the company's 50th anniversary in 1913, there were at least 34 Solvay plants, including an electrolytic plant in Jemeppe-sur-Sambre in Belgium.

As the 19th century progressed, Solvay & Cie was directed toward greater productivity and importance in its market. Despite such impressive growth, the management was not neglecting its workers, a fact about the company's character which should not be overlooked. In addition to his interest in natural science, Ernest Solvay had a strong interest in socioeconomic matters. A proponent of universal suffrage, his social interests led him to the Senate in the 1890's; he had an idealistic view of a future when "justice for all" would be a reality. This vision was realized in concrete terms by the institution of many innovative workers' benefits. By the end of the 19th century, workers for Solvay & Cie were able to take advantage of sick pay, compensation for injury, and the eight-hour work day, which was a Solvay innovation at their Russian plants. His social interests also led him to various contributions to the nation during World War I, after which he was named Minister of State.

While chemical projects and social interests were part of daily business, they were not the only things surrounding Ernest Solvay's company. Since his youth, the founder had a strong interest in intellectual questions which later led to the creation of the Solvay institutes of Physiology and Sociology. His self-teaching also led him to speculations on such abstract physical principles as mass and energy. His interest in matters such as the nature of the universe led to his initiation of the Solvay conference on physics, which drew the greatest minds of the time together: Einstein, Rutherford, and Marie Curie were but a few of the names listed at the first meeting in 1911.

The company's first major setback came at the end of World War I, when its Russian plants were lost in the aftermath of the revolution. Shortly thereafter, in 1922, Ernest Solvay died. His prominence as a citizen was marked by a letter of condolence sent by King Albert of Belgium to their mutual friend Charles Lefébure, with whom they shared an interest for mountain climbing. The company was able to overcome these losses, however, by modernizing many of its plants in the next years and

making moves into certain other areas, such as the exploitation of potassium mining. In the 1930's and 1940's, increasing efforts were directed towards electrolysis, with new plants established in Italy, Greece, and other countries.

World War II again changed the complexion of the company. Many of its important factories were damaged during the conflict; in addition, several of its plants were lost to the Soviet dominated East European countries. While rebuilding its facilities, Solvay did not neglect to make new developments, holding to its policy of careful diversification. The company first produced polyvinyl chloride in 1949, at its plant in Jemeppe. This move into plastics was to be one of the company's most important decisions, opening up a new and very profitable field which did not diverge significantly from the company's basic product lines.

In the 1950's and 1960's Solvay continued to grow, bulding and maintaining its position as a prominent manufacturer of bulk chemicals. The next major changes in the company came in the late 1960's under the direction of Baron Rene Boël. One of the most important changes made by Boël was to place Solvay's shares on the public market, in 1971, for the first time. In addition, he made major structural changes in management. Previously, Solvay & Cie had been organized by a French and Belgian managerial structure known as a "commandité," in which authority was held by a group of five executives. All were required to be members of the Solvay family, into which Boël had married some time earlier. Boël abandoned this form of administration for a more modern corporate structure, paving the way for more clearly defined management responsibility and opening up top management to executives from outside the family. The initial addition of two non-family members was enlarged upon in subsequent years. Many European firms have been forced into similar changes by economic necessity, but Solvay managers said they chose their own time, when the changes made were able to provide significant benefits to the company.

During the same time, the company began to make record expenditures in research and development. It also began looking into new fields for growth. An example of this was its move from being a straightforward plastics manufacturer to a plastic processor as well. Today, Solvay makes plastic bottles and baby seats, and has successfully entered the consumer market as well as the industrial market.

The changes in Solvay's management kept the company financially healthy through the late 1970's when, under the leadership of Jacques Solvay, it was acknowledged as the European leader in the manufacture of polyvinyl chloride. Production on its oldest line, soda ash and caustic soda, was reduced to approximately 20% of the firm's total income. Yet this reliable 20% was to provide the next great challenge for Solvay. In 1976 United States companies began manufacturing soda ash from a natural source, a rock mined in Wyoming, called trona. Suddenly a process was available which was both less expensive and cleaner than the reliable Solvay process. The situation was not helped by increasing environmental restrictions on chlorine and calcium carbonate. As a result, Solvay-method plants began to close.

In 1978 the European management felt the repercussions of this situation. In the wake of a Solvay price hike on soda ash, designed to offset losses at their oldest plants, Belgian glassmakers signed a letter of intent with the FMC Corporation in the United States. Faced with the loss of their contracts and of some 1200 jobs, Solvay asked the Belgian government to intercede, while initiating measures to reduce their prices. Although the glassmakers seemed content to return their business to Solvay, FMC was less satisfied. The dispute led to changes in Solvay policy to suit antitrust laws, and helped support the suspicion that, sometime in the future, artificial means of production would be discontinued for this product, although Solvay still keeps a profitable presence in the business during the present time.

Despite such problems in the oldest branch of the firm, Solvay did not stop looking for new developments. The year 1984 saw the reorganization of its American interests under a new holding company, Solvay America, in an attempt to increase its profile in the United States. Approximately the same time, the company extended its financial outlays, marking $650 million to be dedicated to capital improvements in the period 1985–87. Another profitable move was the company's acqusition of life sciences firms, which began in 1979. Solvay now produces a number of drugs and vaccines for human and animal health care, in plants located in Europe and in the United States.

Solvay's recent history has been somewhat embattled, especially in terms of their old mainline products soda ash and caustic soda. Its newer plastics products have also experienced a difficult time on the market due to a general decrease in plastics sales throughout Europe. However, the firm has managed to maintain its financial position, showing higher sales in 1986 than ever before. In the past 10 years Solvay management has become increasingly aware of the company's vulnerability due to a reliance on bulk chemicals alone, and its diversification, more varied than ever before, shows a calculated response to this pressure. Along with this, changes in management may affect the company in the years ahead. However, the firm is known for its conservative management policy, and no major surprises should be expected. With fully operative plants in Japan, Brazil, Singapore, and Australia, as well as the U.S. and most of the countries in Western Europe, Solvay shows every sign of financial stability, and its diversified interests and increasingly aggressive moves into new areas promise a prosperous future.

Principal Subsidiaries: Solvic & Cie SNC; Mutuelle Solvay SCS; Interox SA; Plavina & Cie SNC; Duphar & Cie SNC; Plastilit & Cie SNC; Solvay-Coordination Internationale des Crédits Commerciaux SA; Enterprise et Gestion Immobilières (Égimo) SA; Vanilia & Cie SNC. The company also lists subsidiaries in the following countries: Australia, Austria, Bermuda, Brazil, France, Italy, The Netherlands, Portugal, Spain, Switzerland, United Kingdom, United States, and West Germany.

SUMITOMO CHEMICAL COMPANY, LTD.

5–15, Kitahama
Higashi-ku, Osaka 541
Japan

Public Company
Incorporated: June 1, 1925 as Sumitomo Fertilizer
Manufacturing Company
Employees: 7,536
Sales: ¥ 658.6 billion (US$ 3.287 billion)
Market value: ¥ 616.8 billion (US$ 3.859 billion)
Stock Index: Tokyo Osaka Nagoya Kyoto Hiroshima
Fukuoka Niigata

The name of Sumitomo is historically associated with copper mining. The original Sumitomo business was established in 1590 as a copper refinery which grew steadily over the next three hundred years to become one of the largest family-run industries in Japan. Early in the 20th century several Sumitomo divisions were made independent corporations in order to attract a greater amount of investor capital. As independent members of a larger Sumitomo industrial group, each of these companies later established itself as a viable coporate entity.

A Sumitomo copper smelter located at Niihama endangered the local population with heavy emissions of sulfur dioxide, a hazardous waste gas. A study was undertaken in 1906 to investigate ways in which the gas could be utilized and the pollution eliminated. A new technology was discovered and in 1913 a facility was added on to the Niihama complex which transformed sulfur dioxide into sulfuric acid and calcium superphosphate, which was then used as a fertilizer.

In 1925 the chemical division of the Niihama copper refinery was made an independent corporation and renamed Sumitomo Fertilizer Manufacturing. When it was incorporated, the company's capitalization was increased through the sale of stock shares to private investors. In 1930 the company broadened its product line to include ammonia and ammonia-related industrial chemicals. When the production of nitric acid was added in 1934, Sumitomo Fertilizer ceased to be an appropriate name and so it was changed to the Sumitomo Chemical Company.

Chemical production is an essential component of any nation's industrial capability. When right-wing militarist elements seized power in Japan during the 1930's, they initiated an industrial mobilization for achieving Japanese economic domination of Asia and the western Pacific. The movement became increasingly belligerent and culminated with the initiation of a full-scale war of conquest in Asia. Sumitomo Chemical was an essential component of the Japanese war effort. The company produced a variety of industrial chemicals used in the manufacture of weapons and military equipment.

Sumitomo Chemical grew rapidly during the war. In 1944 it absorbed the Japan Dyestuff Manufacturing Company, which produced dyes and pharmaceutical products. When the war ended with the Japanese surrender in September of 1945, Sumitomo emerged as the nation's largest chemical concern. The war destroyed almost all of Japan's industrial capability and many Sumitomo factories sustained heavy damage. As a result, the company initially suffered from both an inability to produce certain chemicals and poor market conditions.

After the war the Allied occupation authority outlawed large industrial organizations called *zaibatsu* ("money cliques"). Sumitomo Chemical was a member of the Sumitomo group, one of the largest *zaibatsu* in Japan. As part of the dissolution of the Sumitomo Group, Sumitomo Chemical was forced to change its name to Nisshin Chemical Industries in 1946 and refrain from using the *igeta*, the Sumitomo trademark.

In 1949 Nisshin Chemical acquired Sumitomo Aluminum Reduction, a division of a dissolved affiliate of the Sumitomo group. With the addition of alumina fabrication facilities, Nisshin became an integrated manufacturer of dyestuffs, pharmaceuticals, and aluminum, in addition to a variety of industrial chemicals.

During the Korean War (1950–1952), restrictive Japanese commercial laws were modified to promote greater industrial growth. Many of the prewar *zaibatsu* affiliations were re-established. In 1952 Nisshin Chemical was allowed to change its name back to Sumitomo Chemical and resume use of the *igeta* logo. Other members of the Sumitomo group (particularly banks) purchased substantial minority shares of Sumitomo Chemical. Although the strict vertical organization of the prewar Sumitomo group was not re-instituted, the various Sumitomo companies established a monthly meeting for the coordinatioin of business strategies.

Japan's Ministry for International Trade and Industry (MITI) had a major role in the development of the Japanese chemical industry. During the 1950's most Japanese chemical companies remained largely non-integrated manufacturers. In other words, they specialized in just one stage of chemical production. Larger foreign companies, however, integrated their facilities so that they could produce chemicals more efficiently and at a lower cost. This made it difficult for Japanese companies to compete effectively. In an effort to improve the competitiveness of Japan's chemical industry, MITI directed the merger of numerous non-integrated producers.

Sumitomo Chemical, however, was already an integrated producer. It was also the largest chemical company in Japan. Rather than merge with other companies, the government encouraged Sumitomo to establish new product lines. The company began to produce new fertilizers under a government policy intended to support

Japanese agriculture. In 1958 Sumitomo opened a new plant at Niihama to produce low density polyethylene. In 1961 it established a factory in Nagoya for aluminum production, and the following year completed the Ibaraki Plant in Osaka for the preparation of pharmaceuticals.

Sumitomo Chemical continued its expansion in 1965 when it established the Takatsuki special laboratory facility to conduct research in new chemical technologies. A second petrochemical complex (independently operated until 1975) was built at Chiba, near Tokyo, in 1967, and two years later an aluminum smelter was completed at the Toyama Works. Another research facility called Takarazuka was founded in 1971 to develop new pharmaceutical and pesticide technologies. The company's light metals division was converted into an independent subsidiary called Sumitomo Aluminum Smelting in 1976.

Despite the company's rapid expansion, the management of Sumitomo Chemical failed to respond quickly to deteriorating market conditions. The company's chief competitor, Mitsubishi Chemical Industries, surpassed Sumitomo as the nation's largest chemical company. In 1977 Sumitomo's president, Kaneshige Hasegawa, was "promoted" out of operational management to chairman, and the company's successful managing director, Takeshi Hijikata, was named president. In addition, nine new board members were appointed.

Hijikata demonstrated his abilities as a persuasive and innovative negotiator when he managed to convince the government of Singapore to nationalize a chemical complex, which it was building in partnership with Sumitomo. Hijikata also convinced MITI that the company was capable of reaching a compromise with the Singaporean government without any danger of a diplomatic misunderstanding.

Fertilizer production had become increasingly unprofitable since the oil crisis in 1974. Over the next several years Sumitomo gradually scaled down its production of fertilizer, but continued to expand in the more profitable area of pesticides. In 1978 a new plant was constructed at Masawa for production of pyrethroid insecticides. A pharmaceutical and pesticide research facility was added to the Osaka Works in 1980, and two years later a New

Products and Systems division was established to reinforce the company's development of new products.

Difficult market conditions forced the company to rationalize production. In 1983 production of ethylene and ethylene derivatives at the Ehime Works was curtailed in order to concentrate production at the Chiba plant. The following year Sumitomo Chemical and Inabata & Company jointly established a separate company called Sumitomo Pharmaceuticals to handle both companies' pharmaceutical businesses.

Sumitomo Chemical remains independent of the numerous other Sumitomo group companies. As a member of the Sumitomo group, however, its management affairs and business strategies are shared with other group members, with whom it also shares, to a significant degree, cross-ownership of stock. It it still one of the largest chemical companies in Japan, although market conditions and increasingly well-organized competition have obscured its pre-eminence. In order to deal with this increasing competition Sumitomo is presently devoting a great deal of its resources to the development of new technologies, particularly in the rapidly growing field of biotechnology.

Principal Subsidiaries and Affiliates: Nihon Oxirane Co. Ltd.; Sumitomo Bakelite Co., Ltd.; Japan Exlan Co., Ltd.; Seitetsu Kagaku Co., Ltd.; Japan-Singapore Petrochemicals Co., Ltd.; Nihon Polystyrene Co., Ltd.; Sumitomo Naugatuck Co., Ltd.; Nihon Vinyl Chloride Co., Ltd.; Chiba VCM Co., Ltd.; Nihon Singapore Polyolefin Co., Ltd.; Koei Chemical Co., Ltd.; Japan Lactam Ltd.; Nihon Aklylate Co., Ltd.; Tobu Butadiene Co., Ltd.; Japan Aldehyde Co., Ltd.; Politeno Industria e Comercio S.A.; Nihon Methacryl Monomer Co., Ltd.; Japan Upjohn Ltd.; Sumitomo Bayer Urethane Co., Ltd.; Sakata Shikai, Ltd.; Shinto Paint Co., Ltd.; ICI-Pharma Ltd.; Taoka Chemical Co., Ltd.; Nippon Wellcome K.K.; Nippon Medi-Physics Co., Ltd.; Sumika-Hercules Co., Ltd.; Sumitomo Chemical America, Inc.; Sumitomo Aluminium Smelting Co., Ltd.; Sumitomo Joint Electric Power Co., Ltd.; Sumitomo Chemical Engineering Co., Ltd.; Sumitomo Pharmaceuticals Co., Ltd.; Sumiarco Co., Ltd.

UNION CARBIDE CORPORATION

39 Old Ridgebury Road
Danbury, Connecticut 06817
U.S.A.
(203) 794-2000

Public Company
Incorporated: November 1, 1917
Employees: 91,459
Sales: $6.343 billion
Market value: $3.703 billion
Stock Index: New York Amsterdam Basle Brussels
Frankfurt Geneva Lausanne London Paris Zurich

In 1876, the first carbon arc street light changed light into day in Cleveland, Ohio with the help of Charles F. Brush. As a result of this invention, a company was formed in 1886 to make street light carbons and later carbon electrodes for electric furnaces. Soon the Eveready trademark became a part of this company. Four years later, it produced the first commercial dry cell battery and then, in 1894, built one of the first industrial research laboratories in the United States.

Meanwhile in North Carolina in 1892 two men attempted to make aluminum in an electric furnace. Thomas L. Willson and Major James T. Morehead produced calcium carbide, resulting in acetylene. These two chemicals were considered mere laboratory curiosities at the time, but Morehead convinced several Chicago entrepreneurs in the use of acetylene for city and home lighting, and the Union Carbide Company was formed in 1898 to manufacture calcium carbide. Morehead didn't give up hope for his electric furnace idea. In fact, in 1897, he, with the help of Guillaume de Chalmot, produced America's first commercial high-carbon ferrochrome and furnished ferrochrome for armorplate during the Spanish-American War.

Electric lighting became practical during this time, eliminating any expansion for Union Carbide's acetylene lighting business. But their calcium carbide plants continued to operate in Sault Ste. Marie, Michigan and Niagara Falls, New York. In 1900 their capital stock was $6,000,000, par value $100. Dividends were at 4 percent, with Charles F. Dieterich as president, George O. Knapp as vice president, and A.B. Proal as secretary and treasurer. Their main office was located in Chicago, Illinois. In 1906 the company purchased an alloys business and a metals research laboratory, and established a separate division to produce alloys for steelmaking. Under the direction of Dr.

Fredrick M. Becket, its chief metallurgist, the new company began a line of alloying metals that were respected in the field. One example is their creation of low-carbon ferrochrome, resulting in the development of modern stainless steels.

The discovery in France of a hot metal-cutting flame resulting from burning acetylene in oxygen, created a high demand for such resources. Charles Brush interested several electrode producers in forming the first oxygen-producing company in 1907. This company later became the Corporation's present Linde Division. In 1911, Union Carbide bought interest in the oxygen company, therefore bringing together for the first time the carbon and carbide interests.

Union Carbide's major competitor during this period was the Prest-O-Lite Company, the largest single purchaser of calcium carbide for acetylene lamps for automobiles. When an alternative form of acetylene was requested, Dr. George O. Curme, Jr. was hired by Prest-O-Lite in 1914 to find it. He consulted scientists from the Linde Company and Union Carbide to conduct research on the gas. The cooperative efforts resulted in the formation of the Union Carbide and Carbon Corporation in 1917.

The government's need for ethylene during the World War I regenerated interest in hydrocarbon byproducts. In 1919 the first production of synthetic ethylene began. Dr. Curme and his associate, James A. Rafferty, predicted a future need for synthetic organic chemicals, and America's petrochemical industry and the Corporation's chemicals business were established in 1920. With combined research efforts, new developments occurred rapidly. New products included ethylene glycol (today's Prestone anti-freeze and coolant), batteries for portable radios, quiet flickerless carbons used for the first sound movies, and ferroalloys to improve the steels used to build skyscrapers, bridges, and automobiles. The company's technology included the production of corrosion- and heat-resistant alloys. Six years later it acquired vanadium interests on the Colorado Plateau, which eventually supplied the uranium for atomic energy. Graphite skills were added to the Corporation's carbon activities in 1928 with the Acheson Graphite Corporation. The Chicago World's Fair in 1933 enabled Union Carbide to exhibit more than half of the known chemical elements to the public. Today, Union Carbide works with more than 90 of the 107 chemical elements named by scientists.

With the advent of World War II Union Carbide focused its attention on developing raw material resources and utilization of by-products. Carbide resumed its butadiene studies, begun years before, to succeed in developing a synthetic rubber, and soon acquired the Bakelike Corporation, increasing its technology in the field of plastics. Carbide was also responsible for research on vanadium that eventually involved the Corporation in the government's atomic energy program. Scientists demonstrated that gaseous diffusion could be used to separate quantities of uranium-235. Union Carbide and the Manhattan Engineer District entered into a contract on 18 January 1943 to operate the Oak Ridge Gaseous Diffusion Plant. After intensive research, Linde perfected a refining process for treating uranium concentrates. A plant was built and operated by the Electro Metallurgical Company, presently the Metals Division, to provide extensive emergency metallurgical research, and to manufacture uranium. Graphite products and special carbons were developed and manufactured by National Carbon, presently Carbon products. Uranium-bearing materials were located and provided by the United States Vanadium, now part of the Metals Division, also constructing three plants for treating uranium ores with newly developed processes. Finally, Union Carbide and Carbon Research Laboratories contributed to the development of the atomic weapon itself.

Following World War II, Union Carbide expanded. Polyethylene, a plastic used in squeeze bottles, as well as in films and sheeting, became its largest dollar-volume product. Other materials such as gases and carbon products also continued to succeed.

Restructuring of the Union Carbide Company began during the 1950's. Interest in new fields of technology emerged. The Metals Division was established to handle worldwide ore procurement, and a food casings business, formally the Visking Company, was also established. By 1957 Union Carbide and Carbon Corporation had established some 400 plants in the United States and Canada, in addition to overseas affiliates. The public was becoming increasingly aware of its activities, so the company decided to change its name to the Union Carbide Corporation in 1957. Consumer products such as Eveready batteries and Prestone anti-freeze continued to increase in sales. To accommodate this, a separate division strictly for consumer products was established in 1959. Then in the early 1960's the Glad line of plastic wraps, bags, and straws was introduced and became a leading brand in its field.

International operations of Union Carbide was restructured in 1966 to accommodate new subsidiaries, including Union Carbide Pan America, Inc., Union Carbide Europe, Inc., Union Carbide Eastern, Inc., Union Carbide Africa and Middle East, Inc., and Union Carbide Canada Limited (a 75-% owned subsidiary). A new division was named in 1969—Films-Packaging Division (previously the Visking casings business), consolidating activities in food casings and related products. During the late 1960's and early 1970's, Union Carbide decided to sell and dissolve some of its businesses in order to concentrate on further expansion of certain industries. Among the businesses sold were Neisler Laboratories (acquired in 1965), the Stellite, or Materials Systems Division, Ocean Systems, Inc., a subsidiary underwater work, The Englander Company, Inc. (a bedding company acquired in 1964), most of its oil and gas interests, a pollution-monitoring devices business, a plastic container line, a fibers business, a jewelry line, and an insect repellant business. Other organizational changes came about during this period as well. The New Business Development Department, formed in 1970, merged with the Corporate Technology Department in 1971. Two years later, the Consumer Products Division was elminiated to form a Battery Products Division. Preston and Glad products acquired the Home and Automotive Products Division. The Agricultural Products Division, developed in

1976, began producing Sevin insecticide, Temik pesticide, and similar materials.

In 1972 a comprehensive long-term program was established by Union Carbide with the following objectives: "Strengthening the assignment of individual responsibilities and accountabilities, strengthening business management methods, allocating resources selectively in strategic planning units, and practicing good corporate citizenship at home and abroad." With the advent of new strategies came new materials and processes, including molecular sieve adsorbents and catalysts, specialized electronic materials, foamed plastics, biomedical systems, pollution abatement systems, energy (converting coal to gases and liquids for fuel), miniature batteries, food (chemicals to increase food yield, raising salmon, trout, and other fish species, shrimp fishing off the coast of India), Thornel carbon-graphite fibers (used in aerospace, gold club shafts, tennis rackets, and fishing rods).

In addition to these developments, Union Carbide had established additional pesticide and fertilizer producing plants in particular, Bhopal, India. During the mid-1960's India was experiencing a chronic food shortage. The central government's "Green Revolution" included increasing use of pesticides. When Union Carbide approached New Delhi authorities with an offer to build a plant in Bhopal, they were gladly accepted. In 1975 the Indian government granted Union Carbide a license to manufacture pesticides, and the plant was built, Union Carbide owning 51 percent and India's private companies owning 49 percent. The plant was built on the outskirts of the city, not densely populated at that time. But with construction came more residents: more than 900,000 people eventually lived in this capital of Madhya Pradesh. Union Carbide increased its ties with the local government and helped the city to build a park. The company also hired local residents for management positions.

By the late 1970's, Union Carbide had established itself as having one of the better safety records in the chemical industry throughout all its subsidaries, including India. But a massive disaster at the Bhopal plant in December 1984 led to the deaths of some 2500 people, with a huge additional number possibly permanently disabled. It has been called "the worst industrial accident in history" (*Newsweek*).

After the incident, Bhopal police arrested five senior Indian executives of Union Carbide. In a written statement, Arjun Singh, chief minister of Madhya Pradesh state, charged Warren Anderson, chairman of Union Carbide's board, with "corporate and criminal liability," and accused the Union Carbide management of "cruel and wanton negligence." Many class action suits were filed against Union Carbide on behalf of all the victims by two Florida attorneys, Michael Tobin and Jack Thompson, in association with the San Francisco lawyer Melvin Belli. According to the Cook County Municipal Law Library, these suits were later filed in India. Union officials claim that at least five tons of methyl isocyanate (MIC) seeped out in the 30 minutes before the leaking tank was sealed. The effects of the chemical on humans resemble those of nerve gas (*Newsweek*).

In addition to the human toll, the tragedy halted

business at the $9 billion company, and Union Carbide shut down production and distribution of methyl isocyanate at their plant in Institute, West Virginia. Stock prices plunged 12 points. Union Carbide may never be able to recover from the 1984 Bhopal disaster. As Chairman Warren Anderson concedes, "We have a stigma and we can't avoid it."

Principal Subsidiaries: Amerchol Corporation; Amko Service Company; Bayox, Inc.; Beaucar Minerals, Inc.; BEK III Inc.; Be-Kan, Inc.; Bentley Sales Co. Inc.; Blue Creek Coal Company, Inc.; Catalyst Technology, Inc.; Cellulosic Products, Inc.; Chemicals Marine Fleet, Inc.; Dexter Realty Corporation; Gas Technics Gases and Equipment Centers of Eastern Pennsylvania, Inc.; Gas Technics Gases and Equipment Centers of New Jersey, Inc.; Gas Technics Gases and Equipment Centers of Ohio, Inc.; Global Industrial Corporation; Hampton Roads Welders Supply Company, Inc.; Harvey Company; Innovative Membrane Systems, Inc.; International Cryogenic Equipment Corporation; Iweco, Inc.; Karba Minerals, Inc.; KSC Liquidation, Inc.; KTI Chemicals, Inc.; Linde Homecare Medical Systems, Inc.; Linox Welding Supply Co.; London Chemical Company, Inc.; Media Buyers Inc.; Merritt-Holland Company; Mon-Arc Welding Suppy, Inc.; Nova Tran Corporation; Paulsboro Packaging Inc.; Phoenix Research Corporation; Polysak, Inc.; Prentiss Glycol Company; Presto Hartford, Inc.; Presto Welding Supplies, Inc.; Seadrift Pipeline Corporation; Soilsery, Inc.; South Charleston Sewage Treatment Company; UCAR Capital Corporation; UCAR Energy Services Corporation; UCAR Interam, Inc.; UCAR Louisiana Pipeline Company; UCAR Pipeline Incorporated; UCORE Ltd.; Umetco Minerals Exploration; Umetco Minerals Sales Corporation; Unigas, Inc.; Union Carbide Africa and Middle East, Inc.; Union Carbide Canada Ltd. (74.5%); Union Carbide Caribe, Inc.; Union Carbide Communications Company, Inc.; Union Carbide Engineering and Hydrocarbons Service Company, Inc.; Union Carbide Engineering and Technology Services; Union Carbide Ethylene Oxide/Glycol Company; Union Carbide Europe, Inc.; Union Carbide Films-Packaging, Inc.; Union Carbide Grafito, Inc.; Union Carbide Imaging Systems, Inc.; Union Carbide Industrial Services Company; Union Carbide Inter-America, Inc.; Union Carbide International Capital Corporation; Union Carbide International Sales Corporation; Union Carbide Polyolefins Development Company, Inc.; UNISON Transformer Services, Inc.; Vametco Minerals Corporation; V.B. Anderson Co. (85.33%); Welders Service Center of Nebraska, Inc.; Wolfe Welding Supply Company, Inc. The company also lists subsidiaries in the following countries: Australia, Austria, Belgium, Bermuda, Brazil, Canada, Colombia, Costa Rica, Ecuador, Egypt, France, Ghana, Greece, Guatemala, Hong Kong, India, Indonesia, Iran, Italy, Japan, Kenya, Malaysia, Malawi, Mexico, Netherlands, Netherlands Antilles, New Zealand, Nigeria, Pakistan, Panama, Philippines, Puerto Rico, Singapore, South Africa, South Korea, Spain, Sri Lanka, Sweden, Switzerland, Taiwan, Thailand, Turkey, United Kingdom, U.S. Virgin Islands, Venezuela, West Germany, and Zimbabwe.

Further Reading: Behold the Poison Cloud: Union Carbide's Bhopal Massacre by Larry Everest, Chicago, Banner Press, 1986.

VISTA

VISTA CHEMICAL COMPANY

15990 North Barker's Landing Road
P.O. Box 19020
Houston, Texas 77224
U.S.A.

Public Company
Incorporated: October, 1983
Employees: 1,600
Sales: $560 million
Market value: $491 million
Stock Index: New York

Though the history of Vista proper is actually rather brief, its parent company does have a longer history and in fact dates back almost 40 years (a relatively long time in the chemical industry).

On 20 July 1984 a management-led investment team at Conoco Chemicals Company purchased their company's assets from the Du Pont Corporation which owned Conoco at that time. For almost two years this company (named Vista Chemical Company) remained privately held. In December of 1986 a public offering of the company's stock finally occurred.

The progenitor of Conoco Chemical Company was the Continental Oil Company (which later became Conoco Inc.). In 1949 Continental converted a refinery it controlled in Baltimore to produce a synthetic detergent, alkylate. This alkylate was the major active ingredient in many industrial and household cleaners. This was Continental's first venture into the field of chemicals. Several innovative products came out of Continental during the next decades. In the late 1950's the company developed "the world's first process for selectively manufacturing linear primary alcohols." This product is used as a "plasticizer" and also in household detergents. Continental began mass production of this product in 1961 at their plant in Lake Charles, Louisiana. This same year witnessed the completion of a methyl chloride production unit at the same Lake Charles plant, which constituted further product diversification for Continental.

The early 1960's was a period of growth and innovation for Continental. In 1964 they began production in Baltimore of a detergent alkylate which was biodegradeable, Nalkylene, derived from an earlier biodegradeable detergent developed by the company called LAB (linear alkybenzene).

When Du Pont purchased Conoco in 1981 rumors began to circulate that the former company would sell off some of the latter's chemical operations. Du Pont's emphasis was on specialty chemicals and high technology; accordingly, the commodity business of Conoco's chemical operations constituted a diversification they were not willing to tackle at that time. A group of higher echelon managers from the chemical division of Conoco approached the Du Pont executives with a proposal to buy out the chemical operations in a leveraged buyout. General negotiations surrounding the buyout were friendly: a former Du Pont chairman and member of the board arranged for legal services for the group forming Vista (he was also a member of the law firm eventually involved in the buyout). In addition, Du Pont arranged that all 1200 professionals from the chemical operations could move to Vista or stay with Du Pont in suitable operations.

Du Pont retained several units of Conoco Chemical. The largest of these was a plant in Chocolate Bayou, Texas which produced ethylene, propylene, butadiene, and aromatics. This petrochemical unit was originally a joint venture between Monsanto and Conoco. However, after 1981 it was wholly owned by Du Pont. In addition, Du Pont retained the high density polyethylene unit in Bay City, Texas, the Conoco Drag Reducer business which manufactures agents that increase the flow rate of liquid hydrocarbons in pipe, and the standing interest in Condea Chemie (West Germany). The 50% interest which Du Pont held in Petroquimica Espanola was sold off to the Spanish partner. The remaining chemical operations, out of which Vista was created, were sizeable. The total assets purchased amounted to seven plants in the United States (dealing primarily in detergent additives and polymers), a 50% equity in a manufacturer of alkylates and a 25% equity in a producer of aluminum alkylys, both in Japan, and a 25% interest in a manufacturer of styrene, synthetic rubber, and aromatics in Argentina.

The most notable thing about the buyout is that it was proposed during the worst period of business for the chemical industry since the 1930's. The chemical industry in the United States was operating at around 64% capacity, and because the Middle East oil producing countries were building chemical plants of their own, the future looked even more forboding. However, studies carried out by the consortium putting up the capital for the buyout indicated that the detergent business was virtually immune to recession. Since the buyout was primarily involved with precisely this business, general industry slowdowns would not affect it. In fact, the studies also showed that even in 1982 (the very worst year) Vista (had it existed at that time) could have kept up on its debt.

The financing of the buyout was rather complicated due to the fact that it involved asset based lending. This meant that the buyout group had to purchase the properties individually (instead of en masse). The E. F. Hutton Group served as financial adviser (and part of the backing group) to the Vista buyout team. Manufacturers Hanover Bank put together a group of seven banks and insurance companies to finance the buyout, and the Prudential insurance company was the major financer of the subordinated debt. Initially the buyout team had a difficult time finding financing for their plans and Gordon Cain (who was Conoco Chemicals' chief) claimed that two thirds of the banks and insurance companies approached with the plan balked at the idea.

It was not until almost a year after the initial offers were proposed that Du Pont signed a letter of intent with the buyout group. The buyout group was composed of 39 managers from Conoco's chemicals division.

The chemical division of Conoco Oil Company dates back to the 1930's when Witco Incorporated, a large chemical concern (then known as Wishnick-Tumpeer Inc.) formed Continental Carbon, in association with the Continental Oil Company (as Conoco was known at that time). Continental Oil held only a 20% interest in the chemical operation (i.e. Continental Carbon) for many years after this. The Shamrock Oil and Gas Corporation held a 30% interest in Continental Carbon and supplied the chemical operation with residue gas which was used for the manufacture of carbon black. This continued until 1958 when Continental Blacks Inc. (which was 58% owned by Continental Oil) was merged with Continental Carbon (which, by that point was 40% owned by Continental Oil) to form Continental Carbon Company. The last mentioned company was 51% owned by Continental Oil after the merger. However, by 1980, one year before the merger with Du Pont, Continental Oil Company owned 80% of Continental Carbon Company.

In 1981 there occured the largest merger in history—Du Pont bought Conoco for 7.8 billion dollars. The giant bought out Conoco in order to protect itself from growing oil prices (Conoco held oil sites in Alaska and Alberta). At the time of the takeover, Conoco Inc. was the ninth largest oil producer in the United States. This was the culmination of a takeover battle that had started one year earlier, when Mobil Oil and the Seagrams conglomerate of Canada were turned down by Conoco in an investment bid. However, during this period Du Pont had accepted a Seagrams investment offer and, as a consequence, Seagrams held 19% of Du Pont stock. As a result of the merger with Conoco, Seagrams actually ended up with 20% of Du Pont stock and obviously, an interst in Conoco. However, according to the agreement between Seagrams and Du Pont, the latter company cannot buy more than a 25% interest in the former until 1991.

After this merger, Du Pont began selling some of its new aquisitions in order to pay off some of the money it had to borrow to aquire Conoco. It was in this context that some of the managers of Conoco offered to buy out the chemical operations from Du Pont.

The first five years of Vista's operation proved to be profitable. Operating income rose by almost 500% to 90.8 million in 1986; return of shareholder's equity rose by 100% to 46.6%, and Vista shares rose in value by almost 100% to $30 per share (the average increase in the chemical industry as a whole was only 30%). Perhaps most importantly, the total debt capitalization of Vista was reduced by 25%; after the buyout, approximately 90% of the firm's total capital was debt—currently that figure is down to 65%. This reduction was made possible by the stock offering which occured in December 1986. Vista sold 4.4 million shares of stock for approximately $70 million, which monies were used to redeem all outstanding special preferred stock and to repay part of its indebtedness. One important benefit of this was that the company was able to renegotiate its bank credit agreements at lower interest rates. According to the new credit schedule, interest rates are connected to the company's net worth so that as the worth of the company increases, the interest rates will decline.

Vista made its first purchase five years after its birth. In July 1986 a compounding operation based in Kentucky, Premiere Products, was purchased for the purpose of augmenting the company's line of PVC products. This was followed six months later by the purchase of another compounding production facility, Blane Products, in Massachusetts. This brings the total of Vista's facilities in the United States to nine.

Vista credits its success over the last five years to its policy of switching to high margin specialty chemical products from low margin-high volume more basic products. This change is evident in both the company's PVC production and in its surfactant alcohol business (which is necessary for all types of detergent cleaners). Vista has switched from producing low grade PVC which would be used for pipe manufacture to higher quality PVC which would be used in specialty applications, for instance, automobile manufacturing. At the time of the buyout 70% of Vista's PVC production was pipe grade. In the surfactant field, expansion on the part of Vista has again been in the field of specialty chemicals; for instance, a new customer for Vista in this area is Helene Curtiss a manufacturer of beauty products and shampoos. Since these products require closer attention to quality, Vista formed a department specifically devoted to quality control. This department initiated a company-wide "statistical process control" program.

Vista has not planned major investment in any new plants. When Vista was formed it was one of the top five of 14 PVC producing companies in the United States, and its greatest strength lies in its degree of integration.

Witco

WITCO CORPORATION

520 Madison Avenue
New York, New York 10022
U.S.A.
(212) 805 3800

Public Company
Incorporated: May 6, 1920 as Wishnick-Tumpeer
Chemical Company
Employees: 8,009
Sales: $1.355 billion
Market value: $1.013 billion
Stock Index: New York

Witco Corporation, the highly successful manufacturer of specialty chemicals, petroleum products, and engineered materials, began in 1920 as a small Chicago area chemical distributor. Since that time, Witco's consistent expansion through both acquisitions and internal developments have made the company one of the strongest, if not the largest, chemical companies in the industry.

The company was founded as Wishnick-Tumpeer Chemical Company by Robert I. Wishnick in association with the brothers Julius and David Tumpeer. Wishnick was president, owning 51% of the company's shares, and was Chairman Emeritus of Witco until his death in 1980. It was Wishnick who shaped the company's growth and direction for over half its life. His two original partners, who together owned only 20% of the company's shares, sold their interest shortly after World War II.

Born in Koltchina, Russia in 1892, Robert Wishnick came to the United States to join his father and oldest brother in 1896. At age seven he lost his right arm at the elbow after breaking it badly in a fall. This childhood accident seems only to have hardened Wishnick's determination to make something of himself. He put himself through school, earning one of the first degrees in Chemical Engineering from the Armour Institute of Technology, now the Illinois Institute of Technology. Then, employed days as a chemist, he worked towards a law degree, which he received in 1917 from Kent College of Law.

His first job with the American Magnesium Products Company brought near disaster to his employers, but ironically foretold the successful business strategy Wishnick would follow to bring Witco to its present position in the chemical industry. His company sold a floor wax which complemented its product line of magnasite

floor materials. However, Wishnick thought that the company should produce its own floor wax, rather than reselling floor wax originally purchased elswhere. He had his own mixture of wax and turpentine on a burner when the telephone rang and drew him away. In his absence, the mixture boiled over and set the entire factory on fire, burning it to the ground. This may not have been the most auspicious of beginnings, but it demonstrated clearly Wishnick's drive for independence. From that time Wishnick continually strived to push Witco to self-sufficiency through manufacturing its own products.

In 1920 after working as a sales representative with A. Dager & Company for two years, Wishnick, with Julius Tumpeer, set up Wishnick-Tumpeer as a chemical distributing concern on East Illinois street in Chicago. The company's largest market was in carbon black and various other coloring agents needed by Chicago's vigorous printing industry. Before the company was a year old, however, a recession set in and sales declined considerably. Wishnick responded by cutting costs wherever possible. He reduced his own salary, cut the company's profit margin then worked to increase volume. These measures have been consistently successful for Witco and have been used to great effect whenever the company suffered from changes in the market. It also helped the company record a profit during its first year, despite the recession.

In 1922 the company was able to buy a 20% interest in a carbon black plant in Swartz, Louisiana. Witco then marketed the product on a commission basis in its own area. In 1923 Wishnick felt it was time to expand further and asked Julius Tumpeer to head the company's first New York office, though Wishnick later replaced him.

Also in 1924, Wishnick-Tumpeer purchased its first manufacturing concern, Pioneer Asphalt Company in Lawrenceville, Illinois. By 1926 so much of the company's business was in asphalt products that the board elected to drop Chemical from the company name, making the new name simply Wishnick-Tumpeer Incorporated. The steady growth which had marked the company from its beginnings continued through the 1920's until the crash of 1929.

Once again, Wishnick and his company implemented cost cutting measures. Wishnick reduced wages, salaries and, of course, margins. This strategy worked again and the company managed to turn a profit in each year of the 1930's. During this time, cash flow was a severe problem, but Wishnick had a unique solution. Most of the company's cash flow problems were caused by its customers' late bill payments. Each month Wishnick made a special trip to the accounts payable departments of the company's major accounts. There he left a small gift of candy or flowers with the secretaries and politely suggested that his bill be moved from the bottom of the pile to the top where it could be paid as soon as possible.

In 1933 the company acquired another carbon black plant which, after additional negotiations, led to Wishnick's formation of Continental Carbon Company in association with Continental Oil Company and Shamrock Oil and Gas Company. These two other concerns supplied the needed natural gas for carbon black production and

Wishnick-Tumpeer became the exclusive sales agents for the new company.

In 1935 Witco's first overseas operation was created in Britain: the company acquired an interest in Harold A. Wilson & Company, a supplier of pigments to the United States. Eventually, the entire company was bought by Wishnick. This effort was only the beginning of what are today extensive overseas holdings. Witco now has 12 wholly owned foreign manufacturing operations and part interest in 17 others.

The company's last important move before World War II was to build its first chemical plant in Chicago to produce industrial chemicals and asphalt products. The war brought large amounts of business for Wishnick-Tumpeer. However, it also led to problems of shortages and rationing. Most of the company's business was still in distribution, and at times Wishnick's suppliers were unable to deliver what was needed.

As the war was ending, annual sales were at approximately $7.8 million. The company was larger than ever before, but its future was uncertain. Many of the larger chemical companies Wishnick was accustomed to buying from were developing their own competing sales forces. In 1944 Wishnick changed the name of his company to Witco Chemical Incorporated. Then, in 1945, the board of the new company made official its plans to move as quickly as possible into manufacturing and to leave the distributing business.

Soon thereafter, the Chicago plant was expanded to include the production of metallic stearates, and then a number of new companies were acquired. Franks Chemical Products Inc. was purchased and then moved to less expensive quarters in Perth Amboy, New Jersey. A Los Angeles plant was bought from the India Paint and Varnish division of American Marietta, and new equipment was ordered for the plant to begin production of stearates. In 1954, by the time sales had grown to nearly $20 million, a British stearate plant was also purchased. This steady and extended expansion was not without difficulties, however. There were recurring operating problems in the Perth Amboy plant, some of which William Wishnick, the President's son, was asked to help solve. There was also a major fire in the Chicago plant, and then in 1953 the first strike in Witco's history took place in the Lawrenceville plant.

None of this weakened William Wishnick's resolve, however. In 1955 the decision was announced to end the company's distributing business altogether and to begin moving toward complete self-sufficiency. Witco sales were as high as $30 million, but over a ten year period only 35% of that was from its own manufacturing operations. Some major acquisitions were on the horizon, but not until after a management reorganisation. The Tumpeer brothers were no longer with the company (Julius had retired in 1947 and David had died in 1951). It was then, in 1955, that Robert Wishnick became chairman of the board, and Max Minnig, a long-time senior employee, became president. At that time, William Wishnick rose to the executive vice presidency from his position as vice president and treasurer.

In keeping with its new corporate strategy, Witco spent the next two years making acquisitions and expanding operations. Sales rose to $40 million, 40% of which came from Witco manufacturing facilities. Then, in 1958 Witco went public and sold 150,000 shares of common stock. This expansion continued unabated through the mid-1960's. In 1960 the Sonneborn Chemical and Refinery Company was acquired, bringing sales up to the $100 million mark. International expansion was accelerated as well, with new acquisitions in Belgium, France, and Canada.

In 1964 further administrative changes led the way for even greater expansion. Robert Wishnick became chairman of the finance committee as well as managing director of international activities. Robert's son, William, succeeded him as chairman of the board, and Max Minnig became chief executive officer while maintaining his position as president. As chairman, William initiated the greatest growth period in Witco's history. He began with the 1966 acquisition of Argus Chemical Company at a price of $22 million. This provided Witco with a new plastics operation and one of its senior managers, Bill Setzler. The younger Wishnick also spent considerable sums on plant modernization and research and development. This tendency toward reinvestment of generated capital was to characterize the next two decades of Witco growth. In the period from 1966 to 1975 William Wishnick increased the company's sales by 250%. During this period he also assumed the duties of president and chief executive officer after Max Minnig's retirement in 1971.

In fulfillment of Robert Wishnick's dream, Witco became a firm devoted exclusively to manufacturing chemical products when its 1933 agreement with Continental Carbon Company expired. Witco kept its 20% interest in the company, but did not renew its licensing contract with the company. Witco now sold only Witco-manufactured products.

The recession in 1974 brought the traditional cost-cutting measures at Witco. The recession also brought a fourth-quarter drop of 50% in sales compared to the previous quarter. In addition, there was a sharp earnings drop in early 1975. By the end of 1975 matters had returned to normal, but there was still an overall drop in operating earnings of 23%. Despite this, Witco continued to expand, albeit more slowly. The Waverly Oil Works was purchased and a new $10 million hydrogenation plant was built in Pennsylvania.

1975 witnessed additional administrative changes as highly talented managers from acquired companies rose to executive levels. Henry Sonneborn, brought in when his company was purchased in 1960, assumed the presidency and also became chief executive officer while William Setzler of the Argus division was appointed to the board of directors. William Wishnick returned to the position of Chairman and his father Robert was appointed chairman emeritus, a position he held until his death in 1980.

The period from 1975 to 1986, half of it spent without the founder's presence, was characterized by a marked drop in acquisitions for Witco. The new administration, led by William Wishnick, continued to emphasize expansion of existing operations, research and development, and modernization of equipment and methods. This strategy resulted in slow but steady growth, especially in the Argus division which expanded its operations and opened up new markets for its plastics. By 1985 75% of the $70 million used for reinvestment went to plant modernization.

In October of 1985 Chemical was again dropped from the company name, leaving it as Witco Incorporated. At that time specialty petroleum products made up 53% of the company's business, while specialty chemical products accounted for only 41%. The remaining 6% consisted of engineered materials for special applications.

In 1986 Thomas J. Bickett took over as president and chief executive officer from the retiring William J. Ashe, who had occupied the job since Henry Sonneborn retired. In 1978 Bickett had been asked to join Witco while working for an accounting firm contracted by Witco. His appointment to the position came after he had been with the company for 12 years, serving for much of that time on the board of directors.

The chemical market in the latter half of the 1980's is good for Witco. The company maintains a low profit margin but boasts one of the highest returns on stockholder equity in the business. William Wishnick has less and less to do with the direct management of Witco, but still maintains control over the direction of the company, even if he owns only 7.5% of the company shares. William feels that the future of Witco will be determined by its acquisition strategy. "We are an operating company—not an investment company," he said. "Anything we have a minority interest in is for sale." It remains to be seen if Witco will remain successful without a Wishnick directing the day-to-day operations of the company. However, if Thomas Bickett can continue the Wishnick's traditional emphasis on expansion and frugality, Witco's prospects for the future are very good.

Principal Subsidiaries: Witco Canada Inc.; Baxenden Chemical Co., Ltd. (53½%); Witco SA; Witco Ltd. (60%); Argus Quimica Mexicana SA de CV; Witco BV; Jonk BV; Surpass Chemicals Ltd.; Witco Chemical Australia Pty. Ltd.; Continental Carbon Co.; Enenco, Inc.; Witco International Sales Corp.; Witco Investment Corp.; Witco Foreign Sales Corp.; Witco Nencorp, Inc.; Witco Oil & Gas Corp.

Further Reading: *The Witco Story* by William Wishnick, New York, Newcomen Society in North America, 1976.

CONGLOMERATES

AEG A.G.
ALCO STANDARD CORPORATION
ALLIED-SIGNAL INC.
AMFAC INC.
ARCHER-DANIELS-MIDLAND
    COMPANY
BARLOW RAND LTD.
BAT INDUSTRIES PLC
BTR PLC
C. ITOH & COMPANY, LTD.
COLT INDUSTRIES INC.
ELDERS IXL LTD.
FARLEY NORTHWEST
    INDUSTRIES, INC.
FMC CORPORATION
FUQUA INDUSTRIES, INC.
GREYHOUND CORPORATION
GULF & WESTERN INC.
HITACHI LTD.
IC INDUSTRIES, INC.
INSTITUTO NACIONAL DE INDUSTRIA
INTERNATIONAL TELEPHONE &
    TELEGRAPH CORPORATION
ISTITUTO PER LA RICOSTRUZIONE
    INDUSTRIALE
JARDINE MATHESON HOLDINGS LTD.
KATY INDUSTRIES, INC.

KIDDE, INC.
KOÇ HOLDING A.Ş.
LEAR SIEGLER, INC.
LITTON INDUSTRIES, INC.
LOEWS CORPORATION
LTV CORPORATION
MARUBENI K.K.
McKESSON CORPORATION
MINNESOTA MINING &
    MANUFACTURING COMPANY
MITSUBISHI CORPORATION
MITSUI BUSSAN K.K.
NISSHO IWAI K.K.
OGDEN CORPORATION
SAMSUNG GROUP
SUMITOMO CORPORATION
SWIRE PACIFIC LTD.
TELEDYNE, INC.
TENNECO INC.
TEXTRON INC.
THORN EMI PLC.
TOSHIBA CORPORATION
TRANSAMERICA CORPORATION
TRW INC.
VEBA A.G.
WHITTAKER CORPORATION
W.R. GRACE & COMPANY

AEG

AEG A.G.

Zentralabteilung Finanzierungen
Theodor-Stern-Kai 1
D-6000 Frankfurt am Main 70
Federal Republic of Germany
(069) 600-3188

Public Company
Incorporated: 1883 as Deutsche Edison Gesellschaft für angewandte Elektricität
Employees: 73,760
Sales: DM 10.032 billion (US$5.166 billion)
Market Value: DM 6.111 billion (US$3.147 billion)
Stock Index: Berlin Bremen Düsseldorf Frankfurt Hamburg Hanover Munich Stuttgart Basle Paris Vienna Zurich

Emil Rathenau was the founder of what is now the massive AEG. He was born in Berlin in 1838, and, after the completion of his schooling, served for four years as an apprentice in his uncle's factory. This uncle then gave him enough money to attend the polytechnic in Hanover, but he had to leave because of his activities for student freedom. He completed his degree in mechanical engineering in Zurich, then returned to Berlin where he worked as a draughtsman for a construction firm. This seems to have bored him, for he quit and wandered over to England, where he worked in a number of engineering firms for two years.

Young Emil was called to home and responsibility by his father, who wanted him to be more than just somebody else's employee. Not having any money himself, Emil convinced his friend, Julius Valentin, to help him buy the engineering factory of Webers, which at that time employed some 40 to 50 workers. The factory produced engineering parts for works, including the iron for the Berlin Hoftheater. Now an owner and businessman, and no longer simply a technician, Rathenau began to focus his attention on matters of efficiency. He was one of the first industrialists to introduce assembly-line methods in Germany. His efforts were very successful, he became an important businessman, and married, in 1867, the daughter of a wealthy banker.

The war of 1870–71 brought lucrative contracts to the factory. Other companies were not willing to make the necessary improvements for the work required by the War Office, but Rathenau was, so most of the business came his way. By this time, banks were noticing the company,

and encouraged it to go public, which it did, as the Berliner Union. In this, Rathenau sold out his own interest in the company, for 750,000 marks, but remained as the director. The war was followed by a brief boom which collapsed into an economic crisis throughout Germany. The Berliner Union folded and, though Rathenau himself lost little money, he was branded as a failure. His troubles were increased by the complete failure and suicide of his father-in-law.

Rathenau became disillusioned with engineering but not with industry. Still only in his mid-thirties, he quit working and travelled. He went to the World's Fair of 1876 in Philadelphia, where he was particularly impressed by the Bell Telephone Company's display. Shortly after that, Bell tried to move its business into Germany, but the public objected, calling the telephones the "American Swindle." The Post Office was convinced of the usefulness and profitability of the invention and selected Rathenau to lead the effort to establish it as a business. It was not easy, but finally, in 1880, he had rounded up ten investors and the Berlin Exchange opened for business.

In 1878 Rathenau had visited another World's Fair, this one in Paris, and had seen the wonders of electric street lighting. He met Werner Siemens in Switzerland, and the two men proposed a plan for installing such lamps in Berlin, but the plan came to naught, primarily because Siemens's leading engineer did not want the extra work. The technical problems in the economic production of such lighting were many. In 1879, Thomas Edison's patent of his element finally made possible the inexpensive production of electric lighting on a large scale. Rathenau immediately recognised the value of Edison's invention, but the competition for the patent leases was intense, and Rathenau had trouble getting the backing he needed. Siemens was trying to introduce his own patents, and his many relatives in Deutsche Bank blocked financing of competitors. In 1882 Rathenau and the banker Jacob Landau formed a consortium with Sulzbach, the Nationalbank, and the French Compagnie Continentale, which had the Edison patent licences for France. The consortium, called Studiengesellschaft, was licensed to provide the streetlighting for all of Germany except the Frankfurt and Wiesbaden areas. The group was cautious, and gave Rathenau only six months to make a success of the business. His first customers were the printworks W. Büxenstein and the Bömische Brewery, both large and respected firms. In the winter of 1882–83, the first street in Berlin was lit. Snow is reputed to have fallen and sceptics to have been enchanted by the effect.

The Munich exhibition of 1882 brought a great opportunity for the Studiengesellschaft. Siemens and other companies were too conservative to participate in it, but Rathenau was a great lover of industrial fairs, and his products were well displayed. The company lit a street, had many showrooms of their smaller products, and put on a ballet on an electrically lit stage. This last was highly popular, and the directors of the Munich Hoftheater and the Royal Residence Theater contracted with the consortium to give them similar lights. The exhibition was such a success that banks were now much more willing to provide funding. Some of these banks transferred their support from Siemens, who finally realised that he was missing out on an important new market.

In 1882 Werner Siemens, having lost the chance for the Edison licences in Germany, tried to protect his business by securing them for works in Russia and England. He tried negotiating with the Compagnie Continentale, but it decided that it needed only one ally in Germany and, in 1883, helped Rathenau form Deutsche Edison-Gesellschaft, giving it the sole right to use all Edison patents in Germany. The company began with a capital base of 5 million marks; Compagnie Continentale kept two of its representatives on the board; and Siemens & Halske were forced to drop all of their suits for the Edison patents.

DEG was legally formed on 19 April 1883, with 15 founders. Fourth on the list was Emil Rathenau. He was given the responsibility for the Executive Board, and selected only Felix Deutsch as Secretary. Born in 1858 in Breslau, Deutsch had become a hard-working wunderkind, first in the sugar industry, then in banking.

DEG moved into offices at Leipziger Strasse 96 and began plans for building power stations. Rathenau also made a deal with Julius Springer to publish all technical papers produced during the work of the company. In its first year of operation, DEG installed over 5,000 lights in 27 different locations, mostly factories, but also in steamships. Still finding it difficult to sell the product to a sceptical public, the company used only one million marks of its capital.

Rathenau felt that the company's chief concern should be, not the installation of small generators and lighting, but the construction of central power generating plants. DEG built, after long negotiations, Berlin's first central generating station. This worked well, and a separate company was formed to handle it, the Städtische Elektricitäts-Werke A.G. zu Berlin (1884). Rathenau's idea was that power should not be owned by the consumer, but a guaranteed service.

In spite of the fact that Rathenau was a fanatical worker, in the office from 8.30am to 11pm on most days, the initial growth of DEG was slow. In 1884 the dividends were only 4%. But technical successes finally led to commercial ones. A lightbulb factory was built, producing 150,000 bulbs per year. An arc lamp invented in Belgium was manufactured in DEG factories. The company began to expand beyond the borders of Germany, angering other holders of Edison licences.

The brawls among the Edison patent licencees around the world were continual and were becoming serious. The French holder had over-extended itself and was incurring losses. Siemens was still trying to encroach. The Swan Electric Light Company in England kept claiming that its own inventions did not violate the Edison patents. Nearly all of them were fighting with the American headquarters. The consequential instability and uncertainty severely inhibited co-operative growth, as nobody knew which patent lease agreements would be valid, or for how long.

DEC's business became more shaky. Dividends were low, and the banks refused to allow the company to go public. Assets had sunk and Rathenau's competence was being questioned. But when he threatened his resignation, the board refused to let him go, and he remained with

increased power (Felix Deutsch joined the board). A united front was needed to see DEG through its own brawls with Siemens. The two companies had shared some work and battled over other contracts and licences for so long that the legal situation between them was extremely complicated and looked to lead to a lengthy court battle. Members of both boards met, but usually ended up at odds. Finally, a banker, Adalbert Delbrück, was called in to find a solution. In May 1887 both companies signed the treaty he had written. Under its terms, DEG dissolved its relationship with Compagnie Continentale and was now permitted to expand worldwide; the Berlin Städtischen Elektricitäts-Werke was to be headed by Rathenau's old friend Julius Valentin; DEG would build and run Berlin's two new power stations; the DEG-Siemens 1883 contract was dissolved; either firm could now build power stations but only Siemens could supply the parts; salesmen of the two firms would be friendly with one another; two Siemens representatives would sit on DEG's board; and finally, DEG would change its name to Allgemeine Elektricitäts-Gesellschaft (AEG).

AEG now expanded freely, buying another factory north of Berlin and moving into new offices. Oddly, Rathenau, Deutsch, and Paul Mamroth all chose to live communally above the new offices. Sales offices opened in Paris and Belgium, and AEG bought shares in the small electricity companies of many cities. AEG and Siemens formed a new company, in 1890, to manufacture accumulators for them both. This company also expanded rapidly, building factories in Russia, Finland, Sweden, and Norway.

From 1889 AEG began to be interested in electric trains. The company bought the Sprague Company's above-ground cable system patents for Germany at a cost of $25,000 and 2½% interest. Their first train contract was for the town of Gera. AEG formed Deutsch Strassen un Lokalbahn A.G. with 2.5 million marks to build electric tramways, and won the contracts for systems in Kiev and Breslau. In 1894 AEG formed Gesellschaft für den Bau von Untergrundbahnen to build the underground railway for Berlin. In 1889 it formed, with another company, yet another subsidiary, to manufacture aluminum, but this was never allowed to drain resources from AEG's primary interest of electro-technology.

For the first third of the century, AEG continued to thrive. Emil Rathenau was succeeded by his son, Walter. While they learned to work closely together, AEG and Siemens remained strongly competitive, the latter always far in the lead.

The Second World War brought the extreme disasters that led to the eventual end of AEG's independence. The company lost nearly 90% of its production facilities in East Germany and in the territories taken over by Poland and the Soviet Union. As Germany began to recover, AEG tried, under the chairmanship of Hans Buhler in the 1960's, to force its own recovery with manic growth. Unable to adjust to the idea of a small AEG, it bought more than 50 firms, almost all in the household goods sector, in a period of four years. While Germany prospered and consumers had the income to buy household goods, AEG prospered. With the recession of the early

1970's, AEG's falsely bolstered fortunes began to decline in earnest. AEG had also become heavily involved in the construction of nuclear power stations, which led to additional problems when these contracts were lost. The 1970 profit of 8.4 million Deutsche marks collapsed to a massive loss in 1974 of 664 million, and 960 million in 1979.

AEG certainly did not endure all of this without a fierce struggle to recover. When dividends stopped in 1973, there was a reshuffle of management. Yet another blow came when, in 1977, Jürgen Ponto, head of the Dresdener Bank and on the AEG-Telefunken Board, was murdered by terrorists. The surly and unpopular Dr. Walter Cipa was brought in to trim the fat in 1979, with a program of ferocious rationalisation. The previous year, the company had been forced to sell its stake in Kraftwerk-Union to Siemens, which was thus taking on AEG's nuclear losses. As it became more and more obvious that only a miracle could save the company, the crisis began to affect Germany politically, as the general public began to fear that the company's failure would mean that the boom years of recovery were truly over. In December 1979 a group of West German banks put together a 1 billion Deutsche mark rescue package, and AEG's capital was written down from 930 to 310 million.

It was clear that the only way that the company would be able to survive would be in joint venture schemes, and the search for partners began. In 1981 a video deal was signed with JVC, Thorn-EMI, and Thomson-Brandt, and a telecommunications deal was signed with Bosch. By the end of the year, however, losses were still great, and AEG had to ask banks for more money, to write off some 240 million in loans, and to sell off assets for 700 million in cash. Heinz Dürr was appointed chief executive and immediately began to woo Grundig, United Technologies, and especially the British GEC. Still desperately cutting costs, the company even printed its 1981 annual report on recycled paper, all to no avail.

In August 1982 the company applied to the Frankfurt court for restructuring proceedings under German bankruptcy law, finally admitting insolvency. The proposed settlement was to reduce the workforce from 120,000 to 60,000, and to award creditors only 40% of their claims. Understandably, the many banks involved were not pleased, but neither were they surprised. Often a leader in the field, AEG was one of the first of Germany's many bankruptcies in the 1980's. In September 1984 the bankruptcy proceedings finally ended, and AEG made its final payment of 350 million Deutsche marks to its some 900 creditors. The company had sold off Telefunken Fernseh & Rundfunk to France's Thomson S.A. The number of employees was down to about 75,000. Other sales included 49% of Ant Nachrichtentechnik to Robert Bosch, and all of Mannesmann and Allianz Versicherungs.

AEG survived, in a year when over 7,000 other German companies filed for bankruptcy, with Dürr still at the helm. The following year, Daimler-Benz moved in and bought 56% of AEG, paying 1.77 billion Deutsche marks. All of its debts were wiped out in a trice and the exhausted AEG would never be cash poor again.

Principal Subsidiaries: Olympia Aktiengellschaft, (99%); AEG Kabel Aktiengesellschaft, (98.3%); AEG Kanis GmbH; Dufrost Kuhl-und Gefriergerate GmbH; Eltro GmbH Gesellschaft fur Strahlungstechnik (73.8%); Sachsenwerk Licht-und Kraft-AG; Elekluft Elektronik-und Luftahrtgerate GmbH (74%); Lloyd dynaowerke GmbH; Debeg GmbH; Elektro-Mechanik GmbH; Elektron Versorgunsverwaltung GmbH; AEG Electronica Construction GmbH; ATM Computer GmbH; Hydra Vermogensverwaltung GmbH; AEG Software-Technik GmbH & co. KG; IFM Interntionale Fluggerate und Motoren GmbH (80%); AEG Analgenexportgellschaft mbH; PGS Planungsgesellschaft mbH Architekten Ingenieure; Fabeg GmbH; EAS Assekuranz Vermittlungs-GmbH (54.8%); Werbeagentur Dr. Kuhl GmbH; Elektrochemie GmbH; AEG Software Technik Verwaltungs GmbH; Telefunken Patentverwertungsgellschaft mbH; AEG International AG, (Switzerland); AEG Corporation, Somerville (U.S.A.); Officine Galileo Sicilla S.p.A. (Italy).

ALCO Standard Corporation

ALCO STANDARD CORPORATION

825 Duportail Road
Valley Forge, Pennsylvania 19482
U.S.A.
(215) 296–8000

Public Company
Incorporated: November 24, 1952 as Rainbow Production
Corporation
Employees: 18,400
Sales: $4.161 billion
Market value: $1.045 billion
Stock Index: New York

While the history of Alco Standard as a corporation
began in 1952 with the Rainbow Production Company
(which became Alco Oil and Chemical Corporation after
acquiring a company of that name in 1956), the history of
Alco Standard, the highly diversified conglomerate, began
in 1960 with the formation of V&V Companies, a holding
company established by Tinkham Veale II and two associates.

Veale began V&V Companies with his younger brother
George and a classmate, John Vaughan, at the age of 47,
at which time he was already a millionaire. In 1941 Veale
graduated with a degree in engineering from Case Institute
of Technology. He then married the daughter of A.C.
Ernst of Ernst & Ernst accounting, who in turn helped
Veale and some college associates buy into a wartime
manufacturer of specialty engineered goods in Cleveland.
Ernst tutored his son-in-law in the ways of what Veale
himself calls "wheeling and dealing", and Veale was able
to retire in the late 1940's when he and his associates
dissolved their investment team. Veale invested the capital
his first venture generated and became a millionaire by
1951.

He stayed out of the business world for the next ten
years. While he did keep an eye on his investment
portfolio and served on the board of directors of Alco Oil
and Chemical from 1954, Veale spent most of this time
breeding and racing thoroughbred horses. Then in 1960,
after beginning to feel a need for additional challenges, he
and his associates formed V&V; their first investment was
Alco Oil and Chemical.

V&V purchased a large minority share of Alco, and
realized reasonable profits from its investment until 1965
when the two companies were merged to form a larger

company. Alco had changed its name to Alco Chemical in
1962 to reflect increasing specialization, but after joining
forces with V&V, the company name was changed to Alco
Standard.

By the time Veale and Vaughan became group vice
presidents of the newly formed company in 1965, Alco had
already made some acquisitions of its own in the chemical
field. Miller Chemical and Fertilizer and Union Fertilizer
were the company's earliest acquisitions, followed in 1962
by Higgs and Young and Goulard and Olena, distributors
of fertilizer and agricultural materials. These early
attempts at expansion were successful, but had brought
company profits of only $250,000 a year on sales of $5
million; its shares at that time sold for 13¢.

Meanwhile, V&V had made other investments of its
own including Modern Equipment Company, Gas
Machinery Company, and RMF. These two groups
formed the basis for Alco Standard's impressive expansion
over the course of the 22 years since the merger in 1965.
Before serious growth could begin, however, Alco faced
difficult times. The early 1960's brought financial trouble
to Alco, and only skillful financial handling kept the new
company from bankruptcy. At one point, a 1 for 6 reverse
split of Alco's stock was necessary to bring the price per
share up to $3. This served to boost available capital to the
point where Veale was able to purchase three small
companies with Alco convertible preference shares. He
then made use of these companies' cash reserves to
support further acquisitions. By 1968 profits has risen to
$12.5 million on $140.4 million in sales, and the price per
share had risen to $1.17 after a 2 for 1 split, this time in the
right direction.

This sort of growth can be credited directly to Veale's
rapid but very careful acquisitions. He bought only into
private management-owned companies with sales in the $5
to $10 million range. The management of many of these
companies was kept on and given considerable autonomy,
with Alco acting as a board of directors only. The success
of many of these operations has been attributed by Veale
to Alco's extensive profit-sharing program, through which
his managers own a great deal of stock in the company. In
fact, Alco management owns 45% of the company's
common stock while Veale himself controls only 11%. By
1968, 52 separate companies had been acquired in this
manner and Alco's interests had been expanded into four
distinct areas—chemical, electrical, metallurgical, and
distribution. It is this last area which has developed into
Alco's largest and most profitable division.

In the mid-1960's, several Supreme Court anti-trust
decisions forced many big American paper manufacturers
to divest themselves of paper merchants they had acquired
during the 1950's. Many of these were sold to their own
management and as a result the paper distribution business was fragmented and inefficient. In 1968 Alco acquired
Garrett-Buchanan of Philadelphia and used it as a base
upon which to build the only national paper distribution
organization of its time. Many similar acquisitions were
made, adding to the size and profitability of this growing
division, and by 1970 Alco's distribution business had
grown to the point where outside help was sought in
management. Ray Mundt, now president of Alco, was

brought in from Kimberly Clark to manage the fast-growing division because he had the industry experience needed for the job.

Mundt saw an immediate need for centralized management of his division and was able to implement his plan to create a new company within Alco. Unisource, the national paper distribution operation Veale had imagined, was set up as an operating company for all the smaller distributors. Larger warehouses and computerized ordering, warehousing, and delivery made Unisource the most efficient and cheapest distributor in the United States. By 1981 Unisource alone generated $36 million in income for Alco on $963 million in sales.

The success of Unisource prompted Alco to move into other distribution areas. In 1969 distribution of specialty steel products was added, followed by auto parts, liquor, and glass containers. A health supplies distribution operation was added in 1977 and saw a dramatic rise in profitability within its first four years. By 1981 sales had risen from $83 million to $422 million and profits had gone from $2.8 million to $13 million. Altogether in 1981, $78.5 million were generated in distribution from $1.9 billion in sales accounting for 60% of Alco's profits and 75% of its sales.

Alco's earnings were expected to continue to rise at a rate of 10% or more, but 1983 brought margins that had sunk 2.1% and lowered return on equity. Even though Alco's profits as a whole rose, Veale, who was by then chairman, and Mundt, by then president and chief executive officer, were not happy with the situation. The problem was not in their successful distribution divisions, but in manufacturing. 23 of Alco's producers of plastics, rubber, specialty products, capital equipment, and chemicals, which constituted about 45% of Alco's total manufacturing operations, formed the crux of the problem. They were operating well enough and had good cash flow but were not able, due to the cyclical nature of their businesses, to expand at the rate that other Alco operations had achieved.

In 1984 Alco merged these smaller firms into a single operation named Alco Industries and sold the new company to its managers. Alco still retains a 19% equity in the firm, but has little to do with the company's operation. Without abandoning manufacturing entirely, Alco was able to decrease its dependency on its manufacturing operations to 15% of its sales and less than one third of its profits.

Restructuring of Alco's operations followed this divestiture closely. In 1984 Mundt divided the remaining companies into eight distinct segments including paper products, pharmaceuticals, and food equipment. Each group manager reports directly to Mundt. This new structure was designed to allow Mundt to oversee the over 180 companies owned by Alco while still leaving him free to pay special attention to paper and health products distribution, which remain Alco's strongest divisions.

Since that time Mundt has made six new acquisitions in the paper distribution market, including Saxon Industries, a struggling international distributor valued at $378 million. Alco was able to buy the company which was under backruptcy protection, for only $148 million in 1984. This purchase was a marked departure from Alco's usual policy of buying only companies with sales under $10 million, but as Alco's vice president for acquisitions is reported to have said, "when you are in the paper distribution business, it is not often you find an opportunity to increase yourself by 40%." Alco's only worry in paper distribution is of possible antitrust difficulties.

In the meantime, Mundt is busy expanding Alco's distribution operations in other areas. In 1983 seven office-products distributors were brought in. The revenues of these companies totaled over $70 million in 1982 and there has been little but growth since then. Pharmaceutical products, Alco's second fastest-growing operation, has expanded to fill third place in the industry, behind McKesson and Bergen Brunswig. Moves into electrical products distribution are planned, as is expansion of Alco's food equipment division.

Mundt believes that Southeast Asia's new attraction for fast food restaurants will provide a ready and expanding market for the food equipment division which does a great deal of business with the major companies involved. Other plans for change include possible divestiture of Alco's unprofitable coal business, which is suffering from low coal prices brought on by similarly low oil prices.

Mundt's future plans for Alco would seem to be more of the same. Distribution has proved consistently profitable for the company, and its president is moving toward further expansion of that end of the business in preference to manufacturing. The company's revenues have continued to rise steadily through the 1980's, although net income dropped suddenly in 1985. This was accompanied by rapid reductions in Alco's debt, however, and may not be indicative of hard times ahead.

Principal Subsidiaries: ATI; Alco Foodservice Equipment Co.; Alco Health Services Corp.; Alco-Plant City, Inc.; Alco Standard Petroleum Corp.; Alco Venture Capital Co.; Alexander Mercer & Hunt Co.; Allegheny Wholesale Drug Co., Inc.; Bearing-Belt & Chain Inc.; Big Drum, Inc.; Brown Drug Co.; Carpenter/Offutt Paper, Inc.; Devonshire Corp.; Hampshire Corp.; Kilroy Structural Steel, Inc.; Otto Konigslow Mfg. Co.; MDR Corp.; MLC Leasing Co.; Modern Business Systems, Inc.; Northwest Industries, Inc.; Paper Corporation of America; Partners Securities Co.; Ed Phillips & Sons Co.; Relco Financial Corp.; Reynolds Products, Inc.; Rita-Ann Distributors, Inc.; Spectra Office Concepts, Inc.; United Wine & Spirits Co., Inc.; Upshur Coals Corp. The company also lists subsidiaries in the following countries: Bermuda, Canada, Cayman Islands, England, France, New Zealand, Spain, Sweden, United Arab Emirates, and West Germany.

Further Reading: Alco Standard Corporation, "The Corporate Partnership": A Commitment to Excellence by R.B. Mundt and Tinkham Veale, New York, Newcomen Society, 1980.

ALLIED-SIGNAL INC.

Columbia Road and Park Avenue
Morristown, New Jersey 07960
U.S.A.
(201) 455-2000

Public Company
Incorporated: December 17, 1920 as the Allied Chemical
and Dye Corporation
Employees: 150,000
Sales: $11.794 billion
Market Value: $8.238 billion
Stock Index: New York Toronto

Allied-Signal, formed from the acquisition of Signal Companies, Inc. by Allied Corporation on August 6, 1985, is one of the largest industrial corporations in the United States. The company provides a wide range of products for many industries, including automobile parts, telecommunication equipment, broadcast and studio equipment, plastics, oceanic equipment, housing and construction materials, soaps, paper, commercial printing typography, agricultural fertilizers, paint, aluminum, steel, textiles, and chemicals. It also provides important services for commercial and military aerospace and aviation, petroleum production and refining companies, and the space program. The company has its roots in the chemical industry and has had experiences from its earliest days in acquiring and holding subsidiaries. It may be said that Allied-Signal, formerly Allied, was born large and has been gaining ground ever since.

The outbreak of the First World War convinced several executives in the fledgling American chemical industry that the U.S. should contest the German lead in this field. Among them were Dr. William H. Nichols, a respected chemist and President of General Chemical Company, Eugene Meyer, a publisher and financier, and Meyer's protege, Orlando F. Weber. Meyer's efforts bore fruit on December 17, 1920, with the formation of the Allied Chemical & Dye Corporation, a merger of five companies which among them provided the new company with four basic ingredients of the chemical industry of the day: acids, alkalies, coal tar, and nitrogen. The acids were furnished by General Chemical, founded in 1899, whose president, Dr. Nichols, became Allied's first chairman. The alkalies were contributed by the Solvay Process Company, founded in 1881, and, like General Chemical, the leading American company in its field at the time of the creation of

Allied. The Barrett Company, founded in 1858, was by 1920 the largest manufacturer of coal tar products in the U.S., while Semet-Solvay, founded in 1895, was a builder and operator of coke ovens, a byproduct of which is coal tar. The National Aniline & Chemical Company, founded in 1917, at first merely supplied aniline oil, a substance used in making dyes, but its head, Orlando F. Weber, became Nichols' successor and moved the new company into the production of nitrogen.

Although it was Eugene Meyer's financial genius which had created Allied, it was Weber's personality and management style which influenced Allied's methods of doing business for generations to come, for good and for ill. Orlando Franklin Weber was born on October 6, 1878 in Grafton, Wisconsin. His father was a secretary of the Federated Trades Council in Milwaukee and a socialist labor leader. The younger Weber, however, was drawn to private enterprise. He first opened a bicycle shop and then went into the automobile business, starting an agency in Chicago for the Pope-Toledo car in 1902. From Chicago he moved to Detroit and then to New York where he came to the attention of Meyer. Meyer put Weber in charge of the 1915 reorganization of Maxwell, an early automobile company whose name was to linger in the public mind long after the company folded, thanks to the jokes of Jack Benny. Weber followed Meyer into the War Finance Corporation during World War I and, as a result, became interested in the chemical industry. Since Weber's National Aniline had come through the war in the best financial shape of the five companies which formed Allied, it was only natural that Meyer should turn to his young associate to run the new chemical company.

Weber, first as president then as chairman, appropriated funds for a large plant to be built at Hopewell, Virginia to fix nitrogen from the air for the production of synthetic ammonia. Ammonia could be turned into nitric acid which, when combined with the soda ash made by the Solvay component of Allied, produces sodium nitrate, a substance with an agricultural use as fertilizer and a military use as an ingredient in explosives. By the end of the 1920's Allied was doing a thriving business making and selling basic chemicals to the rest of American industry.

Important as this achievement was, it was on the financial aspect of running the company that Orlando Weber's personality left its most enduring mark. Weber was a mathematical genius who had a grasp of the most complicated and detailed economic theories and who could, when called upon, discuss them by the hour with no notes. He was also highly secretive, keeping vital information about the company locked up in his personal safe and sharing this information with as few people in company management as possible. He was regarded by many of those that knew him as an autocrat who refused to spend any more of his company's money than absolutely necessary.

The beneficial consequences of this unusual collection of personality traits was that, since Weber was a strong believer in a large reserve of liquid assets, Allied was able to survive the Great Depression relatively unscathed. From 1921 through 1939 Allied had no funded debt, never borrowed from banks, and paid a dividend every year, including 1932, the worst year of the Depression. The harmful consequences of Weber's eccentric personality were, first of all, a refusal by Allied to engage in basic research leading to new products. Weber justified this decision by maintaining that he did not want to compete with the companies which were Allied's customers. This policy, however, left Allied with a shrinking share of the market after World War II when new chemical products were introduced. Secondly, Weber's penchant for secrecy got him into trouble with his stockholders, to whom he refused to issue detailed reports, and eventually with the Securities and Exchange Commission which, in 1934, charged him with failing to provide enough information to allow government agencies to determine whether Allied was making or losing money. Weber justified his reticence by claiming that he needed to protect company secrets. However, this secrecy, combined with his autocracy, resulted in the fact that the highest executives in the company were not conversant with the overall operation of the company when he retired in 1935. This gap in expertise was to plague Allied for the next 30 years.

Weber's autocracy took many forms, some petty and other significant. During his tenure, and for several years thereafter, Allied executives were forbidden to have their pictures taken for the media, forbidden to allow their biographies to appear in *Who's Who in America*, and forbidden to take part in meetings of trade associations. More significantly, lateral communication between executives within the company was made cumbersome. If, for example, the plant manager for ammonia wished to speak with the plant manager for soda ash, then each manager had to ask permission from their respective vice presidents in order for the conversation to take place. The vice presidents, in turn, would have to ask Weber. Weber himself could make this system work because he was the original guiding spirit of the company and consequently knew where each piece of the mosaic of company operations fit. When he left, however, Allied's corporate bureaucracy remained in place without anyone of Weber's talents to organize all the pieces.

Weber himself was the cause of this knowledge vacuum, as it were, at Allied. In order to keep Charles Nichols, son of the scholarly Dr. Nichols, and the Solvay family from taking control of the company, Weber put Allied in the hands of accountants. These accountants knew little of the chemical industry but were, according to *Forbes*, the next three chairmen of Allied: Henry Atherton, Fred Emmerich, and Glen B. Miller.

During their term of office, from 1935 to 1959, Allied made money during World War II because basic chemicals were essential to the war effort, but its plants became obsolete. In 1935, under the chairmanship of Emmerich, Allied borrowed $200 million to modernize its plants. Emmerich found himself unable to update company policy, however, because division heads had acquired complete autonomy. No vice president could make any decision without the concurrence of every other vice president.

Glen B. Miller, Emmerich's successor, created the jobs of research vice president and marketing vice president, positions which had not existed at Allied previously. The company continued to drift without any coherent company policy or long term strategy, however, because of the advanced age of its management. Kirby H. Fisk, who had experience in insurance and finance, was put in charge in 1959 and arranged a merger with Union Texas Natural Gas in 1962. Fisk then died of a heart attack, and Allied's board could not agree on a successor. A troika emerged: Chester M. Brown, who had a background in operations, became president and chief executive officer; Harry S. Ferguson, the accountants' champion, became chief administrative officer and chairman of the executive committee; and Howard Marshall, head of Union Texas before the merger, continued to run the petroleum concern but now with a strong voice in Allied's boardroom. Since there was no agreement as to who should be chairman of the board, the position was left vacant. Finally, Frederick Beebe, a member of Allied's board representing the interests of Eugene Meyer (Weber's mentor), set in motion the complicated legal machinery which reorganized the board of directors and brought in John T. Connor, a former Secretary of Commerce under Lyndon Johnson, to be president in 1967 and chairman of the board in 1969.

The accession of Connor marks the beginning of Allied's recovery. Connor found that Allied showed earnings on paper during the terms of his predecessors by means of unorthodox accounting methods, all perfectly legal but masking the fact that Allied had slipped from first to sixth place in the American chemical industry. In the twelve years of his involvement with Allied, Connor improved the corporate staff by hiring his own people, appropriated larger expenditures for the company's more profitable businesses, like oil and gas, and moved the company away from its orientation to basic chemicals and toward intermediate and end products which utilize chemicals.

In May of 1979 the current Chairman of the Board, President, and Chief Executive Officer, Edward L. Hennessy Jr., arrived on the scene to complete Allied's recovery and turn it into Allied-Signal, one of the most dynamic and promising corporations in America today. Whether by accident or design, Allied's board chose a leader whose personality and abilities are similar to those traits of Orlando Weber's which proved beneficial to the company. Like Weber, Hennessy is an expert at mathematics, careful with corporate assets and decisive. Unlike Weber, however, Hennessy is direct and explicit rather than secretive (though at times somewhat brusque) and, more importantly, devoted to the research and development which Weber shunned.

Since taking charge, Hennessy has directed Allied to the forefront of scientific and technological advances, sometimes at the expense of the chemical business conducted by Allied at the time of its formation. In September 1979, for instance, Allied discontinued its operations in coke, coal, and paving materials, selling its paving materials business, its Detroit, Michigan and Ashland, Kentucky coke plants, and two coal mines. Hennessy followed the lead of Connor in this policy, who had sold off the Barrett Company in 1967. These moves were prudent, since more money could be made in other areas, but they so changed the nature of the company's business that it is misleading to think of the modern Allied-Signal as primarily a chemical company.

Hennessy's positive contributions have been largely in the area of acquiring high-tech businesses: Eltra in 1979, Bendix in 1983 (as a result of that company's ill-starred attempt to take over Martin Marietta), and Signal Companies, Inc., in 1985. Allied-Signal's business is now conducted in these three segments: aerospace/electronics, automotive, and engineered materials. In 1985 the aerospace/electronics segment accounted for 39% of Allied-Signal's revenues, the automotive segment for 27%, and the engineered materials segment for 22%.

In 1985 Allied-Signal lost $279 million, the first loss in the company's history. This loss is attributed by Hennessy to the establishment of The Henley Group, Inc., a company formed from all of Allied-Signal's businesses outside the three business segments mentioned above, and to restructuring the bureaucracy of the company to complete its modernization. In spite of this loss, sales in the aerospace/electronics segment rose 27% in 1985 and edged up 1% in the engineered materials segment. Sales in the automotive segment (components for brake systems, air and fuel filters, turbo-charging equipment, and spark plugs) declined by 4%.

Allied-Signal is such a large and diverse company that it appears to be in no danger of further financial difficulties. The company's reorganization and acquisition of other large firms in order to diversify its product line seem to be complete. Only time will tell whether Hennessy's wish to make Allied-Signal one of the leading scientific and technological companies in the world in the field of aerospace and electronics will come true.

Principal Subsidiaries: The Signal Companies, Inc.; The Henley Group, Inc.

Further Reading: *Allied Corporation: Strength Through Diversification* by Edward L. Hennessy, New York, Newcomen Society, 1984.

AMFAC INC.

P.O. Box 7813
San Francisco, California 94120
U.S.A.
(415) 772-3300

Public Company
Incorporated: July 20, 1918 as American Factors, Ltd.
Employees: 22,550
Sales: $2.405 billion
Market Value: $501 million
Stock Index: New York London

In 1849 a German ship captain named Heinrich Hackfeld docked his 156-ton boat *Wilhelmine* in Hawaii after a 238-day journey from Bremen, Germany. After deciding to become a permanent resident, Hackfeld opened a general store which became very popular with the imported laborers who worked on the islands' isolated plantations. Hackfeld's small venture quickly expanded into other lines of business, including boarding houses and real estate. Hackfeld later opened a trading house, exporting Hawaii's primary agricultural product, sugar, and importing building materials. Hackfeld's company became one of the largest in Hawaii, operating retail stores and hotels, trading a wider variety of products, and purchasing thousands of acres of property. Several years later Hackfeld died and ownership of the company passed to his family.

In July of 1918, soon after the United States became involved in World War I, the American Alien Property Custodian confiscated H. Hackfeld & Company on the grounds that it was owned by "enemy aliens." All of the company's assets were taken over by a group of competitors, including Castle & Cook, Alexander & Baldwin and C. Brewer. The company was incorporated and its name was changed to American Factors (a factor is a commissioned agent), and its chain of B.F. Ehlers retailing outlets was renamed "Liberty House." Under the new management American Factors became more involved in sugar production. Demand for sugar remained high during the Depression and World War II, which kept American Factors profitable and allowed it to continue paying dividends to stockholders.

Although it continued to diversify during the 1950's, American Factors remained primarily involved with the production of sugar. However, in 1959, the same year Hawaii was made a state, airline companies acquired long-range passenger jetliners which made Hawaii suddenly more accessible to the American vacationer. Just as suddenly, demand for hotel space and land began to increase. As a major landowner American Factors recognized this as an opportunity to exploit its hotel and lodging interests. Many of its existing properties were improved, additional facilities were constructed, and several parcels of undeveloped land were sold to developers at a sizable profit.

Despite its increased involvement in the Hawaiian tourist industry, a great deal of American Factors' business remained in sugar production. The sugar market had always been cyclical, alternating between periods of strong demand and oversupply. Yet during the 1950's increased competition lowered profit margins, even when markets were strong. In 1964 low demand for sugar and molasses forced the company's operating profits to decline by 43% (it still paid a dividend, however). The first of many changes at American Factors occurred on April 30, 1966. The company's name was changed to Amfac, which was shorter, easier to remember and more "corporate-sounding."

Henry A. Walker, Jr., a native Hawaiian whose father had served for many years as president of American Factors, was himself named president of Amfac in 1967. The board of directors gave Walker three instructions: enlarge the company, decrease the company's dependence on sugar, and geographically diversify its operations. In 1968 Amfac purchased the Fred Harvey hotel chain and later acquired the Island Holiday group on Hawaii. Amfac's Liberty House retail department stores were introduced to the American mainland along with its wholesale distribution network of electrical, medical, industrial and agricultural products. Amfac acquired the family-run Joseph Magnin retail chain for $31 million in 1969. Walker directed the company to sell additional parcels of Hawaiian real estate to help finance acquisitions on the American mainland, which included Pacific Pearl, Wakefield Seafoods and the 1971 purchase of Lamb-Weston, a potato and vegetable processor responsible for a substantial share of American's frozen french fry and mushroom production.

In 1974 the Federal Trade Commission accused Amfac and other suppliers to the C&H sugar consortium of price fixing. The settlement which resulted cost Amfac several million dollars. Although sugar prices that year were high, it was the last time that Amfac would report a profit on its sugar operations for several years; Congress failed to renew the Sugar Act of 1948, which guaranteed a broader degree of price stability by limiting sugar imports.

After several years of poor performance all 48 stores in Amfac's Joseph Magnin chain were sold to the Ross Hall Corporation for $35 million. Although Amfac added 18 stores to the chain, increasing sales from $50 million to $83 million, expected profits failed to materialize. Henry Walker told *Business Week,* "We're getting out of the women's apparel business because we find we're not very good at it." Amfac did, however, retain its 55 highly profitable Liberty House stores, 23 of which were located in Hawaii.

Amfac's earnings declined every year until 1978. Losses

until that time were due primarily to non-operating factors, such as the continued write-off of the Joseph Magnin chain and the company's switch to a uniform "last in, first out" (LIFO) accounting method, which tends to show lower profits, but also provides the company with taxation benefits.

During the period that its profits were depressed Amfac became a takeover target for a number of hostile acquisitions. The takeover attempts failed because Amfac was protected by Gulf & Western, a New York conglomerate which owned 20% of the company's stock. Henry Walker, who incidentally was a Gulf & Western board member, told *Financial World,* "A number of people have tried to acquire Amfac, but they couldn't without first getting control of G&W's block." Gulf & Western was committed to Amfac's independence, maintaining that its substantial interest in Amfac was strictly for "investment purposes." Any hostile bid for the company would almost certainly have encountered strong opposition from Gulf & Western.

Amfac was not, however, protected from a different kind of corporate raid. Sid, Ed, Robert and Lee Bass, four Stanford and Yale-educated brothers from Fort Worth, Texas, announced in 1982 that they had acquired 11% of Amfac's stock, and had filed a "13-D" financial disclosure form with the Securities and Exchange Commission. The Bass brothers did not intend to take over Amfac, but their sudden interest in the company concerned stockholders, particularly Gulf & Western, which at the time owned just under 25% of Amfac's stock. Amfac's management arranged a complex joint venture with the brothers called Fort Associates. The joint venture gave the Bass brothers interests in several hotels and real estate in Texas and Hawaii, in addition to $52 million in cash, while it retrieved half of the Basses' ownership of Amfac's stock. Fort Associates was set up to give the Bass brothers an early return on their investment and Amfac a later return with tax advantages. While the venture remains profitable, Amfac stated that it would rather have resolved the situation differently.

In the meantime, sugar prices began to recover after Congress included sugar in its 1981 Farm Act. Although Amfac was making money on sugar again, Walker continued to reduce the company's exposure to the volatile commodity through a process of continued diversification. Amfac had acquired over 50 companies since 1967, most of which were located on the mainland.

Myron Du Bain, a former chairman and president of Fireman's Fund Insurance, was named president of Amfac on January 1, 1983. Du Bain, who had no previous experience with sugar, directed Amfac's operations from the San Francisco office. Du Bain was hired to "tighten the screws" at Amfac, deciding which businesses should be emphasized and which should be scaled down or sold. Henry Walker remained in Hawaii, where he continued to serve as chairman of the board, managing Amfac's sugar operations.

During Du Bain's first year Amfac sold 12% of its assets for $177 million, but still posted a $68 million loss. In addition, Gulf & Western sold all its stock in Amfac, although with little consequence. The company recovered during 1984, yet lost almost $29 million in the final quarter when its Hotels and Resorts Group was restructured. As a result, Amfac was forced to withhold its quarterly dividend for the first time in 66 years. Amfac sold its commercial nurseries, seafood fisheries, Hawaiian tour business, and its Liberty House outlets in California. By 1985 Du Bain had reduced Amfac's debt by $120 million to $400 million. Du Bain left Amfac in September of that year, taking an early retirement to pursue community and civic activities. He was replaced by Ralph Van Orsdel for an interim period lasting until the following May when Ronald Sloan, who had been with Amfac for 25 years, was named president and cheif executive officer.

Sloan announced that Amfac would continue to phase out its interest in sugar, and that its retailing and resort operations would be scaled down. Perhaps most significant on Sloan's agenda was the revelation that Amfac would reverse its geographical diversification onto the mainland and expand its presence in Hawaii, where it owns over 50,000 acres of land. While reducing the scale of its sugar production, Amfac is shifting its emphasis in agricultural products to commodities such as cocoa and coffee. Investors expressed confidence that, at least in the short term, Amfac would return to its traditional path of stable growth and steady dividends and remain the largest private sector employee in Hawaii.

Principal Subsidiaries: Amfac Distribution Corp.: Amfac Electric Supply Company, Amfac Health Care, Amfac Supply Company; Amfac Foods, Inc.: Fisher Cheese Company, Inc., Lamb-Weston, Inc., Monterey Mushrooms, Inc.; Amfac Hawaii, Inc.: Amfac Properties, Amfac Sugar and Agribusiness, Amfac Stores, Inc.: Liberty House, Village Fashions; Amfac Resorts, Inc.

Further Reading: *Dynasty in the Pacific* by Frederick Simpich, Jr., New York, McGraw-Hill, 1974.

ARCHER-DANIELS-MIDLAND COMPANY

4666 Fories Parkway
P.O. Box 1470
Decatur, Illinois 62525
U.S.A.
(217) 424-5200

Public Company
Incorporated: May 2, 1923
Employees: 10,386
Sales: $5.5 billion
Market Value: $3.3 billion
Stock Index: New York

Archer-Daniels-Midland is a successful company with a quiet and conservative profile. It specializes in purchasing, transporting, storing, processing and merchandising agricultural commodities. The company's attitude is direct and optimistic: "Food is a growth business. Globally there are 85 million more mouths to feed each year; the equivalent of the current population of Mexico, or more than one-third of the U.S. population. ADM plans to participate in this growth."

Archer-Daniels-Midland has always been clearly focused, and has no intentions to diversify outside of the foods related business. Since its early years the company's methods have been consistent—strong research and development which emphasizes new production methods and uses for agricultural products, coupled with a bottom-line mandate for high performance and cost efficiency.

John W. Daniels began crushing flaxseed in Ohio in 1878, and in 1902 he moved to Minneapolis, Minnesota to organize the Daniels Linseed Company. The entire company consisted of one flax crushing plant which made three products, including raw linseed oil, boiled linseed oil, and linseed cake or meal. In 1903 George A. Archer joined the firm, and in a few years it became the Archer-Daniels Linseed Company. Archer also brought experience to the firm because his family had been in the business of crushing flaxseed since the 1830's. Archer and Daniels then hired a young bookkeeper by the name of Samuel Mairs. Mairs would later become the chairman of the board when the business was much larger and significantly more affluent.

These three men had a common goal of "year round production at low margins," a goal which directs the company today. Archer and Daniels used hydraulic presses to process flaxseed, and their linseed oil was essentially the same as that used by the ancient Egyptians. In the early years profits were low, but Archer-Daniels Linseed never finished a year in debt. They also grew slowly, buying the stock of the Toledo Seed & Oil Company, and the Dellwood Elevator Company, a grain elevator firm.

The year 1923 was a turning point because the company purchased the Midland Linseed Products Company and then incorporated as the Archer-Daniels-Midland Company. However, other equally significant changes occurred during the 1920's which were important to the company's future. Archer, Daniels and Mairs began the scientific exploration of ways to alter the chemical structure of linseed oil. This project initiated the company's successful research and development program. Research and development allocations were not commonplace for companies at that time, and the market was startled by the company's slogan: "Creating New Values From America's Harvests."

Throughout the 1920's the company made steady purchases of oil processing companies in the midwest. At the same time, it was also engaged in other agriculturally related activities. It built elevators on Minneapolis loading docks to store grain until it was shipped down the Mississippi to other ports. Then, in 1930, Archer-Daniels-Midland purchased the Commander-Larabee Company, a major flour miller with plants in Minnesota, Kansas, and Missouri. Commander-Larabee was capable of producing 32,000 barrels per day. (Today Archer-Daniels-Midland can produce 165,000 hundredweights of flour per day.) Purchase of Commander-Larabee had two additional advantages; it allowed ADM to coordinate its oil by-product business with Commander-Larabee's feed-stuff by-product business, and the mutual sales effort lowered overhead. During this time, the company also discovered how to extract lecithin from soybean oil, reducing the price of lecithin from ten dollars to one dollar per pound. (Lecithin is widely used as an emulsifier in the food and confectionery industries.) As a result of Archer-Daniels-Midland's growth maneuvers and research, the company had $22.5 million in assets by 1938.

As a linseed oil manufacturer, Archer-Daniels-Midland interacted with more than just the food market. The paint product industry used drying oils in the manufacture of various products, and the three major oils used were linseed, tung and perilla. These oils added critical gloss and hardness properties to paint finishes. The demand for drying oil in the paint industry fluctuated widely because it depended heavily on construction. Demand for domestic drying oil was also affected by the availability and price of foreign oils. (Most oils were imported from the Far East and South America.) Added to these two variables was the quality and size of each year's harvest. Even during the Depression and coping with all these variations in a struggling economy, the company made a profit. This was because Archer-Daniels-Midland had been working on ways to adapt oils to sell to new markets, including soaps, drugs, brake fluids, lubricants, petroleum and chemicals.

Since Archer-Daniels-Midland knew the value of its research department, it appropriated 70% of its earnings (one to two million dollars annually) back into the business for development and expansion. One result was a process whereby the usable fibres (the tow) of flax straw (a waste product up to then) could be used in the manufacture of flax papers. World War II made it impossible to increase the company's facilities as much as it wished; nevertheless, the company's capacities still grew significantly from 1930 to 1945. From a 1929 processing capacity of 20 million bushels of flaxseed per day, the company could process 36.6 million bushels per day by 1945. Wheat flour capacity went from zero to 30 million bushels per day. Grain storage capacity increased from 7.5 million to 50.4 million bushels per day.

The immediate post-World War II years from 1946 through 1949 showed dramatic growth; sales increased 287%, and net income increased 346%. In 1949 sales were $277 million, with a $12 million net profit. Archer-Daniels-Midland was well positioned in several market areas because it supplied basic ingredients to a wide range of industries. The company was the United States' leading processor of linseed oil, the fourth largest flour miller, and it had become the largest soybean processor. It also served the paint, leather, printing, gasoline, paper, cosmetics, pharmaceuticals, rubber, ceramics, munitions and insecticides industries.

The conservative management style had consistently safeguarded the company's success. For instance, whenever possible Archer-Daniels-Midland hedged its purchases of raw products by sales in the futures markets or by forward sales of the completed products. By the end of fiscal year 1949, the company had no bank debt, and it had paid a dividend every year from 1927 onward. All plants were kept at a high state of operating efficiency, using modern, streamlined methods. There had also been a change in the processing level. The company began to put its product through advanced physical processing instead of selling them in a raw or semi-finished state. This increased profit margins. Overall, management estimated that 40% of its increase in sales from 1939 to 1949 was due to new products and methods developed within the company.

Due to the fact that the company supplied core oils used in foundry industries, the outbreak of the Korean War increased demands on production through the early 1950's. The company was also increasing its outlay for whale oil procurement, which it had begun in the 1930's. And it was increasing its production of protein concentrates and marketing them extensively for stock-feeding purposes.

When company president Thomas L. Daniels (son of the founder) and chairman of the board Samuel Mairs celebrated Archer-Daniels-Midland's 50th anniversary in 1952, the company was manufacturing over 700 standard products and had extended its operations overseas. More foreign expansion followed in Peru, Mexico, the Netherlands and Belgium. In these ventures, the company specialized in partnerships with local interests. President Daniels expressed the company's attitude toward foreign involvement in the late 1950's when he said, "ADM looks with particular favor on Western Europe as an area of great chemical producers. . . . All industry there is expanding rapidly, both for local consumption and for export to other parts of the world."

Archer-Daniels-Midland had weathered the Depression and World War II, but ran into trouble during the 1960's. Although it made several grain production and storage purchases in the early 1960's, unstable commodities prices and the company's chemicals operations were causing losses. Net earnings were $75 million in 1963, and then declined to about $60 million in 1964, and then declined even further to $50 million in 1965. By 1965 the company could not cover its dividend. At this time John Daniels, president and grandson of one of the founders, and Shreve M. Archer, Jr., one of the directors, asked a new man to join their leadership team with the purchase of a block of the Archer family stock. His name was Dwayne O. Andreas, and he effectively took control and revolutionized Archer-Daniels-Midland.

Andreas' low profile appealed to the company management, and so did his background. He came from a long-term farm products background, first with his father, and then on his own. One of the first things Andreas did was eliminate a 27 person public relations department. By his own admission, he "almost never talks to analysts or reporters." He is not a stereotyped executive, however, having contributed to both Martin Luther King's Southern Christian Leadership Conference as well as Richard Nixon's presidential campaign. He has also advocated increases in the corporate income tax rate.

Andreas thought that one specific product could do a great deal to turn the company around, namely soybeans. Andreas recalled, "I knew that ADM was a dozen years ahead of everyone else in textured vegetable protein research, and I believed that was where important action was going to be." Whereas scientists advocated an almost pure protein product derived from the soybean, Andreas encouraged the development of textured vegetable protein, a 50% protein soy product which is far more economical to produce. His increasing power in the company (by 1968 he was chairman of the executive committee) made his plans a reality. Andreas described his actions by saying, "One of the first things I did was to take the edible soy out of the lab and construct a plant in Decatur (Illinois) to make all the grades of edible soy protein in 1969." He expected to exceed the plant's capacity by 1976. However, by 1973, with doubled production, the plant was already short of demand. Textured vegetable protein (TVP) was widely used in foodstuffs. And soybean oil is the number one food and cooking oil in use today.

The company also sold its troublesome chemical properties to Ashland Oil & Refining Company for $35 million in 1967. That same year it acquired the Fleischmann Malting Company, which would become a very profitable producer of malts for the food and beverage industry. Andreas proved expert at maintaining a good profit margin on soybeans too. Two or three cents shaved off costs made large differences in this slender-profit-margin item. In this area, Andreas's management rules of efficiency and profitability echoed the founders' practices.

With unprofitable operations sold, profitable ones newly acquired, and the increasing success of the soybean, the company entered another major area of operations. In 1971 it purchased Corn Sweetners, Inc., producer of high fructose syrups, glutens, oil and caramel color. Corn Sweetners resulted in good returns for Archer-Daniels-Midland and increased the company's finished-food capabilities.

Throughout the 1970's the company built textured vegetable protein plants in Europe and South America. In addition, Dwayne Andreas brought three other member of the Andreas family into Archer-Daniels-Midland as the company expanded. These three have become heads of various divisions, although the company still retains one Archer and one Daniels in high-ranking positions.

From the net low of $50 million in earnings in 1965, by 1973 net earnings were near $117 million. This increase paralleled the upward swing in U.S. soybean production and exports from 700 million bushels per day in 1965 to 1.3 billion in 1973.

That growth continued through the 1970's and into the 1980's. Archer-Daniels-Midland has several major subdivisions, the largest of which is the Oilseed Processing division. In this division, soy products long ago outstripped linseed and all others. The next largest, Corn Sweetners division, produces ethanol in addition to high-fructose products. In fact, the Decatur, Illinois plant is the single largest source of ethanol in the United States. Archer-Daniels-Midland Milling Company processes the company's grains, and in 1986 the milling division became even larger when Archer-Daniels-Midland absorbed Growmark, a large midwestern grain merchandising and river terminal cooperative. The new wholly-owned subsidiary is called ADM/Growmark.

Another division, the Columbian Peanut Company acquired in 1981, produces oil and peanut products, and Archer-Daniels-Midland is the leading domestic peanut sheller. Gooch foods is the company's market name for a line of pasta products, which have been in increasing demand since the advent of microwave pasta dishes. Other divisions of Archer-Daniels-Midland include Southern Cotton Oil Company, Fleischmann Malting Company, Inc., American River Transportation Company, Supreme Sugar Company, and the British Arkady Co., Ltd. (this last is a supplier of specialty products to the bakery industry).

The oilseed operations account for 45% of revenues, the corn operations 34%, the wheat and flour operations 12%, and all others 9%. Net earnings for 1986 were $240 million. Instead of being a low profile, moderately successful company, Archer-Daniels-Midland is presently a low profile, extremely successful company. It is one of the world's largest agricultural processors and plans to remain exclusively in the food business, relying on its proven strategy of efficiency, research, and good margins.

Principal Subsidiaries: ADM Milling Co.; American River Transportation Co.; Gooch Foods, Inc.; Supreme Sugar Co., Inc.; Smoot Grain Co.; ADM Transportation Co.; Tabor Grain Co.; ADM Feed Corp.; Columbian Peanut Co.; ADM Grain Co.; Southern Cotton Oil Co.; ADM Investors Services, Inc.; ADM Leasco, Inc. The company also lists subsidiaries in the following countries: Cayman Islands, The Netherlands, United Kingdom, and West Germany.

BARLOW RAND LTD.

P.O. Box 782248
Sandton 2146
South Africa
(011) 801–9111

Public Company
Incorporated: August 29, 1918 as Thomas Barlow & Sons (South Africa) Ltd.
Employees: 143,959
Sales: R 14.62 billion (US$ 6.58 billion)
Market Value: R 3.497 billion (US$ 1.573 billion)
Stock Index: Johannesburg London Paris Brussels Antwerp Frankfurt Zurich Basel Geneva

The original South African Barlow company was founded by Major Ernest Barlow, an Englishman who fought with the British against Dutch and Huguenot Boers in South Africa at the turn of the century. Major Barlow returned to South Africa in 1902 and established an engineering supplies company in Durban. The family-owned "import-indent agency" was incorporated in 1918 under the name Thomas Barlow & Sons (South Africa) Ltd. The original Thomas Barlow & Sons was established as a cotton mill in Lancashire, England during the 18th century, and continued to trade in textiles when Major Barlow borrowed its name for his enterprise in South Africa.

Major Barlow died in 1921. In 1927 the company was taken over by his eldest son Charles, who that year received an engineering degree from Cambridge University. That year Barlow became the South African sales agent for the Caterpillar company, an American manufacturer of heavy machinery. Through its connection with Caterpillar, Barlow & Sons gained expertise in construction and agricultural machinery. Over the following years, strong demand for engineering supplies allowed the company to expand its scale of business.

Barlow escaped destruction during World War II because it was located far from the battlefields of Europe, Asia, and north Africa. The war did, however, disrupt the world economy and cause some hardship in South Africa. Barlow took advantage of several opportunities to grow by supplying provisions to allied forces and taking over production of goods which could no longer be imported.

After the war Barlow expanded its operations in Southwest Africa (Namibia) and Rhodesia (Zimbabwe). Southwest Africa was confiscated by South Africa during World War I, and placed under South African mandate by the Treaty of Versailles. It was also extremely rich in mineral deposits, including diamonds, copper, lead, zinc, and uranium. Rhodesia, a self-administered British colony, was also well-endowed with mineral resources, including gold, copper, chrome, nickel, and tin. As a company, Barlow was in a privileged position to supply mining equipment and develop new mining technologies, but did not directly engage in the operation of any mines.

Barlow eliminated "South Africa" from its corporate name in 1956 when the British Thomas Barlow & Sons ceased to exist. After that time there was no longer a need to distinguish the two companies.

In the early 1960's, the White minority government of Ian Smith in Rhodesia came under increasing pressure from Britain and the United States to integrate its society and permit the Black majority to engage in politics. The government's strong resistance resulted in economic sanctions and guerilla warfare against Rhodesia. As conditions deteriorated in Rhodesia, Barlow began to divest itself of certain properties and businesses there. The operations maintained by Barlow in Rhodesia were originally part of the Rhodesian Development Corporation, which Barlow purchased in the mid-1950's. These assets were placed under a new division of Barlow called Thomas Barlow & Sons (Rhodesia) Ltd. Capital raised from the sale of Rhodesian companies was used to purchase shares of businesses in Britain, as part of an overall strategy to diversify the company geographically as well as operationally.

In April of 1966 Thomas Barlow & Sons Ltd. and South African Breweries exchanged 12 million rand worth of stock. As a result, South African Breweries owned 22% of Barlow, and Barlow owned a substantially higher percentage of South African Breweries. As part of an effort to combine their marketing and resource networks, a number of executives from South African Breweries were admitted to the board of directors at Barlow.

Barlow companies which were losing money in Southwest Africa and Rhodesia were reorganised. Generally, however, Barlow subsidiaries in those states and in Britain continued to perform beyond expectations. The well-established tractor company and the fast-growing forestry division, called Federated Timbers, continued to be Barlow's most profitable companies.

Through its association with the Caterpillar company, Barlow gained expertise in corporate finance and product distribution. By the end of the 1960's, Barlow had diversified into several fields, and continued to sell mining equipment and technical expertise to mining companies. In June of 1971 Barlow purchased Rand Mines Ltd., South Africa's oldest mining house. Rand was acquired for 39 million rand in stock, the largest takeover in South African history. At the time, Barlow was primarily a distributor of industrial products; only 10% of its revenue were derived from manufacturing. Rand Mines, on the other hand, was South Africa's oldest mining house, but in recent years had established a strong presence in primary industries. The new company, Barlow Rand Ltd., was a fully integrated manufacturer and distributor of heavy industrial products.

Shortly after Barlow took control of Rand on June 28, it

was discovered that the companies in the Rand group had been overvalued. Specifically, the Middleburg Steel and Alloys Group was singled out as being "in a disastrous state." After a thorough investigation of asset valuations, liabilities, and contingencies, 17.9 million rand had been written off from the pre-acquisition price.

Charles Barlow expressed his company's grave concern over social conditions in South Africa. Under the government policy of *apartheid*, Black (Bantu), "Coloured" (mulatto, quadroon, octoroon, etc.), and Asian (primarily Indian) people were segregated from the White population and politically disenfranchised. They were also limited to dangerous labor-intensive occupations with low pay, and denied education and opportunities for advancement. Poor working conditions for non-Whites at Barlow Rand inhibited the company's performance. Barlow recognized that rising social tension over *apartheid* could lead to labor strikes and racial violence.

Many industrialists supported social reforms in South Africa. If conditions did not change, they feared that more radical opponents of *apartheid* would exploit the situation for political gains, incite a civil war and cause a revolution. Barlow Rand initiated an advancement program for non-White South Africans, which included better education, higher wages, and the lifting of restrictions on promotion. The measures were, on the whole, generally regarded as inadequate, but indicative of some reform in light of government restrictions on the advancement of non-Whites.

In a continuing effort to reduce its exposure to the increasingly risky business environment in South Africa, Barlow Rand redoubled its efforts to expand in Europe. The government, however, had strict prohibitions on the transfer of capital out of South Africa. Restrictions on exit capital meant that the Barlow Rand could not divest its holdings in South Africa, consequently its foreign subsidiaries would have to achieve greater growth independently.

Under South African laws, Barlow Rand could only offer shares of its own stock in return for shares in European companies it was interested in purchasing. In order to increase the marketability of its shares in Europe, Barlow Rand stock was listed on the Brussels and Antwerp bourses in February of 1972, and on the Paris bourse the following July.

In July of 1974 Charles Barlow announced his company's intention to purchase the Union Corporation, a mining finance group with substantial British holdings. Over the next two months, however, Gold Fields (of South Africa) and General Mining (now called Gencorp) entered the bidding. Barlow Rand withdrew from the competition when it decided the bidding price for Union shares had exceeded a reasonable value. Shortly afterward, General Mining purchased the Union Corporation.

Social conditions began to deteriorate rapidly in Rhodesia, where the minority government was rapidly losing support. When South Africa stopped supplying the Rhodesians with weapons (particularly helicopters), Prime Minister Ian Smith was forced to initiate a program to bring a Black majority government into power within two years. Because it was a South African company, Barlow

Rand's presence in Zimbabwe (Rhodesia) became less welcome, and the company's stock was subsequently delisted from the Harare (Salisbury) stock exchange.

Many nations refused to continue trading with South Africa because of the government's racist social policies. South Africa was widely criticized for *apartheid*, which it claimed was necessary to prevent communists from gaining control of the country. Barlow Rand was not as adversely affected by this development as some smaller, more specialized South African companies. Still, it continued to diversify, in 1978 purchasing a 55% share in the Nampack packaging unit of Reed International, and a 50% share of GEC South Africa. Barlow Rand later sold its wholly-owned packaging division to Nampack. In January of 1980 the company sold Nampak in order to purchase a controlling interest in G.C. Smith, South Africa's largest producer of sugar, as well as a manufacturer of chemicals and flooring.

In 1979 Charles Barlow died. He was succeeded by a highly capable and progressive man name Aanon Michael Rosholt. A protege of Barlow, Rosholt advocated the integration of educational facilities for South Africa's races, and for the eventual elimination of *apartheid*.

As a result of the Wiehahn reforms of 1979, trades unions for non Whites grew in both size and influence. Companies such as Ford, the Anglo-American Corporation, Chloride (S.A.), and Barlow Rand generally supported the growth of the trades unions. The unions, however, targeted these and other pragmatic companies as institutions of the White regime, and deliberately opposed them as such. This led Mike Rosholt to complain that Barlow Rand was being "picked on" as an easy target.

Rosholt undertook a reorganization of the company's industrial relations, under increasing fears that the company's labor force (75% Black and 10% Coloured and Asian) was more likely to strike or become violent. Declaring that, "Labor relations are too important to be left to personnel specialists," Barlow Rand reemphasized internal growth by increasing salaries and establishing 45 literacy centers to facilitate the advancement of non-White workers.

In a speech in 1981, Rosholt said that Black trade unions were a fact of life which "must be seen as bodies which can possible defuse labor problems." He expressed his belief that representation was an internal union matter which employers should not try to influence. The employees' unions, however, continued to regard Barlow Rand with skepticism. The company, however, remained relatively free of labor unrest.

Rosholt became more outspoken about the need for reform of *apartheid*. He told a conference attended by the South African prime minister Pieter Botha, "Business does not believe, as the government appears to, that there us unlimited time for the process of change." Criticism of government policies placed Rosholt in a precarious position, as a member of the English-speaking business establishment, he did not want to be perceived as an enemy by the somewhat suspicious *afrikaans*-speaking government establishment. On the other hand, Rosholt recognized that Barlow Rand could not continue to conduct business in an environment of radical tension and uncertainty.

Continuing to expand, Barlow Rand purchased dealerships for Hyster forklifts in Britain and the southeastern United States. In April of 1982, the company acquired one of South Africa's largest food companies, Tiger Oats. In 1985 Barlow Rand launched a takeover of J. Bibby & Sons, a British industrial and agricultural concern, partially owned by Tiger Oats. The company offered three pounds per share, an amount so generous that 97% of Bibby shareholders sold out, leaving so few English shareholders that the company lost its listing on the London bourse.

Today Barlow Rand is the largest company in South Africa, and an international parent company of businesses in southern Africa, Britain, the United States, and Europe. The groups' operations are divided among eight autonomous divisions: mining; cement, lime and paint; electronics and engineering; heavy equipment; building and construction supplies; packaging, paper and appliances; sugar, food and textiles; and group services.

The company remains committed to the elimination of racist social policies in South Africa, and under the leadership of Michael Rosholt has grown in sales from 3.4 billion rand in 1980 to over 14.6 billion rand. All South African companies, however, have recently experienced serious problems directly related to the government's policy of *apartheid*. Consumer boycotts, difficult economic conditions, and government interference compounded Barlow Rand's problems with its identification as a South African company. Economic sanctions and world political opposition to South Africa, in protest of its society, are certain to have highly adverse effects on Barlow Rand, at least until such time as *apartheid* is ended.

Principal Subsidiaries: (capitalized at over R 500,000) Marico Fluorspar (Pty) Ltd.; Rand Mines, Ltd.; Rand Mines (Mining Services) Ltd.; Rand Mines Properties, Ltd.; Welgedacht Exploration Co., Ltd.; Witbank Colliery, Ltd.; Kohler Sacks, Ltd.; PPC Lime, Ltd.; Pretoria Portland Cement Co., Ltd.; AEI Henley Africa (Pty) Ltd.; ATC (Pty) Ltd.; Fenner (S.A.) (Pty) Ltd.: GEC South Africa (Pty) Ltd.; KSB Pumps (Pty) Ltd.; Reunert, Ltd.; Barlows Manufacturing Co., Ltd.;Belon Industries (Pty) Ltd.; Brollo Africa (Pty) Ltd.; Federated-Blaikie, Ltd.; Federated Timbers, Ltd.; Firststeel, Ltd.; Plascon-Evans Paints, Ltd.; Robor Industrial Holdings, Ltd.; Thesen & Co. (Pty) Ltd.; W.F. Johnstone & Co., Ltd.; Fibre Spinners & Weavers (Pty) Ltd.; Hextex (Pty) Ltd.; Romatex, Ltd.; Veldspun (Pty) Ltd.; Barlan Forms (Pty) Ltd.; Brown, Davis & McCorquodale (Pty) Ltd.; Hypack (Pty) Ltd.; Keartlands-Nasionale Litho (Pty) Ltd.; Metal Box South Africa, Ltd.; Nampak, Ltd.; Nampak Products, Ltd.; Spicers (Pty) Ltd.; Adcock-Ingram, Ltd.; C.G. Smith Foods, Ltd.; C.G. Smith Sugar, Ltd.; Festive Farms (Pty) Ltd.; Harvestime Corp. (Pty) Ltd.; Imperial Cold Storage & Supply Co., Ltd.; Meadow Feed Mills, Ltd.; Natal Cane By-Products, Ltd.; Radue Weir Holdings, Ltd.; S.A. Sea Products, Ltd.; Sabax, Ltd.; Sea Products (S.W.A.) Ltd.; Smithchem (Pty) Ltd.; Tiger Oats, Ltd.; W.G. Brown Investments, Ltd.; J. Bibby & Sons, Plc,; Barlow Rand Properties, Ltd.; Barlows Central Finance Corp., Ltd.; Barlows Mining Holdings & Estates, Ltd.; C.G. Smith, Ltd.; Corner House Investment Co., Ltd.; Rand Mines Holdings, Ltd.

Further Reading: The South African Economy: Its Growth and Change by Jill Natrass, Oxford, Oxford University Press, 1981.

BAT INDUSTRIES PLC

Windsor House
50 Victoria Street
London SW1H 0NL
England
(01) 222–7979

Public Company
Incorporated: September 29, 1902 as British American
Tobacco Company Ltd.
Employees: 197,000 worldwide
Sales: £4.010 billion (US$5.895 billion)
Market value: £4.571 billion (US$6.720 billion)
Stock Index: London Montreal Amsterdam Frankfurt
Hamburg Antwerp Düsseldorf Basle Zurich Paris
Brussels Geneva

BAT Industries, a tobacco-based conglomerate, began as
a compromise between two rival tobacco manufacturers:
one American, and one British. James Buchanan
("Buck") Duke, head of the highly successful American
Tobacco Company, decided in 1901 to make a bid for the
UK market. In response, several smaller independent
British tobacco companies banded together to form the
Imperial Tobacco Company Ltd. It was from these two
tobacco companies that BAT, which today deals all over
the world not only in tobacco products, but also in paper,
retailing, and financial services, was born.

Imperial Tobacco was able to resist American Tobacco's
attempt to capture its native market but only after a
prolonged trade war that proved very expensive for both
participants. American Tobacco having withdrawn from
the English marketplace, Imperial was in a stronger
position and decided to press its advantage.

It was when Imperial started to make moves toward the
American market that chairman Duke saw the need for a
compromise. A truce was called, and the two rival
merchants agreed not to conduct business in each other's
domestic markets. Each company also assigned brand
rights to the other so that consumers who had grown used
to a given brand would not be lost. This deal also initiated
the creation of a new company, British American
Tobacco, of which American owned a two-thirds share
and Duke was the first chairman.

This new company, registered in London in 1902,
acquired the recipes and trademarks of both originating
companies. It also acquired all the export business and
overseas production operations of each company. The new

company's sales and growth potential seemed limited
compared to the successes of Imperial and American. In
time, however, British American Tobacco would grow,
not only to outsell its parent companies, but to become the
world's largest private-sector tobacco concern.

Steady but slow growth occurred during the first decade
of this century. Then in 1911 the United States Supreme
Court ruled that American Tobacco was a monopoly and
therefore illegal. The court, though requiring that Duke
break up his successful American operation, did not want
to deprive the American public of its tobacco or the
American economy of a healthy business. Unable to come
up with a viable solution, the court turned to Duke for
help. The chairman of BAT and of American Tobacco
then devised his own, less damaging dismantling strategy,
which the court accepted fully. American Tobacco cancelled most of its covenants with BAT and Imperial and
sold all of its shares in BAT. Most of the shares sold went
to British investors, and BAT became listed on the
London Stock Exchange.

This left British American Tobacco, still chaired by
Duke, able to sell its product independently all over the
world, except in the United Kingdom where it was still
bound by its covenant with Imperial. Imperial at this time
also retained a one-third share of BAT, but this did little
to impair BAT's success. Duke's operation began rapid
expansion of British exports and overseas operations.
Many new subsidiaries were established around the world
during the brief period between the disentanglement from
American Tobacco and the first World War. Local sources
of raw materials were discovered and developed, and
international sales grew steadily.

The war brought large numbers of women into the
company for the first time. They were primarily employed
in the distribution of cigarettes to the troops abroad, most
of whom had switched to cigarettes from the less convenient pipe. Although brought on by the war, the switch
to cigarettes caught on and became permanent. Many
people never returned to the pipe, and BAT began selling
cigarettes in increasing numbers.

The end of the war brought even greater fortunes for
BAT. Until Duke did so, no commercial enterprise was
able to penetrate the Chinese market farther than the
government coastal trading stations. BAT, now able to
exploit the untapped interior market, achieved record
growth in the years immediately following and maintained
impressive sales levels throughout the rest of Duke's
chairmanship. While chairman, Duke was BAT's pioneer
in growth; the company's next chairman, Sir Hugo
Cunliffe-Owen, was a pioneer of decentralization.

Sir Hugo had been involved with BAT since its inception. Early involvement in the negotiations between
American Tobacco and Imperial endeared him to Duke,
who appointed him director and secretary. He held those
positions until Duke retired in 1923 (he died two years
later) and then succeeded the founder as chairman. When
Sir Hugo inherited the chair, BAT's capitalization had
quadrupled since 1902 and its sales had grown by nearly a
factor of forty. In 1923 BAT's world sales had grown to 50
billion cigarettes per year.

Sir Hugo visited China in 1923 to decentralize one of

BAT's biggest operations. Chinese cigarette consumption had grown from 0.3 trillion in 1902 to 25 trillion in 1920, and to nearly 40 trillion by the time of his visit. Sir Hugo's plan was to restructure BAT China Ltd. into independent regional units which could operate when local conditions deteriorated. As China was a major concern, Sir Hugo also spent a great deal of time and energy over the next two decades lobbying the Chinese government to minimize the taxation of tobacco.

Sir Hugo's decentralizing efforts spread from China to many of BAT's other international operations. The Chairman felt that increased local autonomy would lead to better decisions and improved group performance. This proved true despite skepticism that too much decentralization could produce an unwieldy corporate structure. In 1927 BAT had the resources to enter the US market, monopolized at one time by American Tobacco. Sir Hugo acquired Brown and Williamson, a small tobacco producer in North Carolina. With BAT's help, this modest company has grown to become the third largest cigarette manufacturer in the United States. This pattern of rapid growth from modest beginnings was maintained through the Depression era and steadily through the Second World War. At the end of the war, in 1945, Sir Hugo stepped down from the chairmanship and became simply titular president of BAT.

Without Sir Hugo's active participation, the management of BAT did little other than maintain the company's steady growth through the late 1940's and 1950's. Profitability remained undiminished and the company was able successfully to weather the storm of communist revolution in China, at which time all of BAT China Ltd's assets were nationalized. By 1962, BAT's capitalization was such that it was able to begin major moves toward diversification.

During that year, BAT acquired minority interest in two companies, neither of which was involved in tobacco production or sales. Mardon Packaging International does handle cigarette packaging and was thus a logical choice for BAT. Wiggins Teape Ltd, on the other hand, is a large specialty paper manufacturer. Mardon was not highly successful at first. It was formed from five smaller packaging companies in cooperation with Imperial Tobacco and its first-year turnover was modest. It grew steadily, however, as most of BAT's investments have, and by the end of the 1970's was advancing turnover at a rate of 15% per annum.

The success of these two enterprises, which later became wholly owned subsidiaries of BAT, paved the way for further and greater BAT acquisitions. The groundwork was now laid for BAT's transformation from a large tobacco company to an even larger conglomerate. While other major tobacco companies were attempting to diversify into other packaged goods, BAT wasted little time in moving into unrelated but profitable fields. During the 1960's and early 1970's several major international fragrance and perfume houses were brought in to create a third leg in BAT's group. These included such internationally known concerns as Lentheric, Yardley, and Germaine Monteil.

Once these companies were thoroughly absorbed into BAT's operations, BAT turned its eye toward a West German department store chain called Horten. At first a minority share was held and then, as before, the company was acquired as a whole. This led almost immediately to further department store chain acquisitions. Gimbels and Saks Fifth Avenue were acquired in the U.S., Kohl's and Department Stores International in the U.K., and Argos, the British catalogue store, joined in 1979. Patrick Sheehy, before becoming BAT's present chairman, was involved in one more such acquisition. Marshall Field department stores were the unwilling subject of a takeover bid conducted by the controversial team of Carl Icahn and Alan Clone. Sheehy was able to convince BAT to make a friendly bid for the chain and managed to prevent Icahn from succeeding.

Many of these investments gave BAT a good deal of trouble at first, just as Mardon had before. While Saks Fifth Avenue, which appealed to the upper middle-class consumer, maintained high profitability, Gimbels, despite efforts to bring in wealthier clientele, has had a consistently poor showing. With the exception of Gimbels, BAT has been able to absorb and make a real success of its retailing leg as well as its earlier extension into paper.

In 1972 the treaty of Rome brought the United Kingdom into the EEC and with it an end to the agreements between BAT and Imperial Tobacco. New restraint of trade laws prohibited their arrangement. The companies exchanged brand rights once again, each retaining full ownership of its original brands in the U.K. and Western Europe only. BAT was able to keep its brand and trademark ownership in the rest of the world and in the duty free trade outside Western Europe. Ties with Imperial Tobacco were finally severed in 1980 when that company sold its remaining few shares in BAT after having made major reductions over the preceding decade.

Due to the increasingly diversified nature of British American's interests, the name of the company was officially changed to BAT Industries in 1976 and management was restructured for tighter control. BAT Industries became a holding company for several smaller operating companies organized according to industry. These operating companies in turn controlled the individual manufacturing and retailing enterprises.

Appleton Papers was added to the BAT operation in 1978. This American company established BAT as the world leader in the manufacture of carbonless paper. That year BAT also acquired Pegulan, a large home-improvements company in West Germany, as well as two fruit juice companies in Brazil. Other purchases followed in pulp production in Brazil and Portugal.

Within two years of his 1982 accession to BAT's chairmanship, Patrick Sheehy decided to add a fourth leg to BAT's existing three supports. Eagle Star, a British insurance group, was involved in an unfriendly takeover struggle with the West German firm Allianz when Sheehy contacted its chairman, Sir Denis Mountain, with a friendly proposal. Eagle Star, which had rejected a low bid from Allianz as "grossly inadequate", accepted a similar bid from BAT as Sir Denis felt the two companies could work together well. In fact BAT Industries saw a 26% rise in pre-tax profit during the first half of 1987, 45% of which was due to Eagle Star. Hambro Life Assurance, another large British firm, rounded out BAT's new fourth leg in financial services and became Allied Dunbar when it was acquired by BAT in 1985.

Since the addition of financial services to BAT's portfolio, Sheehy has implemented a policy of "focusing and reshaping the business" rather than continuing to move into new areas. Sheehy feels that BAT should only be involved in companies able to maintain a leadership position in their markets. This has meant some significant divestitures for BAT. In 1984 British American Cosmetics, International Stores, and Kohl's Food Stores were all sold. Mardon Packaging was sold to its own management in 1985 and in 1986 Gimbels and Kohl's (U.S.) department stores were put up for sale. That year 88 Batus retail stores were also divested in the U.S. along with the West German Pegulan. Despite the recent trimming, or perhaps because of it, BAT's sales have continued to rise; 1986 sales were up 12% over 1985.

With the increasing uncertainty of a long-term market in tobacco, Sheehy has also taken steps to decrease BAT's dependence on that industry. In 1986 only 50% of BAT's pre-tax profit came from its tobacco group. This is down from 57% in 1985 and 71% in 1982. This change is not due to a decrease in tobacco sales, however, but to overall growth in the other groups, most notably Eagle Star, which increased its contribution to BAT's profits from 11% in 1985 to 19% in 1986.

Despite increased profitability, BAT's shares are still low rated world wide. This is due more to investor wariness about tobacco and recent fluctuations in the dollar, however, than to weakness in the marketplace.

Michael Dunbar, former deputy chairman of Sedgwick Group insurance brokers, has just taken over as chief executive officer of Eagle Star, which will hopefully lead to further expansion of BAT's financial services operation.

With Sheehy's reorganization a success, the chairman indicates that his next move will be to acquire an American financial services company to further consolidate that area. BAT Industries, under the leadership of Patrick Sheehy, seems bound for a profitable future of indefinite length.

Principal Subsidiaries: Ardath Tobacco Co. Ltd.; BAT Ltd.; BAT Services Ltd.; Argos Distribution Ltd.; Jewellers Guild Ltd.; Marshall Field & Co.; Frederick & Nelson, Inc.; Gimbel Bros, Inc.; J.B. Ivey & Co.; John Breuner Co.; Kohl's Dept. Stores Inc.; Saks & Co.; Crescent Stores, Inc.; Thimbles Speciality Stores; The Wiggins Teape Group Ltd.; Jointline Products Co. Ltd.; Samuel Jones & Co. Ltd.; Spicer-Cowan Ltd.; Eagle Star Holdings plc; Allied Dunbar and Company plc; City of London Insurance Co. Ltd.; Gresham Investment Trust plc; Midland Assurance Ltd.; Shield Insurance Co. Ltd.; Grovewood Securities Ltd. The company also lists subsidiaries in the following countries: Argentina, Australia, Austria, Bangladesh, Belgium, Brazil, Canada, Chile, Costa Rica, Cyprus, El Salvador, Finland, France, Guyana, Honduras, Indonesia, Italy, Japan, Malaysia, The Netherlands, Nicaragua, Panama, Puerto Rico, South Africa, Suriname, Switzerland, United States, Venezuela, West Germany, and Zambia.

BTR PLC

Silvertown House
Vincent Square
London SW1P 2PL
England
(01) 834–3848

Public Company
Incorporated: March 31, 1864 as Silver's India Rubber
Works & Telegraph Cable Company, Ltd.
Employees: 85,400
Sales: £4.01 billion (US$5.895 billion)
Market value: £4.57 billion (US$6.72 billion)
Stock Index: London

BTR, or British Thermoplastics and Rubber, is a London-based conglomerate with substantial worldwide interests, particularly in the United States. The company is involved in the manufacture of a variety of plastic and rubber products, including conveyor belts, artificial limbs, underwater cables, and plastic components in industrial machinery. Over the years, BTR has diversified into construction, engineering, and industrial and consumer manufacturing.

BTR has its origin with Arrowsmith & Silver, a colonial merchant of clothing and other provisions, established in London in 1798. At some point prior to 1823, the company came under the control of Stephen W. Silver, and the company's name was changed to Silver & Company. That year Silver established a waterproof rubber clothing factory in Greenwich as an extension of his enterprise. The factory was moved in 1852 to a part of West Ham which later became known as Silvertown.

By 1862 Silver & Company was involved in the manufacture of various Indian rubber and ebonite products, including insulated telegraph wire. Silver purchased a rubber making facility at Persan-Beaumont from the Franco-American Company in 1864 and incorporated his company as Silver's India Rubber Works & Telegraph Cable Company. The enterprise was subsequently renamed the India Rubber, Gutta Percha & Telegraph Works Company when it entered the field of gutta percha production (gutta percha is a rubber-like substance with a high resin content, and was especially useful for underwater cables and in dentistry). A separate gutta percha factory was established at Silvertown, and Walter Hancock, who was experienced in its production, was placed in charge of the plant in 1864. In December of that year Hancock's independent Gutta Percha Company and West Ham Gutta Percha Company were merged with Silver's operations.

Beginning in 1868, India Rubber experienced a strong increase in demand for its products, especially underwater cables for transoceanic telegraph lines. The company acquired many of its own cable-laying ships, and participated in the establishment of a number of international communications companies, including the Direct Spanish Telegraph Company (1872), West Coast of America Telegraph (1876), and the South American Cable Company (1891). By 1892 the company controlled communications offices across the British Isles.

India Rubber entered the sports and leisure industry in 1888 when it introduced golf balls made of gutta percha. The following year India Rubber began to engineer electrical systems for municipalities in Britain. In 1895 the company took managerial control of Palmer Tyre Ltd., a manufacturer of rubber tires for bicycles and carriages; the company was later acquired and consolidated into India Rubber in 1901. In 1906 the company helped to establish Jointless Rim Ltd., a manufacturer of jointless steel wheel rims at the Arrol works in Birmingham. India Rubber established another operation at Persan in 1909 to produce rubber automobile tires, for which demand had grown in proportion to the rising popularity of automobiles.

Demand for insulated cable waned after 1918, and India Rubber reduced its production volume and closed the Arrol plant. Two years later the company withdrew from the electrical systems business. Strong demand for tires and other rubber products caused an expansion of the Silvertown facility, which covered 16.5 acres in 1923, and sales offices were established in Australia, New Zealand, South Africa, India, and Argentina, in addition to several major British cities.

India Rubber was significantly affected by the establishment in 1924 of the British Goodrich Tyre Company, a subsidiary of the B.F. Goodrich Company of Akron, Ohio. From its headquarters in Leyland, British Goodrich purchased several local companies involved in the production of bearings, rubber tires and hoses, golf balls, and other rubber products. In 1933 British Goodrich acquired a controlling interest in the Silvertown Rubber Company, the principal subsidiary of India Rubber.

British Goodrich relinquished its control over the Silvertown facility in 1934, which subsequently changed its name to the British Tyre and Rubber Company, or BTR. Shortly afterwards, BTR acquired the Danish subsidiary of B.F. Goodrich, and in 1935 gained control of James Lyne Hancock Ltd., Britain's oldest rubber company.

In 1936 BTR acquired a production license from an American company called Stowe Woodward which permitted it to produce "Stonite" printing rollers. In 1937 BTR gained production rights from Bell's Asbestos and Engineering to manufacture "Bestobell" machine belting and "High Test" friction surface belting. Also that year BTR discontinued electric cable and wire production. A.G. Spalding & Brothers, widely known for its golf balls and sports equipment, was acquired by BTR in 1938.

Shortly after World War II began, in 1940 the Silvertown plant was severely damaged by German bombings.

Silvertown was a primary German target because its Palmer Tyre group manufactured a number of products for British warplanes. Another factory, located on Penfold Street in London, was requisitioned so that Palmer could immediately resume production. BTR headquarters was moved to Vincent Square in London. Also in 1940, BTR installed production facilities at Leyland for high pressure reinforced hydraulic hose.

BTR produced a wide variety of products for the allied war effort, and contributed significantly to the victory in 1945. After the war, however, Britain remained in an economic crisis which had a deleterious effect on British industry. BTR gained some relief from these conditions when its new polyvinyl chloride products division experienced strong demand for fire-resistant PVC conveyor belts, which were required by new safety regulations instituted by the National Coal Board.

BTR stopped manufacturing tires in 1956 due to falling demand and low profitability. In order to retain the BTR name, the company conveniently changed its name to British Thermoplastics and Rubber. From 1956 to 1959 BTR acquired companies involved in the production of hoses, polyurethane insulating foam, and packaging materials.

During the early 1960's BTR reorganized its managerial structure and sales operations. Six new operating divisions were created: belting; linings and coverings; general mechanicals; aero products; industrial hose and assemblies; and plastics. Also during this period, Spalding & Brothers was sold, and the J.E. Baxter Company, a manufacturer of industrial respirators, was acquired.

In 1964 BTR closed the Silvertown plant, redistributing its operations to other BTR facilities. BTR expanded its paper manufacturing venture with Stowe Woodward, and also formed a new joint venture company called Bristol-BTR, which produced reinforced plastic aircraft parts.

BTR announced a new corporate identity program in 1965. Under the direction of Chairman Sir David Nicolson and Managing Director Owen Green, BTR started to purchase "niche" businesses, those with a large share of a specialized market or a well-defined position in a large market. Sir David and Green practiced a margin-oriented management style, or a "high profit margin maintained on the back of substantial capital spending and high product quality."

By the mid-1970's BTR acquired companies based in Switzerland, Holland, Australia, and West Germany. BTR offices were also established in Sweden, France, South Africa, Australia, Switzerland, and the United States. Major domestic acquisitions included the Leyland and Birmingham Rubber Company and Miles Redfern, a manufacturer of rubber automobile parts.

BTR became involved in the recovery of oil and gas from the North Sea fields when it helped to establish an equipment manufacturer called Williams Brother Offshore, Ltd., in collaboration with the U.S. Filter Corporation. BTR also purchased its long time American affiliate Stowe Woodward. Between 1970 and 1976 BTR's earnings went from £1.35 million to £11 million, over an eight-fold increase, in nominal terms.

In the later 1970's and early 1980's BTR purchased several larger companies, including the Allied Polymer Group in 1978, which manufactured air/sea survival equipment, hoses, surface treatment equipment, and other plastic products. In 1980 BTR acquired the Huyck Corporation, an international manufacturer of finishing products for printing. The Serck Group, which specialized in electronic engineering for instruments and control systems, was acquired by BTR in 1981.

BTR was re-registered as a public limited company on January 4, 1982, and became ultimately responsible for the management and operations of all BTR subsidiaries.

The company's largest and most important acquisition came after three years of study by BTR management. Thomas Tilling Plc was acquired in 1983 for £637 million. The Tilling group included Tilcon (a quarrying company), Grahams Builders Merchants, Newey and Eyre (electrical wholesalers), Rest Assured (furniture), Intermed (health care), Cornhill Insurance (later divested), Vokes (filters), and Pretty Polly (hosiery). The acquisition of Tilling increased BTR's asset valuation from about £500 million in 1983 to almost £1.4 billion a year later. At the time it was the largest takeover in British industrial history.

Opponents of the merger claimed that with the exception of the electronics division, Tilling's operations had nothing in common with those of BTR. These claims were refuted by BTR management which maintained that the company would not consider any acquisition unless its operations offered "contiguity with an existing group company in either manufacturing, technology, or marketing."

BTR gained control over the Nylex Corporation of Australia in 1984, and Dunlop Holdings, a sports and leisure equipment manufacturer, in 1985. Dunlop Tire (USA) was subsequently sold to its management for $203 million as part of a restructuring program initiated by Dunlop chairman Sir Michael Edwardes. A controversial £1.2 billion bid for Pilkington Brothers failed in 1986, but did not appear to detract from BTR's increasing profitability. In addition, Owen Green (since created Sir Owen), assumed the chairmanship of BTR when Sir David Nicolson returned to the board as a regular member.

The company's operations are currently divided into eight divisions: Transportation; Paper and Publishing; Health Care; Consumer; Financial Services; Construction; Energy and Electrical; and Industrial. BTR owns over 600 companies worldwide, and derives most of its operating income from electrical products and construction.

Principal Subsidiaries: (Construction): Graham Building Services Co.; U.S. Supply, Inc.; Pascon Co.; Pilkington's Tiles Co.; Tilcon Co.; (Energy and Electrical): ADS Anker Co.; Audco; Summers Electric Group; Charlton-Leslie Co.; Dunlop Oil & Marine; Facile Technologies, Ltd.; Maloney Co.; Serck Co.; Worcester Controls UK, Ltd.; (Industrial): BTR Industrial Products Co.; BTR Silvertown Co.; Clarkson Group; DCE; Vokes, Ltd.; Dunlop Hose; Dunlop Ho-Flex Co.; Leyland & Birmingham Co.; Lonstroff-BTR Co.; Peter-BTR Co. (91%); Sarmcol; Hansen Transmissions, Ltd.; Gascoigne Group; Hansen Transmissions, Ltd.; Vacu-Blast Co.; Apex

Belting, Ltd.; (Consumer): Dunlop Aerospace; BTR Kennon, Ltd.; Fatati, Ltd.; Dunlop Automotive; Dunlop Metalastik; Empire Rubber Co.; Hertfordshire-BTR Co.; Rubber & Wheel/Lesteel Co.; International Radiator Services (70%); BTR Permali Co.; Russell Plastics; Dunlop-Beaufort; Dunlop Overseas; Dunlop South Africa (51%); (Health Care): MedVent MedDent; MDH, Ltd.; Bear Medical Systems, Ltd.; Nunc, Ltd.; Hanger Co.; Vessa, Ltd.; Viennatone; (Paper and Printing): Huyck Corp.; Stowe Woodward Co.; Cow Proofings Co.; Dunlop Graphic Products; (other): Shanshin Enterprises (70%); Dunlopillo; Dunlop A.G.; Rest Assured, Ltd.; Pretty Polly, Ltd.; Nylex; Dunlop Slazenger; (Holding and related): BTR, Inc.; BTR Industries; BTR Finance B.V.; BTR Nylex (62%); BTR South Africa (61%); Dunlop Holdings; Thomas Tilling; Audco India (50%); Bestobell, Plc. (24%); Dunlop Nigerian Industries, Ltd. (37%); Harper Gilfillan (50%); Octopus Publishing Group, Plc.

C. ITOH & COMPANY, LTD.

68, Kita-Kyutaromachi 4-chome
Higashi-ku, Osaka 541
Japan
(06) 241-2121

Public Company
Incorporated: December 1, 1949
Employees: 7,473
Sales: ¥ 14.07 trillion (US$ 70.11 billion)
Market Value: ¥ 267.2 billion (US$ 1.331 billion)
Stock Index: Luxembourg Tokyo Osaka Nagoya

Chubei Itoh was born in 1842, the son of a dry goods merchant. In 1853, the year Admiral Perry from the United States "opened" Japan to international trade, Itoh began to accompany his older brother on sales trips to Osaka and Kyoto. By 1859 the younger Itoh was making his own sales trips, selling cloth to merchants in Okayama and Hiroshima. The following year, at the age of 18, he established his own wholesale business and worked diligently to expand his small operation.

The 1860's were a time of upheaval and change in Japan. The 264-year old government of the Tokugawa Shogun was overthrown in 1868 by loyalists of the Meiji Emperor. Itoh's business continued to prosper in spite of the civil war. In 1872 he opened a larger shop in Osaka and within five years was one of the largest textile wholesaler-retailers in the city. A branch was opened in Kyoto in 1883, and the Osaka shop was designated the Itoh *Honten*, or "head office."

Chubei Itoh and his nephew Tetsujiro Sotoumi opened a third shop in Kobe in 1885. The Itoh-Sotoumi Company was primarily involved in the exportation of textile goods through *shokan*, or foreign trading agents. The export trade was very profitable, in spite of the *shokan*, who collected large commissions. Profits from export sales were reinvested in the company's domestic operations. Itoh opened a foreign office in Shanghai in an effort to bypass the *shokan* and their commissions. However, it was a difficult market to enter, and the company's representatives lacked the proper skills needed to deal effectively with Chinese merchants. As a result, the Shanghai office consistently lost money.

Itoh died in 1903 and his second son, also named Chubei, inherited the business. The younger Itoh was well trained and proved to be every bit as adept in business affairs as his father.

A few years before, Japan asserted its political dominance in northeast Asia when it defeated Russia in a war for influence in the region. In particular, Chosen (Korea) became a neo-colonial possession of Japan. In 1898 a new *shokan* called Chosenya was established to handle trade between Japan and the Korean peninsula. It was a lucrative and developing market in which Chosenya had a monopoly. In 1905, however, the younger Itoh once again attempted to bypass the middlemen. He posted two company representatives in Korea, and later opened a full branch office in Seoul.

Itoh's business ventures on the Asian mainland deteriorated during 1907. In Chosen there was increasing dissatisfaction with the "low quality of Japanese products." On the other hand, representatives in Shanghai found it increasingly difficult to manage exchange rate fluctuations between the gold-based yen and the silver-based Chinese currency. Mismanagement at the Shanghai office became so acute that by 1908 it was sold to its employees and severed from the Itoh company.

The company recovered quickly, due mainly to a rapid increase in domestic trading activity. In March of 1910 Chubei Itoh, aged 23, went to London reportedly to study business administration. It is more likely, however, that he spent his time negotiating arrangements with English merchants. He discovered that the *shokan*, who presented themselves as powerful international figures in Japan, were actually small agencies with relatively little influence overseas. Itoh purchased large quantities of high-grade wool and other products directly from wholesalers in London and sent them to his company in Japan. Itoh also discovered that bank loans in London were commonly set at around 2–3%, substantially less than the 11–13% charged by the Yokohama Specie Bank in Japan. Taking advantage of these two factors enhanced Itoh's ability to undersell competitors in Japan and reinvest a larger portion of the company's profits.

Japan was a victorious nation in World War I and, as a result, was awarded substantial commercial and military rights in the Pacific. It was a period of tremendous growth for large Japanese companies, particularly the large conglomerates which had become known as *zaibatsu*, or "money cliques." C. Itoh & Company was not considered a *zaibatsu* like Mitsui, Mitsubishi, or Sumitomo. It was, however, a substantial company, engaged in commercial trading at a time when trade had become extremely important to the continued growth of the Japanese economy.

The strong economy and rising demand for textile products transformed the import trading division of C. Itoh virtually overnight. Demand for Itoh's products continued to grow faster than supply, causing prices (and therefore, profit margins) to rise with them. By 1919 the trading division had grown to twice the size of its parent company, and foreign offices had been established in New York, Calcutta, Manila, and four cities in China. As Itoh's volume of trade grew, so did its variety of products. In addition to textile and agricultural products, the company handled machinery, iron and steel products, and automobiles.

Like most economies which experience strong economic

reversals during periods of rapid expansion, Japan entered a serious recession in 1920 which adversely affected consumer demand. Due to the fact that C. Itoh was still a relatively small company without the full backing of a *zaibatsu* bank, it was forced to borrow heavily in order to cover its obligations and went deeply into debt. The following year the company was forced to reorganize. C. Itoh & Company was restructured and named the Marubeni Company. Another new company called Daido Trading was created from a division of C. Itoh Trading. It had previously been responsible for trade with Southeast Asia and the United States, but was ruined when demand for imports disappeared.

All three Itoh companies were forced to lay off hundreds of workers and suspend stock dividends for several years. Their recovery was slow, but gained momentum later in the 1920's. Ironically, these companies experienced their strongest post-recession growth during the worldwide depression of the 1930's. The Calcutta branch, which was closed in 1921, reopened in 1931. In the following years new offices were opened in Australia, Thailand, and Indonesia. It was during this period that the benevolent one-man-rule of Chubei Itoh II was replaced by a more consensus-oriented presidential form of management.

The decade of the 1930's was a difficult period for Japanese business and politics. Right-wing militarists had terrorized their way to power and threatened not only to nationalize the nation's industries, but to dominate all of East Asia and the western Pacific. In the short term, the *zaibatsu* and other large companies stood to benefit greatly because they were the primary suppliers of machinery, weapons and provisions to the growing Japanese military. In the long term, however, these same militarists had pledged to nationalize the *zaibatsu* and other companies. The Itoh companies were only three of hundreds who were placed in the difficult position of collaborating with the military government.

The militarists led Japan into a war against China in 1937, and later against Britain in 1940, and the United States in 1941. That year Itoh merged with Marubeni & Company and Kishimoto & Company to form a new company called Sanko K.K. The concentration of resources was intended to facilitate greater efficiency and conserve limited resources.

Despite the position of Japanese industry and the military, neither had the ability to mobilize or develop new technologies quickly enough to prevent the Allies from turning the war in their favor. Matters became particularly desperate when the Japanese mainland (and its factories) came within range of American bombers. In 1944, as part of an effort to rationalize Japanese industry, the government ordered Sanko, Daido, and a subsidiary of Itoh called Kureha Textiles to merge. The new company, called Daiken Manufacturing, existed for about a year before Japan surrendered.

After the war, the military occupation authority, "SCAP" (for Supreme Commander of Allied Powers), implemented a complete reorganization of Japanese industry. Many American-style commercial laws were enacted, including an anti-monopoly law which outlawed the *zaibatsu*. Although Daiken (Itoh) was not as large as the *zaibatsu*, SCAP ordered it divided into several companies.

When the reorganization was completed in 1949 Kureha, C. Itoh and Marubeni were made independent companies under separate management groups. Both Itoh and Marubeni were given the authority to conduct both domestic and international business. Itoh exported Japanese textile products on a barter basis in return for foreign grain. The trade was stable and profitable, and enabled the company to establish itself quickly. In 1950 Itoh trade representatives were dispatched to India, Pakistan and the United States. The United Nations war effort in Korea necessitated a change in commercial policies in Japan. On short notice Japanese companies, including Itoh, were contracted to supply food, clothing, and other provisions to United Nations forces in Korea. Itoh, which had already established an international network of suppliers, was quickly prepared to meet the sudden increase in business. The company product line, long dominated by textile products, was diversified to include petroleum, machinery, aircraft and automobiles.

When the Korean War ended in 1952 many of Itoh's military contracts were cancelled. The demobilization in Korea caused a serious recession during 1953 and 1954. Hundreds of smaller trading companies were forced into bankruptcy. C. Itoh, however, was larger and better able to endure the poor economic conditions. It later took over the business of the smaller bankrupt companies and continued to expand its product line.

Unlike the former *zaibatsu* groups, the postwar Itoh companies (C. Itoh, Marubeni, and Kureha) did not merge back together. During this period *zaibatsu* groups circumvented many anti-monopoly laws by coordinating their individual company strategies through bankings groups (called *keiretsu*). C. Itoh was neither a prewar *zaibatsu* nor a member of a postwar *keiretsu* group. During the later 1950's, however, the company accumulated enough capital to begin large-scale lending operations.

C. Itoh & Company and *keiretsu* group leaders such as Mitsui Bussan, Mitsubishi, and Sumitomo were engaged primarily in trading. They became know as *sogo shosha*, or "general trading companies." C. Itoh experienced strong growth during the 1960's, particularly on the strengths of its trading activities. An international information network was created which made the company more responsive to business opportunities around the world.

In the late 1960's Itoh identified an opportunity to develop a nickel and cobalt mine at Greenvale in northeastern Australia. Itoh, in partnership with Australian interests, Mitsubishi and Nissho Iwai, started the project in 1971. Raw materials from the mine were to be sold to Kawasaki Steel and Nisshin Steel, among others, and used to produce stainless steel.

When OPEC countries forced a dramatic increase in the price of oil in 1973, oil-dependent countries such as Japan found themselves seriously vulnerable to inflation and interruptions of supply. C. Itoh recognized this as an area of great opportunity. In coordination with the C. Itoh Fuel Company, Itoh invested heavily in the development of new technologies for petroleum production.

In the mid-1970's the Japanese government became concerned about another trading company called Ataka, which was nearly bankrupt. Ataka had gained a reputation for mismanagement and inefficiency. It was repeatedly warned by banks and the government to practice greater discipline. When it appeared that Ataka's demise was inevitable, the Japanese government stepped in. In order to prevent the failure of such a large company (Ataka was Japan's tenth largest trading firm), the government hastily arranged for a major portion of it to be absorbed by Itoh. When the merger was affected on October 1, 1977, C. Itoh & Company moved from being the fourth to the third largest Japanese trading firm. The merger greatly increased Itoh's interests in steel and chemicals, and further reduced textiles to about 20% of total sales volume.

In addition to its trading activities, C. Itoh has recently been involved in a number of large industrial projects, acting as a coordinator and providing financial support. Itoh's largest foreign projects are the Hassi-R'Mel natural gas plant in Algeria, a cashmere factory in Mongolia, the Baoshan steel complex near Shanghai (led by Nippon Steel), and the Kaduna oil refinery in Nigeria (with Chiyoda Chemical). Early in 1987, however, Itoh backed out of the Greenvale Mine project when it appeared that demand for non-ferrous metals would not recover. The company is also involved in the development of natural resources, including petroleum products and uranium, and metals (despite ending its involvement with Greenvale).

Itoh's primary product is its trading and information network, which enables it to coordinate business projects and see them through from planning a factory to marketing its final product. Unlike many of its competitors, Itoh's expertise lies not in engineering, but in organization, management, and financial planning.

Principal Subsidiaries: Kurita Water Industries, Ltd.; Fuji Oil Co., Ltd.; Daiken Trade and Industry Co., Ltd.; C. Itoh Fuel Co., Ltd.; Takiron Co., Ltd.; Sanko Steel Wire Mfg. Co., Ltd.; Century Research Center Corp. C. Itoh & Company also has subsidiaries in the following countries: The United States, United Kingdom, West Germany, Australia, Hong Kong, Singapore, and Brazil.

Further Reading: The Soga Shosha: Japan's Multinational Trading Companies by Alexander Young, Boulder, Colorado, Westview Press, 1979.

Colt Industries

COLT INDUSTRIES INC.

430 Park Avenue
New York, New York 10022
U.S.A.
(212) 940-0400

Public Company
Incorporated: November 11, 1911 as Pennsylvania Coal &
Coke Corp.
Employees: 19,700
Sales: $1.616 billion
Market value: $405 million
Stock Index: New York

Widely known for its firearms, Colt Industries is more than
a gun company. With 78 manufacturing plants in 25 states
and several foreign countries, Colt is a broadly diversified,
billion dollar conglomerate.

It didn't always look like Colt would be around long
enough to expand into other businesses. The company was
incorporated in 1954 as Penn-Texas Corp., the plaything
of Leopold Silberstein. It was among the first of the
conglomerates, growing entirely through acquisitions. The
company staggered, however, and five years later the
company was renamed Fairbanks Whitney Co. to establish
a fresh identity for itself.

What is today Colt Industries was born in 1962. That
year George A. Strichman left his middle management job
at International Telephone & Telegraph Corp. to become
president and chairman of Fairbanks Whitney. Shortly
after, he described the company as "a case history in
catastrophe." It had been through a decade of mismanagement and wheeler-dealing that ended in a flurry of proxy-
fights and multi-million dollar losses. A few months later,
Strichman recruited David L. Margolis, who had worked
with Strichman at ITT, to be financial vice-president and
treasurer.

The company's profile desperately needed to be
defined. Its operation ranged from Pennsylvania coal
mines and firearms to machine tools and a hodgepodge of
other industrial products. To help the company make the
transition, the company in 1964 adopted the name Colt
Industries.

The new management shied away from making long
term goals because Colt dealt mostly in cyclical business.
But by narrowing its products and markets, the company
registered at impressive rate of earnings growth in its first
few years. By 1966 the company had achieved its second
year in the black. Sales rose to $191 million from $164

million the previous year, and earnings at $1.64 per share
were almost twice that of a year earlier. Most of those
profits came from the manufacture of military products for
the Vietnam War. And that result didn't include the
$600,000 earned on $8 million in sales by the newly
acquired Quincy Compressor Co.

But for a capital goods and defense company in the
midst of booms in both businesses, these earnings were
merely moderate. Colt earned less than 3% on sales at a
time when well-run competitors were making 8% to 10%
and more; even Colt's creditable return on equity of some
13% the previous year was due in large part to the
shrunken book value created by heavy writeoffs in 1962.
But, Strichman told the media, the company was capable
of paying its bills without relying on outside cash.

With the war boosting the company's market, Colt
achieved an earnings peak in 1968, which it would not
surpass for another eight years. It acquired Crucible Steel,
which helped reduce Colt's reliance on military business,
but its large industrial group was actually operating at a
loss during much of this period. By also buying Holley
Caburetor and Central Transformer that year, the
company managed to gain significant market shares in
such product lines as fluid controls, automotive carbure-
tors, aircraft fuel systems, and some types of water and
sewage pumps. Those acquisitions enabled Colt to move
forward while reducing its dependence on steel products.

In 1972 earnings appeared to be on an upward trend
throughout much of the company's 19 divisions, which
were broadly grouped into four categories. The largest
unit, Materials, a producer of stainless steel and high alloy
steel, accounted for about 42% of Colt's sales and more
than 65% of its profits. Demand at Crucible Steel was
strong in all markets. Fluid Control Systems brought in
18% of the company's volume and profits. That group was
made up of Holley Carburetor, the largest imdependent
manufacturer in its field, and Chandler Evans, which
produced aircraft fuel controls, pumps, and valves.

But not all of the Colt's divisions were as healthy. The
Industrial and Power Group, comprised of Central
Moloney Transformer, Pratt & Whitney Tools, Fairbanks
Morse Weighing Systems, and Quincy Compressors,
accounted for 31% of Colt's sales that year but racked up a
loss of close to $7 million. And the Firearm Division,
which produces M16's, police revolvers, and sporting
arms, represented 9% of the company's overall total and
15% of profits.

Colt weathered the 1973–77 recession era, doubling its
sales to $1.5 billion and quadrupling its earnings to $69.6
million. It had achieved that growth despite often sluggish
markets for its specialty steel, machine tools, firearms, and
numerous industrial products. Much of the success rested
with Strichman, who didn't hesitate to prune products that
did not live up to their promise in profits, including large
power generators, electric motors, piston engines, pumps,
and compressors, among others.

In 1977 Colt came under scrutiny by the Justice Department. A broad-scale grand jury investigation looked into
illegal arms and ammunition sales to South Africa by Colt
and the Winchester Group of the Olin Corporation. Both
companies conceded that they had illegally shipped arms

via third parties to South Africa, which was under an arms embargo because of its apartheid policy. The companies fired several employees who were said to have conducted the sales in violation of corporate policy and without knowledge of senior officials.

Colt had adopted a more cautious attitude in recent years. For the five years preceding 1978, it had made no major acquisitions. And Strichman conceded to *Business Week* that he was paying little attention to outside opportunities. As he saw it, either asking prices were too high or built-in problems were too great. "We spent a generation cleaning up our problems. We're not going to pay a premium to buy somebody else's," he told the magazine.

But if Colt was being more conservative about buying new companies, that didn't stop it from playing the market with the companies it had. This prompted *Business Week* to observe that Colt moves "in and out of product lines so often that the company sometimes seems to be run like a floating crap game." That year Colt phased out several models of commercial firearms—the company name derived from its venerable Patent Fire Arms Manufacturing unit. At the same time it was trying to absorb Menasco Manufacturing Co., an aircraft landing gear producer acquired the previous year. By entering industries that cycled at various times, Colt buffered its position against economic downturns. The automotive caburetor business, for instance, is affected by new car sales, but also has a flourishing replacement market to fill the gap when new car sales drop. Sales of Colt's electrical distribution transformers depend largely on the rate of residential and light construction, where market trends do not necessarily coincide with capital spending by such industries as paper, petroleum, and chemicals. The last is Colt's primary customer for alloy tubing and pipe products.

And it was clear that the company's efforts to replace or scrap unprofitable markets or products was beginning to pay off. Fairbanks Morse had established itself as one of the leaders in the highly competitive market of medium-speed diesel engines used by utility and industrial plants. It had attained that position despite competition from at least five other companies, and its dollar volume and backlog were up from one year before. Quincy, an important manufacturer of small air compressors, was competing mainly against Sullair for the bulk of its business. Quincy's orders were also increasing steadily, and its backlog shot up three times from the previous year.

Indeed, Colt's fast-moving strategy was essential if it hoped to cope with the sharp ups and downs that had proven chaotic for many capital goods companies and thwarted their attempt to do long-range planning. Colt wisely chose to enter only industries that rarely cycled together, and by retaining only those companies that come through cycles at higher profit levels than before. And the company was also careful not to expand cyclical operations when they were on the upswing in order to avoid costly excess capacities and inventories on the downswing. This strategy enabled the company to perform successfully, despite a slowing capital goods spending. Colt doubled its sales over the previous five years to $1.7 billion, while its net income grew in that period to $80 million from only $16.3 million.

Many of the company's divisions were in excellent shape. In 1978 Colt's steel business was doing relatively well, producing $650 million in sales and operating profits of $50 million. Sales for the company's industrial and power equipment division exceeded $500 million, while operating profits reached $50 million. Fluid control sales rose to more than $280 million with operating profits over $40 million, making this the most profitable segment of Colt's business. Even the recently acquired Garlock industrial seal business had $230 million in sales with operating profits of $30 million.

As usual, though, not all of Colt's divisions were doing well. Trent Tube, the world's largest producer of welded stainless steel tubing, had an estimated $125 million in sales and $14 million profits. Business had been badly hurt by imports and increasing domestic competition. And Colt firearms, the principal manufacturer of the M16, had been experiencing a downtrend in sales and earnings since 1977 when all production for the U.S. government ended. Exports could have made up the difference, but government approval for export was increasingly difficult to obtain.

In 1981 Penn Central's upper management made an unsuccessful bid to buy Colt Industries. Penn, which had just emerged from a large reorganization as a strong, diversified company, offered $1.4 billion. But a group of Penn's large shareholders owning 22% of the firm's stock balked at the deal, believing it was $400 million too high. Shareholders critical of the proposed deal mounted a $1 million campaign to persuade small stockholders, who would have a large combined vote, to veto the projects. Management barely reacted to the opposition. In the final vote, the deal was sunk by a small margin.

In 1982 Colt announced it would close its big Crucible Stainless & Alloy Division, which represented nearly 25% of the company's sales. That move put 4,500 workers at the Midland, Pennsylvania, plant out of work. Colt had been plagued by the specialty steelmaking division's drain on cash. The year earlier Colt completed a $100 million program to install two new steelmaking furnaces at Midland and to make other improvements. Colt, which made $109.5 million overall on sales of $2.2 billion in 1981, said the division was suffering from substantial losses ($61.8 million) on sales of $500 million. Wall Street analysts heartily approved of Colt's move to either sell or close down the plant.

With Crucible out of the way, the financial outlook for the rest of the company was improved. The company took advantage of its somewhat stronger financial position to buy back 4.7 million shares at a premium rate of $24 a share, about 20% over book value.

In 1985 Colt unloaded another unit, this time Fairbanks Morse Pump Division. A Kansas City-based investor group bought all of the company's assets, including the exclusive use of the trade name Fairbanks Morse which dates back to 1880.

Predicting the outlook for Colt, a company that has never liked long-range planning, is difficult. But one former executive told *Business Week*, "Colt figures the opportunities for exceptional growth in the 1980's are limited." Just as closing plant (part of a major division) and selling a division cut off opportunities, stock buybacks have never been a way to make a business grow.

Principal Subsidiaries: Central Moloney Inc.; Colt Industries Operating Corp.; Delavan Inc.; Garlock Inc.; Stemco Inc.; Menasco Inc. The company also lists subsidiaries in the following countries: Canada, France, Panama, Switzerland, United Kingdom, and West Germany.

Further Reading: The Rampant Colt: The Story of a Trademark by Robert Laurence Wilson, Spencer, Indiana, T. Haas, 1969; *The Colt Heritage: The Official History of Colt Firearms from 1836 to the Present* by Robert Laurence Wilson, New York, Simon and Schuster, 1979.

ELDERS IXL LTD.

One Garden Street
South Yarra, Victoria 3141
Australia
249–2424

Public Company
Incorporated: December 1981
Employees: 45,000
Sales: A$7.658 billion (US$5.081 billion)
Market Value: A$1.485 billion (US$985.7 million)
Stock Index: Melbourne   Sydney Adelaide Brisbane
Perth Hobart London Hong Kong Paris Tokyo Zurich
Frankfurt

Elders IXL is the largest company in Australia. While it may be considered a conglomerate, Elders is particularly strong in brewing. It has a well-established reputation for acquiring companies whose performance is poor and transforming them into highly profitable businesses through the introduction of modern management methods and strict financial control. As a result, the modern Elders group has grown into a large and highly competitive company which has achieved phenomenal growth, averaging an annual 33% increase in pre-tax profits since 1981.

The man primarily responsible for the creation of Elders IXL is John D. Elliott, an honors graduate in commerce who earned an MBA from Melbourne University. After two years working for Broken Hill Proprietary, Elliott spent six years as a consultant with McKinsey & Company, an international management consulting firm. During this period he became familiar with the mining, retailing, and chemical industries, and worked extensively in Australia and the United States.

A large Australian food products company called Henry Jones IXL came to the attention of John Elliott in 1972, after that company solicited McKinsey & Company for advice on ways to strengthen its financial position. Henry Jones IXL suffered from outdated management and poor financial control, and had become vulnerable to a hostile takeover. Recognizing the potential of the company under proper management, Elliott organized a consortium of investors, which by December of 1972 had raised A$30 million to purchase it.

The company Elliott and his group purchased had well-established brand names and was quite well known for its fruit preserves and jams. The company was based in Hobart, Tasmania, where it was established by Sir Henry

Jones in 1889. Sir Henry was unable to read or write, and at the time had no distinguishing title. So, when choosing a name for his company, he selected three letters from the alphabet I, X, and L to convey the message "I excel." When the company was taken over by John Elliott 90 years later, he pledged to retain the three letters for their valuable character.

As managing director of Henry Jones IXL, Elliott immediately implemented new management policies aimed at revitalizing the company. With funds raised through the sale of Henry Jones IXL's lower yielding assets, Elliott engineered the A$6 million takeover of another Tasmanian fruit canning company called Tom Piper Ltd. With the addition of Tom Piper, Henry Jones IXL had doubled its profits by the end of 1973.

When the United Kingdom entered the European Economic community in 1975 it ended many of its preferential trade agreements with Commonwealth countries such as Australia. As a result, many Australian companies were excluded from traditional markets in Britain, damaging the Australian fruit canning industry. Henry Jones IXL's profits fell from A$3.7 million in 1974 to 1.7 million in 1976. The company's recovery from this situation, however, was well-planned and carefully executed.

In 1978 Elliott initiated a three-year program of external growth (growth by acquisition) as part of an effort to diversify into a broader range of operations. That year Henry Jones IXL purchased two smaller firms, Alva Jams Pty. and W.H. Johnson Pty. and the following year took control of J.R. Wyllie and Sons and Provincial Traders Holding Ltd., a large edible oils concern. In 1980 Henry Jones IXL acquired Barrett Burston (a maltster and producer of animal feeds), and the Australian operations of Wattie Pict Ltd., a large frozen foods company based in New Zealand. By 1981 Henry Jones IXL also had acquired interests in engineering, agricultural products, lumber, and media.

During 1981 Elder Smith Goldsbrough Mort (ESGM), a major shareholder in Henry Jones IXL, had become the target of a hostile takeover by the financier Robert Holmes à Court and his company Bell Resources. It was conceivable that, if successful in acquiring ESGM. Bell Resources could easily gain control of Henry Jones IXL. When Bell had accumulated a 19.9% share of ESGM, a group of investors friendly to ESGM (which included Henry Jones IXL) initiated a defense by purchasing a separate 20% share. A bidding war became increasingly undesirable to all parties concerned. At that time a complex agreement was reached wherein a fourth company, Carlton & United Breweries, would acquire ESGM's interest in Henry Jones IXL in addition to Bell Resources' interest in ESGM. ESGM would then "acquire" Henry Jones IXL (the reverse actually occurred), to form a new company called Elders IXL. While ESGM did, in fact, acquire Henry Jones IXL for A$149 million, John Elliott and his management team assumed control of the new company. Carlton and United Breweries emerged from the compromise with a 49.4% "friendly" interest in Elders IXL.

ESGM was originally created by a merger in 1962 between Elder Smith and Goldsbrough Mort & Company. The largest of these concerns, Elder Smith, was established in 1839 by a 24-year old Scotsman named Alexander Lang Elder. Elder Smith was primarily involved in animal husbandry and raising livestock. Goldsbrough Mort, founded in 1888, was a wool trader and dumper (wool dumping is the process of concentrating wool into bales for shipping). When the two companies merged, they created one of the largest pastoral companies in Australia.

Like Henry Jones IXL before John Elliott, ESGM was characterized by outdated and highly conservative management techniques. In the process of creating Elders IXL, Elliott corrected these problems and transformed the ESGM operations into modern and profitable divisions. Within four months of the merger, Elders IXL launched a A$115 million takeover bid for Wood Hall Trust, a British construction firm with significant pastoral interests in Australia and a worldwide network of trading offices. The incorporation of Wood Hall Trust into the Elders Group strengthened the ESGM finance business, consolidated Elders' position in pastoral activities, and provided the group with a strong foothold in international trading. The acquisition also provided Elders IXL with a listing on the London bourse.

In July 1982, only four months after the acquisition of Wood Hall Trust, Elders IXL purchased a 19.9% share of Bridge Oil Ltd. Elders continued to purchase companies through 1983, acquiring Westwools Holdings, F.J. Walker Ltd., Mayfair Foods, and Commercial Bureau (Australia) Pty., which operated a trading office in Moscow.

During the two years since its compromise agreement with Bell Resources, Elders IXL considered its shareholding arrangement with Carlton & United to be undesirable, but had never found an opportune moment to resolve the issue. Suddenly, in November 1983 Elders was threatened by an indirect takeover as a result of its relationship with Carlton & United. An Australian investment company called Industrial Equity Limited (IEL) indicated its intention to take control of Carlton & United, which still held a 49.4% interest in Elders IXL. If successful in acquiring Carlton & United, IEL could easily gain control of Elders.

Elders was forced to mount an immediate defense. Within a week the company raised A$980 million through a syndicated bank loan, and announced its intention to acquire Carlton & United. Elders succeeded in purchasing not only IEL's interest in Carlton & United, but several other large blocks of shares. Elders emerged with a majority of shares, and six months later completed its takeover of Carlton & United with the acquisition of all remaining shares.

Elders paid A$998 million for Carlton & United, using mostly borrowed funds and raising its debt-to-equity ratio to 5.3:1. The acquisition was not, however, purely opportunistic or defensive; brewing had long been identified by Elders management as an area worthy of investment. It also forced Elders to identify which areas were to become its "core" businesses, and to implement a stricter divisional organization. The General Jones processed foods operation was sold in 1984, as were a number of other secondary businesses. Bridge Oil and Elders' 20% share in Kidston Mines were sold to another subsidiary called Mungana Mines (subsequently renamed Elders

Resources). Greater concentration was placed on the brewing industry, and, in particular, creating an international market for Foster's Lager, Carlton & United's most popular beer.

In an attempt to enter markets in the northern hemisphere, Elders management decided to acquire an established company in North America or Europe. During the spring and summer of 1985 Elders accumulated shares of Allied-Lyons, a British beverage company, and in October announced its intention to purchase the company for £1.68 billion. Allied-Lyons took a number of defensive actions and asked the British Monopolies & Mergers Commission to review the matter for possible antitrust violations.

During the MMC investigation, Elders became involved in a takeover battle in Australia which weakened its financial position enough to prevent a successful bid for Allied-Lyons. Early in 1986 Robert Holmes à Court attempted to gain control over Broken Hill Proprietary (BHP), Australia's largest industrial mining concern. Elders and BHP had a common interest in preventing the takeover. In April the two companies agreed to exchange a large enough number of shares to ensure that hostile bidders would not be able to gain control of either company. Elders emerged from the cross-investment scheme with an 18.6% share of BHP.

Elders was given permission to proceed with the takeover on September 3rd, 1986. By that time, however, Elders had abandoned it bid for Allied-Lyons, and instead entered into negotiations with Hanson Trust Plc to purchase Courage, one of Britain's largest breweries, for £1.4 billion. The takeover was completed on September 18, and the ensuing months proved once again the ability of Elders IXL to acquire and revitalize companies much larger than itself.

Six months later Elders raised A$875 million in a rights issue, and almost immediately announced the purchase of a 50.1% share of Carling O'Keefe, the third largest brewing company in Canada, from Rothmans Inc. The remaining shares of Carling O'Keefe were purchased at C$18 per share, bringing the total cost of the acquisition to C$392 million.

By the end of March 1987, Elders IXL had built an international brewing network which consisted of Carlton & United in Australia, Courage in Britain, and Carling O'Keefe in Canada. In achieving this network, however, Elders incurred further debt, depressing its valuation to a level lower than the sum of its individual parts, and creating pressure for a break up of Elders IXL. In order to prevent the break up of Elders IXL, Peter Scanlon, a fromer strategist with Elders, proposed the establishment of several independent Elders companies organized by operation, each controlled by Elders IXL, which would remain head of the group. By listing some of these companies overseas, Elders could reduce its exposure to high rates of taxation in Australia.

Scanlon headed an investment company called AFP (for Australian Forest Products), in which John Elliott was also a partner. In order to prevent corporate raiders from gaining control of Elders and selling its divisions at a premium, AFP began to accumulate options to purchase shares of Elders stock as early as September 1986. By the following August AFP held options to 40% of Elders, which, with the BHP cross-investment, thoroughly protected the company from a hostile takeover.

In August 1987 Elliott announced that Elders IXL would divide its assets among four separate companies. Carlton & United, Courage, and Carling O'Keefe would be placed with a new company called the Elders Brewing Group, listed in London (where the corporate tax is 13% lower than in Australia). Elders' various merchant banks and other financial interests would be placed under another foreign-domiciled company called the Elders Finance Group. The company's pastoral and international trading operations would be placed with the Elders Agribusiness Group, which would remain in Australia. Elders Resources, created in 1985, would remain in charge of Elders' numerous natural resource assets. The following month it was announced that a fifth company called Elders Investments Ltd. would be registered in Hong Kong, and would take over the group's international finance business.

Elders IXL will sell 35% of each new company, with the exception of Elders Resources, in which it plans to retain only a 48.5% share. Capital raised from the sale of these shares will substantially decrease Elders' debt load, and may eventually lead to the resolution of its defensive cross-investment with BHP. Presently, Elders IXL is the sixth largest producer of beer in the world, and is in an excellent position to establish its Foster's Lager as a "world brand."

John Elliott has been an outspoken opponent of government policies toward business (and in particular, corporate taxation) under the Labor Party administration of the Australian Prime Minister Bob Hawke. Elliott has frequently been spoken of as a candidate for national office with the opposition Liberal Party, of which he is treasurer. Members of Elders management, as well as fellow partners at AFP, expressed strong concern that Elliott would be lured away from their companies to enter politics. In October 1987, however, Elliott agreed to remain with these companies through 1990.

Principal Subsidiaries: Prior to the reorganization of Elders IXL in 1987, the company listed 384 subsidiaries; as a result of the reorganization, Elders now lists five subsidiaries: Elders Brewing Ltd. (65%) (U.K.); Elders Finance Ltd. (65%); Elders Agribusiness Pty. (65%); Elders Resources Ltd. (48.5%); Elders Investments Ltd. (65%) (Hong Kong).

FARLEY NORTHWEST INDUSTRIES, INC.

6300 Sears Tower
Chicago, Illinois 60606
U.S.A.
(312) 876-7000

Wholly-owned subsidiary of the Farley/Northwest Holding Corporation
Incorporated: August 3, 1967 as Northwest Industries, Inc.
Employees: 19,000
Sales: $456.1 million

Farley Northwest Industries is a relatively young company when compared to other corporations in America, but "middle-aged" when compared to the many other conglomerates which were created in the 1960's, when one-product companies started to diversify their operations. Companies which produced a narrow range of products diversified in an attempt to insulate themselves from increasingly unstable competition and erratic demand in the marketplace.

Ben W. Heineman had joined the financially troubled Chicago and North Western Railway company in 1952. He was promoted to president in 1956 and given the mission of returning the railroad to profitability. He made the C&NW's commuter trains the most punctual in the country by demanding strict adherence to schedules and by enforcing discipline. In ten years Heineman brought the C&NW from a $5 million deficit to a $26 million operating profit. He failed, however, in an attempt to create a large midwestern railroad network through a process of mergers, and decided instead to widen the scope of the company's business by purchasing two chemical companies. In 1967 he created Northwest Industries as a subsidiary of the railroad. The following April Northwest was converted into a holding company and parent of the C&NW and its other corporate holdings. That same month Northwest Industries purchased the Philadelphia & Reading corporation, whose assets included Lone Star Steel, Acme Boot, Universal Manufacturing, and Union Underwear.

In 1969 Heineman attempted to acquire the tire manufacturer B.F. Goodrich for Northwest Industries. Goodrich mounted a fierce defense which thwarted the takeover. This caused a temporary crisis of confidence among Northwest shareholders which depressed the company's stock value.

Heineman was also fighting a losing battle to maintain the profitability of the railroad. After several years of unsuccessful attempts to sell the C&NW, Heineman announced an agreement to sell the railroad to its employees for about $415 million plus $19 million in notes payable (book value was approximately $734 million). Under railroad tax rules, however, capital losses were equivalent to operating losses, which meant that the sale could generate a tax credit of over $200 million for Northwest. The C&NW also burdened Northwest's balance sheet with $360 million of debt, which discouraged additional infusions of shareholder capital. This, in turn, prevented Northwest from acquiring other more profitable companies. The sale was finalized on June 1, 1972.

Northwest acquired the Buckingham Corporation in May 1971 for $120 million. Buckingham was an importer of wine (Mouton Cadet and Marquisat) and liquor (Cutty Sark and Finlandia vodka). In April 1973 Northwest purchased the General Battery Corporation, a manufacturer of automobile batteries, for about $85 million. In February 1976 the company purchased an 83% share of Microdot Inc., a manufacturer of steel ingot molds and universal-type connecting gears. Remaining shares of Microdot were later purchased, and it was made a wholly owned subsidiary of Northwest at a total cost of $81.5 million. In September the company acquired the BVD underwear label from Rapid American for an undisclosed amount. In November 1977 Northwest purchased a 97.4% stake in the Coca-Cola Bottling Company of Los Angeles (which earlier that year had acquired the Coca-Cola Bottling Company of Mid-America) for $202 million. Despite his record of success during the 1970's, Heineman lost takeover bids for Swift and Home Insurance.

Velsicol, a chemical subsidiary of Northwest Industries, was accused by the Environmental Protection Agency of withholding research information which suggested that two of its pesticide products, Chlordane and Heptachlor, might cause cancer. In an effort to avoid further public relations damage to the company, Northwest entered a plea of no contest to the government's charges. Velsicol was forced to pay additional health settlements stemming from a separate case in which the company mistakenly shipped a flame retardant chemical called polybrominated biphenyl, or PBB, as a livestock feed ingredient.

In June 1981 Northwest sold its Buckingham and Coca-Cola Bottling subsidiaries to Beatrice Foods for $600 million. Northwest received nearly double what it paid for the subsidiaries, and at the same time cleared itself of Buckingham, whose profits declined as consumers began to demand lighter liquors and wines. Lone Star Steel, a Northwest subsidiary which manufactured steel tubing for oil drilling rigs, posed a larger problem. Lone Star was dependent on high oil prices to maintain demand for its products. When oil prices were high, Lone Star was very profitable. But when oil prices stablized and later began to decline in 1981, Lone Star started to lose money and drain profits from Northwest. The company's stock value dropped from $80.50 to $34.75 per share.

In order to raise money, in 1983 the company sold its Microdot subsidiary to a group of investors for $121 million. Despite this, the situation became so serious that

Heineman openly entertained the option of selling his company. In 1984 Donald Kelly and Roger Briggs, two executives who lost their jobs at Esmark when the company was acquired by Beatrice, organized an investment group which offered to purchase Northwest Industries for $1.4 billion, or $50 per share. Kelly and Briggs appointed Frederick Rentschler (no relation to Fred Rentschler of United Aircraft) as the new president of Northwest Industries. The arrangement fell through, however, when banks pledged to support the Kelly-Briggs group withdrew.

It was at this time that an energetic young entrepreneur named William Francis Farley appeared. Farley, who has an MBA and a law degree, was owner of the Chicago-based Farley Industries. He made his fortune by building an industrial empire on leveraged buyouts of other companies. Farley offered to purchase each share of Northwest for $42.50 in cash and $7.50 in preferred stock in the new company, in addition to one share of Lone Star Steel, which he intended to spin off as an independent company. Farley's acquisition of Northwest Industries was completed on July 31, 1985, and 71-year-old Ben Heineman, chairman and chief executive officer of Northwest Industries for 29 years, retired.

Farley Industries is a private corporation. By purchasing Northwest Industries, Farley removed the company from public ownership and changed its name to Farley Northwest Industries, Inc. As a subsidiary of the Farley/ Northwest Holding Corporation it carried a debt load of $1.2 billion, as compared to $410 million under Ben Heineman. Generally, leveraged buyouts require the acquisitor to borrow heavily from banks in order to finance their takeovers. The debt is then secured by offering the company as collateral. But many analysts agreed that the price paid for Northwest was too high.

Bill Farley may have agreed. Shortly after the takeover he announced his intention to sell a small oil and gas drilling venture for $50 million, the company's 26% stake in Pogo Producing for $90 million, various real estate properties for $30 million, and Universal Manufacturing, an electrical transformer company, for $70 million. (What was actually sold varied somewhat.) The company retained its Union Underwear subsidiary, which markets its products mostly under the names BVD and Fruit of the Loom, as well as Acme Boot, makers of Acme, Dingo, Dan Post, and Lucchese footwear. In addition to the General Battery Corporation, Farley Northwest operates lead smelters in Texas and Pennsylvania and cotton mills in Alabama and North Carolina.

Farley Northwest Industries began generating a modest but respectable profit in its first year. That profit, however, was already set aside for reducing the company's considerable debt. However, Bill Farley doesn't have to worry about disaffected shareholders; since it's private the company doesn't have any.

FMC CORPORATION

200 East Randolph Drive
Chicago, Illinois 60601
U.S.A.
(312) 861-6000

Public Company
Incorporated: August 10, 1928 as the John Bean
Manufacturing Company
Employees: 28,064
Sales: $3.229 billion
Market Value: $1.407 billion
Stock Index: New York

The billion-dollar FMC Corporation began as a plant sprayer manufacturer toward the end of the 19th century. This manufacturer of defense, industrial and agricultural equipment, and chemicals fell upon hard times some two decades ago, but two extraordinary leaders have shaped it into the strong multinational corporation that it is today.

The roots of the FMC Corporation lie in the John Bean Spray Pump Company established in California in 1884 when Bean invented the hand spray pump. Over the next 34 years he built his product into the preferred pump in the region. Another prosperous local firm in the 1920's was Frank L. Burrell's cannery. The two merged in 1928 to form the John Bean Manufacturing Company, which changed its name to the Food Machinery Corporation the next year. From this manufacturer of simple food production equipment the diverse FMC was to grow.

Bean, not a businessman by nature, passed the management of the company on to his son-in-law, David Christian Crummey, at a fairly early point in time. Upon the merger, control passed on to his son, John David Crummey. While the younger Crummey was a strong voice leading the firm, the hand of another man was evident in the company's actions. This man was Paul L. Davies, Crummey's own son-in-law, who left a banking vice-presidency to become vice-president of Food Machinery. The policies of growth which Davies put into effect kept the company financially healthy throughout the Depression. Davies recognized the cyclical nature of purely agricultural businesses; they depended too much on crop fluctuations. In 1933, therefore, the firm began to expand by purchasing the Peerless Pump Company, whose inexpensive pumps were in high demand during these lean years. This was the beginning of a policy of diversification

which was to bring the company into increasingly varied and prosperous areas.

Food Machinery not only survived the Depression, it prospered, and emerged in the early 1940's prepared for the consistent growth which was to characterize it under Davies. An aggressive and energetic man who worked consistent 12 hour days, Davies used diversification as both a means of expanding the company's market, and a hedge against cyclical weakness in any one branch. In 1943 the company made its first foray into the chemical market by acquiring the Niagara Sprayer and Chemical Company, a strong independent manufacturer of insecticides and fungicides. This move was followed by the 1948 acquisition of Westvaco Chemical Corporation, which produced industrial chemicals. The Niagara merger left Food Machinery in the position of producing not only sprayers and pumps, but the chemicals to put through them; the later merger, upon which the company became the Food Machinery and Chemical Corporation, expanded their chemical product line even more.

Alongside this chemical expansion, Food Machinery's equipment division prospered in the 1940's due to the Second World War. Some months before the United States entered the war, Food Machinery began producing the "Water Buffalo," an amphibious tank which provided important troop mobility over the next crucial years. Other products were adapted for wartime uses as well, such as the orchard sprayer which was to be used for decontamination purposes if necessary, and nailing machines which produced ammunition boxes at an exceedingly high rate.

After the war, the company's production line returned to its earlier emphasis, although defense contracts continue to play an important role to this day. With the war ended, however, the company was at no loss for customers. Wartime reductions produced a market for expensive and technologically advanced food processing equipment, and Food Machinery's business grew. Other existing products were adapted to peacetime uses as they had been in war, with sprayers, for example, being turned to firefighting uses. A drop in earnings occurred the year after the Westvaco acquisition, but by 1950 the company was back on its prosperous track. Davies continued to put money both into diversification, and into research and engineering which led to new products and continued growth.

Every year between 1950 and 1966 the Food Machinery and Chemical Corporation (which changed its name to the FMC Corporation in 1961) showed a financial gain, and the company was a favorite of investors. Their trend toward diversification continued, most notably with the purchase of the American Viscose Corporation in 1963, despite opposition from the antitrust division of the Justice Department. Davies' vigor, vision, and talent for profitable purchases provided a strong center for the company's rather loose management through 1966. In this year, Davies decided to retire. His strategy was to avoid overstaying his productive years, and to leave a strong successor. The man who replaced him as chief executive officer, who had assumed the presidency some few years back, was engineer James M. Hait. It was Davies' intent to leave this hand-picked officer to continue the company's expansion and growth.

Perhaps the choice was an unfortunate one; perhaps certain market trends made some decline inevitable. What is certain is that, in 1967, FMC's financial growth came to an abrupt halt. While Hait would remain chairman of the company until 1971, he was replaced as chief executive officer in 1967 by Jack M. Pope. This year also marked the company's relocation of its headquarters to Chicago, and its acquisition of the Link-Belt Corporation, an equipment manufacturer which quickly proved to have antiquated plants and serious financial difficulties. This purchase, along with the 1963 Avisco acquisition, became a draining point for FMC's finances, instead of increasing its profitability.

In 1968, with Pope as its leader, FMC did show a brief resumption of its upward growth trend. However, this improvement on the books proved to be largely due to an accounting change, and the health of the company was not restored. The growth which had paid off so strongly for Paul Davies was too much for his successors. Even toward the end of Davies' administration, the loose reins under which he had run the company had been a bit too loose for its ever-increasing size. Now, under new management, the control necessary for an improved financial condition was lost. The status of the company declined among investors as its finances weakened. By 1973 FMC stock had fallen from $44 per share to $15.

By the end of the decade Paul Davies' company was experiencing severe financial difficulties. Its management was unable to maintain profitability. The synthetic fiber branch was losing money, and the recession of 1970–71 caused even the strong machinery division to suffer. FMC's profits fell to $39 million from their 1968 level of $75 million. It was at this point that the company appointed a third successor to Davies, one who would finally bring FMC back to financial prosperity. This successor was a Harvard Business School graduate who had been with FMC for 20 years, Robert H. Malott.

From the time that Malott took control of FMC, it was clear that it would not be an easy task to revive the company. Obviously a change in management strategy was called for in order to turn around the company's decline. For Malott, that change began with a recentralization of management. The company's size and relatively loose management procedures had contributed to its decline, so Malott reorganized FMC by consolidating the many branches of the company into two groups for better administrative control.

Realizing that the mere continuation of former company policy was an unworkable strategy, Malott approached his first years as chief executive officer with a different set of policies. Between 1972 and 1978, FMC disposed of 20 product lines which were either immediate financial drains or were soon to be in danger. This was one step that Hait and Pope had apparently been unwilling to take, but it gave new life to the company. Chief among these sales and closings was the 1976 sale of the fiber division. Price cutting in the synthetics market and competition from cotton and polyester (FMC produced primarily rayon) had made this one of the chief money drains and one of Davies' few

untimely purchases. Malott ended this losing struggle by selling the division to the newly-formed Avtex Fibers Inc. He also made other timely decisions, such as the 1976 closing of a pulp mill in Alaska, in the face of strict environmental controls which were about to be imposed. His evaluation of these branches provided the first step toward FMC's recovery.

Malott's financial policies also began to revive FMC during this period. One such policy was his refusal to reduce prices when faced with competition. Instead, Malott cut production, keeping profit margins up. Another keynote of Malott's financial management was his aggressive capital spending. His outlays in research and development made it possible for new products to be developed. In addition, in the two years prior to 1976, FMC put $400 million into high growth areas, such as petroleum equipment and specialty chemicals. The profitability of Malott's policies was almost immediately apparent; by the spring of 1976, with a personnel increase of only 1000 workers, Malott raised sales from $1.3 billion to $2.3 billion, a much-needed $1 billion increase.

By 1976, FMC's great comeback was obvious. In an April article *Forbes* magazine called the corporation "a stronger, better run company than it was in its heyday." Even with the company well on the road to full recovery, however, management policy did not rest with contentment. In 1977, Malott began to decentralize the administrative control of the company in order to facilitate faster growth. The diversification of the company itself suggested somewhat decentralized management, now that it was financially stable. Malott divided the company into nine well-defined groups, centering around their chemical, equipment, and specialty products. The situation differed from earlier times in that final decisions still rested with top management, and close communication was to be maintained. Lower managers were being trained to think in specific terms, those of a world-wide market. This restructuring was to lead the company into its next significant period of growth and expansion.

The years between 1977 and 1980 were not, however, marked solely by unchecked growth. As in any industry, fluctuations were seen in the demand for FMC products. Four of the nine groups, however, remained the strongest: defense equipment, petroleum equipment, industrial chemicals, and agricultural chemicals. Much of the strength of this last category came from the sales of Furadan, still the most popular pesticide for protecting corn, sugar cane, and some 18 other crops. Fluctuations in chemical markets were one reason that FMC, by 1980, was not reporting a financial return at hoped-for rates.

While management was bringing FMC back to prosperity, there were also periods of intense public scrutiny. As the government became more interested in environmental issues, for example, some of FMC's procedures were called into question. Alleged pollution from such chemicals as carbon tetrachloride gave rise to cease-and-desist orders and plant closings throughout the mid-to-late 1970's. FMC was also involved in the major controversy over phosphates during the first half of the decade. In 1970 the company was the second largest producer of the chemicals, which cause premature aging of natural water sites. Court battles on the subject continued through 1975 when a Chicago ordinance banning the chemicals was upheld. Such environmental conflicts, while not damaging the company directly, forced additional internal changes in production.

FMC is also the primary contractor for an advanced armed personnel carrier called the Bradley Fighting Vehicle, developed during the 1970's to counter the introduction of a similar but less sophisticated Soviet model called the BMP. In the early 1980's the Bradley was criticized for a lack of battlefield survivability. FMC and Pentagon officials responded that even the most heavily armoured tanks are not impervious to attack, but nonetheless began to investigate ways to improve the Bradley. About 3000 Bradleys have been delivered, each capable of defeating enemy tanks and other fighting vehicles while moving at high speeds in any kind of weather.

Despite such conflicts, FMC continued its growth and expansion during the 1980's. Plans for new acquisitions were being announced in 1984, and the following year FMC's stock standing was upgraded to "attractive" by an analyst specializing in chemicals firms, who has for a decade seen the field as only a fair risk. Profits and returns increased to record levels. In 1986, however, the picture began to change. Amid concerns about a possible hostile takeover, FMC began to plan a general restructuring of the entire company. Drops in income, due to some declining defense revenues, left the company vulnerable. Management's recapitalization plan, which cleared with stockholders in May, was formulated to shift the distribution of stock away from the public to company employees. The negative side of the plan was the $2 billion in new debt required to finance the program. FMC's stock declined in desirability due to this move, and management admits that it does not expect its stock to recover until 1991.

Another factor in the recent history of FMC involved the insider trading scandal of 1986. Investor Ivan Boesky used illegally gained information about FMC's restructuring to turn a profit of $975,000. In the process, according to the company, his influence cost FMC some $225 million in additional recapitalization costs. This economic stress has laid an even heavier burden on the threatened company.

The future of FMC is now more dependent than ever before upon fluctuations in interest rates and commodity prices, problems with its defense markets, and possible ill effects of the new debt load. While some Wall Street analysts have doubts, the company's management expresses confidence that it can retain its financial viability. The FMC Corporation faces a period of more uncertainty in the next five years than at any other time in its history. However, if a diversified yet structured product line and the kind of firm, creative management exhibited by Robert Malott offer hope for success, FMC has a promising basis for revival.

Principal Subsidiaries: B S & B Engineering Co., Inc.; Intermountain Realty Corp.; Intertrade Corp.; Wayne Inter-American Corp.; Lithium Corp. of America; Marine MCI Corp. The company also lists subsidiaries in the following countries: Argentina, Australia, Austria, Belgium, Brazil, Cameroon, Canada, France, Gabon, Greece, Guatemala, Italy, Lebanon, The Netherlands, Norway, Philippines, Singapore, South Africa, Spain, Switzerland, Thailand, United Kingdom, and Venezuela.

FUQUA INDUSTRIES, INC.

4900 Georgia Pacific Center
Atlanta, Georgia 30303
U.S.A.
(404) 658-9000

Public Company
Incorporated: reincorporated May 6, 1968 as Fuqua
  Industries, Inc.
Employees: 11,000
Sales: $701 million
Market Value: $691 million
Stock Index: New York

Fuqua Industries is a conglomerate with a history of acquiring, reorganizing and then selling companies. This may seem like an unstable or risky way to conduct a multimillion dollar business, but Fuqua Industries has grown steadily since its inception in 1965. One of the keys to Fuqua's success is that it concentrates on those operations that can hold susbstantial shares of their respective markets. The three most profitable divisions of Fuqua Industries are also the oldest: Snapper brand lawn and garden equipment, Colorcraft wholesale photofinishing, and a network of sporting goods manufacturers. These have been the operating base of Fuqua since 1967.

Fuqua is a thriving corporation because of an innovative management team at the highest executive level. John Brooks Fuqua, the founder and current chairman, astutely identifies profitable financial ventures. Lawrence P. Klamon, the president since 1981, proved himself when he engineered a reconstruction of Fuqua Industries in the early 1980's. Fuqua has previously acquired companies rather aggressively, gauging success almost wholly by annual sales and profits, less so by the coherence of industries or Fuqua's reputation on Wall Street. In the past decade, however, John Brooks Fuqua and Klamon have chosen to invest conservatively in new manufacturing operations, but also to take some risks with a number of sophisticated financial maneuvers.

Raised by his grandparents on a tobacco farm in central Virginia, John Brooks decided early that he did not want to become a farmer. At 14 he ordered a 25-cent pamphlet on operating a ham radio and soon taught himself enough about radio to earn an operators license. After his graduation from high school, he began working for the U.S. Merchant Marines as a radio operator. At 19 John Brooks landed the job of chief engineer at a broadcasting station in South Carolina. During this period, he borrowed books by mail from Duke University on banking, finance and management. He read about business avidly in lieu of going to college. One of the first things he learned from these books was that a successful businessman should know how to use other people's money. Practicing these lessons over and over again, John Brooks bought land, established credit with local banks, borrowed money for construction, and then sold the whole property for a profit.

John Brooks' tenure as a radio station engineer was short-lived. He quickly made up his mind to either own or manage his own station. After evaluating the market in several southern cities, he settled on Augusta, Georgia. With three investors to finance the venture, John Brooks became part owner and manager of the new station, and soon made an initial investment of $250,000 in equipment, expanding the operation into television broadcasting. John Brooks took this station public many years later with Fuqua Industries and finally sold what grew to become a network of stations for $30 million in 1981.

Becoming increasingly skillful at turning assets into profits, John Brooks found an opportunity to test his theory that "buying profits would be faster and less risky than growing profits." He discovered that the owner of a Royal Crown Cola bottling plant had accumulated excess profits and neither paid them out in dividends nor reinvested in the company. Under the current law, such profits would be subject to gross penalty taxes. Persuading the owner that it was in the company's interest, John Brooks purchased the plant with the owner's excess profits. When John Brooks sold the plant three years later, he was already testing other markets. A wholesale baker company and a multimillion dollar auto financing business were sold when he developed political ambitions.

In 1957 John Brooks Fuqua was elected to the Georgia State Legislature. He served as chairman of the Senate Banking and Financing Committee and the House Banking Committee, and from 1962–66 he was chairman of the state Democratic Party. Though he loved politics and recommends that every businessman take a greater interest in government, John Brooks's real ambition was to build a successful conglomerate. Fuqua Industries was founded at this time with the purchase of Natco Corporation for $3 million.

Natco, a brick and tile manufacturer, was the smallest company on the New York Stock Exchange. Despite a downward trend in profits, Natco had a 75 year legacy with solid assets, no debts and a book value double the market value. It served Fuqua Industries primarily as a vehicle for going public; John Brooks served Natco by turning it back into a very profitable company in three years. Although it was sold quickly, Natco launched Fuqua Industries into a period of acquiring interests in a miscellany of industries, including lawn and garden equipment, photofinishing, sporting goods, yachting equipment, trucking, broadcasting, mobile homes, and movie theaters.

Fuqua's stock remained highly valued until 1970 when the recession and increasing market pressure on conglomerates forced stock prices to decline. From 1969–74, Fuqua stock dropped from $41 to $3 a share. John Brooks realized that the conglomerate needed to write off or sell unprofitable companies to reduce Fuqua's debt-to-equity ratio. Fuqua trimmed $70 million in sales from it total revenue by selling the large boat manufacturing division, a host of movie theaters, and some fringe sporting goods companies, taking a $20 million write-off and losing $16 million. Fortunately, the cash inflow of $45 million from the sale of many companies, plus the sale of $60 million in debentures and stock, enabled Fuqua to pay off much of its short-term bank debt and refinance the remainder into long-term debt.

This put Fuqua on a sound financial foundation, despite a continuing burden of debt. The reorganization soon provided Fuqua with the opportunity to test a new investment strategy that emerged when John Brooks sought to buy a widely recognized, multinational company that already held a substantial share of its market. His eye was on Avis Corporation, whose stock had been put up for sale by International Telephone and Telegraph in 1977. John Brooks was outbid by Norton Simon Inc., but his thwarted attempt to acquire this billion dollar company energized the Fuqua staff. Identifying another conglomerate called National Industries that was losing money due to poor management, John Brooks deferred to his staff. "My young tigers wanted to turn National around and be heroes," he said. "I'm not that interested in climbing mountains any more. But they run the company. I try to give them the tools to do it."

Fuqua purchased National Industries in early 1978, paying a 55% premium over the stock price but still acquiring it for a total sum substantially under book value. Fuqua paid $60 million for National, only half of it in cash and the rest in Fuqua stock and debentures. Since the company had $45 million in cash assets, John Brooks claims that he "bought them with their own cash."

National comprised a motley assortment of companies —some profitable, some not. Its primary interests were in oil distribution, a farm equipment retail chain, a dairy industry, and an East coast soft drink company. Immediately after acquisition, Fuqua sold the unprofitable companies. For the companies Fuqua retained, management personnel and strategy was reviewed and, in some cases, changed. Finally, Fuqua trimmed operating costs by $1 million by consolidating National's disparate insurance plans and bank financing under the Fuqua system. This centralization of resources also cut National's overall expenses in tax, legal, accounting, and public relations departments.

Within 18 months after merging, three National subsidiaries were sold for $66 million in cash, more than what Fuqua had paid for the entire holding company. National turned out to be a highly profitable investment, as well as a good financial exercise in divestiture. By 1978 Fuqua's earnings had jumped by 82%, exceeding $2 billion in sales by 1980.

Stock prices were still much lower, however, than what the corporation was worth. This prompted Fuqua's senior vice president of Finance and Administration, Lawrence P. Klamon, to present John Brooks with a proposal to shrink the corporation to one-third its size. The reason for such a drastic divestment, Klamon maintained, was intuition as much as a response to Fuqua's decline on Wall Street. The corporation's diversity threatened its reputation, and the quality of its investments were not consistent: some companies operated within unstable industries, some had constitutionally low profit margins, others had assets valued much higher than their earnings substantiated.

John Brooks agreed to the proposal in 1980 and Fuqua sold its trucking company and three television stations. Lano Corporation, a petroleum distributor, and Hawthorne Mellody were sold in 1981. The remaining movie theaters and the Tractor Supply Corporation, operating a store retail chain, was sold by the close of 1983. None of the operations was unprofitable, but Klamon reasoned that they did not fit Fuqua's new strategy of investing in high-profit, high-quality manufactured products under stable market conditions. Hence the trucking and petroleum companies, while proving themselves to be the greatest contributors to Fuqua's revenue at one point, operated in highly unstable markets. Trucking deregulation was imminent, which would adversely affect profits. Retail operations were inconsistent with Fuqua's aim to invest in manufacturing. The dairy industry's profit margins were too low, while the television stations were too highly valued—they were sold for roughly 20 times earnings. The divestiture was successul; Fuqua's sales had shrunk from over $2 billion to $732 million and stock prices quickly recovered.

During this restructuring phase, John Brooks contemplated going private. After consulting a private investment firm, Forstmann Little, Fuqua proposed a buyout of all outstanding stock at $20 a share, five dollars over the market price. Less than two weeks after the offer, Forstmann Little itself staged a takeover attempt by persuading four top executives to present a proposal to the board of directors offering $25 a share to all stockholders. John Brooks promptly fired the four executives, and although the board rejected the Forstmann Little proposal, the higher bid made Fuqua's offer to buy out at $20 per share impossible. John Brooks abandoned plans to go private but tendered an offer to purchase 20% of the oustanding stock, partly to prevent any future takeover attempts. Surprisingly, Fuqua's offer attracted over twice the number of shares John Brooks had anticipated buying. By 1981 Fuqua had acquired 72% of all outstanding stock at a total cost of $186 million.

Fuqua has since concentrated on its commitment to shareholders to increase the value of its holdings, not the size of the company, by adopting a more conservative approach to new acquisitions and investments. By those standards an eligible company should already hold a substantial share of its market and have a long history or familiar brand name products. Fuqua prefers to invest in products or services that cater to individual consumers, avoiding businesses that are capital intensive, require competitive pricing (e.g., construction), or are dependent on a high level of technical expertise or sophistication. Companies which have established efficient and cost-effective manufacturing plants in or outside of the United States are also favorable Fuqua targets.

Hostile takeovers never played a large role in Fuqua's acquisition strategy; approval of the new company's management is a prerequisite for all Fuqua mergers. "You have to have a feeling that things will mesh," Klamon maintains. "Intuition plays an important role in the overall picture." So with most newly acquired companies, John Brooks and Klamon have no intention of changing business policy or personnel. To demonstrate this, during the first few months following a merger, Fuqua does not initiate communication with the newly acquired company's executives.

During the years 1980–84, profits from longstanding investments tripled. Fuqua's three main divisions have never been unprofitable, but during this period the corporation's financial base and stock prices quadrupled. Snapper (lawn and garden equipment) grew from a company with nearly $10 million in yearly sales in 1967 to $260 million in sales nearly 20 years later. Still headed by the company's original founder, Snapper maintains professional loyalty to its dealers and service centers and refuses to sell through discount or mass merchandisers. As a result, the company carves out a larger share of the market for quality lawn and garden equipment each year. Colorcraft's photofinishing revenues grew from $3 million to over $300 million in a 20 year span. The company continues to grow as it acquires other smaller operations such as Colorfoto Inc., Drewry Photocolor and Berkey Photo Inc. The sporting goods division has wide-ranging interests in camping equipment, boat trailers and various athletic supplies, including exclusive contracts with professional sports teams.

Fuqua's investments since restructuring, however, have not been invariably successful. With the profitability of its three main divisions secure, Fuqua invested heavily in American Seating Company, acquiring it wholly by 1983. Fuqua intended to build it up into another consistent contributor to annual sales. However, prior to the company's sale in early 1987, John Brooks admitted that the venture was a mistake because the company was so badly managed.

In 1986 Fuqua entered the financial services field by acquiring the Georgia Federal Bank. This seems to be an area of business that suits Fuqua and will probably take the place of American Seating as the fourth primary division.

Although annual sales of Fuqua have not increased substantially since the restructuring in the early 1980's, stock prices have remained high—between $25 and $35 per share. Yet Fuqua Industries remains a paradoxical corporation. While it concentrates most of its resources on financially and managerially accountable profitmakers, Fuqua's most important resource, John Brooks himself, is carving out a new way to earn a profit.

Early in 1983 Fuqua purchased a controlling interest in Triton Group Ltd., a floundering real estate investment trust. Though it was never wholly owned by Fuqua and sold in 1986, John Brooks directed Triton into two highly profitable acquisitions, including Simplicity Pattern, maker of home sewing patterns, and Republic Corporation, a metal products enterprise. Fuqua's interest in Triton Group was its eligibility for tax loss carry forwards (amounting to $200 million) that could shelter the company's future profits for a limited period of time, freeing cash to repay debts and make new acquisitions. Concerning this kind of investment strategy John Brooks has said that, "Investing in bankrupt companies is a very sophisticated game. There are still not too many players in that area."

Although John Brooks hinted at retirement in the late 1970's, he currently appears to be as committed as ever to working at the office. Admitting that he has never developed leisure interests outside of reading other companies' balance sheets, John Brooks seems to realize that even in retirement he would be pursuing business ventures.

Principal Subsidiaries: Ajay Enterprises Corp.; Aliso Management, Inc.; American Seating Co.; Colorcraft Corp.; Fuqua Homes, Inc.; Fuqua SHL, Inc.; Fuqua World Trade Corp.; Georgia Federal Banks, FSB; Hutch Sporting Goods, Inc.; Nelson Recreation Products, Inc.; Weather-Rite, Inc.; Willow Hosiery Co., Inc.

Further Reading: The Story of Fuqua Industries Inc. by J.B. Fuqua, New York, Newcomen Society, 1973.

GREYHOUND CORPORATION

Greyhound Tower
Phoenix, Arizona 85077
U.S.A.
(602) 248-4000

Public Company
Incorporated: September 20, 1926
Employees: 36,050
Sales: $2.647 billion
Market Value: $1.401 billion
Stock Index: New York

Greyhound Lines has been the leader in the motorcoach industry since 1930. Through the decades, however, the veteran bus company has had to face a series of formidable competitors: trains, the automobile and inexpensive air travel. In the 1960's Greyhound realized that it was going to have to alter its strategy and diversify into non-motorcoach related areas as airfares decreased and car ownership increased. Greyhound is presently committed to expansion into consumer products and its specialty, the service industry.

The bus company that became Greyhound was founded in 1913 by Carl Wickman. Wickman was an emigrant who settled in Hibbing, Minnesota because the weather there reminded him of his native Sweden. Wickman's first ambition was to be a car salesman, but when he couldn't sell a single seven-passenger "Hupmobile" he founded America's first bus company.

The company started by transporting miners from Hibbing to Alice, Minnesota, where the Mesaba Iron Range was located. The round-trip fare was 25 cents. The secret to Wickman's early success was maximizing ridership, which took the form of stuffing 18 miners into a seven passenger Hupmobile. Wickman's revenues began to increase and he took on partners who helped him invest in larger vehicles. Since there were no buses in 1914, Wickman had large touring cars, mostly Studebakers and Packards, sawed in half and elongated. In 1916 the company, then known as "Hibbing Transportation," had its own bus station which was located in a firehouse.

Carl Eric Wickman and his partners were not the only motor coach entrepreneurs in Hibbing. By 1915 a motorcycle racer named Ralph Bogan began transporting miners from Hibbings to Alice for 50 cents. Hibbing Transport responded by reducing its fares to 40 cents. Thus began the first known price war among bus companies. Wickman eventually offered Bogan a share in Hibbing Transport, establishing a pattern of merging with competitors that would eventually result in the formation of the largest bus company in the world.

By the mid-1920's Wickman's company, renamed Mesaba Transportation Company, was worth several million dollars and had numerous partners. In 1925 the man who had started it all left the company and purchased a fledgling firm known as the White Bus Line. This company merged with others to form the Motor Transit Corporation, nicknamed "Greyhound."

Greyhound came along at a time when the idea of the "vacation" became firmly entrenched in the American psyche. The motorcoach, whose operating costs were a small fraction compared to trains, soon became the transportation of choice for vacationers, salesmen and even jazz bands.

Despite the popularity of this new form of tranportation, Greyhound nearly failed after the stock market crash of 1929. In 1929 Greyhound's net income was $1.3 million, but this dropped to $38,000 in 1930. The present title of the company, Greyhound Corporation, was adopted in 1930, but by 1932 Greyhound was $140,000 in debt. It was the 1933 World's Fair that saved Greyhound by dramatically increasing ridership. Carl Jackson, a historian who has studied Greyhound, claims that ridership also increased after a 1935 movie entitled, "It Happened One Night," was released. In this movie the then famous movie star Claudette Colbert takes a cross-country bus trip.

During the following years Greyhound revenues climbed to four, five and then six million dollars before the end of the decade. In 1939 management of Greyhound anticipated the coming war, and began to stockpile parts. Greyhound suspected both that its buses would have a part in the U.S. war effort and that its supplier, General Motors, would be busy manufacturing jeeps. Both intuitions were correct.

One of Greyhound's principal duties during the war was to transport workers to shipyards and munitions factories. Military personnel were often transported via Greyhound to their bases. Wartime responsibilities and gas shortages made it difficult for Greyhound to serve all its civilian customers, and the company actually used advertisements to discourage ridership. "Serve American Now So You Can See America Later" and "Don't Travel Unless Your Trip Is Essential" were two Greyhound advertisements during World War II.

A 35 m.p.h. speed limit, imposed to save rubber, and a continual shortage of parts annoyed Greyhound management throughout the war. America's most well-known motorcoach company found consolation in its balance sheets however, as profits climbed to $10 million by the mid-1940's. At that time, Greyhound served over six thousand towns and carried one-fourth of all U.S. bus passengers—more than any other company. Its bus routes stretched like a net across the continental U.S. and Canada.

In 1946 Carl Wickman retired as president of Greyhound and returned to Sweden. There he was knighted by King Gustav V "for serving the unserved." Upon Wickman's retirement, Orville Caesar became president of

Greyhound. Orville Caesar lobbied intensely for wider highways to accommodate his buses and fought to change the laws restricting the length of a bus to 35 feet. His new "Scenicruisers" were 40 feet long and illegal in certain states.

The growth of Greyhound slowed to 2% a year in the late 1940's. Postwar prosperity brought with it thousands of new passenger cars, and the increase in cars meant fewer bus patrons. In addition, severe labor problems did not help the company. A series of walkouts in 1950 was prompted by a well-publicized incident in which 19 drivers suspected of skimming fares were lured to a hotel and held there against their will for 36 hours. Labor difficulties were nothing new for Greyhound. During World War II the Navy commandeered shipyard buses when the Greyhound drivers decided to strike.

In 1956 President Arthur Genet decided to move Greyhound into the car rental business. There were several reasons for this move. One reason was that the car rental offices could operate out of Greyhound's urban terminals. The rental business would allow Greyhound to capitalize on something that had been a problem, namely, the popularity of the automobile. There was an unforeseen problem with the car rental strategy, however, and this was that the typical Greyhound bus passenger, to whom the rental business was geared, was not likely to rent a car. Within two years the car rental division was depressing revenues and had to be abandoned.

Not all of Greyhound's early attempts at diversification were as unsuccessful as the car rental business. Beginning in the 1940's Greyhound established a chain of restaurants, called "Post Houses," in its larger terminals. These were successful, as was the package express business, whose implementation cost almost nothing at all.

Until the mid-1960's, Greyhound was primarily a bus company, and company management did everything it could to prevent passengers from defecting to trains or planes. A large proportion of Greyhound's passengers were black, and by the early 1960's Greyhound's marketing strategy was oriented toward blacks. Greyhound was the transportation of choice for the freedom riders, in fact Greyhound buses were even attacked by the Ku Klux Klan. Seregationist laws requiring blacks to ride in the back of the bus were contended by Greyhound.

The company was motivated by economic considerations to promote black ridership, but it must also be noted that Greyhound was one of the first companies to implement something resembling an affirmative action program. Long before the civil rights movement Greyhound could be described as progressive in its hiring policy towards blacks, particularly black bus drivers. In the early 1970's Greyhound began to hire women drivers and, at the present time, blacks and women are represented on the Greyhound board of directors.

Greyhound began to diversify in earnest during the 1960's. Previous to 1961, the company's diversification had been limited to the operation of restaurants in terminals, a van line, a package express service and the manufacture of buses and bus accessories. All of Greyhound's original expansions were connected to its main business, namely, interurban transportation. Even the unsuccessful car

rental business was meant to appeal to bus passengers, who were expected to rent a Greyhound car during their stay in the city. However, after 1962 Greyhound began to diversify into businesses not related to transportation.

In 1962 Greyhound purchased Booth Leasing and soon became the largest industrial leasing company in the world. Among the items offered for leasing were computers, locomotives and jet airplanes. In 1966 a separate computer leasing company was formed. In addition, a money order firm, Traveller's Express, and an insurance company, General Fire and Casualty, were added to Greyhound's list of purchases by 1965. Greyhound's food services were expanded in 1964 with the acquisition of a roadside restaurant chain, Horne's, and Prophet Foods, a large industrial and institutional caterer. In 1967 Greyhound continued to make acquisitions in the service industry. One of these purchases, Aircraft Services International, provided ground handling and janitorial services. Greyhound also began to provide food for the airlines.

The companies purchased by Greyhound during its acquisition program during the 1960's were all small, and the majority of Greyhound profits still came from the operation of buses. Even after its expansion, food services only accounted for 5% of profits, and financial and leasing activities for 20%.

The diversification of Greyhound into non-bus activity was necessary because the motorcoach industry was steadily shrinking, partly in response to an increase in inexpensive airfares. Even with some lucrative acquisitions, Greyhound lost money because profits from the bus line were down. Bus line profits hit a low point in 1967, when riots after the death of Martin Luther King depressed ridership.

Company management thought that a major acquisition would help Greyhound considerably. As a result, in 1970 Greyhound acquired Armour Foods for $400 million. To reduce its investment Greyhound immediately sold $225 million of Armour assets, leaving only the meat-packing and consumer products operations. Armour's pharmaceutical division was sold to Revlon in 1977. Despite some problems with the low-margin meat packing business, the two remaining divisions generated a net income of $25 million on an investment that had been reduced to $100 million. Armour's contribution to Greyhound was superseded, however, by the financial services division with 1978 profits of $25.8 million.

Greyhound's success with its expansion into financial services and its initial success with Armour continued to be overshadowed by difficulties with bus operations throughout the 1970's. Though some decline in ridership was inevitable as people chose the convenience of air travel, many of Greyhound's problems resulted from poor management. One major problem was that Greyhound scheduling and routing favored long-distance ridership, while over 80% of its customers used Greyhound for distances of 200 miles or less. This inappropriate routing and scheduling discouraged some short-haul passengers. So did the bus stations themselves, whose interiors were often regarded as uncomfortable and unpleasant surroundings; in fact, the washrooms were a major passenger complaint. To aggravate matters, rather than making an investment in upgrading facilities the bus division engaged in a costly price and advertising war with Trailways motorcoach company.

In 1978 Greyhound Corporation chief executive officer Gerald Trautman realized that the company's health still depended on its bus operations. Since he wanted to leave the company in good financial condition when he retired, Trautman postponed his retirement, demoted his protégé James Kerrigan, and placed himself in charge of the bus operations that Kerrigan had supervised. After Trautman took charge of the bus line, more attention was paid to details such as clean washrooms and bus maintenance. Measures like these, coupled with the gas shortage (which made car travel less desirable), helped increase bus profits 83% between 1978 and 1979.

In 1982 Trautman decided to retire. His successor, John Teets, while not unappreciative of Trautman's final efforts, had a different approach to the management of Greyhound. Upon becoming chief executive officer Teets immediately began to sell subsidiaries that were not performing well. The meat-packing division, which was earning $10 million on sales of $2 billion, was among the first to be sold. Teets blamed higher than average employee wages for Armour's difficulties; when the unions refused to accept a reduction in pay Teets closed all 29 meat-packing plants in one day.

Teets' handling of the violent 47 day bus driver's strike was no different. This strike was precipitated by management's demand that the drivers accept a 17% cut in wages and benefits. After a bitter series of negotiation meetings, the drivers were forced to swallow a 15% wage reduction. Greyhound had won a major concession, but the price was costly—$25 million dollars in lost revenues. On the whole, however, the corporation responded well to Teets' management. Return on equity climbed to 12% and should continue to rise. Had a customer not defrauded Greyhound leasing of of $19 million dollars, 1985 profits would have been up 12% from the year before.

Greyhound's future plans, according to Teets, involve a larger commitment to food, convention and travel services, and also consumer products. Purex, a food and soap manufacturer, was added to the Armour/Dial consumer products line. Although financial services provide approximately one-third of company profits, Teets does not anticipate any new acquisitions in that area. As for the bus line, it will be downgraded to accommodate the irreversible changes in transportation. Many of the valuable urban terminals have been and will be sold as the company concentrates on providing service for airports and suburban areas.

Principal Subsidiaries: Greyhound Lines, Inc.; Texas, New Mexico & Oklahoma Coaches, Inc.; Vermont Transit Co., Inc.; Motor Coach Industries; Transportation Manufacturing Corp.; Universal Coach Parts, Inc.; Dial Corp.; Armour International Co.; Greyhound Capital Corp.; Greyhound Realty Corp.; MCI Acceptance Corp.; Verex Corp.; Aircraft Service International, Inc.; Consultants & Designers Inc.; Dispatch Services, Inc.; Faber Enterprises, Inc.; Florida Export Tobacco Co., Inc.; Glacier Park, Inc. (80%); Premier Cruise Lines, Ltd. (Cayman Islands); Travelers Express Company, Inc.

Further Reading: Hounds of the Road: A History of the Greyhound Bus Company by Carlton Jackson, Bowling Green, Ohio, Popular Press, 1984; *The Greyhound Story: From Hibbing to Everywhere* by Oscar Schisgall, New York, Doubleday, 1985.

Gulf+Western Inc.

GULF & WESTERN INC.

One Gulf & Western Plaza
New York, New York 10023
U.S.A.
(212) 333-7000

Public Company
Incorporated: April 18, 1967
Employees: 18,800
Sales: $2.290 billion
Market Value: $4.817 billion
Stock Index: New York

After years of conducting operations in everything from auto parts to zinc, Gulf & Western has recently narrowed its focus. Today, its primary businesses are in entertainment, financial services, and consumer products. While the company perhaps no longer lives up to the acquisitive image sometimes attributed to it, Gulf & Western nonetheless remains a large conglomerate with nearly $3 billion in revenue and nearly 20,000 employees. All that for a company whose first business in auto parts, the company founder admitted years later, "never mounted to a hill of beans."

Charles George Bluhdorn had emigrated to the United States from Austria in 1942. After experimenting with some disappointing commodities import-export businesses, he found success importing coffee from Brazil and Africa through his Fortuna Coffee Company. However, the coffee business fluctuated wildly, and Bluhdorn was searching for an acquisition in an industry offering greater security.

The large, rapidly growing auto parts business seemed to offer that security, since auto parts sales volume is nominally affected by economic downturns. During times when car production decreases, drivers run their cars longer and thus use more replacement parts. When car sales increase, auto parts sales to new cars also rise, and there are more cars on the road that will eventually need replacement parts.

Bluhdorn also wanted a publicly traded company whose stock he could use to buy other companies. Michigan Plating & Stamping Company fit both criteria. The Grand Rapids based company, with sales of $8.4 million, had an almost worthless contract to supply rear bumpers to Studebakers and an American Stock Exchange listing.

In 1956 Bluhdorn secured a controlling interest in Michigan Plating and joined its board of directors. The next year Bluhdorn merged Michigan Plating with Beard & Stone Electric Company, a Houston-based auto parts distributor. Later, in 1958 Bluhdorn renamed the company Gulf & Western Corporation, because of the company's location on the Gulf of Mexico and his belief that most of its growth would come in the Western United States, where automobile sales were increasing rapidly.

With Detroit setting postwar production records and the number of cares on the road increasing steadily, Gulf & Western acquired a number of private auto-parts warehouses and distributors.

In 1965, as Gulf & Western's annual sales approached $200 million, Bluhdorn decided the time had come for the company to diversify. He began searching for a company with large cash reserves which he could use to purchase still more companies. Harold U. Zerbe, a Pennsylvania business man who had joined Gulf & Western's board when Bluhdorn bought his regional auto parts distributorship, knew of a company with such assets. New Jersey Zinc, a large mining and chemical company on whose board Zerbe was also a member, had acquired a large amount of cash that management didn't know what to do with. Managers wanted to use the money to expand operations, while the group of controlling owners wanted to enlarge the company's investment portfolio.

In a matter of days Bluhdorn arranged an $84 million loan from Chase Manhattan Bank, and Gulf & Western acquired a large amount of the company's stock. Gulf & Western sided with the company management in the financial dispute, and by early 1966 the conglomerate Gulf & Western was born. The acquisition helped to improve Gulf & Western's total sales from about $180 million to almost $300 million, and almost to triple the company's earnings to $17 million.

Now that Gulf & Western had entered into a field beyond the business of automotive parts, Bluhdorn began looking for companies in any industry whose undervalued assets he could use to borrow against heavily and purchase more companies. In 1966 Paramount Pictures Corporation became his next target.

Like most large movie companies at that time, Paramount was suffering heavy losses on its feature film productions. It had discontinued producing television programs, and it was leasing old movies on poor terms. The company, however, had hidden assets, especially its extensive real estate, including the downtown movie theaters of Famous Players in Canada, and also its old movies which, if negotiated properly, could be sold to television for large profits.

Gulf & Western paid $125 million for Paramount and, in return, Gulf & Western's sales were improved to $450 million, ranking the company in the top 110 U.S. manufacturing companies. Bluhdorn made himself president of Paramount and promoted Martin S. Davis, a Paramount vice president, to executive vice president.

In the meantime, Gulf & Western hadn't neglected its primary business of auto parts. Its operations had grown to 33 auto parts warehouses and 150 auto parts distribution outlets in 28 states by 1966. It also had a franchise operation in Mexico and operations in Nassau. Even as the Paramount negotiations were proceeding, Gulf & Western had acquired a European auto parts distributor in an attempt to gain a large share of that market.

In 1967 Bluhdorn's fondness for commodities again surfaced when Gulf & Western paid $54 million for South Puerto Rico Sugar Company. Most of the company's operations were in the Dominican Republic, where it owned the extensive Romana sugar mill and 300,000 acres of land. Nearly half of the land was used to produce sugar cane and, at the peak of the cane-cutting season, the company employed 19,000 people, making it the country's largest private employer as well as the largest taxpayer and landowner.

The next year Gulf & Western purchased 23 companies, including Consolidated Cigar, its first venture into the consumer products field, E.W. Bliss, Universal American, Brown Company, and Associates Investment Company. With one billion in assets, the Associates Investment Company, in the consumer financing field, became the largest single contributor to Gulf & Western's earnings. Those acquisitions brought the total number of companies that Gulf & Western had acquired since its formation to 130.

In 1968 Gulf & Western's sales surpassed the one billion mark for the first time, reaching $1.3 billion and producing a net income of $69.8 million. Bluhdorn, the company's largest shareholder, watched the value of his one million shares climb to $22 million. Due to its accelerated acquisition program, Gulf & Western's annual sales gains and earnings were much better than other conglomerates, though the price earnings ratio of its securities remained among the lowest.

That year *Fortune* magazine attributed much of Gulf & Western's success to its good management and conservative acquisition strategy. Only 95 people worked at company headquarters, with control resting in the hands of approximately six or eight officers. To manage the large conglomerate, Bluhdorn divided the company into profit centers, and made the vice presidents of each group part of the corporate staff. Bluhdorn financed most of the acquisitions with company securities, believing that "the best buy you can make today is to put out paper and know that twenty years from now you can put out the same amount of money." However, because the company's securities were selling at low price to earnings ratios, it was forced to buy small companies (usually family run) in noncyclic industries and rely on Bluhdorn's business acumen to increase their sales.

Gulf & Western even profited from most of its unsuccessful takeover attempts. In 1968, for instance, the company purchased 8% of Pan Am stock, hoping to exploit the airline's new 747 airplane and its extensive routes, and develop resort complexes around the world. Yet Pan Am chairman and chief executive officer Harold Gray was uninterested. A House Judiciary Subcommittee, however, was interested and within a month announced it was investigating the purchase. Gulf & Western quickly got rid of the Pan Am stock, selling the largest share to Resorts International Inc., while making a significant profit.

During that same year, Gulf & Western attempted to buy Armour Company, whose sales were three times its own. Bluhdorn figured that Armour's non-meatpacking assets were worth more than the market's valuation of the company even if he bought nearly 100% of stock. After being discouraged by the Justice Department and watching Gulf & Western's stock plummet 13 points in three weeks, Bluhdorn dropped the bid and sold the stock at a $16.5 million profit.

Similarly, when Gulf & Western was forced to sell the shares it had purchased in Sinclair because its management resisted the move, Gulf & Western nonetheless profited by selling its interest to Atlantic Richfield for $145 a share when it had originally paid $72.

In the meantime, Gulf & Western had built up a $244 million stock portfolio, which was unusually large for an industrial company. Besides receiving dividends, Gulf & Western benefited from the right to include on its balance sheets a percentage of the profits of any company in which it held more than a 20% stake.

In 1969 Wall Street analysts, congressmen and the media charged that conglomerates inflated their earnings by promotional tricks with their accounting procedures. As a result of this anti-conglomerate sentiment, Gulf & Western's stock dropped 30 points in a short period, costing shareholders $500 million and lowering the company's already dismal price earnings ratio to less than eight times earnings. The combination of depressed stock and the climate in Washington brought Gulf & Western's fast-paced acquisition phase to an end, forcing the company to rely on internal growth, which had been running at 18%.

However, there was also some good news. In 1972 Paramount, which was close to bankruptcy when acquired, recorded its highest box-offices revenues in history. And, generally speaking, during the mid-1970's Gulf & Western managed to keep its earnings mounting when Litton, Fuqua, Bangor Punta, and other conglomerates had fallen on hard times.

In 1975 the company's operations in the Dominican Republic became a source of trouble. The U.S. Securities and Exchange Commission charged the company with illegally withholding more than $38 million in profits owed to the government of the Dominican Republic. The following year, the National Council of Churches proposed unsuccessfully that Gulf & Western disclose detailed data on payrates for sugar workers and relationships with union and government officials. Gulf & Western defeated this proposal, while Bluhdorn said that Gulf & Western paid the highest wages of any U.S. concern with facilities in Latin America.

In 1977 Gulf & Western bought Madison Square Garden for double market price. Bluhdorn was after the company's vastly undervalued real estate, including a Manhattan office building, land around New York's Roosevelt Raceway and Chicago's Washington Park.

Public image problems continued to plague Gulf & Western. In 1978 the company spent $3.3 million to print its annual report in *Time* magazine, hoping to raise its price earnings ratio from a low multiple of four. However, this strategy didn't work. One year later, *Forbes* magazine reported on Bluhdorn's "$400 million credibility gap." According to *Forbes*, due to the fact that Wall Street didn't trust Bluhdorn, the company's stock was probably trading at a price/earnings ratio two points less than it would have under other management, costing shareholders $400 million.

Later that year the SEC mounted a second investigation, accusing Bluhdorn and Don F. Gaston, an executive vice president, of a wide range of misconduct, including charges that the two executives had the company's pension fund make "inappropriate" investments in companies where they had a personal investment. The agency charged that the trading benefited Gulf & Western and its executive officers, but hurt the pension fund.

In 1980 the SEC and management at Gulf & Western reached a settlement in the investigation of the company's Dominican Republic operations originally started in 1975. Gulf & Western agreed to spend $39 million over seven years in order to fund a social and economic development program in the Dominican Republic. The second SEC investigation was settled in 1981. No restitution was called for under the terms of the agreement.

In early 1983 Bluhdorn died of a heart attack at the age of 56 while flying back from a business trip to the Dominican Republic. Martin S. Davis then became Gulf & Western's vice chairman and chief executive officer. Davis immediately set out to streamline the company's operations from seven operating groups into three units, focused on the areas of entertainment, financial services, and consumer products. To accomplish this, he restructured the company's management and sold the company's stock portfolio, bringing in $750 million. At the same time he began selling businesses that didn't fit into the three main units. Within months Gulf & Western sold Consolidated Cigar Company and put up for sale fifty other units representing 20% of sales and assets, including chemicals, concrete equipment, mechanical presses and racetrack operations, resulting in $359 million in cash and notes.

With its cash reserve rapidly increasing, the company had become an attractive takeover target. Consequently, later that year the company's directors authorized a stock repurchase of up to 10 million shares. The company quickly bought back seven million shares from financier Carl Lindner for $29.95 a share, and purchased an additional one million shares off the market.

In 1984 Gulf & Western continued its highly-focused acquisition program, paying $180 million for the remaining 73% of Esquire, Inc. that it didn't already own. The company also acquired Prentice-Hall, Inc. for $710 million and Glen & Company, a publisher, for $100 million. Also that year, Gulf & Western sold its sugar and related holdings in the Dominican Republic and Florida for $200 million, and agreed to sell the site of old Madison Square Gardens for $100 million.

Gulf & Western completed its transformation into a tightly focused company during 1985 by selling its consumer and industrial products group to Wickes Company for $1 billion in cash. The sale left Gulf & Western producing a company with $3.7 billion in entertainment and communication assets and $7 billion in financial service assets. As a result, in a short period of time the company's stock price more than doubled from $18 a share to $41.25.

With the company's operations strictly defined, Gulf & Western's future looks more secure than ever. Davis is said to be interested in acquiring broadcasting and publishing companies. And with more than $3 billion in sales and $400 million in profits, he clearly has a solid base on which to expand.

Principal Subsidiaries: Allyn & Bacon, Inc.; G & W Canada, Inc.; G & W Holding Corp.; Prentice-Hall, Inc.; Gulf & Western Realty Corp.; Madison Square Garden Corp.; Modern Curriculum Press, Inc.; Paramount Pictures Corp.; Simon & Schuster, Inc.; Thirtieth Century Corp.; Esquire, Inc.

Further Reading: The Gulf & Western Story by Charles G. Bluhdorn, New York, Newcomen Society, 1973.

HITACHI LTD.

6, Kanda Surugadai 4-chome
Chiyoda-ku, Tokyo 101
Japan
03 (258) 1111

Public Company
Incorporated: 1920
Employees: 77,135
Sales: ¥2.933 trillion (US$18.428 billion)
Market Value: ¥2.767 trillion (US$17.383 billion)
Stock Index: Luxembourg Frankfurt New York
 Amsterdam Paris Hong Kong Tokyo Osaka Nagoya

Although it is recognized primarily for its stereo components and high-technological telecommunications equipment, Hitachi Limited of Japan is one of the world's largest diversified manufacturers of industrial machinery. Most of its popular consumer items (VCRs, televisions, mircowave ovens) have been spin-offs of its larger operations. Throughout its 77 year history Hitachi has supplied many of Japan's leading industrial corporations. Hitachi produces everything from hydroelectric turbines and state–of–the–art nuclear generators to advanced semi-conductors and electrical locomotives. It has even developed a robot that does ice sculpture.

Hitachi has often been called the General Electric of Japan, and the Hitachi management is proud of the association. There are, in fact, quite a few similarities. General Electric is larger than Hitachi, but not significantly. Hitachi has 151 offices in 39 countries and operates 106 factories which manufacture 40,000 different products. The company has 486 subsidiaries and over 1,000 affiliates, making it one of the world's 30 largest conglomerates. General Electric's and Hitachi's revenues are also close, both around the $30 billion mark. Moreover, Hitachi has imitated General Electric in technological and management training areas.

The story behind Hitachi's rise to success involves a man and his electric motor. In 1910 a Japanese nationalist named Namihei Odaira was upset with the lack of mechanical expertise in his country. Most Japanese industrial companies imported their technology from Europe and the United States, claiming that similar Japanese equipment was unreliable. To prove them wrong Odaira, a recent graduate of the Tokyo Institute of Science, began making his own 5-horsepower electric motors. These were then leased to a copper mine located in the hills above the

fishing village of Hitachi (which means rising sun).

The motors worked efficiently for the copper mine but Odaira had trouble selling them to other Japanese firms. It was not until the outbreak of World War I that Hitachi was able to gain some large customers. A major power company found that, because of the war, it could not obtain the three large turbines it had ordered from Germany and was forced to turn to Hitachi in the absence of a better alternative. Odaira made the best of his opportunity, delivering the 10,000 h.p. power generators in five months. The power company was impressed and sent more orders to Hitachi. Soon other corporations came to Odaira for help in building their industrial sectors.

In the 1920's Hitachi expanded its operations to meet the growing demand of Japan's burgeoning industrial economy. Through the acquisition of other companies, Hitachi became the nation's largest manufacturer of pumps, blowers and other mechanical equipment. The company also became involved in metal working and began manufacturing copper cable and rolling stock. These developments served to consolidate Hitachi's ability to build and supply a major manufacturer without outside help. In 1924 it also built Japan's first electric locomotive.

The coming to power of the Japanese military government in the 1930's forced some changes at Hitachi. Although Hitachi tried to maintain its independence, the company was nonetheless pressured into manufacturing war material, including radar and sonar equipment for the Imperial Navy. Odaira, however, was successful in preventing Hitachi from manufacturing actual weapons. The war itself devastated the company. Many of its factories were destroyed by Allied bombing raids.

Following the war, the American occupational forces tried to disband Hitachi altogether. Odaira himself was removed from the company. After three years of negotiations Hitachi was "allowed" to maintain all but 19 of its manufacturing plants. The cost of such a production shutdown was prohibitive. This was followed by a three month labor strike in 1950 that severely hindered Hitachi's reconstruction efforts. Only the Korean War saved the company from complete collapse. Hitachi and many other struggling Japanese industrial firms benefited from defense contracts offered by the American military.

During the 1950's Chikara Kurata, who had succeeded Odaira as president of Hitachi, directed the company into an era of market expansion. Anticipating the future of electronic engineering, he established technology "tie-ups" with General Electric and RCA. He also initiated a number of licensing agreements which allowed Hitachi to compete, through affiliates, in the worldwide market. In the 1960's the firm also moved into the consumer goods sphere, introducing its own brand of household appliances and entertainment equipment. More importantly, however, Kurata began investing in computer research. In 1957 Hitachi built its first computer and entered into the high-technological age.

During the 1960's Hitachi developed Japan's first online computer system, and emerged as the world's largest producer of analog computers which are used in scientific research to compile complex statistical data.

Despite its technical advances, Hitachi and most other

Japanese electronics companies were still far behind IBM. The Japanese Ministry of International Trade and Industry took direct action to narrow the gap and make Japan competitive. It funded a cooperative research and development effort which involved most of Japan's major technical firms. The goal was to design a computer that could match IBM's top line. Hitachi benefited greatly from this program, and ended its overseas policy of non-confrontation. From that point forward, the high-tech competition between America and Japan, and between IBM and Hitachi in particular, was under way.

Hitachi has long been recognized for its ability to adapt to changing economic conditions. Its flexibility was especially evident during the 1974 OPEC oil crisis that devastated Japan (which imports nearly 95% of its energy) and its industrial sector. Drastic cost-cutting measures were taken to keep the firm financially solvent, and company executives voluntarily took 15% pay-cuts. Following 1975, when the company had its first disappointing fiscal year, sales and profits at Hitachi began to increase dramatically.

Hitachi appeared to be transforming itself into the IBM of the Orient, but perhaps it was trying too hard. In July of 1982, Hitachi and 11 of its employees were indicted on charges of commercial bribery and theft. Apparently some employees at Hitachi had been stealing confidential design secrets from IBM so as not to lose ground in the intense race for technological superiority. The FBI and the U.S. Justice Department arranged an operation which caught Hitachi employees paying for IBM documents.

Penalties for the offence were, on the surface, quite light. Hitachi was fined $24,000 and only two employees were given jail sentences. However, the negative publicity caused by the scandal damaged Hitachi considerably. News of the trial appeared just as the company was beginning a full-scale marketing campaign for its products in the U.S. Many American companies cancelled their orders or refused to receive shipments. According to an out of court settlement, Hitachi also pays IBM $40 to $46 million annually in royalties.

Hitachi recovered from this unfortunate set of circumstances, but is faced with other problems. Marketing has always been the company's weakest department and is presently hampering Hitachi's competitiveness abroad. Profits dropped for the first time in a decade in 1986, down 29% to $884 million. Part of the problem derives from the overly-strong yen, the worldwide decrease in semiconductor sales, and the loss of markets to inexpensively operated Taiwanese and Korean firms.

Yet the real reason behind Hitachi's declining sales is that many of its product lines have either matured or are presently in low demand. The company is simply not positioned well to enter into fast-growing markets. Its profit margins are shrinking. Its two largest sectors, industrial equipment and consumer products, are in trouble; the former because the old industrial companies who are Hitachi's chief customers are ordering less equipment, the latter due to an increase in the variety of VCR's, TVs, etc., on department store shelves and Hitachi's unimpressive marketing efforts. In the growing field of personal computers, for instance, Hitachi is far behind its rivals (NEC, Matsushita, Fujitsu) in sales. Despite building one of the very first personal computers, it now commands only 5% of this lucrative market. Hitachi's brightest spot is its telecommunications operation, which competes strongly with IBM.

Once considered an extremely good investment, Hitachi stock has been performing poorly in the recent past. This was especially evident in 1986 during the record run on the Tokyo Stock Exchange; despite all the activity, Hitachi's share price barely moved. Many investors have sold Hitachi stock in favor of more promising alternatives.

Exports have also fallen off. Debt-ridden Third World countries cannot afford Hitachi's industrial machinery due to the uneven currency exchange; and U.S. and European heavy equipment sales have dropped for the same reasons they have fallen in Japan, namely, because of a deteriorating industrial sector.

To deal with these problems, present Hitachi president Katsushige Mita has sought to change the company's approach to its business. "We cannot live with tradition alone," he says. "I have to make Hitachi a more modern company." To this end, Mita is reorganizing the firm. The production plants themselves are being made more cost-effective. To compete more effectively with Koreans and Taiwanese in the export market, Hitachi is increasing automation of its domestic plants and reducing labor costs. Overseas production plants are also part of Mita's strategy. A VCR plant recently began operations in California, and an auto parts factory is scheduled to be built in Kentucky so as to be closer to Japanese carmakers in Detroit.

Research and development expenditures have been increased to help Hitachi keep pace with the ever-changing cycles of electronic technology. Mita intends to mass market Hitachi's latest high-tech products and move the company away from the heavy industrial equipment. Hitachi officials are particularly excited about their new flat-screened TVs and erasable compact discs, which they hope will revolutionize home entertainment. There is also considerable interest in Hitachi's new video printer that produces extremely clear snap-shot size prints from a television monitor.

Principal Subsidiaries: Asahi Kogyo Co., Ltd.; Babcock-Hitachi K.K.; Hitachi Cable, Ltd.; Hitachi Metals, Ltd.; Hitachi Chemical Co., Ltd.; Hitachi Chemical Co. America Ltd.; Hitachi Construction Machinery Co., Ltd.; Hitachi Maxwell, Ltd.; Hitachi Denshi, Ltd.; Hitachi Heating Appliances Co., Ltd.; Hitachi Kiden Kogyo, Ltd.; Hitachi Lighting, Ltd.; Hitachi Electronics Engineering Co., Ltd.; Hitachi Power Engineering Co., Ltd.; Hitachi Machinery & Engineering Ltd.; Hitachi Ohira Industrial Co., Ltd.; Hitachi Medical Corp.; Hitachi Seiko, Ltd.; Japan Servo Co., Ltd.; Nippo Tsushin Kogyo Co., Ltd.; Hitachi America Ltd.; Hitachi Consumer Products of America, Inc.; Hitachi Instruments, Inc.; Hitachi Semiconductor (America), Inc.; High Voltage Breakers, Inc.; Hydraulic Turbines, Inc.

Further Reading: Multinational Management: Business Strategy and Government Policy by Yoshi Tsurumi, Cambridge, Massachusetts, Ballinger, 1977.

IC Industries

IC INDUSTRIES, INC.

One Illinois Center
111 East Wacker Drive
Chicago, Illinois 60601
U.S.A.
(312) 565–3000

Public Company
Incorporated: August 31, 1962 as Illinois Central
Industries, Inc.
Employees: 43,050
Sales: $4.222 billion
Market Value: $3.325 billion
Stock Index: New York

Illinois Central Industries is the conglomerate that grew out of the Illinois Central Gulf Railroad. The chief engineer of the company's strategy is William B. Johnson, who joined the struggling railroad in 1966 when it had $300 million in revenues. Prior to joining the Chicago-based company, Johnson was a lawyer for the Pennsylvania Railroad and president of Railway Express Agency.

As president of Illinois Central Railroad, Johnson is heir to a company history dating back to 1851 when a group of European bankers decided to take advantage of the growing railroad business in America. At the onset, the railroad was operated only inside Illinois, but just after the U.S. Civil War the company began a vigorous expansion plan, incorporating more than 200 railroads into its system. By 1867 the railroad had crossed the Mississippi into Iowa, eventually stretching southward through Kentucky, Tennessee, Arkansas, Alabama, Mississippi, and on to New Orleans. Additional Illinois Central lines ran to South Dakota, Minnesota, Wisconsin, Indiana, Missouri and Nebraska. For more than a hundred years the Illinois Central Railroad did its job of hauling freight and passengers up and down the Mississippi Valley and throughout the northern portion of the midwest. No evidence existed of the company's future expansion outside of the railroad business.

However, on August 31, 1962 the railroad was incorporated as Illinois Central Industries, Inc. And under William Johnson's leadership the company had a new goal—diversification. The Johnson blueprint called for the building of a consumer and commercial products conglomerate by using company cash and stock to buy other businesses, and company tax credits to shelter their earnings. With the single-mindedness typical of its

president, the company began methodically to work toward that end.

The first dramatic step was taken in 1968 when the company ventured into the nonrail business, purchasing the Abex Corporation. Formerly known as American Brake Shoe and Foundry, the company produced brakes, wheels and couplings for railroad cars, brake linings for cars and trucks, hydraulic systems for airplanes and ships, and specialized metal castings for industrial uses such as sugar mills and locomotives.

Sixteen years after this initial acquisition, Johnson bought the Pneumo Corporation, a Boston-based aerospace, food and drug company, for $593 million. Over a year later he orchestrated the merger of Abex and Pneumo, forming the Pneumo Abex Corporation. The Pneumo purchase was viewed as a means of increasing overall revenue. The subsidiary also provided income from its military contracts, and gave credence to Johnson's theory of growth through acquisition.

In 1970 Illinois Central Industries diversified into the real estate business by becoming a major partner in the Illinois Center. The Center is a complex of office buildings, hotels and condominiums that sprawls across 83 acres of lakefront property in downtown Chicago. In another real estate transaction, the company sold land it owned in New Orleans; the city's Superdome now rests on this property. Yet Illinois Central Industries maintained ownership of 11 adjoining acres for future developments such as the Hyatt Regency hotel. The company has also developed an array of industrial parks in or near Fort Lauderdale, Memphis and New Orleans.

This diversification toward real estate came at a time of increasing debate over what role the traditional railroad business should play in the evolving structure of the company. The faltering operations, on the one hand, were aided by a merger with the Gulf, Mobile and Ohio Railroad, which was a combination of several railroads including: the Gulf, Mobile and Northern; the Mobile and Ohio; and the Chicago and Alton. The merger was formally completed on August 10, 1972 and the new line was named the Illinois Central Gulf Railroad by the parent company.

The sale of some of the company's prime property, on the other hand, indicated movement away from continuing the railroad business. Indeed, by the late 1970's Johnson vacilated back and forth between placing the railroad for sale on the market and then duly removing it. Actually it was the eventual piecemeal sale of the line that proved immensely profitable and solidified Johnson's reputation as an astute businessman.

When the railroad was first placed on the market, no serious purchaser stepped forward, mainly because Johnson had let the railroad deteriorate through lack of maintenance. Johnson then decided to dismantle the line and sell it part by part. This process was greatly aided by capital improvements and rail deregulation during the mid-1980's, and Johnson netted handsome profits for his company.

As Johnson's strategy of diversification unfolded, the company changed its name in 1975 to IC Industries, Inc. Three areas of business were identified as important and company acquisitions fell into these categories: consumer products; commercial products; and railroad activities. The holding company was structured around decentralized management and a growing list of subsidiaries that maintained primarily autonomous operations.

In the consumer products group, a 1978 acquisition brought in the Pet company, the St. Louis, Missouri, firm that produces evaporated milk. Since then the company has expanded into a variety of food products, including Whitman Chocolates and Old El Paso, the best selling brand of Mexican foods in the United States. The enterprise has grown to 30 owned and eight leased manufacturing plants located in America and six foreign countries.

The Hussman Corporation, a manufacturer of refrigeration equipment for food retailers and processors, composed an important branch of IC's commercial products group. In the early part of the 1980's Hussmann suffered a slump in sales and profits, but by 1984 the subsidiary regained its profitable standing and earned about $44 million before taxes. Later that same year, Hussmann acquired Riordan Holdings, Ltd., a top producer of food refrigeration equipment, based in London, which served to heighten Hussmann's overseas profile. There are 20 Hussmann-owned and ten leased manufacturing facilities in the United States, Mexico, the United Kingdom and Canada, as well as three owned and 95 leased branch facilities in these same countries (excluding Mexico) that sell, install and maintain Hussmann products.

The Pneumo Abex Corporation currently manufacturers products that fall into three basic components: aerospace, industrial, and fluid power products. There is stiff competition, particularly in the aerospace business, but IC regards the competition as a challenge to invest more of its dollars and technology in the field, enabling it to compete with larger firms such as Cleveland Pneumatic Company. Industrial products include braking materials for the automotive original equipment and replacement outlets, and safety equipment for recreational vehicles, trucks and automobiles. Products are manufactured for use in mining, earthmoving, steel making and food processing, to name a few. Canadian and United States railroads are markets for iron and composition brake shoes, cast steel wheels and custom-made trackwork manufactured by Pneumo Abex. Fluid power products include complete hydraulic systems that are used in construction and mobile equipment, industrial and marine machinery, materials-handling equipment, off-shore drilling and nuclear power plants. This division also manufactures products for aerospace and general aviation markets, from 33 plants in the United States and 16 in foreign locations.

When market analysts examine William Johnson's formula for corporate success, which entails pruning acquisitions of all but their most profitable divisions, they most often look to Pet. This is now the largest of IC's $1.8 billion consumer division. One year following this acquisition, its pre-tax profits almost tripled to an estimated $85 million in 1984, on a revenue increase of 33%. Part of this carefully crafted plan involves selling low-return operations. Over a six year period, 22 of Pet's units, with sales totalling $400 million, have been sold in order to funnel money into Pet's more profitable products. In line with the increased demand for ethnic foods, channeling funds into the Old El Paso food products line has helped to rank number one in sales. In 1982 Pet acquired the Wm. Underwood Company in the United Kingdom, producers of Red Devil spreads and B & M baked beans and, in the process, secured a share for Pet in the overseas market. In turn, Pet formed an International Group and in early 1984 brought the Old El Paso line to England. The product is distributed through Underwood's Shippams meat products operation. Continuing to expand its international divisions, Pet disclosed that in May of 1987, it acquired Facchin Foods Co. Ltd. Facchin is a pasta manufacturer in Edmonton, Canada, which has become part of Primo Foods Ltd., Pet's Canadian subsidiary. In addition to more than 800 Italian food products, Primo produces Old El Paso Mexican foods and Underwood meat spreads.

Pepsi Cola General Bottlers is the second largest franchise bottler of Pepsi Cola beverages in the United States, claiming the greater share of the soft-drink market in Chicago, Cincinnati, Kansas City and Louisville. This branch of IC's consumer products group also handles other soft-drinks, including Dad's Root Beer, 7-Up, Dr. Pepper, Orange Crush, Canada Dry and Hawaiian Punch. In 1984 Pepsi General garnered only minimal profits, partly because of heavily discounted prices and partly because both Pepsi Cola and Coca Cola introduced new products to the consumer. However, for the next two years Pepsi General's sales growth averaged 7%, outstripping the industry's as a whole.

Another of IC's major consumer product holdings is Midas International, a company that makes automotive exhaust systems, suspension systems and brake services through approximately 2,000 franchised and company-owned Midas shops in America, Canada, England, France, Australia, Belgium, Germany, Austria, Panama and Mexico. Originally specializing in replacement mufflers, Midas has broadened its range to include repairing and replacing brakes and shock absorbers at about 95% of its outlets. The expansion of services accounts for the estimated 9% profit growth shown during 1985-86.

The indefatigable William Johnson has twice deferred his own retirement in order to complete his plans for the company of which he has been chairman since 1968. He envisions IC Industries as an outstanding and reliable investment vehicle—a blue chip company. His conglomerate, which receives at least three-fourth of its revenue from nonrail subsidiaries, has recently attracted Wall Street analysts and investors. In 1985, nine separate sales of branch lines belonging to Illinois Central Gulf Railroad produced in excess of $250 million. That amount was realized by selling parts of nonrail businesses that did not meet IC's profit margin standard, such as Pet's dairy division, Pneumo's food and drug store chains, and five ICG Railroad line segments totaling 1,558 miles of track.

IC Industries, Inc. is now an international diversified holding company. Johnson's timetable calls for the company to concentrate on consumer products and commercial products in the near future, particularly the aerospace bsinesses. In the area of consumer products, Pet plans to introduce new lines and augment its international sales, while Midas has new services and locations on the drawing board. In the area of commercial products, Pneumo Abex will focus on the operations of its aircraft flight control and landing gear business, while Hussmann's future appears solid because of recent European acquisitions.

In keeping with IC's record of making a major acquisition every two years, those elements that will complement existing subsidiaries are under consideration. The IC plan is to continue building its empire through market expansion, rigorous cost containment, and greater productivity.

Principal Subsidiaries: Mid-American Improvement Corp.; Hussmann Distributing Co., Inc.; IC Equities, Inc.; IC Leasing, Inc.; Illinois Center Corp.; Illinois Central Gulf Railroad Co.; La Salle Properties, Inc.; South Properties, Inc.; IC Products Co.; Bubble Up Co., Inc.; Dad's Root Beer Co.; IC Industries International; ICP Holding Corp.; BIH Foodservice, Inc.; Midas International Corp.; Pneumo Abex Corp. The company also lists subsidiaries in the following countries: Australia, Austria, Bermuda, Canada, Denmark, France, Italy, Japan, Mexico, The Netherlands, Sweden, Switzerland, United Kingdom, Venezuela, and West Germany.

Further Reading: IC Industries by William B. Johnson, New York, Newcomen Society, 1973.

INSTITUTO NACIONAL DE INDUSTRIA

Plaza del Marques de Salamanca, 8
28006 Madrid
Spain
(341) 401-4004

State-controlled Holding Company
Founded by government decree: September 25, 1941
INI Group Employees: 198,748
Sales: 1.73 trillion pesetas (US$11.53 billion)

Spain's economy existed on a shaky foundation of regionalism, protectionism, and premodernization longer than that of any country in Europe. By 1939 the foundation was crumbling and Spain's new government, headed by Francisco Franco, was faced with the task of repairing the severely damaged structure. Spain's tradition of extreme protectionist economic policies and political isolationism, coupled with the aftermath of the Spanish Civil War and the outbreak of the Second World War, placed the Franco regime in the unenviable position of reconstructing the economy with very limited resources and no outside help.

The years 1939 to 1959 are known as Spain's period of autarky, establishing a self-sufficient and independent national economy. The period officially started with the passage of The Law of Protection and Development of National Industry in October of 1939. It was drafted by Juan Antonio Suanzes, childhood friend of Spain's new leader Francisco Franco. The law was designed to help Spain compete with the more advanced capitalist nations. Under the law every investment decision required government approval. No new industrial facility could be established and no installation could be modified or relocated without official sanction.

Two year later, the Instituto Nacional de Industria (INI) was created as a state holding company under the direction of Suanzes. INI was modeled after Italy's Instituto per la Ricostruzione Industriale (IRI) created in 1933 to reconstruct Italy's economy during the aftermath of its own civil war. IRI was closely linked to the Fascist regime of Benito Mussolini. Like its Italian counterpart, INI became closely linked with its country's ruler. INI was initially created to improve Spain's military defense and strengthen the economy by making Spanish industries less dependent on imported raw materials.

INI underwent an enormous period of growth during the 1940's. During its first decade, INI specialized in three major areas, including mining, chemical fertilizers, and electricity. In 1944 INI created the Empresa Nacional de Electridad (ENDESA) to construct power stations. Two years later INI formed the Empresa Nacional Hidroelectrica del Ribogorzana (ENHER) to harness the power of the River Noguera-Ribogorzana and its tributaries in the Catalan. Both power companies helped reduce the country's excess demand for electrical power, smoothing the path for industrial development.

Despite progress in the areas of electric and hydroelectric power, the Spanish industry continued to suffer from a shortage of energy. In addition, inadequate transportation and lack of modernization kept industry production below prewar levels until the 1950's.

The decade of the 1950's was a period of economic change with INI at the forefront. The decade began favorably enough with rapid industrial expansion, but ended on a less optimistic note. During this time, INI had interests in most of Spain's major industries, including petroleum, aviation, transportation, engineering, and manufacturing. However, even with all its financial problems, Spain's rate of industrial production between 1951 and 1959 was double that during the reign of its first dictator, Primo de Rivera (1923–30).

To improve the still flagging industrial economy, Spanish manufacturers were encouraged to join forces with foreign interests. INI played a major role in this area, often providing attractive incentives such as low interest loans and other accommodations to foreign investors. In 1950 the Sociedad Espanola de Automoviles de Turismo (SEAT) was founded by INI in partnership with Fiat, the Italian automobile company. Fifty-two percent of SEAT's capital was provided by INI while Fiat initially held 6% of the company's stock.

Franco made the decision after World War II not to participate in the U.S. sponsored Marshall Plan. It was one of the first, but certainly not the last, of Franco's decisions that eventually hurt Spain's economy. In 1951, several years after other European nations had taken advantage of the Marshall Plan, Spain received its first loan from the U.S. government. Later that year Spain and the U.S. signed the Pact of Madrid. Under the terms of agreement, the United States received permission to build military bases in Spain in return for considerable economic aid. In an undoubtedly related incident, many of the United Nations imposed economic sanctions and restrictions (due to Fascist associations and human rights violations) against Spain were lifted, opening the door to foreign investments and markets.

Although significant, these measures were not enough to make Spain's industrial sector equitable with the rest of Europe. As late as 1958, 85% of Spain's industrial structure was comprised of small, nonmodernized companies with low levels of production. Between the years 1950–51 and 1957–58 the country's export/gross domestic product and import/gross domestic product ratios never exceeded 5%, an extremely low figure for any industrialized nation. Also that year, INI ceased to receive budgetary support from the Spanish government and, as a result, the level of self-financing among INI companies fell dramatically from 83% in 1957 to 18% in 1958.

The low export figures, combined with the nation's rising inflation rate, created a volatile situation for Spain's economy and Franco's government. In one year, the nation's rate of inflation rose from an average of 9.1% to 15.5%. In an effort to contain the problem, the Franco regime instituted a series of economic measures collectively known as the "Stabilization Plan." A ceiling of 80,000 million pesetas was imposed on government spending during the coming year. Strict limits were enforced on lending by the banking system to the public sector. Transportation and public utilities prices were increased up to 50%. Limits were also placed on the amount of credit banks could make available to the private sector. Furthermore, additional efforts were made to attract foreign investors.

The effects of the plan were quick and dramatic. By the end of 1960 prices in general had been stabilized and some prices had even started to decrease; investments in the public sector were increased and interest rates were lowered.

As a result of these measures, the 1960's and 1970's were collectively referred to as the "Spanish Miracle." In 1964 the first of three "Plans of Development" was initiated to develop Spain's underdeveloped regional industries. INI's role in this development was relatively small during the first two plans, but was crucial during the third and final plan. During the period between 1968–71, 72% of INI investments were directed towards activities which were either undesirable to or economically unviable for the private sector. This was in keeping with INI's original goal of supplementing the private sector where private business could not fulfill investment needs.

In an effort to bring the company more in line with the rest of the industrial sector, in 1968 INI was placed under the jurisdiction of the Ministry of Industry. Claudio Boada was appointed president of INI in 1970. He was expected to take a more business-like approach to the Institute's finances. One of his first steps was to create a three year reorganizing plan designed to make the company more profitable and less dependent on government subsidies. It was hoped that the plan would force INI's subsidiaries and affiliates to operate more like regular industries, on a profit and loss basis. However, the Institute continued to acquire or create companies that were not economically profitable. In addition, later that year a government subsidy of 3,900 million pesetas was granted to INI's coal mining subsidiary Empresa Nacional Hulleras del Norte (HUNOSA) to meet debts incurred between 1967 and 1970. Also that year, for the first time since 1958, INI received direct budgetary support from the government.

The international steel crisis of the 1970's had a devastating effect on Spain's industrial industry which was dominated by INI companies. In 1973 INI's two major steel companies Ensidesa and Uninsa were merged in an effort to increase productivity. The efforts proved futile. By 1980 Ensidesa, the country's largest state-owned integrated steel company, lost more money than any of INI's other holdings.

Soon after the steel crisis came the international oil crisis of the mid-to-late 1970's. Franco continued to subsidize oil prices despite the rapidly rising costs. As a result, while the rest of Europe and the world was reducing oil consumption, Spain increased oil consumption more than 13% from 1973 to 1979. The ramifications of Franco's decision would be felt in following years.

In 1974 INI was brought into the forefront of the industrial sector by the Institute's newest president, Fernandez Ordonez. By the end of 1974, production by INI companies in the refined petroleum sector amounted to 32% of the national total. In 1974 INI participated directly in 60 companies of which 15 were wholly-owned by the Institute. In 1975 INI and its subsidiaries were responsible for 45% of all steel produced, 92% of ship tonnage launched, and 100% of Spain's major airline activity.

1975 was a significant year for INI and Spain. After almost four decades, the dictatorship of Francisco Franco came to an end with his death in November of that year. Prince Juan Carlos, who had been designated ruler since the monarchy was restored by the 1947 Law of Succession, finally took over on November 22, 1975. King Juan Carlos' ascension did not occur without significant opposition from various conservative parties.

The subsidies of oil prices ceased after Franco's death, just in time for the international oil crisis of the late 1970's. Due to the fact that Spain's oil prices had not reflected the true level of inflation, Spain's prices tripled when the rest of Europe's oil prices merely doubled. In Spain, INI operated the largest amount of oil companies and consequently suffered the largest amount of losses. These losses, coupled with other losses, promoted the new government to consider changing the company's structure.

Despite the oil crisis and its effects on Spain's economy, INI continued to expand. By 1976 INI was responsible for more than 50% of the total production of Spanish cars, ships and aluminum, and coal.

The 1980's will be remembered as INI's period of reconstruction. Fiat, which had born the brunt of the company's losses since its partnership with INI began, decided to sell its interests. Thus INI was completely responsible for SEAT's finances. As a result, in 1980 INI began a five-year investment plan. The investments were anticipated to show profits by 1985 when Spain was scheduled to enter the European Community's Common Market. Projected investment for the years 1981 to 1985 was estimated to be approximately $24 billion.

On the heels of a significant victory towards making INI profitable and self-sufficient, Jose Miguel de la Rica, who took over INI's leadership in 1978 and made valiant efforts to increase INI's profitability, was replaced in 1981 by Carlos Bustello. Under de la Rica's leadership, INI had won the right not to be forced to take over failing companies except by Parliamentary order. Prior to the agreement, INI was required to assume control over companies at the government's request. The new agreement with Parliament would make it harder for INI to absorb ailing companies. Moreover, in an attempt to reduce its losses, INI sold or eliminated a significant number of unprofitable companies in 1984. In 1986, 51% of INI's shares of SEAT were sold to the Volkswagen corporation.

By the end of 1985, Spain's economy appeared to be experiencing its second miracle. Foreign investment increased by significant amounts. The Japanese, which had invested one million dollars in Spain during 1980, invested $100 million during 1985 and over $200 million during 1986. Furthermore, forecasts by the Organization for Economic Cooperation and Development estimated that Spain will add 104,000 more workers to its work force by 1987.

The future of Spain's economy is looking better than it has for several decades. International economists have noted that INI's cost-cutting measures are a step in the right direction. However, it still has a long way to go before its goals for the Spanish economy are accomplished.

Principal Subsidiaries: ENDESA; ENCASUR; ENHER; Gas y Electricidad, SA; Unión Eléctrica de Canarias, SA; ERZ; ENUSA; Empresa Nacional Siderúrgica, SA; FOARSA; PRESUR; Empresa Nacional Hulleras de Norte, SA; Minas de Figaredo, SA; ENADIMSA; BAZAN; Construcciones Aeronáuticas, SA; SANTA BARBARA; ENASA; INISEL; ENOSA; ERIA; Astilleros Españoles, SA; Astilleros y Talleres del Noroeste, SA; Astilleros Canarios, SA; BARRERAS; ATEINSA; Babcock Wilcox Española, SA; Equipos Nucleares, SA; FSC; MTM; INESPAL; ALUMINIO ESPAÑOL SA; ALUMINA ESPAÑOLA SA; ENDIASA; CARCESA; Lactaria Española, SA; Oleaginosas Españolas SA; Pesa Electrónica, SA; Empresa Nacional de Autocamiones, SA; ENFERSA; POTASAS; ALMAGRERA; IBERIA; AVIACO; ELCANO; Compañía Transatlantica Española, SA; INITEC; AUXINI; Empresa Nacional de Celulosas, SA; ARTESPAÑA; GRUPO ALVAREZ; Iniexport, SA; CARBOEX; INFOLEASING, SA; MUSINI; SODIGA; SODICAN; SODIEX; SODIAN; SODICAL; SODIAR; ENISA.

ITT

INTERNATIONAL TELEPHONE & TELEGRAPH CORPORATION

320 Park Avenue
New York, New York 10022
U.S.A.
(212) 752-6000

Public Company
Incorporated: January 31, 1968
Employees: 253,000
Sales: $7.600 billion
Market Value: $9.127 billion
Stock Index: New York London Paris Basle Bern
Frankfurt Tokyo Vienna Geneva Lausanne Brussels
Antwerp Zurich

The history of International Telephone and Telegraph is interwoven with the lives of two men, Col. Sosthenes Behn and Harold Geneen. Behn founded the company in 1920 with the intention of creating an international telephone system modeled after American Telephone and Telegraph. Geneen later took over the corporation and, believing that diversity facilitated growth, molded ITT into one of the world's largest conglomerates. ITT remains one of the world's largest diversified companies under the leadership of current chairman of the board Rand V. Araskog, but is on the verge of eliminating its most high profile operation, namely, telecommunications.

When Lt. Col. Louis Richard Sosthenes Behn and his brother Hernand founded ITT in 1920, they expected to take advantage of an industry market that barely existed outside of the United States. In 1920 the U.S. reported 64 phones per 1,000 inhabitants, while Germany was estimated to have 9 phones per 1,000 inhabitants, Britain 5 per 1,000 and France 3 per 1,000. At that time three companies, Siemens, Ericsson and AT&T, dominated what there was of the world market.

Although a small company, the Behns were well-positioned to compete in the growing international market. They had operated South Puerto Rico Telephone Company since 1905, and Cuban Telephone Company since 1916, and in both cases used ingenuity and skill to transform inefficient companies into well-run, profitable operations with good service records. Sosthenes Behn's tour of duty with the American Expeditionary Force in World War I (where he gained the rank of Lieutenant Colonel) set in motion his vision for an international telephone system. Behn intended to achieve this international system

via ITT, which he and his brother Hernand formed in 1920 as the holding company for their existing companies, and for those they would acquire.

The way ITT expanded into the European market provides an example of the way it would conduct business during most of the Behn era. The combined effects of good timing, well-placed connections and Sosthenes' charm brought ITT the concession for telephone service in Spain in 1924. Timing was crucial due to the fact that before 1924 ITT's securities were a questionable issue on Wall Street. However, the company's consistent growth and steadily expanding earnings, coupled with the support of National City Bank, provided Wall Street analysts with a good reason to support ITT's venture into the Spanish telephone market. Behn provided the rest by placing influential Spaniards on the board of ITT's new company, CTNE, and charming the appropriate members of the Spanish government.

The Spanish concession, operated by CTNE, furnished ITT with an entrance into the European market, one that Behn wasted no time in expanding. Upset with the quality of equipment available to him, he began to search for an equipment manufacturing company to purchase. Timing and connections again helped ITT. In 1925 the U.S. government was pressuring AT&T to divest its overseas operations, which included International Western Electric Company, a European-based manufacturer of telephonic equipment. A National City banker arranged a meeting between Walter Gifford, chairman of bank customers at AT&T, and Sosthenes Behn, which resulted in the sale of the company to ITT on September 30, 1925, along with temporary use of some of AT&T's patents.

After ITT acquired the Spanish concession and the International Western Electric Company, it entered a period of rapid growth. ITT became one of the most highly valued stocks in the bull market of the period, enabling it to acquire numerous companies, mostly in the telecommunications field. Behn's dream for the international telephone system came closer to reality, and his reputation as a cosmopolitan and shrewd businessman increased.

ITT had become an international company holding manufacturing companies and operating concessions in France, Germany, Britain and much of Latin America. National citizens ran ITT's subsidiaries in every country with a facility, while corporate headquarters in New York played a passive management role.

The search for additional companies continued, though Behn's acquisition program placed ITT heavily in debt. The debt seemed manageable in the thriving world economy of the late 1920's, and ITT continued to be a popular stock despite the fact that a recession would hurt the company.

Yet if a recession would hurt ITT, it is to be expected that the Depression nearly put it out of business. The debt accumulated during the 1920's was only part of ITT's problems, as the very nature of the company's business exacerbated its financial difficulties.

As a holding company ITT earned money through dividends and profits remitted by its subsidiaries, most of which were foreign. Most ITT clients were either governments or quasi-nationalized telephone operating companies. However, in the restrictive trade atmosphere of the early part of the Depression, many foreign nations refused to allow American-based ITT to repatriate earnings from its subsidiaries. ITT was therefore deprived of significant revenues and threatened with bankruptcy through much of the Depression, despite eliminating dividends to shareholders. To make matters worse, ITT lost a good manager when Hernand died in 1933.

At the beginning of World War II, in Argentina, Spain and elsewhere, ITT's holdings were in danger of being taken from the company by governments sympathetic to Germany. Profits again became impossible to repatriate. Behn's business acumen enabled him to sell some of ITT's holdings (in Rumania, for instance) and helped avoid having others (particularly SEG and Lorenz in Germany) taken from the company at a time when foreign operations of other major American manufacturers were not treated as well. As much a factor in these matters was Behn's penchant for employing mostly nationals, of whom the head of SEL had some influence with Hitler. Still, these events earned ITT the ire of many Americans, and after the war it was one of several companies accused of collusion with Hitler, an accusation that would linger long afterwards.

ITT's difficulties in the Depression and World War II made Behn determined to reduce its dependence on its non-U.S. companies. Behn abandoned the international telephone system and established ITT's new goal: to derive two-thirds of its revenues from American companies.

This was a goal that was difficult to achieve. ITT had consolidated some operations within the U.S. in response to the war, centered around the earlier acquisition of Federal Electric. Federal's electronics-oriented and military contracts made it a significant revenue earner during the war, and Behn hoped the company could gain a portion of the postwar market for consumer electronics and durables. Such efforts were mixed at best and, as a result, Behn looked to merge ITT with one of several large U.S. companies, including Sylvania, Raytheon, ABC and RCA in order to realize his postwar goal of a company earnings distribution. None of the larger mergers materialized, but those that did, such as Coolerator and Capehart-Farnsworth, drained capital and performed poorly, keeping ITT's stock low in a bull market.

Such domestic difficulties weakened ITT, and Behn's position as leader. Although ITT was once again profitable, the dividend was not restored, and stockholders began to challenge Behn's decisions. A boardroom battle for power occurred which Behn eventually lost, despite having reinstated the dividend in 1951. He remained chairman until he died in 1956, though his power was largely symbolic after 1953.

During this period of time the company's emphasis was on overseas operations, although even the European subsidiaries were posting smaller than expected profits. Some observers commented that the three years spanning Behn's death and Harold Geneen's accession at ITT saw nothing more significant than a change of logo from IT&T to ITT.

If there was a lull in company growth and productivity, it ended in 1959 when Harold Sydney Geneen took over as head of ITT. Geneen's management abilities had been showcased at such firms as American Can, Bell & Howell, Jones & Laughlin, and Raytheon, and at ITT he became almost a synonym for excellence in management. The Geneen method of "Management by Meetings" was popularized and widely imitated.

Geneen had drive, ambition, and seemingly endless energy. He also believed firmly that companies should aim at both short and long-term growth, not stability. These characteristics would help make ITT one of the world's largest conglomerates, controlling Continental Baking, Sheraton Hotels, Avis and the Hartford Insurance group, to name a few of ITT's major acquisitions. However, Geneen did not immediately initiate a program of expansion. He first reorganized the company with a management shake-up and thorough cost-cutting measures. In his first five years, over 30% of the company's executives were replaced, though in keeping with ITT tradition few were fired. Instead, executives regarded as lacking the necessary skills were worked to the point where they would quit. As one said, "Nothing matters to him but the job—not the clock, not your personal life, nothing." So many executives would come and go during the Geneen era that ITT was compared to a revolving door, and a *Forbes* magazine reporter gave it the title of Geneen University.

Geneen instituted his changes to redirect a corporation that, in his mind, left a question of "how long it would have gone on before it cracked wide open." This was not an entirely accurate perception; ITT was a growing company, even if it fell short of its earnings potential. Part of the problem stemmed from the Behn legacy, including the almost complete lack of cohesion among subsidiaries. Geneen worked to correct this, and increased headquarters' role in the affairs of subsidiaries through yearly meetings and required reports.

In 1963 ITT began to make a significant number of acquisitions, averaging one company a month. Geneen promoted the notion of a diversified company as a strong company, one able to weather downturns in a particular sector of the economy through its holdings in other sectors. Such strength made a diversified company the best vehicle for corporate growth, assets could be transferred to the appropriate divisions, and the company would be less dependent on individual clients as well as cyclical markets.

That same year Geneen began to emphasize U.S. operations over European ones, wanting 55% of ITT's revenues to come from U.S. subsidiaries. Several factors influenced this decision: France and Britain began advocating the nationalization of certain ITT subsidiaries, Fidel Castro expropriated Cuban Telephone, and competition intensified in the European telecommunications market.

Emphasizing U.S. operations explains ITT's increased number of acquisitions, for its traditional method of growth-by-acquisition would be the key to an increase in domestic revenues. However, ITT made its move into the U.S. market at the same time as a number of other companies, part of a merger trend that due to its size and complexity caused a large amount of consumer distrust. In a decade that would become increasingly anti-big business, so to speak, multinationals and especially conglomerates became targets of frequent attacks in the nation's press, fueled by books such as *Up the Corporation*. Some people thought that ITT symbolized what was wrong with big business.

Success made the company a convenient target. Geneen's cost-cutting measures and his complementary acquisition program helped ITT meet his first five-year goal, namely, to double earnings and income. In this way ITT became a billion-dollar corporation in 1962, and by 1969 it had quadrupled in size. However, questionable actions both abroad and in the U.S. damaged ITT's reputation as a well-run company.

The year 1968 was a milestone year for ITT. In 1968, 55% of corporate earnings came from U.S. subsidiaries, thanks to several large acquisitions, among them Sheraton Hotels, Levitt Homes, Rayonier, Pennsylvania Glass Sand and Continental Baking. Yet 1968 also saw the first of a series of setbacks for ITT, as it lost its bid to acquire ABC when the U.S. Justice Department challenged the take-over on antitrust grounds.

The Justice Department made several more moves against ITT, which culminated in its litigation attempting to prevent its takeover of Hartford Fire Insurance in 1970. ITT agreed to divest assets equal to those of Hartford's, but far more damaging was the negative publicity that resulted from the two confrontations with the Justice Department.

ITT's image with the U.S. public was further damaged in 1971. In that year ITT was accused of bribing Republican officials into locating the 1968 Republican National Convention at the Harbor Beach Sheraton in San Diego, and also of interfering in the affairs of a foreign government (by opposing Salvador Allende in Chile).

These incidents alone would have cast a shadow over Geneen's final years as head of ITT. Except the acquisitions that put ITT's earnings proportions at 55% domestic and 45% foreign also blemished Geneen's reputation for managerial brilliance. Only the Pennsylvania Glass Sand Company would become an immediate source of profits for ITT, and the purchase of Levitt Homes would eventually prove a disaster.

In 1978 Geneen, 67, stepped down from the chairmanship of ITT, although he remained on the board until 1983. His immediate successor did not remain long and was soon replaced with the little known Rand Vincent Araskog. Araskog was promoted from within ITT and was expected to be Geneen's pawn. This proved a misconception. Araskog began to sell pieces of Geneen's empire to gain the cash which was needed to reduce the huge debts acquired during ITT's takeover phase and also to fund new research and development. Araskog maintained ITT's divisional structure (which Geneen had modeled after Albert Sloan's General Motors) of National Resources, Diversified Services, Telecommunications and Electronics, Engineered Products, and Consumer Products and Services, with emphasis on financial services and telecommunications.

Araskog thought that ITT's System 12 telephone switching exchange would sell well in the U.S. telephone market, as it had in Europe. However, despite a one billion-dollar investment, System 12 proved difficult to adapt from the European to the American system, and in 1986 ITT discarded conversion plans and entered negotiations to sell its telecommunications division to a French telecommunications company under government control.

Should the sale materialize ITT will undergo a fundamental change. Telecommunications provides a quarter of ITT's revenues. The company could shift emphasis to the financial services division, its best performer, and it is conceivable that ITT could do what American Can did, that is, sell its high profile business and concentrate on financial services, thus providing its shareholders with the higher investment returns that many request. Then again, should the sale not materialize, Araskog's moves to reduce debt and sell certain assets should help ITT to remain competitive in its chosen field.

Principal Subsidiaries: ITT Corp.; ITT Holdings Inc.; International Standard Electric Corp.; ITT Communications and Information Services, Inc.; Hartford Fire Insurance Co.; ITT Credit Corp.; ITT Consumer Services Corp.; ITT Financial Corp.; Kellogg Credit Corp.

Further Reading: The Sovereign State of ITT by Anthony Sampson, New York, Stein and Day, 1973; *Tales of ITT: An Insider's Report* by Thomas S. Burns, Boston, Houghton Mifflin, 1974; *When Telecom and ITT Were Young* by Maurice Deloraine, New York, Lehigh, 1976; *ITT: The Management of Opportunity* by Robert Sobel, New York, Times, 1982; *The Politics of International Economic Relations* by Joan E. Spero, New York, St. Martin's Press, 1985.

ISTITUTO PER LA RICOSTRUZIONE INDUSTRIALE

Via Veneto, 89
00187 Roma
Italy
(06) 47271

State-controlled Holding Company
Incorporated: January, 1933
Employees: 472,000
Sales: L 27.159 trillion (US$16.195 billion)
Market Value: L27.159 trillion (US$16.195 billion)
Stock Index: Milan

In 1933 the foreign and domestic markets of hundreds of major Italian companies had been destroyed by the difficult economic conditions of a world-wide Depression. These companies were unable to repay debts they owed to major Italian banks and, in turn, threatened the country with the collapse of its banking system. In order to free the banks from the burden of these debts, the Italian government established the Istituto per la Ricostruzione Industriale to 'buy out' these debts from the banks. It was regarded as an emergency measure to save the Italian banking system.

IRI was originally organized into two sections, the Sezione Smobilizzi Industriali, for managing state-owned shares of private companies, and the Sezione Finanziamenti Industriali, for providing additional long-term industrial financing. A limited economic recovery in 1934 and 1935 resulted in the dissolution of the finance section and the assumption of its duties by a large credit institute called IMI.

During the period from 1933 to 1936, IRI disposed of almost half of the assests it purchased. However, it remained in control of Italy's three most important commercial banks, including Banca Commerciale Italiana, Credito Italiano, and Banco di Roma. During this time IRI became closely tied to the Fascist regime of Benito Mussolini. The directors of IRI, Alberto Beneduce, Francesco Giordani and Donato Menichella, convinced Mussolini to continue state sponsorship of IRI. In 1937 it was declared a permanent agency.

In order to reduce the costs of administration, IRI created semi-autonomous sub-holding companies called *finanziarie* to manage all the company's interests in a specific industry. It created STET in 1933 to operate the telephone interests, Finmare in 1936 to manage shipping,

a new *finanziaria* for it in 1952 called Finelettrica. SIP and Finsider in 1937 for iron and steel.

Holdings and activities which the Fascists had no interest in maintaining were eliminated from the IRI portfolio. IRI's interests in electrical utilities, textiles, agriculture and real estate were sold along with numerous foreign investments. The company's interests in steel, shipping and engineering (the primary sectors of the Italian military/industrial complex) doubled from 26% of total holdings to 54%. Gradually, IRI was transformed into a mechanism for achieving the Fascist regime's goals of economic autarky and military mobilization.

The Fascist government under Mussolini exercised expansionist state policies which resulted in the annexation of Albania and the colonization of sections of Somalia, Ethiopia and Libya. Fascist Italy's military adventurism, social policies and opposition to Bolshevism made it a natural ally of Nazi Germany and Imperial Japan. When the second world war began, Italy became a member of the Axis. In 1943 the country was occupied by German troops who were sent by Hitler to defend Italy against Allied attacks on what Churchill termed "Europe's soft underbelly."

As a result of these allied attacks IRI's substantial merchant shipping properties were completely destroyed. The company's pig iron plants, most of which were located in the Mediterranean combat zone, were heavily bombed. Southern Italy, where most of the company's electrical, telephone and heavy engineering assets were located, was the area most exposed to Allied attacks. By the end of the war IRI was almost completely destroyed.

After the war IRI came under the control of the Allied Control Commission. It was investigated for criminal activities during the war and later cleared. It was originally planned that IRI would be broken up and sold to private investors, but weak capital markets and the company's complete state of ruin forced the company to remain intact. CIR (the Comitato Interministrale per la Ricostruzione) was given overall responsibility for IRI in April of 1946. However, the period from 1945 to 1948 for IRI was described as one of "organizational chaos," with no plan for reconstruction.

IRI had a difficult time generating capital for reinvestment. During the war IRI deliberately employed an excessive number of people to avoid their conscription or deportation to Germany. After the war the company was prevented from laying off workers by labor unions and socialist political organizations. These restrictions slowed the conversion of IRI's shipyards to civilian shipbuilding because it was obligated to continue diverting funds from capital investments to pay employees for whom no work could be found. Overemployment slowed the company's recovery and delayed Italy's postwar reconstruction.

In 1948 IRI was placed under the control of the Italian government's Council of Ministers and given new statutes. A new *finanziaria* called Finmeccanica was created that year to manage the company's engineering subsidiaries. In addition, a campaign was initiated to diversify geographically the company's employment centers which were concentrated in Genoa, Naples, Trieste and Milan.

IRI re-entered the electrical utility business and created

(Società Idroelettrica Piemonte), a subsidiary of Fine-lettrica, controlled a company called RAI which operated the Italian radio broadcasting system. In 1952 IRI took direct control of 75% of RAI, leaving the remainder for SIP. Television services were introduced two years later.

In 1955 the Italian government was faced with a shortage of capital for the construction of roads. It was decided that the construction and operation of selected motorways (or *autostrade*) should be turned over to private investors. Shortly afterwards IRI was awarded a concession for the Autostrade del Sole between Milan and Naples. The following year IRI established the Società Concessioni e Costruzioni Autostrade to manage the Autostrade del Sole and subsequent IRI motorways.

The government ordered IRI to take over the operations of a bankrupt textile company called Manifatture Cotoniere Meridionali in 1956. IRI was given instructions to aid and reorganize MCM, which was the largest cotton concern in southern Italy. The acquisition marked IRI's return to the textile industry.

In 1957 the Italian government forced two Italian telephone companies, TETI and SET, to sell a majority of their shares to IRI, which through STET controlled Italy's other three telephone companies. The following year control was transferred to STET, which in 1964 merged all five telephone companies into SIP (Società Italiana per l'Esercizio Telefonico). Also in 1957, IRI took control of the Italian national airline Alitalia, which was established in 1946 by the Italian government, British European Airways and TWA. The company's shipbuilding assets, recovered during the late 1950's, were placed under the control of a sixth IRI *finanziaria* called Fincantieri.

IRI increased its involvement in the national autostrade system during 1966. A subsidiary called Infrasud was created to manage the system of alternate highways around Naples and various other urban infrastructure ventures in southern Italy. The following year Infrasud and a number of other infrastructure interests were placed under the control of a new IRI subsidiary called Italstate (Società Italiana per la Infrastrutture e l'Assetto del Territoria). Italstate was a consulting agency organized like a *finanziaria*.

In 1957 the Italian parliament passed a law which dictated that state holding groups locate 60% of investments in new industrial enterprises in southern Italy. In observance of the law, IRI located its new steel mill at Taranto in southeastern Italy. In 1959 IRI took over the financially troubled shipyard at Taranto. The company made several more investments in the underdeveloped south, well beyond that stipulated by the law.

In the early 1960's IRI carried out a "rationalization," reducing employment and closing down some less profitable enterprises. However, pressure from unions and local governments prevented IRI from completing its goal of a more complete reduction in the company's size. From this point IRI ceased to be a state-run "hospital for sick firms" and was transformed into an operating company.

During the early 1960's the Italian government became increasingly interested in central planning. As a result, in December of 1962, it nationalized the Italian electrical industry and placed it under the authority of a state-

controlled company called ENEL (Ente Nazionale di Energia Elettrica). The capital which IRI received from the government as compensation for its electric companies was turned over to SIP for modernization of the company's telephone sector.

IRI's shipbuilding, iron and steel, and maritime industries entered a period of prolonged financial crises during the 1970's. Italian heavy industry in general lost its ability to compete with foreign manufacturers, particularly the Japanese. An additional financial burden was created when the Italian government instituted anti-inflationary economic policies which prevented IRI from making necessary tariff adjustments for its telecommunications, air transport and *autostrade* sectors. The government also ordered IRI to take over several ailing subsidiaries from the dissolved EGAM (Ente Gestione Aziende Minerarie).

IRI's unique corporate personality was based on the idea: "make state industries profitable and the private sector will invest." As IRI went further into debt, private investors became less willing to hold shares of either IRI or its subsidiaries. The Italian government was forced to purchase substantial amounts of IRI stock in order to keep private investors interested and to maintain the company's level of capitalization.

The IRI Group, or *Gruppo,* reported losses in 1974 of 68 billion lire. In the following two years the company lost 385 and 445 billion more. The worst year, however, was 1980, during which IRI posted a 2.4 trillion lire loss. In an attempt to forestall further decapitalization in 1981, IRI issued a quarter billion dollars in convertible bonds to the public.

Romano Prodi was elected president of the company by the board of directors in 1982. Prodi presented an intricate plan for IRI's recovery. The plan included reorganizing failing IRI companies and concentrating their resources to create new and more efficient companies. Financially troubled subsidiaries whose product lines were unrelated to IRI's other activities were to be sold. Prodi proposed that IRI and its subsidiaries offer more stock shares to the public to increase the involvement of private capital. Finally, on the managerial level, operational costs were to be more closely monitored and contained.

Prodi's plan also included a reduction in the company's work force, which was larger than the Italian army. The employee role was reduced from almost 600,000 to 472,000 in 1985. During this period IRI increased its expenditures for research and development from $400 million to over $800 million.

The program to elicit greater participation from private shareholders continued through 1986. 18 IRI Group companies were listed on the Milan Stock Exchange. Despite the divestment of several subsidiaries (including the sale of Alfa Romea to Fiat in 1986), IRI remained in control of over 400 companies worldwide. The company's considerable foreign holdings reflect on IRI policy which "considers internationalization as an instrument for growth."

Gruppo IRI is the largest company and the largest employer in Italy. The Finsider subsidiary is the third largest producer of steel in the world (after Nippon Steel and USX), and accounts for 55% of all Italian steel production. Another IRI company, Fincantieri, is responsible for 70% of Italy's shipbuilding output. Finmare accounts for 21% of Italian shipping volume and SIP controls 82% of Italian telecommunication traffic. Forty-five percent of the country's toll highways are operated by Autostrade. Alitalia, the airline subsidiary, covers 91% of the country's commercial air transportation. Selenia and Aeritalia control 55% of the Italian aerospace industry.

A number of large banks, including Banca Commerciale Italiana, Credito Italiano, Banco di Roma and Banco di Santo Spirito, are part of the IRI Group. Together they form the largest banking concern in Europe and account for 20% of Italy's total national lendings.

IRI was created as a government agency to reform and reorganize failing Italian companies. It has been transformed into a successful operating company under the direction of a centralized management bureau. While it is still government-controlled, substantial infusions of private capital into IRI have given it a unique new character. IRI's management board is almost completely divorced from the Italian government; its decisions are not subject to government approval.

Principal Subsidiaries: Banco Commerciale Italiana (65.5%); Credito Italiano (68.1%); Banco di Roma (80.6%); Banco di Santo Spirito (95%); Mediobanco (54.6%); Credito Fondiario (78.9%); Banco di Chiavari (69.9%) Cofiri; SIFA (51%); Finsider; Finmeccanica; STET (84.6%); SIP (70.3%); Italcable (51.3%); Sirti (46.4%); Fincantieri; Italstate; SME (64.4%); Alivar (94%); Ansaldo Trasporti (75%); Dalmine (81.9%); Finmare; Alitalia (77.8%); Aeritalia (84%); Autostrade (87.1%); Cementir (50.1%); Sifa (47.2%) Sofin; RAI; Finsiel; SPI.

Further Reading: The State as Entrepreneur: New Dimensions for Public Enterprise: The IRI State edited by Stuart Holland, London, Weidenfeld and Nicolson, 1972.

JARDINE MATHESON HOLDINGS LTD.

48th Floor, Connaught Center
Connaught Road
Central
Hong Kong
5-8438388

Public Company
Incorporated: April 9, 1984
Employees: 18,000
Sales: HK$10.4 billion (US$1.335 billion)
Market value: HK$9.142 billion (US$1.173 billion)
Stock Index: Hong Kong London

Jardine Matheson is one of the oldest names in East Asia, and has been a highly influential member of the Hong Kong business community since the territory was made a British colony in 1842. It has been a common saying for many years that Hong Kong is run by Jardine Matheson, the Royal Hong Kong Jockey Club, and the colonial government—in that order. In recent years, however, the company's desire to expand in other regions has caused it to lose some influence in Hong Kong.

William Jardine was born in 1784 in Dumfriesshire, Scotland. After studying medicine, Jardine went to work for the British East India Company as a ship's surgeon, but left the East India Company in 1832 to establish a trading company in Canton, China, with James Matheson, the son of a Scottish baronet, who had served for several years as Danish consul in China.

Trading with the Chinese was made extremely difficult by a xenophobic Manchu government, which believed that as the center of the universe, China already possessed everything in abundance and had no need for the products of "foreign barbarians." Among other things, Jardine Matheson & Company was restricted to a small plot of land on the banks of the Pearl River, near Canton, and were prevented from "keeping women" or dealing with Chinese merchants who were not officially sanctioned *co-hongs*. On one occasion, Jardine was struck a blow to the head as he attempted to petition local authorities. Entirely unaffected by the attack, he earned the nickname "iron headed old rat" among the Chinese.

Unable to make money selling manufactured goods to the Chinese, Jardine Matheson began smuggling opium into China aboard ships chartered from Calcutta in British India. Opium clippers sailed under cover of darkness to forbidden ports, while company agents bribed harbor masters and watchmen to prevent being discovered by the authorities. The Chinese government declared the opium trade to be illegal, but was virtually powerless to stop it. Finally, Chinese authorities seized and destroyed 20,000 chests of opium worth $9 million.

Jardine persuaded the British Foreign Secretary Lord Palmerston to send warships to China to enforce a judgment for reparations and to preserve free trade. The hostilities which ensued became known as the First Opium War. The Chinese lost, and were forced to sign a treaty on August 29, 1842, which awarded the British $6 million in reparations, opened the ports of Canton, Amoy, Foochow, Ningpo, and Shanghai, and ceded the island of Hong Kong to Britain.

Jardine Matheson purchased the first plot of land to be sold in Hong Kong, and promptly moved its offices there. The colony's first governor, Sir Henry Pottinger, endorsed the opium trade (in defiance of Queen Victoria), and later won the support of Parliament which viewed the opium trade as a method to reduce the British trade deficit with China. When the company's opium boats sailed into Hong Kong they were greeted by a cannon salute (the cannon is still fired daily, marking the noon hour). Jardine Matheson profited greatly from its privileged position in Hong Kong, and through the strength of its opium trade, began to develop commercial interests throughout the region. Jardine Matheson became known among the local Chinese as a *hong* (the word implies "big company" but has no relation to the name Hong Kong), and its chairman became known as a *taipan*, literally a "big boss."

During this period Thomas Keswick, also from Dumfriesshire, married Jardine's niece and was subsequently taken into the Jardine family business. Their son William Keswick established a Jardine Matheson office in Yokohama, Japan, in 1859, and later became a leading figure in company management. The Keswick family grew in influence within the company, largely displacing the Matheson interests.

Jardine Matheson established trading offices in major Chinese ports, and helped to set up enterprises as diverse as brewing and milling cotton, in addition to trading tea and silk. The company introduced steamboats to China, and in 1876 constructed the first railroad in China, linking Shanghai with Jardine Matheson docks downriver at Woosung.

Continued hostilities between China and Britain resulted in a Second Opium War in 1860 and a war to protect colonial interests in 1898. As victors in both these wars, the British gained trade concessions and colonies throughout China, and won virtually unrestricted commercial rights to conduct business in China. The opium trade, which China had been forced to recognize as legal, had become an extremely sensitive subject. Thousands of addicts (known as "hippies" because they would lie on their hips while smoking opium) had created a serious social problem. Elements in Parliament called for an end to commercial activities which perpetuated the pain and suffering of these addicts. The issue was seized by nationalists who argued for an end to the domination of colonial powers in China, and eventually led to uprisings such as the Boxer Rebellion and the Republican Revolution. For its own protection and business interests, Jardine Matheson was forced to curtail trading opium.

By 1906, the year it incorporated in Hong Kong, Jardine Matheson had expanded into a wider range of operations, but experienced strong competition from another British trading house called Butterfield & Swire, which was also based in Shanghai and Hong Kong. The competition between Jardine Matheson and the Swires began in earnest in 1884 when Butterfield & Swire set up a rival sugar refinery in Hong Kong in an attempt to break Jardine Matheson's monopoly. The competition spread into shipping and trading, but remained on the whole civilized and constructive.

Jardine Matheson continued to operate in China relatively unobstructed by the Nationalist government, which had grown increasingly corrupt. The company continued to expand its interests in China and, with other foreign interests such as Swire and Mitsui, became one of the largest companies in the country.

In the summer of 1937 Japanese forces attacked China in an attempt to expand Japanese commercial and strategic interests on the Asian mainland. Jardine Matheson officials stationed in areas overrun by the Japanese were branded as agents of European imperialism and imprisoned. The company's compradores were scattered, and its factories were looted; approximately 168,000 spindles were stripped from Jardine Matheson textile mills. Japanese military adventurism in China led to the occupation of several more Chinese ports, including Shanghai and Canton, where Jardine Matheson conducted a substantial portion of its business. Tony Keswick, a grandson of William Keswick, managed the company's affairs in Shanghai until 1941, when he moved to Hong Kong after having been shot by a Japanese. He was replaced by his brother John, who himself was forced to flee when the city came under siege. Jardine Matheson had been effectively prevented from doing any further business in China, but continued to operate in Hong Kong which, as British territory, the Japanese were unwilling to invade.

As a member of the anti-Comintern pact, Japan was unofficially allied with Nazi Germany and Fascist Italy in the war in Europe. The increasingly belligerent military leaders in Japan pledged to evict European imperialists from Asia and to establish a trans-Asian "Co-Prosperity Sphere." On December 1, 1941, Japanese forces invaded British colonies in Asia, including Hong Kong. Jardine Matheson officials in the colony were imprisoned with other Europeans at Stanley Prison. John Keswick, however, managed to escape to Ceylon (Sri Lanka), where he served with Admiral Earl Mountbatten's staff.

When the war ended in 1945, the British resumed control of Hong Kong and John Keswick returned to oversee the rebuilding of Jardine Matheson facilities damaged during the war. The company owned a small airline, textile mills, real estate, a brewery, wharves, godowns (warehouses), and cold-storage facilities. In 1949, however, after four years of civil war, Communist forces seized control of the Chinese mainland.

In Shanghai, John Keswick attempted to work with the Communists (who had invited capitalists to help rebuild the economy), in the belief that they would be more orderly and less corrupt than the Nationalists. Keswick argued for British recognition of the new government, and even attempted to run his company's ships past Nationalist blockades. By 1950, however, new government policies were enacted which increased taxes, restricted currency exchanges, and banned layoffs. Ewo Breweries, a Jardine Matheson subsidiary in Shanghai, was ordered to reduce its prices by 17%, despite heavy increases in the cost of raw materials. The government forced Ewo to remain open, despite a $4 million annual loss.

Companies based in Hong Kong were bound to observe a British trade embargo placed against China as a result of the Korean War. Conditions had deteriorated to a point where it was impossible to continue operating in China (on one occasion Keswick was arrested as he attempted to leave Shanghai). Compelled to close its operations in China, Jardine Matheson entered into negotiations with the government, and in 1954 settled the nationalization of its assets in China by writing off $20 million in losses.

Jardine Matheson continued to trade with the seven official Chinese state trading corporations, and attended the bi-annual Canton Trade Fair, where Chinese companies negotiated approximately half their nation's foreign trade.

Many of Jardine Matheson's management traditions changed after the war. While managers continued to be recruited primarily from Oxford and Cambridge, they started placing younger men in higher positions. John Keswick, whose nephews Henry and Simon were too young to run the company, returned to Britain in 1956 to direct the family estate and appointed Michael Young-Herries to manage the operations in Hong Kong.

In the late 1950's John and Tony Keswick enlisted support from three banks in London and purchased the last Jardine family interests in the company. Jardine Matheson became a publicly traded company in 1962 and, with additional capital provided by shareholders, acquired controlling interests in the Indo-China Steam Navigation Company and Henry Waugh Ltd., and established the Australian-based Dominion Far East Line shipping company.

In 1966 China embarked on its second campaign to form a nation of communes. During this campaign, called the "Cultural Revolution," China ceased virtually all trade with Hong Kong. While Jardine Matheson lost a significant amount of trade with the Chinese, its association of textile companies in Hong Kong continued to generate large profits from exports to the United States. The company's greatest achievement during this period was the sale of six Vickers Viscount aircraft to the Chinese. By 1969 the Cultural Revolution had lost its momentum and Jardine Matheson was once again doing business with the Chinese.

In 1972 the Keswick family attempted to install Henry as the new *taipan*, but met considerable resistance from supporters of managing director David Newbigging, the son of a former director of Jardine Matheson. The Keswicks prevailed after winning the support of institutional shareholders in London, and Henry Keswick was named senior managing director, while his father John resumed the chairmanship to ensure that the Keswicks did not lose control of the company.

Three years later Henry stepped down and returned to London, and was replaced by David Newbigging. Henry, remarked *Fortune*, lacked the "panache" of the elder Keswicks, and made "more than a few enemies" through his bold financial maneuvers. Henry did, however, complete a buyout in 1973 of Reunion Properties, a large real estate firm based in London. Keswick financed the takeover by creating an additional 7% of Jardine Matheson equity, but through the acquisition nearly doubled the company's assets. Henry Keswick also oversaw the acquisition of Theo H. Davies & Company that same year. Davies, a large trading company active in the Philippines and Hawaii, controlled 36,000 acres of sugar plantations. A few months after it was purchased by Jardine Matheson, world sugar prices rose dramatically.

At the time David Newbigging assumed the senior directorship of Jardine Matheson, a disturbing trend began to arise in Hong Kong. Throughout its history, Jardine Matheson had operated as a trading agent, or "middleman," arranging sales between producers in one location and consumers in another. Manufacturers in Hong Kong, however, discovered ways to sell their products directly to customers, bypassing agents such as Jardine Matheson. Even Hawker-Siddeley, a British company, managed to arrange the sale of six Trident jetliners to the Chinese without the negotiating expertise of Jardine Matheson.

Between 1975 and 1979, Jardine Matheson's profits grew at an annual rate of only 10% (a poor record for Hong Kong). David Newbigging responded by disposing of under-performing Jardine Matheson subsidiaries outside Hong Kong. He redoubled efforts to increase trade with China (which had only invited the company back into China in 1979), and resumed investments in Hong Kong-based enterprises. Jardine Matheson, however, had little expertise in these enterprises and lost money in almost every venture.

During the 1970's British companies in Hong Kong such as Jardine Matheson, Swire, Hutchison, and Wheelock Marden, were consistently outperformed by local, ethnically Chinese *hongs*. Most of these *hongs* became public companies in the early 1970's, and invested heavily in Hong Kong industries, which experienced strong growth during a decade-long bull market. These companies became serious competitors of the British establishment by the end of the decade.

Cheung Kong Holdings, a local *hong* run by an influential figure named Li Ka Shing, achieved a dominant position in the Hong Kong property market by 1980, threatening the business of Hongkong Land, a development company established in 1889 by William Keswick's brother James Johnstone Keswick, and which remained closely associated with Jardine Matheson. In addition, when the shipping magnate Sir Yue-Kong Pao decided to diversify from ships into property a year earlier, his first move was to outbid Jardine Matheson for the Hongkong & Kowloon Wharf & Godown Company, over which the two groups had previously shared control.

When it was discovered that a secret partner had begun acquiring shares of Jardine Matheson stock in late 1980, many observers suspected that either Li or Pao (or worse, both) were attempting to purchase a large enough share in Jardine Matheson to win control over Hongkong Land. Newbigging announced in early November that Jardine Matheson and Hongkong Land had agreed to increase their interests in each other, so as to make it impossible for any party to gain control of either company. The cross-ownership scheme, however, placed both companies deeply into debt.

The defensive actions required during 1980 forced Jardine Matheson to sell its interest in Reunion Properties in order to raise cash. Newbigging was criticized for being too conservative and placing too much emphasis on local and regional operations. While members of the Keswick family attempted to have Newbigging removed, perhaps no one worked as tirelessly as John Keswick. Newbigging finally stepped down as senior managing director in June of 1983, but retained the titular position of chairman. He was replaced as *taipan* by 40-year-old Simon Keswick.

The election of Simon Keswick, who had not yet proved his business acumen, initially worried many investors of Jardine Matheson. Upon taking control, however, Simon moved decisively to reduce the company's debts and to place Hongkong Land on firmer financial ground. In order to raise cash, he authorized the sale of Jardine Matheson's majority stake in Rennies Consolidated Holdings, a South African hotel, travel, and industries group based in Johannesburg, for $180.1 million. Keswick also established a new decentralized system of managerial control which split operations into a Hong Kong and China division and an international division.

In early 1984 David Newbigging was replaced as chairman by Simon Keswick. With the company now thoroughly under Keswick family control, Simon announced on March 28 that Jardine Matheson & Company would establish a new holding company called Jardine Matheson Holdings, incorporated in Bermuda. The announcement came at an extremely sensitive point in negotiations between the British and Chinese governments on the future of Hong Kong. Many observers regarded Keswick's plan as an attempt to remove Jardine Matheson from the uncertain business environment in Hong Kong, and as a solid display of no confidence in the Sino-British arrangement under which China would resume sovereignty over Hong Kong on July 1, 1997.

In defense of his actions, Simon Keswick admitted that Bermuda provided Jardine Matheson with a more stable operating environment than Hong Kong, but noted that the company was not abandoning its interests in Hong Kong, merely reducing its exposure there from 72% of total assets to a planned 50%. In addition, he pointed out that Bermuda (a British colony since 1612) permitted companies to purchase their own shares, a practice not allowed in Hong Kong.

In 1984 Jardine Matheson disposed of its sugar interests in Hawaii. The following year Keswick announced that after 153 years, Jardine Matheson would leave the shipping business, and that the company's fleet of 21 ships would be sold. By the end of the year many of the assets

Jardine Matheson acquired during the 1970's had been sold, reducing holdings by 28%.

In 1986 Keswick dismantled much of Hongkong Land, selling the company's residential real estate portfolio, and announcing that its Dairy Farm food subsidiary and Mandarin-Oriental Hotels unit would become independent. Keswick's plan to reduce Hongkong Land to real estate alone caused its managing director David J. Davies to resign in protest.

At the final juncture of his experience in Hong Kong, Simon Keswick announced in June of 1987 that he would relinquish the position of senior managing director to a 37-year-old American named Brian M. Powers. Keswick would remain company chairman and manage the family interests from London, as his uncle John did 20 years earlier.

The nomination of Powers to become *taipan* caused great concern among members of the company's more traditional Scottish establishment. Keswick, who had reversed the company's decline with drastic and unpopular measures, and who had yet to demonstrate their success, defended his choice of Powers. He explained that Jardine Matheson was now an international company with Hong Kong interests (rather than the other way around), and that as such, Brian Powers was best qualified to manage its affairs.

Jardine Matheson is primarily a trading company with strong interests in real estate and manufacturing. The company is also involved in finance through its joint venture subsidiary Jardine Fleming, a London-based merchant bank created by Jardine Matheson and Robert Fleming & Company. Despite its announced intention to move toward a more international base of operations, Jardine Matheson will remain intimately associated with business in Hong Kong and China. It has, despite its past, managed to maintain a special relationship with the Chinese government, and continues to be an important institution in arranging greater commercial contacts between China and the industrial West.

Principal Subsidiaries: Jardine Matheson Holdings Ltd. has 88 principal subsidiaries, including Jardine Matheson & Co., Ltd. (Hong Kong); Jardine Asian Holdings, Inc. (Panama); Jardine Davies, Inc. (Philippines) (81%); Gammon (Hong Kong) Ltd. (50%); Jardine Offshore, Inc. (Panama); Allied Guarantee Insurance Co., Inc. (Philippines) (23%); Central Registration Hong Kong, Ltd. (50%); East Point Reinsurance Company of Hong Kong, Ltd. (35%); Jardine Fleming Holdings, Ltd. (Hong Kong) (50%); Hongkong Land Co., Ltd. (26%).

Further Reading: Overseas Investment in the Age of High Imperialism: The United Kingdom 1850–1914 by Michael Edelstein, New York, Columbia University Press, 1982; *The Thistle and the Jade* edited by Maggie Keswick, London, Octopus, 1982.

KATY INDUSTRIES, INC.

KATY INDUSTRIES, INC.

853 Dundee Avenue
Elgin, Illinois 60120
U.S.A.
(312) 379-1121

Public Company
Incorporated: August 24, 1967
Employees: 6,607
Sales: $431 million
Market Value: $148 million
Stock Index: New York

Katy Industries, Incorporated was born out of an acquisition of the Missouri-Kansas-Texas railroad (MKT), a financially troubled operation that was in need of a profitable parent company. Wallace Carroll, whose knowledge of railroads dated back to his job as a section hand that helped pay his way through Boston College became acquainted with MKT many years later when he was persuaded that the ailing railroad had some attractive aspects that outweighed its reputation as a money-loser. In particular, Carroll was attracted by its New York Stock Exchange listing and the $30 million tax loss it would provide for his own company named American Gage.

Katy Industries became the parent holding company of MKT because the railroad company purchased 80% of the stock of Carroll's American Gage. With this purchase, Wallace Carroll became the chairman and majority stock owner of Katy Industries.

Carroll's experience with company acquisitions and expansions began in 1940 when he established a gauge business in Illinois. He had left New England for Chicago in 1936 after he was hired as a salesman for a Rhode Island precision gauge maker. Four years later he was selling gauges on his own. However, producing the gauges seemed a more profitable business than selling them, and thus Carroll borrowed $6,000 and took on a partner to start his manufacturing business. Carroll did not regret moving into the manufacturing business, but he did regret going into a partnership. "I promised myself I'd operate alone from that moment on," he stated, and he has kept his promise to himself ever since.

Carroll's entry into the gauge manufacturing business was timely. As with most manufacturing companies during World War II, Carroll's American Gage grew rapidly because of an "insatiable demand" for gauges. By the end of the war, American Gage was doing so well that Carroll

was able to begin purchasing other small manufacturing businesses. Carroll wisely made his acquisitions based on a peace-time economy. In particular, one of the companies that he bought after the war was a manufacturer of pots and pans. By 1948 Carroll's holdings had grown large enough that he established American Gage and Machine Company, of which he became sole owner, as a way in which to contain his holdings.

During this time Carroll's formula for acquiring companies, as a general rule, was to pay cash. He looked for small, family-owned businesses that produced both a good product and a substantial profit. His preference was to keep the original management, but if the management was comprised of older men then his policy was to make them consultants or honorary officers and hire a younger generation to manage the company.

While Carroll was successfully developing American Gage, the MKT railroad was having its share of problems. Several years before the creation of Katy Industries, MKT was on the verge of bankruptcy. The "Katy," as the railroad is nicknamed, included 2700 miles of damaged roadbed from Missouri to Texas on which derailments were likely to occur if the cars were moving faster than 25mph. Shipment of stock would often be damaged and, very few shippers would allow their products to be transported on the Katy. In March 1965 as a result, only 600 cars were moving on a daily basis.

However, by October of 1965, 1000 cars were moving daily. The cause for this substantial increase in activity on the Katy lines was a "non-stop talker" named John Barriger who came on board to save the railroad from its bankrupt condition. Barriger did not expect that the Katy would ever become a prosperous railroad, but he did hope that he could rebuild it so that a larger railroad company would be enticed into a merger.

Barriger had spent many years around the railroads of the country. After his graduation from MIT in 1921 Barriger worked for the Pennsylvania Railroad and then moved on to Calvin Bullock, Limited, a Wall Street firm where he worked as an industry analyst and inspected the nation's railroads. During World War II he was associate director of the Office of Defense Transportation. After the war he headed the Monon railroad, which was almost bankrupt. When he left in 1953 Barriger had managed not only to save the railroad from bankruptcy, but to establish a sound financial basis for its future operations.

In 1965 Barriger was nearing retirement age at the Pittsburg & Lake Erie Railroad company when he heard that the Katy was in need of talented management. Preferring the excitement of his work and the challenge of the Katy over retirement, he took on the job. As the new president of MKT, Barriger relied on his friends to help improve the railroad. By repairing the roadbeds as much as he could within the first few weeks of his presidency, and by making a deal with his numerous railroad friends that their use of the Katy would be returned through payment of back damage claims and improved service, Barriger was able to increase the number of cars moving on the Katy lines within a short period of time.

The return to creditable service on the Katy was a difficult task. The poor condition of the roadbed meant spending any profits on the railroad. Still, its reputation as a money-loser had not prevented Barriger from saving it from bankruptcy, and although his hope that a merger with a larger railroad would take place was not realized, the railroad company looked strong enough for a parent company to give it the kind of support it needed. Barriger continued his presidency only long enough to get the Katy in a strong operating position.

Katy Industries quickly began to diversify after the acquisition of the MKT. Carroll separated the company into four very different groups: the Electrical Equipment and Products Group, the Industrial Machinery, Equipment and Products Group, the Consumer Products Group, and the Oil Field and other Services Group. By 1972 the company was expanding into European and Canadian markets, particularly within the oil and gas exploration fields.

One of the most important acquisitions for Katy Industries in the late 1960's was that of Bee Gee Shrimp, a collection of companies which operates a 100-trawler fleet off the coast of Georgetown, Guyana, and which harvests and sells shrimp. Bee Gee Shrimp was primarily responsible for doubling the sales and earnings of Katy's Consumer Products Group in 1979, and this allowed Katy a degree of comfort during the recession years.

Even the MKT was showing a profit for the first time since 1963. In 1971 the Katy made a $21,000 profit, which proved its ability to operate on a break-even basis. However, the profits were put back into the railroad, particularly in the area of track maintenance, which was a high 16% of operating costs that year.

By 1971 another man with a reputation of being able to "tackle tough jobs" was at the Katy. Reginald Whitman became president and chairman of MKT in 1969 and is credited for being able to keep the company headed in a profitable direction. Whitman's confidence that the Katy would not only be profitable, but that it would also grow was an important aspect of the future earnings of the company.

By 1973 neither the railroad's negative book value of $9 million nor its net deficit was consolidated in Katy's annual report. The company did not have to write-off the railroad's losses against its consolidated earnings. In addition, Katy no longer had to carry the railroad's large debt on its balance sheet.

For Katy, the railroad provided a shelter that was important to its acquisitions. Between 1970 and 1973 Katy purchased 15 companies for approximately $34 million. Most of the companies were small and privately-owned. Once they were put behind the tax shelter of the railroad their profits increased significantly.

Katy is considered to be a "diversified investment fund" which is different from its kind because it usually owns a majority, if not 100%, of its affiliate's stock. W.H. Murphy, Treasurer of Katy, regards this policy as one which allows a "uniformity of overall corporate policy as well as the exchange of technology, marketing, purchasing, and financial assistance" within the companies.

Katy's formula for acquiring companies has not changed significantly over the years. Carroll still likes to purchase small companies which have good product lines and pre-sent small risks. Says Carroll, "If it is profitable or we could make it profitable, we buy it." It is also Carroll's policy to buy companies which already have good management in order to give the division manager a sizable amount of autonomy. In addition, Katy offers incentives to its subsidiaries which are based on earning increases as a means of keeping the companies productive and efficient.

This formula has been a successful one for Katy. Its net growth increased from $2 million in 1971 to $18 million in 1981. Katy managed to increase sales throughout the recession years of the early 1980's. In fact, its earnings were so good that Katy expanded its pump manufacturing company, LaBour Pump, which is located in Ireland.

In 1983 Katy began to expand into the silverware business. Carroll first purchased Wallace Silversmith Inc. in August, and then purchased Insilco Corporation's international unit around October of the same year. These new acquisitions and investments in the early 1980's represent some of Katy's efforts to offset the uneven earnings of the company's railroad and machinery operations.

By 1985 plans were in the air to sell MKT. Union Pacific had made an offer that required MKT to obtain 60% of the outstanding income certificates on the company. MKT had only purchased 41% by mid-1985. Union Pacific then terminated the offer. Chairman Carroll's comment on this turn of events in early 1986 was that Katy would "keep on running the railroad; it's a good property." What the future holds for the MKT depends greatly on its ability to meet the terms of any future offer.

Katy needed to increase its earnings for 1985. The company had some significant losses which were blamed on the casualty and property insurance business, Midland Insurance. Midland's problems were caused by difficulties in the market. Katy liquidated the insurance company in the early part of 1986, but net sales dropped from $4.3 million in 1984 to $3.9 million in 1985.

In other areas, however, Katy was experiencing new developments. Early in 1985 Katy announced that its subsidiary, Katy-Seghers Incinco Systems Inc., had been awarded its first contract to build a waste-to-energy plant. It had taken the company six years to win a contract since the start of the business in 1979, and the subsidiary was expected to see some profits in 1985. Carroll sees the waste-to-energy plants as the "future direction" of Katy Industries and expects that there will be great demand, and competition, for these plants because of the increased environmental concerns of the nation. Specifically, state and local governments are considering this form of incineration, and if the trend continues in this area, Katy expects to be in the midst of the development of these plants.

With an eye toward future trends and a conservative company policy of acquiring profitable and small-risk companies, Katy is a diversified conglomerate that will continue to grow in the future.

Principal Subsidiaries: Bush Universal, Inc.; W.J. Smith Wood Preserving Co.; Shrimp Group; Sterling Salem Corp. (80%); Peters Machinery Co.; Fulton Iron Works

Co.; Aetna Bearing Co.; Panhandle Industrial Co.; Quality Foods Machinery, Inc.; Bach-Simpson Ltd. (Canada); Elgin Diamond Products Co. (50%); Missouri-Kansas-Texas Railroad Co. (97.77%); American Gage & Machine Co.; Coastal Oil and Gas Ltd. (Newfoundland); Katy Oil Company of Indonesia; Oakes Machine Corp.; Simpson Instruments Sales & Service, Inc.; Katy Export, Inc.; Sahlman Seafoods, Inc.; LaBour International Limited; Wallace International Silversmiths, Inc.; Bee Gee Shrimp, Inc.; Hermann Loewenstein, Inc.; W.H.E. Watch Company, Inc.; Zeugama, Limited; Seacom Sales Company, Inc.; Gilt, Inc.; HMW Industries, Inc. (50%); Data Processing Inc.; Amerad Advertising Inc.; Diamond Stylos Co., Ltd. (30%); B-B Liquidating Co.; C.E.G.F., Inc. (80%); E.R. Liquidating Co., Inc.; Elgin Watch International, Inc.; Empro Manufacturing, Inc.; International Carbide Tool, Inc.; Intrad Imports, Ltd.; KT Air, Inc.; KT-Plas, Inc.; Katy Bearing Corp.; Katy Communications, Inc.; Katy International, Inc.; Katy Seghers Incinco Systems, Inc.; Katy Teleswitch, Inc.; Modern Foods, Inc.; Trans Continental Leathers, Inc.

KIDDE

KIDDE, INC.

Park 80 West, Plaza Two
Box 5555
Saddle Brook, New Jersey 07662
U.S.A.
(201) 368-9000

Wholly-owned subsidiary of Hanson Industries
Incorporated: July 1, 1968 as Walter Kidde & Co., Inc.
Employees: 32,000
Sales: $2.356 billion
Market Value: $769 million
Stock Index: New York

Kidde, Inc. was not always a billion dollar conglomerate. In fact, Walter Kidde began his company in 1900 with only $300 in savings, a degree from Stevens Institute of Technology, and an interest in the construction industry. However, Kidde's business acumen helped push Kidde, Inc. into the ranks of Fortune 500 companies within the United States.

The New York construction company that Walter Kidde established in 1900 grew quickly into another area of interest. Kidde began to expand into the business of fire fighting, which became the catalyst for his company's rapid growth and development. In 1918, Kidde, Inc., then Walter Kidde & Company, purchased the rights to the "Rich" system for detecting fires on board ships. This method of extinguishing fires by steam had one major flaw, namely, steam caused extensive damage to the ship's cargo. Kidde's answer to this problem was to use carbon dioxide instead of steam as a means of smothering the fire without damaging the cargo.

While Kidde had made advances in solving the problems confronting effective fire fighting, he still faced another major hurdle. The carbon dioxide was not being released quickly enough from its container and therefore the extinguishing process was not completely successful. In 1923, Kidde solved this problem by purchasing the patent rights for a siphon device that allowed quick release of the carbon dioxide. With this new addition to the design of its extinguishers, Walter Kidde & Company achieved two manufacturing firsts: in 1924 the first portable carbon dioxide fire extinguisher was produced and in 1925 the first built-in industrial system was installed. In addition, the company began winning government contracts. In 1926 Walter Kidde & Company, along with the Navy, designed a system to protect airplane engines against fires.

With these new developments in the fire extinguisher aspect of the company, Kidde separated the fire-fighting business from the construction business but kept the original name. This was just the beginning of the multi-interest outlook that was later to become the trademark of Kidde, Inc.

The 1930's were profitable years for Walter Kidde & Company. By 1940 the company had 200 sales agencies in the United States and major cities in Europe, South America, Africa and Asia. Subsidiary sales companies were also located in Canada, Germany, and Italy, and two factories were producing products in England.

In particular, World War II had a significant impact on the growth of the company. Prior to the war 30% of the company's extinguisher sales went to the U.S. government. In 1938 Walter Kidde & Company had its best year with sales of $2 million and a work force of 450. It was in this year that Walter Kidde wondered whether or not he was "smart enough to run a $5 million business," as he pondered the inevitable expansion of his company.

Five short years later, sales far exceeded the $5 million mark. By 1943 Walter Kidde & Company was producing $60 million worth of war equipment and the work force had increased to 5,000. The transition to war-time production was not an easy one; however, once the war began, production and demand for Kidde's products grew rapidly. So rapidly, in fact, that production of war equipment could not meet demand, and the company was often behind schedule. This was in part due to the company's need to adapt their peace time products to war uses.

Although production may have been slower than demand, the products manufactured by Walter Kidde & Company did play an important role in the war. In addition to the fire detection and extinguishing equipment for tanks, planes and ships, Walter Kidde & Company also manufactured inflation devices for life rafts and safety belts. The company is credited with manufacturing the automatically inflated rubber life boats from which Captain Eddie Rickenbacker, a World War I hero and flying ace, and his seven companions, were rescued after spending three weeks in the South Pacific when their airplane ran out of fuel.

Walter Kidde's concern over whether he was capable of running a $5 million business was clearly answered by 1943. The company was headed for a profitable future. While Walter Kidde may have been reticent about his potential as a businessman, his ability to discern future trends and developments assisted him in the growth of his own company. In 1939 he predicted the demand for labor-saving machinery, and the future of the "one-man-push-button-controlled plants" that would create individual working efficiency.

Kidde's ability in the private sector was enhanced by his involvement in the public sector. He was chairman of the board of trustees of Stevens Institute of Technology; member of the New Jersey advisory board of the Public Works Administration; and president of the New Jersey Chamber of Commerce from 1935 to 1938. He also declined an offer to be the New Jersey republican candidate for governor in 1927. His interest in making things work is underlined by his success in reorganizing the bankrupt New York, Susquehanna & Western Railroad, of which he was a trustee, and restoring it to a paying basis in 1937. In 1943, the year his company reached peak production figures, Kidde died at the age of 65 from a heart attack, and the company was handed over to his son John Kidde.

As expected, the drop in production at the end of the war caused a dramatic drop in Walter Kidde & Company sales. In the 1950's the company diversified into areas of machinery and tool manufacturing, siphon devices for consumer and medical uses, and aircraft accessories. Fire extinguishers were still an important part of the company. However, in general, the activity of the company had markedly decreased. In 1959 sales reached the $40 million mark and did not change until 1964 when a new president was brought on board.

In January of 1964 there were several new changes at Kidde, changes that would affect the size and outlook of a company that had not experienced many since the war. Although Walter Kidde & Company was considered to be a firmly established company with an excellent reputation, it was also considered to be a company that needed direction.

Fred Sullivan, at that time an officer and director of the large conglomerate Litton Industries, was attracted to the idea of "defining" a new direction for the company. Sullivan was so interested in this new opportunity that he succeeded the late Robert L. Dickson, who had been president of the company since 1961.

Sullivan's rise to Kidde's top leadership is a classic story. He began by working as a $14-a-week clerk during the Depression at Monroe Calculating Machine Company, which was then the number one company of its kind. After 10 years at night school, Sullivan earned his BA degree at Rutgers, and a rare MBA at New York University. At the age of 39 he was president of Monroe. When Monroe merged with Litton Industries in 1958, Sullivan became an officer and director of the company until he left in 1964 to assume a new position at Walter Kidde & Company.

From the time Sullivan began his presidency at Kidde, acquisition and growth were elements of his primary strategy. His management style is described by *Forbes* magazine as "no-frills, tight-with-a-buck, keep it lean and liquid." This style meant reducing the work force by 10% and reorganizing the entire company upon his arrival at Kidde.

Sullivan's reorganization plans included the need to think in terms of customer markets instead of product lines. Prior to Sullivan's presidency, the company had separate lines for burglar alarms and fire protection services. One of the first initiatives of the company reorganization was to combine these two lines. This new definition of the protection field resulted in acquisitions of lock and safe companies by the close of the 1960's.

Under Sullivan's direction Kidde quickly grew from a fire extinguisher concern of $40 million in annual revenues in 1964 to $400 million by 1968, when the company was incorporated as Kidde & Company, Inc. Some of the larger acquisitions of the 1960's included Dura Corporation, which manufactures auto parts and testing equip-

ment; Lighting Corporation of America; and Grove Manufacturing Company, which manufactures hydraulic cranes. In particular, Grove became an important acquisition for Kidde because of its lucrative contracts with the U.S. government in the 1980's.

Kidde's fast rate of growth placed it in a unique position. While most large companies reach the Fortune 500 list after many years of development, Kidde just missed this notable ranking in 1965, a year after Sullivan's move into the company. *Fortune* magazine reported that Kidde was ranked 501 on the list that year and missed being 500 by $60,000, the price of one of Kidde's burglar-alarm systems for a large company. One year later, Kidde not only made it onto the list, but ranked 283.

One of Kidde's most problematic acquisitions was made in 1969 when it purchased U.S. Lines, a major, but financially troubled transportation system. Sullivan was later to label this acquisition, a "grave mistake." It was an acquisition that resulted in eight years of frustration and litigation. The U.S. Lines acquisition was, at the time, an attractive investment for Kidde because of its future earning potential as a container transportation system.

Although Kidde was apparently looking into the future when it made this acquisition, it did not seem to fit the Kidde formula of buying companies with a "proven record of successful growth faster than the GNP." Kidde competitors looked on in disbelief, feeling sure that Kidde had decided incorrectly. However, Sullivan looked past the operating losses of U.S. Lines and into the future of container transportation, which he believed represented a "major building block in a new kind of transportation system that is coming."

When U.S. Lines lost $1.5 million in 1970, Kidde began to look for a buyer. It was not until 1978 that a sale took place, and even though the shipping company had started to earn money again in the 1970's, Kidde was determined to sell it. The buyer was Malcolm McLean, who had founded Sea-Land Service, Inc., one of the U.S. Lines competitors. U.S. Lines was sold for $111 million, and the general analysis of the sale was that Kidde, and Sullivan, had managed to turn a potential disaster into a profit.

Kidde's sale of U.S. Lines was timely. With the emergence of the recession Kidde found itself in the enviable position of being in good in financial condition. This was also due to Kidde's decentralized approach and the careful acquisitions made in the late 1970's. Overall, Kidde purchased ten businesses in 1979, one of which included Victor Comptometer, which was right behind Sharp Electronics, the leader in sales of desktop calculators.

By 1980 the company had adopted Kidde, Inc. as its title and was making solid profits in its recreational and consumer lines, such as Faberware cookery, Jacuzzi water therapy equipment, Bear archery equipment and Sargent Locks. Sullivan was not concerned that the company was too diversified. He believed that his decentralized approach to managing the Kidde subsidiaries helped to keep the subsidiaries "responsible and profitable." The group managers are considered to be corporate-level executives who have offices at the leading corporation within their group, and not at the New Jersey headquarters. This management style allows Sullivan to maintain control of the subsidiaries, but it also allows for decision-making at the local level.

While consumer and recreational products were doing well for the company, Kidde made a move away from this market in 1981 into the energy and industrial markets. Kidde's Grove Manufacturing purchased Oilfield Industrial Lines Inc. that same year and began its oil rig business. Although Kidde was affected when the price of oil dropped in 1982, the company promptly moved into oil and gas exploration as a way in which to establish a market for its own rigs. However, the plan failed, and the blame was placed on the explorers, who were considered to be novices. This failed expansion into oil and gas exploration resulted in the sale of five operating units to compensate for the 1985 losses of $400 million.

While Kidde's entrance into the oil industry was not successful, and its future financial stability is questioned because of such a major loss, the 80 new businesses that have been acquired by the company since Sullivan joined the company in 1964 have established Kidde as a solid, diversified conglomerate. Even though new developments for Kidde Inc. depend on its ability to recover from the oil and gas exploration setback, management's policy of continued diversification and acquisition will play an important role in determining its future earnings.

In July 1987, Sullivan announced that Kidde was studying options such as reorganization or selling off some or all its assets, and in August Hanson Industries, the US arm of Hanson Trust of the UK, bought Kidde in a $1.7 billion deal. Sir Gordon White, the chairman of Hanson Industries, commented on the good match of the two groups' operations, and said that Kidde would be kept largely intact. Some of Hanson's previous takeovers, however, have been paid for in part by disposing of unwanted assets, and it remains to be seen how many of Kidde's assets will be sold.

Principal Subsidiaries: Walter Kidde Sales & Service Co.; S.R. Smith Co., Inc.; Globe Security Systems Inc.; E.J. Burke Security Systems Inc.; Globe Protection Inc.; Inter-State Bureau of Investigation Inc.; Interstate Detective Agency Inc.; Interstate Service Corp.; Interstate Security Services Inc.; W.K. 38, Inc.; Thexnrer, MI.; Tucker Housewares, Ml.; S.R.M. Business Svces, Inc.; S.R.M. Business Svces, Inc.; Oilfield Pipe & Supply Co.; Oilfield Industrial Lines Inc.; Kidde Systems, Inc.; Kidde Recreation Prod., Inc.; Kidde Automated Systems, Inc.; The Jade Corp.; Input/Output, Inc.; Walkers-Roberts Corp.; W.K., Inc.; W.K. 64, Inc.; Republic Creations, Inc.; Total Ltd.; Merit Protective Service Inc.; Reliable Sentry Services Ltd.; Southern Security Services Inc.; Southern Security Devices Inc.; J.H. Sparks Inc.; Deena Products Co.; Devine Lighting Inc.; Dura Steel Products Co.; Fashion Inc.; Jacuzzi Inc.; Jacuzzi Whirlpool Bath Inc.; Jet-Phillips Inc.; Wright Light, Inc.; Keystone Lamp Mfg. Corp.; Kim Lighting Inc.; Marvin Electric Mfg. Co.; Mobilite Inc.; Piedmont Moulding Corp.; Progress Lighting; Rexair Inc.; Circle Steel Corp.; Cook Pump Co.; Grove Manufacturing Co.; Manlift Inc.; National Crane Corp.; South Texas Equipment Co., Inc.; Grove Beco Corp.; Associated Laboratories Inc.; Bayless Stationers, Inc.; Bright Star Industries, Inc.; Business Products Inc.; Chatas Glass Co., Inc.; Craig Systems Corp.; EAM Inc.; Kidde Consultants Inc.; Kidde Credit Corp.; Kidde Consumer Durables Corp.; Tose Inc.; Treher-Montague, Inc.; W.D. Byron & Sons, Inc.; Kidde Holdings, Inc.; Newport Plastics Corp.; Fenwal Inc.; Richards Manufacturing Co.; Shadeco, Inc.; Spartus Corp.; J.H. Spaulding Co.; Whiteway Manufacturing Co.; Vigon Lighting Inc.; The ERTL Co.; Vanity Fair Industries Inc.; Nissen Corp.; Universal Gym Equipment Co.; The Valley Co.

KOÇ HOLDING AŞ

Meclisi Mebusan Caddesi 53
Findliki-Istanbul
Turkey
(1) 143 29 00

Public Company
Incorporated: 1963
Employees: 31,075
Sales (group): TL 1.544 trillion (US$ 2.083 billion)
Market Value (total assets): TL 616 billion (US$830 million)
Stock Index: Istanbul

Koç (pronounced "coach") is a name immediately recognized in Turkey, but virtually unknown elsewhere. It is the name of several of Turkey's most prominent companies, including Koç Holding, the largest private capital firm in Turkey. The founder of the Koç group of companies is Vehbi Koç, the first Turkish businessman to gain national prominence. Known as a generous philanthropist, he is also responsible for introducing a number of modern Western business practices to Turkey.

Vehbi Koç was born and raised in Ankara, at that time a city of 30,000 located in central Anatolia. When he was a boy he recognized that the most prosperous families in Ankara were non-Turkish minorities such as Greeks, Jews, and Armenians. They were successful traders and businessmen, occupations which were discouraged for Moslem Turks. Still, the minorities lived comfortably and many were rich, while Turks lived more modest lives as *hodja* (priests), civil servants, wardens, farmers, and grocers.

In 1917 Vehbi Koç convinced his father, a literary scholar, to help him establish a small grocery store in Ankara. Although he was only 16 years old, Koç recognized that commerce was the only means to wealth for a man such as himself. He pursued his trade diligently and endured the economic hardships of both World War I and the subsequent collapse of the 600-year old Ottoman Empire.

When Turkey became a republic in 1923, President Kemal Atatürk moved the nation's capital from Istanbul to Ankara. Koç entered new lines of business in construction and building supplies, and later won a prestigious contract to replace the roof of the Turkish parliament when the old one was blown away in heavy winds. Vehbi Koç worked tirelessly, often for more than 16 hours a day.

Although he became a millionaire at the age of 26, he continued to display unusual dedication. For eight months during 1930 he labored at a construction site to ensure that a hospital project was completed on schedule.

In 1928, as the company continued to diversify, Koç became a local agent for the Ford Motor Company and established several Ford dealerships throughout the country. Koç signed an exclusive agreement with the Mobil Oil Company in 1931 to search for oil in Turkey, and by 1940 had secured exclusive Turkish import and distribution rights for a variety of European and American products, including Ford cars and Socony Vacuums. During this period the company headquarters were moved to the port city of Istanbul so that trading operations could be more closely monitored.

Turkey was a neutral power during most of World War II and never became directly involved in any military action. Despite this, Koç experienced a significant disruption in its international trading business.

German forces occupied Greece and nearly succeeded in reaching the Caucasus oil fields northeast of Turkey before the war turned in favor of the Allies. After German troops were driven out of southeastern Europe and Germany had fallen, the Soviet Union attempted to gain control over the Dardanelles and Bosporus Straits, strategic Turkish sea lanes which connect the Black Sea and the Mediterranean. Between 1945 and 1947 a number of developments in Yugoslavia and Greece reduced Soviet influence in the area, and a conservative Turkish government with strong ties to the United States came into power. As the government consolidated control, it instituted a series of isolationist commerical policies which were intended to protect the domestic economy.

Foreign companies were obliged to sell their products through local agents such as Koç, who maintained import and distribution rights for foreign products in Turkey. Koç concluded agreements with several companies, including General Electric and Burroughs. Competition was greatly reduced and limited to only a few Turkish companies, operated by *compradore* capitalists like Vehbi Koç, Danis Koper, Uzeyir Avunduk, and Y. Selek, who held a virtual monopoly over imported products which were greatly in demand.

The company's profits were heavily reinvested, helping to make the 1950's a period of impressive growth. Koç became affiliated with United States Rubber and Siemens, and in 1955 purchased a small steel furniture and home appliance manufacturer called Arçelik (Turkish for "pure steel").

Koç was criticized in academic and political circles for allowing Western "imperialist" corporations to drain Turkish capital and foreign exchange which could have been used to develop Turkish industries. Koç, however, did generate a small amount of foreign exchange through its export operations. While defending its role as a net importer, Koç started to expand its domestic production facilities, and eventually negotiated licensing agreements to domestically manufacture products which had previously been imported. While this still required the importation of parts and components, Koç redirected a considerable amount of its production payments to Turkish interests.

In 1963 Vehbi Koç established a holding company for his diverse business interests. Koç Holding was founded as an *anonim şirket* (the Turkish form of incorporation) and designated as the coordinating organ for the 28 companies which comprised the Koç group. In 1966 the company made its first public stock offering. The infusions of private capital further increased the companies' capitalization and made even greater expansion possible.

Vehbi Koç slowly relinquished control of the group to his only son Rahmi, whom he later appointed chairman of the Koç Holding executive committee, and his three daughters. Such a graceful move into retirement was uncommon in Turkey, where patriarchical autocracy is practiced in business as well as family affairs. In fact, the elder Koç did not retire. He maintained a light work schedule and continued to serve as chairman of the board, which preserved his right to veto any decision made by his son's executive committee.

In 1966 a wholly-owned subsidiary of Koç called Otosan began to manufacture an automobile based on the Ford Cortina design. Sold under the name of *Anadol*, it was the first automobile to be completely manufactured in Turkey. Another Koç company called Tofaş continued to assemble Fiat automobiles, sold under the brand name *Murat*.

Offering highly competitive salaries, the Koç group attracted the best qualified managers and businessmen in Turkey from a variety of ethnic and religious backgrounds. Many were educated at West European and American universities and business schools (Rahmi Koç graduated from Johns Hopkins University). They brought with them the latest managerial skills and strategies, and formed an innovative and dynamic group which was largely responsible for the institutionalization of five year plans in 1971 as part of a broader scheme of long range planning.

When import companies purchase materials from a foreign country, they are usually required to pay for them in terms of the foreign country's currency. Companies which have not accumulated enough foreign currency for the transaction are forced to purchase it from commercial or government banks. When their foreign currency reserves are depleted, they are obligated to sell the local currency. This depresses the value of the local currency and makes it even harder to import foreign goods. Koç was a company in just this position. It never accumulated foreign currencies because it imported substantially more than it exported; in other words, Koç was a net importer.

During this period the Koç group continued to experience problems with foreign currencies. As a net importer it was unable to meet its requirements for foreign exchange. In order to meet their obligations to foreign suppliers, Koç companies were forced to drain foreign exchange from government accounts. In time, this became a considerable political liability. Once again Koç began to explore options which would allow them to substitute domestically produced products for those which were imported.

During this period Koç helped to establish a steel alloy plant at Bursa called Asil Çelik. It was planned that Asil Çelik would produce engine blocks and component parts for other Koç group manufacturing operations. Although the plant was built to help reduce the company's depend-

ence on foreign imports, it may also have been intended to win the sympathies of certain politicians and elements in the military who strongly believed that for strategic and economic reasons, Turkey should develop its industrial infrastructure.

Asil Çelik, the centerpiece of the company's import substitution drive, took several years to complete. While progress was made in reducing the company's foreign exchange, the company remained a net importer. The Turkish economy, however, deteriorated so seriously that at one point even government foreign exchange reserves were depleted. Koç, which generated only 10% of its foreign exchange needs, was forced to suspend import payments and temporarily scale down its operations.

In response to the crisis, Rahmi Koç set up a new company agency called Ram diş Ticaret, specifically devoted to the promotion of exports and internal generation of foreign exchange. Koç also won a year long battle with the rival Sabanci group for control over the country's fifth largest bank, the Türkiye Garanti Bankasi. The bank was restructured to perform more international transactions for the Koç group. The Koç companies experienced record growth during 1977 and 1978, the worst years of Turkey's economic crisis. Rahmi Koç redoubled his company's efforts to promote exports, recognizing that "the country cannot be poor while we are making money."

Koç became impatient with what was termed the "sluggish bureaucracy" of government officials in Ankara. He assembled a team of trade representatives from the Koç group to meet with officials from Soviet bloc nations, who were told to narrow their trade surpluses with Turkey by puchasing more Turkish products. Next, Middle Eastern oil-exporting nations were asked to increase their imports of Turkish products. Soon, however, Turkey's economic crisis began directly to affect Koç. The company's growth virtually halted by 1979 and 5000 workers had been laid off.

On September 11, 1980, as the Turkish economy approached a state of virtual chaos, elements of the Turkish armed forces under General Kenan Evren seized control of the government and imposed martial law. As part of the military government's stabilization policy, severe restrictions were placed on foreign exchange payments. As a result, Koç was forced significantly to alter its business strategies. Operations in the group's divisions (many of which were operating at 30% of capacity) were further scaled down, and some were closed completely. The Asil Çelik steel plant was the most seriously affected Koç interest. The plant was closed and later nationalized by the military government.

The Koç financial division, consisting of a bank and an insurance company, were expanded to provide the group with greater foreign exchange services. When the financial division was etablished in the mid-1970's, it ended a 50-year policy of Vehbi Koç that the company remain out of this line of business.

With control restored to the Turkish economy, the military government authorized a general election for the return of civilian government. The Motherland Party led by Turgut Özal came to power in 1983 and began a campaign to "Westernize" the economy by lifting protectionist trade restrictions. Beginning in 1985 foreign companies were permitted to export products directly to Turkey.

Imported Japanese and Soviet automobiles began to compete directly with automobiles manufactured by Koç's Tofaş and Otosan divisions. Koç also faced competition from imports in such areas as refrigerators, office supplies, canned goods and textiles. The company protested strongly, arguing that the sudden implementation of a liberal trade policy would upset the economy and eliminate domestic investment incentives. Prime Minister Özal responded that the people of Turkey were suffering under a trade policy which forced them to purchase inferior goods, and which provided Turkish companies with no incentive to improve their products in order to make them internationally competitive. While presenting Koç with a serious challenge to its livelihood, the trade policy was not considered to be a ruinous development.

Koç maintained its association with a variety of Western corporations, and in 1985 concluded an agreement with American Express to establish a joint venture bank called the Koç-Amerikan Bank. Koç was also a partner in the Istanbul Fruehauf Corporation, which began to produce full and semi-trailers in 1985.

Vehbi Koç took another step into retirement during 1984 when he passed the board chairmanship to his son Rahmi. He continued to advise the executive committee of his opinions and concerns through daily memos. Koç, a strong proponent of free trade and Turkish membership in the European Community, was regarded as a distinguished elder statesman.

Koç Holding and the various group companies have largely succeeded in maintaining profits and growth, despite the government's liberalization of import policies. Rahmi Koç has proved himself to be a highly competent and well-trained business strategist. Based on its past record of success and current managerial talent, Koç promises to remain the most prominent member of Turkey's corporate community.

Principal Subsidiaries: Tofaş Group (Automotive): Bursa Oto, Egemak, Gün Oto, Istanbul Fruehauf, Istanbul Oto, Karsan, Karsan Pazarlama, Opar, Ormak, Otobüs Karoseri, Otokar Pazarlama, Otoyol, Otoyol Pazarlama, Ottar, Setur Oto, Türk Traktör, Tofaş, Tofaş Oto, Tormak, Trakmak; *Otosan Group* (Automotive): Döktaş, Ege Oto, Kuzey Motolari, Motör Ticaret, Otokoç, Otosan, Standard Belde, Nasoto, Otomotor; *Automotive Supplies Group*: Bebimot, Beldesan, Endiksan, Mako, Royal Tevzi, Takosan, Tekersan, Uniroyal Endüstri; *Durable Goods Group*: Alpa, Arçelik, Ardem, Atilim, Beko, Bekoteknik, Destek, Egemen, Gelişim, Hamle, Türk Elektrik Endüstrisi; *Consumer Products Group*: Aymar, Besan, Beytaş, Bozkurt, Bürosan, Düzey, Kav, Kurt Mensucat, Maret, Migros, Tat, Türkay; *Construction and Mining Group*: Demir Export, Garanti Inşaat, Izocam, Kimkat, Koçtaş, Koza, Mavi Çelik, Merkez Ticaret, Türk Demir Döküm, Tarko, Tek-Iz; *Energy and Trade Group*: Ak-Yak, Akpa, Ankara Gaz, Aygaz, Bilar, Bürokur, Bursa Gaz, Gazal, Haliç Antrepoculuk, Koç Burroughs; *Energy and Trade Group*: Lipet, Mobil Gaz, Porsuk Ticaret, Setur, Setur Diners, Setur Avis, Tataş, Turistik Işletmeler; *Financial, Foreign Trade and Siemens Companies*: Koç Yatirim, Şark Sigorta, Etmaş, Hataş, Simko, Günsu, Kofisa Diş Ticaret, Ram. Koç also has interests in 22 non-consolidated companies.

LEAR SIEGLER, INC.

220 South Orange Avenue
Livingston, New Jersey 07039
U.S.A.
(201) 535–9522

Wholly-owned subsidiary of F.L. Industries
Incorporated: December 21, 1950 as Siegler Heating Co.
Employees: 29,725
Sales: $2.3 billion

Lear Siegler does not produce the fancy, executive jets that bear the "Lear" name. Rather, the company's products range from car seats and brakes to weapons control gear for military fighter planes. Its more than $2 billion-a-year annual sales comes from three major areas: aerospace-technology, automotive parts, and industrial-commercial. The company, however, is basically anonymous since its products are either unmarked or bear only the label "LSI." But Lear Siegler, which went private in 1987, is an influential part of the manufacturing industry in the United States.

The company was incorporated in December 1950 as Siegler Heating Company. Originally a maker of climate control equipment, the company changed its name to Siegler Corporation after merging with Siegler Enamel Range Company Inc. in 1954. In that year, John G. Brooks, a flamboyant entrepreneur, and nine other associates bought the Siegler Corporation of Centralia, Illinois, for $3.3 million – $3.2 million of this money was borrowed for 24 hours at a cost of $60,000. Over the next decade and a half Brooks, who became Siegler's first president, established a reputation for supervising numerous startling acquisitions.

In June 1955, seven months after the merger, Hallamore Manufacturing Company, an electronics firm, became Siegler's first acquisition. During the 1960's, the company expanded rapidly. In 1962 Siegler merged with Lear Inc, an aerospace electronics firm, and changed its name to Lear Siegler Incorporated. The deal, which cost Siegler five shares for each seven Lear shares, nearly doubled the company's sales – from $96.2 million in 1961 to $190.8 million by the end of 1962.

In 1965 LSI (the "short" form of the company's name) acquired all assets of Hypro Engineering Inc (today operated as the Hypro Division) in exchange for more than 120,000 common shares. In 1966 it purchased American Metal Products Corporation, an automobile

seating and furniture parts manufacturer, and Home Furnace Company (which today operates as a division of the company). In 1968 LSI purchased National Broach & Machine, a gear machine manufacturer.

LSI acquired Cuckler Steel Span Company (today operated as Cuckler Building Systems Division) in 1970. The purchase of the Haas Corporation (currently the company's plastics division) and American Industrial Manufacturing Company, a manufacturer of thermo, plastic, and fiberglass safety helmets, represented LSI's entry into plastics manufacturing.

In the early 1970's, LSI's luck changed for the worse. In 1971 the company, then a major subcontractor for the Lockheed L-1011 commercial jet programs, saw its earnings plunge when the project was suspended because of problems with the jet's engine supplier, Rolls-Royce. Delays in other government projects, steep start-up costs at a modular housing factory in Hawaii, and a strike at General Motors also damaged the company's profits. By the end of the year Lear found itself involved in a major reorganization which involved consolidating five of its divisions and selling five others.

In January 1971, following a business dinner in Detroit, John G. Brooks had a fatal stroke at the age of 58. He had personally presided over more than three dozen acquisitions of mismatched, marginally profitable businesses which took the company into many different areas. Robert Campion, then company Secretary, followed Brooks as Lear Siegler's president and chief executive officer. Campion's low-key approach permitted the company to fade into relative obscurity.

Campion had come to what was then the Siegler Corporation from Alexander Grant & Company, the company's accounting firm in Chicago in 1957. Campion, a staunch believer in corporate planning, became one of the most successful practitioners of growth through acquisitions and diverstiture. By the time he took charge of the company, however, LSI had acquired the reputation of being overstaffed and under-controlled. One of Campion's goals for the company was to rebuild it, partially through diverse acquisitions and partly by extending its product lines. Campion believed that as an industry reached the end of its natural life cycle, it should be discarded. LSI, as a conglomerate, should periodically shed components that failed to meet productivity and/or profitability standards to prevent the company from stagnating and keep it growth-oriented. Campion wanted $2 back in sales for every $1 of total assets, on which he wanted to net 4 to 5 cents in profits.

Another of Campion goals was to improve LSI's management by re-educating the managers who were specialists in their field to be generalists sensitive to the needs of the whole corporation and concerned with long-range objectives. He took away their numbers and asked for long-range strategies in return.

By the mid-1970's Lear had acquired full ownership of the formerly 50%-owned American Avitron Inc, as well as Central Foam Corporation (now a unit of Foam Products Division). In 1977 and 1978 Lear sold four divisions. Campion anticipated that the troubled automotive industry would pass on their profit losses to their suppliers and divested many holdings in this area. By late 1979 Campion had removed the company from the axle-housing business and had started selling parts of the division that manufactured seats for cars and trucks. By this time, only 8% of LSI's automotive business resulted from the sale of original parts; the rest came from the safer automotive after-market or from selling specialized machine tools. As automakers began restructuring their assembly lines for the production of small vehicles for the 1980's, this machinery became increasingly popular.

In February 1984 LSI paid $282 million for the Bangor Punta Corporation, known primarily for its Piper Aircraft, Smith & Wesson law enforcement equipment, and Starcraft powerboats, camping trailers, and Cal and O'Day sailboats. Starcraft, the largest U.S. manufacturer of aluminum boats, represented Lear's entrance into the recreation industry.

LSI's Automotive Division, whose two major products were replacement glass and brake products, showed record sales in 1984. The Aerospace Division did (and still does) most of its business in the military sector. By 1979 the company had such a backlog of military orders that it seemed invincible to the impending recession. LSI provided digital fly-by-wire flight control systems for both Israel's Lavi fighter aircraft and Sweden's multi-role JAS-39 aircraft. The company expanded its military capabilities even further with the purchase of Developmental Sciences Inc., designer and manufacturer of small remotely piloted vehicles. Most of the company's military business, however, involved retrofitting older aircraft.

In 1984 LSI and ITT's cockpit voice recognizers were flown in Phase I of developmental testing in General Dynamics Advanced Fighter Technology Integration F-16 fighter plane. Budget limitations, however, forced the replacement of ITT's equipment with Texas Instruments' for Phase II of testing. Both systems were considered for communications, navigation, weapons system status reports, and aircraft systems cautions control, which used computer-generated speech fed to the pilot's earphones.

In early 1985 Lear bid on a $5.3 million contract for F-18 fuel tanks. The company, however, learned in February that Israel Military Industries would be awarded the contract. The company protested to the Pentagon, using the argument that the "Buy American" rules should have applied. When the Navy announced it would proceed with the purchase, LSI filed a suit in United States District Court in Los Angeles to block the Navy's actions until the protest had been resolved.

LSI's lawsuit was the first to challenge the administration's decision to disregard the section of the 1984 Competition in Contracting Act that suspends action on a bid award that is under protest. The law – part of an industry-backed effort – was originally designed to increase competition for the lucrative military business by putting impartiality back in the bid process and makes the 25-day deadline on agency response to bid protest investigations a requirement. Both President Reagan and then attorney general William Smith, however, declared this section of the law an unconstitutional breach of the division of powers between the White House and Congress and ordered purchasing agents to disregard the law. The

Navy agreed informally to delay the purchase pending more litigation

By mid-1985 LSI's main contribution to the automotive parts industry was metal seat frames. Lear built a plant within 15 minutes of a major General Motors plant in Michigan to meet the auto industry's growing need for rapid finish car seats that can be delivered within hours of an order. The location allows American automakers to operate with a smaller inventory and to design specifications like their counterparts in Japan.

In June 1986 the Zentec Corporation agreed to purchase LSI's Data Products division, once the leading supplier of low-end dumb terminals. LSI's decision to abandon the market came after its 17% market share in 1980 diminished to about 2 percent in 1985. Pressure from personal computer manufacturers and inexpensive overseas suppliers forced the company initially to shift designing, producing, and packaging of the equipment offshore, and then, finally, to sell.

Also in 1986, St. Clair Industries Inc. (a holding company comprised of four managers at the company) completed a leveraged buyout of National Broach & Machine Company, a gear machine and cutting tools manufacturer and engine builder that primarily served the defense and aerospace industries. Additionally, Nortek Inc. bought Lear's Climco unit, the company's climate control operations.

Since purchasing Piper Aircraft in 1984 as part of the Bangor Punta deal, LSI has had to battle the general depression in the aviation industry. The glut of used planes, low demand, and high product liability insurance forced Piper to close two of its three plants in 1985. Piper was forced to pay over $50 million to cover the increase in its product liability insurance which cut into the company's already shrinking profits. By the end of 1986, LSI, faced with a possible takeover, made plans to sell Piper.

In mid-October the company announced talks with Drexel Burnham Lambert on a massive restructuring plan. In early October, LSI's shares inexplicably increased from the mid-50s to the high-60s. Some analysts speculated that several large traders scattered rumors of a hostile takeover bid to "scare" irregular trading in the company's stocks and to cause LSI to do something that could net quick profits. Other analysts believe that the sharp rise in stock prices, occurring just 13 days before LSI publicly announced restructuring plans, had a hint of impropriety. (In early 1987, Drexel Burnham Lambert was involved in a massive insider trading scandal, in what was referred to by some as "a game of stocks and robbers." Several traders involved with Drexel pleaded guilty to the charges that they profited from early disclosures on restructuring and takeover.)

Analysts had for months prior to the disclosure, however, recommended LSI's shares as a possible restructuring or buyout candidate. By October Drexel indicated that LSI might consider recapitalization along the same lines as Colt Industries Inc., which had earlier in the year accumulated debt and reduced its equity in what was called a public leveraged buyout. LSI had been restructuring on its own since early 1985 by divesting all undesired divisions. By the beginning of November 1986, however,

LSI's chief, Norman A. Barkley, doubted that the company could avoid a takeover.

As a means of protection against hostile bidders, LSI, along with more than ten other industrial conglomerates, reinstated the "poison pill" provision into their by-laws. The clause, designed to discourage raiders from making a hostile takeover bid, gave shareholders in the company the option to buy additional stock or sell their shares at a better than usual market price, thus making the takeover extremely unprofitable. The Securities and Exchanges Commission condemned the measure as not being in the best interest of the stockholder because it often reduced the value of the stock.

In November 1986 Wickes Inc, a clothing, furniture, and bedding manufacturer, made a "friendly" bid of $93 per share for LSI after AFG had offered $85 per share in late October. Wickes, who had agreed to purchase Collins & Aikman Corporation for $1.16 billion the week before, could not find adequate financing for the deal, and was finally forced to withdraw its bid in December. In that same month, Forstmann Little & Company (part of F.L. Industries), a New York investment partnership, launched a leveraged buyout of LSI. Forstmann's offer of $92 per share, or $2.1 billion, was better than AFG by $7 per share and was only $1 less per share than Wickes' offer. Forstmann's advantage over its competitors, however, was its ability to obtain financing and not because its bid was the highest. The funds came from cash pre-committed by institutional investors.

Lear Siegler has seen more than 40 acquisitions and divestitures in its relatively short lifespan. Shaped by John Brooks and Robert Campion, the company grew from a maker of heating equipment to a manufacturer of auto and plane parts, and expanded from serving rural communities into a major subcontractor for the military. Talk of possible break-up plans and management changes are not encouraging for the company that was once thought of as an innovative member of the manufacturing industry.

Principal Subsidiaries: Aviquipo of Britain Ltd.; Aviquipo of Canada Ltd.; Aviquipo Holland B.V.; Aviquipo de Portugal, S.A.; Lear Siegler International Ltd.; Lear Siegler Industries Ltd.; Lear Siegler Properties Inc.; No-Sag Drahtfedern GmbH; No-Sag Spring Company Ltd.; Arroyo Insurance Company.; Brake Specialty Inc.; Bangor Punta Corporation; Bangor Punta International Capital Corporation; Bangor Punta Overseas S.A.; Société Jeanneau Constructions Nautiques S.A.; Producers Cotton Oil Company; South Lake Farms; Starcraft Recreational Products Ltd.; Certified Brake Ltd. (U.K.); Data Products Ltd.; Developmental Sciences Inc.; Developmental Sciences International Corporation; Lear Siegler International Corporation (FSC); Lear Siegler International GmbH; Lear Siegler International Italiana S.r.l.; M.H.E. Contracting Inc.; M.H.E. Contracting Ltd.; Rapistan-Industria e Commercio Ltd. (94% owned); Rapistan Lande GmbH; Rapistan Lande N.V.; Rapistan Lande S.A. (88% owned); Rapistan S.A. de C.V. (70% owned); Rapistan S.A. (89% owned); Rapistan Systems Ltd.; Rapistan van der Lande B.V. (90% owned); Société No-Sag Française (56% owned); Central de Industrias S.A. (40% owned); No-Sag Drahtfedern Spitzer & Company (50% owned); Rapistan Lande S.A. (Spain) (49% owned); LSI Avionic Systems Corporation.

Further Reading: Planning for Growth and Profit: The Success Story of Lear Siegler, Inc. by John G. Brooks, New York, Newcomen Society, 1970.

Litton

LITTON INDUSTRIES, INC.

360 North Crescent Drive
Beverly Hills, California 90210-9990
U.S.A.
(213) 859–5000

Public Company
Incorporated: Nov. 2, 1953 as Electro Dynamics Corp.
Employees: 58,200
Sales: $4.2 billion
Market Value: $2.1 billion
Stock Index: New York Zurich Amsterdam

By the time he founded Litton in 1954, Charles "Tex" Thornton had compiled quite a resumé. Born to a family of modest means, Thornton made his first real estate investment at 14 and owned a filling station and car dealership at the age of 19. Thornton's reputation as an astute businessman was established during World War II when he designed a statistical control system that vastly improved the United States government's ability to procure and allocate military equipment.

Thornton and his associates, who included Robert S. McNamara and Roy Ash, were known as the "Whiz Kids." After the war the entire group was hired by Ford Motor Company. After two years at Ford, however, Thornton went to work for Howard Hughes and helped establish Hughes Aircraft Company in the semiconductor market. When Thornton tired of Howard Hughes's eccentric business practices he decided to form his own company.

When Thornton organized his company he did not have any capital. However, Thornton correctly believed that the U.S. Defense Department would soon be seeking increasingly sophisticated weapons, and that there was room in the defense industry for another large electronics company. Due to the fact that small electronics firms tended eventually to be eliminated or absorbed by larger competitors, Thornton resolved that his company would grow and expand quickly, by making acquisitions if necessary. His company would have to be large if it was to compete with rivals like Howard Hughes.

Thornton believed that the success of his plan depended on surrounding himself with financially astute and technically proficient businessmen. Since he could not offer high salaries, he used stock options to induce people to join him. Over the years, the list of ex-Litton employees reads like a Who's Who of prominent American business-men; several of Thornton's subordinates went on to prominent posts in the U.S. government and to manage firms like Ford.

With the help of Roy Ash and Hugh Jamieson, Thornton formed a company called Electro Dynamics, and immediately set out to find the small electronics company on which they would build their empire. Litton Industries, a vacuum tube manufacturer located near San Francisco, California, seemed the ideal choice. The only problem involved raising the $1.5 million necessary to purchase Litton from its founder Charles Litton. After an agreement with Joseph Kennedy collapsed, Thornton and Ash approached Lehman Brothers, an investment firm. Lehman Brothers had followed Thornton's career since he was a vice president at Hughes Aircraft, and had decided to finance Thornton before he even requested assistance. Joseph Thomas from Lehman Brothers later said that their firm did not invest in Electro Dynamics as much as it invested in the ability of Thornton.

Using borrowed money, Thornton acquired Litton Industries in 1954, and purchased a few smaller electronics firms that same year. Thornton's strategy was to continue purchasing electronics companies with high growth potential, and build Litton into a company that could meet almost any request for advanced technology.

Since Thornton knew Litton stock would eventually increase in value, he paid cash for companies whenever possible. Colleagues claimed that one of Thornton's techniques for arriving at a good price for a company was to continue the negotiations for as long as possible until physical exhaustion caused the other party to yield. After acquiring a company, Thornton allowed the original employees as much freedom as possible, so they could continue conducting the operations that made the company desirable in the first place.

When he purchased Litton Industries, Thornton promised Lehman Brothers that his company, with eight million dollars in sales, would have $100 million in sales by 1959. As it turned out, Litton Industries reached $120 million in sales by that year. In order to reach and exceed his goal, Thornton had merged with Monroe Calculating Machines. Monroe benefited from Litton's technological assets while Litton needed Monroe's sales and service outlets. Besides calculators, Litton was manufacturing inertial guidance systems for aircraft, potentometers, barratons, duplexers, klystroms, and other electronic products. During this period, almost 50% of Litton's business was with the U.S. government.

By 1961 Litton was the fastest growing company on the New York Stock Exchange. Litton's success during this time can be attributed to Thornton's business acumen. Although Thornton had built Hughes Aircraft into a leader in the field of semiconductors, he kept his own company out of that market. The semiconductor market crashed in 1961, confirming Thornton's decision. Thornton also refrained from manufacturing transistors, which overcrowded the market in the early 1960's.

When Litton stock began selling at 33 times earnings (it was later to reach 75) some analysts suggested that the company would soon experience financial difficulties; Litton had acquired 23 companies in eight years. Thornton defended himself by pointing out that he purchased companies on the basis of how well they were managed and then provided the management with the money and freedom it needed to develop new products. The rate of growth for these companies, which averaged 50% a year, was produced internally as well as through acquisitions.

By 1963 sales reached half a billion dollars. An article in *Fortune* magazine suggested that Litton's success lay in going against the current wisdom. For instance, in its defense work, Litton concentrated on procuring contracts for manned aircraft and let other contractors fight over missile contracts. The U.S. Air Force's need for aircraft turned out to be greater than anyone had previously suspected.

One of Litton's most important acquisitions was Ingalls Shipbuilding Corporation, the country's third largest private shipbuilder. The large but ailing company was purchased for eight million dollars in cash and the assumption of nine million dollars in debt. The appeal of the company was that it made submarines and oil-drilling equipment to which Litton's electronic controls could be added.

In the mid-1960's Litton continued to sustain its high rate of growth, even after it passed the one billion dollar mark in sales. Although it continued to acquire more companies, Litton resisted defining itself as a conglomerate; instead, it referred to itself as a "technological company," or a multi-industry manufacturer of products whose common denominator was their technological complexity. Where Stouffer frozen foods and Royal typewriters fit into the picture was not clear. Yet Roy Ash spoke of the electronics empire as "a company that is meaningful as a whole" with "a coherent relationship between its different parts."

After 57 quarters of remarkable growth, Litton reported a decline in earnings of $11 million and, as a result, its shock plummeted. Investors incurred a paper loss of two million dollars. The decline in profits would not have been such a catastrophe if Litton stock had not been selling at 40 times earnings, and if Litton had not conducted a certain type of publicity campaign. Critics charged that Litton's true innovations were in investor relations, rather than in high technology.

Forbes magazine described Litton's annual reports as "a feast for the eye and a famine for the mind." In fact, Litton used unusual, but not illegal, accounting techniques that exaggerated the company's growth. Litton convinced its stockholders to look at the company's "synergy" and its "meaning as a whole" rather than scrutinize figures that would have revealed some money losers among Litton's acquisitions. The company's highly publicized technological innovations and perceived advantage in the market was also exaggerated. For example, the license for Litton's microwave oven was owned by Raytheon, the company that invented it. It was revealed that Litton relied heavily on other companies' research and development of new products. Litton's success resulted from producing other companies' inventions inexpensively; when it had to depend on its own designs the company often ran into difficulties.

Part of Litton's failure to develop better products can be attributed to the company's emphasis on short-term growth. Management often overlooked long-term research and development in favor of immediate financial gains. Although Litton executives envisioned themselves as part of a high technology conglomerate, according to *Business Week* magazine the company was "a mundane manufacturer of capital goods."

In 1972 Litton's credibility was further damaged by Roy Ash's claim that after three years of declining profits, Litton's sales would revive that year. Instead of sales reviving, however, the company recorded a $2.3 million deficit. The division most seriously affected was Ingalls Shipbuilding, which had recently built a large new shipyard. Due to delays in building a number of container ships, Litton was forced to pay a total of five million dollars in penalties. In addition, due to delays by the shipbuilder in meeting a one billion dollar contract for landing helicopter assault ships, the U.S. Navy decided to reduce its initial order from nine to five ships.

In 1973 Fred O'Green, an engineer, was chosen by Thornton to replace the departing president Roy Ash. O'Green was instructed by Thornton to reduce Litton's holdings and improve its technological competence. O'Green was chosen because of his experience with Ingalls Shipbuilding. It was thought that O'Green could use his expertise to correct production and design problems at the shipyard.

O'Green began to analyze Litton's various businesses and separate the profitable ones from the money losers. In 1974 Litton reported $77 million in write-offs in the business systems division, which had lost money for two consecutive years. In 1979 the company sold its Triumph-Adler typewriter business, which had lagged far behind its competitors. The largest write-off was the $333 million of cost overruns Ingalls Shipbuilding absorbed from the five disputed helicopter ships it had built for the U.S. Navy.

As Litton eliminated its losing businesses, the company's more successful ventures became apparent. Western Geophysical emerged as one of Litton's most profitable holdings; its seismic exploration services prospered during the 1970's oil crisis. Western Geophysical had compiled over 200,000 miles of logs charting seismic activity and these logs were a priceless source of information for oil drillers to pinpoint sources for oil. With 30 research ships collecting data around the world, Western Geophysical led the world in providing seismic information to the oil industry.

Another source of profit for Litton was its guidance and control business. Litton's most significant contribution to the high technology field was its inertial guidance system, which helps keep planes on their flight routes. As a direct result of the effectiveness of this system, Litton procured a $1.6 billion contract from the Saudi Arabian Air Force.

Eventually, problems at Ingalls Shipbuilding were corrected. Profits increased from $44 million in 1979 to $78 million in 1983. Due to Litton's large capital investment in the shipyards, Ingalls' success was crucial to the financial stability of the company. The importance of Ingalls Shipbuilding to Litton was underscored when Western Geophysical's profits declined because of a decrease in oil exploration during the early 1980's.

During the 1980's Litton finally became the high technology company it had always regarded itself. Unprofitable high technology businesses and non-related businesses were divested, including business machines, small publishers, medical products, and office furniture. Though earnings dropped in 1983, the company's earnings curve was much higher than it had been in the 1970's. In fact, Litton soon became a possible takeover candidate. The idea that Teledyne owned 26% of Litton's stock was not exactly reassuring to company management. Litton purposefully went deeper into debt to discourage potential buyers and to improve its cash reserves in the event of such a takeover.

In the early 1980's Litton purchased Itek, a defense electronics firm, and Core Laboratories, a natural complement to Western Geophysical. At that time, it appeared Litton was refocusing on defense electronics, seismographic equipment, and industrial automation, especially robotics.

Litton has not escaped controversy. The National Labor Relations Board is investigating allegations that the parent company has a centralized anti-union policy, which also filters down to the subsidiaries. In addition, the U.S. Defense Department recently suspended the company from bidding on new defense contracts when it was reported that a Litton subsidiary defrauded the government of $300 million. To make matters worse, the company's expanded capability radar warning system for the F-16 fighter jets has failed operational tests.

The future for Litton probably means more restructuring. Orion Hoch, who took over as chief executive officer in late 1986, hopes to wean the company away from defense contracts and to improve oil services and industrial automation services. One step in this direction occurred in February 1987 when Litton merged its resource exploration group with the Atlas division of Dresser Industries to offer an expanded high technology oil exploration service. At the same time, Litton purchased Lamb Technicon Corporation, which supplies automated manufacturing systems for the auto industry, to improve its industrial automation services.

Hoch told *Forbes* magazine recently that, "The Litton of the future is essentially in place. Now our job for the next several years is to make what we have perform."

Principal Subsidiaries: Litton Business Systems, Inc.; Litton Industrial Automation Systems, Inc.; Litton Systems, Inc.; Western Geophysical Co. of America. The company also lists subsidiaries in the Cayman Islands, Saudi Arabia, and Switzerland.

Further Reading: Someone Has to Make It Happen: The Inside Story of Tex Thornton, The Man Who Built Litton Industries by Beirne Lay, Englewood Cliffs, New Jersey, Prentice Hall, 1969.

LOEWS CORPORATION

666 Fifth Avenue
New York, New York 10103
U.S.A.
(212) 841-1000

Public Company
Incorporated: November 12, 1969
Employees: 21,900
Sales: $6.7 billion
Market Value: $5.801 billion
Stock Index: New York

The Loews Corporation is a $6.5 billion conglomerate, with extensive interests in tobacco, insurance, movie theaters, watches, and hotels. Recently it has also invested heavily in broadcasting and oil tankers. With such large operations one would expect Loews to be managed like any other conglomerate. However, this is not the case. The Loews Corporation is a family business. The principle owners, Bob (Preston Robert) and Larry Tisch, are brothers. The former is president and chief operating officer; the latter is chairman and chief executive officer. A number of Tisch offspring have also become prominent members of the company's management.

This does not mean that the Tisch family supervises the day-to-day operations of the corporation. Rather, the company functions through a network of divisions which exercise a large degree of autonomy and assume responsibility for performance. Initiative and innovation are encouraged and rewarded. However, when something goes wrong the problem is brought quickly to Bob Tisch's attention. There is no administrative labyrinth in which to lose or hide operational defects. "Loews is a big business run like a small business," Tisch says. "I hope we can keep it that way."

The Tisch brothers were given an early business education by their father, Al, who owned a children's manufacturing plant in Manhattan. Bob and Larry were given the task of making phone sales to retail stores and wholesale distributors. The two brothers also helped operate a few summer camps their parents owned in New Jersey.

This "hands on" experience was coupled with formal training. Bob, after a brief hiatus spent in the Army, graduated with a degree in economics from the University of Michigan in 1948. Larry, at 18, graduated cum laude from New York University's School of Commerce and then went on to receive a Master's in business administra-

tion from the Wharton School in Philadelphia. Later he enrolled in Harvard's law school.

In 1946, Al and Sadye Tisch sold their summer camps and purchased the Laurel-in-the-Pines Hotel in Lakewood, New Jersey. The hotel business went well, and soon became more than the parents could handle alone. As a result, Larry dropped out of Harvard in order to help run the business and Bob soon followed. Soon afterward, the older couple decided to sign over their share of the hotel (worth about $75,000 at the time) to their sons and give them control of the operation.

It was not long before the brothers were leasing two other small New Jersey hotels and making a profit. Then, in 1952, they acquired two grand but old hotels in Atlantic City called the Brighton and the Ambassador. One they tore down to build a motel in its place; the other they quickly resold at a profit. Later, the Tischs liquidated some of their New Jersey investments to purchase their first two hotels in New York City.

In 1956, with only eight years experience in the business, Bob and Larry erected the $17 million Americana Hotel in Bal Harbour, Florida, and paid for it in cash. Although it was subsequently sold to Sheraton, it represents an important step in the success of the brothers. With the Americana, they firmly established themselves among the major hotel operators. Later the brothers obtained such prominent hotels in the United States as the Mark Hopkins, The Drake, the Belmont Plaza, and the Regency.

In 1959 a major anti-trust ruling forced Metro-Goldwyn-Mayer to relinquish ownership of Loew's Theaters. This decision created an opportunity for the Tisch brothers, allowing them to move into a new business area. Six months before MGM was to divest Loew's, Bob and Larry purchased a large amount of stock in the theater chain; by May of 1960 they had gained control of the company.

The brothers did not enter into the theater business because they knew about the motion picture industry. Nor did they purchase Loew's because it was already a profitable operation on its own. On the contrary, Loew's theaters were losing money. They were large, multi-tiered movie houses with high ceilings and interiors reminiscent of another age. They played only one motion picture at a time and were rarely filled to capacity. Television and the proliferation of material coming out of Hollywood meant that theaters would have to cater to various tastes simultaneously in order to secure larger audiences. The old Loew's theaters were not designed for this purpose.

The reason Bob and Larry Tisch purchased Loew's had to do with real estate. The Loew's theaters, though antiquated, were located on valuable city property. It was the opportunity to acquire this valuable property that prompted the brothers to purchase the company.

Almost immediately they began transforming the theaters into liquid assets, demolishing 50 of them in a matter of months and then selling the vacant lots to developers. This, of course, hastened the demise of the palatial movie house, but it was nonetheless a necessary business tactic. Loews (the apostrophe has since been eliminated) remains a prominent participant in the movie industry with theaters in 26 metropolitan areas. However, its 143 screens are located in only 61 facilities. There are often four screens in one building, each showing a different movie.

The Loews name, established and well-recognized, became the corporate title under which all Tisch operations (including hotels) were placed. The new Loews Corporation ran smoothly and efficiently, turning substantial profits every year. By 1968 the brothers again had the capital and the inclination to diversify and invest in a new business sector. This time they acquired Lorillard Industries, America's oldest tobacco manufacturer.

Lorillard, the maker of Kent and Newport cigarettes, had once been a major company with a large share of the tobacco market. However, managerial incompetence and discord had paralyzed the company, almost bringing it to full collapse. Upon assuming control of Lorillard, the first thing Larry Tisch did was examine the firm's subsidiaries, particularly its candy and cat-food divisions which were consuming a disproporionate amount of resources. The brothers discovered that the top executives spent 75% of their time on candy and cat-food, which together made up only 5% of Lorillard's total business. Lorillard divested itself of these interests and the executives who were so fond of them. Larry and Bob Tisch then redirected the company toward its tobacco operations. Market share slippage was reversed, and Lorillard today is America's fifth largest tobacco company.

A similar scenario took place in 1974 when Loews acquired CNA Financial, a large insurance firm. The Chicago-based conglomerate reported a $208 million deficit that year and was looking to lose more. Like Lorillard, its subsidiaries were draining the financial resources of the company. CNA's tangential interests were poorly managed and veritable "money pits." Moreover, there was considerable waste at the top of CNA's corporate structure.

When Loews took charge it "weeded out the bad subsidiaries and concentrated on the ones it could save." The Tisch brothers then took aim at the wastefulness that plagued CNA's headquarters. Money executives were fired as Tisch austerity measures prevailed over past CNA lavishness. The 3,000 square foot suite of the former chairman was rented out, as was the corporate dining room. The streamlining had a dramatic and positive effect. In 1975 CNA earned a $110 million profit, and has been financially sound ever since. It now does over $3 billion in business.

The next major acquisition for Loews was Bulova watches. For $38 million the brothers acquired 93% of the company in 1979. Like the other Loews subsidiaries, Bulova was then a financially troubled company with an image problem. Due to quality control problems it had been supplanted by its chief competitor Seiko. The introduction of Pulsar and similarly priced Timex watches put added strain on Bulova's already dwindling market share.

Its name was simply not recognized by the new generation of consumers.

The Tisch brothers applied their proven method of managerial restructuring, but without total success. The problems went beyond personnel and corporate networks; the product itself needed to be revised. James Tisch, Larry's son, headed the operation and immediately introduced 600 new watch styles, complete with extended warranties. To deal with the image problem an extensive advertising campaign was conducted. The company recovered, but slowly. By 1984 it had cut its losses to $8 million (roughly half of its 1980 total), yet it was still not paying for itself. Not until 1986 was the company able to turn a profit.

When not tending to the operations at Loews, Bob and Larry Tisch lead separate lives. Bob is heavily involved in public service. He is one of New York City's most vocal supporters and has been elected over 15 times to the chairmanship of New York's Convention and Visitors Bureau. It was Bob Tisch and the Bureau's president, Charles Grillett, who came up with the idea of using an old jazz expression, the "big apple", to represent New York City.

In 1986 Bob Tisch unofficially left Loews to accept an appointment as U.S. Postmaster General. Despite the doubts of those who feel his absence will weaken the company's performance, most analysts contend that Bob Tisch's move to Washington D.C. will help Loews, citing the advantages of both political and financial connections.

Late in 1985 Larry Tisch purchased a large amount of CBS stock to help the company fight a takeover attempt by Ted Turner. Throughout 1986 Tisch increased his share holdings in CBS and obtained a seat on the board of directors. In September of that year he was elected president of CBS, much to the pleasure of stockholders and employees who had grown frustrated and uneasy during the Turner takeover attempt.

Tisch's popularity was short-lived, however. Intending to operate CBS as if it were any other business, he took measures to alleviate waste and make CBS more cost-effective. Wage and expenditure reductions, along with wholesale firings, caused a serious rift in the huge broadcasting firm. The news division, traditionally given considerable leeway in regard to fiscal accountability, was especially hard hit. Only time will tell if Tisch will be able to mend CBS without sacrificing the people and principles that once made it the most respected of the three major American broadcasting networks.

Principal Subsidiaries: CNA Holdings, Inc.; Loews Theaters, Inc.; Loews Hotel Holding Corp.; Bulova Watch Co. Inc.; Loews Cinemas, Inc.; Loews Trading Corp.

LTV CORPORATION

2001 Ross Avenue
P.O. Box 225003
Dallas, Texas 75265
U.S.A.
(214) 979-7711

Public Company
Incorporated: May 11, 1956 as Ling Electronics, Inc.
Employees: 37,300
Sales: $8.199 billion
Market Value: $847 million
Stock Index: New York

The man who built LTV from a small electronics firm into one of America's largest corporations was named James J. Ling. Through a process of acquisition and merger Ling created a modern corporate conglomerate. Prior to the 1930's a company such as Ling's would have been regarded as a monopoly.

In 1947 Jimmy Ling invested $2000 in order to establish an electrical construction and engineering firm in Dallas. In 1956, after several successful years in business, the Ling Electric Company merged with L.M. Electronics of California and the name of the company was changed to Ling Electronics. A subsequent merger with Altec Electronics in 1959 changed the name of the company to Ling-Altec. A year later Ling-Altec merged with the Temco Electronics and Missile Company of Dallas. The new company, Ling-Temco, became one of the first major defense companies to be founded after World War II.

In 1961 Ling-Temco merged with the Chance Vought Aircraft Company. Vought was founded in 1917 and became part of the Boeing United Aircraft conglomerate in 1929. After that organization was forced to break up in 1934, Vought became a division of United Aircraft (later United Technologies). A conflict of interest in manufacturing led to United Aircraft's sale of Vought in 1954. Seven years later Ling initiated a difficult takeover of Vought which resulted in his temporary (but voluntary) loss of control over the company and all but 11 shares of company stock. Upon completion of the takeover on August 16, the company's name was again changed to Ling-Temco-Vought.

Ling's notion of what constituted a successful conglomerate was based on the idea that no division should account for more than 30% of the company's sales. In addition, concentration of the company's business in related fields was to be avoided at all costs. It was for that reason that Ling-Temco-Vought became interested in Wilson Foods in 1966. Wilson's primary product was fresh meats, but it also operated two other businesses dependent upon animal by-products including sporting goods and pharmaceuticals. The sporting goods division made (among other things) footballs from pigskin and tennis rackets from animal guts, and the pharmaceuticals division derived hormones, steroids and other drugs from animal organs. Wilson's president Roscoe Haynie knew nothing of Ling's takeover effort until two weeks before it was completed. By January 5, 1967 Ling-Temco-Vought had acquired control of Wilson, and Haynie agreed to move to Dallas and work for Ling. That same year Ling-Temco-Vought was listed number 14 in the Fortune 500 ranking with annual sales of over $1 billion.

Ling divided Wilson into three operating divisions: Wilson & Company (meat), Wilson Sporting Goods, and Wilson Pharmaceutical & Chemical, and shares of stock in the three divisions were sold to the public. On Wall Street the share offerings were greeted with some skepticism. Despite this skepticism, Ling believed the parts of the company were worth more separately than together, and in time he was proved correct. Before long Ling-Temco-Vought's remaining share of the three Wilson companies was worth more than its initial investment.

Ling-Temco-Vought's growth in the five years from 1965 to 1969 was impressive. In 1965 the company had total sales of $36 million. In 1969 that figure had grown by more than 100 times to $3.8 billion. This growth was made possible through "redeployment," Ling's term for offering a minority share of an Ling-Temco-Vought division's stock to the public. Under favorable market conditions, private investors would drive up the price of the stock. This provided Ling-Temco-Vought with more collateral to support larger bank loans which were, in turn, used to finance more takeovers.

In 1968 Ling-Temco-Vought acquired the Greatamerica Corporation from Dallas investor Troy Post in return for $95 million in debentures. Greatamerica was the parent company for Braniff Airways, National Car Rental, and a number of insurance companies. Later that same year the company purchased a majority interest in the Jones & Laughlin Steel Corporation of Pittsburgh. Ling-Temco-Vought's numerous acquisitions led the U.S. Justice Department to initiate an antitrust investigation. Ling managed to avoid a federal lawsuit by agreeing to sell Braniff and the Okonite division, which was acquired in 1965. Despite the legal battles, Ling's strategy of redeployment had been successful.

Unfortunately, redeployment had an even more serious detrimental effect under unfavourable market conditions. When the economy began to decline in 1969 Ling-Temco-Vought's growth abruptly halted. The company was forced to divest itself of several divisions in order to generate enough cash to compensate for its growing debt. Wilson Sporting Goods was sold for $8.7 million and Wilson Pharmaceuticals was sold to American Can for $16 million. Investors subsequently lost confidence in Ling-Temco-Vought. The same stock that traded for $167 in 1967 was now worth $11.

In May of 1970 Ling-Temco-Vought's board of directors voted to remove Ling from the chairmanship. Robert Stewart was named interim chairman until a permanent replacement for Ling could be found. Ling was demoted to president, a position where he had no control over company policy. Six weeks later Ling resigned from the corporation. The board elected W. Paul Thayer of Ling-Temco-Vought's Aerospace division to become the company's new president, and a few months later, its chairman.

Thayer's first objective was to dispose of Ling-Temco-Vought's unprofitable divisions and remove all the others from public trading. Ling-Temco-Vought, which had until this time been more of an investment portfolio than a holding company, was to be converted into an operating company directly involved with its subsidiaries. This reorganization allowed one of the company's divisions to help another financially, something which was not possible under Ling.

Ling-Temco-Vought's debt was restructured and a campaign to acquire the privately-held shares of the company's divisions was launched. On May 5, 1971 Ling-Temco-Vought became the LTV Corporation. Later that month the company acquired the remaining shares of Vought Aircraft from private investors. The investors received $3.2 million and two former Ling-Temco-Vought subsidiaries, LTV Ling Altec (the Altec Corporation) and LTV Electrosystems (now called E-Systems). By November of 1974 LTV had also acquired the minority interests of Wilson & Company and Jones & Laughlin Steel.

LTV's Vought division was subcontracted to manufacture tail sections for a number of aircraft, including Boeing's 747 and McDonnell Douglas' DC-10 and KC-10. Vought also manufactured the A-7 Corsair II fighter and the S-3A antisubmarine airplane. In the mid-1970's, however, Vought's ability to generate a consistent profit was undermined by the Pentagon when it eliminated Vought from several lucrative defense contracts. Vought then attempted to enter civilian markets when it engineered a $34 million "Airtrans" ground transportation system for the Dallas/Ft. Worth Airport. The project was mired in controversy from its inception and a series of problems led Vought to declare a $22.6 million loss on the project. Subsequent orders for the A-7 from the Defense department and the governments of Greece and Pakistan, as well as a contract to produce Lance surface-to-surface missiles, helped to keep Vought in business.

By 1977 LTV was reduced to three principal lines of business: steel (Jones & Laughlin), meat packing (Wilson), and aerospace (Vought). All three lines of business were cyclical (that is, they experience alternating periods of good and then bad market conditions). In 1977 all three of LTV's divisions were suffering from the adverse conditions in their respective markets. LTV lost $39 million on sales of $4.7 billion.

At this time Paul Thayer made a move more characteristic of something Ling would have done. He announced LTV's intention to purchase the Lykes Corporation of New Orleans. Lykes was the parent company of Continental-Emsco, a petroleum equipment supply and service company; the Lykes Brothers Steamship Com-

pany, a cargo shipping company; and Youngstown Sheet & Tube, a financially troubled steel finishing plant. As part of the merger agreement LTV (which was already $1 billion in debt) would also become responsible for Lykes' debt of $659 million.

Upon closer inspection, however, the proposed merger was regarded as quite promising. The Youngstown mill could produce steel less expensively with raw steel from the Jones & Laughlin plant in Aliquippa, Pennsylvania. In addition, transportation costs could be reduced and Jones & Laughlin could transfer its backlogged orders to Youngstown's underutilized plants at Indiana Harbor.

The Justice Department had suspected the merger on antitrust grounds until Attorney General Griffin Bell interceded. Bell held a thorough investigation and later declared that Lykes had no chance of surviving without the merger. Despite considerable opposition from Senator Edward Kennedy (who questioned Bell's authority in the matter), Bell overruled the Justice Department and approved the merger, which was completed on December 5, 1978. The new division was renamed J&L Steel.

In 1981 LTV attempted to perform a similar expansion of its aerospace division. This time the takeover target was the Grumman Corporation. However, opposition from Grumman was considerable. The Federal Trade Commission arranged for an injunction on further purchases of Grumman stock by LTV on the grounds that a merger of the two companies would be anticompetitive in the carrier-based aircraft field. In addition, Grumman's pension fund and an employee investment group (who already held 35% of the company's stock) began buying large amounts of Grumman stock and refused to tender them for an LTV bid. This invited the interest of the U.S. Labor Department which was concerned about fiduciary improprieties. Even the company's founder, 86-year old Leroy Grumman, came out of retirement to campaign for his company's independence. What LTV may have underestimated most was the fierce loyalty of Grumman's employees to their company. Yet it was a U.S. Court of Appeals which prevented LTV's bid from being successful when it ruled against the takeover on antitrust grounds.

Without the additional resources of Grumman, LTV's Vought division was forced to re-equip itself with new equipment in order to meet its 15-year $4 billion contract to produce a Multiple Launch Rocket System for the Defense department. It was a very costly investment which left LTV with liquidity problems at a very bad time.

LTV sold its Wilson subsidiary in June of 1981 (before the Grumman bid) in order to generate cash. The Wilson division's share of revenue was quickly replaced, however, by the newly reorganized Continental-Emsco subsidiary. LTV officials claim to have known in advance that the profitable Continental-Emsco division was about to experience a period of adverse market conditions. However, according to LTV's president Ray Hay, "the business came down so fast we didn't have time to shut off our subcontractors." As a result, Continental-Emsco was left with a year's inventory and was forced to report a substantial operating loss.

Ray Hay came to LTV in 1975 from the Xerox Corporation. He left Xerox out frustration at being passed over for that company's presidency. At the time, Paul Thayer was looking for a man of Hay's talent and ability to be LTV's next president. Hay accepted Thayer's invitation, and when Thayer left LTV in January of 1983 to serve as Deputy Defense Secretary, Hay was elected ceo and chairman of the board.

Thayer's tenure of the Defense department was shortened in 1985 when he and a Dallas stockbroker named Billy Bob Harris were convicted of obstructing a federal investigation into the illegal use of privileged information. The "insider trading" scheme involved LTV and two other companies on whose boards Thayer served during 1981 and 1982.

In 1983 LTV sold the Lykes Steamship division and reorganized the remaining subsidiaries into three product-oriented divisions. The Vought Corporation was combined with a number of smaller divisions and renamed the LTV Aerospace & Defense Company. In addition, Continental-Emsco became the LTV Energy Products Company.

The following year LTV initiated a takeover of Republic Steel. The company was pleased with the relative success of its Jones & Laughlin/Youngstown merger and believed that by absorbing Republic it could achieve similar results. The Justice department, however, withheld its approval of the merger because the combined company would control 50% of the sheet steel market. In addition, the department was concerned about an impending merger between US Steel and National Steel. If both mergers were allowed the two companies would control nearly half of America's steelmaking capacity. However, a month later US Steel cancelled its merger with National and Jones & Laughlin was given permission to merge with Republic on the condition that it sell two of its sheet steel plants. On July 29, 1984 the $770 million takeover was completed with the creation of a new combined subsidiary called the LTV Steel Company.

As a condition to the merger, Republic's chairman Bradley Jones was named ceo of LTV. Furthermore, LTV was forced to offer costly retirement settlements to Republic personnel. The compensation was so attractive that Jones himself decided to take early retirement. He was replaced by LTV's former ceo David Hoag.

During this time the American steel market was inundated with inexpensive imported steel from modern plants in Japan, Europe and Canada. In 1985 foreign producers controlled 30% of the domestic market. This had the effect of closing American steel plants and reducing production capacity to between 50 and 60%.

Attempts to modernize LTV Steel and raise productivity had limited success. At the Aliquippa Works manhours per ton of steel went from eight in 1981 to 3.8 in 1985. And while the company's investments in modernized facilities were generating an annual return of three percent, the debt cost 15% per year to service. In effect, the investments were generating a net loss of 12% annually. In 1985 steel production at Aliquippa was idled and all but 700 workers (out of 9700 in 1981) were laid off. In addition, 3000 white collar jobs were eliminated.

The company's pension fund was turned over to a federal pension insurance agency to which LTV was obligated to make contributions. When LTV requested permission to skip a $175 million payment to the fund, the Pension Benefit Guaranty Corporation asked for and later received a claim on LTV Aerospace for collateral. LTV initiated a $500 million divestiture of most of the non-steel assets it acquired from Republic. In early 1986 the Gulf States Steel and LTV Specialty Products divisions were sold.

LTV was unable to maintain liquidity and on July 17, 1986 applied for protection under Chapter 11 of the bankruptcy code. According to chairman Ray Hay, "We just could not generate cash flow." Under Chapter 11 LTV was temporarily relieved of its annual $319 million debt service and $350 million pension contributions. LTV began to consider either selling its energy division or closing additional steel plants.

There has been a general consensus among industry experts that LTV has been managed very poorly. Many of them have different explanations for LTV's misfortune. Jim Ling, however, is still alive to say "I told you so." Ling, who was paralyzed by Guillain-Barre syndrome in 1981, pointed out that LTV should never have violated the unwritten rule of allowing any one division to account for more than 30% of the company's sales. Steel accounted for 65% in 1985. Most industry analysts believe that if LTV were not so deeply involved in manufacturing products with cyclical and declining markets, it would not be bankrupt.

LTV is using the period of time under bankruptcy protection to implement a massive reorganization program. In the past the bankruptcy laws under Chapter 11 have allowed many companies the opportunity to realign their operations so that they may re-enter the market and perform successfully. What LTV does during its bankruptcy protection remains to be seen.

Principal Subsidiaries: LTV Steel Company; LTV Aerospace and Defence Company; LTV Energy Products Company.

Further Reading: The Age of Giant Corporations by Robert Sobel, Westport, Connecticut, Greenwood, 1972; *LTV Looking Ahead*, Dallas, The Company, 1980.

MARUBENI K.K.

3, Hommachi 3-chome
Higashi-ku, Osaka 541
Japan
(06)266-2111

Public Company
Incorporated: December 1, 1949 as Marubeni Co., Ltd.
Employees: 10,170
Sales: ¥ 14.31 trillion (US$ 79.51 billion)
Market Value: ¥ 417.4 billion (US$ 2.319 billion)
Stock Index: Düsseldorf Frankfurt Amsterdam
   Luxembourg Tokyo Osaka Nagoya Kyoto
   Hiroshima Fukuoka Sapporo Niigata

In 1872 a young merchant named Chubei Itoh established a small store in Osaka to serve as an outlet for his commercial trading business. A symbol for the store was created which placed the word *beni* (Japanese for "red") inside a circle, or *maru*. In 1883, as the Itoh trading company expanded, the Marubeni store was made its head office.

Over the next twenty years, C. Itoh & Company took over an increasing number of duties from foreign trading agents and established its own international trading network. The company experienced particularly strong growth after Japan asserted its military dominance in the region by defeating Chinese armies in 1895 and the Russian navy in 1905. At the outbreak of World War I, C. Itoh & Company took advantage of several opportunities in international trading, created when companies in Europe redirected their energies toward production of war material.

Japan allied itself with the Entente later in the war, and when Germany was defeated in 1919 Japan was awarded German colonies and commercial rights in Asia. Within two years, however, uncontrolled economic expansion caused a serious recession which threatened hundreds of companies with financial collapse. C. Itoh & Company was forced to reorganize in 1921. The company itself was renamed Marubeni Shonten, Ltd., and several divisions belonging to its larger subsidiary C. Itoh Trading became a new company called Daido Trading. Marubeni was mainly involved in textile trading, but expanded over the course of the decade to include a wider variety of industrial and consumer goods.

In the early 1930's a group of right-wing militarists within the Japanese armed forces initiated a rise to political power based on subversion and terrorism. As strong opponents of Communism, these militarists were natural allies of the Nazi and Fascist governments of Germany and Italy. After taking control of the government they declared a "quasi-war economy" in preparation for the Japanese conquest of East Asia and the western Pacific.

Large Japanese conglomerates known as *zaibatsu* (Mitsui, Mitsubishi, and Sumitomo) and companies such as Iwai, C. Itoh, and Marubeni were viewed by the militarists as self-interested institutions of laissez-faire capitalism. One widely recognized goal of the militarists was the nationalization of these companies. At the time, however, nationalization was not possible. These companies were responsible for virtually all the weapons, machinery, and provisions needed to maintain the Japanese occupation of Korea, Manchuria, and China, and to conduct subsequent military campaigns.

In 1941, as part of an effort to increase the scale and raise the efficiency of Japanese industries, Marubeni was merged with C. Itoh Trading and Kishimoto & Company to form a larger firm called Sanko Kabushiki Kaisha. On December 1 of that year Japanese forces attacked British colonies in Asia, and on December 7 attacked American forces in the Philippines and Hawaii.

Initially, Sanko performed better than most Japanese companies in the war economy. Later in the war, however, Japanese forces failed to consolidate their gains and the war turned in favor of the United States. Additional demands were placed on the economy in general and companies such as Sanko in particular. In 1944, the year the Japanese mainland became exposed to American bombing raids, Sanko was forcibly merged with Daido Boeki and Kureha Spinning to form a new company called the Daiken Company. Chubei Itoh II, the son of Marubeni's founder, was placed in charge of Daiken as its president.

The companies which formed Daiken, indeed even those which formed Sanko, were forced to perform under such extraordinary circumstances that none of them had an opportunity fully to integrate their operations with the other companies. Daiken existed more as an industrial group than a company.

When the war ended in the late summer of 1945 most of the country's industrial capacity had been destroyed. An Allied occupation authority under General Douglas MacArthur initiated a plan for reconstruction and the general reorganization of Japanese industry. Large conglomerates, particularly the *zaibatsu*, were divided into hundreds of independent companies in an effort to eliminate monopoly practices and encourage greater competition. In 1949 Daiken, which was not a *zaibatsu*, was redivided into Kureha Spinning, C. Itoh & Company, Marubeni, and a small manufacturer of nails called the Amagasaki company. Marubeni was given authority to conduct international trade. Under the leadership of President Shinobu Ichikawa, the company utilized its strength in textiles to finance diversification into non-textile items such as food, metals, and machinery.

When the Korean War broke out in June of 1950, Marubeni became one of thousands of Japanese companies whose services were urgently needed by the United Nations forces. Marubeni reacted quickly to new opportunities created by the war and, as a result, experienced faster growth than many other companies. The war also transformed Japan's role as a postwar ally of the United States; it was decided that Japan should be developed into an industrial nation.

The Korean War ended in 1953, and many U.N. supply contracts with Japanese companies were terminated. This caused a serious recession in Japan and forced many companies, including Marubeni, to reorganize its operations and management. Nonetheless, the company declared itself fully recovered from both World War II and the recession in 1955.

On February 18, 1955, Marubeni merged with Iida & Company, an established name in Japanese business which operated several large department stores under the name Takashimaya. In order to emphasize its equality with Iida, the Marubeni Company changed its name in September to Marubeni-Iida.

The Ministry for International Trade and Industry (MITI), the Japanese government's coordinating body for the nation's industries, selected Marubeni-Iida to handle trading activities for Yawata Iron & Steel and Fuji Iron & Steel (merged in 1970 to become Nippon Steel). As a result of this decision, Marubeni occupied a leading position in the field of silicon steel and iron sheets, which were being consumed in greater quantities by the growing Japanese appliance and automobile industries.

Marubeni-Iida's newly established machinery trade group was awarded several contracts over a short period during the late 1950's, firmly establishing the company in the area of engineering. These contracts included a nuclear reactor for the Japan Atomic Energy Research Institute, a fleet of aircraft for the Japanese defense agency, and a number of factories which produced components for the electronic industry.

Marubeni-Iida entered the petrochemical industry in 1956 when it helped a leading chemical fertilizer and aluminum company called Showa Denko secure chemical production licenses from American companies. The company fostered relationships with other chemical companies and later became a leading importer of potassium and phosphate rock.

In the ten years from 1949 to 1959 Marubeni had reduced its concentration in textiles from 80% of sales to 50%. During the 1960's Marubeni-Iida acted as a supplier of materials for Japanese companies as well as a marketing agent for their products. In addition to textiles, metal products and chemicals, Marubeni-Iida was active in trading light and heavy machinery and rubber products.

In 1965 Marubeni-Iida merged with the Totsu Company, a leading metal and steel trading firm which was closely associated with Nippon Steel. The merger substantially increased the company's size and strengthened its position in metals. With the addition of Totsu's 1380 employees to Marubeni-Iida's 8000, the new company became a *sogo shosha*, a large general trading firm like the former *zaibatsu* companies. In order to cope with its new position as one of Japan's primary instruments for industrialization and growth, the new Marubeni-Iida initiated a general reorganization of its management and planning systems.

When the reorganization was executed in 1968, the company made greater efforts to develop raw material sources overseas, including petroleum products, coal, metal ores, industrial salt, foodstuffs, and lumber. During this time Marubeni-Iida improved its transportation and marketing networks and also improved upon the coordination of its various trading activities.

President Nixon's decision to remove the U.S. dollar from the gold standard in August 1971 resulted in a worldwide disruption of currency values known as the "Nixon shock," or in Japan, *shokku*. The value of the dollar dropped steeply, which made it more difficult for Japanese companies such as Marubeni-Iida to export products to the United States. The company's operations were so adversely affected that it was again forced to reorganize. The company entered promising new lines of business, emphasized its more profitable existing operations, and divested itself of unprofitable slow-growth enterprises. The following January the company's name was changed to the Marubeni Corporation.

In August of 1973 Marubeni acquired Nanyo Bussan, a trading firm which handled copper, nickel, chrome, and other metals from the Philippines. The acquisition increased Marubeni's share of the nation's copper imports from 0.8% to 7%, and refractories (hard to melt metals) from 0 to 30%. The addition of Nanyo Bussan to Marubeni further diversified the company's operations and strengthened its position in metals.

In February of 1976 it was reported that Marubeni illegally diverted commissions from the sale of Lockheed aircraft to officials of the Japanese government. Marubeni was accused of bribing officials for their support of Lockheed sales in Japan. Marubeni, Lockheed's agent in Japan, initially denied any complicity in the scandal. Marubeni's chairman Hiro Hiyama, however, resigned in an effort to preserve the company's integrity. The former vice chairman of Lockheed, Carl Kotchian, testified that Hiyama advised him to bribe the Japanese officials, in accordance with "Japanese business practices." Hiyama later denied Kotchian's testimony. By July prosecutors arrested nearly 20 officials of Marubeni and All Nippon Airways, including Hiro Hiyama, who was accused of violating Japan's foreign exchange control laws.

The Lockheed scandal came only three years after Marubeni was accused of profiteering in rice by hoarding supplies on the Japanese black market. Marubeni was seriously damaged by its unfavorable public image; over 40 municipalities cancelled contracts with Marubeni, and several international ventures were terminated.

Marubeni's president, Taiichiro Matsuo, who had served in the government's Ministry for International Trade and Industry, assumed the chairman's responsibilities. After declaring that it no longer represented Lockheed, the company implemented a reform of its management structure to improve upon checks and balances at the executive level. In a move toward decentralization, many of the president's administrative responsibilities were redistributed to a board of senior executives.

Marubeni recovered quickly from the Lockheed scandal. In 1977 the company's trading volume was double the figure in 1973. As the third largest of Japan's *sogo shosha*, Marubeni consolidated its international trading network, and expanded its business in the United States, Australia, Brazil, Britain, West Germany, and Sweden. Marubeni also opened or expanded offices in the Soviet Union, the People's Republic of China, the Middle East, and Africa. The company later came to operate offices in over 100 foreign countries.

Through the early 1980's Marubeni was involved in the development of coal mines in the United States and Australia, a copper mine in Papua New Guinea, and non-ferrous metal mines in Australia and the Philippines.

When President Ferdinand Marcos of the Philippines was forced into exile in the United States in February of 1986, he brought with him 2300 pages of documents which were seized by the U.S. government. Officials of the U.S. Congress later revealed that some of these documents detailed illegal payments by Japanese companies to President Marcos and several of his friends and associates. Once again, Marubeni was identified as a major participant.

Called into question was the Japanese "aid-for-trade" policy which promises aid to foreign countries on the condition that Japanese companies perform the work. However, while the Lockheed scandal brought down the government of Kakuei Tanaka and involved several suicides, the Marcos scandal was expected merely to cause damage to Japanese-Philippines relations. For Marubeni it was an unwelcome revelation which further compromised its public image.

Additionally, *Diamond's Japan Business Directory* noted in 1986 that Marubeni has recently suffered a ¥ 900 million appraisal loss due to the company's close association with the financially troubled Sanko Steamship Company. Marubeni also has an outstanding "bad" claim of more than ¥ 4.3 billion. These are regarded as serious impediments to the company's performance, deserving close attention.

Marubeni is a member of the Fuyo Group, an industrial organization consisting of 29 companies, including Hitachi (electronics), Nissan (automobiles), Canon (cameras), Showa Denko (chemicals), Kubota (farm machinery), and Nippon Steel. The Fuyo Group (*Fuyo* is another way of referring to Mount Fuji) was created by several corporate leaders in the early 1960's to promote friendship, share information, and "study projects of mutual interest."

Like the former *zaibatsu* companies, whose operations are centered around a bank, the Fuyo Group is associated with the Fuji Bank. Unlike those companies, however, the Fuyo Group has a relatively short history. Its members are brought together more by prospects for mutual benefit than by historical affiliation. As a result, the Fuyo Group is less rigidly constituted. Representatives of the Fuyo Group members meet in a series of monthly meetings, or *kai* (the Fuyokai, Fujikai, and Fusuikai, as well as a general discussion panel), where planning strategies are formulated.

Marubeni's partners in the Fuyo Group are a source of financial support through their business, providing a diverse mix of products as well as stable producer and consumer markets. As one of the largest general trading companies in Japan, Marubeni is essential to the Japanese economy and may therefore enjoy considerable support from the government.

Principal Subsidiaries (and affiliates): Amatei, Inc.; Benny Steel Co., Ltd.; Sanyo Co., Ltd.; Tomiyasu Co., Ltd.; Marubeni Construction Material Lease Co., Ltd.; Yamatogawa Kokan Co., Ltd.; Ohtsuka Steel Trading Co., Ltd.; Marubeni Metals Corp.; Hitachi Electrical Steel Co., Ltd.; Tokyo Electrical Steel Co., Ltd.; Osaka Electrical Steel Co., Ltd.; Nagoya Electrical Steel Co., Ltd.; Nisshi-Nippon Steel Center Co., Ltd.; Marubeni Machinery Sales Co., Ltd.; Dengensha Manufacturing Co., Ltd.; Okano Valve Mfg. Co., Ltd.; Shinnihon Reiki Co., Ltd.; Macs Co., Ltd.; Marubeni Construction Machinery Sales, Inc.; Benytone Corp.; Marubeni Tekmatex Corp.; Kaji Iron Works, Ltd.; Crimson Line, Ltd.; Koyo Line, Ltd.; Japan Overseas Leasing Corp.; Marubeni Machinery & Engineering Corp.; Asano Engineering Co., Ltd.; Marubeni-Setsubi Co., Ltd.; Shinnihon Doboku Co., Ltd.; Marubeni Fudosan Co., Ltd.; Marubeni Industrial Textiles Co., Ltd.; Marubenitex Corp.; Miyako Knit Co., Ltd.; Toyama Fishing Net Mfg. Co., Ltd.; Sanyo Textile Co., Ltd.; Marubeni Iryo Co., Ltd.; Kyoto Marubeni Co., Ltd.; Marutaka Keito Co., Ltd.; Marubeni Seni Yohin Co., Ltd.; Panther Co., Ltd.; Marubeni Shigyo Co., Ltd.; Minatoya Paper Trading Co., Ltd.; Koa Kogyo Co., Ltd.; Marusumi Paper Mfg. Co., Ltd.; Marubeni Pack Co., Ltd.; Fukuyama Paper Co., Ltd.; Nikko Oil Mills Co., Ltd.; Shinshindo Baking Co., Ltd.; Central Japan Grain Terminal Co., Ltd.; West Japan Grain Terminal Co., Ltd.; South Japan Grain Terminal Co., Ltd.; Marubeni Shiryo Co., Ltd.; Nippon Chunky Co., Ltd.; Okayama Chunky Broiler Co., Ltd.; Ohmiya Ham Co., Ltd.; Marubeni Livestock & Meats, Ltd.; Dairy Queen (Japan) Co., Ltd.; Katakura Chikkarin Co., Ltd.; Marubeni Foods Corp.; Nissan-Marubeni Shoji Co., Ltd.; Toyo Sugar Refining Co., Ltd.; Beniko Corp.; Ebikoh Corp.; Marubeni Reizo Co., Ltd.; Marukoh Fisheries Co., Ltd.; Minami Kyushu Food Products Co., Ltd.; Hinomaru-Nissui Co., Ltd.; Maruseikokosan Corp.; Marubeni Oil Terminal Co., Ltd.; Marubeni Energy Corp.; Nisseki-Marubeni Co., Ltd.; Shin Nippon Lique-fied Gas Co., Ltd.; Ohita Terminal Industries, Ltd.; Marubeni Plastic Products Co., Ltd.; Solvay-Marubeni Chemicals Co., Ltd.; Marubeni Electronics Co., Ltd.; Marubeni Hytech Co., Ltd.; Kokusai Tymshare, Ltd.; Marubeni Information Systems Co., Ltd.; Network Service Co., Ltd.; Japan Voicemail, Inc.; Marubeni Software Co., Ltd.; Nippon Steiner Co., Ltd.; Marubeni Mokuzai-Kenzai Co., Ltd.; Overseas Transport Service Co., Ltd.; Marubeni Credit Corp.; Levene Co., Ltd.; Marubeni Insurance Center Co., Ltd.; Vittel Japan Co., Ltd.; Marubeni Auto-Leasing Co., Ltd.; Marubeni Sports Co., Ltd.; Marubeni Ameria Corp.; Marubeni Australia Ltd.; Marubeni Benelux, S.A. (Belgium); Marubeni Brasil, S.A.; Marubeni Canada, Ltd.; Marubeni Deutsh-land, GmbH (West Germany); Marubeni France, S.A.;

Marubeni Hong Kong, Ltd.; Marubeni Iberia, S.A. (Spain); Marubeni Iran Co., Ltd.; Marubeni Italia S.p.A. (Italy); Marubeni Mexico S.A. de C.V.; Marubeni New Zealand, Ltd.; Marubeni Panama International, S.A.; Marubeni Peru, S.A.; Marubeni Scandinavia A.B. (Sweden); Marubeni UK, Plc.; Marubeni Venezuela C.A.; Heung Hwa Industry Co., Ltd. (South Korea); P.T. Sermani Steel Corp. (Indonesia); Total Steel of Australia Pty, Ltd.; Crest Steel Corp. (USA); Archer Pipe & Tube Co., Inc. (USA); Pioneer Metals Co., Ltd. (Nigeria); Heng Leeng Maruken Metal Leasing Pte, Ltd. (Singapore); Bleim Steel Co. (USA); Marubeni Brasileira de Mineracao Ltda. (Brazil); Marubeni Coal Pty., Ltd. (Australia); Marubeni International Petroleum Co., Ltd. (Hong Kong); Marubeni International Electronics Corp. (USA); Uniphone Ushasama Sdn. Bhd. (Malaysia); Marubeni-Komatsu, Ltd. (U.K.); UMW Acceptance & Credit Sdn. Bhd. (Malaysia); P.T. Komatsu Indonesia; N.V. Nissan Belgium, S.A.; Motores Hino de Guatemala, S.A.; Suzuki, S.A. (Guatemala); Nissan Motor del Peru, S.A.; Pilipinas Hino, Inc. (Philippines); Pilipinas Nissan, Inc. (Philippines); Pilipinas Transport Industries, Inc. (Philippines); Nissan Mexicana S.A. de C.V. (Mexico); Eye Lighting Industries Pty., Ltd. (Australia); Marubeni-Citizen Cincom, Inc. (USA); Deutsch-Japanisches Center, GmbH (West Germany); Marubeni Benelux Development, S.A. (Belgium); Marubeni Brasil Representacoes e Participaceos Ltda. (Brazil); Shanghai International Realty Co., Ltd. (People's Republic of China); Taipyung Development Co., Ltd. (South Korea); Marubeni Saudi Arabia Co., Ltd.; Dampier Salt, Ltd. (Australia); SELEMEX, S.A. (Mexico); P.T. Pralon Corp. (Indonesia); Korea Petrochemical Industry Co., Ltd. (South Korea); Agricultural Chemicals (Malaysia) Sdn. Bdn.; Columbia Grain, Inc. (USA); Exportadora e Importadora Marubeni-Colorado, S.A. (Brazil); MAGRISA Marubeni Agro Industrial, S.A. (Brazil); Bering Sea Fisheries, Inc. (USA); North Pacific Processors, Inc. (USA); Togiak Fisheries, Inc. (USA); LYL Rubber Sdn. Bdn. (Malaysia); California Woodfiber Corp. (USA); Daishowa-Marubeni International, Ltd. (Canada); Capital Veneers Sdn. Bdn. (Malaysia); Canobolas Wood Topmaking Pty., Ltd. (Australia); Marnan Wood Industries Pty., Ltd. (Australia); Kobes do Brasil Industria a Comercio, Ltda. (Brazil); Unitika do Brasil Industria Textile Ltda. (Brazil); P.T. Kurabo Manunggal Textile Industries (Indonesia); P.T. Kuraray Manunggal Fiber Industries (Indonesia); P.T. UNITEX (Indonesia); Textile Industriales de Centro America, S.A. (Costa Rica); Dusit Textile Co., Ltd. (Thailand); Erawan Textile Co., Ltd.; Tokai Dyeing Co., (Thailand) Ltd.; Wateree Textile Corp. (USA).

Further Reading: The Sogu Shosha: Japanese Multinational Trading Companies by Alexander K. Young, Boulder, Colorado, Westview Press, 1979; *Industry and Business in Japan* edited by Kazuo Sato, New York, Croom Helm, 1980.

McKESSON CORPORATION

One Post Street
San Francisco, California 94104
U.S.A.
(415) 983-8300

Public Company
Incorporated: August 4, 1928 as McKesson & Robbins
Employees: 17,200
Sales: $6.285 billion
Market Value: $1.549 billion
Stock Index: New York

McKesson Corporation's journey to the highest ranking position in the wholesale distribution industry occurred over a period of many years. However, the changes in direction as well as management philosophies experienced by McKesson during its 150 years of business have resulted in a company that is resilient and secure in its future direction.

In 1833 John McKesson founded his own wholesale drug company in Manhattan with another partner, and the company was known as Olcott & McKesson. Twenty years and another partner later, the firm changed its name to McKesson & Robbins. Yet this was just the beginning of the changes experienced by McKesson. When John McKesson died in 1893, the McKesson heirs left the company in order to form the New York Quinine and Chemical Works. Subsequently, in 1926, McKesson & Robbins was sold to Frank D. Coster.

Coster was responsible for turning the respected name of McKesson & Robbins into one connected with scandal. Coster's real name was Philip Musica, the son of a New York importer of Italian foods. The Musica family prospered in their import trade primarily by bribing the dock customs weigher to falsify the weight of the shipment. However, the prosperity did not last long and in 1909 the Musica team was arrested. Philip paid a $5,000 fine and served five months in prison for the crime.

The prison experience did not reform the Musicas, however, and when they were again arrested in 1913 the charges were similar. Their hair importing business, started after Philip left prison, was in debt for $500,000 in bank loans. Through a bank investigation it was discovered that the supposedly valuable hair pieces being used for collateral were in fact only worthless ends and short pieces of hair. The Musica family was caught trying to escape on a departing New Orleans ship. Philip was the scapegoat for the family escapades once again and served three years in prison. When he was released in 1916 he worked for the District Attorney's office as an undercover agent named William Johnson.

During World War I Musica began a poultry business, but his entanglement with the law was not over. In 1920, although he was indicted on charges stemming from a murder case, he was never convicted and did not serve a prison sentence. Shortly afterward, Musica changed his business interests from poultry to pharmaceuticals, posing as president of Adelphi Pharmaceutical Manufacturing Company in Brooklyn. This company was actually a front for a bootlegging concern and Musica's partner, Joseph Brandino, would later contribute to Musica's suicide through his blackmail attempts.

Musica changed his name to Frank D. Coster after the close of Adelphi. With his secret past behind him, Coster managed to establish himself as a respectable businessman by starting a hair tonic company that had a supposedly large customer list. With this outwardly attractive collateral, Coster appeared to be a reasonable buyer for McKesson & Robbins in 1926. For 13 years after he purchased McKesson & Robbins, Coster was able to keep his identity a secret; he was even listed in *Who's Who in America* where he was described as a businessman as well as a "practicing physician" from 1912 to 1914.

Coster's true identity was revealed in 1938 when a company treasurer's concern over the way the profits were being handled led to an investigation of McKesson & Robbins. The investigation uncovered that Coster had stolen $3 million from the company through the false customers he had set up and was also paying blackmail fees to his former partner, Brandino, who had discovered Coster's true identity and threatened to expose him. In 1939 Coster shot himself, Brandino was convicted of blackmail, and McKesson & Robbins once again returned to the normal conduct of business.

The company's calm and relatively quiet existence was intruded upon in 1967 when Foremost Dairy of California implemented a hostile takeover. The management of McKesson & Robbins was not pleased with this takeover and this resulted in an unhappy relationship between the two companies for several years after the merger. In fact, it was three years before McKesson offices were even moved to San Francisco, the headquarters of Foremost.

The new company formed by this merger, Foremost-McKesson, Inc. had no company strategy and was moving in several different directions at the same time. Rudolph Drews, head of Foremost-McKesson, is described by *Forbes* magazine as the "freewheeling" president who acquired several diverse companies from "sporting goods to candy" after the merger with McKesson, and who was better at making acquisitions than at managing the company. In 1974 Drews was forced from the corporation after a day long board meeting; his management style was considered the cause for a "flattening" of earnings.

Drews' response, "I'll be back," after he was fired from Foremost-McKesson was no idle threat. Drews established his own corporate-merger consulting business and found an opportunity in 1976 to orchestrate a takeover bid of his former company. Drews' middleman for this takeover bid was Victor Posner, a Miami multimillionaire who saw an opportunity to buy out Foremost-McKesson. William Morison, the new president of Foremost-McKesson, worked hard to resist this bid by Sharon Steel, Posner's Pennsylvania firm. Posner was able to obtain 10% of Foremost-McKesson's stock before Morison began the company's defensive strategy of careful planning, research and public relations moves that produced some valuable information on the Sharon Steel Corporation bid — the company had overstated its earnings for 1975 by 45%.

Posner's bid was unacceptable to Foremost-McKesson not only because of the connection with Drews, but also because of Posner's takeover tactics. *Forbes* states that Posner was "scourged coast to coast" for his tactics as a "corporate marauder." In response to Posner's success at buying 10% of Foremost-McKesson's stock and to guard against any similar activity in the future, Foremost-McKesson stockholders approved a charter change which prohibited any "unsuitable" part from acquiring over 10% of the company's common stock. An unsuitable party was defined as any business that might jeopardize Foremost's liquor or drug licenses.

The attempted takeover by Posner was a problem for Foremost-McKesson for many reasons. While the bid was dropped in April of 1976, the company had lost valuable time in executing the "turnaround plans" devised by the new president William Morison. Morison took over after Drews' departure in 1974 and was determined to make the company a more dynamic, streamlined operation. Up to this point, Foremost-McKesson had been viewed as two companies wedded together with no real direction and no real activity. Morison complained that, "people on he East Coast think of us as McKesson the drug company, and people on the West coast think of us as Foremost the dairy company, and we don't think either one really fits anymore."

With Morison's turnaround plans, Foremost-McKesson was creating a new image for itself. In 1977, Executive Vice President Thomas E. Drohan, compared the company to an elephant that, under the new direction of Morison, was now "off its knees and ambling noisily."

During its $14 million fight with Sharon Steel Corporation in 1976, Foremost-McKesson made two major acquisitions and sold or combined 11 of its less significant operations. Morison wanted to move the company away from its role of middleman as a wholesale distributor of pharmaceutical products, beverages and liquor, and emphasize production of proprietary products such as C.F. Mueller's pasta products. Morison's objective was to streamline the company by selling its low profit operations and investing $200 million into new businesses by 1990. The battle with Posner sidelined many of these goals, nevertheless Foremost's acquisitions of C.F. Mueller Company the country's largest pasta marker, and Gentry International, a processor of onion and garlic, were two significant acquisitions made in 1976 that met the objectives set by Morison.

Before Morison retired in 1978, he reorganized the company into four major operating groups: drugs and health care, wine and spirits, foods, and chemicals, as well as a small homebuilding division. Morison's strategic plan

was the first of its kind for Foremost-McKesson, and it was one factor that placed the company in a more comfortable position for the future.

This strategy continued after Morison's retirement when Thomas P. Drohan took over as president. Drohan's defense against a corporate raider was to maintain a high stock price. And Drohan's style of management was to improve productivity along with saving money. Specifically, he updated the inventory and stock procedures so that computers were used to order stock, allowing Foremost to reduce personnel costs by a third.

Drohan also redefined the role of the middleman by establishing data processing procedures that would be valuable to both suppliers and customers, placing Foremost-McKesson in the position of acting as part of the marketing teams. These practices in the early 1980's put Foremost-McKesson in the position of a leader in wholesale practices. The company's investment in the wholesale business, automating warehousing, and data processing led to an average profit growth of 20% per year compared with the 2% average growth before 1976.

The 1980's saw a different type of company than the one described as "lethargic" only a decade earlier. The acquisitions made in the early part of the 1980's were made to strengthen the company's role as a major distributor of health care products. In 1983, the same year that the company name was changed to McKesson Corporation, $90 million was spent on acquisitions of distributor and distributor-related industries. In 1982 the drug distribution business contributed $2.1 billion to the company's $4 billion in sales. Net sales for the first part of the 1980's increased steadily, with only a slight drop in 1983.

The company diversified within the chemical industry as well. The McKesson chemical group has played an important role in the company's sales. The company purchased its first chemical recycling plant in 1981, with plans to build six additional plants around the country. The chemical solvent recycling was a profitable business because of the strict Resource Conservation and Recovery Act (RCRA) legislated in Congress that mandated environmentally safe disposal processes. McKesson expected to obtain 10% of the 1986 chemical solvent market.

Neil Harlan has been the chairman of McKesson Corporation since 1979. He is a former army captain, Harvard business professor, and McKinsey & Company director. Harlan's approach to management of the company has resulted in selling the pieces of the company that did not fit its distribution image. Specifically, C.F. Mueller was sold in 1983. Harlan stated that his company "erred" when Mueller was purchased in 1976 because Foremost-McKesson had no "east-coast presence in foods" and "few opportunities for combining sales forces, regional offices, or marketing efforts."

McKesson also sold Foremost Diaries in 1983, along with its food processing and homebuilding subsidiaries, all of which were 30% of the "old company's" assets. These subsidiaries no longer fit the "distribution vision" presented by Chairman Harlan.

Acquisition has been a key component of McKesson's management strategy since 1984. Acquisitions have included additional drug and health care product distributors, software firms, and drug and medical equipment distributors. The chemical group is still the least profitable group within the company because the centralized purchasing system applied to the drug and liquor wholesale distribution does not work as well in the chemical industry. Harlan states that he "hopes that our history shows we will not be afraid to make the hard decision [to get out of chemicals] if it's warranted."

Harlan's approach has made McKesson one of the leaders in wholesale distribution. His strategy is two-fold; he believes that "any company that doesn't stick to what it does best is inviting trouble" and that "anybody who doesn't prepare [for a raider] is living in a dreamworld."

With this approach to managing a large corporation such as McKesson, the company has clearly established specific objectives for the future.

Principal Subsidiaries: Alhambra National Water Co., Inc.; California Culinary Academy, Inc.; Corporation of America; D'Amico Foods Co.; Dresden/Davis Organization, Inc.; Foremost Foods, Inc.; Foremost-McKesson Canada, Inc.; Foremost-McKesson Property Co., Inc. The company also lists subsidiaries in the following countries: Ecuador, Italy, Lebanon, The Netherlands, Taiwan, and Thailand.

MINNESOTA MINING & MANUFACTURING COMPANY

3M Center
St. Paul, Minnesota 55144
U.S.A.
(612) 733–1110

Public Company
Incorporated: June 25, 1929
Employees: 85,466
Sales: $779 million
Market Value: $15.055 billion
Stock Index: New York Frankfurt Dusseldorf Geneva
Zurich Basle Amsterdam Tokyo

Observers and outsiders frequently describe Minnesota Mining and Manufacturing in terms approaching awe. 3M earns such respect because of its improbable, almost defiantly non-corporate nature. The company is gigantic, yet it is as innovative and as full of growth potential as though it were a small venture. 3M's very existence is in itself somewhat improbable. It was formed in 1902 to exploit the mineral corundum, a venture that almost bankrupted the company. But 3M learned its lesson the first time, developed a fiercely entrepreneurial spirit, and earned a reputation as a company that does good work, and a good company to work for.

From its beginning, 3M concentrated on industrial wares. Its founders, headed by Minnesota industrialists Lucius P. Ordway and John Ober, planned to mine corundum, a mineral harder than all others save diamonds. Three years after it started, 3M concluded its history as a mining firm with nothing to show but a pile of useless rock (the "corundum" was actually anorthosite).

To go with 3M's pile of rocks was a pile of debts. To nurture the company, Ober went without a salary for its first 11 years, and Ordway poured some $230,000 of his own money into it, much more faith than the company seemed to warrant.

Ordway and Ober were able to use their pile of anorthosite to make sandpaper, which had a large and expanding market, thanks to the midwest's numerous furniture factories and fast-growing industrial economy. While 3M did not turn a profit for several more years, two of the employees it hired in 1907 would ensure its future.

The two employees were William L. McKnight and A.G. Bush. The two worked as a team for some 60 years, and developed the sales system that helped make 3M a success. McKnight ran 3M between 1916 and 1966, serving as president from 1929 to 1949 and chairman of the board from 1949 to 1966. McKnight created the guidelines which seem something of a company creed—diversification, avoiding price cuts, increasing sales by 10% a year, high employee morale, and quality control.

In some ways, the sales system overshadowed the guidelines. McKnight and Bush designed an aggressive, customer-oriented brand of salesmanship. Sales representatives, instead of dealing with a company's purchasing agent, were sent past the purchasing agent and into the shop where they could talk to the people who used the products. Going into the shop enabled 3M salesmen to find out both how products could be improved and what products were needed. This resulted in some of 3M's early innovations. For instance, when Henry Ford's newly motorized assembly lines created too much friction for existing sandpapers, which were designed to sand wood and static objects, a 3M salesman went back to St. Paul with the news. 3M came up with a tougher sandpaper, and thus captured much of the sandpaper market for the growing auto industry. Another salesman noticed that dust from sandpaper use made the shop environment extremely unhealthy. In response, 3M began looking for a way to make waterproof sandpaper. It found a glassworker-cum-inventor with a patent for waterproof (thus substantially dust-free) sandpaper. 3M bought the patent, came out with WetorDry sandpaper, and grew larger. It also hired the inventor as its first full-time researcher. This marked the creation of one of the nation's first corporate research and development divisions.

Sending salesmen into the shops paid off a few years later in an even more significant way, by giving 3M a product line entirely removed from sandpaper. In 1923 a salesman in an auto body painting shop noticed that the process used to paint cars in two tones worked poorly. He promised the painter that 3M could develop an effective way to prevent the paints from running together. It took two years, but the research and development division invented a successful masking tape.

The invention of Scotch tape established 3M as a force for innovation in American industry. As with sandpaper, 3M immediately began to develop different applications of its new technology. Its most famous adaptation came in 1930, when some industrious 3M workers found a way to graft cellophane to Scotch tape, creating a transparent tape.

Transparent Scotch tape provided a major windfall during the depression, helping 3M to grow at a time when most businesses struggled to break even. Another salesman invented a portable tape dispenser, and 3M had its first large-scale consumer product. Consumers used Scotch tape in a variety of ways: to repair torn paper products of all sorts, strengthen book bindings, hold clothes together until they could be sewn, and even remove lint.

By 1932 the new product was doing so well that 3M's main client base shifted from midwestern furniture and automobile factories to Scotch tape and a host of similar office products. During the 1930's 3M funnelled some 45 percent of its profits into new product research; consequently, 3M tripled in size during the worst decade American business had ever endured.

3M continued to grow during World War II. The company did not shift to making military goods, as many U.S. corporations did, but continued to concentrate on understanding its markets and finding a "niche" to fill.

The war did leave 3M with a need to do some rebuilding, and not enough cash on hand to do so. Since its early days, 3M had needed no debt to keep going. Earnings had always financed new plants and equipment. To meet its building needs, in 1947 3M issued its first bond offerings to help fund the program.

Its first stock offering, coupled with its tremendous growth rate, attracted attention to 3M. In 1949, when President McKnight became Chairman of the Board McKnight (with A.G. Bush also moving from daily operations to the boardroom), it marked the end of a tremendous era for 3M. Under McKnight, 3M grew almost 20 times, from $5.4 million to $108 million in sales.

Such growth could not be ignored. Now that 3M was publicly traded, investment bankers took to recommending it as a buy, business magazines sent reporters to write about it, and other companies tried to figure out how 3M grew. One writer argued that 3M's formula was to find an uninhabited market (a niche), fill it, patent the product, and let the lawyers defend its monopoly for as long as possible. If legal work seemed too expensive, said the writer, 3M would enter into licensing agreements to protect profits.

This cynical assessment has some truth to it. 3M did not and does not produce "me-too" products, preferring to develop new products to find the niche. Or, as McKnight's immediate successor as president, Richard Carlton, put it: "we'll make any damn thing we can make money on." Uninhabited markets do not lend themselves to easy discovery. Research and development received money that most companies spent on other things (most companies still did not have such departments by the early 1950's), and the pursuit for ideas was intense.

Carlton kept the company focused on product research (today, 3M rewards its scientists with Carlton Awards), which led to another innovation in the 1950's, the first dry-printing photocopy process, ThermoFax.

3M went through the 1950's in impressive fashion, with 1959 marking the company's 20th consecutive year of increased sales. A *Forbes* article noted that research, patents, and marketing know-how had created a growth environment that seemed unstoppable, and quoted then-president Herbert Buetow as saying "we are virtually recession-proof."

For all its growth and diversity, 3M continued to produce strong profits for its established products. In a way, this was almost to be expected, given 3M's penchant for being in "uninhabited" markets. As noted by John Pitblado, 3M's president of U.S. Operations, "almost everything depends on a coated abrasive during some phase of its manufacture. Your eyeglasses, wrist watches, the printed circuit that's in a TV set, knitting needles . . . all require sandpaper."

In the 1960's 3M went on another growth binge, doubling in size between 1963 and 1967 and becoming a billion-dollar company in the process. Existing product lines did well, and 3M's ventures into magnetic media provided excellent returns. One venture, the backdrops used for some of the spectacular scenes for the 1968 movie *2001: A Space Odyssey*, earned an Academy Award.

But the 1970's brought some obstacles to 3M's seeming odyssey of growth. First, several of the company's top executives resigned when it was revealed that they had operated an illegal slush fund from company money between 1963 and 1975, which included a contribution of some $30,000 to Richard Nixon's 1972 campaign.

Worse than the political embarrassment, sales growth slowed during the decade, particularly in the oil crunch of 1974, ending 3M's phenomenal string of averaging a 15% growth rate every five years. 3M responded to its cost crunch in characteristic fashion: it turned to its employees, who devised ways for the company to cut costs at each plant.

The company also had difficulties with consumer products. Particularly galling was the loss of the cassette tape market, which two Japanese companies, TDK and Maxell, dominated through engaging in price cutting. 3M stuck to its tradition of abandoning markets where it could not set its own prices, and backed off. Eventually, 3M stopped making much of its magnetic media, instead buying from an overseas supplier and putting the 3M label on it. The loss of the magnetic media market, coupled with a shaky performance in computer disks, was not overwhelming: revenues doubled between 1975 and 1980, and in 1976 3M was named one of the Dow Jones Industrial 30.

Unfortunately, price cutting was not the only problem confronting 3M. Major competitors seemed to face it on all fronts, and the niches seemed extinct. Some business writers even speculated that 3M might be taken over and split up. Others wondered whether a company "admirably suited" for the 1950's, 1960's, and 1970's could be transformed into a company for the 1980's. Corporate structure was also becoming a problem. 3M is radically decentralized, particularly for a large company. This accounts for its creativity, but it also results in communication problems and an inability to concentrate resources on a few particularly promising ideas.

These problems faced 3M in the 1980's. Lewis Lehr became company president in 1981. Lehr, who fretted that "there isn't a business where we don't have to come up with a new technology," promptly restructured 3M from 6 divisions into 4 sectors: Industrial and Consumer, Electronic and Information Technologies, Graphic Technologies, and Life Sciences, containing a total of some 40 divisions. He also established a goal of having 25 percent of each division's earnings come from products that did not exist five years prior, a goal 3M met in 1984 and 1985, giving 3M a range of 45,000 to 85,000 products, depending on how many variants of the same idea you count. (Half of its new products are specifically designed for customers or potential customers.)

Lehr's concern was not to keep the company going; 3M was still well respected, with a very low (less than 25%) debt-to-equity ratio and reasonable levels of growth. Shareholders had little to complain about; 1986 marked the 18th consecutive year of increased dividends. Rather,

Lehr wanted to ensure that 3M would continue to develop new ideas.

So far, the major product of the 1980's has been the ubiquitous yellow Post-it, but 3M may have an even bigger idea on the horizon. 3M has developed optical disks, a product with tremendous long-range potential but no true market yet. Meanwhile, in a possible shift in strategy, 3M is sticking with its video tape sector, even engaging in cost-cutting to fend off severe pressure from competitors. At stake is what could become an $8 billion market.

3M is also trying to create more consumer products, as this is a division that accounts for only 10% of company sales. 3M has not tended to do well with consumer products, creating things like the eminently forgettable Mmm What a Tan! 3M made a bold move and brought in outsiders to help create and market consumer products.

The company is committed to its employees, and offers excellent work conditions. 3M views itself as a family, and, accordingly, tries to make working for it enjoyable. From sponsoring employee road races in the Philippines to encouraging corporate clubs, 3M constantly strives to keep its people satisfied and working productively. The process seems to work — most 3M workers and executives, including current chairman Allen Jacobson, never move on to other companies.

3M's concern for people spreads beyond its employees. A number of new products, such as WetorDry sandpaper, were created to improve working conditions. When Thermo-Fax dominated the copier market, 3M established a number of copy centers, which were all run by handicapped people. It designs new plants so they don't infringe on the environment, and works to eliminate environmental abuses before the product reaches the market.

Principal Subsidiaries: Dynacolor Corp.; Media Networks, Inc.; National Advertising Co.; Riker Laboratories, Inc.; Sanns, Inc. The company also has subsidiaries in the following countries: Argentina, Australia, Austria, Belgium, Brazil, Canada, Denmark, Finland, France, Hong Kong, Italy, Japan, Mexico, The Netherlands, Norway, Puerto Rico, Singapore, South Africa, Spain, Sweden, Switzerland, United Kingdom, Venezuela, and West Germany.

Further Reading: Our Story So Far: Notes from the First 75 Years of 3M Company, St. Paul, Minnesota, 3M Public Relations Department, 1977; *In Search of Excellence* by Thomas J. Peters and Robert H. Waterman, Jr., New York, Harper and Row, 1982.

MITSUBISHI CORPORATION

6-3, Marunouchi 2-chome
Chiyoda-ku, Tokyo 100
Japan
(03) 210-2121

Public Company
Incorporated: 1918 as Mitsubishi Shoji
Employees: 9150
Sales: ¥17.22 trillion (US$76.87 billion)
Market Value: ¥823 billion (US$3.279 billion)
Stock Index: Tokyo Osaka Nagoya Kyoto Hiroshima
Fukuoka Sapporo Niigata

The Mitsubishi three diamond logo has become one of the most familiar symbols in the world. As a manufacturer and trader of thousands of items, Mitsubishi Group companies are represented in virtually every country in the world. It has had a dominant presence in the development of eastern Asia since the 1870's and for many people has recently helped Japan to achieve a benign form of the pre-World War II economic plan known as the "Greater East Asia Co-Prosperity Sphere."

Mitsubishi is the family business of the House of Iwasaki. Its founder, Yataro Iwasaki, was born in 1834. He was a peasant who purchased samurai.status with the help of relatives. Despite his rural heritage, Iwasaki developed contacts with a number of urban administrators in Tosa prefecture (or fiefdom). Later, as a Tosa official and member of the administrative class, Iwasaki established a number of personal relationships with influential politicians whose assistance and favoritism would later prove indispensable.

After the restoration of the Meiji emperor in 1868, the new government initiated a national program of industrial modernization. It established and operated several model corporations which were later sold to private investors. At this time, however, the only private interests with enough money to purchase these corporations were established companies run by Japan's richest families. Family companies such as Mitsui, Sumitomo, and Yasuda greatly expanded their financial interests when they took control of the government companies.

Yataro Iwasaki, however, was not from a rich family. However, in 1870, during the first years of the Meiji government, he was able to purchase Tsukumo Shokai, the official Tosa shipping company. In 1873 he changed its name to Mitsubishi, which is Japanese for "three dia-

monds." Iwasaki was dedicated to an occupation as a merchant and to making Japanese shipping companies competitive with the large foreign lines.

Mitsubishi's greatest supporter in government was a close friend of Iwasaki, the Finance Minister Shigenobu Okuma. He lobbied on behalf of Mitsubishi, designating the company for numerous subsidies and privileges. When the Japanese government launched a punitive military expedition against the island of Formosa (Taiwan) in 1874, Okuma saw to it that Mitsubishi was chosen to provide the ships. The government later offered direct subsidies to Mitsubishi *Shokai* (company) to ensure that Japan remained competitive in world shipping. With the active support and protection of the government, Mitsubishi, like Mitsui, Sumitomo and Yasuda, evolved into a *zaibatsu* (literally a "money clique").

By 1877, 80% of Japanese maritime traffic was controlled by the Mitsubishi Shokai. Iwasaki, however, had made a number of political and professional "enemies" as a result of his privileged influence in government and trading practices. On numerous occasions Iwasaki was personally attacked in newspapers for his unscrupulous business practices. The other *zaibatsu*, particularly Mitsui, relied heavily on Mitsubishi for shipping and suffered greatly from its monopoly prices. Customers shipping freight on Shokai boats were obliged to use Mitsubishi warehouses and insure their goods with the Mitsubishi Maritime Insurance Company.

In 1880 Mitsui supported the creation of a rival shipping company called Tokyo Fuhansen. Within a year Mitsubishi had succeeded in driving Fuhansen out of business. However, after Count Okuma died in 1881, his political opponents joined Iwasaki's competitors with the common goal of breaking the Mitsubishi shipping monopoly. The following year Fuhansen was reorganized, merged with several other smaller shipping companies, and renamed Kyodo Unyu (United Transport). Kaoru Inoue, a political enemy of Okuma and close friend of Mitsui's Takashi Masuda, convinced the government to invest heavily in Kyodo Unyu. Thereafter, Mitsubishi and Kyodo Unyu engaged in an extremely costly and intense competition which drained both companies of virtually all their resources.

During the battle with Kyodo Unyu, Mitsubishi attempted to consolidate its operations by securing a guaranteed source of fuel. In 1881 the company purchased the Takashima coal mine. Iwasaki also sent representatives to the northern island of Hokkaido to investigate its potential for coal mining. After gaining control of coal resources, Iwasaki turned his attention to gaining control of a ship supplier. Iwasaki reminded the government that the Russians had just completed a naval base at Vladivostok, while Japan's major shipyard at Nagasaki was barely able to handle minor repairs. Mitsubishi won a contract to lease and later purchase the bankrupt Nagasaki Shipyard from the government.

By 1885 the battle for supremacy in Japanese shipping was deadlocked. That year the director of Kyodo Unyu, Eiichi Shibusawa, invited the government to impose a regulatory monopoly on shipping. Suddenly it was learned that Yataro Iwasaki had acquired a controlling interest in

Kyodo Unyu. In what may have been the world's first hostile takeover, Iwasaki secretly purchased a majority of his competitor's stock. He consolidated both companies into the Nihon Yusen Kaisha, or Japan Shipping Company, and denied managerial roles to both Masuda and Shibusawa who were stunned by their defeat. However, Iwasaki was unable to savor his victory; he died shortly afterward.

Iwasaki's associates, all of whom were samurai, were unable to assert themselves as independent managers until after Iwasaki died. Despite the fact that Mitsubishi was organized as a company, Iwasaki operated it as a family concern and exercised authoritarian control. His younger brother, Yanosuki Iwasaki, assumed the leadership of Mitsubishi Shokai and NYK in 1886.

The following year the Mitsubishi Shipbuilding Company became the first Japanese concern to manufacture a ship made of steel and equipped with a boiler. Japanese production of "black ships" for transportation and the military propelled Japan into a higher class of naval power. The major shipping companies, NYK and OSK (Osaka Shosen Kaisha), expanded their routes to China and Korea, and by 1899 to Europe, North America, India, and Australia.

NYK was a major beneficiary of the Sino-Japanese War (1894-1895), which opened several ports in continental Asia to increased Japanese trade. Like many of the other *zaibatsu*, Mitsubishi participated in Japan's colonization of Korea, Manchuria, and Taiwan. Mitsubishi, however, was primarily involved in establishing shipping links and developing an infrastructure in the colonial territories.

In 1893 Yanosuke Iwasaki initiated a reorganization of Mitsubishi and changed its name to Mitsubishi Goshi Kaisha. Three years later he diversified the company's operations by purchasing the Sado gold mine and Ikuno silver mine. He also purchased and developed a 110 acre swamp which later became some of the most expensive property in the Tokyo business district.

Koyata Iwasaki (who replaced Yanosuke as head of the company in 1916) continued the diversification program. Between 1917 and 1919 Mitsubishi established internal divisions for banking, mining, real estate, shipbuilding, and trading. As a victor in World War I, Japan was legitimized as a major world power with great influence in the Pacific. But this legitimization was owed to the *zaibatsu* (and not least Mitsubishi), who had built Japan into what it was.

In 1918 Mitsubishi was incorporated as a joint-stock company (totally owned by the Iwasaki family). At that time Mitsubishi Shoji Kaisha (Trading Company) was established as a separate business entity. Between 1917 and 1921 several more of the company's divisions were made independent public companies in order to attract investor capital. Mitsubishi Shipbuilding (later Mitsubishi Heavy Industries) was created in 1917, Mitsubishi Bank in 1919, and Mitsubishi Electric in 1921.

In the ensuing decade right-wing nationalist political terrorists gained influence in the military and government. Political assassinations claimed the lives of many moderate and leftist figures. In 1932 terrorists murdered Takuma Dan, head of Mitsubishi's chief rival, Mitsui. Many of the *zaibatsu* tempered their growth during this period to avoid becoming targets of the militarists, who had seized power in Japan.

The militarists envisioned a regional economic regime for eastern Asia called the Greater East Asia Co-Prosperity Sphere. As part of this scheme, Japan would be responsible for industry and management, China for agriculture, Manchuria and Korea for mining and forestry, Indonesia for oil, and the Philippines for fishing. For this reason, the *zaibatsu* were essential partners to the militarists. They alone had the resources and expertise to implement such an ambitous development strategy. Mitsubishi in particular was involved in the most important fields: shipping, shipbuilding, mining, heavy manufacturing, electrical generation, warehousing, and trading.

After the Japanese invasion of China in 1937 Mitsubishi was required to provide the military and occupation forces with warships, aircraft, vehicles, weapons, and provisions. When Japan invaded the rest of eastern Asia and bombed Pearl Harbor in 1941, the uneasy partnership between the *zaibatsu* and the militarists became more important. Companies such as Mitsubishi continued to search for profit. They also comprised the military/industrial complex which perpetuated Japan's ability to make war.

While Mitsubishi Shipbuilding turned out warships, the aircraft division of Mitsubishi Heavy Industries manufactured over 18,000 warplanes, the most important of which was the "Zero." The simple technology of the Zero made it possible for thousands to be built quickly. Its vast numbers and ability to climb and accelerate made it one of the most formidable weapons of the war.

In 1945 Japan surrendered to American forces, which during the previous year had destroyed Japan's major cities, and with them Japan's major factories. What remained of Mitsubishi was left in ruins. The American occupation forces under General Douglas MacArthur formulated an industrial plan for the reconstruction of Japan which included the implementation of American-style anti-monopoly laws. As a result of the legislation, the *zaibatsu* were outlawed and use of their prewar logos was banned. Mitsubishi was divided into 139 independent companies. In addition, severe restrictions prevented the companies from coordinating business strategies and setting up cross ownership of stock.

The communist revolution in China during 1949 and the Korean War (1950-1952) significantly increased the strategic value of Japan as an industrial power and American ally. Many of the punitive laws imposed on Japan by the occupation authority were lifted. Subsequent legislation in Japan weakened the effect of the anti-monopoly laws. Starting in 1950 several of the former Mitsubishi *zaibatsu* companies had been allowed to reassemble. The surviving core of company interests readapted the Mitsubishi Shoji Kaisha name and the triple diamond logo. In 1953 the Mitsubishi Bank (called the Chiyoda Bank during the occupation) started to use its old name and began to coordinate the various former Mitsubishi companies. In 1954 Mitsubishi Shoji merged with three of its former component companies and started to re-establish its worldwide trading network.

A number of associated companies were created during the 1950's, including the Mitsubishi Gas Chemical Company and the Mitsubishi Petrochemical Company. The company's most important foreign associate, the Mitsubishi International Corporation (MIC), was established in the United States in 1954. MIC carefully observed industrial and consumer trends in the United States and played an important part in the formation of Mitsubishi's long-term international planning. MIC also served as a training ground for international representatives of Mitsubishi.

Japan's Ministry of International Trade and Industry (MITI) played an active role in maintaining a healthy balance of monopolistic competition between the new *zaibatsu*, Mitsui, Mitsubishi, Sumitomo and others. MITI is responsible for the excellent coordination of resources, planning and development which allowed Japanese companies to grow and perform successfully in the postwar period. With the new *zaibatsu* as its instrument, MITI prepared Japan for several decades of export-led growth.

As a result of the direction provided by MITI, Mitsubishi anticipated Japan's increasing demand for various mineral commodities. In the 1960's Royal Dutch Shell discovered a large deposit of natural gas in the sultanate of Brunei. At the time, demand for natural gas was increasing rapidly in Japan. Mitsubishi participated with the government of Brunei and Royal Dutch Shell in developing a system whereby natural gas can be compressed into a refrigerated liquid and shipped in specially designed tankers.

Next Mitsubishi turned its attention to the untapped mineral potential of Australia and Papua New Guinea. The company formed a subsidiary called Mitsubishi Australia to participate in a large coal mining project at Bowen Basin in Queensland. Beginning in 1971 raw materials were shipped from Australia to Japan where they were used to produce iron and steel.

In 1969 Mitsubishi helped to create a forestry company called Balikpapan Forest Industries at Sotek, Indonesia. In 1973 Mitsubishi formed a joint venture with the Mexican government to produce salt in Baja California, and with the Kenyan government to develop the tourist industry in that country. In the late 1970's Mitsubishi established a joint marketing agreement with the Chrysler Corporation to sell cars in the United States built by the Mitsubishi Motor Company.

In 1971 Mitsubishi Shoji Kaisha changed its name to Mitsubishi Corporation, an Anglicized name intended to reflect the company's growing internationalization. By this time, however, the amalgamation of the prewar Mitsubishi combine had ceased. Top level managers in the associated Mitsubishi companies were reluctant to give up their independence (and possible their jobs) by placing themselves under the direction of other managers. Consequently there are 19 independent Mitsubishi companies whose directors belong to a monthly meeting group called the Kinyo-kai (Second Friday Conference) where their business strategies are formulated.

Unfortunately, many Japanese companies have ceased to rely on the trading services provided by the *sogo shosha*, or general trading companies. In most cases they have found it more cost effective to develop their own international networks. In addition, it had become harder for Japanese companies to compete internationally because of the rising value of the yen. Mitsubishi, in particular, experienced slower rates of growth. After 18 years as Japan's leading trading firm, Mitsubishi fell to fifth place in 1986. Still, the company's management and business coordination skills are highly regarded. Mitsubishi has a well-established reputation for good organization.

Takeo Kondo was named president of Mitsubishi in June of 1986. A few months later he presented a plan for reorganizing the company and reviewing its operations. In November, however, Kondo suddenly died. He was replaced by Shinroku Morohashi, a vice-president whom Kondo had charged to implement the restructuring plan. The "K-plan," as it has become known, involves the divestiture of unprofitable operations, reorganization of staff, entry into newer, more promising fields such as high technology, and the introduction of more efficient administrative techniques.

Having survived both war and strong international competition, Mitsubishi stands a good chance of remaining one of the most influential companies in both Japan and the world. Unfortunately for all the *sogo shosha*, however, it is not likely that any of them will regain the growth rates they experienced during the 1960's and 1970's.

Operations of the Mitsubishi Corporation are divided into the following groups: Fuels, Metals, Machinery, Food, Chemicals, Textiles, and General Merchandise.

Further Reading: Mitsubishi and the N.Y.K. 1870–1914: Business Strategy in the Japanese Shipping Industry, by William D. Wray, Boston, Harvard University Press, 1984.

MITSUI BUSSAN K.K.

2-1 Ochtemachi 1-chome
Chiyoda-ku, Tokyo
Japan
(03) 285-1111

Public Company
Incorporated: 1947 as Daiichi Bussan Kaisha, Ltd.
Employees: 11,445
Sales: ¥ 18.08 trillion (US$ 90.06 billion)
Market Value: ¥ 464.4 billion (US$ 2.313 billion)
Stock Index: Luxembourg Amsterdam Frankfurt Hong Kong Tokyo Osaka Nagoya Hiroshima Niigata Fukuoka Kyoto Sapporo

The Mitsui family traces its ancestral lineage to about 1100 A.D., and for its first several hundred years produced successive generations of samurai warriors. By 1650, however, the role of the samurai had changed. Sokubei Mitsui, head of the family, became a *chonin*, or merchant. He established a soy and sake brewery whose products first became popular in the red-light district of Edo (Tokyo). The business, which passed to his son Takatoshi, later expanded to include a dry-goods store, a pawnshop and a currency exchange which later evolved into a bank. The dry-goods store (named Echigoya in honor of an ancestor) operated on an innovative "cash only" basis with non-negotiable prices. The bank introduced the concept of money orders to Japan. The various Mitsui business ventures continued to grow through the end of the 17th century, particularly the bank, which was selected by the Tokugawa government to be its fiscal agent in Osaka. In the ensuing 150 years Mitsui enterprises prospered in the cities of Edo and Kyoto as well as Osaka.

During the 1860's the Mitsui financial reserve was nearly depleted. The family took the unprecedented step of hiring an "outsider" named Rizaemon Minomura away from another company in Edo. Minomura was a promising young executive who had demonstrated his talents and had a proven record of success. As an orphan and childhood drifter, he had no allegiance to family or prejudice to social status. Minomura also had a close personal relationship with Kaoru Inoue, a Japanese statesman with considerable influence in government circles. When Mitsui was forced to lend 350,000 ryo (the old Japanese currency) to the failing Tokugawa government Minomura, through his government contacts, managed to secure a government remittance of 320,000 ryo. Having saved the company

from ruin, Minomura was promoted to "head clerk," or chief executive, and given near dictatorial power.

Through an efficient information network, Minomura learned of the impending financial collapse of the Tokugawa government. He redirected support to the opposition Restoration party, a political movement which vowed to reinstate the Meiji government. In return for its support, Mitsui was appointed to manage the party's finances. After the battle of Tobu-Fushimi in 1868, the feudal government fell and the Meiji emperor Matsuhito was restored to power. Mitsui severed its ties with the Tokugawa rebels and continued to develop intimate relations with Meiji politicians. Mitsui became the official Meiji government banker, a position which greatly increased its influence and ability to expand.

Minomura urged that Mitsui relocate its headquarters from Kyoto to the new capital of Tokyo. He encountered strong resistance from the Mitsui family and the people of Kyoto. Arguing that the company needed to be located at the center of activity in order to survive, Minomura eventually won his point and moved the company to Tokyo in 1873.

In Japan at this time, capital and talented entrepreneurs were concentrated in the hands of a few large, well-diversified companies called *zaibatsu*, or "money cliques." The four largest *zaibatsu* were Mitsui, Mitsubishi, Sumitomo, and Yasuda, all of which controlled large banks. In turn, the banks were directed to provide low-cost capital for financing the *zaibatsu's* numerous industrial ventures. In 1874 Mitsui, as the *de facto* Ministry of Finance, held about ¥3.8 million and US$460,000 for the government, free of interest with no minimum reserve level.

The Meiji government initiated an extensive program of national modernization. Students were sent to the United States and Europe to study modern industrial production methods and bring them back to Japan where they would be applied to government-sponsored enterprises. The modernization program encountered difficulties because the government companies were unable to generate capital for investment and lacked managerial expertise. The *zaibatsu* companies, which had money and talent, were invited to participate in the modernization program by managing several of the various state enterprises. While still diversified, Mitsui remained primarily involved in banking, Mitsubishi established a shipping empire, and Sumitomo became a major copper producer.

During a Tokugawa rebellion at Satsuma the government commissioned Mitsui to provide about two-thirds of the army's provisions. Within a year the company's wealth had grown from ¥100,000 to ¥500,000. Hachiroemon Mitsui, the head of the family, was appointed by the government to at least 15 managerial positions in state enterprises. In the meantime, Inoue helped Minomura to consolidate his position in the company by informing him of impending changes in government policy. But while Hachiroemon Mitsui took credit for many of the company's new ventures, it was actually Rizaemon Minomura who planned and executed them.

It is not true that Mitsui was only as successful as it was because of its close relationship with the government. Two other wealthy families from the Tokugawa period, Ono and Shimada, encountered financial difficulties and later collapsed. Mitsui was successful because it was well organized and did not retain incompetent managers just because they were family members.

After Mitsui began to trade internationally in 1874, its business took a turn for the worse. It was unprepared to compete with larger foreign companies which had established trading networks and the benefit of protected colonial markets. By 1876 Minomura considered closing the international venture.

At this time Kaoru Inoue, who had previously left government service to pursue a career in industry, decided to return to politics. In order to avoid an explicit conflict of interest he was forced to sell Senshusha the company he established in 1872. Senshusha did a great deal of business with the government, which was considered an excellent customer. It was also managed by a respected administrator named Takashi Masuda. Inoue offered to sell Senshusha to Mitsui (which was certain to continue funding his political aspirations). It was also considered a personal favor to Minomura. Mitsui, after all, badly needed the talents of Masuda, who had gained considerable experience in international trade while working for an American company.

In July of 1876 Senshusha was merged with Kokusan-gata Karihonten, the Mitsui "temporary" head office for domestic trade located in Tokyo, and renamed Mitsui Bussan Kaisha (the Mitsui Trading Company). Takashi Masuda was placed in charge of the Bussan, and the following year took over as head clerk when Minomura died at the age of 56.

Shortly before Minomura died, Mitsui Bussan was appointed as marketing agent for high grade coal from the government's Miike mine, which it later purchased. In order to facilitate the profitable export of coal to China, the Bussan established a small office in Shanghai, its first foreign outpost.

In 1877 Mitsui Bussan was asked to supply military provisions to government forces in Kyushu during another samurai rebellion called the Seinan War. The conflict generated a ¥200,000 profit for the company, which was later used to finance the opening of additional Bussan branch offices in Hong Kong (1878) and New York (1879).

In 1882 Takeo Yamabe, an agent for the Osaka Textile Company, chose Mitsui to handle a purchasing transaction with two British textile machinery companies. Over the next few years the Bussan continued to purchase British textile machinery, primarily from Platt & Company. It became the exclusive Japanese agent for Platt in 1886. The Bussan's imports of textile machinery (mostly spindles) averaged between ¥25,000 and ¥46,000 in the years 1885–87, but rose to ¥270,000 in 1888.

In order to meet the sudden demand for cotton in Japan, Mitsui began to import cotton from Shanghai in 1887. When less expensive cotton of a higher quality became available from India, Mitsui dispatched an agent to Bombay, where a representative office was opened in 1892. By 1897 Mitsui accounted for over 30% of Japan's cotton imports. In 1900 the Bussan began to import American cotton through its New York office.

Mitsui relied heavily on the shipping services of Mitsubishi. Since it operated a monopoly in maritime transportation, Mitsubishi was free to charge highly inflated rates for its services. Companies such as Mitsui, which were heavily dependent on shipping, suffered greatly at the hands of Mitsubishi. When Eiichi Shibusawa, an "enemy" of Mitsubishi's founder Yataro Iwasaki, decided that he would no longer tolerate the monopoly practices, he proposed to Masuda that Mitsui help him to establish a rival shipping company. What ensued has been described as one of the most publicized and deadly episodes of competition in Japanese economic history.

In 1880 Mitsui participated in the establishment of the Tokyo Fuhansen (Sailing Ship) Company. A year later it appeared that Mitsubishi had succeeded in driving Fuhansen out of business. Determined to prevail, Shibusawa enlisted additional support from Masuda and Kaoru Inoue. In 1882, they arranged the formation of a new company called Kyodo Unyu (United Transport) in which Fuhansen was merged with a number of smaller shipping companies. The previous year Mitsubishi lost its "protector" in the government, Count Okuma. Iwasaki's enemies in government seized upon the Count's death as an opportunity to retaliate against Mitsubishi. The government provided Kyodo Unyu with trained shipping crews and increased the company's capitalization by 75%. Over the next two years fares on the Kobe-Yokohama passenger route dropped from 5.5 to 0.25 yen.

By 1885 the resources of both Mitsubishi and Kyodo Unyu were almost completely depleted. It was at this point that Shibusawa proposed that the government impose regulation of the industry. Unknown to him, however, Yataro Iwasaki had secretly purchased over half of the shares of Kyodo Unyu. He merged the company with Mitsubishi and renamed it the Nihon Yusen Kaisha (Japan Shipping Company), or NYK. Both Shibusawa and Masuda, who remained major shareholders or NYK were denied managerial roles in the new company, and both felt humiliation from their failure to defeat Mitsubishi.

Mitsui Bussan also emerged from the battle with Mitsubishi financially exhausted. Once again Masuda approached Inoue, who managed to secure a government loan to the Mitsui Bank on the condition that Masuda would be replaced by Hikojiro Nakamigawa, a former English teacher at Keio College who had quickly risen to become president of the Sanyo Railway Company. Masuda accepted Inoue's conditions, but remained with the company.

In the meantime, Eiichi Shibusawa continued to challenge NYK by organizing subsequent shipping companies, all of which failed. However, the Oji Paper Company, which he established in 1875, had become quite successful. Shibusawa persuaded Nakamigawa to increase the Bussan's investment in Oji Paper until it acquired a majority in 1890. Almost completely by surprise, Nakamigawa had Shibusawa and his talented nephew Okawa removed from the company. Mitsui took over control of Oji Paper and Shibusawa, defeated a second time, retired.

Chosen to reform Mitsui, Nakamigawa had the company's charter amended in 1896 to include shipping. Two years later several other transport-related operations were added, including warehousing and insurance. Although Nakamigawa died in 1901, his plans for Mitsui to enter maritime transport continued under Masuda. In 1903 a separate division for shipping was established. By the time the Bussan was formally incorporated in 1910, it had entered a number of new businesses; it was no longer just a trading company.

Mitsui Bussan profited greatly during World War I. On several occasions the Mitsui Bank called in outstanding loans from other creditors in order to finance the Bussan's numerous ventures. In 1917 the company created the Mitsui Engineering & Shipbuilding Company which manufactured many ships for the transport division.

As a result of numerous international treaties signed after the war, Japan became a more influential power in Asia. Only 50 years after the Meiji Restoration, Japan began to imitate the industrialized West in another way by "exporting" capital (or making large capital investments in its colonial possessions) to Formosa (Taiwan), Chosen (Korea), and Manchukuo (Manchuria). Mitsui was an active participant in the development of these areas by helping to establish an industrial infrastructure.

Takashi Masuda, who was advancing in age, relinquished his responsibilities to Takuma Dan, a former government engineer from the Miike coal mine. Although he was not trained as a businessman, Dan was a highly disciplined manager. During the 1920's the number of companies under the Bussan's control quadrupled. Toward the end of the decade, however, extreme right-wing militarists initiated a terrorist campaign against the traditional establishment. Mitsui, the largest *zaibatsu*, was frequently attacked because it came to symbolize the democratic capitalist establishment in Japan. In 1932 Takuma Dan was assassinated by a rightist "young officers" group.

Mitsui elected Seihin Ikeda to succeed Dan, but this did not prevent further attacks. Right-wing militarists subsequently assassinated hundreds more moderate politicians, industrialists, and military officers. Perhaps under threat, Mitsui ceased trading a number of agricultural products and offered a substantial amount of stock in its subsidiaries to the public. In 1933 the Bussan established a ¥30 million fund for the promotion of social services and relief of the "distressed." After the February Incident, an isolated but serious mutiny of rightist officers in 1936, the Mitsui family announced that it would cease to participate in the management of the Bussan.

In order to appease critics of "democratic industrialism" who were rapidly coming to power, many of the *zaibatsu* openly participated in the development of a *Junsenji Keizai*, or "quasi-war-time economy." As a result, several *zaibatsu* directly benefitted from the government's increased investment in heavy industry. The military/industrial establishment grew rapidly after Japanese forces invaded China in 1937. That year Mitsui launched the Toyota Motor Corporation and Showa Aircraft Industry Company. Mitsui Bussan had become the largest and most powerful conglomerate in the world, employing 2.8 million people.

Like nearly all Japanese companies, Mitsui played an active role in the Japanese war effort, helping to develop shipping, railways, mining, chemical and metallurgical industries, and electrical generation. The company was active in every country under Japanese occupation. By 1943, however, it was realized that Japan had no chance of winning the war. When the mainland of Japan became exposed to aerial bombings, major factories and industrial enterprises were primary targets.

When the war ended in September of 1945, Japan had been almost completely destroyed. All of Mitsui Bussan's major facilities were severely damaged. The entire nation was placed under the command of a military occupation authority, called "SCAP," for Supreme Commander of Allied Powers. Representatives of the *zaibatsu* convinced President Truman's envoy John Foster Dulles that, if properly administered, a "generous" peace treaty would ensure that Japan would become a reliable American ally in the Far East. Nonetheless, SCAP reorganized Japanese industry on the American model of organization and enacted an "Anti-Monopoly Law." Since they were considered monopolies, the *zaibatsu* were ordered dissolved. Mitsui Bussan was broken into over 180 separate companies, none of which were allowed to use the prewar Mitsui logo.

Mitsui Bussan was divided into the "new" Mitsui Bussan (called the Nitto Warehousing Company), Daiichi Bussan, Nippon Machinery Trading, Tokyo Food Products, and a dozen smaller firms. The Mitsui Bank, which during the war was merged with the Daiichi and Daijugo Banks to form the Teikoku Bank, was split into two banks, Mitsui and Daiichi. Mitsui Mining was reorganized and renamed Mitsui Metal Mining. Nettai Sangyo and Mitsui Wood Vessels dissolved, and Mitsui Lumber was absorbed by the new Bussan. Affiliated companies such as Tokyo Shibaura Electric (later called Toshiba) and Toyota were made fully independent. Finally, all coordination of activities through a *honsha*, or parent company, was strictly prohibited.

Despite the various prohibitions, leaders of the former Mitsui *zaibatsu* companies remained in close contact; 27 of them formed a monthly luncheon group called the Getsuyo-kai (Monday Conference). The anti-monopoly laws were subsequently weakened by Japanese acts of legislation in 1949 and 1953. After the Korean War (1950–1953) the laws were further relaxed and many of the *zaibatsu*, including Mitsui, began to reform under the direction of their former subsidiary banks. Even the Mitsui logo (the Japanese character "three" surrounded by a diagonal square, representing "wellspring") came back into use. Nitto Warehousing began to absorb some of its former component companies in 1951, and in 1952 adopted the name New Mitsui Bussan. Daiichi absorbed the remaining companies between 1951 and 1957, and in 1958 was itself merged with the New Mitsui Bussan, which dropped "New" from its name.

The new *zaibatsu*, called *keiretsu* (banking conglomerates) or *sogo shosha* (trading companies), lacked the strict vertical discipline of the prewar organization. Mitsui completed its reassembly and transition into a *sogo shosha* by 1960.

As the Bussan's various subsidiary industries consolidated their operations, their quasi-*honsha* parent company began to establish offices in many foreign countries, even ones with which Japan had no formal diplomatic ties. As it did before the war, Mitsui's foreign offices functioned as unofficial Japanese consulates.

A second meeting group called the Nimoku-kai was established in 1960. Members of this group later included Toyota, Toshiba, and many of the Getsuyo-kai members. Together with the Getsuyo-kai, which included Toyo Menka Kaisha, Ishikawajima-Harima Heavy Industries, Showa Aircraft, and Oji Paper, among others, the Nimoku-kai enabled Mitsui to coordinate the activities of the former *zaibatsu* affiliates.

In order to expand its heavy industry sector Mitsui purchased the Kinoshita Sansho steel company in 1965. Kinoshita's operations were later merged with Mitsui's Japan Steel Works, Ltd., which was established in 1907. During the 1960's Mitsui helped to develop the Robe River mine in Western Australia, which provides most of the iron ore for the Mitsui steel mills in Japan. Other Australian ventures followed, including another iron ore mine at Mount Newman and a bauxite mine at Gove. These projects led to the creation of a larger joint venture with AMAX in 1973 called Alumax, which produces aluminum in the United States.

Mitsui became a major petrochemical company in 1958. The chemical division, Mitsui Koatsu, sold not only its products, but its production technologies. The Iran Japan Petrochemical Complex at Bandar Khomeini (formerly Bandar-e-Shapur) was begun in 1973. Since 1980, however, it has been a frequent target of Iraqi air strikes. If and when it is ever completed, it promises to be the largest chemical plant in the Middle East.

Several of Mitsui's former subsidiaries, while remaining associated companies, resisted amalgamation with the parent company because each company's management board wanted to avoid interference from Mitsui; they did not want to be placed into a larger industrial scheme which would reduce their independence. Associated companies, such as Onoda Cement, Toyo Manka, Sapporo Breweries, and Oji Paper, which permitted a more embracing relationship with Mitsui, found the amalgamation difficult to bear. Managers of these companies were given subordinate positions in Mitsui and their opinions carried significantly less weight. In 1973 three other companies, Toshiba, Mitsui O.S.K. Lines, and Mitsukoshi, rejoined Mitsui by accepting membership in the Nimoku-kai. Other larger and more successful associated companies, such as Toyota and Ishikawajima-Harima Heavy Industries, are not expected to join the Nimoku-kai as full members.

Mitsui has a strong presence in Brazil, where it is involved in the production of steel, coffee, soybeans, maize, and fertilizer. As an example of Mitsui's diverse mix of products and geography, the company produces lumber and trawls for shrimp in Indonesia, raises chickens in Korea, manufactures chemicals in Belgium, plastics in Portugal, nylon in Kenya, paper in Singapore, refines sugar and makes automobile tires in Thailand, and mines copper in Peru and coal in Australia.

Despite the anti-monopoly laws (many of which are still carried on the books in Japan) Mitsui today has regained virtually all of its prewar grandeur. As one of the world's largest commercial enterprises, Mitsui has both the resources and ability to develop and apply new technologies in any field it wishes to enter. The fact that Mitsui has survived the conditions it has experienced in the last 120 years indicates that it is likely to remain as successful in the future as it has been in the past.

Principal Subsidiaries: (Japan): Toyo Shoji Co.; Toyo Wire, Ltd.; Toyo Officemation, Inc.; Mitsui Liquified Gas Co., Ltd.; Mitsui Oil Co., Ltd.; Kanto Denka Kaisha, Ltd.; Daiichi Reizo Co., Ltd.; K.K. Ichirei; Sangyo Kogyo Co., Ltd.; Mikuni Coca-Cola Bottling Co., Ltd.; Bussan Fudosan K.K.; Mitsui Lumber Co., Ltd.; Mitsui Bussan Forestry Co., Ltd.; Mitsui Concrete Industrial Co., Ltd.; Chita Futo K.K.; Daiichi Tanker Co., Ltd.; Kinoshita & Co., Ltd.; Bussan Credit Co., Ltd.; Fuji Works, Ltd.; Kokusai Oil & Chemical Co., Ltd.; Nihon Dennetsu Co., Ltd.; Mitsui Bussan Machine Tool Co., Ltd.; Kyoto Brass Co., Ltd.; K.K. Shinsei; K.K. Gumma Coil Center; Sanyu Foods Co., Ltd.; Mitsui Knowledge Industry Co., Ltd.

Principal Subsidiaries: (Foreign): Thirty companies in ten countries, including: Mitsui-C.Itoh Iron Pty., Ltd. (Australia); Mitsui Iron Ore Pty., Ltd. (Australia); Mitsui Salt Pty., Ltd. (Australia); Mitsui Tubular Products, Inc. (USA); Ocean Packing Corp. (USA); United Grain Corp. (USA).

Affiliated Companies: Sixty-seven in Japan, including: The Mitsui Bank, Ltd.; Mitsui Mutual Life Insurance Co.; Toyo Menka Kaisha, Ltd.; Taisho Marine & Fire Insurance Co., Ltd.; Ishikawajima-Harima Heavy Industries Co., Ltd.; Toshiba Corp.; Toyota Motor Corp.; Toray Industries, Inc.; Mitsui O.S.K. Lines, Ltd. Twelve in seven foreign countries, including Mitsui & Co. (USA).

Further Reading: Mitsui: Three Centuries of Japanese Business by John G. Roberts, New York, Weatherhill, 1973.

NISSHO IWAI K.K.

2–4–5 Akasaka 2-chome
Minato-ku, Tokyo 107
Japan
03 (588) 4010

Public Company
Incorporated: 1968 as Nissho Iwai Company, Ltd.
Employees: 7303
Sales: ¥9.484 trillion (US$52.8 billion)
Market Value: ¥200.2 billion (US$1.114 billion)
Stock Index: Osaka Tokyo Nagoya Hiroshima Frankfurt

Nissho Iwai was created in 1968 as the result of a merger between Iwai & Company and the Nissho Company. Both Iwai and Nissho had previously existed as independent companies primarily involved in trading and the production of ferrous metals.

Bunsuke Iwai began his life in business as an apprentice at a general store in Osaka called the Kagaya. In 1863, when he was 21, Iwai set up his own shop, specializing in popular imported foreign goods. The shop sold Western glass, oil products, paper, pottery, silk, woolens, and wine.

In 1868 the government of the Tokugawa shogunate was overthrown by forces loyal to the Meiji emperor. The new government sponsored a national modernization program to promote Japanese industry and export enterprises. As elements of the economy engaged in greater specialization, larger amounts of income became available to consumers, which increased their demand for foreign goods. Iwai's business began to grow at a faster rate, and expanded both geographically and in terms of trading volume. In 1877 another young entrepreneur named Iwajiro Suzuki established a similar trading firm called Suzuki & Company.

Iwai & Company came very close to bankruptcy in 1879 when a bank it helped to create became financially insolvent. Within ten years, however, the company had established itself as one of the largest import traders in Osaka, employing over a dozen full-time agents in the port city of Kobe. As a wholesale, Iwai sold over one hundred varieties of goods to merchants across western Honshu and Kyushu.

Japan entered the second stage of its industrialization in the 1890's when modern cotton spinning methods were introduced to Japan. Both Iwai and Suzuki imported materials for cotton production. Iwai was the larger of the two companies and had considerably more capital available for reinvestment. Iwai purchased several factories and converted them to produce goods which the company had been importing.

In 1897 Iwai became associated with a British trading firm called William Duff & Sons, through which Iwai imported a number of European goods. Iwai and Duff dealt directly with each other, eliminating the *shokan*, middlemen with privileged and established international trading networks. The *shokan* attempted to dissuade Iwai from formalizing its direct relationship with companies such as Duff, but failed.

When the Yawata Steel Works began production of iron and steel in 1901, Iwai was designated its primary trading agent. Iwai gained considerable experience in international trading, and by 1906 began to export a variety of Japanese goods (including matches, textiles, sundries, and jute sacks), primarily to India. The following year the company dispatched agents to India and the Netherlands East Indies (Indonesia) to promote sales of Iwai & Company products.

In 1912 Iwai was incorporated and shares of company stock were sold in order to raise capital. The export trade, however, was highly unprofitable and caused the company to grow at a slower rate than other larger trading companies. While Iwai's trade volume amounted to five million yen in 1913, the largest trading company Mitsue registered ¥340 million.

Suzuki remained exclusively involved in the import trade and, as a result, experienced stronger growth. As one of the world's largest sugar brokers, Suzuki maintained offices in London and became only the second Japanese company to be admitted to the Baltic Exchange. During this period Suzuki achieved a level of operation which placed it in a category with major trading companies. Suzuki engaged in trading iron and refined metal products, chemical and agricultural products, and entered heavy industry with the creation of a shipbuilding division.

Much of the credit for Suzuki's rise to prominence is given to two of the company's senior managers, Naokichi Kaneko and Seiichi Takahata. They coordinated foreign suppliers with markets in other countries and, in the process, established Suzuki as one of the world's first international intermediary traders. For example, the company sold Chilean sulphur to Russia and purchased Ukrainian wheat for sale to commodity traders on the Baltic Exchange. Suzuki operated over 20 large ships, transporting cargoes between Europe, Asia, and the Americas.

At approximately the same time, international trading had become highly competitive for Iwai and was increasingly dominated by a few large conglomerates known as *zaibatsu*. In an effort to reduce the company's exposure to international trading and realize the growing economic advantages of domestic production, Iwai created a number of operating subsidiaries to produce goods for import substitution. The company established Dai Nippon Celluloid in 1913, Nippon Steel Plate in 1914, and Tokuyama Soda in 1918. In addition, the company established branch offices in countries around the world to take over the business of agents who were preoccupied by the war.

As one of the victorious nations in World War I, Japan was allowed greater freedom to develop and police eastern Asia as its regional "sphere of influence." Japanese companies were invited by the government to exploit natural resources and develop industries in Chosen (Korea), Taiwan, and Manchuria. The result was that Japan had begun a transformation into a mercantilist economy; it "exported" some of its labor-intensive industrial capacity to other countries and engaged in more active development of a modern heavy industrial sector.

The 1920's was a decade of stagnation and slow economic growth. Japanese companies had a more difficult time competing in international markets because Japan's wartime allies had rededicated their industrial energies to the development of their economies. The companies most seriously affected by the recession were C. Itoh, Iwai, and Suzuki. By 1928 conditions had become so poor for Suzuki that it was forced to reorganize. Many of its properties were taken over by Mitsui, and those that remained were used to form a new organization called the Nissho Company.

Iwai was threatened with bankruptcy in 1930, but recovered when demand for iron and steel increased. The company's profits from foreign trading began to rise sharply in 1933. Two years later Iwai expanded its operations in Korea, China, and the nations of southeast Asia, and later in Latin America, Africa, Egypt, India, and Australia. Nissho opened offices in Los Angeles and New York, and in 1937, in Calcutta.

Japan's domination of Asia grew under the militarist government. In 1937, as part of a plan to establish a regional economic order, Japan launched an invasion of China. The Japanese economy was mobilized to prepare for subsequent military conquests, which increased demand for a wide variety of products, principally steel. Despite the growth experienced during this period, Nissho and Iwai chose not to divide their resources into independent associated companies, as did Mitsui, Mitsubishi, and Sumitomo.

Japanese military adventurism erupted into general war in 1941. Although they were viewed as enemies of those in power, Nissho and Iwai remained principal contributors to the Japanese war effort. After initially making large territorial gains, the war turned against Japan. American bombers came within range of Japanese targets in 1944, and the following year Japan was defeated.

Like many other Japanese companies, both Nissho and Iwai were devastated by damaged facilities and the collapse of the economy. The policies laid down by the Allied occupation authority were particularly harsh for the large *zaibatsu* conglomerates. Mitsui, Mitsubishi, and Sumitomo, among others, were divided into hundreds of independent companies.

In order to prevent the occupation authority from imposing a potentially debilitating reorganization of its operations, Iwai offered to divest itself of seven manufacturing subsidiaries. The offer was accepted, and Iwai's trading division was permitted to remain intact. With foreign markets no longer opened to Japanese companies, Iwai was forced to subsist on the slowly recovering

domestic trade. The insurance and manufacturing divisions of Nissho were detached and re-established as independent companies.

When the *zaibatsu* were dissolved, numerous opportunities were created for Nissho and Iwai to expand their operations. In the postwar years, both companies re-established and expanded their metals divisions and entered the field of machine manufacturing. Nissho created three associated companies in 1949, Nissho Chemical Industry, Nissho Fuel, and Nikkyo Shoji (Trading). The establishment of these companies marked the entry of Nissho into the field of petrochemicals, essential in the production of hundreds of industrial products.

The outbreak of the Korean War in June of 1950 drastically altered Japan's role as a Western ally. The nation's economy was redirected to promote industrial growth which would make Japan self-reliant and impervious to the expansion of communism. Iwai did not benefit from the war as greatly as other companies, but nevertheless did well enough to absorb heavy losses during two recessions in the early 1950's. The growth of both Nissho and Iwai continued on a stable course for the remainder of the 1950's, and was marked by the opening of several more offices throughout the world. The most notable of these was the Nissho American Corporation, opened in 1952.

Many of the prewar *zaibatsu* companies began to reorganize their fragmented organizations around banks which were formerly part of the *zaibatsu* groups. After the war, virtually all the *zaibatsu* organizations engaged in international trading and became known by a new name, *sogo shosha*, or "general trading companies." While neither Nissho nor Iwai were ever considered *zaibatsu*, they were large enough by 1960 to be referred to as *sogo shosha*.

The *sogo shosha* played an important role in acquiring and developing new technologies, and then applying them to goods manufactured for export. Capital accumulated from exports was reinvested to produce newer and larger plants. Nissho and Iwai were mainly involved in steel marketing, the development of new machinery, and construction of new factories. They later branched out into other industries, establishing housing construction and realty ventures, as well as marketing subsidiaries for a variety of consumer products.

The largest trading companies in 1962 were C. Itoh, Mitsubishi, Mitsui, and Marubeni-Iida, each with sales several times larger than Iwai. Iwai was an importer of metal products which other Japanese companies had begun to produce in great volume. As Japan became a net exporter of these products, the gap between Iwai and the larger, more diversified *sogo shosha* expanded even further. Poor management and the overbearing influence of the Iwai family ruined the company's last opportunities to recover. When banks and other lending institutions realized that Iwai's condition was failing and irreversible, they withdrew their financial support.

By comparison, Nissho Trading was well managed and profitable. When it appeared that Iwai would fail, the Japanese government ordered Nissho (the seventh largest trading company in Japan) to merge with Iwai (the tenth largest). Although the merger was directed by the government, both organizations had much to gain. The new company, called Nissho Iwai, had a greatly strengthened intelligence gathering network, and its capitalization was approximately doubled. In addition, the new company had the benefit of a larger market with a rationalized management structure. As a result of the merger, Nissho Iwai became the fifth largest trading company in Japan.

Nissho Iwai maintained a close relationship with the Sanwa and Dai-Ichi Kangyo banking groups. The company also maintained its relationship with Kobe Steel, Ishikawajima-Harima Heavy Industries (formerly Harima Shipbuilding), and Teijin, a large chemical company. Nissho Iwai reduced its exposure to the domestic steel market and increased its export volume. Despite increased growth, Nissho Iwai was surpassed by Sumitomo Trading in 1972 and relegated to the position of the sixth largest trading company in Japan.

The company was implicated in an illegal payments scandal in 1979. Nissho Iwai acted as a sales agent of military aircraft for McDonnell Douglas, Boeing, and Grumman, and was accused of diverting sales commissions to Japanese politicians. One of the company's executives committed suicide and three more were arrested, including the vice president of aircraft sales, Hachiroh Kaifu. Even the chairman of Nissho Iwai resigned. Despite the alleged improprieties, Nissho Iwai nearly doubled its sales volume in 1979. The company did, however, announce that it would withdraw from the aircraft marketing business.

The following year the company's name was changed to the Nissho Iwai Corporation. A new emphasis was placed on acting as a intermediary sales agent between two foreign parties, and contributing to the development of industrial projects with financial participation and technological assistance.

Nissho Iwai remains the sixth largest Japanese *sogo shosha*. It is a principal importer of liquified natural gas and exporter of steel. As the growth of the Japanese economy has slowed in recent years, the growth of Nissho Iwai has been similarly affected. While the company's intermediary trade has recently declined, many of its export divisions have remained financially healthy, particularly Nissho Electronics. Nissho Iwai has also recently acquired large shares of Nihon Sugar and Fuji Seito, a food products company.

Principal Subsidiaries: Goto Drop Forging Co., Ltd.; Hamamatsu Kohan Kako K.K.; Komatsugawa Koki Co., Ltd.; NIK Metal Corp.; Nissho Iwai Steel Corp.; Nissho Iwai Steel Leasing Co., Ltd.; Oyodo Steel Co., Ltd.; Nihon Mining and Concentrating Co., Ltd.; Nissho Iwai Nonferrous Metals Corp.; Kokusai Kisen K.K.; Kokusai Marine K.K.; Nissho Electronics Corp.; Nissho Iwai Aerospace Co., Ltd,; Nissho Iwai Business Automation Corp.; Nissho Medi Science Co., Ltd.; World Aircraft Sales Corp.; Nissho Iwai-titled Apparel Co., Ltd.; Seni Kakoo Co., Ltd.; Chuo Woolen Mills, Ltd.; Sunrock Textile Co., Ltd.; Chuo Tobacco Co., Ltd.; Nike Japan Corp.; Nissho Iwai Sports Corp.; Beisei Tobacco Trading Co., Ltd.; Nissho Iwai-titles Glass Co., Ltd.; Propane & Oil Co., Ltd.; Sekiyu Corp.; Fuji Kako Co., Ltd.; Nippla Chemical Co., Ltd.; Nissho Iwai Polymers & Products Corp.; Sambow Resin Industries Co., Ltd.; Taiyo Kagaku Kogyo Co., Ltd.; Fuji Seito Co., Ltd.; Marusan Co., Ltd.; Nissho Iwai Foods Corp.; Nissho Iwai Delica Corp.; Nissho Iwai Foods Osaka Corp.; Osaka Suehiro Broiler Co., Ltd.; Shin-Meito Co., Ltd. Nissho Iwai also lists subsidiaries in the following countries: Argentina, Australia, Belgium, Brazil, Canada, France, Hong Kong, India, Iran, Italy, Kuwait, New Zealand, Nigeria, Panama, Spain, Sudan, Tanzania, Thailand, the United States, Venezuela, and West Germany.

Further Reading: The Soga Shosha: Japan's Multinational Trading Companies by Alexander Young, Boulder, Colorado, Westview Press, 1979.

OGDEN

■ ■ ■ ■ ■

OGDEN CORPORATION

277 Park Avenue
New York, New York 10172
U.S.A.
(212) 754-4000

Public Company
Incorporated: August 4, 1939
Employees: 39,000
Sales: $800 million
Market Value: $1.340 billion
Stock Index: New York

"Evolutionary adaptation is just as important for a company as it is for organisms." So stated Ralph E. Ablon, the president and directing force behind the Ogden Corporation. This philosophy has taken Ogden from a shaky beginning to a successful present and a promising future.

In 1935 the Utilities Power and Light Corporation was in danger of bankruptcy. The Atlas Corporation, controlled by Floyd Odlum, had been its chief creditor. By 1939 Odlum devised a plan reorganizing all remaining assets of the old utility under the control of a newly established company. This new company, the Ogden Corporation, could then liquidate these lingering assets. By 1951, with the exception of approximately $1,597,000 in cash and a few securities, Ogden sold all of the resources of the old utility. The corporation finally consisted of a rudimentary skeleton which the stockholders then voted to dissolve. It was at this point that Charlie Allen, of Allen & Company, stepped in.

Charlie Allen, the founder and senior partner of Allen & Company, had a sharp mind and a keen awareness of the workings on Wall Street. Starting as a runner on the stock market after quitting high school, he soon became a bond trader. Unable to work within a hierarchy of superiors and bored with his everyday routine, Allen started his own trading room with less than $1000 working capital. Through agressive buying and selling techniques, Allen & Company grew steadily.

In 1951 Allen bought, at liquidation prices, the 80% of the Ogden Corporation that Atlas had previously owned. He then began his revitalization process. Allen first terminated the liquidation proceedings. He then sent his lawyer, Jacob L. Holtzmann, to the Delaware state capital. Holtzmann convinced members of the Delaware Bar to pass a law stating that a two-third stock-holder's

vote could stop dissolution. He pointed out that this provision was recommended by the American Bar Association. Ogden was, for the present, saved.

Allen intended for the Ogden Corporation to be a holding company. His idea was to purchase inexpensive companies, incorporate them under Ogden's, and then sell the companies when the highest profit could be extracted from them. This has been management policy throughout the history of the conglomerate. Over 55 companies have been acquired by Ogden. They are either existing subsidiaries or have merged with the parent company. The first company Ogden purchased is an excellent example of Allen's strategy.

Teleregister Corporation was a manufacturing firm owned by Western Union. They were the top producers of the electronic quote boards used by the various stock exchanges in this country. Computerized data processing had just passed through its initial stage, and the company had an opportunity for remarkable growth. However, Teleregister was able to receive only minimal capital from its parent company for expansion and research. Western Union itself was expanding and it could not spare the capital needed for their subsidiary's expansion. The new opportunities at the end of World War II allowed the company to redirect all of its working capital back into its own projects. At this point Ogden offered Teleregister all of the capital it needed.

In 1953 Ogden purchased Teleregister for $2 million. Teleregister grew so rapidly that new management and an expanded staff of engineers and draftsmen were needed to handle the deluge of incoming orders. The number of employees more than doubled. Ogden allowed Teleregister an opportunity to diversify into data processing systems made specifically for individual companies. For instance, the company offered American Airlines its first computerized ticket reservation system. Teleregister also developed automated banking services.

Ogden continued to acquire companies, although product lines had little to do with Allen's acquisition strategy. In 1955 Ogden purchased all of the capital stock of Commercial Filters Corporation and also acquired Luria Brothers and Company. One year later, Ogden acquired Syntex, S.A. and Caribbean Chemicals, S.A. Syntex, then the leading producer of steroids and cortisone intermediates, was Ogden's first foreign subsidiary. In 1957 Ogden bought EIMCO Corporation, a firm concerned with mining, and its subsidiaries. Ogden sold two subsidiaries in 1958. Both Syntex International, S.A. and Chemical Specialties, Inc. were sold. Ogden then took control of Avondale Marine Ways, Inc., through a subsidiary, as well as all stock in Avoncraft Construction Company in 1959. In addition, the Case Manufacturing Corporation subsidiary merged into the parent corporation in the same year.

Obviously, Ogden had become a company interested in diversifying its holdings. One of its most important divisions was Luria Brothers & Company Inc. Through Luria, Ogden became the largest producer of scrap metal in the world. The Federal Trade Commission had even complained that Ogden excessively dominated the industry.

A major change that took place in 1962 demonstrates Luria's importance to Ogden. The new president and chairman elected to replace Teleregister's Maurice L. Sindeband was the former president of Luria Brothers, Ralph A. Ablon. Ablon had come from a more intellectual than industrial background. After graduating from Ohio State University, he had returned to teach English there. He entered into the Luria Brothers and Company by marrying the heiress to the company. Ablon soon became president of Luria, and retained his position when Ogden purchased it in 1955. In 1962, when Allen had decided to expand Ogden's board of directors and make executive changes, Ablon showed himself to be the man to consolidate Ogden into one operation.

Ablon, however, arrived at a bad time. The demand for scrap was down and prices were low. It took less and less scrap metal to produce steel. Ablon reacted to this situation quickly; he decided Ogden should become a company with many markets with "the flexibility to withstand unexpected shocks." Ablon also decided it was time for a change in Ogden's direction. He brought in highly educated management and continued Ogden's innovative research. He also expanded the company's interests into more demolition and shipping projects. Finally, he added food industry to the conglomerate. By 1969, the results of the changes Ablon had initiated were apparent.

Under the leadership of Ablon, the shipping industry grew to become a large and important operation within Ogden. In 1962 Ogden acquired control of the stock in the International Terminal Operation Company then the largest stevedoring company in the U.S. When the remaining interest in Avondale Shipyards of New Orleans was purchased in 1966 at 450,000 common shares, the yard showed a $130 million backlog of orders at a time when other shipbuilders had difficulty surviving. Avondale has since become one of the most efficient and highly organized shipyards in the industry. And, although many prominent unions have tried, the majority of employees have yet to come under union control.

The food service industry brought many new companies into Ogden's organizational structure befoe 1969. Ogden acquired almost all of the interest in Tillie Lewis Foods, Inc. in 1966 for $14 million. The remainder was purchased in 1967. In addition, Ogden purchased 73,000 common shares in Wilson Foods. In 1968 Ogden bought Western California Canners, Inc. through a subsidiary, and directly acquired Chef's Orchid Airline Caterers, Inc.

Even with these new companies, Ogden continued to rely heavily on its ferrous processing and metal recycling industries for capital. Luria Brothers & Company purchased the voting rights for Jarcho Brothers, Inc. in cash during 1964. Ogden acquired Wabash Alloys, Inc., an aluminium recycling plant, as well as Barth Smelting Corp in 1968. Also in 1968, Ogden acquired Mayville Metal Products Company, producers of parts for various electronic, business, and office machines. Mayville, in turn, purchased some assets of Steelmade, Inc. in 1970.

In 1969 it was apparent that Ablon's restructuring of Ogden had some flaws. The diversification plan resulted in problems, especially within the areas of ship building and food products. Due to mismanagement, Avondale Ship-yard's business began to steadily decrease. Avondale's management took more interest in costly ventures than with controlling worker production or planning future projects. Both the management at Avondale and at Ogden battled for power until Ogden finally gained control in 1971 due to irregularities found in Avondale's order books.

The stress at the power struggle within the company inevitably affected Avondale's productivity. Mechanical expansion at the factories along with poor contract decisions drained much of its potential profits. In 1969, for the first time since Ablon had taken control, Ogden Corporation's earnings fell. This was due not only to Avondale's instability, but to a number of unforeseen circumstances. For instance, a destroyed crop of tomatoes weakened Ogden's food division. Ogden was also forced to write off a large quantity of cyclamates, a salt formerly used in artificial sweeteners, due to the unhealthy side-effects in humans. In addition, Ablon made the unfortunate decision to invest in the Charles Luckman Association.

In 1968 Charles Luckman's architectural design company seemed like a good purchase. Luckman designed such famous buildings as Madison Square Garden, the Phoenix cultural center, and the Lever Building in New York City. Ablon, on the basis of these merits, appointed Luckman as head of Ogden's newly formed development subsidiary. However, by relying on Luckman's architectural fame, Ablon allowed Luckman to control a large amount of Ogden's capital. One of Luckman's major projects, the Broadway Plaza in Los Angeles, ran in excess of $10 million over the estimated budget. It was at this point Ablon gave Ogden's partners control of the project, and started to look a little deeper into Luckman's affairs. What he found was that Luckman had committed Ogden to a lease on a 13-story office building, owned by the Luckman family, on Sunset Boulevard. Instead of receiving the projected $900,000 from the building, Ogden would pay $3 million for improvements. In 1973 Ablon decided to sell the architectural firm back to Luckman for only $1000, and loan Luckman an additional $1 million to aid his revival attempt with the stipulation that Luckman would eventually also pay Ogden $1.5 million in overdue fees. Overall, the Luckman transaction cost Ogden nearly $12.5 million.

In light of what had happened, Ablon changed his criteria for choosing investments. He now chose investments according to an "admissable risk threshold." This meant he judged, prior to investing, how much Ogden would possibly lose if an entire venture failed. If the amount lost in the transaction would not be too large, Ogden would take the risk. If, however, the venture could expose the company to a potentially volatile economic situation, no matter how good it looked initially, Ogden would abandon it.

Whereas once Ablon's response to Ogden's slow profits was diversification, his answer was now consolidation. In the early 1970's Ablon tried to increase Ogden's Corporation's productivity by concentrating on three distinct industries. He predicted that a combination of shipping, ferrous recycling, and food production and services would allow Ogden to weather any recession and energy shortage. His prediction was correct.

After five years of low profits, Ogden showed signs of a revival in 1974. The company seemed in good financial condition. This was due largely to Ogden's mainline industry, scrap metal production. The scrap business was rapidly improving. Ogden, still the world's largest recycler, relied heavily on these steady profits to regain some stability in the corporation. Ogden expanded their industrial division further with the addition of Yuba Heat Transfer Corporation in 1978, and then with Danly Machine Corporation in 1981. With stability in this portion of the company, management could then concentrate on the company's other divisions.

One of the weakest units of Ogden during the early 1970's was the food division. Ogden Food Products Corporation, especially the Tillie Lewis Tomatoes operation, was failing. In 1979, however, Ablon saved this part of Ogden by purchasing the Progresso division of Imasco Foods Corporation for $35 million. Ablon had tried unsuccessfully to buy Progresso for ten years at the firm offer of $35 million. However, in 1979, Ogden acquired through the transaction about $30 million in tangible assets. Earlier, almost half of the $35 million offer represented a goodwill gesture; when the transaction was finalized, however, the goodwill amount Imasco eventually received dwindled to only $2 million in tangible assets.

Ogden purchased other companies to strengthen the food division. Ogden acquired Wometco Coffee Time, a food and beverage vending company, from Wometco Enterprises Inc. in 1979. In 1981 Ogden also purchased Hain Pure Food Company Inc., and Offshore Food Services Inc. These new companies helped Ogden expand its vending service area in addition to its food production industry.

In the 1970's Ogden's third area of concentration, shipping, again began to show increased productivity. By offering credit as an incentive, Avondale shipyards procured many contracts for shipbuilding. By 1979 Avondale's contracts passed the $1 billion mark and the length of the contracts extended to over three years.

Avondale was, at this time, the fourth largest shipyard in the United States and possibly the most productive. Careful controls and scheduling, computer assistance, and satisfied workers were the reasons Avondale brought in nearly half of Ogden's operating income by 1980. This was a remarkable turnaround from less than a decade earlier when Avondale was slipping further into financial difficulties.

In the early part of the 1980's Ablon, as other economic forecasters, realized that the economy of the United States was changing. "We were becoming a post-industrial, or fully developed, society; the requirement of mass consumption was becoming more important than mass production." Consequently, Ablon turned his attentions to developing Ogden as a service industry.

Ogden's first excursion into the service industry was Allied Maintenance Corporation. In 1982 Ogden paid $118 million for Allied, which provided such services as security and plant operations, as well as maintenance for private and public meeting centers. Allied Maintenance and Ogden Services joined in 1985 to form Ogden Allied.

Ogden expanded into yet another direction with waste-to-energy management. The company purchased the rights to the Martin System of incineration in 1983 and formed Ogden Martin Systems. This technique burned waste at 2800 degrees efficiently and cleanly. Cities, crowded by huge waste sites, are beginning to look for new ways to dispose of the tons of waste per year and will look to companies like Ogden in the future. Ogden presently has 15 operational plants with plans for 25 more by 1990.

Although many changes have occurred throughout Ogden Corporation's history, the conglomerate has successfully adapted to them. Ogden adjusted as easily to the waste-management industry as it had to the scrap metal, the shipbuilding, and the food service industries. Ogden, under Ralph Ablon's leadership, must still be considered a driving force in today's industry.

Principal Subsidiaries: Luria Brothers & Co., Inc.; Wabash Alloys, Inc.; Ortner Freight Car Co.; Mayville Metal Products Co.; Avondale Shipyards, Inc.; International Terminal Operating Co. Inc.; Ogden Food Services Corp.; Yuba Heat Transfer Co.; Danly Machine Corp.; Ogden Security, Inc.; Ogden Food Products Corp.; Ogden Martin Systems, Inc.

SAMSUNG GROUP

Samsung Main Building
250 2-ka Taepyung-ro
Chung-ku, Seoul
Korea
7721 1114

Public Company
Incorporated: January, 1952 as the Samsung Company, Ltd.
Employees: 129,039
Sales: W 12.23 trillion (US$ 13.73 billion)
Market Value: W 1.652 trillion (US$ 1.944 billion)
Stock Index: Seoul

The Samsung Group is one of four South Korean trading firms. It has been described as the Korean equivalent to Japanese general trading firms such as Mitsui, Mitsubishi, and Sumitomo. Like these companies, Samsung has been chosen as an instrument of national development by the government.

The Samsung Commercial Company was founded by a young Korean entrepreneur named Byung-Chull Lee. Lee was born in 1910, the second son of a wealthy landlord. He gained his early education in a traditional Confucianist school. Although he never graduated from middle school, he enrolled at Waseda University in Japan where he studied political science and economics. Lee dropped out after a few semesters due to poor health and returned to Korea. He spent the next several years in Seoul, "doing nothing in particular."

In 1936 Byung-Chull Lee moved to Taegu, a city in southeastern Korea, and with an inheritance established a local rice mill. Over the next two years Lee began trading in a wider variety of products, including wool and textiles. In 1938 the company was officially incorporated as the Samsung Commercial Company (Samsung is Korean for "three stars"). The company employed 40 people, continued to expand, and later opened offices in Manchuria, northern China, and the Beijing area.

Korea, however, had been annexed by Japan in 1910 and thereafter was administered as a Japanese colony called Chosen. Manchuria and much of northern China were occupied by Japanese armies. All of these areas were under the authority of a Japanese military administration which limited the activities of Korean companies such as Samsung, and protected larger markets for Japanese firms.

During World War II Korea was spared much of the destruction inflicted upon Japan, but was subjected to acute shortages of food and other products. When the war ended in 1945, Soviet troops occupied the northern half of Korea while American troops occupied southern Korea and Japan. Samsung's operations north of the 38th parallel were subsequently terminated by Soviet authorities, who were transforming nothern Korea into a Marxist state. South Korea, meanwhile, was working to establish its independence and in 1948 declared itself a separate state.

Samsung experienced strong growth during the war and by 1945 had expanded into transportation, real estate, milling, noodle making, brewing, and general domestic trading. Lee moved his company from Taegu to Seoul in 1947, and in November of 1948 established an international trading firm called the Samsung Mulsan Company. The new company was created specifically to import goods for which demand was rapidly increasing in Korea. By 1950 Samsung had grown to become one of Korea's top ten firms.

On June 25, 1950 North Korean armed forces launched a full-scale invasion of South Korea and by August had overrun all but a 4000 square mile area around Pusan. Samsung was devastated; most of the company's operations were either destroyed or behind enemy lines. United Nations forces entered the battle on September 15, and by late October had driven the communist forces north to the Chinese border. At that time several hundred thousand communist Chinese troops attacked the U.N. forces and advanced southward to the 38th parallel, where the war became stalemated. An armistice was concluded on July 27, 1953.

Lee's company was re-established in Pusan in January of 1951 as the Samsung Trading Company. Samsung benefitted significantly from its role as a supplier to the U.N. forces in Korea; during its first year in Pusan the company grew 1700%. Lee recognized that the large-scale importation of foreign goods had a negative effect on the economy, and that several commodities could be produced domestically. In order to reduce the country's dependence on imports, Lee created the Cheil Sugar Company in 1953.

When it was established Cheil Sugar was the only manufacturer of sugar in South Korea. Strong demand for sugar generated large profits and further enhanced the company's monopolist position. By 1954 Cheil Sugar had accumulated enough capital to establish a second company called the Cheil Wool Textile Company.

Cheil Sugar and Cheil Wool Textile were intimately associated with Samsung. All three companies performed so well that by the late 1950's Samsung started to acquire smaller firms and purchase large quantities of commercial bank shares. In 1957 Samsung created Samsung Construction and the Dongbang Life Insurance Company. By the end of the decade Samsung controlled a number of financial intermediaries and had become known as a *chaeböl*, or international conglomerate much like the Japanese *zaibatsu*.

Lee considered entering the fertilizer business, but became discouraged when he was targeted in student protests as a symbol of opportunism. Lee's wealth and close association with the government had become a serious public relations liability.

In 1960 rising political tension in South Korea forced President Syngman Rhee to resign. The social order continued to deteriorate. The following year, in an effort to restore order, General Park Chung Hee seized power and imposed martial law. The military government initiated an official investigation into the illicit accumulation of wealth by certain individuals during the Rhee regime. Byung-Chull Lee, who was in Japan at the time of the coup, was implicated and accused of tax evasion, illegal campaign contributions, and profiteering.

Lee returned to Korea to meet with General Park. The two men reached a compromise which largely absolved Lee of wrongdoing, and enabled him to emerge later as an important leader and representative of South Korean industry. As part of his compromise with General Park, however, Lee was obliged to construct a fertilizer plant for the government. When the government reversed its decision in December of 1963, Lee was forced to pay the government a large fine instead. In August of 1964 Lee finally established his own fertilizer plant at Ulsan called the Han Kook (Korea) Fertilizer Company. It was one of the largest industrial projects at the time and took three years to complete.

In 1966 it was discovered that officials of Han Kook, including one of Lee's own sons, were involved in the illegal smuggling of Japanese saccharin into Korea. Lee's activities were subjected to another investigation, but again he reached a compromise wherein he surrendered 51% ownership of Han Kook to the government. The scandal greatly damaged the public image of both Samsung and Byung-Chull Lee. This did not, however, slow the company's growth. By 1970 Samsung was a large industrial group which had extended into a number of new fields, including department stores, universities, paper, securities, and a newspaper named the Joong-ang Daily News.

Samsung forecasted and then prepared for strong growth in the demand for electronic goods. In 1969 the company, in association with Sanyo, established Samsung Electronics in the city of Suwon. An international network was established to improve the company's export and intelligence gathering capabilities. The partnership with Sanyo was discontinued in 1972, although the two companies continued jointly to manufacture electronic components. Samsung Electronics originally manufactured products for U.S. retailers such as Sears, J.C. Penney, and K-Mart.

In May of 1975 the government introduced a new strategy for export promotion. It designated 13 large trading firms as General Trading Companies, or GTCs. The GTCs are actively supported by the South Korean government (much the same way that Japan's Ministry for International Trade and Industry supports the large Japanese trading companies) which offers advice on international market conditions and helps to strengthen tender offers in international competitions. Samsung was designated as the "number one" GTC.

As part of the development of industry emphasized in the government's fourth Five Year Economic Plan, Samsung created two new major operating companies in the chemical and heavy manufacturing industries.

Samsung Petrochemical was established in 1977 as joint venture with Amoco and Mitsui Petrochemical. Its primary product is purified terephthalic acid (PTA), an essential ingredient in the manufacture of synthetic fibres.

Samsung Shipbuilding was established in 1974 as a major producer of large ships and offshore structures. The division has since been merged with Samsung Heavy Industries and Daesung Heavy Industries, both manufacturers of large equipment and machinery. The new company was renamed Samsung Shipbuilding and Heavy Industries.

Samsung Precision Industries was created in 1977 to overhaul and maintain aircraft engines for the South Korean air force. Its operations have since broadened to include the manufacture of jet engines, industrial robots, and military equipment. The Samsung Group entered the microelectronics industry in 1980 when it purchased the Korea Telecommunications Company. Renamed Samsung Semiconductor and Telecommunications in 1982, this division has grown strongly in the last ten years and is now a major producer of semiconductors and microchips.

With a broad base of manufacturing industries established, Samsung was in excellent shape to begin a more aggressive export campaign. Utilizing Japanese technologies and taking advantage of lower labor costs (75% to 80% lower than in Japan), Samsung started to market its electronic products under its own name in the United States. Samsung entered the "low" end of the market, with an inexpensive and less sophisticated line of products. The company was so successful that several Japanese manufacturers were forced to concede considerable market shares. Once established, Samsung gradually began to introduce higher quality (and therefore more expensive) electronic equipment. The success of this strategy has proven Samsung's ability to react quickly and compete effectively in the international market.

One area where South Korea holds a considerable comparative advantage over Japan is in automobile production. The near collapse of the South Korean auto industry in 1980, however, forced the government to enact legislation in 1982 which limited automobile production to Samsung's rival GTCs, Hyundai and Daewoo. Samsung attempted to circumvent the legislation by proposing a joint venture with the Chrysler Corporation, but that too was ruled unacceptable in 1984.

Unlike other international conglomerates, Samsung is not headed by a holding company. The Samsung Group consists of 26 profit-making institutions (12 publicly traded) each of which hold substantial minority interests in the other Samsung companies. The activities of these companies are coordinated through an advisory board consisting of the various company chairmen.

With 61 offices in 40 countries the Samsung Group is the largest GTC in Korea today. Byung-Chull Lee, however, before his death in 1987, gradually relinquished control of the company to his third son, Kun-Hee Lee. This is highly unusual in Korea, where strong preferences are given to a family's eldest son, but it has been suggested that Lee simply felt his third son was most capable of operating the company. Samsung's success under Kun Lee, however, may not be guaranteed. The company still faces considerable competition in the world market and may sooner or later lose its advantage in labor costs.

Principal Subsidiaries: Samsung Shipbuilding and Heavy Industries Co., Ltd.; Samsung Precision Industries Co., Ltd.; Samsung Electronics Co., Ltd.; Samsung Electronic Parts Co., Ltd.; Samsung Electron Devices Co., Ltd.; Samsung Watch Co., Ltd.; Samsung Semiconductor and Telecommunications Co., Ltd.; Korea Engineering Co., Ltd.; Samsung Corning Co., Ltd.; Cheil Sugar & Co., Ltd.; Cheil Wool Textile Co., Ltd.; Cheil Synthetic Textiles Co., Ltd.; Samsung Construction Co., Ltd.; Joong-ang Development Co., Ltd.; Samsung Petrochemical Co., Ltd.; Chonju Paper Manufacturing Co., Ltd.; Hotel Shilla Co., Ltd.; Chosun Hotel Co., Ltd.; Shinsegae Department Store Co., Ltd.; Dongbang Life Insurance Co., Ltd.; Ankuk Fire & Marine Insurance Co., Ltd.; Yong-in Farmland.

Further Reading: Government, Business, and Entrepreneurship in Economic Development: The Korean Case by Leroy P. Jones and Il Sakong, Cambridge, Massachusetts, Harvard University Press, 1980.

SUMITOMO CORPORATION

2–2, Hitotsubashi 1-chome
Chiyoda-ku, Tokyo 100
Japan
03-217-5000

Public Company
Incorporated: December 24, 1919 as Osaka North Harbor
Co., Ltd.
Employees: 6,485
Sales: ¥ 13.309 trillion (US$ 73.941 billion)
Market Value: ¥ 371.4 billion (US$ 2.063 billion)
Stock Index: Frankfurt Tokyo Osaka Nagoya

Sumitomo is one of the oldest surviving business ventures in the world. It may also be considered one of the most humanistic corporations in the world because of its historical concern for the well-being of employees. The Sumitomo companies have adhered closely to basic principles of conduct in which harmony and patriotism are emphasized.

The "spiritual pillar" of the Sumitomo Corporation is Masatomo Sumitomo, the first head of the family and founder of the business. He was born just north of Kyoto in 1585 and became a Buddhist priest. At the age of 45 he opened a small medicine and book shop called the Fujiya. There he established a set of highly moralistic principles for conducting business which were passed down through subsequent generations to form the basis for the modern Sumitomo company charter.

Since Masatomo's marriage had produced no sons, his brother-in-law Riemon Soga was adopted into the family. Masatomo and Riemon were also related by a common lineage to the noble Heike family. When Masatomo died in 1652, Riemon Soga became head of the House of Sumitomo. As a young man, Riemon worked as an apprentice in a copper refinery. In 1590, at 18, he opened his own shop in Kyoto called the Izumiya, literally the "Fountainhead Shop." For the company's logo he adopted the *igeta*, the ancient character for "well frame."

Japanese refineries at this time lacked the technology to remove small naturally occurring quantities of gold and silver from copper. These precious metals were sold to foreign traders as copper and were later extracted overseas at a great profit. Riemon Soga, however, learned about a refining procedure used by the foreigners (who were called *nanban-jin*, or "southern barbarians") which involved the addition of lead to molten copper and smelting with char-

coal to remove, first silver from copper, and later lead from silver. This method, known as *nanban-buki*, made Riemon and the Izumiya very successful. Contrary to what may have been expected of an entrepreneur, Soga unselfishly instructed his competitors in the *nanban-buki* method.

When Riemon Soga died in 1636, the Izumiya passed to his second son, Chubei. His first son, Tomomochi, married Masatomo's daughter and was adopted by the Sumitomo family. He established a separate copper refinery and crafting shop which was also named Izumiya.

At the age of 16 Tomomochi moved his business from Kyoto to Osaka, which was recovering from damage incurred during a war between Tokugawa and Toyotomi armies. Tomomochi's competitors welcomed him to Osaka in a demonstration of their gratitude to his father. The Izumiya expanded quickly and later absorbed both the Fujiya and the original Izumiya operated by his brother. By the time of Tomomochi's death in 1662, the Izumiya in Osaka had become the center of the Japanese copper industry.

Tomomochi's fifth son, Tomonobu, became the third head of the Sumitomo family at the age of 15. In 1680 he gained permission from the Tokugawa Shogunate to rehabilitate the Yoshioka Copper Mine, which had been worked to exhaustion over a period of centuries. Shortly after Sumitomo commenced revitalization of the Yoshioka mine in 1684, it was discovered that Tomonobu's younger brother Tomosada had committed several serious errors in the management of the family brokerage house, which subsequently was forced to liquidate. This placed the entire family enterprise in jeopardy and the following year obliged Tomonobu, who was a partner in the brokerage operation, to resign all his posts at the age of only 38. He was succeeded as head of the family by his 15-year old son Tomoyoshi. The Izumiya endured several more years of hardship, but eventually recovered. In the meantime, restoration of the Yoshioka site continued.

In June of 1690 the manager of the Yoshioka mine, Jyuemon Tamuke, was approached by a man from the island of Shikoku who quite unexpectedly confided in Jyuemon that he had discovered a promising rock formation on the side of the mountain opposite the Tatsukawa Copper Mine, where he was employed as a miner. An expedition was ordered to investigate the area. The results immediately convinced the Sumitomo family to apply to the Shogunate for permission to mine the site, called Besshi. A permit was granted the following May, and digging commenced in December. Despite a fire in 1694 which claimed the lives of 133 people, Besshi was ambitiously developed and over the next one hundred years produced more copper than any other mine.

The Besshi and Tatsukawa mines continued to operate on both faces of the same mountain but were prevented from coordinating their operations because the Shogunate was opposed to giving one family control over such a large natural resource. In 1749 representatives from both mines convinced the government that the failing Tatsukawa mine could only remain viable if it was placed under Sumitomo management. By 1762 Tatsukawa was again faced with closure unless its operations were fully integrated with

Besshi. That year the government permitted the Sumitomo family to purchase the mine.

During the next century the Sumitomo family remained involved in a variety of business activities. The primary trade, around which all other ventures revolved, was copper production. While the Sumitomo's wealth increased, no innovations were made in the smelting process and no real business acumen was displayed. The Besshi mine became a liability, dependent on government subsidies. In 1867 the family business was renamed Sumitomo Honten (head office) and designated as the central office for all Sumitomo activities.

During 1865 armed forces of the Choshu clan initiated a military campaign against the Tokugawa government, with whom the Sumitomo family had cultivated close ties. Despite its relationship with the Tokugawa Shogunate, the Besshi subsidies were suspended and the Sumitomo family was ordered to remit substantial amounts of money in war taxes to help fund government counteroffensives. Three years later the Choshu were joined by the Tosa and Satsuma clans, and together they succeeded in overthrowing the Shogunate and restoring the Meiji Emperor.

In the process, the Besshi mine was sealed by Tosa forces and the Sumitomo copper warehouses at Osaka were occupied by the Satsuma. Saihei Hirose, who had just been appointed general manager of the Besshi mine, met with the leader of the Tosa forces, Ganyemon Kawada (later president of the Bank of Japan). He persuaded Kawada to evacuate the Sumitomo properties after convincing him that the family unwillingly supported the Shogunate.

Still, the company was in very poor financial condition. The defeated warlords of the Shogunate defaulted on loans from the Sumitomo financial office, and the currencies it held greatly decreased in value. In addition, the Besshi mine had degenerated to the point where it was nearly unworkable. At this point there was strong pressure from within the family to sell the mine.

Hirose was determined to rehabilitate the Besshi mine. He secured new sources of food for the employees, constructed new housing, and even established a day care center. After he settled an ownership dispute with the government, Hirose proceeded with the modernization of the mine. Hirose managed to obtain numerous loans which required him to mortgage most of the family's property. In 1873 he hired a French engineer named Louis Larroque to prepare a study on Besshi with recommendations for its modernization. Hirose did not extend Larroque's two year contract, but instead sent two of his own employees to Europe to study French methods of mining and metallurgy.

Hirose introduced a number of technological innovations to Japanese mining in 1880, including the use of dynamite and jack hammers. He purchased a steam-powered ship and train engine, and incorporated the substitution of coke for charcoal in the smelting process. He established his own sales and supply branches, including an export office. Large areas of woodland were purchased for lumber, and a machine manufacturing and repair shop was established. The productivity of the Besshi

mine rose quickly; annual copper production increased from 420 tons in 1868 to over 1800 tons in 1888.

Saihei Hirose is regarded as the most important figure in Sumitomo's modern history. In addition to being given credit for saving the family enterprise, he successfully asserted the independence of the business from the government and contributed greatly to the development and growth of Osaka. He retired in 1894 and died 20 years later at the age of 86.

Hirose was replaced by his nephew, Teigo Iba, who continued to emphasize the modernization of Besshi, but also advocated the diversification of the Sumitomo family enterprise. Iba formalized the family banking operations in 1895 when he established the Sumitomo Bank.

Iba stepped down in 1904, proclaiming that only younger, more dynamic managers possessed the imagination and courage to implement new strategies and take risks. He was succeeded by Masaya Suzuki, who led the company until his death in 1922. During his tenure Sumitomo was reorganized as a limited partnership, and renamed Sumitomo So-Honten in 1921. Suzuki also re-emphasized Masatomo's founding precepts of moralistic and trustworthy conduct. He is remembered as a highly principled manager who expected nothing less than strict adherence to ethical business practices.

Between 1922 and 1930 two more men served briefly as the top executive, Kinkichi Nakata and Kanchiki Yukawa. During their leadership Sumitomo branched out into several more fields with the creation of new subsidiaries. By this time Sumitomo had grown to become one of Japan's largest industrial concerns. It was one of the country's few but powerful *zaibatsu*, or "money cliques," which emerged after the Meiji Restoration. Unlike the other *zaibatsu*, Mitsui, Mitsubishi, and Furukawa, Sumitomo did not become involved in the purchase of high-growth "model" industries which were established by the Meiji government and later turned over to private enterprise. Sumitomo's prominence had been gained purely on the virtues of its existing operations.

In 1930 Sumitomo appointed Masatune Ogura to serve as director general. He supervised the company's incorporation as Sumitomo Honsha (trading company), Ltd. in 1937. But his 11 years as chief executive were complicated by right-wing nationalists operating within the military. They gained influence in Japanese politics through intimidation and assassination and openly attacked the *zaibatsu* for their preoccupation with self-interest and "lack of sympathy" for the masses. However, of the three *zaibatsu*, Sumitomo was spared most often from militarist terrorism. Whatever his political beliefs, Ogura was drafted into the militarist government in 1941 to serve as a cabinet minister.

Later that year Japan began a full-scale war of conquest in Asia aimed at establishing a regional economic order centered around Japan. For Sumitomo's new chairman, Shunnosuke Furuta, it was an extremely difficult period. He was required to make special efforts in order to keep the company's various divisions together; the unusual circumstances of war had forced Sumitomo's subsidiaries to adopt a more autonomous, presidential form of management. Additionally, the company and its 200,000 employees were not fully prepared for the wartime mobilization.

Japan's fortunes in the war began to change during 1942. Within the year American bombers were within range of targets on the Japanese mainland. Since Sumitomo was a large industrial concern, and therefore essential to the Japanese military, its factories were exposed to frequent bombings. When the war ended in September of 1945, virtually all of Japan's industrial capability had been destroyed.

Japan was placed under the administration of a military occupation authority called SCAP, an acronym for the Supreme Commander of Allied Powers. SCAP imposed a variety of American-style commercial laws, including an anti-monopoly law, which mandated the complete dissolution of all *zaibatsu*. Despite strong criticism from some quarters, Shunnosuke Furuta complied with the edict and supervised the breakup of the Sumitomo *Honsha*, or parent company, into several fully independent firms, all of which were forbidden to use the *igeta* logo.

In the following months thousands of Japanese citizens, including Sumitomo employees who were posted overseas, returned to Japan. It was extremely demoralizing for those who had been fortunate enough to avoid areas of battle. Furuta worked very hard to ensure that all his employees could remain employed and healthy.

The *Honsha* was reorganized in November of 1945. Furuta made the difficult decision to set the company on a new course of business. Under its new name, the Nihon Kensetsu Sangyo, Ltd., was established as a general trading company, or *sogo shosha*.

In the years following World War II, particularly during the Korean War, the restrictive commercial laws were gradually relaxed. The former Sumitomo companies began to establish affiliations through the Sumitomo Bank and limited cross ownership of stock. The *igeta* came back into use and a monthly meeting, the Hakusui-kai, or "White Water Club," was established so that the individual heads of the affiliated Sumitomo companies could coordinate business strategies. This did not, however, mark the reformation of the *zaibatsu*, which had a more disciplined, autocratic management style.

On June 1, 1952 the company officially changed its name to Sumitomo Shoji Kaisha, literally the "Sumitomo Commercial Affairs Company." It became the trading house for the various Sumitomo affiliated companies at a time when Japan was experiencing a period of phenomenal economic growth. As Japan grew in economic importance, Sumitomo Shoji established a number of foreign offices. Products handled by the company soon included iron and steel, non-ferrous metals, electrical and industrial equipment, chemicals, textiles, fuel, and agricultural and marine products, in addition to real estate. Sales transactions rose from $254 million in 1955 to $2.3 billion in 1965, and over $26 billion in 1975.

Due to the fact that the Sumitomo companies are so closely associated and because so much of their activity is centered around the Sumitomo Bank, the entire group has become known as a *keiretsu*, or "banking conglomerate." This type of organization was necessary to prevent hostile takeovers of the Sumitomo companies, most of which were made vulnerable by heavy debt. If, for instance, Sumitomo Heavy Industries was in danger of being purchased by Mitsubishi Heavy Industries, the affiliated Sumitomo companies would collectively refuse to sell their controlling interest.

Today the Sumitomo Corporation has over 125 offices in 83 countries, including such difficult trading environments as Iran, Cuba, Bulgaria, and Libya. The Sumitomo *guruupu*, or group, includes such well-known affiliates as the NEC Corporation, Asahi Breweries, Sumitomo Heavy Industries, Sumitomo Chemical, Mazda Motors, and Mitsui O.S.K. Lines. In all there are 44 *guruupu* companies divided among 14 industry groups. With the Sumitomo Corporation at the head of the group, and with considerable resources made available by the Sumitomo financial companies, the various Sumitomo enterprises will be able to develop new technologies and exploit new markets quite easily in the future.

Principal Subsidiaries: Sumisho Kiden Hanbai Co., Ltd.; Sumisho Machinery Trade Corp.; Sumisho Non-Ferrous Trading Co., Ltd.; Sumisho Kagakuhin Hanbai Kaisha, Ltd.; Fujimoto Sangyo Co., Ltd.; Sumisho Sekiyu Kaisha, Ltd.; Sumichiku, Ltd.; Sumisho Fruits & Vegetables Co., Ltd.; Sumisho Textile Co., Ltd; Sumisho Pulp & Paper Sales Co., Ltd.; Sumisho Building Materials Co., Ltd.; Summit Stores, Inc.; Sumisho Computer Service Corp.; SC Finance Co., Ltd.

Further Reading: The Soga Shosha: Japan's Multinational Trading Company by Alexander Young, Boulder, Colorado, Westview Press, 1979.

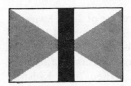

SWIRE PACIFIC LTD.

Swire House
9 Connaught Road
Central
Hong Kong
5-230011

Public Company
Incorporated: 1866 as Butterfield and Swire
Employees: 16,000
Sales: HK$ 13.96 billion (US$ 1.753 billion)
Market Value: HK$ 9.681 billion (US$ 1.240 billion)
Stock Index: Hong Kong

Swire Pacific is one of the most influential companies in Asia. It is an example of the growing significance of Asian industrial conglomerates which will play a major role in advancing the nations of the Pacific Rim to positions of economic prosperity and leadership in the 21st century. As part of the larger London-based Swire Group, Swire Pacific remains located in the British colony of Hong Kong, where the company's predominance was first established.

In Britain during the early 1800's a canal was built which linked the seaport of Liverpool to Halifax, a city in the northeastern county of Yorkshire. The canal introduced international trade to Halifax and in the process seriously damaged local industries which could not compete with cheaper imports. John Swire, the patriarch of the Swire family, moved from Yorkshire to Liverpool where in 1816 he established a general trading house whose primary commodities were American cotton from New Orleans and cheese, pork and wine from Boston and New York. John Swire died in 1847 leaving the business to his two sons, John Samuel and William Hudson Swire.

The John Swire & Sons trading company grew steadily during the next decade. It established interests in a number of Liverpool shipping companies and opened a branch office in Manchester. In 1855 John Samuel Swire traveled to the former British penal colony of Australia. He opened an office in Melbourne to handle Australian imports of his company's cotton. As soon as the business was operating successfully, he turned it over to a local agent and returned to England. His brother William was forced to retire from the company due to persistent ill health. From that time onward, John Samuel Swire was left to run the operation alone.

In 1861 the American Civil War destroyed Swire's cotton trade. Determined to reassert its position in the textile market the company turned to the more stable markets of the Far East where it was already engaged in the trade of tea. Swire became displeased with the performance of his agents in the Far East and decided that the company should run its own affairs there. He traveled to Shanghai in 1866 and later formed a partnership with Richard Shackleton Butterfield of the Butterfield Brothers firm in Bradford, Yorkshire. In 1867 they opened an office together in Shanghai under the name of Butterfield & Swire. The company adopted a Chinese name, *Taikoo,* meaning "great and ancient." Although the partnership was dissolved within two years, the Shanghai office continued to be called Butterfield & Swire.

The company's business in Asia benefited greatly from Japan's restoration of the Meiji leadership in 1868. Under the Meiji, Japan became a modern industrial state. Butterfield & Swire, which opened an office near Tokyo in Yokohama the previous year, was ideally situated to take advantage of the growing strength of the Japanese economy.

By 1871 Swire's headquarters had been moved from Liverpool to London, and a third Far East office was opened in the British Colony of Hong Kong. The company expanded its interest in shipping when it became the Shanghai agent for the Blue Funnel Line. In 1872 Swire created its own shipping concern, the China Navigation Company, which served ports on the Yangtze River and along the Chinese coast. China Navigation's primary competitor on the waterways was another Hong Kong firm called Jardine Matheson & Company. In 1873 Swire established an office in New York where the company had already been handling American imports of tea from Yokohama for several years.

Swire further diversified its business in 1884 when it created the Taikoo Sugar Refinery in Hong Kong with the intention of breaking Jardine Matheson's monopoly on sugar. The two companies competed in a fierce but gentlemanly manner for many years. According to John Samuel Swire, "Don't fight. But if you do fight, go in sharp and win."

In 1866 the Yokohama office, which for years had been dependent on the textile trade, began importing large quantities of sugar from Hong Kong and Taiwan in addition to soya beancake from China. Swire also handled Japanese exports of rice to Australia. In 1887 the company opened a second Japanese office in Kobe. In 1900 Butterfield & Swire founded the Taikoo Dockyard company in Hong Kong. With expanded commercial interests in China, the company also opened a paint factory in Shanghai and a tugboat and barge company in Tianjin. The red, white and blue Swire flag was seen flying over China Navigation ships plying waterways across China and throughout East Asia.

John Samuel Swire died in 1898. His company passed to a third generation of Swires under the direction of his son John. Despite some disruptions of business in China during the Boxer Rebellion in 1900 and the Republican Revolution in 1911, Swire's interests in China, Japan, Australia, and Southeast Asia continued to prosper and expand. John Kidston Swire, grandson of John Samuel

Swire, succeeded his father as director of the company in 1920.

Swire's operations were paralyzed in 1937 when Japan launched its war of expansion against China. The company's interests in northern China and Shanghai were closed. Japanese landings on either side of the Hongkong peninsula isolated the colony from the nearby Chinese city of Guangzhou (Canton), forcing Swire to curtail virtually all of its trading operations with the mainland. On December 1, 1941, six days before the attack on Pearl Harbor, Japanese troops invaded Hong Kong. During the Japanese occupation all of Swire's Far Eastern activities were suspended. By the time of the Japanese surrender in September of 1945 more than half of Swire's ships, the sugar refinery and dockyard had been destroyed.

As soon as World War II ended a civil war erupted in China between the Communists and the Nationalists. The war was won in 1949 by the Communists who renounced all agreements concluded by the Nationalist government. This included Swire's business arrangements with Chinese partners and the Chinese government. In addition, Swire's extensive properties in China were nationalized without compensation. In only a few short years Swire's financial empire had nearly been ruined.

Butterfield & Swire focused attention on rebuilding its operations in Hong Kong. The shipping facilities were rebuilt and new ships were ordered. John Kidston Swire became interested in diversifying his company's transportation interests in the Far East. In 1948 Butterfield & Swire purchased a controlling interest in Cathay Pacific Airways, a small Hong Kong-based airline company with a fleet of two DC-3s.

The company's shipping and airline activities grew rapidly during the 1950's. Shipping officers in Japan were reopened and new connections in Papua New Guinea, Australia, and Korea were established. Cathay Pacific absorbed its local competitor, Hong Kong Airways, purchased newer aircraft, and opened new routes to Singapore, Manila, Bangkok, and Saigon. Butterfield & Swire's involvement in Cathay Pacific led it to invest in a number of other businesses related to aviation, including the Hong Kong Aircraft Engineering Company which operates a virtual monopoly on aircraft maintenance in the colony.

During the 1950's and 1960's the company's expansion was well-planned and largely uneventful, and its name was changed from Butterfield & Swire to Swire Pacific. On occasion, however, profits became depressed when regional or international economic recessions lowered demand for shipping services. Due to the fact that the shipping business was so closely linked to the volatile economic cycles of Pacific nations, Swire Pacific began to diversify its operations. It became interested in property ownership in Hong Kong, where the supply of land was limited and demand was becoming acute. In 1965 Swire Bottlers Limited became the franchised bottler of Coca-Cola and its allied brands.

Additional diversification occurred in the areas of shipping and warehousing services, agriculture, trucking, canning, magnetic tape, and high technology components. Cathay Pacific was continuing to grow at an annual rate of 22% (doubling its size every four years) and began handling air freight. As a result, Cathay Pacific became Swire's most popular subsidiary and was quickly gaining a reputation as "Hong Kong's airline."

John Kidston Swire retired as director of John Swire & Sons in 1968, leaving the company in the care of his two sons named John and Adrian. The fifth generation of Swires oversaw most of the company's diversification and growth, especially in Hong Kong. When John Kidston Swire died in 1983 the parent company of the Swire financial empire, John Swire & Sons, Ltd., remained a privately owned family concern based in London. However, Hong Kong, where the dynamic Swire Pacific subsidiary was located, became the subject of an international debate.

After a series of negotiations the governments of Great Britain and the People's Republic of China agreed to end British colonial authority over Hong Kong on July 1, 1997. This placed into doubt the future of all capitalist enterprises operating in Hong Kong, including Swire Pacific. Jardine Matheson promptly responded by relocating its legal address and much of its business to Bermuda. In an effort to forestall the exit of more companies, the Chinese promised to preserve the unique economic character of Hong Kong after they take control of the territory. When Swire Pacific, which is the only publicly traded Swire company, announced that it was reducing its share of ownership in Cathay Pacific, a Chinese government investment company in Hong Kong purchased 12.5%. The Chinese investment in Cathay Pacific was regarded as evidence of China's sincerity in maintaining the prosperity of Hong Kong.

John Swire & Sons maintains substantial holdings in Britain, Australia, Japan, the United States, South Korea, Papua New Guinea, and Mauritius, in addition to Hong Kong. By remaining in Hong Kong it has demonstrated a willingness to work with the Chinese for the future of Hong Kong. The Swires have survived the Boxer Rebellion, two world wars and a civil war, and it is unlikely that they are worried about a negotiated settlement which has the full support of the British government. Swire has established an excellent relationship with the Chinese which promises to be advantageous when the Chinese economy develops and selected foreign companies such as Swire Pacific are invited to participate.

Principal Subsidiaries: Cathay Pacific Airways (50.23%); Hong Kong Aircraft Engineering Company, Ltd. (42.6%); Swire Air Caterers, Ltd. (52.5%); Taikoo Royal Insurance (44%); Hong Kong United Dockyards (50%); Swire Insurance; Swire Properties. The company also has additional subsidiaries which include 91 with majority interest and 19 with minority interest.

Further Reading: Overseas Investment in the Age of High Imperialism: The United Kingdom 1850–1914 by Michael Edelstein, New York, Columbia University Press, 1982.

TELEDYNE, INC.

1901 Avenue of the Stars
Los Angeles, California 90067
U.S.A.
(213) 277-3311

Public Company
Incorporated: 1960
Employees: 47,200
Sales: $3.241 billion
Market Value: $3.902 billion
Stock Index: New York

It is fitting that Teledyne has located its corporate headquarter's on Avenue of the Stars. During the early 1960's, the company rose out of nowhere to achieve success in the semiconductor business. In five years the company reached *Fortune* 500 proportions, and was recognized as the fastest growing high-technological conglomerate in the United States. However, as Teledyne diversified into other areas it began to lose some of the success it garnered during its early years.

Ever since he was a boy Henry A. Singleton wanted to build a large corporation, "a company like GM, AT&T, Dupont—I want to build a company like that." In 1960, after earning three degrees from MIT and rising to vice-president and general manager of Litton, Singleton decided the time was right. He quite his $35,000 a year job in order to establish his own company. He convinced his assistant and old friend, George Kozmetsky, who had earned a doctor of commercial science from Harvard, to join him in a new business venture.

Singleton, who in five years had increased Litton's electronics equipment division to $80 million in sales, decided that success lay in the semiconductor business. Despite an already crowded market, he nevertheless believed that producing semiconductors, the "basic building block of electronics," would lead to other high technological and high growth inventions.

Singleton and Kozmetsky, using the money they earned from their Litton stock options, each invested $225,000 to start their business. Singleton became chairman and president of the company they named Teledyne, and Kozmetsky became executive vice-president. Their high-technological background and innovative ideas quickly paid off. The company achieved first year sales of $4.5 million and employed nearly 450 people. Second year sales of $10.5 million confirmed their success.

Sales continued on an upward trend when the company embarked on a series of acquisitions, first in electronics and then in geophysics, to increase the company's strength in businesses related to semiconductors. In 1966 Teledyne bought Vasco Metals Corporation, which started a third wave of acquisitions, specialty metals. Vasco, with sales of $43 million, specialized in titanium, molybdenum, beryllium, and vanadium alloys.

Later that year Kozmetsky, whose 130,000 shares of Teledyne were by then worth well over $20 million, retired from the company to become dean of the College of Business Administration at the University of Texas. George A. Roberts, formerly president of Vasco, replaced him as president of Teledyne. Singleton continued on as chairman and chief executive officer.

By the end of that year Teledyne, with sales three times that of the previous year, broke into the *Fortune* 500 ranking. Teledyne's sales of over $256 million ranked it 293.

In 1967 Teledyne seemed headed for even more success. Teledyne's 16,000 employees were busily making micro-electronic integrated circuits, microwave tubes, aircraft instruments, miniature television camera transmitters, hydraulic systems, computers, seismic measuring devices, specialty alloys, and a large variety of other sophisticated products. Singleton's and Kozmetsky's personal worth had prospered along with the company, reaching $30 million.

More good news arrived when the company bested IBM and Texas Instruments in a government contract contest and became the prime contractor for the development of the Integrated Helicopter Avionics System (IHAS). The IHAS was a helicopter control system that used computers to provide the "precise navigation, formation flight, terrain following, and fire control" in virtually any kind of weather. Also that year, in a move *Business Week* magazine called a "coup," Teledyne purchased the Wah Chang Corporation, a leading producer of tungsten and columbkum, and the world's producer of hafnium, zirconium, and other exotic metals.

To increase the company's assets and provide it with leverage if management decided to look for new capital to buy more companies, Teledyne moved into the insurance business by purchasing 21% of United Insurance Company for $40 a share.

In 1969 Teledyne's sales surpassed the billion dollar mark. The company subsequently stopped its aggressive acquisition program and paid off its short term debts. Wall Street analysts predicted that the acquisition phase was over and that Singleton was turning Teledyne into an operating company. Generally, however, Teledyne's financial condition was quite strong. For the ten years previous to 1971, the company led the *Fortune* 500 ranking in earnings and earnings per share growth. And in the early 1970's, while many conglomerates were experiencing financial difficulties, Teledyne's weathered the recession. Sales increased somewhat with inflation, but net profits remained near $60 million.

In 1972, Argonaut, one of Teledyne's six financial companies, decided to expand from the worker's compensation field into the medical malpractice insurance business. At the same time, the frequency and size of malpractice claims were growing, but premiums didn't keep pace. By 1974 Argonaut took a $104 million pretax writeoff, resulting in a $31.2 million net loss in insurance operations and a reduction of Teledyne's net profit for the year to $31.5 million. Nine of Argonauts 11 top officers were fired, and Singleton began running the operations from headquarters in Los Angeles. Argonaut, one of the last large companies in the malpractice market, discontinued underwriting individual policies for the 20,000 physicians it covered. It continued to offer coverage to the 25% of the nation's hospitals it covered, but at higher rates and covering fewer risks. In the meantime, the company collected $170 million in reserves against malpractice cases.

Teledyne's problems were compounded in 1973 when the consumer products division lost $1.8 million, mostly because of its Packard-Bell television production unit which had failed to capture a large enough share of the west cost television market. Teledyne reduced production and narrowed the loss to half a million the next year.

With the insurance unit and consumer unit problems solved, Teledyne's outlook had improved markedly. Net income soared to $101.7 million on sales of $1.71 billion. The largest share of profit came from industrial products such as diesel and gasoline engines and machine tools. Insurance operations had improved and were contributing $19 million. The consumer products division showed a healthy profit of $13.1 million because of Water Pik, which had sold a million shower heads at $25 to $40 each. The closing of the Packard Bell television unit had little effect on earnings since it was accomplished so successfully that no final writedown was taken.

In 1976 the company attempted, for the sixth time since 1972, to buy back its in stock in order to eliminate the possibility of a takeover attempt by someone eager for the cash reserves the company had accumulated. Altogether, the company spent $450 million buying back its stock, leaving $12 million outstanding, compared to $37.4 million at the close of 1972. With many of the company's divisions showing stronger results and fewer shares outstanding, Teledyne's stock increased from a low of $9.50 the year before to $45, becoming the largest gainer on the New York Stock Exchange and overcoming its traditional unpopularity with investors since Singleton refused to pay a cash dividend (instead he offered a 3% stock dividend). Singleton wasn't content to buy back his own stock though. That same year Teledyne purchased 12% of Litton's stock, becoming the company's largest shareholder.

By 1978 Singleton's strategy of bringing in new management to replace underachievers appeared to be working. Only one of the 130 profit centers into which the company was divided was losing money. Without a single acquisition, company sales had soared to $2.2 billion, the result of internal growth at annual rate of 7%. Nearly all of Teledyne's units were reporting continued growth and strong positioning in the market place. Sales from the company's offshore drilling rig had grown to $80 million from $10 million in 1966. Water Pik's sales reached $130 million, up from eight million in 1966. Teledyne had also become an important producer of specialty metal. Allvac,

which vacuum-melts metals, had surpassed $40 million in sales compared with $1.5 million in 1964. Even tiny Merla Manufacturing, purchased for only $80,000 with monthly sales of $30,000 had grown to $7 million. Chang had grown from near bankruptcy in 1967 to over $100 million in 1977. And Packard Bell's business was greater than when it sold televisions.

In the meantime, over a two year period, Singleton took advantage of the company's regained financial strength and used $400 million of the company's earnings to purchase surprisingly large stakes in 11 companies. By 1978, through Teledyne, Singleton had gained effective control of six companies, owning 22% of Litton's common stock, 28.5% of Curtiss-Wright, nearly 20% of Walter Kidde, 22% of Brockway Glass, and 20% of Reichhold Chemicals. In addition, he purchased 8% of GAF, 5.5% of Rexnord, 7% of Federal Paper Board, 5% of Colt Industries, and 8% of Eltra.

Most of money for the purchases was funneled through Unicoa and Argonaut. Almost all insurance companies keep some of their assets in stock, but most have stock holdings less than their net worth. Argonaut, on the other hand, had accumulated seven times its net worth in stock holdings, which is very unusual in the insurance business. Singleton's action quickly caught the attention of the business press and of the management of the companies whose stock he purchased. Rumors abounded about his possible intentions, some of which speculated that he wanted to merge the companies into Teledyne, particularly his former employer, Litton.

In the end, the merger attempts never materialized. However, it was soon apparent that what Singleton had actually purchased were a number of difficulties. As earnings were being channeled into the stock market, Teledyne was putting only 1.5% of manufacturing sales back into research and development and plant and equipment maintainance, more than 25% below the average industry investment. Manufacturing operations, cut off from corporate resources, started to lose competitiveness. As a result, Teledyne's divisions lost market shares, contracts, and technological advantages.

One of the worst problems the company was confronted with occurred in 1980. Until then, its Continental Motors division in Muskegon, Michigan supplied diesel engines to all U.S. military tanks, an important contributor to Teledyne's earnings. When the turbine-powered M1 was introduced that year, however, Continental was relegated to the replacement-engine market for existing tanks.

In addition, Wah Chang, which had once enjoyed a virtual monopoly on the free-world production of zirconium, a crucial metal in building nuclear reactors, had lost a large portion of its market share. The French had walked away with 40% of market. And Westinghouse Electric Corporation's completion of a new plant threatened to reduce Chang's market share to less than half of the $150 million free-world output.

In 1981 the insurance operations, which contributed 25% of Teledyne's total revenue, were once again in trouble. The units, which were not performing well within their industry, lost $79.2 million before taxes.

The stock portfolio, which had been built up at the

expense of the rest of the company, was also in trouble during 1982. Overall, Teledyne's stock portfolios had dropped $380 million during the previous year. That unreported loss almost matched the company's earnings of $412 million on sales of $4.3 billion. Part of Teledyne's stock problems were due to its 16% investment in International Harvester, which over the previous year and a half had lost $100 million on paper.

The manufacturing plants and service companies continued to perform poorly in several important markets. Water Pik was showing a profit, but only by reducing product development, advertising and marketing expenditures drastically. And Ryan Aeronautical, formerly the premier producer of robot aircraft used for military target practice and reconnaissance, lost most of its market share. Ryan's Firebee model controlled 75% of market in the early 1970's. However, Teledyne's emphasis on accumulating cash opened the field to more innovative competitors. Northrop Corporation, for instance, introduced less expensive and easier to launch alternatives that used sophisticated electronics to match the Firebee's capabilities.

With the company financially weakened, Teledyne management appeared to adopt a more aggressive strategy in 1982 by making its first large acquisition bid in 13 years. Continental tried to purchase Chrysler's tank division, which was the prime contractor for the M-1 tank. However, General Dynamics Corporation won the bid with a $336 million offer, exceeding Teledyne's offer by $36 million. According to *Business Week*, Pentagon officials were relieved that Continental lost the bid because they considered Continental to be "stagnating."

In 1983 Teledyne's sales fell from $3.24 billion to $2.86 billion, while net profit fell 37% to $248.7 million. That same year, Teledyne took a $49.1 million dollar write down on its stake in GAF, and in December of 1985 Teledyne sold its 6.7% share in GAF.

With Teledyne's financial troubles fully apparent, discord also began to appear in management. High level executives complained increasingly that Singleton, who once claimed to have no specific business plan for the company, was only involved in management when problems developed.

Wall Street analysts have no doubts that Teledyne can survive its current problems. However, they have also made it clear that Teledyne must narrow its corporate focus. If Teledyne is to remain an important high-technology focus, it must return to improving its primary high-technology businesses and refrain from expending its resources in accumulating a large stock portfolio.

Principal Subsidiaries: Teledyne Industries, Inc.; Argonaut Insurance Co.; Teledyne Exploration Co.; Teledyne Isotopes, Inc.; Teledyne Life Insurance Co.; Trinity Universal Insurance Co.; Unicoa Corp. (98.4%).

TENNECO INC.

Tenneco Building
P.O. Box 2511
Houston, Texas 77002
U.S.A.
(713) 757–2131

Public Company
Incorporated: June 9, 1947 as Tennessee Gas Transmission Company
Employees: 97,000
Sales: $14.5 billion
Market Value: $7.185 billion
Stock Index: New York Toronto

Tenneco is one of the largest diversified companies in the world. Its main interests are in natural resource development, machine manufacturing, and chemical and agricultural products. Much of the company's success is attributed to its first director, a native of Chicago named Henry Gardiner Symonds. Symonds was born in 1903, and acquired a degree in geology from Stanford in 1924 and an MBA (with distinction) from Harvard in 1927. He began his career in Chicago as a banker with what is today the Continental Illinois Bank and Trust Company. In 1930 he began work with a small investment firm and bank subsidiary called the Chicago Corporation. Symonds was very successful, and by 1932 had been promoted to vice president of the division. In 1938, near Corpus Christi, Texas, oil was discovered on land which the Chicago Corporation had purchased for natural gas deposits. Symonds was dispatched to Texas to manage the property, and later that year became a board member of the firm. The Chicago Corporation was unable fully to exploit the large reserves of natural gas it had developed in Texas because the war created shortages of pipeline materials essential for gas transmission. When a shortage of fuel for defense plants in West Virginia developed in 1943, the Chicago Corporation was able to obtain a Federal Power Commission license to operate a pipeline, in addition to a priority order for pipeline materials. Symonds was placed in charge of the construction of a 1265–mile pipeline which linked the gas fields of the Gulf states with factories in the eastern United States.

A company called the Tennessee Gas and Transmission Company, founded in 1940 and acquired by the Chicago Corporation in 1943, was placed in charge of the pipeline. The project was completed in October 1944, but the day after it went into operation the Federal Power Commission moved to regulate the pipeline and ordered the company to reduce its transmission rates. Symonds thought the Federal Power Commission had misled him into believing his company would be allowed to operate without regulation, and that the Commission's actions were unfair to the Chicago Corporation, which organized the project. Symonds declared that he would never again become involved in projects which were subject to government regulation. The Chicago Corporation promptly divested itself of Tennessee Gas after the war, but Symonds remained with the company and was subsequently named its president.

Tennessee Gas continued to add pipelines to its network, planning 3840 additional miles in 1946. A long coal strike that year increased demand for oil- and gas-burning furnaces and other devices. This increase in demand prompted Tennessee Gas to apply for rights to build more gas lines, and for the first time to pump oil through the government-sponsored "big-inch" and "little inch" oil pipeline programs. On July 18 of the following year the company was re-incorporated in Delaware as the Tennessee Gas Transmission Company, but its headquarters remained in Houston.

Symonds used profits from the pipeline operations to establish a separate but complementary subsidiary business in oil and gas exploration. He also advocated the acquisition of existing oil companies during the 1950's, including Sterling Oil, Del-Rey Petroleum, and Bay Petroleum. The company also acquired a number of petrochemical companies during 1955, diversifying the product base and involving Tennessee Gas in industrial plastics.

Fifteen Oil, acquired in 1960, was one of several subsidiaries engaged in oil and gas exploration and production in places as diverse as Alaska, Canada, Latin America, and Africa. A subsidiary called the Tenneco Corporation was formed that year to coordinate the management of several company subsidiaries.

Also in 1960, the chairman of the Federal Power Commission, Jerome Kuykendall, and several other FPC officials were criticized for having met with the general counsel for Tennessee Gas. Symonds contended that the meeting had been widely misunderstood, and refuted allegations that they had privately discussed legally restricted matters.

In February 1961 a corporate restructuring occurred which placed the company's non-utility subsidiaries, principally Tennessee Gas and Bay Petroleum, under the managerial authority of Tenneco. Acquisitions in the chemical industries continued through the 1960's, and included the Heyden Newport Chemical Corporation, forming the core of what later became Tenneco Chemicals, Inc. in March 1965.

The Tenneco division added a new line of business in June 1965 when it purchased the Packaging Corporation of America, a manufacturer of paperboard and packaging materials, with over 400,000 acres of timberland resources. Between September 1950 and March 1966 Tennessee Gas had acquired 22 companies.

A second corporate restructuring took place in April 1966. Tenneco assumed control over all the assets of

Tennessee Gas, which subsequently became a Tenneco subsidiary. Gardiner Symonds was promoted from president and chairman of the board (positions he had occupied since 1958) to chief executive officer and chief policy officer, in addition to being named chairman "for life".

Tenneco's most significant acquisition under Symonds came in August 1967, when it purchased the Kern County Land Company for approximately $430 million. Kern was established in California around 1850 by two lawyers from Kentucky named Lloyd Tevis and James Ben Ali Haggin. Their aim was to purchase land for resale to prospectors drawn to California in search of gold. The scheme failed, but the introduction of irrigation transformed the 2.5 million acres of arid wasteland into arable cropland. It was also discovered that some of the land held oil deposits which Kern lacked the expertise to develop. Tenneco, however, was perfectly suited to develop the sites, but had no immediate interest in Kern's agricultural businesses. Still, those businesses were profitable and could easily be assimilated into Tenneco's existing land management group. The acquisition also included Kern's 53% interest in J.I. Case, a manufacturer of farm and construction machinery located in Wisconsin, and Walker Manufacturing, which produced automotive exhaust systems.

Tenneco was divided into geographical subsidiaries, including Tenneco West (formerly Kern), and Tenneco Virginia, which had grown out of the company's gas transmission business. In September 1968 Tenneco Virginia purchased Newport News Shipbuilding & Drydock Company for about $140 million. Newport News was engaged in the construction of nuclear-powered submarines and aircraft carriers, as well as merchant and commercial ships. The company also repaired and reconditioned ships, and refueled nuclear vessels. It was the nation's largest privately owned shipyard, and it was in serious financial trouble.

Gardiner Symonds died of a heart ailment on June 2, 1971 while still chairman of Tenneco. His method of expansion through diversification was based on three rules: seeing that the company he wished to acquire would benefit from Tenneco management; choosing companies whose operations would complement those of Tenneco; and enforcing standards which kept each division "big enough to stand on its own two feet." Under Symonds's successor, James Lee Ketelson, Tenneco continued to operate on these precepts, but the number and size of subsequent acquisitions were noticeably reduced.

The application of Tenneco management methods to Newport News transformed the shipbuilding division into a successful venture by 1971. Over a period of several years, Tenneco invested nearly $100 million in Newport News. By 1973 the division had accumulated an order backlog of one billion dollars. As a result of increased demand for imported petroleum products, Newport News engaged in the construction of large ships capable of carrying crude oil and liquified natural gas.

From the time that Tenneco purchased Newport News until 1976, it acquired an additional 13 companies, including Albright & Wilson Ltd., a British chemical company, and consolidated its ownership of J.I. Case. The auto-motive parts division of Tenneco experienced strong growth during the 1970's through the acquisition of AB Starlawerken of Sweden in 1974, Monroe Auto Equipment, best known for their line of shock absorbers, in 1977, and Lydex, a Danish company in 1978. Tenneco started to purchase insurance companies in 1978, including Philadephia Life and Southwestern Life Insurance.

In the course of restructuring Newport News Shipbuilding, Tenneco encountered severe disagreements with organized labor and the Occupational Health and Safety Administration (OSHA). Eventually, after a three-month strike, all 16,500 employees of Newport News gained representation by the United Steelworkers. OSHA levied a fine of $786,190 on Newport News, citing 617 cases of deficient medical care, unsafe working conditions, and excessive noise. It was the largest fine OSHA had ever imposed on any company.

Wall Street analysts had consistently advised Tenneco to sell Newport News, warning that the division would require costly modernization and reorganization. Despite its problems, however, Tenneco officials recognized the potential of Newport News, particularly after Navy Secretary John Lehman declared his intention to establish a 600-ship navy in 1981.

Newport News abandoned commercial shipbuilding in favor of government defense contracts. Much of its initial work in this area centered on the *Los Angeles*-class attack submarine, which it designed and has consistently delivered at a profit. Newport News is also the world's only manufacturer of nuclear-powered aircraft carriers, including the *Carl Vinson* and *Theodore Roosevelt*, launched in 1982 and 1986, respectively. Newport News has also planned to construct servicing berths for the larger Trident submarines, currently built exclusively by the Electric Boat division of General Dynamics.

During the early 1980's Tenneco sold its petrochemical and polyvinyl chloride production facilities to Occidental Petroleum. The company dealt with low gas prices and the adverse trends in the gas industry through the formation in 1984 of a new subsidiary called Tenngasco, which was responsible for sales of spot market gas in unregulated intrastate markets. Also in 1984 the Tenneco Packaging Corporation of America acquired Ecko Housewares and Ecko Products from the American Home Products Corporation.

As a result of a severe crisis in the American farming industry throughout the early 1980's, International Harvester was forced to restructure its operations (and subsequently change its name to Navistar). This included the sale of its farm machinery line, which Tenneco purchased in 1985 for $430 million. This division was combined with Case, which was also losing money, and which Tenneco had attempted to sell. Tenneco officials, however, believed that Case could benefit from Harvester's broader product line and stronger dealer network. The new combined group would have a 35% market share for large tractors, a figure second only to Deere & Company with 42%. As a result of restructuring efforts and the temporary closure of several tractor plants, the new Case division registered a modest profit by the end of the year.

Tenneco still derives over 75% of its operating profit from the exploration, processing, transportation, and marketing of oil and natural gas. James Ketelson, who was named chairman and chief executive officer in 1978, was instrumental in the company's decision to convert its refinery at Chalamette, Louisiana to process lower grades of crude oil from Venezuela and Mexico. In response to the reduction in oil prices, Tenneco redirected capital expenditures from oil and gas exploration into finding ways to produce oil at lower prices.

The company also reached a preliminary accord in 1986 to sell its five insurance companies to I.C.H. Corporation for about $1.5 billion.

Tenneco survived a 1982 attempt by stockholders to separate and sell the company's various divisions. Again in 1987, word surfaced that Tenneco might be targeted for a takeover because its debt is high, it is rich in assets, and it is "underperforming." Tenneco has insisted on paying stock dividends rather than reducing its debt or, in some other way, reducing its exposure to corporate raiders. While another major restructuring does not appear imminent, Tenneco's financial condition is highly susceptible to the fluctuations of a volatile energy market.

Principal Subsidiaries: Tenneco Corp.; Tenneco Oil Exploration & Production Co,; Tennessee Gas Transmission Co.; Tenngasco Corp.; Tenneco Oil Processing & Marketing Co.; Newport News Shipbuilding Co.; Tenneco Automotive Co.; J.I.Case Co.; Packaging Corp. of America; Tenneco West Co.; Albright & Wilson, Inc. (England); Tenneco Minerals Co.; Tenneco Europe (England).

Further Reading: The Age of Giant Corporations by Robert Sobel, Westport, Connecticut, Greenwood, 1972; *Tenneco's First 35 Years*, Houston, The Company, 1978.

TEXTRON

TEXTRON INC.

40 Westminster St.
Providence, Rhode Island 02903
U.S.A.
(401) 421-2800

Public Company
Incorporated: April 16, 1928 as Franklin Rayon Corp.
Employees: 56,000
Sales: $5.023 billion
Market Value: $2.694 billion
Stock Index: New York

Textron has made so many changes in its corporate identity that any characterization of it as a business enterprise is subject to revision on rather short notice. It has, however, consistently earned a profit for its stockholders. For that reason, many investors may not care what it does so long as it keeps generating a profit for them, Textron is involved in many industries, but traditionally it has been recognized as an important United States aerospace manufacturer.

The man behind the success of Textron was Royal Little. Little sought practical business experience as an unpaid apprentice at a textile mill after his graduation from Harvard in 1919. He remained in the textile business, working for the Franklin Rayon Yarn Dyeing Corporation. He recognized the serious drawbacks of producing a product in a business vulnerable to volatile market cycles. As far back as the 1920's, Little advocated diversification as a means to insulate a company from occasional slumps in certain lines of business. Specifically, Little advocated "non-related" diversification, that is, simultaneous operation of totally unrelated businesses. The system had to be unrelated so that heavy losses in one business wouldn't affect the profitablity of related industries.

Neither Little nor his company were in a position to implement a general diversification until 1952. The company, which changed its name to Textron eight years earlier, acquired a variety of other smaller companies. Little later recalled in his book, *How to Lose $100,000,000 and Other Valuable Advice* that a banker refused to back his acquisitions until he proved that he could run a textile business. Little successfully completed a hostile takeover of American Woolen in 1955 in what *Fortune* magazine called "the stormiest merger yet." Little's policy for successful takeover bids was to "be sure to pick a company

whose board of directors isn't smart enough" to fight back with a counter-takeover.

In 1956 Royal Little hired a Providence banker, Rupert Thompson, to oversee what he admitted were his irrepressible impulses to acquire more companies. Thompson made sure that Textron's acquisitions were "balanced," or sufficiently spread out so that a depression in any one market wouldn't severely affect the company as a whole. Based on this strategy, Little and Thompson established what has (arguably) been declared the world's first conglomerate.

Textron entered the aerospace industry in 1960 when it purchased the Bell Aircraft company. Bell was best known for its helicopters, but first gained wide recognition shortly after World War II when it built the XP-59 Airacomet, which was the first American jet aircraft. During the war, Bell was a major supplier of aircraft parts to the Army Air Corps. Its founder, Lawrence D. Bell, worked as an engineer for Glenn Martin and later for Donald Douglas. Under the protection of Textron's financial umbrella, the Bell division was able to invest more money into longer term research and development of helicopters and their new specialty, rockets.

Royal Little retired from Textron in 1962 and relinquished his seat on the board of directors. Thompson maintained a strict policy toward Textron's various divisions. The company would sell a particular division at the first sign of adverse performance. Such was the case for Textron's last textile holding in 1963; Amerotron was sold when it "failed to perform."

Rupert Thompson was described as having combined Alfred Sloan's management strategy for General Motors and Little's strategy of growth through acquisition. Textron maintained a consistency for meeting production and financial targets, demanding a 20% return on equity after taxes for the company's various divisions. Thompson was the manager of a company which was perhaps better described as basically an asset portfolio, or "management concept."

Rupert Thompson left Textron in 1968 after he was diagnosed as having cancer. The man he appointed to take his place was the company's president, G. William Miller. The company Miller took over was a well-diversified manufacturer of tools, industrial machines, consumer goods, plastics, appliances and, of course, helicopters.

Only months after he assumed the leadership of Textron, Miller launched an attempted takeover of United Fruit. When the attempt was thwarted Textron returned to less ambitious acquisitions of small firms, particularly zipper and fastener manufacturers. By 1971 Textron was ready for another ambitious takeover, this time of the Kendall Company, which would have placed Textron in the health care business. The attempted takeover of Kendall failed when another company outbid Textron.

Miller's most ambitious takeover attempt came shortly afterward when he tried to engineer a 45% controlling interest in the larger but nearly bankrupt Lockheed Corporation. Lockheed resisted the bid and later brought pressure from Wall Street upon Miller to abandon the takeover.

Miller's attempt to enter into the oil and gas business

was cut short when he left the company in 1977 to take a position with the Carter administration as Federal Reserve chairman, and then later as secretary of the Treasury. One of Miller's best qualities was his insightful recognition of the fact that the United States was rapidly transforming itself into a service-oriented economy. He brought Textron into financial services by acquiring insurance and other financial service companies.

The man who replaced Miller was Joseph Collinson. Collinson's tenure was short-lived, he retired from the company in 1979. He was succeeded by Messrs. Bob Straetz as chairman and Beverly Dolan as president. The new men in charge were quicker to sell divisions which were performing poorly. One of the first to be sold was Polaris, the snowmobile manufacturer.

Straetz and Dolan later divested Textron of divisions not related to aerospace or technology. In effect, Textron was being reconverted into an operating company. They professed impatience with subsidiaries that didn't "perform" and promised to "dump" them without a grace period. Straetz told *Fortune* magazine, "Some of that concept of non-related diversification still exists, but we're trying to make Textron a more focused company." The company operated principally around Bell Aerospace, which accounted for about one quarter of Textron's sales.

Bell's UH-1 Huey helicopter was used extensively during the American involvement in the Vietnam war. After Vietnam, Textron cultivated a strong market for Bell helicopters in Iran. However, this $875 million market was lost with the fall of the Shah. From this turn of events, Straetz and Dolan learned the importance of maintaining a diverse group of customers. They tried next to establish a lucrative commercial market for Bell.

Bell produces a number of light helicopters, characterized by their dragonfly appearance. It competes with Boeing's Vertol, and particularly the Sikorsky division of United Technologies. Sikorsky manufactures larger, heavy duty helicopters, but competes intensely with Bell in the medium sized section of the market. Typical of many recent Pentagon contracts, Sikorsky and Bell have been teamed to jointly develop a "VTOL," or vertical take-off and landing airplane.

Bell is the division which is most responsible for Textron's identity as an aerospace company. That identity has been preserved by the continuing success of Bell. However, while Bell's products are of good quality, a unique management structure must also be credited for the general success of the division and its parent.

Unlike most other firms, an unusual amount of authority is vested with Textron's vice presidents. A vice president is thereby enabled to specialize in a certain area of the operation with the full authority of his office behind him. This also encourages good communication within the top management eschelon, and allows the president and chief executive officer to concentrate on more general matters, such as acquisitions and divestitures. Many American corporations have admitted to copying this style of management.

In 1984 Textron was the object of a hostile takeover bid by Chicago Pacific Corporation. It was the third unsolicited bid for Textron, which had become a target because of its large debt. Chicago Pacific was one-sixth the size of Textron. It had emerged from bankruptcy only months before the bid, selling all its railroad capital, including engines, track and traffic rights. The company had a large amount of cash and was embarking on an acquisition program. Textron, however, mounted a defense which rather easily foiled the takeover bid.

Shortly thereafter, Dolan completed Textron's acquisition of Avco. Avco was formerly the Aviation Corporation of the Americas, one of the three large aeronautic combines of the 1930's, and the company which launched Pan Am and American Airlines. Over the years Avco gradually sold its aircraft interests until, by the time of the Textron acquisition, it was essentially a financial institution centered around the insurance business. Avco was already threatened by a takeover from a smaller company when Textron, Avco's preferred suitor, made its own bid. With the success of the Avco acquisition, Dolan replaced Bob Straetz as chief executive officer.

In 1985 Textron surprised its stockholders by offering to sell its main operating division, Bell Aerospace. Upon closer inspection the stockholders voted in favor of the proposed sale, but it marked a serious change in Textron's stated intention to convert itself from a conglomerate into an operating company. The sale of Bell was intended to raise stockholder's return on equity and eliminate the corporate debt which made it an attractive takeover target.

The sale was postponed following an improvement in the company's financial position. Bell has been retained and reorganized into two operating units: Bell Aerospace, which continues to handle the aeronautic business; and Textron Marine Systems, for (presently unspecified) marine projects.

Twenty-five years after leaving Textron, Royal Little still defends his notion of non-related diversification. He has refused to comment on Textron's current activities. He may be as unsure about their future direction as everyone else. For the benefit of its stockholders, however, Textron can be expected to emphasize its continued financial health and profitability.

Principal Subsidiaries: Textron Canada, Ltd.; Textron Financial Corp.; Textron Pacific, Ltd.; TIH Corp.; Bell Helicopter Textron, Inc.; H R Textron, Inc.; Textron Acceptance Corp.; Dorfinco Corp.; Textron International Finance Corp.; Textron Atlantic Belgium, S.A.; Textron Atlantic SARL; Textron Atlantic, B. V.; Societe Fabrications Bostich; Textron S.A. de C. V.; Avco Corp.

Further Reading: Textron—From the Beginning by Robert S. Eisenhauer, Providence, Rhode Island, The Company, 1979; *How to Lose $100,000,000 and Other Valuable Advice* by Royal Little, Boston, Little Brown, 1979.

THORN EMI PLC

Thorn EMI House
Upper Saint Martin's Lane
London WC2H 9ED
England
01-836-2444

Public Company
Incorporated: March 3, 1980 as a result of the merger of Thorn Electrical Industries Ltd. and EMI Ltd.
Employees: 80,484
Sales: £3.316 billion (US$4.769 billion)
Market Value: £1.683 billion (US$2.42 billion)
Stock Index: London

Jules Thorn was born in Austria in 1899, and as a young man attended the University of Vienna, where he completed a degree in business management. During the 1920's Thorn traveled to England on several occasions as a sales representative for an Austrian gas mantle firm. In 1928, shortly after he moved to England, Thorn established the Electrical Lamp Service Company, which imported light bulbs and radio components from the continent. In 1932 he purchased a controlling share of the Chorlton Metal Company. Thorn operated a radio rental shop, which was established as Lotus Radio in 1933. That same year he purchased Atlas Works, manufacturer of an electric lamp known as the Atlas Lamp. With the profits from these operations, Thorn acquired the Ferguson Radio Corporation in 1936, enabling him to manufacture as well as sell radio sets. The company's operations were subsequently merged that year under the name Thorn Electrical Industries.

Thorn's electronic businesses prospered until 1940 when Britain declared war on Germany. As a result of the war, the British economy was severely affected. Virtually all products, including those manufactured by Thorn, fell under a tightly controlled government rationing program.

When the war ended in 1945, Jules Thorn initiated an ambitious expansion of his company's interests through acquisition. Ecko-Ensign Design and Tricity Cookers, both electrical engineering firms, were purchased in 1950 and 1951, respectively. Throughout the 1950's Thorn Electrical Industries consolidated a firm position in the field of electronics and electrical appliances. Thorn personally supervised every aspect of his company's activities, gaining a reputation for hard work and tireless enthusiasm for profit.

By the end of 1961, Thorn had acquired Philco and Pilot, in addition to Ultra Radio & Television, and interests in HMV and Marconiphone. Through its acquisitions that year, Thorn Electrical Industries had become the largest producer of radio and television sets in Britain. In recognition for his contributions to the British electronics industry Jules Thorn was knighted Sir Jules in 1964.

The transmission of television programs in color did not begin in Britain until December of 1967. Jules Thorn recognized that this development would drastically increase demand for color television sets, the technology and patents of which were difficult to acquire in Britain. Thorn arranged for blank tubes to be imported from the United States and coated with the necessary color-sensitive chemicals in his factories. As a result of Thorn's imaginative and timely solution, Thorn Electrical Industries was able further to consolidate its position in the British television market.

As a result of the merger of Robinson Radio Rentals and Thorn interests, the combined Thorn/Radio Rentals group became the world's largest television rental company, controlling just under one-third of the 7.5 million televisions in Britain.

Other acquisitions during this period reflected the company's continued diversification. Metal Industries was acquired in 1967, KMT Holdings in 1968, Parkinson Cowan in 1971, Clarkson International Tools in 1974, and Cleveland Twist Drill in 1976. By far, however, Thorn's largest takeover bid came in 1979 when an opportunity arose to purchase EMI Ltd., a diversified entertainment and electronic instruments conglomerate.

EMI was itself formed as a result of a merger in 1931, and produced *gramophone* recording equipment. Over the years, EMI organized a line of sophisticated electronic systems, which included early British radar equipment and the BBC's first television system. Along a separate line of development, EMI enlarged its position in the recording and music publishing industries in 1954 when a decision was made to take over Capitol Records in the United States. Tremendous growth was experienced in this division a decade later, largely on the strength of record sales by the Beatles.

By the late 1960's profits from the EMI recording division surpassed those of the electronics division, and enabled EMI to purchase the entertainment organization of Sir Lew Grade, and the cinema business of the Associated British Picture Corporation. As a result, EMI had become one of the largest motion picture entertainment concerns in the world by 1970.

In the early 1970's, however, EMI was burdened by heavy losses from its Capitol Records operation, and a poorly planned investment in an Italian television manufacturer called Voxson. The most significant development for EMI during this period was the introduction of a revolutionary new Computed Tomographic X-ray scanning device in 1972. The fact that EMI had developed this scanner, with no previous experience in X-ray equipment, caused many seriously to reconsider the company's prospects.

Profitable sales of the scanner in the United States were drastically reduced after the Carter Administration restricted government aid to hospitals. In addition, EMI failed to anticipate a strong reaction from its competitors. General Electric subsequently introduced a similar but faster model which effectively removed EMI from the market.

By 1977, serious problems with the medical electronic division caused management to be broken up into three divisions, each responsible for its own profitability. At one point EMI even appeared willing to dispense with its recovering music operations.

Institutional investors, who held a three quarters voting majority in Thorn, expressed concern that a merger of the two companies would be problematic because Thorn and EMI were very different companies. In the event of a merger, Thorn would have to let EMI management run itself, at least for a few years, because it knew so little about EMI's businesses. Another cause for concern was that EMI's new management team, led by the very capable Lord Delfont, had to prove itself under difficult circumstances.

At the end of October 1979 EMI rejected a £145 million bid by Thorn. The offer was resubmitted the following week for £165 million and accepted. The new company's name was changed to Thorn EMI on March 3, 1980.

The various divisions within the old Thorn and EMI organizations continued to operate independently of each other and, to some extent, of the central management group. Management re-implemented a planning model developed by the Boston Consulting Group which provided for the development of new enterprises by channeling funds from profitable operations. This had the effect of starving the successful enterprises within the company of funds needed to maintain a competitive product lines. Just as the model failed in the early 1970's, it was failing again a decade later. Thorn EMI was less like a successful operating company and more like a weak investment portfolio.

In an attempt to raise money and reduce losses during 1980 and 1981, the company sold its medical electronics business, its Hotels and Restaurant division, and parts of the Leisure and Entertainment division. Also at this time, on December 12, 1980 Sir Jules died at the age of 81.

Peter Laister, chairman of Thorn and later Thorn EMI, attempted to create a more efficient operation out of the fragmented organization by acquiring new divisions. Laister wanted to develop an integrated communications and entertainment business with particular emphasis on advanced electronics. INMOS, a microchip manufacturer, was acquired in 1984, but an attempt to purchase British Aerospace that same year failed. Unable to fulfill his plan or shake Thorn EMI out of stagnation, Laister was removed from the board of directors in what was described as a boardroom "coup" in July of 1985.

Laister was replaced by a former non-executive director named Sir Graham Wilkins. Sir Graham advocated a much different approach, emphasizing a return to the basic industries upon which both Thorn and EMI were built: lighting, rental and retail, and various domestic appliances.

According to Sir Graham, the fundamental problem with Thorn EMI at the time was "that it was too broadly based on activities that were loss making and which we could not afford to keep. We had to prune things which had no immediate profit potential." The divestment of these unpromising operations began in earnest during the 1985–86 fiscal year with the disposal of Thorn EMI Screen Entertainment (the expensive films and cinema division), Thorn EMI Heating Ltd., divisions of Metal Industries which had not already been sold, cable television interests, and a portion of its interest in Thames Television Ltd.

As a result of a general restructuring of Thorn EMI, its operations are presently divided into four main operating groups: rental and retail, technology, music and consumer and commercial products. Each group is further divided into a number of divisions which specialize in particular lines of business.

The rental and retail group encompasses television and video recorder rental, and the retailing of recorded music, home entertainment products and consumer durables. The technology group is responsible for defense electronics and telecommunications systems. Music, mostly through EMI and Capitol labels, covers record and video products as well as music publishing. The final group, consumer and commercial products, produces lighting, appliances, and consumer electronics products through divisions such as Kenwood, Ferguson, and Tricity.

The reorganization has given the company a clearer identity and enables top management to establish a more controllable enterprise. Each division now has more operational responsibility and manages its own debt.

Thorn EMI has emerged with a bias toward consumer products. Two-thirds of its trading profits are derived from its High Street record outlets, the rental outlets, and the Rumbelows retail chain. Research, development and advanced engineering remain priorities of the company's lighting business, which holds 50% of the British market. New appliances, such as a halogen heating device, and the introduction of an appliance rent-to-own scheme for the company's 3.5 million credit-tested customers hold great promise for the future.

Under the leadership of Sir Jules, Thorn developed a reputation for developing products without properly evaluating (some would even say ignoring) consumer preferences. Sir Graham, on the other hand, has expressed the need of Thorn EMI "to find out what our customers want and make it for them at a price that gives us a decent profit, and then find out what they are going to want." The company's return to the more stable basic businesses it has historically performed well in has enabled it to overcome the problems of its recent past and regain its position as an industry leader.

Principal Subsidiaries: Thorn EMI Ferguson Ltd.; Thorn EMI Television Rentals Ltd.; Thorn EMI Retail Ltd.; Thorn EMI Domestic Appliances Ltd.; Thorn EMI Lighting Ltd.; Thorn-Ericcson Telecommunications Ltd. (51%); Capitol Industries-EMI Inc. (USA); Thorn EMI Records Ltd.; Thorn EMI Electronics Ltd.; AWA-Thorn Consumer Products Pty. Ltd. (Australia) (20%); Glass Bulbs Ltd. (50%); The Gramophone Company of India Ltd. (40%); Stearn Electric Company Ltd. (50%); JZT Holdings B.V. (Holland) (33%); Thames Television Ltd. (46%); Toshiba-EMI Ltd. (Japan) (50%).

TOSHIBA

TOSHIBA CORPORATION

1-1 Shibaura 1-chome
Minato-ku, Tokyo 105
Japan
(03) 457 2104/5

Public Company
Incorporated: 1896
Employees: 120,000
Sales: ¥2.511 trillion (US$15.774 billion)
Market Value: ¥1.914 trillion (US$12.026 billion)
Stock Index: Tokyo Osaka Nagoya Kyoto Hiroshima
Fukuoka Sapporo Niigata London Paris Amsterdam
Düsseldorf Frankfurt Luxembourg

Toshiba Corporation is one of Japan's largest producers of consumer and electric products. Established in 1904 as Shibaura Engineering Works, Toshiba has promoted the development of a technology which yearly supercedes itself, and has played an active role in Japan's rise to the forefront of international business.

The company had its origins in 1875 in Tokyo, as the first telegraph equipment shop in Japan. The framework in which Toshiba began, however, was far from the climate in which it now operates. During the late 19th century, Japan lagged far behind Britain, France, Germany and the United States in industrial development. Beseiged with economic problems resulting from the overthrow of the Tokugawa government in 1869, and a tremendous influx of imported goods and machinery which threatened her fledgling industries, Japan was at her most vulnerable. Confronted with the task of strengthening its faltering industries, the new government was quick to respond.

In October of 1870 the Ministry of Industry (Kobusho) was formed and subsequently acted as a catalyst for the country's industrial development. In its attempt to integrate contemporary technologies into Japan, the government concentrated on hiring foreign engineers, technicians and scientists to instruct Japanese engineers in operating imported machinery ; the government also sent government engineers abroad to inspect manufacturing techniques with the intent of selecting machinery and manufacturing techniques for use in Japanese industries.

The integration of foreign technologies was first put into practice by Toshiba, then known as Shibaura Seisakusho, whose 1,300 horsepower steam engine, copied from blueprints of an English counterpart, was successfully implemented in a plant in Kanebo, Japan. This venture con-

vinced Japanese industry of its potential for technological advancement through the implementation of foreign technology onto domestic skills and resources.

As a result, in the 1880's an agreement trading technological expertise for payment was adopted by Shibaura as the most expedient means to upgrade its technological capabilities. This process allowed the business to expand and begin manufacture of heavy electrical equipment in the following decade.

By 1902 Shibaura's own technological capabilities had produced a 150-kilowatt 3-phase-current dynamo for the Yokosuka Bay Arsenal, marking one of the initial transformations from foreign to Japanese-based technology, and the beginning of the company's rise to the forefront of international business. In 1909 Shibaura had direct access to those technologies and grew to be a leading manufacturer of electrical equipment.

While Shibaura and other Japanese corporations were growing in strength and increasing their capabilities, they were deeply debilitated by the advent of World War I. As the war began, Japanese manufacturers were cut off from Germany, England, and the US, major suppliers of machines, industrial materials and chemicals, forcing them to turn to one another for necessary materials and machinery to keep their fledgling industries alive. The hardships experienced during this period had long-term advantages however, by forcing Japanese industry into self-sufficiency and paving the way for the country's industrial advancement.

In the interim between world wars, the company continued to grow. By 1939, Shibaura had merged with the Tokyo Electric Company, Ltd. to form Tokyo Shibaura Electric Company, Ltd., or Toshiba, and became established as a central power in the manufacture of electric lighting and broadcast equipment. This corporation was the first to develop 16″ color television, television phones, and hundreds of other innovations responsible for the automation revolution in offices and factories.

With the outbreak of World War II, Japan was once again forced to look to herself for survival. After the devastation of war, the country rebuilt itself with the aid of occupying U.S. forces under the terms of the San Francisco Treaty. With the assistance of the Japanese government and its citizens, the American Occupation Authority instituted social and economic reforms, and poured resources into financial markets. As Japan was readmitted into the international trading community, access to overseas markets for manufactured goods and raw materials was facilitated; the glut of raw materials available at the time enabled Japan to obtain necessary commodities in large quantities at favorable prices and, consequently, to regain its financial and industrial strength.

In this more favorable climate, Toshiba once again began to flourish. By 1949 Toshiba shares were first listed on the Tokyo Stock and Osaka Securities Exchange. Backed by the powerful trading house of the Mitsui Group, the company's financial status was well secured. Starting in the 1950's, Toshiba began a program to strengthen its competitiveness in both the domestic and international markets.

Yet it would be some time before modern business

policies affected the company in any fundamental way. Citing the use of "archaic management practices," Toshiba executives were criticized for their rigid adherence to a feudal system of hierarchy and status. Top officials maintained lax working hours and were far removed from any operational business. An indisputable separation between a superior and his subordinates made the exchange of ideas virtually impossible. To reduce the burden of responsibility on any one executive, numerous signatures were needed to approve a document. Thus innovation was easily stymied in a chain of bureaucracy.

By 1963 management problems were compounded by a recession. In one year Toshiba's pre-tax profits slid from $36 million to $13 million. To halt any further erosion, a radical change was in order. For only the second time in Toshiba's history the company sought an outsider to rectify the ailing business. Toshiwo Doko, chairman of IHI, the world's largest shipbuilder, was hired to fill the position. By facilitating a merger in 1960 between Ishikawajima Heavy Industries and Harima Shipbuilding & Engineering Company, Doko was credited with creating a highly profitable enterprise.

When he joined Toshiba as president in 1965, Doko retained his title as chairman of IHI. The combined status ranked Doko as Japan's leading industrialist. These two companies had shared interests prior to Doko's appointment at Toshiba; IHI owned over ten million shares in Toshiba and Toshiba controlled over four million shares in IHI. After Doko became president, Toshiba raised its stake in IHI as both companies shared executives on their boards and established trade agreements. This exchange strengthened Toshiba's financial standing.

Doko's other corrective measures included the reduction of Toshiba's dependence on borrowed capital. This was aided by the U.S.-based General Electric company's agreement to purchase all of Toshiba's capital issue. General Electric's interest in Toshiba dated back to before World War II, but had been neglected in the intervening years. With this new infusion of capital Toshiba could expand and modernize operations.

The new company president also initiated a comprehensive campaign to export Toshiba products around the world. By establishing independent departments, the company could better facilitate the export of consumer and industrial goods. Major contracts were finalized with U.S. companies to export generators, transformers and motors, as well as televisions and home appliances.

Other streamlining efforts took the form of expanding the sales force, hiring new management, and consolidating operations. By 1967 Toshiba controlled 63 subsidiaries and employed upward of 100,000 people; the company ranked as the largest electronic manufacturer in Japan and the nation's fourth largest company.

Over the next years Toshiba focused its energies on research and development of new products, slowing entering the nascent computer industry and perfecting consumer electronic products. In the 1970's, Sony, Hitachi and Toshiba began to establish a presence in the consumer electronics market, creating a newfound respect for the superiority of Japanese technology with well-made, cost-effective items.

Within the past three decades, Toshiba has continued to expand through a series of joint ventures and agreements with both Japanese and foreign corporations. In October of 1984, Toshiba's growth was augmented with the formation of its Information and Communications Systems Laboratory. The Lab serves to develop and integrate office automation products such as voice recognition systems and digital private branch exchange systems (PBXs) which transmit telephone calls within private buildings. Through a 1986 agreement with AT&T, Toshiba now markets these systems throughout Japan, as well as assisting that corporation with technological insight.

Toshiba's interest and involvement continue to grow as new markets develop. In the computer field, Toshiba has expanded through a series of agreements with American companies, among them Motorola and IBM. In 1986 Toshiba entered into a joint venture with Motorola for its Japanese production of computer memories and microprocessors. The two companies are involved in joint development of microcomputer and memory chips based on exchange of technology, and development of a manufacturing facility in Japan.

In the same year, Toshiba entered into an agreement with IBM-Japan to market their general purpose computers domestically. Through this arrangement, Toshiba markets its own communications equipment with IBM-Japan's computers, selling to governmental agencies, local governments and other institutions to which IBM had previously been blocked. An additional marketing contract with IBM introduced the first PC-compatible laptop computer, the TJ3100, to Japan, and met with great success.

Although Toshiba is best known in America for its computer-related and consumer products, it has a wide range of additional business ventures. Among Japanese corporations, Toshiba is the leader in the production of advanced medical electronic equipment. In 1986 the corporation initiated the supply of blood chemical analyzers, used to detect liver and kidney disease, to Allied corporation, a leading U.S. chemical manufacturer.

Other accomplishments suggest Toshiba's technological foresight in solving global and domestic problems. In 1984 Toshiba was responsible for the world's first direct broadcast satellite, launched in January of that year. Additionally, Toshiba has begun production of equipment for uranium fuel enrichment for use in nuclear power plants, marking an important step towards Japan's acquisition of a domestic nuclear fuel supply.

Other major markets within the company have seen substantial growth in recent years, particularly in the areas of semiconductors and consumer products. Utilized in equipment from stereos to computer memories, semiconductors are an important part of Toshiba's portfolio. In 1986 alone, Toshiba's semiconductor facilities experienced a 55% increase due to contracts in France and West Germany, as well as domestic production. Perhaps the greatest indicator of Toshiba's potential lies in the fact that, for the first time in its history, it has surpassed its closest competitor, Hitachi, as the second largest semiconductor manufacturer in Japan.

In the light of the preceding accomplishments, the area for which Toshiba is best known remains its consumer products division. In acquisition and innovation, this segment is growing at a rapid pace. In April of 1984 Toshiba reorganized the production, marketing and research and development sections of its video and audio products, incorporating them into one centralized location. While sales of standard consumer products such as VCR's, compact disc players, televisions, and personal cassette recorders continue to grow, Toshiba has been quick to capitalize on new markets. In 1986 Toshiba entered the home video market, creating a wholly-owned subsidiary and introducing 110 new video titles to the Japanese market; in the same year, it entered an agreement for the provision of cable equipment to American Television and Communications Corporation.

Perhaps the most exciting and opportunity-charged advances made by Toshiba in recent years involve its entry into the global markets. Toshiba will soon begin provision of its integrated circuit technology to the Chinese Electronics Import and Export Corporation to assist in development of television production. Additionally, Toshiba has accepted a ¥12 billion contract for a color television assembly plant in Russia, marking Moscow's first agreement of this nature with a Japanese company.

Recent events, however, have found the company attempting to mollify a scandal surrounding one of its subsidiaries. According to Washington sources, the subsidiary sold machine tools to the Soviet Union that would help build quieter submarine propellers. This makes detection more difficult and will force NATO to modernize its antisubmarine detection equipment. While Toshiba claims it is not able to control the subsidiary's daily operations, the sale broke a Western law concerning the sale of technologically advanced equipment to Communist countries. Amid a growing protest by a right-wing extremist group in Tokyo, the company president, Sugiichiro Watari, issued a public apology to the United States.

On July 1, 1987, however, both Watari and Chairman Shoichi Saba announced their resignations from the Toshiba Corporation in the wake of a U.S. Senate vote to ban the import of Toshiba products for two years. The Toshiba Corporation is planning its own investigation into the events that led to the sale. While Saba's replacement is as yet unknown, Joichi Aoi, a former senior executive vice president, will assume Watari's position.

In the meantime, two executives at Toshiba Machine, the subsidiary under investigation that is 50% owned by Toshiba Corporation, were arrested and four top-ranking officials resigned. The Japanese government has prohibited the subsidiary from exporting products to the Soviet Union for one year as well as repealed the company's right to sponsor visas for visiting personnel from Eastern-bloc countries. Many industry analysts have noted, however, that these positive measures will not compensate for the loss of the U.S. market over the next two years.

Principal Subsidiaries: Toshiba Electric Equipment Corp.; Tokyo Electric Co., Ltd.; Toshiba Electric Appliances Co., Ltd.; Onkyo Corp.; Toshiba Credit Corp.; Toshiba House and Living Industry Co., Ltd.; Toshiba Heating Appliance Co., Ltd.; Shibaura Engineering Works Co., Ltd.; Kitashiba Electric Co., Ltd.; Marcon Electronics Co., Ltd.; Toshiba Components Co., Ltd.; Toshiba Medical Systems Co., Ltd.; Toshiba Tungaloy Co., Ltd.; Tokyo Optical Co., Ltd.; Toshiba Glass Co., Ltd.; Toshiba Seiki Co., Ltd.; Iwate Toshiba Electronics Co., Ltd.; Nikko Sitsugyo Co., Ltd.; Toshiba Battery Co., Ltd.; Minato Building Co., Ltd. The company also lists subsidiaries in the following countries: Australia, Brazil, Canada, France, Italy, The Netherlands, Panama, Singapore, Sweden, Taiwan, Thailand, United Kingdom, and the United States.

Further Reading: Industry and Business in Japan edited by Kazuo Sato, New York, Croom Helm, 1980.

TRANSAMERICA CORPORATION

600 Montgomery Street
San Francisco, California 94111
U.S.A.
(415) 983-4000

Public Company
Incorporated: October 11, 1928
Employees: 15,600
Sales: $6.080 billion
Market Value: $2.562 billion
Stock Index: New York London Amsterdam Zurich
Geneva

When Peter Amadeo Giannini, the son of Italian immigrants, began dreaming of his career in turn-of-the-century San Francisco, he had not set his heart on building a banking empire. Instead, at the age of 12 he was sneaking out of his home at night to work in his stepfather's produce business and, by the age of 19, was a full partner. His early success at this business allowed him to retire at the age of 31 with a modest, but comfortable, fortune. His foray into the banking world did not begin until several years later when he received a legacy from his father-in-law, Joseph Cuneo, who had made Giannini a director of his Columbus Savings and Loan Society, a building and loan association in San Francisco. Giannini's career in banking lasted for over forty years, and during this time he established the Transamerica Corporation.

After Giannini was appointed a director of Columbus Savings and Loan he became immersed in a number of disagreements with other directors of the bank over policy issues. He consequently left the Savings and Loan Society and established his own banking business which was located directly across the street from Columbus Savings and Loan. Giannini organized the Bank of Italy with $150,000 in capital contributed by his stepfather and ten friends. He envisioned the bank as an institution for the "little fellow," and the bank subsequently made loans to merchants, farmers, and laborers who were mostly of Italian descent.

Ironically, the San Francisco fire and earthquake of 1906 established Giannini's reputation in the banking world. As he stood amid the rubble of his bank on the morning of the earthquake, he was able to salvage over $2 million in gold and securities. In order to avoid the looters who were running through the city, he hid his bank's resources under piles of vegetables in a horse-drawn cart borrowed from

his former produce business. Giannini immediately alerted his depositors that their savings were safe and began making loans to businessmen who had lost their savings and their companies.

Giannini's success as a banker is also clearly evidenced by his anticipation of the 1907 stock market crash, and his accumulation of gold before the crash. When the crash came Giannini was able to pay his depositors in cash while other banks were using certificates for cash. From this experience, Giannini realized that only larger banks would ensure security, and therefore he began purchasing small banks and converting them into branches of the Bank of Italy. With these acquisitions Giannini established the first branch banking policy in California.

The Bank of Italy grew so rapidly that by 1919 Giannini was able to form Bancitaly Corporation to organize the expansion. In 1928 Bancitaly Corporation was followed by Transamerica Corporation, which was formed as a holding company for all Giannini's banking, insurance, and industrial concerns.

Giannini's expansion into other areas of the financial services had established him as a leader in the financial services field. By 1929 he had moved into the New York banking scene and purchased the solidly established Bank of America. The following year after this important acquisition, all of Giannini's banks were consolidated into Bank of America National Trust and Savings Association. Transamerica played the role of parent company throughout this period.

In 1931, just a year after the consolidation of his banks under Bank America, Giannini retired and left the top post to Elisha Walker, a Wall Street investment banker. Walker did his best to break up this "empire" created by Giannini. Not surprisingly, Giannini forced Walker out in a "furious proxy battle" at the 1932 annual meeting.

During the previous few decades Giannini's operations had been closely observed by both Wall Street and regulatory branches of the U.S. Government; Giannini's success had found critics within both these institutions. Throughout the 1930's Transamerica experienced problems with regulatory procedures and changes enacted by the government. In 1937 Transamerica sold 58% of its stock in Bank America, although it still controlled the board of directors. At the time of his death in 1949, Giannini was embroiled in a fight with the Federal Reserve Board as to whether or not Transamerica had violated the Clayton Anti-Trust Act in creating a "credit monopoly" by placing directors on the boards of banks in the huge chain owned by Bank of America. It was the Reserve Board's belief that Transamerica still controlled the bank even after the 1937 split.

The split between Bank of America and Transamerica was present throughout World War II until 1956 when Congress passed the Bank Holding Company Act, which did not allow bank holding companies the right to involve themselves in industrial activities. By this time, Transamerica was a holding company for several industrial concerns as well as the successful Occidental Life Insurance company. As a result of the passage of this Act, Transamerica sold its banks, forming Western Bancorporation, and was left with Occidental Life and other smaller concerns under its direction.

While the litigation continued over Bank of America, Transamerica was resourcefully building up its life insurance business through Occidental Life. By the early 1960's Occidental Life had assets of $751 million. The success of Occidental Life was due largely to its ability to make the most of a sale. In the post war 1930's Occidental was selling term life insurance to Californian families. Since term life insurance carried lower premiums than full life insurance, other insurance companies dismissed this type of sale as a trivial pursuit, but Occidental banked on high volume sales that would eventually be converted into full life insurance as the policyholder's income increased, thus making up for the initially low profit. This method worked. Occidental's insurance sales increased from $1 billion in 1945 to $6 billion in 1955 to $16 billion in 1965.

Due to the success of Occidental Life it is not surprising that in 1959 President Horace W. Brower was interested in expanding the company's financial services and moving toward "modern merchandising techniques." When Brower rose to the chairman's seat, he looked outside the company to find a "hard-nose financial man" who could successfully run the company as president. The man Transamerica found was John R. Beckett, a 42-year old investment banker and vice president of Blyth and Company's San Francisco office. Beckett was considered to be extremely conversant with the world of finance and negotiations, an important quality since Brower was ready to begin a major acquisition program for Transamerica Corporation.

The plan at Transamerica during this time was to create a financial institution where people could do all their business, something of a "department store of finances." It was Beckett's belief that people wanted "convenience and service" and he was willing to provide such banking. Beckett's concern centered on the fact the financial service industry changed quickly and he was determined to stay ahead of his competitors.

Occidental Life was used as a base for changing Transamerica into a holding company not only for insurance but other companies within the service field. Beckett was interested in company's that would "work in harmony with one another in the market place." The first major acquisition after Beckett became president was Pacific Finance Corporation in 1961, and additional acquisitions focused on land, title insurance and mortgage banking companies. New credit card, leasing and life insurance operations were also started during the 1960's. By 1969 Transamerica was considered a large service conglomerate. To his credit, Beckett changed the dependency on Occidental from 75% of the company's profits to just over 50% by 1966.

Beckett saw the transformation of Transamerica not only as a chance for consumers to do business with a "friendly" full-service bank, but as a way to impress upon customers the importance of using these services over and over again. Beckett compared Transamerica with General Electric: "We hope it will be like the family that buys a refrigerator from G.E. If they like the product and the price, and they get good service, they'll go back to G.E. when they need a new stove . . . That's exactly what we're trying to do in financial services."

Beckett's attempts to enlarge Transamerica resulted in the company being labeled a conglomerate, but Beckett strongly disagreed with this image. Beckett saw managers of conglomerates as "opportunists, people who make acquisitions strictly on an ad hoc basis. They move too quickly, pay too much, use funny accounting and don't look for long-range values. Eventually their bubbles will burst." In contrast, Beckett believed that he was acquiring companies slowly and in concert with a plan to provide a full-line financial services company.

According to Beckett's plan, financial services also included leisure time services for consumers such as movies and travel. In 1967 Transamerica acquired United Artists and in 1968 Trans International Airlines and Budget Rent-a-Car. United Artists would prove to be the acquisition of the 1960's that resulted in financial difficulties for Transamerica.

United Artists, created in 1919 by such movie stars as Douglas Fairbanks, Sr., Mary Pickford, Charlie Chaplin, and D.W. Griffith, looked like a profitable acquisition in 1968, but in 1970, two years after Beckett became chairman, Transamerica's earnings dropped by half because of an $18 million loss due to several unsuccessful films. This interest in the movie industry stemmed back to Giannini's days when, just after his acquisition of Bank of America, he provided financial support to film producers when most every other bank in the country was refusing to do so. Beckett, although caught by surprise by the large loss at United Artists, eventually saw the film company turn into a very profitable business by the late 1970's with such successful films as *Rocky*, *Coming Home* and *One Flew Over the Cuckoo's Nest*.

However, along with these successes there was also unrest within United Artists; the management who had initially sold the film company to Transamerica was now interested in buying it back. Beckett fought back, telling *Fortune* magazine that if "the people at United Artists don't like it, they can quit and go off on their own." That is exactly what they did.

Beckett claimed that he would never sell United Artists, but in 1981 it was sold for $380 million under the direction of president James R. Harvey, who took over in January of 1981 when Beckett became chairman. Harvey was an executive vice president under Beckett and had been with the company since 1965. Harvey's goal for Transamerica is to shape the company into a financial services company once again. The sale of United Artists in the early 1980's has been succeeded by the sale of Trans International Airlines and Budget Rent-a-Car in 1986.

In 1982 a $300 million acquisition of Fred S. James and Company, an insurance broker, was made. With this acquisition, President Harvey said that Transamerica was "shaping the prototype of the insurance company of the future." Harvey's acquisition focus is now on financial services which include insurance, consumer finance and equipment leasing, and industrial machinery. In 1986 Transamerica was interested in purchasing a large brokerage house or mutual fund management company to add to its growing financial services line.

Transamerica's success as a major financial services operation has been based on a good understanding of consumer needs. Through a history of changes and growth, Transamerica has maintained its powerful and influential position in the world of finance. It is clear that Transamerica is headed toward a promising future as a full-service financial institution.

Principal Subsidiaries: Transamerica Occidental Life Insurance Co.; Transamerica Insurance Co.; Transamerica Title Insurance Co.; Transamerica Financial Corp.; Transamerica Interway, Inc.; Transamerica Equipment Leasing Co.; Transamerica Airlines, Inc.; Budget Rent a Car Corp.; Transamerica Investment Services, Inc.; Transamerica Development Co.; Transamerica Realty Services; FSJ Holding Company, Inc.; Compass Computer Services (50%); Transamerica Overseas Finance Corp. NV; Transamerica Delaval Inc.; Transamerica Life Companies; Transamerica Real Estate Tax Service.

TRW INC.

1900 Richmond Road
Cleveland, Ohio 44124
U.S.A.

Public Company
Incorporated: 1901 as Thompson Products Co.
Employees: 93,186
Sales: $6.036 billion
Market Value: $2.957 billion
Stock Index: New York

The merging of one of the world's largest auto parts makers and one of the world's leaders in aerospace technology might seem an unlikely combination. But for TRW that mix of the mundane with the high-tech has proven the path to success. The company has achieved the kind of prosperous, stable business that has eluded other conglomerates.

TRW's conglomerate structure is deeply rooted in the company's history. In the early 1950's the Cleveland-based Thompson Products was looking for an acquisition. J. David Wright, the company's general manager, and Horace Shepard, a vice president, thought the auto valve and steering component maker needed more technical sophistication. Thompson, founded in 1901, had made a name for itself in automotive and aircraft engine parts and had become well known by sponsoring the famed Thompson Trophy Race, aeronautical equivalent of auto racing's Indianapolis 500. But in recent years the company was facing a decline in manned aircraft and saw opportunities in aerospace and electronics.

To break into the young high-tech industry, Wright and Shepard tried to buy Hughes Aircraft Co. Hughes was willing to listen to bids but scoffed at the Thompson offer, which was thought to be ten times too low.

Just a few months later, two of Hughes Aircraft's top scientist-executives, Simon Ramo and Dean Woolridge, decided to leave Hughes to form a new electronic systems company, and Thompson put up $500,000 to bankroll the venture. Not long afterward, Ramo-Woolridge Corporation was established in Los Angeles and quickly gained solid standing in the advanced technology business, being awarded the systems engineering and technical direction contracts for such important missile programs as Atlas, Minuteman, Titan, and Thor.

By 1958 Thompson Products had invested $20 million—20% of its net worth at the time—for a 49% interest in Ramo-Woolridge, and the two operations were merged as Thompson-Ramo-Woolridge. Though united on paper, the company maintained separate corporate headquarters, with Woolridge president in Los Angeles and Wright chairman in Cleveland. Ramo and Shepard, a former chief of production procurement for the Air Force, also had an active role in management.

Merger could hardly have started less auspiciously. In the midst of a recession, the Cleveland-based group was hit with a 14% drop in automotive business and a 34% drop in manned aircraft business. When business improved for the Cleveland division, LA got into trouble. Its venture into semiconductors collapsed in 1961, and the McNamara era was beginning at the Pentagon.

The West coast scientists who had only known cost-plus-fixed-fee contracts needed help. They had to learn how to go from spending money to making it. This education was hampered by hard feelings between the two groups. The electronics end wasn't living up to its promise of being the business of the future. In first four years following merger, profit margins that had been at the 4%-plus level in the mid-1950's dropped to an average of barely 2%.

With the company facing such mundane tasks as cost-cutting, Woolridge, who reportedly never really wanted to be a businessman anyway, resigned in 1962. As Woolridge was getting settled in at his new job as a professor at Caltech, Shepard was promoted to president and Ramo named vice-chairman. With Cleveland now in control of the company, the LA scientists were quickly reassured when the new management team instituted a number of reforms to get the company back on its feet, including writing off $3 million in inventory.

In 1963, Shepard and Wright began pruning unprofitable divisions. They sold most of the unprofitable Bumker-Ramo computer division to Martin Marietta. The company retained partial ownership in Bumker-Ramo but no longer played a large role in the company's plans. Shepard and Wright continued hammering out the company's plans for long-term growth, seeking specifically to raise profit margins. To this end, in 1964 they sold the microwave division and the division which made hi-fidelity components, intercoms, and language laboratories.

To shore up the company's auto parts division, they bought Ross Gear & Tool, a maker of mechanical and power steering units, and Marlin-Rockwell, a ball bearings manufacturer. The 7% profit margin of the new acquisitions, which had combined profit of $5.7 million on sales of $76.5 million, helped boost TRW's overall margin to 4% in 1964, up a percentage point from the year earlier.

In 1965, in another look toward the future, Thompson-Ramo-Woolridge adopted a shorter, less cumbersome name, the now household initials TRW. Also that year the company's investment in aerospace and electronics was becoming increasingly clear. In the previous decade, sales in space and electronics shot up from $14 million to $200 million. But despite that dramatic growth, the company's earnings still came mostly from its oldest business, auto-parts. New and replacement parts accounted for 34% of TRW's $553 million in sales and 40% of its earnings. Chief among those products were its steering linkages, valves, and braking devices that it sells to GM, Ford, and Chrysler.

Things improved for TRW in 1966. An auto parts boom was helping the company's profitability. The Cleveland-based automotive group had a return of 6% on sales of $350 million. The equipment group, also in Cleveland, had an increase of sales to $200 million in aerospace and ordinance technology but lower profit margins because of start-up costs for unexpected demand in commercial aircraft. The Los Angeles-based TRW System had $250 million in sales and a 3% profit margin building and designing spacecraft and doing research. Totals were up to $870 million in sales for TRW, producing $36 million in profit for 4.2% return. Even with the upturn in sales, the company was relying less on government contracts, down to about 44% from 70% ten years earlier.

With the company's financial picture on the upturn, the wrangling between Los Angeles and Cleveland declined. As *Business Week* reported, the discord was "under control, if not cured."

The company continued its tightening of operations in 1966. It bought United Car with $122 million in sales and sold its one consumer business, a hi-fi manufacturer.

Nevertheless, TRW had grown into a conglomerate, a term disliked by company management. In 1969 TRW operated six groups that, in turn, administered 55 divisions. The company derived 32% of its revenues from aerospace products and systems and computer software, 28% from vehicle components for autos and trucks, 23% from electronic components and communication, and 17% from industrial products ranging from mechnical fasteners to automated controls.

To manage the increasingly far-flung company, TRW maintained strict management control over all operations. By encouraging communication between all levels of management and holding monthly manager meetings, TRW avoided the problems that had plagued Gulf & Western, which had grown into a rambling giant.

Another of TRW's successful management styles caught *Fortune*'s eye in 1966. The magazine covered in depth the happenings of a TRW management meeting in Vermont, where 49 of the company's top executives had gathered annually since 1952 at an old farmhouse to think about the company's future.

The next year TRW continued beefing up its auto parts business, acquiring Globe Industries, a Dayton-based maker of miniature AC and DC electric motors. At the same time, TRW's electronics group had grown to more than 20 plants in the U.S., Canada, and Mexico. The company continued to evade problems that had plagued other conglomerates, posting a slight pre-tax gain of 16.4%, above the industry average of 13.3%.

1969 saw the naming of a new president of TRW, Ruben F. Mettler. One of his first big projects was a contract for a laboratory that NASA would send on the Viking probe to Mars. TRW won the challenge to provide one black box weighing 33 pounds with complex instruments capable of making biological and chemical tests to detect the most primitive forms of life. The NASA contract was only worth $50 million, not a big financial risk for a multi-billion dollar company like TRW, but the job was impor-

tant for the company's prestige.

The auto parts business, in the meantime, was once again proving to be immune to cyclical trends in car output. The market for new parts was in a slump, but it was made up for by the accompanying increase in demand for replacement cars as consumers kept their cars on the roads longer. TRW also announced a move into business credit reporting, challenging Dun and Bradstreet.

The company's sound financial condition was unmistakable. For the five years preceding 1970, the company had average earning jumps of 27% annually and an average of 23% increase annually in sales. But company officials conceded that the company couldn't keep growing at that rate forever. It had acquired 38 companies through 1968, a pace it wouldn't be able to maintain indefinitely. The company looked for future growth to run about 10%.

The company's skillful management again became apparent in 1971, when TRW was forced to make cuts because of aerospace recession. Its TRW Systems division had to cut the number of employees by 15%. Managers were not spared cuts either; 18% of the professional staff was laid off. The company's open management style enabled TRW to build a strong enough relationship with its employees that two-thirds of them were non-union, perhaps preventing labor squabbles that had appeared in other companies.

TRW made a risky venture in 1976, entering the tricky market of electronic point-of-sale machines. Those machines had boosted profits for retailers, but not for manufacturers. Its proposed 2001 system aimed at the general market and cost $4,000 per unit, similar to competitors. TRW's move into POS's was largely a defensive tactic. The electronic credit authorization business it had pioneered in the 1960's was coming under increasing competition. Then NCR, the overall leader in POS machines, launched a POS system incorporating credit checking in 1975. TRW attempted to enter the market with an established customer base by acquiring the service contracts for the 65,000 customers Singer had built up during its short, ill-fated move into the POS market. TRW remained cautious, however, only delivering 200 to 300 machines in 1976, mostly to the May Co. Altogether that year non-food retailers ordered 24,500 POS terminals worth $94 million, and the market was picking up.

In 1976 TRW achieved the moment of glory it had long awaited with Viking's historic landing on Mars. The company took out full-page newspaper ads proclaiming "That lab is our baby." Appropriately, Mettler, 52, who had pushed for TRW to compete for the Viking contract, was named to succeed Horace A. Shepard as chairman and chief executive officer when Shepard retired the next year.

Aerospace ventures continued to play an important role in the company's finances. In 1977 TRW was still the chief engineer for U.S. intercontinental ballistic missiles. Aerospace and government electronic revenues were providing a cool $60 million in profits on revenue of $440 million. The electronics division had $300 million in sales. The data communications unit was also doing well with over $150 million in sales. It had established a retail credit bureau, a business credit system, and was an international maker of data equipment. But auto and commercial parts were still accounting for twice as much in sales and five times as much in earnings.

In 1980 TRW and Fujitsu Ltd., Japan's largest computer maker, formed a joint venture that aimed to grab a large share of the U.S. market. TRW had a 3,000 person service organization, reportedly the largest independent network in the U.S. for data process maintenance, with a special team to develop software. Each company invested $100 million, with Fujitsu keeping a 51% share and TRW 45%. TRW initiated the venture, seeking a foreign partner to perform maintenance work for its POS's. Fujitsu, which gets 68% of its revenue from data processing, was eager to expand overseas to increase its economy of scale to compete with IBM back home. Fujitsu named a majority of the directors of the new company so it could qualify for Japanese export and financing tax breaks. But TRW took charge of running it. One of new company's first moves was to buy TRW's ailing POS and ATM maker division. The company, hoping in the beginning to capture a large segment of the small and medium size computer market, predicted sales of $500 million to $1 billion by the decade's end.

Despite TRW's careful planning, the POS and Fujitsu deals both proved unsuccessful. The competition from established POS makers, particularly IBM and NCR, was too great. Nonetheless, TRW remained a strong, highly visible company. *Forbes* in 1983 called it "a paragon" for other conglomerates. It had by then grown to $5 billion in sales spread across 47 different businesses, and had 300 locations in 25 countries. It had also grown to be the number one producer of valves for automobiles and aircraft plus a wide range of other products. With a 16% return on stockholders' equity as proof, *Forbes* called TRW one of the best managed, most successful American companies. The company has had only four chief executive officers in fifty years.

In 1985 TRW reaffirmed its allegiance to its oldest division by completing two joint overseas operations in auto parts. One was in South Korea and one in Malaysia, both to produce steering and suspension components.

TRW's highly defined business strategy and excellent management have earned it the reputation for being the best run of the conglomerates. If the company continues its past tradition, and there are no signs to the contrary, TRW should strengthen its already considerable position in acrospace research and technology and the automotive and commercial parts industry.

Principal Subsidiaries: ESL Inc.; TRW Automotive Products Inc.; TRW International Finance Corp.; SMP Inc.; TRW Electronic Products Inc.; TRW International Sales Corp. The company also lists subsidiaries in the following countries: Brazil, Canada, Japan, the United Kingdom, and West Germany.

Further Reading: The Little Brown Hen That Could: The Growth Story of TRW Inc. by Ruben F. Mettler, New York, Newcomen Society, 1982.

VEBA A.G.

Karl-Arnold-Platz 3
D-4000 Dusseldorf 30
Federal Republic of Germany
(0211) 4579–1

Public Company
Incorporated: 1929
Employees: 68,683
Sales: DM35.890 billion (US$18.481 billion)
Market Value: DM11.778 (US$6.065 billion)
Stock Index: Berlin Hanover Munich Hamburg
Dusseldorf Frankfurt

In 1855 a rather unusual path of immigration was followed when William Thomas Mulvaney, an Irishman, moved from London to Germany. Mulvaney was born in Northern Ireland in 1806 and began his working life as a surveyor in London. In the great restructuring of the British Civil Service, Mulvaney was among the many who were made redundant. In Germany he used his surveying skills to select for purchase a number of coal fields in Westphalia. He employed new procedures for the construction of extremely efficient mine shafts, which put his mines ahead of others in production. By 1865 his 1230 miners were mining 330,000 tons of coal per year, much more than others with the same number of miners. After the war of 1870–72, coal prices fell and Mulvaney's Irish shareholders sold out. In 1873 he formed, with two German banks, the Hibernia & Shamrock-Bergwerksgesellschaft zu Berlin, with 5.6 million marks as capital. Mulvaney served as the chairman of the board until his death in 1885.

Mulvaney was followed by Leo Gräff, who saw the company through the depression of the 1880's and a strike in May 1889 when 80,000 miners walked out. Shortly after the end of the strike, Gräff died and was replaced by Carl Behrens, who led the company through a period of expansion. In 1904 the Prussian state acquired 46% of the shares in Hibernia, against a large and organised opposition of banks and mining groups. In 1917 the state bought the rest of the shares.

The Prussian state had bought up a number of companies, and, in 1929, formed Vereinigte Elektrizitäts und Bergwerke A.G. (VEBA) out of three of them: Hibernia, the Preussischen Bergwerks- und Hütten AG (Preussag), and the company the state had formed in 1927, the Preussischen Elektrizitäts-AG (Preussenelektra). The purpose of the formation of VEBA was to entice inter-national financing for the companies. No foreign capital was invested, though some internal investments were obtained.

At the same time, a businessman named Hugo Stinnes was creating what would become the biggest business concern in German history. Born in 1870, Stinnes was the grandson of the successful coal merchant Mathias Stinnes. Hugo learned business in Coblenz, and the trade in the mines of Wiethe, where he worked for a few months, and then in the School of Mines in Berlin. Upon graduating, he was taken into his grandfather's firm. He left when he was 23 and, with a capital of 50,000 marks founded his own firm, Hugo Stinnes A.G.

Initially, Hugo Stinnes followed the same business path as Mathias. He bought mines, built ships, and set up coal depots throughout the North, Baltic, and Mediterranean seas. He founded in 1897, with August Thyssen, Mülheimer Bergwerksvereins in order to acquire more mines. He bought into the huge Deutsch-Luxemburgische Bergwerks- und Hütten A.G., a company which had grown from 1 million marks at its founding in 1901 to over 100 million in 1910. Its growth was largely due to its voracious appetite for other companies. Stinnes was also involved in the massive expansion by amalgamation of the gas and electricity supplier Rheinisch-Westfälische Elektrizitätswerk A.G. From 1909, he had begun to build up a trading centre for his businesses in Hamburg, and it was here that he was most active during World War I.

Under the guise of the patriotic industrialist helping his country's cause, Stinnes took over every business he could. He was a welcome guest at official functions and served as an advisor and supplier to the government. Thus given free rein, he bought out, in 1916, Eduard Woermann and acquired the Hamburg-Amerika and the Norddeutscher-Lloyd, and the shares in the Woermann and German East African lines. The following year he bought the entire business of the coal merchants H.W. Heidmann. He then bought a couple of hotels, one of which he turned into offices for his empire. After wiping out his competitors at home, he moved toward those in the occupied countries of Belgium and France, amalgamating and incorporating at will, and encouraging the German government to deport Belgian workers. After the war, Stinnes was accused by Erzberger of deliberately causing the ruin of the French coal mines and of robbing the Belgian workshops. Erzberger was later murdered by a revolutionary gang.

Stinnes, unperturbed by the damage done to his business by the peace terms, continued after the war as he had done before. The Deutsch-Luxemburg concern had been most seriously damaged, so in 1920 Stinnes arranged for its merger with the Gelsenkirchener Bergwerks A.G., founded in 1873 by Emil and Adolf Kirdorf, to form the Rheinelbe Union. He linked this with the Siemens-Konzern, which dealt in electrical appliances, instruments, automobiles, and trucks. The huge Siemens-Rheinelbe-Schuckert-Union now had absolute control of both supply and market. With a capital of 615 million marks, it was bigger than even the Klöchner group, and made Stinnes the most powerful businessman in Germany, if not in Europe.

Stinnes may have sensed a lack of popularity, particularly with the press. He tried to woo them by purchasing book publishers, paper mills, book binders, printers, and, finally, a few newspapers. For variety, he bought an automobile factory, the Esplanade Hotel in Berlin, and a few other hotels in Thüringen. Lastly, he began to move into banking, where he met his greatest opposition.

Stinnes once said that he worked so hard in order to make money for his children. If so, it did them no good. Within a year after his death, in 1924, his sons had argued with the directors of the empire and with the banks their father had offended, and the whole concern collapsed. Hugo Stinnes Jr. did get some American backing to form a couple of new companies, the Hugo Stinnes Corporation in New York, and Hugo Stinnes Industries. The last remains of his father's empire can be found in Rheinisch-Westfälische Elektrizitätswerk A.G., Essen (RWE).

While VEBA's Hibernia did not profit so much from the First World War as did Stinnes's business, it survived, as a state-owned business, very well in the 1930's. In 1933 the company was politicised, and in 1935 Wilhelm Tengelmann was appointed chairman of the board. Hibernia was a major participant in the Third Reich's Four Year Plan, and converted some of its works into armaments factories. It managed to avoid bombing by the Allies until 1944, and by the end of 1945 the works were all repaired and in full operation again. After the War, most of the members of the board were arrested; one managed to disappear.

For the rest of the 1940's, the board was not permitted to act independently. In 1952 a new board was formed, with 21 members, and a period of expansion began. There were major extensions to chemical works and power plants. In 1956, because of the high cost of coal production, VEBA turned to oil production. At this time, Hibernia and Stinnes were discussing a merger, but it was not until 1965 that Hugo Stinnes A.G. joined VEBA. Preussag did not recover so quickly and, in 1959, was partly privatised, with VEBA retaining only 22.4% of the shares. Again, in the 1960's, when VEBA experienced financial difficulties, it was decided to sell some shares to the public, and to use the money to finance the subsidiaries. Initially, share prices were high, but when they dropped VEBA bought quite a few of its own shares. This led to an investigation, which was dropped. The court was satisfied not only that VEBA needed to buy its own shares, but that it had committed no crime in failing to mention its purchases in the annual report for that year.

Soon afterward, another VEBA subsidiary built the first nuclear power plant in West Germany.

Rudolf von Bennigsen-Foerder was appointed chairman of the board in 1971. He immediately tried to improve VEBA's image, and embarked upon a grand reorganization scheme. One part of this scheme involved the disbanding of Hibernia, and of putting nearly all of its shares into VEBA Chemie A.G. Soon after, Hibernia's name was deleted from the public register of companies. VEBA was restructured along four main lines of operation: the supply of energy, chemicals, glass, and trade-transport services. The concern seems to have inherited some of Hugo Stinnes's talents, for twice, in 1973 and then in 1979, the Federal Antitrust Commission ruled against VEBA's share dealings. In both cases, the Commission's ruling was ignored and the deals permitted by means of "ministerial permission." By this time, VEBA had some 900,000 shareholders, and was the biggest joint stock company in Europe.

Rudolf von Benningsen-Foerder remains at the helm, occasionally selling off a company or two or buying a few others. In 1987 the government's last 25.55% was sold and VEBA became a public company. Finally free of government ownership, the group hopes it is also free of political, particularly anti-nuclear, parties. The net group profit for the first half of 1986 was DM303 million, and a pre-tax profit of DM778 million. If it ever can get approval, the group hopes to invest some of this money in the proposed Borken nuclear power plant. The next five year plan includes expansion in existing areas of business as well as experimentation in new ones.

Principal Subsidiaries: Chemie-Verwaltungs A.G..; Chemtrans Gesellschaft für den Transport Petrochemichser Flüssigkeiten mbH Duisburg; Gesellschaft für Energiebeteiligung mbH; Gewerkschaft ver. Klosterbusch; Gewerkschaft Morgenglück; Hannover-Braunschweigisch Stromversorgungs A.G.; Hibernia Industriewerte GmbH; Huls A.G.; Induboden GmbH; Indupark Grundstucksverwertung GmbH; Kommanditgesellschaft Unitrakt Bauträger- und Verwaltungsgesellschaft mgB & Co.; Preussische Elektrizitäts A.G.; Ruhrkohle A.G.; Stinnes A.G. The company also lists subsidiaries in the following countries: Australia, Austria, Belgium, Brazil, Denmark, France, Greece, Italy, Ivory Coast, Japan, The Netherlands, Norway, Senegal, South Africa, Spain, Sweden, Switzerland, United Kingdom, and the United States.

WHITTAKER CORPORATION

10880 Wilshire Boulevard
Los Angeles, California 90024
U.S.A.
(213) 475-9411

Public Company
Incorporated: July 31, 1947
Employees: 8,600
Sales: $1.124 billion
Market Value: $367 million
Stock Index: New York

The Whittaker Corporation grew from a manufacturer of aircraft valves in the 1940's to a conglomerate of nearly 140 widely diversified businesses. Until Joseph F. Alibrandi stepped in as president in 1970, the company faced impending bankruptcy. Although it is now much smaller and more manageable in size, nevertheless, Whittaker continues to struggle with maintaining a continuous and stable product line.

In 1947 engineer William R. Whittaker borrowed $4,800 to begin the manufacture of aircraft valves. Later he broadened the product line through an acquisition to include the production of guidance instruments. In 1956 the company merged with one of the first commuter software companies and the newly formed company assumed the name of one partner—the Telecomputing Corporation. Despite the reorganization, William R. Whittaker remained the top executive and principal shareholder of the company.

The further acquisitions of Monrovia Aviation Corporation and Narmco Industries allowed the company to enter into the manufacture of metal and non-metal materials. This shift in product orientation is attributed to Whittaker's desire to diversify away from its dependence on U.S. military contracts. Although the company had grown into a $60 million manufacturer of aerospace components, it remained vulnerable to trends in defense industry expenditures. In addition to the acquisitions, Whittaker's growth strategy included implementing cost control measures and performance records. The company now adopted the name of its founder and became the Whittaker Corporation.

To guide the company through this period of reorientation and growth, William Whittaker looked for a new president. He found his ideal executive in 1964 in the person of William Meng Duke, a Ph.D. in engineering from UCLA. Duke's previous management positions included senior vice presidency at Los Angeles' Space Technology Laboratories and head of International Telephone & Telegraph Corporation's U.S. Defense Group. Possessing both an impressive amount of scientific knowledge and a talent for business, Duke's leadership potential seemed well matched to Whittaker's goals. As the company founder moved up to the position of chairman, Duke attempted to prove his business acumen.

In the next five years, through an aggressive and expansive program of acquisition, Whittaker grew from an obscure Los Angeles-based company to a complex of 80 diverse companies with a total annual sales of $753.4 million in 1969. Although Whittaker's business ranged from manufacturing pleasure boats to industrial chemicals, Duke did not consider his company a conglomerate. According to Duke, 70% of Whittaker's products remained related to some aspect of the integrated manufacture of metal and non-metal materials. Whether in processing alloys, chemicals or ceramics, Duke claimed his company could produce not only a variety of materials but also could construct a product tailored to a customer's particular needs.

Wall Street analysts observed the spectacular rise in Whittaker's stock price. From less than $1 a share in 1964, the stock price rose to $46 a share in 1967. Despite such growth, however, a number of problems began to surface. As late as 1967 nearly one-third of Whittaker's business remained tied to military contracts. In particular, $30 million in volume was generated from products, such as helicopter blades, used in Vietnam. Moreover, the management of such a wide variety of businesses became troublesome. At the Columbus-Milpar subsidiary, for example, an undetected problem in inventory build-up and quality control caused a major profit loss. And finally, the number of acquisitions had put tremendous financial strain on Whittaker's resources.

By 1970 the company was operating on a $332 million debt. Stock prices dropped to $6 a share. To remedy the situation Joseph F. Alibrandi, a 41 year old executive from the missile's systems divisions at the Raytheon Company, assumed the position of president. Alibrandi took immediate action by selling nearly a quarter of the 135 aquisitions. The company's net income rose and long term debt was significantly reduced. While these improvements brought tangible results, a number of surprise setbacks illustrated the types of difficulties facing the new top executive. One setback involved the attempted sale of the Crown Aluminium subsidiary. A $6 million inventory shortage cancelled the sale and forced Whittaker into the embarrassing situation of regaining control of the subsidiary. Another problem surfaced when Whittaker's housing subsidiaries falsely anticipated a $2.8 million profit.

Despite these setbacks Alibrandi continued his five-year program to restructure the company. Strict financial and organization guidelines were mandated to all levels of operation. The assiduous young executive was soon promoted to chief executive officer. The son of Italian immigrants, Alibrandi exhibited shrewd leadership skills while refusing the many perks associated with his high-level position. Of the 50 remaining businesses at Whittaker, Alibrandi planned to concentrate on five areas of growth, including technology, industrial chemicals, recreational products, transportation, and metals. These distinct areas were eventually absorbed into wholly owned divisions.

By 1976 Wall Street analysts once again looked favorably on Whittaker's performance record. A welcomed increase to Whittaker's business came with a $100 million contract from Saudi Arabia to establish a health care program. Alibrandi had made prior contacts with the Saudis during his employment at Raytheon; he had managed the Hawk missile installation project. Using these former contacts, Alibrandi proposed the health-care management contract to the Saudi Arabian ministry of defence.

In the marine division the company constructed a line of recreational yachts. The Columbia division manufactured luxury sailing yachts requiring costly hand labor. Although these boats were sold at high prices, the division reported a $5.6 million loss. While many crticized Alibrandi for investing in an area of business that did not fit well with Whittaker's other operations, the president defended the division as a future profit maker.

Although the original five-year plan actually required seven, by 1977 the company reported two consecutive years of earnings growth. This achievement occurred despite major obstacles in two areas of business. A hydraulic device plant in France experienced difficult labor problems and a freight-car manufacturing operation depleted its order backlog. Whittaker's greatest source of profits emerged from the life sciences group. The renewed Saudi Arabian contract contributed $150 million over the next two years and products developed out of cancer research generated approximately $1 million.

As Whittaker's product lines continued to strengthen their performance, the metal division emerged as the company's largest operation. Moving into a highly diversified business of metal products, the group generated 42% of total sales in 1978. Included in this division was the manufacture of railroad freights, which now held a backlog of orders worth $200 million. The technology division volume, comprised of the hydraulic equipment business and the aerospace component operation, increased due to a growing demand for products. In the marine division, Whittaker became one of the largest producers of commercial fishing vessels and recreational boats.

Despite these gains Alibrandi's major business thrust remained in the life sciences and chemical groups. Through the Saudi contract Whittaker was now the United States' largest healthcare service supplier to a foreign country. A $10 million contract to build a hospital in Abu Dhabi increased Whittaker's overseas presence. To augment growth Alibrandi planned future expansion in the areas of biomedical testing, healthcare management consulting, and specialty chemicals. By 1980 five new chemical companies subsidiaries joined the division. In addition, Alibrandi sold the less profitable chemical operations and hired a new group of executives.

In 1981 Alibrandi announced a strengthened commitment to healthcare. In an effort to alleviate the company's dependence on the cyclical markets of chemicals, metals and marine vessels, Alibrandi planned to make healthcare Whittaker's major line of business. Through a number of acquisitions the president and chief executive officer hoped to construct an integrated hospital supply and management company.

Even as the company experienced disappointments over the next several years, Alibrandi continued to expand the company's orientation toward healthcare. Several successful acquisitions reported less impressive performance records than was anticipated and two attempted acquisitions failed. Even more disturbing was the fact that the Saudi Arabian contract was awarded to a competitor. Despite these setbacks, Alibrandi invested $100 million in building a nation-wide network of Health Maintenance Organizations; an investment, it is said, that he hoped would become the foundation of Whittaker's business. The first of these HMOs was purchased in Norfolk, Virginia, and Alibrandi hoped to acquire ten similar organizations by the end of 1985.

Although Health Maintenance Organizations represented Whittaker's new market strategy, the pursuit of growth through specialty chemicals and aerospace equipment was not abandoned; between 1985 and 1986 Whittaker acquired five additional chemical subsidiaries and five defense electronic and aerospace subsidiaries. Ranging from manufacturers of enamel stripping to producers of coil coating, these new businesses attempted to strengthen Whittaker's diversified technologies.

A surprising turn of events in recent years have significantly changed Whittaker's business orientation. The company suddenly announced it was selling its HMO businesses to the Travelers Corporation. Although Alibrandi claimed he never planned to remain in the health maintenance field on his own, analysts attribute the abrupt shift to cost overruns. Critics now accused the company of lacking a stable product line. Furthermore, the hospital supply business reported disappointing figures, the chemical division continued to suffer from cyclical markets, and the aerospace operations remained subject to trends in defense spending.

In the most recent episode of Whittaker's shifting market orientations, the company stated it would sell all of its healthcare and metal production businesses and concentrate on chemicals. Wall Street analysts applauded this decision as an attempt to regain a company focus. The purchase of Du Pont's adhesive business, for example, increased Whittaker's sale of adhesives to 25% of total sales in chemicals. The company also announced it would buy back 6 million of its 12.8 million outstanding shares. While some analysts interpret this action as a protective move by management to defend against a possible takeover attempt, other analysts interpret it in the opposite way where the stock repurchase represents an attempt to attract a potential suitor. While Whittaker maintains it is not a takeover target, the company's precise business orientation remains a question of the future.

Principal Subsidiaries: Acrodyne Industries, Inc.; Bennes Marrel S.A.; Cochran Systems, Inc.; Compass Financial

Corp.; Falcon Research Col.; Great American Chemical Corp.; Holborn Reinsurance Co.; Holex Inc.; Medical Systems Export Corp.; Metropolitan Financial Services Corp.; Riva Boats International S.p.A. (Italy); Thixon, Inc.; ToxiGenics, Inc.; Whittaker Controls, Inc.; Whittaker General Medical Corp.; Whittaker Health Services, Inc.; Whittaker Healthcare Ltd. (Cayman Islands); Whittaker International N.V. (Netherlands Antilles); Whittaker International Services Co.; Whittaker Life Sciences International, Ltd.; Whittaker Life Sciences, Ltd. (U.K.); Whittaker M.A. Bioproducts, Inc.; Whittaker Marine Export Corp.; Whittaker Medical International Ltd. (U.K.); Whittaker Metals Corp.; Whittaker Metals, Inc.; Whittaker Oil & Gas Corp.; Whittaker Purchasing Services Ltd.; Whittaker Survival Systems (U.K.) Ltd. (U.K.); Whittaker Technical Products Export Corp.

GRACE

W.R. GRACE & COMPANY

1114 Avenue of the Americas
New York, New York 10036
U.S.A.
(212) 819–5500

Public Company
Incorporated: June 20, 1899
Employees: 78,523
Sales: $3.726 billion
Market Value: $2.617 billion
Stock Index: New York Amsterdam Basle Hamburg
Geneva Lausanne Zurich London Paris Frankfurt

J. Peter Grace, W.R. Grace & Company's chairman and grandson of the founder, has a habit of buying companies on a whim. On a trip to Washington, D.C., he purchased 80% of The American Cafe after eating one meal there. However, it's doubtful that anyone at the company was surprised by Grace's action. He had previously purchased Far West Restaurants after eating at a branch in Phoenix and Coco's restaurants after eating at an outlet in Newport Beach. Over the past 41 years Grace, the longest reigning chief executive officer at any major company, has bought and sold 150 companies. At one time or another the company, in addition to its current role as fifth largest chemical company, has been the world's largest distributor of spaghetti, a cowboy apparel retailer, and owner of an airline. It may be hard to believe that W.R. Grace & Company started out shipping guano, or bird droppings, from South America.

In 1854 William Russell Grace and his father James Grace travelled to Callao, Peru. James, a prosperous Irish landowner, wanted to establish an Irish agricultural community. He hoped to rebuild the family fortune which had been depleted during the Irish famine of 1847–48 when he provided employment to a large number of people from the countryside around his estate. Not finding the prospects he had hoped for in Peru, James soon returned to Ireland.

William, however, remained in Peru and became a clerk in the trading firm of Bryce & Company. His value to the company was recognized after a few years when he was made a partner in the firm, which was then renamed Bryce, Grace & Company. Under William's direction the commercial house soon became the largest in the country.

Poor health forced William to retire from the Peruvian business in 1865. He returned to New York City where he

had spent a year during his youth. His brother, Michael P. Grace, who had joined him earlier in South America, remained behind to manage the growing family business in Peru which was soon named Grace Brothers & Company.

With his health fully recovered, William established W.R. Grace & Company in New York. William had long been a confidant of the Peruvian president, and through this connection the company became the Peruvian government's agent for the sale of nitrate of soda.

The Chile-Peruvian war of 1887–81 severely weakened Peru's economy, and the government had difficulty repaying its foreign debt. In 1887 a group of foreign bondholders in the Peruvian government, mostly British, called on Grace Brothers & Co. to attempt a settlement of the debt. Michael accepted the offer and in the settlement he negotiated, known as the Grace-Donoughmore Contract, two Peruvian bond issues amounting to $250 million were cancelled in exchange for equally valuable concessions to the bondholders. Bondholders received shares in a newly-established company, The Peruvian Corporation, which received the rights to two state-owned railroads for 66 years, all Peruvian guano output up to 3 million tons (except for that on Chincha Island), a government promise to pay shareholders 80,000 pounds sterling annually for thirty years, and ownership of the lucrative Cerro de Pasco silver mines. In return, the shareholders agreed to finish uncompleted railroads and repair existing ones within certain time limits. (Most of the contracts for supplying the railroad building program went to the Grace company).

At the time of the company's incorporation in Connecticut in 1899, Grace listed capital of $6 million. The amount, however, undervalued the company's worth since it did not include Grace Brothers & Co. Limited in London and its branches in San Francisco, Lima, and Callo, Peru as well as Valparaiso, Santiago, and Concepcion Chile.

When William Grace died in 1904 control of the company passed to Michael who became chairman. In 1907 he negotiated a new agreement with the Peruvian government anulling the terms of the previous agreements and extending the Peruvian Corporation's lease for 17 years. The government agreed to continue paying £80,000 annually to shareholders for 30 years, but made claims to one half of the company's net proceeds.

William's son Joseph, who started working for the company's corporate offices in New York in 1894 when he graduated from Columbia University, became President in 1909. The company underwent a period of rapid growth during Joseph's presidency and in the process greatly expanded South American production and trade.

In 1929, the year Joseph became chairman of the board, W.R. Grace and Pan American Airways together established the first international air service down the west coast of South America, Pan American Grace Airways otherwise known as Panagra.

After suffering from a stroke in 1946 Joseph retired. A feud subsequently broke out among family members over who should run the company. Eventually Joseph prevailed and his son J. Peter, after some misgivings of his own, became president.

At the age of 32 Peter inherited a company with $93 million in assets and whose primary interests were in

Grace Steamship Lines, Grace National Bank, Panagra, sugar plantations and cotton mills in Peru and Chile. The company also produced paper and biscuits, mined tin, and grew coffee.

From the very beginning Peter was concerned about the political and economic instability of South American nations that he believed threatened Grace's operations. In particular, many companies had shown resistance to U.S. domination of their economies. With what proved to be remarkable foresight, Peter embarked on a plan of diversifying into U.S. and European investments, seeking to reduce South American investments from 100% to 5%. To raise the capital necessary for his expansion the company went public in 1953. The board of directors resisted his plan of broadening investment and, though the Grace family owned more than one half of the company's stock, he nearly lost his position as chief executive officer.

Attracted by profits achieved by Dupont, Peter began searching for investments in the chemical industry. He purchased two major chemical companies which made Grace the nation's fifth largest chemical producer. In 1954 Grace completed a merger with Davison Chemical Corporation, a manufacturer of agricultural and industrial chemicals. Later that year Grace purchased Dewey & Almy Chemical Company, an investment one industry analyst later called "among the greatest acquisitions of all time." A producer of sealing compounds and batteries, Dewey and Almy grew rapidly and earnings quickly surpassed the $35 million purchase price. This became the foundation for one of the world's largest specialty chemical operations. Over the next 11 years Grace acquired 23 more chemical companies for four million shares of stock.

Seeking to enter markets which could compensate for the cyclic nature of the fertilizer industry, Grace set out to build the "General Foods of Europe." Over the decade Peter Grace purchased a chocolate producer in the Netherlands, a Danish ice cream maker, and an Italian pasta company. Critics charge that he was searching for companies he could shape and manage himself, attempting to prove he was his ancestors' equal as an entrepreneur.

Peter continued selling the company's old businesses and using the money to acquire new ones. In August of 1965 he sold Grace National Bank to what is now Marine Midland Bank. The next year he acquired a 53% interest in Miller Brewing Company. And in 1967 Peter sold the company's 50% interest in Pan American Grace Airways to Braniff Airways for $15 million.

The late 1960's proved a difficult time for Grace. The fertilizer market became severely depressed, once a source of substantial profit. Facing falling profits Grace attempted to boost efficiency by closing marginal plants, but in the process the company incurred huge losses.

In the meantime, relations between Grace and Miller Brewery's minority stockholder, an heir to the company's founder, had turned for the worse. Peter realized he would never be able to buy the rest of the company. Thus, in 1969 Grace sold its holdings in Miller for $130 million, resulting in a net profit of $53.9 million.

In the early 1960's the company management had reversed its previous policy in regard to South American investment and began pouring funds into paper, food and

chemical companies. Later that year, however, Grace's fears about these investments came true when the Peruvian government seized the company's sugar mills and a 25,000 acre sugar plantation. Earnings on South American operations tumbled from $12 million the previous year to zero on sales of $256 million. Peter, not discounting the possibility of pulling completely out of the region, said that company investments in future would be made on the attitude of each individual country.

In the early 1970's, Grace made a move into consumer goods. In 1970 the company purchased Baker & Taylor, a supplier of books to libraries, as well as F.A.O. Schwarz, the New York toy store. And hoping to cash in on America's love affair with leisure-time activities, the company acquired Herman's World of Sporting, a landmark in New York's financial district.

Grace saw a chance for substantial returns in the sporting goods business. Involvement in the market was especially attractive since there were no national sporting goods chain stores. Department stores, preferring the profits and turnover of apparel and other "soft" product lines, had shunned sporting goods. The company sought to expand Herman's from 3 stores with $10 million in sales into the first national chain. As part of the plan Grace bought Mooney's of Boston, Atlas of Washington, and Klein's of Chicago and converted them to Herman's sporting goods stores.

In 1971, the year Peter became chairman, the company's profit was at its lowest point in years after hitting a high of $82 million in 1966, and its return on equity was well below that of other conglomerates. Extraordinary (or one time only) writeoffs, became such a regular part of the company's financial statements (just that year the company wrote off $7.8 million from closing fertilizer plants) that some security analysts had come to consider them a regular part of Grace's operations. Consequently it was not surprising that in 1972 company executives produced a 700 page memo establishing twenty criteria for acquiring a new business. Most importantly, these executives decided that in order to be purchased a company must have $20 million in sales and $1 million in profits.

In 1974 Peter began to reduce the company's holdings by selling a grocery products venture, and began to concentrate company investments in three areas: consumer goods, chemicals, and natural resources. Fertilizer profits had rebounded because of low supply and high worldwide demand, but the consumer groups showed lackluster profits even with large sales in sporting goods. In addition, Grace's final investment in Peru was severed later in the year. The Peruvian government nationalized its paper and chemical operations, leading to a loss of $11.5 million for the company, despite $23.6 million in compensation from the government.

By 1976 the company was ready to continue its move into consumer goods and services. Later in the year, when the company was about to make a public stock offering to raise capital for further expansion, it received an offer from Peter's old friend Friedrich Karl Flick, who during the 1950's had worked for Grace National Bank for three years. Flick, head of Friedrich Flick Industrial Corporation, Germany's largest family owned company, was looking for somewhere to invest the $900 million it had recently made from the sale of its 29% interest in Daimler-Benz to Deutsche Bank.. Wanting to take advantage of German laws that granted tax free capital gains and dividends earned on investments of more than 25% ownership in foreign companies, Flick eventually bought a 30% stake in Grace.

Though the Grace family interest in the company had dwindled to 3%, Peter made it clear that Flick would not run the company. Receiving seats for only 3 of the company's 35 directors, Flick nonetheless obliged since he was concerned with his own business ventures in Europe.

The consumer divisions' growth accompanied increasing internal strife at the company. In 1979, after years of watching the company's stock trading at low earnings multiples, management proposed splitting up the company into seven or eight separate companies which would command higher stock prices. Worried about the company's increasing reliance on consumer products, they also suggested selling the energy division whose market value could have been as much as $1 billion over book value. Peter, unwilling to give up his control of the company which might also have resulted from these proposals, rejected both ideas.

At the beginning of the 1980's Grace's move into natural resources appeared as if it was going to be as profitable as its venture into chemicals. The company's energy reserves had grown to 73 million barrels of oil, 300 billion cubic feet of natural gas and 239 million tons of coal. Specialty chemicals sales and earnings, meanwhile, rose an average of 15% annually over the last decade. The company had 85 product lines from plastic packaging materials to petroleum cracking catalysts, many of which were market leaders.

However, the company suffered with falling energy prices in 1981. Moreover, in 1982 the combination of a poor natural resources profit and a further decline in the fertilizer business led to a 50% decrease in the company's profitability. As a result, Grace petroleum was put up for sale in 1984. The retail and consumer goods divisions, which were returning just 14% of profits on 36% of sales, looked like they might be next.

The company's problems were compounded in 1984 when Flick became the target of a government bribery scandal and was forced to confront a $260 million dollar tax bill. Rumors abounded in West Germany that Flick was looking for someone to buy the family business, putting Grace at risk of a hostile takeover.

The rumors about Flick proved true when Deutsche Bank acquired the company and put its holdings in Grace on the market. The company immediately seized the attention of takeover specialists, since Grace's assets could be sold at a profit of $20 to $25 more than the market price. GAF Corporation Chairman J. Heyman approached Grace about a friendly takeover, causing Grace's stock to rise 30%.

Peter, fearing a takeover, was forced to buy Flick's holdings for $598 million, though already severely strapped for cash. The acquisition put Grace's debt at $2.6 billion and caused a downgrade of Grace's credit rating.

Critics, both inside and outside the company, regarded this as an unthinking decision. Complaints about Peter's domination of the company and an incoherent business strategy put mounting pressure on him to sell the consumer division. Since Grace was desperate for cash, this forced Peter to comply. Energy and fertilizer investments were reduced. Herman's was sold to Dee Corporation for $227 million, realizing a profit of $144 million. The remaining consumer goods businesses were sold for $500 million, but because of high expansion costs at the 317-store home center operations, Grace barely broke even on the sale. In addition, Peter agreed to selling 51% of the restaurant division to its management in a leveraged buyout. In light of these events, speculation arose that Peter might resign.

For the moment Grace's days of rapid expansion and wide diversification are at a halt. Management has called for selling all energy and fertilizer investments and concentrating on specialty chemicals, where the company has been losing some of its market lead in recent years. As a result, executives say that the company is undergoing a transformation from being one of the last of the family controlled companies to being a more conventionally-managed corporation.

Principal Subsidiaries: Akapaw Inc.; Alewife Boston Ltd.; Alewife Land Corp.; Amargosa Pipeline Corp.; American Carry Products Corp.; Amicon Far East, Ltd.; Annie's Santa Fe of Kansas, Inc.; Antilles Chemical Co.; Arrow Inter-American Corp.; Axial Basin Coal Corp.; Beckett Golf Club, Inc.; Bermanns Far East Ltd.; Berry Gas Co.; Booker Drilling Co., Inc.; Camillus Acres, Inc.; Caribe Nitrogen Corp.; Carrows Beverages, Inc.; Carrows Restaurants, Inc.; Chomerics, Inc.; Coalgrace, Inc.; Commercial Sites, Inc.; Cox Marketing, Inc.; Cramer Advertising Associates; Creative Food 'N Fun Co.; Creative Restaurant Concepts, Inc.; Darex Puerto Rico, Inc.; Daylin-Summitt, Inc.; Devcoa Inc.; Dewey and Almy Co.; De Zaan, Inc.; Drilling Mid. Inc.; Duncan, Lagnese and Associates, Inc.; Ecarg, Inc.; Ecotrol, Inc.; ELF Aviation, Inc.; E L Liquidating Corp.; Elson T. Killam Associates, Inc.; El Torito/Milwaukee, Inc.; Food Distributing Corp.; F.P. Ott's/Madison, Inc.; Gilbert/Robinson, Inc.; GPC Marketing Co.; GPC Transporter, Inc.; Gracoal, Inc.; G/R Texas Enterprises, Inc.; F/R of Penn, Inc.; GRC Ice Cream Co.; Hanover Square Corp.; Momco International, Inc.; HTIG Interiors Inc.; Hungry Tiger Inc.; J.B. Robinson Jewelers, Inc.; Jet and Go, Inc.; Killam-Dearborn Environmental Engineers, Inc.; Leather Bottle NO. 1, Inc.; Liquor Lounges, Inc.; Lobster House; LKS Enterprises, Inc.; Mar-Ral, Inc.; M-B Food Distributing Co., Inc.; Metaramics; Monolith Enterprises, Inc. (80% owned); Mount Bundey Mining, Inc.; New American Restaurant Corp.; NRG Eastern Coal Development, Inc.; Ochoa Fertilizer Co., Inc.; Offshore Fisheries, Inc.; Ole's, Inc.; Ole's Nevada, Inc.; One Hundred West of St. Louis, Inc.; Panana Inc.; Process Evaluation and Development Corp.; Red Steer, Inc.; Restaurant Supply, Inc.; Ridgewood Chemical Corp.; Ridgewood Phosphate Corp.; Sam Wilson's/Kansas, Inc.; Seriglif, Inc.; Seven Hanover Square Corp.; Sheplers Catalogue Sales, Inc.; Sourgasco II Corp.; Southern Oil, Resin & Fiberglass,

Inc.; Standard TransPipe Corp.; Stantrans, Inc.; Stopover Restaurants, Inc.; Support Terminal Services, Inc.; Toco Villa, Inc. (83.5% owned); Tia Marie-Washington, Inc.; TVS Merger Corp.; 2701 Corp.; Ven-Tech One, Inc.; Water Street Corp.; Woodward Chemicals Corp.; Woolwich Sewer Co., Inc.; Woolwich Water Co., Inc.; W.R.C.

Technical Ventures, Inc. W.R. Grace also has subsidiaries in many European countries.

Further reading: "Arms, Guano, and Shipping: The W.R. Grace Interests in Peru, 1865–1885" by C. Alexander G. de Secada, in *Business History Review* (Boston), 59, 1985.

CONSTRUCTION

A. JOHNSON & COMPANY H.B.
BARRATT DEVELOPMENTS PLC
BECHTEL GROUP, INC.
BILFINGER & BERGER BAU A.G.
BOUYGUES
DILLINGHAM CORPORATION
FAIRCLOUGH CONSTRUCTION
  GROUP PLC
FLUOR CORPORATION
JOHN BROWN PLC
JOHN LAING PLC

KAJIMA CORPORATION
KUMAGAI GUMI COMPANY, LTD.
LINDE A.G.
MELLON-STUART COMPANY
OHBAYASHI CORPORATION
THE PENINSULAR & ORIENTAL STEAM
  NAVIGATION COMPANY
  (BOVIS DIVISION)
TAYLOR WOODROW PLC
WOOD HALL TRUST PLC

✕ THE AXEL JOHNSON GROUP

A. JOHNSON & COMPANY H.B. (since 1988: AXEL JOHNSON GROUP AB)

Jakobsbergsgatan 7
S–103 75
Stockholm
Sweden
08 788 50 00

Private Company
Founded: 1873
Employees: 3,383
Sales: Skr17.00 billion (US$2.50 billion)

The Axel Johnson Group of Stockholm comprises two legally and financially independent companies, Axel Johnson & Co. HAB, also of Stockholm, and Axel Johnson & Co., Inc. of New York. All North American activities of the Group are conducted by the New York company, and interests in the rest of the world (there are subsidiaries and offices in some 30 countries) are controlled from Stockholm. The Group's business is in five distinct areas: raw materials (oil, coal, ore and metals); engineering and industrial products (through Johnson Construction Company, a subsidiary of Nordstjernan AB, the Group is very active within construction); electronics; industrial investments; and global marketing and distribution.

The company's beginnings can be traced back to 1873 when Axel Johnson, then in his 30th year, officially established himself with the Stockholm Board of Commerce as an agent for foreign companies. "In addition to the chemical house in London," he wrote his brother in August 1873, "I have an agency for harvesting machines and one for clothing, also one from Cologne for scrubbing brushes, one from Dresden for textiles, two from Bremen for wool tape and one from Berlin for aniline dyes." Axel Johnson had obtained some of the agencies from W. Ullberg & Co., a leading Stockholm store, for whom he had worked for about three years, latterly as head clerk and silk importer. Before long, he discontinued several of the Ullberg lines but added cheese, wine and cognac. The wine company, Musotte & Girard of Bordeaux, failed soon thereafter but Johnson held the cheese agency for about ten years.

In July 1874, still struggling to make a living from his business, Axel became engaged; ten months later, he was married. By this time, his agency was advertising imports such as Portland cement, coal, coke, chemicals for paper and glassworks, and saltpetre. Many of these products came from Great Britain, and it was to this country, and to Russia and Germany, that Johnson directed much of his attention. An office in London, set up by an associate, Lorentz Tidén, facilitated Johnson's many dealings with British firms. Of notable importance was Johnson's connection with the South Yorkshire Steam Coal Owners Association; both Johnson and Tidén recognized the increasing importance of coal imports to Sweden. The firm's first shipments of the high quality Yorkshire coal were made in the spring of 1875 and within a year Johnson had estalished his firm as a prominent coal importer. Before the end of the decade, A. Johnson & Company was also importing Newcastle coal.

A depression in the late 1870's led to many bankruptcies in Stockholm, but Johnson's diligence kept his company afloat. His major concern was the credit-worthiness of some of the companies he supplied; if several of his clients failed, he would too. The firm's major disappointment was in sales of matches. In his second year of operation, Johnson had purchased an interest in a Swedish match company, but overproduction had outstripped demand.

But while Johnson's match business remained a problem, his representation of Swedish ironworks became a significant and · profitable part of his business, largely because of his connection with the Avesta ironworks in southern Dalarna. Johnson had first established contacts with the company in 1875, and four years later he formalized an agreement with the ironworks management. He was granted, with certain restrictions, exclusive agency rights in many Swedish cities for the Avesta plant's thin steel sheets which were in great demand in Sweden's construction industry. At the same time, the Avesta company agreed to fill all of its coal requirements through A. Johnson & Co., provided his prices remained in line with those of other coal suppliers. Soon Johnson was importing other essential items for steel mills—ferromanganese, silicon, pig iron, cement and fire bricks from Great Britain, and coke from Germany.

But despite the ever increasing amount of business, Johnson, who was both enterprising and cautious, kept his office staff to a minimum. He also maintained irreproachable relations with his bankers and was extremely solicitous of his firm's reputation. His careful business practices paid off, and during the 1880's, the firm began to prosper. Johnson finally decided to increase the number of his staff and improved his sometimes unsatisfactory bookkeeping system.

As Johnson accumulated liquid assets, he began to invest in real estate in the Stockholm area and formed the Hornsberg Land Company with three other investors. He was also instrumental in the establishment of the Stockholm Southern Transportation Company, and in 1883, his firm acquired a two-thirds stake in a lumber yard in the southern part of Stockholm where Johnson had lived with his wife and son since 1877. (The son, Axel II, was born in the previous year).

By the autumn of 1882, Johnson and his family (now there were four sons) were installed in a new and fashionable residence befitting Johnson's increasing prominence in the business world. It was a time of greater prosperity and Johnson's enterprises flourished.

There was a modest fall in profits in mid-decade, but as the 1880's drew to a close, results were better than ever. Johnson's holdings by 1890 were ten times what they had been in 1880. Throughout the period, Yorkshire coal accounted for almost half of the firm's purchases, and business connected with Avesta Jernverks AB (the steel company had been reorganized in 1883) remained brisk. By early 1884, Johnson was selling Avesta steel in parts of Britain.

However, by 1890, business between Avesta and A. Johnson & Co. dropped to almost nothing (Johnson's attempts in the 1880's to gain control of the ailing steel company had not been successful) and Johnson turned his attentions to shipping, an area in which he had plenty of experience.

The company's first freighter, purchased in 1885, did not make money and was sold in less than three years. But the Annie Therese, acquired in 1890, became the founding vessel of the Johnson Line. The Annie Therese plied her trade between the Baltic and the North Sea with timber and iron for Britain and coal on the homeward run. By 1905, A. Johnson & Co. owned a North Sea freighter fleet and had become involved in the development of a transatlantic shipping company. At this time, Johnson, now something of a magnate, realised an aim which had eluded him for years; he purchased Avesta Jernverks.

Axel Johnson, who had not enjoyed good health, died in 1910 and his son, Axel II, took over the company reins. One of his first acquisitions was an oil refinery which produced fuel for the firm's ships (the Johnson fleet was the first to be powered entirely by diesel engines). While he had been provided with a solid financial base, Axel II had to contend with the economic upheaval of two world wars and the Great Depression.

At first, A. Johnson & Co., like most Swedish firms, benefitted from World War I. As a neutral power and a major exporter of raw materials, Sweden traded vigorously with both sides; however, as Swedish stocks were rapidly depleted, numerous exports became subject to licence and the company grew concerned that both its export/import business, and its shippping interests, would be seriously affected. An agreement with Great Britain in March 1918 provided for limited imports of vital British goods in exchange for the loan of a large part of the Swedish merchant fleet; A. Johnson & Company was kept busy.

After the war, as Sweden recovered economically in step with the rest of the world, the company expanded. It built more ships, acquired a shipyard, and purchased several civil and mechanical engineering firms. The Depression, and grave labor conflicts in Sweden naturally had a profound effect on the company; but the younger Johnson's expansionist policies and the continuation of his father's efforts to diversify, helped the company to weather harshly adverse conditions.

Again neutral in World War II, Sweden tried to protect itself from isolation, and as early as December 1939 it reached a war trade agreement with Great Britain. But the German invasion of Denmark and Norway put Sweden and its industries in a very difficult position. A. Johnson & Company, along with many other Swedish firms, carried on as best as it could and waited anxiously for the end of hostilities.

As an international trader, A. Johnson & Company was particularly concerned by Sweden's isolation during times of European hostilities. Axel Johnson II therefore built on his father's activities in the U.S. market, and sent his son, Axel III (born in 1910, the year his grandfather died), to New York to strengthen the company's ties there. Meanwhile, Axel II tackled the job of rebuilding the company after the devastations of the war. It was no easy task. European recuperation was unexpectedly slow and the temporary elimination of Germany from world trade seriously affected Sweden's recovery program; indeed the country experienced an economic crisis which led to massive cuts in Swedish imports.

By 1951 however, there were signs of major improvements and during the next 15 years, Sweden's total production increased by 66%; in the same period, home consumption rose by 50%. There was good news too for the company in the U.S. Axel III had successfully expanded the American part of the business, and in 1953 he returned to Stockholm to help his father. In 1956 he assumed the presidency of Nordstjernan, a separately administered company which controls, among other things, the important Johnson shipping interests. Upon the death of his father in 1958, Axel III also became president of the parent company.

The third generation Johnson ran the family business for a little over two decades; he retired in 1979 because of failing health and died in February 1988. His period in office was a time of continuing expansion and diversification; while interests in shipping and exports of raw products remained strong, the company reflected the growing importance to Sweden of its manufactured exports. As in the past, A. Johnson & Company invested heavily in the industries it represented as a marketing agent or shipper.

In part, the company's increasing interests in electronics, medical instruments, chemicals and industrial products were developed to offset the problems besetting the petroleum industry. The financial crisis of 1974 and the subsequent economic uncertainties following in the wake of numerous OPEC decisions, as well as the now-entrenched difficulties of heavy industrial operations, were causes for alarm; Johnson suffered some serious setbacks.

In 1986, the Group's raw materials operations reported unsatisfactory earnings; oil business was particularly low since the company decided against trading in a market with sharply declining prices. Activities in stainless steel, chemicals and electronic components also suffered, but the operations of Axel Johnson Instrument AB had a successful year, with increasing sales and favorable profitability.

The present chairman of the newly-named Axel Johnson Group is Antonia Johnson; born in 1943, she is the daughter of Axel Johnson III. Axel Johnson & Co. HAB, Stockholm is presided over by Göran Ennerfelt, and his counterpart at Axel Johnson & Co. Inc., New York is John Priesing. The days when the company was confused with wax floor polish and baby powder are over, and the present administration looks to the future with cautious optimism.

Principal Subsidiaries: Araliace AB; Axel Johnson International AB; AB Kratos; Nortex Electronics AB; Nynas AB; Rederi AB; Lexi R. Ribbert AB; KAB Kjellberger AB; AB Axel E. Madsen; J.P. Myhre Son Eftr Ab; Nordick Electra AB; Svensk Teknisk Byra AB; Fastighets AB Vildmannen (66%). The company also lists subsidiaries in the following countries: Brazil, Canada, Denmark, Finland, France, Greece, Mexico, Norway, Singapore, South Africa, Spain, Switzerland, United Kingdom, United States, and West Germany.

BARRATT DEVELOPMENTS PLC

Wingrove House
Newcastle upon Tyne NE5 3DP
England
091–286–6811

Public Company
Incorporated: 1958
Employees: 4,340
Sales: £444.3 million (US$602 million)
Market value: £277.6 million (US$408.1 million)

Barratt Developments plc is one of the smaller companies in the construction industry. Yet the firm's size is no reflection upon its growing importance. While building houses is the company's primary business, in recent years Barratt has become involved in a broad range of projects. The most successful of these new activities are the urban renewal operations and the leisure property developments.

The company was founded in Britain in 1958 by Sir Lawrie Barratt. Barratt's original intention was to provide private housing for first-time buyers. This strategy proved to be very lucrative: after a slow start, between 1977 and 1979 alone turnover increased from £99.3 million to £163.2 million. The impressive rise in sales propelled Barratt to the forefront of the British housing industry.

For years prior to Barratt's success, over one-third of new construction activity in Britain had been subsidized by the government. By early 1980, however, this situation had changed; the Thatcher administration drastically reduced appropriations for all building programs, especially public housing. Although the company was initially hurt by the decision, later it was compensated by Thatcher's tax incentives to private homeowners. By 1982 sales surpassed £300 million and the company had built over 1,000 units more than its closest competitor, Wimpey's plc.

By the mid-1980's, Barratt decided to expand its product line. After conducting an exhaustive review of the British housing market, Barratt developed a range of individually designed houses. This series, called the Premier Collection, offered over 60 different house types from which to choose, including retirement and luxury residences.

Barratt management also decided to shift its marketing emphasis away from first-time customers in order to attract second and third-time homeowners. Because of escalating land prices due to the lack of available residential space, Lawrie Barratt thought it too difficult for the company to meet the needs of first-time buyers. As a result, Barratt would concentrate on satisfying the growing consumer demand for larger homes.

However, at the same time the company began building larger private residences, it also initiated a number of successful projects designed to rehabilitate existing urban properties. Joint ventures with city councils, organizations and lending institutions led to affordable housing for urban residents while halting the deterioration of inner-city properties.

In addition to these renovation projects, Barratt also participated in novel development programs for cities throughout Britain. One such plan included offering shared ownership of dwellings through housing associations and subsidized rents for low-income tenants. Another effort, the Charlotte Square development in Newcastle upon Tyne, resulted in the construction of inexpensive and attractive modern housing within the city's ancient walls. This marked the first time an industry leader in building private homes committed such large resources to urban renewal.

In 1980, the company created Barratt American Inc., a California-based subsidiary. The U.S. was chosen as a site for expansion due to its thriving housing market and economic stability. Through direct sales, identifiable market segmentation, and low prices, it quickly entered the highly competitve market. In a few years, Barratt successfully established itself as one of the leading firms in the American housing industry.

The most innovating aspect of Barratt's U.S. marketing strategy is the package deal available to first-time buyers. The company offers everything from domestic furnishings to trade-in deals on old homes, and American customers often need only make a small downpayment in order to become residents of a Barratt house.

Barratt sells its products through Sears, Roebuck & Company where potential customers can browse through a fully furnished condominium display. By selling small, inexpensive units in this way, the company has provided a new opportunity for consumers formerly excluded from purchasing a home. While the average price of a California house hovers around $120,000, a Barratt unit can be purchased for $50,000. With these marketing programs, Barratt hopes its trademark becomes as recognizable as that of an American car manufacturer.

Yet, while Barratt's American subsidiary has captured a significant portion of the housing market in southern California, it has recently experienced difficult times. Rising unemployment, high interest rates, low housing starts and the lengthy approval process to secure planning permission to sell some of its units have all contributed to a decrease in sales. Nonetheless, Barratt remains confident that California's rising population and its growing affluence will work in favor of the company's U.S. investment.

In addition to its U.S. subsidiary, Barratt has home-building operations in 40 locations around Scotland and England. In addition to these holdings, Barratt has lately exhibited a talent for the development of leisure properties. Seven luxury resorts, constructed by Barratt Multi-Ownership and Hotels Limited, are located in attractive settings of the Scottish Highlands, Snowdonia and the New Forest. Furthermore, Barratt's timeshare apartments in Costa Del Sol, Spain have had an impressive market reception. This led the company to construct two new resorts on the Mediterranean coast. These developments offer vacationers attractive dwellings in addition to generous amenities. Today, Barratt stands as Europe's market leader in timeshare apartments.

Barratt also participates in an area within the industry known as property investment and construction. By concentrating on specialist building contracts in the industrial and commercial sectors, the company has gained a large financial return. Successful projects include the construction of an office building of bronze tinted glass and natural stone in Glasgow and the completion of factory units at the Stoneywood Industrial Park in Aberdeen.

While the company has a long way to go in achieving its goal of ranking first in the U.S. homebuilding market, Barratt continues to perform well overall. Having grown in just under 30 years from a small operation into a network of subsidiaries both in the United Kingdom and California, Barratt has a very promising future in the worldwide construction industry.

Principal Subsidiaries: Barratt Scotland Ltd.; Barratt Northern Ltd.; Barratt Midlands Ltd.; Barratt Southern Ltd.; Barratt South East Ltd.; Barratt American Inc.

BECHTEL GROUP, INC.

P.O. Box 3965
San Francisco, California 94119
U.S.A.
(415) 768–1234

Private Company
Incorporated: 1925
Employees: 25,000
Sales: $6.8 billion

One industry analyst has noted that Bechtel's achievements as the largest United States construction and engineering firm have reshaped more of the earth's landscape than virtually any other human efforts in history. As a private and predominantly family-controlled company, Bechtel has long been averse to publicity, an attitude which has sometimes been problematic in light of the firm's numerous links to prominent U.S. government officials. Although as a private company Bechtel is not required to publish financial information about its operations, 1985 estimates suggest the company generated $8.6 billion in revenues.

Most of Bechtel's business comes from building traditional electric utility plants, although the company has also played a key role in the development of the domestic and foreign nuclear power industries. The downturn in the economy during the early 1980's, and the concurrent recession in energy-related industry, compelled Bechtel to consolidate its operations by reducing the workforce, diversifying into areas outside its traditional markets, contracting jobs previously considered too small, and providing operating services for existing power plants.

In 1884 when he was 12 years old, Warren A. Bechtel moved with his family from a farm in Illinois to the frontier area of Peabody, Kansas. After graduating from high school, Bechtel ventured unsuccessfully into a music career. When "The Ladies Band" failed, Bechtel's father wired return fare to the stranded slide trombonist. The disappointed musician went back to work on the family farm. Some years later poor farming conditions left Bechtel virtually without any possessions other than a team of 14 healthy mules. When the Chicago Rock Island and Peoria Railway Company pushed westward in 1889, Bechtel gathered up his mule team and worked his way across the continent grading railbed for frontier train lines.

Bechtel eventually sold his mule team, but he continued working for the rail industry in a variety of manual labor positions. He managed to accumulate a small fortune and formed the W. A. Bechtel Company with his three sons and his brother. The young company began many new ventures, including construction of the Northern California Highway and the Bowman Dam, which was at the time the second largest rock-fill dam in the world. By the time the company incorporated in 1925, Bechtel was the largest construction firm in the Western U.S. When a six-company consortium received the $49 million contract for construction of the Hoover Dam, Warren Bechtel became president of the group. Work on the enormous dam lasted from 1931 to 1936. Warren Bechtel did not live to see the project completed, however; he died suddenly in 1933 at age 61.

Stephen Bechtel, one of the founder's three sons, took over the presidency in 1935. He had previously been a vice president. The young executive directed the company to new financial and industrial heights, supervising completion of the Hoover Dam as well as work on the San Francisco-Oakland Bay Bridge, a hydrogeneration plant, and the Mene Grande Pipeline in Venezuela.

As the United States entered World War II, an already established partnership between Bechtel and John McCone, a steel salesman, grew to encompass a syndicate of companies participating in the construction of large shipyards. McCone and Stephen Bechtel had met at the University of California and had become business associates during work on the Hoover Dam. As an employee of Consolidated Steel, McCone secured the supply of necessary support structures for Bechtel. The business association proved so successful that after the dam was finished the former classmates formed a partnership. By 1940 McCone secured contracts for the partnership to build ships and tankers, and to modify aircraft for the war effort. Later the partnership developed the syndicate that built the Calship and Marinship yards in California, as well as a total of 500 ships. When McCone took a postwar position as undersecretary of defense, it was revealed that the directors of Calship earned 440 times their initial investment of $100,000—a profit of $44 million.

Bechtel's operations continued to expand in the years following the war. The 1100-mile Trans-Arabian Pipeline, completed in 1947, is regarded as the first major structure of its kind. The South Korean Power Project effectively doubled that nation's energy output in one move. In 1951 the pioneering company developed the first electricity-generating nuclear power plant, in Arco, Idaho. Later the company built a nuclear fuel reprocessing plant there. By the end of the 1950's Bechtel had construction and engineering projects on six continents and was ready to take advantage of the emerging market for nuclear power.

In 1960 Stephen Bechtel became chairman of the board, and Stephen Jr., a Stanford Business School graduate and grandson of the founder, stepped into the chief executive officer post. A 1978 estimate suggested that the two men controlled at least 40% of company stock. In the likely event of the younger Stephen one day inheriting his father's wealth, it is estimated that he could become the richest person in the U.S. (The other 60% of Bechtel stock is held by some 60 top executives who have agreed to sell back their shares when they leave the company or die.)

With a new generation of leadership in place, the company sought to gain hegemony in the emerging nuclear power industry. In 1960 Bechtel completed the nation's first commercial nuclear station, in Dresden, Illinois. Two years later the company built Canada's first nuclear power plant. Construction in foreign markets began to increase almost immediately thereafter. Although the nuclear power industry subsequently ran into difficulties such as cost overruns, questions about environmental safety, and stiff regulatory measures, Bechtel still continues to promote nuclear energy as a necessary option to conventionally generated power.

Bechtel's construction projects in the 1960's and 1970's included the San Francisco Bay Area Rapid Transit system (BART), the subway transit system in and around Washington, D.C., a slurry pipe in Brazil, and an innovative tar sands project in Alberta, Canada.

In the 1970's two former Nixon cabinet members took executive posts at the company. Later both men, George Shultz and Caspar Weinberger, would leave Bechtel for positions in the Reagan Administration. Bechtel has actively cultivated its ties to the federal government, and employs several former high officials—a fact which bothers critics of the company.

In 1976 Bechtel unveiled plans for its Jubail Project, the largest undertaking ever attempted by a construction company. On Saudi Arabia's Persian Gulf coast, the company is building a futuristic industrial community on the site of an ancient fishing village. The project is expected to be completed in 1996 at an estimated cost of $100 billion. The new city will be the home of Saudi Arabia's integrated petrochemical industry. A 1973 meeting between Stephen Bechtel, Jr. and King Faisal was the catalyst for the plan to haul off 370 million cubic meters of sand and build a modern city complete with a five-million-gallon desalination plant, modular homes, a sex-segregated swimming marina, and a number of factories.

Due in part to a broad political effort aimed at halting the use of nuclear power in the U.S., in recent years the company has had to turn away from nuclear energy to less controversial markets. However, problems in the nuclear power industry persist. A 1978 lawsuit concerning malfunctions at the Palisades nuclear generator in Michigan cost Bechtel $14 million in settlement fees. In addition, a 1984 *Mother Jones* magazine article suggested that in attempting to secure nuclear power contracts in South Korea the company may have violated the 1977 Foreign Corrupt Practices Act through the use of irregular payments. The article also argued that certain Bechtel executives who later became top U.S. government officials may have known the payments warranted investigations by the Federal Bureau of Investigation and the Justice Department but said nothing. (The company issued its employees a point-by-point rebuttal of the article.)

The company was in the limelight several times during he 1970's. A 1972 class-action suit alleging sex discrimination at Bechtel settled out of court for $1.4 million. A bribery scheme involving construction of a New Jersey pipeline led to convictions for four Bechtel employees. Further unwanted publicity arose from the revelation that Bechtel had installed a 420-ton nuclear-reactor vessel backward. Finally, in 1975 the U.S. Justice Department sued Bechtel for allegedly participating in an Arab boycott of Israel, a charge the company denied.

The decade was also a turning point for Bechtel's traditional business in construction and engineering. Prompted by increased government regulation and changing economic conditions, Bechtel embarked on a new program of financing and operational services. Soon after they began, the new divisions contributed 66% of total revenues. To defray increasing construction costs, the company now secures financing for its customers, and in some cases even puts up its own money. Bechtels diversification program also included acquiring a 15% share of the Peabody Coal Company and a major interest in the prestigious Dillon, Read & Company investment firm. By 1982 over half the company's business involved overseas markets.

During the Reagan presidency Bechtel's ties to the federal government increased considerably. Shultz left the presidency of Bechtel Corporation to become Secretary of State after Alexander Haig, former chairman of United Technologies, left the post in 1982. Weinberger, previously the Bechtel general counsel, was Secretary of Defense for the first seven years of the Reagan administration. By 1984 Bechtel's connections in Washington also included CIA director William Casey, Middle East special envoy Philip Habib and former CIA director Richard Helms, all of whom had worked for the company either as employees or as consultants in the past.

Stephen Bechtel, Jr. is now chairman of the board. Alden P. Yates, Bechtel president, has led the firm into numerous projects previously regarded as too small for Bechtel. These include finishing jobs abandoned by the company's competitors and actively seeking contracts, even those as small as $2 million. Furthermore, remodification and modernization efforts at existing plants offset the lack of contracts for new construction. Finally, the company's operating services division keeps skilled experts at work in their fields, mostly in ongoing maintenance of existing facilities. Despite measures to locate new sources of income, Bechtel had to cut its workforce in 1984 to 35,000 (from 45,000 in 1982).

With new Bechtel offices open in New Delhi and Beijing, and a large amount of construction underway in the Pacific Basin, industry analysts predict that in the future approximately 70% of the company's business will be abroad. While Bechtel consolidates its business and enters new markets, it continues to maintain an impressive presence within the international construction industry.

Principal Subsidiaries: Bechtel Western Power Corp.; Bechtel Eastern Power Corp.; Bechtel Inc.; Bechtel National, Inc.; Bechtel Limited; Hydro & Community Facilities Division. The company also has subsidiaries in Argentina, Australia, Brazil, Canada, Chile, China, Egypt, France, Indonesia, Korea, Saudia Arabia and Spain.

Further Reading: The Bechtel Story: Seventy Years of Accomplishment in Engineering and Construction, San Francisco, The Company, 1968.

BILFINGER & BERGER BAU A.G.

Carl-Reiss-Platz 1-5
Mannheim, Bad-Wuertt 6800
Federal Republic of Germany

Public Company
Incorporated: 1975
Employees: 22,300
Sales: DM3.922 billion (US$2.019 billion)
Market value: DM2.119 billion (US$1.091 billion)
Stock Index: Berlin Düsseldorf Munich Hamburg

Bilfinger & Berger, a large West German construction company, is an amalgamation of smaller enterprises that were all founded around the turn of the century. The constituent firms' combined capabilities give Bilfinger & Berger the potential to bid worldwide on projects virtually of any scale. The company is well known for using the most current design and construction methods creatively. Indeed, it and its predecessors helped develop many of these techniques.

The company's present structure is the result of the 1975 merger of Grün and Bilfinger A.G. and Julius Berger-Bauboag A.G. Founded in 1892, Grün and Bilfinger incorporated in 1906. Berger-Bauboag was itself the product of a 1969 merger. Bauboag was founded in 1890 as a public construction firm named Berlinische Bodengesellschaft; it built thousands of apartments and many banks, stores and shopping centers. Julius Berger, also founded in 1890, incorporated in 1892 as Julius Berger-Civil Engineers.

In his first ten years in business, Julius Berger concentrated on railway, road and bridge construction. He quickly earned a solid reputation with the government and received contracts for hundreds of miles of railways and roads. In 1893 alone he built 22 stretches of railroad across Germany. August Grün was co-director of a successful company with experience in water-related civil engineering projects. When Grün's partner left the firm in 1892, Paul Bilfinger, an engineer working for the government, stepped in. At that time the company already employed 250 people and had accumulated equipment and experience in a broad range of construction areas.

From the start of their partnership, Grün and Bilfinger bid on a wide variety of engineering projects. The firm entered the international arena in 1907 when it built a 45-mile stretch of railway in Hungary. In the same year, Berger's firm began work on jobs outside its previous

focus, building a canal in Hamburg, a dam and power station in Blesen, and hydraulic control installations on several German rivers and canals. In 1909 the two firms collaborated on a project for the first time, widening the 61-mile Kiel Canal, an important shipping route connecting the North and Baltic Seas.

Both firms landed major foreign contracts in 1911. Grün and Bilfinger entered a joint venture with another enterprise to build ship-landing stages at Swakopmund. Julius-Berger won an international competition for the five-year contract to construct the five-mile Hauenstein Tunnel in Switzerland. By 1913, both firms had expanded their international activities to less developed countries. Grün and Bilfinger began excavation work in Tanga (German East Africa) and Cameroon in 1912, and Julius Berger began surveying for road projects in southwest Africa, Costa Rica and Colombia the following year. Between that time and the firms' merger in 1975, their combined efforts accounted for a large share of the road, rail, bridge and dam development in Africa, southwest and southeast Asia, and Central and South America. Both firms specialized in modernization of inter-city travel and efficient re-direction of busy inner-city routes. The merged entity has continued the effort.

Julius Berger made a crucial move in 1914 when it launched its own mining activities. From then on the firm's standard practice in international contracts was to set up its own mining operations on or near each construction site. The firm would adapt its established formulas to fit the local supply. Julius Berger has saved millions of marks on materials over the years by collecting its own ores and soils instead of buying from suppliers.

Both firms frequently played vital roles in the German government's travel systems improvement plans. Along with their traditional work on roads and railways, the firms received several subway building contracts, beginning with one for the Berlin underground in 1915. They undertook many water-related jobs as well, including widening and re-channeling rivers, digging and dredging canals, and building locks and dams.

In the period between the world wars, both firms saw rapid growth in the international market. Among the larger projects Julius Berger engaged in during this time were the Trans-Persian railway in Iran (1923) and the Benha Bridge across the Nile in Egypt (1930). Grün and Bilfinger worked on a sewage system for Salonika, Greece (1926); reinforced concrete roads in the center of Montevideo, Uruguay (1926); an underground railway in Athens (1927); 16 miles of tunnels for a drainage system and subway in Buenos Aires (1928); and the Carioba Dam in Brazil (1934), among others.

The burst of international activity declined to a near halt after 1935. The slowdown lasted through the end of World War II, but the two firms sustained themselves with work on the projects Adolf Hitler had begun in 1933 in an effort to ease unemployment in Germany. Hitler's programs included construction of the autobahns, a network of asphalt and concrete highways that would crisscross the nation. Both firms were at the top of the list of bidders, and they received several contracts. Many stretches of the autobahns called for long and high bridge sections, each requiring individual planning and, often, creative designs. The challenging requirements kept engineers who had been working in exotic locales and unusual terrain stimulated.

During World War II both Julius Berger and Grün and Bilfinger built several airports and naval installations. Like most other German companies, they spent the two years after the war clearing rubble, making emergency track and bridge repairs, and repairing damaged railway stations, roads, dikes, and housing and industrial properties.

By 1950 Julius Berger had resumed its activities abroad, building pumping stations in Egypt and the Managil Canal in the Sudan. Also in 1950, Grün and Bilfinger employed a new method in bridgebuilding, using prestressed concrete for the first time on a railway bridge in Heilbronn. The method of pouring concrete around metal-cable frames quickly became the most popular and effective use of concrete, and is still common.

The German post-war administration hired both Julius Berger and Grün and Bilfinger to build series of telecommunications towers. The first went up in 1952, and the projects soon became a staple in the companies' logbooks. Between 1969 and 1977, they built a total of 18 of the structures. At the same time the companies began constructing numerous hydro-electric power plants, usually in conjunction with a dam or barrage. Julius Berger was a leader in modifying the technology involved in hydro-electric power.

Both companies also continued to be innovators in bridge construction technology, and through the late 1950's were leaders in water-related engineering projects, building dams, bridges, port installations, locks and power stations around the world. One of their biggest accomplishments during the era was a joint venture formed to build the 5.5-mile prestressed concrete Lake Maracaibo Bridge in Venezuela.

After World War I the Bauboag firm had changed its building focus from apartments to commercial and industrial structures. Through the 1950's and 1960's it built stores and malls, universities, and industrial plants. Julius Berger wanted to enter the field, but rather than expand from within, it merged with Bauboag in 1969. The marriage was immediately successful; later the same year Julius Berger-Bauboag received contracts to build the National Library in Berlin and to do stuctural work at Munich's Olympic Stadium. The stadium job included a cycle-racing track, flyover access roads and a new metropolitan train station.

In 1968 another joint effort would bring Grün and Bilfinger together with Julius Berger on a work site. The success of the project, a long autobahn tunnel in Hamburg, led in 1970 to Grün and Bilfinger acquiring a majority holding in Julius Berger-Bauboag. The two enterprises merged formally on December 29, 1975 and took the name Bilfinger & Berger Bau A.G.

Although a recession hit the international building industry in 1973, Bilfinger & Berger flourished throughout the 1970's. The two larger constituent companies began building nuclear power stations and offshore oil-drilling rigs early in the decade. In addition, since 1975 the merged Bilfinger & Berger has received sustained funding from the European Community and West Germany's Federal Ministry of Research and Technology to develop its innovative concrete articulated tower, which consists of a ball-and-socket joint between a drilling tower and its foundation on the ocean floor. The structure greatly reduces the stress caused by wind and waves. The firm has also built some of Europe's largest sewage treatment plants over the past 20 years.

The international division of Bilfinger & Berger is very active. The United States subsidiary is Fru-Con Corp. of Baldwin, Missouri. Some of the better known projects it has worked on since 1975 are two nuclear power plants in Illinois (at Clinton and Baldwin), subway systems in Washington, D.C. and Atlanta, and the space shuttle launching complex in Vandenberg, California. The subsidiary Julius Berger Nigeria, Ltd., based in Lagos, has modernized much of the transportation infrastructure in that country since 1970. The firm has also been involved in the design and construction of the new Nigerian capital at Abuja. Bilfinger & Berger has completed roadwork totalling over 330 miles in the Tripoli area in Libya in the past decade. Through the 1980's projects abroad have accounted for 60% to 70% of the firm's total construction volume.

Bilfinger & Berger is a classical example of a successful civil engineering and construction firm. The company has taken on projects of all scales by solving the problems at hand efficiently, combining existing methods with its own creative new ideas wherever necessary. Bilfinger & Berger has left its mark around the world and is likely to continue making an impact with new construction technologies.

Principle Subsidiaries: BBSE Systems Engineering GmbH; B&B Vorspanntechnik GmbH; Gottlieb Tesch GmbH; GBF-Fertigbau-Gesellschaft mbH; GKW Consult; **GKW Ingenieure; Grund- und Pfahlbau GmbH;** Propria Bauträger-und Verwaitungs-gesellschaft mbH; Modernbau GmbH; Sönnichsen & Görtz; Wilhelm Scheidt. The company also lists subsidiaries in England, Indonesia, Italy, Malaysia, the Netherlands, Nigeria, Saudi Arabia, and the United States.

BOUYGUES

381 Avenue du General-De-Gaulle
Clamart Cedex
France 92142
33–630–23–11

Private Company
Incorporated: 1952
Employees: 15,900
Sales: FFr45.02 billion (US$7.00 billion)

The rise of Bouygues in the French construction industry may be attributed to the personal attention its founder has given to each of the company's projects. Francis Bouygues (pronounced 'Bweeg') has built his company through dedication and a commitment to expansion. The company has completed numerous large-scale construction projects both in France and around the world and, while the industry is currently weathering a recession, Bouygues has been able to maintain its growth by pursuing more diverse and profitable lines of operation.

Prior to 1952, Francis Bouygues worked alongside Eugène Freyssinet, a construction pioneer who revolutionzed the industry through the introduction of prestressed concrete. With a sense of vision inspired by the works of Freyssinet, and an entrepreneurial spirit which would become his trademark, the young engineer used a $1700 loan acquired from his family to set up a small firm which operated from his apartment.

Much of Bouygues' work lacked the glamour of his future achievements. Yet Bouygues immersed himself in every aspect of his business, from driving a truck to managing construction sites. His first construction jobs included the renovation of old factories and pre-dawn repair work at the Lido cabaret.

It was not long before Bouygues had made a name for himself; positive trends in the industry afforded Bouygues many opportunities to demonstrate his business acumen. To ensure the ready identification of the company's projects, Bouygues became one of the first firms to paint its equipment uniformly in one color, "minimum orange."

As the construction industry expanded during the 1950's and 1960's, due mainly to large public works projects, the rate of employee turnover became problematic. Competition among companies to hire workers was so acute that employees of Bouygues worked an average of only six months. In order to halt this trend, Bouygues created an elite corps of workers in 1963 called the *Compagnons du*

Min-orange. Identified by the company color, this cadre of membership-only employees displayed greater dedication to the company, were less likely to leave Bouygues, and asked for fewer salary increases.

Membership in the *Compagnons* requires nomination by a site manager and approval by a committee of *Compagnons.* Only one in ten nominees gain admittance. Members of the corps wear uniforms with badges or stars indicating rank. Although membership assures job security, members can be demoted, should they prove unworthy of their rank. *Compagnons* are rewarded with long weekend holidays to such vacation spots as Sardinia, Istanbul, and Dubrovnik. Bouygues' plan has worked well; employee turnover decreased noticeably.

With a force of committed workers in place, Bouygues proceeded to make impressive gains in the industry. During the 1950's and 1960's the company erected several subsidized housing projects in Paris. The company's first large-scale project was the Parc des Princes soccer stadium, awarded to Bouygues in 1969. While the contract marked Bouygues' entrance to the higher ranks of the industry, Francis Bouygues' enthusiasm failed to conceal a certain degree of inexperience.

An extremely complex design, combined with the need for custom-made precast concrete, threatened the project from the start. When the first column erected began to slide, a school near the construction site was evacuated. With his reputation at stake, Bouygues quickly assumed personal control of the project and instituted corrective measures. When the project was completed (ahead of schedule), Bouygues' profit from the job was negligible. However, Bouygues earned great respect for its efforts, and soon new orders began to accumulate.

Unlike industry competitors, Francis Bouygues insists on complete control of his projects. And even though he was compelled to form partnerships on several occasions, he nevertheless avoids these arrangements as much as possible. In one instance, a joint highway contract placed Bouygues at one end of a road and the company's partner at the other end. Joint work commenced only when the two roads were connected.

Another example of Francis Bouygues' management style is shown by his decision to create a company union in 1968. This came at a time when the industry was plagued with labor disagreement and strikes. As members of a separate union, Bouygues employees never joined these strikes. Bouygues later encouraged his employees to gain affiliation with the Force Ouvrière, a politically conservative nationwide union, largely opposed to the more militant Confédération Générale du Travail. Force Ouvrière organized many of Bouygues' employees, although as late as 1982, 70% elected to remain exclusively with the company union. Even more significant than its lack of union organization, Bouygues employees have very few grievances; all are generally well-paid.

Bouygues' successes in and around Paris continued to grow as the company completed power plants, an airport passenger terminal, a conference center and numerous skyscrapers. By the mid-1970's Bouygues announced plans to expand on two fronts: in the remainder of France, and overseas. Domestic operations centered on the private home building industry. The Maison Bouygues division built homes to satisfy individual tastes at inexpensive prices. By the early 1980's Bouygues had become the largest home builder in France.

The company's late entrance into overseas markets compelled Bouygues to bid lower than its competitors for an Iranian contract to build the 1974 Asian Games stadium in Teheran. Bouygues' price was 30 to 40% less than those of larger industry veterans such as Bechtel—Bouygues won the contract. This project led to further contracts to build residences in Iran and to perform repairs on the Shah's palace. Using the revolutionary concrete truss design of the Asian Games stadium, Bouygues went on to complete the 1.5-mile Bubiyan Bridge in Kuwait. Business expanded to Iraq, where the company constructed a nuclear power plant (destroyed by Israeli bombing in 1984). In addition, Bouygues constructed a mosque in Jeddah, Saudi Arabia. Outside the Middle East, the company secured contracts to build power plants and universities in West Africa.

As eager as it was to enter foreign markets, Bouygues was prevented from doing so by strict financial policies which were intended to protect the company from losses in unstable countries. Francis Bouygues refused to work on credit in these high-risk markets, and always remained ready to leave them on short notice; during the Iranian revolution in 1978, Bouygues moved out without incurring any losses.

One exception to Bouygues' reluctance to work with partners came in the late 1970's, when the Saudi Arabian government opened bidding for the construction of King Saud University in Riyadh. Bouygues' desire to maintain his independence was overridden by his ambition; when the Saudi government informed Bouygues that his company was too small to win the contract alone, he formed a partnership with Alabama-based Blount, Inc. Still, Bouygues insisted on a 55% controlling interest in the partnership, which gave him the final approval in all decisions. The 40-month deadline set by the Saudis for the completion of the project discouraged most bidders. By the time the $2 billion contract was to be awarded, all but two contenders had dropped out of the competition. When the contract was finally awarded to the Bouygues-Blount partnership in 1981, it was the largest fixed-price construction agreement ever. Because the two companies stood to lose money if the construction fell behind schedule, Bouygues and Blount completed the project on time and collected an additional $50 million windfall.

Bouygues entered the 1980's with impressive financial credentials and great prestige. Yet changes in both the French and world economies forced the company to change its business strategy. High interest rates, falling oil prices, and a shrinking construction market forced Bouygues to reduce its work force. President François Mitterand's social policies reduced the amount of government funds available for large public works projects. To compensate for the changing economic conditions, Bouygues was also forced to alter its financing methods for overseas projects; the Nigerian government paid the company four months late for a $620 million power plant.

Bouygues initiated a program of diversification in order to mitigate the effects of the beleaguered construction market. An attempt to purchase Druout, a French insurance company, was thwarted when that company's former owners sued to halt the takeover. Later, Bouygues acquired a 55% share of Amrep S.A., an oil services company. In an attempt to broaden its presence in the United States, Bouygues purchased a number of engineering firms and re-organized them as an Omaha-based consortium called HDR, Inc. A larger holding company, called the Centerra Corporation, was also formed to perform work in design, engineering, financing, and construction. Centerra's first large project was construction of the New World Center in Seattle.

Other successful acquisitions included operations in offshore drilling, electrical engineering, battery manufacturing, retailing, and water services. However, the largest of all Bouygues purchases was in the area of construction. France's second largest construction group, SCREG, accumulated a massive debt which made it vulnerable to a takeover. With the addition of SCREG, Bouygues' revenues increased to nearly $7 billion. Through SCREG, which is operated as a subsidiary, Bouygues became involved in the road construction industry.

As Bouygues continues to expand, industry analysts have raised the question of the company's future without its assiduous founder. In 1986 many believed Bouygues' eldest son Nicolas was being prepared to assume leadership of the company, but he suddenly left his father's firm and started his own business. Three other children, including Bouygues' daughter are currently employed with Bouygues. Still, the question of succession remains largely unanswered. Although he has lost a lung to cancer, Francis Bouygues has yet to reduce his work load.

Recently, the company failed to take over Spie-Batignolles, a large French contractor in which Bouygues claimed it had an original 10% interest. Not only was the attempted takeover particularly acrimonious, it resulted in an inquiry in which Bouygues was accused of failing to declare a major corporate interest. [French law requires investors to declare any corporate interest in excess of 10%.] The Commission des Operations de Bourse, the French stock market regulatory committee, later charged Bouygues with failing to declare a 24% interest in Spie-Batignolles.

In April of 1987 Bouygues and a consortium of private investors acquired a controlling interest in TF-1, the leading French national television network. In order to augment its minority share of CGCT, a French telecommunications firm, Bouygues announced plans to expand into the radio telephone market. Bouygues's entry into the broadcasting and communications industry came as its offshore oil operations registered significant financial losses. This diversification effort promises to be Francis Bouygues' greatest challenge; the entrepreneur has not excluded the possibility of entering the publishing industry. How successful Francis Bouygues will be in an industry so different from his original construction business remains to be seen.

Principle Subsidiaries: GTB; Kesser; Mistral Travaux; Norpac; Enterprise Quille; Elan; GFC; GTFC; GCA; Les

Longs Reages; SCREG; HDR, Inc.; Sam Clam; Bafir; Bouygues Offshore; GIE CIG; Bisseuil; Texim et Cie.; Pertuy; Stim; Bouygues Iran; SETAO (74.37%); Univest; Revex; Etudes et Prefabrication Industrielle EPI.

DILLINGHAM CORPORATION

1441 Kapiolani Blvd.
P.O. Box 3468
Honolulu, Hawaii 96801
U.S.A.

Private Company
Incorporated: 1961
Employees: 12,000
Sales: $1.5 billion

The Dillingham company was established in the Hawaiian islands when they were still an independent kingdom known as the Sandwich Islands. As the Hawaiian economy grew, Dillingham expanded from sugar refining and railroad transportation into construction. By the time the company reverted to private ownership in 1983, it had become one of the largest construction companies in the United States, with numerous projects completed worldwide.

Among the first Americans to settle in the Sandwich Islands were a group of New England missionaries, who arrived in 1820. They established themselves in positions of economic and political power, and began a crusade to convert the Polynesian natives to Christianity. From this group of *haole* (Caucasian) settlers emerged five dominant family-run mercantile companies known as "The Big Five." These five companies established commercial interests in every aspect of the Hawaiian economy.

It was in this environment that Benjamin Franklin Dillingham unexpectedly found himself in 1865. Dillingham, a Cape Cod schooner captain, was stranded in the Sandwich Islands after losing his life's savings in a failed commercial venture to ship bananas to California. Temporarily disabled with a broken leg, Dillingham took a job as a clerk in a local hardware store, and within two years the enterprising seaman had become co-owner of the business.

Dillingham married into the *haole* establishment by taking a missionary's daughter for his wife. Still, he was unable to purchase arable land for an agricultural venture; the Big Five maintained a strict monopoly on land. He did, however, manage to buy a tract of wasteland on the island of Oahu. He organized a group of investors to develop the land for sugar cane cultivation, and built a railroad to connect the inland plantation with a wharf. The Oahu Railway & Land Company, as it became known, was highly successful. The company added more real estate and expanded its trackage—Dillingham even started to transport his competitors' sugar.

The native Queen Liliuokalani was deposed in 1893, and a year later the Republic of Hawaii was established with Sanford B. Dole as its president (Dole's cousin Jim founded the Dole pineapple label in 1898). Dillingham gained greater acceptance in the commercial establishment, and attempted to build a second railway on the island of Hawaii. But construction costs mounted quickly, and soon the company was severely in debt. Benjamin Dillingham summoned his son Walter to interrupt his studies at Harvard and return to Hawaii to manage the crisis.

Hawaii was annexed by the United States in 1898, and made a territory two years later. The islands' increased exposure to American shipping traffic led Walter Dillingham to establish a new family venture; with a $5000 loan, he founded the Hawaiian Dredging & Construction Company in 1902. The company's first contract called for the dredging of Honolulu Harbor and Pearl Harbor and, by 1910, had generated enough profit to bring the company out of debt. The coral and sediment drawn from the harbors was used to fill a 5000-acre swamp on the island of Oahu, which made possible a Dole pineapple plantation, a tourist development (later known as Waikiki Beach), and, some years later, an airport.

Dillingham's company diversified into pier services, warehousing, barge transportation, and land development. After the Japanese bombing of Pearl Harbor in 1941, the company joined a 14-member consortium of construction companies whose job it was to build air bases on islands captured from the Japanese.

After the war, Dillingham's companies performed construction work in foreign countries. It was involved in widening the Suez Canal, constructing a harbor in Kuwait, and building a variety of structures in Australia. In the United States, Hawaiian Dredging maintained harbors in the Pacific, and established a strong presence in the mainland construction industry. The company's principal owner, Walter Dillingham, became one of the richest men in Hawaii by the late 1950's. Dillingham's success, however, did not go unchallenged.

For many years the mainland Permanente Cement Company enjoyed a monopoly in Hawaii. Its proprietor, an outspoken 72-year old entrepreneur named Henry J. Kaiser, had done a great deal of business with Dillingham. But, when Dillingham decided to participate in establishing a local competitor, Kaiser returned the challenge. He announced plans to build a cement plant in the islands and, furthermore, to establish a dredging business in Hawaii. The conflict between Kaiser and Dillingham degenerated into personal attacks; Kaiser accused Dillingham of disrupting his business with underhanded tactics. Dillingham called Kaiser an "outsider," and maintained that he had no business being in Hawaii.

Dillingham found itself at the fore of a disturbing trend: Hawaiian markets were no longer isolated from mainland interests. The local establishment was forced to adopt more aggressive business strategies in order to maintain its historical competitive advantages. On many levels Hawaiian businesses banded together in self interest.

Walter Dillingham served on the boards of five major companies, including a newspaper and the Bank of Hawaii. Later, he was appointed to the board of American Factors (a Big Five sugar and real estate conglomerate now called Amfac). Dillingham opposed statehood for Hawaii because he felt the islands would be dominated by the International Longshoremen's and Warehousemen's Union, which he believed was controlled by communists. [In 1949 the union led a strike which paralyzed the Hawaiian economy for 179 days.] In 1959, as Dillingham began to emerge as the victor in its battles with Kaiser, Hawaii was inducted as the 50th state.

Walter Dillingham gradually relinquished managerial responsibilities to his son Lowell. Only one philosophy course short of a degree from Harvard, Lowell returned to Hawaii in 1934 to learn every aspect of the family business. He was named president of Hawaiian Dredging in 1955, and of the Oahu Railway in 1960. In 1961 he oversaw the merger of his two companies to form the Dillingham Corporation, and the transformation of the family business into a public company.

The company began construction of buildings in 1959. One of its largest projects was the $30 million Ala Moana Center, a large shopping complex which nearly doubled the amount of store space in downtown Honolulu. Having decided that the company should pursue a more global perspective, Lowell Dillingham initiated the "Dilco" plan, under which Dillingham would aggressively seek new projects outside of Hawaii. As a result of the program, Dillingham won contracts to build the 43-story Wells Fargo Building in San Francisco, water works in Vietnam, a large hotel in the Philippines, airfields in Thailand, and numerous other structures in Australia. Dillingham also performed harbor improvments in Iran and established a group of seven subsidiaries in Australia, New Zealand, and Papua New Guinea.

The Dilco plan proved enormously successful—profits had risen from $48 million in 1962 to $325 million in 1968. While the Dillingham family was undoubtedly the greatest beneficiary of this growth (they retained 41% ownership of the company), private investors also found Dillingham an excellent investment. After Dillingham gained a listing on the Pacific Exchange, management strived to expand even further in anticipation of a second listing on the larger New York Exchange.

In order to spur growth through diversification, Dillingham acquired two large California-based construction companies, a supplier of liquefied petroleum gas, and a Canadian tug boat company. Dillingham also entered into joint ventures in mining in Canada and Australia but failed in its attempt to gain control of the United Fruit Company. Nevertheless, Herbert C. Cornuelle, a former president of both United Fruit and the Dole Corporation, joined Dillingham as an executive vice president. Cornuelle later became the first non-family executive to serve as company president.

The diversification program encountered problems when it was realized that the company had grown too fast for effective consolidation or efficient management. By 1970 Dillingham had acquired over 30 companies and, while revenues increased 1000%, return on equity fell by 3.9%. As president, Cornuelle had the dual task of raising short term profits while maintaining the company's expansion. He elected to dispense with all marginally-performing assets, and to invest the proceeds in more profitable maritime and natural resource ventures—areas more closely related to Dillingham's established operations.

Dillingham was made more competitive as a result of Cornuelle's strategy. But, because its new profits had not been used to reduce its debt, Dillingham unknowingly became vulnerable to a hostile takeover.

A controversial financier named Harry Weinberg announced that he had acquired a 10% interest in Dillingham. Weinberg demanded representation on the board of directors, complaining that Dillingham's stock was under-valued and that the company's real estate holdings had been under-exploited. Cornuelle responded by reducing the number of board seats from 15 to three. With the situation deadlocked, Weinberg later agreed to purchase some of Dillingham's most promising real estate. Ownership of these properties, which included the Ala Moana Center, was transferred to a limited partnership owned by Weinberg and a group of other shareholders. The partnership later split up the portfolio and sold the properties at a substantial premium over its original investment in Dillingham.

Cornuelle's takeover defense was successful, but Dillingham had lost its most profitable division. In order to support the company's share price, Dillingham's other three divisions—construction, maritime operations, and energy—would have to become more profitable. Management was particularly optimistic about expansion of the energy division, which conducted oil and gas exploration, produced liquefied petroleum gas, and transported oilfield equipment.

Share prices, however, remained weak and, as Dillingham was failing to gain the attention of investors on Wall Street, the company became the apparent target of another takeover. Kuo International, a Singapore-based company run by petroleum interests, announced in 1983 that it had increased its holdings in Dillingham to 7%. Unable to mount a second defense without seriously dismembering the company, Dillingham turned to the investment banking of firm Kohlberg Kravis Roberts & Company for advice. Kohlberg Kravis recommended that Dillingham return to private ownership; as a private company, it would no longer be subject to hostile takeovers or share performance evaluations. A group of institutional investors was created to purchase all of Dillingham's outstanding shares of $350 million (including $30 million for Harry Weinberg's interest). Dillingham management retained a 12% interest in this group, and appointed J. Joseph Casey president and chief executive officer.

Casey has emphasized Dillingham's expertise in construction, and has encouraged greater involvement in higher-risk projects. While this shift in emphasis is expected to incur larger debts in the short term, it will provide the company with greater operational mobility. With plans to acquire a small engineering firm, Dillingham hopes to gain greater involvement in industrial projects. At that time, Dillingham will have regained its position as a fully integrated construction company.

Principal Subsidiaries: Dillingham Corp.; Dillingham Land Co.; Dillingham Construction Corp.

Fairclough

FAIRCLOUGH CONSTRUCTION GROUP PLC

28 Southampton Lane
London WC2A 1AR
England

Public Company
Incorporated: 1959
Employees: 17,000
Sales: £635 million (US$1.04 billion)
Market value: £473 million (US$695 million)
Stock Index: London

Fairclough Construction Group is one of Britain's prominent construction companies. Its growth from a small, local stone mason firm into the nation's most important public works and civil engineering contractor has been a steady, if slow and gradual, process.

Leonard Fairclough was born on November 17, 1853 in Adlington, Lancashire. He apprenticed with a local builder, eventually qualifying as a craftsman mason. By the age of 30 he started his own business in a tiny workshop in Adlington. Within 10 years, however, Fairclough employed enough people to justify building houses for them, a common practice in that era.

Gradually increasing the size of his contracts and expanding the region in which he operated, Fairclough picked up jobs in textile-producing towns and villages all across Lancashire. Monument and artistic masonry was the primary emphasis during the company's early years, along with the construction of chapels, schools, mills, shops, clubs, and small roads and bridges. While building an extension to a public building in Chorley, Fairclough was appointed main contractor and placed in charge of subcontracting. This is one of the first instances of a contracting system now standard in the industry.

At the turn of the century, Leonard Miller Fairclough joined his father's company as an apprentice and worked 12-hour days in its stone quarries. Working his way up the management ladder, Leonard Jr. became a director of Fairclough in 1917. Leonard Sr. died in 1927, and his son was then named governing director of the company, a position he held until 1959. Leonard M. Fairclough is usually credited with directing the company's gradual transition from a regional masonry operation into an influential civil engineering contractor.

Although Fairclough was constantly expanding,

throughout the 1920's most of its business consisted of relatively small-scale projects. In the 1930's, however, this changed. Working with local utility authorities to replace antiquated sewage systems across the countryside, the company laid pipes, dug trenches and dredged canals. Fairclough also won contracts for upgrading and maintaining power stations and factories, and building bridges of increasing size.

During World War II, Leonard M. Fairclough was appointed a regional leader under the Ministry of Works Emergency Organization. His responsibilities including training and directing demolition and engineering teams to deal with the immense damage caused by enemy bombing raids. Also, the government contracted the company to build camps for housing prisoners of war.

Fairclough was kept extremely busy after World War II, as the nation turned to the construction industry for help in repairing its war-torn infrastructure. The newly nationalized operations, including coal, gas, and electrical utilities and railway systems, were funded by massive government reconstruction programs. One large contract for Fairclough involved remodeling 31 railway bridges near Manchester, built as part of the system's conversion from steam to electric power.

Fairclough built its first bridge in Lancashire in 1904, and by the 1950's had accumulated a wealth of experience in the field. For this reason, the British government chose the company to build the small but significant inaugural strip of its planned network of Motorways, near Preston, Lancashire. The company's house journal confidently stated that, "An ounce of Lancashire experience on this eight and one-half miles with its 23 bridges is worth tons of theoretical argy-bargy about the pros and cons of Motorways." This experience quickly paid off as Fairclough was awarded contract after contract to design and construct miles of motorways, including scores of bridges.

By 1983, the company had completed more than 300 miles and over 1000 bridges on the Motorway project. Two of these bridges, noted for their engineering and construction, span the River Mersey, linking Cheshire and Lancashire: the Thelwall Viaduct, a one and one-quarter mile bridge which soars 75 feet above ground to cross the Mersey and the Manchester Ship Canal in one stretch, and the Widnes-Runcorn bridge, the longest single-arched steel span in the United Kingdom.

For all of its large-scale projects, Fairclough remained in the crowded echelon of mid-sized construction companies throughout the 1960's and most of its business was still confined to the northwest region of England. However, having become a public company in 1959, and increasing its capital by the issue of stock over a 10-year period, Fairclough bought C.V. Buchan & Company, of Stone, Staffordshire in October 1970. This firm had worldwide experience in tunnelling, as well as a successful precast concrete plant; Fairclough management turned it into the largest concrete-segment producer in the U.K. The Fram Group, purchased in 1972, expanded Fairclough's range of operations into mechanical engineering, increased its geographical boundaries, and doubled the company's revenues. Sir Lindsay Parkinson & Company was acquired in 1974, adding marine experience and opencast mining to

Fairclough's list of services. Parkinson helped to expand the company's overseas operations to include more projects in Africa and Eurasia, and also brought ownership of the Wentworth Golf Club in Surrey. In 1978, the firm procured the constructional engineering firm Robert Watson & Company Ltd., of Bolton, Manchester and Bristol, Avon. This transaction led Fairclough into manufacturing structural steel and platework; one of the largest contracts in recent years involved the erection of a new terminal at London's Heathrow Airport.

These four acquisitions during the 1970's led to the development of eight divisions: Fairclough International Construction; Fairclough Scotland; Fairclough–Parkinson Mining; Fairclough Engineering; Fairclough Civil Engineering; Fairclough Precast; Fairclough Building; and Fairclough Projects. Between the early 1970's and 1980's, Fairclough's Civil Engineering division alone constructed the United Kingdom's largest sewage system in Glasgow, drove its largest-diameter water tunnel at Sheffield, and developed its largest service reservoir at Prescott. Leonard M. Fairclough, having left his post as director in 1959, lived to see only a part of this impressive growth. He died in 1976.

In 1970 Fairclough had pretax profits of £1.2 million, turnover of £23 million, and assets under £3 million; by 1981 pretax profits were £13.4 million, turnover £245.5 million, and assets a healthy £59.5 million. In 1982 Fairclough achieved record profits, despite the worldwide recession. This success resulted in an increase in the amount of cash available, which is why the company bought a 15.3% interest in French Keir and approximately 14% in William Press, two British construction firms, in the early 1980's.

In November 1982, a holding company for Fairclough and William Press was formed, and a board of six directors was drawn up, three from each company. Called AMEC, it looked like a successful merger; a London *Times* correspondent envisaged, " . . . Press's strong presence in the industrial sector complementing Fairclough's experience in work for the public and private sectors." The merger created the fifth largest construction firm in Britain in terms of capitalization.

The rationale for a merger was that Press had a much larger international client base than Fairclough: international contracts accounted for 30% of its total business in 1982 as compared to Fairclough's 15%. The company was also heavily involved in the British energy industry's conversion from coal to natural gas, and has built some of the largest oil terminals and pipelines in the U.K. In addition, it operates over 70% of Britain's offshore field developments in the North Sea.

Nonetheless, despite its promise, the holding company achieved negligible profits during its first three years. There were two reasons for this: the reduced amount of work available in the offshore and process engineering sectors, areas where slumping gas prices helped to delay the arrival of the recession; and Press's apparent mistakes in management and financial accounting at one of its subsidiaries during the early 1980's, which accounted for millions of pounds in losses due to either late or incompleted projects.

Generally, Press and Fairclough operate as independent companies, thus despite Press's lingering financial difficulties, Fairclough's continued profit growth accounted for AMEC's slight annual increase. Beginning with 1986, however, the group emerged from its doldrums when pretax profits jumped more than £5 million to £30.5 million. Bill Morgan, current chairman of AMEC, has reported that both Press and Fairclough have full order books for the late 1980's, and although there has been a slight downward trend in contracts for the public sector over the last few years, growth in power plant construction and the defense industry contracts should more than compensate for the difference.

Principal Subsidiaries of Fairclough Construction Group plc: Fairclough Building Ltd.; Fairclough Civil Engineering Ltd.; Fairclough Estates Ltd.; Fairclough Parkinson Mining Ltd.; London Fairclough (Hotels) Ltd., Cyprus (75%); Rearden Plant Ltd.; Robert Watson & Co., Ltd.; Wentworth Club Ltd.; John Howard & Co. Ltd. (41.3%); Howard Doris Ltd., Scotland (25%); Gulliver Consolidated Ltd., Zimbabwe (45%).

FLUOR CORPORATION

3333 Michelson Drive
Irvine, California 92730
U.S.A.
(714) 975–2000

Public Company
Incorporated: April 28, 1924
Employees: 22,309
Sales: $4.17 billion
Market value: $1.268 billion
Stock Index: New York Amsterdam London Geneva
Basle Zurich

The Fluor Corporation entered the 1980's as one of the world's premier builders of large and complex projects. However, the company's $2.2 billion purchase of St. Joe Minerals in 1981 proved to be a devastatingly costly move. Combined with a highly volatile energy market and falling oil prices, the acquisition brought Fluor serious financial trouble. As a result, the company sold assets, reorganized, and combined subsidiaries in an effort to reduce its losses. Reversing its past strategy of broad diversification, Fluor narrowed its interests to two basic areas. The firm now focuses on engineering and construction services, and natural resources management.

Fluor's story begins with a Swiss emigré who when he arrived in the United States knew only one English word—"Hello." Born in 1867, John Simon Fluor was a carpenter who had gained engineering experience while serving in the Swiss army. Fluor emigrated in 1888, age 21, joining his two older brothers who had settled in Oshkosh, Wisconsin. The three pooled their money in 1890 to start a saw and paper mill called Rudolph Fluor & Brother. J. Simon Fluor's contribution was $100; he served as manager at the mill.

In 1903 the company name changed to Fluor Brothers Construction Company, with J. Simon Fluor as president. Nine years later he traveled on his own to California and started a general construction business under his own name. With innovative methods and precise work, Fluor built his venture's reputation quickly. The Southern California Gas Company asked him to build an office and numerous meter shops in 1915, and afterward Fluor received a contract for a compressor station from Industrial Fuel Supply Company. Fluor recognized that the emerging California petroleum industry held enormous potential, so in 1921 he began to tailor his engineering and construction work to meet the demands of the field.

Fluor received a contract to erect a cooling tower in 1921. Believing that those in use at the time were inefficient and wasteful, he designed the "Buddha tower," a radical advancement which not only cooled water more efficiently but reduced water loss. The name came from the tower's resemblance to Buddhist shrines. Fluor soon began manufacturing the towers. The oil and gas companies quickly recognized the Buddha towers' merit, and used them at many installations.

Fluor incorporated his business as Fluor Construction Company in 1924 with a capital investment of $100,000. He began manufacturing large engine mufflers, expanding the company from strictly engineering to engineering and construction. After outgrowing two different facilities, Fluor built new quarters in Los Angeles and consolidated all general offices in one building in 1927.

In the mid-1920's, Fluor started involving his sons in the family business. He retained the presidency until 1943, although his sons ran the company. Peter Earl Fluor, older of the sons, became executive vice president and general manager. Peter Fluor seemed to be a born salesman, and associates called him "the company engine,". He led Fluor's development through the Depression and World War II.

Fluor's business continued increasing until the stock market crashed in October 1929. Between 1924 and 1929 annual sales grew from $100,000 to $1.5 million. In need of additional capital in 1929, the company reincorporated and changed its name to Fluor Corporation, Ltd. to reflect its involvement in fields outside construction. At the time of the reincorporation, Peter Fluor and his brother J. Simon Fluor, Jr. encouraged company employees to take advantage of the company's success by offering them Fluor stock at one dollar per month per share. The brothers initiated many employee benefit programs and were considered enlightened employers.

Until 1930 Fluor operated primarily within California. That year, Peter Fluor pushed for expansion, contrary to his father's wishes, and sold Fluor's services to the Panhandle Eastern Pipeline Company. The contract was for construction of compressor stations on an oil pipeline from Texas to Indiana. The company also opened a Kansas City office. Fluor's expansion got another boost later that year when the Shell Oil Company hired the firm to build a $100,000 refining unit in Illinois. It was the company's largest refining contract to date and helped establish Fluor as a major competitor in the refining construction field.

Fluor's business decreased sharply during the Depression years, but the company's leadership wanted to keep its skilled personnel on the payroll. Thus many Fluor employees with sophisticated expertise worked as laborers until business improved. Also during the Depression, Fluor registered patents on two of the company founder's inventions. They were the Fluor aerator tower, patented in 1932; and the Fluor air-cooler muffler, patented in 1938.

The pressures and energy needs of World War II led Fluor into more new work areas. Early in the war years, Fluor had only a few months to develop facilities and personnel capable of producing high-octane gasoline and synthetic rubber. Later, Sinclair Oil Company selected Fluor to design and build a sulfuric alkylation plant at its California refinery. Between 1940 and 1943, Fluor facilities produced more than a third of all 100% octane gasoline in the United States, and the Fluor staff developed three patented procedures to improve oil and gas processing.

In 1944 Simon J. Fluor died. Peter Fluor succeeded him as president, and J. Simon Fluor, Jr. became executive vice president. Peter Fluor died unexpectedly in 1947 at age 52. An interim officer followed him in the presidency, and in 1949 the permanent successor, Donald Darnell, took over. After a few years of declines in business, Fluor turned to the U.S. government for contracts in the early 1950's, and thus entered another new area of work. The company participated in construction of a large materials testing reactor for the Atomic Energy Commission in Arco, Idaho. Many more assignments in the nuclear field followed.

The immediate postwar years were a time of significant international expansion for the company; the firm secured contracts for refineries and natural gas plants in Canada and Venezuela. In 1946 a contract for a grassroots refinery in Montana solidified Fluor's reputation as a refinery engineering firm and helped lead to an assignment to expand the Aramco facilities in Saudi Arabia. The company formed its Gas-Gasoline Division in Houston in 1948.

By the time the Korean War created massive petroleum product needs in 1950, Fluor's reputation was so widespread that it was a natural choice for many energy-producing projects. In the first half of the decade, Fluor actively diversified its operations. It contracted work for the U.S. Air Force at Dhahran Air Base and for refineries in Puerto Rico. More projects followed, including designing and building plants for the petrochemical industry in Canada, Scotland, Australia and South Africa. A London office opened in 1957. In the late 1950's Fluor's expertise in building helium plants gained the company contracts with Britain's Bureau of Mines and Office of Saline Water.

In the early 1950's Fluor introduced a new technique that has since become standard in the industry: using scale models in the design of process facilities. The models helped Fluor staff become specialists in lifting large vessels at job sites. Today Fluor maintains a model shop at each engineering office.

During this period of rapid expansion and large international contracts, Darnell became chairman of the company, J. Simon Fluor, Jr. became president and chief executive officer, and J. Robert Fluor (the founder's grandson) became executive vice president.

As the company grew, Fluor's leadership recognized the critical value of recruiting a staff trained in the most current, sophisticated construction methods. Because the marketplace during the 1950's was short of workers with the skills Fluor demanded, the company established in-house training and college tuition reimbursement programs, both of which are still in use.

In 1962 J. Robert Fluor, an engineer and former U.S. Air Force pilot who bred thoroughbred horses, became president and chief executive officer of the company. His tenure was significant for Fluor Corporation in four major ways: internationalization, computerization, acquisitions in the offshore oil drilling industry, and mining acquisitions.

In the first case, Fluor built refineries in Korea and Iran, extending its operations into two more nations. Second, during the decade the company began using computers throughout its offices for both engineering projects and management needs.

Third was extensive diversification into offshore drilling, beginning in 1967 with a merger of five companies into Fluor under the divisional name Coral Drilling. Around the same time Fluor established a new subsidiary called Deep Oil Technology for deep-ocean recovery of oil. In 1968 the company created Fluor Ocean Services, an umbrella management company headquartered in Houston. Ocean Services quickly became a worldwide company. Fluor's largest offshore drilling acquisition occurred in 1969, when the company took over the Pike Corporation of America. Pike consisted of three major divisions: a drilling operation (Western Offshore Drilling and Exploration Company), an equipment distributor (Republic Supply Company of California), and a specialty tubing and pipe distributor (Kilsby Tubesupply).

Fluor's involvement with the mining and metals industry also began in 1969. The company purchased Utah Construction and Mining Company, forming the subsidiary Fluor Mining & Metals, Inc. Fluor Australia, another mining interest, was set up soon afterward. In later years mining would become a significant interest for Fluor.

The company's activities in the 1970's focused heavily on the international natural resources industries: oil, gas and nuclear power. Fluor also set up subsidiaries and management organizations in Europe, Indonesia, South Africa, Alaska and Saudi Arabia, the last being a $5 billion gas program. In 1973 Fluor consolidated its oil and gas activities to form Fluor Oil and Gas Corporation. It completed the world's largest offshore facility for natural gas in Java in 1976.

The financial figures for three consecutive years demonstrate the rate of the company's expansion: 1973, $1.3 billion; 1974, $4.4 billion; 1975, $9 billion. New corporate offices opened in Houston and Irvine to accommodate the company's rapidly growing staff. Fluor executives attributed a large part of the company's success to its task force management concept, under which every Fluor project received all the tools, personnel and resources to get the job done, and the project director had full authority and responsibility for the entire project.

In the late 1970's the Saudi Arabian minister of industry asked company president J. Robert Fluor to help improve Saudi Arabia's poor image in the U.S. At that time Fluor chaired the board of trustees at the University of Southern California. He asked executives of 40 major companies that dealt with the Saudis to fund a $22 million Middle East Studies Center at the university. The center was to be run by a former oil company employee and controlled by the donors. The university faculty and the Los Angeles Jewish community blocked the project because of the irregularity of its intended relationship with its fund sources. Fluor Corporation's public relations department said the affair had been distorted by the "Jewish Press."

Along with Fluor's extensive and sometimes controversial international involvement, the company also made a significant domestic expansion by acquiring the Daniel

International Corporation in 1977. Daniel was an industrial contractor with revenues over $1 billion a year that in many ways complemented the Fluor portfolio. Daniel's operations were primarily based in the U.S., whereas Fluor worked largely overseas. The two had different client lists and were involved in different kinds of projects. Most Fluor employees were members of labor unions, but most of Daniel's employees were not. Despite, and in some cases because of, their differences, the two companies integrated efficiently.

This was not the case, however, with the purchase of St. Joe Minerals in 1981. The acquisition happened at a time when Fluor had a good cash flow because its engineering and construction sectors were both growing. Management knew about the mining industry from its experience building facilities for mines. Fluor executives determined that metals prices ran counter-cyclically to the market variations in the construction industry, making mining the perfect complement to building. Thus the company successfully bid $2.2 billion for St. Joe.

In the next several years Fluor posted significant losses. The company was not prepared for the crash in metals prices of the early 1980's. The fall was compounded by a deep recession, a reduced inflation rate, and a collapse in petrochemical plant building because of the oversupply of oil. From a high of $71 in 1981, Fluor stock fell to lower than $20 by 1985, and the company accumulated $724 million in debt.

After J. Robert Fluor's death in 1984, David S. Tappan, Jr. moved up from the Fluor presidency to become chief executive officer. Tappan brought a great deal of international experience to the position and looked for ways to ease the company's dependence on oil contracts.

As the company continued to lose money from 1983 through 1986, it earnestly sought a return to profitability, finally deciding it must divest some of its holdings and restructure the entire enterprise. Fluor sold all the oil properties and some of the gold affiliated with its St. Joe Minerals operation (approximately $370 million), all its offshore drilling facilities ($17.5 million), and some of the corporate offices it had built during the 1970's.

The company also divested its South African operations in 1986. Fluor's stated political position on the issue was that the company "still believes sanctions and withdrawal of U.S. firms from South Africa are counterproductive to achieving a peaceful solution to the problems of racial inequality. But as uncertainties of continued operation in South Africa escalate, we felt that an orderly transfer of ownership at this time would be in the best interests of all concerned." Fluor retained a repurchase option on the divested South African assets.

In 1986 Fluor's two largest divisions merged. Fluor Engineers, Inc. and Daniel International became a single worldwide operating unit, Fluor Daniel. The company called the merger a move toward greater flexibility. The merged entity offers fully integrated construction services —including feasibility studies, concept design, project management, engineering, construction, procurement and maintenance—from each of its 54 offices around the world.

Fluor's major divisions in 1987 were Fluor Daniel, Fluor Constructors International, Inc., and St. Joe Minerals Corporation, each with several subsidiaries. Two other significant divisions are American Equipment Company, Inc. and Fluor Venture Group. The latter is a source of financial backing for engineering and construction projects.

Fluor's total assets in 1981 were $4.5 billion; in 1986 they were down to $2.6 billion. Similarly, whereas the company employed 44,000 people in 1981, five years later there were half as many employees. Pared down to its two main divisions, engineering and construction and natural resources management, Fluor is currently working to rebuild the remarkable success it enjoyed for decades prior to the crisis of the early 1980's.

Principal Subsidiaries: Fluor Engineering and Construction Group, Inc.; Fluor Engineers, Inc.; Fluor Construction International, Inc.; Daniel International Corp.; St. Joe Minerals Corp.; A.T. Masseu Coal Co., Inc.; St. Joe Domestic Metals Corp.; St. Joe International Corp.; Fluor Oil and Gas Corp.; Fluor Drilling Services, Inc.; Western Offshore Drilling and Exploration Co.

Further Reading: Fluor Corporation: A 65-Year History, by J. Robert Fluor, New York, Newcomen Society, 1978.

JOHN BROWN

JOHN BROWN PLC

John Brown House
20 Eastbourne Terrace
London W2 6LE
England

Wholly-owned subsidiary of Trafalgar House plc
Incorporated: April 1, 1864
Employees: 10,050
Sales: £457.6 million (US$672.7 million)
Market value: £65.3 million (US$96 million)

Since its founding 150 years ago, John Brown has changed its emphasis several times. It began manufacturing steel files, shifted to rails and rail coach springs, then to shipcladding and shipbuilding, and finally, in the 1950's to general construction. John Brown has been a consistent leader within its various realms and has weathered depressions and other financial crises successfully. However, in the late 1970's and early 1980's the company's fortunes fluctuated dramatically, eventually leading to a near collapse. Trafalgar House—the British construction, natural resources, and shipping and aviation conglomerate—resuscitated John Brown in 1986 with an £80 million takeover.

Born in Sheffield, England in 1816, the company founder was the son of a slater. John Brown attended a local school, and when he was fourteen his father pushed him to learn the linen drapery craft. John Brown refused flatly; he wanted to be a merchant, and to that end entered the local firm of Earle Horton & Co. as an unwaged apprentice.

Earle Horton & Co. went into the steel business and offered Brown a partnership in 1837. Unable to collect the capital needed to join the firm, he had to refuse the offer. The firm's owners then made a second offer: for £500, Brown could be the firm's sales agent. Brown convinced a local bank to back him this time, and at age 21 he became a traveling salesman with a horse and gig. He carried his cutlery samples and drummed up so much business that he made enough money to start his own enterprise. Brown resigned from Earle Horton & Co. and set up the Atlas Steel Works, manufacturing crucible steel files.

In the 1840's the railways' rapid expansion gave great impetus to the steel industry in England. More tracks were being laid and more coaches built all the time, creating a seemingly unlimited demand for steel. In 1848, Brown invented and patented the conical spring buffer for railway coaches, which increased both safety and comfort. His invention made Brown's name and fortune; he worked a representation of it into the company seal and later, when he was knighted, into his crest. The successful Atlas Steel Works continued growing, and in 1856 Brown transferred all of his works to a larger site he had purchased from a failed business. That year he renamed the firm Atlas Steel & Spring Works.

In the following years Brown began manufacturing iron from ore in his own six puddling furnaces. The other, typically conservative, merchants in the area thought he was crazy not to order the iron needed for steel production from Sweden and Russia, the main sources at the time. Nevertheless, Brown's iron was good and cheap, and he was soon producing 100 tons a week.

The last of Brown's three remarkable innovations was adoption, in 1858, of the Bessemer process for converting iron to steel. Once again the move went against conservative opinion, and again it was successful and lucrative. Brown began selling Bessemer-made steel rails in 1861.

Shortly after introducing the new rails, Brown made a secret examination of a French warship to inspect the French "iron cladding," which usually consisted either of several thin pieces of plate riveted together or of single rolled-iron plates. Determining that he could do the job better, John Brown built a rolling mill, and in 1863 was the first steelmaker to roll 12-inch armor plate for warships. After files, then rails and springs, the company had now embarked on its third phase, shipcladding, which would develop into shipbuilding. The *HMS Warrior* was the first battleship to sail with Brown's armor. Brown spent over £200,000 developing the armor plate manufacturing business, and expanded his works to 21 acres. During the decade beginning in 1857, Brown's workforce grew from 200 to 4,000. Turnover expanded from an initial £3,000 to nearly £1 million in 1867, when John Brown was cladding three quarters of Britain's warships in iron.

In 1859 Brown took two partners. The move had excellent results for the company but ended in personal disaster for Brown himself. William Bragge was an engineer, and John Devonshire Ellis was from a family of successful brass founders in Birmingham. By 1864 they had turned the firm into a limited company called John Brown & Co., with a capital of £1 million. Ellis contributed his own invention, the compound armor plate of rolled iron with a steel face. He also knew how to run a company, which Brown did not. Brown considered the company his own; after all, it had been his innovation and energy that founded the venture that now bore his name. Brown disliked working with people he considered outsiders—though they were, of course, shareholders—and having the directors criticize his decisions on expenditures. The increased tension damaged both the company and John Brown's health. In 1871 Brown resigned, leaving J.D. Ellis to take over as head of the firm. In the next several years Brown tried to form a few other companies, all of which failed. He died, impoverished, at age 80 in 1896, to the expressed sadness of his old partners.

J.D. Ellis remained chairman until retiring in 1906. During his tenure he brought both his sons, Charles Ellis and William Henry Ellis, into the company. The former took over as managing director from his father in 1892 and held the post until 1928. Under J.D. Ellis the company bought a joint interest in Spanish iron mines in 1872 to secure a steady supply of iron ore. John Brown later bought the Aldwarke Main & Car House Collieries and started mining coal.

In the last decades of the nineteenth century, several factors threatened John Brown's success. The British railway companies began to import cheaper supplies from foreign companies, new labor laws reduced workers' hours and raised their wages slightly, Britain had a rail strike, coal prices were depressed, and finally, there was a long coal strike. John Brown survived all these difficulties and the depression of 1894–5 through careful management, and at times managed to do quite well.

The company bought the Clydebank Engineering & Shipbuilding Co., the most successful shipyards in the United Kingdom, in 1899. With this acquisition John Brown entered the shipbuilding industry, shifting its focus yet again. The next year the company produced a Japanese battleship, a Cunard steamship, and five destroyers. Ships John Brown built later included the *Lusitania*, the *Aquitania*, the *Tiger*, the *Repulse*, and the *Hood*.

John Brown and another Sheffield steel company, Thomas Firth & Sons, exchanged shares in 1902 and agreed to work together. While the companies continued under separate management until they merged in 1930, their boards shared many directors. In 1908, the firms established the Brown Firth Research Laboratory in Brearley, where chrome stainless steel and "Staybrite" stainless steel were developed. The latter is still used throughout the world.

The company bought the Coventry Ordnance Works in 1904 but saw little profit from the enterprise until the First Lord of the Admiralty, Winston Churchill, began to place orders for gun mountings on warships in 1910. Business was good through World War I, after which John Brown sold the Ordnance Works and bought Craven Tasker Ltd., makers of several kinds of vehicles.

Ship and gun orders dropped drastically in the years after the war, of course. Foreign competition in the steel industry and workers' strikes in industry in general compounded Brown's difficulties. Ironically, with everyone else in the world hoping for continued peace, John Brown was worried about where to get more orders for ships and armaments. A few came from Australia, but it was not until the 1931 order from Cunard Lines for the *Queen Mary* that John Brown's fortunes would begin to improve. Canadian Pacific soon ordered a liner, Cunard ordered the *Queen Elizabeth*, and the British government ordered two sloops, two destroyers, and a 9,000-ton cruiser. Profits were over £100,000 for 1934.

The company made a move into another new realm in 1936 when it bought a large block of shares in Westland Aircraft Ltd. at Yeovil. The following year John Brown purchased the Markham & Co., Ltd., engineering firm. Markham was well known for its machinery, especially its tunnelling machines, which were used in excavations for the London and Moscow Undergrounds and the Paris Métro. Throughout World War II, John Brown and Markham were, not surprisingly, at full production. The former built ships totalling a third of a million tons, and the latter made midget submarines.

As a result of the British government's nationalization of the collieries after the end of the war, Brown consisted mainly of steel and tool works, a shipyard, and Markham Engineering. The company faced the need for modernization and conversion to some sort of peacetime production. Shell, gun and bomb manufacturing came to a halt. John Brown converted its armor plate shops to handle heavy engineering weldments and manufacturing. In 1947 the company formed a Canadian subsidiary and purchased Hispeed Tools and A. Wickman. A new division formed to build oil refineries took the name Constructors John Brown (CJB). The shipyard remained the largest part of the company, employing over 6,000 people and building, among other craft, the royal yacht *Britannia*. In the 1950's Brown's Cravens subsidiary produced rolling stock cars for railways around the world. It began making modern cars for the London Underground in 1959. The company expanded into Australia, South Africa, the United States, and Zimbabwe (then Rhodesia) in that period.

By the end of the 1950's, the company's profits had climbed to almost £2 million, where they hovered until 1965, when Japanese shipbuilding began to threaten Brown's market. John Brown responded by modernizing its Clydebank shipyards and by beginning to make gas turbines and pipelines, as well as by increasing its emphasis on general construction. In the second half of the 1960's, Brown received the order for the *QEII*, and CJB was building factories in Sweden and the USSR. Nevertheless, by 1971 profits were only up to £3 million. Three years later, CJB posted huge losses on three fixed-price contracts, causing a group loss of £2 million. By 1978, the losses had turned around and Brown had a cash reserve of nearly £20 million.

The company's seesawing fortunes continued for some years, with large contracts followed by sudden losses. Eventually the company became known in financial circles for its dramatic rises and falls. In 1982 Brown announced deals worth £104 million and bought Olofsson, a U.S. machine tool manufacturer, for £44 million. Profits for 1982 were £14.2 million, much higher than at any time in the previous decade. However, the company's £25 million share issue that year was a failure. Furthermore, reorganization and layoff costs, and the loss of contracts in Argentina during the Falkland Islands War wiped out most of the record profits. The next year, pre-tax losses were £9 million, and the company began to try to sell part of John Brown Engineering. By the middle of the year, losses for the group totalled £26.7 million and the chairman resigned. Many of the company's problems were results of the U.S. government's opposition to western firms working on the Soviet pipeline; Brown had several large contracts to supply for and build lengths of the pipeline.

After the near collapse, a rescue package was put together, involving new management, a £70 million recapitalization, asset sales, and layoffs of more than 7,000 workers. Key to the rescue was the £80 million takeover by Trafalgar House in 1986.

Brown's engineering and construction divisions remain its largest. In 1986 Brown received contracts to build two British Nuclear Fuels plants, as well as one for a polypropylene project for the USSR. The latter is a plant with a 100,000-ton annual capacity to be situated near Stavropol. Scheduled for completion in 1990, it will increase the Soviet Union's polyester fiber production by 40% within its first two years of operation. Also in 1986, the Markham division provided large-scale tunnelling equipment for main sewer bores in Cairo. Based largely on that unit's efficiency, Markham received a contract to build two even larger units for excavation of the rail tunnel under the English Channel.

At the same time, the engineering division compiled its best order list in many years; its most notable project was a large gas turbine order for China. In addition, the division hoped privatization of power in Britain would open up a major new market. Toward that end, it began to develop new business areas such as flue gas desulphurization.

In September 1987 Brown announced it would sell its Craven Tasker and East Lancashire Coachbuilders units, its only ventures in the road transport industry. Though the two had combined annual revenues of £25 million, Brown managers had determined that the road transportation industry was now outside its major business areas.

The plastics machinery business has become the fastest growing part of the group. The weak dollar of the late 1980's allowed the plastics division to make important inroads into the U.S. market.

John Brown has fared well since Trafalgar House acquired the company in 1986, but given Trafalgar's policy of letting its constituent companies carry on their own management, it cannot yet be said with certainty that Brown's troubles are over. However, with the support of such a powerful new owner, the company undoubtedly has a better prospect for the future than it would have had left on its own.

Principal Subsidiaries: Bone Markham Ltd.; Brecon Construction Co., Ltd.; John Brown Engineering Ltd.; Carmodine Ltd.; Dollain Ltd.; Firth Brown Tools Ltd.; Eric Johnson, Stubbs & Co., Ltd.; Penroyson Ltd.; Roxby Power Engineering Ltd.; Sanctuary Holdings Ltd.; Wickman Ltd.

Further Reading: Steel & Ships: The Story of John Brown's, by Sir Allen Grant, London, Michael Joseph, 1950; *Family Engineers,* by Eric Mensforth, London, Ward Lock, 1981.

LAING

JOHN LAING PLC

Page Street
London NW7 2ER
England
01–959–3636

Public Company
Incorporated: 1920
Employees: 11,300
Sales: £875.5 million (US$1.287 billion)
Market value: £219.7 million (US$323 million)
Stock Index: London

Around 1800 a Scot named David Laing moved south to Cumberland, in England, and built a house for himself and his bride. With that simple construction project, Laing started in a business his family has stayed in for more than 180 years. Today Martin Laing, fifth-generation descendant of David Laing, presides over Britain's largest construction firm.

After building his first house, David Laing worked in the village repairing the church, digging wells and engaging in other small jobs to maintain his livelihood. His eldest son, James, born in 1816, joined him upon finishing school. It appears that James Laing would have been content to carry on as a repairman and minor builder like his father, but his marriage in 1841 to Ann Graham, who had her eyes on the future, changed James Laing's life. She convinced him to hire permanent employees and buy a plot of land for £20. In his spare time, Laing built a house on the plot; Ann helped by leading a team of their children in hauling rocks up the hill from a river bed. He finished the house in 1848 and sold it the same year, thus giving birth to the Laing construction firm.

The £150 proceeds from that first sale financed construction of two more houses on the same piece of land. James and Ann raised their family in one of the houses and sold the other. It is uncertain why in 1867 James sold everything and moved the family to Carlisle, where he worked as a laborer until he managed to start another business of his own. Again the eldest son joined his father in business; John Laing, born in 1842, worked as a stonecarver for his father.

When James Laing died in 1882, John Laing took over the business and began to procure larger contracts for public projects such as the Carlisle electricity works and repairs on the local castle. Under John Laing, the business began to produce its own building materials. Laborers dug clay, made bricks by hand, and fired them in a kiln on the construction site. The business remained relatively small and confined to the Carlisle area until the fourth Laing took over.

John Laing's son John William Laing, born in 1879, was active in the business before he was 20 years old, so active that the firm changed its name to John Laing and Son. Ann Laing, by now quite advanced in age and feeling that her family was suitably established, wanted her grandson to go into a more genteel field than construction. Unaware that the young man was a budding construction tycoon, she tried to keep him out of the business. In a peculiar reversal of the norm, John William Laing rebelled against his grandmother by staying in the family firm.

The construction industry in Great Britain experienced great growth in the first decade of this century. During this period Laing procured many contracts for public works, including the Uldale reservoir and the Barrow sewer.

By 1910 John William Laing was the sole proprietor of the firm and had begun to organize it into the successful international business it is today. He hired more employees and started accepting larger and more distant contracts, especially for factory construction. Laing was very concerned about preparing accurate cost estimates, maintaining strict control over the construction workers, and using scientific methods. He wanted to know about every aspect of construction, even at times living on building sites and learning such skills as bricklaying, masonry and how to inspect each laborer's work.

Laing devised his cost estimating technique with William Sirey, a clerk in the firm. It consisted of sending trained estimators to the site to prepare a detailed analysis of every phase of the job. As a result, Laing's quotes were more accurate than those of his competitors. The system additionally helped the firm reduce the builder's standard problem of surprise costs surfacing during construction. Estimators remain important in the company that was among the first to apply cost-control procedures systematically.

During World War I the company received a series of British government contracts for war works. Laing built naval armament testing stations, an armament factory and workers' accommodations in Gretna, an aerodrome, and a riveting school. By the end of the war, John Laing & Son was a substantially larger firm with an intricate and invaluable web of contacts in government departments.

In 1920 the firm became a limited company and opened offices in London. Two years later the headquarters moved from Carlisle to a 13-acre site in Northwest London at Mill Hill. Now in national competition for construction work, the company won contracts for the Middlesex County Hospital, the Federation of British Industries House, office blocks, pumping stations, power stations and an army camp.

The postwar housing shortage also brought significant profits. The company built many public housing blocks for the Local Authorities; it also built houses for sale to the public. A subsidiary company, Laing's Properties Ltd., owned and managed large blocks of Laing-built flats. Laing's largest source of work, however, was the Air Ministry, for which the company built aerodromes, airfields, equipment depots and the underground head-quarters for the Bomber Command of World War II. The company began construction of three new aerodromes in October 1939, and on 14 more the next year. In the process Laing developed expertise in runway construction that would prove lucrative during the war years.

World War II brought contracts for a total of 54 aerodromes, including hangars, runways, offices and housing. Work on ordnance factories, power stations, coal mines and part of the floating harbor used in the D-Day invasion of France also made significant contributions to Laing profits during the war.

The fifth generation of Laings, William Kirby Laing and James Maurice Laing, joined the firm before World War II. In 1950 the company established its first regional center, in Bristol. Two years later the company went public and took the name John Laing & Sons (Holdings) Ltd. The family and its trusts and charities held the bulk of the shares. John Laing became the chairman, and his sons became joint managing directors. By this time, the number of employees was up to 10,000, and every site had a quality supervisor.

Postwar contracts included schools, the Prestwick and Glasgow airports, factories, the Windscale and Berkeley nuclear power stations, and more than 10,000 houses. The firm continued the coal mining it had begun during the war, extracting 12,555 tons in 1947. In 1953, net assets reached £6.6 million, and the company employed 15,000 people at its building sites and offices.

John Laing retired in 1957 and was knighted two years later. Paternalistic and devout, he served as president of the London Bible College, helped establish the Salisbury Bible House in what is now Harare, Zimbabwe, and had his company build the Coventry Cathedral and return the profits to the church. While he was known during his time at the helm of the firm for providing every construction site a welfare officer to look after meals, movies, whist drives and religious services for the laborers, it was reported that he could also be harsh. He once reportedly fined a man for going to the pub during lunch. He died in 1978 at age 98.

Under William Kirby Laing and James Maurice Laing, the company continued on the successful path the men's father had planned, winning contracts for more power stations and expanding into road construction while continuing to build houses. In 1985 Martin Laing, of the family's sixth generation in construction, became chairman. That year, the company won contracts totalling almost £27 million.

Martin Laing determined that the company, now Britain's largest construction firm, should begin to diversify. With an £84 million cash reserve, Laing had room to experiment. Diversification projects included building supermarkets at airports and creating a new water treatment company, called Water Services, set up as a joint venture with the French company Lyonnaise des Eaux. Martin Laing believed the skills the company gained from the experience of installing its own elaborate computer system could be the basis of a profitable service. Consequently, in 1987 the company established its Energy, Technology and Environment division which offers high-technology services, from computer-aided road design to nuclear waste processing. The new division is expected to provide 10% of Laing's profits by 1990.

The company's other divisions continue to be successful as well. Profits have risen steadily in the 1980's, from £30.3 million in 1984 to £38.1 in 1986, with each subsidiary doing correspondingly well. Housebuilding in the United Kingdom, Saudi Arabia, Oman, the United Arab Emirates, Iraq, Spain and California is now one of the major sources of growth, though there have been some problems with non-payment by clients in Saudi Arabia. This has depressed share prices somewhat. Nevertheless, the company's participation in several major projects the British government plans for the late 1980's and early 1990's, as well as the lucrative new technology division, should preserve Laing's leadership of the Untied Kingdom construction industry for the next several years, at least.

Principal Subsidiaries: John Laing Construction Limited; Laing Industrial Engineering & Construction Limited; Laing Management Contracting Limited; Laing Management Contracting (Scotland) Limited; Laing-Loy Management Contracting Limited (50%); Holloway White Allom Limited; Degremont Laing Limited (50%); Water Services Limited (50%); John Laing Properties Limited; Scot Projects Limited; Laing Homes Limited; Super Homes Limited; Laing Land Limited; John Laing Developments Limited; Laing Teesland Limited (50%); SBD Construction Products Limited; OC Summers Limited; Esk Manufacturing Company Limited; Victoria Joinery Limited; Beechdale Engineering Limited; EPL International Limited; John Laing Services Limited; Elstree Computing Limited; JL Property Holdings Limited Overseas; John Laing International Limited; Laing Projects Limited (Jersey, CI); Laing Projects BV (Holland); Laing SA (Spain); Laing Wimpey Alireza Limited; Wimpey Laing Limited (50%); Laing Holdings Inc. (USA); John Laing Homes Inc. (USA).

Further Reading: Life and Belief in the Experience of John W. Laing, CBE, by Godfrey Harrison, London, Hodder and Stoughton, 1954; *The Biography of Sir John W. Laing, CBE,* by Roy Coad, London, Hodder and Stoughton, 1979.

KAJIMA CORPORATION

2−7, Motoakasaka 1−chome
Minato-ku, Tokyo 107
Japan
(03)404−3311

Public Company
Incorporated: February 22, 1930 as the Kajima
Construction Company
Employees: 15,365
Sales: ¥ 1.021 trillion (US$5.320 billion)
Market Value: ¥ 1.186 trillion (US$6.177 billion)
Stock Index: Tokyo Osaka Nagoya

The Kajima Corporation is one of the oldest and largest construction companies in Japan. It was founded in 1840 by Iwakichi Kajima, an innovative carpenter and designer. Construction remained the family trade of Kajima's sons, who witnessed the transformation of Japan from a isolated nation into a developing regional power after the Meiji Restoration in 1868.

The industrial modernization policies of the Meiji government created a demand for newer and larger factories and buildings as well as railroad lines and tunnels. Kajima built the first European-style commercial building in Japan, an office structure for the Hong Kong-based Jardine Matheson & Company, and entered the field of railroad construction in 1880 under the name Kajima Gumi. The company quickly established a reputation for excellence in railroad bed construction and tunneling. As Japanese industry continued to grow, Kajima Gumi completed a greater number of industrial and infrastructural projects.

Kajima Gumi began construction of hydroelectric dams during the 1920's. Relatively unaffected by the worldwide economic depression, Kajima Gumi became a public company on February 22, 1930, capitalized at three million yen. With the involvement of private stockholders, the company was able to devote more capital to larger projects. With a larger scale of operations, Kajima Gumi became active as an industrial contractor.

Extreme right-wing elements of the Japanese military rose to power during the 1930's, advocating a neo-mercantilist economy and Japanese colonial domination of East Asia and the western Pacific. As part of their "quasi-war economy," large industrial projects were undertaken which were intended to augment Japan's war making capabilities. Like many other Japanese companies,

Kajima Gumi attempted to remain divorced from politics. However, because of the nature of its business, and the overwhelming coercive power of the militarists, the company became an active participant in the Japanese was effort.

Japan was so completely devastated by the war that it was largely unable to feed or rebuild itself. This created great opportunities for construction companies such as Kajima Gumi, who were needed to build new structures and repair others which had been damaged.

Kajima Gumi was reorganized under the commercial laws imposed by the Allied occupation commander, and reestablished in 1947 as the Kajima Construction Company. Two years later, the company established the Kajima Institute of Construction Technology (KICT) where new construction materials and engineering technologies could be developed. The Institute, located in Tokyo's Chuo ward, employed 233 specialists and was the first private research institution of its kind in Japan.

In the early 1950's Kajima began to design nuclear reactor complexes, which necessitated the expansion of the research institute. In 1956 the Institute was relocated to the Tokyo suburb of Chobu. The following year Kajima built the Number 1 reactor at the Japan Atomic Energy Research Institute's Ibarakiken complex.

Kajima completed Japan's first skyscraper, the 36-story Kasumigaseki Mitsui Building in 1956. Part of that building consisted of a Large Structure Testing (LST) laboratory, which helped Kajima to formulate new technologies for other larger, earthquake-resistant skyscrapers, such as the Shinjuku Mitsui Building (55 stories) and the Sunshine 60 Building (60 stories).

During the 1960's the company undertook an increasing number of projects outside Japan, constructing buildings and dams in Burma, Vietnam, and Indonesia. After establishing its reputation of excellence overseas, Kajima was chosen to complete a variety of projects in Taiwan, South Korea, the Philippines, Malaysia, Thailand, and Hong Kong.

The company's name was changed to the Kajima Corporation in 1970 to better reflect its international character and wide range of engineering services. New technologies developed by KICT were continually applied, particularly in the area of aseismic structures. The Institute built an "earthquake simulator" in 1974. A year later a hydraulics laboratory was established, which placed Kajima in a leading position among Japanese companies in dam, breakwater, and ocean platform construction.

Kajima was given full responsibility by the East German government to build the International Trade Center Building in East Berlin, free of government restrictions or demands that local companies be involved in the project. This project marked Kajima's emergence from East Asia. Projects in the United States, Turkey, Algeria, and Zaire followed.

As early as the 1960's Kajima used shield tunnel borers, but KICT introduced new processes which improved the safety and efficiency of established tunneling methods, using water jets and concrete-spraying robots. Kajima also developed a shield tunnel borer capable of making sharp turns, and it was one of several companies involved in the construction of the 54 kilometer Seikan Tunnel, linking the Japanese islands of Honshu and Hokkaido.

In 1982 the Kajima Corporation was awarded the Deming Prize for engineering excellence. Since that time it has continually been given recognition for its achievements. Kajima holds almost 1100 Japanese patents, 72 of which are registered in foreign countries.

In addition to its other major construction activities, Kajima is currently building a floating oil storage facility near Nagasaki capable of holding six million kiloliters (32.4 million barrels) of oil. The company is also working on an integrated method for decommissioning aging nuclear power plants, a service which will become increasingly important as nuclear power plants near the end of their 40–year life spans.

Kajima has remained under family management since its inception. Several years ago, however, when Seiichi Kajima's marriage produced no sons, his daughter Ume married Morino Suke, a career diplomat and scholar who was adopted into the family and given the name Kajima. His first son, Shoichi Kajima, is the company's current president, and a brother-in-law of both the chairman and honorary chairman.

Due to its years of experience, the Kajima Corporation is extremely competitive in railroad, dam, and other civil engineering projects. It also remains one of the strongest Japanese companies in the overseas markets. Kajima has maintained an excellent financial situation with few liabilities and high earnings. The company's research institute and continued strength in the construction of nuclear power plants and earthquake-resistant skyscrapers are indispensable assets which should secure the company's position as Japan's number one civil engineering firm for many years.

Principal Subsidiaries: Toa Co., Ltd.; Taiko Trading Co., Ltd.; Kajima Road Co., Ltd.; Chemical Grouting Co., Ltd.; Kajima Publishing Co., Ltd.; Kajima Productions, Ltd.; Japan Foundation Engineering Co., Ltd.; Japan Sea Works Co., Ltd.; Kajima Services Co., Ltd.; Sanei Real Estate Co., Ltd.; Hotel Kajima No Mori; Kajima Leasing Corp.; Creative Life Corp.; Yaesu Book Center, Inc.; Ilya Corp.; KOCAMB Co., Ltd.; Kajima Tenant Planning Co., Ltd.; Kajima International, Inc. (USA); East West Development Corp. (USA); Kajima Development Corp. (USA); Kajima Engineering and Construction, Inc. (USA); P.T. Waskita-Kajima Corp.; ChungOLu (Sino-Kajima) Construction Co., Ltd. (Taiwan); Kajima GmbH (West Germany); Thai Kajima Co., Ltd. (Thailand); Kajima Corporation Australia Pty., Ltd. (Australia).

KUMAGAI GUMI COMPANY, LTD.

17–1 Tsukudo-cho
Shinjuku-ku, Tokyo
Japan
260-2111

Public Company
Incorporated: January 6, 1938
Employees: 7,931
Sales: ¥ 841 billion (US$ 5.26 billion)
Market Value: ¥ 571.2 billion (US$ 3.573 billion)
Stock Index: Hong Kong Tokyo Osaka

Santaro Kumagai began his career in construction in 1898 as an employee of a private contracting firm. In 1902 Kumagai undertook his first independent project, the Kyoto Electric Power station. When it was completed Kumagai had proved himself a competent manager, capable of resolving complicated design and materials problems. Through subsequent projects, such as the Nakagawa Canal in Nagoya, Kumagai found his expertise in ever greater demand. His still small but growing company was selected to construct the Sanshin Railway (now the Iida Line of the Japanese National Railways). Sanshin was a difficult seven year project which required the development of a new tunnelling method.

The rapid growth and expansion of the Japanese economy, particularly after World War I, created a large demand for new buildings and other structures in Japan. During this period in his career, Santaro Kumagai directly benefitted from the nation's strong economic growth. His company was selected to manage the construction of an increasingly diverse number of residential, industrial, and infrastructural projects.

In the early 1930's militarists seized control of the Japanese government. They declared a "quasi-war economy" and initiated a national mobilization in preparation for the establishment of a "Greater East Asia Co-Prosperity Sphere," economically centered around Japan. The government invested heavily in new construction projects to support the Japanese military and the growing imperialist system of commerce. This created strong demand for Kumagai's services.

A talented business manager named Jinichi Makita joined Kumagai on January 1, 1938. Five days later the company was officially incorporated as Kumagai Gumi, with Santaro Kumagai as its president. Makita was named senior managing director, and Kumagai's son Tasaburo was promoted to vice president.

Diplomatic tension between Japan and Western nations increased dramatically after the Japanese invasion of China in 1937, and continued to grow until the outbreak of war in 1941. Like many companies which were a part of the Japanese military/industrial complex, Kumagai does not discuss its involvement in the Japanese war effort. It may be assumed, however, that during the war Kumagai had little choice but to place its resources at the disposal of the Japanese government.

Japan was heavily bombed during the war. When the war ended in 1945 most of the country's factories and infrastructure had been completely ruined. In order to provide fully integrated construction services, Kumagai Gumi established an architectural design division in 1946. However, while there was a need to rebuild the nation, there were few sources of capital available to invest in new construction.

When the Korean War broke out in 1950, the United States recognized the strategic value of Japan. The formation of new factories and ports was actively encouraged by the Japanese Ministry for International Trade and Investment and elements supporting the United Nations forces in Korea. On May 1, 1951, during a period of heavy activity in construction, Santaro Kumagai died.

Under the continuing leadership of Jinichi Makita, Kumagai Gumi became involved in the construction of highways, hydroelectric dams, and railways. The company contributed significantly to the development of new tunnelling methods. In 1952 Kumagai independently manufactured Japan's first shield tunnel borer, a large tubular device with soil and rock pulverizers mounted on a circular forward shield. The machine is capable of creating a tunnel with a diameter of several meters. In 1958 Kumagai founded a new division called the Toyokawa Works to manufacture specialty construction equipment.

Kumagai Gumi gained a reputation for structurally sound and efficient buildings. In 1960 the company was awarded the Building Contractor's Society Prize for the design and construction of the Nagano Shimin Kaikan (People's Hall) and the Todofuken Kaikan (Prefectural Hall). Kumagai remained active in industrial projects, and completed several more housing, water, and railway tunnel projects. In 1961 Kumagai Gumi accepted its first overseas project, the construction of water reservoirs at Plover Cove and Hebe Haven in Hong Kong.

Tasaburo Kumagai resigned from the presidency on November 28, 1967 to serve as a senator in the Japanese Diet, but remained a company director. Jinichi Makita, who had served as company chairman since 1964, took over the presidency. After only a year Kumagai decided to leave politics and return to the company, where he was named chairman.

Kumagai Gumi continued to expand both in Japan and abroad. The company's Toyokawa and architectural research facilities developed a number of new engineering and design techniques which greatly improved the company's abilities and further enhanced its reputation. In 1969 Kumagai was chosen by the Republican Chinese government on Taiwan to construct the Tachien hydroelectric dam (the highest dam in Asia) for the Taiwan Power Company, and was later chosen to expand Hong Kong's Kai Tak Airport and develop the Castle Peak Highway.

In November of 1970 Tasaburo Kumagai's son Taichiro was named managing director of the company. Two years later when Taichiro Kumagai was promoted to vice president, Jinichi Makita's son Shinichiro was named a company director. That same year, 1972, Kumagai Gumi was listed on the Hong Kong Stock Exchange and a subsidiary called P.D. Kadi International was established in Indonesia.

In keeping with the growing volume of work Kumagai was performing in Hong Kong, a subsidiary was established there in 1973. Kumagai Gumi subsequently incorporated subsidiaries in Taiwan (1974), the Philippines (1976), Iran (1977), the United States (1980), and Australia (1983).

In 1975 Kumagai Gumi undertook its first high-rise building project, the Shinjuku Nomura building in Tokyo. Completed in 1978, the building has 53 stories and stands 210 meters high. In 1976 the company became the first in Japan to employ successfully the New Austrian Tunnelling Method (NATM). The NATM involves driving support rods deep into rock surrounding the tunnel and then spraying concrete onto the tunnel walls. This combination of measures virtually eliminates any later contraction in the tunnel's size due to soft or unstable rock. Since Kumagai introduced NATM, almost all the tunnels it builds utilizes this method.

Kumagai Gumi was awarded a contract to construct a water supply tunnel at Isfahan in Iran. Although the project was initiated by the Shah, subsequent regimes under the revolutionary government of the Ayatollah Khomeini elected to continue the project.

On December 22, 1978 a series of management changes were made. Jinichi Makita was named chairman, Taichiro Kumagai was promoted to president, and Shinichiro Makita became a vice president. Tasaburo Kumagai continued to serve as a director and special consultant.

Kumagai has expanded its involvement in tall buildings, bridges, and industrial infrastructures, while remaining a leading name in tunnel construction. Some of the company's more spectacular building projects include the Victoria Central Development Project in Australia, the Columbus Circle Condominium in Manhattan, and the Bank of China Building (designed by I.M. Pei & Partners) in Hong Kong. The Onaruto Bridge located in southern Japan, with a total length of 1629 meters, is Kumagai's longest suspension bridge. Kumagai Gumi tunnels include the submerged Mass Transit Railway tunnel beneath Hong Kong Harbor, the Rogers Pass Tunnel in Canada, and the 53.8-kilometer Seikan railway tunnel which connects the Japanese islands of Honshu and Hokkaido.

On November 12, 1986, Jinichi Makita died at the age of 94. Makita was known for his willingness to involve the company in difficult projects, which in turn helped to establish Kumagai's reputation as one of the world's most capable construction firms. Today, Kumagai Gumi is Japan's largest construction company and ranks among the top 20 worldwide.

Principal Subsidiaries: Kumagai Doro Co., Ltd.; Sampo Special Construction Co., Ltd.; Port Island Housing Co., Ltd.; Nippon Pressed Concrete Co., Ltd.; Kyowa Takuken Development Co., Ltd.; Tochi Kogyo Co., Ltd.; Kumagai Gumi (Hong Kong) Ltd.; Kumagai International, Ltd. (Hong Kong); Everbright-Kumagai Development Co., Ltd. (Hong Kong); Shenzhen Kumagai Co., Ltd. (China); P.T. Kadi International (Indonesia); Taiwan Kumagai Co., Ltd.; Summa Kumagai, Inc. (Philippines); Kumagai-Zenecon Construction Pte. Ltd. (Singapore); Zenecon-Kumagai Sdn. Bhd. (Malaysia); Kumagai (N.S.W.) Pty. Ltd. (Australia); Kumagai Australia Finance Ltd.; Kumam Corporation (USA); KG Land California Corp. (USA); Kumagai International USA Corporation; KG Land New York Corp. (USA); KG (Hawaii) Corporation (USA); Kumagai Properties , Inc. (USA); Kumagai Construction, Ltd. (Canada); Kumagai Overseas (Curacao) N.V. (Netherlands Antilles); Kumagai Gumi U.K., Ltd.

LINDE A.G.

Abraham Lincoln Strasse 21
6200 Wiesbaden 1
Federal Republic of West Germany
(061) 217701

Public Company
Incorporated: 1879
Employees: 15,000
Sales: DM2.619 billion (US$1.349 billion)
Market Value: DM3.4 billion (US$1.751 billion)
Stock Index: Berlin Frankfurt Munich Düsseldorf
Hamburg

Carle von Linde invented his refrigeration machine in 1875, and formed his own company four years later. Ever since, Linde A.G. has been involved in a wide variety of engineering endeavors, from manufacturing refrigeration and air conditioning systems to the production of rare gases and the construction of an array of industrial plants.

Linde was born in Berndorf on June 11, 1842. He became professor of mechanical engineering at the College of Technology in Munich at the age of 26 and retained that position until he was 68. Linde made the most of his time spent at the school and undertook research in the areas of refrigeration and air and gas liquification processes. For the first ten years of his company's existence, Linde took a sabbatical from teaching and was its sole director. After the firm was well on its way to success, however, Linde returned and directed its operations from the college. He died on November 16, 1934.

Linde consists of four divisions managed by the executive board of directors in Wiesbaden: the refrigeration and shop equipment division; the industrial gases division; the process plant engineering and construction division; and the hydraulic and materials handling equipment division. The present divisional breakdown of the company did not formally occur until 1972, but these operations have traditionally followed separate paths of development.

Linde's first scientific breakthrough, which occurred in 1875, was an ammonia compression machine used for manufacturing ice. Four years later, Linde founded Gesellschaft für Linde's Eismachinen. Initially, orders for refrigeration machines were "almost distressingly slow." Looking for possible business alternatives, his solution was to engineer and supply ice factories in which his refrigeration machines would be installed. By 1890, over 700 of his machines were employed in 445 breweries across western Europe.

Soon thereafter, the company changed its emphasis from planning ice factories to building and operating cold stores. Linde co-founded Gesellschaft für Markt-und Kühlhallen in Berlin to use his refrigeration technology and expand the cold stores operations. Yet, for over 50 years, even though other firms purchased Linde's refrigeration systems, and most of the company's ice factories had been sold, the cold storage operations were never a financial success. As a result, Linde sold all of its holdings in that area during 1982 and 1983.

It was only after 1920 that the company's sales of refrigeration equipment skyrocketed, due primarily to the acquisition of two major competitors. Industriegas GmbH., located in Mannheim, designed oxygen generators. The value of the purchase for Linde, however, was in the Industriegas subsidiary, Maschinenfabrik Sürth. Sürth, situated near Cologne, was well-known as the first German company to manufacture transportation containers for compressed and liquified gases, and also for the production of various components for refrigeration units. The second significant acquisition was Kulmöbelwerk G.H. Walb and Company of Mainz-Kostheim, a manufacturer of large commercial items such as refrigerated grocery counters.

After their assimilation by Linde, and throughout the 1930's, the Sürth works built components and systems units for commercial refrigeration, while G.H. Walb made smaller units and domestic products. Commercial production continued through World War II, although these plants were required to provide mining and compression units to the armed forces. Near the end of the war, both the Sürth and the G.H. Walb works were entirely destroyed. By 1949, however, a new machine shop had been built at the Sürth facility, and by 1960 the operation had been completely reconstructed. Soon afterwards, Linde established its entire refrigeration engineering department at this factory. The branches at Sürth and G.H. Walb were then combined in 1964 to form the present refrigeration and shop equipment division.

Carl von Linde's 1895 invention for producing liquid air led to the growth of the TVT München division of process plant engineering and construction. In addition, his related research with other rare gases laid the groundwork for what is presently the industrial gases division. The separation of these divisions was more for administrative purposes than for anything else, since their operations significantly overlap.

Linde's initial plan was systematically to improve the design and production of air liquifiers, and he devoted much of his time in Munich to the development of new gas liquification processes. In 1902, the company built the first oxygen production plant and in 1904 constructed the first plant for the production of pure nitrogen. Linde also built the first double-column rectifier, which allowed pure oxygen and nitrogen to be produced in the same apparatus without using any extra energy.

During this time, Linde also built gas production plants in Düsseldorf, Mülheim, Nürnberg, and Dresden. Expanding throughout Europe, the company built plants in Antwerp, Toulouse, Paris, Barcelona, Stockholm,

Vienna, and London. In 1907 Linde established the Linde Air Products Company in Cleveland, Ohio. (This plant was extremely successful; eventually acquired by Union Carbide, it is presently called the Linde division.)

Until World War II, Linde was deeply involved in expanding its existing plants. During the war, however, both the plant engineering and construction and industrial gases facilities within Germany were heavily damaged; as a result, they had difficulty re-establishing their operations both at home and abroad. However, the economic prosperity in West Germany during the late 1950's and early 1960's led to a rise in domestic demand for liquid oxygen and nitrogen, and contracts with former partners overseas were also renewed.

Linde built the world's first heavy water nuclear energy plant in 1955 and the first system to separate radioactive elements from nuclear reactor gases in 1959. It also constructed, in 1964, the world's largest air separation unit in West Germany; two years later the company built the world's largest ammonia-synthesis plant in the U.S.; in 1970, it devised Europe's most extensive helium refrigeration system.

The Güldner Aschaffenburg division had its beginnings very early in the century when Linde needed engines to drive the refrigeration machines his firm was manufacturing. He formed a partnership with Dr. Hugo Güldner, a chief design engineer, and Dr. Georg von Krauss, a locomotive manufacturer. The first diesel engines were built at the Güldner works in 1907; by this time, Linde controlled the majority of company stock.

During World War I, the factory was retooled entirely for the war effort, manufacturing iron shells, motor vehicles and aircraft engines. The company recovered quickly in the 1920's, and expanded its product line to include engines for agricultural equipment and components for the repair of locomotives, railcars, and boats. The Güldner facilities were taken over completely by Linde in 1929 and thereafter concentrated on producing small diesel engines and tractors.

The plant in Aschaffenburg was totally destroyed during an Allied air raid in World War II, but the works were fully functional once again by 1950. A new era for the company began in 1955 with the production of the Hydrocar, a platform truck with hydrostatic transmission. Linde then acquired the hydraulics department of Gusswerk Paul Saalmann & Sohne in 1958. By 1969, the Aschaffenburg factory discontinued the production of tractors and diesel engines and concentrated entirely on fork-lift trucks and hydraulic equipment.

There have been a number of important developments during the 1980's. The refrigeration and shop equipment division has designed its units for energy conservation as well as individually customized them to match contemporary store styles throughout the world. The current product line covers a comprehensive selection of refrigerated and freezer display cases, refrigeration systems, and energy monitoring and control systems. Besides the impressive growth in orders from Arab countries, industrial users, whose needs range from switchgears and transformers to computer rooms and brewery storage, have also contributed to increased profits for Linde.

Much of the innovative research in the utilization of wastewater and sewage has been conducted at Linde's process plant engineering and construction division. The new techniques it has developed during the 1980's include the highly economical DS process for storing and utilizing sewage sludge and the Laran process for anaerobic decomposition of contaminated wastewaters. Additional environmental protection research has been conducted in the purification of flue gases, including the mechanism known as smokestack "scrubbers."

The industrial gases division has maintained a strong market position: stricter environmental protection measures in many countries have led to increased use of oxygen in the steel industry, at foundries, and in the manufacture of electrodes; the wastewater purification field has grown sizably in the past decade; and demand for high-purity gases has increased dramatically in the semiconductor and glass-fiber industries.

The improvement in the Güldner Aschaffenburg division's sales, due largely to new drive and transmission systems developed in recent years, has been mostly in the form of exports to foreign companies manufacturing agricultural and construction equipment. In addition, in 1985 this division also produced a small, three-ton capacity, fork-lift truck which has helped to increase sales. However, continued growth in this area is limited due to competition, lower prices, and a worldwide overcapacity.

The breakdown of division size in terms of sales is approximately: refrigeration and shop equipment, 19%; process plant engineering and construction, 25%; industrial gases, 21%; hydraulics and materials handling, 35%. Linde's long-term goals are to increase inventory turnover, maintain nearly full employment of its facilities, and retain the company's reputation as a world leader in the construction industry.

Principal Subsidiaries: Still GmbH; Matra-Werke GmbH; Linde Technische Gase Berlin; °Celsior GmbH; Selas-Kirchner GmbH; Mapag Maschinenfabrik GmbH; Tega-Technische Gase and Gasetechnik GmbH; Rheinkälte GmbH; Wohnungsbau Linde GmbH; Commercium Versicherungsagenfur und Immobilien GmbH; Werburg and Messebau GmbH; Markt-und Külhallen Aktiengesellschaft; Wagner Fördertechnik GmbH & Co.; Société d'Application des Techniques Linde S.A.R.L.; Linde Froid et Climatisation S.A.R.L.; Fenwick-Linde S.A.R.L.; Fenwick Location S.A.; Still S.A.; Airgaz S.A.R.L.; Abello, Oxigeno- Linde S.A.; Carretillas E Hidraulica, S.A.; Walter Stöcklin S.A.E.; Linde Technische Gase GmbH; Linde Kältetechnik GmbH; TEGA-Technische Gase GmbH; Linde Refrigeration Ltd.; Linde Hydraulics Ltd.; Linde Kältetechnik AG; Linde Fördertechnik AG; Linde Holding AG; Pangas, Likos AG; Linde K.T. Italiana S.p.a.; Linde Güldner Italiana S.p.a.; Still Italia S.p.a.; Sarca N.V.; Still N.V.; L'Oxyhydrique Internationale S.A.; Still Intern Transport B.V.; Linde International B.V.; Airgas Nederland B.V.; N.V.W.A. Hoek's Machine-en Zuurstoffabrief; A/S Dansk Ilt- & Brintfabrik; Linde K.T. Norge A/S; Linde-Hellas E.P.E.; Linarco Ltd., Saudi Arabia; Fedgas (Pty) Ltd., South

Africa; Linde Far East Engineering, Ltd., Japan; Linde (Australia) Pty. Ltd.; Linde Gas Pty. Ltd.; Lotepro Corp.; Selas Fluid Processing Corp.; Baker Material Handling Corp.; Linde Hydraulics Corp.; Lagus Capital Corp.; Lotepro Plants Ltd., Canada; Linde do Brasil Ltda., Brazil; Aeroton Gases Industrials Ltda., Brazil.

Mellon Stuart Company

MELLON-STUART COMPANY

One NorthShore Center
Pittsburgh, Pennsylvania
U.S.A.
(412) 323-4600

Private Company
Incorporated: December 31, 1917
Employees: 1500
Sales: $949.5 million

One of the oldest construction companies in the United States, the Mellon-Stuart Company is involved in general contracting; construction management; and industrial, mining, heavy and highway construction. In the past two decades Mellon-Stuart has experienced tremendous growth, and is now one of the top ten builders in the nation. Though the company's work traditionally has been concentrated in the eastern states, Mellon-Stuart has in recent years begun to expand its realm to encompass the entire continental U.S.

In the early 1900's, Thomas A. Mellon of Pittsburgh decided on a career outside the prominent family banking business. With associate Robert Grace and uncles Andrew W. Mellon and Richard B. Mellon, he organized a firm which specialized in railroad, tunnel and bridge construction. The firm, called the Robert Grace Contracting Company, was responsible for large construction jobs for the Cleveland Belt Line, the Erie Railroad, and the Baltimore & Ohio, Erie and Pennsylvania. Thomas Mellon became president of the firm several years later after buying Grace's interest. In 1917 the company merged with the Stuart Company, which specialized in reinforced concrete work and erecting office buildings and power plants. Stuart had built several large office buildings in the Pittsburgh area, most notably the Oliver Building and the City-County Building. James L. Stuart served as president of the merged Mellon-Stuart firm for two years. Upon his retirement in 1919 due to failing health, he sold his interest in the enterprise to Thomas Mellon. By 1921 Mellon was the president and sole owner of Mellon-Stuart.

In the early years, the firm's activities were primarily in heavy industrial construction, especially railroad and bridge work. Railroads that contracted with Mellon-Stuart were the Illinois Central; Delaware, Lackawanna & Western; Baltimore & Ohio; Norfolk & Western; and Erie and Pennsylvania. The majority of the company's non-railroad work was in Pittsburgh, but Mellon-Stuart also maintained offices in New York and Chicago. The Chicago area was the more active of the two; in that city the firm built, among other projects, the massive Union Station in 1925 and the exclusive Standard Club. (Al Capone worked for Mellon-Stuart as a laborer on the Union Station job.) In the New York area the company concentrated on commercial construction; two important projects were the Pren-Brook Apartment Building and the Flatbush Industrial Building.

In the 1920's and 1930's Mellon-Stuart erected many distinctive buildings in Pittsburgh, including the Mellon Bank headquarters (completed in 1921), the Koppers Building (1929—at that time the city's tallest), the Gulf Oil Corporation headquarters (1933), and the Mellon Institute (1937). The Mellon Institute was a scientific research center established by the two uncles who had helped Thomas Mellon get started in construction, both members of the banking part of the family. Begun in 1913 as part of the University of Pittsburgh, from 1927 to 1967 it functioned as an independent entity. In 1967 it joined the Carnegie Tech to form Carnegie Mellon University. Construction of the facility lasted from 1930 to 1937 and entailed solving some unusual engineering problems. Designed to echo classical Greek architecture, the building is ringed with 62 columns and has five below-ground levels (to keep the facade low, in keeping with its Greek precedents). To ensure that the 42-foot columns would not chip when lowered into place, Mellon-Stuart engineers had enormous blocks of ice positioned on the precise spot where each column was to rest, then placed the column atop the ice. As the ice melted, the column gradually dropped into place. Construction of the building required 269 traincar loads of limestone and 62 of granite.

The New York and Chicago offices closed in 1930 as the company began feeling the effects of the Depression. In 1933 Mellon-Stuart let its construction permits in those cities expire. During the Depression the company also sold all its heavy construction equipment. From then on, Mellon-Stuart no longer engaged in bridge, railroad or tunnel construction, concentrating instead on commercial, institutional, industrial and industrial housing activities.

The firm's third president, E.P. "Ned" Mellon, the son of Thomas Mellon, began his tenure with the company in November 1930, though not in a management capacity; he worked an air hammer on the Mellon Institute construction job. A Mellon-Stuart foreman had bet the younger Mellon $50 that he could not operate an air hammer for 60 days at the bottom of a 4.5-foot diameter caisson. By the time Mellon collected his money, he had dug to 42 feet below the bottom floor of the Mellon Institute.

In 1936 Ned Mellon took a vice presidency in the firm. He assumed the presidency in 1947 when his father became chairman of the board. The elder Mellon retired later the same year because of ill health. Ned Mellon moved into the chairmanship at that time, and another vice president, James B. Kelly, took the presidency. Two years later, in 1951, Mellon-Stuart recruited Donald C. Peters to replace Kelly. Peters had been the director and vice president of Crump, Inc., another Pittsburgh firm. Ned Mellon remained the chairman, and the two men controlled Mellon-Stuart together until 1975. Bob Peters took the presidency in 1975, when his older brother Donald became chairman of the board. Five years later Bob Peters replaced his brother as chairman; he stayed in the post until 1986.

Defense contracts were plentiful during World War II. Mellon-Stuart received six large-scale contracts, the largest being one for more than $17 million to build Camp Reynolds (with a capacity of 20,000 troops) outside Greenville, Pennsylvania. After the war Mellon-Stuart offices opened outside Pittsburgh again. The first were in Youngstown, Ohio; Fairmont, West Virginia; and Owensboro, Kentucky. Contracts during the late 1940's ranged in size from the $8.5 million western area headquarters building for Bell Telephone of Pennsylvania to small jobs for as little as a thousand dollars.

Mellon-Stuart undertook several internal innovations during the 1950's. These included an employee incentive plan, quarterly salary bonuses and a comprehensive budget control program. The first two have been quite successful, enabling the firm to boast that its annual personnel turnover at the managerial level has been lower than 5% during the life of the company. The third was a cost estimating and control system called Advanced Budget Control, under which bidding for all jobs to be done by contractors is handled in the order the tasks will follow in the construction process. Bidding begins during the design process, though bids for some later phases are not received until after construction has begun. Standard practice dictated taking all bids at once, and only after the design phase is complete. Mellon-Stuart's method shortened the time between design and construction.

David Figgins joined Mellon-Stuart as a trainee estimator during the 1950's; he is now chairman of the board. In 1954 Figgins emigrated to the United States from Ireland to pursue a career in singing. He only managed to earn $68 a week as a professional vocalist, however, so he took a job as a field engineer for a Toronto construction firm. Figgins signed on with Mellon-Stuart at Bob Peters' request in 1956. He worked as a project engineer, field engineer and project manager, until in 1964 he became a vice president of the firm. In 1980 he would take the Mellon-Stuart presidency.

In the 1960's, Mellon-Stuart established an Employee Stock Ownership Plan, but initially few employees participated. Indeed, by 1970 all stock in the company was held by just eight managers. At one point, Donald Peters owned 50% of the stock, and his brother held another 30%. Retirement by people holding such large interests would clearly create cash strains, because they would take their equity with them. In fact, it was rumored that Bob Peters was asked to delay his retirement precisely because of the prospect of a cash problem. Subsequent changes in the plan have made it impossible for individuals to hold more than 10% of Mellon-Stuart's stock. At present the company is entirely employee-owned.

Mellon-Stuart reorganized as a holding company and expanded its activities greatly during the 1970's. The company especially sought contracts outside the Pittsburgh area, primarily because of the decline of Pennsylvania's steel-based economy. At the same time Mellon-Stuart reopened an office in Chicago, and it now operates a total of five offices in the United States. In 1972 the company entered the mining business when it formed Badger Construction, a mine construction division. At the beginning of the 1980's the construction industry magazine *Engineering New Record* ranked Mellon-Stuart 192nd in its list of the top 400 contractors in the U.S.

The current president of Mellon-Stuart, Edward Poth, left the presidency of Paschen Contractors Inc. of Chicago to join the company in 1986. Paschen's rank in the industry was much higher than Mellon-Stuart's and the majority of its jobs have been competitively bid public works projects. Figgins, who is now chairman, has stated that this is the direction in which Mellon-Stuart management wants to move. The firm hopes to achieve an equal blend of competitive bids and negotiated contracts. Since Poth joined the company, it has reduced its number of ongoing jobs and begun to concentrate on projects of a larger scale. Figgins has said the company should have 15 continuing projects in its portfolio at any given time, and that it will only seek jobs in the $10 million to $40 million range.

In recent years Mellon-Stuart has attempted to tighten control over its operations, in part because several projects went badly in the mid-1980's. For instance, the company lost over $2 million on a Pittsburgh renovation project when the developer went into bankruptcy. Also, though the company will continue to operate regional offices, all operations are under central control. Reorganization within Mellon-Stuart in the past few years has entailed consolidating operations and streamlining the managerial organization, resulting in the elimination of jobs, changes in the structure of responsibility and reassignment of personnel. In the current structure, each officer of the company is responsible for developing a long-term relationship with at least one repeat client or promising prospect.

Today Mellon-Stuart is the ninth largest general builder in the U.S. It ranks as the country's 24th largest contractor and the 35th construction manager. In the future, the firm's management hopes to enter more joint ventures and broaden Mellon-Stuart's geographic scope to encompass the entire continental U.S.

Principal Subsidiaries: Cameron Construction; Carnegie Properties, Inc.

OHBAYASHI CORPORATION

3 Kanda Tsukasacho 2-chome
Chiyoda-ku
Tokyo 101
Japan
(03) 292-1111

Public Company
Incorporated: 1919 as Ohbayashi Gumi
Employees: 10,409
Sales: ¥ 770.5 billion (US$3.057 billion)
Market Value: ¥ 157.7 billion (US$625.6 million)
Stock Index: Osaka Toyko Nagoya

The Ohbayashi Corporation is one of the largest general construction companies in the world, integrating engineering, design, contracting, construction and management. It has gained a reputation for solving difficult engineering problems by developing new methods and technologies for specific projects. Hundreds of structures in Japan and throughout the Pacific Rim stand as monuments to Ohbayashi's engineering ability.

Japan embarked on a national program of modernization after the Meiji Restoration in 1868 which stimulated demand for newer, larger and more durable buildings. Yoshigoro Ohbayashi took advantage of the favorable market conditions in 1892 and opened a small construction business in Osaka. After six years, completing modest construction jobs, he was joined by a talented young man named Kanezo Shirasugi. Ohbayashi and Shirasugi completed several more projects while refining their engineering and construction skills. In 1901 Ohbayashi was awarded its first major contract: the grounds and buildings for Osaka's Fifth National Industry Fair, completed in 1904. The following year Japan and Russia went to war for control over Manchuria and, in turn, dominance in the Far East. Ohbayashi erected 100 barracks and 10 field hospitals for the Japanese army in only three weeks, helping to contribute to the subsequent Japanese victory.

The company was reorganized as a limited partnership in 1909. Shortly afterwards, Ohbayashi finished building the landmark Tokyo railroad station, which was one of the few structures to withstand the Great Kanto Earthquake in 1923. Soon the company was awarded its first heavy construction contract to build a railroad tunnel linking Osaka and Nara. Yoshigoro Ohbayashi's son Yoshio was placed in charge of the company in 1916 while still a 22-year old student at Wasedo University. Two years later the company was incorporated and its name changed to Ohbayashi Gumi.

In the early 1920's Ohbayashi executives were invited by the Fluor Company to study modern construction methods in the United States. These executives brought back the technology learned in the U.S. to Japan where it was assimilated by Ohbayashi's design engineers. Ohbayashi erected three major structures during this period, including the Mainichi Newspaper Office, the Sumitomo building in Osaka, and the Merchant Marine Building in Kobe, all of which are still standing today.

The earthquake in 1923 leveled much of Tokyo and created a firestorm which destroyed many more buildings. Ohbayashi was called upon to construct new buildings which were both earthquake-resistant and fireproof. The demand for Ohbayashi's modern buildings helped the company to expand rapidly. One of its products is Koshien Stadium near Osaka, popular for its bi-annual high school baseball tournaments.

When Japanese militarists came to power in Japan a decade later, Ohbayashi was employed to complete a considerable number of building projects for the state. The company does not discuss its role in the Japanese war effort.

After the war Yoshio Ohbayashi turned the company over to his son-in-law because his marriage had not produced any male offspring. His daughter's husband Yoshiro adopted the family name and subsequently became head of the house of Ohbayashi. The practice of a man taking his wife's name in marriage is common in Japan when a family has no blood relative male descendants.

During the American occupation of the immediate postwar period, reconstruction was slow. Japan was forced to remit war reparations which reduced the amount of capital available for construction. However, when North Korean military forces invaded South Korea in 1950, Japan's role in the Western alliance was changed. The country was to be reconstructed as a modern industrial ally in an effort to balance Western strategic interests in Asia with communist China and Soviet interests. Ohbayashi was in an ideal position to benefit from the accelerated demand for new construction. The company won contracts for the Japan Broadcasting Corporation, the Tokyo railroad station annex, and the Mainichi Osaka Center completed in 1956. Also during the 1950's, Ohbayashi completed its first hydroelectric dam.

In 1961 Ohbayashi developed a new method for building concrete walls with technology adapted from Soletanche Company of France. The technology, called *OWS* (for Ohbayashi Wet Screen), was first used in the construction of the New Osaka building and remains an integral part of Ohbayashi's construction method. The company further diversified its scope of operations in 1964 when it laid its first highway. Ohbayashi has had a major role in the construction of every major expressway in Japan ever since.

When the island of Singapore declared its independence from the Malaysian union in 1956, a massive land reclamation project was planned for the island's east coast. Ohbayashi was chosen to execute the engineering and five of the project's seven phases. By the time the reclamation was completed in 1984, Ohbayashi moved 100 million cubic meters of earth to reclaim 2170 hectares (8.37 square miles) of land, upon which were built several housing projects and Singapore's Changi International Airport.

During the 1970's Ohbayashi developed an innovative new tunneling method and a light weight air membrane dome roof. In 1978 Ohbayashi constructed its headquarters in Osaka with the intention of showcasing the company's expertise in energy-efficient designs. A second facility, the Technical Research Institute, is considered the most energy-efficient building in the world.

Ohbayashi recently completed work on the world's largest liquid natural gas storage facility at Sodegaura, and an underground drainage and reservoir system near Osaka designed to hold flood waters from the Hirano River. Ohbayashi also engineered an earthquake-proof "dynamic" floor for the Sumitomo Bank which is designed to insulate sensitive computers from violent geologic activity. Numerous other construction projects are completed each year, including the restoration of national treasures like the Katsura Rikyu Detached Villa, building nuclear power plant containment vessels, and manufacturing concrete tiles for "Bullet" trains.

Ohbayashi not only completes hundreds of projects each year in Japan, but also an increasingly large number of projects overseas. In 1984 the company's name was anglicized (from Ohbayashi Gumi to Ohbayashi Corporation) to reflect its growing internationalization. The Ohbayashi Corporation was chosen to supervise the renovation of Shanghai International Airport in China. Over 60 dams have been built by Ohbayashi in a number of southeast Asian nations. The city of San Francisco chose Ohbayashi to install a major sewer main under difficult conditions through soft and unstable soil. Other American projects include the Toyota automobile plant in Georgetown, Kentucky and an irrigation tunnel for farmland in Utah. Since it became a member of the U.S. Civil Engineering Society in 1986, Ohbayashi is expected to become eligible for even more projects in the United States.

Yoshiro Ohbayashi believes his company will continue to be a leader in the construction industry for many years. "A well-built building," he says, "will last anywhere from 25 to 250 years. As contractors and architects, we must be able to envision what life will be like, and design structures to match."

Architectural critics have generally given Ohbayashi excellent marks in all phases of its work. With an impressive portfolio of accomplishments and with a worldwide network of offices, Ohbayashi can be expected to remain one of the leading construction corporations in the world.

Principal Subsidiaries: Thai Ohbayashi Corporation, Ltd. (Thailand); P.T. Jaya-Ohbayashi Corporation (Jakarta, Indonesia); Ohbayashi Malaysia SDN. BHD (Malaysia); Ohbayashi America Corporation; United Development Corporation (USA); James E. Roberts-Ohbayashi Corporation (California, USA); Ohbayashi Hawaii Corporation (Hawaii, USA); Ohbayashi Associates Hawaii, Inc. (Hawaii, USA); Kauai Development Corporation (Honolulu, USA); Saudi Japan Construction Company, Ltd (Riyadh, Saudi Arabia); PM Ohbayashi (B) SDN. RHD (Brunei); Citadel Corporation (USA); Ohbayashi Europe B.V. (Netherlands).

Bovis

THE PENINSULAR & ORIENTAL STEAM NAVIGATION COMPANY (BOVIS DIVISION)

79 Pall Mall
London SW1Y 5EJ
England
(01) 930-4343

Incorporated: 1928
Employees: 2,400
Sales: £618 million (US$877 million)

Bovis was a small and relatively unremarkable building enterprise for its first 60 years of operation, but in the years following World War I energetic management and a series of progressive innovations began to expand the firm into a diversified builder. Bovis suffered a financial setback engendered by an aggressive acquisitions spree in the early 1970's, leading to a takeover by the Peninsular & Oriental Steam Navigation Company in 1974. Carefully controlled growth in the 1980's has made Bovis Britain's fourth largest builder.

In 1885 a Mr. Saunders sold the small building business he had founded thirty years before to C.W. Bovis, who changed the enterprise's name to his own. Bovis spent nearly 25 years nurturing the business before he decided to retire. In 1929 he sold the company to Sidney Glyn and Samuel Joseph. The company continued quietly for another ten years.

V.E. Vincent, Glyn's younger brother, joined the company at the end of World War I. He redesigned the nameboards displayed on construction sites to attract more attention to the firm and took Bovis into furniture making with the design of a wardrobe for men called the Compactom. A now defunct subsidiary by the same name manufactured and sold the units.

An important innovation in the firm's construction operations during the 1920's was the "Bovis System" of negotiating a contract. At the time many builders were struggling with the high and often unpredictable costs of construction, as well as with the intense competition for contracts. While some created precise techniques for estimating the cost of building to a given design, Bovis suggested instead that clients bring in the builder from the beginning. The builder would then base its estimate on the mutually developed design. The plan greatly reduced the likelihood of surprise costs arising after work was under-

way. It also enabled Bovis to get an early lead on competitors interested in a particular construction job but not prepared to participate in the design phase. In 1927 Marks & Spencer was Bovis's first customer under the procedure. In later years there would be many more.

Bovis Ltd. went public in 1928 but remained both a parent and an operating company. Glyn, Joseph and Vincent rotated yearly in the executive positions. As the Depression took hold, the company formed a subsidiary called Multiple Properties and hired a property scout to find and purchase suitable sites for Bovis-built shopping centers. Other subsidiaries were created at the same time to take over specialized functions: Nox Ltd. competed for contracts for which the Bovis System was not suitable; and Yeomans & Partners Ltd. handled small jobs. Bovis also established its own school to train builders for the firm.

Like most construction companies, Bovis benefitted from World War II. It won the contract for moving the entire Woolwich Arsenal to Staffordshire in 1940 and later worked with Laing and others on the floating Mulberry Harbours used in the D-Day invasion. Nox build several airfields, and Yeomans & Partners repaired London buildings and works damaged by bombs.

Soon after the war ended, Joseph died (he had been Lord Mayor of London for a time) and Vincent retired. Glyn remained as chairman and named Paul Gilbert managing director. Gilbert immediately formed another subsidiary, Gilbert-Ash Ltd., to specialize in civil engineering and overseas work.

The company expanded rapidly overseas, primarily in Africa, where most British construction companies sought work after the war. At home in England, Gilbert-Ash also took advantage of the prefabricated housing boom. In 1951 the division started erecting schools and other public buildings with a pre-stressed concrete system called Integrid. Another Bovis invention, the plastic window, appeared at this time, but it did not succeed.

By 1959, fifty years after Glyn and his partners had purchased Bovis, they had built it from a small company into an international group of semi-autonomous and often competitive subsidiaries. Glyn retired that year. After the sudden death of Gilbert in 1960, Bovis made administrative changes designed to ensure tighter financial control and accountability and more flexible senior management. The company also bought two housing development companies. The acquisitions boosted the group's profits from £750,000 in 1967 to £13.5 million in 1972.

Bovis then went on a buying spree, but without changing management practices to accommodate growth. The firm acquired many companies in the U.K., one in Canada, one in Southeast Asia, and property developing sites in Europe. Overextended and somewhat vague about management of the various interests, Bovis began suffering an inward collapse. Profits dropped from the 1972 high to a loss of £12 million in 1973. The company was now an easy target for a takeover; the next year it became a wholly-owned subsidiary of the Peninsular & Oriental Steam Navigation Company (P & O).

After extensive reorganization by P & O, Bovis's profits crept back up to £7.7 million in 1975. Excess properties were sold, and the construction and civil engineering divisions expanded. Two years later, profits had risen to £8.5 million. However, by 1978 the number of employees had dropped to 2,854 from nearly 10,000 in theearly 1970's.

In the 1980's Bovis has maintained steady, controlled growth, eventually becoming Britain's fourth largest builder. In this decade the firm has received major contracts for the Westminster Conference Centre, a prison in Cambridge, and the rebuilding of the Lloyds headquarters.

Principal Subsidiaries: Gilbert-Ash Ltd.; Audley Properties Ltd.; Bovis Construction Ltd.; Bovis International Inc.; Constructional Units Ltd.; Sepec Securities Ltd.; Wysegroup Ltd.; Yeomans & Partners Ltd.

TAYLOR WOODROW

TAYLOR WOODROW PLC

10 Park Street
London W1Y 4DD
England
(01) 499-8871

Public Company
Incorporated: 1921
Employees: 9,649
Sales: £927 million (US$1.316 billion)
Market Value: £526 million (US$746 million)
Stock Index: London

Frank Taylor, the founder of Taylor Woodrow, was a shopkeeper's son who became a tycoon and a peer of the realm. He was born in Hadfield, near Glossop, Derbyshire in 1905. His family lived in a small house with the front room converted into a fruit shop; by the age of eleven, Frank was operating the business alone.

While Frank was still a teenager the family moved to Blackpool and his father set himself up as a fruit wholesaler. Frank learned the business by working for a rival wholesaler. By 1921 his father decided to buy a house, but he was unable to secure a loan. Sixteen-year-old Frank offered the following arrangement: he would put up £30, his father £70, and the bank, with whom Frank had negotiated, a £400 loan. Frank proposed to build two houses with the money, including one for his uncle. In the event, Frank with his family sold the newly-completed houses, realizing a handsome profit.

Frank soon began building small developments of 20 to 30 houses. His plan was to make enough money to open a fruit wholesale business in California, but his early successes persuaded him to remain in the construction industry.

After a few years in business, government authorities realized that Frank was still a minor, and ruled that his land and property deals were illegal. Frank's uncle Jack agreed to serve as his adult partner, but Jack's sole contribution was the addition of his surname, Woodrow, to the company's title.

In 1930, Frank Taylor moved his business to London where he purchased some marshy land near a proposed factory. After arranging another loan, he installed a pumping station to drain the land and built houses for the new factory's employees. He sold 50 houses in the first week at an average cost of £450 each. The estate, Grange Park, took three years to complete and comprised 1,200 homes. By 1934, Taylor Woodrow's profits were £54,000 and the firm was building estates throughout the home counties and southern England.

The company went public the following year with a capitalization of £400,000. Taylor, the managing director, then established a housing and apartment development company on Long Island, New York. Returning to London, Taylor purchased 100 acres of land along the Grand Union Canal and built new company headquarters; the offices were designed so that they could be converted into houses if extra funds were needed.

Shortly before World War II, Taylor Woodrow received contracts from the war office to build military installations, and after war was declared, the company constructed gunnery camps, anti-torpedo boat gun emplacements, land and sea defense works, hospitals, factories, caissons, and an aerodrome. When schedules were threatened because most of the workforce had been enlisted, Taylor hired laborers from Ireland, a technically neutral country. With workers and government contracts in plentiful supply, the company expanded dramatically.

After the war, many buildings had to be replaced and demobilization created a demand for new homes. In concert with other builders, Taylor Woodrow funded the research and design of Arcon, a prefabricated housing system. The Ministry of Works ordered 43,000 of these units.

In spite of the amount of work available in Britain, Taylor Woodrow had grown so large that it needed to expand overseas. In a joint venture with Unilever, the company extended operations into West Africa where it erected Arcon tubular steel frames to which walls of a variety of local materials could be added. In 1947, Taylor Woodrow (East Africa) was formed to build 127 miles of oil pipeline in Tanganyika. For three years, company teams constructed pipeline, erected a sawmill, and built prefabricated houses; but dissatisfied with the project's central management, Taylor Woodrow withdrew.

The West African, South African, American, and United Kingdom projects were more successful. In Africa, the company built entire towns, from housing to sewers and breweries; in the United States, the firm continued its apartment complexes; in Britain, Taylor Woodrow erected factories and added bridge and tunnel construction and opencast coalmining to its activities.

Since the end of the war, Taylor Woodrow has built several energy plants in England, including the Battersea Power Station and another near Castle Donington. It completed the world's first full-scale nuclear power station at Calder Hill in 1955. In conjunction with other companies, Taylor Woodrow also built the Hinkley, Sizewell and Heysham nuclear power stations.

The company received the prestigious Queen's Award for Industry in 1966 for its development of a new pile driver, the Pilemaster. The firm also designed the first spherical prestressed concrete pressure vessels, initially used for a power station at Wylfa.

The building slump in Britain during the 1970's did not create any serious problems for Taylor Woodrow since it was operating very successfully in developing countries, particularly in the Middle East. Profits rose steadily throughout the decade to £24 million by 1979. Six years later, in 1985, profits had more than doubled to £53.7 million.

Frank Taylor resigned as managing director in 1979 and became Life President; already knighted, he was elevated to the peerage in 1982 and assumed the title Baron Taylor of Hadfield. Throughout its history, the company has largely avoided the effects of recessions, and today's management hopes that it can continue to maintain impressive financial returns.

Principal Subsidiaries: Taylor Woodrow Construction Ltd.; Taylor Woodrow International Ltd.; Taylor Woodrow Property Co., Ltd.; Greenham Group Ltd.; Greenham Trading Ltd.; E & D Taylor Ltd.; Cymru Building Ltd.; Myton Ltd.; Phillips Consultants, Ltd.; Terresearch Ltd.; Jonathan James Ltd. The company also lists subsidiaries in the Bahamas, Belgium, Canada, Cayman Islands, Denmark, Ghana, Gibraltar, the Netherlands, Indonesia, Oman, Singapore, Tanzania, and the United States.

WOOD HALL TRUST PLC

Greenly House
Dukes Place
London EC3
England
(01) 283-0911

Wholly-owned subsidiary of Elders IXL, Ltd.
Employees: 2,000
Sales: £812 million (US$1.193 billion)

Wood Hall Trust is a company in the process of disposing of its assets. A large and diversified company with interests in construction, shipping, and mercantile operations, Wood Hall Trust was acquired in 1982 by Elders IXL, the Australian conglomerate. Acquired for its more profitable enterprises, which have been merged into those of the new parent company, Wood Hall Trust is now systematically selling or closing down its remaining, less profitable operations.

Wood Hall Trust was formed in 1951 when the Ocean Salvage and Towage Company, a small and bankrupt maritime enterprise, was purchased by the Singer and Friedlander merchant banking company. As a condition of the sale, all five of the Ocean Salvage's directors were required to leave the company. They were replaced by a new board, with Michael Richards serving as chairman. Shortly after the sale, Richards and two other directors purchased 70% of the shares held by Singer and Friedlander and changed the company's name to Wood Hall Trust. The new company was intended to function as a trust for investments in the wine and spirits industries—the original operations in boat salvage and towing were abandoned altogether.

The new directors were highly astute investors. Within five years of taking control of the company, they had brought two important subsidiaries into the trust: the David Sandeman Group and Hart, Son and Company, merchant bankers. Drawing principally on the skills of Hart, the trust went on to acquire a variety of companies involved in construction, import/export trading, bill brokering, and advertising.

Speculative investment of this kind has often led to uncoordinated growth. The directors of Wood Hall Trust, however, closely monitored their investments and were ready immediately to dispose of any asset that failed to perform well. Although still small, Wood Hall Trust became, by the mid-1960's, one of the most successful investment houses in the City of London. Among the companies acquired by the trust during this period were Bendicks (a chocolate manufacturer) and Tilgate Pallets. Wood Hall Trust entered the construction industry in 1964 when it purchased Cableform, an electrical engineering concern, and Hornibrook, an Australian civil engineering contractor.

The trust's interests in construction were later expanded when they acquired Davis Estates and H. Fairweather and Company. Davis Estates was a major real estate development company involved in council and private housing projects throughout the United Kingdom. The Fairweather and Hornibrook groups were involved in a broader range of construction jobs—office and public buildings and civil engineering projects. Most notably, Hornibrook had a major role in the construction of the Sydney Opera House.

One of the Wood Hall Trust's most interesting acquisitions during the 1960's was that of the Paterson Simons Group (later called Paterson Newark). Paterson Simons was established in Singapore during the 1850's by a group of colonial merchants. One of the company's founders, William Ker, fostered a strong personal relationship with Temenggong of Johore, and by 1853 he had been placed in charge of the Malay ruler's finances. The relationship led to special business privileges for Ker and his partners, William Paterson and Henry Minchin Simons. The company traded in a variety of commodities, including camphor, vanilla, cinnamon, sea slugs, shark fins, tin, coffee, and pearls. Taking note of the profitable opium trade being conducted by companies such as Jardine Matheson, the partnership began shipping opium to China.

The partnership eventually adopted the name Patent Slip and Dock Company, but its name was changed to Paterson, Simons & Company in 1859, when Ker retired. The company re-established its port monopoly in Johore in 1899, following a merger with the Tanjong Pagar Dock Company. Six years later the port operation was expropriated by the British government, but the company retained its interests in shipping and in maritime and property insurance and continued to act as agents for the East India Coal Company and for a number of shipping lines—and thereafter, despite its colorful past, continued to operate uneventfully until the time it was acquired by Wood Hall Trust.

The 1970's was a decade of stable growth for the Trust, particularly in Australia, where its mercantile and construction interests gained the attention of another investment trust, Elders IXL. Like Wood Hall Trust, Elders—and its constituent company Henry Jones IXL—had a long history. Initially involved in pastoral interests (fruit jam production, among other things), Elders was eventually acquired by a group of investors who transformed the company into a classic international financial conglomerate which launched often hostile takeovers of marginally performing and undervalued companies. Once acquired, these companies were either dismantled and sold for cash or other assets, or rehabilitated by Elders to be more competitive.

Elders made a hostile bid for Wood Hall Trust in 1982

and gained control of the company shortly after offering to pay £90 million for all outstanding shares. Unwilling to work with Elders after its raid, Michael Richards retired and was replaced by fellow board member Alastair Ennand. Ennand, however, retired soon after Richards, and a third man, Bob Stickens, was named chairman.

In the years that followed, Elders acquired a number of other large companies and reorganized its management structure. It was decided that Wood Hall Trust's operations would be sold or absorbed by other subsidiaries of Elders. This plan precipitated the retirement of Stickens and the absorption of other Wood Hall Trust board members into the Elders organization. Many of the Wood Hall Trust's mercantile interests have now been taken over by the Elders Agribusiness group, and its assets in Africa, Asia, and the Middle East have been transferred to Elders International. The Wood Hall Trust building group, once the most prominent division of the company, is currently being "wound down," concluding or selling maintenance contracts and selling many of its real estate holdings.

It is possible that Wood Hall Trust will have ceased to exist by the mid-1990's.

Principal Subsidiaries: Wood Hall Building Group Ltd.; K.E. Millard & Co. Ltd.; One St. James's Ltd.; Vogan & Co. Ltd.; Osborne & Stevens Group Ltd.; A.J. Phillips Ltd.; Wood Hall Pty. (Australia); Paterson Ewart Group Ltd.

CONTAINERS ———————————————

BALL CORPORATION
CONTINENTAL GROUP COMPANY
CROWN, CORK & SEAL COMPANY
METAL BOX PLC

NATIONAL CAN CORPORATION
OWENS-ILLINOIS, INC.
PRIMERICA CORPORATION
TOYO SEIKAN KAISHA, LTD.

BALL CORPORATION

345 South High Street
Muncie, Indiana 47305
U.S.A.

Public Company
Incorporated: in 1922
Employees: 9,000
Sales: $1.4 billion
Market Value: $932 million
Stock Index: New York

The Ball Corporation is one of the few large companies that is more widely known in the American Midwest than in New York City. Ever since the five Ball brothers discovered that John Mason's patent on canning jars had expired in the mid-1800's, Ball has been making the preferred canning equipment in America. Five generations have preserved everything from pickle relish and apricots to cherry jam and tomatoes in the distinctive jars. The design has virtually gone unchanged for over 100 years.

When the name Ball is mentioned most Americans think of fruit jars. But in fact, home canning equipment makes up less than 10% of Ball's total sales. The bulk of revenues come from such diverse sectors as solar sensors, plastic soft drink bottles, satellite instrument systems and aluminum beer cans. Ball has secured numerous U.S. Defense Department contracts and participates in the Space Shuttle Program of the National Aeronautics and Space Administration (NASA).

The Ball Corporation began in 1880 when the five Ball brothers went into the business of making tin-jacketed glass containers for kerosene lamps. From this type of operation it was an easy shift to the manufacture of canning jars and lids. Moreover, it was wise business strategy. Thomas Edison had just invented the incandescent lightbulb and turned the kerosene lamp into an antique. The glass jar, on the other hand, had a great future.

The Ball Corporation is based in Muncie, Indiana and the present chief executive officer Richard M. Ringoen is only the fifth president in the company's 107-year history, and the first who was not a member of the Ball family. Though Ball finally went public in 1972, 60% of the company's stock is still owned by the family.

Until the end of World War II Ball was primarily a jar and bottle manufacturer with few other interests. In the late 1940's, however, a problem had to be confronted — nearly 70% of the company's glass production facilities were in need of modernization. Ball had either to diversify and grow in order to underwrite necessary modernization costs or liquidate the company. The family decided to diversify the company, and under president Edmund F. Ball, they made a number of key acquisitions, but none in the glass container field. A 1947 antitrust ruling prohibited Ball from purchasing more glass subsidiaries. Before the company ventured too far afield, Ball hired a New York management consulting team to help establish a long-range program. In the words of Edmund Ball's successor, John Fisher, "We wanted to plan for growth, not just hope for it."

The significant changes at Ball, those which have molded the company into what it is today, took place in the late 1950's and early 1960's. The launching of Sputnik by the Soviets in 1958 ushered in the Space Age and created many new opportunities in the field of aerospace; Ball raising eyebrows in corporate America, decided to take advantage of the situation. "We got into the space field because it was the beginning of the biggest scientific effort in our nation's history," said Fisher. "We knew it could be profitable for us, and that we could get commercial 'fall-out' from it."

The Ball management proved itself correct on both counts. Fully one-fourth of the company's business presently comes from the sale of computer components, pointing controls for NASA satellites, electronic data display devices, and many related items such as Sound-Guard, a preservative for phonograph records that is a derivative of a lubricant developed for spacecraft. The company also built the cameras for the Viking I and II spacecraft that were used to determine the landing site on Mars; the Space Shuttle tether system, which allows small payloads to trail up to 65 miles away from the parent ship; and the telescope on the Infrared Astronomical Satellite launched in 1983 that has helped scientists to determine more precisely the size of the Milky Way galaxy. Ball Corporation procured $180 million in defense contracts alone by 1987. Chief Executive Officer Richard Ringoen hopes the company's "strong position in infrared and ultraviolet instrumentation will continue to allow it to compete favorably with larger aerospace firms like General Dynamics."

Ironically enough, Ball had entered the high-tech market almost by mistake. In the 1950's the company hired a small engineering firm in Boulder, Colorado to develop a device that would more accurately weigh glass batch materials. The original device was never developed, but Ball was impressed enough by the technical skill of the small operation to purchase it. From this small start Ball invested heavily in research and development and made this sector a vital part of the company's overall business.

The 1960's were years of unparalleled growth in the container industry, especially in the consumer beverage area. Americans began drinking more beer and soft drinks than ever before, and innovations such as the pop-top can and the non-returnable bottle allowed container companies to make large profits. While not being a large-volume can manufacturer on the order of American Can or Continental, Ball has nonetheless been extremely successful in this competitive market. Cans now make up two-thirds of the company's packaging sales, supplanting jars and bottles as the company's primary container product.

Ball's present success in this area can be traced back to 1968 when the firm made an early switch to two-piece cans. The two-piece can, which is lighter, less expensive, and faster to make, is now used to package 70% of all soft drinks and 94% of all beer. Since Ball was already in the container industry, it was able to win manufacturing contracts from such important customers as Pepsi, Coca-Cola, Dr. Pepper, Stroh's Beer and Budweiser. In fact, Anheuser-Busch and Ball constructed a $32 million plant in New England that manufactures two-piece alumium cans for the brewer on an exclusive basis. While Ball controls less than 1% of the total can market, it has 7% to 8% of the two-piece can market.

Ball's diversification efforts during the 1950's and 1960's were bold in concept but still fairly modest in scope; the company was still very much a family operation. The man responsible for creating the widely diversified company that the Ball Corporation is today is John W. Fisher, who became president and chief executive officer in 1971. It was Fisher who directed the company into such fields as petroleum engineering equipment, photo-engraving, and plastics, and established the company as a leading manufacturer of computer components and high-tech hardware for defense and space.

Fisher, the last company president to be a member of the Ball family (his wife is the daughter of one of the five founding Ball brothers), resisted the traditionalists within his firm and pushed Ball into new markets all over the world. In 1972 Fisher acquired a Singapore-based petroleum equipment company that built and sold production gear and provided engineering expertise to oil firms in the Pacific. This purchase gave Ball subsidiary operations in Singapore, Malaysia, Indonesia, Panama and Japan. The following year the Ball-Bartoe Aircraft Corporation was established in Boulder, Colorado. It is presently involved in the development of an experimental STOL (short take-off and landing) military jet.

Next came agricultural systems and prefabricated housing. Fisher established a Ball Corporation division in Boulder devoted solely to the production and sale of "turnkey" irrigation packages for agricultural development in arid but arable areas of Libya and other nations in the Middle East. Ball also designed a modular home that could be erected on-site in a little more than six hours. In desert nations where building materials are scarce and therefore expensive, Ball has succeeded in selling a large number of these "kit" houses.

Then, in 1974, Fisher acquired a small California computer company. This concern was expanded into today's Ball Computer Products Division based in Sunnyvale, California, in the heart of Silicon Valley.

Following Ball's success in the foreign petroleum engineering equipment business, Fisher established similar operations in the United States. However, stiff competition, higher technological standards and prohibitive start-up costs thwarted this venture from the start. Fisher wasted no time in selling it in 1976 for a mere 40 cents per share. In the mid-1970's Ball also developed and introduced Freshware food containers. Made of plastic with tight-fitting lids, these were presented as a challenge to Tupperware. The product was never actually marketed and Ball had to write it off as a loss, phasing out the project in a matter of months.

These were relatively small setbacks. Fisher's management strategy was long-term and he was willing to bear the burden of brief and small-scale problems. The two large obstacles he never surmounted, however, were the company's image and the stock market's ambivalent reaction to it. Despite its interesting acquisitions, the American public still associated Ball almost exclusively with its glass jars.

Ball Corporation went public in 1972 for two reasons. The company management wanted to establish accurately the market value of the Ball family holdings, and they intended to raise equity money to finance the company's diversification efforts. But despite its impressive history, Ball's stock price did not significantly increase.

Fisher's efforts to give Ball a more technological image, his trips across the United States to speak with investors, and his dedication to growth have not changed the minds of many people. Fisher could not understand why a profitable company would not be an attractive stock purchase. He remarked, "We live in a world where products must be packaged, in good times or bad. This is all a bit mystifying to me."

When Fisher retired in 1981 he was replaced by Richard Ringoen. Ringoen in recent years has primarily concentrated in two areas—technology and packaging. Many of the other sectors, while being neither divested not disregarded, have been left to operate on their own. In particular, Ball Corporation under Ringoen is attempting to develop and market the "plastic-can." Plastic soda-pop bottles of the two-liter, half-liter and 12-ounce varieties have already proved popular with consumers. Beer in such containers, Ringoen contends, could be next. "The technology is there for plastic cans that will hold their shape at the high temperatures you need for pasteurization." Ball has spent millions of dollars in the past five years on plastics and is now poised for an entry into the market "if it should come."

Principal Subsidiaries: Ball Agricultural Sales Corp.; Ball Packaging Products, Inc.; Ball International Sales Corp.; Pantek Corp.; Muncie & Western Railroad Co. The company also lists subsidiaries in the following countries: Bermuda, France, Switzerland, United Kingdom, and West Germany.

CONTINENTAL GROUP COMPANY

Riverpark
800 Connecticut Ave.
Norwalk, Connecticut 06856
U.S.A.
(314) 577-2000

Wholly-owned subsidiary of Kiewit Investors Corporation
Incorporated: January 17, 1913

Sales: $4.8 billion

The Continental Group has long been a financially stable container company. Engaged in the mature and traditionally slow growth industry of canmaking, its revenues have increased every year without interruption since 1923. The company has overcome the problems endemic to canmaking (small profit margins, shrinking domestic market, large capital outlays for industrial machinery, etc.) through astute and careful management. However, the tranquil atmosphere at Continental was disrupted in 1984 when the company began accepting offers for a possible takeover. It was ultimately purchased by the Omaha, Nebraska construction firm of Peter Kiewit Sons and since then it has been completely restructured.

Incorporated during 1913 in New York, the company was acquired by the Los Angeles Can Company in 1926 and then merged with the Continental Can Company of California. As cans gradually became the preferred method of packaging and preserving consumer products, Continental's business grew impressively. By the 1930's it was also producing corrugated paper boxes and crown bottle caps and had emerged as the second largest container company in the United States, behind American Can.

The decade of the 1930's was particularly important for Continental. It expanded outside the United States and began licencing equipment and expertise to affiliate companies in Europe. These holdings were then subsequently increased after World War II, providing Continental a strong foothold in the burgeoning European can market and a large competitive edge over American Can. In fact, Continental went from being just half the size of American Can Company in 1942 to being slightly larger in 1956, with most of the growth coming in the ten year period between 1945 and 1955 when Europe was experiencing its post-war boom.

Not all the news was good, however. Both Continental and American suffered a setback in 1950. Up until that year these two companies had offered volume discounts to their larger customers, thereby significantly underselling their smaller competitors. In 1950 a Federal Court struck down this practice and also demanded that the two companies offer canmaking machinery for sale. Prior to this, Continental and American would only lease machinery to other canmakers. This also served to weaken the grip of the "big two" on the industry.

Because the business was opened more widely to competition, prices and profit margins began to decrease, and many of the major can customers began to see the benefits of manufacturing their own cans. The most vivid example of this was Campbell's Soup which, despite only making cans for its own products, became the third largest canmaker in the world.

This situation left Continental Can two choices: either invest heavily in research and development to make the technology of competitors and defecting customers obsolete, or diversify into other markets to mitigate the drop in can profits. Company management decided to do both. The traditional three-piece, soldered-seam tin can was gradually being replaced by cans of lighter metals such as aluminum and other steel alloys. While the new cans required a more complex manufacturing process and more expensive materials, their lighter weight made them popular with consumers and less expensive to transport. This represented the future of canmaking, and Continental was quick to prepare for it.

In 1956 the company made its first major ventures outside canmaking. In that year Continental merged with the Hazel-Atlas Glass Company and a few months later purchased the Robert Gair Paper Company. However, no sooner had Continental finalized the agreements than it was charged with an anti-trust suit. The litigation lasted for a number of years, ultimately reaching the Supreme Court where the mergers were declared lawful. The Justice Department could not prove that the Continental-Hazel-Gair agreements adversely affected competition. But between the court costs and three successive years of subpar performance, both Gair and Hazel-Atlas were proving to be costly financial ventures. Less than a year after the mergers had been pronounced legal, Continental divested itself of both companies.

In 1963 a simple but ingenious feature was introduced to cans—the pop-top tab opener. Though it is unclear who thought of the idea first (both Amcan and Alcoa have patents on somewhat similar designs), it did not take long for most major can producers to introduce the new pop-tab cans. The industry was virtually revolutionized overnight. The era of the "six-pack" had started. The new cans, which were light, easy to open, easy to store, and unbreakable, helped ward off a challenge from the nonreturnable bottle which was so popular at the time. Due in large part to the new can, beer and soda pop consumption in the United States increased dramatically in the 1960's. Continental, which had always considered itself an industrial container corporation, began to manufacture consumer beverage cans and flourished.

The various brewers and soft drink bottlers were

eventually consolidated under a few large companies, thus reviving the trend towards the self-manufacture of cans. A corporation such as Schlitz, by building "on-site" can plants instead of contracting a company to make and transport their cans, could save a large amount of money. Container technology was also changing. Aluminum, despite its higher price, was emerging as the canmaking "staple" by replacing the heavier and less popular tin can. And for the first time the storage and container potential of plastics began to be recognized. To keep up with the shifting topography of the industry the old canmaking companies, American Can and Continental, were forced to make huge capital outlays for modernization programs in the early 1970's.

The first thing Continental did was develop the Conoplan program where, in an effort to keep its customers and slow the trend toward self-manufacturing, Continental would construct a canmaking operation within the client's factory, thereby eliminating all transporation costs. In addition, Continental chief executive officer Robert Hatfield closed 15 plants which were considered too distant from customers. He then spent over $100 million to modify existing plants so that they could produce the newer and more profitable two-piece can which was quickly replacing the older three-piece can.

However, these measures were not enough. In order to achieve more substantial growth, Continental accelerated its diversification program and more firmly established itself in foreign markets. The company developed and marketed its paper products with considerable success, and also moved into the non-container fields of oil and gas. In 1969 it established the Europemballage container holding company which in a matter of years became the largest canmaker in Europe's Common Market. So large, in fact, that the Common Market principals sued Europemballage for anti-trust violations and succeeded in restricting the holding company from acquiring affiliates in new markets. Despite this setback, Continental was able to take advantage of Europe's move toward supermarkets and canned perishables and reap large financial rewards.

In 1976 Continental Can, reflecting its more diverse corporate personality, changed its name to the Continental Group. And as if to prove its reorientation, the company spent $370 million to purchase the Richmond Corporation, a $1.1 billion life, title, and casualty insurer. The idea behind the acquisition was to integrate the capital intensive packaging sectors with a sector that had low capital requirements but plenty of liquid assets. These assets were then redeployed to such areas as oil and gas exploration.

In 1981, Robert Hatfield retired and S. Bruce Smart took over as chairman. Smart continued most of Hatfield's programs and procedures, and like his predecessor regarded energy, not consumer retail goods, as the prime growth industry of the future. He planned to spend $800 million over a five year period on energy exploration, research, and transportation.

Continental continued its slow but steady growth and gradually increased its lead over American Can. Despite its continuing success, however, the company's stock was markedly undervalued. In 1984 a British financier, James Goldsmith made an offer to buy the Continental Group. Soon Continental had attracted a number of potential suitors, both foreign and domestic. Smart and the management at Continental ultimately sold the company to Peter Kiewit Sons Inc., a construction firm based in Omaha, Nebraska. Kiewit paid $3.5 billion in cash and assumed debt to finalize the agreement.

Smart apparently thought that a Nebraska construction company one third the size of Continental would be easier to deal with than financial professionals like Goldsmith. At a banquet dinner given to celebrate the finalization of the sale, Smart said, "I don't think we'll have anyone from Nebraska coming all the way to Connecticut to tell us how to make cans."

The full irony of the statement was not felt until a year later. If the people at Kiewit did not change the way Continental made cans, they changed everything else. Under the direction of Donald Strum, Kiewit dismantled the sprawling Continental Group in an effort to make the operation even more profitable. His two goals were: to sell Continental's properties until only the can operations and the timberlands were left; and to eliminate the corporate management "dead wood" which had become conservative and complacent. In the matter of a year Strum sold $1.6 billion worth of insurance, gas pipelines, and oil and gas reserves. Staff at the Stamford, Connecticut corporate headquarters was reduced from 500 to 40. Among those relieved of their duties was S. Bruce Smart himself, who later accepted a job with the Reagan Administration as Secretary of International Commerce.

Apart from those in higher management, however, no one else suffered from the changes brought on by the dismantling and restructuring of the company. The real winners in the deal were the Continental stock-holders. The sale to Kiewit raised share-prices and the selling of Continental properties brought impressive dividends.

The Continental Group of today barely resembles the diversified company of the late 1970's. For the first time since the mid-1950's Continental is once again a can and box manufacturer, and though the container industry is considered "mature," Continental is well situated for continued profitability. Many of the can plants have been modernized and more thoroughly automated to reduce labor costs, and the company's overseas ventures are developing impressively. The new Continental Group will be very active in the container industry during the years ahead.

Principal Subsidiaries: Continental Bondware, Inc.; Continental Container System; Continental Can International Corp.; Continental P.E.T.; Continental Plastic Containers; Continental Plastics Industries of Europe, Inc.; Continental White Cap, Inc.

CROWN, CORK & SEAL COMPANY

9300 Ashton Road
Philadelphia, Pennsylvania 19136
U.S.A.
(215) 698-5100

Public Company
Incorporated: 1927
Employees: 12,523
Sales: $1.619 billion
Market Value: $1.266 billion
Stock Index: New York

Although it is the fourth largest canmaker in the United States, the Crown Cork & Seal Company of Philadephia commands only 4% of the can market in America. Continental Group and American Can are the largest companies in the industry, followed distantly by National Can. Campbell's Soup and a number of other major can purchasers now manufacture their own containers and also take up a portion of the market. In fact, Campbell's makes more cans privately than either National or Crown Cork do commercially.

However, the Crown Cork & Seal Company, as its name indicates, is much more than a small domestic can manufacturer. Nearly half of its sales come from closures and crowns (bottle-caps). It ranks first in this area, manufacturing tops and caps for everything from anti perspirant to ginger ale. Crown Cork also builds high-speed filling, handling and packaging machinery for cans and bottles. It sells or leases this equipment to private companies.

Crown Cork's origins date back to 1927 when it was incorporated in New York City as a consolidation of New Process Cork Company Inc. and New York Improved Patents Corporation. The following year the company expanded its operation to include plants overseas. It formed the Crown Cork International Corporation as a holding company for subsidiaries engaged in bottle crown and other cork business outside the United States. This early entry into the foreign market gave Crown Cork an advantage over its competitors in the container and closure fields, an edge which it still holds today. In fact, Crown has more plants outside the United States than within it. There are 64 factories spread out over Africa, Europe, and Latin America as compared to just 26 in the U.S.

Oddly enough, Crown Cork did not even venture into the canmaking business until 1936 when it purchased the Acme Can Company and began building its first large can plant in Philadephia under the name of Crown Can. While the middle of the Depression would seem to be the worst possible time to enter a capital intensive industry, Crown's can operation was successful right from the start. Processed canning was quickly taking the place of home canning as the preferred way to preserve and store perishable goods. For this reason the container industry, until very recently, has been immune to the economic cycles which plague most other types of businesses, industrial or otherwise.

Within the container business Crown Cork & Seal is somewhat of an enigma, because it has achieved financial results which seem to contradict industry logic. Profit margins in can manufacturing have been small and shrinking for decades, and canmakers like American and Continental have been relying on diversification and economies of scale to create profits. Crown Cork & Seal, on the other hand, has neither expanded into non-container fields nor sought to augment its own canmaking program by purchasing other small can operations. Yet it has managed to maintain an earnings growth rate of 20% a year. How does it do this?

The answer can be traced back to 1957. In that year an Irishman named John F. Connelly became its president. At that time Crown Cork was dangerously close to bankruptcy court, and lacked leadership. It suffered a first quarter loss of over $600,000 and Bankers Trust was calling in a $2.5 million loan, and an additional $4.5 million was due by the end of the year.

Connelly took dramatic measures. He halted can production altogether and filled the remaining orders with a large stockpile of unpurchased cans that had been allowed to accumulate. The customers did not object, and the money saved by selling old inventory instead of producing new cans brought Crown Cork close to solvency. In addition, unprofitable and unpromising product lines, such as ice-cube trays, were immediately discontinued.

Connelly also reduced overhead costs, particularly those incurred by redundant labor. In one 20 month span the payroll was cut by 25%, pink slips being issued to managers and unskilled workers alike. The moves were drastic but necessary. By the end of 1957 the company was making both cans and profits.

Once the initial bankruptcy crisis had passed, Connelly directed Crown Cork & Seal with renewed energy into two areas within which Crown had traditionally held a positioned advantage: aerosol cans and foreign container markets. In the years immediately preceding Connelly's tenure the company, while not neglecting these markets, had not pursued them with the vigor they warranted.

Crown Cork & Seal had pioneered the aerosol can in 1946 and Connelly was shrewd enough to recognize its potential. Hair spray, bathroom cleaning supplies, insecticides, and many other household products would come to be staples for the American consumer and would be marketed in aerosol dispensers.

In 1963, for example, Crown installed two aerosol can product lines in its Toronto factory, thinking that it would take the market five years to absorb the output. Within a year, however, another plant was required to handle the orders. A decade later, the same situation was repeated in Mexico. Only in the late 1970's and 1980's, when the negative environmental impact of aerosol cans became widely known (it was discovered that aerosol containers expel fluorocarbons into the air which destroy the earth's fragile ozone layer), did Crown to re-examine this sector of its business. The company was among the first to develop an aerosol can which did not propel fluorocarbons into the atmosphere.

Connelly invested considerable amounts of capital to reclaim Crown's pre eminence overseas in closures and cans. Between 1955 and 1960 the company received what were called "pioneer rights" from many foreign governments wanting to build up the industrial sectors of their countries. These "rights" gave Crown first chance at any new can or closure business being introduced into these developing nations. This kind of leverage permitted the company to make large profits while using industrial equipment that was, by American standards, obsolete. Moreover, the pioneer rights allowed Crown to pay no taxes for up to 10 years.

Crown's foreign operations are managed and staffed only by citizens and residents of the country concerned. That is to say, there are no Americans on Crown's payroll outside the United States. Connelly sent the foreign plants outdated but still functioning equipment and let them begin. Crown profited from its disposal of antiquated machinery and created a far-ranging network of semi-autonomous subsidiaries in the process.

In the early 1960's the can industry was losing more and more ground to the non-returnable bottle. It appeared that cans would never be able to capture the lion's share of the beverage container market. For this reason American Can and Continental began experimenting with large scale diversification into non-container fields. Crown Cork, however, did not follow the example; in fact Connelly went against the prevailing wisdom and entrenched Crown Cork still further into the consumer product can business, spending $121 million on a capital improvement program initiated in 1962.

In 1963, just as the canmaking industry was experiencing its first recession in decades, the pull-tab pop-top was introduced. In the words of one canmaker at the time, the new and seemingly simple innovation made opening a can "as easy as pulling the ring off a grenade, and a lot safer." The new pull-tab opener revolutionized the industry while helping to dramatically increase canned beverage consumption. At the same time, Americans began drinking more beer and soft drinks than ever before, and the can industry experienced a seven year period of unprecedented growth. Crown Cork, an early entrant in the pull-tab can market, performed even better than American Can and Continental and its year-to-year profits increased by double digit percentage points.

In the early 1970's the beverage can market leveled out, with many of the major brewers and soft drink producers developing facilities to manufacture their own cans. A number of can companies, particularly American and Continental, did not adjust well to the diminishing growth in beverage can demand. They were overextended and operating at a greater capacity than necessary. Crown Cork, which did not rely as heavily on can customers like Schlitz or Pepsi, was not as severely affected when beverage companies began manufacturing their own cans. Furthermore, Crown's foreign enterprises, which were accounting for close to 40% of total sales, were expanding rapidly. They more than compensated for any domesic decrease in revenues. Crown also became involved in the printing aspect of the industry by acquiring the R. Hoe & Company metal decorating firm in 1970. With this addition to its operation, Crown had the equipment necessary for imprinting color lithography upon its cans and bottle caps. By 1974 Crown had a consolidated net profit of over $39 million—double that of its 1967 results.

The first widespread production of two-piece aluminum cans began in the mid-1970's. Aluminum was relatively expensive, but simpler to manufacture, lighter for the consumer, and since it was recyclable, it met with the approval of environmental groups.

Connelly, however, once again went against industry trends. Just as he had refused to participate in the diversification trend years before, he steered Crown Cork clear of the aluminum two-piece can. He decided instead to concentrate on the old-style three-piece steel can which had been the mainstay of the industry for years. Many industry analysts regarded this strategy as particularly risky since the Food and Drug Administration had indicated that it might outlaw the three-piece can. The lead used to solder the three seams of the can was considered a health hazard. To circumvent this problem Crown began welding rather than soldering its cans.

Connelly was against switching from steel to aluminum for two reasons. First, by relying on the steel can the company was relieved of the high research and development costs necessary for changing to aluminum can manufacturing. Secondly, Connelly realized that there were only a handful of corporations selling aluminum in bulk. This meant that the canmakers would be paying a premium price for their raw materials. Crown, by using steel, could play the various steel producers off one another and drive the price of its materials down. The strategy worked, and Crown's company was making profits while his larger and supposedly more "progressive" competitors spent hundreds of millions of dollars on retooling for aluminum cans.

Connelly, it seems, has made very few mistakes. In all of his years as president, the company has never suffered a quarterly loss; it is virtually debt-free. And by judicious buying of Crown Cork shares, Connelly owns more than 14% of the company—an investment worth about $150 million.

Recently, a small New Jersey juke-box, vending machine, and steel cable firm called Triangle Industries has entered the container industry. Owners Norman Pelz and Peter May have already purchased National Can and a large canning division of American Can in leveraged buyouts. Some Wall Street analysts speculate that it may be looking to acquire Crown Cork & Seal as well. However, those close to Connelly say that he will never sell.

Crown Cork & Seal lists subsidiaries in the following countries: Argentina, Belgium, Brazil, Canada, Chile, East Africa, Ecuador, Ethiopia, France, Italy, Malaysia, Mexico, Morocco, The Netherlands, Nigeria, Peru, Portugal, Puerto Rico, Singapore, Switzerland, Thailand, Venezuela, West Germany, Zaire, and Zambia.

METAL BOX PLC

Queen's House, Forbury Road
Reading RG1 3JH
England
0734 581177

Public Company
Incorporated: November 29, 1921 as Allied Tin Box
Makers, Ltd.
Employees: 28,707
Sales: $1.154 billion (US$1.697 billion)
Market Value: $794.5 million (US$1.168 billion)
Stock Index: London

The canning of foods, or "tinning" as it is often called in Britain, has been a common method for preserving food for about a century. Before that time, all foods had to be purchased fresh, salted, or dried. The industry that developed to produce these cans, or "tins," in Britain was originally controlled by numerous family firms, each with a small tin can making factory in which workers could turn out 200 cans in an hour. These family concerns were small, profitable, and only mildly competitive in such a large market.

One of the family can makers was initially a printing business established in 1855 by Robert Barclay, a Quaker. His main customer was Barclay's Bank (owned by distant relatives) for whom he printed checks. Barclay's brother-in-law, John Fry, joined him as a partner in 1867, and their company, Barclay & Fry, became Britain's largest check printer. With the help of some technical information sold to him by an early industrial spy in France, Barclay developed the process of offset lithography and tried to sell it to many other firms. He died of a stroke in 1876 before any sale could be finalized.

The new printing process ended up being leased to Huntley, Boorne & Stevens, tin box makers for the biscuit company, Huntley & Palmer (the two Huntleys were also related). Huntley & Palmer was the first manufacturer to use the offset process to print designs on their own tins; prior to that their tins had been hand painted. Soon, Carr's Biscuits were also using printed tins; these were manufactured by their Quaker relatives, Hudson Scott & Sons. Some time during the 1890's, Barclay & Fry decided to use their offset process themselves, but they remained primarily stationery printers.

Decorated biscuit tins were very popular throughout Great Britain and many homes had quite large collections of them. There were Alice in Wonderland designs, tins to commemorate every grand occasion, and tins resembling miniature cottages or featuring birds, books or beauty spots. The tin making industry grew and since labor costs were low, profits were high. Soon, the Trade Boards Act required tin manufacturers to improve worker conditions and wages, and this caused some of the employers to form the British Tin Box Manufacturers Federation in order to protect their interests.

The First World War brought more business to the industry; a new product had to be manufactured—the ration tin used by British troops. Due to government restrictions on tin, many of the companies in the Federation cooperated closely, and after the war, in 1921, four of these tin box makers, Hudson Scott, F. Atkins & Co., Henry Grant & Co., and Barclay & Fry, formed the Allied Tin Box Makers Ltd. A year later they changed their name to Metal Box & Printing Industries. From the beginning it was understood that each of the member companies would remain private, but that all would cooperate in controlling the market and making acquisitions.

Before long, however, the group's comfortable control of their market was threatened by the importation of an American method of semi-automatic can making that could produce 200 cans every minute. G.E. Williamson's family firm, which had refused to join the manufacturers' group, purchased the new American machinery in 1927 and began to produce cans for the government's Fruit & Vegetable Research Station in Gloucestershire. The research organization was interested in advanced canning methods in order to increase the markets for British farm produce.

Inevitably, with its superior technology, the American canning industry quickly became interested in the British market. American Can moved in first by purchasing a small independent company and renaming it the British Can Company, Ltd. It then attempted to acquire Metal Box & Printing Industries. However, in its determination to resist a takeover, Metal Box arranged a partnership that not only kept it independent, but defined and nurtured its growth. The company signed an agreement with American Can's U.S. rival, Continental Can. The two firms exchanged stock shares and Metal Box was given the exclusive right in Great Britain to purchase canning machinery, technical advice, training, and patent licenses from Continental Can. This effectively eliminated the competition as no other British company was able to purchase the technology. In little more than a year, British Can was in disarray. Metal Box agreed to buy it out on the condition that American Can stayed out of Great Britain and Ireland for the next 21 years.

These deals, illegal under today's business laws, had been arranged by Metal Box's Robert Barlow. Still under 40, Barlow was now the head of Britain's canning monopoly and determined to make it even larger. But his aggressive managerial style alienated most of the old family leaders of the group's companies, and many resigned from the board of directors. Barlow wanted to bring all member companies under one authority and ignored those on the board who opposed him. He set up an executive committee with two others, Hepworth and Crabtree, to make policy decisions and, essentially, to circumvent the board.

In 1931, Barlow's committee instituted a single accounting system for all member companies in an attempt to force some kind of uniformity on them under a newly created head office. The managing director of Barclay & Fry tried to have Barlow fired, but Barlow called a meeting of the entire board and convinced them that his plan would make the company stronger still. As Barlow consolidated his position he banished some of his detractors to plants in South Africa and demanded the resignations of others. By 1935 he was in complete control of Metal Box and had largely succeeded in centralizing sales and supplies, and rationalizing production functions, for all the company's plants.

Metal Box experienced nothing but success during the Depression. As smaller canmakers collapsed, the company purchased them, and by 1937, Metal Box was selling 335 million cans a year. Following the American example, Metal Box had begun to manufacture the equipment needed to seal the cans on site and sold this machinery to its customers. Metal Box was not interested in expanding into the field of food production, but it did open a publicity department to increase interest in canned foods. Whenever there were difficulties, either with suppliers or customers, Metal Box considered a takeover. For example, inefficient management at a tin plate supplier in South Wales led Metal Box, with the help of Continental Can, to purchase the company.

Surprisingly, Metal Box's income from security check printing combined with turnover from machine manufacturing and interests in mining, etc. was double that of its income from the cans themselves. Profits rose dramatically for Metal Box in the 1930's—from £103,480 in 1931 to £316,368 in 1939.

Throughout the decade Barlow had maintained a strong interest in foreign markets. Partnerships or subsidiaries had been formed in France, the Netherlands, Belgium, India, and South Africa. Continental Can was still Metal Box's mentor and main partner and the two essentially divided up the world markets between themselves. Metal Box was to expand within Europe and the British colonies, while Continental Can would develop interests in the rest of the world.

In the late 1930's, the innovative company planned to produce new forms of packaging such as card containers with metal ends and cans with wax lining for beer. However, the onslaught of World War II curtailed new production in favor of equipment for the troops. Containers for gas masks were easy to make in tin box factories, and Metal Box produced 140 million of them for the government. The paint tin production lines were adapted to produce casings for anti-tank mines. Shell casings and ration tins were also produced by the millions. Even so, due to strict government controls, company profits fell to £242,428 in 1945.

In 1943, as the war turned in the Allies' favor, Barlow established a committee to plan new forms of packaging that could be exploited as soon as the war was over. Consequently, Metal Box was an innovator in the field, quickly moving toward paper, foil and plastic container products as the post-war economy began to improve. But Metal Box still dominated the British can and carton market. Between 1941 and 1961, eight new factories were built or purchased, and by the 1960's, Metal Box was the leading packaging supplier to some of the largest companies in the world, including Unilever, Nestlés, Heinz, Imperial Tobacco, BAT, ICI, Hoechst, and Shell.

After the war, Metal Box was more than ready for further organizational changes. The accounting department was restructured and a financial comptroller was appointed. Additionally, administrative functions were more clearly defined and brought under central control, and subsidiaries were also made more accountable to central management. Barlow retained his position as executive chairman, but in 1946, he brought in D.W. Brough as his managing director. Brough had been in charge of operations in South Africa; however, he lasted less than two years. Barlow replaced him with two executives, G.S. Samways and D. Ducat, and these two men served as joint managing directors until Samways' resignation in 1954; Ducat then served alone, but Barlow still maintained overall control until his retirement in 1961.

In the late 1940's, the U.S. Department of Justice had filed an antitrust suit against Continental Can and began to investigate its arrangements with Metal Box. The two companies hastily modified their agreement in 1950 and cooperation between them is now restricted to machinery and technical information; all mutual ventures and attempts at market controls were dropped. The modified agreement was renewed and slightly expanded in 1970 and will continue until 1990.

Up to 1970, Metal Box had continued to expand both at home and abroad. In Britain, Wallis Tin Stamping Co., Brown Bibby & Gregory, and Flexible Packaging were all acquired, widening Metal Box's product line to include plastic film, aerosols, central heating, and engineering. The company established facilities or subsidiaries in Italy, Malaysia, Tanzania, Japan, and Iran, and upgraded the older plants in India, France, and South Africa. Even so, Metal Box still conducted three-quarters of its business in the United Kingdom.

In 1967 the Board of Trade referred the British can industry to the Monopolies Commission which ruled that Metal Box was operating a monopoly—supplying 77% of all metal containers, 63% of aerosols, and 80% of open-top cans. However, the Commission concluded that the company's monopoly did not harm the public interest and did not find Metal Box lacking in efficiency, innovations or service. Its report even praised Metal Box for passing on savings to its customers. But the company was instructed to terminate all of its exclusive arrangements, both with customers and with suppliers. Thus, in one stroke, Barlow's market control procedures were ended.

Like the rest of the industry, Metal Box suffered from the recessions of the 1970's but its strength in the British market has continued to serve it well. The drastic reductions in its work force in the 1970's, and the sale of subsidiaries and properties, have given the company a leaner look. It owes much of its success to the long and tough administration of Robert Barlow, and it continues to be Britain's largest can manufacturer.

Principal Subsidiaries: Risdon Ltd.; Metal Box Overseas Ltd.; Venesta Packaging Group Ltd.; Stelrad Group Ltd.; Stelrad Overseas Ltd. The company also lists subsidiaries in the following countries: Belgium, Bermuda, France, Ireland, Italy, Jamaica, Kenya, The Netherlands, Nigeria, Tanzania, United States, West Germany, and Zimbabwe.

Further Reading: *Metal Box: A History* by W.J. Reader, London, Heinemann, 1976.

NATIONAL CAN CORPORATION

8101 Higgins Road
Chicago, Illinois 60631
U.S.A.
(312) 399-3000

Wholly-owned subsidiary of Triangle Industries, Inc.
Incorporated: 1929 as Metal Package Corporation
Employees: 10,541
Sales: $1.9 billion

The National Can Corporation has for decades been the third largest can manufacturer in the container industry. Yet because it is so much smaller than American Can and the Continental Group (about one-sixth their size), National is both more flexible and responsive to changes in the industry. Even so, the company had 1985 revenues in excess of $1.9 billion and was producing cans in over 30 foreign countries.

The "big two" traditionally looked upon National Can with benign indifference. It controlled just enough of the market (8% compared to 30% for American Can and Continental) to keep anti-trust laws from being used against American Can and Continental. However, this ambivalent relationship has changed in the last 20 years to become one that is more competitive. In fact, National Can's growth rate is better than those of all major canmakers except Crown, Cork & Seal. Moreover, it has done this with the unwilling assistance of American Can and Continental.

Most major can customers will not rely exclusively on one container company; and rather than play one rival against another and risk angering both, the clients will contract the majority of their can orders to either Continental or American Can and then assign what is left over to a smaller third party. As a result, the intense competition between American Can and Continental provides a lot of business for National. The company also benefits from the technology of its rivals. Customers usually insist that their cans all be made in uniform fashion. This means that the large canmakers, to their chagrin, are almost obligated to sell their technology to those small companies which are completing the order. This saves a corporation like National significant amounts of money in research and development costs.

National Can has used its strategic position to advantage since 1952 when the struggling Chicago-based firm merged with Cans Inc., a small Chicago canmaking company owned and operated by Robert Solinsky. Solinsky had founded Cans Inc. in 1939, and after the merger he became chairman of the new National Can. He had a reputation as a man who won and kept customers with his personal approach to salesmanship, and for implementing effective corporate austerity measures. Solinsky made a point of keeping payroll and other overhead costs within the company's means.

In the early 1960's Solinsky directed National Can's attention and resources toward the small but burgeoning beverage can market. With the introduction of the pull-tab opener, the beverage can market exploded in the 1960's and National Can, more than any other canmaker, took advantage of the "six-pack" revolution.

The rapid growth in the beverage can market predictably slowed toward the end of the 1960's. Many major can users began to produce their own cans, thereby cutting into the profits of the container companies. National Can, like its competitors, diversified; but it remained closer to areas related to canmaking. Anticipating the industry shift to lightweight metal cans and renewed consumer demand for glass bottles, it purchased the Aluminum Can Company in 1967, and two glass companies in 1970. Also in 1967, National Can established can plants in Great Britain and Greece, and formed a wholesale grocery products division. The following year the company entered into the retail buiness by acquiring a fruit company and a dog food company, both of which were can users.

Canmakers also took measures to impede the trend towards "in-house" can production by major container clients. American Can and Continental agreed to build "on-site" plants for customers in an effort to reduce their transportation costs and dissuade them from notions of self-manufacture. National Can took a different approach, choosing instead to build "feeder" plants near steel mills that would shear, coat, and lithograph body sheets and can ends. These would then be transported to satellite facilities near the customer's factories for final fabrication. This process was more cost effective because it was less expensive to freight flat metal than finished cans.

Despite the efforts of can producers to maintain control of their industry, it became clear that the business was changing fundamentally. Canmaking had been virtually immune to volatile economic cycles, canned goods being such a large part of the American way of life as to almost assure stability. In the 1970's, however, the container industry showed itself to be subject to market fluctuations.

Self-manufacture of cans was the most important factor, but also contributing to the worsening state of affairs were overcapacity and changes in technology. The latter had the effect of making many container factories obsolete. Canmakers found the cost of re-equipping their plants to be so expensive that both Continental and American Can began to accelerate their diversification programs, reducing their dependence upon cans. National Can, though its uninterrupted year-to-year growth was halted in 1971, was positioned better than most companies within the industry as it had been following a careful program of modernization since the mid-1960's. Before anyone else, National Can was producing the new two-piece can which was gradually replacing the old three-piece soldered seam can.

Canmakers also had to confront political challenges. Environmental groups cited the container industry as a chief contributor to the proliferation of litter. In 1971 both Vermont and Oregon passed laws requiring a mandatory deposit on most beverage containers; five years later similar legislation was effected in both Maine and Michigan. Recycling was the requisite measure, and aluminum cans and refillable bottles became more popular. A recycled aluminum can uses 89% less energy than a can made of virgin metal, and a bottle refilled 10 times over reduces the waste of the "one-way" non-returnable bottle by two-thirds. Tinplate steel cans became almost obsolete in the beverage market as the recycling process was complex and expensive.

In 1973 Frank Considine was appointed chief executive officer at National Can when Robert S. Stuart, who had been chairman since 1967, retired. Stuart was Robert Solinsky's son and had changed his name upon his father's insistence. From Stuart, Considine inherited a financially healthy, but potentially troubled company. Early investments in two-piece canmaking machinery and aluminum had allowed National Can to respond effectively to the industry's changing complexion, but the diversification program was proving to be troublesome. Following the leads of American Can and Continental, National Can had initially planned to reduce its can sales to 50% of total revenues by branching out into other fields. However, the canned grocery and dog food business was more than National could handle. Competing with such formidable corporations as General Foods and Ralston-Purina proved to be beyond the abilities of the can company.

Considine quickly set about the task of reorienting National Can back towards the manufacturing of cans. In the eyes of those within the industry this move was both courageous and suspect. Many of these people, including the heads of both Continental and American Can, thought that Considine was taking National in the wrong direction; but Considine was steadfast. On the issue of diversification he once said, "We won't buy a piano to see if we can play it."

All of National Can's business interests peripheral to the basic canmaking operation were sold, and the liquid capital from these sales was put into container production, particularly two-piece can manufacturing. Considine realized that the production problems which had traditionally hampered a full conversion to the two-piece can did not require increased research and development (at which National Can was not adept), but rather was a matter of process refinement, an engineering task at which National Can was experienced and skilled.

Considine hoped that by upgrading National Can's bottle, plastic container, can, and bottle-cap operations it would be able to obtain those areas of the market ignored or abandoned by Continental and American. While the "big two" were closing down can plant after can plant, National was building new factories, mostly in the Sunbelt states of the southwestern United States where it had a firm market share and where beverage sales were particularly strong.

National Can was so eager to hasten the departure of Continental and American from the canmaking industry that it often agreed to unprofitable contracts. For example, it agreed to deliver cans to a customer in Kansas by a wholly unrealistic date. To make the deadline, National had to transport cans from a plant in Tampa, Florida, incurring prohibitive freight costs. Considine soon realized that forced growth in an industry with slim profit-margins could not be maintained, and that grossly under-selling competitors in order to procure business is a dangerous tactic.

Considine has become known as one of the most "hands-on" corporate managers in business, involving himself deeply with the day-to-day affairs of the factories and the people who work in them. This allows National Can to retain the feel of a small, family operation while gradually growing into a $2 billion a year business.

In 1985 National Can became involved in the wave of takeover battles that has enveloped corporate America in recent years. Miami Beach investor and raider Victor Posner sought to increase his share holding in the company to obtain control of management. Considine was open to Posner's offers at first until he realized the hostile nature of the takeover attempt. Considine and National Can then delayed the takeover in the hope that a better suitor would come along. The following November National was purchased by Triangle Industries of New Jersey in a leveraged buy out that cost close to half a billion dollars. Triangle Industries is a juke-box and vending machine maker owned by Nelson Pelz and Peter May with revenues under $300 million. Pelz and May acquired the much larger National by selling "junk bonds" and borrowing a great deal of capital, successfully making the purchase without putting up much of their own money.

In 1986 Triangle Industries purchased all of American Can's (recently renamed Primerica) U.S. packaging businesses. Primerica's shift away from packaging and toward financial services and specialty retailing prompted an enthusiastic response to Triangle's offer. Thus, while the change in National Can's ownership raises questions about the company's future, its commitment to the business of canning remains strong.

Principal Subsidiaries: NCC International Sales Corp.; National Protein Corp.; Consolidated Cork International Corp.; A & Q Corp.; Apache Container Corp.; Clermont Fruit Packers, Inc.; Clermont West, Inc.; National Trading Corp.; Dura Closures, Inc.; McGhee Harris Corp.; M-H Packaging Systems, Inc.; NATADCO, Inc.; National Seed & Feed Co.; NCC Food Corp.; Packaging Systems, Inc.; NACANCO Service Corp.

OWENS-ILLINOIS, INC.

One Sea Gate
Toledo, Ohio 43666
U.S.A.
(419) 247-5000

Wholly-owned subsidiary of Kohlberg, Kravis, Roberts & Company
Incorporated: December 16, 1907 as The Owens Bottle Machine Corporation
Employees: 44,048
Sales: $3.5 billion

Owens-Illinois is the world's largest manufacturer of glass bottles and other glass products such as television picture tubes, telescope lenses, laboratory equipment and tableware. It controls nearly 33% of both the domestic and foreign bottle markets, a market share comparable to those of American Can and Continental, the two largest companies in the can industry. With $3.5 billion in revenues, it dwarfs even its closest competitors, Anchor-Hocking and Glass Containers Corporation.

While glass sales constitute close to 50% of its total sales, Owens-Illinois also relies heavily on its non-glass operations, both in and outside the container business. The company is number one in plastics and the production of corrugated shipping boxes. It is also a major manufacturer of plywood and has recently involved itself in health services and financial consulting. With diverse interests worldwide Owens-Illinois is a model modern corporation.

The Toledo-based company was incorporated in 1907. It was the product of a merger between the Owens Bottle Company and the Illinois Glass Company of Alton, Illinois, a small manufacturer of glass products for the drug and medical fields. Like most can and bottle making companies, Owens-Illinois weathered the years of the Depression without a production slowdown. Throughout the 20th century the container industry as a whole has proved itself to be almost unaffected by dramatic swings in the economy.

In 1935 Owens-Illinois acquired the Libbey-Glass Company and entered the consumer tableware field. The Libbey division was responsible for making tumblers, glass pitchers, dishes and bowls. Soon afterward Owens began conducting experiments with glass fibers, and learned that one of its chief competitors, Corning Glass, was doing similar research. The two firms agreed to cooperate and formed Owens-Corning Fiberglas in 1938. Development of marketable fiberglas products quickly followed. Corning and Owens, with their virtual monopoly on fiberglass technology, profited greatly. At the present time, fiberglas in loose constructions is weaved into textiles and insulation material (the famous pink "cotton candy" foam that lines America's attics); and when "packed" tightly in rigid sheets it is used, among other things, to manufacture car and boat bodies.

During the period immediately following World War II, Owens-Illinois remained primarily a glass maker, its few deviations from the bottle business being limited to those areas on the immediate periphery of glass containers. This was all soon to change. A number of anti-trust rulings in the late 1940's restricted companies like Owens-Illinois from increasing market share through wholesale acquisitions of subsidiaries in their respective industries. Growth, it seemed would have to come from fields outside glass.

The first significant move came in 1956 when Owens purchased National Container Corporation, America's third-largest box maker at the time. The move into forest products, though gradual, was as predictable as it was necessary. It made good economic sense to make a forest products company part of the Owens-Illinois holdings. Not only was the parent firm supplied cardboard boxes at reduced rates, but the paper and pulp sector turned profits of its own. Lily-Tulip, the company's consumer paper division, makes everything from wax-lined milk cartons to disposable cups.

In the 1950's Owens-Illinois took another step outside the glass container field, into a promising new area—plastics. The company had for some time made plastic caps and closures, but up until the mid-1950's the technology for making plastic containers was not available. This changed very fast.

Most popular at that time was the plastic squeeze-bottle which could be used as a container for prepared mustard and other sauces. Owens-Illinois, however, directed its energy toward semi-rigid plastic containers. The strategy was successful. In 1958 Owens-Illinois persuaded a number of large bleach and laundry detergent companies to switch to the new bottles. They were immediately popular with consumers and have continued to be popular until the present time. Each year plastic containers claim a more substantial share of counter space in American supermarkets.

Despite the important advances in paper and plastics, the company was still very much committed to glass manufacturing. The 1960's were years of tremendous growth in both can and bottle manufacturing. Although the two industries were rivals for the growing consumer beverage market, there was enough soft beverage and beer business for all the container companies. The intense competition was for the "lion's share," and the initial demand for the new pop-top can seemed to relegate glass containers to a distant second place.

However, the ever-bothersome returnable bottle, with its thick glass and mandatory deposit, gave way to the lighter "one-way" bottle. The new construction ushered in a renaissance for the glass industry, allowing it to challenge the can industry more effectively. Since the one-way bottle was not returned for refilling it could be made of thinner glass. This meant production cost and production time were reduced, thereby increasing profit margins. Although many industry analysts thought the glass beverage container was destined to failure in the early 1960's it did not surrender its market share to the pull-tab can; bottle sales tripled during that decade.

Still, Owens-Illinois was aware that diversification efforts would have to be accelerated if growth was to continue. The 1960's burgeoning of the beverage market was not to be repeated and expansion in glass manufacturing slowed considerably. The company involved itself in such far-removed fields as sugar cane farming in the Bahamas and phosphate rock mining in Florida. Moves such as these prompted Owens-Illinois to drop the word "glass" from its corporate name.

As beverage sales leveled off in the 1970's, the container industry found itself in the midst of a worldwide recession. Many large can and bottle customers, which included large breweries and soft drink companies, began manufacturing their own containers. Many can and bottle manufacturers had unwisely increased the size of their container-producing facilities and were now confronted with over-capacity, an unwieldy workforce, and tumbling prices. The problem was particularly acute in bottle manufacturing where production is more labor intensive.

Owens-Illinois attempted to solve this problem technologically, investing in new industrial equipment that could make 20 bottles in the time it used to take to make six, and therefore cutting labor costs. Also, the company dedicated more factory space, often entire plants, to single product lines for one customer. However, these were "stop-gap" measures and did not solve the overall problem. Wholesale modernization was necessary.

As Owens-Illinois entered the 1980's its production costs advantage, once the envy of the industry, had been eroded. While the company developed revolutionary new container machinery, it allowed the majority of is conventional glass plants to deteriorate. Edwin D. Dodd, the company's chief executive officer, divested marginal interests which were draining resources and performing poorly, and supervised a $911 million four-year plant modernization program.

More importantly, the company's attitude toward its own industry changed, particularly regarding bottle manufacturing. Historically a large volume dealer concerned with maintaining its huge market share, Owen-Illinois began to emphasize profit margins rather than its portion of the bottle manufacturing market. Unprofitable plants, even relatively new ones, were closed or sold, production of the two-way returnable bottle was discontinued in favor of the exclusive manufacture of the "one-way" bottle; and the minimum order level was raised while the customer base was reduced to a number of large-volume, "blue-chip" customers. The results of this policy were impressive. Capacity was reduced by 24% and the work force was cut by 30%. Owens-Illinois was again able to reclaim its productive edge over competitors.

Owens-Illinois regard for the natural environment has drawn the attention and praise of consumer advocate Ralph Nader. In his 1971 study on water pollution, Nader cited Owens-Illinois as the industrial company with the best record on environmental issues. The compliment was well deserved. Its glass factories are among the safest and cleanest in the business; it leads the industry in recycling; and has advocated a national system of resource recovery to deal with the mounting solid waste problem.

Owens-Illinois environmental policies came about largely through the work of a former chief executive officer, Raymond Mulford who died in 1973. He encouraged community participation on behalf of his staff and factory workers, and devoted nearly half of his time in later years to social and environmental programs. Most company plants are located in small towns and Mulford insisted they be an asset, not a liability, to the community. This meant confronting the issue of pollution control long before it was a national concern.

The modernized Owens-Illinois company is the most formidable member of the glass container industry. It presently out-produces its competitors by 33%. Yet, to increase profit margins and efficiency, company operations were streamlined. The company invested heavily in research and developed production methods that reduced the labor content of a finished glass product from 40% to 20%. A total of 48 plants were closed and 17,000 workers laid off. The jobs of 46,000 other employees, however, were saved.

Many of Owens-Illinois' rivals have not spent the money necessary to compete. Thatcher Glass, once number two in the industry, went bankrupt in 1981. Its failure was the product of a poorly executed leveraged buy-out and an unwillingness to rebuild old furnaces and install new technology. Other manufacturers, such as Anchor-Hocking and Glass Containers Corporation have found themselves in similar predicaments.

Robert Lanigan, the present chief executive officer of Owens-Illinois, has emphasized the manufacture of plastic bottles and the increasingly popular plastic-shield glass bottle. He has also continued the diversification program and has acquired two nursing home chains and the Alliance Mortgage Company. Owens-Illinois' policies have been aimed at reducing the company's vulnerability to a takeover. Since the container industry is a mature, slow-growth one, return on stockholder's equity was, in the mid-1980's, less than 10%. Thus its stock price was well below book value; at the same time, it had an attractive annual cash flow of $300 million.

While Lanigan's efforts have undoubtedly benefitted the company, he has not succeeded in avoiding a takeover. On December 11, 1986, Kohlberg, Kravis, Roberts & Company, a holding company which specializes in taking firms private, offered to purchase Owens-Illinois for $55 per share. Owens-Illinois refused the offer and threatened to initiate a reorganization, including the sale of over $1 billion in assets, in order to protect the company from subsequent takeover attempts. Kohlberg, Kravis responded by raising its bid to $60 per share. When investment houses acting on behalf of Owens-Illinois failed to find buyers willing to outbid Kohlberg, Kravis, Owens-Illinois officials were forced to negotiate.

In mid-February 1987, Owens-Illinois announced that it had agreed to be acquired by a Kohlberg, Kravis subsidiary, the Oil Acquisition Corporation, for $60.50 per share, or about $3.6 billion. In order to finance the buyout a number of banks agreed to extend a short-term, or "bridge" loan of $600 million to Kohlberg, Kravis, to be paid back over 18 months through an issue of high-yield bonds.

Kohlberg, Kravis, Roberts & Company first established a relationship with Owens-Illinois in 1981 when it purchased the Lily Tulip Company from Owens-Illinois. While some members of the Owens-Illinois board opposed the takeover (and becoming a private company), it was generally agreed that the short-term interests of the stockholders were served. At the time of the takeover, there was speculation that Kohlberg, Kravis would be forced to sell certain divisions of Owens-Illinois in order to finance the debt it incurred as a result of the acquisition.

Principal Subsidiaries: Marinette, Tomahawk & Western Railroad Co.; Owens-Illinois Development Corp.; Owens Illinois Finance Corp.; Sabine River and Northern Railroad Co.; Treitler-Owens, Inc.; Valdosta Southern Railroad Co.; Automatic Inspection Devices; Universal Materials Inc.; Andover Controls; Health Care and Retirement Corp. of America; Prudent Supply Inc.; L.E. Smith Glass Co.; Alliance Mortgage Co. The company also lists subsidiaries in the following countries: Brazil, Bermuda, France, Indonesia, Italy, Spain, Switzerland, Venezuela, West Germany, and the United Kingdom.

PRIMERICA

PRIMERICA CORPORATION

(formerly American Can Company)
American Lane
P.O. Box 3610
Greenwich, Connecticut 06836–3610
U.S.A.
(203) 552-2000

Public Company
Incorporated: 1901
Employees: 25,600
Sales: $2.864 billion
Market Value: $2.737 billion
Stock Index: New York

Throughout the 20th century, the American Can Company has been making containers for everything from green beans to soda pop and soup. However, its product line goes well beyond the manufacture of cans. The company has recently put a great deal of research and resources into plastics. In 1984, for example, Amcan developed the plastic "squeeze-bottle" for Heinz Ketchup. Since its introduction to the marketplace, grocers have not been able to keep enough of them on the shelves.

Once the dominant canmaker in a fairly closed industry (only the Continental Can Company was a serious rival), American Can has seen a gradual decline in its market share over the last 30 years. Yet it remains a very large operation with annual gross sales exceeding $4.3 billion. More than 50% of its revenues come from such areas as specialty retailing, direct marketing, record distributing, insurance sales, and a number of financial services. In the words of American Can's recently retired chairman, William S. Woodside, "When I started with this company in 1950 cans were the prima donna of the opera. Thirty-one years later, they're the last row of the chorus."

American Can's metamorphosis from being a large and exclusively one-industry corporation to one with formidable interests in a handful of unrelated fields is reflective of a more general business trend toward diversification, especially among corporations involved in capital intensive production. However, the change did not happen quickly.

Incorporated in New Jersey in 1901, American Can emerged as one of the "twin giants" of the canmaking industry, the other being Continental Can. Throughout the 1920's and 1930's, canning became the most effective way of containing, preserving, and storing both industrial and consumer goods. American Can's business grew even during the Depression, becoming twice the size of its nearest rival.

Despite wartime rationing measures and often unpredictable supplies of metal resources, Amcan continued to prosper during the 1940's. Continental and Amcan were so much larger than their other competitors that both were able to offer large volume discounts to the major can customers. This had the effect of putting even greater distance between these two companies and the smaller canmaking operations which constituted the rest of the industry.

This arrangement of the industry's structure was challenged by the United States federal government and ultimately dismantled. In 1950 a federal court struck down the volume discount practice employed by Amcan and Continental, reducing the leverage of the two can making companies over their smaller rivals. This particular ruling altered the complexion of the canmaking industry forever. Not only was competition reintroduced to the business but many major can customers, no longer able, to receive volume discounts on their containers, began manufacturing their own cans to consolidate their operations.

All of these developments spelled trouble for American Can. Canmaking, because it is so capital intensive, needs wide profit margins to be a perennially successful enterprise. More competition, loss of revenues due to "self-manufacturing" of cans by large clients, and higher labor costs due to unionization (American Can employees belong to the United Steel Workers labor association) made such margins difficult to obtain. In addition, there were changes in the technology of the industry itself that required large capital outlays by the company if it was to maintain its position. This involved a definite shift away from tin and steel cans to those of lighter metals such as aluminum. Moreover, the recycle value of glass and plastic was also recognized. This meant that the canmaking plants themselves would have to be modernized or at least modified to keep pace with changing consumer demand. It became clear to the directors at American Can that the cost of surviving on the can business alone would have been so high as to financially damage the company. The only alternative, therefore, was to diversify.

American Can's first step outside canmaking was a large one. In 1957 it purchased the forest products operations of Dixie and Marathon paper products, the company which makes Dixie cups, Brawny and Aurora paper towels, a variety of types of toilet tissue, and a number of other related items. The purchase proved to be a good one; the growth potential of the paper industry was much better than that of cans and containers. However, after this initial success, American Can's diversification record was marred by a number of failures. During the 1960's the company ventured into chemicals, commercial printing, and glass bottle making. Company management had neither experience nor expertise in these spheres. As a result, the company was forced to divest from all of these operations.

The 1960's were not all bad, however. In fact, the sixties were the "Golden Years" of the can industry. In 1963 the pop-top or ring-tab can opener was introduced. This innovation revolutionized the beverage can business and ushered in what has been called the "era of the six-pack."

Consumers no longer had to look for the can opener or poke holes in their beer cans with screw drivers, knives, and ball-point pens. The hole was already built into the can, one had only to pull the ring. Beer and soft drink sales, spurred on by the new, more convenient can, increased markedly, and the canmakers enjoyed their most profitable decade ever. Yet, even with this increased profitability, it became clear once again that can manufacturing alone would not sustain American Can. Due to "in-house" can operations by former customers and increased competition from other canmakers, the company lost a substantial portion of its market share.

By early 1970 there was no denying that American Can needed a new approach to both diversification and the business of canmaking if it was to remain competitive. The job of reorientation fell to chief executive officer William May. His plan called for a company "think-tank" which would attract the best young business and technical minds in the country. Within the container industry and others, American Can was to become *the* innovative and creative corporation. In order to bring this about, May hired a group of talented business theorists who, though short on practical experience, were supposed to lead American Can into the 1980's.

These men led American Can into the areas of aluminum recycling and resource recovery, both of which enjoyed a period of growth in the late 1970's when ecology and environmentalism were in vogue. These operations, however, have since stagnated. The new leadership at American Can also encouraged the company to invest in smaller fields such as records and mail order retail products so as to benefit from the excellent short-term returns these businesses were enjoying. Consequently, American Can purchased Pickwick record distributing in 1975 and Fingerhut direct marketing in 1978. The latter became the only successful investment in May's diversification portfolio, while the former continues to be an unprofitable business venture.

May hoped to arrange the company's various operations so that by the end of his tenure the container manufacturing portion would be less than 50% of the business. Yet future acquisitions in other sectors depended upon a healthy canmaking operation. It was can manufacturing, by way of the stock market, which generated the capital necessary to invest in other things. Hence, May took the difficult but necessary steps to modernize American Can's aging canmaking network. In 1972 he began selling and closing those plants considered to be antiquated and beyond modification. Throughout the decade, approximately 105 factories which annually produced $1.2 billion in sales were shut down or sold; in the process, the company incurred $300 million in total write-downs. The old system was supplanted by a new network of 62 plants. Eight of these, at a total cost of $200 million, were built to make the newer, more cost-effective two-piece can (which two-piece can (which requires only one seam) that was quickly replacing the old style three-piece can (which requires two).

At first May's strategies were successful and paid out considerable dividends to investors. 1974 represented one of the best business years in company history. American Can posted both record sales and record earnings, and the future indicated both continued growth and profitability. However, this was soon to change.

The major area of concern was the recently purchased Pickwick company, the world's largest record distributor and retailer. Pickwick's problems began when the bottom fell out of the record buying market in the late 1970's and early 1980's. Record prices increased significantly during this period, alienating younger customers (who make up the bulk of the industry's clientele) and leading them to record borrowed albums on blank cassette tapes rather than buy them new in the stores. Despite the stabilization of record prices in recent years, the trend toward home recording technology has kept Pickwick from recovering completely. It is a $500 million a year operation that has trouble making a profit.

To make matters worse, the Sam Goody record store chain, part of Pickwick's retail network, was investigated by the Justice Department. A number of the top officials at Goody were indicted for allegedly dealing in counterfeit records and tapes. American Can reported the improprieties quickly and in good faith, but the damage had been done. Many Wall Street analysts and members of the container industry thought American Can had gone too far afield in entering the record business and that it was unsound financial planning. The Goody scandal seemed to confirm these misgivings and shake the confidence of investors in American Can's ability to make successful acquisitions.

Fingerhut, the direct-marketing firm purchased by the company at the height of the mail-order retail explosion, carved out a market for itself by catering to a group often overlooked by others in the industry, namely, the low to medium income household. Fingerhut developed computerized profiles of each of its four million customers and then marketed products corresponding to their demands. This established for Fingerhut a loyal (and growing) consumer block.

In the meantime, the corrective modernization measures taken by May were not enough to keep the company from losing more and more of its market share. In the beverage can market alone, American Can's portion dropped from 28% in 1971 to approximately 18% in the 1980's. The company was still lagging behind Continental Can and others in the shift away from steel to aluminum and plastics. Moreover, recycling laws of various types were passed in a number of states, resulting in greater consumer interest in glass which is cheaper and easier to "send through the mill" a second time. These things served to worsen American Can's already unstable financial situation and depressed employee morale.

In 1980 William May retired to become the dean of New York University's Graduate School of Business. Taking his place and inheriting his problems was William Woodside, a man with a reputation for being a brilliant business strategist and a tough administrator. Woodside joined American Can in 1950 as an economist, and then later became the marketing director at Dixie Paper in 1962. In 1975 he moved back to the home company to become second in command at American Can under May.

When Woodside took the helm of American Can he

soon learned that his largest problem was money; he did not have enough of it to keep the company from lapsing into permanent stagnation. American Can's 1980 profits were off 33% and it was having trouble making even 5% on its assets. Woodside was faced with a dilemma: American Can needed growth via acquisitions in order to generate investment funds, but these acquisitions required capital outlays that the company simply did not have.

Rather than circumvent this problem, Woodside developed a plan designed to overcome it. He called it "asset redeployment," a program in which tangential and unprofitable business would be sold so as to generate the liquid capital needed to invest in areas of greater growth potential.

Woodside's first significant move in this direction was to put up for sale the company's forest products operations, worth almost $1 billion. Both the Dixie-Marathon paper operation and the American Can container plants were highly capital intensive. Woodside understood that no company could withstand the financial strain and resource costs of maintaining large interests in two such industries. One of them had to be sold, and there was really little choice as to which it was going to be. Dixie had been marginally profitable throughout its history, despite losing ground to competitors like Northern Paper, and timberlands were highly regarded by Wall Street at the time; selling Dixie-Marathon would not be difficult. The company's can operation, on the other hand, was considered part of a dying industry; what is more, it maintained a very costly labor pension plan. "We simply would not be able to unload it," said Woodside.

The sale of Dixie, however, was not as smooth as American Can had hoped. Woodside waited too long before accepting offers from potential buyers and before long interest in timberlands began to wane. Ultimately the company sold its forest operations for $423 million, a figure far below what most analysts thought them to be worth. Woodside, too, recognized the error in strategy. "If ever there was a bad time to sell those assets, we picked it."

Before the sale of Dixie was finalized Woodside sought to acquire new businesses, particularly those in the sectors of financial services and insurance. In fact, American Can bought Associated Madison Insurance for $140 million in 1981 before it had received any payment on its forest operations. Woodside was encouraged to make the purchase by Gerald Tsai, the "boy wonder" of the stock market who had financial interests in Madison.

Tsai, who was born in Shanghai and then educated in the United States at Boston University, made a reputation for himself on Wall Street during the 1960's. As an expert trader he made a great deal of money in a short period of time. In 1966 he started the Manhattan Fund, raising millions of dollars by convincing investors he would yield them high returns. The project turned out badly, however. Tsai lost most of the money and the confidence of investors.

Following this fall from grace, Tsai spent 12 years positioning himself for a possible comeback. He quietly became a major force in the insurance trade; and associating with American Can was just what he needed to make his return. By 1983 Tsai was a vice chairman and major stockholder at American Can, and proved to be an indispensable ally to Woodside in his sometimes unpopular attempts to redirect American Can's capital into financial services. Indeed, between 1982 and 1986 Tsai and Woodside spent $800 million to acquire all or part of five major insurance companies, including American General Capital Corporation which runs $4.3 billion worth of mutual funds. These acquisitions paid off handsomely. In 1984 American Can reported $4.1 billion in revenues and $100 million in net income, the company's best figures in years.

Tsai, who became chairman at American Can in 1986 when Woodside retired, claimed that direct marketing and financial services would soon make up 75% of its business, further relieving the company of its dependence upon canmaking. This figure was an understatement. When Triangle Industries, National Can's new parent company, approached American about purchasing all its U.S. packaging businesses, Tsai responded enthusiastically. The sale earned American $600 million in cash and stock and completely divested the company from the last of its packaging operations.

In keeping with its growing image as a financial services and specialty retailing conglomerate, American changed its name to Primerica. The company is now the largest underwriter of individual life insurance and the largest retailer of audio and video products in the United States. Other areas of increasing activity include the management of mutual funds and home mortgages.

Primerica continues to use the two billion dollars earned from the sale of all its paper and packaging operations to acquire new businesses. Using American Express as a model of a successful diversified financial services company, Tsai announced his company would purchase Smith Barney, a Wall Street investment firm. This action marks Tsai's return to the position of his former years as a mutual fund manager on Wall Street.

By infusing capital into Smith Barney's operations, Tsai hopes the firm will expand its international business and corporate financing services. Although this latest acquisition marks the last major purchase that Tsai claims his company is able to manage for the time being, Primerica is well on its way to becoming a leader in the financial services industry.

Principal Subsidiaries: Associated Madison Companies, Inc.; AC Insurance Co.; AC Securities Inc.; American Capitol Corp.; American Services Associates; Associated Direct Marketing Services Inc.; Berg Enterprises, Inc.; Mass Marketing Systems International; PennCorp Financial Inc.; Voyager Group Inc.; Performance Plastics Packaging; Worldwide Metal Packaging; Fingerhut Companies; Sam Goody Inc.; The Musicland Group, Inc.

TOYO SEIKAN KAISHA, LTD.

Saiwai Building
3-1 Uchisaiwai-cho, 1-chome
Chiyoda-ku, Tokyo 100
Japan
(03) 508-2111

Public Company
Incorporated: July 1941
Employees: 5963
Sales: ¥375.1 billion (US$2.286 billion)
Market Value: ¥360.8 billion (US$2.266 billion)
Stock Index: Tokyo Osaka

Toyo Seikan Kaisha is the largest container company in Japan and occupies a dominant position in the market. The company was founded in 1933 by a Japanese entrepreneur named Tatsunosuke Takasaki. Toyo Seikan was the successor of another packaging company which originally purchased its canning technology from the American Can Company in 1912. Other canning technologies were subsequently acquired from Continental Can. Takasaki placed a high value on the public good, pledging in his company's founding precepts to place those obligations above all other aspects of business, including profit. Takasaki was also a strong supporter of education in his field. In April 1938 he founded the Oriental Canning Institute, where new canning technologies could be developed in an academic atmosphere.

Toyo Seikan entered the canning business during a difficult period in Japanese history. Ultra-nationalist elements of the Japanese army were rapidly coming to power, advocating Japanese military and economic domnation of East Asia. Toyo Seikan became a joint stock company in July 1941. During this period, the government encouraged industrial concerns to reinvest and expand (often by merger) so that resources could be more efficiently used. Toyo Seikan, however, remained independent throughout the war. Japanese military adventurism in Asia may have created stronger demand for canned products, such as troop rations. While Toyo Seikan does not discuss its activities during the war, its production was probably monitored or coordinated by a state planning authority.

When the war ended in September 1945, much of Japan's industrial capacity had been complete destroyed. A new industrial policy introduced by the Allied occupation authority caused thousands of companies to undergo substantial reorganization. Toyo Seikan was no exception; its changes were completed in May 1949, and shares of stock were listed for public trading.

Toyo Seikan resumed its successful canning operations, and in 1953 introduced aerosol loading for pressurized spray products. During the 1950's Toyo Seikan became associated with a number of other smaller packaging companies, and formed the core of an informal business organization which became known as the Toyo Seikan Group. These companies started to produce flexible packaging in 1960 and introduced plastic container production in 1961.

In April 1961 Toyo Seikan established the Toyo Junior College of Food Technology as a successor to the Oriental Canning Institute. The institute was upgraded to a junior college in order to expand the school facilities and attract more skilled instructors. The Toyo Seikan Group established strong relationships with other food research institutes, including the Toyo Food Research Institute and the Composite Research and Development Center.

An increasing number of packaging companies became associated with the Toyo Seikan Group during the 1960's and 1970's. At that time most of Toyo Seikan's foreign sales were derived indirectly through exports. Later, the company established joint enterprises in Korea, Singapore, Thailand, Nigeria, and Indonesia to produce metal containers, glass products and bottle crowns. Toyo Seikan also began to license container technologies developed by its research institutes to foreign counterparts. Toyo Seikan currently licenses several of its packaging methods to 25 companies in 13 foreign countries. The company is associated through technical agreements with the Continental Group, Owens-Illinois, and Metal Closures.

The Toyo Seikan Group derives most of its operating income from the sale of metal, glass, and plastic containers to Japanese and foreign customers (approximately 50% of Toyo Seikan Kaisha's sales come from the production of cans for beverages). The Group is also deeply involved in the manufacture and sale of packaging machinery, such as integrated bottling devices.

The most identifiable Toyo Seikan product is the curved PET can it produces exclusively for Sapporo Beer. The popularity of the PET can be attributed to the novelty of its odd shape and the slightly larger than standard volume of beer it contains. The Toyo Seikan Group consists of 25 subsidiaries and affiliated companies, including the Toyo Kohan Company (involved in the production of steel products), Toyo Glass (glass bottles and machinery), and Tokan Kogyo (paper and plastic containers). Members of the Takasaki family have remained intimately involved in the affairs of Toyo Seikan. The current president of Toyo Seikan Kaisha is Yoshiro Takasaki, son of the founder.

Principal Subsidiaries: Toyo Kohan Co., Ltd.; Toyo Glass Co., Ltd.; Tokan Kogyo Co., Ltd.; Japan Crown Cork Co., Ltd.; Toyo Food Equipment Co., Ltd.; Toyo Aerosol Industry Co., Ltd.; Ferro Enamels (Japan), Ltd.; Honshu Seikan Kaisha, Ltd.; Shikoku Seikan Kaisha, Ltd.; Ryukyu Seikan Kaisha, Ltd.; Toyo Yoki Kaisha, Ltd.; Daito Seikan Kaisha, Ltd.; Toyo Denkai Kaisha, Ltd.; Osaka Denkai Kaisha, Ltd.; Toyo Seihan Co., Ltd.;

Fukuoka Packaging Co., Ltd.; Tokan Unyu Kaisha, Ltd.; Toyo Unso Kaisha, Ltd.; Tokan Unso Co., Ltd.; Saiwai Shoji & Co., Ltd.; Tokan Kyoei Kaisha, Ltd.; Toyo Seikyu Kaisha, Ltd.; Toyo Kikai Hambai Kaisha, Ltd.; Tokan Soko Kaisha, Ltd.; Fiji Can Co., Ltd. (Fiji); P.T. United Can Co., Ltd. (Indonesia); Doosan Glass Co., Ltd. (South Korea); Sam Hwa Can Making Co., Ltd. (South Korea); Metal Box Toyo Glass Nigeria Limited (Nigeria); Toyo Glass Machinery Singapore (PTE), Ltd. (Singapore); Crown Seal Co., Ltd. (Thailand).

DRUGS

ABBOTT LABORATORIES
AMERICAN HOME PRODUCTS
A.B. ASTRA
BAXTER INTERNATIONAL
BECTON, DICKINSON & COMPANY
CIBA-GEIGY LTD.
FUJISAWA PHARMACEUTICAL
   COMPANY, LTD.
GENENTECH, INC.
GLAXO HOLDINGS PLC
F. HOFFMANN-LA ROCHE
   & COMPANY A.G.
ELI LILLY & COMPANY
MARION LABORATORIES, INC.
MERCK & COMPANY
MILES LABORATORIES
MYLAN LABORATORIES
NOVO INDUSTRI A/S
PFIZER INC.
PHARMACIA A.B.

RORER GROUP
ROUSSEL-UCLAF
SANDOZ LTD.
SANKYO COMPANY, LTD.
SANOFI GROUP
R.P. SCHERER
SCHERING A.G.
SCHERING-PLOUGH
G.D. SEARLE & COMPANY
SIGMA-ALDRICH
SMITHKLINE BECKMAN
   CORPORATION
SQUIBB CORPORATION
STERLING DRUG, INC.
SYNTEX CORPORATION
TAKEDA CHEMICAL INDUSTRIES, LTD.
THE UPJOHN COMPANY
WARNER-LAMBERT
THE WELLCOME FOUNDATION LTD.

ABBOTT LABORATORIES

Abbott Park
North Chicago, Illinois
U.S.A.
(312) 937-6100

Public Company
Incorporated: March 6, 1900 as Abbott Alkaloidal
Company
Employees: 33,500
Sales: $3.808 billion
Market Value: $14.617 billion
Stock Index: New York London Zurich Basle Geneva
Lausanne

Abbott Laboratories is one of the oldest and most successful of America's pharmaceutical companies. The man most responsible for the company's current impressive performance in the market place is Robert A. Schoellhorn. When Schoellhorn joined Abbott in 1973 (after 27 years with American Cyanamid), he found the company in an unprecedented state of disarray. Three years earlier the Food and Drug Administration had banned production of cyclamates, an artificial sweetener of which Abbott was a major producer; the FDA had also ordered the company to recall 3.4 million bottles of a contaminated intravenous solution. Though only a divisional vice-president at the time, Schoellhorn would later prove crucial to Abbott's impressive comeback. Today Abbott's prospects have never looked so good—it is one of the few drug manufacturers recommended as an investment by Wall Street brokers.

Abbott Laboratories has its origin in the late 19th century in a small pharmaceutical operation run from the kitchen of a Chicago physician named Wallace Calvin Abbott. As did other physicians of the time, Dr.Abbott commonly prescribed morphine, quinine, strychnine and codeine—all of which were liquid alkaloid extracts—for his patients. Because they existed only in a liquid form, these drugs were prone to spoilage over time, mitigating their effectiveness as treatments. In 1888 Dr. Abbott heard that a Belgian surgeon had developed alkaloids in solid form. Alkaloid pills soon became available in Chicago, but Dr. Abbott was dissatisfied with their quality, and he decided to manufacture his own.

Dr. Abbott began to advertise his products to other doctors in 1891. So successful was his business that he eventually sold shares to other doctors and incorporated his operation in 1900 as the Abbott Alkaloidal Company. By 1905 annual sales had grown to $200,000.

During World War I Abbott's company was essential to the medical community: several important drugs, manufactured exclusively by German companies, were no longer available in the United States. Abbott developed procaine, a substitute for the German novacaine, and barbital, a replacement for veneral.

After the war, Abbott continued to concentrate on the research and development of new drugs. In 1921 the company established a laboratory at Rocky Mount, North Carolina which developed a number of new drugs, including sedatives, tranquilizers, and vitamins. Despite Dr. Abbott's death that year, the company continued to invest heavily in new product development and aggressive marketing campaigns.

DeWitt Clough was named president of the company in 1933, ending a period of somewhat stale communal leadership. A more dynamic character than any since Dr. Abbott, Clough is best remembered for the inauguration of the company magazine, *What's New?* The publication had such a positive impact on worker morale and public opinion that several of Abbott's competitors started similar publications.

During World War II Abbott once again played an important role in battlefield and hospital health care. By this time American pharmaceutical companies such as Abbott were much less dependent on Germany companies, particularly the IG Farben—a conglomeration of the world's most advanced drug manufacturers. After the war much of the IG Farben's research was turned over to American manufacturers. Abbott, however, had little to gain from this information; it was already a worthy competitor on its own.

After the departure of DeWitt Clough in 1945, Abbott shifted its attention to the development of antibiotics. The company developed erythromycin, which, under the brand names Erythrocin and E.E.S., constituted a significant portion of Abbott's prescription drug sales for several decades—even after the expiration of its 17-year patent. Sales of the drug increased dramatically when it was found to be an effective treatment for Legionnaire's Disease.

Abbott stumbled onto a lucrative new product when one of its researchers accidentally discovered that a chemical with which he had been working had a sweet taste. The chemical, a cyclamate, could be used as an artificial sweetener. Initially, from 1950, it was marketed to diabetics, but in the 1960's, as Americans became more health and diet conscious, it was increasingly used as a sugar substitute in a wide variety of foods.

By 1965 Abbott had gone several years without a major breakthrough in research and, worse yet, none was projected at any time in the immediate future. Two years later Edward J. Ledder was named president of the company. He advocated a reduction in Abbott's emphasis on pharmaceuticals by diversifying into other fields. In the years that followed, Abbott introduced an array of consumer products, including Pream non-dairy creamer, Glad Hands rubber gloves, Faultless golf balls, and Sucaryl, a cyclamate sugar substitute. In an effort to insure the success of Abbott's consumer product line, Ledder placed

Melvin Birnbaum, a highly experienced and able manager he had hired away from Revlon, in charge of the division.

Ledder's policy of diversification laid the groundwork for more flexible corporate strategies. No longer exposed exclusively within the pharmaceuticals market, Abbott was able to cross-subsidize failing operations until they could be rehabilitated. Despite this flexibility, Abbott soon realized new obstacles to its growth.

The company's hospital products competed in a limited, institutional market. New drugs had greater profit margins, but were subject to government approval procedures that kept companies waiting for several years before they could market their discoveries. Consumer products, on the other hand, involved more expensive marketing and generated less profit than pharmaceuticals. Unable to increase profits without substantial risk, Abbott's management decided to maintain the strategies that were in place.

Cyclamate sales had grown so dramatically that by 1969 they accounted for one-third of Abbott's consumer product revenues—or about $50 million. The increasing popularity of cyclamates as an ingredient in diet foods, however, led the FDA to conduct an investigation of possible side-effects from their overuse. The FDA's research was widely criticized as "fragmentary" and "fatally flawed," but it was nonetheless used as evidence that cyclamates were carcinogenic. The market collapsed in August 1970 when the FDA banned domestic sales of cyclamates. Abbott, which overnight had suffered the loss of one of its most profitable operations, protested the ban, but was unable to reverse the decision. Although the company has continued to petition the FDA, subsequent studies have confirmed that metabolization of cyclamates can lead to chromosome breakage and bladder cancer.

Less than a year after cyclamates were banned, Abbott was forced to recall 3.4 million bottles of intravenous solution. The bottles were sealed with a varnished paper called Gilsonite, which, it was discovered, harbored bacteria. The contamination was discovered only when health care workers noticed and then investigated the high incidence of infection in patients who had been administered Abbott's intravenous solutions. The Center for Disease Control linked the contaminated solutions to at least 434 infections and 49 deaths. With litigation imminent and sales down from $17.9 million to $3 million, Abbott's share price began to fall. Abbott moved quickly to replace its Gilsonite seals with synthetic rubber, but then the company faced the larger problem of regaining market share.

The crises of the early 1970's left the company's upper echelon of management weakened and vulnerable to criticism. Although Edward Ledder was recognized for the success of his diversification program (and largely excused for his inability to prevent either the cyclamate ban or the intravenous solution crisis), conditions were obviously ripe for the expression of talent by a new manager. Robert Schoellhorn, a veteran of the chemical industry, was just such a manager. His efforts as a vice-president in the hospital products division at Abbott resulted in a revenue increase of 139% for that division between 1974 and 1979. He correctly predicted that the next most profitable trend in health care would be toward cost-effective analysis and treatment. Schoellhorn was later promoted to president and chief operating office of the company.

Abbott Laboratories registered an annual sales growth rate of 15.5% and an earnings growth rate of 16.5% by 1979. This expansion was attributed by financial analysts to the company's increased productivity, reduced costs, expansion into foreign markets, and greater involvement in hospital nutritionals and diagnostic testing equipment. The company also introduced three new drugs in 1979—Depakene, an anticonvulsant, Tranxene, a mild tranquilizer, and Abbokinase, a treatment for blood clots in the lungs. All three products were the direct result of the company's increased investment in research and development in the mid-1970's.

Utilizing its knowledge of intravenous solution production, vitamin therapy, and infant formula (Abbott holds one-half of the market for infant formula with Simulac), Abbott developed a comprehensive nutritional therapy program to speed the recovery of hospital patients and thereby reduce medical care costs. As many as 65% of all hospital patients suffer from some form of malnutrition, and Abbott has been highly successful in marketing their program. Another advantage of adult nutritional products is that they have a place in the growing home care market.

Abbott has had similar success marketing its lines of diagnostic equipment. Electronic testing devices developed by Abbott are more accurate than manual procedures. In order to strengthen the technical end of its diagnostic equipment research, Abbott hired two top executives away from Texas Instruments to head the division. Some of the products currently under development by Abbott include a device that can detect cancer from a blood test as well as fibers to be used to transmit surgical laser beams.

Robert Schoellhorn, now chairman and chief executive officer, has continued to emphasize investment in pharmaceutical research and development—seven new drugs introduced in 1982 accounted for 17% of sales in 1985. Foreign operations also remain extremely important to Abbott (the company has 77 foreign subsidiaries and manufacturing facilities in 28 countries). Schoellhorn continues to support Ledder's original diversification policy. The introduction of Murine eye-care products and Selsan Blue dandruff shampoo has served to expand the domestic consumer product line and promises to provide earning stability in the event of a downturn in any of the company's other markets.

While other hospital product companies struggle to compete in the new cost-conscious market, Abbott Laboratories has successfully engineered the smooth transition into the 1980's and looks superbly positioned to continue to grow in the 1990's.

Principal Subsidiaries: Abbott Diagnostics Inc.; Abbott **Pharmaceuticals Inc.; Oximetrix de Puerto Rico Inc.**; Hemostatix Inc.; CMM Transportation Inc.; Haven Leasing Corp. (80%); Murine Co. Inc.; M & R Diatetic Laboratories Inc.; Oximetrix Inc.; Ross Laboratories Inc.; Sorenson Research Co. Inc.; Swan-Meyers Inc.; Tobal

Products Inc.; Takeda-Abbott Products Inc. (50%). The company also owns subsidiaries in the following countries: Argentina, Australia, Austria, Belgium, Bermuda, Brazil, **Canada, Chile, Colombia, Denmark, Ecuador, El Salva**-dor, England, France, Greece, Guatemala, Hong Kong, Ireland, Italy, Jamaica, Japan, Lebanon, Mexico, Mozambique, The Netherlands, Panama, Peru, Philip-pines, Portugal, Singapore, South Africa, Spain, Sweden, Switzerland, Thailand, Uruguay, Venezuela, and West Germany.

Further Reading: *The Long White Line: The Story of Abbott Laboratories* by Herman Kogan, New York, Random House, 1963.

AMERICAN HOME PRODUCTS

685 Third Avenue
New York, New York 10017
U.S.A.
(212) 986-1000

Public Company
Incorporated: February 4, 1926
Employees: 47,298
Sales: $4.927 billion
Market Value: $13.514 billion
Stock Index: New York

American Home Products, one of the largest pharmaceutical concerns in the United States and a conglomerate that includes food and household-product divisions, is often referred to as "Anonymous Home Products" or the "withdrawn corporate giant." Though the company markets such familiar products as Black Flag insecticides, Easy-Off over cleaner, Woolite, and Chef-Boy-Ar-Dee, as well as ethical and proprietary drugs (including Anacin), the corporate name never appears on product labels. Public relations is considered such a low priority that until recently switchboard operators answered the phone with the company phone number instead of the company name. And although executives at American Home Products have made no effort (until recently) to influence Wall Street analysts, the company's 32 consecutive years of increased sales and earnings make AHP shares a very popular investment.

This unusual combination of anonymity and financial success stems from a history of competent management, product diversification through acquisition, and close-fisted expenditures on virtually everything except advertising,. AHP has been able to strike a balance between the aggressive advertising of its consumer package goods and maintaining a reputable name within the medical community, which is often reluctant to accept the idea of ethical drugs supported by the pressure of advertising.

AHP's strict management policy allows for a minimal margin of error. If a product does not show promise before money is spent on promotion, it is dropped. If a division does not increase sales and earnings by 10% annually, a division president could be out of a job. Until recently, AHP found little reason to invest in research, preferring to wait for competitors to release innovative products, and then launching its own improved line. Or, failing that, it would simply buy the competitor.

Expenditures are so closely monitored at AHP that in 1983 employees at the Whitehall division paid $20 each to attend their own Christmas party. A journalist from *Business Week*, researching a rumor in 1970 that then AHP chairman and president William F. LaPorte had reduced the size of the toilet paper in the executive washrooms to save money, discovered that, in fact, the paper *was* 9/16-inch narrower than regulation size. As late as 1980 LaPorte was personally approving any expenditures of more than $500, including anything from the purchase of a typewriter to a secretarial pay rise.

American Home Products' knack for acquiring little-known products and companies at a reduced price and turning them into money-makers dates back to AHP's earliest years. In 1926 a group of executives associated with Sterling Products Inc. and Household Products Inc. consolidated several independent nostrum makers into a holding company. Its subsidiaries sold such medicinal products as Hill's Cascara Quinine, St. Jacob's Oil, Wyeth's Sage and Sulphur, Kolynos dental cream, and Old English No Rubbing Floor Polish.

W.H. Kirn was named chairman of the new company in 1930 and served until 1935, when Alvin G. Brush, a salesman of Dr. Lyon's toothpaste, took over as president and chief executive officer, a position he held for the next 30 years. Brush's penchant for expansion through acquisition, while maintaining a sizable amount of cash in reserve, set the pattern for AHP's operating style. In his first eight years as president, Brush acquired 34 food and drug companies for a total of $25.6 million in cash and stock. One of AHP's earliest prizes was the acquisition of a sunburn oil in 1935 that the company transformed into Preparation H, now one of the world's best selling hemorrhoid treatments. Other purchases included the 3-in-One Oil Company in early 1936 and later that year Affiliated Products Inc., which made cosmetics and toiletries under such names as Outdoor Girl, Kissproof, and Neet.

In 1938 AHP acquired Eff Laboratories, a manufacturer of commercial vitamin products, and S.M.A. Corporation, a producer of infant foods and vitamins. In 1939 the Black Flag Company came under the AHP umbrella, followed in 1943 by the G. Washington Coffee Refining Company, a manufacturer of grocery specialties. In 1946 another grocery-specialties firm, Chef-Boy-Ar-Dee Quality Foods Inc., came aboard.

AHP's marketing genius transformed the products of these companies into household words. Preparation H is a good example. By 1981, Preparation H had captured 64% of the hemorrhoid-treatment market, and its success was attributable exclusively to the company's aggressive advertising. In 1968 AHP spent more than $2 million on radio spots and $6 million on television advertising for Preparation H. These amounts may seem exorbitant for a single product; the figures become even more impressive when one realizes that the radio code standards only re-admitted the controversial advertisements for hemorrhoidal medications in 1965 and that the National Association of Broadcasters continued to debate approval for television. AHP advocated a broadened scope of code approval even as it appropriated more funds for advertising on noncode television stations.

The struggle for an expanded consumer audience was fought not only over advertising codes for personal products; AHP's aggressive marketing style also brought investigations of the company's advertising copy. In 1967 the Federal Trade Commission ordered AHP and three other companies to refrain from making false claims with regard to the therapeutic value of their hemorrhoid treatments. Citing the advertisements' unsubstantiated claims, the FTC prohibited any future misrepresentation.

Company executives were not intimidated by the FTC ruling. AHP, deeming the commission's findings "capricious" and "arbitrary," asked for a review before a federal appeals court. The company continued to run advertisements in more than 1,100 newspapers, 700 radio stations, and 100 television stations. In response, the FTC temporarily enjoined AHP from continuing to run the advertisements. The court finally upheld most of the commission's findings, and the advertising copy for Preparation H had to be permanently modified.

Throughout this controversy AHP executives remained characteristically unavailable for comment. This combination of persistent product promotion (at the risk of damaging company reputation) and a united but anonymous executive front came to the fore in the promotion of another AHP product. In 1930 the company had purchased the rights to manufacture a little-known painkiller called Anacin, previously promoted through samples to dentists. AHP's Anacin grew in popularity and became the nation's leading over-the-counter analgesic. As with Preparation H, it took aggressive marketing to propel Anacin into this position.

By 1971 AHP had spent more money on the promotion of Anacin than had any other analgesic manufacturer on a comparable product. Total costs for radio advertising reached $1.5 million, and for television advertising surpassed $25 million. In 1972 the FTC charged that AHP and two other analgesic manufacturers were promoting their products through misleading and unsubstantiated claims. Because no reliable scientific evidence existed as to the superiority of one brand over another, or the ability of analgesics to relieve nervous tension, the FTC disputed therapeutic claims and advertisements that did not identify generic ingredients such as aspirin and caffeine.

AHP and the other manufacturers refused to negotiate consent agreements, and so the FTC issued formal complaints and ordered hearings before an FTC administrative judge. The case was finally settled in 1981 and permanent limits were placed on misleading claims in Anacin advertisements. In 1982 a federal appeals court upheld the FTC ruling after AHP attempted to have it overturned.

During the hearings on aspirin advertisements, Johnson & Johnson's Tylenol made its market appearance. To maintain their market share, AHP and other aspirin manufacturers launched a campaign to promote aspirin's anti-inflammatory action. After several suits and countersuits between AHP and Johnson & Johnson, a federal court judge in 1978 ordered the discontinuance of the advertising of Anacin's anti-inflammatory property as a claim of superiority over Tylenol.

Competition in the pain-reliever market was intensified by the introduction of ibuprofen. The new drug is a non-steroidal anti-inflammatory agent that is as effective as aspirin and aspirin substitutes, but without the side effect of digestive-tract irritation. AHP marketed its ibuprofen under the name Advil. Industry analysts suggest that ibuprofen could capture as much as 30% of the pain-reliever market.

The pattern of controversy and investigation established in the marketing for Preparation H and Anacin continued with several other AHP products. Easy-Off oven cleaner, Black Flag insecticide, Easy-On starch, and Aero Wax were all involved in an FTC investigation into deceptive advertising. Yet, for all of the controversy, no one can dispute AHP's success in capturing markets and acquiring products that have become household staples.

AHP's advertising budget for 1985 was estimated at more than $412 million. Despite or perhaps because of this great expenditure, AHP is notorious among advertising agencies as a demanding and uncompromising client. Paying the lowest possible commission rates, the company will, nonetheless, demand the best price for prime-time spots on television and expect promotion to be effective on strict budgets. In 1967, Ted Bates & Company, the fifth largest advertising agency in the world at that time, resigned AHP's $20 million account because of "differences in business policy." This was not the first time an AHP account had been abandoned by an agency. Grey Advertising Inc. and J. Walter Thompson similarly dropped the demanding company's account. The Bates agency was replaced with an in-house agency (AHP-owned) called the John F. Murray Company. At the time of the replacement, industry-owned agencies were already highly anachronistic.

By 1983 AHP grudgingly began to change its attitude toward promotion. The company hired world-renowned photographer Richard Avedon and actress Catherine Deneuve to promote its line of Youth Garde cosmetics. But despite this willingness to "upscale" its advertising, AHP was voted as one of the ten worst clients of 1983 by *Adweek.*

The success of AHP's proprietary goods has overshadowed the company's position as a leading manufacturer of ethical drugs. In 1932 AHP acquired Wyeth Chemical Company (now Wyeth Laboratories), a pharmaceutical manufacturer with a long history, under unusual circumstances. Wyeth was run by family descendants until the death of Stuart Wyeth, a bachelor. He bequeathed the laboratory to Harvard, his alma mater, and the university in turn sold the company to AHP at a generous price. In the early 1940's AHP also acquired two other pharmaceutical laboratories, Ives and Ayerst.

AHP's prescription drugs and medical supplies accounted for 47% of sales and 62% of profits in 1983. Among the ethical drugs AHP produces are Ovral, a low-dosage oral contraceptive, and Inderal, a drug that reduces blood pressure and slows the heartbeat. Inderal was introduced in 1968, and by 1983 supplied more than half of the U.S. market for beta-blocker drugs. The company is also busy developing new pharmaceuticals: AHP filed 21 new drug applications with the Food and Drug Administration in 1985 alone.

In 1981 company president John W. Culligan was promoted to chairman and chief executive officer. LaPorte, who had been chairman since 1965, continued as chairman of the executive committee. Culligan, 64 years old at the time of the promotion, had been with the company since 1937. John R. Stafford, a lawyer recruited from Hoffmann-LaRoche in 1970 as general counsel, was named company president on December 1, 1986. Despite the change in leadership, it is uncertain whether AHP can change LaPorte's highly centralized style of management and financial control. For a company with more than $4 billion in annual sales, this style contradicts every modern theory of corporate management.

Nevertheless, this anachronistic approach has guaranteed shareholders a handsome return on investment. In 1982, *Fortune* magazine's directory of the 500 largest U.S. industrial corporations ranked American Home Products 76th in sales and 24th in profits. The company has no long-term debt, and it pays out 60% of earnings in dividends.

In 1983 AHP spent $425 million to buy the Sherwood Medical Group. Sherwood is a manufacturer of medical supplies and places AHP in a competitive position to capture the lion's share of the growing medical-device market. But despite recent increases, the company's research and development funding continues to fall short of expenditures by other companies its size. In an industry the lifeblood of which is innovation, AHP's reluctance to invest in research can only hinder long-term growth. Because its operating margins for food and household products are lower than those for prescription drugs, many industry analysts now think that AHP should sell some of its peripheral products and concentrate on pharmaceuticals.

Principal Subsidiaries: American Home Foods Inc.; Ayerst Laboratories Inc.; Household Research Institute; Ives Laboratories Inc.; John F. Murray Advertising Agency Inc.; Sherwood Medical Co.; Whitehall Laboratories Inc.; Wyeth Laboratories Inc.; Wyeth Nutritionals Inc. The company also lists subsidiaries in the following countries: Belgium, Brazil, Canada, England, France, Japan, Philippines, South Africa, and West Germany.

A.B. ASTRA

S-151 85 Södertälje
Sweden
(0755) 329 80

Public Company
Incorporated: 1913
Employees: 6,405
Sales: SKr4.435 billion (US$584.6 million)
Market Value: SKr2.256 billion (US$297.4 million)
Stock Index: Stockholm London

Astra is the leading pharmaceutical company in Scandinavia. Long recognized by the Swedish scientific community for its strong emphasis on research and development, the company is currently increasing its international presence through licensing agreements and joint ventures with foreign firms. The name Astra is now recognized well beyond the boundaries of Sweden.

Prior to 1913 Swedish law limited the manufacture of pharmaceuticals to registered apothecaries. With the ratification of an amendment to the statute in 1913, it became possible for industrial companies to manufacture drugs. Astra was formed by the initiative of more than 400 doctors and apothecaries who joined together to establish the company and to become its first shareholders.

Principal among these early participants were a number of accomplished men who also assumed leadership positions in the new company. Prof. Hans von Euler, who was later to be the recipient of the 1929 Nobel Prize in Chemistry, joined Astra as its scientific adviser. Dr. Adolf Rising, a former employee of Ciba, the Swiss pharmaceutical concern, became Astra's first production manager. Dr. Sven Carlsson, owner of another Swedish company, provided financial support and secured a production site, a factory manager's house in Södertälje. Carlsson eventually assumed the chairmanship of the company.

Two products—Digitotal, a heart medication, and Glukofos, a nutritional supplement—emerged from Astra's facilities in 1914, and the company began to prosper. When the apothecary Hjalmar Andersson Tesch joined Astra in 1915 as the company's new president he brought with him a number of his own pharmaceuticals; Astra's product line now comprised a variety of medicines and chemical compounds. Government war-time restrictions on imports created a demand for Astra's products, and the company bought new factory buildings to meet that demand. By the end of World War I Astra was reporting handsome profits.

The years following the war proved less successful. In an attempt to create a company of international stature, the Swedish chemical company AB Svensk Färgämnesindustri acquired Astra's entire capital stock. The directors of Svensk incorrectly assumed that the shortage of raw materials during the war would persist in the post-war years. They invested in equipment for the manufacture of artificial sweeteners (a lucrative product for Astra during the war) and acetylsalicylic acid, the chemical base for aspirin. But prices for raw materials dropped as war shortages disappeared. The company faced imminent bankruptcy as its manufacturing costs grew larger than the prices its products could command in the marketplace.

A solution seemed possible when Sweden's first socialist government announced plans to create a nationalized pharmaceutical monopoly. Despite harsh criticism from the apothecaries, the press, and opposition members of parliament, the government authorized the state liquor monopoly to purchase Svensk Färgämnesindustri. Dr. Ivan Bratt, former leader of that monopoly, became Astra's new chairman, and the company seemed ready to assume a major role in the proposed pharmaceutical monopoly. Yet, within months, the socialist government fell, and its successor was staunchly opposed to the new monopoly. From 1921 until 1925 the government sought a private buyer who would release the state from its responsibilities—even the employees of Astra were approached as potential buyers. A purchaser was finally found in the form of a private consortium, and Astra became an independent company once again. Meanwhile, Astra's running deficit had cost the state millions of kroner.

The company's new board members included Erik Kistner and Richard Julin, a merchant and a banker respectively, whose business acumen helped to stop Astra's seemingly endless losses. In 1927 Börje Gabrielsson became company president; he remained in this position until 1957. The new hierarchy reorganized many of Astra's operations. The most important of these changes allowed for the formation of the company's own distribution network. In just a few years the company was again profitable.

With the establishment of research and development facilities in the 1930's, Astra began to create more innovative products. Hepaforte, marketed in 1937, offered treatment for sufferers of pernicious anemia. Another important drug to emerge from Astra's laboratories was Nitropent, a medication for angina pectoris.

Astra's growth during the years prior to World War II resulted not only from its development of new products but also from its aggressive expansion and acquisition strategy. By 1940, company subsidiaries were operating in Finland, Latvia, Stockholm and Hässleholm.

Restricted imports and shortages of raw materials during World War II once again placed Astra's products at a premium, and once again profits increased. The company constructed a new modern central laboratory and established a subsidiary to supervise the management of, and distribution to, Astra's numerous branch offices. The company established new subsidiaries in Denmark, Argentina and the United States.

In the post-war years a number of successful pharmaceuticals emerged from Astra's laboratories. Ferrigen, an iron preparation, and Sulfadital, a sulfa medication, were two products of many that were well received in the marketplace. The most important of all Astra's products developed during this period was Xylocaine, a local anesthetic that even today remains one of Astra's most popular products. Yet Xylocaine might never have happened if it had not been for Astra's strong relationship with the academic community and its commitment to research.

In 1943 two chemists from the University of Stockholm, Nils Lofgren and Bengt Lundqvist, approached Astra with a discovery they thought worth further investigation. The chemists had offered their compound to other companies, but only Astra demonstrated the ultimate interest of financial support. After five years of clinical testing in Astra's laboratories, Xylocaine appeared on the market, and its immediate success confirmed the chemists' and Astra's belief that they had produced the best local anesthetic available. Xylocaine's quality was soon recognized in foreign markets as well, and Astra's reputation as one of the world's most important pharmaceutical manufacturers grew accordingly. By 1984, local anesthetics constituted 24% of Astra's total group sales, with Xylocaine alone contributing SKr 696 million.

The worldwide production of Xylocaine began in earnest during the 1950's, and during that decade Astra broadened its overseas activities with an international network of subsidiaries and foreign licensees. Domestically, Astra consolidated its holdings to forestall the problems usually associated with quick growth, overhauled its pharmaceutical line to remove any unprofitable products, and confined all drug manufacturing to the Södertälje plant. The company continued to modernize its facilities and increase the size of its sales organization. By far the most important of Astra's measures during this period was its significant increase in research and development spending. As a result of this commitment, the company produced a number of successful new products throughout the 1950's, including Secergan (an anti-ulcer medication), Ascoxal (a treatment for oral infections), Jectofer (an injectable iron preparation), and Citanest (another local anesthetic).

Throughout the 1960's Astra continued to expand both at home and abroad. The company acquired a manufacturer of nutritional products and a distributor of medical supplies. It created and built new operations in Western Europe, South and Central America, and Australia. It joined with England's Beecham Research Laboratories in an attempt to develop synthetic penicillins. By 1983, 80% of Astra's sales were generated from overseas markets.

By the 1970's Astra's diverse activities required the company to form separate divisions. In addition to the variety of drugs developed in the past, the pharmaceutical division now manufactured cardiovascular and anti-asthmatic drugs. The chemical products division produced agricultural products, nutritional products, cleansers, and recreational items. The varia division was responsible for medical equipment and rust prevention products. By the end of the decade, however, Astra announced that it would henceforth concentrate solely on the production of pharmaceuticals and, as a result, the company sold all of its other holdings.

With a renewed commitment to the manufacture of pharmaceuticals, Astra's unique and highly efficient research units emerged as the company's strongest assets. One notable pharmaceutical to emerge from Astra's laboratories in recent years is Seloken, now a very successful medication for heart disease. By 1984 Astra's three most important products—Seloken, Xylocaine and Bricanyl (a bronchodilator)—generated 52% of the company's revenues; specifically, Seloken had become Astra's best selling drug as well as one of the best selling drugs in the world.

Astra now has a number of promising products still in the development stage—including drugs to treat viral infections, gastro-intestinal agents, and drugs for the central nervous system. Ulf Widengren, Astra's current chief executive officer and president, now projects an annual growth in profits of between 16 and 22%.

Another notable achievement has been Astra's record of good labor relations. The company operates a profit-sharing plan, and has subsidized the post-secondary education of one-third of its staff.

With subsidiaries in 21 countries (West Germany is Astra's largest foreign market), the company earned more than one billion kroner for the first time in 1985. Large foreign companies, particularly in the United States and Japan, now compete for the right to market pharmaceutical products developed by Astra, and foreign investors have become increasingly interested in Astra's shares. With its efficient worldwide organization, its line of proved products, its commitment to excellence in research and development, and with a new array of drugs about to enter the market place, Astra seems ready for a secure and profitable future.

Principal Subsidiaries: AB Draco; AB Tika; AB Hassle; Hassle Lakemedel AB; Astra Pharmaceutical; Production AB; Astra Pharmaceuticals; International Ab; Astra Development AB; Astra Pharmaceuticals AB; Astra Medictec AB; Astra Tech AB; Astra Chemical Products AB; Astra Fondaktiebolag; Astra-Merck (U.S.A.); Copthorne Insurance, Bermuda. Astra also has subsidiaries in the following countries: Argentina, Australia, Austria, Canada, Denmark, Finland, France, Ireland, Italy, Japan, Malaysia, Mexico, Netherlands, Norway, Philippines, Switzerland, United Kingdom, United States, and West Germany.

BAXTER INTERNATIONAL

One Baxter Parkway
Deerfield, Illinois 60015
U.S.A.
(312) 948-2000

Public Company
Incorporated: October 19, 1931
Employees: 32,000
Sales: $5.543 billion
Market Value: $5.490 billion
Stock Index: New York

In 1931 two Iowa doctors launched the Don Baxter Intravenous Products Company to distribute intravenous solutions commercially to hospitals in the midwestern United States. Their company survived the economic strains of the 1930's and grew to become one of the world's largest and most profitable manufacturers and suppliers of medical care products and services.

Dr. Ralph Falk and Dr. Donald Baxter knew that the intravenous solutions available at the time were of variable quality and limited in quantity; they planned to overcome these problems by manufacturing large, closely controlled supplies of solutions and packing them in evacuated containers. (Prior to Baxter's founding, only large research and teaching hospitals had the facilities to produce intravenous solutions.) In 1933 the company opened a plant in Glenview, a Chicago suburb, with a staff of six employees who produced Baxter's complete line of five solutions and packaged them in glass containers. The American Hospital Supply Corporation, also based in Chicago, distributed the Baxter products.

Falk bought his partner's interest in 1935 and soon thereafter established a research and development division. Two years later he built a second manufacturing facility, in Canada. The company was then known as Baxter Laboratories Inc. In 1976 it became Baxter Travenol Laboratories Inc., and in 1987 it became Baxter International two years after a merger with the American Hospital Supply Corporation.

In 1939 Baxter introduced the Transfuso-Vac blood collection system, a sterile vacuum-type collection and storage unit that made 21-day blood storage possible. Previously, blood could be kept for only a few hours. The Transfuso-Vac gave rise to blood-banking. In 1941 Baxter went a step further by introducing the Plasma-Vac container, which enabled the medical community to separate plasma from whole blood and store the plasma for later use.

During World War II Baxter was a provider of blood collection products and intravenous solutions to the U.S. armed forces. The company opened a number of temporary facilities in order to meet the military's increasing demand; after the war these operations were consolidated in the Glenview plant. Late in the 1940's the company expanded into a new office and production facility in the Chicago suburb of Morton Grove. Today that facility houses research and materials management operations.

Baxter formed a pharmaceutical specialties division under the name Travenol Laboratories in 1949. The division was responsible for developing and marketing chemical compounds and medical equipment.

Willem Kolff, a Dutch physician, applied dialysis procedures to treatment of kidney failures during the 1940's, and Baxter made commercial use of his methods in the U.S. In 1948 Fenwal Laboratories introduced an unbreakable plastic container for blood storage; the container became part of Baxter's product line. Its successor was the Viaflex plastic IV bag. Later, the product would be a basis for the development of a plastic delivery system for dialysis solutions.

The company expanded considerably during the 1950's. It opened a facility in Cleveland, Mississippi which today produces intravenous and irrigating solutions, needles, dialysis solutions, respiratory therapy products, and many disposable devices used in medical treatment. In addition, Baxter made several important acquisitions during the decade, including Hyland Laboratories of Los Angeles in 1952; and Flint, Eaton and Company and Fenwal Laboratories of Boston in 1959. In 1959 the company also established its international division. Today the international operations are controlled by two separate divisions, Travenol Europe and the Americas-Pacific Division. The two have manufacturing facilities in 17 countries and distribute products in more than 100.

Perhaps the most significant development of the decade for Baxter was William B. Graham's appointment as president and chief executive officer in 1953. Graham was responsible for the decision to support Dr. Willem Kolff's research effort to produce a working artificial kidney. In 1956 Baxter introduced the first commercially-built kidney dialysis system, making the first move into a realm in which the company would continue to be an innovator.

Baxter shares began trading on the New York Stock Exchange in 1961. Because of the company's steady growth during subsequent years, shareholders voted several two-for-one stock splits during the 1960's. Baxter ended its 30-year-old distribution contract with American Hospital Supply in 1963 and thereafter developed its own sales force.

The company built two Arkansas facilities during the 1960's. In 1962 Baxter acquired Disposable Hospital Products, and in 1967 it purchased Dayton Flexible Products Company and Cyclo Chemical Corporation. Meanwhile, the company's international operations were making extensive inroads into European markets, especially through the development of its wholly-owned subsidiaries.

In the 1960's and 1970's Baxter introduced several important technological innovations, beginning in 1962 with the first disposable total bypass oxygenator for open-heart surgery. The contemporary version of the TMO membrane oxygenator system closely simulates the functions of the heart and lungs. In 1968 Baxter introduced the Hemofil antihemophilic factor, which was six times as powerful as any similar product on the market at that time. Later the company would develop another important innovation in the treatment of hemophilia, the Autoplex anti-inhibitor coagulant. In 1979 Baxter offered Continuous Ambulatory Peritoneal Dialysis (CAPD) as an alternative to hemodialysis for kidney failure. CAPD can be performed at home by the patient, is less costly than hospital treatment, provides more uniform results, and allows increased patient mobility.

Baxter's sales totalled $242 million in 1972, securing the company a spot on the *Fortune 500* list. By 1978 sales had grown to $1 billion, and the company could boast an earnings growth rate of 21% for the preceding 24 continuous years. During the 1970's Baxter built a new plant in North Carolina and a new corporate headquarters in Deerfield, Illinois, and made a series of acquisitions. The company bought American Instrument Company and Surgitool in 1970, Vicra Sterile Products in 1974, and Clinical Assays in 1976. In 1976 Baxter shareholders voted to adopt the name Baxter Travenol for the parent company, with Travenol Laboratories as the major domestic operating subsidiary.

In 1980 Vernon R. Loucks replaced William Graham as president and chief executive officer; he was elected chairman of the board of directors in 1987.

Though in the early 1980's the U.S. government and private agencies were demanding stricter cost control of medical care, Loucks and other leaders of Baxter felt the company could continue to achieve accelerated growth if health care products and therapies were shifted away from their traditional focus on hospitals and toward alternative environments such as small clinics and private homes. Loucks directed the company into the growing markets for home health care and alternate-site care.

At that time, industry analysts were predicting a continued strong demand for intravenous solutions and equipment, kidney dialysis equipment, and various blood-derived products, all market areas that Baxter dominated. The company's earnings per share rose steadily, from $1.86 in 1980 to $2.64 in 1982, and further rises were expected. Worldwide manufacturing facilities, development of "mini-bags" of pre-mixed drugs, and domination of the CAPD market were all factors favoring the company's continued growth.

In 1982 Baxter acquired Medcom Inc., a medical education and information company, and in 1984 it acquired two computer software firms specializing in health management applications. In late 1983 the company formed a partnership with Genentech Inc. to develop, manufacture and market products in the human diagnostics field.

Loucks also initiated a comprehensive cost-cutting program to direct the company toward becoming the lowest-cost supplier of medical products and services. Loucks turned the company's research and development away from sophisticated, expensive items toward cost-cutting products such as pre-mixed drugs. A key focus of the new research and development programs, many of them launched in cooperation with other firms, was adaptation of traditionally expensive products for less costly use in the home.

When the federal government announced reductions in the fees it would pay for kidney dialysis treatment in 1982, industry observers predicted that Baxter would take the lead in home dialysis methods. Baxter's sales of home dialysis products had risen 40% since 1978, when the company introduced CAPD. The company had even developed a device called an ultraviolet germicidal chamber to reduce the risk of infection from tactile contamination.

Though these and other indicators seemed to point toward a bright future for Baxter in the mid-1980's, 1984 turned out to be a disastrous year for the company. By the end of 1983 Baxter announced that its earnings in 1984 were likely to be below the average of previous years. Net sales for 1984 were in fact down 2.3% from 1983 levels, net income dropped a precipitous 86.7%, and the average price for Baxter common stock was down 29%. These results were directly attributable to a special charge of $116.1 million after taxes, the results of consolidations (three manufacturing facilities were closed) and asset revaluations.

Several market trends led to Baxter's decline in 1984. Among them were a drop in demand from hospitals for the company's traditional hospital-oriented products. Hospitals undertook cost containment efforts in response to pressure from government and private insurance companies; these efforts restrained day-to-day hospital activity, which in turn dampened demand. Despite having anticipated many of the changes in the market and having shifted its research into growth areas, the company was unable to offset the slackened demand from hospitals as well as the effect of increasingly competitive pricing in the industry. The high investment in research and development of products for Baxter's new non-hospital products and services had not yet begun to pay off, adding to the general financial malaise.

One of Baxter's most significant adjustments to the new attitude in the medical industry was its development of a "package deal" of products and services for hospitals. The plan combines the company's traditional products (intravenous supplies, blood therapy products, hemodialysis and urological goods) with consulting services to help the hospital reduce costs. It is designed to establish contacts with hospitals which are setting up home health care systems that encourage patients to recuperate at home rather than in hospital. However, to make a profit in home health care, an organization must be able to rely on a large patient pool, particularly because many patients are short-term. Baxter did not have access to such a pool.

A further problem facing Baxter is that it maintains extensive production facilities for its products, even though these products, especially intravenous solutions and equipment, are sold in domestic markets in which demand is decreasing. Demand remains strong in international markets, but conducting business in foreign territory has its drawbacks, as Baxter's departure from the Philippines in 1985 illustrated. Labor strikes in that country caused turmoil in the company's intravenous operation; an eventual withdrawal from the country cost Baxter its $10 million investment in the facility.

In the late 1980's both the perceived danger and the slight real risk of Aids contamination from blood transfusions have depressed the demand for blood therapy products. Though a blood screening test was developed relatively quickly, analysts have predicted that a return to earlier levels of use of blood therapy products is unlikely in the near future. This slow down will certainly affect Baxter.

Company operations are divided into two segments: medical and non-medical care. The former accounted for 99% of Baxter's sales in 1984. It is organized according to categories of products and services. Parenteral Therapy includes intravenous solutions, scts, catheters, and flow control devices, irrigation solutions, and enteral nutrition products. Sales of these products declined by 7% in 1984. The company attributed the decline in large part to the public's fear of contracting Aids. Renal and Urological Therapy includes products for the treatment of kidney failure, such as hemodialysis and peritoneal dialysis, and for the treatment of urinary tract conditions, such as irrigating solutions, drainage bags and catheters. Sales of these products declined 1% in 1984. Medical Products encompasses diagnostic products, respiratory therapy products and services, physical therapy services, medical gloves, specialized pharmaceutical products in the endocrine and surgery fields, cardiopulmonary products, surgical trays and specialty needles, health and medical education and train-ing programs, computerized health care information systems, and hospital management consulting systems. Sales of these products rose by 9% in 1984, primarily in respiratory therapy and hospital information services.

In 1985 Baxter acquired its old partner, American Hospital Supply Company, for $51 per share in cash and securities. Although earnings were diluted by the takeover, investors were confident about the future of the company. Stock rose 35% as assimilation of American progressed. There were rumors that the merger had created difficulty for the two companies in trying to coalesce their divergent "corporate cultures," but the only visible sign of trouble was the resignation of three top-level American executives. In 1987 the company took its new name, Baxter International, and named William H. Gantz president. Formerly the executive vice-president and chief operating officer, Gantz now shares an "office of the chairman" with Loucks. **The position of chief operating officer no longer exists.**

The combining of assets of the two companies signals a leviathan effort on their part to meet a large portion of the world's demand for hospital products. With new emphasis on high profit products, including diagnostic equipment and computer software for hospitals, the Baxter-American merger promises increased competition in a crowded market.

Principal Subsidiaries: Entertainment Partner, Inc.; **MedTrain, Inc.; AHS Realoo, Inc.; AKL Corp.; Baxter** Travenol Finance World Trade Corp.; Baxter Travenol World Trade Corp.; Travenol Laboratories Inc.

BECTON DICKINSON

BECTON, DICKINSON & COMPANY

One Becton Road
Franklin Lakes, New Jersey 07417
U.S.A.
(201) 848-6800

Public Company
Incorporated: 13 November, 1906
Employees: 17,600
Sales: $1.39 billion
Market Value: $2.666 billion
Stock Index: New York

Becton Dickinson is one of the medical industry's major suppliers, largely as a result of its strong position in the field of diagnostic technology. Yet, despite a long and reputable history, the company has in recent years struggled to rectify a weakened financial position caused by a poorly timed expansion in the industry. As a result, Becton Dickinson management has been working to consolidate existing operations and reduce costs in order to maintain earnings growth and investor interest.

The company was founded in 1898 by two salesmen, named Maxwell W. Becton and Fairleigh S. Dickinson, as a venture to manufacture medical thermometers. The enterprise remained a conservatively managed, family-run business throughout its first 50 years. Becton Dickinson entered the affluent postwar years with a solid market share in medical supplies and was well prepared for a major expansion. Fortunately, it was recognized that the company's traditional approach to business would not be appropriate for the future. So in 1948 the sons of the founders, Henry P. Becton and Fairleigh Dickinson, Jr.—both astute businessmen, assumed managerial control of the company.

With Dickinson as chief executive officer and Becton serving in a variety of other capacities during the 1950's, Becton Dickinson gradually expanded its product line. By 1964 over 8000 products were being manufactured by Becton Dickinson, including a broad line of medical supplies of superior diagnostic accuracy. In the course of an acquisition program (intended to speed external expansion), Becton Dickinson purchased several specialized research laboratories, in addition to Carworth Inc., the leading producer of laboratory mice. The company divided its business into four operating divisions—medical health, laboratory, animal research and testing, and overseas sales. Increasingly, however, Becton Dickinson's strongest growth was experienced in the market for disposable items. In 1964 products such as disposable syringes and needles accounted for 60% of the company's $70 million in sales.

During the 1970's Becton Dickinson continued to make gains in the medical supplies business, despite increasingly difficult market conditions. The world oil crisis of 1973–74 caused a reduction in petrochemical feedstocks which, in turn, made medical raw materials difficult to obtain. In addition, the Food and Drug Administration adopted the same strict certification standards for diagnostic equipment as it had applied to pharmaceuticals. This delayed the commercial introduction of new products and, with technological advances, exposed them to higher rates of obsolescence. While these conditions lessened Wall Street's interest in companies in the medical industry, Becton Dickinson remained highly optimistic. With sales figures doubling every five years—and with 19% of all sales derived from overseas, Dickinson declared to shareholders that the company did not fear the impending device regulation, but instead was helping the FDA to formulate its new regulations.

When the FDA's Medical Device Act was enacted, Becton Dickinson found, to some dismay, that 85% of its products were subject to the new regulation. Wesley J. Howe, who succeeded Dickinson as president and chief executive officer in 1974, was confident that the company's products would be able to meet all the new FDA requirements; to be sure, he hired a team of legal and technical experts to guarantee standardization.

Despite growing regulation, the early years of Howe's direction were marked by a continuity of policies; Howe was handpicked by Dickinson and dedicated to the same conservative style of management. To increase efficiency, Howe automated and integrated more of the company's facilities and reduced his staff by 13%. In order to consolidate his greater influence, he also replaced 14 of the company's 17 division presidents.

Howe's leadership was proving highly effective. In one area, Becton Dickinson's marketing approach was particularly effective: targeting insulin users through doctors, diabetes associations, camps, pharmacies, and pharmacy schools. With control of almost 100% of the insulin syringe market, Becton Dickinson's sales increased to $456 million in 1975.

This success, however, was greatly compromised in the boardroom by Fairleigh Dickinson, who despite having relinquished his posts voluntarily, continued to demand managerial control. At the heart of the matter was a conflict between family interests, determined to maintain family control, and board members who favored control by a more professional corporate elite. While Howe remained above this conflict, several other important managers did not; ultimately, Dickinson would order Howe to fire them. In 1977 four board members resigned. With morale an increasingly serious problem, Howe asserted his position. Four new, "unprejudiced" board members were named to the board and Dickinson was relegated to the ceremonial post of chairman. But the power struggle was not over.

Dickinson was asked to approach the Salomon Brothers investment banking firm and initiate a study on a company Howe wanted Becton Dickinson to acquire. When completed, the study warned of numerous problems with the takeover. Howe maintained that Dickinson had sabotaged the study and, when the situation became unresolvable, ordered Dickinson removed from the payroll.

Dickinson then resorted to another strategy. With 4.5% of the company's stock, Dickinson authorized Salomon Brothers to line up additional investors to lead a takeover of Becton Dickinson. A Salomon agent named Kenneth Lipper approached several companies, including Avon, American Home Products, Monsanto, and Squibb, in an effort to set up a takeover. Becton Dickinson's attorneys warned Lipper that his action was illegal. But rather than call off the search for buyers, Lipper challenged the attorneys to stop him in court—cognizant that a well-publicized court battle would only gain more attention for his cause.

On January 16, 1978, before Lipper could be stopped, Becton Dickinson learned that the Philadelphia-based Sun oil company, had acquired 34% of its stock. (Like Becton Dickinson, Sun had just emerged from an important battle against founding family interests.) The transaction lasted only 15 minutes and involved 6.5 million shares at a purchase price of $45 each—well above the trading price of $33. Sun created a special subsidiary called LHIW (for "Let's Hope It Works") to manage the shares until a controlling majority of shares could be acquired.

The takeover had severe consequences. H. Robert Sharbaugh, chief executive officer of Sun, came into strong disagreement over the takeover with the founding Pew family and was eventually forced out of the company. Becton Dickinson, in the meantime, learned that Sun's purchase had been conducted off the trading floor, in violation of numerous laws. Finally, three Becton Dickinson shareholders sued Fairleigh Dickinson, complaining that they had been excluded from Sun's tender offer.

The New York Stock Exchange refused to file charges against Salomon (an important customer), and instead turned the matter over to the Securities and Exchange Commission. At this point, Sun offered to indemnify Salomon against any liabilities resulting from court action. The legality of the takeover was no longer in question. Instead, the question revolved around the manner in which Sun's interest in Becton Dickinson should be disposed of. With Sun no longer in pursuit of Becton Dickinson, the only clear beneficiaries of the takeover were the lawyers left to pick up the pieces.

Ironically, Sun and Becton Dickinson had a common interest in the divestiture. If the 34% share was placed on the market in one parcel, share prices would plummet and Sun would lose millions. Becton Dickinson, on the other hand, opposed summary disposal because large blocks of its shares could fall under the control of still other hostile acquisitors. An agreement was finally reached in December 1979, under which Sun would distribute a 25-year debenture convertible into Becton Dickinson shares. The unprecedented agreement ensured both a gradual spin-off of Becton Dickinson shares and the maintenance of stable share prices. While the agreement was said to have cost Sun

extremely large sums of money, it was satisfied with the arrangement.

Fairleigh Dickinson continued to seek injunctive relief from the SEC, and remained under attack from Becton Dickinson shareholders demanding the return of their $15 million profit from the original Sun tender offer. Sun's board at this time was nervously awaiting the response of its shareholders to the costly defense of Salomon Brothers.

American Home Products made a brief and uncharacteristic hostile bid for 2.5% of Becton Dickinson—by comparison with Sun, a minor incident. Ironically, Sun's debenture scheme prevented any company from gaining greater control of Becton Dickinson.

The first order of business, according to Wesley Howe, was to position Becton Dickinson for future growth. With company profits rising, Howe arranged to reinvest cash on hand into new projects. He reorganized the company into 42 units so that each division's performance could be more accurately scrutinized. Unprofitable operations, such as a computer parts manufacturer, were either sold or closed down. Older products were reassessed, and in some cases improved; insulin syringes were redesigned for more accurate dosages. Foreign sales were stepped up and, despite a negative effect on earnings, an expansion of the product line was carried out. While some new products were added by takeovers, others, such as the balloon catheter, were developed internally.

The expansion had been justified to ensure future viability, but by 1983 bad investments had cost the company $75 million in writeoffs—$23 million alone from a failed immuno-assay instrument division. Bad planning caused production stoppages and cost overruns. Howe then came under criticism for failing to invest heavily enough in research and development. With remedial measures in place, the company's financial condition had improved greatly by 1985. That year the company declared an $88 million profit on sales of $1.44 billion. Much of this turnaround, however, came from non-operating profits resulting from the sale of unprofitable divisions and a reduction in overhead. Nonetheless, productivity was up, and new product development emphasized more cost-effective diagnostic equipment.

Howe's new strategy involves slower growth rates, and raised productivity. To balance this more modest business plan, Howe allocated a 5.1% share of revenue to research and development and purchased a 12% share of a company which manufactures equipment for synthesizing DNA. But, while one may be optimistic about Becton Dickinson's prospects—the company continues to hold a majority of the European and American syringe markets—the difficulties of the last decade will continue to be felt.

Principal Subsidiaries: Becton Dickinson Electronic Co.; Becton Dickinson Overseas, Inc.; Johnson Laboratories, Inc.; Hynson Westcott and Dunning, Inc. The company also lists subsidiaries in the following countries: Canada, France, Mexico, Panama, and Puerto Rico.

CIBA–GEIGY

CIBA-GEIGY LTD.

Klybecstrasse 141
Basle, Baslestadt 4002
Switzerland

Public Company
Incorporated: 1884
Employees: 81,012
Sales: SFr14.434 billion (US$8.869 billion)
Market Value: SFr11.503 billion (US$7.079 billion)
Stock Index: Geneva Zurich Basle

Ciba-Geigy is the largest chemical company in Switzerland. But since the country offers only a limited market and lacks many essential raw materials, Swiss chemical companies have been forced to enter foreign markets; and in order to compete successfully, they have had to lead the world in certain technologies.

In the early years of this century, the world's strongest chemical industries were in Germany, the United States, and Switzerland. German companies, fearful of losing their leading position to rapidly advancing American firms, openly colluded and coordinated business strategies. After World War I the German companies formed a cartel, the notorious IG Farben. In order to maintain competitiveness with the Germans, the three largest Swiss chemical companies, Ciba Ltd, J.R. Geigy S.A., and Sandoz Ltd., formed a similar cartel called the Basle A.G. This trust lasted from 1918 to 1951. By 1970, however, market conditions led Ciba and Geigy to merge, forming one of the world's leading pharmaceutical and specialty chemical companies.

Geigy is the older of the two companies—one family member was in the drug business as early as 1758. Through several generations, the Geigy family had married into the prosperous silk manufacturing establishment in Basle and then became established in the dye trade in 1883. Only a few years later, the Geigy family set itself apart from other dyers in Basle by embracing newly discovered synthetic dying processes.

A few years earlier, in 1859, a French silk weaver named Alexander Clavel moved to Basle, where he established a dyeworks called the Gesellschaft für Chemische Industrie im Basle, or "CIBA." In 1884 Clavel abandoned silk dying for a more lucrative trade in dyestuff manufacturing. Ciba gained a reputation for Fuchsine, a reddish purple dye, and Martius yellow.

By 1900 Ciba was the largest chemical company in Switz-

erland. With a major alkali works located at Monthey, it was one of the only Swiss manufacturers of inorganic dyes. Ciba, however, started a limited diversification into the pharmaceutical business with the introduction of an antiseptic called Vioform. Between 1900 and 1913 net assets quadrupled while profits nearly tripled. Geigy, during this period, remained steadfastly committed to organic dye production, some of which were still derived from coal tar.

Early in the century both Ciba and Geigy established factories in Germany, due in part to a labor shortage in Switzerland, but also to avoid enforcement of environmental laws designed to reduce pollution in the River Rhine.

Until World War I, German chemical companies dominated the world dye trade with a 90% market share. Those companies, including BASF, Hoechst and Bayer, could easily have run Swiss competitors out of business through price competition; they had proven their ability to hold back the American chemical industry in its infancy. Instead, Ciba and Geigy developed practices that would permit international expansion while not provoking the Germans. Central to this strategy was the abandonment of bulk dye production (the German specialty) in favor of more expensive specialty dyes.

In time, the German companies developed a vested interest in the survival of their Swiss counterparts. Eighty percent of the raw materials used by the Swiss companies came from Germany. In eliminating Swiss competitors, the German companies would eliminate customers whose capacity they could not economically absorb. Furthermore, competition among German companies to fill a sudden void left by the Swiss could have destabilized the careful balance maintained by the cartel. As Swiss companies became acclimated to the German system, they were accorded certain privileges, such as an exclusive right to export to Germany. Cooperation between Swiss and German companies also took the form of an occasional profit sharing pool, as existed between Geigy, Bayer and BASF for black dye.

The hostilities that began in Europe in 1914 severely upset the equilibrium that had existed between Ciba, Geigy, and their German counterparts. Unable to secure raw materials and chemical intermediaries from German suppliers, factories in Basle were forced to suspend dye production. The Swiss later negotiated an agreement with the British, who had been dependent on German dyes and were unprepared for their trade embargo. The British agreed to supply the Swiss with raw materials on the condition that Swiss dyes would be sold preferentially to Britain. While Swiss factories in Baden were seized by the German government, The Swiss were free to export to the lucrative (and formerly German) markets in Britain and the United States and to establish factories in France and Russia.

Ciba's profits increased dramatically, from SFr3 million in 1913 to SFr15 million in 1917. The end of the war, however, reopened world markets, but left the industry in a severe state of overcapacity. By 1921 Ciba's profits had fallen to SFr1 million. At this time the German companies decided to reform their cartel, this time under the aegis of a large holding company called the IG Farben. Ciba, Sandoz and Geigy were invited to join the IG Farben but, true to Swiss neutrality, elected instead to form their own cartel, the Basle AG.

The Basle AG, founded in 1918, was fashioned after the IG Farben. The group consisted of Ciba, Geigy, and Sandoz—virtually the entire Swiss chemical industry. The agreement mandated that all competition between the three companies would cease, technical knowledge would be freely shared, and all profits would be pooled. Ciba would receive 52% of the group's profits, while Geigy and Sandoz would each be entitled to 24%. Any sales between the companies were to be invoiced at cost, raw materials would be purchased jointly, and the manufacture of any product would be assigned to whichever company could produce it at the lowest cost.

From the cartel's inception, Geigy's weak market position was a source of tension for its partners. It still produced vegetable dyes, which were gradually losing market share to organic dyestuffs. Despite Sandoz's contention that it was being forced to subsidize Geigy, the Basle AG remained stable. In fact, it was considered more successful than the larger and more powerful IG Farben. All three firms invested their profits into a broader range of chemical interests, including chemicals and pharmaceuticals. By 1930, these divisions contributed over one quarter of the group's profits. A joint venture between Sandoz and Geigy led to the establishment of the Cincinnati Chemical Works, a subsidiary which gave the Basle AG a tariff-free foothold in the American market.

In 1929, placing profit before independence, the Basle AG joined with the IG Farben to create the Dual Cartel. French dyemakers joined the group shortly afterwards, forming the Tripartite Cartel. In 1932, with the addition of the British cartel Imperial Chemical Industries, the group was again renamed the Quadrapartite Cartel. This pan-European cartel existed until 1939 when World War II forced its dissolution.

Due to the secrecy characteristic of Swiss firms, little is known about the Basle AG's activities during the war; the company had subsidiaries in both Allied and Axis nations. At one point, Ciba angered its partners by placing its shares in Cincinnati Chemical Works under the custody of an American trust. Apparently fearing the eventual seizure of those shares by the alien property custodian, Geigy and Sandoz protested in American courts, but were unable to retrieve Ciba's shares.

In 1940 Dr. Paul Mueller, a researcher with Geigy, discovered the insecticidal properties of DDT. Originally thought safe enough to be sprayed directly on refugees to eradicate lice, DDT was considered a "wonder chemical." Research during the war led to the development of several ethical drugs, including Privine, a treatment for hay fever, and Nupercaine, a spinal anesthetic used in childbirth. The companies also developed drugs for treatment of high blood pressure and heart disease.

After the war Ciba notified Geigy and Sandoz that as a result of American antitrust laws, the 1918 agreement could not be respected among subsidiaries in the United States. Geigy made a similar declaration in 1947, regarding American assets. Two years later Sandoz again raised the issue of cross-subsidization and proposed that the cartel be dissolved. Geigy opposed the motion, but Ciba, unwilling to abandon its lucrative markets in the United States, eventually sided with Sandoz; the postwar environment no longer justified cartelization for self-protection. The Basle AG was finally dissolved in 1951.

Geigy's poor financial performance called into question its survivability outside the cartel. During the 1950's, however, the full market potential of DDT was realized. Suddenly profitable, Geigy expanded its market in agrichemicals by introducing a corn herbicide called triazine.

Both Ciba and Geigy grew steadily during the 1950's. Between 1950 and 1959, Ciba's sales grew from SFr531 million to SFr1026 million, and Geigy's grew from SFr260 million to SFr738 million. By 1960 both Ciba and Geigy were diversified manufacturers, competing directly in pharmaceuticals, dyes, plastics, textile auxiliaries, and agricultural and specialty chemicals. Each year Geigy's sales grew stronger, until in 1967 the company overtook Ciba.

Although older than Ciba by 25 years, Geigy maintained a more youthful image. While Ciba sold itself as the company "where research is the tradition." Geigy recruited engineers with the slogan, "future with Geigy." But in 1970, while Ciba and Geigy personnel were quibbling over their respective talents, the leaders of both companies were discussing a possible merger.

The idea to merge was first raised when the two companies jointly established a factory at Toms River, New Jersey. With increasingly difficult conditions in export markets—particularly the United States—officials of the two companies began to explore the benefits of combining their textile and pharmaceutical research; Geigy's strength in agricultural chemicals complemented Ciba's leading position in synthetic resins and petrochemicals.

Ciba and Geigy were both in excellent financial condition. However, some of the same market conditions that had led them to form the Basle AG in 1918 were once again prevalent. Competition against German companies in export markets had intensified. But it was as a defense against emerging petrochemical industries in oil-rich Persian Gulf states that the merger was most attractive.

The largest obstacle to a merger between Ciba and Geigy was American antitrust legislation. Antitrust sentiment in the United States was so strong that federal prosecutors vowed to block the merger in Switzerland if it threatened to restrain American trade in any way. In order to win approval in the United States, Ciba agreed to sell its American dyeworks to Crompton and Knowles and Geigy its American pharmaceutical holdings to Revlon. Despite further challenges, including one from the consumer advocate Ralph Nader, the merger was approved.

Mechanically, the merger consisted of a takeover of Ciba by Geigy. This was done to minimize tax penalties amounting to SFr55 million. Geigy's chairman, Dr. van Planta, assumed the chairmanship of the new company, with Ciba's chairman, Dr. Kappeli, serving as honorary chairman.

As promised, the Ciba-Geigy merger has proven "synergistic." The more profitable, but less diversified, Geigy has benefited from Ciba's research capabilities. Ciba, on the other hand, has profited from Geigy's more modern approach to marketing and management. In the United States, the company's American subsidiary passed the one billion dollar sales mark in 1978, and doubled that figure only six years later. The company's worldwide sales that year were SFr17.5 billion, 30% of which came from U.S. operations. Despite a 14% drop in profits between 1978 and 1980, Ciba-Geigy has maintained strong annual sales growth since 1981; profits as a percentage of sales was 8.1% in 1985.

In contrast to its impressive performance on the balance sheet, Ciba-Geigy has suffered a few problems with its public image. In the mid-1970's a Ciba-Geigy product marketed in Africa as an ordinary analgesic produced a horrifying side-effect: the loss of large pieces of flesh. More recently, the plant at Toms River recently discontinued production of Posgene in response to a Greenpeace campaign which warned the community of a possible accident similar in magnitude to the tragedy in Bhopal, India.

Ciba-Geigy is one of the five largest chemical companies in the world. And, while it is widely diversified within the industry, it has maintained a steady emphasis on sophisticated chemicals—whether they are pharmaceuticals, plastics, pigments, or pesticides. (Until it was sold, Airwick, which made air fresheners and other consumer products, was one of Ciba-Geigy's very few low-tech ventures.) The company plans to strengthen existing product lines and limit diversification to compatible high-technology operations in biotechnology, laser applications, and diagnostics.

Principal Subsidiaries: Ciba-Geigy lists subsidiaries in the following countries: Argentina, Australia, Austria, **Belgium, Brazil, Canada, Chile, Colombia, Denmark,** France, Italy, Japan, Korea, Lebanon, The Netherlands, Portugal, Spain, Sweden, United Kingdom, and the United States.

Further Reading: The Basle Marriage: History of the Ciba-Geigy Merger, by Paul Erni, Zurich, Neue Zurcher Zeitung, 1979.

FUJISAWA PHARMACEUTICAL COMPANY, LTD.

3 Doshomachi 4-chome
Higashi-ku, Osaka 541
Japan
06-202-1141

Public Company
Incorporated: 1930
Employees: 5,746
Sales: ¥204 billion (US$1.13 billion)
Market Value: ¥147 billion (US$816 million)
Stock Index: Tokyo Nagoya Osaka

Fujisawa Pharmaceutical Company is one of Japan's oldest and largest drug manufacturers. Although management positions continue to be held by descendents of founder Tomokichi Fujisawa, the nearly 100-year-old company operates as a modern corporation. Innovative technology, coupled with an international orientation, are the major elements in Fujisawa's successful business approach.

In 1894 Fujisawa Shoten opened in Osaka as a private dealership in medicinal herbs. The business expanded rapidly during the early decades of this century, its success based on the production of such widely used compounds as Camphor, a stimulant, and Santonin, a treatment for intestinal worms. Even though the company faced shortages of ingredients during World War II, it continued to prosper. It adopted its current name in 1943.

Along with the rest of the pharmaceutical industry, Fujisawa experienced unprecedented growth in postwar Japan, mainly as a producer of antibiotics (by 1961 antibiotics accounted for 10.3% of Japan's total drug production). Because Japan had no effective patent laws, and the results of highly expensive research and development could be easily pirated, Japanese pharmaceutical companies tended to import the technology to manufacture antibiotics and other medicines from abroad.

Fujisawa has always shown an impressive ability to establish good working relations with foreign firms. In 1953 Fujisawa signed a contract with the Italian company Carlo Erba to sell a broad spectrum antibiotic, Kemicetine, in Japan. Other such licensing arrangements have involved Irgapyrin, an anti-arthritic drug from Geigy of Switzerland, and a local anesthetic, Xylocaine, from the laboratories of Astra in Sweden. Fujisawa has also developed a number of successful drugs on its own—for example, Trichomycin, an antibiotic used in the treatment of candidiasis and trichomoniasis.

Besides the production and sale of antibiotics, Fujisawa has been notable for its work with vitamin preparations. The pure synthesis of thioctic acid in company laboratories led to a highly successful product marketed as Tioctan. Neuvita, a longer-acting vitamin preparation, was added to the product line in 1961 after the firm developed a process to combine thioctic acid with vitamin B1. This new product, helpful in the treatment of liver disease, was well received by both physicians and the general public.

At the forefront of producing and marketing antibiotics and vitamins, Fujisawa reaped financial rewards. With antibiotics accounting for more than 10.3% and vitamins totaling more than 20% of the Japanese pharmaceutical industry's entire drug production in 1962, Fujisawa enjoyed an increase in profits of 2.5 times its 1961 results.

In the late 1950's and throughout the 1960's Fujisawa continued to expand its product line, expanding, too, into non-pharmaceutical items, such as antioxidative food additives. The company's continued expansion in the 1960's—like that of many other Japanese pharmaceutical concerns—can also be attributed to the regulations of the National Health Insurance System established by the government in the early part of the decade. With the implementation of this program, the burden of public health costs fell upon the government; people began to visit their doctors more frequently. With more patients, doctors prescribed more drugs. Because doctors operated their own drug dispensaries, the Ministry of Health and Welfare set official prices at which they would be reimbursed. These official prices were often higher than the purchase price: the profit involved obviously did not discourage doctors from generously prescribing drugs.

Even as Fujisawa experienced record growth and profits, it continued, as did other Japanese pharmaceutical firms, to depend on foreign research and production technology. The result was a huge trade deficit between imported and exported drugs. The government, recognizing the potential of an active domestic pharmaceutical industry, implemented a number of measures to encourage export and to ensure that Japanese companies could withstand foreign competition. These measures included the tightening of patent laws and a restructuring of official drug pricing, which put innovative drugs at a premium.

Fujisawa's expenditure for research and development thereafter increased dramatically as it searched for lucrative patentable products. Two new drugs to emerge from company laboratories at this time were Pyroace, an antibiotic, and Padrin, an antiseptic. By 1966 company profits were nine times what they had been a decade before, with newly-developed products accounting for between 40 to 50% of total sales.

Fujisawa now looked to foreign markets as a means of recouping its huge investments in new products. A technical co-operation agreement with Delagrange in France led to Fujisawa's licensing the manufacture and sale of the drug Primperan. In the non-pharmaceutical division, the company began to export a leavening agent for baked goods. Both of these products were well received in foreign markets.

As technology began flowing from East to West, foreign companies became particularly interested in a new class of potent antibiotics developed by the Japanese. Known as third-generation cephalosporins, these antibiotics are particularly important for their ability to combat the highly-resistant strains of bacteria found in hospitals. In 1970 Fujisawa became the third company in the world to develop the cephalosporin "Cefamezin." Their new drug, called Cefazolin, was introduced in 1971. A joint venture between Fujisawa and SmithKline Beckman in 1977 has led to the introduction of Cefazolin and other Fujisawa antibiotics on the American market. This agreement also entitled Fujisawa to sell innovative SmithKline drugs in the Japanese market—including Tagamet, SmithKline's well-known anti-ulcer drug, and Auranofin, its popular anti-arthritic medication.

Fujisawa opened an American subsidiary in 1977 and established a London office in 1979, and it was during this time that Mutsuya Ajisaka, Fujisawa's director of planning and co-ordination, outlined a new company strategy. Although much of the firm's overseas success had so far been achieved through licensing arrangements, henceforth Fujisawa would participate in more direct marketing of its products. Ajisaka also felt that antibiotics, including cephalosporins, though continuing to achieve huge sales, had saturated the market; the company should concentrate its research in other areas. Within a few years, calcium blockers, a new class of potent drugs, emerged from Fujisawa's laboratories. These pharmaceuticals, which prevent blood vessels from constricting, are used to treat angina pectoris and hypertension.

By 1982 the per capita drug bill in Japan had reached the equivalent a nearly $100. In an effort to counter excessive profiteering and to alleviate national expenditures on medicine, the government began reducing the price of drugs. By 1987 prices had dropped 50%, and patients were now required to pay 10% of examination costs.

This structural change in the National Health Insurance System almost immediately affected Fujisawa. Profits declined because demand declined. In 1985 alone the drug price decrease led to an average 5% reduction in demand for Fujisawa's products. Against this background, Fujisawa also found itself competing in a more crowded marketplace and suffering, with other pharmaceutical companies, increased costs for research and development.

Despite these difficulties, Fujisawa remains a strong and innovative competitor within the international pharmaceutical industry. The company introduced six new drugs in 1986, and it is now strongly committed to developing a new class of drugs appropriate for Japan's growing geriatric population. One such drug, Gramalil, is used to treat psychotic disturbances in the elderly. Fujisawa has also recently developed an anti-tumor substance from soil bacteria, a drug that has been shown to be effective in treating leukemia and melanoma in laboratory animals.

Principal Subsidiaries: Doei Co. Ltd.; Fujihan Co. Ltd.; **Hoshienu Pharmaceutical Co. Ltd.; Izumisha Co. Ltd.;** Hoei Pharmaceutical Co. Ltd.; Daiichi Yakuten Co. Ltd.; Imasan Sangyu Co. Ltd.; Shinwa Building Co. Ltd.; Fuji Tanso Co. Ltd.; Daisan Kogyo Co. Ltd.; Smithkline and Fujisawa K.K.; Klinge Pharma GmbH.

GENENTECH, INC.

460 Point San Bruno Blvd.
San Francisco, California 94080
U.S.A.

Public Company
Incorporated: 1976
Employees: 900
Sales: $43.5 million
Market Value: $49 million
Stock Index: NASDAQ

Genentech Inc. develops and manufactures products to alleviate life-threatening diseases. An acknowledged leader in biotechnology, the company fabricates organisms from gene cells, organisms that are not ordinarily produced by the cells. Conceivably this process, referred to as gene splicing or recombinant DNA, may lead to cures for cancer or Aids. The potential success of this young science causes it to flourish, attracting entrepreneurs and investors. Founded in 1976, Genentech was financed by Kleinman, Perkins, Caufield and Byers, a San Francisco high-tech venture capital firm, and by its co-founders, Robert Swanson and Herbert Boyer.

Swanson, a graduate of the Sloan School of Management at MIT, was employed by Kleinman, Perkins, where he learned of the achievements of Cetus, a biotechnology firm founded in 1971; he decided to investigate the prospect of marketing DNA products. Initially, the concept was met with little enthusiasm, but in Herbert Boyer, a distinguished academic scientist, Swanson found someone who enthusiastically supported his plan. One of the first scientists to synthesize life (he had created gene cells with Stanley Cohen), Boyer wanted to take his research further and to create new cells.

Boyer and Swanson decided to leave their respective jobs and to found Genentech (genetic engineering technology). Thomas J. Perkins, a partner with Kleinman Perkins, who became Genentech's chairman, suggested that the new company contract out its early research. Swanson followed Perkins's advice, and contracted the City of Hope National Medical Center to conduct the company's initial research project.

Boyer and Swanson wanted to exhibit their grasp of the relevant technology before they attempted to market products—to achieve credibility for Genentech. To accomplish this goal, Boyer intentionally selected an easily replicated cell with a simple composition, Somatostatin. The first experiment with Somatostatin required seven months of research. Scientists on the project placed the hormone inside a bacteria E. coli, found in the human intestine. The anticipated result was that the bacteria would produce useful proteins that duplicated Somatostatin, but that did not happen. Then a scientist working on the project hypothesized that proteins in the bacteria were attacking the hormone. Somatostatin was protected, and the cell was successfully produced. Although it established credibility for the company, the experiment brought no real financial returns. Boyer and Swanson intended to produce human insulin as Genentech's first product.

Early in the summer of 1978 Genentech experienced its first breakthrough in recreating the insulin gene. This development required an expenditure of approximately $100 million and 1,000 human years of labor. By 1982 the company had won approval from the Food and Drug Administration. Eli Lilly, the world's largest and oldest manufacturer of synthetic insulin, commanded 75% of the American insulin market, and Swanson knew that Genentech stood little chance of competing with them. He informed Lilly's directors of Genentech's accomplishments, hoping to attract their attention: he believed that the mere threat of a potentially better product would entice Lilly to purchase licensing rights to the product, and he was correct. Lilly bought the rights. This manuever provided ample capital for Genentech to continue its work. By 1987 the company was earning $5 million in licensing fees from Lilly.

Swanson pursued a similar strategy with the company's next product, Alpha Interferon, Hoffmann-La Roche purchased the rights to Interferon and paid approximately $5 million dollars in royalties to Genentech in 1987. Revenues from these agreements helped to underwrite the costs of new product development, which can run from $25 to $50 million per product prior to FDA approval.

The only product independently marketed by Genentech, human growth hormone (HGH), generated $43.6 million dollars in sales in 1986. Approved by the FDA in 1985, HGH helps to prevent dwarfism in abnormal children. As the medical profession learns more about the drug's capabilities, demand for HGH should increase. Genentech's entry into the market was facilitated by an FDA decision to ban the drug's predecessor because it was contaminated with a virus. A "new and improved" version of HGH patented by Eli Lilly has also received approval from the FDA. Lilly's drug, unlike Genentech's version, actually replicates the growth hormone found in the human body. To counter this potential threat to their market, Genentech sued the FDA to force the agency to determine which company holds exclusive rights to the product.

Such legal disputes are not unusual for biotechnology firms still in their infancy. Because the products of the industry duplicate substances found in nature, they challenge existing legal theories. Traditionally, products and discoveries determined as not evident in nature receive patent awards. Biotechnology firms contest these standards in the courtroom, attempting to force alterations in the law, to make it conform to the needs of the industry. Companies apply for broad patents to secure against technological innovations that could undermine their niche in the marketplace. For start-up firms like Genentech, patent battles consume large sums of money in both domestic and foreign disputes.

In Britain, Genentech recently lost its exclusive rights on t-PA, or tissue plasminogen activator. The British firm Wellcome challenged Genentech's patent in the British courts, claiming it was overly broad. This decision against the company, viewed more as an annoyance than a serious blow, may be reversed on appeal. A far more serious setback for Genentech occurred when the FDA refused to approve t-PA for the American market.

Activase (t-PA) helps to break down fibris, which causes blood clots, and is used to treat heart attack victims. Delay in approval for the drug, expected in 1988, resulted from the failure of Genentech's evidence to prove the drug prolonged the lives of heart attack victims. Clinical data showed serious side effects to the drug, such as severe internal bleeding in patients treated with high dosages.

In anticipation of FDA approval, Genentech manufactured large amounts of t-PA to ensure an adequate supply for the anticipated demand. But Activase, considered far superior to similar products, faces stiff competition when it enters the market. Delays in approval give competitors like Biogen and Integrated Genetics the opportunity catch up with the industry leader. A dozen or so companies have filed patents for similar drugs. Genentech cannot expect to easily secure foreign markets for its new drug either. Competition is stiff; this relatively new industry has had little time to carve out established markets, and there are important competitors, particularly in Western Europe and Japan. Germany's BASF has appealed to the courts for the right to market its own version of t-PA.

The FDA compounded Genentech's setback when it recommended approval for the intravenous method used to administer Activase for a competing drug, Skreptokinase. Skreptokinase, currently injected into the coronary artery by catheter, costs about $200 dollars per dose. The cost of Activase, approximately $3,000, holds little appeal for hospitals: the slower acting Skreptokinase apparently produces similar effects to those of Activase at much less cost.

Genentech faces other critical challenges. Unwilling to ignore the projected billion dollar sales potential of the products of the biotechnology industry, large pharmaceutical and chemical companies aggressively seek to establish a presence in the same marketplace. Because of their size, these companies react slowly when initiating research projects, yet they face fewer capital constraints. The evolution of biotechnology requires companies to manufacture as well as develop products if they expect to remain competitive. The big companies have the capability to meet this requirement. Other factors favor the big companies. They face fewer staffing limitations; they already employ large numbers of employees engaged in marketing and manufacturing. For these reasons, only a small number of the smaller biotechnology firms is expected to survive mergers or acquisitions by the large firms. The others, forced out of manufacturing and product development, will survive as contract researchers.

Though the future looks bleak for the smaller, less well-established biotechnology firms, they do retain some advantages. The start-up firms tended to cultivate close working relations with the universities. This relationship has allowed the "start-ups" to maintain a superior research position as well as an advantage in attracting academic talent. The financial benefits offered by the start-up companies present great financial opportunities to academic scientists in exchange for their services. Through stock options, many have the opportunity to become wealthy overnight.

During 1987 start-up biotechnology firms rasied $1.1 billion dollars in 50 share offerings. In 1980, when Genentech went public, the value of its shares soared because Wall Street investors were willing to gamble on the promise of the company. Genentech's share price more than doubled, from $35 to $82. Financial analysts suggested that over-enthusiastic investors were pushing the value of Genentech shares—and those of other biotechnology firms—well above the real value of the companies, and cautioned that a decline was inevitable. Following the FDA's failure to approve Activase, Genentech's share price did decline. Because the company is considered the industry leader, that decline rippled throughout Wall Street, causing the value of many other start-up firms to decline as well.

Despite recent difficulties, Genentech earned $6.6 million in interest on capital on hand and, although criticized on many fronts, the company's management continues to command a positive cash flow. The creative financial manuevers initiated by Swanson have secured the company against recent setbacks. Current estimates suggest that Activase will be earning $250 million a year by 1990.

The applications of biotechnology extend beyond health care; they also affect the agricultural and chemical industries. Agriculture still remains a dominant industry in the United States, and experiments in cell replication could transform that industry. Technological innovations affect not only farmers but also food processors, plant-oil manufacturers, the forestry industry and the ornamental and floral industries. Over the next thirty years the discoveries of biotechnology will alter human existence. At the forefront, Genentech helps to establish new precedents for the field, yet it suffers the consequences of its position. The company has shown it has the capability to regroup, plan effective strategies and move on to find revolutionary solutions to both medical and social problems.

Principal Subsidiaries: Genentech Development Corp.; Genentech Venture.

Glaxo

GLAXO HOLDINGS PLC

Clarges House
6–12 Clarges Street
London W1Y 8DH
England
(01) 493-4060

Public Company
Incorporated: March, 1972
Employees: 25,634
Sales: £1.412 billion (US$2.03 billion)
Market Value: £4.888 billion (US$7.03 billion)
Stock Index: New York London

Much of the recent glamour surrounding Glaxo Holdings is the result of the great success of its anti-ulcer drug—Zantac. Commanding more than half the world market for anti-ulcer medication, Zantac is now the largest selling prescription drug in the world. Despite such success, Glaxo executives are quick to refute any suggestion that the company's future depends solely on the strength of one product. Instead they point to Glaxo's long history in drug innovation, its strong emphasis on research and development, and new products soon to be released on the market.

Glaxo began life as a merchant trader. After a New Zealand partnership between Joseph Nathan and his brother-in-law was dissolved in 1873, the English-born entrepreneur started an independent company under the name Joseph Nathan & Company. Importing and exporting goods ranging from whalebone to patent medicines, Joseph Nathan prospered. He eventually returned to London in order to supervise his growing business there, while his sons remained in Wellington to manage the company activities in New Zealand.

While on a purchasing trip in London one of the Nathan sons discovered an American process to dry milk. After securing the rights to this process, the company began production of dried milk at Bunnythorpe factory in New Zealand. Research on the sanitary quality of the milk soon caught the attention of the medical establishment; sales of the product, however, proved disappointing. The most promising market emerged in infant food. Thus began production of Glaxo baby food products.

Alec, the youngest Nathan son, moved from New Zealand to London to supervise an expansion of the baby food business there. Much of the sales momentum Alec thereafter achieved is attributed to his *Glaxo Baby Book*,

an informative yet familiar guide to child care. In it could be found the Glaxo slogan, "Builds Bonnie Babies," which would soon become famous. Only a year after the product registered its first impressive sales figures, Joseph Nathan died and the chairmanship passed to his son Louis. Those sales continued to grow, and within a relatively short period of time Glaxo Baby Foods had become an important U.K.-based manufacturer.

By the outbreak of World War I production demands compelled the company to build a more modern facility and to hire new staff: Ernest Rose joined the company to supervise manufacturing processes, and Harry Jephcott was placed in charge of Glaxo's rudimentary laboratory. With the completion of Glaxo House, the company's new headquarters, Jephcott's laboratory grew and employed a staff of eight scientists including two women.

In the years that followed Harry Jephcott moved up the ranks from chemist to company chairman. Born in 1891, the son of a train driver, Jephcott received his education in pharmacy. When first hired by the Nathan family he was regarded as "Alec's folly," but he quickly proved his worth and became indispensable to Glaxo's success. Standing more than six-and-a-half feet tall, Jephcott was an imposing figure. As a top executive he was known for his firm leadership and business acumen—a perfect complement to Alec Nathan and his concern with worker welfare. Jephcott's accomplishments eventually were rewarded with a knighthood.

The sale of Glaxo Baby Foods continued to grow in the years following World War I, and the company expanded into such markets as India and South America. Jephcott's 1923 visit to the International Dairy Congress in Washington, D.C. soon changed the course of Glaxo's history. There he observed Professor Elmer V. McCollum's and Dr. Theodore Zucker's original work in identifying and extracting Vitamin D. Recognizing the huge market potential in fortifying Glaxo products with this anti-rachitic, Jephcott persuaded the company's directors to secure a process license. After achieving an immediate success with Vitamin D fortified products, Glaxo moved on to produce a pharmaceutical item, Ostelin Liquid, Britain's first commercial vitamin-concentrate. Ostelin products eventually included a comprehensive line of vitamin preparations.

In the 1930's Glaxo's major advancements included the production of Adexolin (Vitamins A and D) and Ostermilk, a retail version of Glaxo's vitamin fortified milk that soon surpassed the pharmaceutical version in sales. Because of increased business overseas, the company built a factory in India, established a company in Italy, and secured distributorships in Greece, Malaya and China. In an effort to strengthen the company's increasing activity in pharmaceuticals, that Glaxo department was organized into a separate subsidiary called Glaxo Laboratories Ltd.

During World War II, the company concentrated on producing pharmaceuticals for the war effort—anesthetics, penicillin and a variety of vitamin supplements. After the war Glaxo began the mass production of penicillin in earnest, using the American process of deep fermentation. Several long-time Glaxo employees retired. Harry Jephcott became chairman of the company on Alec Nathan's retirement. Ida Townsend, Glaxo's successful export manager, joined the board in 1947, the company's first woman director. Changes occurred not only in personnel but also in structure: Glaxo's parent company, Joseph Nathan & Company, was dissolved, and Glaxo became an independent public company. All Joseph Nathan's diversified interests, from butter importing to fencing exporting, were sold to finance Glaxo's growth.

By far the most important of Glaxo's post war achievements was the isolation of vitamin B12. Along with their American counterparts at Merck, who had achieved the same feat virtually simultaneously, Glaxo had made a major advance in the treatment of pernicious anaemia. Of similar magnitude was Glaxo's synthesis of the hormone necessary for the treatment of hypothroidism.

In the 1950's Glaxo grew through acquisition and consolidation. The company acquired both a chemical and a medical supply subsidiary and established an independent veterinary department to meet the increasing demand for animal pharmaceuticals. Through a merger Glaxo joined forces with Allen & Hanbury's, one of Britain's oldest pharmaceutical manufacturers. Britain's first commercial cortisone product emerged from Glaxo's laboratories during this time. The discovery of sisal as an abundant source of an important steroid led to the commercial synthesis of a series of corticosteroids.

Glaxo's growth continued into the 1960's. To monitor this growth, the directors formed a new parent company, Glaxo Group Limited. Jephcott assumed the title of chairman for the holding company. In 1963 he retired from this position and became Glaxo's first honorary president. The physicist Sir Alan Wilson assumed the chairmanship. Glaxo's scientists worked to develop Betnovate, a new corticosteroid. Through a licensing agreement with Schering U.S.A., a pharmaceutical company engaged in original research in corticosteroids, Glaxo developed a production process essential to the manufacture of the drug.

During the next decade, Beecham, an industry competitor, attempted the largest takeover in British history by making an unfriendly bid for Glaxo. To protect its independence, Glaxo management sought to increase its holdings through a merger with a company of similar interests. Thus Glaxo and Boots, another competitor, planned to combine their company resources. Yet neither the takeover nor the merger ever happened. The Monopolies Commissioners ruled against the proceedings on the grounds that innovation declines as companies grow above a certain size. In the wake of the aborted takeover the company renamed itself Glaxo Holdings.

In 1973 Sir Alan Wilson retired and Austin Bide, a long-time Glaxo employee, assumed the titles of chairman and chief executive officer. Other changes during the 1970's included the establishment of a U.S. subsidiary. Domestic consolidation brought all Glaxo's UK operations under one holding company. In pharmaceuticals Glaxo's innovative research in cephalosporins resulted in the development of Zinacef.

Near the end of the 1970's Glaxo suffered from the effects of inflation. Citing Glaxo's continuing dependence on export trade, its failure to expand significantly beyond the British and Commonwealth markets, and its persistent reputation for poor marketing decisions, City analysts projected slower growth in the company's future. What industry observers did not know was that the company would soon release a drug destined to become highly successful throughout the world. Zantac, Glaxo's trade-name for its anti-ulcer drug ranitidine, was still in testing during this time. However, based on the emerging results of these tests, Glaxo knew that Zantac was ready to present a competitive challenge to SmithKline's Tagamet, then the pre-eminent anti-ulcer medication and best selling drug in the world.

Soon after Sir Austin retired as chief executive officer, Zantac was launched in several European markets with a high degree of success. Paul Girolami, a long-time Glaxo employee who had formerly served as Group Financial Director, assumed Sir Austin's position. Over the next several years Girolami established himself as the architect of Zantac's marketing policy in the United States and Japan. In a joint venture with Hoffmann-La Roche, the Swiss pharmaceutical concern responsible for developing the world's two best selling tranquilizers, Glaxo introduced Zantac to the U.S. market.

By 1984 Zantac had captured 25% of the new prescription market. Glaxo announced plans to build a $40 million plant in North Carolina to manufacture the drug in the United States. Joseph J. Ruvane, Jr., president of Glaxo's U.S. company, claimed Glaxo would become one of America's top ten pharmaceutical firms. The company's actively traded shares increased in price from £2.40 a share in 1980 to £10.25 after a two-for-one split. Despite such spectacular results, Girolami claimed Zantac would never account for more than half of Glaxo's total sales. New products, including an anti-hypertensive and a treatment for migraine headaches, were in experimental stages. The company sold its interests outside of prescription drugs and increased its research and development allocations. Ceftazidime, a profitable new injectable antibiotic, received a strong market reception in Japan.

Zantac's arrival in Japan, however, was a less resounding success. Japan involved major competition, an anti-ulcer drug discovered by the Japanese Yamanouchi Company. Yet in other markets, including the U.S., Zantac now commands a 50% share. Glaxo now plans to introduce its products in Taiwan, Korea and Indonesia, and the **company's shares will soon be listed on both the Japanese and the New York exchanges. Recently, however, Glaxo's** share price failed to reach market expectations. Nevertheless, industry observers and the company's directors alike remain confident that Glaxo's continuing success will not reside in the fluctuating appeal of its stock, but rather in its long history of developing noteworthy pharmaceuticals and effectively marketing them.

Principal Subsidiaries of Glaxo Group Ltd: Glaxo Group Ltd. (U.K.); Eschmann Bros. & Walsh Ltd. (U.K.); Evans Medical Ltd. (U.K.); Farely Health Products Ltd. (U.K.); Glaxo Animal Health Ltd. (U.K.); Glaxochem Ltd. (U.K.); Glaxo Group Research Ltd. (U.K.); Glaxo Operations UK Ltd. (U.K.); Glaxo Pharmaceuticals Ltd.

(U.K.); Glaxomed Ltd. (U.K.); W.H. Deane (High Wycombe) Ltd. (U.K.); Macfarlen Smith Ltd. (U.K.); Glaxo Export Ltd. (U.S.) (U.K.); Matburn (Holdings) Ltd. (U.K.); Glaxo Inc. (U.S.); Glaxo also has subsidiaries in the following countries: Argentina, Australia, Austria, Belgium, Bermuda, Brazil, Canada, Chile, Colombia, Denmark, Finland, France, Greece, Hong Kong, Ireland, Italy, Kenya, Malaysia, Mexico, Netherlands, New Zealand, Norway, Pakistan, Panama, Peru, Philippines, Portugal, Singapore, South Africa, Spain, Sri Lanka, Sweden, Switzerland, Thailand, United States, Uruguay, Venezuela and West Germany.

Further Reading: *The Economics of the Pharmaceutical Industry* by Duncan W. Reekie, London, Macmillan, 1975.

F.HOFFMANN-LA ROCHE & COMPANY A.G.

Grenzarcherstr 122
Basle, Baslestadt
Switzerland 4058
62 292

Public Company
Incorporated: 1919
Employees: 45,477
Sales: SFr14.549 billion (US$8.94 billion)
Market Value: SFr15.186 billion (US$9.331 billion)
Stock Index: Basle Zurich Geneva

At the beginning of this century Fritz Hoffmann-La Roche, the son of a wealthy Basle silk merchant, joined a local pharmaceutical company. Originally his family had hoped that he would become a scientist, but when he showed no interest in such a career they decided he should enter the business world. When his father bought a partnership in the company, the younger Hoffmann found himself promoted to a senior management position.

Although the weight of family wealth did him no harm, Fritz Hoffmann was a talented enterpreneur who soon proved a success in his own right—and ahead of his time. He was committed to standardized packaging, equally committed to maintaining product quality. He recognized the importance of forming ties between the pharmaceutical industry and the community of academic scientists. To this day Hoffmann-La Roche remains firmly committed to research. Company research is very generously funded, and various of the company's facilities around the world offer scientists a freedom in experimentation usually associated only with university laboratories.

Despite such well-intentioned policies, the young company experienced hardship in its early years; after only a few years in business, Hoffmann faced bankruptcy. Disregarding his father's dying wish that he abandon the pharmaceutical business, Fritz arranged for recapitalization (mainly from his own family) and started again. This time the company enjoyed almost immediate success. Dr. Emil Barell, a young employee, developed several successful drugs: Thiocal, a cough medicine, and Digalen, an extract from the digitalis plant used in the treatment of heart disease; both products are still available today. Other products included Pantopon, a pain killer, and Sirolin, a cough syrup.

By the eve of World War I Hoffmann's products could be

found on four continents. It was at this point that Hoffmann's wife's maiden name, Roche (Swiss custom combines both the husband and wife's surnames), appeared on several products. To standardize the marketing of products, the company adopted that name as its world trademark. The future looked promising. Yet World War I created a number of complications that threatened all the success of the recent past.

The company's new factory in Germany, at Grenzach, produced a major share of Roche pharmaceuticals. But the Germans boycotted the company because they suspected it was supplying France; meanwhile, French doctors accused the company of being pro-German. In Britain, Roche products were blacklisted when the rumor spread that the company was producing poison gas for the German Army. Most devastating of all, the company lost more than a million francs in uncollected receivables in Russia during the Revolution.

This series of disasters forced the company to go public. Of the four million francs of paid-in capital used to reorganize the company, three million was supplied by Fritz Hoffmann; the remainder came from his brother-in-law, two associates, and Dr. Barell. The following year, 1920, the company asked shareholders to double their subscriptions. That marked the last time that Hoffmann-La Roche has resorted to the capital market; since then the company has relied solely on the strength of its profits for its funding. As late as 1971, heirs of the original shareholders continued to hold more than half of the voting shares and non-voting shares. Today, Hoffmann-La Roche remains a public company, but the combined family interests effectively control the company. Because of the scarcity of voting shares in the marketplace, and because of the very sound financial position of the company (there is virtually no long-term debt), Hoffmann-La Roche shares command a premium.

The year 1920 also marked the death of Fritz Hoffmann. Barell assumed the role of president and ushered in a new era of growth and expansion. Then a tragedy in the Hoffmann family changed the course of control in the company. Emanuel, Fritz' eldest son, died in a car accident. In the late 1930's his widow married Paul Sacher, founder and conductor of the Basle Chamber Orchestra. Sacher is now responsible for voting 49% of the shares, which include the interests of his wife, his stepson Lukas Hoffmann (executive vice-president of the World Wildlife Fund), and his stepson-in-law, Jakob Oeri, a Basle surgeon. All three men sit on the board of directors.

At the same time that Barell became president of the company, the American Elmer H. Bobst became general manager of its U.S. subsidiary. The American branch had been established in 1905, and Bobst had initially joined the company as a sales representative. Bobst's advancement was rapid, and his regime a resounding success: under his leadership the company introduced Allonal, a pain reliever, which became the company's first million dollar product.

In the years preceding World War II the company's strategy shifted; it gradually moved from extracting medicines from natural sources to synthesizing them, and its most important breakthrough came in the large-scale production of synthetic bulk vitamins. Barell obtained a process for synthesizing vitamin C as early as 1933. Later successes included vitamins A and E. Today, Roche's plant in New Jersey is the world's largest producer of vitamin C. In 1971 the company enjoyed between 50 and 70% of the world market for vitamins, and production continues to grow.

As World War II approached, Roche's American subsidiary assumed greater importance. In 1928, Nutley, New Jersey had become the site of the company's American headquarters; when war and possible Nazi invasion of Switzerland threatened, the company prepared to expand the Nutley site. Company interests were also transferred to a Canadian holding company called Sapac. This arrangement, originally meant to protect the company from the effects of war, remains in existence today. Thus, today's shareholder actually owns an interest in two companies—Hoffmann-La Roche and Sapac. Though American operations in Nutley remain under the administration of Sapac, its vast production and research operations now make it virtually an independent company.

Not only were assets transferred in the early 1940's; Emil Barell himself moved to Nutley until the end of the war. Differences in their personalities and their approaches to business caused Bobst and Barell to disagree constantly, and in 1944 Bobst resigned. He went on to assume control of the struggling Warner-Lambert Company and directed one of the most impressive comebacks in the pharmaceutical industry.

When Bobst left the company, Barell hired Lawrence Barney to be president of the American branch. Recruited from the prestigious Wisconsin Alumni Research Foundation, he remained at Roche for the next 20 years. Emil Barell died in 1953 at the age of 79. His successor, Albert Caflisch, served until 1965. Yet the years between 1945 and 1965 were important to the company not only in terms of new executive personalities but also because of its innovations in research and development.

For this was the period during which Hoffmann-La Roche released its line of benzodiazepines, destined to be phenomenally successful. Many years of research, under the direction of the scientist Leo Sternbach, led to the development of drugs that are now household words, Valium and Librium.

Librium was introduced in 1960. This new tranquilizer was revolutionary in its ability to relieve tension without simultaneously causing apathy. Before long, the company was barely able to keep up with demand; it now held the patent to the one of the best-selling prescription drugs in the world—*the* best-selling drug in the United States. In 1963 Hoffmann-La Roche introduced Valium to the market, and by 1969 it exceeded Librium in popularity. Never before had a pharmaceutical company introduced two significant market successes in so short a time. By 1971 some 500 million patients, generating an estimated $2 billion in sales, had used one or the other of the drugs. With several years to go before patents expired, the two drugs continued to break sales records.

The company's success in developing benzodiazepine tranquilizers, however, was no protection from the vicissitudes inherent in the daily operations of a large multi-national company. Hoffmann-La Roche's pricing policy came under attack when the British Monopolies Commission discovered that Roche Products Ltd., the U.K. subsidiary of Hoffmann-La Roche, was paying the parent company the sums of $925 a kilo for Librium and $2,300 a kilo for Valium. In Italy, a country in which there are no drug patents, the costs per kilo were $22.50 and $50 respectively. Based on these findings, the Monopolies Commission ordered the company to reduce its prices in the U.K. 50 to 60% and to repay excess profit estimated at $30 million.

In response, the company petitioned the House of Lords to overturn the government order. Adolf Jann, head of Hoffmann-La Roche since Caflisch's death in 1965, vigorously defended the company's pricing policies. Formerly known for its unwillingness to disclose financial information, the company now put its financial cards on the table, running full-page newspaper advertisements defending its prices on the basis of its traditionally high costs for research and development. Information about company sales and profits were made public for the first time (in 1973 $500 million of the $1.2 billion volume at Hoffmann-La Roche was attributable to the sale of Valium and Librium).

Among consumers increasingly alarmed about the escalating costs of drugs, the company's arguments were generally ignored, and Germany, the Netherlands, Australia, Sweden, and South Africa began investigations of their own.

By 1980, after years of litigation, Hoffmann-La Roche had emerged from the controversy virtually unscathed, having agreed to adhere thereafter to a system of voluntary price restraints.

The tumultuous price wars of the 1970's were not the only source of difficulties for the company. In 1976 a poison cloud of TCDD, a dioxin found in Agent Orange, escaped from Icmesa, an Italian chemical factory owned by Hoffmann-La Roche. TCDD is an unwanted byproduct of trichloropenol, a drug produced by Icmesa. Although the cause of the poison cloud remains speculative, experts believe that on the day of the accident the temperature in the reactor was accidentally allowed to rise to 300 degrees centigrade, 125 degrees more than the safe temperature for production.

Nearly 80,000 domestic fowl and half the pigs in the area died as a result of the accident. Six days after the blast the first case of chloracne, a human skin disease caused by TCDD, was reported. The company alerted the authorities by supplying a map of the area that they believed to be contaminated and advising that the area should be evacuated. The Italian government, with the full assistance of the company, initiated investigative procedures and decided to evacuate 267 acres on which some 700 people lived. An additional 5,000 people, living in the periphery of the area, were instructed in preventive measures. Despite these precautions, there were finally 136 confirmed cases of chloracne. Hoffmann-La Roche paid more than $17 million in 1978 to cover the costs of decontamination and the relocation and settlement of displaced people; in 1980, the company paid Italian authorities a further $114 million in compensation.

Recent developments at Hoffmann-La Roche have involved a joint venture with Glaxo, the British pharmaceutical company, to market Zantac, an anti-ulcer drug. Using 750 Hoffmann-La Roche salesmen, the two companies have challenged SmithKline's popular drug Tagamet, and their aggressive marketing strategies have caused Zantac to capture 25% of the market in just over six months. Hoffmann-La Roche has also been at the forefront of genetic engineering, particularly in its production of interferons. Roferon-A, released on the market in June of 1986, is marketed as a treatment for rare forms of cancer.

As the company enters the 1990's, Hoffmann-La Roche's most immediate problem must be the expiration of its patents for Valium and Librium. The first of these patents expired in the mid-1970's; the last major one—the American patent of Valium—expired in early 1985. With generic substitutes now on the market, the company's sales have begun to fall. In the short term, then, because there has been no compensation in the form of major new drugs, Hoffmann-La Roche seems destined for retrenchment. Yet Hoffmann-La Roche can be expected to retain its eminence in both marketing and research, insuring that that it will maximize its sales effort on its existing product line at the same time as it strives to develop new products, insuring, too, that it will remain one of the pre-eminent pharmaceutical companies in the world.

Principal Subsidiaries: F. Hoffmann-La Roche & Co. Ltd. Co.; Roche AG; Teranol AG; Lauduna AG; Biological and Medical Research Institute Ltd., Laboratoires Sauter S.A.; Givaudan S.A.; Givaudan Dubendorf A.G.; Givaudan Research Co. Ltd.; Kontron Holding AG; Kontron Electronic AG; Tegimenta AG; W + W Electronic AG; Dr. R. Maag AG; Socar AG. Hoffmann-La Roche also has subsidiaries in the following countries: Argentina, Austrialia, Austria, Belgium, Bolivia, Canada, Chile, Colombia, Costa Rica, Denmark, Dominican Republic, Ecuador, Egypt, Finland, France, Germany, Great Britain, Greece, Guatemala, Hong Kong, India, Indonesia, Iran, Ireland, Italy, Japan, Malaysia, Mexico, Morocco, The Netherlands, New Zealand, Nigeria, Norway, Pakistan, Panama, Peru, Philippines, Portugal, Puerto Rico, Singapore, South Africa, South Korea, Sweden, Taiwan, Thailand, Turkey, Uruguay, United States and Venezuela.

ELI LILLY & COMPANY

307 E. McCarty Street
Indianapolis, Indiana 46285
U.S.A.
(317) 261-2000

Public Company
Incorporated: January 17, 1901
Employees: 28,000
Sales: $3.710 billion
Market Value: $13.210 billion
Stock Index: New York Basle Geneva Zurich

Although Eli Lilly & Company has in recent years been embroiled in controversy and been the target of numerous lawsuits related to its products, the Indianapolis-based giant is still among the leaders in the pharmaceutical industry. In a *Fortune* magazine survey of corporate performance, Lilly moved from seventh to sixth place in the industry's rankings during 1986. And despite involvement in more than one allegedly unscrupulous drug promotional campaign, the company remains one of the most profitable manufacturers of ethical drugs in the world.

Lilly manufactures human health, agricultural, and cosmetic products in 18 plants and facilities in the United States, including its Indianapolis headquarters, and in 32 plants in 28 countries around the world. The company's products are sold in more than 130 countries. Lilly commands more than 300 wholesale distribution outlets and employs about 1,300 salaried sales representatives in the United States, and at least as many abroad.

Despite these huge domestic and international operations, Lilly jealously guards its American heartland values and wields significant influence in its native city. For instance, in 1971 *Forbes* magazine prepared a company profile, but because Lilly did not want the article published, an Indianapolis newspaper refused to sell *Forbes* photographs of the Lilly family.

Much of this community loyalty stems from Lilly's long history of paternalism and generosity. In 1876 Colonel Eli Lilly, a Civil War veteran, acquired a laboratory in Indianapolis and began to manufacture drugs. The business established itself successfully with the innovation of gelatin-coated capsules, and it wasn't long before Colonel Lilly used company profits to benefit the community. He donated money to build a children's hospital and chaired a committee that helped indigents during the financial panic of 1893.

This civic consciousness was inherited by the second generation of Lilly management. During the Depression, the Colonel's grandson, Eli Lilly, refused to lay off any employees. Instead, he had them help with general maintenance of the facility until they could return to their normal jobs.

Lilly established the Lilly Endowment to provide financial support for educational institutions. The family donated $5 million worth of rare books to Indiana University, and later donated a coin collection worth $5.5 million to the Smithsonian Institution. The foundation also funded new buildings, music schools, student centers, and laboratories in every college and university in Indiana and in several around the country.

Lilly also laid the foundations for its reputation for marketing ingenuity in those early years. After the 1906 San Francisco earthquake Lilly did not wait for requests for medicine to arrive; the company sent as much of its stock as it could to the disaster area. Since then the ready availability of Lilly's products has been central to its marketing strategy. That and aggressive advertising campaigns, plus its large, eager sales force, have been the keys to its marketing success.

Besides being a pioneer in pharmaceutical marketing, Lilly has been notable for its development of many important drugs. In the 1920's the company developed insulin from a hormone extracted from the pancreas of pigs. Today Lilly is the leading manufacturer of insulin, commanding at least 75% of the American market. Later in the decade the company produced a liver extract for the treatment of pernicious anemia. In the 1930's Lilly laboratories synthesized barbituric acids, essential to the production of drugs used in surgery and obstetrics. In 1955 Lilly manufactured 60% of the Salk polio vaccine. But the company's greatest contribution to human health has been in production of penicillins and other antibiotics that revolutionized the treatment of disease.

Throughout this era of innovation and expansion, and up until recently, Lilly's management remained a constant. Every president and almost every member of the board of directors was either a direct descendant of Colonel Lilly or a native of the Midwest, if not of Indiana. After the Colonel's death in 1898, his son, Josiah Lilly, ran the company for the next 34 years. He was succeeded by son Eli and later by Josiah Jr. During the 16-year presidency of Eli Lilly, sales rose from $13 million in 1932 to $117 million in 1948. After Eli relinquished his executive powers to his brother, he became the titular chairman of the company. Upon his death at age 91, he had lived to see the company reach $1 billion in sales.

Josiah Jr.'s presidency marked the last reign of a direct family descendant. Richard Wood, the current chief executive officer, is only the second of six presidents to be an "outsider." He was, of course, born and raised in Indiana and is a longtime Lilly employee.

Not only is the company's clannishness evident in the executive branch, it is also apparent in Lilly's management style. In 1971, of the $4 billion worth of company stock, members and descendants of the Lilly family owned $1 billion of that stock, while the Lilly Endowment (controlled by the family) owned $900 million worth. Furthermore, the foundation has resisted making large disbursements, and it was not until the 1969 Tax Reform Act that the foundation was forced to loosen its 25% hold on stock. Yet in 1979 the foundation continued to hold 18.6% of company shares.

Lilly's conservative management paralleled its outspoken ideology. During the 1960's the Lilly endowment professed a specific political mission. The foundation was to support an understanding of "anti-communism, free enterprise, [and] limited government."

Despite what some have called an anachronistic approach to business, no one can dispute Lilly's financial success. In the 1970's, while the rest of the drug industry was depressed, Lilly doubled in size. When the pharmaceutical business was hit hard by competition from generic drugs that flooded the marketplace after the expiration of patents for drugs discovered in the 1950's and '60s, Lilly diversified into agricultural chemicals, animal-health products, medical instruments, and beauty-care products.

Meanwhile, Lilly increased its expenditure on research and development of pharmaceuticals, spending $235 million in those areas in 1981 alone. The immediate result was three new drugs: Ceclor, an oral cephalosporin antibiotic; Dobutrex, a heart-failure treatment; and Mandol, an injectable cephalosporin effective against a broad spectrum of hospital-acquired infections. The release of the new cephalosporins represented a significant step for Lilly. The company had always been dominant in the antibiotic market, but competition from Merck, SmithKline, and foreign drug companies threatened Lilly's supremacy. With the new drugs, the company was able to recapture hegemony of the cephalosporin market; of the $3.27 billion in company sales in 1985, $1.05 billion was from the sale of antibiotics.

A similar success story resulted after the company bought Elizabeth Arden for $38 million in 1971. At first glance, the purchase of the beauty-care company seemed an unwise move. Elizabeth Arden had been a money loser and continued to lose money for five years after Lilly acquired it. Lilly management seemed to have no idea of the intense competition in the beauty industry. But, in an unusual move, Lilly hired outsiders to fill its subsidiary's top executive positions, and by 1982 Elizabeth Arden's sales were up 90% from 1978, with profits doubling to nearly $30 million.

The introduction of several new drugs in the late 1970's increased Lilly's sales and challenged the market boundaries of competing products. Lilly released Nalfon, an antiinflammatory drug, to compete with Merck's number-one-selling Indocin. In addition, the company introduced Cinobac, an antibacterial agent used to treat urinary-tract infections; Eldisine, a treatment for childhood leukemia; Moxam, a potent new antibiotic licensed from Shionogi, a Japanese drug company; and Benoxaprofen, an antiarthritic introduced in the United Kingdom. Moreover, using groundbreaking recombinant DNA technology, Lilly was among the first to produce human insulin from bacteria. This breakthrough promised to protect Lilly's majority share of the insulin market.

The initial flurry over the possible hazardous side effects of a popular analgesic called Darvon seemed to have subsided. Critics had charged that the drug was both ineffective and had the dangerous potential for abuse, but Lilly mounted an educational campaign on proper use of the drug and continued to hold 80% of the prescription analgesic market. Darvon generated annual sales of $100 million.

With a 19% increase in sales in 1978, a 24% return on equity, and impressive results from President Wood's foreign-market campaign, Lilly's prospects seemed excellent. Then, however, company growth began to fall short of projected figures.

In 1982, a miscalculation of inventory and expected sales caused Lilly to produce far more Treflan (a soybean herbicide) than it could sell. With the patents expiring on Treflan and two animal products, and with the overproduction of Treflan, income from agricultural products suddenly did not look as promising as it once had.

Furthermore, profits from Moxam had to be shared with Shionogi, the Japanese partner in the joint venture. And the patent on Keflin, an injectable cephalosporin that had been generating $100 million in sales, expired in November 1982.

Lilly's diversification into medical instruments through the acquisition of IVAC Corporation, a manufacturer of vital-signs-monitoring systems and intravenous-fluid-infusion equipment, and Cardiac Pacemaker, a manufacturer of heart pacemakers, cost Lilly $286 million in stock, a significant investment with an unknown potential for profits. And since the combined assets of its medical instrument subsidiaries and Elizabeth Arden represented only 20% of the entire company, their projected profits were not expected to have a substantial effect on company profits as a whole.

Of more concern, however, was the re-emerging specter of Darvon's addictive qualities. Ralph Nader's consumer-advocacy group demanded a ban on Darvon because of its alleged associations with suicides, overdoses, and misuse by addicts. Joseph Califano, the U.S. Secretary of Health, Education and Welfare, harshly criticized the sincerity of Lilly's educational campaign. He went so far as to recommend that Darvon and other propoxyphene products not be prescribed "unless there really isn't an alternative, and then only with care." The FDA charged that Lilly's educational campaign actually amounted to ingenious marketing. (Lilly sales representatives not only gave doctors educational material that emphasized the drug's positive attributes, they also conveniently left samples.)

To the company's dismay, Darvon was not the only drug to cause a controversy. Oraflex, the American version of Benoxaprofen, was withdrawn from the market in August 1982. Only one month after the FDA approved Oraflex, a British medical journal documented five cases of death due to jaundice in patients taking the drug. The FDA accused Lilly of suppressing "unfavorable research findings." Initial warnings about the possibility of inconsequential side effects were later amended to include the threat of jaundice, but only after the company had already applied for FDA approval.

At a time when drug-regulation reform would have allowed companies to interpret the results of their own lab tests, the Oraflex controversy represented a major disaster. Furthermore, publicity for the drug, which was projected to be a $100 million seller (prescriptions for Oraflex increased by 194,000 in just one month), had been unwittingly distorted. Reports from outside the company had falsely claimed that the drug could cure arthritis.

On August 21, 1985, the Oraflex controversy culminated when the U.S. Justice Department filed criminal charges against Lilly and Dr. William Ian H. Shedden, the former vice-president and chief medical officer of Lilly Research Laboratories. The Justice Department accused the defendants of failing to inform the government about four deaths and six illnesses related to Oraflex. Lilly pleaded guilty to 25 criminal counts that resulted in a $25,000 fine. Shedden pleaded no contest to 15 criminal counts and was fined $15,000. All 40 counts were misdemeanors; there was no charge against Lilly of intentional deception.

Lilly has also been cited as a defendant in a lawsuit filed agains drug manufacturers and distributors of diethylstilbestrol (DES). The drug, which was prescribed to pregnant women during the 1940's and 1950's to prevent miscarriages, caused vaginal cancer and related problems in their children. Lilly was the first and largest manufacturer of DES, and it is estimated that 40% of the drug came from Lilly production facilities. In 1981 a court ordered the company to pay $500,000 in damages to one plaintiff, and in 1985 Lilly was ordered to pay $400,000 to the first male seeking damages in a DES-related case. Other claims are asking for damages totaling in the billions of dollars.

Of all Lilly's projected successes, human insulin manufactured using recombinant DNA technology has the greatest potential. Although recombinant techniques remain costly because of their infancy, manufacturing will eventually be on a much larger scale than that of traditional methods of obtaining insulin. The 1986 acquisition of Hybritech, a genetic engineering company, emphasizes Lilly's commitment to the future of biotechnology.

That commitment, plus its aggressive marketing techniques, small army of sales representatives, and efficient wholesale distribution network, should keep Lilly near the top of the pharmaceutical industry.

Principal Subsidiaries: Eli Lilly International Corp.; Elizabeth Arden, Inc.; Bethco Fragrances, Inc.; Philip Kingsley Products, Inc.; ELCO Management Corp.; Cardiac Pacemakers, Inc.; Physio-Control Corp.; IVAC Corp.; Advanced Cardiovascular Systems, Inc. The company also lists subsidiaries in the following countries: Australia, Austria, Belgium, Brazil, Bermuda, Canada, Denmark, England, France, Finland, Guatemala, Italy, Japan, Korea, Malaysia, Mexico, The Netherlands, Spain, Sweden, Switzerland, Taiwan, Venezuela, and West Germany.

Further Reading: *Threescore Years and Ten: A Narrative of the First Seventy Years of Eli Lilly & Company* by Roscoe Collins Clark, Chicago, R.R. Donnelly, 1946.

MARION LABORATORIES, INC.

9300 Ward Pkwy
Kansas City, Missouri 64114
U.S.A.
(816) 966-4000

Public Company
Incorporated: 1964
Employees: 2,567
Sales: $474 million
Market Value: $5.332 billion
Stock Index: New York

One of the smaller yet financially sound companies in the health care industry, Marion Laboratories develops, manufactures and markets pharmaceutical, hospital and laboratory products. Formally incorporated in 1964, the company spends relatively small amounts on research and development, a unique strategy for a drug company. This practice reflects positively in the company's financial health—Marion Laboratories currently owes no substantial long-term debt, and its shares are increasingly attractive to investors. The success of the company reflects the character of its founder and current chairman, Erwing M. Kauffman.

After serving as an officer in the U.S. Navy during World War II, Kauffman took a job as a salesman with a pharmaceutical company in Decatur, Illinois. Energetic and aggressive, Kauffman flourished. Within a year his commissions made him the highest paid employee of the company, even including the company's president. Amazingly, Kauffman was punished for his success: the company reduced the size of his territory and trimmed his commissions. Kauffman resigned and started his own company.

At its inception, in 1950, the company had $4,000 in capital. To hold overheads, Kauffman operated from the basement of his house. The one and only product he manufactured was a calcium supplement made from crushed oyster shells. Kauffman operated alone: during the day he made and packaged the product and made sales calls; in the evenings he typed orders and labels for the packages. His company grew until it had achieved 40% of the $100 million a year market.

Marion Laboratories, incorporated in 1964, succeeded the original company. To attract valuable people, Kauffman offered both share options and a profit sharing plan. During the 1950's the plan purchased shares in the company, which allowed four Marion employees to retire with a net worth of more than one million dollars.

During its first decade the new company actively pursued a policy of acquisitions; the fruits of diversification eventually accounted for 40% of the company's sales.

The hugh expenditure required for research and development of a new product—about $60 million dollars—inhibited many companies from introducing new drugs in the 1970's. Marion Laboratories basked in the luxury of not investing millions of dollars on product research. The hope of discovering a miracle drug and making a fortune failed to entice Kauffman. A natural at sales, Erwing Kauffman influenced the company to spend little on developing original products; rather, he sought to establish a niche in the marketplace through existing products. In 1974 the company spent nothing on original research. Instead, Marion spent $1.8 million on reformulating and developing products discovered but rejected by other companies.

In 1964 Marion earned $130,000; by 1974 earnings on sales were $12 million, and the company enjoyed a 36% return on equity. Although analysts projected stagnation or decline in the share price, the company has continued to perform well and currently enjoys one of the highest ratings among health and drug companies.

In 1978 Marion Laboratories established its consumer products division. During the same year the company introduced Gaviscon, an over-the-counter antacid. Marketed in chewable tablet form, the product provides for the temporary relief of heartburn. It was immediately successful, and accounted for 6% of the company's net sales in 1986.

The company continues to maintain its interest in drugs that treat ailments related to the influence of calcium on the body. The largest percentage of net sales, 47% in 1986, came from Cardizem. The drug slows calcium buildup and prevents the artery muscles from being blocked by calcium deposits. Cardizem is used in the treatment of stable and unstable angina. The Food and Drug Administration has granted approval for Marion to release Caridizem in tablet form. Similar compounds were submitted to the FDA for approval by other companies in the latter part of 1986. How much of a threat these products pose to Marion Laboratories remains unknown.

Marion's ulcer drug, Carafate, gained FDA approval in 1982. The product represented a "new mode of therapy" in ulcer treatment. Carafate forms a protective barrier preventing further damage to mucosal tissues blocking the diffusion of gastric acid and pepsin in ulcer craters. The drug poses no threat to healthy tissue where proteins are bound.

Both Carafate and Cardizem originated from research conducted by the Japanese company, Tanabe Seiyaku, and Marion pays licensing fees to Tanabe. The mutual interests of both companies have grown, and in 1984 they entered into a joint venture to manufacture and market Tanabe products in the United States and Canada.

Marion Laboratories now markets the following products: Sivadone, a cream used to prevent infections in cases of second- and third-degree burns; Ditropan tablets and syrup, a urological agent that treats certain bladder conditions; Nito-Bid Capsules and Ointment, which manages angina pectoris or chest pain caused by insufficient blood-flow to the heart (this product accounted for 6% of the net sales in 1986). The hospital products division sells diagnostic products such as Culturette, a disposable, 10-minute culture transport system used by hospitals and clinics to diagnose Group A streptococci. Another product, Toxi-Lab, a broad spectrum drug detection system, may find new users other than hospitals as concern about drug abuse increases. Ard, another hospital division product, speeds the identification of bacteria in the blood stream that can cause infection in patients using antibiotics. Bac-T-Screen also detects bacteria.

Marion Laboratories is also notable for its concerns with community services. The company has instituted STAR—Students Taught Awareness and Resistance. The aim of this educational program is to help reduce drug abuse in young children in Kansas City. The Kauffman Foundation contributes three-quarters of the funding for the five year, $5 million project; Marion Laboratories contributes the rest. Erwing Kauffman instigated the educational campaign after a 1983 drug scandal involving the Kansas City Royals baseball team, which he owns. Kauffman and his wife Muriel also support an ongoing project aimed at teaching life-saving techniques such as cardiopulmonary resuscitation.

American pharmaceutical companies face stiff international competition, and their enormous expenditures on research and legal fees for patents can severely dilute profits. In this context Marion Laboratories holds a unique position among its peers. These financial drains have been historically avoided by the company, which now finds itself in a healthy position. The company continues to reflect the entrepreneurial spirit of its founder, not following the trends of other companies but creating its own means to success.

Principal Subsidiaries: Marion Laboratories lists all subsidiaries under four wholly owned divisions: Consumer Products Division; International Division; Professional Products Division; Scientific Products Division.

MERCK & COMPANY

Rahway, New Jersey 07065
U.S.A.
(201) 574-4000

Public Company
Incorporated: June 27, 1927
Employees: 34,800
Sales: $4.129 billion
Market Value: $22.336 billion
Stock Index: New York

While Merck currently stands as one of the most profitable pharmaceutical companies in the U.S., its beginnings can be traced back to Freidrich Jacob Merck's purchase, in 1668, of an apothecary in Darmstadt, Germany. Located next to a castle moat, this store remained in the Merck family for generations.

In 1827 Heinrich Emmanuel Merck began manufacturing drugs. His first product was morphine. By the time he died, in 1855, Merck products were used worldwide. To ensure the quality of drugs being manufactured in the U.S. George Merck, the 24 year old grandson of Heinrich Emmanuel Merck, traveled to the New World and eventually established his own business venture. In 1899 George Merck and his business partner, the German chemist Theodore Weicker, acquired a plant site in Rahway, New Jersey.

The manufacturing of drugs and chemicals at this site began in 1903. Today this same location houses the corporate headquarters of Merck and Company and four of its divisions, as well as research laboratories and chemical production facilities. Once known as "Merck Woods," the land surrounding the original plant was used to hunt wild game and corral domestic animals. In fact, George Merck kept a flock of 15 to 20 sheep on the grounds to test the effectiveness of an animal disinfectant. The sheep have become a permanent part of the Rahway landscape.

The year 1899 also marks the first year the "Merck Manual Of Diagnosis and Therapy" was published. In 1983 the manual entered its 14th edition. A *New York Times* review rated it "the most widely used medical text in the world."

During World War I George Merck, fearing anti-German sentiment, turned over a sizable portion of Merck stock to the Alien Property Custodian of the United States. This portion represented the company interest held by Merck's German cousins. At the end of the war Merck was rewarded for his patriotic leadership; the Alien Property Custodian sold Merck shares, worth three million dollars, to the public. George Merck retained control of the corporation and by 1919 the company was, once again, entirely public owned.

In 1926, the year George Merck died, his son George W. Merck had been acting president for over a year. During the next 25 years he initiated and directed the current Merck legacy for pioneering research and development. In 1933 he established a large laboratory and recruited prominent chemists and biologists to produce new pharmaceutical products. Their efforts had far-reaching effects. En route to researching cures for pernicious anemia, Merck scientists discovered vitamin B12. Its sales, both as a therapeutic drug and as a constituent of animal feed have been massive.

The 1940's continued to be a decade of discoveries in drug research. In the early 1940's a Merck chemist synthesized cortisone from ox bile which led to the discovery of cortisone's anti-inflammation properties. In 1943, streptomycin, a revolutionary antibiotic used for tuberculosis and other infections, was isolated by a Merck scientist.

Despite the pioneering efforts and research success under George Merck's leadership, the company struggled during the postwar years. There were no promising new drugs to speak of, and there was intense competition from foreign companies underselling Merck products, and from former domestic consumers beginning to manufacture their own drugs. Merck found itself in a precarious financial position.

A solution was found in 1953 when Merck merged with Sharp and Dohme, Incorporated, a drug company with a similar history and reputation. Sharp and Dohme began as an apothecary shop in 1845 in Baltimore, Maryland. Its success in the research and development of such important products as sulfa drugs, vaccines, and blood plasma products matched the successes of Merck. However, the merger was more than the combination of two industry leaders. It provided Merck with a new distribution network and marketing facilities to secure major customers. For the first time Merck could market and sell drugs under its own name.

At the time of George Merck's death in 1957, company sales had surpassed $100 million annually. Although Albert W. Merck, a direct descendant of Friedrich Jacob Merck, sits on the board of directors today, the office of chief executive has never again been held by a Merck family member.

In 1976 John J. Honran succeeded the eleven year reign of Henry W. Gadsen. Honran was a quiet, unassuming man who had entered Merck as a legal counselor and then became the corporate director of public relations. But Honran's unobtrusive manner belied an aggressive management style.

With pragmatic determination Honran not only continued the Merck tradition for innovation in drug research, but also improved a poor performance record on new product introduction to the market. This problem was most apparent in the marketing of Aldomet, an antihypertensive agent. Once the research was completed,

Merck planned to exploit the discovery by introducing an improved beta-blocker called Blocadren. Yet Merck was beaten to the market by its competitors. Furthermore, because the 17 year patent protection on a new drug discovery was about to expire, Aldomet was threatened by generic manufacturers. This failure to beat its competitors to the market is said to have cost the company $200 million in future sales. A similar sequence of events occurred with Indocin and Clinoril, two anti-inflammation drugs for arthritis.

Under Honran's regime, the company introduced a hepatitis vaccine, a treatment for glaucoma called Timoptic, and Ivomac, an antiparasitic for animals. And while Honran remained strongly committed to financing a highly productive research organization, Merck began making improvements on research already performed by competitors. In 1979, for example, Merck began to market Enalapril, a high-blood pressure inhibitor, similar to the drug Capoten which is manufactured by Squibb. Sales for Enalapril reached $550 million in 1986. Honran also embarked on a more aggressive program for licensing foreign products. Merck purchased rights to sell products from Astra, a Swedish company, and Shionogi of Japan.

Honran's strategy proved very effective. Between 1981 and 1985 the company experienced a 9% growth rate, and in 1985 the *Wall Street Transcript* awarded Honran the gold award for excellence in the ethical drug industry. He was commended for the company's advanced marketing techniques and its increased production. At the time of the award, projections indicated a company growth rate for the next five years of double the present rate.

In 1984 Honran claimed Merck had become the largest U.S. based manufacturer of drugs in the three largest markets—the U.S., Japan, and Europe. He attributed this success to three factors: a productive research organization; manufacturing capability which allows for cost efficient, high-quality production; and an excellent marketing organization.

The following year Honran resigned as chief executive officer. In 1986, his successor, P.R. Vagelos, was also awarded the ethical drug industry's gold award.

Although Merck's public image has generally been good, it has had its share of controversy. In 1974 a $35 million lawsuit was filed against Merck and 28 other drug manufacturers and distributors of diethylstilbestrol (DES). This drug, prescribed to pregnant women in the late 1940's and up until the early 1960's, ostensibly prevented miscarriages. The 16 original plaintiffs claimed that they developed vaginal cancer and other related difficulties because their mothers had taken the drug. Furthermore, the suit charged that DES was derived from Stilbene, a known carcinogen, and that no reasonable basis existed for claiming the drugs were effective in preventing miscarriages. (A year before the suit, the Federal Drug Administration banned the use of DES hormones as growth stimulants for cattle because tests revealed cancer-causing residues of the substance in some of the animals' livers. The FDA, however, did not conduct public hearings on this issue; consequently, a federal court overturned the ban.)

Under the plaintiffs' directive the court asked the de-fendants to notify other possible victims, and to establish early detection and treatment centers. More than 350 plaintiffs have subsequently sought damages totalling some $350 billion.

Merck was not only beleaguered by the DES lawsuit. In 1975 the company's name was added to a growing list of U.S. companies involved in illegal payments abroad. The payoffs, issued to increase sales in certain African and Middle Eastern countries, came to the attention of Merck executives through the investigation of the Securities and Exchange Commission. While sales amounted to $40.4 million for that year in those areas of the foreign market, the report uncovered a total of $140,000 in bribes. Once the SEC revealed its report, Merck initiated an internal investigation and took immediate steps to prevent future illegal payments.

More recently, Merck has found itself beset with new difficulties. In its attempt to win hegemony in Japan—the second largest pharmaceutical market in the world, Merck purchased more than 50% of the Banyu Pharmaceutical Company of Tokyo. Partners since 1954 under a joint business venture called Nippon Merck-Banyu (NMB), the companies used Japanese detail men (or pharmaceutical sales representatives) to promote Merck products.

However, when NMB proved inefficient, Merck bought out its partner for $315.5 million—more than 30 times Banyu's annual earnings. The acquisition was made in 1982 and Merck is still in the process of bringing Banyu into line with its more aggressive and imaginative management style.

Problems in labor relations surfaced during the spring of 1985 when Merck locked out 730 union employees at the Rahway plant after failing to agree to a new contract. For three months prior to the expiration of three union contracts, involving 4,000 employees, both sides negotiated a new settlement. However, when talks stalled the company responded by locking out employees. The unresolved issues involved both wages and benefits.

By June 5th, all 4000 employees participated in a strike involving the Rahway plant and six other facilities across the nation. In West Point, Virginia operations were halted when union picketers prevented non-striking employees from entering the plant. Merck, however, was able to win a court-ordered injunction limiting picketing.

The strike proved to be the longest in Merck's history; but after 15 weeks an agreement was finally reached. A company request for the adoption of a two-tier wage system which would permanently pay new employees lower wages was rejected, as was a union demand for wage increases and cost-of-living adjustments during the first year.

The $3.5 billion earned in 1986 ranks Merck second in sales in the U.S. pharmaceutical industry. In the coming decades it is likely that Merck will maintain its position as a top ranking manufacturer of drugs.

Principal Subsidiaries: British United Turkeys of America, Inc.; Calgon Carbon Corp.; Hubbard Farms, Inc.; Kelco Co.; Merck Farms, Inc.; Merck Sharp & Dohme Corp.; **INTERX Research Corp.** The company also lists subsidiaries in the following countries: Australia, Austria, Belgium, Bermuda, Brazil, Canada, Denmark, England, Finland, France, Italy, Japan, Lebanon, Mexico, The Netherlands, Norway, Panama, Portugal, Spain, Sweden, Switzerland, Venezuela, West Germany, and Zimbabwe.

MILES LABORATORIES

1127 Myrtle Street
Elkhart, Indiana 46515
U.S.A.
(219) 264-8111

Subsidiary of Bayer A.G.
Incorporated: June 30, 1922
Employees: 12,000
Sales: $1.152 billion

Miles Laboratories is best known for Alka-Seltzer. Since the 1930's, and particularly in the last two decades, Alka-Seltzer has been the subject of some particularly innovative advertising, and there is now hardly a consumer in the Western world who hadn't heard of the product. Yet Miles is also a leading manufacturer of a number of other very successful pharmaceutical and consumer products. Since 1977 Miles Laboratories has been a subsidiary of Bayer, the huge West German manufacturer, Miles Laboratories is now the focal point of Bayer's growing operations in the United States.

Dr. Miles' Medical Company, incorporated by Dr. Franklin Miles of Elkhart, Indiana in 1885, was the predecessor of Miles Laboratories. Soon after the company was formed Dr. Miles was joined by two colleagues, George Compton and Albert Beardsley. These three men directed the early years of Miles Laboratories, and even today their descendants hold important executive positions within the company. Five years after its founding the company was operating at a profit, and it went on to produce a full line of medical preparations (as well as its own promotional literature) at the Elkhart plant. Until the mid-1930's a sedative called Dr. Miles Restorative Nervine accounted for a major portion of company sales.

Andrew "Hub" Beardsley, the nephew of Albert Beardsley, spent 35 years with the company, rising from bottle-washer to first chairman of the board in 1925, and it was he who provided the impetus for the company's movement away from sedatives to new and innovative drugs. During the mid-1920's pharmaceutical companies became increasingly interested in the possibilities of effervescence and in producing medicines in tablet form. "Hub" encouraged one of his research scientists to work on transforming Nervine into an innovative combination, an effervescent tablet. Before development of the product had gone very far, "Hub" suggested a change of direction. He had observed that reporters on the *Elkhart Truth* successfully resisted

colds by daily drinking a mixture of aspirin and bicarbonate of soda; he decided that it was an effervescent aspirin/bicarbonate of soda tablet that he wanted his chemists to create. After years of experimentation, Miles Laboratories achieved Hub's vision, and Alka-Seltzer was introduced to the marketplace in 1931.

Its immediate and increasing success had much to do with the repeal of prohibition. Alka-Seltzer relieved headaches and upset stomachs, and as the incidence of hangovers increased, so did consumption of Alka-Seltzer. Even today Alka-Seltzer remains the world's number one cure for the hangover: it is now sold in more than 100 countries and generates $90 million in sales each year.

From its founding to the present time, Miles Laboratories has also been notable for its concentration on advertising and for the skill with which some of that advertising has been presented. Between 1902 and 1942 the company issued more than one billion publications—not only advertising leaflets but also almanacs, calendars and a popular series called the "Little Books." In 1933, Charles Beardsley (a future president of Miles) initiated a radio campaign for Alka-Seltzer, sponsoring the popular *Saturday Night Barn Dance*; and in 1949, with its sponsorship of *The Quiz Kids*, Miles was one of the first companies to support the new medium of television. The common denominator of both the company's radio and subsequent television commercials has been humor—memorable and amusing jingles for radio, exaggerated and often hilarious depictions of the "before and after" Alka-Seltzer patient for television. By 1971 total sales of Miles Laboratories products amounted to $322 million, but the company entered that decade confronting a number of difficulties. Costly promotional outlays—the Alka-Seltzer commercials were obviously the best that money could buy—were diminishing profit margins. And a decrease in consumer spending was reducing sales of the company's limited range of products. To solve these problems, the company's management decided to diversify into a greater range of products. Dr. Walter Ames Compton, president of Miles from 1964 to 1973, initiated a development program emphasizing nutrition and diagnostics. He was an advocate of diet and preventive therapy, and he made it company strategy to develop products for compensive health care.

With this goal in mind, Miles acquired the Worthington Foods Company, a pioneer in the development of vegetable protein substitutes—particularly soybeans. An efficient source of nutrition, soybeans are easy to grow, are an abundant source of protein, and have none of the disadvantages of meat, which is costly to produce and is high in cholesterol. With meat prices on the rise and consumers increasingly concerned about their intake of fat, Miles hoped to take advantage of a growing market for alternative protein sources. Morningstar meat substitutes seemed likely to be able to capture a sizable portion of that market.

Additional new products introduced in the late 1960's and early 1970's as part of Miles' modern health care agenda included a full range of supplementary vitamins, from children's vitamins (Chocks, Flinstones, and Bugs Bunny brands) to the popular One-a-Day vitamins, first marketed in 1943 but now improved to include minerals and iron.

Miles' Professional Product Group demonstrated fast growth: this group produced a broad range of health care products, from diagnostic agents and ethical drugs for the treatment of allergies and skin conditions, to laboratory supplies, to electronic instruments. The group soon accounted for one-fifth of total sales and an even higher percentage of earnings.

Yet, even though the company did achieve its objective of diversification, the years between 1972 and 1977 seemed to involve a kind of lull in its fortunes. Reliance on consumer products had diminished: they now accounted for less than one-half of sales (as opposed to three-quarters in 1961), and Alka-Seltzer generated only 13% of total sales volume. But a program of capital spending to bolster Miles' facilities for effective manufacturing in the future had cut significantly into the company's limited funds. Each year $4 to $5 million of a total of $15 to $17 million in net sales was consumed by interest. By 1974 research and development and promotional spending for Morningstar products had reached $33.4 million. Although these products generated $20 million in sales by 1976, it would be some time before the meat substitutes were profitable enough to begin repaying their developmental costs.

Alka-Seltzer, still the company's biggest single product, did not perform as well as expected. Sales of the product declined 14% in the first nine months of 1974, almost certainly the result of publicity surrounding a Food and Drug Administration review of over-the-counter products. Calling the drug an "irrational" mixture of aspirin (a stomach irritant) and antacid ingredients, the FDA as well as one of Ralph Nader's consumer groups questioned Alka-Seltzer's ability to settle upset stomachs. In response, Miles introduced a new non-aspirin tablet and emphasized Alka-Seltzer's ability to provide relief from headaches as well as indigestion. But total sales of the product continued to slip.

The company's bankers, increasingly critical of family management, used their infuence to install Rowland G. Rose as new company president in 1977. Descendants of the founders continued to serve on the board, but from 1977 outsiders took an increasingly greater role in company management. Rose came to the company just as its prospects were improving. Dome Laboratories, the ethical drug division, introduced new products for the treatment of allergies, skin conditions, and mental illness. Miles' production of specialty enzymes experienced a 15% increase in one year. With the building program completed, capital spending began to decrease. Rose was himself committed to a "profit consciousness" for the company that would guide Miles into a decade of growth.

Rose was barely given a chance to initiate his new program, however, before the company suddenly found itself the object of a takeover bid. In October 1977 Bayer AG of West Germany, the world's fourth largest chemical producer, offered $40 cash for each of the company's 5.4 million shares. Share prices had risen from $24 to $41 a share once rumors of a takeover had begun circulating, and in the end Bayer paid $47 a share, or a total of $253 million, the most expensive acquisition by a foreign chemical or pharmaceutical company ever made in the United States.

Analysts now agree that the Bayer takeover was simply the most dramatic occurrence in a growing industry trend of established European companies entering the U.S. market by acquiring medium-sized American companies. Rather than build their own distribution systems, foreign companies save a great deal of trouble and money by buying American firms in the same business that have already developed successful operations. While maintaining its identity, Miles Laboratories in Elkhart effectively became Bayer's headquarters for its U.S. pharmaceutical operations (in 1986 Bayer headquarters was established in Pittsburgh).

Miles' distribution facilities were not the only attraction. At the time of the takeover, production of hospital products in three of Miles' divisions were generating a growing percentage of company earnings. Diagnostic equipment accounted for 32% of sales and 50% of earnings.

It is in this area of diagnostics, as well as pharmaceuticals and biotechnology, that Bayer has directed its subsidiary. First under T.H. Heinrichs, the new chief executive officer in 1979, and then under Dr. Klaus H. Risse from 1985, Miles' health care products gained precedence over the company's other products. In 1984 Bayer arranged a contract between Miles and Genetic System Corporation, a biotech firm, that will allow Miles to manufacture and market monoclonal antibodies, products of genetic engineering.

The years of heavy debt for Bayer, the result of its expansion in the American market, are now past; the company is presently enjoying the benefits of its effective planning. In 1985 some seven American companies, now all subsidiaries of Bayer, reported a total of $203 million in pre-tax profits, an increase of 6.8% over the previous year. Of all its investments, however, Miles Laboratories remains the most prized of Bayer's acquisitions. Its sales have grown impressively since the takeover, and it now generates one third of its income from overseas markets.

Miles is now also in a position to market all of the extensive Bayer product list. Formerly, Bayer would license its best-selling drugs to its own competitors, to take advantage of their superior sales and marketing organizations. Dr. Risse says it is unlikely they will ever do so again. Miles is now financially stable, its reorganized sales force is effective, and Miles has become highly competitive in the pharmaceutical marketplace.

Miles Laboratories' access to Bayer drugs is obviously important to the company's development. As well, the company can be expected to produce its own innovative drugs. Bayer's global research budget in 1986 amounted to an astronomical $750 million, and each of its American subsidiaries had access to this fund. Miles' research budget for 1985 alone was $100 million (it amounted to $25 million per annum before the takeover). By investing heavily in research, Bayer hopes to encourage innovation and to maintain its edge in the pharmaceutical market. Breakthrough technologies and drugs have historically created huge profits for the industry: Bayer is acutely aware, then, of the importance of research and development, and wishes its constituent companies actively to participate in the process.

The future of Miles Laboratories is therefore closely linked with that of its parent company in West Germany. Just how successful the marriage between Elkhart and West

Germany ultimately proves will serve as a model for other companies contemplating a move into the American market using the same formula. For now, at least, neither management nor investors can quarrel with Miles' impressive performance and Bayer's very satisfying profit margins.

Principal Subsidiaries: Cutter Laboratories Overseas Corp.; Miles Export Sales Co., Inc.; Miles International Inc.; Miles International Management Co., Inc. The company also has subsidiaries in the following countries: Argentina, Australia, Brazil, Canada, France, Japan, England, Mexico, Italy, Spain, Switzerland and West Germany.

Further Reading: *Serving Needs in Health and Nutrition: The Story of Miles Laboratories* by Walter Ames Compton, New York, Newcomen Society, 1973.

MYLAN LABORATORIES

1030 Century Building
Pittsburgh, Pennsylvania 15222
U.S.A.
(412) 232-0100

Public Company
Founded: 1961
Employees: 288
Sales: $91•million
Market Value: $559 million
Stock Index: New York

When Roy McKnight, the 55-year old president of a manufacturer's representative company, was brought in as chief executive of Mylan Laboratories in 1976, even he had his doubts. He had no previous experience in the drug industry, and he faced a formidable challenge. McKnight now recalls: "We had $1.9 million in accounts payable, with 70% of that more than 150 days old. We owed more than $400,000 in delinquent withholding and FICA taxes. We had 320 production people out on strike, even though we didn't even have a union! Our inventories were overstated by $2 million, and we had a negative net worth of $900,000." In short, "the company was facing imminent bankruptcy." Could it be turned around? "Back in 1976," says McKnight, "that was an open question."

Although Milan Puskar, one of the original founders of the company, had resigned in the early 1970's, frustrated by the direction the company was taking, he continued to believe that the generic pharmaceutical industry had great potential and that Mylan Laboratories had a future. It was he who convinced McKnight to have a try. Together with Frank Beber, a former partner with the accountants Alexander Grant and Company, they took on the task of curing a very sick company. Today, 12 years later, Mylan Laboratories ranks as one of the top manufacturers in the growing generic drug market.

Back in 1976 Mylan Laboratories set itself the goal of becoming a leading company in the manufacture of pharmaceuticals under their chemical names. More practically, before that goal could be reached, its new executive team set about repairing the almost terminally struggling company they had inherited. They acted immediately on what they saw as the causes of the crisis: the company had expanded too fast into too many products, and it was being overwhelmed by high production costs. McKnight took the necessary remedial action: he persuaded the company's

bankers to extend more credit (personally guaranteed by members of the Mylan board); he settled the strike by allowing workers to unionize but simultaneously reduced the workforce by one-third; he encouraged more aggressive marketing campaigns; and he discontinued all products that were unprofitable. One year later, the company was operating in the black.

It has continued to grow because of management's innovations. Instead of employing an army of salesmen to contact physicians and pharmacists directly, Mylan used just four salesmen to sell commodity generics under their chemical names directly to bulk buyers—drugstore chains, mail-order houses and distributors. Mylan also entered the growing market for branded generics—drugs on which patent protection has expired and the market has accordingly declined, drugs that large pharmaceutical companies generally farm out to others to manufacture. Because consumers are willing to pay more for a brand-name generic, McKnight realized that these products could involve great potential for his company. Today, branded generics account for 40% of Mylan's sales.

Mylan concentrated too on new product introduction—though, with generic drugs, this is a tricky strategy. Market shares can never really be protected; as drugs come off patent, competing companies are sure to quickly manufacture their own generic versions. Mylan's experience with Lasix, the best-selling diuretic in the country, provides a good example. On 27 August 1981 the company received approval to manufacture furosemide, the generic equivalent. By the close of business that day the company had recorded $1 million in sales; within three days, they had doubled that number. For a company that then had annual sales of only $31.8 million, such response was extraordinary. Yet within two months there was competition in the marketplace. That scenario is typical in the generic industry. Mylan Laboratories, however, has had remarkable success in weathering competition. By 1982 there were nearly 100 products on the company's list, and only one other manufacturer of generics came close to posting similar profits.

Much of Mylan's success, as that of other generic manufacturers, can be traced to a change in consumer attitudes over the last two decades. Consumers has begun to rebel against the high cost of prescription drugs; so, too, have insurance companies and the federal government, eager to limit the rising cost of health care. The generic drug companies, and the discount drug chains, have tried to respond to that challenge. But a potentially large marketplace also breeds a potentially large number of competitors, which can in turn can lead to both price-cutting and diminished profits, and Mylan has had to act with particular cunning to achieve its success. Management has realized that it can expect overwhelming response—as with furosemide or with indomethacin (for which sales reached $1.5 million in the first week after Food and Drug Administration approval)—only in the first few months the generic is on the market. By choosing to prepare generics for drugs with two to three years left on their patents, Mylan has been successful in completing the requisite FDA tests, in setting up its manufacturing facilities, and in producing enough inventory so as to make an immediate entrance in the marketplace as soon as the patent has expired.

Generic products have not been Mylan's only success. The company has also made notable advances in the development of innovative drugs. In 1984, after spending $5 million on research and five years on clinical tests, the company received FDA approval to market Maxzide, a diuretic hypertensive. Maxzide was in direct competition with SmithKline's Dyazide, the third best-selling patented drug in the U.S., but Mylan's product was not a generic version but rather a new formulation of chemicals. McKnight described the FDA approval of the newly developed drug as the "single most important event in Mylan's history." Aside from marking the company's entrance into the field of drug development, Maxzide promised to gain wide market acceptance. The reformulation solved problems of bio-availability as well as offering a convenient once-a-day dosage. Using the Lederle Laboratories sales force to distribute the drug, Mylan predicted that sales of the diuretic would reach $100 million by 1987–88.

Despite such accomplishments, the generic market continues to be the mainstay of Mylan's business. In September 1985 the company received FDA approval to market diazepam, the generic version of Valium, the phenomenally successful Hoffmann-La Roche tranquilizer. Eager to protect its threatened monopoly, Hoffmann-La Roche sponsored a study that claimed that generic versions of Valium were less effective. Yet Mylan, along with several other companies marketing diazepam, remained confident about the drug's acceptance in the marketplace.

During the last decade the best selling and most profitable drugs have increasingly come under the threat of generic competition. Further, passage of the Drug Price Competition and Patent Term Restoration Act in 1984 enables generic producers to gain quicker FDA approval by allowing these companies easier access to drugs for which patents had expired. To the chagrin of not only Hoffmann-La Roche but also many other large pharmaceutical companies who feared for their own very successful products, some 21% of Valium's $310 million market was whittled away by diazepam in the first few months following its introduction.

To protect themselves against the growing threat of generic competition, a number of the large companies have engaged in an energetic and often vituperative campaign to discredit generics. These efforts, though costly, have been mainly ineffective. By the end of 1986 sales of generic drugs had reached $3 billion.

For Mylan Laboratories in particular, 1985–86 was a record-breaking year. Besides having won approval for diazepam, the company received FDA approval to market seven new generics, including Flurazepam-HCL, a generic version of Hoffmann-La Roche's sleeping pill Dalmane. On Wall Street, Mylan shares sold at 40 times earnings; between 1979 and 1985 Mylan shares had been split six times. In a 1986 *Financial World* survey, Mylan Laboratories ranked 37th on the magazine's list of the 70 top growth companies.

Although the share price of generic drug companies increased almost 300% between the years 1983 and 1985, Wall Street analysts began warning in late 1985 that it was unlikely that the generic companies could continue to post such gains; the warnings themselves had the effect of reducing many share prices. The analysts' main worry was that it would be increasingly unlikely that the generic companies could continue to post such impressive gains when the gains themselves were acting as an incentive to draw more competition into the marketplace. Yet, established generic drug companies have shown remarkable resiliency—none more than Mylan.

Mylan Laboratories will of course face competition from other generic drug companies; the large drug companies will probably provide even greater competition. With their huge expenditures on research and marketing, these companies will continue to have the superior means to develop new products and market them effectively. Yet McKnight and his colleagues are no strangers to solving difficult problems. Modest about his own achievements, McKnight denies that he and his colleagues are "miracle workers." "We would not have achieved what we did," he says, "if Mylan Laboratories hadn't had one foot in the grave." One is tempted to add that, after bringing the company back from the dead and making it the most successful generic drug maker in America, meeting the competition of even the largest pharmaceutical companies seems only a minor challenge.

Principal Subsidiaries: Mylan Pharmaceuticals Inc.

NOVO

NOVO INDUSTRI A/S

Novo Alle, Bagsvaerd
Denmark 2880
(02) 982333

Public Company
Incorporated: 1940
Employees: 4,800
Sales: Dkr 4.118 billion (US$459 million)
Market Value: Dkr 1.88 billion (US$210 million)
Stock Index: Copenhagen London New York

Novo Industri produces approximately one-third of the world's supply of insulin and one-half of its supply of industrial enzymes. Although the Danish company is engaged in a variety of pharmaceutical and chemical activities, the production of insulin and enzymes remain the core of Novo's diverse enterprises. The company's current international stature evolved out of refining long-established skills and acquiring expertise within these specific fields.

August Krogh, a Danish physiologist and Nobel prize recipient, informed his colleagues of innovative drug research taking place in Toronto. There scientists were using pancreas extracts as a treatment for diabetes. Inspired by Krogh's enthusiasm, a number of Danes engaged in further investigation of this revolutionary hormone called insulin. Among these early converts were Harald Pedersen, a mechanical engineer, and his brother Thorvald, a pharmacist. Together they established a rudimentary production facility in the basement of Harald's home in Copenhagen. In 1925, just four years after the discovery of insulin, the Pedersen brothers were producing a stable, commercially viable, solution called "Insulin Novo."

By 1931 production demands required the Pedersen's to leave their cellar and rent space in a former dairy factory. Eventually the brothers purchased the building along with property surrounding the plant. Growing in just 10 years from a fledgling basement operation into a large scale enterprise, the company sold insulin in 40 countries. Pancreas from oxen, calves and swine were procured from slaughterhouses across Europe and transported to Novo first by refrigerated car, then by railway van, and finally by lorries. To satisfy Novo's growing need for space Arne Jacobsen, the renowned Danish architect, was contracted to design modern factories.

Research and development remained a priority from the very beginning of the company's history. Profits from insulin sales were reinvested to fund the company's laboratories. Novo opened the Hvidore Hospital for the exclusive treatment of diabetic patients and as additional facility for investigating the uses of insulin. Yet it was not until Knud Hallas-Moller joined Novo in 1937, immediately after graduating in pharmacy, that the company's research activities accelerated. As head of a new research team comprised mostly of former classmates, Hallas' first project involved investigating methods of improving insulin yields and prolonging its effectiveness.

The result of Hallas' years of study became the foundation for Novo's Lente series of insulins. Based on his discovery that auxiliary substances were not necessary to produce sustained effects, at present the Lente series remains one of the most widely used insulin preparations around the world. Hallas' research garnered him a doctorate from the University of Copenhagen. Later, Hallas received an honorary doctorate from the University of Toronto where insulin was first discovered. In 1977 he received the H.C. Orsted Gold Medal for his significant scientific contribution and in 1981, the year he retired as president to become chairman of the board, Hallas was elevated to the First Class of the order of Knights of the Dannebrog. Hallas met his wife, Gudrun Hallas-Moller, while still working as a researcher; she is the daughter of founder Harald Pedersen.

An additional product line was added to Novo's operations in 1938, thus expanding the company's activities outside the exclusive task of manufacturing insulin. Sterilizing and autoclaving sheep guts produced a versatile surgical thread called Catgut. The popularity of this product kept Novo Facilities occupied over the course of many years; however, in the 1950's when new methods of suturing wounds supplanted the need for Catgut, production was abandoned.

Novo introduced another product during this time that marked a significant step in the direction of developing biochemicals. When the company began competing with the tanning industry for animal glands during World War II, Novo decided to extract both insulin and trypsin, an enzyme necessary for batting hides. The combined manufacture of these two products complemented each other well; once insulin was extracted, trypsin could be produced from the gland residues. From the first production of trypsin in the dark cellar of the insulin factory, Novo proceeded to manufacture a wide range of enzymes which eventually led to its becoming one of the world's leading manufacturers of enzymes.

At the same time Novo pursued this early enzyme production, the company possessed basic knowledge of fermentation techniques. This knowledge soon proved useful both for the future manufacture of enzymes and the immediate need for penicillin. During World War II there was increased pressure on the scientific community to produce mass quantities of the recently isolated bacterial combatant. Novo, eager to contribute, ordered its employees to examine anything from old ski boots and jam jars in order to find the correct fungi. While yields varied as Novo attempted to improve its technology, it was not until Hallas' postwar visit to the U.S. that the company finally perfected production.

Observing the superior qualities of crystalline penicillin developed at Cornell University, Hallas encouraged Novo to develop its own method of crystallization. By 1947 Novo researchers obtained the desired results and the company became one of the first to commercially produce this stable form of penicillin. With this success Novo proceeded to extend its operations to include the manufacture of second generation antibiotics. Today these pharmaceuticals remain indispensible for the treatment of patients with penicillin allergies and for fighting bacteria resistant to penicillin.

The following decade saw the introduction of Heparin Novo, a notable drug used in the treatment of blood clots. As trypsin is a necessary ingredient in the manufacture of this new product, heparin fitted well with Novo's established activities. Using organ tissue from oxen or pigs as raw materials, Novo packaged heparin in small disposable syringes enabling doctors to closely monitor the dosage.

In addition to the manufacture of heparin, the 1950's brought significant structural changes to the growing company. Under Hallas' encouragement, the Pedersen brothers created the Novo Foundation as a receptacle for all Novo's non-negotiable shares. Prior to this decision, control of the company remained in the hands of the founding family. As the Pedersens neared retirement, a solution was sought to protect Novo's future as an independent company. By establishing a foundation with a voting majority, the company acquired an important defense against hostile takeovers as well as a source for contributing to humanitarian projects.

By acquiring expertise in fermentation technology through the manufacture of penicillin, Novo stood well prepared to initiate enzyme production by fermentation of micro-organisms. The first product of this technology was amylase, an industrial enzyme used in the manufacture of textiles. Over the next 15 years a number of enzymes emerged from Novo's laboratories that no longer required animal organs for raw materials. The most successful of these products was Alcalase, an enzyme used in detergents. In the mid-1960's these types of enzymes became popular around the world and propelled Novo to the forefront of the industry.

A major setback in 1970, however, caused enzyme sales to drop precipitously. A campaign in the U.S. to expose alleged health hazards for users of enzymes brought Novo under harsh criticism. After just having completed three new fermentation plants, the company was forced to lay off 400 workers as millions of kroner were lost in sales. Only when the National Academy of Sciences dismissed evidence of health risks did enzyme sales in the U.S. regain some of its lost momentum. In 1979 Novo completed an enzyme factory in North Carolina for the production of fructose sugar. Increasing demand for this product resulted in the recent expansion of this facility.

In 1955 Novo purchased a piece of land in Bagsvaerd, an area north of Copenhagen. Over the course of the next several years Novo built an array of facilities on this site and Bagsvaerd became the center of administrative and production activities. Also during this period several new lines of pharmaceuticals augmented Novo's traditional businesses. These included steroid products for gynecological applications and Glucagon, a diagnostic aid.

Despite these successful additions, the improvement of insulin products remained a company priority. In a major scientific breakthrough, Novo introduced Monocomponent insulins, the purest preparation of insulin available. For the first time in the treatment of diabetes insulin could be administered without the presence of contaminants found in other preparations. Other improvements included the basal/bolus concept of treatment whereby a diabetic could simulate the natural patterns of short- and long-acting insulin. The compact NovoPen, an injection device based on this concept, allows diabetics more freedom in their lifestyles.

Novo's most recent innovation in insulin products involved the 1982 introduction of the first commercially produced human insulins. Aware that porcine insulin differs from human insulin by only one amino acid, Novo discovered a chemical process to transform porcine insulin into an identical copy of that found in the human body. Today, Novo's industry competitors have successfully developed human insulin produced through genetic engineering. In response to this and other technological developments in the industry, Novo organized its own genetic laboratory to manufacture both enzymes and hormones.

The need for capital to support Novo's growth over the past years resulted in the company's stock being listed first on the Copenhagen and later on the London and New York exchanges. In 1975, to celebrate Novo's 50th anniversary, company employees were allowed the opportunity to become co-owners through the purchase of stock at nominal value. Some 90% of Novo's employees are shareholders. While Novo's stock presently remains an attractive investment, recent fluctuations in exchange rates caused earnings per share to decline between 1984 and 1986. Nevertheless, sales for human insulin more than doubled during the same time period.

Novo factories now operate in the U.S., Japan, France, South Africa, and Switzerland with plans underway to construct new facilities around the world. In 1981 a jointly owned company was initiated with E.R. Squibb & Sons, a large U.S. pharmaceutical concern. Research and development, always a company priority, is funded through the annual reinvestment of an average 10% of sales. In addition to insulin research, the company is currently engaged in developing a broad range of innovative applications for enzymes. These applications include such diverse areas as pollution control, fuel alcohol projects, and food protein sources.

Principal Subsidiaries: Novo industries (Pharmaceuticals) (Pty.) Ltd.; Novo Industri A/S; Novo Laboratories, Inc.; Novo Biochemical Industries, Inc.; Novo Industri Oy; Novo Farmaka A/S; Novo Industri B.V.; Novo Laboratories Pty. Ltd.; CSL-Novo Pty. Ltd.; Novo Industrie Enzymes S.A.; Novo Diagnostic Systems A/S; Novo Industri A/S Ltd.; Novo Laboratories Ltd.; Novo Enzyme Products Limited.; Novo Laboratories Ltd.; Novo Industri Limited; Alfred Jorgensen Laboratory of Fermentation

Ltd.; Hermedico A/S. The company also has subsidiaries in the following countries: Brazil, France, Ireland, Italy, Greece, Japan, Netherlands, Portugal, Spain, Sweden, United Kingdom and West Germany.

PFIZER INC.

235 E. 42nd Street
New York, New York 10017
U.S.A.
(212) 573-2323

Public Company
Incorporated: April 21, 1900
Employees: 40,000
Sales: $4.476 billion
Market Value: $12.417 billion
Stock Index: New York London Basle Lausanne Paris
Brussels Zurich Geneva

Recently, Pfizer has reported $4 billion in sales, projected $500 million for research and development by 1988, and commanded one of the largest overseas operations in the industry. All of this, of course, did not happen overnight. After almost one hundred years of quietly manufacturing fine chemicals, the revolution in medical care through the development of penicillin led Pfizer to important innovation within the industry.

In 1849 Charles Pfizer, a chemist, and Charles Erhart, a confectioner, began a partnership in Brooklyn to manufacture bulk chemicals. While producing iodine preparation and boric and tartaric acids, Pfizer pioneered the production of critric acid. To this day, Pfizer sells citric acid to soft drink companies, using large-scale fermentation technology.

While Pfizer technicians became experts in fermentation technology, across the ocean Sir Alexander Fleming made his historic discovery of penicillin in 1928. Recognizing penicillin's potential to revolutionize health care, scientists struggled for years to produce both a high quality and large quantity of the drug. Experimentation with production became an imperative during the Nazi air raids of London during World War II. In a desperate attempt to solicit help from the community of United States scientists, Dr. Howard Florey of Oxford University travelled to America to ask the U.S. government to mobilize its scientific resources.

Due to their expertise in fermentation, the government approached Pfizer. Soon afterward, Dr. Jasper Kane from the company laboratory began his own experiments. Initially using large glass flasks, Dr. Kane's experimentation then led to deep-tank fermentation. Later, the company announced its entrance into large-scale production with the purchase of an old ice plant in Brooklyn.

Refusing government money, the company paid the entire $3 million for the purchase and within four months John McKeen (future chairman and president) had converted the ancient plant into the largest facility for manufacturing penicillin in the world.

However, early production was not without its difficulties. The first yields of penicillin required constant supervision, and yet quality and quantity remained low and inconsistent. In one of those inexplicable quirks of history, however, a government researcher browsing in a fruit market in Peoria, Illinois discovered a variant of the "Penicillium" mold on an over-ripe cantaloupe. Using this variant, production suddenly increased from 10 units per millimeter to 2,000 units per millimeter. By 1942 Pfizer divided the first flask of penicillin into vials for the medical departments of the Army and Navy; this flask was valued at $150,000. It was Pfizer penicillin that arrived with the Allied Forces on the beaches of Normandy in 1944.

Even as the government controlled production of the drug for the sole use of the Armed Forces the public, aroused by miraculous results of penicillin, asked Pfizer to release the drug domestically. In 1943 John L. Smith, Pfizer president, and John McKeen, against the explicit regulations of the federal government, supplied penicillin to a doctor at the Brooklyn Jewish Hospital. Dr. Leo Lowe administered what was thought of as massive dosages of penicillin to a number of patients and cured, among others, a child suffering from an acute bacterial infection and a paralysed and comatose woman. Smith and McKeen, visiting the hospital on Saturdays and Sundays, were witness to penicillin's curative effects on the patients.

Nevertheless, it was not until the end of the war when the federal government realized its mistake in restricting production of the drug. In 1946 Pfizer purchased Groton Victory Yard, a World War II shipyard, in order to renovate it for mass production of the new publicly accessible medicine. This marked Pfizer's first official entrance into the manufacturing of pharmaceuticals. In a few years the five story high building, equiped with 10,000 gallon tanks, produced enough penicillin to supply 85% of the national market and 50% of the world market. In 1946 sales had already reached $43 million.

Competition from 20 other companies manufacturing penicillin soon resulted in severe price reductions. The price for 100,000 units dropped from $20 to less than 2 cents. Furthermore, while the company could boast ownership of fermentation tanks "exceeded in size only by those in the beer industry," Pfizer's bulk chemical business decreased as former customers began establishing production facilities of their own. Pfizer's instrumental role in developing antibiotics proved beneficial to society, but a poor business venture.

All this was to change drastically under the new direction of president John McKeen. In 1949 McKeen, whose career at Pfizer began the day after he graduated from the Brooklyn Polytechnic Institute in 1926, was elevated to president and later chairman of the company. Already responsible for increasing sales by an impressive 800% between 1939 and 1950, McKeen's business acumen became even more evident during the Terramycin campaign. In the postwar years, pharmaceutical companies searched for new broad-spectrum antibiotics useful in the treatment of a wide number of bacterial infections. Penicillin and streptomycin, while helping to expand the frontier of medical knowledge, actually offered a cure for only a limited number of infections. Pfizer's breakthrough came with the discovery of oxytetracycline, a broad range antibiotic that would soon prove effective against some 100 diseases.

The drug's remarkable capture of a sizeable portion of the market was not due entirely to its inherent curative powers. Rather it took McKeen's ability to promote the new drug that actually propelled Pfizer into the ranks of top industry competitors. McKeen's first accomplishment was the timely decision to market the antibiotic under a Pfizer trademark. Thus Terramycin, the drug's chosen name, launched Pfizer into its first ethical drug campaign. Lacking the resources other pharmaceutical companies had to promote their drugs, McKeen announced the "Pfizer blitz" whereby the company's small sales force used an unusual array of marketing strategies.

For the first time, the company circumvented traditional drug distributing companies and began selling Terramycin directly to hospitals and retailers. Pfizer's miniscule detail force (pharmaceutical salesmen) would target one small region at a time and promote their product to every accessible healthcare professional. The salesmen left generous samples of the drug at every sales call, sponsored golf tournaments, and ran noisy hospitality suites at conventions. Surprised at the success of this tiny band of salesmen which would eventually grow into a 4000 man army, industry competitors reluctantly increased their own sales forces and similarly began promoting their products directly to physicians.

Taking the calculated risks of insulting the entire medical community, Pfizer ran lavish advertisements in the conservative *Journal of the American Medical Association*. The ad was greeted with a large degree of reservation and threatened the drug industry's abhorrence of "hard sell" marketing. In an unprecedented move, the company had paid a prohibitive $500,000 to run the multi-page ad. In two years the entire Terramycin campaign cost $7.5 million and Pfizer became the largest advertiser in the American Medical Association's journal.

After twelve months on the market, Terramycin's sales accounted for one-fourth of Pfizer's total $60 million sales. Yet problems with the company's advertising strategy were soon to surface. In 1957, while promoting the reputability of a new antibiotic called sigmamycin, a Pfizer advertisement used the professional cards of eight physicians to endorse the drug. John Lear, science editor of the Saturday Review, denounced this advertisement in a scathing attack. Not only were the names of the eight physicians fictitious, Lear claimed, but the code of Pharmaceutical Manufacturers Association prohibited soliciting endorsements from physicians. Moreover, Lear used the Pfizer ad to underscore and criticize what he saw as a trend towards the overprescription of antibiotics, exaggerated claims on drug effects, and concealment of possible side effects.

Pfizer was quick to defend their advertisement. The company upheld the reputability of the ad agency, William Douglas McAdams Inc., a highly respected firm responsible for the Sigmamycin campaign. While defending the drug and the clinical reports supporting the drug's efficacy, Pfizer admitted that the business cards were purely symbolic and therefore fictitious and, as a result, may have been misleading. The company accordingly changed the campaign.

John Lear's final attack on Pfizer expressed an unspoken industry complaint. Not only was it disturbing that such "hard sell" marketing should actually prove successful, but since Pfizer's recent past was in bulk chemical production this added "insult to injury," so to speak. Being a newcomer to the industry of ethical drugs, Lear argued that the young company should have shown respect for the industry's formal and restrained method of conducting business. However, Pfizer was not intimidated by the industry's attitude toward its advertising campaign; it was interested in claiming and maintaining a share of the market. If it meant breaking tradition, it was clear Pfizer was not going to hesitate.

Aside from its modern marketing campaigns, Pfizer was very successful at developing a diversified line of pharmaceuticals. While many companies concentrated their efforts on developing innovative drugs, Pfizer generously borrowed research from its competitors and released variants of these drugs. While all companies participated in this process of "molecular manipulation," whereby a slight variance is produced in a given molecule to develop greater potency and decreased side effects in a drug, Pfizer was particularly adept at developing these drugs and aggressively seizing a share of the market. Thus, the company was able to reduce its dependence on sales of antibiotics by releasing a variety of other pharmaceuticals.

At the same time Pfizer's domestic sales increased dramatically, the company was quietly improving its presence on the foreign market. Under the methodical directive of John J. Powers, head of international operations and future president and chief executive officer, Pfizer's foreign market expanded into 100 countries and accounted for $175 million in sales by 1965. It would be years before any competitor came close to commanding a similar share of the foreign market. Pfizer's 1965 worldwide sales figures of $220 million indicated that the company might possibly be the largest pharmaceutical manufacturer in the U.S. By 1980 Pfizer was one of two U.S. companies among the top 10 pharmaceutical companies in Europe, and the largest foreign health care and agricultural product manufacturer in Asia.

Pfizer's crowning success to its unorthodox business proceedures involved McKeen's quest for diversification through acquisition. While competing companies within the industry preferred to keep between $50 and $70 million in savings, Pfizer not only kept a meager $25 million in cash, but was the only major pharmaceutical to use common equity to borrow capital. "Not to have your cash working is a sort of economic sin," McKeen candidly stated. Between 1961 and 1965 the company paid $130 million in stock or cash and acquired 14 companies, including manufacturers of vitamins, antibiotics for animals, chemicals, and Coty cosmetics.

McKeen defended this diversification strategy by

claiming that prodigious growth had decreased overall profits while competitors, on the other hand, had neither grown nor profited from their conservative investments. Furthermore, Pfizer's largest selling drug, Terramycin, generated only $15 to $20 million a year and therefore freed the company from a dependence on one product for all its profits.

In 1962 Pfizer allotted $17 million for research and that same year McKeen announced plans for his "five by five" program which included $500 million in sales by 1965. Obviously, sales would not come from new pharmaceuticals, but from the company's accelerated rate of acquisitions.

McKeen never actually saw the company reach this goal during his presidency. In 1964 sales did surpass $480 million, but the following year Powers replaced McKeen as chief executive officer and president, and inherited a company with almost half its sales generated from foreign markets and wide product diversification from 38 subsidiaries.

For the next seven years Powers continued to preside over the company's comfortable profits and sizeable growth. In the absence of McKeen's style of conducting business, Powers directed Pfizer towards the more conservative and methodical approach of manufacturing and marketing pharmaceuticals.

Powers guided the company in a new direction with an increased emphasis on research and development. With increased funds allocated for research in the laboratories, Pfizer joined the ranks of other pharmaceutical companies searching for the innovative, and therefore profit making, drugs. Vibramycin, an antibiotic developed in the 1960's, was very profitable; by 1981 it generated sales of $250 million.

In the early 1970's Edmund Pratt Jr. stepped in as company chairman and Gerald Laubach took over as Pfizer president. While company assets reached $1.5 billion and sales generated $2 billion by 1977, Pfizer's overall growth was much slower through the period of the late 1970's and early 1980's. Increased oil prices caused comparable increases in prices for raw materials; low incidents of respiratory infections slowed sales for antibiotics; and even a cool summer in Europe reduced demands for soft drinks and, consequently, the need for Pfizer citric acids. All of these factors contributed to the company's slow rate of growth.

In the light of this, the two new top executives significantly changed company strategy. First, funds for research and development reached $190 million by 1981; this marked a 100% increase in funding from 1977. Secondly, Pfizer began a comprehensive licensing program with foreign pharmaceutical companies to pay royalties in exchange for marketing rights on newly developed drugs. This represented a noticeable change from the years Powers supervised international operations. Under his directive Pfizer choose to market its own drugs on the foreign market and establish joint ventures or partnerships only if no other option was available.

The two new drugs, one called Procardia, a treatment for angina licensed from Bayer AG in Germany for its exclusive sale in the U.S., and the other called Cefobid, an antibiotic licensed from a Japanese pharmaceutical, promised to be highly profitable items. Furthermore, drugs discovered from Pfizer's own research resulted in large profits. Sales for Minipress, an antihypertensive, reached $80 million in three years, and Feldene, an anti-inflammatory, generated $314 million by 1982.

By 1983 sales reached $3.5 billion and Pfizer was spending one of the largest amounts of money in the industry on research ($197 million in 83). Pratt, in a final move to shed Pfizer of its former idiosyncrasies, began selling some of its more unprofitable acquisitions.

It is interesting to note that one Pfizer product acquired through a company acquisition in the 1960's experienced a market rediscovery during the 1980's. Ben Gay, an ancient liniment marketed for relief of arthritis pains through the late 1970's, found new patrons in the health-conscious 1980's. Discovering that sales for Ben Gay were increasing when marketed as a fitness aid, Pfizer began an advertising campaign by employing athletic superstars to endorse the drug. This campaign cost the company $6.3 million in 1982.

With a projected budget of $500 million for research and development in 1988, a comprehensive line of new drugs, and a reduction of diversification through sales of unprofitable acquisitions, Pfizer is well prepared for the future.

Principal Subsidiaries: Radiologic Sciences, Inc.; Shiley Inc.; Valleylab, Inc.; Composite Metal Products, Inc.; Redmond Holding Co.; Pfizer Hospital Products Group, Inc.; Site Realty, Inc.; Pfizer Pigments Inc.; Pfizer Genetics Inc.; American Medical Systems, Inc.; Quigley Company, Inc.; Adforce Inc.; Myerson Tooth Corp. The company also lists subsidiaries in the following countries: France, Ireland, Italy, and Japan.

PHARMACIA A.B.

S-751 82 Uppsala
Sweden
46 18 16 30 00

Public Company
Incorporated: 1921
Employees: 5,566
Sales: SKr3.481 billion (US$511.8 million)
Market Value: SKr9.691 billion (US$1.414 billion)
Stock Index: Stockholm

Pharmacia began in 1911 in Stockholm with one product, the phospho-energon energy pills made from animal products. The recipe for the energy pills was created by C.M.de Kunwald and was patented in 1910. Phospho-energon sold so well that the turnover during Pharmacia's first year was above 20,000 crowns. From 1912 to 1962 phospho-energon, in various forms, was sold in Finland, Russia, the United States, Denmark, Norway, and England, and remained throughout that time a strong 30% of Pharmacia's total production.

While Pharmacia began with one product, it had never been the intention to rely on a single product. From the outset, the 21 people who invested 32,100 crowns in initial shares were told that the new company would produce medicines on a commercial scale. In 1912 Pharmacia took on the production of cedar oil, from cedar wood from Lebanon. The cedar oil was used in the production of Cedrolinol, an ointment used for rheumatic complaints. In 1913 another product, Sodamint, to be used against "throatache" and stomach complaints, was launched. Paraform, which contained formaldehyde, was another product Pharmacia made to fight throat infections.

In that year, foreign competition was pressing hard upon Pharmacia and other Swedish companies, and the former invested in heavy use of the advertising slogan "Favour the Swedish preparations." Anachronistically, Pharmacia continued its expensive advertising campaign, sending marketing managers to the United States and Russia, and sending detailed brochures on Pharmacia products to each and every doctor in Scandinavia. By 1915 the company had suffered tremendous losses, all due to this campaign, most of it for the promotion of phospho-energon.

During these years, the company, perhaps consequently, was always on the move. In 1912 the lease on the original building expired, and Pharmacia moved to a new building. In 1916 it moved again, to a larger factory where it could produce 500 tablets per hour. It later sold that building for a profit and, in 1920, moved to south Stockholm.

Pharmacia was adventurous in business as well as in products and advertising. It tried selling chocolate and cocoa with phospho-energon in it; and in 1920 it began selling Quina Laroche, a type of Chinese wine. In 1919 another pharmaceutical firm, Malmsten & Bergvalls, had grown so quickly since its formation in 1914 that it wanted access to Pharmacia's larger production capacity. The two companies decided to co-operate, using one another's resources, but not sharing chemists directly. Pharmacia would buy raw materials from Malmsten & Bergvalls, and would serve as its exclusive agent in New York and Paris, while Malmsten & Bergvalls would buy Pharmacia's partially finished products needed for its own production.

The leading pharmaceutical companies of Sweden felt that the state should establish a central laboratory for the development of medicines. In October 1920 it was agreed that the state would underwrite such a laboratory. The new enterprise, called Apotekarnes Droghandel AB, was officially formed in March 1921, and included the majority of the country's leading chemists, including Pharmacia's Grönfeldt.

Pharmacia continued in its struggle between growth and marketing, and with the eternal problem of cashflow. In 1922 it was still expanding, with ever larger orders, but the profits were so low that all employees had to take a cut in wages. The next year the company began producing laxatives, a product with a proven market. After its marketing splurge, the company remained somewhat timid about promotions and concentrated on product development. After the laxatives came the 1926 launch of Kreosan Simplex, used in the treatment of bronchitis and tuberculosis. In 1927 it started to produce vitamins.

At this time one of the founding chemists, Grönfeldt, stepped down as managing director because of ill health, and was replaced by Carl Erik Häggert, a former vice president of the company. Nils Winckler, the Information Chief, was later proposed as the head of development and research. The company spent 15,000 crowns on building a new alkaloid facility and, in 1933, started a Drogfarmen on which to grow its own ingredients for morphine, opiates, and belladonna. Expansion and production within the country were less vulnerable to internal competition as there was a high degree of co-operation among the companies. The medicine manufacturers met very often to discuss "rationalization of production" so as not to overlap, and so that each could have its own specialty. These meetings lasted until the 1950's, when a new, more official, union was formed, the Läkemedels-Industri Föreningen (LIF).

Prior to the Second World War the research department of Pharmacia received the increased resources that came in from the dramatic new product created by Nanna Svartz of the Karolinska Institutet. Her interest in the treatment of rheumatic diseases and her brilliant research with sulpha led to the launch of Salazopyrin, a product which is still used, now in the treatment of ulcerative colitis. With the proceeds from this and other sulpha products, Pharmacia could afford to launch, with Uppsala University, another major product. Professor T. Svedberg and Arne Tiselius, both Nobel Prize-winners, had been asked by sugar manufacturers to do research on the sugar beet. Björn Ingelmann, a student, worked with them on the project, and it was he, in 1941, who identified and separated dextrose. During the Second World War the team developed from this Dextran, a plasma substitute, which was in use by 1943.

Sweden is a country with a small population, and so Pharmacia was under constant pressure to expand and export its production. In 1955, in conjunction with the Danish AS Pharmacia and the Dutch Organon, it launched and marketed until 1969 a line in hormones. The market in the United States was actively pursued by Gösta Virding and L. Arling Elwinger. In 1948 they established Pharmacia Laboratories Inc. in New York, with Elis Göth as director and Nathan Katz as secretary and financial advisor. This company sold Salazopyrin in the United States and reported on its research results in the Mayo Clinic Bulletin, encouraging many other doctors to try it in the treatment of ulcerative colitis.

At home, Pharmacia moved first to a building shared with Apotekarnes Droghandel AB, then to Uppsala, its final home. There, it had many good contacts with chemists at Uppsala University, with the added advantage that Uppsala was a growing "new industry" town.

Bjorn Ingelmann began working on pectin as well as dextrin. In the 1950's he had developed a separation process, using a centrifuge, that had been unsatisfactory. Later, Jerker Porath and Per Flodin developed a new separation method using a cellulose powder which eventually was marketed as Sephardex. This was a big success and took Pharmacia into the new production area of aids for research. Pharmacia Fine Chemicals AB was formed in 1967, with Bertil Gelotte as director, to produce separation products. In 1985 Bioteknik-Gruppen (BTG) was formed, to spend 826 million crowns to develop and market aids for biotechnical research and industrial cleaning. BioSensor AB was formed to concentrate on work in molecular biology, particularly DNA technology.

As Pharmacia expanded, it licenced the manufacture of its products in foreign countries, allowing for foreign expansion through subsidiaries. Pharmacia GB Ltd. was formed in Great Britain to produce Dextran, Macrodex, and Rheomacrodex, and for the sale of Sepharon. The same pattern was followed in Japan when, in 1960, Pharmacia co-operated with Green Cross KK. In 1971 Pharmacia KK was finally formed, withdrawing from Green Cross KK and working on its own. To control these and other licencing requirements, a separate company, Pharmacia International, was formed in 1967. These subsidiaries led to contacts with foreign chemists and clinics, particularly in the United Kingdom, but also elsewhere. In 1980 a Hungarian, Endre Balazs, developed for Pharmacia Healon a remarkable product used in eye surgery, now one of the company's biggest sellers.

Pharmacia adopted a major restructural plan in 1985. This divided the company's business interests into four large groups: biotechnology, health care, opthamology, and diagnostics. It also included a firm commitment to expansion, and, in 1986, Pharmacia acquired AB Leo, LKB-Produkter AB, and assets of Intermedics Intraocular Inc. Its largest selling products for 1986 include some of the old familiar names, such as Salazopyrin and FPLC, a descendant of the separation systems, as well as Healon, the allergy test Phadebas RAST, and Intraocular lenses. Net sales for 1986 were up 7% to 3,646 million crowns, and income rose 11% for the same year. The group employs over 6,000 people in more than 22 countries. Concentrating on the new industries of genetically engineered pharmaceuticals and diagnostic products, and expanding into the information technology necessary to support and control this work, Pharmacia seems to be preparing for control of the field by the end of the century.

Principal Subsidiaries: Meda AB; Pharmacia Biosensor AB; Pharmacia Biotech AB; Pharmacia Biotechnology International AB; Pharmacia Diagnostics AB; Pharmacia Fine Chemicals AB; Pharmacia Food AB; Pharmacia Infusion AB; Pharmacia International AB; Pharmacia Pharmaceuticals AB. The company also lists subsidiaries in the following countries: Australia, Austria, Belgium, Brazil, Canada, Denmark, Finland, France, Italy, Japan, the Netherlands, Switzerland, the United Kingdom, and the United States.

RORER GROUP

500 Virginia Drive
Fort Washington, Pennsylvania 19034
U.S.A.
(215) 628–6541

Public Company
Incorporated: 1968
Employees: 6,000
Sales: $845 million
Market Value: $535 million
Stock Index: New York

Rorer Group is less recognized as a major drug researcher than as an intelligent pharmaceutical concern persistent in its ability to foil takeover attempts. What so attracts would-be purchasers is Rorer's small size relative to its broad line of products. Though once described as a single-product enterprise, Rorer reduced its dependence on sales of the antacid Maalox by initiating an aggressive program of acquisition and internal development. Thus far Rorer has been successful in maintaining its independence; how much longer it can continue this is uncertain.

William H. Rorer, founder of William H. Rorer, Inc., established his pharmaceutical business in Pennsylvannia at the beginning of the 20th century. The small business was passed from father to son when Gerald F. Rorer assumed responsibility in administrating the company. The younger Rorer, graduating from Haverford College in 1929 and the Philadelphia College of Pharmacy and Science in 1931, is responsible for transforming the family-run company into a large publicly owned corporation. By 1950 Gerald Rorer served as company president and two years later he became company chairman as well.

Rorer's major pharmaceutical contribution was the discovery of the antacid Maalox in the early 1950's. While Maalox's anti-ulcer therapy was replaced by the revolutionary treatment available in the more recent drug called Tagamet, Maalox's continued popularity is evident since the product remains a household staple. When Maalox was first introduced it was an immediate success. Yet Gerald Rorer realized that his company's reliance on this product's sales also signified an area of vulnerability. Should a similar product compete directly with Maalox's market, company profits could be seriously jeopardized.

Consequently, in 1968 Gerald Rorer decided to merge his company with Amchem Products, Inc., an agricultural and specialty chemical manufacturer. Amchen, also located in Pennsylvania, pioneered the development of herbicides. The combined interests of the two companies now offered a diversified product line and a broadened earnings base. The 1969 profit figures for the merger, however, were disappointing. Sales of Amiben, one of Amchem's most important herbicides, were hurt by liquidations of trade inventories. The 8% drop in profits was also a result of higher taxes and operating costs.

By 1970 Rorer-Amchem registered a record high for sales and earnings. The $1.28 earnings per share of stock on $133 million sales was generated from the increased demands for Rorer pharmaceuticals and the new penetration of foreign markets. Long term prospects looked favorable as the company invested in research, an expanded agricultural chemical sales force, and new acquisitions.

Despite such a promising future, however, the Rorer-Amchem merger was laden with difficulties. In the following years Rorer's Maalox registered higher and higher profits. Amchem, on the other hand, went through a series of cyclical gains and losses. For this reason, in 1975 Rorer-Amchem stock sold at $20 per share, a figure which represented only ten times predicted earnings. Compared to other pharmaceutical companies Rorer-Amchem stock was not highly recommended.

In February of 1976 Gerald Rorer died. He was 68 years old and had served as president of the Pharmaceutical Manufacturing Association and as vice chairman of the Academy of Natural Sciences. Probably in deference to the late president's role in organizing the merger, divestiture from the unprofitable enterprise did not take place until the September following his death. Rorer-Amchem management agreed to sell the Amchem division to Union Carbide. This large chemical company had enough money and resources to re-establish Amiben's diminishing market share; the larger companies such as Lilly, Monsanto, and Bayer A.G. had already encroached on the sales of the herbicide by marketing similar products.

On the one hand, Rorer's reduced operations meant reduced sales. On the other hand, it meant a higher rating on Wall Street. The agreement to sell the chemical division resulted in an improvement on the company balance sheet. Without any longterm debts, and guarding a comfortable amount of cash in revenue, the Rorer Group was prepared to expand into health care markets. By concentrating on the field it knew best Rorer positioned itself to become a full-line pharmaceutical manufacturer.

Rorer's new chairman, John Eckman, directed the company's era of growth and expansion. Maalox sales continued to increase (in 1975 Eckman boasted that Maalox had outsold the very popular Alka-Seltzer). Interestingly enough, under Eckman's directive Maalox became the focal point of Rorer's marketing strategy. Unlike the past where a concerted effort had been made to shift the company's image of dependence away from sales of the antacid, Eckman, through a sophisticated advertising campaign, actually increased the product's visibility. "Piggyback" products such as Maalox Plus and Maalox Therapeutic Concentrate were released on the market.

The most important reason why Rorer was no longer reluctant to promote this product, and why Rorer actually used Maalox to embark on its first major venture into consumer advertising, was that through an aggresssive policy of acquisition the company was gaining respect as a leader in the health care field. By the end of 1979 sales peaked at $260.5 million, a 16.1% increase from sales in 1978. Aside from the ever popular antacid, several small, profitable and well-timed acquisitions, including Dooner Labs, a manufacturer of proprietary drugs, contributed to increased earnings.

During this time a number of recently developed drugs received encouraging market reception. One Rorer drug released as a Maalox-aspirin combination, called Ascriptin, captured 25% more of the market in 1979 than in 1978. Slo-Phyllin, a treatment for asthma, generated $7 million in sales, representing an increase of 70% over the previous year. The Quaalude sedative-hypnotic product line, a controversial favorite of illegal drug-users, was discontinued because of adverse publicity. In addition to the market entrance of new drugs, Rorer's increased funding for research and development resulted in a number of drugs which promised to be very lucrative. Lidamidine, an antidiarrheal drug awaiting market approval, was expected to capture an impressive portion of the $90 million market. Other drugs in the preliminary testing stage included a treatment for cardiac arrythmias, an anti-fungal drug, and an anti-inflammatory drug.

International operations grew by 22% in 1979, including the acquisition of a major interest in Japan's Kyoritsu Pharmaceutical Industry Company. Plans were under way to market Maalox in Spain and the U.K. Rorer's Richard Manufacturing Company subsidiary, a supplier of surgical equipment, posted a domestic and foreign sales figure of $44 million in 1978. Richard's otological products included joint replacements for hips, knees and ankles, while products used in middle-ear surgery represented an exciting area of growth. Surgical products from the Sonometrics Inc., Dyonics Inc., and Cryomedics Inc., all Rorer subsidiaries, reported close to a $11 million sales figure for 1978.

As the company entered the 1980's overall earnings and sales figures indicated that the company might be one of the fastest growing pharmaceutical manufacturers in the industry. Pharmaceuticals continued to contribute to a major portion of sales and profits with stomach aids accounting for some 50% of the totals. Ascriptin quickly became Rorer's fastest selling drug with sales gains averaging 30% annually. Dyonics surgical equipment subsidiary became the only manufacturer of a complete line of highly innovative materials used in "closed" orthopedic surgery. This revolutionary technique is used frequently by athletes, but is increasingly available to the general public. It employs fiber optic techniques to heal damaged cartilage. The growing demand for this revolutionary procedure found Dyonic products at a market premium.

While Rorer continued to increase earnings and profits while maintaining small longterm debts, Eckman simply could not rest on his laurels. Instead he prepared himself to thwart any attempt of a hostile takeover. In 1983 a group of stockholders owning 13% of the company hired the investment firm of Oppenheimer & Company in an attempt to sell Rorer to an interested customer.

While this was not the first time rumors of takeover bids had reached Eckman (according to him every major pharmaceutical company had approached the idea of acquiring Rorer at some point in the past), this new attempt marked a concerted effort by Rorer stockholders. One interested stockholder was George Behrakis, a founder of Dooner Laboratories, who became an owner of Rorer stock when his company was acquired by the pharmaceutical manufacturer. He felt dissatisfied with the performance of his asthma treatment drug since it had been purchased by Rorer, Eckman, however, appeared unperturbed by the stockholder revolt; according to him hostile takeovers were inappropriate in the pharmaceutical industry. Nonetheless, he asked for the approval of a 66% increase in authorized shares; this action could effectively prevent any takeover attempt by making the company large enough to become too expensive to purchase.

In 1984 Rorer celebrated its 75th year in business. Sales in 1983 had reached $475 million and projections suggested the figure would reach one-half billion by the end of that year. New acquisitions included: Kremers-Urban, a pharmaceutical concern that manufactured an ointment to control angina, the medical products division of Black & Decker, and Omni Hearing Aid Systems.

Despite continued growth, by 1985 a full-fledged proxy fight to acquire Rorer and replace management put Eckman on the defensive. Parker Montgomery, chairman and chief executive officer of Cooper Laboratories, attempted to persuade Rorer shareholders over to his side for a possible takeover. Sales at Cooper Labs, a manufacturer of contact-lens and eye-care products, had reached $256 million. Apparently, merger proposals had been offered by both Eckman and Montgomery, but when personalities clashed and disagreements over terms became insurmountable the negotiations were discontinued. Cooper then filed, for the second time, an antitrust notice announcing an intention to increase its 4.96% share of stock to 15% in Rorer.

In order to prevent this Rorer's board members adopted a "Poison Pill," otherwise called a Share Purchase Rights Plan. This plan deterred hostile takeover bids by forcing the purchasing company to issue stock of its own to stockholders of the targeted company at a price worth twice what it would be getting in return. Should Cooper offer Rorer stockholders $40 a share, for example, the complete deal would not cost a projected $840 million to acquire the total 21 million shares, but rather a prohibitive $1.9 billion due to the prescribed rules of the "Poison Pill."

Eckman, claiming the "plan" protected shareholders from "uneven treatment by a corporate raider," issued the plan on February 25th. While a shareholders meeting scheduled for late April would vote on the Montgomery "anti-pill" referendum, that very same day in February Cooper sought reprisal by suing Rorer in an attempt to invalidate the "pill" in court. Securities and Exchange Commission attorneys had recently argued that similar plans effectively "entrench management and usurp . . . to (a company's) board the shareholders right to determine who will manage the company." Montgomery hoped this same argument could be used to render Rorer's "Poison Pill" ineffective.

On April 23, at Rorer's annual stockholder's meeting, of 82% of the shares voted 51.46% favored Montgomery's "anti-poison pill" resolution while 42.08% voted against the plan in favor of management. Although the resolution was "non-binding," stock prices jumped two points in anticipation of what many believed would be an imminent decision made by the board in favor of the "anti-pill." Montgomery interpreted the vote as an unequivocal victory; his $1.5 million proxy battle had, according to him, been a successful fight to maintain "corporate democracy."

By January of 1986, however, over six months after Eckman had retired as chief executive officer (while still maintaining his position as chairman of the board), Rorer's directors chose to ignore Montgomery's slim majority and continue to utilize the "Poison Pill." Montgomery's takeover attempt, for the time being, was defeated. Yet no sooner had this ended, when rumors of another takeover attempt put Rorer management back on the defensive. Even though the company's balance sheet now reported a $735 million long-term debt due to the recent purchase of Pantry Pride, Revlon's ethical drug unit, the company's huge drug volume made it an attractive takeover candidate. Arrangements for the takeover were tentatively made by a wide range of potential suitors. Included in the list were: Alan Clore, a British investor who had recently made a $50 million profit from his 6.5% stake in the Revlon sale to Rorer; Parker Montgomery, now searching for possible support from a larger company (those rumored as possibilities were Beecham Group, Glaxo Holdings or Boots Company); international companies seeking to secure a foothold in the U.S. market; and domestic companies such as Pfizer. Rorer spun around in a vortex of increasing rumors and growing speculation. However, the new chief executive officer Robert Cawthorn, remained calm. His company, he claimed, had been the subject of many rumors in the past, but never yet had the situation reached a "bidding stage."

Rorer management has been criticized for its tactics in preventing takeovers. Cawthorn, however, has replied that it is in the best interest of the shareholders for the company to maintain its independence. Since earnings were depressed due to the company's recent purchases, shareholders will not begin to benefit from Rorer's growth until 1987. Yet stockholders, knowing a possible $50 per share could be earned in the event of a takeover, may now be less willing to wait for earnings to increase and more inclined to favor the immediate benefits accrued from selling their independence.

Principal Subsidiaries: William H. Rorer, Inc; Surgical Products; Rorer International Corp.

ROUSSEL UCLAF

35 Boulevard de Invalides
7500 Paris
France
(1) 45-55-91-55

The company is 54.5% owned by Hoechst A.G. and 40%
owned by the French State
Incorporated: 1961
Employees: 17,266
Sales: FFr 10.86 billion (US$1.392 billion)

In the recent past Roussel Uclaf, one of the most important pharmaceutical companies in France, has been the subject of a vigorous debate on nationalization and the growing presence of foreign concerns on the domestic market. As a manufacturer of a variety of pharmaceuticals and biotechnological products, Roussel Uclaf remains a source of pride for the French despite the fact that Hoechst A.G., a West German company, holds a major interest in the French firm.

In 1920 Dr. Gaston Roussel established the Institut de Sérothérapie Hémopoiétique (I.S.H.) for the production of Hémostyl. Later he directed the fledgling company toward the area of chemotherapy. The 1928 establishment of the Laboratoires Français de Chimiothérapie and of U.C.L.A.F. (Société des Usines Chimiques des Laboratoires Français) strengthened the company in this area. Over the course of the next several years the company grew through acquisition and expansion. Subsidiaries in Mexico, Brazil, and Argentina began operation and a second factory in France at Vertolaye was acquired.

Upon Dr. Gaston Roussel's death in 1947, Jean-Claude Roussel, the founder's son, took over the leadership of the growing company. Although already well established both in France and abroad, Roussel Uclaf's vast expansion subsequent to the founder's death is attributed to his son's business acumen. As a successful industrialist, Jean-Claude Roussel managed the company virtually by himself and expanded operations into a diverse array of businesses. These included such widely disparate activities as chemicals and aviation. The chemical operations are now organized into Nobel-Bozel, a distinct arm of the group's activities.

By 1961 production demands required the company to restructure its operations. To streamline various scientific, industrial and commercial operations, the Roussel Uclaf Group was formed as the subsidiary holdings of the Roussel Uclaf Company. Today the Roussel Uclaf Group engages in such diverse activities as health care, agricultural products, bulk chemicals and consumer products.

Jean-Claude Roussel continued his single-handed management of the Company until a 1968 vacation in the south of France where he was introduced to a senior Hoechst director. The successes of the family enterprise had become a source of pride for the French population. This encounter, however, inspired Roussel to pursue a policy to "Europeanize" his company. The result of this meeting led to the West German company purchasing a 43% stake in the Chimio holding company which controlled Roussel Uclaf.

This agreement represented an historical undertaking; never before had two private European companies cooperated under the auspice of the Common Market. Despite the implications such a purchase held for the French pharmaceutical industry, Roussel reassured the French government that certain agreements would protect the market from ever completely losing the industry to a foreign company. These agreements provided the French government with authority to decide on the future sale of shares, and also stipulated that Hoechst would never attempt to enlarge its holdings. In addition, it was also agreed that Roussel himself would never sell his personal holdings.

The result of Roussel Uclaf's association with the large West German concern proved useful to both parties. Both companies' chemical operations benefitted by the establishment of the joint venture Nobel-Hoechst Chimie. Furthermore, the association enabled the French company to make use of Hoechst's marketing structure in the Far East and in North America as well as to form its own marketing company within Germany. Hoechst, on the other hand, benefitted from Roussel's successful research in the area of steroids. By far the most beneficial aspect of this partnership, however, was the development of products through joint research. In 1969, Claforan, a third-generation antibiotic, represented the joint efforts of these two companies. Launched on the European, U.S., and Japanese markets, the drug generated over $100 million in 1982.

Yet the original agreement established between the two companies was destined to change. An unfortunate chain of events allowed Hoechst to gain a majority interest in its French partner. In 1972 Jean-Claude Roussel and several company executives were travelling in a helicopter manufactured by Roussel Uclaf's aviation division. En route to Roussel's summer home the helicopter hit a cable line killing all the passengers aboard.

The Roussel family, still a major shareholder, was suddenly faced with the disposition of Jean-Claude's estate. Since most of Roussel's estate was intimately connected with the activities of Roussel-Nobel, this posed financial problems. In order to remedy these extenuating circumstances a number of immediate changes went into effect. A five-man executive team called the "collegiate management" took over all decision making responsibilities formerly held by Roussel. It has been suggested that this structure afforded the German company greater influence over Roussel Uclaf's activities.

Soon after this restructure took effect, the Roussel family announced that financial demands to meet the disposition of the estate compelled them to sell a large amount of voting stock in Chimio. This announcement came at a time of renewed debate on nationalizing the French pharmaceutical industry. With the election awarding victory to a socialist government, the communist minister of health, Jack Ralite, spoke in favor of including Roussel in a nationalized industry. At the same time the French ministry was attempting to find "French solutions" to solve the growing problem of foreign company takeovers. Thus, to keep Roussel Uclaf "French" the government solicited the aid of Rhone-Poulenc, France's largest chemical concern, and Elf-Aquitaine, the state-controlled chemical company. Neither company, however, expressed interest in the purchase of the Roussel shares of stock.

Although the resulting sale found the French government gaining half the seats on the company's supervisory board as well as increasing its holdings in the company to 33%, the purchasing party was neither a competing French company nor the state. Instead, Hoechst had increased its holdings to 51%. Many people reacted to this state of affairs with disappointment; foreign participation in the French pharmaceutical industry now surpassed 50% and drugs patented by international concerns accounted for over 75% of all pharmaceuticals on the domestic market.

Notwithstanding the turn of events, the government's solution represented a pragmatic approach to limit the costs of its expensive program of nationalization. At the same time, Hoechst benefitted from Roussel's research in agricultural products and the French company continued to benefit from their partner's marketing organization. Some 65% of Roussel's total sales in 1981 came from overseas markets, a figure that was greatly supported by Hoechst's marketing organization. Furthermore, joint research and development would enhance the already successful area of antibiotics.

To appease those members of the French population that opposed Hoechst's increased holdings, the French government issued a statement to the effect that it would eventually increase its interest in Roussel Uclaf; in 1982 the government succeeded in acquiring a 40% share. Throughout these proceedings the management of Hoechst maintained that Roussel would always remain an independent entity. One major exception to this occurred with the 1974 creation of a joint subsidiary in the United States.

Roussel's growth subsequent to the agreement was impressive. In 1975 the company diversified into the perfume industry with the purchase of a major interest in Parfums Rochas. Several years later Roussel entered the sunglass industry through the purchase of a French company and Foster Grant, the American manufacturer. In addition, Roussel Laboratories, the subsidiary established in the United Kingdom during the 1930's, had grown into a preeminent British concern.

Total research and development expenditures in 1983 amounted to over $110 million which represented a 22% increase over the previous year. The company entered the field of biotechnology through the creation of a genetic engineering unit. Using biochemical fermentation, Roussel's Romainville Centre is said to be the greatest molecular biosynthesis installation in the world. Here the company concentrates on the production of vitamin B12, antibiotics, and veterinary products. At two other sites, one in France and one in Brazil, the company is engaged in multistage synthesis through chemical fermentation. Here corticosteroids and norsteroids are produced.

In addition to these products Roussel manufactures a broad array of successful pharmaceuticals and chemical products. Cefotaxime, a potent antibiotic, continues to generate profits from the United States and Japanese markets. It is also likely that Surgam, an anti-inflammatory drug, will be Roussel's third largest selling product and Rythmodan, a cardiac rhythm regulator, accounts for 58% of the world sales for this type of pharmaceutical. Furthermore, the company manufactures Deltamethrin, an active ingredient in a biodegradable group of products found in agricultural insecticides. This group is said to be the most powerful but least toxic of all agricultural products on the market.

During the present time Roussel's research continues in such diverse areas as cardiovascular diseases, nervous system disorders, dermatology, psychotropics, and infectious diseases. Furthermore, Roussel's activities outside the area of human health care, including veterinary medicines, consumer goods, chemicals, and agricultural products, continue to produce successful products. The French company's penetration of foreign markets has been very successful with Japan and the United States representing major market thrusts. Overall, the association between Roussel and Hoechst has been mutually beneficial and both companies appear satisfied with the arrangement.

Principal Subsidiaries: Application des Matières Plastiques S.A., Sté, d' (SAMP); Applications Scientifiques et Medicales S.A., Sté d' (SAMS); Applications Tehniques de l'Ouest S.A. (ATO); Carusa (Cia.Agropecuaria) S.A. (Guatemala); Centramite de Courtage, Sté.; Collectorgane S.A.; Delax Farmaceutica Ltda. (Portugal); Distriphar S.A.; Distrivet S.A.; Farquimia S.A. (Argentina); Foster Grant Corp. (U.S.A.); Grupo Roussel México S.A.; Immobilière du 3 Square Desaix S.A.; Laboratoires Cassenne S.A.; Laboratoires Cassenne Takeda S.A.; Laboratoires Diamant S.A.; Laboratoires Lutsia S.A.; Les Laboratoires Roussel & Cie.S.N.C.; Les Laboratoires Roussel S.A.; Larpe S.A. (Peru); Nippon-Roussel K.K. (Japan); Nippon-Uclaf K.K. (Japan); Ormobia S.A. (Italy); Parfums Rochas S.A. (France); Procida S.A. (France); Quimio S.A. (Brazil); Rilab S.A. (Spain); Union Chimique Continentale S.A. The company also has principal subsidiaries in the following countries: Argentina, Belgium, Bolivia, Ecuador, Finland, Greece, Japan, Netherlands, Philippines, Portugal, Spain, Sweden, Switzerland, United Kingdom, United States, Uruguay, Venezuela, and Vietnam.

SANDOZ

SANDOZ LTD.

Lichtstrasse 35
4002 Basle
Switzerland
41 61 24 11 11

Public Company
Incorporated: July 18, 1895
Employees: 40,166
Sales: SFr7.562 billion (US$4.647 billion)
Market Value: SFr5.343 billion (US$3.283 billion)
Stock Index: Basle Zurich Geneva

In 1886 two Swiss men, Dr. Alfred Kern and Mr. Edouard Sandoz, established a company in Basle in order to manufacture and sell synthetic dyes. Thirty years earlier the English chemist, William Henry Perkin, while trying to synthesize quinine from coal tar, came up with a purple dye instead. Two years later a Frenchman used a similar process to produce a magenta dye, and a new industry was born, ending the reliance upon purely animal, vegetable or mineral dyes. The new dyes were more brilliant than the old and lasted longer. They worked better on synthetic fabrics and they allowed for the development of new dye colors. It was an industry that many recognized as potentially very profitable.

Dr. Kern was 36 when the business was formed and was well known as a chemist specializing in dyestuffs trade. The two men purchased 11,000 square meters on the west bank of the Rhine River, built a manufacturing plant, and registered their business under the name of Kern & Sandoz, beginning work on the July 1, 1886. They had ten workmen and a 15 horsepower steam engine, and a certainty that they would succeed. There were some early setbacks: the dyes they originally had intended to produce, including Auramine, Victoria Blue, and Crystal Violet, required a process originated by Kern and an old partner, but that partner would not release his patent rights; another dye, Alizarine Blue, caused a reaction kettle to explode.

The company managed not only to survive but to expand. Kern developed new dyes and Sandoz traveled extensively, searching for more customers and markets for their products. In five years, from 1887 to 1892, their production increased from 13,000 kilograms of six different types of dyes to 380,000 kilograms of 28 dyes.

In 1893 the company began to change considerably. Dr. Kern collapsed and died of heart failure and, though

Sandoz tried to run the company himself, two years later he was compelled to retire from active management for health reasons. In 1895 Sandoz and Company was converted into a limited company called Chemische Fabrik vormals Sandoz (Chemical Works formerly Sandoz) with a share capital of two million francs and with Edouard Sandoz as the first chairman of the board. At this point, the company was fortunate in its selection of managers and chemists to replace the founders; it was these people who, over the next 30 years, provided the company with direction and enabled it to expand. On the technical side, Arnold Steiner and Melchior Boniger developed and produced new products such as sulphur and azo dyes. Two talented sales managers, Werner Stauffacher and Georg Wagner, built a worldwide sales organization that expanded up to and even through World War I.

Although the company was fortunate in the appointment of its managers, it had many misfortunes, particularly from 1903 to 1909 (known among insiders as the "seven lean years") when serious consideration was given by members of the board to the possibility of a merger or even liquidation. Prices for manufactured goods kept falling while those for raw materials increased. There were very expensive patent litigations with competitors as well. However, by 1910 profits began to increase again, reaching one half million francs in 1913, the year after the company's shares first appeared on the Basle Stock Exchange.

The First World War, and Switzerland's isolation, resulted in some intriguing, and later profitable, opportunities for Sandoz. Germany prohibited all exports and, as a means to this end, blocked transit traffic so that everything from fuel to raw materials was in short supply. Wood, transported to Sandoz's plant in horse drawn carts, was used instead of coal throughout the war. Intermediates, which had formerly been imported, were now blocked, but buyers somehow managed to get those purchased in England and the United States into Switzerland. The company's own chemists were able to produce the others. After the war, the world chemical market that had formerly been dominated by the Germans was soon open to competition.

Sandoz profited under these circumstances. It purchased the Rothaus estate in Muttenz, just in case land was needed for expansion. In 1918, to circumvent the protectionist legislation in other countries which, in turn, inhibited Sandoz's international expansion, Sandoz, Ciba, and Geigy formed the Association (Interessengemeinschaft) of Basle Dyestuff Manufacturers. They used this association primarily to establish jointly owned factories in many countries, although they also pooled profits to ensure that none of the members would be forced to declare bankruptcy. The original charter of the Association was for 50 years, but it was amicably dissolved after 33. In 1911 Sandoz had established its first subsidiary in England, and in 1919 established another in New York. In Switzerland the technical departments were restructured by Dr. Hermann Leeman (later president of the company from 1952 to 1963). The previous organization had been a system under which any chemist might be assigned to work simultaneously in research, manufacturing, and application. According to the restructuring, these three functions became separate departments, with the addition of a patent department.

A difficult period of time was again experienced during the early 1920's when a crisis in the textile industry caused a recession in the dependent dyestuffs industry. The workforce was at first put on part-time employment, but in 1921 nearly 30% of the employees had to be laid off. By 1929 business had been severely affected. However, partly due to the protection afforded by the Association, and partly to the company's lead in research and development, Sandoz was able to set up numerous subsidiaries around the world providing a protective network against the failure of any one subsidiary. More significantly, the company embarked on a program of diversification into chemical agents for use by the textile, leather and paper industries, and later for the agricultural industry. Research in these areas produced industrial cleansers, soaps, softening agents, mercerizers, bleaches and, after World War II, fungicides, herbicides, insecticides and rodenticides.

The most interesting part of the company's diversification program began with the establishment, under Dr. Arthur Stoll, of a pharmaceuticals department. Already well-known for his work on chlorophylls, Dr. Stoll now became world famous for the development of a process for the isolation and for the discovery of the importance of ergotamine, an alkaloid of the rye fungus called ergot. The products developed from ergotamine were numerous and sold steadily, so that the pharmaceuticals department gave stability to the company's sales.

When World War II started Sandoz Ltd., as it had been named in 1939, was financially secure with fully stocked warehouses, production sites and sales agencies throughout the world. Transportation of supplies would not be the problem it had been during the previous war, as supplies were now stocked near company plants. Fuel alone remained a problem. Mr. Leeman is credited with having advised the purchase of an old brown-coal mine. This purchase was finalized and, mining 18,000 tons of fuel for itself during the war, the company had solved its fuel problem. As soon as the war was over the Muttenz site was put to use, with a large plant for chemical and agrochemical production being built there. Little is known of Sandoz's contribution, if any, to either side's war effort, but from 1933 to 1948 company profits increased from SFr48 to SFr253 million.

The international postwar expansion did not exclude Sandoz. The company's only difficulty involved increasing production to keep pace with demand. In 1949 Professor Stoll was promoted to managing director. New headquarters were built which altered Basle's skyline. In addition, automation was introduced in the production facilities. And in 1964 annual sales surpassed one billion francs for the first time. Each of the three divisions, including dyes, pharmaceuticals, and chemicals, prospered individually. The dyes division created dyes for the new plastics, paints and synthetic fibers now in demand, as well as the new foron dyes for polyester, and dyestuffs for mass dyeing.

The developments within the pharmaceuticals division caught the world's attention. Sandoz concentrated heavily on its recently discovered synthetic compounds for the treatment of mental disease and migraine. Most of the products developed were based on ergotamine and included such drugs as Methergin, which stopped post partum hemorrhage, and Gynergen, which when injected early enough relieved the pain of migraine headaches. Certainly the most famous of these drugs was Delysid, also called LSD 25. In 1961 the company's Jubilee Volume proudly reported the drug's ability to cause "disturbances in the perception of space and time, depersonalization and color hallucinations" and that "it was destined to play a great role in experimental psychiatry." Research in the hallucinogen called mescaline, derived from the Mexican peyote cactus, and in psilocybin, derived from certain mushrooms, was also aimed at producing drugs which might be used in conjunction with psychotherapy and, in particular, psychoanalysis.

Although the use of Delysid was strictly controlled, and issued only to authorized research centers, within fifteen years of its discovery in 1942 it was being produced illegally all over America and Europe as a "recreational drug." The consequences of a large number of people across the Western world experiencing what the Jubilee Volume referred to as "model psychosis" from LSD have yet to be fully understood. The company quickly curtailed its research into hallucinogens, but it will always be remembered as the company which "invented acid."

The late 1960's and early 1970's continued to be a period of growth for the company; sales doubled from SFr1,977 million to SFr3,616 million. The massive size of the company required further organizational revisions. As a result, an executive committee took over management. In 1968 the dyes and chemicals divisions were amalgamated and a new agro-chemical division was created. The company's diversification also continued during this time. In 1967 a merger with Wander Limited of Berne added a nutrition department. Two years later, the takeover of Durand & Huguenin eliminated a neighboring competitor in dyes manufacturing. A hospital supply business was acquired and its activities combined, during 1976, with those of Rhone-Poulenc in a joint venture. These acquisitions and mergers were engineered by one of the few non-chemist presidents of the company, Carl Maurice Jacotett, a lawyer's son from Neuchatel who had studied theology and philosophy before going into business. During his short presidency, from 1968 to 1976, the workforce increased from 6,345 to over 33,000 people, making Sandoz one of the world's largest pharmaceutical companies.

The oil crisis of 1973, and the consequent rise in prices for raw materials and energy, dramatically affected Sandoz and other manufacturers who could not possible raise the prices of products high enough to cover costs. In 1975 a five year recession began, which led to another review of company structure, this time to reduce overhead and streamline organization. A steady reduction in the number of personnel and a firm control of wage increases helped to decrease losses. Continued diversification and acquisitions soon increased both equity and profit. Sandoz entered the seed business with the acquisition of Rogers Brothers and Northrup King Company (U.S.A.) and Zaadunie B.V. (Netherlands). In 1982 Wasa (Sweden) was acquired, Sodyeco and Zoecon (U.S.A.) in 1983, and Master Builders (U.S.A.) in 1985, the last introducing the company into yet another market, that of chemicals for the construction industry.

By 1975 a department of ecology and safety had been set up in Basle to establish and supervise guidelines throughout the company and its holdings. An effort to develop products with low environmental impacts was also initiated. However, Sandoz has recently received bad publicity for an environmental disaster at one of its Basle plants. Near the end of 1986, when the company was celebrating its centennial, a large amount of toxic chemicals spilled into the Rhine River killing fish and shore life from Switzerland through West Germany to The Netherlands. The public's demand for legislation to ban the production and sale of 129 dangerous chemicals may or may not be satisfied. However, it is undoubtedly the case that some restrictions, even if self-imposed, will have an effect on the company's chemical production.

Sandoz entered 1987 with sales over SFr8 billion, profits over SFr500 million, and an equity of more than SFr4.5 billion. In regard to the future, Sandoz's president, Dr. Marc Moret, has said that the company will continue its strong commitment to research and development. As Sandoz embarks on its second century, the remaining question is what to acquire next.

Principal Subsidiaries: Sandoz lists over 130 subsidiaries worldwide.

SANKYO COMPANY, LTD.

2-7-12
Ginza, Chuo–ku, Tokyo 104
Japan
03-562-0411

Public Company
Incorporated: 1913
Employees: 5,444
Sales: ¥243.1 billion (US$1.210 billion)
Market Value: ¥166.4 billion (US$829.2 million)
Stock Index: Tokyo Osaka Nagoya Fukuoka Niigata
Sapporo

Sankyo is Japan's second largest pharmaceutical company. It also ranks as one of the nation's oldest and most comprehensive drug companies. Sankyo's current participation in developing innovative drugs has led to a demand for the company's products not only in Japan but also in foreign markets around the world.

While living in the United States Dr. Jokichi Takamine discovered a digestive enzyme and called the product Taka-Diastase. In order to import and sell the digestant in Japan, a company under the name of Sankyo Shoten was established in 1899. Contracting a sales agreement with Parke, Davis & Company, a United States drug firm, the product was manufactured in the United States, imported to Japan, and then distributed by Sankyo Shoten. Three years later, in 1905, the company began manufacturing Taka-Diastase in Japan. To augment production Sankyo's first plant was constructed in Shinagawa, Tokyo in 1908.

Other items were soon added to the product line. Dr. Umetaro Suzuki's vitamin B1 discovery in 1910 was marketed under the name Oryzanin. A cough depressant by the name of Brocin and a disinfectant called Oxyfull were added to Sankyo's product line in the early 1900's. By 1913 the growing business was reorganized as a joint stock company and incorporated as the Sankyo Company, Limited. Dr. Takamine assumed the title of president. Later achievements included the production of salicylic acid, used as a mild antiseptic or pain reliever and Dr. Hata's development of Arsaminol, an arsphenamine used as a treatment for syphilis and other infections.

In the 1920's production expanded into new areas. The Wakodo Company, established as a subsidiary, became an industry leader in infant care products. During this period Sankyo also initiated the research into and production of agricultural chemicals and enzymatics. Even the production of yeast for bakers was incorporated as a product item in 1932.

The Japanese pharmaceutical industry experienced unprecedented growth in the post-war years due to a new sense of health consciousness. In particular, worldwide breakthrough discoveries in medicine resulted in antibiotics amounting to over 10% of Japan's total pharmaceutical production by 1963. Japanese pharmaceutical companies, however, did not actually participate in these discoveries; meaningful patent protection laws were significantly absent, making innovation subject to pirating. For this reason companies, allotting negligible amounts of money for research and development, depended on their foreign counterparts for innovative drugs. More recent industry developments have led· to foreign companies seeking out Japan's expertise in antibiotics; in the interim, however, Sankyo played a major role in importing antibiotics.

Through a new licensing agreement with Parke, Davis & Company, Sankyo imported Chloromycetin, the tradename for antibiotic chloramphenicol. By 1950 Sankyo gained the necessary technical expertise from its foreign licensor to begin manufacturing Chloromycetin domestically. By 1966 this drug accounted for 80% of Sankyo's sales in antibiotics. As Japan's sole manufacturer of this popular pharmaceutical, Sankyo built a vast reserve of cash earned on large profits.

The establishment of the National Health Insurance system in the 1960's was not only important to Sankyo, but to the Japanese pharmaceutical industry at large. Under the new system patients were required to pay a fraction of prescription fees while the government assumed the majority of costs. Moreover, the system encouraged the generous prescription of medications since doctors profited from the difference between the official reimbursement price set by the Ministry of Health and the actual price for which the drugs were purchased. For this reason, the drug industry became one of Japan's most profitable industries. By 1961 the industry's annual growth rate reached 21%.

Sankyo benefited from these changes. Profits increased nearly 18% in 1963 due to the increase in sales of external medicines, food products, central nervous system drugs, and farm chemicals. Biotamin, a newly developed vitamin B1, recorded a monthly average sale of ¥150 million, making the sale of antibiotics and vitamins nearly half Sankyo's annual sales. At this time, the company's food product line included a non-caloric synthetic sweetener and a fruit juice clarification enzyme. Sankyo's agricultural chemical division produced more products than any other pharmaceutical company in Japan. Tachigaren, a soil fungicide and seed disinfectant developed by Sankyo, was awarded the Okochi Prize in 1969.

Sankyo's entry into foreign markets paralleled its growth in business. Joint ventures with overseas companies grew to include projects with AKZO, a pharmaceutical company in Holland, Miles Laboratories and Air Products, two companies in the U.S., and pharmaceutical companies in Taiwan and India. Biotamin was well received on foreign markets and Cytochrone-C (sometimes spelled Titochrome C or Tytochrome C), an innovative new drug for the treatment of high blood pressure, was scheduled to be marketed abroad. This innovation marked one of Sankyo's first major discovery that did not employ technical assistance from foreign companies.

The sale of Biotamin, Chloromycetin, and the newly developed Cytochrome now accounted for Sankyo's three major products. Biotamin became a popular item in overseas markets and Sankyo provided manufacturing knowledge to companies in France and Portugal. While the basic patent right for Chloromycetin was scheduled to expire in 1966, Sankyo's market preeminence through affiliated patents mitigated the effects of losing exclusive marketing rights to this drug.

To facilitate growth two new plants were scheduled for construction. The Fukuroi site was chosen for the manufacture of soft drinks and seasonings and the Hiratsuka plant would house the manufacture of pharmaceuticals. Due to the fact that the main plant at Shinagawa was operating at capacity, the Hiratsuka site was designated the new main plant.

Further changes in the pharmaceutical industry resulted in Japanese companies significantly increasing their research and development expenditures. The enactment of the 1976 patent protection laws marked an important date for the industry. Rather than depending on their foreign counterparts to develop drugs, Japanese pharmaceutical companies could invest in research without fear of pirating. Furthermore, an altered pricing system, placing newly developed drugs at a premium, suddenly made innovative drug research a highly lucrative business. The products of this research not only served to benefit the quality of domestic health care, but also began reversing the flow of technology from West to East.

Sankyo actively participated in this new development. During the 1970's Sankyo took a leading role in the development and production of drugs for the nervous system. The tranquilizer, Serenal, was developed with the intention of serving a growing number of people who experienced the stressful demands of modern lifestyles. The company submitted patent applications for the manufacture of the tranquilizer in over 40 countries. Furthermore, upon the completion of the Hiratsuka plant, the company alloted funds to significantly increase research and development expenditures. Meanwhile, several other promising drugs existed in the development stage.

Prior to this new emphasis on research and development, a vast trade deficit existed between the large number of imported pharmaceuticals and the comparatively smaller number of drugs exported. Even as late as 1982 almost 80% of the drugs sold in Japan continued to be manufactured abroad or domestically with technology developed overseas. Recognizing the potential in developing a drug export trade, the government implemented further industry incentives with the 1980 Pharmaceutical Affairs Act of 1980. This act extended from three to six the number of years a company is ensured exclusive licensing rights with foreign companies. The new atmosphere encouraging industry export, coupled with the rising cost of research and development, compelled pharmaceutical companies to aggressively pursue foreign markets. Since millions of dollars were now spent on the development of a single drug, companies looked to foreign licensing as an attractive means of recovering investments in research and development.

Sankyo strengthened its long involvement with foreign markets during this period. In addition to the overseas introduction of Serenal, a joint venture in India was established. Uni-Sankyo supplied bulk medicine to the Indian market and also exported products to Asia and Africa. By 1986 Sankyo's licensing program and joint ventures grew to include agreements with Sandoz in Switzerland, Glaxo Holdings in the United Kingdom, and Du Pont, Squibb, and Upjohn in the U.S. In a recent move to heighten the company's presence in the United States, Sankyo opened an office in New York.

Of the many drugs developed in Japan and actively pursued by foreign companies, a new family of highly effective third-generation antibiotics represented the drugs most in demand. Sankyo participated in the development and distribution of these medicines through the sale of Cefmetazon, a cephamycin-allied antibiotic, that will be sold in the United States through a license agreement with Upjohn. Of similar technological importance is Sankyo's involvement in the development of drugs called enzyme inhibitors. By discovering the inhibitor for the enzyme instrumental in the synthesis of cholesterol, Sankyo developed a drug to inhibit heart disease. As licensee to Sankyo, Squibb's salesforce is waiting for the results of clinical testing in the United States before marketing this cholesterol reducer.

Other lucrative products developed or marketed by Sankyo included an anticancer agent introduced in 1984. Sankyo acquired the rights to sell this agent, called Kurestin, which was developed by the Kureha Chemical Industry. In addition, Captoril, a promising anti-hypertensive drug, promises a source of future income.

As the company expanded its business through innovation and overseas market penetration, the pharmaceutical industry underwent major changes. The per-capita drug bill by 1983 reached $95. To combat accusations of excessive profiting and to reduce the burden of national expenditures, official drug prices were reduced by over 50% and patients were required for the first time to pay 10% of examination costs. As a result, nationwide drug production deceased for the first time since World War II and profits were negligible. Sankyo's net profits in relation to sales dropped from 3.9% in 1982 to 3.64% in 1983. Research and development expenditures, nevertheless, continued to increase. For this reason, by 1985 profits did not increase from the previous year despite the successful market introduction of Kurestin and a new anti-ulcer agent. Despite the changing configuration of the National Health Insurance system, Sankyo will remain influential in both domestic and foreign markets.

Principal Subsidiaries: Sankyo Organic Chemical Co.; Nippon Nyukazai Co. Ltd.; Sankyo Chemical Inc.; Kinjo Yakuhin Co. Ltd.; Dewa Yakuhin Co. Ltd.; Sankyo Pharmacy Co.; Kyushu Sankyo Co.; Utsunomiya Chemical Co.; Fuji Flour Milling Co. Ltd.; Nihon Dia-Valve Co. Ltd.; Meguro Chemical Industry Co. Ltd.; Sankyo Foods Co.; Hokkai Sankyo Co. Ltd.; Wakodo Co. Ltd.

SANOFI GROUP

40 Avenue George-V
75008 Paris
France
(1)47-23-01-50

Public Company
Incorporated: 1973
Employees: 21,286
Sales: FFr 14.5 billion (US$1.91 billion)
Market Value: FFr 4.827 billion (US$639 million)
Stock Index: Paris

The history of the Sanofi Group begins with the 1973 merger of a number of cosmetic, health care, and animal nutrition firms into a corporate subsidiary of the French state-owned Elf Aquitaine oil company. This undertaking marked an ambitious program of diversification that created a state enterprise capable of competing in the health care industry on an international scale. Today Elf Aquitaine maintains a 63.2% interest in the company. Sanofi grew from a moderate concern into the second largest pharmaceutical company in France; it was chosen to coordinate all Elf Aquitaine's biotechnology activities.

René Sautier assumed the responsibility of running both the Sanofi Group and Atochem, Elf Aquitaine's recently acquired chemical operation. Although Sautier's position was subordinate to that of Michel Pecqueur, the president of the state-owned oil company, a program of rationalization restructured the company into five decentralized divisions and allowed Sautier a certain degree of independence in running the company. Much of Sanofi's success is attributed to his business acumen.

Although Sanofi was created in order to form an amalgamation of companies, it was only in 1979 that all its pharmaceutical activities were regrouped under a single organization. This tactic represented an effort to strengthen research activities and overseas market penetration. Three companies including Labaz, Parcor and Galor, all previously affiliated with Sanofi, were now wholly absorbed, and for the first time Sanofi gained a separate stock market quotation through the issuing of public stock on the Paris exchange.

While currency exchange fluctuations caused Parcor to register a profit decline in 1979, that same year Sanofi reported an overall increase in company profits. The following year Sanofi increased its holdings by merging with the Clin-Midy division of CM Industries, a manu-

facturer of pharmaceuticals, veterinary, chemical, medical-surgical and food products. This action significantly increased Sanofi's research and development budget and expanded the company's size by 50%. Sanofi now ranked among the leading pharmaceutical companies in France.

By mid-1980 Sanofi's profits reached unprecedented heights. A 56% increase over the previous year's figures was attributed to benefits gained from the reorganization. Although the sale of pharmaceuticals accounted for a majority of Sanofi's activities, a significant increase was generated from the sale of cosmetics and veterinary products.

Between the years 1978 and 1982 Sanofi's international sales improved by 275%. By gaining access to two of the world's most important markets, the United States and Japan, Sanofi's overseas activities generated nearly half of the company's consolidated revenues. A joint subsidiary formed in 1981 with the U.S. based American Home Products company was followed by a similar agreement established with the Japanese groups Meiji-Seika-Kaisha and Taisho. Through the operations of these joint ventures $104 million was generated from the sale of just three drugs. In addition to expanding pharmaceutical operations, Sanofi was successful in tripling its foreign sales in the cosmetics division.

Sanofi's research and development activities, supported by a 34% increase in expenditures during 1982, produced a number of potentially profit making drugs. Among the products undergoing clinical testing were an anti-arrhythmic, a third-generation cephalosporin and a treatment for certain forms of cancer. In addition, research proceeded on a psychotropic drug and on an anti-convulsion drug. Sanofi's pharmaceutical research takes place at five laboratories in France as well as at facilities in Brussels and Milan.

One of the most important developments in Sanofi's research activities was the 1983 inauguration of a biotechnology center in Labège, the largest of its kind in France. At the same time the company acquired a minority interest in Entremont, a dairy products firm engaged in researching biotechnological applications. In particular, Sanofi was interested in Entremont's investigation into the production of milk compounds through biotechnology. These two developments marked an important step towards building Sanofi's future position as the biotechnological center of all Elf Aquitaine's activities.

In addition to advances in the field of biotechnology, Sanofi continued its program of acquisition. In 1983 Choay, a pharmaceutical company specializing in the area of venous thrombosis, was acquired by Sanofi. Sanofi now gained access to a new line of important pharmaceuticals. The animal health division also increased its holdings through the acquisition of Institut Ronchèse, a manufacturer of vaccines and other veterinary medicines.

By 1984 Elf Aquitaine's increasing biotechnological activities compelled the state-owned oil group to reorganize its company structure. Chairman Pecqueur transferred most of Elf Aquitaine's activities in this area, from health care to agricultural products, to the control of Sanofi. While Atochem, Elf Aquitaine's chemical subsidiary, maintained control of biotechnological activities in the area of industrial products, Sanofi solidified its role as the center of Elf Aquitaine's innovative technologies.

As a first step in creating Sanofi Elf Bio Industries, Sanofi merged with Rousselot, a gelatine, protein, and glue producer in which Elf Aquitaine formerly held a majority interest. Through the action of this merger, Elf Aquitaine's stake in Sanofi increased to 62%. To increase the financial standing of Elf Aquitaine's biotechnological developments, Pecqueur announced plans to double the company budget in this area to $22 million.

By 1985 Sanofi posted an annual sales figure of FFr15 billion. This marked an significant increase from the FFr2 billion generated yearly during the 1970's. Yet Sautier, commenting on the weak European market and price controls for pharmaceuticals on the domestic market, initiated a program of internationalization in hopes of recouping investments on foreign markets. Two important targets of this overseas market penetration were the U.S. and Japan. Thus, a sizeable amount of cash savings was set aside for any acquisition suitable for this expansion. Additional foreign acquisitions included a Brazilian subsidiary of Revlon, as well as a 50% interest in a South Korean company.

Other significant events which occurred during 1985 included the introduction of the first low molecular weight heparin. This product, developed by the Choay subsidiary, marked a significant step in the prevention of thromboembolic diseases. In addition, Diagnostics Pasteur, a subsidiary in the area of medical equipment, released the Elavia test for detecting the antibody to LAV, a virus associated with AIDS.

Two successful U.S. acquisitions following Sautier's plans for expansion included the Dairyland Food Laboratories, a Wisconsin dairy company, and Dahlgren, a large crop seed producer. Both companies managed a successful biotechnology program. The following year a 35% bid for Barberet & Blanc, an Antibes-based specialist in carnations and gerberas, further strengthened Sanofi's operations in plant and genetic technologies. Barberet & Blanc, a small family operation located on the French Riviera, had developed expertise in "in vitro" plant-growing techniques as well as creating new carnation varieties resistant to deadly fungus.

Thus, through a series of acquisitions of small but high-technology concerns, Sanofi has gained expertise in the area of biotechnological processes in food additives, dairy products and large crop seed sectors. Some 25.8% of Sanofi's 1985 sales resulted from products developed out of these technologies. In addition to benefits from this product orientation, Pecqueur's plan to internationalize Sanofi's operation resulted in 50% of the company's sales being generated from foreign markets.

During the same time that successful biotechnological products emerged from Sanofi's laboratories, the sale of pharmaceuticals continued to account for 46.8% of group sales. In the United States, the Food and Drug Administration recently approved the marketing of Cordarone, a major anti-arrhythmic drug. This drug is marketed through a joint venture between Sanofi and American Home Products.

As Sanofi continued to broaden its activities and generate profits through the sale of health care products, cosmetics, additives, seed sectors, and animal pharmaceuticals, the company implemented an employee profit-sharing program. Recently, a company savings plan and a share purchase option completed this program.

The future of Sanofi depends on the company's continuing success in developing innovative products and penetrating foreign markets. The company today maintains a strong position as a leading French pharmaceutical concern. As Sanofi's diverse activities suggest, the company will continue to hold this position in the years to come.

Principal Subsidiaries: Centre Pharmaceutique Européen (C.P.E.); Centre de Recherches Clin-Midy (C.R.C.M.); Diagnostics Pasteur; Diphac; Distrithera; Farmadis; Francis SpA (Italy); Francopia; Labaz GmbH (West Germany); Labaz-Sanofi NV (Belgium); Laboratoires Choay; Laboratoires Clin-Midy; Laboratoires Labaz; Laboratoires Lafarge; Laboratoires Millot-Solac; Laboratoires Pharmygiène; Laboratoires Robilliart; Laboratoires Roland-Marie; Laboratoires Sauba; Laboratoires Labaz (Spain); Midy Arzneimittel GmbH (West Germany); Midyfarm; Midy SpA (Italy); Moehs (Spain); Opiaramon; Parcor; Produits Dentaires Pierre Rolland; Prophac; Sapchim; Sempa Chimie; Sintebras (Brazil); Ceva Laboratories Inc. (USA); Cie Rousselot; C.M. Aromatics Inc. (USA); Dairyland Food Laboratories Inc. (USA); Dahlgren (USA); Eurogat; Fondoirs de la Moselle; Méro-Rousselot-Satia; Rousselot Bénélux (Belgium); Rousselot Ltd (U.K.); Sanofi Elf Bio Industries; Société Anonyme de Récupération Industrielle & Agricole (S.A.R.I.A.); Création et Diffusion Internationale de Parfumerie (C.D.I.P.); Omnium de la Parfumerie de Luxe (Parfums Van Cleef & Arpels); Parfums Charles Jourdan; Parfums de Molyneux; Roger & Gallet; Sanofi Beauté; Secta Laboratoires de Cosmetologie Yves Rocher; Stendhal. Sanofi also has subsidiaries in the following countries: Brazil, Mexico, Netherlands, Switzerland and the United Kingdom.

R.P. SCHERER

2075 West Big Beaver Road
P.O. Box 160
Troy, Michigan 48099
U.S.A.
(313) 649-0900

Public Company
Incorporated: as Gelatin Products Corporation in 1944
Employees: 2,400
Sales: $167 million
Market Value: $131 million
Stock Index: NASDAQ

The R.P. Scherer Corporation manufactures encapsulation products for the pharmaceutical and nutritional health industries. With a long history of industry expertise, the company commands over 60% of the worldwide market for soft elastic gelatin capsules. Scherer similarly produces a major share of two-piece fused hardshell capsules, popular among drug companies as pharmaceutical encasements. In recent years, however, competition from drug companies manufacturing their own capsules has reduced Scherer's hardshell business. The increasing demand for soft-shell capsules, principally through the growing vitamin market, partially compensated for the decrease in sales. Acquisitions outside the area of capsules also served to broaden the earnings base. Yet internal management disputes and unreliable markets have prevented the company from regaining its former position. Only with the recent introduction of MaxEPA, a highly regarded fish-oil capsule, has there been hope of improvement.

Robert Pauli Scherer was born in 1907, the son of an eye specialist. In 1930 he received a degree in chemical engineering from the University of Michigan. After a brief period of employment in a pharmaceutical company Scherer resigned and devoted himself to developing a capsuling machine. Working in his father's basement metal shop for three years, Scherer eventually patented his machine and revolutionized the pharmaceutical industry. A model of Scherer's rotary die process machine is presently on exhibit at the Smithsonian Institution in Washington.

Using his newly invented machine, Scherer formed the Gelatin Products Company. Immediately successful, the new company soon secured business with a growing list of pharmaceutical manufacturers and in 1947 adopted its present name. While claiming nothing he had ever accomplished could be considered "work," the young company leader found himself managing a multinational corporation with subsidiaries operating in Canada, Europe, and South America. Always searching for new products to encapsulate, Scherer's entrepreneurial spirit led him to experiment with such unusual mediums as insect repellent and lighter fluid.

At the age of 53 Scherer died, passing company leadership to his son Robert P. Scherer Jr. From that time until the mid-1970's the operation of the Scherer corporation seemed secure. Its virtual monopoly on the soft gelatin market increased the company's stock to a high of $40 per share.

As events would soon show, however, Scherer's control of the market became threatened when the rising cost of gelatin compelled pharmaceutical companies to seek less expensive ways to compress their products. Similarly, an expected sales increase resulting from the company's own product, Vitamin E, did not materialize, and a strong dollar overseas had adverse effects on the nearly 51% net income derived from foreign operations. In response to a plunging stock price and a leveling of profit margins earned from encapsulation, Robert Scherer embarked on a program of diversification through acquisition. In search of purchases which provided access into the growing medical equipment market, Robert Scherer's company soon acquired Storz Instruments Company and Surgical Mechanical Research Inc. This latter purchase incurred, for the first time, a long-term debt totaling $1.6 million.

In addition to medical equipment, the company also operated a hair care business. To augment growth in new areas, Robert Scherer hired a management team recruited from large industry competitors. James A. Cormack, former chairman of Johnson & Johnson's Ethicon division, joined Scherer in 1976 as president and chief operating officer. Other recruited executives came from such diverse companies as Miles Laboratories and American Natural Resources Company.

By 1977 Scherer's gelatin capsule operations, increasingly dependent on the nutritional health industry, experienced a revived market participation. Some 73% of the gelatin capsule sales came from vitamins produced in Scherer facilities. Similarly, profits from the Storz Instruments subsidiary exhibited a profit increase of 23% in the third quarter. A 1979 purchase of First Texas Pharmaceuticals included the addition of new products for encapsulation as well as an opportunity to market vitamins for the first time under a brand name. In an apparent show of company support, Robert Scherer purchased 22,600 shares of his company's stock which increased his personal holdings to a 10% interest. Several other Scherer executives followed the chairman's lead in purchasing common shares.

Despite such a promising outlook, internal disputes soon exposed numerous company problems. An unfortunate purchase of a hardshell capsule factory formerly owned by Scherer officer and director Stephen Lukas was beset with problems concerning inventory and quality control. Consequently, an unusual countersuit between Lukas and the company alleging such unseemly occurrences as price-fixing and delinquent payments resulted in an acrimonious exchange of accusations. While all claims were eventually dropped, the damage surrounding company credibility lost numerous customers.

Not only was the company reputation damaged during this period of upheaval but discontentment about Robert Scherer's job performance surfaced in an unusual public announcement. Although the holdings of the chairman and his family together comprised a 74% interest, and a noticeable portion of Scherer's board of directors were family members, nevertheless Robert Scherer was not protected from being ousted by the board. Increasingly critical of Scherer's allegedly indifferent attitude towards the business, including the frequent use of the company's Lear Jet for non-business purposes, the board took action by arranging to split the company in two. The board gave Robert Scherer control of a small privately held company comprised of Scherer's medical equipment and hair care subsidiaries in exchange for the chairman's 21% interest. Since these subsidiaries represented a 21% contribution to sales and earnings, the agreement offered a fitting solution to a growing quandary.

One person especially in favor of the company split was Heiner Koepff, the 49% owner of Scherer's West German gelatin supply operation. In 1979 nearly half of Scherer's profits were generated from the West German facility. Thus Robert Scherer's program of diversification resulted in a business entirely unlike and separated from the foundation laid down by his father. Peter R. Fink, Wharton graduate and son-in-law of the later Robert Pauli Scherer, now assumed the role of president while Wilbur Mack assumed the vacated chairman's position.

As president Fink turned his attention to the immediate rectification of the company's earnings figures. He invested $70 million in upgrading and expanding operations and increased Scherer's research expenditures to $2.5 million. Although confronting a growing long-term debt, nevertheless the company registered a 6% earnings gain on sales between 1981 and 1982 and an almost doubled profit margin. Wall Street analysts suddenly showed renewed interest in the company.

No sooner had the new management started attending to business, however, when the company was forced to fight a takeover attempt. In July of 1982 FMC Corporation, a large Chicago conglomerate, offered $22 a share to acquire 4.1 million or 52% of the total common stock. While some of the founding family members showed interest in the bid, Fink successfully prevented any such action; his proposal requiring an 80% shareholders approval for a merger to occur received ratification.

After the merger episode had subsided, Scherer stock began trading at 13 times earnings; this was in response to the excitement generated from an agreement with Merck to develop suppositories for drugs previously available in injection form. At the same time, the company benefited from a bizarre and tragic event. In September of 1982 Johnson & Johnson, a hard-shell capsule customer of Scherer's for years, became the victim of product sabotage when it was discovered that the extra-strength analgesic Tylenol had been laced with cyanide. While only 15% of Scherer's total volume was generated from the hard-shell business, nonetheless, Johnson & Johnson's decision to stop manufacturing Tylenol did have its repercussions for the encapsulation manufacturer.

Due to the fact that soft one-piece capsules represented a virtual tamper-proof casing, Scherer's market position as the largest manufacturer of soft elastic gelatin capsules took on new significance. Should pharmaceutical companies search for new protective methods of packaging their products, Scherer was prepared to meet the increased demand. Wall Street analysts, recognizing the company's potential expansion, began predicting an annual growth rate of 15-20%. By 1984, however, disappointment replaced optimism. Citing extenuating circumstances surrounding the strength of the dollar on the foreign market and initial expenditures invested to start new facilities in Utah and the United Kingdom, Scherer reported a 42% decline in earnings for the first quarter.

While the financial community became increasing skeptical, Fink remained confident in his company's future. The initially large investments for the new facilities decreased. Furthermore, the market for health and nutritional products, now comprising a major portion of Scherer's sales, was said to be increasing. Some 80% of Scherer's sales were in the soft capsule business, of which 75% were used to encapsulate vitamins and health foods in the U.S. Approximately 25% of total sales came exclusively from the sale of Vitamin E.

Fink's optimism, however, could not prevent the mounting skepticism. The nutritional market, inherently more cyclical than the pharmaceutical market, represented a fluctuating array of trends. When pharmaceutical companies began to rely less and less on Scherer's products and more in favor of synthesizing their own tablet form of vitamins, Scherer was forced to depend more heavily on the health food market. Yet when, for example, the Vitamin E trend collapsed, Scherer experienced a 43% decline in sales of their formerly popular product.

In regard to ethical drugs, a 1986 estimate reported that only 2% of all oral medications were packaged in soft-shell capsules. The Tylenol tragedy did not, as was hoped, increase demand. With Johnson & Johnson's decision to sell the analgesic in tablet or "caplet" (capsule-shaped tablets) form only, the announcement all but extinguished predictions of a soft-shell encapsulation increase. Hard-shell capsules remained more popular among pharmaceutical companies. Yet intensified competition between companies manufacturing hard-shells, including the recent participation of the Warner-Lambert Company and Eli Lilly, resulted in a price-cutting war. After this intense competition had ended, Scherer posted a $3.5 million charge against earnings for closing its new Utah plant. Another area of significant vulnerability surrounded Scherer's 70% volume on foreign markets, making the company increasingly subject to fluctuations in monetary rates.

In order to remedy such glaring deficiencies company management implemented a consolidation program. By reducing overhead costs and diversifying production through the recent purchase of the Lorvic Corporation, a manufacturer of dental supplies, Scherer hoped to regain lost ground. Fink's plan to make further acquisitions in the health care field indicated a shift away from dependence on the sale of soft-shell capsules. Furthermore, the remaining encapsulation business was now directed toward the proprietary and over-the-counter drug markets such as cough-syrups and antacids as well as prescription drugs. Research on freeze-dried tablets that dissolve quickly represented a potential new market for children and the elderly.

Scherer's most promising product, however, is the innovative new health food product called MaxEPA. This encapsulation of fish oil is generating a good deal of excitement in the medical community as numerous studies now reveal that a diet high in fish oil can help prevent hardening of the arteries as well as offer relief to sufferers of a wide array of ailments, including arthritis and cancer of the breast and prostate gland. Receiving rather encouraging support from 13 medical journals, the widening recognition of MaxEPA's potential therapeutic qualities sent Scherer's stock up to $15 per share from a low $9 per share.

With the company poised to introduce MaxEPA in numerous overseas markets, industry analysts presently believe that in a short matter of time Scherer will be arranging its worldwide business with a major drug company. This future partnership could signify Scherer's maturity as a fully integrated health care company. In a significant shift from just several years prior to MaxEPA's market entrance, Scherer's stock is now recommended as a high-growth investment. It will be a few years, however, before the new nutritional supplement's true market potential is revealed.

Principal Subsidiaries: The Lorvic Corporation; Franz Pohl GmbH (W.Ger.). R.P. Scherer also has subsidiaries in the following countries: Argentina, Australia, England, France, Italy, Canada, Brazil, Hong Kong, and Korea.

SCHERING AG

SCHERING A.G.

Postfach 650311
1000 Berlin 65
Germany
(030)-468-0

Public Company
Incorporated: 1871
Employees: 23,884
Sales: DM4.167 billion (US$2.146 billion)
Market Value: DM3.885 billion (US$2.001 billion)
Stock Index: Zurich Basle Hamburg Berlin Munich
Hanover Dusseldorf Geneva

Schering AG, the West German chemical and pharmaceutical company, operates worldwide production facilities for agrichemicals, fine chemicals, electroplating, industrial chemicals, and ethical drugs. Although, at the present time, the company maintains a formidable presence in the United States, this was not always the case. Schering's initial U.S. operations fell victim to the vicissitudes wrought by two world wars. The company's first U.S. subsidiary was dissolved during World War I and after being re-established in 1929 was then seized by the Alien Property Custodian during World War II. To Schering's chagrin, the subsidiary was eventually sold to private investors and severed completely from its parent company. Having no other recourse, the West German firm occupied itself with rebuilding its virtually decimated facilities at home. In the years that followed, however, Schering has regained its lost markets and has expanded to become a worldwide industry leader.

In 1851 on Chaussee Strasse 21, now located in East Berlin, Ernst Schering opened his pharmacy called Gruene Apotheke. Twenty years later the founder incorporated the business as a stock company. The first specialty product to emerge from Chemische Fabrik auf Actien was a medication for gout. In 1902 the company's operations expanded into the area of electroplating. To facilitate the process of plating decorative metal, Chemische Fabrik manufactured baths and electrolytes. Later these operations would expand to include the production of complete electroplating equipment as well as chemical compounds and machinery for printed-circuit manufacture.

At the turn of the century the German company also expanded into such diverse areas as industrial and laboratory chemicals. In the 1920's agrichemicals were added to

Chemische Fabrik's product line and by the end of the decade the company made its first foray into an area that would become increasingly important in the future, namely, female sex hormones. A 1937 merger with a coke and chemical company resulted in the adoption of the current name, Schering AG.

As Germany entered World War II, Schering was widely recognized as a world leader in innovative chemical production and the extent of its operations. Exploratory work on sulfonamides and X-ray contrast media, as well as steroid hormones, positioned the company on the cutting-edge of new technologies. Schering's successful innovations matched their expanding operations; some 30 foreign subsidiaries operated worldwide.

This expansion, however impressive, experienced some setbacks. One of Schering's oldest subsidiaries, Schering & Glatz, was established in the United States in 1876 to distribute Schering products such as diphtheria medication. Yet during World War I, because it was affiliated with Germany, the operation was dissolved. By 1929 the company had reestablished its presence in the U.S. and created the Schering Corporation in New York City. This subsidiary specialized in recent developments in hormone research as company scientists became experts in synthesizing steroid drugs. These products accounted for 75% of total sales for the U.S. subsidiary.

Their expertise eventually led to the development of anti-conceptional products in the 1960's. During World War II, however, their coveted knowledge became the object of espionage reports. Believing Schering research excelled in the area of corticosteriods, or hormones extracted from the renal cortex, a secret investigation conducted by the U.S. government led to the accusation that the company used this knowledge to develop highly sophisticated drugs to further the Nazi cause. Pilots under the alleged influence of a corticosteriods were said to withstand extremely high altitudes which enabled them to fly well above the anti-aircraft flak.

As it happened, corticosteroids was one area where Schering research was not highly developed, and only after the espionage reports made their accusation did Schering begin intense experimentation in this area. Charges of military collusion with the Nazi regime aside, nothing could have prepared the company for its losses suffered after World War II. All of the company's foreign holdings disappeared. In the United States Leo Crowley, acting as the Alien Property Custodian, seized assets to all German properties, including Schering's, within its borders. Almost ten years later, the Attorney General annnounced that the company's U.S. subsidiary was for sale and a group of private investors headed by Merrill Lynch made the purchase. Schering Corporation, as a completely independent business in the U.S., went on to post impressive financial gains with the discovery of two new corticosteriods that became the envy of the drug industry.

As if this were not enough, Schering AG also lost valuable patents as well as the rights to its name in all 30 of its subsidiaries. The Schering factories in Germany were all but destroyed. The remaining employees searched the rubble for machine parts and usable wreckage. After three years of scavenging the company miraculously released a finished product, yet soon afterwards their property was seized in East Germany by the new Communist regime. Nevertheless, in several years Schering succeeded in rebuilding its operations and eventually bought back many of its former subsidiaries.

One former holding that was never repurchased was Schering Corporation in the U.S. As industry observers watched the newly formed company increase its financial success, the management at Schering AG realized, not without remorse, that its former subsidiary had grown too large to purchase back. Access to the use of the shared trademark in the U.S. remained an issue of contention between the two Scherings; in 1983 their grievances, as yet unresolved, led them to engage in a protracted legal battle. Berlex, Schering AG's pharmaceutical subsidiary in the U.S., allegedly infringed on Schering-Plough's (the company formed from the merger between Schering Corporation and a manufacturer of proprietary drugs) trademark. The German company contends, however, that the company namesake which stems from founder Ernst Schering is widely recognized in Europe. Barring its use in the U.S., as Schering AG states, subjects the company to unfair competition. Although litigation affords public scrutiny of the West German company's role in World War II (including the admission that two executives were Nazi party members), Schering AG denies it ever produced war materials.

These difficulties notwithstanding, Schering AG proceeded with its program of reconstruction. Manufacturing such products as lice powder and penicillin, the company soon exhibited signs of revitalization. Interestingly enough, by retaining headquarters in the city of its origins, Schering was the only company with a multinational orientation to remain in Berlin after World War II. Board members committed to staying in their home city influenced the company's decision not to move. Main headquarters presently stand three blocks from the wall that separates East from West Berlin. For security reasons Schering maintains a second corporate office, along with all its business records, in Bergkamen—200 miles west of the East German border.

A major step in Schering's postwar expansion involved pioneering work in anti-conceptional products. Using their expertise in steroid research, the company introduced the first birth-control pill on the European market in 1961. By 1972 the company was responsible for supplying over 50% of the world market, excluding the U.S., with hormonal contraceptives. The success of the "Pill," however, represented only one segment of Schering's diversified product line. Of the $383 million in total sales, 65% came from a broad spectrum of pharmaceuticals, including 30% from X-ray contrast media and psycho-pharmaceuticals, 12% from phyto-pharmaceuticals, 18% from specialty industrial chemicals, and 5% from electroplating. While the Berlin facilities remained the center of all research, administrative, and some packaging operations, fifty subsidiaries operating throughout Europe, Asia and Latin America finished and distributed Schering products worldwide.

One area of company pride involved the emphasis placed on quality research. Expenditures increased to 11.2% of sales and one of every 10 employees worked on research and development. With such an impressive performance record, the West German company prepared to make yet another entrance into the coveted U.S. market. By purchasing a 50% interest in Knoll Pharmaceutical, a New Jersey firm, Schering was just beginning. Between the years 1976 and 1980, five U.S. subsidiaries joined Schering's holdings. The companies purchased included Nepera Chemical, Sherex Chemical, Berlex Laboratories (renamed from Cooper Laboratories), Chemcut and Nor-Am Agricultural Products. The acquisitions directly corresponded to Schering's five divisions: a unit for drugs, industrial chemicals, fine chemicals, agri-chemicals, and electroplating.

Horst Kramp, a 51 year old executive board member of the six-man Vorstand, directed Schering's U.S. operations. The unusual management structure, which did not allow a position for president, placed Kramp on equal footing with his five colleagues. While each Vorstand member holds a distinct function, all policies, dating back to the 1950's, were decided on by consensus. Kramp, whose administrative abilities includes marketing and sales, joined Schering in 1964 as a domestic sales manager. In the 1960's he travelled to the U.S. to work at Nor-Am only later to return to Germany and become the only nonchemist on the Vorstand.

By 1982, while Schering sales grew by 4%, the U.S. subsidiaries registered negligible earnings figures. The Vorstand members remained unconcerned, citing the time necessary before the companies could turn a profit. An effort to remove unprofitable operations became the next step. Facilities manufacturing such products as adhesive chemicals or sulfuric chemicals were sold. In the meantime, $22.5 million was appropriated for the expansion of the U.S. subsidiaries, including the building of new headquarters and research facilities. Similarly, management at Schering has been conscientious in the provision and support of research expenditures for the U.S. holdings, investing as much as 14% of the company's gross income.

The West German company's meticulous and well-planned reappearance in the U.S. reflects a detailed program of long-term planning. Executives remain laconic about predicting future success; unlike many U.S. companies Schering AG rejects the usefulness of short-term profit goals. One subsidiary, however, with decidedly ambitious goals is Berlex. Its president and chief executive officer, Robert E. Ivy, has hopes that the subsidiary will become one of the top competing pharmaceutical companies in the United States.

Principal Subsidiaries: ASAG Inc., USA; Berlinmed Ltda, Brazil; Industrias Farmaceuticas Alemanas, S.A.; Productos Quimicas Naturales, S.A., Mexico; Berlimed (Pty.) UC Ltd., So. Africa; FBC Holdings (Pty.) Ltd. Chloorkop, So.Africa; Asche AG, Germany; CHEBAG Beteiligungs-AG, Germany; Chemiewerk, Curtius Verwaltungs Gesellschaft mbH, Germany; Germapharm GmbH, Germany; REWO Chemische Werke GmbH, Germany; Scherax Arzneimittel GmbH, Germany.

SCHERING-PLOUGH

One Giralda Farms
Madison, New Jersey 07940
U.S.A.
(201) 577–2000

Public Company
Incorporated: July 28, 1970
Employees: 23,800
Sales: $2.399 billion
Market Value: $5.901 billion
Stock Index: New York

Frank Brown, Schering Corporation's first U.S. chief executive officer, at one time rejected a deal with Revlon to market certain Schering pharmaceuticals as high-volume items. This would have meant high-profile marketing through television advertisement. Brown's successful but conservative business style, however, did not make him receptive to the combination of drug and cosmetic advertisement and marketing. Interestingly enough, it is this very combination of drugs and consumer products that has contributed to the longevity of the company.

In 1971 Abe Plough, the founder and marketing genius behind Plough, Inc., a proprietary drug and consumer product company, approved of a merger between his company and the Schering Corporation. The 80 year old man, with a colorful entrepreneurial history, was looking for a successor to run his firm. A solution was found in his unlikely friendship with Willibald Hermann Cozen, the German-born chief executive officer of Schering.

It was Cozen who actually designed the merger and, as a result, became the chief executive officer of Schering-Plough. The merger combined the comprehensive manufacturing of Schering's antibiotics, antihistamines, and other ethical drugs, and Plough's household consumer products with names as common as Coppertone and Di-Gel. While Schering-Plough is not generally recognized at the present time as a heavyweight in the pharmaceutical industry, it has enjoyed steady growth and comfortable profit margins throughout its history.

Long before the merger the Schering Corporation began as a drug manufacturer in Berlin. In 1894 the company started to export diphtheria medication to the United States and an American branch of the German company opened in New York in 1929. Until the end of World War II a sex hormone accounted for up to 75% of Schering's sales. The event of the war, however, changed the course of the company's history forever. Frank Brown, a New Deal lawyer with no previous experience in the pharmaceutical business, was dealt a hand that would bind his future to Schering.

Brown's legal career involved participating in government projects during the 1930's. He joined the Federal Deposit Insurance Corporation, a creation of Roosevelt's New Deal policies, and acted as legal counsel to Leo Crowley. During the war the United States seized assets of all German owned businesses operating within the country. Leo Crowley was appointed the Alien Property Custodian and Brown was given the job of managing the Schering Company. He immediately filled vacated executive positions with associates from the FDIC. In 1943 Brown was formally appointed president of Schering and under his direction the company soon proved a financial success.

Brown realized that research and development was the key to a company's success in the industry. To this end Brown immediately began the development of a research department and, like many other pharmaceutical companies, conducted talent searches for those scientists and students on the verge of new discoveries or noteworthy scientific contributions from medical colleges and universities across the country. Established in 1944, the Schering student competition fund has found many worthy recipients over the years.

At a time when the post-war years marked a reduced demand for sex hormones, the newly expanded research department could not have found a better moment to discover a new antihistamine. Marketed as a proprietary drug (a drug directly advertised to consumers) under the name Trimeton, and marketed also as an ethical drug (a drug only advertised to health care professionals) under the name Chlor-Trimeton, the antihistamine marked a turning point in the history of the Schering Corporation. By 1951 profits had quadrupled with sales reaching over $15 million.

That same year the U.S. Attorney General put the company up for sale. A syndicate headed by Merrill Lynch outbid other prospective buyers and proceeded to sell $1.7 million of stock to the public. However, the investors asked Brown to remain on as company president. He accepted the offer and directed Schering to even greater profitability through the discovery of Meticorten and Meticortelone, two new corticosteroids that became the envy of the drug industry.

The discovery of synthetic cortisone dates back to 1949 when Merck & Co., an industry competitor, first made public its historic findings. Yet while the wonder drug's discovery rightfully belonged to Merck, the process for synthesizing the drug conflicted with several other patents for producing sex hormones. Schering was the owner of one of these patents, and through a "cross-licensing" agreement the company gained access to information about cortisone production.

Soon after production of cortisone began, Schering and its competitors raced to discover an improved line of the drug that would eliminate some of the side effects associated with the steroid. They all hoped to modify the cortisone molecule to find a more effective drug and, at the same time, eliminate hypertension, edema (water retention), and osteoporosis (a bone disease), all side effects connected with cortisone therapy.

Using microorganisms to convert one chemical into another Schering scientists discovered a drug in 1954 that fit the desired guidelines. Clinical testing of the drug brought excellent results. But when Schering was confronted with the prospect of fullscale production, the company realized it had no previous experience in manufacturing by fermentation, the process used to make the new drug. So Schering first tried fermentation in a 150 gallon stainless steel container and later in a 1000 gallon and finally a 22,000 gallon fermenter. This last container used $100,000 worth of cortisone and a few hundred gallons of microorganisms. Having established a successful manufacturing technique, Schering released Meticorten in 1955 and Meticortelone soon afterwards. Almost unbelievably, sales for the drugs jumped to over $20 million by the end of the year, $1 million more than total sales in 1954. By the end of 1955 sales for these drugs reached a new high of almost $46 million and by 1957 exceeded $80 million.

Other pharmaceutical companies manufacturing steroids immediately attempted to profit from Schering's success. Lederle, Upjohn, and Merck all developed similar drugs, and soon Schering found itself embroiled in lawsuits over patent and licensing rights. Merck's product arrived on the market only three months after Schering's, but because Schering had spent heavily on advertising it managed to retain a major share of the market. Furthermore, while Schering was forced to arrange licensing agreements with other companies, Brown demanded what other companies regarded as overpriced royalty payments. Although this initiated new litigation, it also allowed Schering profits to remain at an all time high while agreements were worked out in time-consuming court processes.

Unrelated to Schering's historical development, a consumer product company in Memphis, Tennessee won recognition for its own success story. Abe Plough, founder of Plough, Inc., began his career in marketing in 1908. He borrowed $125 from his father to create a concoction of linseed oil, carbolic acid, and camphor and sold the potion door-to-door from a horse-drawn buggy as a cure for "any ill of man or beast." Plough's inventory expanded to include a mysteriously named C-2223. This relief for rheumatics became an immediate success; after four years Plough had sold 150,000 packages.

What he later claimed to be his shrewdest purchase occurred in 1915: Plough paid $900 for the inventory of a bankrupt drug company. He netted a profit of $34,000 peddling the stock in the back woods where there was still a large demand for oxidine chill tonic. In 1920 he bought the St. Joseph Company of Chattanooga, Tennessee and began manufacturing children's aspirin. By the 1950's Plough realized that the huge sales figures for the popular aspirin was partially due to children taking overdoses of the product. To prevent this from reoccurring Plough ordered child-proof caps added to the aspirin at a time when safety regulations were almost nonexistent. He went on to purchase 27 other companies during the course of his

lifetime. In addition to being talented at making important acquisitions, he was also very adept at marketing: 25% of all income from sales was routinely spent on advertising. And the success of radio advertising, in particular, convinced Plough to buy five AM and FM stations. In Plough's own community he is best remembered for his philanthropic contributions. Upon his death in 1984 at age 92, flags throughout Memphis were lowered to half-mast.

Years before his death, however, the unlikely friendship between Willibald Hermann Cozen, chief executive officer of Schering in 1966, and Abe Plough, was the antecedent to a company merger. At 17, after graduating from Kaiserin Augusta Gymnasium in Koblenz, Cozen began working for Schering A.G., the German parent company. When the U.S. company was seized during World War II and eventually sold to the public, Cozen became the chief executive officer of the new independent company.

When the merger of the two companies was finally completed, combined sales reached $500 million in 1971. This marked the fastest sales growth for any merger in the industry. Yet despite an earnings multiple of 46, Cozen, in his typically reserved style, spoke guardedly of continued expansion. The sales for Garamycin, an antibiotic introduced in 1966 as a treatment for urinary tract infections and burn victims, reached $90 million by 1972. This income accounted for almost half of both companies' growth for the period. The large profits, however, ironically concealed in an "Achilles' heel." Garamycin's patent, scheduled to expire in 1980, signified the beginning of generic competition and the end of Schering-Plough's control over the manufacturing of this drug. The sound of competitors footsteps could be heard following closely behind; Cozen's cautious remarks on continued expansion were well founded.

In 1974 reduced sales for Garamycin already effected company profit margins. In 1975 the return on equity dropped from 31% to 27% and stock dropped 10% from the previous year. Schering-Plough endured the ensuing decline in profits and increased funding for research and development. In 1974 several newly released drugs accounted for $100 million in sales. Similarly, Maybelline cosmetics, a Plough subsidiary, introduced a new line of makeup. The "Fresh and Lovely" cosmetic product line promised to catapult Maybelline into a competitive full-line makeup company.

These moves, however, were not remedies for the ailing profit margin. In 1979 Richard J. Bennet took over as chief executive officer and continued to try and solve the Garamycin conundrum. Schering-Plough has historically been a conservative company with no major debts, maintaining an asset to liability ratio of 2.2 to 1 and a $350 million cash excess after seven acquisitions. Yet Schering-Plough continued to look like a "one product" company because of its heavy reliance on Garamycin sales.

In 1979 40% of all profits, or $220 million, was generated solely from Garamycin. Cozen's ineffective attempt to establish company profitability on the sales of a variety of drugs rather than a single product became Bennet's new challenge. Under his management the company released Netromycin, an antibiotic more potent that Garamycin but with fewer side effects. To ensure continued sales of

Garamycin when the patent expiration date arrived, the company announced a discount plan to entice former customers into future contracts. Meanwhile, large sums of money continued to pour into the research facilities in the hope of discovering new drugs. And finally, in order to bolster consumer product sales, Schering-Plough purchased Scholl, Inc. (a well established footcare company) for $30 million.

Unfortunately, all these maneuvers had only a limited effect on the company. Since doctors had already perfected methods for controlling Garamycin's side effects, they actually preferred to wait for generic and therefore cheaper versions of the drug rather than switch to Netromycin. Similarly, despite $75 million a year spent on research and development, no new discoveries were announced. Furthermore, while Scholl Inc. had yearly revenues of $250 million and earnings of $12 million, its profits had barely kept pace with inflation since 1973.

Of all the disappointments, however, one consumer product did exhibit strong signs of financial success. Maybelline, once known as a manufacturer of "me-too" or imitation products, matured into an aggressive full-line cosmetic company. Bennet claimed in 1980 that Maybelline held 34% of the mascara market and 24% of the eye shadow market. Estimated sales for 1980 jumped to $150 million from $75 million in 1976.

On May 28, 1980, the day the patent on Garamycin expired, Schering-Plough executives appeared unperturbed. In fact, stock on that day jumped from 39⅛ to 45. Not only was Netromycin on the market, but 80% of the hospitals who were previous customers of Garamycin had signed up for the deferred discount plan. More importantly, however, Schering-Plough had paid $12 million for a 14% equity stake in a Swiss genetic engineering company called Biogen. Schering-Plough's interest in the company was significant because it provided them with worldwide rights to the synthesis of human leukocyte interferons using recombinant DNA. The possibilities for using the interferon, a chemical produced naturally in the body to fight viruses, were immense. It was hoped that the synthetic drug could be used to treat anything from cancer to the common cold. Moreover, gene-splicing promised to be highly cost-effective; this new method, on the cutting-edge of biotechnology, could produce the same amount of purer proteins in a week than old methods could in a year. Here was the long awaited breakthrough.

By 1985, in an uncharacteristic move, Schering-Plough had made a more expensive investment in biotechnology than any of its competitors. Expenditures surpassed $100 million. In 1982 Schering-Plough, having reached an agreement to spend $31.5 million over 10 years, formed a partnership with West Berlin politicians to establish a research institute on genetic engineering in Berlin. At the same time plans were announced to build a fermentation and purification plant in Ireland to market the first commercial interferon. Schering-Plough also purchased another biotech firm in Palo Alto, California called DNAX Research Institute. Clearly, Schering-Plough announced to the world where the future of its company resides.

Even with all this fanfare, biotechnology proved considerably less spectacular than originally hoped. Intron A, an alpha-2 interferon released in Ireland, is a useful treatment only for a rare form of cancer called hairy-celled leukemia rather than against more common tumors of the breast or lung it was originally expected to treat. And although R.P. Luciano, vice-president of Schering-Plough, cured his own cold with an interferon nasal spray, side effects such as nasal stuffiness and bloody mucus were generally commonplace.

While Schering-Plough was the first to market a commercial Interferon, patent problems with competitors gave Hoffmann-La Roche rights to market alpha interferons in the U.S. On June 4, 1986, the Federal Drug Administration approved Schering-Plough's Intron A and Hoffmann-La Roche's Rofeon=A for the U.S. market. Projected market sales for the interferon is $200 million in the U.S. and $150 million in Europe. More conservative estimates project only $50 million a year sales worldwide.

While interferon has yet to make a significant mark in Schering-Plough's history, the company continues to enjoy a comfortable profit margin. A conservative fiscal policy is the basis of the company's success. Even if breakthrough technologies are not forthcoming in the near future, the $616 million in cash left over from the Garamycin profits in 1982, the lack of long term debts, and the high credit rating promise to keep Schering-Plough financially sound for years to come.

Principal Subsidiaries: Schering Corp.; Artra Cosmetics, Inc.; Schering Antibiotic Corp.; Plough Export, Inc.; Plough Trading Corp.; Schering Realty Corp.; Schering Pharmaceutical Corp.; Schering Export Corp.; White Laboratories, Inc.; The Emko Company; Plough Inc.; Plough Sales Corp.; Plough Advertising Corp.; Maybelline Co.; Maybelline Sales Corp.; Plough Broadcasting Co., Inc.; Coppertone Corp.; Schering Industries, Inc.; Schering Transamerica Corp.; Plough Laboratories, Inc.; Sheroid, Inc.; Schering Biochem Corp.; Manati Holdings Corp.; Burns-Biotec Laboratories Inc.; Wesley-Jessen, Inc.; Scholl, Inc.; Schering-Plough Investments, Ltd. Schering-Plough also has subsidiaries in the following countries: Australia, Brazil, Canada, Chile, India, Luxembourg, New Zealand, Puerto Rico, South Africa, Switzerland and the United Kingdom.

SEARLE

G.D. SEARLE & COMPANY

P.O. Box 1045
Skokie, Illinois 60076
U.S.A.
(312) 982-7000

Wholly-owned subsidiary of Monsanto Company
Incorporated: April 10, 1908
Employees: 15,000
Sales: $1.24 billion

Four generations of management at G.D. Searle, a pharmaceutical company based in Illinois, descended from the company founder. From 1888 until 1977 the company's highest executive positions passed from father to son. In the intervening years Searle grew from a small Chicago company to an important industry contributor.

When John G. Searle became president and chief executive officer of the company in 1936 he inherited a business started by his grandfather, Gideon D. Searle, in 1889 on the corner of Ohio and Wells streets in Chicago. Initially the small firm sold a wide variety of products. Yet under the direction of Gideon Searle the company soon reduced its product line to highly specialized and profitable items. In order to develop these items, Searle's laboratory research concentrated on innovating drugs for the treatment of cardiovascular diseases, central nervous system and mental disorders. In 1941 company headquarters moved to Skokie, a northern Chicago suburb. One of the most successful products to emerge from Searle laboratories was the 1949 discovery of Dramamine, the first motion sickness pill. In 1966 Dramamine remained a leader in motion sickness medications; today the drug has become a household staple.

By 1960 the company's reputation as a manufacturer of quality drugs corresponded to its growing profits. Increasing sales by one to two million dollars annually, the company had sales in 1960 of $37 million. Searle's former successes, however, offered no indication of the large profits to come with the introduction of one of the most revolutionary drugs of the decade—oral contraceptives. Under the direction of Dr. Albert L. Raymond, head of Searle's research department since the 1930's, pioneering work with synthetic hormones in 1951 led to Searle's development of Enovid, the first contraceptive of its kind to reach the market. Just four years after "The Pill's" 1960 introduction, the company's sales figure increased 135% to $87 million with a 38% return on stockholder's equity.

Moreover, almost half of the $73 million in total assets existed in cash and marketable securities, long-term debts were virtually non-existent, and Searle stock traded at 34 times earnings.

Despite three stock offerings between the years 1950 and 1966, the Searle family held a 46% interest. Upon John G. Searle's death in January of 1978, the family had become one of Chicago's wealthiest with an estimated net worth of $250 million. John Searle's descendents were not only destined to become wealthy men, but his two sons would eventually assume positions of company leadership. Interestingly enough, however, in early 1963 a proposed merger between G.D. Searle and Abbott Laboratories, arranged by the two company presidents, was said to be inspired by John Searle's lack of confidence in his offspring's business acumen. The golfing partners arrived at a tentative agreement over drinks in Chicago's exclusive Old Elm golf club. According to the arrangement, no plans were made to include top management positions for John Searle's sons.

The proposed merger never occurred. One explanation cited John Searle's realization that the amount of bickering on the golf course between him and Abbott's George Cain was an indication of how poorly they would get along as business partners. A more likely explanation pointed to the complications arising from the younger Searles' sizeable holdings in the merged company. At any rate, John Searle went into semi-retirement during 1966 in the wake of the aborted merger; he assumed the title of chairman and his two sons moved into executive positions. William L. Searle became vice-president of marketing while his older brother, Daniel Searle, a Harvard Business School graduate, succeeded his father as president with the additional title of chief operating officer. Daniel now inherited the leadership of one of the most profitable pharmaceutical companies in the industry.

Yet even before the leadership had changed, a number of industry developments foreshadowed an era of growing problems. Competition from other manufacturers producing birth-control pills, including Upjohn and Johnson & Johnson, reduced Searle's share of the market. Furthermore, a concern about side effects associated with oral contraceptives slowed management's decision to increase production and prolonged the Food & Drug Administration's market approval of Searle's Ovulen, a second generation contraceptive. And finally, the increasing cost of research, coupled with its unpredictable results, meant that company scientists were unable to bring to fruition a new product line. By 1965 earnings decreased to $23.2 million, down from $24.2 million the previous year; while industry competitors posted net profit increases of 19.4%, Searle's dropped 4.4%.

It was under these circumstances that Daniel Searle initiated an ill-fated policy of acquisition. Purchasing a dozen small companies with a wide variety of products, including nuclear instrumentation, medical electronics, and veterinary and agricultural products, Searle operations diversified into unfamiliar waters. While industry competitors made similar purchases outside the business of ethical drugs, few companies were less fortunate in their choices. By 1977 the company reported a $95 million write-off; sales had increased to $844 million yet the return on equity dropped from 50% to 11%. The acquisitions outside the area of pharmaceuticals accounted for 57% of sales but only 13% of profits. G.D. Searle's profitability decreased sharply.

In addition to a new generation of family executives, the year 1966 brought Dr. Raymond's tenure as director of the research department to an end. Dr. Thomas P. Carney, former director of research at Eli Lilly, succeeded Raymond as head of the Searle laboratories. Carney's background in both chemical engineering and organic chemistry, as well as his success in developing profitable agricultural chemicals for Lilly, promised to facilitate the development of new innovative drugs for Searle. Aldactone and Aldactazide, two diuretics used in the treatment of hypertension, and Flagyl, a drug to cure reproductive tract infections, awaited and received FDA approval.

By 1971 an estimated 80% of company profits resulted from sales of pharmaceuticals other than oral contraceptives. The previous year profits had actually risen 12%, but only on the company's ability to use its Puerto Rican operations as a tax shelter; while profits before taxes actually fell $5 million, Searle's tax bill was reduced by $9 million. Long-term debt was now reported at $49 million.

By 1973 sales of Aldactone and Aldactazide alone contributed to 18% of revenues, surpassing revenues generated from the birth control pill for the first time. Research at Searle laboratories, with expenditures increased 33%, led to the development of a new artificial sweetener. Discovered seven years earlier, aspartame's unique structure resulted from the combination of two naturally occurring amino acids. While the company awaited approval to market the product as a food additive, production was planned using the expertise of Ajinomoto, a Japanese company experienced in the manufacture of amino acids. With cyclamates removed from the market and questions circulating about the safety of saccharin, Searle's new product represented the possibility of a large market share. In addition to developing the sweetener, the company moved into new areas of birth control. A copper intrauterine contraceptive was introduced in England and awaited market approval in the United States.

The FDA approval of Aspartame's use as a table top sweetener, as well as a food additive in a number of items, resulted in a minor victory for Searle. Sugar prices had recently tripled and the market for low calorie products began expanding significantly. Furthermore, aspartame lacked the bitter after taste of saccharin with only about .5% of the calories of sugar. Yet several disadvantages in the new product caused industry analysts to remain cautious in their assessment of aspartame's future. The projected cost for the new sweetener was many times greater than that of saccharin, and its short shelf life—it loses its sweetness after several months—precluded any speedy acceptance in the profitable soft drink market. Bottlers would resort to a more stable, less expensive product before they would turn to aspartame. Nevertheless, Searle persevered in the test marketing of Equa, the consumer brand name for its new product.

Despite such hopeful products emerging from Searle laboratories, many industry analysts remained skeptical about the company's future. Diluted earnings, resulting in part from the company's numerous acquisitions, aspartame's unclear future, and the expiration of a number of important patents all contributed to this attitude. Yet, apart from these problems, Searle management could never have been prepared for the series of blows dealt them in a televised hearing involving an FDA challenge to their reputation. A Senate subcommittee on health, headed by Edward Kennedy, sought to investigate allegations about questionable research surrounding the safety of both Aldactone and Flagyl. A 1972 article in the *Journal of the National Cancer Institute*, with the support of numerous subsequent independent studies, cited an increased incidence of lung tumors in mice treated with Flagyl. Similar cancer risks, not evident in Searle's research data, appeared in tests of Aldactone.

While conceding that "clerical errors" had occurred, Searle categorically denied any surpression of lab tests. The company did embark on a public relations campaign to improve its image of social responsibility. The price of company stock, however, dropped from around $25 to $15 per share as analysts estimated that sales of Flagyl, Aldactone, and Aldactazide would be reduced by half its previous volume. With a new strategy of public relations, Searle's problems were hardly over. Only several months later in December of 1975, in an unprecedented move, the FDA suspended permission to market aspartame based on an audit of Searle's new drug applications filed since 1968.

The FDA actions resulted in more delays than actual damage. While labels warning about cancer risks appeared on the investigated products, sales for Aldactone and Aldactazide actually rose 24% on the last quarter of 1975; Flagyl's increased 12%. Aspartame remained under investigation only to receive market approval seven years later. The $29 million already invested in its production was left in abeyance.

While the assault on Searle's corporate integrity marred the company's public image, internal problems threatened to disrupt its very operations. By 1977 money borrowed in the U.S. against the $420 million saved in the Puerto Rican tax shelter, translated into an interest payment of $24 million; earnings from this same tax haven amounted to only $17 million. This, in turn, had some affect on overall company earnings so that shares gaining $1.56 in 1975 gained only $.57 in 1977.

To remedy the situation, an outsider was called in to assume control of the company. Donald H. Rumsfeld, a former congressman, presidential aide and defense secretary, agreed to step in as president and chief executive officer ending the four generations of family management. Daniel Searle, moving up to chairman, had met Rumsfeld 15 years earlier and had actually supported him in his congressional election bid. Their friendship gave impetus to Rumsfeld's mid-life career change. While refusing to state he had given up public life for good, the accomplished politician rose to the challenge of correcting the company's numerous problems.

Searle's turnabout was almost immediate. By repatriating Puerto Rican dollars, bringing in new staff, selling unprofitable divsons, and announcing a massive write-off, Rumsfeld cleared the way for major changes in the company. An optical retailing business, under the name Vision Centers, represented a profitable new acquisition. In 1978 this retailer of eyeware contributed $91 million; a five year estimate placed contibutions at $400 million. While long-term debt now stood at $350 million, Vision Center's profits were necessary to improve the company's performance.

By 1981 Searle reported the second-highest profit margin among 30 leading U.S. drug firms. Furthermore, an FDA announcement ended aspartame's years-old struggle to win market approval. Rumsfeld's revitalization of the research department through the infusion of $100 million promised a new line of pharmaceuticals from anti-ulcer medication to treatments for herpes. An aggressive policy of licensing and joint ventures generated income to supplement the research costs. Long term debt was reduced to $89 million as Pearle Vision Centers moved to the top of the optical retailing business.

In 1983 a 39% drop in earnings during the first quarter resulted in a decision to sell the eyecare subsidiary. Ostensibly, the generated income would help improve pharmaceutical research which had yet to produce an extremely lucrative drug. Drug research, however, did not produce the sought after profits; instead, industry analysts were surprised as sales of aspartame reached record break-ing figures. As a tabletop sweetener and a food additive in cold cereals and dry drink mixes, sales between 1981 and 1982 increased from $13 million to $74 million. As the product was ready to enter into the immensely profit-able soft drink market, Searle invested $25 million to expand production in the U.S. Once Searle received the expanded FDA approval, carbonated drink companies lined up to secure contracts. By the end of 1983 virtually all major bottlers became Searle customers, and with the marketing plan to print the consumer name on all pro-ducts using the sweetener, NutraSweet became a household name.

Despite this expansion after 17 years of testing, fears of aspartame's side effects were not completely dispelled. One study cited changes in behavior after large quantities of carbohydrates and aspartame had been ingested. Woodrow Monte, director of the Food Sciences & Nutri-tion Laboratory at Arizona State University, along with several consumer groups challenged NutraSweet's safety by pointing to its production at high temperatures of methanol, a compound associated with poisoning. The FDA reasserted aspartame's safety by pointing to the existence of methanol in fruit juices.

While sales of aspartame reached $336 million in 1983, the continuing question of its safety was not the only issue to concern Searle management. The sweetener's patent was scheduled to expire in 1987; forthcoming competition threatened the sales figure. Even more disturbing was the lack of new pharmaceuticals. One observer facetiously predicted that the company, like its new campaign to sweeten sodas exclusively with NutraSweet as opposed to a combination with saccharin, was in danger of itself becoming 100% NutraSweet.

As sales of NutraSweet edged towards its maximum market potential the Searle family, still holding a 34% interest, announced its decision to diversify its holdings.

Industry analysts, noting the timing of this announcement, predicted that the family could collect as much as $75 per share. Four months after the announcement, not one company had tendered an offer. The financial burden of running NutraSweet's huge operations, as well as an Internal Revenue Service investigation into allegedly deficient taxes paid by the Puerto Rican subsidiary, deterred potential suitors. Liability for the contested taxes was estimated at $381 million.

Only two months later, the announcement to withdraw the offer to sell Searle seemed to indicate a new effort to remain independent. The company purchased 7.5 million of the Searle family shares, reducing their holdings to 21%. Rumsfeld succeeded Daniel as chairman, which further solidified independent management. No sooner had these events taken place when Monsanto chemical company announced it planned to purchase Searle for an agreed $2.7 billion. For Monsanto the acquisition repre-sented an end to its long search for an ethical drug company, but also included the added advantage of generating income to aid its maturing agricultural chemical products. Searle's experienced marketing and sales staff, its experience in biotechnology, and the attractive market potential of its new antiulcer, called Cytotec, would be highly beneficial to Monsanto.

Along with Searle's attractive qualitites, Monsanto also accepted the drug company's tax dispute liabilities. What the new parent company did not expect, however, was to become embroiled in another controversy. Searle's Copper 7, the most widely used intrauterine contracep-tive, was suddenly accused of causing pelvic infections and infertility. Even more disturbing was a major business magazine's disclosure that the company distorted infor-mation surrounding the IUD's safety. The final version of the company's lab results did not state that some cells in the test monkeys developed "premalignant transforma-tions," but only referred to cell modification. Similarly, Searle's human test results may not have accurately reported the rate of pelvic inflammatory disease developed by users. On January 3, 1986, facing 305 pending lawsuits out of a total 775 claims, Searle withdrew the Copper 7. While continuing to defend the product's safety, the company stated it acted to preempt growing litigation costs; Searle's defense already cost $1.5 million. While the company claims it won eight of the ten trials, the specter of events surrounding the Dalkon Shield, an IUD manu-factured by A.H. Robins, expedited Searle's removal of the device from the market. Litigation costs surrounding alleged infections and ailments suffered by users of the Dalkon Shield eventually caused the company to reorgan-ize under the Chapter 11 bankruptcy clause.

Hundreds of new claims are now being filed against Searle, including shareholders charging the company with failing to inform them of the IUD suits. The cost to the company could run into the millions. While NutraSweet's patent has been extended until 1992, the potential out-come of Copper 7 litigation can hardly be reassuring to its new parent company. The earlier hope of employing Searle's pharmaceutical experience to develop profitable new drugs is sure to be postponed as company manage-ment concentrates on the ensuing court battles.

Principal Subsidiaries: Akwell Industries, Inc.; Dental Health Services of Tampa, Inc.; G.D. Searle Inter-American Co.; LARO, Inc.; SCI Corp.; Searle Cardio-Pulmonary Systems, Inc.; Searle Chemicals, Inc.; Searle Food Resources, Inc.; Searle Optical Inc.; Texas State Optical, Inc.; Pearle Vision Center, Ltd. (United Kingdom). The company also lists subsidiaries in the following countries: Argentina, Australia, Bangladesh, Belgium, Bermuda, Brazil, Canada, Denmark, Finland, France, Greece, Hong Kong, India, Ireland, Japan, Korea, Malaysia, Mexico, The Netherlands, New Zealand, Norway, Pakistan, Panama, Philippines, Portugal, Puerto Rico, Singapore, South Africa, Spain, Sweden, Switzerland, Thailand, United Kingdom, Venezuela, and Zambia.

SIGMA-ALDRICH

3050 Spruce Street
St. Louis, Missouri 63103
U.S.A.
(314) 771-5765

Public Company
Incorporated: 1945
Employees: 2,181
Sales: $215 million
Market Value: $791 million
Stock Index: NASDAQ

Sigma-Aldrich Corporation is the result of a merger between two specialty chemical companies, one which manufactured biochemicals and another which manufactured organic chemicals. While offering divergent products, both companies regarded high-quality products and customer service a priority. The merger, therefore, represented a convergence of business strategy as well as the creation of a diversified product line that ranks Sigma-Aldrich at the top of the specialty chemical industry. In particular, because of the scientific community's involvement in the growing field of biomedical research, Sigma-Aldrich's product catalogue has become a standard issue in pharmaceutical laboratories around the world.

The Sigma Chemical Company was started in 1945 in St. Louis. At a time when sugar was scarce Dan Broida, a biochemist, began a storefront business to manufacture saccharin. The company later went on to produce biochemicals and diagnostic products. And Sigma's customers ranged from hospitals to university laboratories. Scientific fields concerned with the study of life sciences as well as disease diagnostics use biochemicals as the basic substances to develop pharmaceuticals and diagnostic tests.

Aldrich Chemical Company, founded by the Harvard educated chemist Dr. Alfred R. Bader, began manufacturing organic chemicals in a Milwaukee garage six years after Broida established Sigma. Aldrich's first products were those chemicals not offered by Eastman Kodak, a leader in the chemical industry. Bader soon decided that his company could engage in direct competition with larger companies, and he began offering a broad line of organics sold to research laboratories of pharmaceutical companies. The company did exceedingly well and its customer list soon included the likes of Abbott Laboratories and Ciba-Geigy.

The 1975 merger between the two companies matched skill for skill and talent for talent. Broida assumed the role of chairman and Bader took the position of company president. While the combined company interests still remained small compared to those of the larger industry firms, the business acumen of Sigma-Aldrich's management went a long way in securing an impressive percentage of the specialty chemical research market. By 1979 the company laid claim to between 30 and 40% of the $100 million research market. Sales climbed to $68 million representing an annual increase of 15%. Earnings jumped 24% to $9.2 million causing Wall Street analysts to predict a continued growth of 20% a year.

Sigma-Aldrich's marketing success, achieved by neither a large sales force nor expensive advertising outlays, relied on the distribution of catalogues. In addition to advertising products available on a phone-order basis, the catalogue offered (and continues to offer) detailed information about the physical properties of the marketed chemicals. The value of the catalogue as a reference source as well as an advertising tool was evident, and it soon became a company trademark. Initially compiled by Bader in the early 1950's as a one-page, one-chemical listing, the catalogue grew to include 40,000 chemicals. Sigma-Aldrich's small sales force distributed 300,000 free copies of the catalogue in 1979.

The company's reputation among chemists as a manufacturer of quality products matches a distribution network that ensures most orders can be filled in 24 hours. Interestingly enough, in the early years of Sigma-Aldrich's business an average order amounted to less than $100. This indicated a customer profile of academicians or laboratory researchers experimenting with relatively small quantities of chemicals. Although this profile has been altered somewhat due to the increasing pressure to supply bulk commerical chemicals, Sigma-Aldrich fiercely defends its business as first and foremost a service to the research community.

Overseas expansion in the late 1970's found 125 countries purchasing Sigma-Aldrich's products with company subsidiaries operating in Canada, the U.K., Japan, Germany and Israel. Nearly 40% of sales in 1979 resulted from overseas business.

As the company entered the 1980's its growth matched the explosion in the U.S. biomedical research market. Despite such gains Sigma-Aldrich's management, much to the chagrin of some industry analysts, refused to alter the strategy that laid the framework for previous company growth. Rather than set long-term goals or exploit the bulk chemical market as some observers suggested, Broida defended his company's straightforward "opportunistic" policy of keeping pace with state-of-the-art developments in the scientific fields of immunology, microbiology and endocrinology. By supplying chemicals in small quantities to research centers, Sigma-Aldrich's growth and profits corresponded to breakthrough research in the development of pharmaceuticals from recombinant DNA.

Wall Street analysts also criticised the company's B-Line Systems Inc. subsidiary. Manufacturing metal frameworks for industrial plants, the subsidiary was criticised for competing in the business of specialty chemicals on the one hand, and for contributing small profit margins on the other. Despite such criticism, however, the company's lack of long term debt, its sparkling earnings record, and its annual profit increase of 20 to 25% mitigates the seriousness of such complaints.

Upon Dan Broida's death several changes in policy and management affected the company structure. Tom Cori, a nine year Sigma veteran, became company president. Common stock, formerly controlled by a 50% insiders interest, now became more widely held. In 1985, 2.2 million of the 8.68 million outstanding shares were sold for $129.5 million. Most of this stock had been held by relatives of Broida and the sale reduced their holdings to 1.3 million shares. This new figure represented approximately the same interest held by the Bader family.

Of the 2.2 million shares sold the company purchased 500,000. Apparently Bader had been opposed to the company purchase partially on the grounds that $13 million were borrowed to finance the transaction. Company indebtedness now totaled $32.4 million in short-term loans due in part to a $16 million expansion program started in 1980. Some five million shares, on the other hand, were now estimated to be available for trade in the over-the-counter market. Price per share between July and September of 1985 ranged from $60.50 to $71, well over the company's $14 per share book value. A three-for-one stock split was soon in order.

By 1986 some 1.5 million company catalogues circulated yearly. Sigma-Aldrich's orders continued to average less than $150 each; on the other hand company profits totaled $29 million on volume of $215 million. Although president of a company with such impressive achievements, Cori will not be able to rest on his laurels. Limited governmental funds for scientific research as well as the effect of the strong dollar on overseas sales offer some cause for concern. To facilitate expansion by broadening Sigma-Aldrich's product line, the company purchased Pathfinder Laboratories. The new subsidiary, costing $1.5 million in stock during 1984, manufactures radioactive chemicals.

For all the changes brought about by its rapid growth, Sigma-Aldrich remains a chemist's company. Every year 3,000 products are replaced by new ones through customer recommendations. While Broida's home phone number no longer appears in the catalogue, customers are still able to call collect and place orders or simply ask questions about the company's products. In an age of corporate anonymity, an orientation towards servicing customers needs is no mean accomplishment.

Principal Subsidiaries: Aldrich-Boranes, Inc.; Aldrich Chemical Co. (Canada) Ltd.; EGA Chemie K.G.; R.N. Emanuel, Ltd.

SmithKline Beckman
CORPORATION

SMITHKLINE BECKMAN CORPORATION

One Franklin Plaza
Philadelphia, Pennsylvannia 19101
U.S.A.
(215) 751-4000

Public Company
Incorporated: June 29, 1929
Employees: 30,500
Sales: $3.257 billion
Market Value: $6.854 billion
Stock Index: New York Geneva Basle Zurich Paris

SmithKline Beckman, a pharmaceutical company that rose from relative obscurity to become a manufacturer of one of the largest selling drugs in the history of the industry, has entered the 1980's confronting such problems as falling stock prices and decreased earnings estimates. Wall Street analysts have presently become critical of the company that once generated "Tagamania," a phrase coined from the unprecedented performance of the company's ulcer-curing drug called Tagamet.

Long before Tagamet had been developed John K. Smith, along with his partner John Gilbert, opened an apothecary in Philadelphia in 1830. Aside from manufacturing extracts, elixirs, syrups, tablets and pills, the company sold a variety of consumer products, including paint, varnish oil, chemicals, window glass and vials. John K. Smith was later joined by his brother George K. Smith who became one of the earliest advocates of product purity and treatment reliability. He was also one of the first pharmacists to market drugs directly to doctors.

In 1846, during the U.S. war against Mexico, George K. Smith & Company supplied quinine and other pharmaceuticals to U.S. troops. During the Civil War the company's drugs found their way to Bull Run, Antietam and Gettysburg. With the promotion of Mahlon Kline, an employee who moved from bookkeeper to eventual partner in the firm, the company name changed to Smith, Kline & Company. Mahlon Kline's influence in both the company and the industry at large led him to become president of the Philadephia Drug Exchange. By 1887 company sales reached $700,000.

Several years later Smith, Kline & Company merged with French and Richards & Company to become Smith, Kline & French Company. During World War I the newly formed company supplied, among other drugs, 50,000 bottles of aromatic spirits of ammonia to U.S. troops. Smith, Kline & Company pharmaceuticals were also indispensable in the war against the influenza epidemic on the home front. Even as one-third of their own employees suffered from the epidemic, the company efficiently distributed the medication.

By the early 1930's Smith Kline & French (a new name inadvertently adopted when, in the process of reorganization, a comma was accidentally dropped) was on the verge of releasing a new line of pharmaceuticals. In 1932 Benzedine Inhaler, a nasal inhaler, was introduced to the market, and by 1936 company sales were between $8 and $9 million. Then in 1944 Dexedrine, a modified amphetamine, was released.

However, Smith Kline & French's greatest contribution at the time was the development of Thorazine. Using research from Rhone-Poulenc, a French pharmaceutical manufacturer, Smith Kline & French released this drug for use in neuropsychiatry. After an initial display of skepticsm from the psychoanalytic community, Thorazine proved an actual corrective of mental malfunctioning. From 1954 onward, the year the drug was released, the number of institutionalized mental patients decreased significantly.

Despite pioneering psychoactive drugs, and even despite record company sales and earning figures, Smith Kline & French did not fare well in the 1950's and 1960's. No new discoveries promised to replace Thorazine once its patent ran out in 1970. Furthermore, company management seemed divided about the future of the firm while overseas operations remained weak and largely ineffectual. During this period of time hundreds of employees were fired.

By the 1970's a young group of executives emerged to lead the company out of its decline and into a decade of achievement yet to be matched by an industry competitor. Henry Wendt, eventual chief executive officer of the now renamed SmithKline Corporation, joined the company in 1955 with a B.A. in diplomatic history. With overseas responsibilities carrying him to such faraway places as Hawaii, Montreal, Thailand, Hong Kong, what is now called Malaysia, and Japan, Wendt worked his way up through the ranks to become president and chief operating officer in 1976.

The same year, Robert F. Dee, former vice president of the company, was promoted to chairman and chief executive officer. Under the leadership of these two men SmithKline was transformed from a struggling firm into the envy of every industry competitor. Dee's first move was to provide millions of dollars for SmithKline's research and development facilities. Secondly, he increased the overseas sales force from 400 to almost 1500 men. Moreover, Dee reorganized the structure of the company along product lines to facilitate easier marketability.

Most importantly, however, company dependence on sales of amphetamines was significantly lessened. In 1976 less than $10 million of the total $675 million in sales was generated from amphetamines. Several new drugs were introduced to increase sales figures. New entries included three diuretics which promised to capture a portion of the growing anti-hypertensive market, and a cephalosporin antibiotic introduced in 1973 which increased 31% in worldwide sales by 1975.

Product diversification similarly contributed to increasing sales figures. Subsidiaries in animal health, medical diagnostics, and consumer products showed promising returns in the early 1970's. Contac cold tablets and A.R.M. allergy medicine were the most successful of the consumer products. Love cosmetics, an earlier attempt to capture some of Revlon's market, did not perform as well. However, due to consistent profit loss the company finally abandoned its foray into cosmetics.

Despite such a promising turnaround, Wall Street analysts only began taking notice of the change with SmithKline's introduction of Tagamet. Research on the drug started in 1964 at the SmithKline lab in Welwyn Garden City, England. The team of scientists, including Dr. James W. Black, revolutionized the process for discovering new drugs by conducting experiments under the premise that "receptor sites" existed on cells and that disease-causing agents could be blocked by preventing messages from reaching these sites. Previously, research for new drugs involved random testing of chemical compounds without a fundamental understanding of the biological process.

Due to the fact that the late 1960's were not particularly lucrative years for the company, research on the new drug was almost abandoned. Fortunately, positive results filtered back to SmithKline executives before the project was cancelled. The histamine receptor anatagonist concept behind Tagamet promised to provide relief to thousands of ulcer patients. Owing to the revolutionary nature of the drug, the Food & Drug Administration shortened the approval process for new drugs.

The success of the new drug was as much a surprise to SmithKline executives as it was to outside observers. Initially, sales for the drug were conservatively estimated at $150 to $200 million by 1980. Comparing the "speed and magnitude of its acceptance" on the market to the Xerox 914 and the Ford Mustang, sales for Tagamet surpassed $580 million by 1980—nearly equaling the entire gross revenue in 1975. Profits for 1979 amounted to $234 million, or a 266% increase in four years, making Tagamet the second largest selling drug. By 1981 Tagamet replaced Valium as the largest selling drug when sales for the drug surpassed $600 million. Stock for the company selling from as low as $10.81 a share in 1975 rose to as high as $65.25 a share in 1980.

With an untapped market in Japan (the world's largest ulcer-suffering population), overseas sales generated 60% of revenues. An estimated 15 million people sought relief from ulcers by taking Tagamet. The addition of new production facilities and a larger sales force, as well as being poised to enter the Japanese market, promised that sales for Tagamet were sure to increase.

Rather than rest on its laurels, SmithKline executives moved swiftly to ensure the company a healthy future. Large sums of money generated from sales of the drug were poured back into research and development. One drug developed in company laboratories, an anti-hypertensive called Selacryn, proved a disaster. A recall was

issued when reports linked the drug to liver disorders and several deaths. By 1985 the product had been linked to 35 deaths and generated 373 claims for liability. Although most of these cases are now settled, nevertheless, the company was sentenced to two years probation.

A drug that SmithKline is presently promoting, hopefully with better results than Selacryn, is Ridaura. This rheumatoid arthritis pill has gold as an active ingredient. It appears that the new drug actually has the ability to halt the degenerative process of arthritis rather than merely treat the symptoms. Once introduced, Auranofin has the potential for capturing a large proportion of the arthritis market.

Aside from new drug research, SmithKline has invested a large amount of its profits into an ambitious acquisition program. Diversifying into the diagnostic equipment field, the company acquired Mediscan and Acoustic Emission Technology. Similarly, by adding two eye-care manufacturers, Humphrey Instruments and Allergan Pharmaceuticals, SmithKline created a competitive new division to enter a growing market.

By 1982 executives at SmithKline predicted that the $800 million in sales of Tagamet would reach the billion dollar mark by the end of that year. Ironically, it is the very success of Tagamet that now places the company in a precarious position. As late as 1984 Tagamet contributed more than half of SmithKline's $489.5 million in profits. Upon closer inspection, however, this impressive figure reveals an "Achilles heel." While SmithKline has wisely used profits generated from sales of the drug to fund research for new pharmaceuticals and to diversify through acquisition, nevertheless, the company continues to depend heavily on Tagamet's performance for a sizeable portion of its income.

Competition for Tagamet's market appeared sooner than company executives had hoped. While Tagamet's patent will not expire until 1994, several new drugs, particularly one called Zantac developed by Glaxo Holdings, uses an original formula and claims fewer side effects, higher potency, and a convenient twice-a-day dosage. By emphasizing Tagamet's potential to produce side effects such as gynecomastia (swollen breasts in men), impotence, and mental confusion in rare cases of higher than usual dosage, Glaxo (along with the addition of a Hoffmann-La Roche salesforce) planned to capture up to 30% of Tagamet's U.S. market. Hoffman-La Roche, the Swiss pharmaceutical company responsible for Valium, is recognized for is aggressive marketing style, and its unique deal with Glaxo Holdings signaled a formidable challenge.

Already capturing well over 30% of the market in several European countries, Zantac was ready to enter the U.S. market. In preparation to meet the challenge this drug posed to their share of the markets, SmithKline increased its salesforce and trained them in more effective marketing skills. Furthermore, by using information that refuted the reported side effects of Tagamet, SmithKline stood by the effectiveness of its drug. And finally, although acknowledging the convenience of Zantac's twice a day dosage over Tagamet's four times a day dosage, SmithKline executives nonetheless hoped Zantac's 20% price increase over Tagamet would mitigate the attractiveness of a smaller dosage.

Despite SmithKline's concerted effort to meet the challenge of the new drug, Wall Street analysts did not believe the company would be successful. Stock prices dropped in 1983 from a high of $76.50 to $66 a share. Similarly, management's conservative estimate of Zantac's ability to capture between 10% and 25% of the market in the first year soon proved a miscalculation; the new drug easily commanded 25% of the new prescription market. More seriously, reports on the effectiveness of Zantac due to its higher potency represented shorter hospital stays and reduced medical costs over the long term. Henry Wendt, the chief executive officer of SmithKline, never saw his prediction of a one billion dollar sales of Tagamet materialize.

The recent acquisition of Beckman Instruments, a manufacturer of sophisticated diagnostic equipment, was made with the intention of entering into the emerging diagnostics market and reducing the company's dependence on pharmaceuticals. By exchanging a hefty $1.01 billion worth of stock and by agreeing to include the newly acquired company in its name, SmithKline Beckman was positioning itself to remain competitive after Tagamet lost some of its momentum. Wendt stood by the decision and ignored criticism that the large dollar exchange would dilute earnings.

What SmithKline executives were not planning on, however, was a sudden cost-consciousness in hospital spending. The Reagan Administration's order for stricter reimbursement procedures in regard to Medicare payments denied hospitals their former ability to earn cost plus profit from government funds. Instead Medicare paid preset fixed amounts of money for specific ailments. In response, hospitals reduced spending on expensive medical equipment. And as a result, cancellations on orders for Beckman chemical analytic systems increased at the company. SmithKline accordingly shifted its emphasis toward smaller, less expensive devices and the growing demand for diagnostics in private practice. In 1984, however, Beckman's workforce was reduced by 400 and SmithKline instituted a wage freeze for five months.

Company management had hoped that the release of several new drugs would solve the problems of depressed earnings and falling stock prices. Ridaura, the arthritis drug with a gold compound, still required FDA approval in early 1984. The delay, to Wendt's chagrin, was related to two recalls of anti-arthritic drugs manufactured by competing companies. Monocid, an even more lucrative antibiotic, is said to be so effective that patients can be treated on an outpatient basis. If this is the case, Monocid promises to be a financial success. SmithKline has also applied for a more potent version of Tagamet to reduce dosages to twice-a-day.

Notwithstanding these attempts to anticipate possible long term problems, SmithKline's future remains a question mark. Wall Street analysts hesitate to recommend the company and management is now left to its own devices in order to proved SmithKline's viability. In a public show of confidence the company announced in 1984 that it would purchase as many as three million of its own shares. However, the future appeal of SmithKline Beckman on Wall Street remains uncertain.

Principal Subsidiaries: Allergan Pharmaceuticals, Inc.; Beckman Instruments, Inc.; Humphrey Instruments Inc.; SKB Ltd. The company also lists subsidiaries in the following countries: Argentina, Australia, Austria, Belgium, Bermuda, Brazil, Canada, Chile, Colombia, France, Hong Kong, Ireland, Japan, Mexico, The Netherlands, New Zealand, Nigeria, Panama, Philippines, South Africa, Spain, Sweden, Switzerland, United Kingdom, Venezuela, and West Germany.

Further Reading: Beckman Instruments, Inc: There Is No Substitute for Excellence by Arnold O. Beckman, New York, Newcomen Society, 1976; *The Fine Old House* by John F. Maroon, Philadelphia, SmithKline, 1980.

SQUIBB

SQUIBB CORPORATION

P.O. Box 4000
Princeton, New Jersey 08540
U.S.A.
(609) 921–4000

Public Company
Incorporated: 1967
Employees: 24,100
Sales: $1.785 billion
Market Value: $8.397 billion
Stock Index: New York

Squibb Corporation, established in 1858, is one of the oldest drug manufacturers in the United States. The company's nearly 130 years of business is a testimony to its consistency in producing quality drugs. While over one-half of its sales are generated by pharmaceuticals, the company also owns a very profitable cosmetic subsidiary whose brand names include Jean Nate and, until recently, Charles of the Ritz products.

Despite such a good product record, however, Squibb's financial performance, until recently, was not a fair reflection of the company's potential profits. With sales increasing for Capoten, a new antihypertensive drug initially greeted by limited FDA approval, and the sale of a long string of unprofitable mergers and subsidiaries, Squibb's successes have only recently begun to reflect an impressive increase in profits. Yet with competition intensifying in the area of cardiovascular drugs and antibiotics, it will be difficult for Squibb to maintain these figures.

Edwin Robinson Squibb, founder of the company, began his career as a Navy doctor. After originating the process for making pure ether, Squibb left the Navy and established his business in Brooklyn. The young pharmaceutical company, whose products included the manufacturing of chloroform, performed well in the early years. Squibb's two sons operated the company for some time before selling it in 1905. The new owners, Theodore Weicker, a German chemist, and Lowell M. Palmer, an industrialist, led the company through an era of unmatched prosperity. By 1951 annual sales had reached $100 million and Squibb represented one of the largest pharmaceutical concerns in the United States.

These glowing figures are what convinced Thomas S. Nichols, chairman-president of Mathieson Chemical Corporation, to propose the idea of a merger. Under Nichols' leadership the chemical company's assets had quadrupled in the four years between 1948 and 1952. By moving into the fields of agricultural chemicals, organic chemicals and ultimately drugs and cosmetics, Nichols hoped that a merger agreement arrived at between Weicker, Palmer and himself, would continue to support his company's successful expansion.

The proposed merger ostensibly held benefits for Squibb as well. While Weicker and Palmer were relegated to advisory positions, Squibb as a whole was to remain a separate independent division maintaining its own name and policies. At another level, Squibb's antibiotic production, representing a major area in the company's pharmaceutical products, had been experiencing intensified competition in the postwar years. The support offered by merging with the fastest growing chemical company in the industry would compensate for some of the losses suffered by this competition. With Palmer controlling 30% of Squibb stock and the Weicker family also holding a sizeable interest, the merger was completed as proposed without stockholder dissent.

In 1956 the E.R. Squibb Division of the newly formed Olin Mathieson Company (born out of a merger with Olin, a munitions manufacturer), decided to move its production plant of 98 years from Brooklyn to New Brunswick, New Jersey. Representing the first and largest of all Squibb's facilities, the Brooklyn plant was said to be outmoded and inefficient.

The late 1960's launched an era of mixed blessings for Squibb. By 1966 sales had reached $233 million with 40% of it coming from overseas markets; on the other hand, profits had only amounted to $19 million. Beset by cost and quality control problems, an operational overhaul was in order. In order to facilitate such a massive reorganization, Richard M. Furlaud, an Olin lawyer, suggested spinning-off Squibb and merging it with Beech-Nut, a manufacturer of infant food, Life Savers, candy rolls and other confectionery goods.

The impetus behind Furlaud's suggestion was the lackluster performance of Olin's stock. At the time, company stock was selling at 13 times earnings, an unimpressive figure relative to competitors in the drug industry whose stock sold at over 20 times earnings. By allowing Squibb to become an independent company, Olin stockholders could benefit from the realization of Squibb's true earnings potential. Future events would show that as an independent company Squibb stock rose to an earnings multiple of nearly 18.

In addition to spinning Squibb off from Olin, the merger of the independent drug company with Beech-Nut was suggested with the implication that it would create a well-balanced structure through product diversification and broad market strength. Squibb's strong overseas operations could facilitate expansion of Beech-Nut products and the pharmaceutical company's medical knowledge could contribute to the pediatric formula market. Beech-Nut, on the other hand, operated a highly developed distribution network that could expand the market for some of Squibb's products.

Thus the spin-off and merger were completed and Furlaud became the president and chief executive officer of the newly formed Squibb Beech-Nut company. Furlaud believed that his company was now fit to compete with the likes of American Home Products, Bristol-Meyers, and Warner-Lambert, three large pharmaceutical companies also producing consumer goods. Although Furlaud's company was a long way from establishing the financial security and reputation of his competitors, by 1969 Squibb Beech-Nut was showing strong signs of growth. Under tightened production controls, labor and inventory costs had been reduced. Sales for pharmaceuticals surpassed $240 million; another $241 million came from sales of foods and confections including Life Savers, baby foods, tea, and chewing gum.

Under a restructured research program $22 million was relegated for the study of steroids, anti-infectives, and central nervous system drugs. Recently introduced on the market were a number of promising new pharmaceuticals such as a cancer treatment agent, an injectable anti-depressant, and a semi-synthetic pencillin.

Despite such gains in sales and earnings, however, some industry observers remained skeptical about Furlaud's company ever producing the figures initially projected. By 1970 Squibb Beech-Nut stock was selling at around 24 times earnings, a highly respectable price in the drug industry. The problems lay in the profitability spread between Squibb and Beech-Nut products. While Beech-Nut contributed to 40% of total sales, its earnings remained negligible. Industry analysts attributed this discrepancy to outmoded marketing techniques, and Furlaud's appointment of several new Beech-Nut managers confirmed this.

By 1973 Squibb had sold several of its operations. Setting high quotes for profits and earnings, management decided to terminate its coffee, tea and baby food operations. The only remaining divisions of Beech-Nut not sold were the Life Savers candy operation and Dobbs House, an airport catering facility. These subsidiaries, combined with a 1971 acquisition of the cosmetic company Lanvin-Charles of the Ritz, represented, according to Executive Vice President George Maginness, the "right profile." Squibb management felt they had finally reached the long sought-after balance between profit yield and diversification.

Investors held the company in high regard as earnings increased between 11 and 14% from 1969 to 1973. The price/earnings multiple reached a high of 30. By 1975 sales had passed the one billion dollar mark with pharmaceuticals accounting for $546 million. Two new drugs on the market received an impressive response. Velosef, a cephalosporin antibiotic, recorded $9 million in sales on a $200 million market. Halog, an anti-inflammatory used to treat skin disorders, also did exceedingly well, and helped to strengthen Squibb's position as the leading manufacturer of topical steroids. The company's preeminent position in the diagnostic field evolved from the development and acquisition of a broad range of radiopharmaceuticals and contrast agents. Sales for these diagnostics were expected to pass $40 million.

The Squibb Institute of Medical Research, the company's most important department for research, received a $50 million budget to support the continuing study of a successful line of pharmaceuticals that included cardio-vasculars, antidepressants, antibiotics and proprietary items. By 1975, 12% of the total drug sales resulted from products under five years old; this marked the most substantial product flow in the industry. Overseas operations had been established in 36 countries and continued to contribute to a large portion of sales.

The Life Savers division benefited from a nationwide advertising campaign to introduce a new generation to the candy enjoyed by their grandparents. Between 1970 and 1973 Lifesavers sales jumped 40% and the subsidiary controlled over 50% of the domestic market for those types of products. Furthermore, Squibb gained a stronghold in the chewing gum market through the sales of Care Free products. Dobbs House and Lanvin-Charles of the Ritz appeared to be the only major areas of disappointment for Squibb; the poor economic condition of the air travel industry adversely affected the performance of Dobbs, and the cosmetic subsidiary experienced intense competition from the growing presence of Revlon, Norell and Estée Lauder.

The company was now poised on the edge of a new era in pharmaceutical development that would revolutionize the entire industry. By capitalizing on research into the foundation of biological processes, company scientists conducted drug research using more precise methodological techniques. Prior to this research experimental technique amounted to a random testing of only partially understood processes. The first and most dramatic result of molecular manipulation was SmithKline Beckman's development of Tagamet, an anti-ulcer drug that attacked the disease by intercepting a chemical messenger at a cell's "receptor site."

Squibb, along with many industry competitors, began conducting its research of new pharmaceuticals within this theoretical framework. Miguel A. Ondetti, director of a newly created department of biological chemistry at the Squibb Institute for Medical Research in 1976, first started working on an antihypertensive in 1968. The Argentinian chemist who joined Squibb in 1960 derived an enzyme potentially useful in controlling high blood pressure; this nonapeptide was extracted from the venom of an extremely poisonous Brazilian pit viper. Using a nearly abandoned theory that proposed an intricate relationship between kidney functioning and high-blood pressure, Squibb scientists attempted to capitalize on the venom discovery. Unfortunately, only a millionth of a gram of the precious substance could be extracted from a gram of venom and even then it could only be absorbed in an injected form.

The entire project was almost abandoned before the scientists thought of a way to circumvent the problem. Since the chemical they were working with broke down in the digestive tract, they knew any variant of it would do the same. The problem was identifying and intercepting the messenger enzyme produced by the lungs that causes high blood pressure when it modifies another protein. After guessing the shape of the enzyme, the scientists then constructed a new substance to fit into it and inactivate the "message." That new substance was called Capoten and its success gave rise to the description of it as the "Eureka compound."

Not only did the scientific community marvel in awe of Capoten's potential uses, but Wall Street analysts responded to the discovery of the drug in the same way. With estimates reporting that one in every six Americans suffer from hypertension, analysts like David Paisley of Merrill Lynch predicted Capoten's annual sales could reach $500 million. As a result, Squibb's stock increased 60% between 1978 and 1979.

Such a promising product, Furlaud began to think, would make Squibb one of the pre-eminent health-care companies in the world. His company's future, however, would not simply depend on the promise of Capoten; the Charles of Ritz fragrance business now recorded $243 million in sales with Enjoli and Jean Nate ranked in the top four U.S. fragrances. (In 1986, however, Yves Saint Laurent purchased Squibb's Charles of the Ritz product line.) Similarly, Opium, an expensive perfume, had become the fastest-growing product of its kind in the world. Furthermore, between 1978 and 1980 four companies in the diagnostics field had been acquired.

However, some industry analysts remained skeptical about Squibb's future. Recent efforts to improve profitability and upgrade plant operations had cost the company $75 million. To support the newly acquired subsidiaries a large amount of cash was required. The selling of the unprofitable Dobbs House offered some relief, but analysts suggested this was not enough. Capoten was seen by some analysts as not only a scientific achievement but also an essential product for the company's viability. Without all the speculation surrounding Capoten, one analyst claimed, Squibb's stock would drop by 20%.

To the surprise of company management this is exactly what happened. Until the middle of 1980 Capoten was still being tested and as results were monitored a number of side effects appeared. Some patients developed a mild rash or a temporary loss of taste. Several seriously ill patients receiving the drug exhibited an increased risk of kidney damage or injury to bone marrow. By August 1980 the Federal Drug Administration advisory committee had considered Capoten's application and recommended its administration only to those patients who had failed to respond to other medications. Squibb officials had hoped the FDA would note that the severe side effects appeared only in the most seriously ill patients and that those side effects were "dramatically" reduced when the drug was taken in smaller doses. Nevertheless, the FDA panel was not convinced; two days later Squibb stock dropped 20%.

By April the FDA issued a formal pronouncement approving Capoten's use as a drug "of last resort." Its healthy market reception, however, has renewed hope that Squibb may be able to convince the FDA of Capoten's safety not only for conjestive heart failure but also for the treatment of moderate hypertension. Should Squibb gain FDA approval for the drug, analysts project annual sales could reach as high as $300 million. By the end of 1982 Squibb submitted a supplement to the original application in an effort to gain such approval.

Squibb's performance over the next years was erratic. By 1983 sales of Capoten had doubled. Similarly, Corgard, a beta-blocker used to treat hypertension, had also increased its volume by 52%. Yet, despite such impressive figures, the area of cardiovasculars had become increasingly competitive. Moreover, aztreonam, a highly acclaimed Squibb antibiotic, promised sales of $100 million, yet this market also experienced increased competition. A new project involved the marketing of human insulin through a joint venture with Denmark's Novo Industri.

Squibb has been named defendant in a number of DES cases alleging the company's involvement in the manufacturing of an anti-miscarriage drug prescribed between the 1940's and the 1960's said to cause cancer in offspring of women who ingested the drug during pregnancy. In 1979 a case was settled out of court involving a child born with severe abnormalities. Squibb has successfully defended itself in three lawsuits, but has lost a $2.1 million case in 1982 to a woman who developed vaginal cancer. During a recent case in February 1986 the California State Supreme Court ruled in favor of Squibb by stating that the company's 10% control of the DES market did not constitute a "substantial share."

Squibb remains a consistent and reliable manufacturer of pharmaceuticals both in the United States and abroad. However, its long history of unprofitable partners and subsidiaries, as well as the more recent struggle over Capoten, has forced company management to review its long and short-term strategy. Even its recent additions in obstetrical diagnostics have raised doubts among several industry analysts concerned about Squibb's lack of expertise in the area. Many of these analysts maintain that the future growth of Squibb is dependent upon whether or not the company concentrates on what it knows best, namely, the manufacture of pharmaceuticals.

Principal Subsidiaries: E.R. Squibb & Sons, Inc.; Advanced Technology Laboratories, Inc.; Spacelabs, Inc.

Further Reading: Doctor Squibb: The Life and Times of a Rugged Idealist by Lawrence Goldfree Blochman, New York, Simon and Schuster, 1958.

STERLING DRUG, INC.

90 Park Avenue
New York, New York 10016
U.S.A.
(212) 907-2000

Public Company
Incorporated: April 9, 1932
Employees: 27,336
Sales: $1.990 billion
Market Value: $3.377 billion
Stock Index: New York

It is only in recent years that Sterling Drug, Inc. has developed innovative ethical drugs through its own research. For a company that manufactures Bayer aspirin, the leading American aspirin brand, this seems like an unusual occurrence. Yet the company's success has always relied more heavily on growth through acquisition and advertising rather than on research and development. While this approach to business has made the company vulnerable to anti-trust suits and the scrutiny of the Federal Trade Commission, Sterling Drug has nonetheless managed to forge a comfortable niche in the pharmaceutical industry.

William Erhard Weiss began his career in pharmaceuticals as a clerk in a drugstore. Initially selling products on horseback, Weiss later decided to begin his own company. In 1901, with Albert H. Diebold, he established the Neuralgyline Company (the forerunner of Sterling Drug) in West Virginia. The two men immediately laid the foundation for a style of aggressive marketing that would distinguish the company for years to come. The partners posted signs on fences and trees along the West Virginia roadways in order to advertise the merits of their pain reliever Neuralgine. After one year of business, the company sold $10,000 worth of the product. Instead of saving it, however, Weiss and Diebold reinvested total profits, along with additional funds from outside investors, for advertising promotions in Pittsburgh newspapers. By 1907 they had accumulated enough profits to purchase the Sterling Remedy Company, and changed the company name accordingly.

During the same period of time a West German chemical company accomplished a scientific breakthrough by inventing aspirin. In 1893 Felix Hoffman, of Friedrich Bayer and Company, synthesized salicylates, which are naturally occurring chemicals in willows and other plants, and created an effective pain reliever. By the turn of the century the drug was launched on the world market. However, scientific discoveries sometimes become the objects of twists in history. At the end of World War I the Sterling product line consisted of Neuralgyline, Danderine, Casaets, and California Syrup of Figs. This sparse product line was soon strengthened when Francis P. Garvan, the Alien Property Custodian, decided to auction the American Bayer company. Since Bayer was German-owned the U.S. government had seized it and other properties during the war. Sterling offered a prohibitive $5.3 million to acquire Bayer's holdings in the U.S. and became the owner of the Bayer aspirin patent.

In a 1921 ruling that had far reaching consequences for the pharmaceutical industry Judge Learned Hand approved generic use for the word "aspirin." As a result, Sterling resorted to using "Bayer" in their product name in order to maintain a trademark for their product. Thus, at the beginning of the decade Sterling held a major portion of the worldwide aspirin market.

It was not long before the company began competing with its German counterpart. In Latin America, representing at the time a vast untapped market for the Western pharmaceutical industry, the two companies competed for the same market with a confusing tangle of trademarks. To avoid litigation, and to gain access to expensive ethical drug research as well, Sterling signed an agreement with I.G. Farben, Bayer's new parent company. In the 1923 agreement Sterling gave Bayer 50% of its stock in Winthrop Laboratories, a Sterling subsidiary, in exchange for Bayer's manufacturing information and the transfer of Bayer patent and technical data for future discoveries. The Latin American market had been carefully divided in order to create a balance of power between the two pharmaceutical companies.

The cartel represented a huge profit potential for Sterling Drug. Management estimated the value of the agreement in the range of $50 to $100 million. In the 1920's cartels with German companies were condoned as a means of helping Germany's beleaguered post-war economy. Yet, as argued in 1942 *Fortune* magazine article, it was at this early stage that the German government laid the foundation for a policy of economic fascism. At the roots of the struggle over "a simple glassine envelope containing two aspirin-compound tablets" was "Germany's attempt to reduce a continent to the economic and political status of a colony."

Whatever real or imagined designs Germany had in regard to its Latin American market, however, it soon became apparent that it was neither economically nor politically viable for Sterling to continue conducting business with Farben. Coming within a hairsbreadth of suffering U.S. government action, two Sterling subsidiaries in Latin America, Winthrop Products, Inc. and the Sydney Ross Co., suddenly became the advanced guard for a U.S. trade-war policy against Germany. In other words, an all out economic war to gain hegemony over the Latin American market was waged against Farben; as far as Sterling was concerned the cartel ceased to exist.

This sudden turnaround seemed inconsistent in light of the previous intimate business dealings between the two companies. The initial agreement of 1923 called for Sterling to supply aspirin to the Latin American market only if Farben were at any time unable to do so. Yet as late as 1941, during the British blockade of Nazi occupied Europe, Farben asked Sterling to violate the agreement between the two companies and send Winthrop ethical drugs to Latin America. After two and a half days of debate William Erhard Weiss (at that time chairman of the board) ordered the shipment sent.

Weiss' decision soon proved disastrous; the U.S. Government Interdepartmental Committee, composed of members of the Departments of State, Justice, and Treasury, ordered the resignation of Sterling management. In spite of Sterling Drug being placed on a British blacklist for Weiss' compliance with Farben's requested shipment, the company continued the process of establishing new companies in Latin America to protect both itself and Farben from the possibility of expropriation during the war. These activities of the company, in addition to German ownership of portions of Sterling subsidiaries and stock, severely compromised its position during a mounting U.S. war effort.

U.S. government action against Sterling could have taken the form of antitrust litigation or the severing of all Sterling subsidiaries with any connection to Farben. Yet before any such action was initiated a young group of Sterling executives reached an agreement with the government to use the Sterling-Farben relationship as a newly declared battleground for Allied economic policy. Tom and David Corcoran, two executives at the Sterling Ross subsidiary in Latin America, enthusiastically enlisted government support for the offensive against Farben. A short time later Sterling emerged from its near brush with government sanctions as one of the bastions of free trade enterprise.

After the forced resignation of Weiss, Diebold and 48 former employees, the newly installed executives devised a successful company strategy and emerged from the war with unprecedented profit margins. Sterling's victory in this battle of trade-war territory can be attributed to its advertising technique which had been perfected during its forty year period of existence. By distributing 80 million copies of hand material and 27 million samples of products, Sterling's 1000-man sales force canvassed the smallest towns. The Sydney Ross subsidiary purchased the largest amount of radio airtime up to that time and, as a result, in 1942 Latin Americans were exposed to 5 million advertisements for Sterling products. Besides the radio ads, use of sound trucks, soap operas and religious calendars were just a few examples of the variety of marketing approaches. Moreover, these approaches were by no means futile; after one year Sydney Ross subsidiary sold more aspirin than Farben did in either 1940 or 1941.

Sterling's victory over Farben was viewed as a microcosm of the Allied victory over Germany. In 1945 when all German properties were again seized by the U.S. government, Sterling paid $9.5 million to buy out the one-half German interest in its Winthrop subsidiary. Yet the animosity between the two companies did not end. In 1952 the West German company, through its American subsidiaries Shenley Laboratories and Norex Laboratories, filed

an antitrust suit against Sterling demanding that the company either pay royalties on the now illegal 1923 and 1926 agreements or allow the American subsidiaries to manufacture and sell Bayer products in the U.S. based on a previous 1949 agreement.

Sterling was not financially harmed by this litigation. By the early 1970's sales for Bayer aspirin were more than $50 million a year. Today, Sterling Drug retains exclusive rights to the use of the Bayer trademark for its aspirin product in the U.S., while the German company and its U.S. subsidiaries manufacture an assortment of industrial items under the same name. Outside the U.S. and its territories and Canada, use of the Bayer trademark belongs solely to the German company.

In addition to the sale of proprietary drugs that included a new arsenal of pain relievers (Cope, Vanquish, Measurin, and Midol), Sterling had entered the consumer product market and had become the most diversified member of the pharmaceutical industry. The product line for consumer items ranged from cosmetics and Beacon Wax to fragrances and d-Con insecticides. Sterling also manufactured chemicals and animal health products.

In the early 1970's Sterling began researching and developing their own ethical drugs. As well as marketing Neo-Synephrine nasal decongestant, NeGram, an antibiotic used to treat urinary tract infections, Sulfamylon, a cream used on severe burns, and pHisoHex, an antibacterial skin cleanser, Sterling also released pentazocine, a prescription analgesic (trademarked under the name Talwin) potentially regarded as highly profitable in the future. During this period total sales for Sterling products reached over $500 million a year.

While the early 1970's initiated an era of comfortable growth for Sterling, the company was not expanding without its share of setbacks. Arguing that control of health care, beauty and home products lay in the hands of a small number of companies, Federal Trade Commission attorneys (in an appeal on a previously failed anti-trust suit) brought suit against the 1969 Sterling Drug-Lehn & Fink merger. According to the FTC, the combinations of Lehn & Fink, the manufacturers of Lysol products, and Sterling Drug represented a reduction in competition among packaged goods advertisers. With the companies spending a disproportionately large amount of money on advertising (compared to the amount of money generated from sales) the attorneys claimed consumers were denied a fair review of products.

While Lehn & Fink continues today to be a Sterling subsidiary, this encounter with the FTC was not the only problem facing Sterling. In late 1971 the Food and Drug Administration, concerned about possible adverse effects of hexachlorophene, ordered all products containing this chemical to be sold on a prescription basis only. This sharply reduced the sales of Sterling's pHisoHex which had become the largest-selling anti-bacterial cleanser.

The hardest blow to strike Sterling was the growing competition in its virtual monopoly of the aspirin market. It was not until 1971 that scientists finally understood exactly how aspirin works in the body. At the same time, however, Johnson & Johnson released is nonaspirin

Tylenol and marketed it as a superior product without the possible side effect of an upset stomach ordinarily associated with aspirin. Then came Bufferin, Excedrin Extra-Strength, and other analgesic compounds claiming faster relief, higher potency, and no upset stomach. By 1983 Bayer aspirin held only 10% of the $1.3 billion aspirin market.

Soon afterwards Sterling began its own series of aggressive advertisements to strengthen its entire product line. Spending some $153 million in 1973 alone, Sterling became one of the nation's largest advertisers. While Dr. Mark Hiebert, chairman and chief executive officer of Sterling until 1974, was trained as a physician, his real ability was in marketing. Under Hiebert's direction several Sterling household products performed exceedingly well. Yet at the end of his term the FTC began an investigation into misleading analgesic advertisements. The FTC, citing Sterling, Bristol-Meyers, and American Home Products, claimed the companies had made unqualified statements of comparative effectiveness and required further proof of clinical testing. Dr. Hiebert, however, stood by the Bayer aspirin advertisements claiming the product was promoted "in good conscience and with facts."

With the retirement of Dr. Hiebert, a new group of executives stood at the company helm. Clark Wescoe, new president and chief executive officer, Robert K. Pfister, vice chairman, and Glenn W. Johnston, president, directed a tightly controlled administration. Rearranging the three major Sterling divisions which included pharmaceuticals, over-the-counter proprietary drugs, and consumer goods, Wescoe made sure no product crossovers existed. Thoroughly scrutinizing costs and expenditures, Sterling executives directed the company into a period of new growth. By 1974 worldwide sales were estimated at $950 million with a return on equity at 22% and a consistent gain on earnings over the past 24 years.

Consumer products such as Lysol and Beacon Wax generated sales of $123 million and $30 million, respectively. Bayer aspirin continued to maintain the lead with 1973 sales at $70 million. Furthermore, Wescoe's medical background (he was dean of the medical school at the University of Kansas) prompted him to overhaul Sterling's research facilities. Due to Wescoe's influence several promising ethical drugs emerged from Sterling labs.

By 1978 the dispute over controversial advertisements reappeared. The Food and Drug Administration claimed Sterling had distorted one of their reports on the safety of pain-killers. Since Sterling had only partially revealed the report findings, the FDA accused the company of misrepresentation. The company agreed to remove the advertisements, but the dispute was not over. In 1981, based on the complaint filed in 1973, a FTC administrative law judge ordered Sterling to "refrain from making claims about its nonprescription drug products' efficacy or superiority unless those claims are based on competent and reliable scientific evidence."

Besides the FTC order Sterling was confronted with other difficulties. In 1982 when Tylenol was removed from the shelves due to the tragic cyanide poisoning of seven people, Panadol, a Sterling acetaminophen used outside the U.S., could successfully have captured a large portion of the vacated market. Yet Sterling had not planned on introducing the drug in the U.S. until the following year and by then Tylenol recaptured four-fifths of its former market. In addition, Sterling faced new competition from ibuprofen, a generic name for a former prescription pain-reliever. Receiving FDA approval to market the drug over-the-counter, American Home Products and Upjohn entered the ibuprofen market and threatened to take away sales from Sterling's Rufen and Motrin.

Under the new President John M. Pietruski several new products were launched on the market to regain earlier losses. A broadened line of pain-relievers including extra-strength Bayer and an arthritis Bayer, as well as new pharmaceuticals including a radiodiagnostic agent, an aerosol asthma treatment, and a gonorrhea treatment, all helped to increase Sterling sales.

Sterling's most promising drug awaiting approval is milrinone, a treatment for congestive heart failure. After abandoning an attempt to gain FDA approval for a similar drug, amrinone, when a decreased count of platelets or blood clotting mechanisms were found in test patients, Sterling subsequently developed milrinone. This new drug is being promoted as a drug which has the potential for capturing a large market share. Its capability of increasing the heart's ability to contract may have a beneficial effect on a patient's daily existence.

Yet despite milrinone's potential, Sterling's lackluster performance in the mid-1980's has disappointed investors. Overseas earnings were hurt by the strong U.S. dollar and ibuprofen continues to make inroads in Bayer's market. While milrinone's potential for huge profits may have caused Sterling stock to increase in 1985, one Wall Street analyst attributed the rise in price to a rumor of a company takeover.

Principal Subsidiaries: Sterling Pharmaceutical Group; Winthrop-Brown Laboratories; Glenbrook Laboratories; Cook-Waite Laboratories, Inc.; Lehn and Fink Products Group; Minwax Company, Inc.; The d-Con Company, Inc. Sterling Drug also has subsidiaries in the following countries: Australia, Canada, England, Japan, New Zealand, and Switzerland.

SYNTEX CORPORATION

3401 Hillview Avenue
Palo Alto, California 94304
U.S.A.
(415) 855–5050

Public Company
Incorporated: June 25, 1957
Employees: 11,000
Sales: $1.054 billion
Market Value: $4.740 billion
Stock Index: New York

Although a relative latecomer to the business of pharmaceuticals, Syntex Corporation is nevertheless responsible for holding large market portions of the oral contraceptive and anti-inflammatory drug markets. While Syntex presently enjoys comfortable margins as a mid-ranking pharmaceutical manufacturer (it has finally achieved its one billion dollar sales goal set in 1978), the company achieved Wall Street notoriety in the early 1960's when stock prices reached as much as 100 times earnings.

The company quietly posted increased earnings as its product line expanded to include new drugs, but the true impetus behind Syntex's reception on Wall Street was the workings of a financier named Charles Allen. Originally Syntex was founded in Mexico in 1944 by two German refugees. Company scientists concentrated their efforts on manufacturing bulk steroid chemicals and research. After the war, however, the direction of the business was changed by two new employees named George Rosenkranz and Carl Djerassi. While the two new executives pioneered the development of oral contraceptives, Syntex's original owners wanted to continue producing bulk chemicals. At this point Charles Allen, Jr., senior partner in Allen & Company, stepped into the picture. As head of one of the leading investment banker firms in the country, Allen was respected not only for his financial prowess but also for his ability to predict industry trends and evaluate securities. Wall Street investors followed Allen with the loyalty of an army behind its commander.

In 1951 Allen became half-owner of the Ogden Corporation. Several companies were added to the corporation as subsidiaries, including Syntex. The acquisition of Syntex, however, created tax problems. As a result, Syntex was sold in 1958 to Ogden stockholders for only two dollars a share. Allen & Company ended up with about 40% or over one million of the 4.5 million Syntex shares outstanding.

Syntex is actually registered as a Panamanian company. Tax advantages convinced company management to re-establish business in Central America where much of its products are shipped through Panama's free zone. When Rosenkrantz, a Hungarian-born naturalized Mexican citizen, became the company president, he kept headquarters in Mexico City even as Syntex's growing U.S. concern shifted the company's geographic emphasis. The company's independent stature enabled it to reach an agreement with Eli Lilly and Company, one of the industry leaders. Syntex's experience with producing bulk steroid chemicals (sex hormones had been extracted from the Mexican barbasco root) prepared it to enter the growing contraceptive market. The arrangement with Lilly paid for half of certain research costs at Syntex in exchange for Lilly's rights to market the results of that research. Instead of asking for royalties or fixed-price contracts from other major drug firms, Syntex arranged an innovative agreement where it earned a percentage of what those firms earned. Thus Syntex gained quick access not only to Lilly, but to Johnson & Johnson, to Schering and to Ciba-Geigy, all major manufacturers of oral contraceptives.

By 1964 Syntex became a case in point of the virtues and vices of "a bubbling speculative market." Since the company was financed by such a prominent Wall Street figure, since contraceptives had become the new glamour item, and finally since 150,000 shares on file for registration in Washington promised a future stock option program, this resulted in a stock price increase from a low in 1962 of 11 to a high of 190 in 1964. This enthusiasm was bolstered by a 3-for-1 split and a *Wall Street Journal* cover story on birth control. To the horror of some financial experts, the company market value peaked at $855 million while sales for the year were only $16 million.

Problems began to arise during the 1970 Senate hearings on the adverse affects of birth control pills. Sales dropped 10% and earnings fell almost 50%. The price of Syntex stock mirrored these trends; it slipped from over $80 to less than $20 a share. Although prices did eventually climb to another high of $113, this would not be the last time Syntex stockholders would experience such a volatile period of stock market valuations. Syntex management realized that the Senate hearing had seriously threatened the company's viability. Action was necessary in order to ensure that future company profits were no longer dependent on one product, namely, the sales of contraceptives. At this point, Syntex embarked on an effort to expand into a full-line manufacturer of pharmaceuticals.

In the mid-1960's the company began marketing products under its own label. In 1973 an independent marketing team was established with 400 salespeople operating in the U.S. and foreign subsidiaries. Product expansion continued into the topical corticoid market and Aarane, an antiasthma drug, was also introduced on the market. Naproxen, an antiarthritic, was released abroad and in one year had become the best selling product in its field in Mexico.

Through acquisitions Syntex moved into the fields of animal health and dental equipment. By 1973 the dental division accounted for 6.5% of sales and the animal health division generated 22% of sales. One successful product in the animal health division was Synovex, a natural cattle hormone that captured more than 50% of the market when diethylstilbestrol (DES), a synthetic hormone, was banned by the Food & Drug Administration.

As a result of these measures the company reported increased sales figures. In 1972 sales reached $130 million or a nearly 30% increase from 1971. Net income surpassed $18 million and Syntex boasted of a 21% profit margin— the highest in the industry for that year. Oral contraceptives accounted for only 28% of sales and 35% of profits (in 1966 they accounted for 47% of profits).

Syntex's Palo Alto research center became the focal point for the company's expansion. Located near Stanford University the highly respected research center displayed the title of Syntex's U.S. headquarters. Domestic operations accounted for 60% of Syntex's sales. Research Director Djerassi earned the company even greater respect when he strengthened the research organization by recruiting talent through post-doctoral fellowships.

By the mid-1970's Syntex's plan to expand the product line and increase profits through two new drugs named Aarane and Naprosyn did not progress according to schedule. Due to the fact that sales of steroid drugs had reached a peak, Syntex executives had planned on Aarane capturing up to 75% or $40 million of the market. However, Aarane sales only reached $6 million annually by 1976. For this reason the sale of Naprosyn became a company imperative.

The new antiarthritic was released in the U.S. during May 1976. Although sales registered at a high of $20 million annually, the timing for the release of this drug could not have been less fortunate for Syntex executives. The FDA, under pressure from consumer and Congressional criticism, began to regulate drug testing procedures more strictly. The agency charged that lab tests for Naprosyn, conducted by an independent contractor, were invalid. By failing to investigate fully laboratory tests revealing long-term animal toxicity, the FDA argued that the administration of these tests had not adhered to proper federal guidelines.

With the price of its stock declining, company president Albert Bowers traveled to Washington confident that he could delay the FDA's plan to hold a hearing on Naprosyn. While the FDA did agree to allow Syntex a 24-month period to conduct a replacement study in support of Naprosyn's safety, company earnings declined for five consecutive quarters as a factor of the FDA encounter. With the end of the FDA investigation in sight, however, renewed promotional efforts behind the sale of Naprosyn as well as an overall operating increase helped Syntex to resume its expansion and growth. At this time the drug was being marketed throughout the world with the exception of Japan, and this country represented a major untapped market. With the Japanese government awaiting FDA approval, worldwide sales of Naprosyn promised large financial returns.

By 1978 Bowers boasted of a "strong resumption of growth in earnings" as both sales and profits reached record levels. With sales reaching $400 million, Bowers could point to Naprosyn as a large contributing factor to these impressive figures. The FDA, still awaiting test results on toxicity of the drug, continued to threaten Syntex with removal of the drug from the market should the results be unsatisfactory. With an approval for marketing the drug in Japan, however, and a new drug application submitted to the FDA for naproxen sodium (a drug useful not only in the treatment of soft tissue inflammation and dysmenorrhea, but also as an analgesic), Bowers announced a $1 billion sales goal for the mid-1980's.

The year 1979, while continuing to record increased earnings, marked a period of lawsuits. A large number of British women filed suit against Syntex contending they had been harmed by using the company's birth control pill. One plaintiff charged the company with withholding information about dangerous side effects after she suffered a severe stroke. She sought $1 million in damages because, as her counsel argued, she was unable to lead a normal life.

That same year Syntex agreed to settle out of court all pending lawsuits with Syntex shareholders and Industrial Bio-Test Laboratories, the independent lab responsible for the Naprosyn testing. The class action lawsuit alleged that IBT laboratories were inefficient in performing and reporting a study of the drug. While the company admitted no wrongdoing and was still awaiting FDA response to its resubmitted tests, a $2.75 million settlement fund was established. Syntex contributed $575,000 along with contributions from IBT and Syntex's insurance company.

The lawsuits did not seem to affect worldwide sales of the drug. By 1979 sales for Naprosyn reached $27.7 million in the second quarter and $56 million in the first half of the year. International sales of the drug accounted for 60% of total sales. By June a merger was completed with Den-Tal-Ez, a dental equipment manufacturer. With one lawsuit settled Syntex's future looked promising.

In the early 1980's, however, Syntex was confronted with a new problem. The U.S. House of Representatives Subcommittee on Oversight and Investigations charged the company with failing to take action to protect the health of infants when reports linked Syntex manufactured baby formulas to metabolic alkalosis. The company had removed salt from Neo-Mull-Soy and Cho-Free in response to a belief that salt intake by infants could lead to hypertension as adults. Reports that babies were failing to gain weight and had lost their appetites led to a product recall in August of 1979. As a result, the National Institute of Health began a five-year follow-up study on the health of the afflicted children.

In 1985 a $27 million verdict was awarded to two boys who sustained brain damage allegedly due to the salt removal from the formulas. The verdict represented the largest personal injury sum awarded in Illinois. While the company has settled more than 100 cases involving the recall, it is currently considering an appeal. A Syntex spokeswoman said the company would accept responsibility only if brain damage was proven to be the result of the infant formula.

Throughout this period Syntex continued to expand. The Den-Tal-Ez acquisition contributed to a third of total sales in 1980 and Polycon contact lenses, still in the test stage, were predicted to earn $5–10 million in sales. Anaprox, the brand name for naproxen sodium, was selling quite well in foreign markets while awaiting FDA approval. The French pharmaceutical manufacturer, Laroche Navarron, was purchased and Syntex also announced plans to establish a subsidiary in Osaka.

Albert Bowers was named the new chief executive officer in 1980. A Ph.D. in organic chemistry, the 24-year employee was said to be highly qualified for the position vacated by Rosenkranz. Bowers claimed that his move from the laboratory to the executive office was challenging, but that his strong background in chemical research was an essential ingredient in the effectiveness of his leadership.

Syntex has recently been moving into the growing field of genetic engineering. However, this area of drug manufacturing has caused the company some problems. When the president of Syntex's diagnostics division viewed the laboratory work of several Seattle microbiologists, he suggested a contract be drawn up where Syntex would pay $3 million for their research in exchange for the rights to manufacture and market tests developed for sexually transmissible diseases. When the agreement produced four successful products, a new venture was organized called Oncogen where Syntex and the microbiologists split profits 50–50. Later Bristol-Meyers was invited to join the venture by contributing $12 million. Eventually, however, the scientists sold their entire interest to Bristol-Meyers for $300 million. Bowers then proceeded to sell Syntex's portion of the venture to Bristol-Meyers and now concentrates on in-house cancer research.

Syntex entered the business of pharmaceuticals and was greeted by industry analysts with a good amount of excitement. For years the company was one of the favorites of Wall Street while its stock climbed to new heights. However, much of the publicity seems to have faded as the company matured into a fully integrated pharmaceutical company. While Syntex continues to increase sales and profits, the recent $27 million dollar court verdict and the aborted venture into biotechnology finds management facing some important decisions about the company's future direction.

Principal Subsidiaries: Syntex Laboratories; Brazil Diamond Laboratories; Star Dental Manufacturing Co., Inc.; Starlite Dental, Inc.; Syntex Energy, Research, Inc. The company also has subsidiaries in the following countries: Mexico, Canada, Switzerland, Brazil, Spain and the United Kingdom.

TAKEDA CHEMICAL INDUSTRIES, LTD.

27 Doshomachi 2-Chome
Higashiku, Osaka 541
Japan
(06) 204-2111

Public Company
Incorporated: January, 1925
Employees: 10,998
Sales: ¥240 billion (US$1.19 billion)
Market Value: ¥167 billion (US$ 860 million)
Stock Index: Tokyo Osaka Nagoya Hiroshima Fukuoka Niigata Sapporo

Takeda Chemical Industries is Japan's largest pharmaceutical company and one of the largest 20 drug firms worldwide. Until recently Takeda's name was virtually unrecognized outside the borders of its own nation. However, with the increasing presence of Japanese companies on the U.S. market, Takeda's reputation has gained wider recognition.

Takeda's corporate headquarters are located in the same city of its origins—Doshomachi, Osaka. In the mid-18th century this urban center was the focus of the nation's drug business. Ohmiya Chobei, the company founder, established a small firm in 1783 to sell Japanese and Chinese medicines. During the Meiji Era the firm's products expanded to include imported medicines from the west. After the company's first factory was completed in 1895, production began on manufactured pharmaceuticals. Fine chemicals were added to the production line in 1909 and four years later a modern factory was constructed to facilitate growth.

From the start of the Showa Era in 1925 the company's operations expanded significantly and transformed it from a local business to a major pharmaceutical concern. An important innovation during this period of growth was the successful synthesis of Vitamin C in 1937 and Vitamin B1 in 1938. Takeda marketed the product of this innovative research under the name Metabolin-Strong and became the manufacturer of Japan's first synthetic vitamin preparation. During the postwar years Japanese citizens expressed a new health consciousness. A vigorous orientation toward health and hygiene found Takeda's products in great demand. By 1962, 30% of the nation's drug sales were generated from the sale of vitamin preparations; Takeda supplied nearly 50% of the total, earning the title of "Takeda of Vitamin Fame."

In the 1940's the company changed its name to its current title, Takeda Chemical Industries Limited, and absorbed two other firms, Konishi Pharmaceutical and Radium Pharmacy, into its operations. The company's experience with vitamin production increased with the successful synthesis of a thiol derivative of thiamine, otherwise known as a long-acting Vitamin B1 preparation. Alinamin, the brand name of this synthesized product, became one of Takeda's most popular items. In 1952 Takeda's food division was established under the name Takeda Food Industry. This division grew to include the manufacture of enriched foods, food additives and beverages. Six years later Takeda's research activity was strengthened by the completion of new laboratory facilities.

Besides the manufacture of synthetic vitamins, Takeda's pharmaceutical products included tranquilizers, treatments for nervous disorders, and antibiotics. In the food product division, manufactured items included Plussy, a soft drink enriched with vitamin C, and Ino-Ichiban, a popular condiment. Takeda's formidable expansion allowed the company to invest unprecedented amounts of money into new equipment and facilities. Even more significant was Takeda's role in the inception of the drug export trade; by exporting manufacturing techniques for Alinamin, Takeda led the Japanese pharmaceutical industry towards international expansion.

In the early 1960's the Japanese drug industry experienced an annual growth rate exceeding 20%, making it one of the fastest growing industries in the nation. In addition, sweeping changes in government regulation would soon make the industry one of the most profitable. Takeda was well-positioned to capitalize on these changes; no one single industry competitor came close to challenging Takeda's preeminence in sales and marketing.

The 1961 implementation of the Japanese National Health Insurance system marked an important date for the pharmaceutical industry. Under this system the patient's prescription costs were almost completely covered by the insurance program. In addition, the official drug pricing system allowed doctors full reimbursement for the cost of dispensing drugs. This structure, therefore, encouraged the generous prescription of drugs because doctors profited from the difference between the price at which they purchased drugs and the higher official price, set by the Ministry of Health and Welfare, at which they were reimbursed. For this reason the pharmaceutical industry experienced unprecedented financial success.

Takeda's growth matched the expansion of the industry and the health insurance system. Under the leadership of Ohmiya Chobei Takeda VI, decendant of the company founder, Takeda operated as a holding company for numerous subsidiaries including Yoshitomi Pharmaceutical, Teikoku Hormone and Biofermin Pharmaceutical. As profits increased the company established subsidiaries in Taiwan, Hong Kong, Thailand, the Philippines, Indonesia, West Germany, the United States and Mexico. By 1970, 10% of the total national production of pharmaceuticals was traceable to Takeda operations. Moreover, while Japan's industry share of drug exports remained only 2.9% of total sales, export figures increased

34.7% between 1968 and 1970 with Takeda's business accounting not only for 25% of total pharmaceutical exports but also for 25% of food additives and industrial chemicals exports.

Despite movement toward export expansion, the trade deficit in pharmaceuticals remained sizeable; as late as 1982, 80% of the drugs sold in Japan continued to be manufactured overseas or with technology developed abroad. It was precisely this trade deficit that compelled the government to implement changes. One cause for this imbalance was traceable to Japan's lack of strict patent laws in the industry which, in turn, made research and innovation unprofitable. To encourage the industry to be less reliant on foreign technology the government passed stronger patent protection laws and altered the drug pricing system. By establishing high prices for innovative products, the development of new drugs suddenly became a highly lucrative business. Pharmaceutical companies immediately invested money in research and development and for the first time technology began moving from Japan to foreign markets. By 1977 Japan had received 1,700 drug and related product patents in the U.S. alone, ranking it second among all foreign recipients of U.S. drug patents.

Takeda participated actively in this new orientation toward innovation. Between 1970 and 1974 research expenditures increased and a new plant in Kashima was built to strengthen these efforts. The number of patents received locally and abroad for products developed in Takeda laboratories surpassed 3,000. As leadership passed from Chobei Takeda to Shinbei Konishi, the new company president made the development of pharmaceuticals a priority along with the continued expansion into foreign markets. In addition, a new food company was established with the intent of raising the company's food industry market share to 12%. Konishi's strategy proved successful. While the sales of vitamins increased nearly four times between 1960 and 1964, the 1970's found Takeda instrumental in developing innovative antibiotics. A majority of Takeda's $1.8 billion in sales was generated from the sale of vitamins and antibiotics in the early 1980's. By 1982 cephalosporins, a powerful third-generation antibiotic, accounted for 24% of Japan's domestic drug sales.

The Japanese pharmaceutical industry's increasing emphasis on research served not only to strengthen the domestic market but also to facilitate growth overseas. On the one hand, because large expenditures were now needed to support the industry-wide effort, drug companies initiated a concerted expansion into foreign markets as a means of recouping the millions of dollars necessary to develop one drug. On the other hand, Japan's innovation in antibiotics compelled foreign companies to solicit their expertise. Thus began the popular trend of securing foreign licensing agreements between Japanese drug companies and their foreign counterparts. Between 1970 and 1980 drug-licensing increased nearly four times. The enactment of the Pharmaceutical Affairs Act, effectively extending the time a Japanese company can market a drug under exclusive license, encouraged further agreements. Takeda, representing the largest of the Japanese pharmaceutical concerns, contributed largely to this increase. By

1983 the company was involved in agreements with over 20 companies, including the licensing of a cephalosporin antibiotic with Abbott Laboratories.

As industry analysts are keen to observe, licensing agreements with foreign companies are often just the first step in establishing independent foreign operations. Since agreements generally pay the licensee an initial fee and between 2 and 7% in royalties, a more lucrative endeavour is often pursued as a next step in securing overseas markets. Therefore, Takeda initiated a joint venture with Abbott Laboratories where profits were split 50–50. Calling the venture Takeda Abbott Products, the two partners worked to develop and market four new products, including a treatment for diabetes. Takeda's efforts to gain access to the U.S. market were not always easy. The Food and Drug Administration's long approval process often frustrated company officials. Similarly, Takeda experienced difficulty securing a U.S. producer for Nicholin, a treatment for unconsciousness caused by brain damage.

For the most part, however, Takeda's foreign expansion was successful and the company received further impetus to pursue overseas partners when the National Health Insurance system was reformed in the 1980's. By 1982 the per capita drug bill for Japanese citizens reached $95, making the Japanese drug market the second largest in the world. In an effort to halt escalating healthcare costs, the government reduced official drug prices by a total of nearly 50% and required elderly and insured workers to carry some of the costs of treatment. To maintain their respective market shares, companies reduced prices while continuing to allot generous sums for research. Thus foreign markets as a means of alleviating deteriorated domestic profit margins offered even greater appeal. In 1985, for example, Takeda opened a North Carolina plant to produce vitamin B1 in the United States.

Even as Takeda continued pursuing foreign ventures, domestic sales were hurt drastically by the government reforms. Two of the best selling antibiotics, Pansporin and Bestcall, were given between a 12 and 13% price reduction and total sales of antibiotics dropped from 18.4% to 16%. Similarly, vitamins, once accounting for close to 40% of sales, represented a mere 9% of the total. To ameliorate this trend, company president Ikushiro Kurabayashi shifted Takeda's domestic market orientation toward the growing population of aged people. According to a government sponsored research study, one of every four Japanese will be at least 65 in the year 2020. For this reason Takeda's research now concentrates on drugs for geriatric diseases. One such drug, called Avan, treats senile dementia. Having entered the market in early 1987, Avan already generates ¥1 billion a month. Following Avan, Takeda plans to release an anti-osteoporosis drug aimed at treating the 4.3 million sufferers of this disease.

Takeda's research and development expenditures for 1985 reached ¥31.5 billion. This represented the highest budget allotment among all Japanese pharmaceutical companies. Aside from the drugs for geriatric diseases, the company is developing an antidiabetic agent and a high blood pressure treatment drug. Furthermore, Takeda's research makes the company a world leader in biotechnology. Due to the fact that Takeda also excels in fermentation technology, foreign companies are pursuing this expertise as a means of manufacturing products of biotechnology on a large scale. Although company profits suffered from the changes in the health insurance program, these trends suggest Takeda will remain one of the world's most successful pharmaceutical manufacturers.

Principal Subsidiaries: Import-Export, Germany; Century Chemical Works, Malaysia; Paiboon Watana Co, Thailand; Fatec Quimica Industrial S.A., Brazil. Takeda also owns principal subsidiaries in Germany, Taiwan, Mexico, the Philippines, France, and Indonesia.

THE UPJOHN COMPANY

7000 Portage Road
Kalamazoo, Michigan 49001
U.S.A.
(616) 323–4000

Public Company
Incorporated: November 26, 1958
Employees: 20,600
Sales: $2.280 billion
Market Value: $8.163 billion
Stock Index: New York

Upjohn, a large multi-national drug company, is one of the largest ethical drug manufacturers in the United States. Headquartered in Kalamazoo, Michigan, Upjohn manufactures an extensive line of prescription drugs used in the treatment of such conditions as heart disease, cancer, and arthritis, as well as disorders and diseases of the central nervous system. Many of these drugs were discovered and developed in Upjohn's own laboratories since the company's establishment one hundred years ago.

It is not inaccurate to describe Upjohn's Victorian beginnings as marking the origin of modern pharmaceuticals in general. In the nineteenth century, physicians who wished to prescribe medication for their patients were limited to two unsatisfactory choices. One possibility was to administer fluid extracts of unstable and varying potency. The only other alternative was to prescribe drugs in pill form. Although pills at least were of relatively standard potency, they had the disadvantage of being so hard that they could be hammered into a board without doing damage to their coating (as one of Upjohn's early advertising gimmicks showed); such pills did not dissolve even in the stomach and were often passed by the patient. In 1885 Dr. William Upjohn solved these problems and revolutionized the drug industry when he patented a tedious process for the making of a "friable" pill capable of crumbling under the pressure of an individual's thumb.

The image of Dr. Upjohn's thumb crushing a pill eventually became a trademark of the Upjohn Pill and Granule Co., founded in Kalamazoo in 1886 by Upjohn and his brother Henry. A talent for promoting its products ensured the company's steady growth through the turn of the century. By 1893 Upjohn could be seen at the Chicago World's Fair distributing souvenirs of its exhibit—an enormous bottle filled with colored pills. In 1903 the company shortened its name to The Upjohn Company.

Quinine pills and "Phenolax Wafers" (the first candy laxative) were two of the early and successful products made by Upjohn. By 1924 the extremely popular wafers were bringing in $795,000 a year or 21 percent of Upjohn's sales revenue.

From the very beginning, however, Upjohn not only emphasized the marketing of drugs, but also the research and development of new compounds. In 1913 the company hired its first research scientist, a chemistry professor named Dr. Frederick W. Heyl. Dr. Heyl proved to be a sound investment for Upjohn. One of his developments, Citro-carbonate, an effervescent antacid, reached sales of one million dollars in 1926. Heyl was also responsible for patenting a digitalis tablet called Digitora, which is used in the treatment of heart disease, and which is still sold by Upjohn today.

William Upjohn, who was largely responsible for the firm's early research orientation as well as its entrepreneurial adventuresomeness, was an extraordinary man whose interests extended well beyond the bottom line of his company's profit sheet. An avid gardener, he grew 1,000 varieties of peonies (and even authored a book on them) in addition to the medicinal herbs and flowers he cultivated at his country home in Augusta, Michigan. His interest in horticulture led him to donate a 17 acre park to the city of Kalamazoo and to "shorten" the workday at Upjohn to seven hours during the summer in order to enable employees to go home and water their lawns. Dr. Upjohn's interests in the lives of his workers were not merely aesthetic, however; his posting of signs in the Upjohn plant reading "Keep the Quality Up" signified his commitment to responsible citizenship as well as to responsible craftsmanship. In keeping with his own injunction, Dr. Upjohn himself worked hard to improve the conditions under which his employees labored. In 1911 a soup lunch program was initiated at the Upjohn plant. In 1915 Upjohn instituted a group life insurance and benefit program. At the time of his death, he was working on the development of his farm properties in an attempt to create a method of employment insurance for the people of Kalamazoo, most of whom worked for the Upjohn Company. He even served as Kalamazoo's first mayor under a form of commission-city manager style of government which he himself had played a critical role in bringing about.

The Upjohn Company's attachment to Kalamazoo has been strengthened by the fact that the company has remained largely a family affair. When William Upjohn, eulogized as "Kalamazoo's First Citizen," died in 1932, the job of running the company fell to his nephew, Dr. Lawrence N. Upjohn. In 1944 Lawrence Upjohn retired and Donald S. Gilmore became president. Gilmore, whose family owned Gilmore Brother's, a huge midwestern department store, brought to the company valuable experience as a corporate executive from the business world, but even he was by no means an outsider. In fact, he was both the step-son and the son-in-law of William Upjohn. Ray T. Parfet, who has been president of the company since 1961, also married into the family. The company has been so tightly held that until 1968 no one who was not a family member or employee of Upjohn was permitted to sit on its board of directors.

During the 1930's and 1940's, under the guidance of Lawrence Upjohn and later under Gilmore, the company expanded its research and manufacturing facilities, and added twelve more research scientists. This expansion paid off when Upjohn became the first to market an adreno-cortical hormone product in 1935. However, the actual impetus for the company's success occurred during World War II when Upjohn, like many other drug companies, developed a broad line of antibiotics, including penicillin and streptomycin. Upjohn was fortunate enough to be selected by the armed forces to process human serum albumin and penicillin. By 1958 Upjohn was the sixth largest manufacturer of antibiotics, with sales of $22,598,000 worth of antibiotics. Two important drugs in the antibiotic field that are produced by the company today are Lincocin, an antibiotic useful for patients who are allergic to certain other antibiotics, and Cleocin Phosphate, an injectable form of clindamycin used in the treatment of life-threatening anaerobic infections. The company also markets tetracycline, erythromycin, and erythromycin ethylsuccinate, under the names Panmycin, E-Mycin, and E-Mycin E. Another antibiotic produced by Upjohn, Trobicin, has proven useful as an alternative to penicillin in the treatment of gonorrhea.

In addition to antibiotics, Upjohn also developed a product called Gelfoam during the period of World War II. A substance made from beef bone gelatin, Gelfoam is a porous, spongelike material which, when used during surgery, absorbs many times its volume in fluid and is itself absorbed by body tissues. Besides being valuable in surgery, Gelfoam is also useful in the treatment of hemophiliacs. Manufactured in a powder form which can be swallowed, Gelfoam is used to stop internal hemorrhaging that occurs in the digestive tract.

In 1957 the Upjohn Company introduced the first oral antidiabetes agent called Orinase. Many physicians and patients considered Orinase to be the greatest advancement in the treatment of adult-onset diabetes since insulin. Studies conducted in the 1970's, however, linked the drug with heart disease, and its use was subsequently discouraged by the National Institute of Health. Yet Upjohn continues to produce a line of oral antidiabetes agents which currently includes Tolinase and the more potent Micronase.

Another successful product for the Upjohn Company during the post-war period has been the injectable contraceptive Depo-Provera. This drug, which provides protection against pregnancy for about 90 days, has been marketed in over 80 foreign countries through subsidiaries organized by the company around the world. Upjohn has yet to gain FDA approval for the sale of Depo-Provera as a contraceptive in the United States, largely because studies have linked it to serious side-effects including cancer. However, Depo-Provera *has* been approved for the treatment of advanced uterine cancer, and a 1975 study revealed that doctors had prescribed the drug as a contraceptive for some 10,000 women in that year alone.

Upjohn's international expansion during the 1950's was critical not only in allowing it to compete with other large drug manufacturers in foreign markets, but also in enabling it to make genuine advances in the area of research. Nowhere is this clearer than in the story of how Upjohn was able to develop the range of cortisone products for which it is known today. Challenged by Merck, who introduced cortisone onto the market, Upjohn joined forces with S.B. Penick & Co. on an expedition to Africa in 1949–1950 in search of a plant that could provide a cheaper source of the drug. This venture ended in failure, but the company was fortunate enough to discover by accident a mold growing on a petri dish in the Kalamazoo laboratory which was capable of fermenting progesterone, the basic building block for cortisone, out of diosgenin. Upjohn was able to capitalize on their discovery by forming a partnership with a Mexican firm, Syntex, who isolated diosgenin from yams. A number of new hormones now available, including Depo-Provera, were made possible by Upjohn's international initiatives.

During the 1980's Upjohn has continued to expand internationally, forming a new Japanese subsidiary in 1985 while selling its worldwide polymer chemical business to Dow Chemical Co. for $232 million. In 1985 foreign markets accounted for 30% of Upjohn's total sales. Perhaps the most significant recent development for the company, however, has been the emergence of a major challenge in the market for its most lucrative drug, Motrin, which as of 1984 accounted for 40% of its earnings. Motrin, an anti-inflammatory agent widely prescribed in the treatment of arthritis and menstrual cramps, was introduced into the U.S. in 1974 when Boots Co. of Britain licensed Upjohn to sell ibuprofen (Motrin's active ingredient). In 1977, however, Boots entered the U.S. market itself, even while continuing to license Upjohn, and in 1981 began a price war by selling its version of the drug at 20–30% less than Upjohn. By 1984 both companies had extended their battle by producing over-the-counter ibuprofen pills Nuprin and Advil. As a result of this competition, Upjohn's dominant market position has been eroded: by mid-1984 Boots had gained 25% of the market share of prescriptions for ibuprofen.

Despite these setbacks, Upjohn's earnings picture over the last ten years has been good, with retained earnings and dividends increasing steadily between 1979 and 1985. An important factor in Upjohn's recent prosperity has been the success of its anti-anxiety agent, Xanax, whose sales increased 85% in 1985 from $82.2 million to $152.4 million. The outlook for the company's future is promising, largely because of the potential for two particular kinds of drugs under development in its laboratories. The first of these is prostaglandin, a compound believed to be effective against a broad spectrum of illnesses. Presently, Upjohn has produced two prostaglandin products, one for cardiovascular disorders and the other an abortion agent. The second exciting area of potential profit for Upjohn lies in the introduction, expected within the next few years, of an anti-baldness drug called Monoxidil. Originally intended for the treatment of heart disease, Monoxidil was found to produce unwanted hair-growth in patients for whom it was prescribed. Upjohn is now awaiting FDA approval for a topical form of the drug, but the huge demand for this product has already been demonstrated. In 1984, when rumors spread about Monoxidil's hair-restoring power, sales of the drug doubled. With 40 million Americans suffering from baldness, and with an estimated cost of $85 per month for the drug, industry analysts predict that by the early 1990s Monoxidil could bring in a billion dollars in sales for Upjohn.

Principal Subsidiaries: Upjohn Inter-American Corp.; Asgrow International Corp.; Asgrow Seed Company; California Health Care Services Inc.; Homemakers Licensing Corp.; Cobb, Incorporated; Centennial Collection Corp.; Asgrow Florida Co.; O's Gold Seed Co. Upjohn also has subsidiaries in the following countries: Argentina, Australia, Brazil, Belgium, Canada, Chile, Columbia, England, France, Greece, Guatemala, Indonesia, Italy, Japan, Korea, Mexico, Netherlands Antilles, Panama, Philippines, Portugal, South Africa, Spain, Sweden, Taiwan, Thailand, Venezuela, and West Germany.

WARNER-LAMBERT

201 Tabor Road,
Morris Plains, New Jersey 07950
U.S.A.
(201) 540-2000

Public Company
Incorporated: November 8, 1920 as William R. Warner & Co.
Employees: 45,000
Sales: $3.103 billion
Market Value: $5.583 billion
Stock Index: New York Zurich Paris London Frankfurt Brussels

Warner-Lambert is the product of a long history of mergers and acquisitions. The company name reflects the combined assets of two businesses, including the William R. Warner Company, a pharmaceutical and cosmetic concern with a history that dates back to 1856, and Lambert-Pharmacal, the manufacturers of Listerine oral antiseptic. There is only one person, however, who can be credited with transforming the small company into a large multi-national corporation. His name is Elmer Holmes Bobst.

Bobst arrived at William R. Warner & Company in 1945, already a veteran executive of the pharmaceutical industry. His talent as president of Hoffmann-La Roche's U.S. office was instrumental in acquiring for the Swiss company a large share of the U.S. drug market. In addition to making a name for himself as a brilliant business strategist, Bobst earned 5% of the company profits which made him a multimillionaire. For a man that was fond of entertaining Vice President Nixon on his private yacht, Bobst's move to the ailing Warner Company seemed highly unusual.

At the time Bobst was 61 years old and could easily have settled into a comfortable retirement. Instead, when Gustave A. Pfeiffer, chairman of Warner and the only surviving member of the original founding family, approached Bobst with an offer of employment, he accepted the position. As it happened, Pfeiffer had initially asked Bobst to join the company as the head of Warner's pharmaceutical division in 1918. However, because the family refused to sell Bobst any of the company stock (the family held all the common stock), he declined the offer. Twenty-seven years later, after Bobst had proven his ability at Hoffmann-La Roche, Pfeiffer readily offered the job on Bobst's terms; Bobst was hired

and allowed to purchase 11% of the common stock. By 1955 Bobst's holdings were worth over three million dollars.

What Bobst inherited with his new position, however, was a family operated company suffering from an aging product line and decaying physical properties. Pfeiffer's 1916 acquisition of the Hudnut cosmetic line accounted for most of the $25 million sales; yet that same product line barely turned a profit. In an effort to improve the image of the cosmetics production, Bobst renamed the firm Warner-Hudnut in 1950.

Renaming the company was just the first in a series of moves to reorganize the business. Bobst's previous experience with high-level industry and political affairs enabled him to hire accomplished executives and public figures. By hiring such recognized professionals as successful investment bankers, business executives, and political officials (Anna Rosenberg, the company's manager of industrial and public relations, was once the Assistant Secretary of Defense, and Alfred Driscoll, the company president, was the governor of New Jersey for seven years), the company management was filled with new talent.

Despite these developments, one aspect of the company remained the same. Pfeiffer's business had not grown by the accomplishments of its own creativity, but rather by a steady series of acquisitions. In fact, the original Gustavus A. Pfeiffer & Company, a patent medicine company from St. Louis, acquired the Warner Company in 1908. William Warner, a Philadelphia pharmacist, earned a fortune by inventing sugar-coated pills before the Civil War. When Pfeiffer purchased the company he moved the headquarters to New York and kept the company name. Then, in addition to buying the Hudnut line, Pfeiffer also acquired the DuBarry cosmetic company. By the time Bobst assumed the presidency, some 50-odd companies had been acquired during the 99 years of the Warner company's history.

Bobst's managerial style was well suited to this company program. In 1952 he made his first major acquisition by purchasing the New Jersey Chilcott Laboratories, Inc. Chilcott earned its reputation as a manufacturer of ethical drugs largely through its development of Peritrate, a long-acting vasodilator. The drug enlarges constricted blood vessels, and by 1966 an estimated 56% of 3.1 million people afflicted by heart disease used it. While the sales of Peritrate became Warner-Hudnut's mark of excellence in the pharmaceutical industry, its success was also cause for some controversy.

In 1959, because the drug proved to be useful in a wider application of treatments than originally allowed, the Food & Drug Administration approved of Peritrate's "new drug" usages. By 1966, however, the government, under the directive of the FDA, seized a shipment of the drug. Due to a controversial Peritrate advertising campaign, the FDA brought charges against the company's unapproved advocacy of an even wider usage for the drug.

Appearing in several medical journals, including the *Journal of the American Medical Association*, the ten page ads advocated the use of Peritrate not only for the treatment of angina, but as a "life-prolonging" prophylactic for all cardiac patients. The advertisement, based on the results of one study, was released at a time when the FDA had initiated an increasingly aggressive policy of evaluating claims for drug effectiveness. Even as the director of the study refuted the advertisement claims, Warner-Lambert executives stood by the claims for the effectiveness of their drug.

Only a few years after the acquisition of Chilcott, Bobst arranged a merger between his company and Lambert. The merger was the result of an encounter between the two company presidents at a meeting of the American Foundation for Pharmaceutical Education. The two companies complemented each other well. Their two ethical drug laboratories produced different but reputable products, and Lambert's Listerine sales, which accounted for over 50% of the company's total sales, guaranteed a large share of the oral antiseptic market.

However, Bobst had a larger interest in ensuring the outcome of the proposed merger. Lambert's well-organized distribution network reflected modern marketing techniques which were never incorporated into Warner-Hudnut's antiquated sales approach. Furthermore, Lambert company president Edward Williams's strong background in the management of pharmaceutical companies complemented Bobst's accomplished but inexperienced (within the industry, at least) executives. Thus when the merger became a reality, Williams new position in the company led to ex-Governor Driscoll's entrance into the pharmaceutical business as president of the new merger.

One of the most attractive aspects of the merger, however, was the success of Listerine. With publicly accessible information on its formula available since 1879 (it has no patent), and its virtually unchanged brown-paper packaging, Listerine's popularity nevertheless continued to grow. Much of its success is traceable to the advertising strategy of Gordon Seagrove. Recruited by Lambert in 1926, and taken away from his job as a Calliope-player in the circus, Seagrove made Listerine a household staple by promoting its ability to cure halitosis, sore throats, and dandruff. The advertising copy for one magazine shows a man encouraging a woman to continue massaging Listerine into his head, "Tear into it, Honey—It's Infectious Dandruff!"

Listerine continued to increase in popularity over the next decades; by 1975 the oral antiseptic held a sizeable portion of the $300 million market. Similarly, the Listerine producers continued to pay large amounts of money for advertisements. Yet Warner-Lambert's promotional investments in Listerine were not without their difficulties. For years the company advertised the mouthwash's ability to prevent colds and sore throats. During the Asian flu epidemic in 1957 Bobst placed an ad in *Life* magazine promoting Listerine's ability to resist the sickness; Warner-Lambert's own advertising agency had earlier balked at using the ad. However, sales for the mouthwash that year increased to $26 million.

By 1975 the Federal Trade Commission began to investigate the Listerine advertisements. Using its untested powers to order corrective advertisements, the FTC disputed the cold prevention claims of Listerine as unsupportable and ordered the company to embark on a

$10 million disclaimer campaign. This figure was based on the amount equal to the company's average annual advertising expenditure between 1962 and 1972. Attacking the decades-long cold remedy advertisements, the FTC argued that only corrective disclaimers could educate the consumer. In 1978 the Supreme Court upheld the FTC's order.

The merger between the makers of Listerine and the Warner company was followed by a series of additional acquisitions. Emerson Drug (makers of Bromo-Seltzer), Smith Brothers (makers of cough-drops), American Optical, Schick Shaving, Parke Davis, and American Chicle (makers of Chiclets) were all purchased. To acquire Chicle, Warner-Lambert used 7.8 million of its own shares, worth about $200 million. Many industry analysts criticized the high price paid for the gum manufacturer; in 1962 its net income for the year was under $10 million. By 1983, however, after expanding into foreign markets, the Chicle sales were reaching the one billion dollar mark. Ward S. Hagan, chairman of the company, called the gum and mint business "the largest in the world".

The merger of Parke, Davis & Company with Warner-Lambert in 1970 was not subject to the same criticism. It was, however, investigated by the Antitrust Division of the Justice Department. The merger, according to the chairman of the House Judiciary Committee, raised "serious problems" because it had the potential to limit competition and create a monopoly. Upon approval the merger would result in a combined revenue of $1.7 billion and would rank the new company among the 100 largest industrial companies in the U.S.

On November 12, 1970 the Justice Department announced it would not challenge the merger despite the Antitrust Division's recommendation to the contrary. The department referred the matter to the Federal Trade Commission which holds concurrent authority to enforce the Clayton Act. A day later the merger was completed. By 1976, however, the FTC ordered the company to sell several units of its Parke, Davis subsidiary that produced specified drugs. Those units producing thyroid preparations, cough remedies, cough drops and lozenges, normal albumin serum and tetanus immune globulin would have to be sold in order to restore competition in those product lines.

While S. Burke Giblin, the chairman and chief executive officer of Warner-Lambert at the time of the ruling, welcomed the decision because it permitted Parke, Davis to continue in the area of drug development, several other difficulties faced the company. In 1976 Warner-Lambert disclosed figures to the Securities and Exchange Commission concerning illegal payments abroad. Becoming the ninth company to admit bribe pay-offs, Warner-Lambert announced that more than $2.2 million "in questionable payments" had been uncovered in 14 of the 140 countries in which it conducted business.

Only months later an explosion at an American Chicle plant in Queens, New York killed six people and injured 55. One year later a grand jury indicted the company and four of its officials on charges of reckless manslaughter and criminally negligent homicide. The charges were based on reports that the fire department had warned the company about the explosive potential of magnesium stearate dust used as a gum-machine lubricant. Calling the charges "outrageous" and unwarranted, company executives appealed the case. In 1978 a state judge dismissed the charges citing "crystal clear and voluminous evidence" that the company had tried to eliminate the danger of an explosion. In 1979, however, the New York State court's appellate division voted to restore the indictments. Finally, in 1980, the state's highest court dismissed once again all charges in connection with the explosion.

In 1981 a settlement was finally reached on the sale of Warner-Lambert's Benylin cough syrup. After seven years of deliberation, the Food and Drug Administration approved the reinstated over-the-counter sale of the drug. In 1975 the company had made the drug available without a prescription, but the FDA ordered the drug back on a prescription-only status after questions were raised about its effectiveness.

In 1978 Warner-Lambert purchased Entenmann's Bakery, for $243 million in cash. The purchase soon proved fortuitous; by 1982 it had become Warner-Lambert's most profitable consumer division with sales reaching $333 million and an annual growth rate of 19%. At some point in the late 1970's, however, a rumor was started that Entenmann's profits were supporting Reverend Sun Myung Moon's Unification Church. The source of the rumor was said to come from Westchester county in New York; as a result, Warner-Lambert responded by taking out an ad in the county newspaper denying the alleged connection.

Nevertheless, the rumor continued to circulate and actually received a large amount of publicity in the Boston, Massachusetts area. It was reported in some places that delivery and sales people were being harassed, and one Rhode Island church even urged a boycott. When sales growth began to slip, Warner-Lambert mailed a letter to 1,600 churches in New England describing Entenmann's history as a family-owned business for 80 years before it was purchased. Whether the information campaign was successful or not, Warner-Lambert sold the bakery in 1982 to General Foods for $315 million.

Damaging rumors and criminal indictments aside, Warner-Lambert went through the late 1970's with a poor operating performance. Profit margins were off by 40% in 1979 and most of the company revenues came from the sale of consumer goods. Once Ward S. Hagan replaced Bobst as chairman, he embarked on a restructuring program to revitalize the pharmaceutical operations. American Optical, an unprofitable subsidiary, was sold and Hagan closed or consolidated 24 plants in foreign and domestic locations while reducing the company labor force by 29%. Research for new drugs at the Parke, Davis division was supported by a 20% increase in budgetary funds during 1983 to $180 million. Several newly approved drugs had brought $50 million in domestic sales.

Despite the improved operating performance and a predicted earnings growth of 10 to 15%, Warner-Lambert's unexpected purchase of IMED, a small hospital supply manufacturer, caused Wall Street analysts to shake their heads in disbelief. While IMED's 35% hold on sales in the hospital supply field made it the market leader and while sales continued to grow annually at an unmatchable 50%, a closer look revealed a company beset with problems.

IMED's executives apparently concentrated on short-term sales goals, at the expense of new product development. In fact, a management conflict between IMED's manufacturing and research and development executives caused many important employees to resign in frustration. Thus Warner-Lambert's $468 million purchase, signifying a price at 23 times IMED's earnings, was largely criticized. Yet Hagan defended the acquisition by arguing that the company is now competitively positioned to exploit the growing market.

Whether IMED's purchase proves shortsighted or not, company sales increased 2% in 1985 to $3.2 billion with a return on equity at 16% (over an 11% five-year average). Interestingly enough, Capsugel, the Warner-Lambert division that is the world's largest supplier of unfilled gelatin capsules, overhauled its production operation using Japanese batch manufacturing techniques. These revolutionary measures for streamlining production **without risking safety are said to have saved the company** $300 million a year. The company also saved $125 million in potential purchases of new machinery. By using Japanese techniques, the machines whose designs date back as far as 1916 were able to increase output by 90%.

Principal Subsidiaries: American Chicle Co.; American Food Industries, Inc.; Chicle Adams, Inc.; Euronett, Inc.; Family Products Corp.; IMED Corp.; Keystone Cemurgic Corp.; Parke, Davis & Co.; Tabor Corp.; Warner-Chilcott Inc. The company also lists subsidiaries in the following countries: Argentina, Austria, Belgium, Brazil, Canada, **Chile, Costa Rica, France, Guatemala, Italy, Japan,** Mexico, The Netherlands, Philippines, Spain, Switzerland, Thailand, United Kingdom, and Venezuela.

Wellcome

THE WELLCOME FOUNDATION LTD.

P.O. Box 129
The Wellcome Building
183 Euston Road
London NW1 2BP
England
(01) 387 4477

Wholly-owned by the Wellcome Trust
Incorporated: 1924
Employees: 18,342
Sales: £998 million (US$1.467 billion)

"Wherever the British Lion goes, there goes the Unicorn which represents Burroughs Wellcome & Co. You will always find the two together, whether it is in the heart of darkest Africa or at either of the two Poles." Just as the unicorn assured good health in the days of old, so it is today. Wherever that horn is seen, whether fighting a common cold or a deadly disease, there is the most up-to-date medical formulation that can be prepared. Wellcome plc continues to offer a progressive line of research and medicine to the whole world.

In 1879 Silas M. Burroughs offered Henry S. Wellcome partnership in a growing pharmaceutical company. Both Burroughs and Wellcome had graduated from the Philadelphia College of Pharmacy. Burroughs had gone to London to represent John Wyeth & Bro. and had then created his own business. Wellcome became a travelling representative for McKesson & Robbins, America's largest drug house. Wellcome sailed for Britain in 1880 and accepted Burroughs's offer, bringing with him the exclusive rights to sell McKesson & Robbins preparations outside the American continent. Burroughs Wellcome & Co. was created on 27 September 1880 with a deed of partnership naming Wellcome as a junior partner. Burrough's initial investment was £1200, Wellcome's £800.

Burroughs had always been a man of action. He was also a kind man, often thinking of his employees, offering them the best possible environment to work in. His factories provided well-lit, open working areas; factory grounds more closely resembled parks than manufacturing sites. Wellcome, however, was a rational man interested in details. His organizational skill and ability to remain calm complemented Burroughs's personality very well.

The strong character of each man could be seen in their early attempts to establish the company on firm ground.

Burroughs showed his more expansive nature by carrying representative product samples throughout the world. Beginning in Spain and Portugal, he traversed the Mediterranean countries through Turkey and Egypt to India, Australia, New Zealand, and the United States. Wellcome balanced this restlessness with his sure organization and development of the business in Britain. The headquarters were set up in Snow Hill, London in 1883. The primary business of the new company was to represent novel powders and pills of American companies (including John Wyeth & Bro. and McKesson & Robbins). In 1982, Burroughs Wellcome & Co. began manufacturing their own products.

In choosing a manufacturing site, the two partners encountered their first clash of interests. While Burroughs had been travelling for two years, Wellcome had become more and more frustrated by the stamp duty placed on products imported from America. This duty spoiled the excellent business opportunity Britain's efficient shipping offered. It took some convincing to make Burroughs see the logic behind manufacturing in Britain. Burroughs was finally persuaded, however, and in 1883 their first factory was acquired on the Thames at Wandsworth.

The high standard of quality, precise and innovative formulation, and thoughtful promotion offered Burroughs Wellcome & Co. assured success. Refined ingredients together with highly accurate machinery yielded compressed products ranging from one thousandth of one grain to over sixty grains in dosage. Many trademarks were registered in this initial phase, the most important being the Tabloid, conceived by Wellcome in 1884. Numerous awards of excellence were acquired at trade shows and scientific exhibitions. Wellcome profited from the excellent publicity these awards brought. He also took advantage of publicity gained through medical chests supplied to notable people, e.g., the explorer Henry M. Stanley. Wellcome was the first man to offer pharmaceutical training with his products.

Success loomed, but due to personal differences the partnership was never stable. In the same year they opened their first Associated House in Australia (1886), Wellcome's health deteriorated and he spent a year recuperating in the USA. When he returned in 1887, Burroughs demanded that the partnership be dissolved due to the neglect Wellcome had shown. Burroughs had always been a highly emotional partner, often making accusations he would later regret, and Wellcome refused to allow the company to be split, successfully defending his rights in a law suit. Despite these difficulties a larger factory site was opened in 1889 at the old Phoenix Mills in Dartford, Kent. This factory was renamed the Wellcome Chemical Works. The site is still the major production center of the Group. In 1894 Wellcome established the Physiological Research Laboratories (WPRL). In less than one year the lab had produced an anti-diptheria serum.

In 1895 a decisive event occurred affecting the direction that Burroughs Wellcome & Co. would follow. Just as negotiations to dissolve the partnership had begun, Burroughs died, and although Mrs. Burroughs attempted to gain some control of the company, Wellcome took over. He continued to run the company alone for another thirty years. In the early 1900's, a great expansion occurred.

Between 1900 and 1904 Wellcome fought to regain control of the Tabloid trademark from competitors through legal action. New associated houses were opened in South Africa (1902), Italy (1905), Canada (1906), the U.S. (1906), China (1908), Argentina (1910), and India (1912). Sales rose from £218,625 to £323,772 at home and from £71,711 to £136,846 overseas between 1904 and 1915.

While sales increased, so did the company's research. The Wellcome Chemical Research Laboratories (WCRL) was opened in Snow Hill in 1896. The director, Dr. Frederick B. Power, had befriended Wellcome at Philadelphia College. In 1901 WPRL became the first private institution in Britain to be allowed legally to experiment on live animals. Wellcome helped establish the Tropical Research Laboratories at Gordon Memorial College in Khartoum in 1903. The Wellcome Bureau of Scientific Research (WBSR) established in 1913, assumed control over all of Wellcome's research laboratories. Also in 1913, Wellcome opened the Wellcome Historical Medical Museum with a collection that had been created over some ten years.

With the start of World War I, Wellcome offered the control of the company to the government. Vaccines and sera, especially the gas-gangrene and the tetanus antitoxin sera, were developed and produced by the WPRL. The WBSR became a source for knowledge of tropical infections and treatments. Drugs and chemicals that had formerly been produced in Germany were developed by the WCRL. Wellcome even helped the government with aid in transportation and laboratories. The war brought business to £440,064 at home and £326,901 abroad.

The 1920's brought few changes to the company. No new foreign houses were established, though two depots were set up in the Dutch East Indies (1920) and Sweden (1921). In 1920 the Wellcome Entomological Field Laboratory was established. Finally, the Dartford plant began producing insulin in 1923 and was modernized.

The initial expansion that marked the beginning of Burroughs Wellcome & Co. had ended. The company had come upon a time of consolidation. Wellcome, no longer interested in the chore of controlling his commercial enterprises, united the nine Burroughs Wellcome associated houses, the research institutions, and the museums into one private company, the Wellcome Foundation Ltd., in 1924 with £1 million. Making himself the governing director, he left most of the daily decisions to his general manager, George E. Pearson. Wellcome devoted more and more time and profits to the Historical Medical Museum, only entering affairs of business when a figurehead was necessary. As more money and time went to the museum, less innovation and expansion occurred. The company began to stagnate.

Wellcome's final act of consolidation was the Wellcome Research Institution, finished in 1932. The cost was £250,000. Originally housing the Wellcome collection and some laboratories, the building in Euston Road is now the Wellcome building, headquarters of the group since enemy action destroyed the Snow Hill building in 1941.

In 1933, in the midst of the worldwide depression, Wellcome personally planned an exhibit for the Century of Progress Chicago Fair. In the best space in the Hall of Science, 24 displays were set up illustrating the history of the company. This proved to be the highlight of the company's next few years.

In 1936, Sir Henry S. Wellcome died. In order to be sure that the company would maintain the ideals he had established, Wellcome left a will dividing the shares of the Wellcome Foundation among five trustees: G. Hudson Lyall, Sir Henry Dale, Professor T.R. Elliott, L.C. Bullock, and Martin Price. These Trustees, along with a board of directors, were to continue the activities of the Foundation, directing all profits to charitable purposes, research in medicine and those sciences pertaining to it, and maintenance of museums dedicated to this research and the history of medicine. The will also made provisions for the employees' welfare fund and yearly payments to designated persons. Finally he made provisions for a library, sports field, and gymnasium to be built attached to a school in Garden City, Minnesota, Wellcome's home town, in memory of his parents.

Overall, Wellcome left a company in poor shape. Provision for his death duties was inadequate, and the company had failed to fund research and development. What research continued did not always have cogent objectives. Only the United States and Australian houses offered any kind of useful income. The Wellcome Foundation had sunk to a state of disunity and apathy.

In 1940 George Pearson was replaced by T.R.G. Bennett. Bennett realized the need to unify the Foundation, but could not succeed with the plans he tried because of the wartime restrictions on capital. By 1948, the company had sunk to its lowest point. An accountant, H.E. Sier, was named as a new Chairman, and two managing directors, C. Gordon Oakes and Denis E. Wheeler, were appointed. In 1953, Michael Perrin assumed the retiring Sier's position as Chairman. By that time, the crisis had ended.

The 1950's brought a spirit of revitalization to Wellcome. The Board of Directors developed a long-term plan to increase revenue, improve the range of the company's products, and expand the market for these new products. The company first and foremost needed capital to work with. Crucial initial capital was gained through the sale of the Empirin range of analgesics through the United States company. The Board then attempted to improve the marketing of the existing line of products, and sales between 1949 and 1952 increased by 75 per cent.

The Board's second change dealt with Wellcome's outdated product range. The company had fallen behind in competitive research, completely ignoring the growing field of chemotherapy. Corrective action was taken by both Dr. Kellaway at the end of the 1940's and Dr. Adamson, the new Research Director appointed in 1953. A variety of synthetic drugs and medical and veterinary vaccines was developed. These were commercially successful. Septrin, an antibacterial treatment, and Zyloric, an anti-gout preparation, were especially important in the 1960's. Government intervention in drug testing in the 1970's eventually slowed the growing product line. However, combinations of drugs proved to be successful. Actifed, of major importance commercially, was developed as a combination of Actidil, an antihistamine, and other market drugs.

Now an expansive market was needed to absorb the new capital and the extensive, more balanced, product line.

New associated houses were opened in New Zealand (1954), Brazil (1955), Kenya (1955), and Pakistan (1956). In 1959 Cooper McDougall & Robertson Ltd. was acquired. This not only opened up a greater number of trading posts throughout the world but also added animal health products to the Foundation's range of medicine. Calmic Ltd. and its overseas connections were acquired in 1967. This British-based company offered consumer and medical products as well as a hygiene service. Hadleigh-Crowther, a manufacturer of dairy hygienic products, was purchased in 1969, Macdonald Taylor, specialising in surgical dressings, in 1971, and Jensen Salsbery, another animal health laboratory, in 1979.

Further expansion into Europe was achieved by the acquisition of seven companies in the 1960's and four more in the 1970's. Other companies were established near the Mediterranean and in Asia at this time as well. In these new territories the company would work through local agents until enough merchandise was being sold to warrant Wellcome's creating a company.

Much of the growth of the company was due to the energetic leadership coming from the enthusiastic Board. Sir Michael Perrin attempted to unify company activity in order to keep one main objective. In 1967 three new deputy chairmen were brought in: Denis Wheeler centralized group activities, such as research or development. Dr. Fred Wrigley, the new Chairman of Calmic, was crucial to the expansion in Europe, and A.A. Gray became responsible for veterinary medicine and Chairman of Cooper McDougall & Robertson. With Gray's promotion to Chairman of Wellcome in 1971, a more diversified regional network was incorporated into the management hierarchy. A.J. Shepperd, Gray's successor and the current Chairman, attempted to strengthen Wellcome's export markets by creating a new export division.

The final procedure Wellcome had to endure was a modernization of its structure. An increasing demand for upper management to organize and centralize the various companies called for increased activity in hiring and updated training. Dartford was a site built over 50 years before the expansion of the world market occurred. Almost half of the buildings were either demolished or reassigned for other duties in order to make room for modern facilities. Rebuilding, extending, and reallocating buildings went ahead at many sites in Europe, Africa, and Asia. Most of the United States company moved from New York to two sites in North Carolina.

Of all the people who braved this transition period, it was the shareholders who endured the hardest times. Seventy per cent of the net profit was reinvested into the company between 1950 and 1980. Their patience paid off when the business boomed.

Today Wellcome is struggling with the formidable disease Aids. Once again Wellcome is attempting to tackle current medical problems.

Further Reading: The Wellcome Research Institution and the Affiliated Research Laboratories and Museums, London, Wellcome Foundation, 1933; *Physic and Philanthropy: A History of The Wellcome Trust 1936–1986* by A. Rupert Hall and B.A. Bembridge, London, Cambridge University Press, 1986.

INDEX TO COMPANIES AND PERSONS _____

Listings are arranged in alphabetical order under the full company name, so that Eli Lilly & Company will be found under the letter E; definite articles (The) and forms of incorporation (A.B.) that precede the name are ignored for alphabetical purposes. Company names appearing in **bold** have separate entries on the page numbers appearing in **bold**.